THE IRWIN SERIES IN
INSURANCE AND ECONOMIC SECURITY

DAVIS W. GREGG

Consulting Editor

Books *in the*
IRWIN SERIES IN INSURANCE AND ECONOMIC SECURITY

ATHEARN   *General Insurance Agency Management*

BICKELHAUPT & MAGEE   *General Insurance*   8th ed.

BLACK, KEIR, & SURREY   *Cases in Life Insurance*

BOWE   *Estate Planning and Taxation*   3d C.L.U. ed.

BRAINARD   *Automobile Insurance*

DICKERSON   *Health Insurance*   3d ed.

DONALDSON   *Casualty Claim Practice*   rev. ed.

EILERS & CROWE   *Group Insurance Handbook*

FOLLMANN   *Medical Care and Health Insurance: A Study in Social Progress*

FRAINE   *Valuation of Securities Holdings of Life Insurance Companies*

GOSHAY   *Information Technology in the Insurance Industry*

GREGG & LUCAS (eds.)   *Life and Health Insurance Handbook*   3d ed.

GREIDER & BEADLES   *Law and the Life Insurance Contract*   rev. ed.

HABER & COHEN   *Social Security: Programs, Problems, and Policies*

HABER & MURRAY   *Unemployment Insurance in the American Economy*

KELLISON   *The Theory of Interest*

LONG & GREGG   *Property and Liability Insurance Handbook*

McGILL   *Legal Aspects of Life Insurance*

McGILL   *Life Insurance*   rev. ed.

MAGEE   *Life Insurance*   3d ed.

MAGEE & SERBEIN   *Property and Liability Insurance*   4th ed.

MEHR & CAMMACK   *Principles of Insurance*   5th ed.

MEHR & HEDGES   *Risk Management in the Business Enterprise*

MELONE & ALLEN   *Pension Planning: Pensions, Profit Sharing, and Other Deferred Compensation Plans*   rev. ed.

MYERS   *Social Insurance and Allied Government Programs*

NOBACK   *Life Insurance Accounting: A Study of the Financial Statements of Life Insurance Companies in the United States and Canada*

REDEKER & REID   *Life Insurance Settlement Options*   rev. ed.

ROKES   *Human Relations in Handling Insurance Claims*

SNIDER   *Readings in Property and Casualty Insurance*

STALNAKER   *Life Insurance Agency Financial Management*   rev. ed.

Life and Health Insurance Handbook

Life and Health Insurance Handbook

Planned and Edited by

DAVIS W. GREGG, C.L.U.
President, The American College of Life Underwriters

and

VANE B. LUCAS, C.L.U.
Senior Vice President for Academic Affairs,
The American College of Life Underwriters

with the Cooperation of
One Hundred and Twenty-One Outstanding
American Insurance Authorities

1973 · Third Edition

RICHARD D. IRWIN, INC.   *Homewood, Illinois 60430*

IRWIN-DORSEY LIMITED   *Georgetown, Ontario L7G 4B3*

Third Edition
9 0 11 12 13 14 15 16 17 18 K 5 4 3 2 1 0 9 8

ISBN 0-256-00169-3
Library of Congress Catalog Card No. 70-190540
Printed in the United States of America

To
M., C., and B. and J., C., and V.
—two families offering continuing
inspiration, and families so
typical of the precious relationships
which are the foundation of life and
health insurance the world over

Preface

THE PROTECTION, accumulation, conservation, and distribution of economic values associated with human life are among the most important functions in modern society. Premature death, disability, and superannuation are risks faced by every man. Most of the economic consequences of these risks are subject to scientific treatment with a resultant decrease in many of life's uncertainties.

The treatment of human life value risks is the principal responsibility of the life and health insurance business of the United States and Canada. The scope of the business—for all practical purposes only about 100 years old—has reached major proportions. In the neighborhood of 800,000 persons are directly involved as company employees, field underwriters, corporate buyers, regulatory personnel, and the like. About 1,900 life and health insurance companies operate in the United States and Canada. More than 155 million persons in the United States and Canada are covered by some form of life insurance, while substantially more (about 185 million) have some type of private health insurance coverage. In 1972, approximately $46 billion, or about 5 percent of the total national income of the two countries, was paid in premiums to this branch of insurance. Adding the $43 billion in social security contributions and the $10 billion in noninsured pension plan contributions gives a total of $99 billion, or about 10 percent of the total national income, set aside annually to cope with life value risks.

Such is the scope of life insurance, health insurance, pensions, estate planning, and the like; such is the breadth of the field with which this *Handbook* is concerned.

The third edition of the *Handbook* is a comprehensive reference source on all major phases of life and health insurance, including the increasingly important fields of pensions, profit sharing, and estate planning. It is a highly practical tool for insurance practitioners, lawyers, accountants, trust officers, risk managers, actuaries, pension planners, and others vitally concerned from day to day with life and health insurance. Although designed as a handbook, it also provides an orderly, integrated volume of principles subject to textbook treatment by the serious student of life and health insurance.

A total of 123 outstanding insurance authorities contributed to the

ix

Handbook, 75 serving as Contributing Authors and 48 as Consulting Editors. Each author wrote his chapter within the carefully conceived master plan for the entire book and against a basic plan for each chapter. The volume is designed so that most chapters stand on their own, thus adding to the effectiveness of the *Handbook* as a reference tool.

The *Handbook* is divided into ten basic sections: Part I—Economic Security and Insurance; Part II—Individual Life Insurance and Annuities; Part III—Variable Life Insurance, Annuities, and Mutual Funds; Part IV—Individual Health Insurance; Part V—Group Life and Health Insurance; Part VI—Pensions and Other Qualified Deferred Compensation Plans; Part VII—Business Uses of Life and Health Insurance; Part VIII—Government Benefits—Protection and Retirement; Part IX—Planning Small and Large Estates; and Part X—Company Operations and Institutional Aspects. The Appendixes contain a variety of contracts, riders, forms, and other materials of practical value.

The basic objective of the Irwin Series in Insurance and Economic Security, initiated in 1949, has been to create literature useful not only to college and university classes but also to the insurance institution in all its dimensions. From the beginning, the need for a comprehensive reference volume on insurance was perceived. Originally, it was thought that a single handbook in insurance should be prepared but, as the design of the volume took shape, it became obvious that a one-volume work was not practicable. It was then decided that two handbooks would be published and, in 1958, preparation of the first edition of the *Life and Health Insurance Handbook* was begun. This volume, published in 1959, proved to be highly useful in the United States and in many foreign countries. Its success indicated the need for subsequent revisions and for the completion of its companion volume, the *Property and Liability Insurance Handbook.* The latter volume, planned and edited in conjunction with Professor John D. Long of Indiana University, was published in 1965.

The first edition of this *Handbook* was based on the notion that an immense amount of intelligent and capable writing talent existed among insurance authorities, but that time and work pressures foreclosed the opportunity for most of them to ponder and to articulate their thoughts for text purposes. It was believed that limiting the writing assignment to a chapter or a part of a volume would permit scores of able persons to make creative contributions to insurance literature. The validity of this thought is recorded on the pages of the previous editions and of this current volume.

In the preface to the first edition, reference was made to the problems of inconsistent terminology. Hope was expressed that future editions would reflect improved insurance language. While progress is reflected in the terminology in this edition of the *Handbook,* much remains to be done. The reader is asked to have patience in regard to the terminological inconsistencies he will encounter. It is believed that the language and thoughts are clear even though terminology used may differ among authors.

To acknowledge properly the help received from so many outstanding persons would require a very long preface indeed. It is hoped that the Contributing Authors and Consulting Editors, listed on subsequent pages, will gain personal satisfaction in the wide use of their ideas. Such is the true compensation to any creative mind; our sincere gratitude to them seems small beside it.

Many very good friends have "walked the extra mile" in developing this edition and we are deeply grateful to them. Everett T. Allen, Jr., E. J. Moorhead, and William G. Williams were especially helpful not only as Contributing Authors but in their assistance in determining the content of certain portions of the *Handbook*. Three of our associates at the American College provided especially valuable assistance in refining the structure of the third edition and in editorial assistance with particular parts. We record our gratitude to Dr. Barnie E. Abelle, Herbert Chasman, and Dr. William H. Rabel. Their knowledge and editorial skill added substantially to the quality of the chapters which had their attention. Mrs. Marjorie A. Fletcher, also of the College faculty, provided helpful assistance in compiling reference materials.

Creative editorial assistance on selected chapters and appendixes was provided by John A. Tuck of the Canadian Life Insurance Association; A. M. Rihouey of the Equitable Life Assurance Society of the United States; H. W. B. Manning of the Great-West Life Assurance Company; Ashby Bladen of the Guardian Life Insurance Company of America; John P. Hanna of the Health Insurance Association of America; Milton Amsel, Dr. Harold Edrich, and William E. Kingsley of the Institute of Life Insurance; Dr. Paul W. Thayer of the Life Insurance Agency Management Association; Dr. Charles Moeller, Jr., of the Metropolitan Life Insurance Company; Joseph C. Sibigtroth of the New York Life Insurance Company; and Dr. J. Robert Ferrari, Richard J. Mellman, and Erwin Rode of the Prudential Insurance Company of America.

Others not named elsewhere who have given much-appreciated help on the project are: William T. Gibb, III, of the American Life Insurance Association; Roger S. Gray, Robert B. Proctor, and Gerald J. Randall of the Connecticut Mutual Life Insurance Company; James A. Attwood, Neil M. DeVries, Milton J. Goldberg, Alan D. Grant, Robert F. Link, and Ray Waters of the Equitable Life Assurance Society of the United States; Roy W. Spear of the Guardian Life Insurance Company of America; John M. Briggs of the Home Life Insurance Company; Robert N. Chiappetta and Fred DeLuca of the Institute of Life Insurance; Bill Diman of the John Hancock Mutual Life Insurance Company; Michael F. Dimond of the Life Underwriter Training Council; H. James Douds of the National Association of Life Underwriters; James E. MacElwee of the North American Life Assurance Company; Karl H. Anderson, Mrs. Daphne D. Bartlett, Raymond A. Bierschbach, C. Donald Hankin, Anthony E. Meehl, and H. Dixon Trueblood of the Occidental Life Insurance Company of California; Robert W. Byron, Robert G. Hill, Kenneth P. Lord, and Robert C. Nuding of the Security Mutual Life Insurance Company of New York; and Selden Davey, John Haessler, and Frederick R. Rickers of the Woodman Accident and Life Company.

Further, the contributions of the authors and editors of previous editions of this *Handbook* who have not participated in this edition are thankfully acknowledged. Whatever the reason for their nonparticipation—whether retirement, change in structure of the volume, or some other factor—their previous help is greatly appreciated.

Acknowledgment is made to Charles J. Zimmerman, Honorary Chairman of the Board of Trustees of the American College; to Dr. John T. Fey, Chairman of the Board of the College; to William D. Grant, Vice Chairman of the Board of the American College; and to others on the College's Board of Trustees. This project, and other projects finished and yet to be finished, could never come to pass were it not for the determination of these men that the College will take its place among the outstanding educational institutions of the United States, that the College will give true educational leadership in economic security and insurance, and that the faculty of the College will devote as much time as possible to writing, research and other creative endeavors. Effective insurance literature comes into existence more easily in this kind of environment.

Helen L. Schmidt, our colleague at the College, has carried the organization and administrative responsibility of the *Handbook* in a brilliantly effective manner. The realization that well over 2,000 letters have been exchanged with authors and editors suggests that very unusual resourcefulness and ingenuity characterized her work. The additional fact that most of the *Handbook* work was carried on during evening or weekend hours adds to our appreciation. It is no exaggeration to say that this *Handbook* could not have been done without her; such is our appreciation to her.

In reflecting on the great amount of time devoted to this project and the resulting disruptions in the lives of our families, we must emphasize the truth in the thought that, "They also serve who only stand and wait." Our families' patience in permitting us the several hundred uninterrupted hours has helped greatly in bringing this project to a successful close. Let us be thankful that after these many months we all still have our life and health.

Bryn Mawr, Pennsylvania   DAVIS W. GREGG
June, 1973   VANE B. LUCAS

Contributing Authors
and Consulting Editors

DR. BARNIE E. ABELLE, C.L.U., Professor of Economics, American College of Life Underwriters, Bryn Mawr, Pennsylvania

LAURENCE J. ACKERMAN, President, Norwich Savings Society, Norwich, Connecticut

EVERETT T. ALLEN, JR., Consultant, Towers, Perrin, Forster & Crosby, Philadelphia, Pennsylvania

JOHN C. ANGLE, F.S.A., Vice President and Actuary, Woodmen Accident and Life Company, Lincoln, Nebraska

VERNE J. ARENDS, Superintendent of Pension Research, Northwestern Mutual Life Insurance Company, Milwaukee, Wisconsin

HOWARD E. BARNHILL, C.L.U., President, North American Life and Casualty Company, Minneapolis, Minnesota

EDWARD B. BATES, C.L.U., President, Connecticut Mutual Life Insurance Company, Hartford, Connecticut

DR. WILLIAM T. BEADLES, C.L.U., Professor of Insurance, Emeritus, Illinois Wesleyan University, Bloomington, Illinois

DR. JOSEPH M. BELTH, C.L.U., C.P.C.U., Professor of Insurance, Graduate School of Business, Indiana University, Bloomington, Indiana

ROBERT M. BEST, C.L.U., President, Security Mutual Life Insurance Company of New York, Binghamton, New York

DR. KENNETH BLACK, JR., C.L.U., Dean, School of Business Administration, Georgia State University, Atlanta, Georgia

B. FRANKLIN BLAIR, F.S.A., Senior Vice President and Actuary, Provident Mutual Life Insurance Company, Philadelphia, Pennsylvania

ROBERT G. BOECKNER, F.S.A., Actuary, Crown Life Insurance Company, Toronto, Canada

HERBERT J. BOOTHROYD, F.S.A., Vice President, New England Mutual Life Insurance Company, Boston, Massachusetts

LAWRENCE R. BROWN, JR., Assistant General Counsel, Provident Mutual Life Insurance Company of Philadelphia, Pennsylvania

J. W. BURNS, President, The Great-West Life Assurance Company, Winnipeg, Canada

PAUL A. CAMPBELL, F.S.A., Associate Actuary, Connecticut General Life Insurance Company, Hartford, Connecticut

BROOKS CHANDLER, Executive Vice President, Provident Life and Accident Insurance Company, Chattanooga, Tennessee

HERBERT CHASMAN, C.L.U., Professor of Taxation and Estate Planning, American College of Life Underwriters, Bryn Mawr, Pennsylvania

EARL CLARK, C.L.U., Chairman, Occidental Life Insurance Company of California, Los Angeles, California

DONALD D. CODY, F.S.A., Senior Vice President, New England Mutual Life Insurance Company, Boston, Massachusetts

DR. GEORGE T. CONKLIN, JR., President, Guardian Life Insurance Company of America, New York, New York

RICHARD P. COOLEY, Secretary, Public Affairs Department, The Travelers Insurance Company, Hartford, Connecticut

PAUL R. CRAIG, Second Vice President, John Hancock Mutual Life Insurance Company, Boston, Massachusetts

DR. ROBERT M. CROWE, C.L.U., C.P.C.U., Dean, College of Business Administration, University of Tulsa, Tulsa, Oklahoma

FRED J. DOPHEIDE, C.L.U., Director of Continuing Education, American Society of Chartered Life Underwriters/American College of Life Underwriters, Bryn Mawr, Pennsylvania

JOHN K. DYER, JR., F.S.A., Consulting Actuary, Beach Haven, New Jersey

RICHARD A. EDWARDS, Vice President-Government Relations, Metropolitan Life Insurance Company, New York, New York

DARRELL D. EICHHOFF, C.L.U., Executive Vice President, Metropolitan Life Insurance Company, New York, New York

DR. ROBERT D. EILERS, C.L.U., Executive Director, The Leonard Davis Institute of Health Economics, University of Pennsylvania, Philadelphia, Pennsylvania

COY G. EKLUND, C.L.U., President, Equitable Life Assurance Society of the United States, New York, New York

JARVIS FARLEY, Chairman of the Board, Massachusetts Indemnity and Life Insurance Company, Wellesley, Massachusetts

E. J. FAULKNER, President, Woodmen Accident and Life Company, Lincoln, Nebraska

DR. JOHN T. FEY, President, National Life Insurance Company, Montpelier, Vermont

JOHN H. FILER, Chairman, Aetna Life & Casualty, Hartford, Connecticut

ROBERT J. FITZWILLIAM, Counsel, New England Mutual Life Insurance Company, Boston, Massachusetts

J. F. FOLLMANN, JR., Vice President, Information and Research Division, Health Insurance Association of America, New York, New York

BENJAMIN M. GASTON, C.L.U., Consultant, American College of Life Underwriters, Bryn Mawr, Pennsylvania

JEROME S. GOLDEN, F.S.A., Actuary, Equitable Variable Life Insurance Company, New York, New York

W. D. GRANT, C.L.U., Chairman, BMA Corporation, Kansas City, Missouri

DR. DAVIS W. GREGG, C.L.U., President, American College of Life Underwriters, Bryn Mawr, Pennsylvania

JANICE E. GREIDER, C.L.U., Counsel, State Farm Life & Accident Assurance Company, Bloomington, Illinois

RALPH L. GUSTIN, JR., Senior Vice President and General Counsel, John Hancock Mutual Life Insurance Company, Boston, Massachusetts

STANTON G. HALE, Chairman of the Board, Pacific Mutual Life Insurance Company, Los Angeles, California

DR. CHARLES P. HALL, JR., C.L.U., C.P.C.U., Professor of Insurance and Risk, School of Business Administration, Temple University, Philadelphia, Pennsylvania

WILLIAM B. HARMAN, JR., Vice President-Law, American Life Insurance Association, Washington, D. C.

WILLIAM HARMELIN, C.L.U., President, Business & Estate Planning Consultants, Inc., New York, New York

LESLIE P. HEMRY, President, Health Insurance Association of America, Washington, D. C.

CHARLES C. HINCKLEY, Walsh & Hinckley Company, Detroit, Michigan

BURKETT W. HUEY, President, Life Insurance Agency Management Association, Hartford, Connecticut

W. R. HUEY, JR., C.L.U., President, Research & Review Service of America, Inc., Indianapolis, Indiana

DOUGLAS B. HUNTER, Second Vice President, Group Pension Department, Connecticut General Life Insurance Company, Hartford, Connecticut

G. DAVID HURD, Vice President, Bankers Life Company, Des Moines, Iowa

JAMES B. IRVINE, JR., C.L.U., President, The Irvine Company, Inc., Chattanooga, Tennessee

PAUL H. JACKSON, F.S.A., Actuary, The Wyatt Company, Washington, D. C.

ROBERT T. JACKSON, F.S.A., President, Phoenix Mutual Life Insurance Company, Hartford, Connecticut

JAMES B. JACOBSON, C.L.U., Senior Vice President, Prudential Insurance Company of America, Newark, New Jersey

DEAN W. JEFFERS, General Chairman and Chief Executive Officer, Nationwide Insurance Companies, Columbus, Ohio

T. H. KIRKPATRICK, F.S.A., Vice President and Senior Actuary, Paul Revere Life Insurance Company, Worcester, Massachusetts

LAWRENCE G. KNECHT, Kiefer, Hunter, Knecht & Williams, Cleveland, Ohio

DR. JOHN D. LONG, C.L.U., C.P.C.U., Professor of Insurance, Graduate School of Business, Indiana University, Bloomington, Indiana

DR. VANE B. LUCAS, C.L.U., C.P.C.U., Senior Vice President for Academic Affairs, American College of Life Underwriters, Bryn Mawr, Pennsylvania

WILLIAM B. LYNCH, C.L.U., Lynch & Nelson, Los Angeles, California

CHARLES B. McCAFFREY, C.L.U., Lecturer on Insurance, The Wharton School of the University of Pennsylvania, Philadelphia, Pennsylvania

JOHN J. McCUISTION, Second Vice President for Health Underwriting, Woodmen Accident and Life Company, Lincoln, Nebraska

DR. DAN M. McGILL, C.L.U., Frederick H. Ecker Professor of Life Insurance, The Wharton School of the University of Pennsylvania, Philadelphia, Pennsylvania

MILES W. MCNALLY, C.L.U., President, McNally, Inc., Minneapolis, Minnesota

FRANK B. MAHER, President, John Hancock Mutual Life Insurance Company, Boston, Massachusetts

DR. ROBERT I. MEHR, Professor of Finance, College of Commerce and Business Administration, University of Illinois at Urbana-Champaign, Illinois

DR. JOSEPH J. MELONE, C.L.U., C.P.C.U., Vice President, Prudential Insurance Company of America, Boston, Massachusetts

MORTON D. MILLER, F.S.A., Executive Vice President and Chief Actuary, Equitable Life Assurance Society of the United States, New York, New York

PAUL S. MILLS, C.L.U., Executive Vice President and Managing Director, American Society of Chartered Life Underwriters, Bryn Mawr, Pennsylvania

STUART A. MONROE, C.L.U., Consultant, Winnetka, Illinois

E. J. MOORHEAD, F.S.A., Vice President (retired), Integon Life Insurance Corporation, Winston-Salem, North Carolina

ROBERT J. MYERS, F.S.A., Professor of Actuarial Science, Temple University, Philadelphia, Pennsylvania

BLAKE T. NEWTON, JR., President, Institute of Life Insurance, New York, New York

PAUL A. NORTON, C.L.U., Executive Vice President, New York Life Insurance Company, New York, New York

GAYLORD L. PAINE, C.L.U., Senior Vice President, Connecticut Mutual Life Insurance Company, Hartford, Connecticut

WILLIAM K. PAYNTER, Executive Vice President, Institute of Life Insurance, New York, New York

HARRY PHILLIPS, III, C.L.U., C.P.C.U., H & R Phillips, Inc., New York, New York

JOHN J. PLUMB, C.L.U., President, Channing Company, Inc., Houston, Texas

JAMES P. POOLE, C.L.U., President, James P. Poole and Company, Inc., Atlanta, Georgia

LORAN E. POWELL, C.L.U., President, Life Underwriter Training Council, Washington, D. C.

DR. WILLIAM H. RABEL, C.L.U., Economic Affairs Officer, Insurance Branch, United Nations Conference on Trade and Development, Geneva, Switzerland

CHARLES F. B. RICHARDSON, F.S.A., A.I.A., Vice President and Actuary, H. W. Black & Associates, Inc., Nashville, Tennessee

GORDON K. ROSE, C.L.U., Vice President for Student Development, American College of Life Underwriters, Bryn Mawr, Pennsylvania

GERALD K. RUGGER, F.S.A., President, Home Life Insurance Company, New York, New York

FRANK P. SAMFORD, JR., C.L.U., President, Liberty National Life Insurance Company, Birmingham, Alabama

WILLIAM H. SCHMIDT, F.S.A., Associate Professor of Actuarial Science, School of Business Administration, Georgia State University, Atlanta, Georgia

DR. STUART SCHWARZSCHILD, C.L.U., C.P.C.U., Professor of Insurance, School of Business Administration, Georgia State University, Atlanta, Georgia

RICHARD M. SELLERS, F.S.A., President, Commonwealth Life Insurance Company, Louisville, Kentucky

GERALD H. SHERMAN, Silverstein & Mullens, Washington, D. C.

W. LEE SHIELD, President, American Life Insurance Association, Washington, D. C.

WALTER SHUR, F.S.A., Senior Vice President in Charge of Individual Insurance Operations, New York Life Insurance Company, New York, New York

LEONARD SILVERSTEIN, Silverstein & Mullens, Washington, D. C.

THOMAS C. SIMONS, C.L.U., Senior Vice President, Connecticut General Life Insurance Company, Hartford, Connecticut

*BENJAMIN F. SMALL, Executive Vice President, American Life Insurance Association, Washington, D. C.

C. CARNEY SMITH, C.L.U., Executive Vice President, National Association of Life Underwriters, Washington, D. C.

J. CARLTON SMITH, C.L.U., Vice President and Educational Director, Southwestern Life Insurance Company, Dallas, Texas

THAXTER P. SPENCER, Vice President and Assistant Secretary, New England Mutual Life Insurance Company, Boston, Massachusetts

DR. ARMAND C. STALNAKER, C.L.U., President, General American Life Insurance Company, St. Louis, Missouri

WALTER W. STEFFEN, F.S.A., Senior Vice President, Lincoln National Life Insurance Company, Fort Wayne, Indiana

L. G. STEINBECK, C.L.U., Senior Vice President and Treasurer, American College of Life Underwriters, Bryn Mawr, Pennsylvania

*CHARLES M. STERNHELL, F.S.A., Executive Vice President, New York Life Insurance Company, New York, New York

GORDON W. THOMAS, C.L.U., Vice President, John Hancock Mutual Life Insurance Company, Boston, Massachusetts

JOHN S. THOMPSON, JR., F.S.A., Vice President and Actuary, North American Company for Life and Health Insurance, Chicago, Illinois

JOHN O. TODD, C.L.U., Senior Partner, The John O. Todd Organization, Northwestern Mutual Life Insurance Company, Evanston, Illinois

RAYMOND F. TRIPLETT, C.L.U., Field Underwriter, New York Life Insurance Company, San Jose, California

CHARLES L. TROWBRIDGE, F.S.A., Chief Actuary, Social Security Administration, Department of Health, Education, and Welfare, Washington, D. C.

JULIUS VOGEL, F.S.A., Vice President and Actuary, Prudential Insurance Company of America, Newark, New Jersey

LELAND T. WAGGONER, C.L.U., Senior Vice President, Home Life Insurance Company, New York, New York

HARRY WALKER, F.S.A., President, Equitable Variable Life Insurance Company, New York, New York

CHARLES B. H. WATSON, F.S.A., Actuary, The Wyatt Company, Washington, D. C.

DR. C. ARTHUR WILLIAMS, JR., Dean, School of Business Administration, University of Minnesota, Minneapolis, Minnesota

JAMES R. WILLIAMS, Vice President and General Manager, Health Insurance Institute, New York, New York

WILLIAM G. WILLIAMS, Director, Group Sales Research, Provident Mutual Life Insurance Company, Philadelphia, Pennsylvania

PAUL L. WISE, Vice President and Counsel, Fidelity Mutual Life Insurance Company, Philadelphia, Pennsylvania

FREDERICK R. H. WITHERBY, Vice President and General Counsel, New England Mutual Life Insurance Company, Boston, Massachusetts

MARSHALL I. WOLPER, C.L.U., President, The Marshall Wolper Company, Miami, Florida

ARTHUR J. WOJTA, C.L.U., Superintendent of Advanced Underwriting, Northwestern Mutual Life Insurance Company, Milwaukee, Wisconsin

V. N. WOOLFOLK, Attorney at Law, New York, New York

DR. EDMUND L. ZALINSKI, C.L.U., President, Zalinski, Lloyd and Pahl, Inc., Drexel Hill, Pennsylvania

DR. JAMES B. ZISCHKE, Chairman, The Zischke Organization, Inc., San Francisco, California

---

*Deceased.

Contents

List of Illustrations   xxxv

Part I
ECONOMIC SECURITY AND INSURANCE   1

1. **Economic Security: Patterns and Philosophies,** *Davis W. Gregg*   3

   The Meaning of Security. Man's Hierarchy of Needs. Human Needs and Economic Security. The American Economic Security System: *An Arbitrary Definition. The Tripod of American Economic Security. Security Expenditures 1950-70.* Issues and Unanswered Questions: *A Wide-Angle Perceptual Lens.*

2. **Human Life Values,** *Kenneth Black, Jr.*   17

   The Concept of Human Capital: *Current Economic Interest. Significance of Human Capital Valuation. Early Efforts to Estimate Economic Value of Human Life.* The Human Life Value Concept: *Human Life Value Defined. Human Life Values and Property Values. Appraising Human Life Values.*

3. **Protection Functions of Life and Health Insurance,** *William T. Beadles*   27

   Pooling of Risks and Law of Large Numbers. Insurance versus Gambling. Protection for Individual and Business Needs: *Estate Clearance Fund. Income for the Family. Disability Income. Medical Expenses. Business Insurance.* The "Life Will." Life Insurance as Property: *Immediate Estate Creation Feature. Creditor Protection. Tax Treatment. Guaranteed Value at Death. Significance.*

4. **Savings Functions of Life Insurance,** *Vane B. Lucas*   39

   Nature of the Life Insurance Savings Element: *Level Premium Concept. Valuation of Reserves and Cash Surrender Values. Semicompulsory Nature of Premium Payments.* Characteristics of the Life Insurance Savings Element: *Safety of Principal. Liquidity. Yield. Maintenance of Credit. Special Characteristics.* Special Uses of Life Insurance Savings: *Gifts of Life Insurance. Business Uses of Life Insurance.* Savings-Investment Priorities and Life Insurance: *Balanced Savings-Investment Program. Life Insurance and Broadened Financial Services.*

Part II
INDIVIDUAL LIFE INSURANCE AND ANNUITIES   53

√ 5. **Contracts—Term Insurance,** *William T. Beadles*   55   5/13/79

   Nature of Term Insurance: *Duration. Term Riders and Policy Forms. Renewable Term Insurance. Convertible Term Insurance. Term Policy Features. Higher Mortality on Term Insurance. Premiums.* Advantages and Disadvantages to the Insured. "Buy Term and Invest the Difference."

✓6.   **Contracts—Whole Life and Endowment, *C. Arthur Williams, Jr.*   66**

Whole Life Insurance: *Types of Whole Life Contracts. The Level Premium Concept. Flexible Provisions in Whole Life Contracts. Uses of Straight Life Insurance. Uses of Limited-Payment Life Insurance. Modified Life and Graded-Premium Contracts. Preferred Risks Contracts and "Specials."* Endowment Insurance: *Endowment Concepts. Types of Endowment Insurance Policies. Uses of Endowment Insurance. Misuse of Endowment Insurance.*

✓7.   **Contracts—Annuities, *Robert I. Mehr*   78**

The Annuity Principle. Classification of Annuities: *Method of Paying Premiums. Disposition of Proceeds. Date Benefits Begin. Number of Lives Covered. Units in Which Pay-Out Benefits Are Expressed.* The Annuity Policy. Uses of Annuities. Limitations of Annuities.

8.   **Contracts for Special Needs, *Julius Vogel*   92**

Need for Special Contracts. Contracts for Use Where Current Insurance Needs Exceed Probable Future Insurance Needs: *Level Term Coverage. Decreasing Term Coverage.* Contracts for Use Where Current Insurance Needs Are Less Than Probable Future Insurance Needs: *Jumping Juvenile Policy. Guaranteed Insurability Rider.* Contracts Oriented toward Savings or Retirement: *Juvenile Educational Endowment Policy. Retirement Annuity Contract. Retirement Income Contract.* Contracts That Minimize Initial Premium Outlay: *Modified, Step-Rate, or Graded Premium Plan. High Early Cash Value Policy. Interim Term Insurance.* Family Policies. Other Special Contracts: *Variations of Participating Contracts. Variations of Nonparticipating Contracts. Contracts with Special Change Provisions. Return of Premium Policy and Return of Cash Value Policy. Tailor-Made Term Insurance Policy. Graded Death Benefit Policy. Joint Life Policy.*

9.   **Legal Concepts and Contract Provisions, *Janice E. Greider*   106**

The Formation of a Contract: *Competent Parties. Mutual Assent. Consideration. Form Required by Law. Insurable Interest Required.* Insurable Interest. Misrepresentation, Concealment, and Warranty: *Concealment. Representations and Warranties. Special Statutes.* Waiver and Estoppel: *Waiver. Estoppel.* The Incontestable Clause: *Interpretation and Development. When the Contestable Period Starts Running. The Meaning of a "Contest." Reformation. Incontestability and Fraud.* Other Required Policy Provisions: *Entire Contract Provision. Grace Period Provision. Misstatement-of-Age Provision. Reinstatement Provision.* Other Basic Policy Provisions: *Suicide Provision. Assignment Provision. Ownership Provision. War Clauses. Payor Clause. Policy Change Provisions.*

10.   **Probability, Mortality, and Money Concepts, *Charles M. Sternhell and Walter Shur*   121**

Probability Theory. *Definition of Probability. Rules of Probability. Law of Large Numbers. Distribution of Insurance Claims.* Mortality: *Mortality Rates. Factors Affecting Mortality Rates. Mortality Tables. Expectation of Life.* Money Concepts: *Accumulated Value of Money. Discounted or Present Value of Money. Annuities.* Combination of Probability, Mortality, and Money Concepts.

11.   **Gross Premiums, *Robert G. Boeckner*   140**

Gross Premiums for Nonparticipating Life Insurance: *Background. Basic Considerations and Requirements. Factors and Assumptions for Life Insurance Premiums. Gross Premium Formulas. Calculation and Testing of Gross Premiums.* Gross Premiums for Participating Policies: *Relationship of Premiums and Dividends. Comparison with Nonparticipating Insurance. Assumptions. General Considerations. Interrelationships. Testing. Developing the Final Scale of Premiums.* Gross Premiums for Annuities: *Single-Premium Immediate Annuities. Deferred Annuities.* Significance of Gross Premiums.

12. **Reserves,** *William H. Schmidt* **158**

Level Premium Reserves: *Calculating the Annual Premium. The Reserve Calculated Prospectively. The Reserve Calculated Retrospectively. Initial, Terminal, and Mean Reserves.* Reserves Based on Nonlevel Valuation Premiums: *Full Preliminary Term Method. Modified Preliminary Term Reserves.* Effect on Reserves of Changes in Assumptions: *Changes in Interest Rate. Change in Mortality Table. Other Changes in Assumptions.* Other Reserves and Related Considerations: *Deficiency Reserves. Natural Reserves. Cash Values and Reserves. Company Reserves as a Measure of Solvency.* Summary.

13. **Nonforfeiture Values and Policy Loans,** *Charles F. B. Richardson* **173**

Historical Development of Nonforfeiture Legislation. Concepts Underlying Current Nonforfeiture Value Practices. Nonforfeiture Values (Options): *Cash Surrender Values. Extended Term Insurance. Reduced Paid-Up Insurance.* Related Values: *Policy Loans. Automatic Premium Loans.*

14. **Surplus and Dividends,** *Robert T. Jackson* **184**

Definitions. Nature of Policyowner Dividends. Determination of Divisible Surplus. Individual Dividends: *Three-Factor Method. The Three-Factor Formula. Terminal Dividends. Statutory Requirements. Practical Considerations.* Dividend Options. Health Insurance Dividends.

15. **Risk Selection and Substandard Risks,** *Gaylord L. Paine* **194**

Selection Objectives: *Antiselection. Standard; Substandard; Unacceptable Risks. Individual Company Objectives. Social Objectives.* Factors of Selection: *Mortality Classes. Age. Sex. Family History. Build (Height and Weight). Medical History and Impairments. Occupation and Avocation. Aviation. Military Service. Foreign Residence. Recent Immigration. Use of Alcohol and Drugs. Driving Record. Departure from Social Mores. Financial Considerations.* The Tools of Selection: *Application. Agents' Reports. Consumer Investigative Reports. Attending Physicians' Statements. Medical Information Bureau.* Pricing Systems for Extra Mortality: *Patterns of Mortality. Substandard Pricing Methods.* Significance.

16. **Contract Cost and Benefit Comparisons,** *E. J. Moorhead* **211**

Ways in Which Contracts Differ: *Participating and Nonparticipating Contracts. Benefits Other Than Death Benefits.* Comparing New Contracts That Are Similar: *Current Dividend Scales and Dividend Histories. Traditional Method of Cost Comparison—Description and Criticisms. Methods of Cost Comparison Proposed in Response to Criticisms. Industry Study: The Interest-Adjusted Method. Rationale of Comparison Methods Other Than the Traditional Method.* Checklist of Factors Requiring Attention. Comparing New Contracts That Are Dissimilar: *Term and Permanent Contracts. Endowment and Whole Life Contracts. Participating and Nonparticipating Contracts. Collateral Contract Features.* Comparing New Contracts with Contracts in Force: *Nature of the Problem. Regulation.* Conclusion.

Part III
VARIABLE LIFE INSURANCE, VARIABLE ANNUITIES,
AND MUTUAL FUNDS **225**

17. **Variable Life Insurance,** *Harry Walker and Jerome G. Golden* **227**

Development in Other Countries. Early Development in the United States. Contract Design: *Alternative Approaches. Special Contract Provisions.* Gross Premiums. Underwriting and Administrative Aspects. State and Federal Regulation. Outlook.

18. **Variable Annuities—Principles and Practices,** *Paul A. Campbell* **240**

Nature of Variable Annuities: *Variable Annuity Concept. Early Variable Annuity Plans.* Types of Variable Annuities: *Individual and Group Variable Annuities. Single-Premium Immediate Variable Annuity. Single-Premium Deferred Variable Annuity. Periodic-Payment Variable Annuity.* Guarantees: *Consumer Protection and Service.* Variable Annuity Contract Provisions. Variable Annuity Regulatory Environment: *Federal Regulation. Regulation by State Insurance Departments. Impact of Regulation on Variable Annuity Operations. Corporate Structure and Management of Variable Annuities. Role of Segregated Accounts. Pricing Aspects of Variable Annuities. Installation and Administration of Variable Annuities.* Potential Variable Annuity Markets. The Significance of Variable Annuities: *To the Consumer. To the Life Underwriter. To the Company.*

19. **Mutual Funds—Principles and Practices,** *John J. Plumb* **257**

Growth of the Mutual Fund Industry. Definition and Purpose of a Mutual Fund Company. Classification of Mutual Fund Companies by Investment Objective. Organization and Structure of a Mutual Fund Company: *The Mutual Fund Company. The Investment Advisor (or Management Company). The Custodian. The National Distributor (or Underwriter).* How Mutual Funds are Purchased and Accumulated: *Bid Price and Asked Price. Three Ways to Purchase Mutual Fund Shares.* Special Features and Services: *Quantity Discounts. Right of Accumulation. Redemption Privilege. Exchange or Conversion Privilege. Reinvestments of Income Dividends and Capital Gains Distributions. Regular Withdrawal Plans. Custodial Accounts under the Keogh Act. Prototype Corporate Retirement Plans.* Mutual Funds and Income Taxes: *Mutual Fund Companies. The Shareholder's Tax Liability on Income Dividends and Net Realized Capital Gains.* How Mutual Fund Companies Are Regulated: *The Federal Securities Act of 1933. The Federal Securities Exchange Act of 1934. The Investment Company Act of 1940. State Laws. The Securities and Exchange Commission Statement of Policy.* Financial Planning and Mutual Funds: *Mutual Funds in Programming Personal Needs. Mutual Funds in Estate Planning. Mutual Funds and Business Organizations. Mutual Funds and Institutions.* Sales of Mutual Funds by Life Underwriters.

Part IV
INDIVIDUAL HEALTH INSURANCE **273**

20. **Individual Disability Income Insurance,** *Brooks Chandler* **275**

History and Development. Extent of Coverage. Basic Provisions: *Insuring Agreement and Definition of Disability. Elimination Period and Payment Duration. Benefit Amounts.* Other Provisions: *Overinsurance Provisions. Exclusions. Guaranteed Insurability Provisions.* Special Forms: *Waiver of Premium Disability Income Benefits under Life Policies. Franchise Disability Insurance. Nonoccupational Coverage. Mortgage Protection. Industrial Disability Insurance. Health Care Supplements. Modified Premium Plans.* Underwriting: *Underwriting Standard Risks. Underwriting Substandard Risks.* Renewal Provisions: *Cancellable Contracts. Guaranteed Renewable with the Right of the Insurer to Change Premiums by Class. Noncancellable Policies.* Administration of Benefit Payments. Recent Developments: *Business Overhead Insurance. Business Interest Purchase. Cash Value and Return of Premium Provisions. Inflation Benefit.*

21. **Individual Medical Expense Insurance,** *John S. Thompson, Jr.* **290**

Development. Forms of Medical Expense Insurance: *Hospital Expense Benefit. Surgical Expense Benefit. In-Hospital Medical Expense Benefit. Nursing Expense Benefit. Extended Care Benefit. Hospital Indemnity Benefit. Major Medical Expense Insurance. Comprehensive Medical Expense Insurance.* Characteristics of Medical Expense Policies: *Renewability and Term. Probationary Period. Definition of Hospital. Successive Periods of Hospitalization. Exclusions.* Risk Selection. Summary.

22. **Legal Concepts and Contract Provisions,** *Richard P. Cooley*   **303**

Contract Principles Applicable. Formation of Contract. Policy Contract: *Face or Filing Back. Insuring Clause. Consideration Clause. Renewability Clause. Payment of Premiums. Eligibility, Additional Family Members, and Termination. Benefit Clause. Exceptions and Reductions. Preexisting Conditions.* Uniform Policy Provisions: *Required Statutory Provisions. Optional Statutory Provisions.* Nature of the Contract upon Renewal.

23. **Premiums and Reserves,** *T. H. Kirkpatrick*   **320**

Net Premiums. Reserves: *Active Life Reserve. Disabled Life Reserve. Other Claims Reserves. Deficiency Reserve. Practical Considerations.* Verification of Claims Assumptions: *Loss Ratios. Actual to Expected. New Experience Tables.* Gross Premiums for Noncancellable Policies: *Basic Elements Affecting Premiums. Methods of Calculation.* Substandard Premiums. Practical Problems in Rate Making: *Lack of Experience Data. Adaptation of Table to Specific Policy. Practical Limits on Expenses. Conservative versus Realistic Assumptions. Secular Trends. Provision for Catastrophes. Completion of Premium Schedules.* Regulation.

24. **Risk Selection and Substandard Risks,** *John C. Angle and John J. McCuistion*   **333**

Nature of Health Insurance Underwriting. Selection Outcomes. Substandard Risks: *Impairment Exclusion Riders. Extra Premiums. Modification of Coverage. Evaluating Experience.* Risk Selection Factors: *Applicant's Health. Occupation. Habits. Portion of Income Insurable. Moral Hazard.* Sources of Information: *Application. Attending Physician's Statement. Medical Examination. Other Sources of Information.*

**Part V
GROUP LIFE AND HEALTH INSURANCE**   **349**

25. **Fundamental Characteristics of Group Insurance,** *Davis W. Gregg*   **351**

Group and Individual Contrasted. Types of Group Life and Health Insurance: *Group Life Insurance. Group Health Insurance.* Basic Features: *Eligible Groups. Size Specifications. Benefit Schedules. Financing.* Group Selection: *Theory of Group Selection. Departures from Group Selection Theory.* Growth and Significance: *Scope of Group Coverages. Forces Underlying Growth. Significance.*

26. **Group Life Insurance,** *William G. Williams*   **372**

Group Term Life Insurance: *Employee Coverage. Dependent Coverage. Advantages and Limitations of Group Term Life Insurance.* Group Creditor Life Insurance: *Eligible Creditors, Loans, and Purchases. Creditor Modifications of Conventional Term Plan.* Group Paid-Up: *Allocation of Cost and Treatment of Cash Values. Provisions for Continuing Protection. Advantages and Limitations.* Group Ordinary Life Insurance: *Tax Aspects. Provisions for Continuing Protection. Advantages and Limitations.* Group Survivor Income Benefit Insurance: *Coverage and Benefits. Provisions for Continuing Protection. Assignment. Advantages and Limitations.* Group Accidental Death and Dismemberment Insurance: *Provisions for Continuing Protection. Limitations.* Voluntary Accidental Death and Dismemberment Insurance: *Limitations. Related Factors.* Federal Employees' Group Life Insurance Plan: *Benefit Structure and Amounts. Eligibility and Enrollment. Cost. Insurers. Provisions for Continuing Protection.* Servicemen's Group Life Insurance Plan: *Eligibility and Enrollment. Benefit Structure and Amounts. Cost. Insurers. Provisions for Continuing Protection.*

27. Group Disability Income Insurance, *Morton D. Miller*   392

Nature and Development. Short-Term Disability Income: *Definition of Disability. Duration of Benefits. Amount of Benefits. Exclusion and Limitations. Occupational Supplement. Termination of Coverage. Cost Control Procedures.* Long-Term Disability Income: *Definition of Disability. Duration of Benefits. Amount of Benefits. Integration with Social Security. Exclusions and Limitations. Termination of Coverage.* State Statutory Disability Income Plans. Group Creditor Disability Insurance: *Determination and Duration of Benefits. Exclusions and Limitations.*

28. Group Medical Expense Insurance, *Charles P. Hall, Jr.*   413

Nature and Development: *Origins. Growth and Competition. Merging Philosophies. Prepaid Group Practice.* Evolving Group Concepts. Basic Medical Expense Coverages: *Group Hospital Expense Insurance. Group Surgical Expense Insurance. Other Medical Expense Charges. Other Group Health Insurance Benefits.* Broad Medical Expense Coverages: *Major Medical Expense Insurance. Comprehensive Medical Expense Insurance. Patterns of Integration.* Prospective Future Developments: *Persons Covered. Breadth and Extent of Coverage. Costs. Co-operation.*

29. Group Underwriting and Reinsurance, *Gordon W. Thomas*   433

Group Underwriting: *Statutory Requirements. Nonstatutory Underwriting Factors: Characteristics of Acceptable Groups. Plan Design. Underwriting Variations by Type of Policyholder.* Underwriting Variations by Coverage: *Group Life Insurance. Disability Income Plans. Medical Expense Plans.* Group Creditor Life and Disability Insurance. Group Reinsurance: *Catastrophic Accident Risk. Sharing Portion of Normal Risk. Sharing Business for Nonrisk Reasons. The Treaty.*

30. Legal Concepts and Taxation, *William H. Rabel*   450

Regulation: *State Insurance Departments. Regulatory Jurisdiction. Group Life Insurance Regulation. Group Health Insurance Regulation. Other Group Insurance Regulation.* Master Contract and Certificate: *Formation, Amendment, and Termination of the Contract. Policyholder's Provisions. Insured's Provisions. Claim Provisions.* Taxation: *Group Term Life Insurance. Permanent Forms of Group Life Insurance. Group Health Insurance.*

31. Group Premiums, Experience Rating, and Reserves, *Donald D. Cody and Herbert J. Boothroyd*   471

The Group Insurance Product. General Theory of Pricing in Group Insurance. Initial Premium Rates: *Group Life Insurance. Group Health Coverages. Recognition of Expenses by Size of Case. Extended Rate Guarantees.* Experience Rating: *Factors in Experience Rating. Experience Rating Formulas. Treatment of High Limits. Renewal Rating of Group Insurance. Rating of Transfer Cases. Dividends and Retrospective Rate Credits.* Group Reserves: *Reserves for Annual Statements. Reserves for Experience Rating.* Other Group Rating and Reserve Concepts: *Funding of Life Insurance for Retired Employees. Minimum Premium Plans. Modified Premium—Dividend Plans.* Illustrative Calculations.

32. Group Insurance Marketing, *James B. Jacobson*   494

Nature of the Group Market: *Importance and Growth. Characteristics. Description of the Market.* The Marketing System: *Group Buyer. Brokers and Consultants. Insurance Company Agents. Group Insurance Administrators. Group Representatives. Direct Marketing. Marketing by Mail and Other Mass Media.* Group Insurance Compensation: *Commission Levels. Types of Commissions. Small Case Commissions. Group Permanent Commissions.* The Sales Process: *Factors Motivating the Group Insurance Purchase. Steps Leading to the Group Insurance Purchase. After the Purchase.* Insurance Company Organizational Structure: *General Considerations. Home Office. Field.* Entering the Group Market: *Reasons for Entry. Problems to Be Considered.*

Part VI
PENSIONS AND OTHER QUALIFIED DEFERRED
COMPENSATION PLANS 511

33. **Nature and Development of Private Pensions,** *Joseph J. Melone* 513

Economic Problem of Old Age: *Increasing Longevity. Nature of Risk of Excessive Longevity. Employment Opportunities. Capacity to Save.* Rationale of Private Pensions. Development of Industrial Pension Plans. Current Scope of Private Pensions: *Coverage of Plans. Benefit Levels. Security of Benefits. Funding Plan Benefits.* Pension Plan Disclosure Laws: *Federal Welfare and Pension Plans Disclosure Act. State Disclosure Acts.* Accounting for Pension Costs.

34. **Pension Plan Design and Funding Considerations,** *Everett T. Allen, Jr.* 529

Basic Plan Features: *Eligibility Requirements. Retirement Ages. Retirement Benefits. Death Benefits. Disability Benefits. Severance of Employment Benefits. Employee Contributions. General Plan Provisions.* Actuarial Cost Considerations: *Estimated Cost versus Ultimate Cost of Plan. Cost Assumptions. Choice of Assumptions. Actuarial Cost Methods.*

35. **Profit Sharing and Thrift Savings Plans,** *James B. Zischke* 548

Profit Sharing Plans: *Differences between Pension and Profit Sharing Plans. Investment of Plan Funds. Combination Pension-Profit Sharing Programs.* Thrift Savings Plans: *Standard Thrift Savings Plans. Satellite or Voluntary Thrift Savings Plans. Investment Provisions. Advantages of Thrift Savings Plans.*

36. **Pensions and Profit Sharing for the Self-Employed,** *Thaxter P. Spencer* 562

Nature of Plans: *Choice of Funding Methods and Vehicles. Definitions. Contributions and Deductions. Excess Contributions. Plan Design. Limitations on Form and Methods of Payment. Prohibited Transactions. Taxation. Discontinuance of Contributions and Disposition of Plan Assets.* Continuing Significance of Plans for the Self-Employed.

37. **Tax Deferred Annuities,** *Charles C. Hinckley* 575

Benefits Available. Eligible Employers: *Internal Revenue Code Description. Regulations. Determining Tax Exempt Status. Employees of Government Institutions Other Than Public Schools.* Eligible Employees. Contracts. Tax Deferment and Exclusion Allowance Formula: *Definition of Benefit. Exclusion Allowance Formula. Includable Compensation. Years of Service. Adjustments for Contributions to Tax-Free Retirement Plan in Previous Years. Practical Considerations.* Additional Income, Estate, and Gift Tax Benefits: *$5,000 Income Exclusion. Estate Tax Exclusion. Gift Tax Exclusion. Tax Deferred Appreciation.* The Problems of Funding; Salary Reductions. Income Taxation upon Receipt under a Tax Deferred Annuity: *Annuity without Incidental Life Insurance. Annuity with Incidental Life Insurance.* Terminal Retirement Funding. Termination of Employment. Conclusion.

38. **Funding Instruments—Individual Policy and Combination Plans,** *Verne J. Arends* 587

Individual Policies: *Nature of Individual Policies. Types of Policies.* Combination Plans. Important Considerations: *Trust Agreement. Effect of Investment Experience. Effect of Employee Turnover. Employer's Options and Actions. Individual Policies for Nonqualified Plans.*

39. **Funding Instruments—Group Permanent and Group Deferred Annuity Contracts,** *G. David Hurd*   596

Group Permanent Contracts: *Original Plans. Group Permanent Retirement Income Contract. Group Permanent Whole Life and Conversion Fund.* Group Deferred Annuities: *Classical Group Deferred Annuity. Money Purchase Plans. Funding for the Individual Employee. Variations of the Group Deferred Annuity.*

40. **Funding Instruments—Deposit Administration Contracts and Separate Accounts,** *Douglas B. Hunter*   614

Plan Specifications: *Eligibility. Employee Contributions. Retirement Age. Pension Benefits. Withdrawal Benefits. Death Benefits. Disability Benefits. Discontinuance Provisions.* Underwriting and Contractual Provisions: *Contract Holder. Minimums and Maximums. Inclusion of Plan Specifications. Contributory Plans. Deposit Administration Fund. Guarantees. Discontinuance of Contributions.* Experience Rating. Immediate Participation Guarantee. Supplementary Deposit Administration. Separate Accounts. Split Funding. Accumulator.

41. **Funding Instruments—Trust Fund Plans,** *Paul H. Jackson*   627

Nature of the Trust Agreement: *Investment of the Trust Fund. Powers of the Trustee. Payments from the Trust. Record Keeping. Miscellaneous Provisions. Amendment and Termination.* Plan Document: *General Rules. Benefit Formula. Early Retirement. Disability Retirement. Death after Retirement. Death before Retirement. Vested Rights. Adjustments to Benefits after Retirement. Plan Termination. Past Service. Labor Agreement.* Actuarial Aspects: *Funding Methods. Actuarial Valuation. Valuation of Assets. Measurement of Investment Performance.* Responsibility: *The Actuary. The Employer. The Union. Multiemployer Plans.* Current Problem Areas. Significance.

Part VII
BUSINESS USES OF LIFE AND HEALTH INSURANCE   645

42. **Key Man Protection,** *J. Carlton Smith*   647

The Nature of Key Man Life Insurance: *A Form of Business Insurance. The Human Factor in Business Success. Factors That Make a Key Man.* Services of Key Man Life Insurance: *Provides Indemnity in Case of Loss. Accumulates a Business Emergency Fund. Strengthens the Credit of the Firm. Provides a Means of Funding a Deferred Compensation Arrangement for the Key Man.* Key Man Life Insurance Arrangements: *The Policy Provisions. Use of Existing Life Insurance. Disposition of the Policy if the Key Man Leaves the Firm. Insurable Interest. Valuation of a Key Man for Insurance Purposes.* Taxation of Key Man Life Insurance: *Federal Income Tax. Federal Estate Tax.* Key Man Health Insurance: *The Need. Purpose of Key Man Health Insurance. Indemnification for Loss through Life Insurance. Indemnity for Loss through Health Insurance. Indemnity through Health Insurance—An Example. The Indemnity Motive—Practical Limitations. The Indemnity Motive—Conclusions. Key Man Disability Indemnification —Conclusions.*

43. **Nonqualified Deferred Compensation Plans,** *Charles B. McCaffrey*   662

Nature of Deferred Compensation. Contracts and Provisions. Income Tax Considerations: *Constructive Receipt. Economic Benefit. Bare Promise versus Commerical Annuity. Cash and Accrual Accounting. Rights Vested or Contingent.* Funding the Deferred Compensation Agreement: *Intra-Company Funding. Use of Life Insurance.* Cost Considerations: *What It Costs the Corporation. Employee Benefits.* Summary.

44. Split-Dollar Plans, *William B. Lynch*   676

Background. How Split-Dollar Works: *Basic Patterns. Pattern Variations.* Major Systems: *Collateral Assignment System. Endorsement System.* Putting the Plan Together. Taxation: *Income Taxation. Estate Taxation. Gift Taxation.* Case Examples of Split-Dollar Plans.

45. Business Continuation—Unincorporated Business Interest, *Arthur J. Wojta*   690

The Proprietorship: *A Family Business. The Disability Hazard. The Mature Proprietorship—A Crossroads. Sale to a Key Man. Keeping the Business in the Family. Liquidating the Business. Planning for the Sale of the Business at the Death of the Proprietor. Establishing Value of the Business. Reporting Gain from Sale of the Proprietorship. Other Provisions in the Buy-Sell Agreement.* The Partnership: *A Shared Responsibility. Formalizing the Agreement. Federal Income Tax Aspects. Continuing the Partnership—A Matter of Planning. Problems of Liquidation. Effects of the Death of a Partner. Alternatives to Liquidation at Death. The Buy-Sell Agreement. Selecting the Buy-Out Method. Income Tax Treatment of Purchase and Sale of a Partnership Interest. Funding the Buy-Sell Agreement. Other Considerations.* The Professional.

46. Business Continuation—Corporate Business Interest, *Stuart A. Monroe*   703

Nature of the Corporation. Problems Caused by Death of Principal Stockholder. Basic Elements of a Share of Stock: *The Minority Stockholder Situation. The Majority Stockholder Situation. The Equal Stockholder Situation. The Situations Reversed.* Importance of Situation Analysis. Retention of Stock Interest by the Family: *Valuation of Stock Interest—If Retained. Estate Liquidity Problem Where Stock Interest Is Retained.* Disposing of Stock Interest through Formal Agreement: *Parties. Stock Redemption versus Cross-Purchase. Special Family Situations.* Advantages of the Buy-and-Sell Agreement.

47. Income Protection for Business Continuation, *William Harmelin* 718

Effect of Disability on a Business: *Sole Proprietorship. Partnership. Close Corporation.* Solutions to Disability Problems without Disability Income Insurance: *The Sole Proprietorship. The Partnership. The Close Corporation.* Solutions to Disability Problems with Disability Income Insurance: *The Sole Proprietorship. The Partnership. The Close Corporation.* A Check List of Important Points to Be Covered in the Disability Buy-and-Sell Portion of a Business Agreement: *1. Definition of Disability. 2. Amount of Salary during Disability before Buy-Out. 3. When Buy-Out Becomes Mandatory. 4. Source of Funds for Buy-Out. 5. Number of Installments to Effect the Buy-Out. 6. Disposition of Business Life Insurance Policies on the Healthy and Disabled Partners When Disability Buy-Out Becomes Effective. 7. Provision for Contingency of Death during Period Disability Buy-Out Payments Are Being Made.* Conclusion.

48. Professional Corporations, *Herbert Chasman*   731

In the Beginning: *Kintner Case. State Law Governs. A Federal Question Once Again. The IRS Agrees to Corporate Tax Treatment for Professionals.* Tax Advantages of Professional Corporations: *Creation of a New Taxpayer. Tax Favored Employee Fringe Benefits. Marginal Efficiency of Profits.* Nontax Advantages of Professional Corporations: *Limited Liability. Centralized Management. Continuity of Life and Ease of Transferability.* Problem Areas for Professional Corporations: *One-Man Professional Corporation. Personal Holding Company Tax. Reasonableness of Compensation. Unreasonable Accumulation of Earnings Tax.* A Look into the Future.

Part VIII
GOVERNMENT BENEFITS—PROTECTION AND
RETIREMENT   749

49. Social Security Benefits for Retirement, Disability, and Survivorship, *Robert J. Myers*   751

Coverage Provisions of OASDI System: *Nonfarm Self-Employed. Farm Operators. Ministers. Employees of Nonfarm Private Employers. Employees of Nonprofit Organizations. Employees of State and Local Governments. Employees of Federal Government. Employees of Foreign Governments and International Agencies. Farm Workers. Domestic Workers. Tips Received by Employees. Employment Abroad. Military Service Wage Credits.* OASDI Insured Status Conditions. OASDI Beneficiary Categories: *Old-Age Beneficiaries. Disability Benefits. Supplementary Benefits. Survivor Benefits. Lump-Sum Death Payments. Special Age-72 Benefits. General Benefit Provisions.* OASDI Benefit Amounts: *Average Monthly Wage. Benefit Formula. Minimum and Maximum Family Benefits.* OASDI Earnings Test: *Payments of OASDI Benefits Abroad.* OASDI Financing Provisions. Basic Principles of OASDI System: *Benefits Based on Presumptive Need. Floor-of-Protection Concept. Earnings-Related Benefits. Individual Equity and Social Adequacy. Self-Supporting Contributory Financing.* Development of OASDI System.

50. Medicare and Other Government Health Benefits, *Robert J. Myers*   769

Hospital Insurance under Medicare: *Coverage and Eligibility. Benefits. Financing. Administration.* Supplementary Medical Insurance under Medicare: *Coverage and Eligibility. Benefits. Financing. Administration.* Medicaid Program. Military and Veterans' Programs. Workmen's Compensation Programs. Temporary Disability Insurance Programs. State and Local Government Health Plans.

51. Servicemen's and Veterans' Benefits, *Barnie E. Abelle*   780

Government Life Insurance: *Brief History. General Policy Provisions. Guaranteed Values. Reinstatement. Conversion and Change of Plans. Dividends. Beneficiary Designations. Settlement Options. Disability Coverage.* Servicemen's Group Life Insurance. Compensation and Pension Benefits: *Disability Compensation. Disability Pension. Death Compensation. Death Pension.* Orphans', Wives', and Widows' Education Benefits. Other Benefit Considerations: *Social Security. Other Death Benefits. Changes in Benefits.*

Part IX
PLANNING SMALL AND LARGE ESTATES   795

52. Concepts of Programming, *Leland T. Waggoner*   797

Programming Defined. Human Life Value Approach to Programming. Estate Creation, Conservation, and Distribution. Programming Process: *Analyze Relevant Factors. Determine the Goals of the Client. Prepare a Specific Plan to Meet the Client's Goals. Program the Life Insurance. Provide for the Creation, Conservation, and Distribution of the Estate.* Analysis of Needs: *Cash Needs. Income Needs.* Preparation of Programming Chart. Health Insurance Programming: *Preparation of a Health Insurance Programming Chart.* Key Concepts of Programming: *Ability to Pay. Self-Disclosure. Concept of Service. Need for Program Review. Providing Monthly Income by Means of Settlement Options. Need for Flexibility.* Programming in the Future.

53. **Ownership Provisions and Beneficiary Designations,** *Paul L. Wise* 816

Ownership Provisions: *Third Party Ownership. Case Law. Multiple Owners. Transfer of Ownership May Not Affect Death Benefits.* Beneficiary Designations: *Revocable and Irrevocable Beneficiaries. Primary and Contingent Beneficiaries. Insurable Interest. Identity of the Beneficiary. "Per Stirpes" or "Per Capita"? Business Organizations. Trustees. Minor Beneficiaries. How to Designate and Change Beneficiaries. Simultaneous Death Clauses. State Creditor Exemption Statutes and Their Effect. Spendthrift Clauses and Their Use. Federal Tax Liens.* Collateral Assignments: *Types of Assignments. ABA Assignment Form. Notice of Assignment to the Insurance Company. Need the Beneficiary Be Changed before Assignment of the Policy?* Importance of Keeping Current.

54. **Settlement Options,** *Lawrence R. Brown, Jr.* 833

Settlement Options Defined: *The Lump Sum Settlement. The Interest Option. The Fixed-Period Option. The Fixed-Amount Option. The Life Income Options.* Special Arrangements and Policies. Use of Settlement Options: *Cash Funds. Regular Income for the Family. Income for Children. Educational Funds. Special Purpose Funds.* Some General Rules: *Election of Settlement Options. Basic Company Rules for Using Options. Requesting Settlement Agreements.*

55. **Estate Planning Principles,** *Laurence J. Ackerman* 844

Cautions Regarding Estate Planning. Estate Planning Not New. Forces of Estate Impairment. Estate Planning Process: *1. Getting the Facts. 2. Evaluating Estate Impairment Items. 3. Designing the Plan. 4. Testing the Plan. 5. Executing Legal Documents. 6. Periodic Review.* Advantages of Planned Estate. The Estate Planning Team.

56. **Trusts and Their Uses,** *V. N. Woolfolk* 856

The Trust Relationship. Types of Trusts: *Life Insurance Trusts. Uses for Living Life Insurance Trusts. The Unfunded Life Insurance Trust. The Revocable Unfunded Life Insurance Trust. The Irrevocable Unfunded Life Insurance Trust. Funded Life Insurance Trusts.* Summary.

57. **Income Taxation of Life and Health Insurance,** *Fred J. Dopheide* 866

General Rules: *Life Insurance Death Benefits. Life Insurance Living Benefits. Health Insurance Benefits. Income Tax Treatment of Premiums.* Life Insurance Arrangements Giving Rise to Tax Consequences: *Transfer for Value. Lack of Insurable Interest. Proceeds as Corporate Distributions. Creditor-Debtor Situations. Charitable Contributions. Separation and Divorce. Additional Compensation. Group Term Life Insurance. Split Dollar Life Insurance.* Summary.

58. **Estate and Gift Taxation of Life Insurance,** *Leonard L. Silverstein and Gerald H. Sherman* 882

Federal Estate Tax: *Identity of Beneficiary. Owner of Policy. Payor of Premiums. Relationship to Qualified Retirement Plans.* Federal Gift Tax: *Taxable Value and Tax Rates. Annual and Lifetime Exclusions and Exemptions. Donor's Marital Status. Inadvertent Gift.*

59. **Gifts of Life Insurance,** *W. R. Huey, Jr.* 892

Family Gifts of Life Insurance: *Tax Savings Available. Tax Advantages of Life Insurance Gift to Donee. Nontax Advantages of the Life Insurance Gift. Direct Gifts. The Gift of Insurance Policies in Trust. Gifts of Life Insurance to Minors in Custodianship.* Charitable Gifts of Life Insurance: *Advantages of Life Insurance as a Charitable Gift. Significant Tax Advantages. Insurance Gift Made in Lieu of Current Cash Gifts. Charitable Bequest at Death. Existing Policy Given to a Charitable Institution. Group Support of a Charitable Institution. Gift Combined with Additional Personal Life Insurance.*

60. Estate Planning—An Illustration, *Lawrence G. Knecht*   **907**

Analysis of the Case—Establishing the Facts: *General Observations. Data of the Illustrative Case. Running the Hypothetical Probate.* Finding the Obstacles or Problems: *General Observations. The Specific Problems.* Designing a Plan: *Testing the Plan. Implementing the Plan. Periodic Reviews.*

Part X
COMPANY OPERATIONS AND INSTITUTIONAL ASPECTS   921

61. Scope and Structure of Life and Health Insurance, *Blake T. Newton, Jr.*   **923**

Scope of Coverage and Benefits:*Life Insurance Growth. Life Insurance Purchases. Pension Plans. Broader Financial Services. Health Insurance Growth. Personal Insurance Benefits. Health Insurance Purchases.* Insurance Companies and Carriers: *Life Insurance Companies. Health Insurance Carriers.* Organizations in the Business. Organizations Related to the Business. Economic and Social Contributions: *Guaranteeing Family Plans. Investing in the National Economy. Insurers as Employers.* What of the Future?

62. Regulation of Life and Health Insurance, *W. Lee Shield*   **936**

Objectives of Regulation. Development of State Insurance Supervision. Modern State Statutes and Regulations: *Insurance Department. Insurance Companies. Agents' Qualification and Licensing. Insurance Contracts.* Challenges to State Regulation. Applicable Federal Laws and Regulations. The Future.

63. Company Organization and Management, *Edmund L. Zalinski* **951**

Special Characteristics. Company Formation. Form of Organization: *Levels of Authority. Departmentalization. Board of Directors. Officers. Committees.* Organization Structure: *Organization Chart. Lines of Business. Group Department. Individual Department. Direct Supporting Operations. Sales Departments. Actuarial Departments. Underwriting Departments. Administration Departments. Claims Departments. Staff Operations. Other Financial Services.*

64. Individual Insurance Marketing, *Burkett W. Huey*   **964**

History of Growth. The Career of Selling Life Insurance: *Income. Satisfaction and Prestige. Education and Training. Security and Opportunity. Likes and Dislikes. The Sales Process.* Marketing Methods: *Career Distributors. Independent Distributors. Special Systems.* Health Insurance.

65. Legal and Professional Responsibilities of the Life Underwriter, *Frederick R.H. Witherby and Robert J. Fitzwilliam*   **976**

One Man, Many Parts. Company's Contract Liability for Acts of the Agent. Company's Tort Liability for Acts of the Agent. Agent's Tort Liability for His Acts. Field Underwriter as a Professional. Rules of the Business. Protection for the Life Underwriter.

66. Reinsurance, *Walter W. Steffen*   **991**

Indemnity Reinsurance: *Reinsurance Defined. Values of Reinsurance. Retention Limit. Relationship of Insurer and Reinsurer. Life Reinsurance Plans. Automatic and Facultative Methods of Ceding Reinsurance. Individual Health Reinsurance. Nonproportional Reinsurance. Group Reinsurance.* Assumption Reinsurance. Glossary of Important Reinsurance Terms.

67. Claims Administration, *Paul R. Craig*   **1007**

Nature and Functions of Claims Administration. Role of the Claims Administrator. General Claims Procedures: *Claim Proofs. Claims Examination.* Life Insurance Claims Administration: *Claims for Death Benefits. Accidental Death Claims. Multiple Indemnity Benefits for Accidental Death. Suicide. Hazardous Occupations. War. Termination of Coverage. Apparent Errors in Age.* Health Insurance Claims Administration: *Total and Permanent Disability Benefits. Long-Term and Short-Term Disability Benefits. Dismemberment Benefits. Medical Expense Benefits. Major Medical Expense Claims. Duplicate Coverage. Duration of Claims.* Claims Payment. Other Payments. Aids in Claims Administration.

68. Company Investments, *George T. Conklin, Jr.*   **1022**

Considerations Influencing Investment Policies: *Long-Term and Predictable Nature of Liability and Cash Flow. Guaranteed Interest Rate on Policy Reserves. Limited Surplus. Competition to Reduce Net Cost. Regulation. The Going-Concern Method of Valuing Assets. Mandatory Securities Valuation Reserve. Federal Income Tax. Liquidity Needs.* Special Characteristics of the Investment Process in Life Insurance: *Forward Commitments. Direct Placements. Diversification.* Distribution of Life Insurance Company Assets: *Mortgages. Corporate Bonds. Government Securities. Equities. Policy Loans.* Broadening Range of Financial Services Offered by Life Insurance Companies: *Separate Accounts. Variable Annuities and Variable Life Insurance.*

69. Company Financial Statements, *B. Franklin Blair*   **1036**

Annual Statement Filed with Insurance Department. Technical Terms: *Ledger Assets. Nonledger Assets. Admitted Assets. Nonadmitted Assets. Amortized Basis. Nonamortizable Securities. Accrued or Revenue Basis; Cash Basis. Supplementary Contracts.* Balance Sheet: *Assets. Liabilities. Capital and Surplus.* Summary of Operations: *Income. Deductions from Income. Net Gain from Operations and Dividends to Policyowners. Treatment of Federal Income Tax. Surplus Account.* Separate Account Blank. Exhibits and Schedules in the Convention Blank: *Exhibits. Schedules.* Annual Reports to Policyowners and Stockholders: *Differences between Annual Report and Convention Blank.* Differences between Life Insurance Accounting and Generally Accepted Accounting Practices. "Adjusted" Figures for Stock Insurance Companies. The Strength of a Company as Revealed by Its Annual Statement: *How Realistic Are Balance Sheets? Measures of the Strength of a Company.*

70. Taxation of Companies, *William B. Harman, Jr.*   **1055**

Federal Taxation: *History of Federal Income Taxation of Life Insurance Companies. Basic Outline of the 1959 Act. Illustration of Gain from Operations Tax Base. Purpose of Determining Taxable Investment Income Base. Taxable Investment Income. Life Insurance Company Taxable Income. Tax-Deferred Account.* Controlled Foreign Corporations. Interest Equalization Tax. Policies Issued by Foreign Insurers. State Taxation: *Premium Tax. Retaliatory Taxes. Other State Taxes.* Local Taxation.

71. Canadian Life Insurance—Important Variations, *J. W. Burns*   **1075**

Government Regulation of Life Insurance. Policy Contract: *Beneficiaries. Incontestability. Reinstatement. Cash Values and Nonforfeiture Provisions. Juvenile Insurance. Miscellaneous Provisions.* Taxation of Life Insurance: *Federal Income Tax. Annuities.* Taxation of Life Insurance Companies.

72. A Brief History, *Paul A. Norton*   **1089**

Life Insurance: *Industrialization Sets the Stage. Early Years. Rise of Mutuals. New Sales Techniques. Mid-Century Growth. Business in Crisis. Beginnings of State Regulation. New Policies, New Methods, New Growth. Armstrong Investigation. Depression Decade. Modern Quest for Security. Premium Payments and National Progress.* Expansion of Group Insurance. Health Insurance.

APPENDIXES

A. Historic Dates in the Development of Life and Health Insurance in the United States — 1103

B. Application for Life Insurance Policy, Including Medical Examiner's Report — 1108

C. Specimen Inspection Report—Life Form and Health Form — 1112

D. Specimen Individual Life Insurance Contract (Straight Life) — 1116

E. Death Rates and Expectation of Life under Various Mortality and Annuity Tables — 1131

F. Selected Compound Interest Values at Various Interest Rates — 1134

G. Net Level Premiums at 2½ and 3 Percent, Curtate Functions, under the 1958 CSO Table at Quinquennial Ages for Various Plans of Insurance — 1141

H. Securities and Exchange Commission Policy on Variable Life Contracts, 1973 — 1142

I. The 1950 Uniform Individual Accident and Sickness Policy Provisions Law—NAIC — 1145

J. Seventh Status Report on Overinsurance for the Subcommittee on Overinsurance of the Accident and Health Committee, National Association of Insurance Commissioners, November 22, 1963 — 1159

K. National Association of Insurance Commissioners Model Group Life Insurance Bill — 1166

L. Specimen Group Term Life Insurance Policy — 1171

M. Specimen Group Life Employee's Certificate Booklet — 1186

N. Model Blanket Accident and Sickness Insurance Bill — 1195

O. Model Franchise Accident and Health Insurance Bill — 1199

P. NAIC Model Rules and Regulations for Group Coverage Discontinuance and Replacement — 1200

Q. Revenue Ruling 64–328, 1964–2 CBU, Pertaining to Split-Dollar Life Insurance — 1204

R. Provisions of Disability Buy-and-Sell Agreement (Close Corporation) — 1208

S. Specimen Agreement for Change of Beneficiary — 1220

T. Specimen Agreement for Election of Method of Settlement — 1223

U. National Statement of Principles of Cooperation between Life Underwriters and Lawyers — 1227

V. Statement of Guiding Principles for Relationships between Life Underwriters and Trustmen — 1231

W. Personal Life Insurance Trust Agreements   1233

X. NAIC Model Act Relating to Unfair Methods of Competition and Unfair and Deceptive Acts and Practices in the Business of Insurance (Revised 1972)   1243

Y. Reinsurance Agreement   1252

INDEXES   1283

Index of Names   1285

Index of Subjects   1289

List of Illustrations

FIGURES

1–1. Economic Security Expenditures for 1940 and 1971 for Individual,Group, and Social Approaches — 10

1–2. Total Security Expenditures for Life, Health and Retirement Coverages — 11

1–3. Distribution of Security Expenditures in Selected Years According to Type of Coverage and Type of Recipient — 11

1–4. Security Expenditures as a Percent of Augmented Disposable Personal Income — 13

4–1. Relative Combinations of Protection and Savings Elements by Type of Life Insurance — 40

4–2. Comparison of Yearly Renewable Term Premium with Level Premium for a Straight Whole Life Policy, Issued at Age 25 — 41

4–3. Proportion of Protection and Investment Elements in a $100,000 Straight Whole Life Contract, Issued as of Age 25, (1958 C.S.O. table and 2½ percent interest) — 42

7–1. Classification of Annuities — 81

8–1. Illustration of Basic Structure of Family Maintenance Policy — 94

8–2. Illustration of Basic Structure of Family Income Policy — 94

8–3. Illustration of Basic Structure of Retirement Annuity Contract — 97

8–4. Illustration of Basic Structure of Retirement Income Contract — 99

10–1. Proportion of Heads in Sequence of One Hundred Coin Tosses — 124

10–2. Variation of Actual Claims from Expected Claims as a Percentage of Expected Claims (for selected numbers of lives insured for one year where probability of death in that year is 0.01) — 126

10–3. Accumulated Value of $1 at End of Various Years at Selected Interest Rates — 135

10–4. Computation of Discounted Value of an Annuity Certain at 3 Percent Interest — 136

18–1. Comparison of Industrial Stock Prices and the Cost of Living, 1900-70 — 242

28–1. Group Medical Expense Insurance Plan Approaches — 426

31–1. Group Life Insurance Rate Calculation—CSG Basis — 489

31–2. Development of Census Factors for Medical Rate — 490

31–3.   Rate Calculation for Comprehensive Medical Plan   491
31–4.   Sample Dividend Calculation   492
32–1.   Company Group Insurance Department Functional Organization   507
39–1.   Illustration of Group Permanent Retirement Income Coverage Issued at Age 30 with Normal Retirement at Age 65   599
39–2.   Illustration of How Dividends Reduce Premiums on Group Permanent Retirement Income Coverages   601
39–3.   Illustration of Funding Pattern for Group Permanent Plan in Which Older Employees Retire and Are Replaced by Younger Employees   602
39–4.   Illustration of Level Pension Benefit Credits under a Defined Benefit Plan   610
39–5.   Illustration of Single-Premium Contributions under a Defined Benefit Plan   610
39–6.   Illustration of Pension Credits for Each Year from a Constant Single Premium under a Defined Contribution Plan   611
39–7.   Illustration of Single-Premium Level Contribution under a Defined Contribution Plan   611
44–1.   Comparison of Collateral Assignment and Endorsement Split-Dollar Systems   681
44–2.   Open-End Note and Work Sheet for Collateral Assignment Split-Dollar System (age 40, $100,000 straight life, gross annual premium $2,783)   683
44–3.   Work Sheet for Endorsement Split-Dollar System (age 40, $100,000 straight life, gross annual premium $2,783)
48–1.   Comparison of the Flexibility of Provisions of Corporate Qualified Plans and Unincorporated Qualified Plans (HR-10)   738
48–2.   Comparison of Professional Partnership and Professional Corporation with Respect to Available Current Spendable Income and Amount Set Aside for Retirement   742
52–1.   Illustrative Confidential Programming Survey and Analysis Form   801–8
52–2.   Life Insurance Programming Chart   812
52–3.   Health Insurance Programming Chart   813
53–1.   ABA-10 Collateral Assignment Form   830
61–1.   Life Insurance in Force in the United States   924
61–2.   Growth of Life Insurance by Types   925
61–3.   Total Health Insurance Premiums as a Percentage of Disposable Income   927
61–4.   Life Insurance Payments, 1971   928
61–5.   Summary of Persons Covered by Type of Private Health Insurance, 1971   929
63–1.   Organization Chart of a Medium-Sized Life and Health Insurance Company   957
66–1.   Certificate of Assumption   1003
68–1.   Distribution of Assets of U.S. Life Insurance Companies, January 1, 1972   1030

TABLES

1-1. Percentage Distribution of Total Security Expenditures by Type of Recipient   12

2-1. Human Life Values (assumed retirement age 65, varying average net future income and age of valuation, interest at 4 percent per annum)   25

6-1. Nonparticipating Annual Premium Rates per $1,000 Charged Males by a Leading Insurer for Some Representative $10,000 Contracts   67

6-2. Net Premium Rates per $1,000 of Straight Life Insurance Issued at Age 35 and Yearly Renewable Term Insurance at Various Ages (1958 CSO Mortality Table, 3 percent interest)   68

6-3. Cash Values per $1,000 Insurance Provided under Five Nonparticipating Whole Life Contracts Issued by a Leading Insurer to an Insured Age 35   70

10-1. Simple Illustration of Mortality Rate Calculation   127

10-2. 1958 Commissioners Standard Ordinary Mortality Table   131

10-3. Growth of $1 Left on Deposit at 3 Percent Interest Compounded Annually   134

10-4. Discounted Value of $1 Payable at the End of Various Years at Selected Interest Rates   136

10-5. Amortization Schedule for an Annuity at 3 Percent Interest   137

10-6. $1,000 Whole Life Policy Issued at Age 80 (using 1958 CSO Mortality Table and 3 percent interest)   138

12-1. Hypothetical Mortality and 3 Percent Interest for Illustrative Premium and Reserve Calculations   160

12-2. Calculation of Reserve by the Prospective Method, Five-Year Endowment for $1,000 Mortality and Interest as in Table 12-1   163

12-3. Calculation of Reserve by the Retrospective Method, Five-Year Endowment for $1,000 Mortality and Interest as in Table 12-1   164

12-4. Comparison of Terminal Reserves per $1,000 Face Amount (straight life (male), age 35)   167

12-5. Comparison of Terminal Reserves per $1,000 Face Amount (straight life (male), age 35)   168

12-6. Comparison of Terminal Reserves per $1,000 Face Amount (straight life (male), age 35)   169

16-1. Comparative Results by Traditional and Interest-Adjusted Methods for Ten Policies   217

16-2. Data on Two of the Policies Exhibited in Table 16-1   217

17-1. Illustrative Death Benefits and Reserves under Three Proposed Variable while Life Insurance Contract Designs (male issue age 35, $1,000 initial death benefit)   231

18-1. Illustration of Periodic-Payment Variable Annuity Account Growth   246

20-1. Number of Persons with Disability Income Protection by Type of Program in the United States (000 omitted)   278

21–1. Number of People with Medical Expense Protection under Individual Policies of Insurance Companies (000 omitted) — 291

23–1. Continuance Table at Age 35 Showing Number Disabled at Stated Durations (per 100,000 lives exposed) — 322

24–1. Illustrative Selection Action Taken on 100 Individual Life and Health Insurance Applications — 336

25–1. Group Life Insurance in Force in the United States, 1911-71 — 364

25–2. Average Size Group Certificate and Average Ordinary and Industrial Policy in Force in the United States, 1920-70 — 365

25–3. Comparative Growth of Group, Ordinary, and Industrial Life Insurance in Force in the United States, 1920-71 — 365

25–4. Number and Proportion of Population with Health Insurance Protection, 1970 — 366

25–5. Number of Persons with Private Health Insurance Protection by Type of Coverage in the United States — 367

25–6. Number of Persons Enrolled in Private Health Insurance Plans, by Type of Plan and Type of Medical Expense Coverage, December 31, 1970 — 368

25–7. Percentage Distribution of Persons Enrolled in Private Health Insurance Plans among Insurers, December 31, 1970 — 369

27–1. Group Disability Income Insurance in the United States, 1935-71 — 394

27–2. Group Disability Income Insurance in the United States by Type of Program, 1963-71 — 395

27–3. Group Credit Disability Income Insurance in the United States, 1967-71 — 395

27–4. Annual Disability Experience (per 1,000 male employees) — 398

27–5. Relationship of Long-Term Disability Benefit to Net Earnings — 405

28–1. Schedule of Surgical Procedures (selected examples) — 422

28–2. Blue Cross Benefits in 1971 (number of plans providing stated benefits under two categories of group certificates) — 428

28–3. Types of Benefits Provided under Blue Shield Comprehensive Contract — 429

28–4. Illustrative Group Comprehensive Medical Expense Insurance Plan (brief description of plan) — 429

30–1. Uniform Premiums for $1,000 of Group Term Insurance Protection — 466

31–1. Commissioners Standard Group (CSG) Monthly Life Rates (per $1,000) (illustrated for decennial ages only) — 473

31–2. Illustrative Credibility Factors for Group Insurance Dividends by Size of Group — 479

31–3. Credibility Factors for Group Insurance Renewal Rating (by size of group and length of period insured) — 480

31–4. Typical Claims Reserves as a Percentage of Annual Premium — 486

32–1. Group Life Insurance in Force by Type of Insured Group— 1968 (excludes dependent coverage, group credit life, Federal Employees' Group Life and Servicemen's Group Life) — 498

39–1.   Number of Insured Plans and Persons Covered under Certain Allocated and Unallocated Funding Instruments   597

41–1.   Assets of All Private Pension Funds, 1961-71 (book value, in billions of dollars)   628

43–1.   Funded versus Unfunded Deferred Compensation Plan—A Cost Comparison.   672

44–1.   Split-Dollar Insurance Ledger Illustration Using Dividends to Reduce Premiums (age 40, $100,000 straight life, gross annual premium $2,783)   678

44–2.   Split-Dollar Insurance Ledger Illustration Using Dividends to Purchase One-Year Term Insurance and Reduce Premiums (age 40, $100,000 straight life, gross annual premium $2,783)   679

44–3.   Revenue Ruling 64-328 and 66-110 Uniform One-Year Term Premiums for $1,000 Life Insurance Protection (Table of P.S.-58 one-year term rates)   686

46–1.   Illustrative Life Insurance Arrangement in a Cross-Purchase Plan for Close Corporation   712

49–1.   Primary Insurance Amounts Computed under Method of 1939 Act   758

49–2.   Illustrative Monthly Benefits under OASDI System for Various Family Categories, Based on Earnings after 1950 (all figures rounded to nearest dollar)   759

49–3.   Past and Future Financing Provisions of OASDI System   761

49–4.   Past and Future Financing Provisions of OASDI and H1 Systems   762

51–1.   Government Insurance Programs   782

66–1.   Illustrative Premium Computations for Risk Premium Reinsurance Plan   994

66–2.   Illustrative Risk Premium Reinsurance Premium Rates per $1,000 (35-year-old risk)   995

66–3.   Comparison of Distinctive Features of Risk Premium Reinsurance, Coinsurance, and Modified Coinsurance Plans   999

70–1.   Outline of Items Comprising Gain (or Loss) from Operations   1058

70–2.   Outline of Items Comprising Taxable Investment Income   1062

70–3.   Items Includable in Policy and Other Contract Liability Requirements   1064

70–4.   Illustration of Current, Deferred and Total Tax Bases of Life Insurance Companies   1066

part I

Economic Security and Insurance

MOST MEN have a compelling need for security. Adventure and risk-taking propensities are balanced by strong instincts for stability and certainty. All insurance and particularly those schemes related to death, disability, and retirement are rooted in basic human needs.

Part I is concerned with the nature of security, with its relation to man's basic needs and wants, and with emerging patterns and philosophies of a rapidly developing private and public economic security system.

The concept of human capital, with particular emphasis on the human life value analysis as part of human capital theory, is examined. Then, the fundamental protection functions of life and health insurance are analyzed and related to the reduction of economic uncertainty.

The final chapter in this Part is concerned with the savings functions of life insurance. Life insurance is one of the nation's oldest and soundest thrift institutions. Increasing opportunities and responsibilities in this service dimension are now emerging.

1

Economic Security: Patterns and Philosophies

By DAVIS W. GREGG

ECONOMIC SECURITY is a compelling goal for most persons. The goal can be defined only for a given person at a given time. For a nation or a society, criteria of economic security will vary with economic development. While merely adequate food, clothing, and shelter may be the goal for most persons in an underdeveloped nation, far more may be expected and even demanded by persons in an affluent society.

The wealth of a nation and the distribution of its wealth are critical elements in evaluating the relative achievement of economic security. The economic health and growth of a society and the full employment of its economic resources, especially the employable human resources, are of major significance.

THE MEANING OF SECURITY

Security is a many-faceted thing. It has economic, social, psychological and other cultural and personal dimensions. To a young lad in a popular newspaper cartoon, security is "a thumb and a blanket." To one of immense wealth, it may be yachts, planes, castles, and jewels.

The etymology of "security," the Latin *securus*, meaning "without care," is suggestive of broad human implications. Security can be thought of as peace of mind and freedom from uncertainty. Insecurity is characterized by feelings of doubt, anxiety, fear, worry, and apprehension.

There is strong evidence that most men have a preference for security. The Swiss philosopher, Tournier, argues that this preference is traceable to a universal principle applicable to the whole of nature: there is a tendency for all things to continue in their mode of existence. In the physical world, there is the law of inertia. In biology, there is the dominance of habit and reflexes. Tournier speaks of the two instincts of man: one being the instinct "of adventure, movement, discovery, risk-taking and progress"; the other, the instinct "of repose, repetition, security and stability." He goes on to tell us that, "customs, usages, and the whole of

3

civilization rest on the instinct of stability" and observes that the "modern social ideal of security and the tremendous increase in insurance express this urge to eliminate all kinds of risk."[1]

Whatever the genesis of man's instincts for security, it appears that his behavior is inexorably related to his needs and wants. Thus, one is led to speculate that personal insecurity results from the inability or the uncertainty of individuals, whatever their situations, regarding the satisfaction of one or more of their needs or wants.

Two general observations seem pertinent. First, man's needs, desires and wants are of an infinite quantity. One eminent social scientist observed that, "Man is a wanting animal and rarely reaches a state of complete satisfaction except for a short time. As one desire is satisfied, another one pops up to take its place. When this is satisfied, still another comes into the foreground. It is a characteristic of the human being throughout his whole life that he is practically always desiring something."[2] Thus, if we accept the concept that insecurity derives from the individual's inability or uncertainty regarding the satisfaction of his needs, we must conclude that man will always be faced with problems of insecurity—a conclusion that seems consistent with the realities of life.

Life at both extremes of the security scale, total insecurity and perfect security, seems unrealistic—and probably undesirable if attainable. The real issues for human growth and happiness and for societal advancement relate to the optimal degree of security and the optimal methods of achieving that objective.

A second observation is that any analysis of security in terms of needs or wants is incomplete without recognition of a ranking, a hierarchy, or a priority of human needs. Human motivation is highly complex. Yet, a carefully developed and widely recognized theory of human motivation, articulated by the brilliant psychologist Abraham Maslow, sheds meaningful light on man's quest for economic security.[3]

Accepting the fact that man is a perpetually wanting animal, Maslow argues that the appearance of a need rests on prior situations, on other prepotent needs, and that needs and desires, to be understood, should be arranged in hierarchies of prepotency. Graphically, he argues that, "We should never have the desire to compose music or create mathematical systems, or to adorn our homes, or to be well-dressed, if our stomachs were empty most of the time, or if we were continually dying of thirst, or if we were continually threatened by an always impending catastrophe, or if everyone hated us."[4]

---

[1] Paul Tournier, *The Adventure of Living* (New York: Harper & Row, 1965), p. 156.

[2] A. H. Maslow, "Preface to Motivation Theory," *Psychosomatic Medicine*, Vol. 5 (1943), p. 87.

[3] The single most complete statement of Maslow's theory of human motivation is found in his volume, *Motivation and Personality*, 2d ed. (New York: Harper & Row, 1970). This volume also contains an extensive bibliography of his and others' works in this area of human knowledge.

[4] Maslow, *Psychosomatic Medicine*, p. 88.

MAN'S HIERARCHY OF NEEDS

Maslow's hierarchy of needs theory suggests the following order of prepotency:

    I.   Physiological needs.
   II.   Safety needs.
  III.   Love and acceptance needs.
  IV.   Esteem needs.
   V.   Self-fulfillment needs.

The needs scale begins with the *physiological* needs. Food, water, sleep, sex, clothing, and shelter are basic for the human—and for most all living things. A starving man is obsessed with the idea of food. All other needs are irrelevant until such a primary need is met. Man lives by bread alone—when there is no bread. But what happens when there is plenty of bread and his belly is chronically filled? "At once, other and higher needs emerge and these, rather than physiological hungers, dominate the organism."[5]

When the physiological needs are reasonably satisfied, man seeks to satisfy the next higher level of needs, usually referred to as *safety* (or protection) needs. All men need protection from harm, physical and psychological. Stability, structure, law, and order are manifestations of this need. Man is entirely willing to take risks, but when he feels threatened or dependent, his greatest need is for protection, for security. The human instinct of self-preservation is one of the most powerful elements of this need. It includes protection "against pain, against danger of life, against jeopardy of bodily integrity, against overwhelming threats. There is usually a further component in this desire for safety in that it implies a world that can be counted on, that is familiar, and that is manageable. In a word, a world that does not threaten and that is not dangerous."[6]

Having satisfied the need for safety, man's behavior is motivated largely by *love and acceptance* needs. These are such needs as those for belonging, for acceptance by one's family and fellowman, for having a place in the group, for giving and receiving friendship and love. Few men are antisocial in the pure sense, and, if so, this behavior often is attributable to the fact that their more primary needs are not being met.

Next in the scale are *esteem* needs. Two dimensions of esteem needs are suggested. First, man has the desire for strength, for achievement, for confidence, for independence and freedom. Second, there is the need for reputation, prestige, status, fame and glory, recognition, importance, dignity, and appreciation.[7]

It has been observed that, "Unlike the lower needs, these [esteem] needs are rarely satisfied; man seeks indefinitely for more satisfaction of

---

[5] Maslow, *Motivation and Personality*, p. 38.
[6] Maslow, *Psychosomatic Medicine*, p. 91.
[7] Maslow, *Motivation and Personality*, p. 45.

these needs once they have become important to him."[8] It also is argued that this level of needs does not usually appear in any significant way for most humans until the lower order of needs are reasonably satisfied.

At the peak of the scale are the *self-fulfillment* needs. Maslow used the term "self-actualization" to describe these needs. He refers to "working out one's own fundamental personality, the fulfillment of its potentialities, the use of its capacities, the tendency to be the most that one is capable of being."[9] The specific form of these needs varies greatly from person to person in that in one case the desire is to be an ideal mother, in another to be a fine musician, in another to be an excellent golfer. To be at peace with himself, man must be what he can be. It has been argued that "the conditions of modern industrial life give only limited opportunity for these relatively dormant human needs to find expression. The deprivation most people experience with respect to other lower-level needs directs their energies to the struggle to satisfy those needs, and the needs for self-fulfillment remain below the level of consciousness."[10]

HUMAN NEEDS AND ECONOMIC SECURITY

Economists, as well as psychologists and other social scientists, also are concerned with the nature and satisfaction of human needs. As an academic discipline, economics is defined as the study of how men and societies can and do choose to allocate and use their limited resources to produce, distribute and consume goods to satisfy human needs.[11]

It has been noted that man naturally strives to attain some desired level or degree of personal security, and in this quest he engages in many varied efforts. Economic activities are included among this vast array of security-oriented activities. He takes risks, he works, he consumes, and he saves in order to fulfill human needs. The obtaining of economic goods for immediate use or to hold as part of his personal wealth command a great deal of man's time and energy. The economic aspect of one's lifetime endeavors is quite great. Economists speak exclusively in terms of economic needs of man whereas psychologists and social scientists identify a hierarchy of human needs. However, there is no conflict here. The hierarchy of needs approach gives meaning and depth to the single perspective of the economists. In short, man engages in economic activities for a variety of reasons other than sustenance of himself and his family.

In view of this discussion, several matters become self-evident. First, all economic actions taken by man are for the ultimate purpose of satisfying human needs and thus providing him with some degree of security. Second, economic security can be defined as the attainment of feeling of certainty, peace of mind, comfort and fulfillment through the acquisi-

---

[8] Douglas MacGregor, *The Human Side of Enterprise* (New York: McGraw-Hill Book Co., 1960, p. 36.

[9] Maslow, *Psychosomatic Medicine*, p. 91.

[10] MacGregor, *The Human Side of Enterprise*, pp. 36–39.

[11] Paul A. Samuelson, *Economics*, 8th ed. (New York: McGraw-Hill Book Co., 1970), p. 4.

tion, ownership, and use of economic goods. Third, the extent to which man's needs are being met and he attains personal feelings of security will vary over time and will vary among individuals as of any given point in time. Fourth, this search of man for personal security for himself and his family is inextricably related to all his various types of needs in a most complex manner. Moreover, the economic dimension of security is related to all his needs in a very direct manner, some more than others.

Category I, the physiological needs, are sought by man for himself and his family. He will do what is necessary—work, create, even steal—to fill these needs. But note two additional dimensions to this and the higher needs that are readily apparent in our advanced society. First, the minimum standards of fulfilling certain of these most basic needs tend to increase as living standards increase. Enough food is not satisfactory: rather, steak, lobster, or other special cuisine may become standard. Second, as immediate needs in this category are met, man tends to think of meeting these same needs for himself and his family in the future. He puts something aside "for the rainy day." Hence, even a man of very limited means is receptive to minimum economic security devices such as money in a savings account in the event he finds himself out of work, life insurance for his family, or an elemental social security system that will give him assurance of some income after he retires.

Category II, the safety needs, are those that cause man to surround himself with protective devices and mechanisms, especially if he is uncertain about the imminence of danger and deprivation. Fear of a housebreaker sharpens the need for a gun, a dog, or stronger window and door latches. Fear of unemployment sharpens the need for some protective help from the employer, the union, the community, or the nation. A man facing the reality of a serious illness or surgery would be expected to have an intensified interest in life and health insurance.[12] Perhaps the intrinsic longing for peace is the ultimate reflection of this human need.

Categories III and IV, the needs for love and acceptance, for esteem and recognition, take on increasing value for man as his lower needs are satisfied. Again, he seeks means to assure the maintenance of friends, fellowship, fraternity, self-confidence, autonomy, and the like. The means by which he satisfies these needs tends to escalate in quantity and quality as his style and standard of life improves. He normally wants the continuance of "his own world" for himself and for his family before and after retirement, and in spite of disability or death during his working years. His interest in life insurance, retirement plans, health insurance, and the like, are among the manifestations of this perception of need and want.

Category V, the needs for self-fulfillment and self-expression, are the most refined and, in most instances, those sought and met only after the other needs have received attention. These needs seem less meaningful to people in a culture struggling for survival. In an advanced and affluent society like ours they take on increasing significance. Man's deep de-

---

[12] Maslow, *Motivation and Personality*, p. 41.

sire to grow through cultural pursuits, to enjoy life through recreational activities, to stretch his mind and consciousness through travel, to learn new things through advanced education, all become increasingly important in an affluent society. It would seem that freedom, in addition to economic affluence, is significant in this category. Pericles spoke of the "true freedoms of man" as "to do all of which he is capable, to realize his full potential within his society, to speak what is in his mind, and to go his own way without interference from other men," all of which are a very real part of self-fulfillment and self-expression.

This brief analysis suggests that:

1. Economic security mechanisms have an elemental role to play in satisfying most of man's basic needs, whatever the level of priority or prepotency;
2. On each level of human need, the minimum tends to increase with man's economic growth:
3. Man is concerned not only with present needs but with future needs;
4. Man is concerned not only with his personal needs but those of his family, church, college, community, and the like;
5. Man's needs are relative and as he moves up the ladder of living standards, he seeks increased protection through economic security mechanisms to prevent a fall from this higher point as he ventures to satisfy the next level of needs; and
6. Any institution, private or public, concerned primarily with serving the needs of man through economic means should include in its perspective all these aspects of the concept of security.

THE AMERICAN ECONOMIC SECURITY SYSTEM

An Arbitrary Definition

One of the most significant developments in 20th-century American history has been the immense growth in what might be called our economic security system. Any definition of this system must be arbitrary. It is recognized that, broadly, the economic security of the people of this nation is related to the relative real growth of our economy, assuming reasonable distribution of its goods and services. A definition more useful for the purposes of this chapter is limited to income maintenance systems involving death, disability, and retirement; and involving individual life and health insurance, employee benefit plans, and social insurance.

In 1970, annual premiums for all forms of private insurance, premiums and contributions for all forms of insured and uninsured employee benefit plans, and contributions or taxes to the federal social security system (excluding the state/federal unemployment compensation system) totaled about $110 billion. This is approximately 18 times the amount so allocated in 1940. It represented about 14 percent of gross national income for 1970 as contrasted to about 7 percent in 1940. In 1970, it represented about $535 for each man, woman and child, and $1,280 for each member of the labor force.

The Tripod of American Economic Security

The American economic security establishment is a unique blending of private enterprise and government activity. The platform of economic security that has been built for the more than 200 million U.S. citizens rests upon the three supports of individual or personal effort, group or corporate effort, and social or government effort. These efforts, in turn, are reflected in large measure in the growth and development of the three basic segments of private and government insurance, namely, individual, group, and social insurance.

Individual or personal insurance represents the oldest of these segments. Its growth and development has come essentially from voluntary decisions of individuals to allocate funds for various insurance coverages based upon individual awareness of security needs and ability to pay premiums.

Group insurance, broadly defined to include insured and uninsured pensions, group life and health insurance, and other elements of employee benefit plans, has been developed through business, union, and other group action on behalf of well-defined groups, usually employees.

Social insurance, initiated in Germany about a century ago but of relatively recent development in the United States, has evolved through action by government, mostly on the federal level.

The economic security system can be likened to a platform resting upon a tripod. Only one leg of the security tripod was of significance in the United States at the turn of the century. The second leg was added early in the century in the form of private pensions and group insurance. The third leg, social insurance, received its major thrust with the passage of the Social Security Act of 1935.

The three legs of this tripod of security have grown remarkably in the past 30 years—from a total outlay of about $6 billion in 1940 to about $107 billion in 1971.[13] The rate of growth, however, has been in inverse relationship to the order in which they were introduced. Figure 1–1 depicts the absolute growth as well as the relative change of the three segments during this period.

1. *Individual.* In 1940, the annual premiums for individual life insurance, health insurance, and annuities amounted to about $4 billion. This was 65 percent of the total "security dollar." For 1971, these premiums had increased to about $23 billion, but this amount represented only about 20 percent of the security dollar.

2. *Group.* The group aspect of the security tripod, as reflected in the annual premiums and contributions for group life and health insurance and all retirement plans and private pensions other than social security, amounted to about $1.5 billion in 1940, or about 25 percent of the security

---

[13] The data used to show growth and change in our "economic security system" or "security expenditures" are not exactly comparable among sources or years. A careful delineation and reconciliation is unnecessarily complicating for the purpose of this chapter.

FIGURE 1–1. **Economic Security Expenditures for 1940 and 1971 for Individual, Group, and Social Approaches**

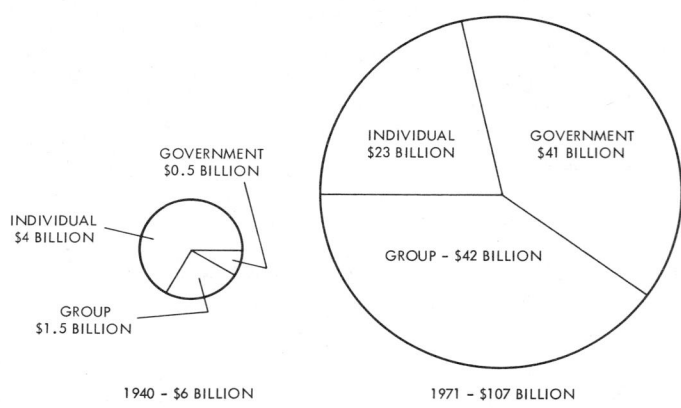

dollar. Thirty years later, for 1971, the amount had increased to $43 billion and represented about 40 percent of the security dollar.

3. *Social.* In 1940, the contributions to the federal social security system amounted to a little less than $650 million, or about 10 percent of the total security dollar in that year. In 1971, these contributions had increased to about $41 billion and represented about 40 percent of the security dollar.

In summary, then, the economic security system in 1971 revealed an individual segment of 20 percent, a group segment of 40 percent, and a social or government segment of 40 percent. In some 30 years, these percentages have changed from individual representing 65 percent, group 25 percent, and social 10 percent. The private sector composed of individual and group decreased during this period from some 90 percent to 60 percent and the government sector increased from 10 percent to 40 percent. During the same period the personal or individualized segment of the security dollar decreased from 65 percent to 20 percent, and the institutionalized segment (group and government) increased from 35 percent to 80 percent.

Security Expenditures 1950–70

Another revealing analysis of security expenditures in the United States for a 20-year period points up trends in security expenditures among life, health, and retirement coverages, the distribution of security expenditures as between private and government programs for these three types of coverages, and security expenditures related to personal income.[14]

---

[14] Life Insurance Agency Management Association, *Security Expenditures in the United States 1950–1965,* Research Report 1967–5 (File 910); and *Security Expenditures in the United States 1950–1970,* Research Report 1972–6 (File 910). Hartford, Connecticut.

FIGURE 1–2. Total Security Expenditures for Life, Health and Retirement Coverages

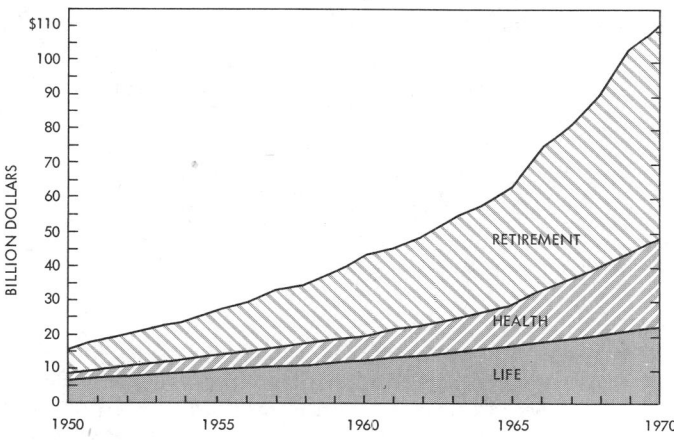

Source: Life Insurance Agency Management Association.

This research indicates that total expenditures have grown from $16 billion in 1950 to $111 billion in 1970. Figure 1–2 shows total security expenditures for life, health, and retirement during the period 1950–70 and reveals clearly the sharply increased share of total security payments going to retirement and health coverages during this period, and particularly in the past five years.

Figure 1–3 shows the distribution of security expenditures in quinquennial years beginning in 1950 by type of coverage with expenditures for each type of coverage being shown for government and private programs. The relative growth of the government programs as contrasted to

FIGURE 1–3. Distribution of Security Expenditures in Selected Years According to Type of Coverage and Type of Recipient

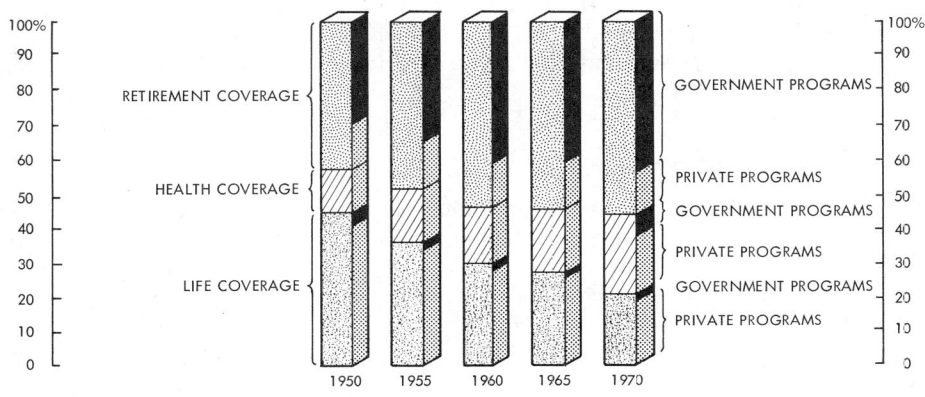

Source: Life Insurance Agency Management Association.

TABLE 1–1. Percentage Distribution of Total Security Expenditures by Type of Recipient

	Percent				
	1950	1955	1960	1965	1970
Life insurance companies (legal reserve)	51	47	40	39	32
Other private insurers and programs	15	17	18	20	19
Government programs	34	36	42	41	49

Source: Life Insurance Agency Management Association.

the private programs is shown to be very substantial for retirement and health coverages. Dollar payments for all government-administered programs have grown more than 900 percent since 1950, from $5.4 billion to $54.1 billion, and have more than doubled since 1965 alone when they amounted to $25.8 billion. Dollar payments to life insurance companies have not kept pace with the government programs but have increased substantially. Since 1950, life insurance companies' premium income from security expenditures has grown nearly 350 percent.

Table 1–1 shows the percentage distribution of total security expenditures by type of recipient for quinquennial years 1950 to 1970. In 1950, legal reserve life insurance companies received 51 percent of the total, other private insurers and programs (fraternals, savings bank life, uninsured pensions, et al.) received 15 percent, and government programs received 34 percent. By 1970, the government programs had increased their share to 49 percent and the share of life insurance companies had decreased to 32 percent.

As reflected in Figure 1–4, the proportion of augmented disposable personal income[15] allocated to security expenditures increased from 7.5 percent in 1950 to 15 percent in 1970. The life insurance companies' share of the augmented disposable personal income moved from 3.86 percent in 1950 to 4.74 percent in 1970. The government programs' share of augmented disposable personal income moved from 3.63 percent in 1950 to 10.22 percent in 1970.

ISSUES AND UNANSWERED QUESTIONS

The patterns and trends of economic security in the United States are clear. Private and public programs are rapidly expanding. Institutional-

---

15 Augmented disposable personal income figures are used rather than the regular disposable personal income figures published by the Department of Commerce because the latter exclude payments for veterans' insurance, payments to railroad and government employee retirement systems, and compensation funds, as well as all social security taxes. For the analysis here, the disposable personal income figures are augmented by payments to these programs by employees and employers. The Department of Commerce figures include payments by employers to private group plans and therefore no adjustments are necessary to include these.

FIGURE 1–4.   **Security Expenditures as a Percent of Augmented Disposable Personal Income**

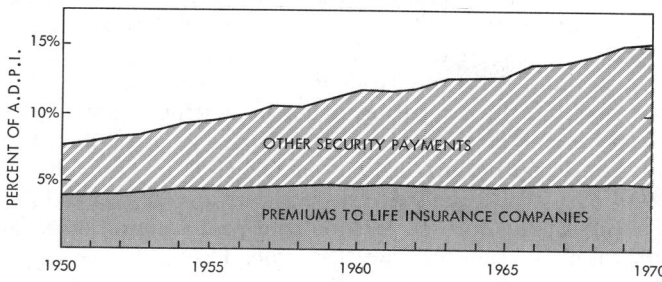

Source: Life Insurance Agency Management Association.

ized programs, private and public, are growing most rapidly. This growth, and possibly this pattern of growth, is in response to man's needs, wants, and desires, and his capacity to fill these needs. Future trends and patterns and their impact are not clear.

In contradiction to the American tradition of seeking individual solutions to problems, there is emerging evidence that attitudes are changing and institutional solutions to problems are sought. For example, the proportion of people who think the individual alone should be responsible for his life insurance needs has declined, the proportion believing the individual should provide the major part of his retirement income has declined, and relatively fewer people are opposed to the expansion of government financial security services—particularly in areas where they feel they have little control.

Changing patterns and philosophies of economic security suggest that all citizens and institutions, and particularly those in the private and government sectors concerned with economic security, should seek philosophical and pragmatic answers to questions that may reveal future dimensions of economic security. Massive and unseen implications to the economic and social forms of the nation are involved.

Question: What is man's attitude toward security—and insecurity? Intuitively, security is garbed in the "white hat," as something good and productive, while insecurity is clothed in the "black hat," as something bad and unproductive. The truth of the matter is that few efforts have been made to define security, to seek its true meaning in human behavior. It can be argued that *insecurity* may be a powerful motivator for man to work, to produce, to create. On the other hand, it seems reasonable to believe that some minimum degree of security is highly desirable if we are to carry out our tasks in our world of specialization. Much needs to be defined and discussed about the relationships of man's basic needs and wants and the design and development of the private and public security mechanisms of the future.

Question: What is the proportion of national income that should be allocated to public security programs? Should the proportion increase, decrease, or remain constant in relation to an expanding national income?

One can argue that as aggregate real income increases, individuals are better able to meet their security needs through personal decision making and, therefore, percentage allocations of national income to public programs should decrease with expansions in the economy. On the other hand, it can be, and is, argued that the affluence of an expanding economy makes possible the allocation of an increasing share of national income to government economic security programs, and thus the relative role of the group and individual approaches should diminish.

Question: Do institutionalized security arrangements reduce the motivation of individuals to build personalized protection and savings plans? The argument is commonly made that social security, group insurance, and pensions are gradually eliminating the need for individual and personal security plans and, based on the trends cited earlier, this may be happening. Yet, there is evidence in recent studies of consumer behavior that achievement of a portion of an attainable goal provides a powerful motivation to pursue that goal; that what is called a "recognition effect" stimulates persons to save personally for retirement because they realize that a fair degree of financial independence is actually attainable as a result of social security and group arrangements.[16] Is it possible that the goal of financial and economic security is such a powerful and persistent one that it will continue to climb with our increasing economic affluence and that individualistic solutions will be stimulated by the institutionalized or societal solutions?

Question: Can institutionalized security mechanisms provide for the higher, individualistic needs of man? By definition, a program of social insurance is universal; practically all persons are included by law and most must make contributions to its cost during their productive years. Is it possible for that which is designed for *all* to provide at the same time for the specialized and personalized needs of individuals and families? The same question can be raised regarding group insurance and pensions although the fitting of benefit to need usually is closer than in social insurance and efforts are being made to offer group insureds greater choice in benefit design.

Question: How significant to our economic system is the accumulation of capital through the individual and group security mechanisms? It is generally accepted that only through continued economic growth over the long run can we achieve the higher goals of our society. Also, if we are to have increasing productivity in our economy, it is agreed that we must have increasing capital accumulation—savings instead of consumption. We know that capital accumulation through the individual and group security mechanisms (life insurance, annuities, and pensions) are a major source of capital. In 1971, the assets of life insurance companies exceeded $225 billion and noninsured pension plans had reserves of about

---

[16] Phillip Cagan, *The Effect of Pension Plans on Aggregate Savings: Evidence from a Sample Survey,* Occasional Paper 95 (New York: National Bureau of Economic Research, 1965). George Katona, *Private Pensions and Individual Saving* (Ann Arbor, Mich.: Survey Research Center of the University of Michigan, 1965). Roger F. Murray, "The Future of Private Pensions: Some Economic Aspects," paper presented to 1966 annual meeting of the American Risk and Insurance Association.

$100 billion. Since most government programs are essentially tax-supported and nonfunded and thus do not accumulate capital for investment, a diminishing role for the private sector may have long-range economic implications.

Question: Are there limits to the expansion of social insurance and group schemes because of their cost to those who ultimately must pay for them? For example, to what extent are persons participating in the payment for social and group insurance through payroll deductions actually aware of their payments? Is it possible that many workers do not realize and do not care about deductions from their base compensation, but rather concentrate only on their "take-home pay"? Stated differently, might the percentage and amount of wages and salaries devoted to social insurance and group insurance be steadily increased over the years without the workers involved becoming disenchanted if the earnings level rises faster than the deductions?

Evidence is accumulating that social security contributions or taxes are becoming real concerns of workers, unions, businesses, and politicians. As the social security tax for the worker at or above the wage base has increased from $45 in 1950 to $144 in 1960, to $632 in 1973 (with these amounts matched by the employer), protests have begun to mount. The expansion of the system by legislation in 1972, with the impact of the taxes first felt in January 1973, resulted in protests to Congress and wide discussion in the nation's news media. The chairman of the powerful House Ways and Means Committee is reported to have responded to the question of, "How high can the payroll tax for social security go without reaching the breaking point?" by saying that, "We're already there, or at least almost there." Since the unfunded system requires that "the young pay for the old," in that benefits can only be paid if those working (and their employers) make adequate contributions, it seems likely that future expansion proposals will be subject to greater study and public debate than has occurred in the past. In addition, it is likely that there will be increasing discussion of the critical question of at least partial funding of social security benefits from general revenues of the federal government.

Question: If it is true that self-fulfillment is man's ultimate need, want, and desire, and if it is true that those needs lower in the hierarchy are increasingly being satisfied in our affluent society through the social and group mechanisms, then should increased attention be given to shaping the individualistic approach toward meeting man's higher level needs? Individuals are different in ambition, energy, creativity, initiative, maturity, education, and the like. Individual differences must be subordinated in public programs designed for all and can be recognized only partly in corporate and group programs. These differences can be fully recognized in individual insurance and in personal savings and investment decisions.

Question: Although it seems reasonable to expect that there will be a major role for all parts of the tripod of economic security—social, group, and individual—shouldn't the advocates of the social approach study the significance of the group and individual approaches; shouldn't the advocates of the group approach look to the strengths of the social and individual approaches; and shouldn't those who believe in the individual approach understand the role of the social and group mechanisms? Understanding, each of the other, might not greatly lessen the enthusiasm of each for his own beliefs but surely it would lead to the kind of dialogue and communication that would strengthen the total economic security establishment.

A Wide-Angle Perceptual Lens

In this chapter, concerned with the nature of security, with man's basic needs and wants, with the role of economic security in fulfilling many of these needs and wants, and with the patterns and philosophies of a rapidly developing private and public economic security system, an effort has been made to suggest in a macro frame of reference the complex of forces that impact upon life and health insurance. A true understanding of this huge financial service institution is not possible without such a wide-angle perceptual lens.

Likewise, those who as individuals, as citizens, and as consumers would seek to understand economic and financial security must develop a full awareness of the varied functions of the business of life and health insurance, of the service roles of those who are a direct or indirect part of this business institution, and of the contributions to customers and to society of these people and this business. In the many chapters of this volume, both the student and reference seeker will find answers provided by experienced and authoritative minds.

SELECTED REFERENCES

Goodman, Mary Ellen. *The Individual and Culture.* Homewood, Ill.: The Dorsey Press, 1967.

Gregg, Davis W. *The Tripod of American Economic Security.* 1965 William Elliott Lecture presented at The Pennsylvania State University.

————. "Security and Insurance: Some Issues and Unanswered Questions," *C.L.U. Journal,* Vol. 21 (January 1967), pp. 13–18.

————. "Freedom and Security," *C.L.U. Forum Report, 1970.* Bryn Mawr, Pa.: American Society of Chartered Life Underwriters, 1971.

Life Insurance Agency Management Association. *Security Expenditures in the United States 1950–1970.* Research Report 1972–6 (File 910). Hartford, Connecticut.

Maslow, Abraham H. "Preface to Motivation Theory," *Psychosomatic Medicine,* Vol. 5 (1943).

————. *Motivation and Personality.* 2d ed. New York: Harper & Row, 1970.

2

Human Life Values

By KENNETH BLACK, JR.

THERE IS GENERAL AGREEMENT that man is most human at the point of choice or when he is engaged in decision-making. It is this ability to make conscious choices based on understanding of past events and prediction of future consequences that distinguishes man most markedly from other animals. Man is vastly superior to other animals in his capacity to visualize the long-range consequences of alternative courses of action.[1] It is the ability, the right and the freedom to make decisions and influence outcomes that permit a man to maintain his individual identity, to develop a self-image based upon a matrix of values—an individual value system—all his own. His individual reaction to varying degrees of uncertainty which influence his choice and decisions again provides him individualistic identity.

From an economic viewpoint, this process of individual decision-making necessitates that an individual *appraise* the consequences of his actions. For example, in many of the purchases he makes from day to day, a man is placing a value on the expected benefits he will derive from the purchases. If he estimates that the present cost is equal to or below the value to him of the future benefits from the expenditure, he makes the purchase. Thus, when an individual buys a home, he must decide that the use of that home has a value to him and his family at least equal to the purchase price.

Similarly, when an employer hires an additional employee, that decision requires the employer to determine the value of the employee's future services. The employer is projecting into the future the value of the services to be performed and comparing them with the total he must pay.

The concept of appraising and comparing future values is inherent in all decision-making. As will be brought out below, the same economic and statistical principles are applicable whether one is concerned with the appraisal of the value of property or of the earning capacity of human beings. In recent years increasing attention has focused upon the analogy

---

[1] All animals are choice-making organisms. They all learn and make appropriate choices based on learning.

between the productive power of human beings and the productive power of such capital assets as business machinery, factories, and equipment.[2]

THE CONCEPT OF HUMAN CAPITAL

Current Economic Interest

Recent years have witnessed intensive concern with research by economists on *investment* in human capital. The main motivating factor probably has been a realization that the growth of physical capital, at least as conventionally measured, explains a relatively small part of the growth of income in most countries. Investment in human capital (e.g., education) has come to be one of the most cogent explanations for the differences in rates of economic growth experienced from country to country.[3]

Traditionally, economists have shied away from the explicit analysis of investment in human capital. The thought of investment in human beings has been offensive to many. Our values and beliefs inhibit us from looking upon human beings as capital goods, except in slavery, and this we abhor. But surely there is nothing in the concept of human capital contrary to the idea that wealth exists only for the advantage of people. By investing in themselves, people can enlarge the range of choices available to them. It is one way free men can enhance their welfare.

In the 1960s, the Joint Economic Committee of the Congress expressed concern with the general inadequacy of available information about the economic effects of investment in human resources.

Although speculation about the money value of human beings began to appear in economic literature as early as the seventeenth century, it is only with the last several years that economists have undertaken specific analysis in this area.[4]

Economists today are clearly interested in this area and increasingly sophisticated research activity and resulting literature are available.

The significance of human capital was dramatically demonstrated in the rapid postwar recovery of countries that had suffered severe destruction of plants and equipment during the war. The toll from bombing was all too visible in the flattened factories; wrecked railroad yards, bridges, and harbors; and the cities in ruin. Structures, equipment, and inventories were heaps of rubble. Not so visible, yet large, was the toll from wartime depletion of the physical plant that escaped destruction by bombs. Econ-

---

[2] See Stuart M. Speiser, *Recovery for Wrongful Death—Economic Handbook* (Rochester, N.Y.: The Lawyers Co-Operative Publishing Co., 1970).

[3] See Mark Blaug, *Economics of Education, A Selected Annotated Bibliography*, 2d ed. (New York: Pergamon Press, 1970).

[4] *Federal Programs for the Development of Human Resources*, Joint Economic Committee, Congress of the United States, Vol. 1, Part 1, p. 3. See also Theodore W. Schultz, "Investment in Human Capital," *American Economic Review*, Vol. LI, March, 1961, p. 2; B. F. Kiker, "The Historic Roots of the Concept of Human Capital," *Journal of Political Economy*, Vol. LXXIV, October, 1966, pp. 481–99; Burton A. Weisbrod, "The Valuation of Human Capital," *Journal of Political Economy*, Vol. LXIX, October 1961, pp. 425–26.

omists were called upon to assess the implications of these wartime losses for recovery. In retrospect, it is clear that they overestimated the prospective retarding effects of these losses. The explanation that is now clear is that they gave altogether too much weight to nonhuman capital in making these assessments. They did not consider adequately the concept of *all* capital and, therefore, failed to account sufficiently for human capital and the important part that it plays in production in the modern economy.

Human resources obviously have both quantitative and qualitative dimensions. How can the magnitude of human investment be estimated? The practice followed in connection with physical capital goods is to estimate the magnitude of capital formation by expenditures made to produce the capital goods. This practice would suffice also for the formation of human capital. For human capital, however, there is an additional problem that is less pressing for physical capital goods: How to distinguish between expenditures for consumption and for investment.

Much of what is called *consumption* constitutes investment in human capital. Direct expenditures on education, health, and internal migration to take advantage of better job opportunities are clear examples, as are earnings foregone by mature students attending school and by workers acquiring on-the-job training. In these and similar ways the *quality* of human effort can be greatly improved and its *productivity* enhanced. Most of the relevant activities are partly consumption and partly investment.

In principle there is an alternative method for estimating human capital, namely by its yield, rather than by its cost. While any capability produced by human investment becomes part of the human agent and hence cannot be sold, it nevertheless is "in touch with the market place" by affecting the wages and salaries that a human agent can earn. The resulting increase in earnings is the yield on the investment (in principle, the value of the investment can be determined by discounting the potential future earnings at yield just as the value of physical capital goods can be determined by discounting its income stream).

Significance of Human Capital Valuation

Estimates of the value of human capital to society are potentially useful for a variety of purposes. Rational population and immigration policies would involve consideration of the productive value of additional people. Assessment of public health, highway construction, and flood control policies would be enhanced by the knowledge of the value of the human capital preserved through such expenditures. One of the benefits of these public projects is in the form of reduced mortality—that is, reduced losses of human capital—from diseases, highway accidents, and floods.[5] Estimates of human capital values also would aid in developing national policies affecting interregional migration. Similarly, as mentioned earlier, education and vocational rehabilitation policies should reflect considera-

---

[5] See Roy L. Lassiter, Jr., and Jordan B. Ray, "Some Implications of Negligence Law for Resource and the Conservation of Human Capital," *Land Economics*, Vol. 44, 275–81, 1968.

tion of how the quality and, hence, the value of human capital can be increased through appropriate expenditures. And the desirability of using per capita human-capital values as the welfare index, instead of per capita current income, seems to merit exploration.

Early Efforts to Estimate Economic Value of Human Life

One of the first, quite detailed, attempts to develop a scheme for estimating the economic value of the human life was done by Dublin and Lotka.[6] Employed as statisticians by a life insurance company, they were primarily interested in estimating the economic loss which a family suffers when the wage earner dies. This was measured by the present value of the future net earnings had the individual lived his normal life expectancy. Net earnings were defined as gross earnings less that part of earnings which the wage earner would have expended on himself.

In order to predict future earnings for an individual at a given age, smooth curves were fitted to cross-sectional age and income data for several income classes representing different levels of skill. Then future income for an individual within a certain skill class was predicted from the appropriate fitted curve. Taking data for annual expenditures on such items as food, clothing, and medical care for a child of a certain age and weighing these by the corresponding expenditures for the adult, an "adult consumption unit" for each child is derived. Totaling these for each child and the adults then gives the number of adult consumption units in the family. Then gross income minus savings and income taxes, divided by the number of adult consumption units for the family, gives a cost of living figure for the male adult. Most expenses (housing, furniture, automobile, and the like) were simply proportioned equally among the members of the family.

Another study, following very closely the estimating procedure used by Dublin and Lotka, was made by Miller and Honrath.[7] The major difference between the two studies was that the latter used more current income data and provided for the growth of salaries over time. The present value of future estimated gross earnings was computed using four different income growth rates and four different discount rates. Based on an estimate that it would cost $1,000 annually to provide food, clothing, and the like, for a male wage earner of a family of five with an annual income of $6,000, a second figure was computed as the present value of future maintenance costs using the figure of $1,000, $2,000, or $3,000 for personal maintenance cost per year. These present value figures are computed and tabulated according to age, race, and selected educational and occupational levels for adult, male wage earners.

A further attempt to estimate the economic value of a human life was made by Rice and Cooper.[8] This study was quite similar to the previous

---

[6] See Louis I. Dublin and Alfred J. Lotka, *The Money Value of a Man*, rev. ed. (New York: The Ronald Press Company, 1946).

[7] U.S. Bureau of the Census, *Present Value of Estimated Lifetime Earnings*, Technical Paper No. 16 (Washington, D.C.: U.S. Government Printing Office, 1967).

[8] D. P. Rice and B. S. Cooper, "The Economic Value of a Human Life," *American Journal of Public Health*, 1967.

study except sex was used as a classification and type of occupation was not considered. The present value of lifetime earnings is presented by age, race, sex, and years of schooling completed. While the method used in this study to estimate earnings is not explicitly explained, cross-sectional data on 1964 earnings are used.[9] Also, since a growth rate in earnings of 3 percent and a discount rate of 7 percent will reduce to approximately 4 percent $\left(\dfrac{1.07}{1.03} = 1.039\right)$, 4 percent was used as the discount rate in this study.

The three studies summarized above are fairly representative of the procedures used historically to estimate the value of a human life, either to the family concerned or to society as a whole. All of these studies used one technique or another to predict future earnings for an individual from cross-sectional data on individuals with similar education and/or occupational experience.

There are a number of more theoretical approaches to predict the future income of an individual that have grown out of the work begun by Becker in the late 50s. These theoretical models are beyond the scope of this discussion but are important developments in improving the capacity to work effectively in this area.[10]

THE HUMAN LIFE VALUE CONCEPT

The human life value concept is one segment of the general theory of human capital. While this general area of inquiry has been under discussion for over four centuries, only in recent times has the interrelationship between human capital and life insurance been acknowledged. Some semblance of the idea existed in the old Anglo-Saxon law where it was used to determine the compensation to be allowed to the relatives of an individual who was killed by a third party. In recent years the valuation of a human life in connection with legal actions seeking recovery for wrongful death or disability has gained prominence. A considerable body of literature has developed in this area, contributing to a more scientific approach to the calculation of damages (including human life values) in wrongful death cases.[11]

Human Life Value Defined

The human life value may be defined, quantitatively, as the capitalized value of the net future earnings of an individual. The preceding sections have indicated that the human life value concept can be used for diverse purposes. It is important to remember that there is not one human life value, but several. A given human life value is a function of its purpose.

In determining the human life value of an individual for inclusion in national wealth (human capital stock), one would have to discount the

---

[9] Cross-sectional data refer to data at a specific point in time whereas time series data are taken at different points in time.

[10] See Gary S. Becker, *Human Capital* (New York: Columbia University Press, 1964).

[11] Speiser, *Recovery for Wrongful Death*.

earnings for many factors *including mortality*. If, on the other hand, one is interested in determining the human life value of an individual to his wife for life insurance purposes, *mortality would not be a discount factor*. One would not discount for mortality because the object of the insurance is to replace that portion of a man's income that would normally go to his wife had he lived. To discount for mortality, then, is to discount for the very factor being insured against. In contrast, in wrongful death cases, one would discount for mortality as well as other factors because here account should be taken of the chance that the individual would not have lived to earn future income.

Again, in estimating the individual human life value, if only 94 percent of a given homogeneous group (as to profession, age, health, locality, and the like) are employed, then the average future gross earnings of this group should be discounted for this factor in determining the individual member's human life value. This is done because there is only a .94 probability of an individual earning this wage.

It is important, then, to define a given human value carefully with cognizance of its intended use. It may be noted that in our society, the capital value of a man or woman is primarily, though not entirely, to other family members. Even to the extent that the capital value of a person is a value to his or her family, other people may still have a strong interest in the maintenance and improvement of the value because of benefits which may accrue to them. Persons outside the family may be called upon to give aid to a distressed family, or may pay indirectly through the effects of high crime rates. If a person with a high human life value is in temporary financial difficulty, he may be able to borrow on the strength of his future. For a person with a low human life value this may be impossible.

Human Life Values and Property Values

The significance of human life values (human capital) in our society may be emphasized by a comparison of such values with our stock of property values. For example, the human capital value for the United States (males) in 1950 has been compared with the dollar value of tangible (nonhuman) assets in the United States in 1949.[12] The human capital values (net of personal consumption expenditures) were $1,055 billion at a 10 percent rate of discount, and $2,218 billion at a 4 percent rate of discount. The dollar value of tangible assets were estimated at $881 billion. By contrast the magnitude of our human capital stock seems impressive.

Economic theory and business and accounting practice often treat human beings and property in ways that make the two seem very similar. For example, classical economic theory refers typically to four factors of production, four resources that are used in the production of almost any good or service throughout the economy. The four resources are land, labor, capital, and entrepreneurship. This means that the services of land,

---

[12] Weisbrod, "The Valuation of Human Capital," pp. 433–34.

labor, and capital equipment are essential to production, and from this point of view they are treated as being essentially alike.

No one, of course, would deny that there are differences between humans and property resources, but these differences are not important from the perspectives with which we are dealing. Nevertheless, we recognize that unlike machines and factories, human beings are not owned. Human beings cannot be bought and sold.[13] It must be kept in mind that the important similarities between human beings and physical assets are emphasized for purposes of economic evaluation. The similarities are not meant to obscure differences which, for other purposes, are crucial.

The similarities between human beings and physical assets are strikingly persuasive. Consider the following:[14]

1. The work-life expectancy of a man or a woman is equivalent to the productive life of a physical asset.
2. The employer's payment of the future expected earnings of a person is equivalent to the future returns expected from employment of a physical asset.
3. The projected personal expenditures of a decedent are equivalent to the projected depreciation and maintenance costs of a physical asset.
4. The services of both physical assets and persons are bought and sold in markets.
5. There is sufficient stability in the expected return of each of these factors of production for there to be purchases and sales of capital assets and of labor services.
6. There is sufficient stability in the expected costs of money, that is, in the discount rate, for a present value to be calculated for the future returns attributable to human resources and property resources.
7. In the vast majority of business decisions with respect to investment, a direct comparison of the present value of physical assets must be made with the present value of human services.

Appraising Human Life Values

The same economic and statistical principles are applicable whether one is concerned with the appraisal of the value of property or of the earning capacity of human beings. The general elements of appraising potential earnings for an individual require a projection over his expected work life of such items as *basic earnings, incentive earnings,* and *fringe benefits.* These elements generally may be expected to vary with such criteria as occupation and industry, age, sex, race, residence, education, mobility, marital status, and number of dependents. The process is still further complicated by the necessity to project change in each of these considerations. For purposes of this discussion, a simplified model will be utilized, but it should be noted that considerable research and develop-

---

[13] For an exception, see Simon Rottenberg, "The Baseball Player's Labor Market," *Journal of Political Economy,* Vol. LXIV (1956), pp. 242–58.
[14] Speiser, *Recovery for Wrongful Death,* pp. 45–47.

ment presently under way is likely to see increasingly sophisticated approaches to the appraisal of human life values.[15]

The name most often associated with the human life value concept is that of Dr. S. S. Huebner. It was mainly through his efforts that the concept gained widespread recognition in the 1920s and 1930s. Dr. Huebner's first written discussion of this concept was in his *Life Insurance* textbook published in 1915.[16] Dr. Huebner developed his human life value concept further in 1927 with the publication of his *Economics of Life Insurance*.[17] In this volume he discussed the human life value concept as the economic basis of life insurance, the monetary importance of human life values, the need for scientific treatment, and methods of appraisal.

Dr. Huebner's method of appraisal was to: (1) determine how much of a man's income is devoted to his family; (2) determine the individual's life expectancy or the number of years between the present age and the contemplated age of retirement, using the shorter period; and (3) multiply (1) by the present value of $1.00 per annum for the period determined in (2). This method, which is limited by the assumption of a continuation of present income into the future and also by discounting for mortality, nevertheless was conceptually easy to grasp and involved only simple arithmetic calculations. Thus, while increasingly sophisticated methods of valuing human capital and individual human life values are available to use in specific areas, for general purposes individual human life values can be estimated through a relatively simple process. It is necessary to determine four quantitative factors:

1. Estimate the individual's expected annual earnings net after taxes;
2. Estimate the amount of his expected annual personal maintenance expenses;
3. Estimate his working life expectancy; and
4. Select an appropriate capitalization rate.

Then, the human life value may be calculated by subtracting personal maintenance expenses (2) from his expected net annual earnings (1) and capitalizing this net amount at the selected rate (4) for the working life expectancy (3).

Assume, for example, that a 35-year-old man is earning $16,000 annually and expects his earnings to remain at this level, that he has a work-life expectancy[18] of 28.6 years, that his expected income tax liability is $2,000, and that his expected annual personal maintenance expenses will be $4,000, 25 percent of his gross earnings. Based on these assumptions, this individual's family can be expected to receive $10,000 a year for 28.6

---

[15] U.S. Bureau of the Census, *Present Value of Estimated Lifetime Earnings,* Technical Paper No. 16 (Washington, D.C.: U.S. Government Printing Office, 1967). See also John E. Brown, "A Study of the Economic Variables Affecting the Valuation of a Human Life in Legal Decisions," (unpublished Ph.D. thesis, Department of Economics, North Carolina State University, 1971).

[16] S. S. Huebner, *Life Insurance* (New York: D. Appleton and Company, 1915).

[17] S. S. Huebner, *Economics of Life Insurance* (New York: D. Appleton and Company, 1927).

[18] The average number of years a person is expected to be both alive *and* in the work force.

TABLE 2–1.   Human Life Values (assumed retirement age 65, varying average net future income and age of valuation, interest at 4 percent per annum)

| Age | Average Net Future Income | | | |
---	$10,000	$15,000	$20,000	$25,000
25	$197,928	$296,892	$395,856	$494,820
30	186,646	279,969	373,292	466,615
35	172,920	259,380	345,840	432,300
40	156,221	234,332	312,442	390,553
45	135,903	203,855	271,806	339,758

years, the work-life expectancy of the working male, age 35, as computed by the Bureau of Labor Statistics. If it is assumed that 5 percent is the appropriate capitalization rate,[19] the present value of one dollar per annum payable in twelve equal monthly installments for 28.6 years is 15.38. The present value of $10,000 per year would then be 15.38 times $10,000, or $153,000, the human life value of the individual in question. In effect, this calculation says this man's discounted future net earnings which would be lost in the event of his death today are $153,000. This value is, in most cases, the most significant value available to a man or his family and deserves careful management and protection as with all important property values. It is important to remember that had this calculation been made for life insurance purposes, "work expectancy" would have been a function of the period until contemplated retirement and no discount for mortality would have been considered.

Table 2–1 presents illustrative human life values with income level and present age as variables. The calculations assume constant future income and maintenance factors (shown net), a retirement age of 65, and a capitalization rate of 4 percent.

The assumption of constant future income and self maintenance costs in the above simplified examples are unrealistic and, as pointed out earlier, complex economic analysis is involved in projecting future net earnings for specific purposes. Consider further the special problems involved in dealing with professional practitioners, key corporate executives, partners, housewives, and other occupational groups with unique characteristics.[20] Nevertheless, this present simplified example does communicate the concept of the human life value (valuing future net earnings) and the significant magnitude of the values at stake.

SELECTED REFERENCES

Blaug, Mark. *Economics of Education, A Selected Annotated Bibliography*, 2d ed. New York: Pergamon Press, 1970.

---

[19] See Lassiter and Ray, *Land Economics*, for a brief discussion of the "proper" rate.

[20] Roy L. Lassiter, Jr., "Estimating the Monetary Value of Damages in Negligence Cases Involving Death," *University of Florida Law Review* (1962), pp. 384–99.

Dublin, Louis I., and Lotka, Alfred J. *The Money Value of a Man.* Rev. ed. New York: The Ronald Press Company, 1946.

Hofflander, Al E. "The Human Life Value: An Historical Perspective," *The Journal of Risk and Insurance,* Vol. XXXIII, No. 3 (September, 1966), pp. 381–91.

Huebner, S. S., and Black, Kenneth, Jr. *Life Insurance* 8th ed. New York: Appleton-Century-Crofts, Inc., 1972.

Speiser, Stuart M. *Recovery for Wrongful Death—Economic Handbook.* Rochester, N.Y.: The Lawyers Co-operative Publishing Company, 1970.

U.S. Bureau of the Census. *Present Value of Estimated Lifetime Earnings,* Technical Paper No. 16. Washington, D.C.: U.S. Government Printing Office, 1967.

3

Protection Functions of Life and Health Insurance

By WILLIAM T. BEADLES

In 1970, John Doe, a 46-year-old businessman, purchased a $10,000 life insurance policy from the Ajax Life Insurance Company, the initial monthly premium being $6.55. Mr. Doe died of a heart attack just 19 days after the policy was issued and his beneficiary was paid $10,122 by Ajax. Also in 1970, Richard Roe, a 28-year-old laborer purchased a $10,000 life insurance policy from Ajax. The initial premium paid by Roe was $80.13. Roe's policy had a "double indemnity" or, more correctly, an "accidental death benefits" rider. Following Roe's death in an auto accident eight months later, Ajax paid his beneficiary $20,147.15. A third Ajax insured in 1970 paid an initial premium of $90.00 for a $50,000 life insurance policy. He died of a heart attack just three months after this policy went into effect and Ajax paid $50,203.70 to the beneficiary.[1]

The above are three illustrations of the 237 "first year" death claims paid by Ajax during 1970. Ajax received a total of $25,446.84 in premiums for these 237 policies which were issued in 1970. In turn, Ajax paid out $3,322,273.03 in that same year in death claims to the beneficiaries of these 237 insureds. To put it differently, Ajax paid out approximately $140 for every $1 of premium which it received on these policies.

A study of the first-year death claims of any large insurer would show that a very large proportion of those early deaths are classified as "accidents." Of these, auto accidents are by far the most numerous. Other accidental causes are lightning, drowning, infant suffocation, train accidents, and motorcycle accidents.

These are striking illustrations of the "protection functions" of life insurance. By purchasing these policies and paying a relatively small premium to put the insurance in force, each of these 237 persons either created a new death estate or increased his present one so that, collectively,

---

[1] All names are fictitious, but all illustrations are factual.

the group of beneficiaries received almost $3⅓ million following the death of these insureds, not one cent of which would have been received had the life insurance not been in force. This was truly "life insurance in action."

How could Ajax, or any life insurance company, do this—pay out over a period of just one year approximately $140 for every $1 of premium it received? Two things are certain: one, there is no private mint to create money out of the blue sky; two, every life insurance company must be prepared to pay the face amount of every policy it issues whenever the insured dies while the policy is in force.

POOLING OF RISKS AND LAW
OF LARGE NUMBERS

While a policy is in force, how can a life insurance company agree to pay *whenever* an insured dies? First is the fact that all insurance is a matter of pooling, of group sharing of losses. Although Ajax had 237 first-year death claims, it issued tens of thousands of new policies that year.[2] In addition, it received premiums that same year from hundreds of thousands of policyowners whose policies had been issued in earlier years and which were still in force on a premium-paying basis.[3]

It is contrary to the pooling principle to consider only the premiums received from the relatively small number of insureds who became first-year death claims to that same group. For every Ajax insured who died in 1970, there were thousands of other Ajax insureds who did not die and who paid premiums for that year.

In addition to the pooling principle, life insurance relies on the ability of the insurer to predict with reasonable accuracy the number of death claims it can expect to have in a given year. This surprising result arises partly from the operation of what is called "the law of large numbers." Obviously, it is not possible to predict when any one person will die, unless he is literally on his death bed, and even then the predictions may not be very accurate. Yet, while the life insurers cannot predict the time of death of any single insured, they are able to predict the approximate number of deaths in a certain period from a given large number of insureds. That which is impossible in relation to any one individual is entirely feasible when a sufficiently large number of persons is considered.

Life insurers make use of widely and carefully compiled mortality statistics. These might show, for example, that among insured persons age 40, and on the basis of past experience, two out of every thousand could be expected to die during the year. This would indicate the probability of death, and experience has shown that, within broad limits, the greater the number in the group, the closer would the actual experience approximate the probable experience.

By using probabilities based upon sufficiently conservative mortality statistics and by insuring enough lives for the law of large numbers to be relied upon, insurers are able to do the apparently impossible. Unfortu-

---

[2] Actually, it issued policies amounting to over $2.5 billion in 1970.
[3] The premiums earned in 1970 amounted to $154,807,042.43.

nately, a significant proportion of the population still does not understand the fundamental purpose of life insurance and how the insurance technique works. The basic, fundamental purpose of life insurance (the one to which all others are subordinate) is to create during life, an ultimate death estate of what has been traditionally a fixed number of dollars, payable whenever death occurs and provided only that the insured's policy be in full effect at the time of death.

INSURANCE VERSUS GAMBLING

The first reaction of many to illustrations such as those used at the beginning of this chapter is that life insurance is perhaps the most outstanding example of gambling. To correct that impression, it is important to show how, in fact, life insurance is the opposite of gambling. It is easy for intelligent people to say of the earlier John Doe illustration, "Well, John bet $6.55, the insurer bet $10,000, and John (or his beneficiaries) won—he died!" But that connotes wagering when actually there was none.

What is the essence of gambling? Whatever one person wins from a wager is lost by the other wagering party. Of greater significance to this discussion is that one cannot make a wager or enter into a gambling agreement of any sort without creating immediately a risk of loss for himself.[4] Before the gambler wagered on the throw of the dice, he couldn't have lost one cent, whatever the result. As soon as he had made a wager, he created a risk of loss to himself where no such risk had existed previously.

The same analysis shows that what one insured gains is not at the expense of another insured. Basically, it can be said that the entire group of insureds provides, through the premiums paid, the funds which make possible the payment of all claims. The purchase of insurance does not create a new and theretofore nonexisting risk of loss to the purchaser, as is always true when one enters into a gambling agreement. Instead, the only intelligent reason for purchasing insurance is that the purchaser faces an already existing risk of economic loss.

For life insurance, the risk arises out of the possibility of premature death, resulting in economic loss to those who may be dependent upon the insured for all or part of their monetary income. The one who faces this risk finds that the insurance mechanism may be used to transfer to the insured group, through the insurer, the risk of the loss arising from his death. In effect the insurer says, "You pay me a reasonable fee (the premium) and I'll assume this risk; if your death occurs while the insurance is in force, I'll pay the stipulated amount (face of the policy) to your beneficiaries so they will not suffer the loss that would otherwise be theirs."

Similarly, the buyer of health insurance may be interested primarily in the fact that his future disability will cause additional expense if he is hospitalized. So he buys some form of hospital insurance to take care of that loss (or extra expense) when it occurs. Or he may be concerned that

---

[4] It must be assumed that the cards are not marked, the dice not loaded, the game not fixed. The wager must be an honest one on both sides.

a future disability may make it impossible for him to perform his job and to continue to receive his pay. This man buys disability income insurance so that if he is totally disabled, his insurer will continue to pay him a stipulated amount each month for as long as the disability continues and possibly for as long as he lives.

Hospital insurance provides funds for extra expenses when hospitalized. Disability income insurance replaces the lost income resulting from the destruction of the earning power of the insured by either accident or sickness. Similarly, life insurance offsets the financial loss that would otherwise result to the beneficiaries in the event of the insured's premature death. In all situations, insurance is purchased because there is a present risk of financial loss upon the occurrence of a future event—hospitalization, total disability, premature death.

Insurance and gambling are similar in only one respect. Both in wagering agreements and in insurance contracts, one party promises to pay a given sum to the other upon the occurrence of a given future event, the promise being conditioned upon the payment of, or agreement to pay, a stipulated amount by the other party to the contract. This means that in either case, one party may receive more, much more, than he paid or agreed to pay. At this point, similarity ceases between gambling and insurance.

State laws in this country recognize this basic difference between insurance and gambling. No reasonable person would buy life or health insurance unless he faced an already existing risk of loss, or the possibility of such, if a given future event occurs. In addition, state laws typically require that such possibility of loss be present (in the form of what is known as an insurable interest) before an insurance contract can be valid.[5]

PROTECTION FOR INDIVIDUAL
AND BUSINESS NEEDS

The specific needs for which life and health insurance are purchased can be grouped under five headings: (1) estate clearance fund, (2) income for the family, (3) disability income, (4) medical expenses, and (5) funds for a business or its owners. As has been indicated, meeting each of these needs involves making provision for a given sum of money to be paid following the occurrence of a stipulated future event—the death or disability of the insured while the policy is in force.

Estate Clearance Fund

The act of dying produces a need for money which would not have been necessary at that time if death had not occurred. From an economic point of view, the other property owned by the decedent goes into his estate, to be used by his executor or administrator to pay all debts owed

---

[5] See Chapter 9 for a discussion of insurable interest and other legal aspects of the insurance contract.

by the decedent and his estate. Any remaining property is to be distributed according either to the will of the decedent or to the applicable state law.

At the time of death, the estate may not have the necessary cash, and it may be a most inappropriate time to liquidate other estate assets to provide funds for the estate clearance purpose. Life insurance can be used most appropriately to provide these needed dollars immediately following death.

Among the different purposes for which funds will be needed almost immediately or soon after death are hospital, medical, and surgical expenses prior to death; funeral and burial expenses; all debts owed by the decedent at the moment of death; death taxes (including federal estate tax and the various state inheritance and estate taxes); property and income taxes accrued at the time of death; and the necessary expenses incurred in the process of settling the estate. Possession of adequate amounts of health insurance (such as major medical) may reduce the amount of funds to be provided by life insurance for estate clearance purposes.

Therefore, it is suggested that perhaps the initial need for life insurance for most people is to provide dollars immediately following death, estimated to be sufficient in amount to assure that the executor or administrator will have adequate funds to pay all of the estate liabilities.

Income for the Family

With funds sufficient for estate clearance purposes, attention should turn to the financial needs of dependents following the death of the insured breadwinner. Typically, these needs are in the nature of a flow of income rather than an immediate cash sum. They can be classified as (1) income during a period for readjustment; (2) income while the children are growing up; (3) a continuing income, perhaps for life, to the widow after the children are presumed to have become self-supporting, including income to supplement or to fill in gaps in the social security benefits; and (4) income for miscellaneous purposes, such as a college education for the children or funds to pay off the mortgage on the family home.

Readjustment Period Income. Concurrent with the need for an estate clearance fund is the need for what is called a readjustment income.

Seldom will the insurance on the life of the breadwinner be sufficient to allow the surviving dependents to live on the same economic level as that to which they had been accustomed. The function of the readjustment fund is to provide a sufficient sum so that the survivors will have some time to recover from the severe emotional shock before they have to adjust their scale of living downward. Funds might be provided to continue the income to which the family was accustomed for a period of time, such as 6 to 18 months. Thus, if the family had been living on $1,000 a month, life insurance of approximately $6,000 to $18,000 would provide a monthly income to the survivors of $1,000 a month from 6 to 18 months.

During the period that the readjustment income is being received, the family will have time to make intelligent plans for moving to the lower level of income which will be available during the rest of the time the children are growing up.

Insurance While the Children Are in School.   The death of the father has stopped the flow of his earnings to the family. The mother may or may not be able to earn income for the support of the family. Even if she is able to work and can secure a job, that income may be much less than the amount needed to support the family at the accustomed level. Further, the situation may be such that the mother should be a full-time mother to the children whose father is no longer living.

Whatever the situation, a major risk of loss facing the father while alive is that his family probably will need additional income for a number of years following his death, should he die while his children are young. Hence, the need for a family income while the children are growing up and until they can be expected to be self-supporting.

Living Expenses for the Widow.   After one has arranged for funds for the clearance of his estate and for both a readjustment period and an income for the family while the children are in school, he then faces his widow's need for income during the rest of her life. She was his wife while he lived; she will be his widow if he predeceases her. The typical husband believes that his marriage vows create an obligation to provide economic support to his wife for so long as she lives, not just while he is living and earning an income.

Although social security provides a significant base for the protection of the family of a deceased covered worker, the survivorship benefits typically are not sufficient to enable the survivors to live as the deceased would have desired. Therefore, most family breadwinners feel that it is necessary to supplement social security benefits. Likewise, since these benefits are not intended to cover all the financial needs of the survivors, there are situations for which social security provides no benefits. A major one of these gaps is the widow's need for income from the time the youngest child is no longer eligible for benefits until the time she can qualify for retirement benefits. This period is called, appropriately, the social security "blackout" period.

Special Family Needs.[6]   Two of the major special needs for which life insurance funds are useful are college education and mortgage payment. Suppose that a breadwinner has planned for his estate clearance fund, for both a readjustment period and an adequate income to the family while the children are in school, for a life income to his widow, and in all of these plans has considered the need for supplementing the social security benefits and for filling in some of their gaps. There still is no specific provision for funds for the college education of his children or for paying off the mortgage on the family home.

---

[6] Personal and family uses of life insurance will be discussed in greater detail in Chapter 52. The planning of all the details for life insurance for these purposes is called "programming." This includes careful analysis of the amount of funds needed for each applicable purpose, the kind of insurance to be purchased, the ownership of the policy, the naming of the beneficiaries, and even consideration of whether the funds should be provided under settlement option and if so, the specific one or ones. Obviously, the programming process is not a simple one. The services of a well-trained life and health insurance underwriter are required.

Technically there is no such thing as a college education insurance policy or a mortgage protection policy. Many types of contracts may be purchased for either or both of these special purposes. Any contract that guarantees to pay its proceeds if death occurs during the period of the mortgage can be used to provide funds to pay off the mortgage. Similarly, any contract that provides for the proceeds to be paid if the insured dies before the children can be assumed to be through college can be used to provide college education funds.

Disability Income

One principal cost resulting from disability is the loss of earned income by the disabled person. Disability income insurance responds to the need for the individual to replace for himself and his dependents the value of this earning power should he suffer serious illness or accident. Disability income protection may be obtained through "riders" attached to life insurance contracts, through disability income contracts, or through health insurance contracts covering loss of income along with medical expenses.

Medical Expenses

Accidents and illness may result in hospital, surgical, and additional medical expenses that erode family savings and dissipate income earmarked for other needs. Thus, the risk of financial loss due to injury or sickness should be recognized through the purchase of health insurance. Because the increasing costs of intensive or prolonged care can reach catastrophic proportions for the family, special emphasis is often placed on the acquisition of health insurance protection against major medical expenses.

Business Insurance

Basically there are three different types of needs for funds to be made available to the business or its owners following the disability or death of an owner or of someone else: (1) key man protection, (2) business continuation, and (3) debtor-creditor protection.

Key Man Protection.[7] Most businesses have one or more so-called "key men." These are employees whose services are especially crucial in connection with the income or profits of the business. To the extent that there is such an employee, it is obvious that the premature death or the total disability of that key employee could have disastrous effects upon the earnings of the business. Equally obvious is the fact that life insurance on the life of the key employee, the insurance being owned by the business and with the business the beneficiary of the policy, is prescribed. Then, following the premature death of the key employee, the insurance proceeds serve to reduce substantially the otherwise severe financial loss to the business. Similarly, the business would want to purchase disability income insurance on the life of the key employee, with the business named as beneficiary of the policy.

---

[7] Chapter 42 provides a full discussion of key man business needs.

Business Continuation.[8]   Whether the business is a sole proprietorship, a partnership, or a closely held corporation, there usually is need for planning to offset the loss to the family or heirs of the disabled or deceased partner or owner, and the loss to the surviving partners or owners. The protection functions of life insurance and disability income insurance can provide sufficient funds to assure the continuation of the business operation.

Debtor-Creditor Protection.   Also in the realm of business needs for life insurance is the debtor-creditor situation. Because the essential nature of insurance is the guarantee of a fixed payment during the disability or following the death of the insured, it is an ideal technique for protecting the creditor from loss should the debtor become disabled or die before the debt is repaid.

As an inducement to the making of the loan, the debtor may offer to make available to the creditor a life insurance policy on the life of the debtor, sufficient in amount to protect the creditor should the debtor die while the loan is unpaid. In group situations, such as the debtors of a loan company or a bank, the insurance usually is issued to the creditor and is set up so that at all times it is exactly equal to the unpaid balance on the loan.

In individual situations where group insurance is not used, the face of the policy typically is a level amount at least equal to the original balance of the loan. The interests of both the debtor and the creditor in the policy are recognized by providing that, following the death of the debtor, the creditor's claim upon the insurance proceeds is equal only to the unpaid balance of the debt owing to him. Any balance of the proceeds remaining after the creditor's interest has been satisfied goes to the estate of the deceased debtor or to his named beneficiary.

In the absence of credit insurance, the creditor may find himself in any one of several undesirable situations when the debtor dies before the debt is paid. If the debt was unsecured, it may be difficult or impossible for the creditor to secure payment. If the creditor has to take legal action against the estate of the deceased, such action will be expensive, time consuming, and is likely to generate ill will. Advance planning requires that the debtor provide the creditor with an interest in a life insurance policy on the life of the debtor so that the balance of the debt will be paid off immediately following death with the funds made available by the life insurance. Disability income insurance can be used similarly in this situation.[9]

THE "LIFE WILL"

The suggestion that the life insurance policy be considered as a "life will" was popularized by the late Dr. Solomon S. Huebner. He pointed out that a life insurance policy could be looked upon as the contract or instru-

---

[8] See Chapters 45 and 46 for a comprehensive consideration of business continuation needs and how to meet them.

[9] See Chapters 20 and 27 for greater detail concerning the ways in which disability income insurance and life insurance may be designed to provide debtor-creditor protection.

ment by which the insured "bequeathed" his human life value, or any portion of it, to his dependents following his death.

The concept of the human life value leads directly to the idea of the "life will."[10] If it is granted that there is human life value in respect to lives which are earning an income, then it must be agreed that this value, whatever it is, will vanish at the death of the one whose life is thus valued. While he lives and continues to produce an income, that income is available for the support of his dependents. Premature death stops the flow of income to those dependents.

The "life will" concept assumes that prudent financial management requires the individual whose life has economic value to act in relation to that value just the same as he would in relation to tangible property which he owns. If he owns valuable buildings, he insures them against fire and other hazards which might destroy them and their value. If they are burned to the ground and their value destroyed, assuming adequate insurance, the insurer will reimburse the insured-owner for what would otherwise have been a total loss.

The same logic can be applied to the human life value. As fire is a major hazard to property values, so is premature death a major hazard to the human life value. One cannot, literally, insure his life value. But he can estimate the value and then insure his life for, or up to, that amount. Then, just as the fire insurer indemnifies the insurer-owner for the lost value of the building, so does the life insurer pay for the lost human life value.

There is logic to this analysis, although the analogy is not exactly parallel. It is the property owner who is paid for the lost value of his building which has burned. Such payment cannot be made by the life insurer to the one whose life value is destroyed by death. The point is that it is the death of the owner which destroys his life value. That difference accounts in part for the real significance of this concept. In the absence of life insurance, the dependents of the one whose life has value for them are deprived of all the possible future economic benefits they could have expected to receive from the continued existence of the life. Thus, through his life insurance, one can guarantee that his dependents will continue to receive after his death whatever benefits he wishes to provide them for his life value, even though that life value has been destroyed by his death.

This is the relationship that is said to exist between the human life value and life insurance. Where does the "life will" come into the picture? It is simply the legal device, the life insurance policy, by which one effects the guarantees referred to above. It provides the funds, in whole or in part, to continue to the dependents the income they would no longer receive after the death of the one on whose life they were dependent.

Although the concept of the "life will" has no legal standing, it is a logical way of looking at life insurance policies. They can be considered as the instruments by which the insured "bequeaths" the equivalent of his human life value to his heirs. The analogy is not far-fetched. One of the most significant ways to appreciate what a life insurance policy does

---

[10] The human life value concept is discussed fully in Chapter 2.

is to look upon it as a "life will." From this point of view, life insurance can be said to provide a degree of immortality to one's life value, which would otherwise vanish into thin air at the moment of death.

If a person's life has at this moment a value of $500,000 to his dependents, that is the present value of the amount they would be denied over the future years if his death were to occur today. If, at the time of death, he has $100,000 of life insurance payable to his dependents, then it is clear that in effect he has insured 20 percent of his life value for their benefit. Although his life value has vanished, an amount equal to 20 percent of that value has been continued to them.

The life insurance policy is not a "life will." A will is an instrument which is defined very precisely in state law. The law does not recognize the existence of a "life will." The whole idea is simply a very enlightened way of looking at one's life insurance policy which is made payable to or is arranged for the benefit of his dependents.

Further appreciation for the "life will" concept is gained when it is compared with the typical property will. That portion of the human life value which is insured and distributed to the beneficiaries of the deceased is received by them immediately, without any shrinkage for court costs and legal fees, and without any necessary publicity. The property will, on the other hand, must be probated, with resultant legal costs, with a substantial delay between death and the receipt of the proceeds and with necessary publicity.

It is possible to arrange the "life will" in such a manner that the proceeds can pass to the beneficiary without liability for some death taxes. All of the property which passes under the property will is subject to one or more death taxes.

It is possible to arrange the "life will" in such a manner that the proceeds can pass to the beneficiary free of claims of creditors of the deceased. All property which passes under the property will, however, is subject first to claims of the creditors of the estate of the deceased. The nature of the "life will" is such that the payments to the beneficiary typically may be made under any one or a combination of several different installment options, with the payments possibly being guaranteed for the remaining life of the beneficiary. The beneficiary of property receives whatever property is available for distribution after the estate debts are paid. He receives the actual property itself and there is no possibility of instalment payments being guaranteed for life or for any substantial period of time.

LIFE INSURANCE AS PROPERTY

It may be significant to consider the life insurance policy as property and to compare it with other property which the deceased insured owned at the time of his death. One's "life insurance" does not transfer to heirs or beneficiaries. Rather, death transforms the life insurance policy, which during lifetime was only a bundle of promises, into cash. Whereas a decedent leaves his land and buildings, his stocks and bonds to his heirs, life insurance on his life cannot be given to anyone after his death. Instead, he leaves them the cash into which the policy has been transformed.

Immediate Estate Creation Feature

One of the most significant aspects of the protection functions of life insurance is the immediate estate creation feature. The point is very simple and is characteristic of every life insurance policy. The full amount of the death estate is always created immediately, that is, at the moment the contract goes into effect following the payment of the first premium.

This feature of every life insurance policy might be characterized as the "new-fashioned" method of creating an estate while one is living, for the benefit of his heirs following his death. It is the "create and save" method. The death estate, that portion of it which is to come from life insurance, is created immediately. As was illustrated at the beginning of this chapter, a death estate of $50,000 or more was created by paying less than $100 as the first premium. Once thus created, the death estate is kept in force by the timely payment of future premiums as they become due.

This new-fashioned method contrasts with the old-fashioned method of creating a death estate. This is the "save and create" method. Here the individual saves each year whatever amount he chooses, say $500. His savings are invested in well-chosen securities or placed in a savings account in a bank or a savings and loan association. At the end of the first year, his death estate (which has been created by saving first) amounts to $500 plus interest. Depending upon his age, it will take several times ten years before the estate which results from the "save and create" method can equal the one which he could have created immediately and have had in effect all of those years, had he used the new-fashioned method of creating first and then keeping what was thus created in effect by continued saving through the years.

If a relatively substantial death estate is needed immediately, there seems to be only one way to create it and guarantee it—through life insurance kept in force by the timely payment of premiums.

Creditor Protection

One significant element in the protection functions of a life insurance policy is that the policy proceeds may be arranged in such a manner that they cannot be attached by the creditors of the deceased insured. States typically have what are called exemption statutes. These statutes set up the conditions under which life insurance proceeds may go to the beneficiaries without being subject to claims of the insured's creditors.

A typical example of an exemption statute provides, in effect, that so long as the beneficiary is someone other than the insured or his estate, the beneficiary is entitled to the life insurance proceeds, without limit, free of claims of creditors of the insured. Some states provide a similar freedom from attachment of proceeds by creditors of the insured, regardless of the beneficiary designation, for all proceeds for which the annual premium does not exceed, say, $500. Other states provide the exemption, again without limit, so long as the beneficiary is a named person who is a close relative of the insured.

The operation of the exemption statutes makes life insurance a most preferred form of property. There are few, if any, other forms of property that one can own at the moment of his death which are not more or less automatically subject to the claims of his creditors and must be used to satisfy those claims.

Tax Treatment

In addition to state exemption statutes, typically each state provides special exemptions for life insurance proceeds from the state death taxes. There are no special exemptions for life insurance under the federal estate tax. For this tax, life insurance is treated exactly as any other property of the deceased. Any property which he owned at his death is subject to federal estate tax. The proceeds of any life insurance policy in which he held what the law calls "any incidents of ownership" are taxed in his estate just as is all other property which he owned. Under the federal income tax, the proceeds of any life insurance policy which are paid by reason of the death of the insured are not considered as income to the beneficiary.

Guaranteed Value at Death

When the life insurance on one's life is compared, as property, with the other forms of property which are owned, one significant difference stands out. It is that the value of the life insurance policy is always guaranteed to be its maximum (the face of the policy) at the moment the death of the insured occurs. This characteristic—the value of the property at death—can never be known in advance for other property which one may own during his lifetime. It is true of life insurance, whether the policy was purchased today or 40 years ago, and whether death occurs today or 40 years hence.

Significance

The insured can count on his life insurance. He can use it as the foundation for the support of his dependents after his death. Furthermore, health insurance provides a method for reducing the uncertainty of economic loss due to illness or disability. The protection functions of life and health insurance are among the most important elements in making economic security an achievable goal for individuals and their families.

SELECTED REFERENCES

Greider, Janice E. and Beadles, William T. *Law and the Life Insurance Contract.* Rev. ed. Homewood, Ill.: Richard D. Irwin, Inc., 1968.

————. *Principles of Life Insurance,* Vol. 1. Rev. ed. Homewood, Ill.: Richard D. Irwin, Inc., 1972.

Huebner, S. S. *Economics of Life Insurance.* 3d ed. New York: Appleton-Century-Crofts, Inc., 1959.

Mehr, Robert I. *Life Insurance Theory and Practice.* 4th ed. Austin, Texas: Business Publications, Inc., 1970.

4

Savings Functions of Life Insurance

By VANE B. LUCAS

THROUGH the medium of life insurance, millions of individuals have accumulated savings while providing financial protection for their families. These savings are pooled by insurance companies and injected back into the financial bloodstream of the economy in the form of investments. Life insurance is one of the largest thrift institutions in the United States, along with savings and loan associations, savings banks, and commercial banks.

The savings element is present in insured pension plans and certain forms of group life insurance. However, a much larger proportion of savings is accumulated through the ownership of life insurance by individuals. This chapter will focus on the savings functions of individual life insurance.

Term life insurance basically provides death benefits for the period of the contract. In contrast, cash value life insurance provides death benefits plus other rights and benefits of value to the policyowner, including that of an orderly and effective means of accumulating savings. Life insurance benefit payments in the United States in 1971 totaled $17.1 billion of which 57 percent was in the form of living benefits for the policyowner and 43 percent in death benefits.[1] Obviously, there is a substantial use of life insurance for family financial needs during the lifetime of the policyowner, including annuities for retirement income, matured endowments, surrender values, policy dividends, and disability payments.

NATURE OF THE LIFE INSURANCE SAVINGS ELEMENT

Figure 4–1 depicts the nature of relative savings accumulation in the basic types of individual life insurance. *Straight life insurance*, whole life insurance under which premiums are payable for the remainder of the insured's life, is the most popular type of cash value (permanent) con-

---

[1] Institute of Life Insurance, *Life Insurance Fact Book, 1972.* New York, N.Y.

FIGURE 4–1.   Relative Combinations of Protection and Savings Elements by Type of Life Insurance

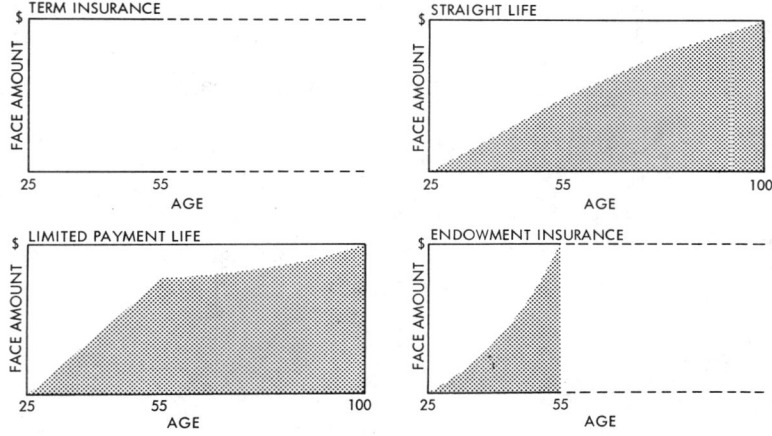

White space illustrates protection and black space illustrates savings. Term insurance is 5-year term renewable to age 55. Limited payment life premiums are assumed payable for 30 years. Endowment proceeds are assumed payable at age 55.

tract.[2] Compared to straight life insurance, *limited payment whole life insurance* results in a more rapid accumulation of savings. Likewise, savings are generated at an even more accelerated pace in *endowment insurance*, in which the emphasis is on savings rather than protection.

Annuities are a means of liquidating funds and technically are not a type of life insurance. However, they are sold by life insurance companies as companion thrift products that provide for a series of income payments periodically over a specified number of years or for life. Most annuity contract forms feature an accumulation period as well as a distribution period.

Although there are many other kinds of life insurance contracts, virtually all of them are variations or combinations of term, whole life, endowment, and annuity plans. The savings element in cash value forms of life insurance is a by-product of the level premium concept.

Level Premium Concept

Premiums for yearly renewable term insurance increase each year to reflect the fact that mortality rates are increasing with the age of the insured. Under level premium life insurance, premiums do not rise from year to year as the probability of death increases. Instead, they remain constant throughout the premium-paying period. The premiums in the early years of the contract must be more than sufficient to meet current

---

[2] "Permanent life insurance" is the description most often used to identify all forms of life insurance that feature a cash value savings element. However, certain permanent contracts are designed to mature in a relatively short time, such as an endowment policy that matures at age 50. In this chapter, therefore, all forms of life insurance with a cash value savings element are referred to as cash value insurance.

death claims in order to provide funds for later years when premiums will be less than adequate to meet death claims. This is the essence of the level premium concept.

Figure 4–2 indicates the relationship between a yearly renewable term premium and a level premium. The chief significance of the level premium concept lies in the fact that the redundant premiums in the early years of cash value contracts create a fund which is held by the insurer for the benefit and to the credit of the policyowners. Earnings (principally interest) are produced by investing the fund. The accumulated fund, improved by earnings, is used to pay out the benefit amounts provided for under the contract. Thus, the level premium is the only arrangement under which it is possible to provide insurance protection to the uppermost limits of the human life-span without the premium per unit of face amount increasing as age advances and eventually becoming prohibitive for most individuals.

FIGURE 4–2.   Comparison of Yearly Renewable Term Premium with Level Premium for a Straight Whole Life Policy, Issued at Age 25

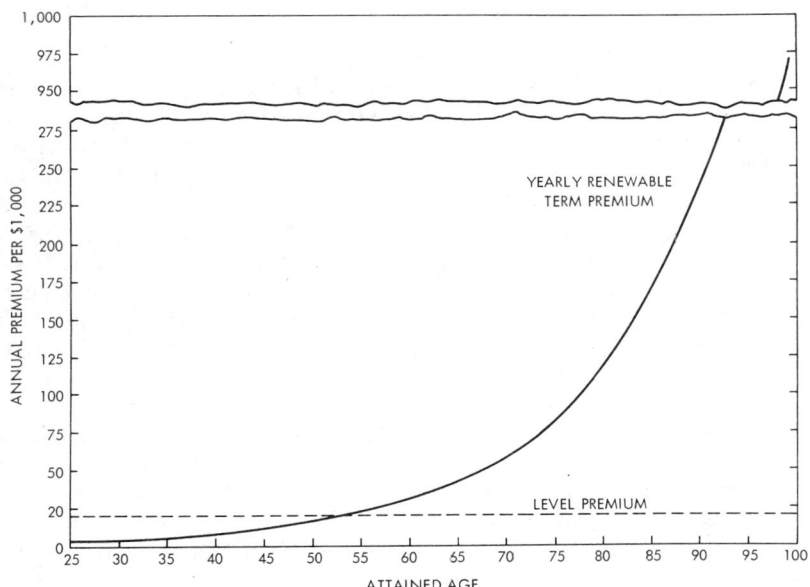

From the standpoint of the insurance company, the pure "protection" element is the difference between the face amount of the life insurance contract and the reserve. Technically speaking, this difference is the "net amount at risk." As the reserve increases from year to year, the amount at risk decreases. Figure 4–3 shows how the combination of protection and savings changes as the contract remains in force over time.

The characteristic flexibility of the life insurance contract is due in large part to the level premium concept that underlies the system of cash surrender values.

FIGURE 4–3.   Proportion of Protection and Investment Elements in a $100,000 Straight Whole Life Contract, Issued As of Age 25, (1958 C.S.O. table and 2½ percent interest)

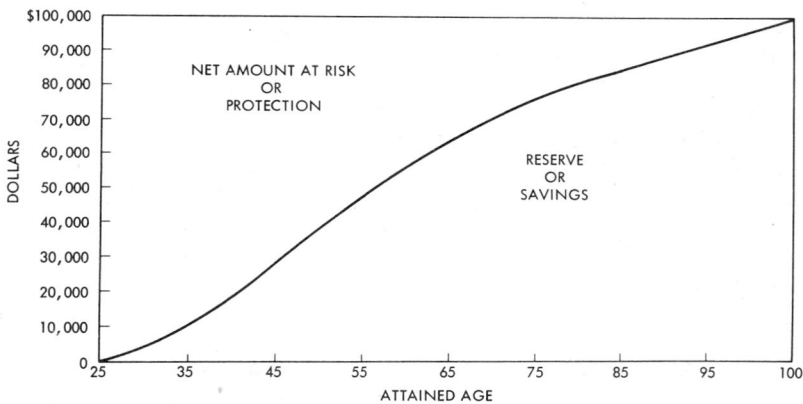

Valuation of Reserves and Cash Surrender Values

The reserve of a life insurance contract is a liability item representing the difference between the actuarially determined value of future benefits payable and future premiums receivable. The funds accumulated in support of these reserves are invested by the insurance company in assets that are the property of the company. Cash surrender values in life insurance contracts represent the insurance company's obligation to the policyowner in the event he desires to surrender the contract. Thus, while cash surrender values arise out of the level premium concept, they are not necessarily equal to the reserve in any particular policy year. Minimum cash surrender values are specified by law.[3] Many life insurance companies, however, provide surrender values in excess of those required by law.

Schedules of cash values are incorporated in life insurance contracts and become obligations binding on the company. Thus, although the pooled life insurance assets in which accumulated funds are invested are the property of the company, the cash surrender value of each contract is a liability of the company and an asset of the policyowner. The principal sum accumulated as cash values is guaranteed. This "guaranteed valuation of principal" is one of the most attractive features of life insurance.

Semicompulsory Nature of Premium Payments

Everyone has wants that represent alternative uses of his limited income stream. Persons with the highest expectations for the regular accumulation of savings often alter their commitment and fall short of their personal goals. Life insurance offers at least a partial solution to this intensely practical problem through the combination of savings accumulation with

---

[3] The Standard Nonforfeiture Law, which became effective in individual states (with few exceptions) on January 1, 1948, applies to minimum surrender values.

the protection feature. In the interest of protecting their families, individuals tend to pay life insurance premiums regularly even when other financial plans must be changed. There is evidence that during the severe economic depression of the 1930s and in subsequent recessions, premium payments have been continued despite the reduction or suspension of other expenditures. This semicompulsory or disciplined saving that characterizes the willingness to pay life insurance premiums has resulted in the fulfillment of thrift expectations of millions of individuals who otherwise might have accumulated little or nothing out of income.

CHARACTERISTICS OF THE LIFE INSURANCE SAVINGS ELEMENT

Safety of principal, liquidity, and yield (from income and capital appreciation) are three basic savings and investment objectives, each of which may be long term or short term in nature. These objectives are not mutually exclusive. Authorities generally agree that no one financial vehicle can maximize all three. For example, if a high yield is considered relatively more desirable, typically the investor must accept the greater likelihood of not being able to liquidate his investment on favorable terms. If safety of principal is of paramount importance, one should not expect the same instrument to provide a high yield to hedge against inflation. By the same token, a priority on liquidity usually will reduce the potential for yield and long-term growth.

Maintenance of credit is another important financial objective for most individuals. The savings element in life insurance relates to all these objectives and also has significant special characteristics.

Safety of Principal

As a thrift institution, life insurance has compiled a remarkable solvency record through years of inflation, wars, recessions, and depressions. In the past half century, among legal reserve life insurance companies admitted to do business in New York State, for example, policyowners have not lost one dollar due to insolvency.[4] Only by investing exclusively in government bonds could the individual investor hope to achieve such a level of safety.

A result of the life insurance technique is that companies are characterized by regularity of premium income, relatively stable investment income, and recurring cash flows from maturing investments. This makes possible long-term, high-yielding investments that are diversified as to type of industry, geographical distribution, maturity, and size. Concentration of investment funds in high-grade corporate bonds and real estate mortgages has been a major factor in the extraordinary performance of the life insurance business with respect to safeguarding principal.

---

[4] Life insurance companies are subject to stringent regulation, primarily by the states in which they do business. New York is one of the states noted for its strict regulatory standards and, further, it requires all companies licensed to do business in the state to "comply substantially" with New York requirements in all other states in which they may operate.

Liquidity

An asset has liquidity if the owner is able to get his cash out, in a hurry, without loss of value. The individual policyowner's life insurance savings element, or cash value, is fully guaranteed and can be withdrawn at any time by giving notice to the company. He may elect to surrender his contract, in which case his protection ceases, or he may elect to withdraw funds through policy loans at contract interest rates. In either case, the cash value is readily available and requires no collateral or statement of the policyowner's financial condition.

Although it is difficult to place a specific value on financial liquidity, it is well known that the ready availability of cash funds during periods of economic downturn often has helped avoid financial stress. Furthermore, liquidity at such times has permitted individuals to take advantage of additional favorable investment opportunities in a "buyer's market."

Yield

The rate of return on any form of savings or investment arises out of the interest (or income) on the principal and the capital gain or loss (appreciation or depreciation) of principal. The dollar value of the life insurance savings element is fixed by contract. Thus, there is no benefit from capital gains or adverse effects from capital loss. In this respect, the savings element of life insurance resembles bank deposits, savings and loan shares, and other fixed-dollar thrift instruments.

The minimum interest rate is guaranteed by the life insurance contract. Because of the long-term nature of life insurance contracts, the minimum rate of return is conservative—usually between 2½ and 3½ percent. However, virtually all policyowners earn a higher effective rate of return on cash values than the guaranteed rate specified in the contract. As explained below, one reason for the higher effective rate of return is associated with the presence of the protection element in the contract. Another reason is the income tax treatment of the investment return on funds being held by the life insurance company for the benefit of the policyowner.

Efficiency of the Protection Element in the Cash Value Contract. Because of two factors, the protection element in life insurance usually costs less in cash value insurance than when it is purchased separately on a temporary basis. One factor is the reduced expense of issuing and maintaining a single life insurance policy when the amount at risk is combined with the savings element. The other factor is the lower mortality rate among owners of cash value life insurance. Relatively high mortality under term insurance results as healthy lives tend to drop their coverage and successive renewals require increasingly higher premium rates. As this adverse selection against the company occurs, the higher mortality costs on impaired lives result in higher premium rates.

Tax Status of Return on Invested Funds. Unlike most other savings and investment media, the interest earned by the accumulating life insurance cash value savings element is not currently taxable and thus not re-

portable by policyowners for federal income tax purposes.[5] It follows that
the *gross* return on alternative taxable savings and investment instruments
necessarily must be higher to equal the *net* return available through the
life insurance contract. This highly important factor should be kept in
mind when yield comparisons are being made.

Another yield factor of considerable significance is the stability of the
rate of return earned by life insurance companies. Life insurance contracts
reflect the long-term nature of the pooling of life contingencies. Likewise,
the investment portfolios of companies represent an accumulation of purchases over an extended period, including long-term bonds and mortgages.
Acquisition of investments at favorable rates is enhanced by the fact that
policyowners will tend to pay life insurance premiums despite economic
adversity. The regular flow of cash to insurance companies normally exceeds the amount of cash required to pay death claims, meet expenses, and
provide living benefits for policyowners and annuitants. This means that
the forced liquidation of investments is minimized or eliminated, and cash
generally is available for the acquisition of bonds, mortgages, and other
securities at current rates.

Several variables make it difficult to generalize with respect to the comparative rates of return on life insurance. These variables include the type
of contract, age at issue of the contract, assumed dividend scale for participating contracts, years the contract has been in force at the time of valuation, and the nature and cost of the term contract with which premium
rates are being compared.

Using a variety of assumptions to compare the cost of pure protection
provided through term insurance, several authorities have measured the
rate of return on the accumulated savings element in permanent life insurance contracts presumed to remain in force for a number of years.
Typically, the *net* rate of return has ranged from about 4 percent to 6 percent or more. For example, Linton's comparisons of selected companies
have shown that a 4.78 percent *net* yield would have to be realized on a
separate savings or investment fund (on which interest is taxable as ordinary income each year) if it were to accumulate at the end of 20 years to
the 20th year guaranteed cash value for a straight whole life insurance
contract issued at age 35.[6]

---

[5] Except for proceeds paid in case of death, most of the earnings on reserves of
life insurance contracts are eventually taxed to the policyowner but usually at a time
when he is in a lower tax bracket.

[6] Albert M. Linton, "Life Insurance As an Investment," *Life and Health Insurance
Handbook* (2d ed.; Homewood, Ill.: Richard D. Irwin, Inc., 1964), p. 238. For the
analysis, figures were obtained from 10 mutual life insurance companies using their
1963 dividend scales. Illustrative term insurance costs were obtained from a company
using relatively low renewable term insurance premium rates.

Several authorities have noted the difficulty in generalizing with respect to rates of
return on life insurance. For an evaluation and critique of the Linton studies, see
Stuart Schwarzschild, "A Model for Determining the Rate of Return on Investment in
Life Insurance Policies," *Journal of Risk and Insurance*, Vol. 34, No. 3 (September
1967), pp. 435–44; J. Robert Ferrari, "Investment Life Insurance versus Term Insurance and Separate Investment," *Journal of Risk and Insurance*, Vol. 35, No. 2 (June

Remembering that the 4.78 percent return in this illustration is *net* of income taxes, it is evident that the effective rate of return on the savings element of the life insurance contract is equivalent to:

—a 7.03 percent gross rate of return if the policyowner is in the 32 percent tax bracket

—an 8.24 percent gross rate of return if the policyowner is in the 42 percent tax bracket

—a 9.56 percent rate if the policyowner is in the 50 percent tax bracket.[7]

It should be emphasized that determining the investment return for the policyowner is more complicated than simply comparing a given company's cash value contract with its term insurance contract. For example, by pitching its term premium at a relatively high level, a company could raise the apparent rate of return on its cash value contract without any real change in its earnings on investments. In other words, if company A's straight life contract yields 5 percent relative to its term contract, and company B's straight life contract yields 4 percent relative to its term contract, one should not infer that investment in company A's straight life contract yields 25 percent more than the investment in company B's straight life contract. The two straight life contracts must be compared to the same term contract.[8]

Maintenance of Credit

An essential key to sound financial planning is the ability to obtain credit when it is needed. Virtually every person, regardless of the nature or amount of his assets, needs or seeks credit on several occasions at various stages in his personal life or business career. The impact of inflation has encouraged larger numbers of individuals to take "funded" positions, by purchasing property, goods, and services with today's borrowed dollars and paying off the loans with tomorrow's presumably cheaper dollars.

Life insurance is property. Thus, the life insurance contract can serve as collateral for loans and as evidence of the borrower's awareness of the need to protect his most valuable source of financial stability—his income stream. Cash value life insurance is permanent property with a savings element that is measurable and readily available. Cash value life insurance contracts may be used to convert commercial loans into secured collateral loans. Through the life insurance technique, the volume of potential credit can be maintained and enhanced so that borrowing power is available when it is most advantageous.

1968), pp. 181–98; Joseph M. Belth, "The Rate of Return on the Savings Elements in Cash-Value Life Insurance," *Journal of Risk and Insurance,* Vol. 35, No. 4 (December 1968), pp. 569–81; Joseph M. Belth, "The Relationship between Benefits and Premiums in Life Insurance," *Journal of Risk and Insurance,* Vol. 36, No. 1 (March 1969), pp. 19–39.

[7] These federal income tax brackets are the marginal rate on the "last" or highest dollars of income; actually, the policyowner's average income tax rate on total annual income will be considerably less.

[8] See Schwarzschild, "Model for Determining the Rate of Return."

Special Characteristics

The life insurance contract has a number of unique features that contribute to its flexibility as an instrument through which savings and financial planning are enhanced. In addition, several special considerations arise from the manner in which lawmakers and the courts have attached significance to life insurance proceeds.

Policy Loan Privilege. The availability of cash values gives rise to the policy loan privilege, under which the insurance company will advance on the security of the contract an amount that, with interest as specified in the contract, will not exceed the guaranteed cash value. The interest rate on such loans usually is no more than 5 or 6 percent. This rate exceeds the rate of return guaranteed for accumulating cash values for several reasons, one of which is the administrative expense of handling policy loans. But financial planners who understand the nature of the guaranteed cash values recognize that the contract's savings element continues to grow even while it is in use by the policyowner on a borrowed basis. This factor cannot be overemphasized because it means that the life insurance contract is a highly flexible source of personal liquidity as the guaranteed accumulation continues. The due date of the policy loan is at maturity of the contract or anytime prior to this date at the option of the borrower.

The contracts of many companies include a provision for automatic premium loans. This provision protects against the unintentional lapse of the contract by advancing, in the form of a policy loan, the unpaid amount of a premium due. The automatic premium loan is advantageous to the policyowner because it helps to continue the contract and all its features in full force and effect.

Dividend Options. Life insurance contracts may be "participating" or "nonparticipating." Participating contracts are characterized by higher annual premiums based on relatively conservative mortality, investment earnings, and expense assumptions. If actual results are better than assumed, the difference is reflected in surplus. This surplus is available for return to policyowners. The amount returned to the policyowners is determined annually and is called a "policy dividend." These dividends are a means for the insurance company to refund the premium redundancy and should not be confused with dividends payable to corporate stockholders.[9]

Policy dividends usually are made available annually on the anniversary date of the participating life insurance contract. The dividend may be taken in one of four basic forms at the option of the policyowner: in cash; applied toward the payment of the next premium under the contract; applied to the purchase of a paid-up addition to the contract; or left on deposit with the company to accumulate at interest. In addition, many companies offer a fifth option, under which all or part of the dividend may be used to buy one-year term insurance.

The first two options essentially amount to a straight refund of the premium overcharge. The other dividend options have certain savings features of importance to policyowners. Under the option to purchase paid-up

[9] See Chapter 14.

additions, the dividend is applied as a net single premium at the insured's attained age to purchase as much paid-up insurance as possible payable under the same conditions as the basic permanent contract. It is particularly significant that paid-up additions typically are available at net valuation rates, thereby leading to possible savings for the policyowner through the proportionally lower costs of adding to the combined protection and savings elements. Usually the paid-up additions are participating as well.

The fourth option provides that policy dividends may be left to accumulate with the company at a stipulated minimum rate of interest.[10] In addition, dividend accumulations participate in the interest earnings of the company in excess of the stipulated minimum rate. In the event of death or surrender of the policy, the accumulated dividends plus interest are added to the policy proceeds.

Many contracts permit paid-up additions or accumulated dividend deposits to be used to convert premium paying insurance into fully paid insurance.

Surrender Options.   The savings feature in cash value life insurance also gives rise to the availability of surrender benefits should the policyowner wish or need to discontinue his insurance coverage. Surrender benefits may be received at the option of the policyowner in one of three forms: cash, paid-up insurance for a reduced amount, or extended term insurance.

Supplementary Benefits. The *waiver of premium* benefit, a form of disability insurance, is offered for a modest additional charge by virtually all companies in connection with the life insurance contracts they issue. The waiver of premium provision becomes operative whenever the insured becomes totally and permanently disabled as defined in the contract. He then becomes entitled to have waived any premium falling due after the disability commences. Of particular significance in connection with the savings functions of life insurance is the fact that the waiver of premium does not affect any other provision of the policy. Under participating permanent insurance contracts, for example, cash values would continue to increase, dividends would be payable, and policy loan privileges would continue in accordance with the original contract.

For an extra premium charge, many life insurance companies offer *disability income* coverage with their life insurance contracts. The coverage is intended to provide regular cash income, usually monthly, to the insured person who becomes totally and permanently disabled before a specific age as defined in the provision. This form of disability coverage in connection with life insurance usually is available only under certain life insurance contracts containing the cash value savings element.

Exemption from Claims of Creditors.   Protection against the claims of the insured's creditors or the beneficiary's creditors, or both, is available through the life insurance contract itself or through state legislation. Al-

---

[10] Interest on dividends left to accumulate is taxable in the year credited, whereas the increase in the cash values of the paid-up additions is not. Thus, the net value to the policyowner of the additions is nearly always in excess of that of the accumulations, in spite of the fact that paid-up additions also provide additional insurance.

though the nature of nonstatutory protection varies, the avoidance of claims of creditors can be of great practical importance in preserving savings for the purposes intended.

Legislative protection takes the form of state exemption statutes in all states. These laws generally reflect the public policy of placing a higher priority on an individual's obligation to his family than to his creditors. The broadest statutes exempt all types of life insurance benefits from attachment by all types of creditors, while some statutes exempt only a modest amount of proceeds payable to the widow and children of the insured.

Federal Income Tax Treatment. It is beyond the scope of this chapter to discuss fully the income tax treatment of life insurance and annuities.[11] However, several aspects of the income taxation of life insurance related to financial planning should be acknowledged.

Of major significance is the fact that proceeds of life insurance paid by reason of a death generally are income tax exempt if paid in a single sum. Portions of installment payments representing the interest earned on proceeds held and invested by the company generally are taxable with one exception. The surviving spouse is entitled to exclude from taxable income up to $1,000 of interest annually received as part of installment payments. This exclusion does not apply to the interest earned on other amounts held by the insurer on deposit. Such interest is fully includable in gross income for income tax purposes.

Endowment proceeds and cash surrender values, received other than by reason of death, are includable in gross income to the extent that they exceed the aggregate net premiums or other considerations paid. State income tax with respect to life insurance generally follows the federal rules. The major exception is that most states fully exempt proceeds paid by reason of death of the insured, whether paid in installments or in a single sum.

Dividends on participating life insurance policies are regarded as a return of premium. Such dividends are not includable in gross income for income tax purposes. However, interest earned on dividend deposits is taxable.

SPECIAL USES OF LIFE INSURANCE SAVINGS

Gifts of Life Insurance

Large amounts of funds are transferred each year in the form of gifts to family members, friends, charities, colleges, universities, and other eligible institutions. The unique combination of protection and savings in cash value life insurance lends itself to creative giving. The cash value in the contract is deductible to the donor in the year the gift is made, and subsequent premiums thereon are deductible in the year paid. The donee has the benefit of a growing source of funds while the contract remains in

---

[11] See Chapter 57, "Income Taxation of Life and Health Insurance."

force, and the protection element assures eventual receipt of the face amount of the contract. Gifts of life insurance offer other attractive features described elsewhere.[12]

A pitfall to avoid in contracts owned by someone other than the insured is the inadvertent gift of proceeds that occurs on the maturity of the policy by reason of death or otherwise if a person other than the owner is named beneficiary. In these cases, it is a good general rule that the owner should always name himself beneficiary.

Business Uses of Life Insurance

Life insurance savings have a special role in the financial health of business enterprises. Funds accumulated through life insurance are well suited to many of the special needs of business operation and continuation.[13]

Cash value life insurance on the lives of active business owners and key executives can provide an effective method for the gradual accumulation of a contingency fund. The same guarantees and flexibilities with respect to collateral loans and policy loans generally apply as well for business purposes as for individuals. Furthermore, the accumulation of cash values through key man insurance on the lives of employees of a firm provides an effective means of funding a deferred compensation plan.

One of the most valuable business applications of the life insurance technique is in conjunction with agreements to assure the effective transfer of ownership upon the death, disability, or voluntary retirement of a sole proprietor, partner in a partnership, or stockholders in a corporation. Cash value life insurance provides the ideal means of funding these agreements because there is a regular accumulation of funds at favorable rates and because the protection element allows the funding to be self-completing no matter how soon the death of the owner may occur.

SAVINGS-INVESTMENT PRIORITIES AND LIFE INSURANCE

Balanced Savings-Investment Program

Two major sources of financial security are earned income and accumulated assets or capital. Certain assets are of a fixed-dollar type such as savings accounts, government securities and corporate bonds held to maturity, life insurance cash values, savings and loan shares, and certificates of deposit. Fixed-dollar assets typically represent the "debt" of the government or business, and are characterized by safety of principal, liquidity, and fixed return, but no capital appreciation. Other assets are of the equity or variable dollar type such as common stock, variable annuities, mutual

---

[12] See Chapter 59, "Gifts of Life Insurance."

[13] Business uses of life insurance are discussed elsewhere. See Chapter 42, "Key Man Protection"; Chapter 43, "Nonqualified Deferred Compensation Plans"; Chapter 44, "Split-Dollar Plans"; Chapter 45, "Business Continuation—Unincorporated Business Interest"; Chapter 46, "Business Continuation—Corporate Business Interest"; Chapter 47, "Income Protection for Business Continuation"; and Chapter 48, "Professional Corporations."

funds, real estate, and ownership of a business. Equity or variable dollar investments usually are "ownership" investments, and are characterized by greater risk, variable return, and the possibility of capital appreciation or depreciation.

Studies show that virtually all individuals desire some balance among the objectives of safety, yield and liquidity in their savings and investment activities.[14] Perception as to what is balance seems to have been distorted in the inflationary period over the past three decades. The inflation expectancy psychology has tended to create in the minds of many the urgency of "inflation hedges" without a real awareness of the ingredients of a balanced program of savings.

The typical family has a number of variable dollar "inflation hedges":

—*Earning power* is an income stream and an "asset" that may be the most accurate reflection of the cost of living because inflation pressure is likely to drive up salaries and wages, while recessions often will curb or reduce earnings;
—*Social security benefits* have been adjusted upward in the period of continued inflation and almost certainly will continue to increase if inflation continues;
—*Company pension and profit sharing benefits* often include built-in inflation hedges;
—The *residence* owned by the family is a major "variable investment" because values tend to appreciate or depreciate in times of inflation or deflation;
—*Business interests* often may be characterized as inflation hedges in the sense that the dollar volume of income and assets often tends to increase with inflation.

In addition to these variable dollar elements, how else should discretionary income and accumulated capital be applied to seek an appropriate savings-investment mix? Several other investment vehicles are available, such as mutual funds, variable annuities, common stocks, and real estate. However, the concept of a balanced savings-investment program also calls for a significant segment of assets in forms that minimize volatility. Most financial advisors suggest that a substantial portion of savings-investment dollars should be applied to assets featuring high safety of principal, liquidity, and a good dependable rate of return.

Among the essentially fixed-dollar type assets mentioned above, cash value life insurance—with its proven record of safety, liquidity and dependable net rate of return—is one of the effective vehicles to provide balance in the savings and investment plans of individuals. This is one reason why life insurance is owned by 8 out of 10 American families, and that there are more than 140 million individual policyowners in the nation. One half of the $1.5 trillion of life insurance in force is cash value life insurance.[15]

---

[14] G. Katona, et al., *1969 Survey of Consumer Finance* (Ann Arbor, Mich.: University of Michigan, 1970).

[15] Institute of Life Insurance, *Life Insurance Fact Book, 1972* (New York: 1972).

Life Insurance and Broadened Financial Services

Increasing levels of discretionary income, the long period of inflation, and other factors have encouraged larger proportions of American families to place more of their savings into investments whose values may appreciate with rising costs and prices. In response to these forces, a growing number of life insurance companies have broadened their financial services to include equity-based products such as variable annuities and mutual funds. Many observers also believe that variable life insurance will become a significant financial vehicle in the years ahead. Thus, it is becoming increasingly clear that life insurance and certain equity products are compatible financial instruments.

Virtually all financial advisors recommend a comprehensive program of life insurance to provide protection for the income stream of individuals during their productive lifetime. The versatility of the savings element in cash value insurance and the combination of safety, liquidity, tax-deferred return, and credit enhancement recommend life insurance as an appropriate depository for part of the fixed-dollar portion of many personal savings and investment portfolios. While life insurance companies probably will continue to broaden their financial services to include a wider range of savings and investment programs, traditional cash value life insurance no doubt will continue to hold a place of primary importance in the financial plans of American families.

SELECTED REFERENCES

Belth, Joseph M. "The Rate of Return on the Savings Elements in Cash-Value Life Insurance," *Journal of Risk and Insurance*, Vol. 35, No. 4 (December 1968).

————. "The Relationship between Benefits and Premiums in Life Insurance," *Journal of Risk and Insurance*, Vol. 36, No. 1 (March 1969).

Ferrari, J. Robert. "Investment Life Insurance versus Term Insurance and Separate Investment," *Journal of Risk and Insurance*, Vol. 35, No. 2 (June, 1968).

Huebner, S. S. *The Economics of Life Insurance*. 3d ed. New York: Appleton-Century-Crofts, Inc., 1959.

Linton, M. Albert. *How Life Insurance Can Serve You*. New York: Harper & Bros., 1958.

McGill, Dan M. *Life Insurance*. Rev. ed. Homewood, Ill.: Richard D. Irwin, Inc., 1967.

Mehr, Robert I. *Life Insurance: Theory and Practice*. 4th ed. Austin, Texas: Business Publications, Inc., 1970.

Schwarzschild, Stuart. "A Model for Determining the Rate of Return on Investment in Life Insurance Policies," *Journal of Risk and Insurance*, Vol. 34, No. 3 (September 1967).

part II

Individual
Life Insurance
and Annuities

THE OLDEST and most widely owned forms of life coverages are individual life insurance and annuities. The basic types of individual contracts—term, whole life, endowment, and the annuity—are analyzed in Part II. Consideration is given to contract design, benefit provisions, and the most common uses of each type. The special types of policies that combine components of basic coverages for special needs also are described. The more significant legal concepts and contract provisions are discussed.

To understand how individual life insurance works, several chapters in this Part are concerned with probability, mortality, and money concepts; with the pricing factors involved; with reserves and nonforfeiture values; and with surplus and dividends. The mathematical concepts are relatively simple; the actuarial and financial application of these concepts is more involved. An essentially nontechnical analysis is followed.

The Part concludes with two chapters of particular significance to the consumer and to the student of life insurance. One chapter describes the factors that determine whether and how life insurance can be issued to cover a particular applicant. The final chapter is devoted to an analysis of contract cost and benefit comparisons.

5

Contracts—Term Insurance

By WILLIAM T. BEADLES

THE EARLIEST life insurance policy of which any known record exists was dated June 18, 1583, and provided insurance upon the life of William Gybbons for a period of 12 months from the date of underwriting.[1] Many policies written during the 1700s provided protection for a period of only six months.

NATURE OF TERM INSURANCE

The above-mentioned policies were all term insurance, which, as the name indicates, gives protection for only a definite and limited period of time. If death occurs during the term for which the policy is written, the proceeds are payable to the beneficiary. If the insured survives the term, the policy expires. In this event, the insured has received the full value for which he paid his premiums. Throughout the entire term, he has known that his death at any time during that period would result in the insurer paying the policy proceeds to the beneficiary. This is the protection which he purchased.

Duration

It is possible to have about as many different durations of term insurance as there are identifiable periods of time following the issuance of the policy. Among the more common forms are 1-year term; 2-, 3-, 4-, and 5-year term; 10-year term; 20-year term; and term to age 60 or 65. Some insurers issue what is called a term expectancy or a life expectancy contract, although there is no uniformity in the use of these names. The ex-

---

[1] Perhaps the only reason there is evidence of the existence of this early policy is that the insurer contested the payment of the proceeds at the death of the insured within the apparent term of the policy. Mr. Gybbons died on May 28, 1584. The insurer contended that the "12 months" of insurance protection meant 12 lunar months of 28 days each, in which event the policy would have expired before the death. The court disagreed and so the first life insurance policy of which we know today ended as a disputed claim. Not exactly an auspicious beginning for the life insurance business.

pectancy policy continues in force for the period of the insured's expectation of life as determined by the mortality table in use at the time the policy was issued.[2] At all ages, according to the Commissioners 1958 Standard Ordinary Mortality Table, the average expectation of life is to an age beyond 65.

At the other end of the scale, preliminary or initial term insurance is available for periods as short as a month. This insurance is usually restricted to situations in which it is desired to put insurance in force immediately, with the policy having an effective date, as far as future premiums are concerned, of one or more months in the future.

Term Riders and Policy Forms

Term insurance also is available in the form of riders, which are attached to cash value insurance policies or to other term policies. The protection afforded by the rider continues only for a stipulated period of time. Frequently, the rider is integrated into the basic contract and does not appear separately.

The most widely used is the *decreasing term* rider. For the period during which the rider is effective, the protection decreases each year (sometimes each month) in accordance with a predetermined schedule. More often than not, decreasing term insurance is in the form of a rider, although over 100 insurers are listed as writing a mortgage protection policy which is nothing more than decreasing term insurance. Decreasing term insurance also is an important element of the popular family income policy.[3]

It is customary to establish a level premium for a decreasing term policy. Whether the decreasing insurance is provided by a policy or by a rider, the rate of decrease can be on a straight line basis (such as $100 a year for each $1,000 of original amount) or on almost any kind of schedule (such as in accordance with the rate at which the unpaid balance of an amortized mortgage is scheduled to decrease).

Increasing term insurance has come to be used more widely in recent years. The amount of insurance payable in the event of death of the in-

---

[2] Technically, the term "expectation of life" is completely without meaning in relation to any one person. It has significance only to a large number of insureds of a given age. In other words, mortality tables do not show the life expectancy of any particular person.

[3] For a discussion of the family income policy, see Chapter 8. Frequently, decreasing term insurance, used without the related nonterm insurance, is called, although quite incorrectly, a "family income policy." This practice of naming a decreasing term policy on the basis of the purpose for which the policy was purchased is both a common and a regrettable one. The problem is that such names as "mortgage protection policy" or "family income policy" do not adequately describe the nature of the contract. The only proper generic name for a decreasing term insurance policy is "decreasing term insurance." The person who buys a so-called mortgage protection policy cannot tell from the name whether it is a decreasing term policy or a combination policy made up of some kind of cash value insurance plus a decreasing term rider. Similarly, a family income policy of one insurer may be just a decreasing term policy, while another insurer may offer a policy with the same name which is a combination of whole life and a decreasing term rider. It would help if insurers would identify their decreasing term policies by that name, leaving it to the life underwriter and the insured to work out suitable situations for which that policy would be applicable.

sured rises during the period of coverage. This type of coverage seems to be available chiefly as a rider, with only a very few insurers in 1970 offering increasing term insurance as a separate policy. One insurer is reported to offer an increasing term policy in a minimum amount of $100,000. As was true with decreasing term insurance, it is customary to establish a level premium for increasing term insurance protection.

The principal use for an increasing term rider is in those policies which promise to return the premiums, in addition to the proceeds, if the insured dies within the term. Such a rider could be added to any policy, although it is usually integrated into the basic policy and does not appear separately. The operation of this return premium rider is quite simple. There is enough term insurance the first year to equal one annual premium. During the second year the term insurance increases to equal two annual premiums. It continues to increase in this manner for whatever period the return premium feature is to be effective, although seldom for more than 20 years. Another similar example of the use of an increasing term rider is in those policies which promise to pay a death benefit equal to the policy face plus the cash value of the policy if death occurs prior to a certain age.

A recent development is the use of an increasing term rider to make possible an automatic "cost-of-living" adjustment at a stipulated rate of increase in the guaranteed death benefit. An assumption that the cost of living will continue to increase for the next 20 years at the rate of 4 percent a year could be met by a basic policy with an increasing term rider which would increase the original face amount by the required percentage each year.

Level term policies and riders also are available. Probably the most common example has been found in the family maintenance policy, which comprises a basic cash value policy plus a level term rider. In this form of combination policy, the rider provides a level amount of insurance protection throughout its term, in addition to the coverage afforded by the basic policy. The same benefits could be made available by using a straight life policy with a separate level term policy.

Renewable Term Insurance

Term insurance expires automatically if the insured is living at the end of the policy term. In order to overcome this disadvantage to the insured who may need to have his coverage continue for a longer period, most companies provide term policies which are renewable at the option of the insured. No term policy is renewable unless the contract so states. If it is renewable, the insurer must renew at the request of the owner, regardless of the insurability status of the insured at the time of renewal.

Other things equal, a nonrenewable term policy will require a smaller premium than will a renewable one, since under the latter the insurer could be forced to continue on the risk for people who would not be insurable at the same rating classification under a new policy.

When a term policy is renewed, it usually carries the premium of the new policy issued at the attained age. If the insured is no longer a standard risk, or if he is uninsurable, then the renewable feature may be of great value if the owner wishes to have the protection continue. Even if the insured is still insurable at standard rates, the renewable feature has value because the suicide and incontestable clauses do not run anew.

Different companies have different restrictions upon the number of times a policy can be renewed. Of the approximately 50 companies issuing 1-year renewable term, about one half will renew for 9 years, others will renew each year to age 64 or 65 and a few to age 69 or 70. There is much greater uniformity in practice relative to 5-year renewable term policies. Most of the companies will renew this policy to age 60, 64, or 65, with some offering renewal to age 70. The protection under a typical renewable term policy cannot extend beyond age 65.

Convertible Term Insurance

Another important feature of most term contracts is convertibility. This gives the insured the right to convert his policy to any form of cash value insurance which the company is issuing at the time of conversion. Although most term policies are convertible, any given one is convertible only if the contract so stipulates.

Frequently, there will be certain restrictions upon the conversion privilege. The most common has been that which sets a date prior to the expiration of the original term, by which time the conversion must be effected. A 10-year term policy thus might be convertible at any time prior to the end of its eighth year. Where such restrictions exist, their purpose is to avoid some of the adverse selection that might otherwise occur by reason of a deterioration in the health of the insured just prior to the expiration of the term policy. The use of a restriction of this type to discourage adverse selection may be of decreasing significance. An increasing number of insurers are permitting conversion at any time prior to the expiration of the term policy.

The insurer must convert when requested to do so by the owner within the time limits set by the contract. It makes no difference what the state of health of the insured is; if his term contract is convertible, he may exercise that privilege simply by asking for conversion and by following one of the two procedures outlined in the following paragraphs.

Most convertible contracts may be converted either currently or retroactively, that is, either as of the attained age of the insured at the date of the conversion or as of the date of issue of the original term contract, or some intermediate date. Conversion as of the attained age is the simpler of the procedures and is the one which is more widely used. Here the insured indicates his desire to convert to, say, a straight life contract. The term contract is canceled, the straight life is issued, and the insured pays premiums henceforth at the current rate for his present age. In other words, although he does not have to make a new application and prove insurability, if he is insurable the result is the same as if he had canceled his term policy and had made a new application for his straight life policy (except that the time periods for the suicide and incontestable clauses run from the date of the original policy). It is when he is no longer a standard risk, or is uninsurable, that the conversion privilege becomes of greatest value to the insured.

Retroactive conversion (to the age of original issue) is more complicated, since the insured is asking the company to convert to a policy which carries the same premium he would have paid had he taken the cash value policy at the original date of the term contract. Assume a 10-year term policy issued at age 25, the insured now being age 32, and suppose that he wishes to convert retroactively to a straight life policy. The insured will find his premium on the new policy will be the same as if he had taken it out originally at age 25. Although the new contract is dated back to the earlier age, the policy form may be either the one which the insurer is currently issuing at the time of the conversion or the form which was being issued at the time of the original application, depending upon the contractual provision in the term policy.

Since the insured in this example has been paying only the term premium for the past seven years, a financial adjustment must be made if he is to receive a straight life policy with all of the guaranteed values as of the end of its seventh year. The payment which the insured must make is calculated in various ways. One procedure is to determine the difference between the gross premiums for the term policy, minus dividends received, and the net amount which would have been paid for the policy into which the conversion is being made. To this is added interest compounded at, say, 5 percent for each year the term policy was in force. Many companies, on the other hand, simply ask for the payment of the difference in the reserves or cash values of the two policies, sometimes with a charge of 5 percent of the difference.

Fundamentally, the financial adjustment in connection with this retroactive type of conversion is aimed at putting both the insurer and the insured in approximately the same financial situation as if the permanent policy had been acquired originally. The result is that the insured has had the protection thus far for a smaller annual outlay and still is in a position to acquire a permanent policy with the advantage of the lower premium rate as of the date of original issue.

A study of over 20,000 term policies issued by 5 life insurance companies showed that over 50 percent were converted. The same study showed that over 95 percent of all conversions were effected on the attained-age basis.[4]

The general practice among insurers is to make the converted insurance available under the policy series or forms currently being issued by that insurer. One reason is that, between the dates of original issue and the conversion, the insurer may have introduced a new series of policies to replace the older series. In this situation, the issuance of the new policy in the conversion procedure is not just a matter of convenience for the insurer. Some states require that when a new series of policies is approved for issue within that state, the former policy series must be withdrawn, with no more of the former policies being issued.

It is not uncommon to restrict retroactive conversion to a date not more than five years earlier than the current date on which the conversion is being effected. One reason for such contractual restriction is the practical one that this type of conversion is seldom requested when the policy has been in force for a longer period. Also, there is more likelihood that the

---

[4] Arthur L. Williams, "Some Empirical Observations on Term Life Insurance," *Journal of Risk and Insurance*, Vol. 31 (1964), p. 445.

policyowner will get the exact policy he would have acquired had he purchased the permanent insurance in the first place, since with a shorter period, there is less probability that a new policy series will have been introduced.

Some insurers provide only for convertibility at the attained age. Some of these insurers may offer a "change of plan" provision in term policies which could go back to the original age. If it is a "change of plan" instead of "convertible provision," then evidence of insurability may be required. The change of plan provision in a term policy is quite different from the provision with the same name in a straight life policy. In the latter, a contractual right is given to change the policy to a higher premium, one without evidence of insurability. (Many insurers will allow this as a matter of company policy, without a contract provision.) In a term policy, the contract may provide for the right to change to a permanent type, with the insurer having the right to require evidence of insurability. The reason for requiring evidence is that the owner is changing from a policy which covered only a specific period of time, to one which could remain in force until the death of the insured, whenever that occurred.

It should be mentioned that decreasing term contracts are characterized by somewhat different conversion features. In the first place, they are seldom convertible for the original amount of the decreasing term insurance; instead, conversion is in relation to the amount of insurance in force at the time of the conversion. Many insurers will permit the conversion of decreasing term insurance to an amount of cash value insurance equal to a percentage, say 75 percent, of the amount of insurance then in force. Obviously, this means that decreasing term is convertible only on the attained-age basis.

Several companies issue term policies which are nonrenewable but which are automatically convertible. If the insured does not choose to convert earlier, the policy converts to some preselected form of cash value insurance at the expiration of its original term. These policies typically are issued for one, two, three, four, or five years. Their significance seems to lie in the fact that the insured does not have to take positive action in order to get his insurance converted. The conversion is automatic.

It should be obvious that from the viewpoint of the insured, the ideal term policy is one which is both renewable and convertible. This is true even though the right to renew or convert makes the policy cost a little more. These rights give the insured the greatest possible flexibility in connection with this insurance and help offset the most serious defect of the term coverage, namely, the fact that both the term, and the accompanying protection, will expire if the insured outlives them. The danger in relying upon term insurance is that the need for insurance may not vanish at the expiration of the original term. Therefore, if the policy is both renewable and convertible, the insured is in a position to continue his protection, regardless of his insurability status.[5]

---

[5] In addition to providing permanent coverage, another reason for converting term insurance is to reduce the cost of pure protection while taking advantage of the savings element in cash value insurance. See Chapter 4.

Term Policy Features

There are very few differences in the contract provisions of term policies and cash value policies.[6] About the only fundamental differences are in the nonforfeiture values and the dividend options. Term policies of 15 or fewer years typically will have no nonforfeiture values. The statutes of a number of states provide that nonforfeiture values are not required in any term policy running for 15 or fewer years and which expires before age 66. Some states have similar statutes requiring such values only for policies which run for 20 years or longer. Longer term policies have some cash values, although they usually start later than those in permanent policies issued at the same age. They usually rise for a few years, and always decline to zero by the end of the policy term.

For term policies with no nonforfeiture values, obviously there can be no loan provision in the contract. Typically, even long-term policies which have a nonforfeiture value will not have provision for loan values since there could be the possibility that the loan might be continued in force until the end of the term, at which time there would be no nonforfeiture value to support the loan. Since there is usually no loan provision, one would not expect to find in any term policy the so-called "indebtedness" provision which typically is found in all permanent life insurance policies.

Term policies may be either participating or nonparticipating. Participating policies normally have no dividend option to provide for paid-up additions, although there is no reason why this could not be done. At least one insurer has a term policy with a dividend option which provides that the dividend may be used to purchase paid-up whole life insurance.

The waiver-of-premium clause, when operative in connection with a term policy, frequently produces a unique benefit. In event of the total disability of the insured, as defined in the policy, the waiver operates in the usual manner to the end of the policy term. At that time, the term policy is converted into permanent insurance, a straight life policy, with the new higher premiums continuing to be waived, with dividends being paid on the new policy, if it is a participating one, and with the regular nonforfeiture values being available. Whether a given term policy has this kind of a waiver-of-premium clause can be determined only by an analysis of the contract.

Higher Mortality on Term Insurance

A significant fact about term insurance is that experience generally has shown a higher rate of mortality among term insureds than for those who have permanent insurance. An actuarial report from one large company stated that "the mortality under term policies of large amount was nearly half again as great as that under [whole] life and endowment insurance." Another study in a large company compared the term mortality experience with the entire experience of the company over the same period. This comparison showed 18 percent higher mortality by amounts of insurance for those who were insured under 5-year term, and 11 percent higher for the

---

[6] See Appendix D for a specimen individual life insurance contract.

first 5 years of those insured under 10-year term. Another company showed 13 percent higher mortality for 5-year convertible but nonrenewable term as compared with standard (nonterm), medically examined business for the same years of issue and observation.

A comparison of intercompany studies of the mortality on policies for large amounts (defined as policies with a face amount of at least $50,000) shows that the extra mortality experienced on term insurance has declined in relation to that for permanent insurance, although the mortality ratio for term policies continues to be higher.[7]

A number of different factors may help to account for the higher mortality under term insurance. It has been suggested many times that a person who knows that he is in poor health, although still insurable, will be inclined to select a plan of insurance which carries the lowest premium—term.

Renewable term offers a further possibility for adverse mortality experience. Healthier lives will be inclined to convert to cash value plans, to purchase cash value insurance with another insurer, or to let their policies lapse. Those who have become uninsurable can obtain continuing insurance only by converting or by renewing; and, of course, renewing is the cheaper of these alternatives, in terms of immediate cash outlay. This could help to explain why renewed term insurance tends to have higher mortality experience.

Some companies are said to be more strict in their underwriting requirements for applicants for term plans than for cash value insurance. It is known that many insurers will not issue term policies on a table of mortality ratings as high as that on which they will issue cash value life insurance policies. Perhaps a more common practice in connection with term insurance is to increase the loading for anticipated extra mortality, or to alter the dividend formula of term policies to allow for extra mortality.

More conservative companies may decline to issue term to some applicants and offer instead some form of cash value coverage. This situation by itself tends to improve term mortality. When term shows a higher mortality, in spite of this practice, the conclusion must be that adverse selection forces are at work. Further evidence of the inherently higher mortality under some types of term insurance is furnished by many studies of the extra mortality experienced in connection with policies which go under the extended term nonforfeiture option. Twenty-seven companies showed, over a 12-year period, a 26 percent higher mortality among these policies than that experienced on standard cash value insurance over the same years. One large company's studies showed, over an 8-year period, a 41 percent higher mortality on extended term insurance than its ultimate experience on standard policies issued during the same years.

---

[7] See *Transactions of the Society of Actuaries* for 1959, 1964 and 1971 (Chicago, Ill.). The latest reported study showed the mortality ratio to be 87 percent for permanent and 96 percent for term. This is a much smaller spread than was reported in the 1959 and 1964 studies.

Premiums

Since term insurance is basically an "if" type, which promises to pay only if the insured dies within the term, at any given age its rate always will be less than for any "when" insurance, which promises to pay whenever the insured dies. Likewise, it will be less than that for any endowment insurance, which promises to pay if the insured dies within the term or if he is living at the expiration of the term. Since only death benefits are paid, and only for those deaths which occur within the term, there is no building-up on substantial cash values or reserve liabilities. When a term policy expires, there is no reserve; there are no cash values. In regard to annual outlay, term insurance is always the least costly form of life insurance which may be purchased by any person.

ADVANTAGES AND DISADVANTAGES TO THE INSURED

The preceding analysis indicates the greatest advantage of term insurance. It involves the smallest possible annual outlay. Any person who finds himself in need of life insurance and without sufficient free funds to purchase the amount needed on a permanent basis will find term insurance particularly attractive. Whatever the sum of money which is available for life insurance, it will always purchase a larger amount of term insurance than of any other kind. The result is that many young families find themselves with a greater amount of protection than would be possible otherwise, simply because of the availability of low-premium term insurance.

However, it is possible to overemphasize the premium outlay aspect of term insurance. Actually, it is low in cost only if the insured dies during the term of the policy protection. If the insured survives, then the term insurance will prove to have been the most expensive form of life insurance that could have been purchased—expensive, that is, in regard to total net outlay. This makes term insurance both the least costly and the most expensive form of insurance. Since the low-outlay aspect has been considered above, the following analysis will show that term insurance is the most expensive, if the insured survives the term.

Assume a person aged 30 (the exact age makes no difference) who decides that he needs an additional $10,000 of life insurance for just the next 10 years. This appears to be an ideal situation for the use of a 10-year term policy. There are, however, other methods by which he could secure protection for this period. For example, he could buy a straight life policy (any policy other than term will do), pay premiums on it for 10 years, and then surrender it for its 10th-year cash value. If these two methods are to be compared, it will be necessary to cash in the straight life policy, since the term policy would expire automatically at the end of 10 years.

With either policy, the insurer promises to pay $10,000 to the beneficiary should the insured die within the 10-year period. In other words, the purpose of the insured is to buy 10-year protection with one or the other of these policies. In nearly every instance the *net outlay* for the protection for the 10-year period will be less with the straight life contract, as the following illustration will show.

One company's rate for 10-year term at age 30 is $8.97 per $1,000. This is a total gross premium, for the $10,000 policy, of $897 over the 10 years. Its rate for straight life at the same age is $22.48, or $2,248 total gross premium for the 10 years. The latter policy has a guaranteed cash value of $1,637.30 at the end of the 10 years. Determined by the traditional method, the 10-year net cost of the straight life, then, is $2,248 minus $1,637.30, or $610.70, as compared with $897 for the term. This saving of $286.30 ignores the effect of dividends and also of compound interest on the difference in premiums.

If the dividends on the above policies are considered, the difference is more striking. The net outlay for the term is brought down to $534.40, while that of the straight life becomes $72.80, a comparative saving over the 10-year period of $461.60. Many will want to consider interest on the difference in premiums each year as part of the cost of purchasing the straight life instead of the term policy. The effect of this consideration is to lower considerably the difference in net cost of straight life and term insurance.[8]

As mentioned above, another feature of term insurance which should be considered carefully by the prospective purchaser is that it is temporary protection only. Even though the policy may be renewable, there is always an ultimate time limit beyond which all protection ceases unless the conversion right is available and exercised. If temporary protection is all that is needed, then term insurance can fill the bill completely and at the lowest annual outlay. The basic problem in this connection is that temporary needs have an almost universal tendency either to continue beyond the originally anticipated term or, if they vanish as planned, to be replaced by some other need. In either of these situations, reliance upon temporary protection may be disastrous.

If the policy is renewable, it may be continued in force at a higher premium at each renewal date. At the younger ages the premium does not increase greatly at each 5- or 10-year interval. After the so-called "middle" ages are passed, the rates begin to jump significantly—so much so that it is quite possible the insured will find his term premium much higher than what he would be paying had he purchased a straight life policy originally.[9]

---

[8] It may be misleading to draw generalized conclusions based on cost comparisons between different types of contracts offered by the same company. See Chapter 4. For a further discussion of cost and benefit comparisons of life insurance contracts, see Chapter 16.

[9] In addition to the higher premium, the net outlay may be even more for the term, as the following example shows. It is assumed that a person aged 20 purchases both a five-year renewable term contract for $10,000 and a straight life policy for the same face amount. Using current rates, dividends, and cash values of one participating insurer, it is assumed that dividends are used to reduce the premiums and that the term contract is renewed at each succeeding five-year interval, through age 60. Then, at age 65, it is seen that the total net payments for the term insurance amount to $5,063.20, as compared with total net payments to age 65 of $3,245 for the straight life policy. The straight life policy required $1,818.20 less net payments than did the term. In addition, although the term policy had no cash value at age 65, the straight

The final point for the insured to consider is that term insurance usually has no built-in values, such as cash or loan values. This is a result of the nature of term insurance and its low premium rate. These so-called "built-in" values, which require more in terms of annual outlay, are present in all permanent policies.

"BUY TERM AND INVEST THE DIFFERENCE"

One theory which has received wide publicity over recent years is the advice to the insured to buy term insurance and to invest separately the difference between the premium for the term and the premium for the same amount of cash value insurance. If the insured dies during the term, the beneficiary under the term policy will have not only the insurance proceeds but also whatever amount there is in the separate investment fund. If the total annual payment had been used to buy cash value insurance of the same face amount, then at death the beneficiary will have only the insurance proceeds.

This advice may be good for some people; however, it has certain aspects which need to be considered carefully. It was pointed out earlier than if a person knows that he is going to die within the next five years, then five-year term will be the cheapest form of insurance for him to buy. The same conclusion applies here. If death occurs within the term, there is no question that a greater amount can be provided for one's beneficiary by buying term and "investing the difference" rather than by putting the same total premium into cash value insurance. The "difference" which is thus invested separately carries the advantage of higher potential yield if invested in equities of some form. However, it generally lacks the advantages which are inherent in the investment portion of the cash value insurance contract, such as safety of principal, guaranteed rate of compound interest, nonfluctuation in value, creditor protection, ready marketability at par, guaranteed loan values with the loan never callable while the policy is in force, and no income tax on the interest as it is compounding.

SELECTED REFERENCES

Huebner, S. S., and Black, Kenneth, Jr. *Life Insurance*. 8th ed. New York: Appleton-Century-Crofts, Inc., 1972.

Linton, M. Albert. *How Life Insurance Can Serve You*, Chap. 3. New York: Harper & Bros., 1958.

Mehr, Robert I. *Life Insurance Theory and Practice*. Austin, Texas: Business Publications, Inc., 1970.

National Underwriter Company. *Who Writes What?* 29th ed. Cincinnati, Ohio, 1970.

---

life policy had a guaranteed cash value of $6,506.30 at age 65. The term policy expires at age 65, while the other policy may be kept in force by continued payment of premiums or under one of the nonforfeiture options. Obviously, this illustration considers only net outlays for the policies and ignores compound interest on the difference in premiums. Also, the comparison would be affected by revisions in the assumed dividend scale.

6

Contracts—Whole Life and Endowment

By C. ARTHUR WILLIAMS, JR.

WHOLE LIFE INSURANCE, unlike term insurance, provides permanent protection. The insurer promises to pay the face value of the contract *when* the insured dies, not *if* the insured dies within a stated period. Endowment insurance provides for (1) payment of the face amount upon the death of the insured within a specified period and (2) payment of the face amount at the end of the period if the insured survives.

WHOLE LIFE INSURANCE

Almost two thirds of the ordinary life insurance in force is whole life insurance sold separately or as part of the combination contracts discussed in Chapter 8.[1]

Types of Whole Life Contracts

Whole life contracts can be divided into two major types: (1) straight life contracts and (2) limited-payment life contracts. The promise of the insurer to pay the face amount upon death is the same for both types of contracts. The major difference between the two categories is the premium payment period.

Under policies of the first type, the premiums are payable for the remainder of the insured's life. The terms "straight life," "ordinary life," "whole life," and "continuous-premium whole life" are used interchangeably to denote this type of contract. The term "ordinary life" is used most frequently but is apt to create some confusion because "ordinary insurance" is also used to denote that branch of insurance which is neither credit insurance, group insurance, nor industrial insurance. The term "straight life" is used in this chapter.

Under policies of the second type, the premiums are payable for the remainder of the insured's life or until the expiration of a stated period,

---

[1] *Life Insurance Fact Book* (New York: Institute of Life Insurance, issued annually).

TABLE 6–1. Nonparticipating Annual Premium Rates per $1,000 Charged Males by a Leading Insurer for Some Representative $10,000 Contracts

Age	Five-Year Term	Straight Life	Paid up at 65	20-Pay Life	Endowment at 65	20-Year Endowment
25 ....$ 5.33		$13.35	$14.86	$22.07	$ 18.55	$42.69
35 .... 6.04		18.61	21.93	27.93	27.71	43.63
45 .... 10.08		27.58	36.49	36.49	46.67	46.67
55 .... 21.05		41.57	79.10	49.25	102.88	54.14

if earlier. Examples are a 20-payment whole life policy, more commonly known as a 20-pay life contract, a 30-payment life contract, and a life paid-up-at-65 contract. An extreme example in this category is the single-payment life contract, under which the insured pays only one premium at the beginning of the policy period.

The differences in the level annual premium outlays for a straight life contract, a paid-up-at-65 contract, and a 20-pay life contract are indicated in Table 6–1, which presents the nonparticipating premium rates charged by one leading insurer.[2] For comparison purposes, premium rates are also presented for five-year renewable and convertible term insurance, an endowment-at-65 policy, and a 20-year endowment policy. The table also indicates the effect of the age at issue upon the various premium rates.

Females pay lower rates than those presented in Table 6–1 for males. For example, a female, aged 35, would pay $16.75 per $1,000 for a $10,000 straight life policy.

The premium rates also depend upon the face amount of the insurance policy because this insurer, like most others, recognizes in its premium rate structure that many of its expenses do not increase proportionately with the amount of insurance purchased. For example, the premium rates per $1,000 of this insurer, for a male aged 35 for a $5,000 straight life insurance contract, would be $19.61, and for a $20,000 contract $18.11. Instead of grading premiums by size of policy, some insurers have chosen to achieve the same effect by grading dividends on their participating insurance.[3]

The Level Premium Concept

Under a straight life insurance contract the insured may pay a level premium rate for the rest of his life. If one-year term policies were issued

---

[2] Nonparticipating annual premium rates are presented in order partly to offset the effect of dividends. The premiums the same insurer would charge a male, aged 35, for $10,000 participating contracts are as follows: $7.75 for five-year term insurance, $23.95 for straight life insurance, $28.47 for paid-up insurance at 65, $35.34 for 20-pay life insurance, $33.42 for an endowment at 65, and $49.20 for a 20-year endowment.

[3] The major difference between the two approaches is that the gradation in the initial premiums is guaranteed, while the gradation of dividends is not. On the other hand, proponents of graded dividends argue that it is easier to adjust inequities that may appear through the dividend structure. See Chapter 8.

which were renewable for life, these term policies would pay the same face amount in case of death as the straight life contract, but the premium rate would increase each year. Table 6–2 compares the net level premium rate that would be paid for straight life insurance issued at age 35 with the net premium rates that would be payable at selected ages for the yearly renewable term insurance.[4]

TABLE 6–2.   Net Premium Rates per $1,000 of Straight Life Insurance Issued at Age 35 and Yearly Renewable Term Insurance at Various Ages (1958 CSO Mortality Table, 3 percent interest)

Age	Straight Life	Yearly Renewable Rates
35	$16.29	$ 2.44
40	16.29	3.43
45	16.29	5.19
50	16.29	8.08
55	16.29	12.62
60	16.29	19.75
65	16.29	30.83
70	16.29	48.33
75	16.29	71.23
80	16.29	106.77
85	16.29	156.44
90	16.29	221.49
95	16.29	341.01

Up to age 58, in this illustration, the annual net premium paid for the term protection would be less than the annual net premium paid for the straight life contract. After this age, the yearly renewable term rate increases so rapidly that at age 70 the total net premiums paid for the yearly renewable term contract would exceed the total net premiums paid for the straight life protection. The rapid increase in the annual rates at advanced ages explains why it is not feasible to issue term policies renewable for life. In practice, the increase would have to be even greater than indicated in Table 6–2 because only those insureds in poor health

---

[4] The net premium is based only upon expected mortality experience and interest earnings. The mortality and interest assumptions here are the 1958 CSO Mortality Table and 3 percent interest. The gross premium is the net premium plus an expense loading. Because the insured must pay a gross premium, it would be preferable to compare in this illustration the gross premiums charged by a representative insurer; but insurers do not issue term policies that are renewable for life. However, it is apparent from the rates in Table 6–1 that the gross premium for five-year renewable term insurance would exceed the $18.61 gross premium for straight life insurance before age 55 and that the total premiums paid for term insurance would exceed those paid for straight life insurance at an earlier age than 70.

Net premium rates are used in the illustration in order to eliminate the complicating effect of expense loadings and because actual gross premium rates for term insurance at the advanced ages are not available.

would be likely to renew their term policies. Consequently, one advantage of the level premium method of payment is that if the insured lives to an advanced age, the net premiums paid for the protection will be less than if yearly renewable term rates had been charged. At some age this is true even after allowance is made for the fact that the extra premium dollars paid in the early years might have been invested elsewhere at a reasonable rate of return.

A much more important advantage of the level premium method is that a savings or investment element is created which is not part of a yearly renewable term contract. As already noted, the net level premiums exceed the cost of protection (based on the assumed mortality and interest rates) in the early years of the straight life contract. On the other hand, the expense loading in the gross premium is not large enough to pay the very high first-year expenses. As a result, the gross premium less the first-year expenses may be (and probably will be) less than the cost of the protection. After the first year, however, the expense loading is more than sufficient to pay expenses and provide a margin for contingencies. The gross premium paid the second year will therefore exceed the cost of protection and the necessary provision for expenses and contingencies in that year. If the remainder of the second-year gross premium exceeds the deficiency in the first-year gross premium accumulated at a specified rate of interest for one year, the difference is accumulated by the insurer at the specified interest rate for one year. This accumulated amount is known as the cash value and is available to the insured upon request.[5] Moreover, if the insured dies, this cash value is part of the face value paid to his beneficiary.

If the second-year gross premium, less the cost of protection and necessary provision for expenses and contingencies in that year, is less than the accumulated deficiency in the first year's premium, that deficiency is reduced, and the reduced amount is accumulated for one year at the specified rate of interest. The same procedure is followed during the third, fourth, and following years. Cash values usually become available no later than the end of the second year.

As stated above, when the insured dies, the cash value is part of the face amount paid to his beneficiary. Because the pure protection element in the policy (called the net amount at risk) is thus less than the face amount of the policy, the cost of the pure protection is less than it would be for a yearly renewable term contract of the same face amount as the straight life contract.

Except for insureds less than nine years of age, the mortality rate increases each year, thus tending to increase the cost of the pure protection. However, once there is a cash value, this cash value increases each year, thereby reducing the pure protection element and reducing its cost over what it would be if the protection were for the full policy face. Initially, the increases in the mortality rate will be the dominant factor, and the cost of the pure protection will increase. The cost of the pure protection

---

[5] Some insurers do not charge the entire first-year expenses against the first gross premium. As a result, cash values may become available at the end of the first year.

and the necessary provision for expenses and contingencies may in fact exceed the gross level premium during some years, but the assumed interest earnings during those years are always sufficient to produce a continuous increase in the cash values. Eventually, the decreasing amount of pure protection becomes the dominant element, and the cost of the pure protection begins to decline. If the assumed mortality rates are those in the 1958 CSO Mortality Table (and this has been the assumption in this illustration), at age 100 the cash value is the face value of the policy, and the cost of the pure protection for deaths during the preceding year is zero. This must be the case because under this table it is assumed that a person aged 99 will die before reaching age 100. Therefore, on the basis of the usual actuarial assumption that death benefits are paid at the end of the year, the face value must be on hand at age 100 for each insured who is aged 99 at the beginning of the year.

Straight life insurance, then, may be considered to be a combination of decreasing term insurance (the pure protection element) and an increasing savings or investment element which equals the face value at age 100.

Other forms of whole life insurance and endowment insurance may be viewed in the same way, except that the savings element will be more important and the cost of pure protection correspondingly less because the higher premiums are level over a period which may be less than the whole of life. Table 6–3 makes it possible to compare the actual cash values under the five whole life and endowment contracts for which premium rates were presented in Table 6–1. Note first that the cash values are zero at the end of the first year, for the reason indicated in the preceding discussion. Note, second, that the cash values under the limited-payment contracts continue to grow after the last premium has been paid because the interest on the cash value exceeds the cost of the pure protection and expenses. Third, after the last premium has been paid on the paid-up-at-65 contract, the cash value is the same as that under the 20-pay life contract, which has a shorter premium payment period. Fourth, the cash value under all three whole life contracts at age 100 is the face value of the contract. Fifth, the cash value under the two endowment policies becomes the face amount at the end of the endowment period.

TABLE 6–3.   Cash Values per $1,000 Insurance Provided under Five Nonparticipating Whole Life Contracts Issued by a Leading Insurer to an Insured Age 35

End of Policy Year	Straight Life	Paid up at 65	20-Pay Life	Endowment at 65	20-Year Endowment
1	...	...	...	...	...
2	$ ...	$ 4	$ 12	$ 12	$ 35
3	16	23	36	36	75
5	48	62	86	87	157
10	137	168	226	226	389
15	235	288	386	386	665
20	342	423	574	573	1,000
Age 65	522	690	690	1,000	
Age 100	1,000	1,000	1,000		

Flexible Provisions in Whole Life Contracts

Certain provisions in whole life insurance contracts make them highly flexible. (See Appendix D for specimen individual life insurance contract.) These provisions are also found in endowment contracts, but some of the provisions, such as the nonforfeiture options and the conversion privilege, provide more flexibility under whole life contracts.[6]

The nonforfeiture options provide a great deal of flexibility. If the insured should at any time wish to discontinue paying premiums, he may surrender the policy for its cash value or request that the insurance be continued as reduced paid-up insurance or as extended term insurance. The paid-up insurance option would provide permanent insurance protection of a reduced amount, while the extended term insurance option would continue the face amount of insurance (less outstanding policy loans and plus dividend credits) in force for some limited term.

This flexibility is increased when the insurer permits the insured to receive the cash surrender value according to the terms of one of the settlement options. For example, the insurer may permit the insured to withdraw the cash value in the form of a monthly income for the insured and his wife as long as they both shall live, with a reduced amount continuing for the lifetime of the survivor. An important feature of such options is that the conversion is made at net rates. Most insurers permit the withdrawal of the cash value according to the terms of some settlement option.

Dividend options, where available, provide even further flexibility because the dividends may be used, among other things, to convert the policy to a paid-up policy at an earlier date.

The loan provision also adds to the flexibility of the policy. Because of this provision, the insured may borrow some or all of the cash value at any time. Also, if the automatic premium loan provision is in effect, its operation may prevent the inadvertent lapse of the policy.

Finally, whole life policies usually permit the insured, without evidence of insurability, to convert the policy to some other contract with a larger savings element. This right provides the greatest flexibility when the whole life contract is a straight life contract because the range of alternatives is greatest.

Uses of Straight Life Insurance

Because straight life insurance provides permanent protection, combines savings with pure protection, and has so many flexible features, it has many uses. In fact, for most families, this policy is more satisfactory than any other basic form. It should be emphasized, however, that the most satisfactory contract depends upon individual needs and preferences, and that some combination of basic forms, such as those described in Chapter 8, may produce the most appropriate contract.

---

[6] For example, reduced paid-up or extended term insurance under an endowment policy cannot extend beyond the period of the endowment. Also, conversion from an endowment policy to a whole life policy is seldom, if ever, allowed without evidence of insurability.

Straight life insurance provides permanent insurance protection at the lowest annual cost. Consequently, in addition to meeting needs that may decline with the passage of time, straight life insurance is a useful way for insureds to provide the necessary lifetime protection against such needs as probate costs and estate taxes. For the same reason, straight life insurance may be a convenient way for an insured to leave a legacy to some person or organization, regardless of the date of death.

Straight life insurance is also useful if the insured wishes to accumulate a savings fund for retirement or any other purpose without sacrificing too much protection against premature death losses. Straight life insurance provides less premature death protection for a given premium outlay than term insurance, which has practically no savings element. On the other hand, straight life insurance provides more premature death protection for a given premium outlay than limited-payment policies and endowment policies, which place more emphasis on the savings element than the straight life insurance contract does. This characteristic of straight life insurance makes it attractive to persons in lower income groups who cannot afford to pay sizable premiums for the protection they need or desire, but who wish to accumulate some savings as part of their insurance protection. This characteristic also may attract persons in higher income groups who desire to accumulate some savings in conjunction with their protection program, but who have alternative uses for some of their savings and who therefore wish to purchase low-cost permanent insurance.

The principal limitation of straight life insurance arises out of one of its strong points. Because the straight life contract enables the insured to compromise between varying objectives, it is not as satisfactory as some other policy when the insured definitely wants to give primary emphasis to any one of these objectives. For example, term insurance may be more appropriate when the insured definitely wants to maximize the amount of insurance available for a given premium. Endowment insurance may be more satisfactory if the insured wishes to emphasize the savings element by providing a smaller amount of protection for a given premium. Needs change, however, and the straight life contract may still be the best in the long run, since it offers the maximum amount of protection, with some savings, on a permanent basis.

Straight life insurance is sometimes criticized on the ground that premiums *must* be paid for life. This, of course, is not true, as has already been demonstrated in the discussion of its flexible provisions. A related criticism is that while a person who wishes to discontinue premium payments after he retires at, say, age 65 may do so, the price is a reduction in the amount of his protection. In many instances, this situation poses a most difficult decision for the insured. One way to avoid this problem would be to convert his straight life insurance to a paid-up-at-65 contract prior to his retirement.

Uses of Limited-Payment Life Insurance

Limited-payment life insurance contracts emphasize savings more than straight life contracts. They also make it possible for the insured to stop paying premiums at the expiration of a certain period without any reduction in the face amount of the contract. Therefore, these contracts are useful in situations where either of these two features is important. Some examples follow.

The paid-up-at-65 contract is attractive when the insured wants permanent protection but does not want the premiums to continue beyond the end of his normal earnings period. This contract also provides a larger savings element in the early years than straight life insurance, as already demonstrated; and at the younger ages the additional premium is slight, as shown in Table 6–1.

Policies with shorter payment periods may prove useful when a person's earning career or the most important part of his earning career covers a relatively short time as in the case of a professional athlete or airline pilot. If the insured can purchase an adequate amount of protection under a policy with premium payments limited to this short period, he has the advantage of knowing that his insurance program will be completed at the end of that time and that a sizable savings component is accumulating. However, if the insured cannot purchase an adequate amount of limited-payment insurance to meet his protection needs, he may be better off with a straight life contract because he can buy more insurance and later take advantage of the nonforfeiture insurance options.

Limited-payment contracts are often used as gifts because the premium payments can be completed within a stated period. The gift may be made for estate planning purposes. For example, a 10-pay life contract may be purchased with the income from a short-term reversionary trust. There are tax advantages to such an arrangement if the grantor is in a high tax bracket and the policy is not on his life because the trust income will be taxed at the lower rates applicable to the trust.

Because interest credited on the savings component of an insurance policy is not taxable in the year in which it is credited, limited-payment contracts may also be used to great advantage by persons in the upper income tax brackets to accumulate savings and to provide protection in case of death.

The principal limitation of limited-payment contracts when compared with straight life contracts is the smaller amount of protection purchased with each premium dollar. Many insureds who buy limited-payment contracts underestimate their protection needs. In addition, many of these insureds place too much emphasis on the fact that premiums cease at the end of a certain period. They may be better able to continue paying premiums at the end of that period than at the beginning. However, an insured with a limited-payment contract generally cannot lengthen his premium payment period except by proving insurability and buying a new contract.

Modified Life and Graded-Premium Contracts

Insurers often issue a whole life contract called a modified life contract, for which the premiums are not level over the premium payment period. Instead, the premium is lower than the level premium during the early years of the premium payment period and, in order to be actuarially equivalent, greater thereafter. The lower premium during the early years, however, is always greater than the term insurance premium would be for those years.

A graded-premium contract is a slightly different contract with non-level premiums. The premium increases each year during the early years of the contract (usually five years) and remains the same after that time. The initial premium is less than the equivalent level premium for a straight life contract at the age of issue, while the final premium is more.

Modified life and graded-premium life contracts are useful compromises between straight life insurance and convertible term insurance. The premium is less than that for straight life insurance in the early years. On the other hand, the insured is accumulating some cash values, he need not decide to convert term insurance or act upon this decision, and the premium increase is not so great as it would be with convertible term insurance. However, the premium does increase either annually for a period or at the end of some period, and the insured should be made clearly aware of this fact. Presumably, his income will increase over the years and the increasing premium will not be a financial burden, but this may not be the case.[7]

Preferred Risk Contracts and "Specials"

Many insurers, especially since World War II, have issued one or more of their whole life contracts (usually the straight life contract or a paid-up-at-85 contract) as a "preferred risk" or "special" policy at reduced rates. "Preferred risk" was the more popular term for these policies as long as they were issued only to persons meeting superior underwriting standards and as long as this was the major justification for the reduced premium. Today the term "special" is more frequently used because the insured is not always required to meet superior underwriting standards. Moreover, other factors, to be noted below, are usually more responsible for the reduced premium than expected mortality savings.

Specials are usually issued with high minimum amounts. Because an insurer's expenses do not increase proportionately with the size of the policy, requiring the special to be at least a certain size enables the insurer to charge a lower rate for this contract.

In addition to the minimum-amount requirement and (possibly) selective underwriting, the reduction in premiums for some specials may also be justified by one or more of the following factors: (1) a reduction in the agent's commission rate; (2) a requirement that premiums be paid annually; (3) reduced cash values; (4) a reduction in the number of settlement options or in the amounts available under a settlement option; (5) dividends payable only if the insured survives a specified period and terminates his policy at the expiration of that time; (6) a reduction in policy services, such as the right to receive the cash value according to the terms of one of the settlement options; and (7) anticipated lower lapse rates because of the economic and personal characteristics of insureds buying specials.

---

[7] Some insurers have used participating modified life and graded-premium contracts partly as a competitive tool to offset the appeal of lower nonparticipating initial premiums. Because dividends usually increase as the policy gets older, they may offset part of the premium increase.

ENDOWMENT INSURANCE

Endowment insurance accounts for about 5 percent of the life insurance in force. Unlike straight life insurance, of which there is about the same amount of insurance in force as there was a decade ago, endowment insurance is now a smaller share of the insurance in force.

Endowment Concepts

There are two concepts of endowment insurance, i.e., the mathematical concept and the economic concept.

Mathematical Concept. The insurance company makes two basic promises under endowment insurance that are exactly opposite in nature. First, it promises to pay the face amount in the event the insured dies during the endowment period. Second, it promises to pay the face amount in the event the insured survives to the end of the endowment period. The first promise is identical with that made under a level term policy for an equivalent amount and period. The second represents a different concept, that of the "pure endowment." A *pure endowment* is defined as a contract which promises to pay the face amount only if the insured is living at the end of the period specified, nothing being paid in case of prior death.

Economic Concept. The above analysis is correct and convenient for purposes of mathematical computation, but another and perhaps more logical and meaningful analysis of endowment insurance has been developed which is consistent with the earlier description of straight life insurance as a combination of decreasing term insurance and an increasing savings or investment element. Under this economic concept, the investment element increases gradually over the endowment period, reaching the face amount at the end of the period. At any time prior to the end of the endowment period, the decreasing term insurance component is equal to the difference between the face amount and the investment accumulation on that date.

Types of Endowment Insurance Policies

An examination of the contracts issued by different insurers shows many variations in the use of endowment insurance. Such policies may be made payable in 10, 15, 20, 25, 30 or more years, or the length of the term may be so arranged as to cause the policy to mature at certain ages, such as 60, 65, 70, and others. When written for a short term, the purpose of the policy usually is to combine immediate protection with heavy savings. If written for a long term, or to mature at an advanced age, the object is usually to combine death protection with provision for old age. Table 6–1 presents illustrative rates for an endowment at 65 and a 20-year endowment contract. Note that the rates for these two contracts at age 45 are the same because at that age these two contracts are equivalent.

The term "endowment" is also sometimes applied to "retirement income" contracts. Under such contracts the amount payable on survival is greater than the face amount, and the amount payable on death is the face amount or the cash value, whichever is greater.

Uses of Endowment Insurance

Broadly, the endowment insurance contract serves as an effective way to accumulate a specific sum of money over a period of time, with the savings program protected by insurance against the contingency of premature death. Such a contract, functionally, serves three purposes: (1) as a method of systematic semicompulsory savings, (2) as an investment, and (3) as a hedge against the savings period being cut short by death.

The endowment insurance contract can be applied to any need for funds which are to be saved over a period of time. For example, funds for education, old age, debt retirement, and other purposes can be accumulated through the purchase of an appropriate endowment insurance contract.

Educational Funds. One of the most popular uses of endowment insurance contracts is to accumulate funds for the higher education of children. The contract may be written on the life of a parent or the child. If the insurance is written on the life of the child, it is advisable to attach a so-called *payor clause,* which provides that premiums are to be waived in the event the premium payor named in the clause should die or become disabled.

Consideration should not be given to insuring the lives of children until the father or other income producer has an adequate life insurance program. Since few men have an adequate program, it is generally desirable to place the insurance on the life of the parent even when the objective is to accumulate funds for educational purposes. If the child dies, the funds will not be needed. If the parent dies, the proceeds may be used for educational purposes or perhaps food and shelter, depending upon the circumstances.

Old Age. Another important use of endowment insurance is to provide funds for retirement purposes. Endowment insurance, if the term is so selected as to make the policy mature at or near anticipated retirement (e.g., 60, 65, or 70), serves as an excellent method of accumulating a fund for support in old age. Many who oppose endowments maturing at earlier ages because of their greater premium per $1,000 support long-term endowments maturing at an age when a man's earning capacity usually ceases and when he normally expects to retire from actual work.

Other Purposes. Endowment insurance also may be utilized to accumulate a fund for other specific purposes such as a grant to a college, hospital, or church, or to finance a long-awaited trip abroad.

Misuse of Endowment Insurance

The above discussion has indicated the usefulness of endowment insurance, but it can be and has been misused. It is essentially a savings plan with insurance to protect the savings program against premature death. Its primary purpose is *not* to provide protection. Due to the heavy savings element, the premiums are the largest of any comparable life insurance plan but provide the smallest amount of protection for each dollar of premium paid. Consequently, endowments should not be used where there is a great need for protection.

Most men have limited funds available and need a life insurance program with emphasis on the protection element. Therefore, the purchase of endowment insurance, particularly with a short term, may soak up available funds without providing the amount of needed protection. Younger men with no responsibilities frequently purchase endowments and then later, when their responsibilities increase, find they are not able to purchase additional protection since their limited funds are already committed to high-premium endowments. It may be possible to exchange an endowment contract for a lower premium, whole life contract at a later date; but where such a privilege is permitted, by contract right or by company practice, it is necessary to furnish evidence of insurability. This is not always possible.

It is important to note that the endowment insurance policy is subject to the limitations of term insurance as far as protection is concerned. It normally should not be recommended to cover a need which is permanent or could run beyond the term of the endowment.

SELECTED REFERENCES

Huebner, S. S., and Black, Kenneth, Jr.   *Life Insurance,* chs. vi, vii. 8th ed. New York: Appleton-Century-Crofts, Inc., 1972.

Maclean, Joseph B.   *Life Insurance,* ch. ii. 9th ed. New York: McGraw-Hill Book Co., Inc., 1962.

McGill, Dan M.   *Life Insurance,* chs. iv, v. Rev. ed. Homewood, Ill.: Richard D. Irwin, Inc., 1967.

Mehr, Robert I.   *Life Insurance: Theory and Practice,* chs. 4, 5. Austin, Tex.: Business Publications, Inc., 1970.

7

Contracts—Annuities

By ROBERT I. MEHR

THE ANNUITY has been called the "upside-down application of the life insurance principle." While this description is not strictly accurate, it does serve as a springboard for a discussion of annuities. This concept is based on the notion that the purpose of life insurance is the scientific creation of an estate, whereas the purpose of the annuity is the scientific liquidation of an estate. Under a life insurance contract the estate is created at death. Under the annuity contract the estate is fully liquidated by death. Reduced to its ultimate simplicity, the idea can be expressed by comparing the nature of the two types of agreements. In exchange for his premium the purchaser of life insurance expects his insurer to pay his beneficiary a specified sum upon his death. For his premium the purchaser of an annuity expects his insurer to pay him a periodic income as long as he lives. Thus, under a life insurance contract the insurer *starts* paying upon the death of the insured, whereas under an annuity contract the insurer *stops* paying upon the death of the insured.

THE ANNUITY PRINCIPLE

The important aspects of insurance are twofold: the reduction of uncertainty and the sharing of losses. The uncertainty facing the purchaser of an annuity is the length of his life. Although the insurance company does not know how long any given individual will live, it does know how to apply the law of large numbers to the experience of a given group of annuitants so as to approximate the actual result for that group. Therefore, when the savings or investments of a large number of individuals are combined into a group or joint account, each member can be paid an annual or monthly amount actuarially calculated to assure that no one will outlive his capital, yet the capital will be paid out and not hoarded. Thus, uncertainty is reduced, and losses (the costs of "living too long") are shared. The amount of periodic income received by each member of the group is determined not only by his contribution but also by his age, sex, type of annuity contract purchased, and sometimes by his health. The older a person is when his annuity income begins, the greater will be his

periodic payments per dollar of contribution. A man will receive more
periodically than a woman of the same age per dollar of contribution.
And if the annuitant is willing to have his payments terminated at his
death, he will receive a higher periodic income than if he insisted on a
guaranteed minimum number of payments. Where the rating formula
considers the physical condition of the annuitant, more will be paid per
period to the unhealthy annuitant than to the healthy one.

The periodic income paid under an annuity contract is composed of
three parts: principal, investment income, and a survivorship or insurance
benefit. The amount allocated to each part from any given periodic payment can be computed easily. For purposes of illustration, assume an
annuity of $1,000 a year issued to a man aged 65, first payment one year
from date of issue. Assume further that the cost of the annuity is figured
on the basis of 3 percent interest and the 1949 Annuity Table. The net
single premium for this annuity under these assumptions would be
$11,013. If the annuity were purchased one year later (age 66), the net
single premium would be $10,611. Thus, in the first year, $402 of the original capital would have been liquidated in the case of the annuity purchased at age 65.

The breakdown of the *first* $1,000 periodic payment into principal, in-
terest, and survivorship benefit can be accomplished as follows:

Initial investment at age 65 (net)	$11,013.00
Interest assumed (3 percent) ....+	330.39
Total amount available	$11,343.39
Annuity payment ....−	1,000.00
Amount remaining without survivorship benefit	$10,343.39

Note that the net cost of the annuity at age 66 would be $10,611.00, but
that only $10,343.39 is available. How is the deficiency of $267.61 made
up? Not all of the 65-year-old annuitants will survive the one-year period
to collect their first $1,000.00. Those who die will release their investment
to be spread among the survivors. Each survivor's share will amount to
$267.61, which is the deficiency in the fund available at the beginning of
the second year.

Thus, for this annuity at age 65, the first annuity payment of $1,000.00
breaks down as follows:

Interest income	$ 330.39	($11,013.00 at 3 percent)
Capital liquidation	402.00	($11,013.00 − $10,611.00)
Survivorship benefit	267.61	($10,611.00 − $10,343.39)
Total	$1,000.00	

Each successive year the survivorship benefit will increase, and the interest income and amount of capital liquidation will decrease. For example,
the annuity payment for the second year will consist of:

Interest income ....$	318.92	($10,611.00 at 3 percent)
Capital liquidation	401.00	($10,611.00 — $10,210.00°)
Survivorship benefit	280.67	($10,210.00° — $9,929.33†)
Total	$1,000.00	

° $10,210.00 is the cost of the annuity at age 67.

† $9,929.33 is the amount remaining from the initial fund plus interest after the $1,000.00 payment is made.

The division of payment for each successive year can be worked out using the method applied above. The formulas for each part are as follows:

Interest income = Net single premium at the beginning of the year times the interest rate assumed

Capital liquidation = Net single premium at the beginning of the year minus net single premium one year later

Survivorship benefit = Net single premium one year later minus (net single premium at beginning of the year plus interest minus annuity payment)

CLASSIFICATION OF ANNUITIES

Up to this point, we have been concerned with the annuity in its simplest form, the single-premium life annuity contract. Under this contract the insurance company promises to pay a given amount each period, usually monthly, to the annuitant during his lifetime in exchange for a single premium which immediately becomes the property of the company, no part of which is returnable in the event of the annuitant's death.

The single-premium life annuity contract, however, does not meet the economic or psychological needs of most purchasers of individual annuities as distinguished from purchasers of group annuities. Some buyers want to pay for their retirement annuities through a series of level annual premiums during their preretirement years. Some do not like the idea of loss to their estates of premiums not returned in annuity payments in the event of early death following retirement. A few purchasers would like to have the annuity payments contingent upon the lives of more than one person. Also, some would like to have the payments expressed in units other than dollars. Because of the variety of interests among annuity customers, a number of variations in annuity forms has developed.

Anyone looking at the wide array of different types of annuities available in the market could become completely baffled without a systematic method of classifying them. Annuities may be classified on at least five different bases: method of paying premiums, disposition of proceeds, date benefits begin, number of lives covered, and units in which pay-out benefits are expressed. These classifications, however, are not mutually exclusive, since every annuity will fall into all five classes. Figure 7–1 is a useful device for viewing the annuity types as a unit.

Method of Paying Premiums

Annuities may be purchased with either a single premium or through a series of installment premiums.

FIGURE 7–1. Classification of Annuities

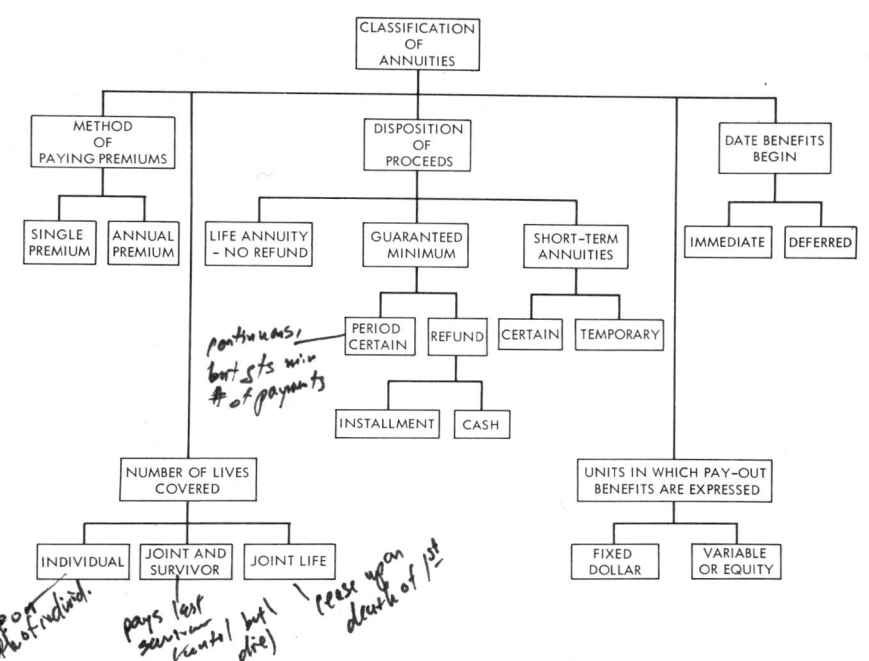

Single-Premium Annuities. An annuity purchased by one lump sum is known as a single-premium annuity. Frequently, life insurance cash values or death proceeds are liquidated as an annuity. Here the cash values or proceeds are used to fund a single-premium annuity at rates guaranteed in the policy. Some insurers offer what is known as an annuity option under which the cash value or proceeds of the policy can be applied to purchase a nonparticipating straight life annuity contract at current rates. (This option gives the insured or the beneficiary that benefit of any change in interest or mortality assumptions that may be favorable to them at the time of election.) The amount of each annuity payment is increased by 3 percent (in some companies, 4 percent) over that paid under a similar annuity policy because there are no additional commissions and taxes to pay.[1]

Aside from its use as a method of liquidating life insurance cash values and proceeds, the single-premium annuity is used in qualified pension and profit sharing plans to fund retirement benefits at the time an employee retires. Nearly all group annuities are written as single-premium annuities.[2] Since nearly 80 percent of all annuity income is written under group contracts or life insurance settlement options, the single-premium annuity is the predominant form of annuity.

Annual-Premium Annuities. By far the most popular type of annuity written on an individual basis is the annual-premium annuity. Here the

---

[1] See Chapter 54 for a discussion of life insurance settlement options.

[2] Group annuities are discussed in Chapter 39.

premiums are paid in periodic installments over the years prior to the date on which the annuity income begins. This type of annuity is a flexible instrument. It is usually written as a savings contract during the period of accumulation. The net premiums, accumulated at interest, are not forfeited either at death or on surrender during this period. Consequently, the death of the annuitant or the surrender of the annuity during the accumulation period does not increase the benefits of the remaining annuitants. Whenever the annuitant wishes to cease paying premiums, he may select a paid-up annuity for a reduced amount or withdraw the surrender value. If he should die before the contract passes from the accumulation to the liquidation period, his beneficiaries are entitled to a death benefit equal to the cash value of the contract or the amount of premiums paid in, whichever is higher. The contract has one further flexible feature. Usually, the annuitant may elect to have his income payments started earlier or postponed until later, with an appropriate actuarial adjustment in the amount of the benefit. The annual-premium annuity appeals to one who wishes to use the annuity instrument as a vehicle for estate accumulation as well as for estate liquidation. And by its use, he is guaranteed an annuity income in the future at today's annuity rate.

Buyers of annual-premium annuities can accomplish their objective by purchasing a series of single-premium deferred annuities. In this event, premiums paid each year would be used to purchase fully-paid annuities with income payments beginning at some designated age. Annuity rate structures favor single-premium deferred annuities over annual-premium annuities. Thus a series of single-premium deferred annuities purchased beginning at age 45 for a premium of $1,000 each year for 20 years would produce a retirement income at age 65 in excess of that produced by an annual-premium annuity requiring a premium of $1,000 a year for 20 years *if* the rates on single-premium annuities are not increased during the 20-year period. However, insurance agents prefer to sell the annual-premium annuity, not only because of their respect for guarantees, but also because commission rates paid on annual-premium annuities are higher than those paid on single-premium annuities. Since higher minimum premiums are required for single-premium than for annual-premium annuities, not all buyers of annual-premium annuities qualify for single-premium annuities.

Disposition of Proceeds

Annuities may be classified further on the basis of the time at which benefits stop. Under this classification there are four types of annuities: the life annuity—no refund, the guaranteed minimum annuity, the annuity certain, and the temporary life annuity.

The Life Annuity—No Refund. Under the life annuity—no refund, the annuitant is paid an income throughout his lifetime. Upon his death, there is no further equity in the contract, regardless of how few benefit payments have been received. This is the purest form of life annuity and offers the annuitant the largest income payment per dollar of purchase price. No financial arrangement can equal the conventional no-refund life annuity in providing the largest, and at the same time certain, dollar income for life.

This contract, commonly called a straight life annuity, is used frequently in group annuities but not so often in individual annuities. Annuitants in many cases fail to understand the insurance principle involved in annuities. If they are willing to sacrifice their unused principal at their death for the benefit of the other annuitants who survive them, they in turn will benefit from the release of similar funds by those whom they survive. The benefit of survival is highest in the straight life annuity. Be this as it may, few annuitants want to expose their principal to full dissipation in the event of early death following retirement.

Guaranteed Minimum Annuities. To meet the psychological and economic objections to the straight life annuity, two forms of guaranteed minimum annuities have been developed: period certain and refund. Refund annuities may be classified further into installment refund and cash refund.

Under a *life annuity, period certain* contract, the annuitant is promised an income for life but is guaranteed a minimum number of payments, such as 120 or 240. If the annuitant dies before the minimum number of guaranteed payments has been made, the payments are continued to his beneficiary for the remainder of the stipulated (certain) period. If the annuitant survives the guaranteed payment period, the benefits continue until his death. For example, if the annuitant owning a 120 months' guarantee dies after five years (60 months), his beneficiary will continue to receive the benefits for 60 months, or she may choose instead to take the commuted value. If the annuitant lives beyond the 120 months, he will continue to collect payments until his death; following the death of the annuitant, his beneficiary will not be entitled to anything.

The cost of the period certain guarantee depends upon the age of the annuitant when benefits commence. For example, a 120 months' guarantee for a female aged 65 would cost about 4.5 percent more than a no-refund annuity. At age 55, the difference in cost would be about 1.2 percent more for the guarantee, whereas at age 45 the difference would be about 0.7 percent.

A *refund annuity* may be either an installment refund or a cash refund annuity. An *installment refund annuity* promises to continue the periodic payments after the death of the annuitant until the combined benefits paid to the annuitant and his beneficiary have equaled the purchase price of the annuity. A *cash refund annuity* agrees, upon the death of the annuitant, to return in cash the difference between benefits drawn and the purchase price paid by the annuitant. If the annuitant himself lives long enough to collect the purchase price in income payments, then upon his death all benefits and values terminate. For example, a $100 a month installment refund annuity would cost about $16,500 for a woman aged 65. If she died after having received 40 monthly installments, her beneficiary would be entitled to 125 more installments, making the total pay-out $16,500, which is the purchase price of the annuity. If this were a cash refund annuity, the cost would be about $16,865. In the event of the annuitant's death after having received 40 monthly payments ($4,000), her beneficiary would be entitled to collect $12,865 in cash, thus completing the total pay-out of $16,865. When the refund is made in cash instead of installments, interest on the decreasing principal not yet paid is sacrificed by the company. Therefore, the cash refund annuity is more expensive than the installment refund. If this were a life annuity—no refund, the cost would have been only about $15,350. If this were a life annuity, 10 years certain, the cost would have been about $16,000.

The choice between a guaranteed minimum annuity and a life annuity—no refund depends upon two considerations: (1) the age at which the annuity payments are to start, and (2) whether there is a need to provide for dependents in the event of the early death of the annuitant. The difference between the cost of a guaranteed minimum annuity and a life annuity—no refund is so insignificant for annuities commencing at early ages that it is uneconomic to purchase the life annuity—no refund. However, at later ages the straight life annuity has significant cost advantages and should be given serious consideration unless there is a need for a refund to provide for dependents in the event of early death. In fact, annuities of any type beginning at early ages seem to be uneconomic, since the return on a safe, direct, interest-bearing or dividend-yielding security is likely to be about as good, without the cost of capital liquidation. For example, at age 30, female, an annuity of $100 monthly guaranteed for 15 years would cost about $30,000. This amounts to a return of about 4 percent, with part of it consisting of a return of principal. The would-be annuitant would not have to look very far today to find a safe direct investment yielding in excess of 5 percent. The low survival benefits at early ages account for the relatively low income from annuities at these ages.

The Annuity Certain. The annuity certain is a contract which provides the annuitant a given income for a specified number of years, independent of his life or death. Upon the termination of these years, the payments cease. Life expectancy is in no way a factor. Therefore, following the prior death of the annuitant, the payments continue to the end of the stipulated period. This form of annuity is commonly used as a method of paying out life insurance proceeds to a beneficiary under the fixed-period or fixed-amount options. For example, the insured might wish to use the $10,000 proceeds of a life insurance policy to pay his beneficiary an annuity certain of $179 a month for five years. If the beneficiary dies before he has received the income for five years, the payments continue to a secondary beneficiary until the end of the five-year period. The discounted value of these payments often is the method of settlement made with the secondary beneficiary.

Temporary Life Annuities. Temporary life annuities are similar to the annuity certain except that payments cease upon the death of the annuitant. A 10-year temporary life annuity will provide monthly payments for 10 years or until the prior death of the annuitant. These annuities are not popular and therefore are rarely seen. Their uses are limited. One use is to provide an income to fill a gap until an income from another source becomes available. For example, a widow aged 50, with no dependent children, might purchase a 10-year temporary life annuity to provide herself an income until her social security benefits start at age 60, 10 years hence.

Date Benefits Begin

Benefits may be payable immediately after the contract is purchased, or they may be deferred until a number of years later.

The Immediate Annuity. The immediate annuity is purchased with a single premium, and benefits begin at the end of the first income period. For example, under certain interest and mortality assumptions, a man aged 65 could purchase a nonparticipating immediate annuity of $100 a month for about $13,000. The monthly benefit will begin one month after purchase. If benefits are to start at the beginning of the first income period, the annuity is called an *annuity due*. The annuity due is used when life insurance proceeds or cash values are converted into life annuity payments, as, for example, under the life income settlement option. With the exception of settlement options under life insurance contracts, few immediate annuities are purchased on an individual basis.[3]

The Deferred Annuity. The deferred annuity may be purchased with either a single premium or an installment premium. The benefit payments begin at the end of a given number of years or at optional ages established in the contract. Thus, for example, a man aged 44 might purchase, with a single premium of about $9,200, a $100-a-month installment refund annuity to begin at age 65. Or he might purchase the annuity for a series of 21 annual premiums of slightly more than $600. If a benefit is payable upon death during the accumulation period, the annuitant may shorten the deferred period, if he wishes, by accepting a smaller annuity. At age 55, for example, he would accept an annuity of about $59 a month if he has a single-premium deferred annuity, or one of about $36 a month if his annuity is an annual-premium annuity. An age 50 starting date would reduce the annuities to about $47 and $16, respectively.

The deferred period may also be lengthened under some deferred annuity contracts. A limitation usually restricts the extension to a given maximum age or to a given maximum number of years beyond the maturity date. In annual-premium deferred annuities, where an extension is allowed, the contract usually provides that no premiums shall be payable on or after the maturity date. An extension of the deferred period produces, of course, a higher annuity payment.

Under the annual-premium deferred annuity, if the annuitant wishes to discontinue his premium payments before the annuity matures, he may do so by agreeing to accept a smaller annuity at age 65. To illustrate, in the foregoing case the annuitant can discontinue premium payments at age 54 and take a paid-up deferred annuity at age 65 of about $55 a

---

[3] On a group basis, immediate annuities are used in connection with deposit administration and immediate participation guarantee plans in pension administration. These plans are discussed in Chapter 40.

month. If he discontinues premium payments at age 59, his paid-up annuity would amount to about $77 a month.

Deferred annuities have two periods: the deferred period and the liquidation or pay-out period. Minimum guarantees can be made available in one of these periods, in both, or in neither. For example, assume a single-premium deferred annuity of $100 a month commencing at age 65, issued at age 25, male. The premium for this annuity would be only about $3,500 if it were written without any guaranteed minimums, that is, if no death benefits were payable during either the deferred period or the period of liquidation. If the annuity guaranteed a return of the premium or cash value, if greater, upon death during the deferred period but was written on a life income only—no refund basis during the period of liquidation, the cost would be about $4,500. But if the annuity not only guaranteed a return of premium or cash value at death during the deferred period but also guaranteed a minimum of 120 payments during the period of liquidation, the cost would increase to about $4,900. It is customary, in writing deferred annuities on an individual basis, to guarantee a refund at death during the deferred period. Whether there is to be any guaranteed minimum during the period of liquidation, and, if so, the nature of any guarantee, is left to the discretion of the annuitant. Frequently, this guarantee feature is flexible, and the annuitant can make his choice at any time before the annuity commences. Of course, the higher the guaranteed minimum selected, the lower will be the amount of each annuity payment. It is common to find group annuities written as pure deferred annuities, that is, annuities written with no death benefits before retirement. Also with group contracts, single-premium deferred annuities are common, whereas most individual annuities are annual-premium deferred annuities.

Number of Lives Covered

The usual annuity covers only one life. Situations do arise, however, when it is desirable to make annuity payments contingent upon several lives. The most popular type of annuity covering more than one life is the joint-and-last-survivorship annuity. Under this contract, income is payable throughout the joint lifetimes of two or more annuitants and continues throughout the lifetime of the last survivor. Sometimes the contract will provide for a reduction in income payments upon the death of the first annuitant, say a one-third reduction, with two thirds continuing to the survivor. For example, a man aged 65 and a woman aged 61 could purchase a joint-and-last-survivorship annuity in the amount of $100 a month for about $19,750. This contract will pay $100 a month as long as either of them is alive. If it is felt that two cannot live as cheaply as one, the couple could arrange to have $114 a month paid during their joint lifetimes and $76 a month during the lifetime of the survivor. In this example, this can be done without any change in premium. Commonly, joint-and-last-survivorship annuities are written on two lives—usually husband and wife—in order to guarantee income to both as long as either may live.

A type of annuity not frequently written is the joint life annuity. This annuity contract provides for payments which continue throughout the joint lifetime of two people but cease upon the death of the first. This type of annuity is valuable when there is an independent income sufficient to support one member of the family but insufficient for both.

Units in Which Pay-out Benefits Are Expressed

Annuities under this classification are of two types: fixed and variable. The terms "fixed" and "variable" have reference to dollars and not to purchasing power. The fixed-dollar annuity, sometimes referred to as the conventional annuity, guarantees the annuitant a fixed, minimum number of dollars during each pay-out period. The variable annuity expresses its promise in terms of a fixed number of units, the dollar value of which fluctuates periodically according to the experience of the company. In some variable annuity plans, these fluctuations are limited to investment experience only, whereas in others they include mortality and expense experience as well.

If the annuitant wishes a guaranteed fixed-dollar income and is willing to accept the risk of decreased purchasing power brought on by inflation, then he will purchase the fixed-dollar annuity. If he does not want to rely on the stability of the dollar and is willing to have his money income fluctuate in the hope that as a result his real income will fluctuate less, he will purchase a variable annuity.[4]

As stated, the various types of annuities described in this chapter are not mutually exclusive. For example, every annuity will have characteristics from each class. To illustrate, there can be a single-premium immediate joint-and-last-survivorship refund fixed-dollar annuity, or an annual-premium deferred life annuity—no refund variable annuity, or any other combination taking one characteristic from each of the five classes.

THE ANNUITY POLICY

The annuity policy itself is a simple instrument. It states that the company will pay the designated annuity to the annuitant and that the payment will be subject to the provisions in the document which constitutes the entire contract. The contract then presents certain information about the annuitant: his date of birth, sex, and age last birthday.[5] This information is necessary to determine the premium. The policy also sets forth certain information about the annuity itself: maturity date, amount of the annuity, maturity value, table of guaranteed values in the event of surrender or death, amount of the premium, premium due dates, and whether the contract is participating.

The annuity contract contains an ownership clause and provisions for change in ownership, as customarily found in life insurance policies. Other clauses typical of life insurance policies found in the usual annuity

---

[4] Variable annuities are discussed in detail in Chapter 18.
[5] A number of companies issue contracts specifying age based on nearest birthday.

contract are those dealing with the grace period for paying premiums, incontestability, deferment of payment of cash values, policy loans, consideration, and beneficiary designation and change.

The contract has the customary assignment clause found in life insurance policies: "The company shall not be charged with notice of any assignment of any interest in the contract until the original assignment or certified copy has been filed with the company at its home office. The company assumes no responsibility as to the validity or effect of any assignment and may rely solely on the assignee's statement as to the amount of his interest." Not all annuity contracts are assignable. In order to qualify for special treatment granted by the federal income tax law to certain qualified individuals, the annuity must be nontransferable. The typical misstatement-of-age clause found in the annuity policy is: "If the annuitant's age or date of birth as recorded has been misstated, the amount of the annuity payments under the contract shall be such as the premium would have purchased at the correct age or date of birth. Any overpayments by the company will be deducted from the payment or payments next succeeding correction of age."

Annuity contracts written on a participating basis offer the owner the options of using the dividend to buy paid-up additions or of applying it toward the payment of the premium rather than taking the dividend in cash. Where a death benefit is available, the annuity contract will usually contain a number of settlement options similar to those found in life insurance policies. A waiver-of-premium benefit in the event of disability and an accidental death benefit, also similar to those written with life insurance, may be found as riders to some annuity contracts.

USES OF ANNUITIES

The principal use of the life annuity is to arrange an income for old age. When a man reaches that stage in life when he can no longer earn his living, he must live off earnings he has accumulated from the past. Unless that fund is large enough to provide a sufficient income from interest and dividends alone, it will have to be liquidated to supplement the periodic income. As the principal is reduced, income will decline, making it necessary to liquidate the fund at an increasing rate if a steady periodic payment is to be maintained. The fund eventually will expire. If the liquidator expires before the fund, there will be no problem. There is, however, a chance that the fund will expire before the liquidator, leaving an old man without an income. It is the function of the annuity to protect against this risk.

The fundamental purpose of a life annuity is to provide a vehicle for the scientific liquidation of capital. It is to assure a person an income he cannot outlive, an income well in excess of that to be derived from investing the cost of the annuity in safe, interest-bearing or dividend-yielding securities. The application of the annuity principle can be used to liquidate an estate created through life insurance contracts, investments in stocks and bonds, savings accounts, or the annuity contract itself. As long as there is a fund available for liquidation, the annuity principle is available to liquidate it scientifically.

Because of high prices, high taxes, and the desire to maintain a high standard of living, today more people than ever are faced with the problem of capital creation, not with the idea of preserving it to pass it along to heirs, but to finance a livable income for their old age by liquidating it systematically through the annuity principle. For example, a young man aged 25 who can save $50 a month toward his retirement would find that at a liberal 4 percent net return compounded annually after allowances for income taxes and investment expenses, he would have accumulated about $58,000 at age 65. This amount would yield a retirement income of about $240 a month, assuming a 5 percent return on the investment fund after retirement. If the same $50 a month were put into an annual-premium retirement annuity, the guaranteed monthly income at retirement would be about $310, an increase of about 30 percent over the direct investment plan.

Even when a person has amassed a fortune large enough to provide a livable income from investment return alone, he may well find a use for the annuity. The substitution of an annuity income for a direct investment income can free some capital for other uses without reducing the amount of the income. For example, it takes a capital sum of $100,000 to provide an income of $5,000 a year at 5 percent interest. An income of $5,000 a year, however, can be provided at age 65, male, by means of a single-premium life annuity, for about $54,000, just slightly more than one half of the amount needed under the direct investment plan. Some or all of the released capital can be used by the annuitant to finance a philanthropic interest or to pass on to his heirs while he is living and at a time when it might do them the most good. Also, the donor will have the satisfaction and pleasure of seeing his heirs put to good use the money he has accumulated for them. In addition, living gifts may have some tax advantages over transfer at death.[6]

Annuities have certain tax advantages which might appeal to some investors. Assume that the foregoing investor purchases the $5,000 annuity at age 65. How will these payments be taxed? According to the annuity tables put out by the United States Treasury Department, the life expectancy of a male aged 65 is 15 years. Since this is an annual annuity rather than a monthly annuity, the regulations require that this expectancy factor be adjusted downward by 0.5. This makes the adjusted expectancy period 14.5 years, and the expected return $72,500 (14.5 × $5,000). The purchase price of $54,000 represents 74.5 percent of the expected return. Therefore, 74.5 percent of each $5,000 annuity payment is viewed by the Internal Revenue Service as a return of invested capital, and only 25.5 percent is considered taxable income. Thus, in this example, only $1,275 is reportable as income, whereas the entire $5,000 would be subject to income taxation under the direct investment plan. Where the investor is in high surtax brackets, the annuity can have a real income tax advantage.

---

[6] Estate planning is discussed in Chapters 55 and 60.

Purchase of the annuity for $54,000 also reduces the gross estate for estate tax purposes. If the taxable estate before the annuity was purchased had a value of $100,000, the federal estate tax would amount to $20,700. Since the purchase of the annuity would reduce the taxable estate to $46,000, such a purchase would also reduce the federal estate tax liability to $6,120. The resulting tax savings is $14,580. So, in effect, the investor is able to purchase an annuity worth $54,000 for what is in effect only $39,420.

The deferred annuity also has income tax advantages during the period of accumulation. The investment earnings are not reportable as income during the year earned. Instead, they act to reduce the purchase price of the annuity in calculating the exclusion ratio for income tax purposes at the time of distribution. The effect of this procedure is to postpone the tax until the period of retirement when income is likely to be lower, the retirement income credit may be available, and the double exemption is allowed.

LIMITATIONS OF ANNUITIES

For psychological—and sometimes economic—reasons, old people do not like to use up their capital in providing themselves a retirement income. They like to leave some of it behind for their heirs. Some are content to live on an income well below that to which their savings entitle them in order that they may conserve their estates.

In any discussion of the limitations of annuities, there must be a clear separation between the fixed-dollar annuity and the variable annuity. Since a separate chapter is devoted exclusively to the variable annuity, this discussion will confine itself to the fixed-dollar annuity. While in some quarters the fixed-dollar annuity is still looked upon as a safe means for arranging a dependable retirement income, in others there is an increasing awareness of the dangers involved in tying long-range investment programs to a fixed number of dollars. Unlike the units used in weights and measures, the dollar has not proved itself to be a dependable measuring rod. The dollar fluctuates in value so widely that it becomes impossible for anyone to determine how many dollars will be needed in the future to cover his retirement income needs. Although the annuity has the advantage of safety insofar as the financial risk is concerned, it leaves its holders miserably exposed to the purchasing power risk. Of course, if price levels decline, the annuitant has gained by accepting this risk. But if, on the other hand, price levels rise, as is likely to be the case, the annuitant has lost part of the security he thought he had purchased.

Activity of a number of insurers and their agents in developing and selling annuities to employees of Section 501(c)(3) organizations and of public schools as a tax shelter has given renewed interest in individual annuities. Activities growing out of the Keogh-Smathers Act also have extended the interest in individual annuities for self-employed, but the interest is limited only to these tax-sheltered markets. Likewise, the formation of professional corporations has stimulated interest in individual annuities. Before the tax-shelter market was made available for individual annuities, these annuities declined both in the amount written and the number in force, the decline beginning in the mid-1950s.

SELECTED REFERENCES

Huebner, S. S., and Black, Kenneth, Jr. *Life Insurance*, ch. 8. 8th ed. New York: Appleton-Century-Crofts, Inc., 1972.

Mehr, Robert I. *Life Insurance Theory and Practice*, ch. 6. Austin, Tex.: Business Publications, Inc., 1970.

8

Contracts for Special Needs

By JULIUS VOGEL

THE RANGE of needs for life insurance protection, and for continuation of income after retirement, can be met rather straightforwardly by the purchase of one or more term policies, whole life and endowment policies, or annuities. However, combinations or unusual arrangements of these basic building blocks sometimes are used to make attractive packages to fit the special needs of the insuring public.[1]

Need for Special Contracts

An advantage of designing policies for special needs is the administrative saving that results from providing several benefits in one policy instead of in a number of separate contracts. On the other hand, a policy containing a package of benefits designed to satisfy a special insurance need perceived at issue may not be as flexible in responding to changing circumstances over the insured's lifetime as several simple basic policies might have been. The agent can best serve the interests of his client by having a clear understanding of his client's present and probable future needs and the components of any special policies that are available, so that he may recommend an insurance program that is most likely to prove satisfactory over the years.

There are several distinct markets or categories of need for which special contracts have been designed. The typical breadwinner has insurance needs which change over time; policies are designed to anticipate changes in needs and ability to pay, or to provide options which the insured can exercise from time to time to reflect his changing situation. Business relationships present another category of need for which life insurance companies have developed special policies.[2] A third market with unique needs for special contracts is the juvenile market.

---

[1] Chapters 5, 6, 7, and 21 discuss certain combinations of term, whole life and endowment, annuity, and disability income insurance forms, respectively.

[2] For a complete discussion of business insurance needs, see Chapters 42–48.

Descriptions of special contracts in this chapter will be limited to those most commonly offered. A convenient classification is as follows:

1. Contracts for use where current insurance needs exceed probable future insurance needs.
2. Contracts for use where current insurance needs are less than probable future insurance needs.
3. Contracts oriented toward savings or retirement.
4. Contracts that minimize initial premium outlay.
5. Family policies.
6. Other special contracts.

CONTRACTS FOR USE WHERE CURRENT INSURANCE NEEDS EXCEED PROBABLE FUTURE INSURANCE NEEDS

This section is concerned with special policies that provide a level or decreasing term element in addition to some form of permanent insurance.

Level Term Coverage

A layer of level term coverage for a number of years may be provided through a *multiple protection policy,* such as a double or triple protection policy. For every $1,000 of ultimate face amount, the multiple protection policy typically provides $2,000 or $3,000 of death benefit for some initial period of years, such as 20, or to some age, such as 65. Thereafter, the death benefit reduces to the ultimate face amount.

There is clearly very little substantive difference between a multiple protection policy and a policy of permanent insurance to which a level term rider has been attached. In the case of the ridered policy, the agent and the insured have some options as to the amount of the term insurance coverage and the length of the term period. In the case of the multiple protection policy, these elements of design are fixed in advance. However, the multiple protection policy may spread premiums evenly over the entire period, while the ridered policy will not do so.

Some companies have designed multiple protection policies under which proceeds of death claims occurring during the multiple protection period automatically are paid in the form of installments. This kind of multiple protection policy is sometimes referred to as a *family maintenance policy* (see Figure 8–1).

Decreasing Term Coverage

The *family income policy* is designed to meet the insurance needs of young family heads (see Figure 8–2). It is intended to guarantee an income for those years during which there will be dependent children, and provides decreasing term insurance for a stated number of years, such as 20 or 25, or to some age, such as 65. The term coverage is used to provide monthly installment payments of a stated amount in the event of the insured's death. The installments are paid from the month of death to the end of the original term period. For example, if the period of term cover-

**FIGURE 8–1.   Illustration of Basic Structure of Family
Maintenance Policy**

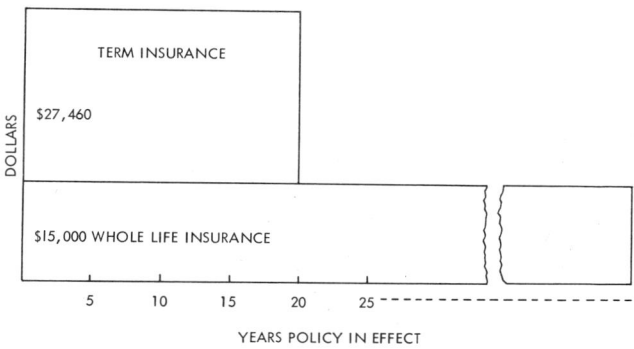

Relative proportions of whole life and term insurance in
a family maintenance policy where the benefit in the event
of death during the first 20 years is a series of monthly installments of $200 payable for 25 years from the date of death.
The death benefit after 20 years is a cash payment of $15,000.

age is 25 years and death occurs at the end of the eighth year of coverage,
installment payments are made for the next 17 years. The basic face
amount generally is payable upon death, although it can be placed under
the settlement options and used to supplement the installment payments.
On the other hand, some companies automatically provide for the basic
face amount to be held by the company at interest to the end of the in-

**FIGURE 8–2.   Illustration of Basic Structure of Family
Income Policy**

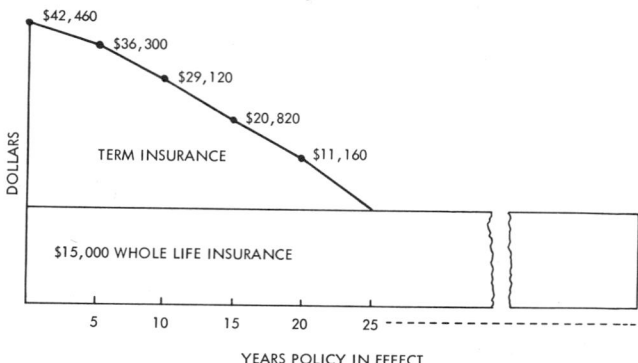

Relative proportion of whole life and term insurance in a
family income policy where the benefit in the event of death
during the first 25 years is a cash payment of $15,000 plus a
series of monthly installments of $200 payable from the date
of death until the 25th policy anniversary. The death benefit
after 25 years is a cash payment of $15,000.

stallment period. The interest is paid as part of the installment payments. This arrangement reduces both the cost of the policy and the amount of protection it provides.

Decreasing term riders are also available under which the amount of insurance is payable in one sum at death rather than as a series of installments. These riders typically are intended to pay off a home mortgage in the event of the insured's death.

It is not unusual for companies to establish a premium-paying period for a decreasing term rider that is shorter than the term of the rider. For example, the premium for a 25-year decreasing term rider may be payable for only 20 years. The premiums thus are "heaped" or concentrated toward the beginning of the term period to reflect the larger benefits payable in the earlier years.

Many companies have designed policies which automatically provide some form of decreasing term coverage in addition to permanent insurance. Other companies prefer the use of decreasing term riders which may be added optionally to many permanent insurance policies in their portfolios. There is no important difference between these two approaches. A company will offer the approach it believes is competitive and can be administered most effectively.

CONTRACTS FOR USE WHERE CURRENT INSURANCE NEEDS ARE LESS THAN PROBABLE FUTURE INSURANCE NEEDS

There are situations where the need for insurance is expected to increase over time. Some of these situations and the special policies intended to meet them are described below.

Jumping Juvenile Policy

A special children's policy, the "jumping juvenile," provides increasing insurance as the need for insurance increases. This policy is sold from birth to age 14. Generally, one unit of coverage provides $1,000 to $1,500 of coverage prior to age 21, and $5,000 of coverage at age 21 and later. Some plans provide for an intermediate jump in coverage, such as to $3,000, around age 15.

The premium for the jumping juvenile policy is level and normally is payable to age 65. The premium level is high in relation to the initial coverage and low in relation to the ultimate coverage. This arrangement produces relatively large cash and loan values during the period of initial coverage, so that this contract also provides a systematic means of saving for education or other purposes.

Guaranteed Insurability Rider

A supplemental agreement or rider has been included in the portfolios of many insurers which permits the insured to purchase additional insurance at one or more specified "option dates" in the future without submitting new evidence of insurability at that time. This feature, which may be added to most policies, has been given a variety of names such as guaranteed insurability rider, insurability option, and option to purchase additional insurance. A small extra premium is charged for the guaranteed insurability rider to compensate the insurer for the extra mortality expected on business issued without any underwriting.

In general, guaranteed insurability riders have the following characteristics: (1) the option may be added to policies issued to new insureds below some maximum age, typically 40; (2) the insured is permitted to purchase additional insurance at specific option dates in the future—for example, when he attains ages 25, 28, 31, 34, 37, and 40; (3) the new insurance is provided at standard rates at the attained age of the insured on the option date; (4) the amount of the additional insurance that can be purchased on any option date varies among companies according to the specific terms of the option, and usually is related to the face amount of the base policy; (5) some agreements permit the insured to accelerate the option dates following specific events, such as marriage or the birth of a child; and (6) an unexercised option may not be carried forward to another date, although subsequent options will not be lost.

For example, on March 1, 1972, a man age 29 purchases a $10,000 life paid-up at 65 policy with a $10,000 guaranteed insurability rider. Assume that the regular option dates will occur at attained age 31, 34, 37, and 40 and there is also a marriage and stork (birth of child) option. On March 1, 1974, the insured is eligible to exercise the first option under the rider. He may purchase up to $10,000 of insurance, usually on any whole life, limited payment life, or endowment plan regularly issued by the insurer at that time for that amount of insurance. Evidence of insurability is not required. The insured usually is given 30 to 60 days to exercise his option. If the insured marries on June 15, 1974, he has the option to purchase another $10,000 of insurance within the next 60 to 90 days. If he does purchase a new policy under this marriage option, the next regular option date (March 1, 1977) will be cancelled.

CONTRACTS ORIENTED TOWARD SAVINGS OR RETIREMENT

Endowment policies and annuity contracts, discussed in Chapters 6 and 7, are primarily designed for accumulation of savings or distribution of proceeds at retirement. Several types of policies and contracts with special or unusual features are described in this section.

Juvenile Educational Endowment Policy

The juvenile educational endowment policy provides a systematic means of accumulating funds for the expenses of a college education. These policies may have a few special features that differ from other endowment policies. For example, some have a special supplementary benefit similar to a guaranteed insurability rider or a conversion privilege. This provision becomes effective when the policy matures and allows the insured to purchase a new permanent plan of insurance without having to submit new evidence of insurability. Juvenile educational en-

FIGURE 8–3. Illustration of Basic Structure of Retirement Annuity Contract

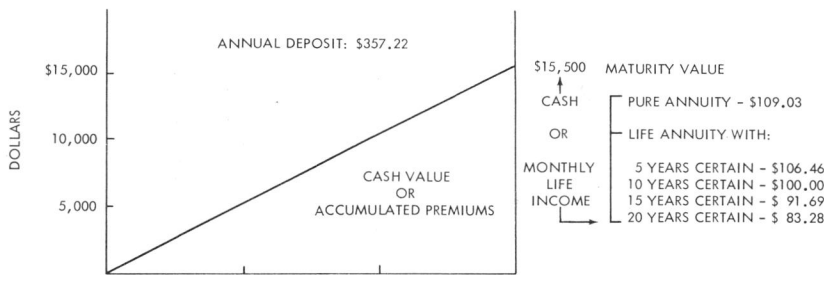

Basic structure of a retirement annuity contract issued to a man age 35 and maturing at age 65. The death benefit prior to maturity equals the accumulated gross premiums during the first eight years and the cash value thereafter.

dowment policies typically provide that the maturity value will be paid in installments while the insured is attending college. However, most regular endowment policies also would include this method of distributing the proceeds as an optional mode of settlement. For a relatively small extra premium, most companies offer an additional benefit, called a payor clause, which waives all future premiums on the death or total and permanent disability of the applicant for the insurance (usually the father).

Of course, the payor clause can be attached to any juvenile policy. When it is attached to a whole life policy, however, it would waive all premiums due before the insured reaches a stated age, such as 21 or 25, rather than all future premiums for the whole of life.

Retirement Annuity Contract

The purchaser of a retirement annuity may pay for his contract either with one payment or with a series of payments over a period of years (see Figure 8–3). Normally a retirement date when annuity payments are to begin is specified in the contract. If the purchaser does not make all the payments required under the contract, he has two options available to him. He can take a cash surrender value, which is essentially the accumulation at interest of the purchase payments he has made less an allowance for the costs the company has incurred in handling his contract; or he can take a reduced annuity which will begin on the retirement date specified in the contract. If the purchaser dies before he receives the first annuity payment, the contract provides a death benefit equal to the greater of the total purchase payments made to date or the cash surrender value of the contract on the date of death. If the annuitant dies shortly after the annuity payments begin, there still will be a death benefit in most cases, since it is customary for the annuities to guarantee five or more annual payments.

Retirement Income Contract

Like the retirement annuity, the retirement income contract offers a systematic means of accumulating funds to provide a retirement income. Unlike the retirement annuity, however, it also provides life insurance benefits during the initial years of coverage (see Figure 8–4). The retirement contract is sold in units, each of which provides some face amount of insurance, usually $1,000 for each $10 per month of lifetime income commencing at a specified age, such as 65. If the cash value of a retirement income contract exceeds the face amount of insurance which generally occurs a few years before the retirement age is reached, the death benefit is increased to equal the cash value.

FIGURE 8–4.   Illustration of Basic Structure of Retirement Income Contract

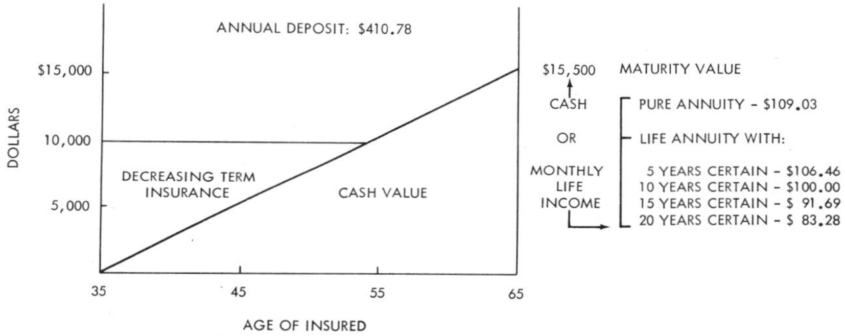

Basic structure of a $10,000 retirement income contract issued to a man age 35 and maturing at age 65. The death benefit equals $10,000 until age 57 and the cash value thereafter.

CONTRACTS THAT MINIMIZE
INITIAL PREMIUM OUTLAY

Many insurance buyers, especially young heads of families who expect their incomes to increase in the future, find they need or want more insurance than they can afford at the regular rates for their age. Accordingly, insurance companies have developed products which allow an insurance program to be started at relatively lower premium rates. Of course, this initial advantage in premium rates must be offset by the use of higher premium rates after the insurance has been in force for a period of time.

Modified, Step-Rate, or Graded Premium Plan

The modified, step-rate, or graded premium policies provide a given amount of insurance at premium rates which are unusually low for some initial period after issue, and correspondingly higher for the remainder of the premium-paying period.[3] Typically, the initial period when premium rates are at a reduced level is 3, 5, or 10 years.

---

[3] Chapter 6 also discusses these modified contracts.

There are some policies in which the premium rate increases more than once. For example, there may be one increase at the end of the 5th policy year and another at the end of the 10th year. Or there may be a premium increase each year for a given period of years such as 10, after which the premium remains level.

High Early Cash Value Policy

A high early cash value policy provides cash and loan values in the first policy year and somewhat higher than normal cash and loan values thereafter. Generally this policy is sold only in high minimum amounts, such as $25,000 or $50,000.

The high early loan values on these policies can be used to pay a substantial portion of the premiums due in the first and later policy years. If this procedure is followed, the increase in the policy loan from year to year results in decreasing protection since the death benefit at any point in time is the face amount of the policy less any policy loan then outstanding. Accordingly, some companies allow participating policy dividends to be used to purchase one-year term insurance for an amount equal to the cash value of the policy, thus overcoming the problem of decreasing insurance. However, the cost of term insurance increases as the insured grows older, and if the policy loan continues to increase from year to year, a point may be reached when the dividend is not sufficient to purchase one-year term insurance equal to the full policy loan. From this point forward, the protection coverage tends to decrease.

This type of program is not well suited to many insurance buyers. It is best suited to individuals in higher income tax brackets who benefit most from the tax deductibility, under certain conditions, of the loan interest paid.[4] Other insurance buyers who are seeking a relatively large amount of coverage for a small initial premium outlay may do better by purchasing regular term insurance, particularly if the need for protection is of a short duration.[5] In any event, it is likely that a variety of contracts emphasizing reduced initial cost or premium outlay will continue to emerge.[6]

---

[4] Chapter 55 considers the implications of these "minimum deposit" plans.

[5] Of course, the insured need not use high early cash values to minimize his premium outlay. He may prefer a policy of this type merely because of the larger cash and loan values it offers, should he desire to use them.

[6] EDITOR'S NOTE: A recently introduced arrangement called "split life" insurance is a linkup of a one-year renewable term insurance contract and an annual premium retirement annuity. The term insurance can be obtained only in conjunction with the annuity, and thus the concept must be viewed as a term-plus-annuity package. Proponents of split life insurance emphasize its flexibility in addition to the relatively low cash outlay (in comparison with whole life insurance) at the earlier durations. The arrangement allows the annuity to be on the life of one person and the term insurance on another, the term coverage can be spread over a number of lives and can be switched among lives, and the life insurance can be continued after the annuity portion is in use for retirement purposes.

The viability and acceptability of split life insurance are yet to be proven. There has been much opposition to the arrangement, both from regulatory authorities and the insurance business. A number of state insurance departments have questioned the

Interim Term Insurance

Sometimes an insurance applicant desires immediate insurance protection, but also desires to defer the contract date of his policy for a period of months. Interim term insurance, also called preliminary term insurance, is frequently used in this situation to provide coverage from the date of the application to the future contract date of the policy. Normally insurers allow interim term insurance to defer the policy date from 1 to 11 months. The premium for interim term insurance is based on the insured's age at the date of application, whereas the premium for the principal policy is based on the insured's age at the end of the interim term period.

FAMILY POLICIES

Since a great deal of life insurance is sold to heads of young families, and since young families have many insurance needs in common, it is not surprising that the insurance industry has designed special policies to provide coverage for the entire family. For young families these policies form the foundation on which their entire insurance program may be built.

The idea behind the family policy is to make available, in a single life insurance contract, a modest amount of protection on all members of the family. This accomplishes several important objectives. These include concentrating most of the premium dollar on the father's life where it is most needed, providing insurance adequate to cover last expenses of other family members without the expense of issuing and administering separate policies, and guaranteeing the insurability of present and future dependent children at the lowest possible cost.

The family policy generally provides permanent insurance on the head of the family on a plan such as whole life, endowment at age 85, life paid-up at age 65 or endowment at age 65; term insurance is usually provided on the other members of the family. Each unit of coverage under the typical policy provides $5,000 of insurance on the head of the family, $1,250 on the spouse, and $1,000 on each child. Smaller amounts per unit, such as $3,000 on the head of the family, also are sold.

The term insurance on the spouse usually runs for 20 years or until the head of the family reaches age 65 or 85. Sometimes permanent rather than term insurance is provided for the spouse; an endowment benefit may be provided at the expiration of the term if the husband's plan is an endowment plan.

The premium for the family policy is computed on the assumption that the wife is the same age as the husband. If, as is usually the case, the husband and wife are not the same age, the predetermined premium will be used to purchase whatever amount of insurance is appropriate at her actual age. If the wife is younger than her husband, the amount of insurance on her life will be somewhat more than the $1,250 per unit; if she is older, her coverage will be somewhat less than $1,250.

---

linkage of two contracts, or suggested the need for deficiency reserves, or indicated that split life may be misleading to the consumer.

Normally the spouse's coverage remains constant, but some plans provide coverage on the wife which decreases as the policy grows older. This reflects the assumption that the financial burden placed on the family by the death of the wife and mother decreases as the family matures. Also, most companies issue policies insuring only one parent to meet the situation where the spouse is already dead, uninsurable, or adequately insured, or where divorce or separation has occurred.

For covered children, the term insurance expires at a specified age, such as 21 or 25, but generally no later than the end of the premium payment period for the policy. Children born after the policy is issued usually are included automatically as soon as they are two weeks old.

Many companies issue family policies providing multiples of up to three to five times the unit benefits described. The premium for a unit depends only on the age of the head of the family, generally the husband, and not on the age of the spouse nor on the number and ages of the children.

At the death of the head of the family, all dependents' unexpired term insurance usually becomes fully paid up. Some companies include a benefit which waives premiums for the entire policy if the head of the family becomes totally and permanently disabled. Several companies include accidental death benefits on the head of the family and on the spouse, and in addition provide benefits for loss of eyesight or limbs.

At the expiry of each dependent's term insurance, a conversion privilege is usually available. The spouse may convert her insurance to a permanent policy of the same amount without evidence of insurability. Children usually may convert to permanent insurance up to five times the amount of their term insurance. The converted policies are issued at premium rates for the attained age at the time of conversion.

There are two common policy provisions to meet the situation where the wife dies during her husband's lifetime and before the expiry of her insurance. One of these provides for a reduction in premiums. The other provides additional term insurance on the husband's life to be provided by that portion of the premium previously used to provide the wife's insurance.

In the past, most companies provided all the above benefits in one integrated or packaged policy. There is a growing trend, however, for companies to issue riders providing benefits similar to those described above for the spouse and children. These companies permit such riders to be attached to new or, in some instances, existing policies on the life of the head of the family. This practice tends to provide greater flexibility in satisfying needs because riders may be added to most policies (other than term) regardless of size or type.

OTHER SPECIAL CONTRACTS

Variations of Participating Contracts

The primary advantage that nonparticipating policies have over participating policies is a lower initial or "going-in" premium rate. Thus, the amount of insurance coverage available per dollar of premium is greater at issue for nonparticipating policies.

Modified or step-rate premium policies, having a reduced initial premium, often are used by mutual companies to compete with nonparticipating insurance. In the selling process, the participating company illustrates how future dividends can be used to offset the scheduled future increases in premiums. Of course, the participating company cannot guarantee that future dividends in fact will offset future premium increases, but it can demonstrate results based on its current dividend scale.

Another relatively new kind of participating policy, designed primarily to compete with the low going-in and guaranteed total premium cost of nonparticipating insurance, is issued in units of coverage where each unit provides $1,000 of initial coverage but a smaller amount of ultimate guaranteed coverage. Each unit is a combination of the ultimate guaranteed coverage—typically permanent whole life insurance—plus a temporary amount of level term insurance equal to the difference between $1,000 and the lower ultimate amount of coverage. The term insurance expires at the end of the policy year in which the first dividend is payable, normally the second or third policy year. When the term insurance expires, the guaranteed amount of insurance reduces to its ultimate value and a special dividend option begins to operate. This option provides a combination of paid-up additional insurance and one-year term insurance such that the sum of the ultimate insurance, paid-up additional insurance, and one-year term insurance equals the initial unit face amount of $1,000. The amount of each year's dividend that is used to purchase paid-up additional insurance and the amount used to purchase one-year term insurance depends upon the attained age of the insured and the amount of paid-up additional insurance purchased by previous dividends.

Premiums are level for the life of the policy. If dividends are sufficient, the insured is covered for the initial amount of insurance throughout the entire life of the policy at a level premium rate that is comparable to that for a nonparticipating policy. However, the level of future dividends cannot be guaranteed. The actual dividends credited may be too small to maintain the initial amount of coverage. On the other hand, the actual dividends credited may be large enough to generate coverage that exceeds the initial amount.

Variations of Nonparticipating Contracts

The primary advantage of participating policies over nonparticipating policies is the payment of policy dividends after a participating policy has been in force for one or more years. Some companies have issued nonparticipating policies which provide annual payments to the insured that are guaranteed as to amount and time of payment. These payments may be taken in cash, left with the company to accumulate at interest, or applied to purchase paid-up additional insurance. The options resemble those available for dividends on participating policies. Of course, since these payments are guaranteed by the insurer, a charge for them must be included in the premium. It follows that the premium for a nonparticipating policy that provides for annual payments to the insured must be greater than the premium for an otherwise similar policy without such payments.

There is also available on the market a nonparticipating policy which closely parallels a participating policy for which dividends are used to reduce premiums. This nonparticipating policy has an adjustable premium feature which permits the insurer to decrease or increase the premium from year to year. The premium, however, may not exceed a guaranteed maximum. The premium varies in accordance with the emerging experience of the insurer, much as the dividend on a participating policy.

Contracts with Special Change Provisions

Most insurers allow a policyowner to make a reasonable change in his plan of insurance after it has been issued. If the change is to a higher premium plan of insurance (for example, changing from a whole life policy to a 20-pay life policy), the insurer will charge the policyowner for the change. If the change is to a lower premium plan of insurance (for example, changing from a 20-pay life policy to a whole life policy), the insurer will grant the policyowner an allowance. Satisfactory evidence of insurability usually is required when changing to a lower premium plan because of the increase in risk involved. The charge or allowance is determined so that the insurer is in essentially the same financial position after the change as it would have been if the policyowner always had been insured under the new plan.

Frequently a substantial sum of money must be charged in order to change to a higher premium plan of insurance. Therefore, some insurers have designed special policies that allow one or more specified changes to higher premium plans where the charge for the change is not paid in one sum at the time of the change. Instead, the charge is amortized over the premium-paying period remaining after the change. Some policies permit this change only at specified option dates, while other policies permit the change at any time, subject to a minimum number of years during which premiums on the new policy will be payable. The change of plan arrangement permitted normally is specified in the original policy.

Return of Premium Policy and Return of Cash Value Policy

It is possible, subject to some rather broad constraints, to design a policy that can provide almost any kind of benefits desired. Accordingly, some companies have designed policies that provide a death benefit equal to the face amount of insurance plus all premiums paid to date, or equal to the face amount plus the cash surrender value at the time of death. Since both the aggregate of premiums paid to date and the cash surrender value increase over time, a policy which provides for the return of premiums or cash surrender value at death is in effect providing a continually increasing amount of insurance. Premiums for such policies necessarily reflect a charge for the additional protection.

Tailor-Made Term Insurance Policy

Tailor-made term insurance is a recent innovation in special insurance policies. It owes its existence to computer facilities now available to most

companies. Tailor-made term insurance provides a pattern of death benefits and premium payments designed by the agent and the insured in the
light of the insured's anticipated insurance needs and ability to pay. The
pattern of death benefits can be level, increasing, decreasing, or any combination of these. Similarly, premiums can be level, increasing, decreasing,
or any combination. There are, however, limits within which the pattern
of benefits and premiums must be confined. For example, there may be
limits on the amount of increase or decrease in death benefits from year
to year, and the maximum amount of insurance may have to bear some
reasonable relationship to the initial amount.

Tailor-made term policies may allow conversion and renewal privileges
similar to those in a regular term policy. Accidental death benefits and
waiver of premium benefits also may be included.

Graded Death Benefit Policy

Graded death benefit policies are special contracts designed for substandard risks. The higher mortality costs are provided for by reducing
the level of insurance per unit of coverage. In a graded death benefit
policy the amount of insurance provided per unit depends on the mortality class of the insured and the duration of the policy. For example, a
graded death benefit policy issued to an applicant whose mortality classification is 200 percent of standard might provide an initial death benefit
of only $500 per $1,000 of face amount. This death benefit would slowly
increase to $1,000 over a period of many years.

The graded death benefit policy has the same premium rate as its
standard policy counterpart. The cash values, dividends and nonforfeiture benefits also are the same as, or very close to, those for a standard
policy. This kind of policy is issued primarily in conjunction with qualified pension programs where the employer is more concerned with providing standard cash and retirement values at standard premium rates
than with providing a standard level of death benefits. In fact, the statutes
of some states preclude issuance of such policies except in conjunction
with such programs. In many situations graded death benefit policies can
be issued to otherwise uninsurable lives.

Joint Life Policy

Most life insurance policies are payable in the event of the death of a
single individual—the insured. However, there are instances where it may
be desirable to write a policy that pays the insurance when the first of
two or more covered persons dies. For example, two partners in a business firm may want such coverage so the surviving partner can use the
proceeds of the insurance to buy the deceased partner's share of the
business.

Many companies offer joint life insurance on a limited number of
plans—typically whole life and limited-pay life and endowments. A few
companies issue joint term insurance policies. Some companies provide
that the surviving insured may convert his coverage under certain conditions, but others terminate all coverage when the first death occurs.

The premium for $1,000 of joint life insurance on two lives is always less than the sum of the premiums for $1,000 of insurance on each individual life. On the other hand, it is always greater than the premium for $1,000 of insurance on either single life. Normally, joint life plans cover two lives. Theoretically, any number of lives could be covered, but three or four lives is the practical limit.

SELECTED REFERENCES

Huebner, S. S., and Black, Kenneth, Jr.   *Life Insurance*. 8th ed. New York: Appleton-Century-Crofts, Inc., 1972.

McGill, Dan M.   *Life Insurance*. Rev. ed. Homewood, Ill.: Richard D. Irwin, Inc., 1967.

National Underwriter Company.   *Who Writes What?* 1971 edition. Cincinnati, Ohio.

Sarnoff, Paul E.   "The Valuation of the Family Policy," *Transactions of the Society of Actuaries,* Vol. 10 (1958), pp. 25–31.

9

Legal Concepts and Contract Provisions

By JANICE E. GREIDER

A LIFE INSURANCE contract must meet the same basic legal requirements as any other contract. As an insuring agreement, it also is governed by other legal principles which relate specifically to insurance contracts. These include special rules concerning concealment, misrepresentation, and warranty, and have resulted in the extensive use of the doctrines of waiver and estoppel by the courts. The incontestable clause is closely related to these concepts but represents a complete departure from principles long recognized in general contract law. These basic legal concepts and important life insurance contract provisions will be discussed in this chapter.

THE FORMATION OF A CONTRACT

Insurance requires a valid contract in the general sense of the word. This is ordinarily achieved in life insurance, as with most other contracts, when competent parties express mutual assent to a promise or promises, with legally adequate consideration. If a particular form is required by law, that form must be followed, and there must exist neither a statute nor a court decision declaring such contracts illegal.

Competent Parties

As a basic principle, everyone is presumed to be capable of making a valid contract. However, certain classes of people have only limited contractual power. These include insane persons, intoxicated persons, married women (though their limitations have largely been removed), and persons who have not reached the required legal age (minors or infants). The most important of these in any consideration of the life insurance contract are minors.

In the absence of a statute to the contrary, the age at which one attains contractual capacity is 21. In recent years, however, there has been a definite trend toward establishing a lower age, such as 18, and statutes to this effect have been enacted in many of the states.

The contracts of a minor are generally said to be "not void but voidable." This means that they may be carried out according to their terms if both parties wish. With a few exceptions, however, a minor may avoid any contract he has previously made—that is, declare it ineffective—at any time during his minority or within a reasonable length of time thereafter. The result is that an adult contracting with a minor is bound by the contract; the minor ordinarily is not.

In the absence of legislation to the contrary, a life insurance contract applied for and issued to a minor is subject to this same general rule. The life insurance company is bound, but at any time until he attains his majority and for a reasonable time after that, the minor has the privilege of disaffirming the contract. In most jurisdictions, he may recover all the premiums he has paid.

Many of the states have enacted statutes removing the limitations of minority with respect to life insurance contracts applied for by minors who have attained a specified age, typically 15 or 16. Frequently, such statutes provide that the insurance must be for the benefit of the minor himself or someone closely related to him.

Mutual Assent

Mutual assent is ordinarily achieved when one party makes an offer or proposal which is accepted by the other. In life insurance the application is traditionally considered to be an offer. However, it is not an offer in the legal sense of the term unless the initial premium accompanies it. In that case the application and the premium constitute the offer, which is accepted when the company issues a policy as applied for. If the policy is issued other than as applied for, the company is considered to have rejected the offer and made a counteroffer. The counteroffer must then be accepted by the applicant before a contract will have been completed.

If the premium is not paid at the time of the application, the application is only an invitation for an offer. The offer is made when the company issues and delivers a policy to the applicant, and it is accepted when the applicant pays the initial premium.

In most instances today, the life insurance agent is authorized to issue a premium receipt (usually a conditional premium receipt, but sometimes a binding receipt) if the applicant pays the initial premium when the application is submitted. In addition to acknowledging that the initial premium has been paid, most such commonly used receipts provide that insurance will become effective at an earlier date than would otherwise be true, if certain conditions are met. Premium receipts are worded differently, circumstances differ from case to case, and court decisions on the subject are not always reconcilable. Generally, however, premium receipts fall into one of three groups: conditional receipts of the insurability type, conditional receipts of the approval type, and binding receipts.

Conditional receipts of the *insurability type* typically provide that insurance will become effective as of the date of the receipt (or of the medical examination, if that is later) if the proposed insured is found to have been insurable as of that date, in accordance with the insurer's standards of risk selection.

The *approval type* of conditional premium receipt, essentially a variation of the insurability type, provides that insurance will become effective as of the date of the receipt (or of the medical examination if that is later) if the application is approved. It should be noted, however, that because of the differences in language among the various types of receipts, it is sometimes difficult to determine into which of these general categories a given receipt actually falls.

A third type of premium receipt provides that insurance will be effective immediately (within the limitations provided in the receipt) subject to the insurer's right to terminate the coverage later, if the proposed insured is found not to meet the company's underwriting standards. This form of receipt is generally classified as a true *binding receipt* and, until recently, was only occasionally used. During the past few years, however, receipts of this kind have been introduced by some of the major American life insurers.

The legal effect of these different receipts can best be explained by illustration. Assume that the death of a proposed insured occurs after his application has been submitted but prior to its being approved or declined in the home office, and assume also that he has been medically examined. Under the insurability type of conditional premium receipt, the application will be considered even after the death of the insured. If he is found to have been insurable as required by the terms of the receipt, the insurance will have been effective on the date of his death, and the claim will be paid.

The approval type of receipt, however, provides that insurance will be effective only if the application is approved. Under receipts of this kind, it has sometimes been contended that insurance was not effective on the date of death if the insured died prior to consideration of the application, since the application had not been approved on that date. This type of receipt, in particular, has been involved in a substantial amount of litigation. The insurability type, therefore, is more widely used at the present time.

Under a binding receipt, insurance is effective in accordance with the terms of the receipt until the application is declined. Under the facts above outlined, therefore, if a binding receipt had been issued, the insurance would have been effective on the date of the insured's death, and the claim also would have been paid.

It is customary to specify in the application that, except as provided in any conditional or binding receipt that may have been issued, insurance will not take effect until and unless a policy has been issued and delivered. Generally speaking, delivery is accomplished whenever the company takes definite action to place the policy out of its legal control. This is done if the policy is manually handed over to the policyowner; however, it is also accomplished constructively when a policy is mailed to the applicant or when it is mailed to the soliciting agent for delivery, if no further action is to be taken except to make such delivery.

Consideration

Consideration may be defined as the price given or asked in exchange for a promise. It is a technical requirement, growing out of the fact that the law will not generally enforce a promise unless something of value has been given in exchange for it. Life insurance policies frequently state that the insurance is granted "in consideration" of the application and payment of the premiums. This is generally held to mean payment of the initial premium. In the language of the law, this is adequate consideration. It puts the insurance into effect and thus is the price the promisor bargained for and was willing to accept.

Form Required by Law

Although most states do not specifically require that the life insurance contract be in writing, they do require that policy forms be filed with a regulatory official of the state before being used. In practice, therefore, a written policy is essential.

Insurable Interest Required

As a matter of public policy, certain insurable interest requirements must be met or an insurance contract will be void. Thus, the presence of an insurable interest is of major concern in any consideration of the life insurance contract.

INSURABLE INTEREST

An insurable interest is one of the most basic of all requirements in insurance. Without it, the contract is a mere wagering agreement; with it, it is a contract whose social and economic importance is so generally acknowledged that it has an almost unique position in the business world.

In property insurance, the applicant is generally considered to have an insurable interest if he has a reasonable expectation of profit or gain from the continued existence of the property to be insured or loss from its destruction. However, the term has a somewhat broader meaning in connection with life insurance.

In life insurance, there are two major situations: (1) the situation where one applies for insurance on his own life, and (2) the situation where he applies for insurance on the life of someone else. It is sometimes said that everyone has an unlimited insurable interest in his own life. Alternatively, it is said that the insurable interest requirement does not apply in this situation. Regardless of the reason, an application for insurance on one's own life does not usually present an insurable interest question.

When one applies for insurance on the life of another for his own benefit, however, he must have an insurable interest in the life of that person. This means an expectation of benefit from the continued life of the proposed insured, but not necessarily a pecuniary benefit. The general rule is that love and affection growing out of a close relationship by blood or marriage is sufficient. Thus a wife has an insurable interest in the life of her husband; a husband, in the life of his wife.

In the absence of a close relationship of this kind, the applicant-beneficiary must show an insurable interest of a pecuniary nature in the life to be insured—that is, a risk of actual monetary loss from the death of the proposed insured. Business relationships furnish the clearest examples of this. The employer, for instance, has a definite risk of loss from the death of a key employee. A creditor has a risk of loss resulting from the death of his debtor.

If an insurable interest is present at the time a life insurance contract is formed, the validity of the contract will not be affected by the fact that the insurable interest may have vanished before the proceeds become payable. This rule may be contrasted with the property insurance rule, which holds that the insurable interest must be present at the time of loss.

MISREPRESENTATION, CONCEALMENT, AND WARRANTY

Insurance contracts differ from the majority of business contracts in one very basic sense—the exchange of values. Most business contracts are commutative agreements, which provide for the exchange of relatively equivalent values. Insurance contracts, however, are aleatory in nature, which means that they may involve the exchange of widely varying values. Proceeds are frequently paid under policies on which only a very few premiums have been paid, for it is of the essence of insurance that no one knows when the contingency insured against will happen with respect to any individual risk. The handling of risk, therefore, is essential to the business of insurance, and several legal principles are derived from this fact.

When the early contracts of marine insurance were formed, in the days when underwriters frequented the coffee shops of 18th-century England, the risk to be assumed was evaluated almost entirely in reliance on information furnished by the applicant. Often the ship was far away and could not be inspected. In any case, it was the owner who was best acquainted with the condition of the ship, the circumstances of the voyage, and other matters which vitally affected the degree of risk involved. As a result, insurance was early declared to be a contract of the highest good faith, and the insurer was held to be entitled to rely upon the information submitted to him. Legal concepts relating to concealment, misrepresentation, and warranty, therefore, as they applied to insurance, were first developed in connection with marine insurance. In any consideration of their application to the life insurance contract, it is important to bear this fact in mind.

Concealment

The early marine insurance contracts were made between businessmen. The buyer was interested in the most favorable rate he could obtain, and the underwriters were entitled to a fair description of the risk. It was reasonable to require a full disclosure of all facts material to a consideration of the risk. The applicant's failure to disclose such information, therefore, was considered fraudulent, and the insurer was justified in avoiding the contract.

For several reasons, this principle was modified in this country as it applied to the life insurance contract. For one thing, life insurers ordinarily require completion of a detailed application form and, often, a medical examination. Thus the applicant would seem to be justified in assuming that the insurer has asked for all the information it deems material to a consideration of the risk. Consequently, the rule in this country is that concealment of a material fact in connection with the application for a life insurance contract will justify the rescission of the contract, and hence denial of a claim, only if it is made with actual intent to deceive. In other words, the applicant has a duty to volunteer information only in situations where it would amount to bad faith to withhold it.

Representations and Warranties

The terms "representations" and "warranties" both refer to statements made by the applicant in the process of forming an insurance contract. A warranty is a statement made by the insured which is contained in and made a part of the contract itself and which must be true in every respect or the contract will be voidable by the insurer. Thus the owner of a ship might warrant its classification. The insurer is entitled to rely upon this information, and if it is not literally true, the contract can be avoided. The parties must intend that a statement be a warranty, however, and it must be included as a part of the contract.

Representations, on the other hand, are statements made by the applicant at or before the time the contract is formed. They are made to influence the insurer to accept the risk, and they may or may not be a part of the contract. False representations will justify the insurer in avoiding the contract, but only if they concern matters material to the risk. The test of materiality is whether, knowing the truth, the insurer would have declined the application or accepted it only on different terms.

Representations are liberally construed by the courts. This means that they need only be substantially true. Warranties, by contrast, must be literally true, or the contract will fail.

Special Statutes

Many of the states have enacted laws modifying the harshness of the law of warranties. With respect to life insurance, the distinction between warranties and representations has been abolished entirely in some states. In others, warranties are defined and their legal effect limited in such a way that their effect is much the same as that of representations. The New York Insurance Law, for instance, provides as follows: "All statements made by, or by the authority of, the applicant for the issuance, reinstatement, or renewal of a policy of life, accident or health insurance or annuity contract shall be deemed representations and not warranties, anything in such policy, contract or application to the contrary notwithstanding."[1]

WAIVER AND ESTOPPEL

The special statutes noted above helped to modify the harsh operation of the doctrine of warranty. In the courts, two other devices—the doctrines

---

[1] New York Insurance Law, Sec. 142, par. 3.

of waiver and estoppel—frequently have been used in connection with problems arising out of the life insurance contract, to bring about a more equitable solution than would be permitted by the strict application of the insurance rules of concealment and warranty.

Waiver

Waiver has been defined as "an intentional relinquishment of a known right."[2] Thus a company may have the right to declare a policy void for breach of a condition specifically set forth in the contract. If, knowing of the breach, an authorized officer of the company expresses an intention not to enforce the right, the right is said to have been waived. For example, the company officer who grants an extension of time for the payment of a premium is waiving the company's right to require payment of the premium on the due date or within the grace period. A right, once waived, cannot afterward be revived except by another agreement.

Estoppel

Estoppel is a different concept from waiver, but the result is much the same. Under an estoppel the company is precluded, because of some action or inaction on its part, from relying on an otherwise available defense. Used in this sense, estoppel has been defined as follows: "The principle is that where one party has by his representation or his conduct induced the other party to a transaction to give him an advantage which it would be against equity and good conscience for him to assert, he would not in a court of justice be permitted to avail himself of that advantage."[3]

Thus, where a general agent delivered a life insurance policy with knowledge that the insured had recently been injured in an automobile accident, the company was held estopped to rely on the policy provision that no liability would exist "unless and until the policy be delivered, and the first premium paid during the lifetime and sound health of the insured."[4]

THE INCONTESTABLE CLAUSE

As the business of life insurance grew, it became evident to insurers as well as courts and legislatures that the strict marine doctrines of concealment and warranty were not appropriate in life insurance. Unlike marine agreements, the life insurance contracts were not made and enforced between businessmen. In life insurance, disputes ordinarily arose only after the insured had died. Thus the best witness was unavailable, and the beneficiary often knew little, if anything, about the circumstances surrounding the application. Often, premiums had been paid over many

---

[2] William R. Vance, *Handbook on the Law of Insurance* (3d ed. by Buist M. Anderson; St. Paul: West Publishing Co., 1951), p. 479.

[3] *Union Mutual Life Insurance Company* v. *Wilkinson*, 13 Wall 222, 20 L. ed. 617 (1872).

[4] *Musette* v. *Monarch Life Insurance Company*, 309 Ill. App. 224, 32 NE(2d) 1004 (1941).

years in reliance on a contract only to have its validity challenged on highly technical grounds at the time the benefit was payable. The result was a growing distrust of life insurers generally, on the part of the insuring public.

As a means of assuring the public of their good faith, life insurance companies began, in the second half of the 19th century, to include in their policies provisions which declared that the contract would not be disputed or contested as to matters relating to its issuance after it had been in force for a specified period of time. The standard policy provisions law, adopted by many of the states in the early years of this century, specifically required an incontestable provision; and today, it is included in the life insurance contract as a matter of course.

The present New York law requires an incontestable provision, as follows:

A provision that the policy shall be incontestable after it has been in force during the lifetime of the insured for a period of two years from its date of issue, except for nonpayment of premiums and except for violation of the conditions of the policy relating to military or naval service; and at the option of the insurer, provisions relating to benefits in the event of total and permanent disability, and provisions which grant additional insurance specifically against death by accident or accidental means may also be excepted.[5]

Companies may use their own wording if it is equally liberal. Thus a typical clause today might read as follows: "This policy shall be incontestable after it has been in force during the lifetime of the insured for two years from the date of issue."

Interpretation and Development

Originally, the statutory wording of the incontestable clause did not include the words "during the lifetime of the insured," and it was generally believed that death of the insured during the contestable period stopped the running of the clause. In 1918, however, the Illinois Supreme Court held that even though the insured died within the contestable period, the policy became incontestable after two years from its issue date.[6] Unless a court action was initiated, therefore, the policy became incontestable at the end of the period.

This decision was followed by other courts, and in 1921 the National Association of Insurance Commissioners recommended the inclusion of the phrase "during the lifetime of the insured." When this wording is used, any defense available to the company if the insured dies during the period continues to be available, even though suit is not brought until the period expires.

At first, the original law generally was not thought to apply to provisions for disability benefits, although they were not specifically excepted from its operation. Later, court decisions held that the incontestable

---

[5] New York Insurance Law, Sec. 155, 1(*b*).

[6] *Monahan* v. *Metropolitan Life Insurance Company*, 283 Ill. 136, 119 NE 68 (1918).

clause applied also to any disability benefits granted in connection with the policy. In 1922, therefore, the National Association of Insurance Commissioners recommended a statutory amendment permitting exceptions for disability benefits and benefits in the event of death by accidental means. Today, however, the New York Insurance Law requires that provisions for disability benefits be incontestable after three years.

When the Contestable Period Starts Running

According to the statute, the contestable period runs from the date of issue of the policy. Where different dates are concerned, however, this may not always be true. For instance, the policy date may be different from the issue date, and the date the first premium is paid may be different yet. Since ambiguities are interpreted in favor of the policyowner or beneficiary, if the insurance actually becomes effective on a date prior to the date of issue, the contestable period has sometimes been computed from the earlier date. Nevertheless, when the policy is dated back six months to obtain the benefit of a lower age and lower premium, it has been held that the contestable period runs from the date of issue and not the effective date of the coverage.[7]

The New York Insurance Department expressly requires that the contestable period of a policy issued under the terms of a guaranteed insurability option run from the issue date of the policy which included the option. Any such policy issued more than two years after the option becomes effective, therefore, is incontestable from date of issue.

The Meaning of a "Contest"

Some of the early life insurance policies provided that nonpayment of premiums made the policy *void ab initio,* that is, void from the beginning. It was necessary, therefore, to except nonpayment of premiums from the otherwise general effect of the clause. Today, if a premium is not paid on its due date or within the grace period, the unpaid premium may be paid by the automatic premium loan; the policyowner may be entitled to a waiver benefit; one of the nonforfeiture benefits may become effective; or the policy may lapse. The exact result as of any given point in time, as well as the rights of the policyowner, will be set forth in the policy; but the policy will not be *void ab initio.* Nevertheless, the wording of the incontestable clause remains. As a result, there has been some confusion with respect to the meaning of the word "contest."

It is very generally accepted that a life insurance policy is not contested when the insurer denies a claim on the grounds that the insured took his own life within the suicide period or that the death was, for other reasons, a risk not assumed under the terms of the policy. It is contested only when the validity of the contract itself is challenged. This is clearly stated in a case which arose out of a dispute concerning the approval of an aviation exclusion rider by the then Superintendent of Insurance of New York. The Superintendent disapproved the rider, stating that it con-

---

[7] *Forrest* v. *Mutual Benefit Life Insurance Company,* 195 Misc. 12, 86 NYS(2d) 910, affirmed 275 App. Div. 939, 89 NYS(2d) 488 (2d Dept. [1949]).

flicted with the statutory provision requiring an incontestable clause. Justice Benjamin Cardozo said:

The provision that a policy shall be incontestable after it has been in force during the lifetime of the insured for a period of two years is not a mandate as to coverage, a definition of the hazards to be borne by the insurer. It means only this, that within the limits of the coverage the policy shall stand, unaffected by any defense that it was invalid in its inception, or thereafter became invalid by reason of a condition broken.[8]

In order to comply with the requirement for a contest within the contestable period, a court action must be commenced by the company. This may be for the purpose of canceling the policy during the lifetime of the insured or as a defense to a claim after his death.

Reformation

Courts generally permit a contract to be reformed to carry out the intention of the parties if a mutual error has been made. There have been instances when the insured has contended that the incontestable clause prevents the insurer from having the policy reformed. It is generally held, however, that reformation is not a contest of the policy and thus is not prevented by the incontestable clause.

Incontestability and Fraud

As a general rule, fraud is said to vitiate a contract. In the early cases, therefore, the incontestable clause was sometimes held not to apply if fraud was involved. Today, the clause is generally held to bar a defense of fraud as well as any other defense going to the validity of the contract.[9] In fact, the incontestable clause has sometimes been criticized on the basis that it permits a fraudulent contract to be enforced after the expiration of the contestable period.

In answer, it should be pointed out that the clause does not so much condone fraud as limit the time in which the company may discover the fraudulent conduct and take appropriate action to cancel the contract. There are also a few exceptions, even after the period has run. Thus, if the application for the insurance were part of a criminal conspiracy or against public policy, or if someone other than the insured took the medical examination, these facts may be brought out as a defense in spite of the incontestable clause, and so may lack of an insurable interest at the inception of the contract, as a general rule.

The purpose of the incontestable clause is to assure that after the specified period, the policyowner may rely upon the company to carry out the terms of the contract, regardless of irregularities in connection with the application which may later be discovered. The fact that having given this assurance, the company may occasionally be precluded from inter-

---

[8] *Metropolitan Life Insurance Company* v. *Conway*, 252 NY 449, 169 NE 642 (1930).

[9] The rule is different in Canada, where the contract is contestable because of fraud at any time. See Chapter 71, "Canadian Life Insurance—Important Variations."

posing a defense based on fraud generally is considered justified by the sense of security given policyowners and beneficiaries by reason of the clause.

OTHER REQUIRED POLICY PROVISIONS

In addition to the incontestable provision, the Uniform Standard Policy Provisions Law requires the inclusion of several other basic provisions in a life insurance policy. Among these are an "entire contract" provision, a grace period provision, a misstatement-of-age provision, and a reinstatement provision. These provisions will be discussed in that order.

Entire Contract Provision

Most states require the life insurance contract to provide specifically that the policy and the application, a copy of which is attached to the policy, shall constitute the entire contract between the insurance company and the policyowner. This is generally referred to as the "entire contract" provision.

In the very early days of life insurance, insuring organizations sometimes included in life insurance contracts, by reference, the provisions of such documents as the charter and bylaws of the organization. This had the legal effect of making the indicated provisions of the charter and bylaws a part of the life insurance contract, although there was no way to know the content of such provisions without examining the documents themselves. Since most policyowners did not have access to these documents, their rights and privileges under the life insurance contract could be significantly modified in this way without any opportunity on their part to know the extent of such modifications. The purpose of the entire contract provision was to assure the policyowner that the policy itself would include the complete text of his contract with the company. Often the entire contract provision is combined with provisions concerning representations and warranties, to read as follows:

> This policy and the application, a copy of which is attached and made a part of the policy, constitute the entire contract. All statements in the application shall, in the absence of fraud, be deemed representations and not warranties. No statement shall avoid this policy or be used in defense of a claim under it unless contained in the application.

Grace Period Provision

Many life insurance companies had voluntarily included a grace period provision in their life insurance policies for a number of years before the Uniform Standard Policy Provisions Law was enacted. A typical grace period provision reads as follows:

> A grace period of thirty-one days shall be allowed for payment of a premium in default. This policy shall continue in full force during the grace period. If the insured dies during the grace period, the premium in default shall be deducted from the proceeds of this policy.

The purpose of the grace period provision is to give the policyowner an additional period of time in which to pay a premium he has not paid on or before the due date. In addition, the provision clarifies the respective rights of the beneficiary and the insurance company if the insured dies after the due date of the unpaid premium but within the grace period. In that event, the insurance is considered to be in force on the same basis as if the premium had been paid, but the insurance company is entitled to deduct the unpaid premium from the proceeds before making settlement.

Misstatement-of-Age Provision

The age of the insured is of basic importance in determining the correct premium rate for life insurance. If his age has been misstated, no matter how innocently, the result may be a significant error in the amount of premiums paid as compared to the premium that should have been paid. Such errors could be corrected either by appropriate premium adjustment or by adjusting the amount of insurance. The required provision specifies the latter method, and an illustrative misstatement-of-age provision reads as follows:

If the age of the insured has been misstated, the amount payable shall be such as the premium paid would have purchased at the correct age.

The incontestable clause generally is held not to apply to misstatements of age, and adjustments in the amount of insurance payable therefore may be made even after the incontestable period has expired. Actually, there has been little controversy on this point, a fact that has been explained on the basis that the age adjustment practice was well established prior to the introduction of the incontestable clause.

Reinstatement Provision

The life insurance contract is also required to include a provision concerning reinstatement. Typically, such a provision reads as follows:

This policy may be reinstated at any time within three years after the due date of a premium in default if it has not been surrendered for its cash value. Reinstatement is subject to:

a) receipt of evidence of insurability of the insured satisfactory to the company,

b) payment of all overdue premiums with interest from the due date of each at the rate of 5 percent per annum, and

c) payment or reinstatement of any indebtedness existing on the date of premium default, with interest from that date.

The purpose of the reinstatement provision is to clarify the requirements for restoring a policy to premium-paying status after it has been permitted to lapse. Most state statutes require that the policyowner be permitted to reinstate his policy, subject to the quoted conditions, any time within three years after the date of the first premium in default. A five-year period, being more favorable to the policyowner, is frequently used.

"Evidence of insurability" generally is held to be a considerably broader phrase than "evidence of good health" and includes such other factors as the insured's occupation, habits, financial condition, and other risk selection factors.

The effect of the incontestable clause upon a reinstated policy sometimes presents a problem if the original contestable period has expired before the policy has lapsed and is reinstated. However, the majority of court decisions have held that the incontestable clause applies to the reinstatement agreement just as it did to the original formation of the contract. That is, the reinstatement agreement may be contested during the same length of time as the policy itself. Statutes to this effect have been enacted in some states.

OTHER BASIC POLICY PROVISIONS

In addition to the provisions that are required by law to be included in the life insurance contract, several provisions customarily are included for other reasons, though they are not required. Among these are the suicide provision, an assignment provision, an ownership provision, a war clause occasionally, a payor clause in policies insuring the lives of children, and a provision concerning the policyowner's right to change his plan of insurance.

Suicide Provision

In the absence of a specific policy exclusion, the proceeds of a life insurance policy would be payable in the event of the suicide of the insured just as they would be on his death from any other cause. However, to permit a person to apply for life insurance with the intention of taking his own life in order to bring about the payment of the proceeds to his beneficiary would violate a basic insurance principle—that the loss insured against must be fortuitous. Life insurance companies, therefore, are permitted (though not required) to include a suicide clause in their policies; and it is customary to do so. An illustrative provision reads as follows:

If within two years from the date of issue the Insured shall die by suicide, whether sane or insane, the amount payable by the company shall be the premiums paid.

Most state statutes concerning the suicide provision require that the exclusion be limited to two years. This period is thought sufficient to avoid the possibility that an application for life insurance will be submitted by a person who specifically contemplates taking his own life. At the same time, treating suicide of the insured after two years from the issue date on the same basis as any other death protects the interest of the beneficiary or beneficiaries, whose needs, in most instances, prompted the purchase of the insurance.

At one time, the incontestable clause and the suicide clause were sometimes considered to be in conflict. Ordinarily, the two periods run concurrently for a period of two years from the policy issue date. The suicide clause, however, merely defines the risk the insurer is willing to assume. Denial of a claim because the insured's death resulted from suicide within the suicide period, therefore, is not a contest of the policy.

Assignment Provision

It is customary also to include in individual life insurance contracts a provision relating to assignment. An illustrative assignment provision reads as follows:

The company assumes no responsibility for the validity or effect of any assignment of this policy, and no assignment will be recognized until it has been duly filed with the company.

In the absence of a specific policy provision to the contrary, a policyowner is assumed to have the right to assign his life insurance contract if and as he wishes. The usual assignment provision, therefore, is included to clarify the responsibilities of the company in the event the policy is assigned.

Ownership Provision

An ownership provision is sometimes included in a life insurance policy to clarify the rights of the owner and the circumstances under which those rights may be exercised. The exact wording of such provisions differs widely from company to company, but the following provision is illustrative:

The owner is as designated in the application for this policy unless otherwise provided by endorsement. The owner shall, during the lifetime of the insured, have the sole right to exercise any privilege and to receive every benefit under this policy, subject to the rights of any irrevocably designated beneficiary.

War Clauses

Policy provisions that exclude war deaths from the coverage provided by the policy generally are referred to as war clauses. Life insurance companies usually do not make use of such clauses except in time of war or when war is imminent; and when the war emergency has ended, the clauses usually have been cancelled.

It is customary to divide war clauses into two general classes—"status" clauses and "results" clauses. A status clause provides that if the insured's death occurs *while* he is in military service, the company's liability will be limited to the amount of premiums paid or the policy reserve, if larger. A "results" clause limits the company's liability to the larger of the amount of premiums paid or the reserve, if the insured's death occurs *as the result* of war. The results clause, being the more liberal, is more widely used than the status clause.

Payor Clause

Most life insurance companies offer a waiver of premium benefit, often called a payor benefit, which may be added to a life insurance policy insuring the life of a child. This benefit is available for a small additional premium and is provided in an endorsement or rider, to be attached to the policy insuring the child. Such a clause provides that the premiums on the child's insurance will be waived in the event the premium payor (usually a parent of the insured child) dies or becomes totally disabled (as defined in the coverage) prior to the child's attainment of a specified age, such as 21 or 25. (The benefit is sometimes provided only in the event of the death of the payor before the specified age of the child.)

The purpose of payor clauses is to assure that the insurance on the life of the child will be kept in force until the child reaches the specified age even though the premium payor may die or become totally disabled prior to that time.

Policy Change Provisions

Most life insurance contracts can be changed, with the consent of the company, to a different plan of insurance, if the owner wishes. Policy provisions granting this right range from very simple to relatively complex. The purpose of such provisions, however, is to set forth the conditions governing such changes. Usually, a change may be made to higher premium plans for the same or a smaller amount of insurance without evidence of insurability, although the owner customarily will be required to pay the difference in cash values or reserves between the policy he is exchanging and the one he is receiving. If the change is to a lower premium plan, it is customary to require satisfactory evidence of insurability, and the difference in the reserves for the two plans is usually refunded by the company.

SELECTED REFERENCES

Greider, Janice E., and Beadles, William T. *Law and the Life Insurance Contract.* Rev. ed. Homewood, Ill.: Richard D. Irwin, Inc., 1968.

Krueger, Harry, and Waggoner, Leland T. (eds.). *The Life Insurance Policy Contract.* Boston, Mass.: Little, Brown & Co., 1953.

Vance, William R. *Handbook on the Law of Insurance.* 3d ed. by Buist M. Anderson. St. Paul, Minn.: West Publishing Co., 1951.

10

Probability, Mortality,
and Money Concepts

By CHARLES M. STERNHELL and
WALTER SHUR

TAKE A SET of mortality rates, an interest rate, a dash of probability theory and compound interest theory, mix well, add an appropriate loading for expenses—and the result will be an actuarially sound premium rate for a life insurance contract. Of course, this recipe will produce a satisfactory result only if the ingredients are of the highest quality, and only if the blending is carried out with the necessary mathematical precision. The purpose of this chapter is to analyze the various ingredients called for by the recipe, and to explain the process by which they are blended into the final product.

PROBABILITY THEORY

A writer on insurance once said: "There is nothing more uncertain than life and nothing more certain than life insurance."[1] Obviously, an insurance company has no way of determining when any particular one of its policyowners will die. Yet, if the company is insuring a large enough number of policyowners, it can predict with a high degree of accuracy the mortality experience for the group as a whole. Who will die in a given year is a matter of complete uncertainty; how many will die is a matter of near certainty.

The phenomenon just described has been most commonly referred to as "the law of averages" or "the law of large numbers." This law, which is the very foundation of the insurance concept, is derived from the mathematical theory of probability. A complete exposition of this theory and proof of the law of large numbers are clearly beyond the scope of this chapter. However, an elementary knowledge of probability theory is helpful in understanding and appreciating the actuarial calculation of premium rates and the operation of the law of large numbers.

---

[1] Miles Dawson, *The Business of Life Insurance* (New York: Barnes & Co., 1911).

121

The theory of probability had a somewhat tainted origin, having developed as a result of efforts to apply mathematics to certain gambling problems. In French society during the middle of the 17th century, gambling was a very popular and fashionable sport. An inveterate gambler, the Chevalier de Mere, consulted a famous French mathematician, Blaise Pascal, on some questions connected with various games of chance. This led to further correspondence between Pascal and some of his mathematical friends, principally Pierre Fermat. It was this correspondence which led eventually to the theory of probability as it is known today.

Definition of Probability

Most persons have some idea as to the meaning of the term "probability." This is reflected in statements such as "it probably will rain today," or "there is a good chance that the Dodgers will win the pennant this year," or "there is not much chance of winning the Irish Sweepstakes." The theory of probability attempts to sharpen this general kind of statement by deriving a numerical measure of the chance that a particular event will occur. The numerical measure, or number, that is associated with an event is called the "probability" of that event.

Suppose that a coin is tossed. What is the probability that it will turn up "heads?" From general observation of the coin, it would not appear that a head is any more or less likely than a tail; and one would expect that in the long run, heads will occur about half the time. It is natural, then, to assign the number 1/2 as the probability of heads. Similarly, it would be expected that the toss of a single die would result in the number 2 about one sixth of the time, as each of the six numbers on the die is just as likely to come up as any other. Hence, we assign the number 1/6 as the probability of tossing a 2. For the probability of an even number when a single die is tossed, it is noted that there are three favorable results, 2, 4, or 6, out of the six equally likely total possible results. Hence, the number $3/6 = 1/2$ should be assigned as the probability of an even number. These few simple examples lead to the following more formal definition of probability:

Definition of Probability. If an experiment must result in one of n equally likely cases, and if the event A includes m of these cases, then the probability of the event A is equal to the fraction m/n.

Stated less carefully, but perhaps more understandably, the probability of an event is equal to the number of favorable cases divided by the total number of cases, provided all cases are equally likely. It is apparent from this definition that the probability of any event is a number between 0 and 1, with 0 meaning impossibility and 1 meaning certainty.

Rules of Probability

For combining probabilities, there are two simple rules associated with calculating the probabilities of more complicated events than those illustrated so far. These rules are called the "addition rule" and the "multiplication rule."

Addition Rule. If A and B are two *mutually exclusive* events, the probability that *at least one* of these two events occurs is equal to the sum of their respective probabilities. ("Mutually exclusive" means that the occurrence of one of the events precludes the possibility of the other.)

As an example of the addition rule, consider the drawing of a card from a standard deck of 52 cards. The probability of drawing an ace is 4/52. The probability of drawing a red king is 2/52. Therefore the probability of drawing either an ace or a red king is equal to

$$4/52 + 2/52 = 6/52 = 3/26$$

Multiplication Rule. If A and B are two *independent* events, the probability that *both* these events occur is equal to the product of their respective probabilities. ("Independent" means that the occurrence or nonoccurrence of one of the events does not affect the chance of the other event occurring.)

To illustrate the multiplication rule, let A be the event that a head occurs when a coin is tossed, and let B be the event that a 6 occurs when a die is tossed. The probability of heads on the coin is 1/2, and the probability of a 6 on the die is 1/6. Therefore, the probability of a head on the coin *and* a 6 on the die is equal to

$$1/2 \times 1/6 = 1/12$$

The calculation of more complicated probabilities usually requires the use of both the addition and multiplication rules. For example, suppose that Mr. A and Mr. B both fire at a target. The probability that A hits the target is given as 1/3, and the probability that B hits the target is given as 3/5. What is the probability that the target is hit exactly one time?

To solve this problem, it will be noted that the desired result can occur in two mutually exclusive ways: (1) A hits the target, and B misses; and (2) B hits the target, and A misses. We note further that the probability that A misses the target is 2/3 (i.e., $1 - \frac{1}{3}$) and the probability that B misses the target is 2/5 (i.e., $1 - \frac{3}{5}$). The answer to the problem is then calculated as follows:

Probability that A hits *and* B misses:
$$1/3 \times 2/5 = 2/15 \text{ (multiplication rule)}$$
Probability that B hits *and* A misses:
$$3/5 \times 2/3 = 6/15 \text{ (multiplication rule)}$$
Probability that target is hit exactly once:
$$2/15 + 6/15 = 8/15 \text{ (addition rule)}$$

Law of Large Numbers

If a coin is tossed a large number of times, it is expected that the proportion of heads obtained will be close to 1/2, which is the probability that a single toss results in heads. As more and more tosses are made, one expects that the proportion of heads will get closer and closer to 1/2.

Figure 10–1 is a chart showing the results obtained by tossing a coin 100 times. It clearly shows the tendency of the proportion of heads to "settle down" at 1/2 as the number of tosses increases. Of course, there is

**FIGURE 10–1.   Proportion of Heads in Sequence of One
Hundred Coin Tosses**

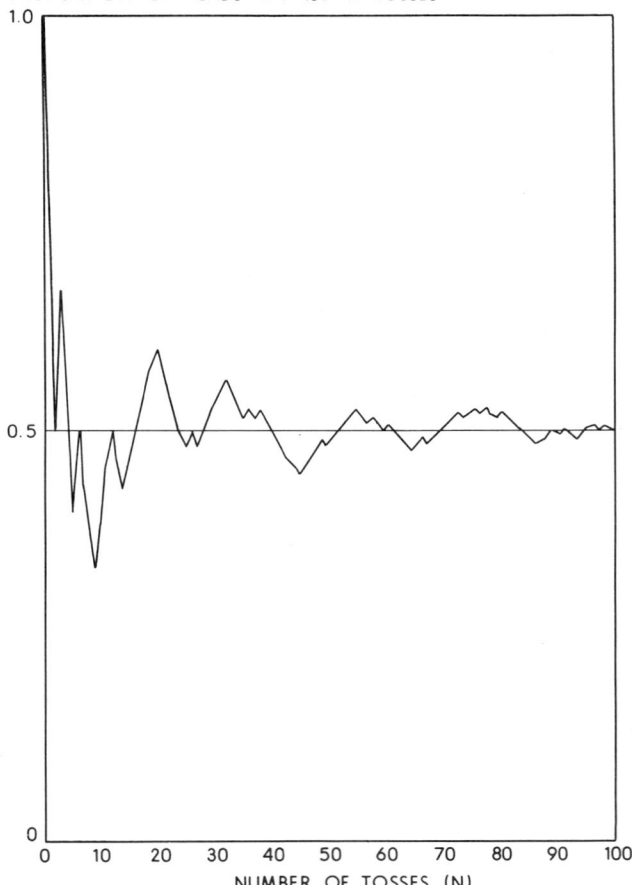

PROPORTION OF HEADS IN FIRST N TOSSES

NUMBER OF TOSSES (N)

no absolute guarantee that this will happen. For example, it is entirely
possible that 100 tosses of a coin will result in 100 heads. The law of large
numbers indicates, however, that as the number of tosses increases, the
probability of a proportion of heads very much different from 1/2 becomes extremely unlikely. Following is an accurate statement of the law
of large numbers in nontechnical language:

Law of Large Numbers   If p is the probability of success for a particular
experiment, and more and more trials of the experiment are performed, the
probability approaches certainty that the actual proportion of successes obtained will be close to p *within any specified degree of accuracy.*

For example, if the proportion of heads obtained in a sequence of coin
tosses is to be between 0.45 and 0.55, the law of large numbers specifies

that the probability of this occurring approaches certainty as the number of tosses increases. For example, on the basis of mathematical calculations, it can be determined that the probability that the proportion of heads lies between 0.45 and 0.55 is 24.6 percent if a coin is tossed 10 times, 72.9 percent if a coin is tossed 100 times, and 99.9 percent if a coin is tossed 1,000 times. If it is said that the proportion of heads is to be within a narrower range, say between 0.499 and 0.501, the law of large numbers specifies that the probability of this occurring also approaches certainty as the number of coin tosses increases still further. For example, if a coin is tossed 1,000 times, the probability that the proportion of heads is between the narrow limits of 0.499 and 0.501 is only 7.2 percent. If the coin is tossed 1,000,000 times, however, this probability becomes 95.5 percent.

Distribution of Insurance Claims

Suppose that a hypothetical life insurance company insures the lives of a certain number of persons in a single year, and that the probability that any one of the insureds will die in that year is 1/100. The insurance company will expect a certain number of claims (namely, 1 percent of all the insureds), but its actual claims may be more or less than the expected number. According to the law of large numbers, if the number of insureds is large enough, the actual claims will very likely show only a small relative deviation from the expected claims. By means of the theory of probability, one can calculate the probabilities of various deviations from the expected claims, depending on the number of insureds.

Figure 10–2 shows the probability of various deviations where the number of lives insured is 1,000, 10,000, and 100,000. If as few as 1,000 lives are insured, there is a good chance that actual claims will be relatively high or low compared to expected claims. This is indicated by the fact that in the "1,000 lives insured" section of the chart the bars in the left and right sections are almost as large as the bars in the center. Where 10,000 lives are insured, the bars are more prominent in the center of the chart, and there is more assurance that actual claims will be relatively close to expected claims. The bottom section of Figure 10–2 shows that if 100,000 lives are insured, it is very likely that actual claims will be relatively close to expected claims.

In particular, Figure 10–2 shows that the probability of actual claims being within 5 percent of expected claims is 12.7 percent if 1,000 lives are insured, 38.3 percent if 10,000 lives are insured, and 88.8 percent if 100,000 lives are insured. Although not shown in the chart, the probability of actual claims being within 5 percent of expected claims is greater than 99.99 percent if 1,000,000 lives are insured.

Thanks to the theory of probability and to the law of large numbers, it truly can be said that "there is nothing more uncertain than life and nothing more certain than life insurance."

MORTALITY

The business of life insurance is concerned with a particular kind of probability, the probability of death. This kind of probability cannot be

FIGURE 10–2.   Variation of Actual Claims from Expected Claims as a Percentage of Expected Claims (for selected numbers of lives insured for one year where probability of death in that year is 0.01)

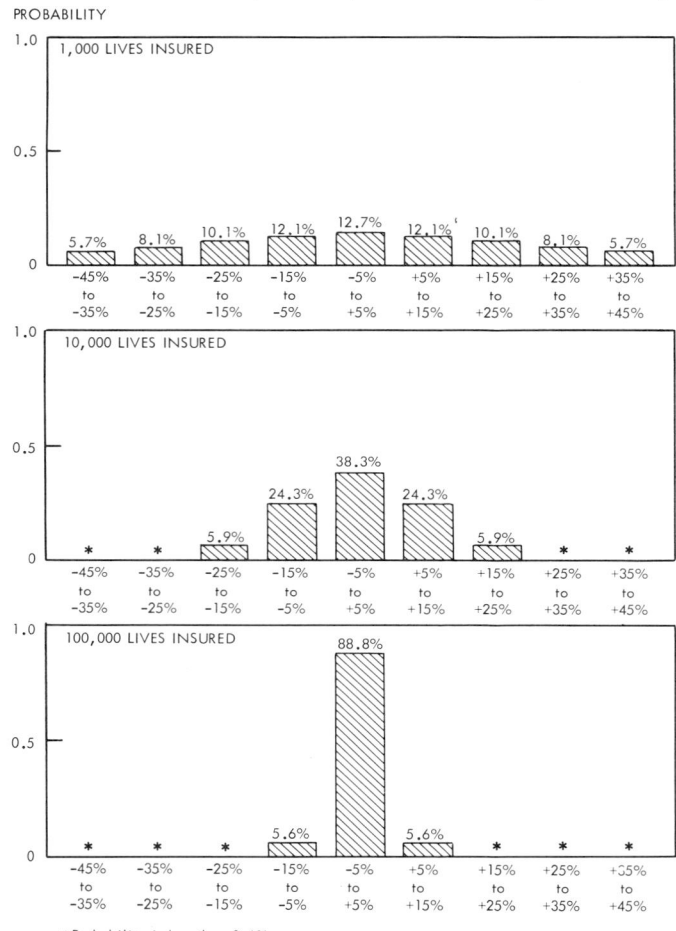

PROBABILITY

*Probability is less than 0.6%

determined by the type of theoretical argument used in the case of coins or dice, where simple conditions of symmetry justify the assumption of equally likely events and lead directly to a theoretical calculation of the desired probabilities.

There are many other types of situations where probabilities cannot be deduced on the basis of theoretical considerations. In many of these situations, however, it is possible to estimate probabilities on the basis of statistical analyses of past experience. For example, the probability that it will rain on a particular day in a given city can be estimated from historical weather records for that city. The probability that a baseball player will obtain a hit in his next time at bat can be estimated on the basis of his recent batting average.

Similarly, the solution to the problem of estimating the probability of death is to analyze past mortality experience. This means keeping track of a large number of people for a particular period of time and determining the number of people who die during that period and the number who survive.

Mortality Rates

As a matter of convenience, the probability of death is generally measured over a period of one year. The term "mortality rate" can then be defined as the probability that an individual will die within one year.

In many respects, the problem of determining a mortality rate is very similar to that of calculating a batting average. Assume that a closed group of 1,000 people is being observed for a period of five years. Each person alive at the beginning of the year represents one "time at bat" and each death represents a "hit." The mortality rate for this group of people would be calculated in exactly the same way as a batting average is calculated, that is, by dividing the number of "hits" by the number of "times at bat."

This calculation is illustrated as shown in Table 10–1.

TABLE 10–1. Simple Illustration of Mortality Rate Calculation

Year	Number of People Alive at Beginning of Year ("Times at Bat")	Number of Deaths during Year ("Hits")
1	1,000	10
2	990	15
3	975	10
4	965	5
5	960	10
Total	4,890	50

The average annual mortality rate for this group of 1,000 people over the five-year period would be 0.01022 (i.e., 50 ÷ 4,890). Another way of expressing this average annual mortality rate is to say that 10.22 out of each 1,000 people alive at the beginning of a year are expected to die within one year.

While this example illustrates the basic concept underlying mortality rates, it is an oversimplification of the actual problems involved in the determination of mortality rates. For example, in many cases people enter or leave the group under observation during the year and have to be counted as fractional "times at bat." In addition, the probability of death depends on many factors, such as age, sex, occupation, state of health, and many others, and the actuary must determine mortality rates that will reflect these factors. The analysis of mortality experience is a far more complex problem than might appear at first glance, and requires considerable care and judgment on the part of the actuary.

Factors Affecting Mortality Rates

The first step in planning a mortality study is to specify the purpose for which the mortality rates are to be calculated. This will determine the particular group to be studied, the time period during which the group is to be observed, and the detailed classifications of the data that will be used in computing the actual mortality ratès. Among the more important factors that must be considered are the following:

1. *General Population versus Insured Lives.* People who purchase life insurance policies are generally in the higher economic and social classes, receive a higher level of medical care, and are judged to be in satisfactory health at the time they are insured (by the insurance company either through a medical examination or through other sources of information); as a result, they experience lower mortality than the population as a whole. *Mortality tables used by life insurance companies are practically always based on the mortality experience of insured lives rather than on the mortality experience of the population as a whole.*

2. *Life Insurance versus Annuity Mortality.* People who purchase annuity policies usually believe themselves to be in excellent health and expect to live a long time. Apparently, their judgments are quite good, on the average, because the mortality of persons who purchase annuity policies is substantially lower than the mortality of persons insured under life insurance policies. A mortality table suitable for use in connection with life insurance policies would be entirely inappropriate for use in connection with annuity policies.

3. *Standard versus Substandard Insurance.* An insurance company underwrites all applications for new individual insurance policies, that is, it makes a judgment as to the degree of risk it will assume if it approves the application. If the applicant has a serious medical impairment, engages in a hazardous occupation or recreation, or appears in any other way to be subject to an extra mortality hazard, he is offered a substandard policy at an extra premium, or, in rare cases, is declined for insurance. It is obvious, then, that a mortality study must carefully distinguish between those who have been insured at an extra premium and those who have been accepted at standard rates.

4. *Age.* Age is one of the most significant factors affecting mortality. The probability of death is relatively high at birth, decreases to a low at about age 10, and then generally increases throughout the remainder of life. A mortality study invariably requires classification of the data by age.

5. *Sex.* Men may be stronger than women, but the fair sex exhibits mortality rates that are well below the corresponding rates for men. If a company charges the same premium rates for men and women, it would use mortality rates that represent an averaging of male and female mortality experience. However, the prevailing practice now is to charge lower premium rates for women, reflecting their better mortality experi-

ence; in these cases, separate studies of male and female mortality experience are required.

6. *Effects of Selection.* Because applicants for insurance are examined either medically or through other sources of information, mortality rates of insured lives are unusually low for a period of at least five years, usually longer, after a policy is issued. For many purposes, it is desirable to have a mortality table that reflects the level of mortality reached after this initial period. Such a table is referred to as an "ultimate" mortality table, as it represents the ultimate level of mortality reached after the effects of the initial selection process have worn off.

7. *Period of Observation.* Because mortality has been improving with advances in medical science and a generally higher quality of medical care, the period of observation must be a fairly recent one if it is to represent current mortality levels. It must also be a long enough period to include a sufficient body of data to produce statistically reliable results. If the period selected embraced any abnormal events such as a war, an epidemic, or an economic depression, the mortality rates derived from the study may be distorted unless steps are taken to adjust for the abnormality. For example, deaths resulting from an act of war are generally excluded from a mortality study.

The decisions that were made in the construction of the 1958 Commissioners Standard Ordinary Mortality Table (referred to as the 1958 CSO Table) provide a specific illustration of the foregoing considerations. This table was based on the mortality experience of lives *insured* under *standard ordinary* policies in 15 large companies. It is an *ultimate table,* excluding experience during the first five policy years. The table is based on mortality experience during the period between 1950 and 1954 policy anniversaries, as this period provided a large volume of homogeneous data and was representative of recent experience. War deaths arising from the Korean War were excluded. The table is based on *combined male and female* experience, but the new legislation that accompanied the introduction of the table officially recognized lower female mortality by permitting, for females, the use of an age not more than three years younger than the actual age of the insured.

The completion of a mortality study along the lines described will produce observed mortality rates for each age based on the average experience of the companies included in the study. Either or both of two further steps must be taken before these mortality rates can be used as the basis of a mortality table for general company use.

The observed mortality rates will normally not grade smoothly by age because of statistical fluctuations and will have to be adjusted by mathematical techniques (referred to as "graduation") to produce a set of mortality rates that grade smoothly by age and that are reasonably close to the observed rates.

The second step, necessary if the table is to be used to calculate policy reserves, is to add appropriate "mortality margins," that is, safety factors that reflect the margins required to cover the range of individual company variations in mortality rates, to these average experience mortality rates in order to produce mortality rates that will be "safe" for use by all companies in the industry. Margins of a particular kind that will increase reserves as well as premiums are necessary in a mortality table such as the 1958 CSO Table because it is designed to serve as a valuation standard; that is, it is used by life insurance companies to calculate the reserves they are required by law to hold.

Mortality Tables

A mortality table generally shows mortality rates for each age. Each mortality rate represents the probability that a person at that exact age will die during the following year.

In order to facilitate calculations involving the probability of dying or surviving during a period of years, two additional columns usually are included in the mortality table. These columns are designated as the "number living" and the "number dying."

Table 10–2 shows the 1958 CSO Mortality Table, an important modern table.[2] Column 1 of Table 10–2 shows the number of persons reaching each year of age out of 10 million persons starting at age zero. The figure of 10 million is an arbitrary one selected for convenience and is referred to as the "radix" of the table. Column 2 shows the number of persons dying during each year of age out of the original 10 million. The figures in columns 1 and 2 are computed as follows:

a) Number living at age zero: 10,000,000 (radix)
b) Mortality rate at age zero: 0.00708
c) Number dying between age zero and age one: (*a*) × (*b*) = 70,800
d) Number living at age one: (*a*) − (*c*) = 9,929,200
e) Mortality rate at age one: 0.00176
f) Number dying between age one and age two: (*d*) × (*e*) = 17,475
g) Number living at age two: (*d*) − (*f*) = 9,911,725
h) And so forth.

Many probabilities can be computed from a mortality table such as the one shown in Table 10–2. The probability that a person aged zero will survive to age 15 is obtained by noting that of the 10,000,000 persons starting at age zero, 9,743,175 reach age 15; hence the probability is 9,743,175/10,000,000 = 0.97432. Similarly, the probability that a person aged 5 will survive to age 85 is 1,311,348/9,868,375 = 0.13288.

The probability that a person aged 20 will die between the ages of 85 and 86 is equal to 211,311/9,664,994 = 0.02186, since the table shows that 211,311 persons will die between ages 85 and 86 out of the 9,664,994 who are alive at age 20. A final illustration is the probability that a person aged 10 will die before age 65. Table 10–2 shows that of 9,805,870 persons living at age 10, only 6,800,531 survive to age 65. Hence, there will be

---

[2] It is not the purpose here to discuss exactly how life insurance companies use mortality tables. However, the 1958 CSO Table will be used to illustrate the interrelationship of probability, mortality, and money concepts in the determination of premiums. Actually, as noted above, the table is used by life insurance companies to calculate the reserve which they are required to hold by law and it often is not used to determine the appropriate level of gross premiums.

TABLE 10–2.   1958 Commissioners Standard Ordinary Mortality Table

Age	(1) Number Living	(2) Number Dying	(3) Mortality Rate per 1,000	Age	(4) Number Living	(5) Number Dying	(6) Mortality Rate per 1,000
0	10,000,000	70,800	7.08	50	8,762,306	72,902	8.32
1	9,929,200	17,475	1.76	51	8,689,404	79,160	9.11
2	9,911,725	15,066	1.52	52	8,610,244	85,758	9.96
3	9,896,659	14,449	1.46	53	8,524,486	92,832	10.89
4	9,882,210	13,835	1.40	54	8,431,654	100,337	11.90
5	9,868,375	13,322	1.35	55	8,331,317	108,307	13.00
6	9,855,053	12,812	1.30	56	8,223,010	116,849	14.21
7	9,842,241	12,401	1.26	57	8,106,161	125,970	15.54
8	9,829,840	12,091	1.23	58	7,980,191	135,663	17.00
9	9,817,749	11,879	1.21	59	7,844,528	145,830	18.59
10	9,805,870	11,865	1.21	60	7,698,698	156,592	20.34
11	9,794,005	12,047	1.23	61	7,542,106	167,736	22.24
12	9,781,958	12,325	1.26	62	7,374,370	179,271	24.31
13	9,769,633	12,896	1.32	63	7,195,099	191,174	26.57
14	9,756,737	13,562	1.39	64	7,003,925	203,394	29.04
15	9,743,175	14,225	1.46	65	6,800,531	215,917	31.75
16	9,728,950	14,983	1.54	66	6,584,614	228,749	34.74
17	9,713,967	15,737	1.62	67	6,355,865	241,777	38.04
18	9,698,230	16,390	1.69	68	6,114,088	254,835	41.68
19	9,681,840	16,846	1.74	69	5,859,253	267,241	45.61
20	9,664,994	17,300	1.79	70	5,592,012	278,426	49.79
21	9,647,694	17,655	1.83	71	5,313,586	287,731	54.15
22	9,630,039	17,912	1.86	72	5,025,855	294,766	58.65
23	9,612,127	18,167	1.89	73	4,731,089	299,289	63.26
24	9,593,960	18,324	1.91	74	4,431,800	301,894	68.12
25	9,575,636	18,481	1.93	75	4,129,906	303,011	73.37
26	9,557,155	18,732	1.96	76	3,826,895	303,014	79.18
27	9,538,423	18,981	1.99	77	3,523,881	301,997	85.70
28	9,519,442	19,324	2.03	78	3,221,884	299,829	93.06
29	9,500,118	19,760	2.08	79	2,922,055	295,683	101.19
30	9,480,358	20,193	2.13	80	2,626,372	288,848	109.98
31	9,460,165	20,718	2.19	81	2,337,524	278,983	119.35
32	9,439,447	21,239	2.25	82	2,058,541	265,902	129.17
33	9,418,208	21,850	2.32	83	1,792,639	249,858	139.38
34	9,396,358	22,551	2.40	84	1,542,781	231,433	150.01
35	9,373,807	23,528	2.51	85	1,311,348	211,311	161.14
36	9,350,279	24,685	2.64	86	1,100,037	190,108	172.82
37	9,325,594	26,112	2.80	87	909,929	168,455	185.13
38	9,299,482	27,991	3.01	88	741,474	146,997	198.25
39	9,271,491	30,132	3.25	89	594,477	126,303	212.46
40	9,241,359	32,622	3.53	90	468,174	106,809	228.14
41	9,208,737	35,362	3.84	91	361,365	88,813	245.77
42	9,173,375	38,253	4.17	92	272,552	72,480	265.93
43	9,135,122	41,382	4.53	93	200,072	57,881	289.30
44	9,093,740	44,741	4.92	94	142,191	45,026	316.66
45	9,048,999	48,412	5.35	95	97,165	34,128	351.24
46	9,000,587	52,473	5.83	96	63,037	25,250	400.56
47	8,948,114	56,910	6.36	97	37,787	18,456	488.42
48	8,891,204	61,794	6.95	98	19,331	12,916	668.15
49	8,829,410	67,104	7.60	99	6,415	6,415	1,000.00

Note: Mortality rates in this table are considerably heavier than those to be expected on standard insured lives. See text of this chapter, and also the comparison in Appendix E.

3,005,339 (i.e., 9,805,870 − 6,800,531) deaths prior to age 65, and the probability that a person aged 10 will die before reaching age 65 is 0.30648 (i.e., 3,005,339/9,805,870).

Expectation of Life

According to the 1958 CSO Table, the expectation of life at age zero is 68.3 years. This figure is computed from the mortality table by finding the total number of years lived by all 10,000,000 persons starting at age zero, and dividing that number by 10,000,000 to obtain an "average number of years lived per person," more commonly referred to as the expectation of life. The total number of years lived is obtained by noting that 70,800 persons will die between ages zero and one and live one-half year, on the average; that 17,475 persons will die between the ages of one and two and live 1½ years, on the average; and so on throughout the remainder of the table. Then these results are combined to obtain the total number of years lived by all persons, namely:

$$(70,800 \times \tfrac{1}{2}) + (17,475 \times 1\tfrac{1}{2}) + (15,066 \times 2\tfrac{1}{2}) + \ldots$$
$$+ (18,456 \times 97\tfrac{1}{2}) + (12,916 \times 98\tfrac{1}{2}) + (6,415 \times 99\tfrac{1}{2}) = 682,966,865 \text{ years.}$$

Dividing this figure by 10,000,000, the figure of 68.3 years is obtained for the expectation of life at age zero.

The expectation of life for a person at an age other than zero would be computed in similar fashion. For example, the expectation of life for a person aged 50 is 23.63 years, obtained as follows from the figures in Table 10–2:

$$(72,902 \times \tfrac{1}{2}) + (79,160 \times 1\tfrac{1}{2}) + (85,758 \times 2\tfrac{1}{2}) + \ldots$$
$$+ (18,456 \times 47\tfrac{1}{2}) + (12,916 \times 48\tfrac{1}{2}) + (6,415 \times 49\tfrac{1}{2}) = 207,052,871 \text{ years.}$$
$$207,052,871 \text{ years} \div 8,762,306 = 23.63 \text{ years}$$

The expectation of life is a convenient index of the general mortality level indicated by a particular mortality table and is useful in comparing the mortality levels of different tables.[3] However, the expectation of life is an average figure and, as such, cannot be used to determine the life expectancy of a particular individual. Similarly, the expectation of life cannot be used by the actuary in his calculations of premium rates, reserves, and other values. Because of the importance of interest earnings, the actuary also must take account of the exact time when each premium dollar will be received and each benefit dollar will be paid. This leads directly to the subject of the next section, "Money Concepts."

MONEY CONCEPTS

Straight life insurance policies call for a level premium to be paid throughout life. Because the rate of mortality generally increases with age, the level premiums are greater than the amount of death benefits paid in the early years and less than the amount of death benefits paid in the later

---

[3] See Appendix E for death rates and expectation of life under various mortality and annuity tables.

years. The excess funds generated in the early years will be needed in the later years to augment the level premiums paid at that time. These funds that a life insurance company holds do not remain idle, but are invested to produce a return to the company in the form of "investment income" or "interest earnings" that are used to reduce the cost of insurance to policy-owners.

Interest earnings are a very important source of income to life insurance companies, as evidenced by the fact that they accounted for about one fifth of all income received by United States life insurance companies during 1971.[4] It is obvious that the calculation of a premium rate must take account of interest. The means of doing this rests on the theory of interest.

Accumulated Value of Money

Anyone who works with interest theory soon develops a concept of money at work very similar to the picture of a snowball growing in size as it rolls through the snow. He thinks of each dollar as something that grows and grows as it passes through time into the future. For example, consider a dollar that is deposited in a bank at a 3 percent interest rate, compounded annually. This means that at the end of one year the bank will credit $0.03 interest, and the depositor will have $1.03 in his account. If that amount is left on deposit for another year, the bank will again credit 3 percent interest, but this time on the larger amount of $1.03. Hence the interest credited at the end of the second year will be 3 percent of $1.03, or $0.0309, and the amount on deposit will have grown to $1.0609 ($1.00 + $0.03 + $0.0309). Table 10–3 shows the results of continuing this process for 50 years.

The rapid growth of a dollar at 3 percent interest is apparent—it has doubled in 25 years and more than quadrupled in 50 years. While these may seem like long periods of time, many life insurance contracts are in force for over 50 years. For this reason, the rate of interest is a very important ingredient in the calculation of premiums, and a difference of as little as one percentage point in the interest rate will affect the premium rate significantly. Figure 10–3 compares the accumulated value of $1 for several different interest rates and shows the importance of a one percentage point differential in the interest rate.

Discounted or Present Value of Money

Table 10–3 shows that $1 accumulates to $1.8061 at the end of 20 years at 3 percent interest. Hence, $0.5537 at 3 percent interest accumulates to $1 at the end of 20 years ($0.5537 × 1.8061). It may be said, then, that "under a 3 percent interest assumption, $0.5537 today is equivalent to $1 in 20 years," or "the discounted or present value of $1 payable in 20 years, at 3 percent interest, is $0.5537." Discounting is the reverse process of accumulating. When one thinks about accumulating a dollar deposited now, he pictures the dollar growing as it moves into the future; when one thinks about discounting a dollar payable in the future, he pictures the

---

[4] Institute of Life Insurance, *Life Insurance Fact Book* (New York, 1972).

TABLE 10–3.   Growth of $1 Left on Deposit at 3 Percent Interest Compounded Annually

Year	(1) Amount on Deposit at Beginning of Year	(2) Interest Credited 3% × (1)	(3) Amount on Deposit at End of Year (1) + (2)
1	$1.0000	$0.0300	$1.0300
2	1.0300	0.0309	1.0609
3	1.0609	0.0318	1.0927
4	1.0927	0.0328	1.1255
5	1.1255	0.0338	1.1593
6	1.1593	0.0348	1.1941
7	1.1941	0.0358	1.2299
8	1.2299	0.0369	1.2668
9	1.2668	0.0380	1.3048
10	1.3048	0.0391	1.3439
15	1.5126	0.0454	1.5580
20	1.7535	0.0526	1.8061
25	2.0328	0.0610	2.0938
30	2.3566	0.0707	2.4273
35	2.7319	0.0820	2.8139
40	3.1670	0.0950	3.2620
45	3.6715	0.1101	3.7816
50	4.2562	0.1277	4.3839

dollar shrinking as it comes back to the present. Table 10–4 shows the discounted or present value, for several interest rates, of $1 payable at various times in the future.[5]

Annuities

An annuity is a series of payments made at certain specified intervals. Usually, the payment is a constant amount, and the intervals are regular, as, for example, $10 payable at the end of each month for 5 years, or $2,000 payable at the end of each year for 10 years. The annuity payments may be certain, or they may be contingent on a particular person being alive. The former are called "annuities certain"; the latter are called "life annuities." The theory of annuities plays an important role in actuarial calculations because the premium payments for a life insurance policy constitute an annuity *to* the insurance company.

Consider an annuity certain of $1 per year, payable at the end of each of the next five years. This annuity is not worth $5 today because each of the dollars payable in the future is worth less today; that is, each must be discounted back to the present. The amount of discount will, of course, depend on the rate of interest. Figure 10–4 illustrates the method of calculating the discounted value of an annuity at 3 percent interest. Each of

---

[5] See Appendix F for selected compound interest and discount functions.

FIGURE 10–3.   Accumulated Value of $1 at End of Various Years at Selected Interest Rates

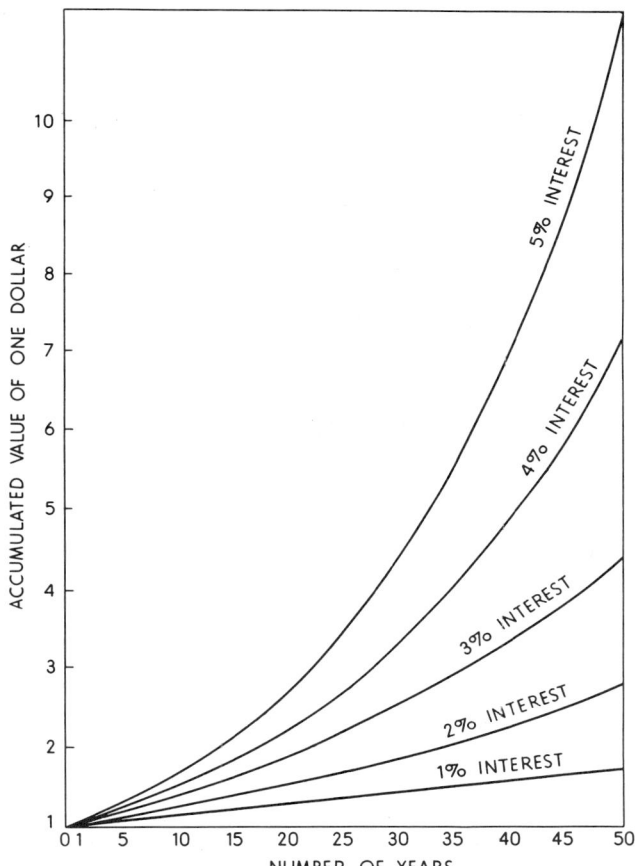

the discounted values shown in Figure 10–4 can be found in Table 10–4 under the 3 percent column. The sum of the discounted values, $4.5797, is the discounted value of the entire annuity, or, as it is frequently called, the present value of the annuity.

Another way of interpreting the present value of an annuity is to note that if the $4.5797 were deposited in a bank at 3 percent interest, and $1 were drawn from the account at the end of each year for five years, the account would end up at exactly zero when the last dollar was drawn. The way this would work out is shown in Table 10–5, which is sometimes referred to as an amortization schedule.

Frequently, it is necessary to find the amount of regular periodic payment which is provided by a single sum of money. For example, one might want to determine the payment that could be made at the end of each

TABLE 10–4.   Discounted Value of $1 Payable at the End of Various Years at Selected Interest Rates

Year	1 Percent	2 Percent	3 Percent	4 Percent	5 Percent
			Interest Rate		
1	$0.9901	$0.9804	$0.9709	$0.9615	$0.9524
2	0.9803	0.9612	0.9426	0.9246	0.9070
3	0.9706	0.9423	0.9151	0.8890	0.8638
4	0.9610	0.9238	0.8885	0.8548	0.8227
5	0.9515	0.9057	0.8626	0.8219	0.7835
6	0.9420	0.8880	0.8375	0.7903	0.7462
7	0.9327	0.8706	0.8131	0.7599	0.7107
8	0.9235	0.8535	0.7894	0.7307	0.6768
9	0.9143	0.8368	0.7664	0.7026	0.6446
10	0.9053	0.8203	0.7441	0.6756	0.6139
20	0.8195	0.6730	0.5537	0.4564	0.3769
30	0.7419	0.5521	0.4120	0.3083	0.2314
40	0.6717	0.4529	0.3066	0.2083	0.1420
50	0.6080	0.3715	0.2281	0.1407	0.0872

of the next five years, in exchange for a single sum of $1 paid now, if money is worth 3 percent. From calculations already made in this section, it is known that a single sum of $4.5797 would provide, at 3 percent interest, a $1 payment at the end of each of the next five years. For a single sum of $1, then, the annual payment provided would be equal to $1.00 ÷ 4.5797, or $0.2184.

FIGURE 10–4.   Computation of Discounted Value of an Annuity Certain at 3 Percent Interest

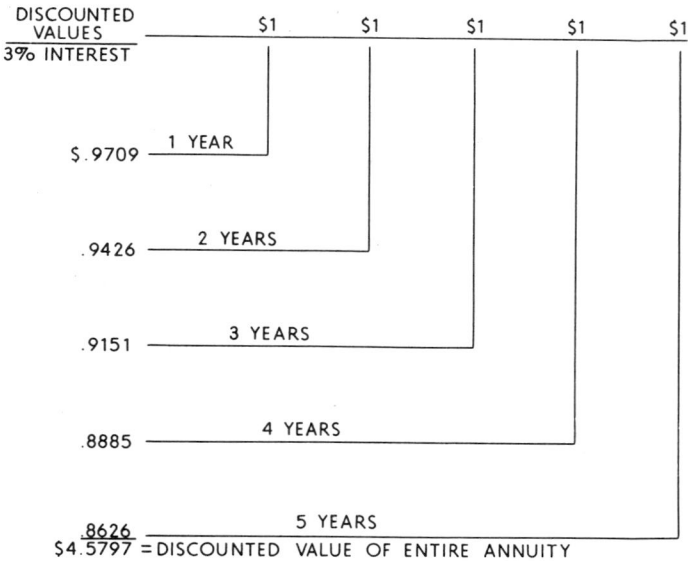

TABLE 10–5.   Amortization Schedule for an Annuity at 3 Percent Interest

	(1)	(2)	(3)	(4)	(5)
			Amount on Deposit at		Amount on Deposit at
	Amount on Deposit at Beginning	Interest Credited	End of Year before Annuity Payment	Annuity Payment at End	End of Year after Annuity Payment
Year	of Year	3% × (1)	(1) + (2)	of Year	(3) − (4)
1	$4.5797	$0.1374	$4.7171	$1.00	$3.7171
2	3.7171	0.1115	3.8286	1.00	2.8286
3	2.8286	0.0849	2.9135	1.00	1.9135
4	1.9135	0.0574	1.9709	1.00	0.9709
5	0.9709	0.0291	1.0000	1.00	0.0000

COMBINATION OF PROBABILITY, MORTALITY, AND MONEY CONCEPTS

Interest theory indicates that a dollar payable at a specified time in the future is worth less than a dollar now. This is true even if the future payment of the dollar is a certainty. The process of obtaining the present value of the dollar is referred to as "discounting for interest." Suppose now that the payment of the dollar in the future is not a certainty, but that it depends on some insured being alive at that time. It is apparent in this case that discounting for interest alone is not sufficient. It is necessary to reduce the present value of the future dollar still further, reflecting the probability that the insured will be alive to pay it. This is referred to as "discounting for mortality."

For example, suppose that a dollar is payable in 10 years if a person now aged 80 is alive at that time. From Table 10–4, it is known that discounting for interest at a 3 percent rate reduces the present value of the future dollar to $0.744. From the mortality table (Table 10–2), it may be observed that the probability that a person aged 80 will live 10 years is $468,174/2,626,372 = 0.178$. Discounting for mortality only, one would say that the present value of the future dollar is $0.178. However, it is necessary to discount for both interest and mortality, and the present value of the future dollar is found to be $0.744 × 0.178 = 0.132.

If expenses are ignored and the net premium rate for a life insurance policy is calculated, the present value of all future premiums must be equal to the present value of all future benefits, where the present values are obtained by discounting for both interest and mortality. In the form of an equation, this reads:

Present value of future premiums = Present value of future benefits

The way in which this equation works out is illustrated in Table 10–6 for a $1,000 whole life policy issued at age 80.[6]

---

[6] Issuance of a policy at the advanced age of 80 is unrealistic. However, the illustration serves to show how the present value of future premiums equals the present value of future benefits from age 80 to the end of the mortality table.

TABLE 10–6. $1,000 Whole Life Policy Issued at Age 80 (using 1958 CSO Mortality Table and 3 percent interest)*

		Premiums					Benefits			
Attained Age	Level Annual Premium (1)	Discount for		Present Value of Premium (4) [(1) × (2) × (3)]	Death Benefit (per survivor) (5)	Discount for		Present Value of Benefit (8) [(5) × (6) × (7)]
		Interest (2)	Mortality (3)			Interest (6)	Mortality (7)	
80	$147.72	1.0000	1.0000	$147.72	$ 109.98	0.9709	1.0000	$106.78
81	147.72	0.9709	0.8900	127.64	119.35	0.9426	0.8900	100.12
82	147.72	0.9426	0.7838	109.14	129.17	0.9151	0.7838	92.65
83	147.72	0.9151	0.6826	92.27	139.38	0.8885	0.6826	84.53
84	147.72	0.8885	0.5874	77.10	150.01	0.8626	0.5874	76.01
85	147.72	0.8626	0.4993	63.62	161.14	0.8375	0.4993	67.38
86	147.72	0.8375	0.4188	51.81	172.82	0.8131	0.4188	58.85
87	147.72	0.8131	0.3465	41.62	185.13	0.7894	0.3465	50.64
88	147.72	0.7894	0.2823	32.92	198.25	0.7664	0.2823	42.89
89	147.72	0.7664	0.2263	25.62	212.46	0.7441	0.2263	35.78
90	147.72	0.7441	0.1783	19.60	228.14	0.7224	0.1783	29.39
91	147.72	0.7224	0.1376	14.68	245.77	0.7014	0.1376	23.72
92	147.72	0.7014	0.1038	10.75	265.93	0.6810	0.1038	18.80
93	147.72	0.6810	0.0762	7.67	289.30	0.6661	0.0762	14.68
94	147.72	0.6661	0.0541	5.32	316.66	0.6419	0.0541	11.00
95	147.72	0.6419	0.0370	3.51	351.24	0.6232	0.0370	8.10
96	147.72	0.6232	0.0240	2.21	400.56	0.6050	0.0240	5.82
97	147.72	0.6050	0.0144	1.29	488.42	0.5874	0.0144	4.13
98	147.72	0.5874	0.0074	0.64	668.15	0.5703	0.0074	2.82
99	147.72	0.5703	0.0024	0.20	1,000.00	0.5537	0.0024	1.33
			Present value of premiums = $835.30**				Present value of benefits = $835.30**	

* Issuance of a policy at the advanced age of 80 is unrealistic. However, the illustration serves to show how the present value of future benefits equals the present value of future premiums from age 80 to the end of the mortality table.
** Totals adjusted by $0.03 (premiums) and $0.12 (benefits) to correct for rounding differences.

Column 1 shows the level net annual premium which is paid at the beginning of each year if the insured is then alive.[7] Columns 2 and 3 show the discounts for interest and mortality, while column 4 shows the present value of each future premium payment. The figures which appear on the line for attained age 90 are those used in the illustration earlier in this section. The total of $835.30 at the bottom of column 4 is the present value of all future premiums.

Column 5 shows the benefit payable (per survivor) in each future year. For example, the proportion of survivors who die between ages 90 and 91 is 0.22814, which is obtained from column 3 of Table 10–2. Since the death benefit is $1,000, the benefit per survivor is $1,000 × 0.22814 = $228.14, the figure which appears in column 5 of Table 10–6 on the line for attained age 90. The figures in column 6, the discounts for interest, are slightly smaller than the corresponding figures in column 2 because it has been assumed that the death benefit is paid at the end of the year, but that the premiums are paid at the beginning of the year; hence the death benefits are discounted one more year than the premiums. Column 7 is the same as column 3, and column 8 shows the present value of each future benefit. The total of $835.30 at the foot of column 8 is the present value of all future benefits, and is precisely the same as the present value of all future premiums.

Table 10–6 shows that the net premium reflects a blending of probability, mortality, and money concepts. Each of these ingredients has been included in its proper place and has been combined with the other ingredients according to a precise mathematical recipe. The result is that, based on given assumptions as to mortality and interest, an insurance contract represents an equal exchange between the insured and the company. The present value of future benefits is the insured's expectation, while the present value of future net premiums is the company's expectation; it is the actuarial blending process which makes these two expectations precisely equal.

SELECTED REFERENCES

Butcher, Marjorie V. and Nesbitt, Cecil J. *Mathematics of Compound Interest.* Ann Arbor, Mich.: Ulrich's Books, N.D.

Encyclopædia Britannica. "Probability Theory." Vol. 18, p. 574. Chicago: Encyclopædia Britannica, Inc., 1971.

Harper, F., and Workman, L. *Fundamental Mathematics of Life Insurance.* Homewood, Ill.: Richard D. Irwin, Inc., 1970.

Kellison, Stephen G. *The Theory of Interest.* Homewood, Ill.: Richard D. Irwin, Inc., 1970.

Larson, Robert E., and Gaumnitz, Erwin A. *Life Insurance Mathematics.* New York: John Wiley & Sons, Inc., 1951.

Pedoe, Arthur. *Life Insurance, Annuities and Pensions.* 2d ed. Toronto, Canada: University of Toronto Press, 1965.

---

[7] The method of determining premiums actually charged by a life insurance company, that is, gross premiums, will be covered in the next chapter.

11

Gross Premiums

By ROBERT G. BOECKNER

THE PURPOSE of this chapter is to introduce the subject of gross premiums, to discuss the basic considerations that enter into the establishment of gross premiums, and to discuss specifically the factors, assumptions, and methods involved in the establishment of gross premiums for individual life insurance policies and annuities.

Determination of gross premiums requires judgment as well as mathematical calculations because assumptions concerning mortality, interest, withdrawals, and expenses must be sufficiently conservative to permit wide fluctuations in these factors during the long period of years that life insurance policies and annuities may be in force. At the same time, premiums must be competitive.

GROSS PREMIUMS FOR NONPARTICIPATING LIFE INSURANCE

Background

Since World War II, competition among life insurance companies has increased steadily. Not only have many new companies been formed, but established companies have tended to become more aggressive in their marketing activities. This intensely competitive atmosphere has resulted in more frequent changes in premium scales[1] and in the introduction of new plans of insurance.

During the early part of this period, mortality improved substantially and the rate of yield obtained by life insurance companies on investments climbed steadily. These changes allowed frequent reductions in life insurance prices, despite the tendency of expenses to increase. A steady rise in the average size of policies issued also helped to offset increasing expenses. The wide use of computers during the last two decades has permitted premium scales to be adjusted more rapidly and more sophisticated methods to be used in their calculation.

---

[1] Competition also has resulted in frequent changes in dividend scales for participating life insurance, discussed below.

The trend of life insurance prices in the future is, however, unclear. Mortality seems to have stabilized in the last decade and it is the opinion of many that interest rates on new investments have peaked. Since expenses are increasing relatively rapidly, future adjustments in premium rates may very well be upward.

Basic Considerations and Requirements

Adequacy. Adequacy is the most important requirement of a gross premium scale since the adequacy, or inadequacy, of a company's premiums will determine the ultimate solvency of the company.

For a defined "block" of business on the average, the total premiums collected and the investment income earned at least should equal the total of benefits and expenses paid. Theoretically, the final test of adequacy cannot be made until the last policy in the "block" has been discharged from the accounts of the company.

Since premiums are fixed at issue, it is necessary to apply adequacy tests at the time a gross premium scale is established.

Most actuaries agree that each and every premium rate of a scale should be sufficient to pass the adequacy test. Occasionally, it is possible to justify some premium rates that are not adequate according to the strict definition of the word. As an example, short-term juvenile endowments may not be able to bear their theoretical share of expenses and still be attractive to the potential buyer. Since this is generally considered desirable business (it may lead to future sales) and since sales tend to be limited, premiums that cover a lesser share of expenses might be justified. This amounts to an arbitrary adjustment in the distribution of expenses so that other business bears more than its theoretical share.

Equity. Equity in a premium scale is primarily for the benefit of the policyowner. For practical reasons, it is impossible to achieve theoretically complete equity but some degree of equity is required to reflect the value to the policyowner of the benefits guaranteed by his policy. There usually is more refinement in the premium classes for individual life insurance than for health insurance, group insurance or social insurance. Premiums for individual life insurance policies generally vary by plan, age, sex, and size.

Legal Limitations. Gross premiums charged by a company must not be in conflict with any law. Currently, Wisconsin is the only state which limits gross premiums directly by specifying in the law the maximum premium that may be charged. The laws of other states may specify limitations which require subjective judgment. As an example, Section 213(10) of the New York Insurance Law provides that a company shall not issue life insurance or annuity contracts which do not appear to be self-supporting on reasonable assumptions as to interest, mortality, and expense.

Other legal requirements which do not limit gross premiums directly may influence premium levels for practical reasons. States have deficiency reserve statutes which require companies to establish additional reserves for those policies with gross premiums less than the net valuation premiums. These additional reserves result in a surplus strain which for some companies will have the effect of requiring some premium rates to be pegged above their "true" level. With the introduction of the 1958 CSO Mortality Table as a standard for valuation, this has become less of a problem.

Minimum cash value statutes in some instances may require cash values which are greater than the asset shares.[2] The result is that premiums must be increased to offset the additional benefits payable upon withdrawal.

Competition and Company Objectives. Competitiveness is a *requirement* of a gross premium scale to the extent that, if a company is to experience reasonable growth, its premium rates cannot be too much higher than the corresponding rates of other companies. Beyond this, the degree to which competition will further affect a company's premium rates will depend upon the results of an analysis of company growth or profit objectives.

In this discussion of the effect of competition on gross premiums, it should not be concluded that a company's rates must be equal to or less than those of other companies. In the first place, this may be impossible in view of the requirement of adequacy. Second, competitive premiums are not always necessary. Personal relationships, service and company image often are more important than low premiums. Also, some companies operate primarily in a local or specialized market in which there is little or no competition and in which the cost of providing insurance may very well be higher than in other markets.

A company may prefer to sell particular plans of insurance such as term insurance, or sell to particular age groups. Consequently, its premiums may be relatively low for these plans or ages. Differences probably reflect the degree of competition in the individual market, or markets, in which the company wishes to sell, or they may reflect the company's ability, or inability, to invest assets at suitable rates of yield.

Competition among life insurance companies applies to agents, as well as policyowners. A company may believe that relatively high commissions will attract good agents, and this additional commission expense, of course, would be reflected in its gross premiums. However, commissions are subject to state regulation. Those companies operating in New York are restricted in this respect by the limitations on compensation to agents contained in the New York Insurance Law.

Factors and Assumptions for
Life Insurance Premiums

The primary factors involved in the calculation and testing of gross premiums are mortality, interest, withdrawal, and expenses. Because the selection of assumptions for these factors can be so important to the future of a company, the actuary must approach the task with a great deal of caution.

It sometimes is implied that gross premiums are directly related to net valuation premiums. There are, in fact, only indirect relationships. Defi-

---

[2] The asset share—the actual fund on hand arising from premium income, less expenses, less cost of benefits—is discussed in Chapter 13.

ciency reserve requirements might have the effect of making some gross premiums equal to the net valuation premiums. In addition, cash values, which are directly related to gross premiums, are related effectively to the reserve basis through the application of the Standard Valuation Law and the Standard Nonforfeiture Law.

Mortality. The long-term trend in rates of mortality experienced by companies under conventionally underwritten individual life insurance policies has been downward. Because the rate of improvement in experienced mortality has been declining steadily, an examination of recent trends probably is more useful for forecasting than a study of long-term trends.

Mortality experience of the past 5 to 10 years might be used as a realistic mortality assumption for calculations of life insurance gross premiums.

Mortality experience can vary substantially from company to company. These variations reflect differences in underwriting rules and practices, and in marketing. On the basis of experience, it generally is assumed that mortality under nonmedically underwritten policies will be higher than mortality under medically underwritten policies. Marketing will affect mortality to the extent that one can expect more antiselection when insurance is sold by mail or by brokers than when it is sold by full-time agents or salaried employees. A number of actuaries also believe that high rates of withdrawal will result in relatively higher rates of mortality. Considerations such as these suggest that, unless a major change in underwriting or marketing policy is contemplated, a company should use its own experience to construct mortality tables for gross premium calculations. However, most companies do not have sufficient recent experience for this purpose, so that many actuaries must look to the experience of other companies or to published mortality tables for assumptions. Of course, the actuary can modify such tables on the basis of his own judgment.

Most companies vary gross premiums by sex. This practice implies greater equity since females have experienced lower mortality than males. A number of companies use the same basic scale of gross premiums for both males and females; but an age setback, generally three years, is then applied for females. The age setback for females cannot be used for those plans of insurance where it would have the effect of altering the premium-paying period or the maturity, expiry, or change date. For example, the method can be used for whole life, but not for life paid-up at age 65. When the practice of setting back the age for females is followed, the mortality assumption for the basic premium scale should be based on male experience. A number of companies construct a completely independent scale of premiums for females, using a mortality table based on the experience of female lives.

Interest. In the selection of interest assumptions for the calculation of gross premiums an actuary generally will consider:

1. The current rate of yield of his company on new investments and on all investments.

2. Short-term trends in his company's rate of yield on new investments and on all investments.
3. The short-term outlook for future investment policy.
4. Contemplated changes in his company's investment policy.
5. Federal income taxes as they apply to the investment earnings of his company.
6. Trends in the investment yields of other companies.

The selection of interest assumptions is a more difficult problem than that of selecting mortality assumptions in that long-term trends in investment yields are not readily discernible, and short-term trends in the past have been both up and down. Since regulation of the economy on the federal level has been increasing steadily, past experience may not be at all indicative of future interest rates.

The yield on new investments will fluctuate more widely from year to year than the average yield on all investments of a company. This compounds the problem since premiums received in the future will be invested at rates available for new investments at the time they are received. However, the yield on all investments tends to follow the yield on new investments, with the lag depending upon the rate of change in the new investment yield rate, the rate at which the portfolio turns over and the volume of inflow of new funds to be invested.

Investment yields will vary from company to company, which may reflect differences in investment policy, or possibly because the insurance laws of some states allow more latitude than those of other states in the type of investments permissible for life insurance companies.

Prior to the enactment of the Life Insurance Company Income Tax Act of 1959, most actuaries reflected federal income taxes in premium calculations by use of interest assumptions based on investment earnings after deducting federal income taxes. There are many companies for which this method of reflecting federal income taxes in premium calculations is still valid. For a rather large number of companies, the tax is based on taxable investment income less $250,000.

Because there is no reliable basis for long-term predictions, most actuaries tend to be conservative in their long-term interest assumptions. On the other hand, very few are predicting any significant decreases in investment yields during the next few years. A number of companies currently are using interest rates that decrease in steps with policy duration for gross premium calculations.

Withdrawals.   Since 1925, the Life Insurance Agency Management Association (LIAMA) has accumulated withdrawal statistics from a number of companies. The results indicate that withdrawal or policy lapse rates definitely are affected by economic conditions.

Actuaries are not too concerned with long-term forecasting of withdrawal rates since withdrawals, except for the early policy years when asset shares are negative or significantly below cash values, usually have little effect on gross premium rates. Therefore, withdrawal assumptions generally can be based on recent experience.

The LIAMA surveys show substantial differences among companies in first-year withdrawal rates. Causes of these differences include variations among companies in distribution of business by age, sex, policy size, and premium payment method; characteristics of agents; characteristics of policyowners; sales training practices; and conservation practices. Persistency is affected by all these factors in addition to economic conditions.

The fact that withdrawal rates vary significantly by company suggests that a company should use its own experience as a basis for withdrawal rates for gross premium calculations. Lacking significant experience, as is the case for new companies and many small companies, the actuary must look to the experience of other companies or to published tables of withdrawal rates, modified to reflect his own judgment.

In practice, it is common to use withdrawal rates which vary only by policy year for premium calculations. Some companies use withdrawal rates which also reflect variation by age at issue, which is often significant. Other companies use different withdrawal rates for different plan groups. As an example, higher withdrawal rates might be used for term plans.

Expenses. The long-term trend of expenses definitely is upward, which is primarily a reflection of the inflationary trend associated with the economy in general. Because of the intensely competitive atmosphere, those expenses associated with the selling, underwriting, and issuance of policies have increased more rapidly than other expenses for most companies. However, long-term expense assumptions are primarily concerned with those expenses incurred in connection with maintaining insurance in force. These are generally relatively small compared with initial expenses, and it is possible that more extensive use of computers will help to offset the effect of inflation with respect to these costs.

Expenses vary significantly by company. Although there are many exceptions, in general the unit expenses of a small company will be higher than those of a large company for the simple reason that certain fixed expenses common to both can be spread over a larger number of units in the case of the large company.

For the purpose of gross premium calculations, expenses can be segregated into four types: acquisition, agents' compensation, maintenance, and termination. Acquisition expenses can be thought of as those expenses which are incurred prior to delivery of the policy and payment of the first premium and would include sales management, underwriting, and policy issue expenses. With respect to agent compensation expenses, one must consider the effect of production and/or persistency requirements for part of the compensation. Maintenance expenses are associated with keeping the insurance in force and would include the cost of premium collection, accounting, valuation, premium taxes, and policyowners' service. Termination expenses are those costs associated with the termination of policies and payment of proceeds, and would include claim investigation expenses. Overhead expenses, such as rent and executive salaries, must be included in the appropriate category. The form of the factors which might be used for the four types of expenses is as follows:

Type	*Form of Factors*
Acquisition	Percentage of premium for first policy year.
	Dollars per unit of insurance for first policy year.
	Dollars per policy for first policy year.
Agent compensation	Percentage of premiums for each policy year (this assumes that all compensation is a function of premiums paid which may not be true).
Maintenance	Percentage of premiums for each policy year.
	Dollars per policy for each policy year (for limited-payment policies, this factor will reduce at the end of the premium-paying period).
Termination	Dollars per claim (and possibly "dollars per unit of insurance" to recognize additional expenses associated with large claims).
	Dollars per withdrawal.

The maintenance expense factor, "dollars per policy for each policy year," is of particular interest. Until the latter part of the 1950s, most actuaries reflected this type of expense in premium calculations by using an assumed average policy size to convert it to "dollars per unit of insurance for each policy year." Since then, most companies have adopted different gross premium rates for different policy sizes. The two methods in general use are referred to as the "band system" and "policy fee system." In general, the band system implies a different scale of gross premium rates for each policy size group, with per policy expenses converted to expenses per unit of insurance for that group by means of the average policy size within it. An example of a policy size group would be one including policies with a face amount in the range of $5,000 to $9,999. Under the policy fee system, the premium for a specific policy is determined by multiplying the number of units of insurance under the policy by a basic premium rate per unit, and then adding a policy fee, such as $10. A number of arguments for the use of each have been presented by proponents of the two systems, but these arguments are largely a matter of opinion as to salability. The only real difference between the two systems is the use of "grouping" in the band system.

Included in the maintenance expense factor, "dollars per policy for each policy year," is a class of expenses which should actually be in the form of a factor, "dollars per premium billed (or collected)." In other words, it is generally more expensive to maintain a policy in force when premiums are paid more frequently than once a year. However, premium scales usually are calculated assuming that premiums are to be paid annually, and formulas are later developed for converting annual premium rates to premium rates for other methods of payment.

Profit. In the discussion of adequacy, it was implied that premiums are adequate so long as the total of the premiums collected and investment income earned is not less than the benefits and expenses paid. A more proper definition of adequacy would require that premiums collected and investment income earned be in excess of benefits and expenses paid since the management of most companies expects frequent additions to surplus and, in the case of a stock company, shareholders expect dividends or an increase in the value of their stock. Therefore, profit is a necessary factor of the premium formula. Sometimes this element is referred to as a contingency loading since the primary purpose of surplus (to which profit is credited) is to protect policyowners from the financial impact of unexpected events or contingencies such as catastrophies, epidemics or a sharp drop in interest rates.

Profit need not be a specific item in the premium formula. Some actuaries prefer to use conservative assumptions for one or more of the primary factors and ignore profit as a specific item. Because of competitive pressures and other considerations, it is not always possible to set premiums at the level necessary to meet the desired profit objectives. Most actuaries prefer to use realistic mortality, interest, withdrawal, and expense assumptions in their final test of a premium scale in order to observe both the expected amount and incidence of profit.

In the calculation and testing of premiums, profit objectives can be expressed in different ways. Some examples are as follows:

1. The present value of profits at issue per unit of insurance is equal to a specified amount.
2. The asset share per unit of insurance exceeds the cash value (or the reserve) by a specified amount at the end of a particular policy year.
3. The average annual profit per unit of insurance issued or in force is equal to a specified amount.

There is considerable difference of opinion among actuaries as well as company management as to what is a reasonable profit.

While it is apparent that there is an inverse relationship between unit profits and competitiveness (assuming other factors are constant), one should realize that more competitive premiums may lead to an increase in new business with the possible result that total profits of a company may increase even though unit profits are decreased.

Gross Premium Formulas

Premium formulas are of two types which will be referred to as the "equation type" and "accumulation type."

The *equation type* formulas equate the present value of premiums to the present value of benefits, expenses, and profit.

Accumulation type formulas involve a hypothetical premium, an accumulation process and an adjustment of the hypothetical premium to meet the profit objective.

Each of the two types of formulas has advantages and disadvantages. The equation type formula produces premiums directly and involves fewer calculations, but it does not give the actuary any insight into the incidence of profits. The accumulation type formula, on the other hand, gives the actuary an indication of when profits develop. It is also more flexible when it is necessary to adjust trial premiums for one reason or another. The major disadvantage of the accumulation type formula is the large number of calculations involved which may make it impractical unless it is programmed for a computer.

Calculation and Testing of Gross Premiums

Actuaries differ in their approach to the calculation of a scale of gross premiums. Generally, the following steps will be performed:

1. Decide upon assumptions for the primary factors and upon the profit objective.
2. Choose a premium formula and calculate trial premium rates for representative plans and issue ages. If an accumulation type formula is used, trial premiums which meet the desired profit objective are obtained directly. If an equation type formula is used, test the trial premiums for profit objective by asset share accumulations or similar studies. If any of the trial premiums are too low to meet the desired profit objective, change one or more of the factors in the premium formula and repeat the calculation and testing steps.
3. Test the trial premiums for competitiveness by comparing them with the corresponding premiums of those companies from which most competition is expected. If a few of the trial rates should be adjusted downward for competitive reasons, make "judgment" adjustments and test the new rates for adequacy by asset share accumulations or a similar study; and, at the same time, note the effect on profits as compared to the original objectives. If it is felt that most of the trial rates do not meet the competitiveness test, the only recourse is to alter the profit objective and repeat the above steps.
4. Calculate premium rates for all plans and issue ages.
5. Test the final complete scale of premiums for consistency and make minor adjustments where necessary.
6. If the company writes insurance in the state of Wisconsin, test a sample of the new premium rates to see that they are not in excess of the maximum rates prescribed in the Wisconsin insurance statutes.
7. If the company writes insurance in a state which requires deficiency reserves, compare a representative sample of the new premiums to the corresponding net valuation premiums. If, in any case, the net valuation premium is in excess of the gross premium, decide whether or not the company is willing to set up deficiency reserves. If not, increase the gross premiums so they are equal to the net valuation premiums in all cases where they were deficient.

If trial premiums are to be tested by asset share accumulations or similar studies, they are often calculated by using a simplified version of the equation type formula. Minor expense factors such as dollars per claim and dollars per withdrawal could be eliminated, or withdrawals could be ignored. The other primary factor assumptions could be adjusted to compensate for these simplifications.

Assumptions different from those used to calculate trial premiums often are used for testing purposes. An actuary might test the trial premiums by more than one set of assumptions to observe the effect on profit objectives. As an example, he might be interested in the effect on profits of a change in the interest assumption.

Experience beyond the 20th policy year often is ignored in the calculation and/or testing of gross premiums. Many actuaries feel that the reliability of long-term predictions is questionable past 20 years. Although a premium scale is guaranteed for the life of the policies issued under it, the cumulative effect of withdrawals and deaths results in a substantial reduction in the proportion of policies still in force after a period of time.

GROSS PREMIUMS FOR PARTICIPATING POLICIES

Relationship of Premiums and Dividends

The subjects of surplus distribution and policyowners' dividends are covered in another part of this *Handbook*.[3] It is necessary, however to consider policyowner dividends in any discussion of gross premiums for participating policies.

Since most companies publish dividend illustrations (based on their "current dividend scale") along with premium rates, a scale of dividends is determined at the same time that a scale of gross premiums is established for participating policies. One actuary may calculate first a premium scale and then calculate a dividend scale, while another actuary may start with a hypothetical dividend scale and then determine the gross premiums that must be charged to pay these dividends. In this chapter, the latter approach generally will be taken. This suggests that dividends be treated as expenses, which can be adjusted after the insurance is in force.

Comparison with Nonparticipating Insurance

The approach to the establishment of a scale of gross premiums for participating policies is generally much different in practice from the approach to the determination of premiums for nonparticipating policies. A consideration of adequacy and equity will serve to clarify this difference.

The principle of participating insurance is to fix the gross premium at a level sufficiently conservative to be adequate under the most adverse conditions which can reasonably be expected. Therefore, such a premium will include a considerable margin for various possible contingencies, and to the extent that this margin proves redundant it is then returned to the policyowner in the form of a dividend. It is desirable that not only the rate structure as a whole be adequate but that the rates for each plan and at each age be adequate, given enough exposure to eliminate the effect of accidental fluctuations. Periodic checks of adequacy can be carried out after issue, and adjustments to maintain adequacy can be made within the latitude afforded by the dividend scale.

Equity is maintained among participating policyowners via the surplus distribution process. It follows that the margins included in the gross

---

[3] See Chapter 14.

premium should be sufficiently large to allow for substantial latitude in the size of the dividends to recognize the variations in experience among policyowners.

It is necessary to study the expected experience and the necessary margin separately for each important component of the premium, such as interest, mortality, and expense, to ensure the adequacy and equity of the premium under various possible future conditions. Nevertheless, it should be kept in mind that it is the total premium which is guaranteed by the company. If the margin for one component (for example, expense) is eliminated or even becomes negative, the margins for the other elements can be and are used to make up the loss.

Assumptions

Interest. A margin for interest is invariably provided for by a reduction in the assumed rate of interest. Currently, the maximum valuation interest rate required by law in the United States is well below earned interest rates for most companies. Since there is a considerable advantage in basing participating gross premiums on valuation assumptions, this difference provides an automatic interest margin.

If we define the interest margin included in the gross premium as the increase in such premium due to the reduction made in the interest rate to provide such a margin, then it should be noted that not all of this margin is necessarily available to increase dividends and/or surplus in the year that each such gross premium is paid. Reserves and cash values generally are based upon the same rate of interest used in calculating the premiums and, therefore, a substantial portion of the interest margin is required initially to build up higher reserves and higher cash values. Of course, in later policy years these margins are returned in the form of excess interest on the reserve, provided the interest actually earned by the company measures up to the expected rate before deduction of the margin.

Mortality. The mortality table used is assumed to contain sufficient margin to cover the highest long-range level of mortality that may, within reason, be experienced during the lifetime of the policy. It need not, however, cover the highest mortality possible in *any one year* such as may be experienced in case of war or a severe epidemic. A modest portion of the mortality margin should not be paid out in dividends in years of favorable experience but accumulated in a contingency fund to cover catastrophic losses.

In order to ensure the orderly release of mortality margins, the table used for valuation purposes should produce reserves which bear a reasonable relationship by duration to the funds accumulated on the basis of current mortality experience. The 1958 CSO Mortality Table satisfies this condition and it is used currently by many companies both to determine gross participating life insurance premiums and to value participating policies. An equitable scale of dividends is easier to design with a modern table, and a modern table is also preferable from a public relations point of view. Furthermore, competition among mutual companies is forcing participating gross premiums downward, making a modern table all the more desirable.

Expenses. The results of a current or recent expense analysis should be used to establish current levels of expenses. With the sharp rise in expenses in recent years, it is becoming increasingly difficult to charge an appropriate amount for current expenses plus a margin for future increases in renewal expenses, and still arrive at gross premiums that are not significantly higher than other companies.

Once the desired expense charge has been established, a simple loading formula generally is obtained to calculate participating gross premiums. For example, the gross premium might be the valuation net premium plus a constant, divided by a percentage. Such a formula, with its advantage of simplicity, can be used because the expense charge in the dividend formula will take care of the more detailed distinctions in expenses actually incurred.

General Considerations

In addition to being adequate to provide for most contingencies, a proposed scale of gross premiums generally must satisfy a number of tests of a more general and practical nature, such as the following:

1. Is the scale in conformity with the company's policy as to the general level of its premium rates?[4]
2. Does the scale conform closely to the premiums charged by those companies from which most competition is expected?
3. Does the new premium scale provide for a scale of dividends which is in conformity with the company's policy as to the general level and slope of its dividend scale?

Interrelationships

The determination of gross premiums for participating insurance is not an independent exercise. Decisions as to scales of cash values, proposed dividends and valuation bases are intertwined with, and inseparable from, the determination of gross premiums, and all must be considered together. For example, given identical gross premium and dividend levels and identical experience assumptions, a lower scale of cash surrender values would provide higher termination profits and therefore higher dividends. That is, to the extent that funds are not required to pay cash surrenders, they become available to increase dividends.

It should be noted particularly that there are compelling practical advantages in making the valuation and gross premium assumptions as to interest and mortality identical. For example, gross premiums may be

---

[4] Some companies feel that for participating policies, a relatively high dividend scale with correspondingly high premiums is more salable than low dividends and low premiums. High premiums have the obvious advantage of a greater margin for adverse experience. On the other hand, those expenses which are a percentage of premiums, such as commissions and premium taxes, will be greater for the same amount of insurance.

obtained by applying a simple loading formula to net valuation premiums. The interest and mortality components of the dividend may be based directly on valuation reserves. Therefore, the effect of a proposed change in such factors may be estimated easily from valuation summaries. In fact, a majority of actuaries use identical interest and mortality assumptions for gross premiums and valuation reserves for participating insurance.

Testing

In actual practice, no final decision as to gross premiums, dividends, nonforfeiture values or valuation bases can be made on purely theoretical grounds. Extensive testing needs to be carried out to ascertain that funds will be released as required to provide the desired dividends. One method to do this might be to develop asset shares on various different sets of assumptions and for various alternative scales of gross premiums but excluding dividend "expense." By deducting from the asset shares so obtained the reserves at various durations and various alternative surplus accumulation objectives, the funds available for annual dividend distribution are obtained.

Developing the Final Scale of Premiums

The following approach might be used in practice to calculate a scale of gross premiums for participating policies:

1. Choose a set of assumptions for the primary factors (mortality, interest and expenses).
2. Using an equation type formula, calculate a set of "nonparticipating" (no-dividend "expense") trial premiums for representative plans and issue ages.
3. Test the trial premiums for conformity with the company's policy as to the general level of its premium rates and for conformity with the premium scales of those companies from which most competition is expected. Make "judgment" adjustments to bring the trial rates into conformity.
4. Using the trial premiums, calculate a set of dividends based on "realistic" assumptions as to mortality, interest, and expenses.
5. Test the trial premium and dividend scales for profit objectives (contributions to policyowners' surplus and, in the case of a stock company, to shareholders' surplus and/or dividends) by asset share accumulations or similar studies. Any adjustments necessary to meet the desired objectives probably will be made in the dividend scale.
6. Calculate premium rates for all plans and issue ages by developing a simple formula which, when applied to the net valuation premiums (or to net premiums on some different basis), will reproduce approximately the trial premium rates.
7. Test the final premium scale for legal requirements and, perhaps, consistency; although the latter is generally unnecessary unless the loading formula referred to in (6) varies by plan or age at issue.

GROSS PREMIUMS FOR ANNUITIES

Single-Premium Immediate Annuities

General. Single-premium immediate annuities are issued on both a single life and a joint life basis, with or without a "refund" feature such as cash refund, installment refund, or a specified number of years and life thereafter. A few companies sell temporary life annuities and/or temporary annuities certain. Practically all companies, including mutual companies, issue only nonparticipating single-premium immediate annuity contracts. This is done primarily for competitive reasons since a larger guaranteed annuity income seems to have more appeal to buyers than a smaller guaranteed income with the possibility of additional income from dividends.

Annuity "premiums" are sometimes referred to as "stipulated payments" or "considerations," and the term "contract" is often used in lieu of "policy."

Mortality Assumptions. The mortality rates experienced by insurance companies under individual annuity contracts have always been considerably less than the mortality rates experienced under individual life insurance policies. However, the trend of annuitant mortality rates has tended to parallel the downward trend of rates of mortality experienced under individual life insurance policies.

It is preferable to base mortality assumptions for annuities on the experience of an individual company. In practice, very few companies have sufficient experience for this purpose, so it is necessary to base mortality assumptions for gross premium calculations on a published mortality table and/or the intercompany experience reported by the Society of Actuaries' Committee on Mortality.

Because mortality improvement in the case of annuities decreases future company profits, it is essential that some provision be made for the continuation of the downward trend in annuitant mortality rates when determining the mortality basis for annuity gross premiums. In practice, most actuaries use the projection methods contained in actuarial studies or a projection scale based on more recent experience of either the company concerned or a group of companies. Conservative interest assumptions have also been used as a means of compensating for future mortality improvements.

As a mortality basis for single-premium immediate annuity premiums, some actuaries, by using projections, develop a mortality table that will apply for some year of experience in the future, such as 1985. Until 1985, the actual mortality is expected to be higher than that assumed, and after 1985 it is expected to be lower than that assumed. Another method used by many actuaries is to assume that all annuities sold according to the premium scale being developed will be effective during a single year, such as 1973.

Recent mortality studies have made it evident that annuitant mortality is highly select and, therefore, current rate revisions of a number of companies have been based on select mortality assumptions, rather than aggregate mortality. Such select assumptions tend to increase premiums, especially at the older issue ages.

Independent mortality assumptions are generally used for gross premiums for male and female lives. Some actuaries prefer to calculate a scale of gross premiums for male lives only and use an age setback to obtain gross premiums for female lives.

Results of the latest intercompany investigation of annuitant mortality indicate that annuitant mortality is antiselective by amount: Actual to expected ratios were substantially lower in the case of contracts providing annual incomes of $2,500 or more than for contracts providing less than that amount.

Interest Assumptions. Since there are no future premiums to invest in the case of single-premium plans, it is common practice to base the interest assumption for gross premiums on the rate of yield obtained by the company on new investments adjusted, if necessary, for federal income taxes. There is, of course, the strong possibility that funds will have to be reinvested at a lower rate sometime in the future. As a means of allowing for this contingency, many actuaries assume a lower rate of interest after a number of policy, or contract, years. In any event, it is desirable to have some margin in the interest assumption.

Expense Assumptions and Premium Formulas. The types of expense associated with single-premium immediate annuities are acquisition, agents' compensation, and maintenance. In the case of annuities, maintenance expenses include the cost of making the annuity payments, accounting, and valuation. The form of the expense factors that might be used for the calculation of gross premiums is as follows:

Type	Form of Factors
Acquisition	Percentage of the gross premium.
	Dollars per contract.
Agents' compensation	Percentage of the gross premium.
Maintenance	Percentage of the gross premium.

In practice, mortality and interest assumptions are selected and net single premiums are calculated. The gross premiums are equal to these net premiums plus a "loading" which consists primarily of a percentage of the gross premium. A constant is sometimes included in the loading to reflect the "dollars per contract" expenses by using average contract size to convert them to "dollars per unit of annuity." Most companies, however, use a policy fee system or a version of the band system to reflect this expense factor in the gross premium structure. The loading formula should also include an element for profit or contingencies which may be a percentage of the gross premium.

Most companies reflect differences in state premium tax rates in the gross premium scale for single-premium annuities. This is done by publishing with the premium rates a table of percentage reduction or addition factors which vary by state.

To convert the amount of monthly annuity payment per $1,000 of single premium to the amount of annual (or quarterly or semiannual) payment per $1,000 of single premium, one method is to use constants which do not vary by issue age or plan.

Substandard Annuities.   A few companies issue annuities at a reduced rate to substandard lives. The usual basis for substandard annuities is a rating-up in age. A rating of more than five years is not usually granted and no annuity will be rated at the very high ages.

There has been much discussion as to whether rated annuities should be issued. Annuitant mortality tables are based on all lives, both good and bad, and while it appears possible to obtain a favorable mortality in the substandard section of a company's business, the result is that the standard section includes a disproportionate share of superselect lives, so that a mortality experience unfavorable to the company results. Annuities should not be issued to very poor risks since, if there is no death benefit, the relatives of the annuitant, after his death, will always feel that the company has dealt unfairly with him, and if there is a death benefit, such as return of the balance of the premium, the company may sustain a loss. In any case, only certain major impairments of a permanent nature, such as heart trouble and kidney ailments, should be rated.

Deferred Annuities

General.   Deferred annuities are generally issued on both a single premium and an annual premium (or fractional premium) basis. Surrender values and a death benefit equal to the total of premiums paid or the cash value, if greater, are provided during the deferred period. The annuity payable at maturity is generally based on the settlement option life annuity rates contained in the company's individual life insurance policies. A few companies use special annuity rates, particularly for single-premium deferred annuities. The cash values are generally equal to a series of net premiums accumulated with interest and without survivorship.

Interest Assumptions.   The considerations involved in the selection of an interest assumption for gross premiums for single-premium immediate annuities will also apply in the case of single-premium deferred annuities. However, account should be taken of the possibility of having to liquidate assets at a loss in order to pay surrender values during the deferred period. In addition, a long deferred period increases the risk of having to reinvest funds at a lower rate sometime in the future. The interest assumptions for annual-premium deferred annuity premiums will tend to be the same as those for individual life insurance policies. Many companies issue participating deferred annuity contracts, in which case a margin should be included in the interest assumption for contingencies and dividends. Participation is usually limited to the period of deferment and the dividends usually reflect only the experience with respect to interest and expense.

Expense Assumptions and Premium Formulas.   The approach to the calculation of gross premiums for single-premium deferred annuities is generally the same as that for single-premium immediate annuities. The net single premium can be determined by first calculating the maturity value per unit of annuity. To obtain the net single premium, this maturity value is discounted for the deferred period using the assumed interest rate. The loading formula used to determine the gross premium can be of the same type as the loading formula used for single-premium immediate annuities.

The approach to the calculation of gross premiums for annual-premium deferred annuities generally parallels the method used for single-premium deferred annuities. The net annual premiums can be such that, when accumulated with interest at the assumed rate, they will equal the desired maturity value at the maturity date. The first-year net premiums should be lower than the renewal net premiums to allow for the recovery of the larger expenses incurred during the first year in the event of withdrawal during the early contract years. The expense factors, which are of the same general type as those for individual life insurance policies, can then be converted to a loading formula which, when applied to the renewal net premiums, will produce the gross premiums. A number of companies use either the policy fee system or a version of the band system to reflect in the premium structure certain of the maintenance expenses.

SIGNIFICANCE OF GROSS PREMIUMS

Many considerations go into the complicated determination of gross premiums. Assumptions must be made concerning mortality, interest, withdrawals, and expenses. The inherent conservatism dictated by the long period of years that life insurance contracts and annuities may be in force is tempered by the hard realities of competition among over 1,800 life insurance companies in the United States.

The result of these elements is the pricing structure for one of the most important financial techniques ever devised.[5] In return for their life insurance premium dollars, millions of families benefit from a systematic savings program and from protection against the risk of premature death.

SELECTED REFERENCES

Anderson, James C. H. "Gross Premium Calculations and Profit Measurement for Nonparticipating Insurance," *Transactions of the Society of Activities,* Vol. 11 (1959), p. 357.

Belth, Joseph M. *The Retail Price Structure in American Life Insurance.* Bloomington, Ind.: Bureau of Business Research, Indiana University, 1966.

Fisher, H. F. *Actuarial Practice of Life Assurance.* Cambridge, Eng.: Cambridge University Press, 1965.

Harper, Floyd S. and Workman, Lewis C. *Fundamental Mathematics of Life Insurance.* Homewood, Ill.: Richard D. Irwin, Inc., 1970.

McGill, Dan M. *Life Insurance.* Rev. ed. Homewood, Ill.: Richard D. Irwin, Inc., 1967.

---

[5] See Chapter 16 for a discussion of life insurance costs and benefit comparisons.

Menge, Walter O. and Fischer, Carl H.   *The Mathematics of Life Insurance.* 2d ed. New York: Macmillan Co., 1965.

Stein, Mel.   "A Direct Comprehensive Approach to the Calculation of Gross Nonparticipating Premiums," *Transactions of the Society of Actuaries,* Vol. XVII (1965), p. 235.

12

Reserves

By WILLIAM H. SCHMIDT

THE LIFE INSURANCE business is an important economic force because of the large amount of assets that it accumulates and is continuously investing. Most of the assets of a company are needed to provide the backing for the company's financial guarantee that it will be able to meet its contractual obligations. These obligations are measured by the policy reserves and other insurance reserves.

Policy reserves and the assets behind them arise because, under the level premium approach, the gross premiums paid in the early policy years usually exceed the expenses, cash values, and death claims in those years. These "overpayments" in the early years are accumulated and invested in order to offset the effect of the increasing mortality costs in the later years.

Policy reserves have significance only in the aggregate. For example, if a company sells only $1,000 one-year term policies, it should have a reserve of $1,000 for each person who will die during the year and needs no reserve at all for those who will not. Since it cannot know in advance the identity of the individuals in each category, it uses the death rates shown in a mortality table to determine the aggregate amount that must be paid to the beneficiaries of policyowners who die. This amount, when related to each $1,000 policy purchased, is known as the reserve per $1,000 policy. It is also known as the average reserve per $1,000.

Thus, the average reserve is merely a convenient device for permitting a company to determine the extent of its liabilities *under certain given assumptions* about interest rates and mortality rates. The purpose of a policy reserve calculation is to arrive at a reasonable, usually conservative, estimate as to how much of the existing assets *must* be conserved to assure payment of future policy benefits, and how much might be spent, perhaps as dividends to policyowners or stockholders, without endangering the company's ability to meet its policy obligations. If the assumptions are changed, the reserves will be increased or decreased. On the other hand, the assets of a company are more readily and objectively valued. Accordingly, the surplus to policyowners and stockholders (i.e., the difference between assets and liabilities) is affected significantly by the assumptions that underlie reserve computations.

158

To establish a uniform and objective basis for ascertaining a company's surplus, Massachusetts in 1858 passed a law empowering its commissioner of insurance to establish minimum reserve standards. The traditional actuarial calculations for premiums and reserves assume that level annual premiums usually will be paid. For this reason the commissioner promulgated level premium reserves (based on the "Combined" or "Actuaries" table of mortality and 4 percent interest) as a minimum standard. Other methods of computing reserves are now permissible, and will be discussed later.

Thus, the mortality table and the rate of interest to be used in the calculation of policy reserves must be determined by a company pursuant to state law. The statutes specify certain mortality tables and rates of interest for use as minimum reserve standards, and such laws usually give the insurance commissioner authority to approve other mortality tables. The insurance company, therefore, is not completely free in its choice of assumptions for determining the value of its liabilities. In this respect, the situation is different from the freedom available to the company in the choice of mortality and interest assumptions used in the calculation of gross premiums.

LEVEL PREMIUM RESERVES

Premiums for valuation purposes—that is, premiums used for reserve calculations—are computed in the same general manner as are gross premiums (see Chapter 11), but with five exceptions: (1) a statutory mortality table, conservatively designed to produce larger premiums and reserves than a "realistic table," is used (for example, the Commissioners' 1958 Standard Ordinary Mortality Table, generally referred to as the 1958 CSO Table); (2) a conservative (lower) interest rate is used; and (3) lapsation, (4) expense, and (5) profit are all disregarded.

Additional assumptions also frequently made in the calculation of premiums for valuation purposes are that (1) premiums, usually level, will be paid annually at the beginning of each policy year; (2) all death claims will be paid by the insurance company at the end of the policy year in which death occurs; and (3) no portion of the annual premium is refundable in the event of death during the policy year. Some companies do not make these assumptions. Among the more common alternate assumptions are: (1) death claims are paid when proofs of death are received; (2) premiums are paid other than annually; and (3) the unearned portion of a premium is refunded at death. Any one of these alternate assumptions will cause minor variations in the individual policy reserve, but these technicalities are beyond the scope of this chapter.

The computation of a reserve is illustrated here by calculations for five-year endowment policies of $1,000 each issued to 100 people who are assumed to be subject to some highly hypothetical mortality rates such that one of these people dies during each of the five years. These calculations will be made at 3 percent interest.

A policy reserve can be computed in either of two ways: *prospectively* (looking ahead) or *retrospectively* (looking backward). First, the steps

TABLE 12-1. Hypothetical Mortality and 3 Percent Interest for Illustrative Premium and Reserve Calculations

(1) Year	Mortality Information			Interest Factors (Present Values)		Interest Factors Combined with Mortality Data
	(2) Number Living at Beginning of Each Year	(3) Number Dying during Year	(4) Number Living at End of Fifth Year	(5) Present Value of $1 Payable at Beginning of Year	(6) Present Value of $1 Payable at End of Year	(7) Col. (2) × Col. (5) × 100
1	100	1		1.000	.971	10,000
2	99	1		.971	.943	9,613
3	98	1		.943	.915	9,241
4	97	1		.915	.888	8,876
5	96	1	95	.888	.863	8,525
			Totals	4.717	4.580	46,255

in arriving at a net valuation premium will be shown. Then, this net valuation premium will be used in the prospective and retrospective reserve calculations.

The mortality and interest data needed are set forth in Table 12–1.

Calculating the Annual Premium

To arrive at the net valuation premium, answers to the following three pairs of questions about these 100 five-year endowment policies of $1,000 each must be sought:

1a. How much will paid in *death benefits?*
    Answer: $5,000 (see column [3] of Table 12–1).
1b. What is the discounted value of this $5,000?
    Answer: $4,580.[1] (Multiply each figure in column [3] by $1,000 and also by the corresponding figure in column [6], and add the results.)
2a. How much will be paid in *endowment benefits?*
    Answer: $95,000 (see column [4]).
2b. What is the discounted value of this $95,000?
    Answer: $81,947.[2] (Multiply the figure in column [4] by $1,000 and also by the corresponding figure in column [6].)
3a. What *premium* will the company receive if each insured pays $100 a year?
    Answer: $49,000. (Add column [2] and multiply by $100).
3b. What is the discounted value of these premiums of $100 each?
    Answer: The discounted value of five premiums of $100 each is $46,255.[3] (Multiply each figure in column [2] by $100 and also by the corresponding figure in column [5] and add the results.)

Now, combining 1b and 2b, it will be seen that the company needs premiums that will have a discounted value of $4,580 plus $81,947, that is, $86,527. Premiums of $100 a year are not large enough because their discounted value is only $46,255. So, by proportion, the needed annual valuation premium calculation must be:

$$\frac{\$86,527}{\$46,255} \times 100, \text{ which is } \$187.06.$$

The Reserve Calculated Prospectively

The prospective method of calculation looks forward and asks: "Taking into consideration the premiums we expect to collect in the future, how much money should we have on hand at the end of any selected policy year for each $1,000 policy currently in force to permit us to meet our obligations as they fall due?"

---

[1] The reader who checks these figures and the figures in Tables 12–2 and 12–3 from the information given in Table 12–1 will encounter small discrepancies. These arise because the calculations were carried out to more decimal places than those shown in columns (5) and (6) of Table 12–1. Had this not been done, Tables 12–2 and 12–3 would have failed to produce consistent results. See Appendix F for more precise interest factors than are given in Table 12–1.

[2] See footnote 1.

[3] See footnote 1.

Looking ahead, the reserve liability (to meet which a corresponding amount of assets must be on hand), is obtained by the relationship:

Reserve = Discounted value of future benefits less discounted value of future premiums.

These discounted values are obtained in exactly the same way as the discounted values to calculate the $187.06 annual premium were computed. The reserve calculations for all five policy years (as well as for the reserve at the date of issue which is zero) are shown in Table 12–2.

The Reserve Calculated Retrospectively

The retrospective method of calculation looks backward and asks: "What has happened to the assumed valuation premiums since the policy was issued? As a result, what is the company's reserve liability with respect to each $1,000 of insurance?"

In the first policy year 100 people would pay premiums of $187.06 each. To this would be added 3 percent interest, and the death benefit payable as a result of one death would be subtracted. The amount remaining is the reserve at the end of the first policy year.

The calculations for all five policy years are shown in Table 12–3. The reserves they produce are identical with those obtained by the prospective method in Table 12–2.

While reserve calculations on this basis have the appearance of dealing with "funds," it is important to keep in mind that this is intended to produce a conservative estimate of the corporate *liability* to a particular group of policyowners. It does not represent the actual investment of the *assets* arising from the gross premiums actually paid (against which are charged expenses and other disbursements, as well as death claims).

Initial, Terminal, and Mean Reserves

The above examples show the calculation of the *terminal* reserve of a policy, that is, the reserve at the *end* of each policy year. The *initial* reserve, that is, the reserve at the *beginning* of each policy year, is the sum of the terminal reserve at the end of the previous policy year, plus the annual valuation premium payable at the beginning of the current year. The theoretical reserve at any point during the policy year is approximated by interpolating between the initial and the terminal reserve.

In order to obtain the total policy reserve liabilities of a company as of December 31, the date of its annual statement, it is usual to assume that its policies have been issued steadily throughout the year. This is equivalent, on the average, to the assumption that all policies were issued on July 1. Accordingly, the appropriate *mean* reserve, that is, the midpoint between the initial and the terminal reserve, is determined for each policy in force. The sum of the mean reserves of all policies in force represents the aggregate reserve liability of the company.[4]

---

[4] The reserve liabilities thus calculated assume that all premiums are payable annually and have been collected. Under actual conditions, an offsetting asset item must be computed, that is, "valuation premiums deferred and uncollected."

TABLE 12–2. Calculation of Reserve by the Prospective Method, Five-Year Endowment for $1,000 Mortality and Interest as in Table 12–1 (but see footnote 1)

(1) End of Year	(2) Amount of Insurance in Force	(3) Discounted Value of Future Benefits — Death	(4) Discounted Value of Future Benefits — Endowment	(5) Discounted Value of Future Premiums	(6) Reserve (3) + (4) − (5)	(7) Reserve per $1,000 (6) ÷ (2)
0	$100,000	$4,580	$81,947	$86,527	$ 0	$ 0
1	99,000	3,717	84,406	69,855	18,268	184.52
2	98,000	2,829	86,938	52,876	36,891	376.44
3	97,000	1,913	89,547	35,580	55,880	576.08
4	96,000	971	92,233	17,958	75,246	783.81
5	95,000	0	95,000	0	95,000	1,000.00

TABLE 12-3. Calculation of Reserve by the Retrospective Method, Five-Year Endowment for $1,000 Mortality and Interest as in Table 12-1 (but see footnote 1)

(1) Year	(2) Insurance in Force At Beginning of Year	(3) Insurance in Force At End of Year	(4) Premiums Received 187.06 × Col. (2)	(5) Col. (4) Plus Col. (8) of Prior Year	(6) Interest on Amount in Col. (5)	(7) Death Benefits	(8) Reserve (5) + (6) − (7)	(9) Reserve per $1,000 (8) ÷ (3)
1	$100,000	$99,000	$18,706	$18,706	$ 562	$1,000	$18,268	$ 184.52
2	99,000	98,000	18,519	36,787	1,104	1,000	36,891	376.44
3	98,000	97,000	18,332	55,223	1,657	1,000	55,880	576.08
4	97,000	96,000	18,145	74,025	2,221	1,000	75,246	783.81
5	96,000	95,000	17,958	93,204	2,796	1,000	95,000	1,000.00

The three types of reserves have different uses. For the annual statement blank required by the regulatory bodies, mean reserves are computed. For participating policy dividend scales, the initial reserve often is used in computing the "excess interest" element, and the terminal reserve (which, subtracted from the face amount, gives the "net amount at risk") is needed for estimating the "mortality savings" element.

RESERVES BASED ON NONLEVEL VALUATION PREMIUMS

The reserve basis just described assumes that a level valuation premium is available annually for reserve purposes, for all policies calling for a level gross premium.

However, relatively heavy expenses are incurred in the first policy year. After deducting these expenses from the gross premium, the balance left is smaller than the level valuation premium. Hence, to set up a level premium reserve in the first year, a life insurance company must reduce its surplus. Most of the younger companies (and some older ones) avoid some or all of this strain on their surplus by using one of several modifications in calculating policy reserves. All the modifications assume that the initial valuation premium is smaller than, and that subsequent valuation premiums are larger than, the level valuation premium.

Full Preliminary Term Method

The full preliminary term reserve method assumes that the first-year valuation premium is equal to the one-year term premium needed to meet the first year's death claims. Future valuation premiums would be the same as if the level premium system were used and the policy had been issued one year later, that is, at one year of age higher.

At age 35, for example, the level annual valuation premium for a $1,000 whole life policy (1958 CSO 2.5 percent) is $17.67. Under the full preliminary term method, only the one-year term premium of $2.45 is needed during the first year, but an increased valuation premium of $18.34 is assumed in all subsequent years.

Modified Preliminary Term Reserves

The full preliminary term method, in other words, provides an additional first-year expense allowance equal to the excess of the full annual valuation premium over the one-year term premium required under the valuation assumptions. For straight life and other relatively low level-premium policies, this is reasonable. For higher level-premium policies, however, the resulting expense allowance is larger than should be needed. Historically, state statutes have limited this allowance, and several reserve valuation methods have been used to meet this situation. The one in most common use today was developed by the National Association of Insurance Commissioners as a part of the Standard Valuation Law.

The *Commissioners Reserve Valuation Method* is the same as the full preliminary term method for policies with level valuation premiums not greater than the 20-payment life level valuation premium at the same age. For higher premium policies, the expense allowance, amortized by larger valuation premiums after the first, is equal to the expense allowance for a 20-payment life policy.

The above approach is merely a variation of earlier methods. The *Illinois Standard* is the same as the Commissioners Reserve Valuation Method except that in the case of higher premium policies the expense allowance must be amortized within the first 20 years if the premium payment period is longer than 20 years.

The *Canadian* method is less liberal. The expense allowance cannot exceed that for a straight life policy, but is amortized over the premium-paying period.

The *Ohio* and *New Jersey* methods are other variants of less importance than the above. The "select and ultimate" reserve method was another and earlier attempt to solve the problem of level premiums and non-level expenses. All these methods, except the Commissioners Reserve Valuation Method, are now only of historical interest in the United States.

EFFECT ON RESERVES OF CHANGES IN ASSUMPTIONS

The size of the individual policy reserve depends upon the assumptions inherent in its computation. For policies other than term, all reserve bases lead ultimately to the same point, that is, $1,000 at the end of the period of insurance.

Change in Interest Rate

Under given mortality assumptions, an increase in the interest rate assumed (for example, from 2½ to 3 percent) will reduce the required annual valuation premium. The assets supporting the liabilities are assumed to earn interest at a higher rate, and the amount of death claims is identical. Looking at the situation "retrospectively," collecting the full 2.5 percent valuation premium will result in accumulating assets more than sufficient to meet the policy benefits, if it is assumed that 3 percent is actually earned on the assets. For example, the 1958 CSO 2.5 percent valuation premium for a straight life policy on a male aged 35 is $17.67, 8.4 percent greater than the corresponding 1958 CSO 3 percent valuation premium of $16.29. Thus, 2.5 percent reserves are larger than 3 percent reserves. The percentage difference, however, is not uniform by policy duration. The percentage difference is greatest when the policy has many years to run. It gradually diminishes and at the termination of the contract the reserves are identical. Table 12–4 illustrates these points.

For the average company's aggregate reserves, the effect of a change in interest rate has been found to be remarkably predictable. For a reasonably mature policy portfolio, a change of one percentage point in the interest rate assumed in the reserve calculations will change aggregate reserves by approximately 10 percent, that is, the percentage change in aggregate reserves will be in the opposite direction and 10 times the percentage point change in the assumed interest rate. This fact was recognized in the development of the Life Insurance Company Income Tax Act of 1959. One of its calculations requires a revaluation of the company's reserves, using the current earnings rate (or a five-year average rate) on

TABLE 12–4.   Comparison of Terminal Reserves per $1,000 Face Amount (straight life (male), age 35)

	Annual Valuation Premiums
1958 CSO 2½ Percent	$17.67
1958 CSO 3 Percent	16.29

Years in Force	Terminal Reserves		Difference as Percentage of 3 Percent Reserve (Percent)
	2½ Percent	3 Percent	
5	$ 81.05	$ 74.72	8
10	167.90	156.29	7
15	259.12	243.48	6
20	352.54	334.23	5
25	445.78	426.20	5
30	535.77	516.21	4
35	618.77	600.25	3
40	692.16	675.36	2
45	757.75	743.20	2
50	811.36	799.12	2
55	857.35	847.43	1
60	905.46	898.40	1
65°	1,000.00	1,000.00	0

° At this duration, under the 1958 CSO mortality table, the last surviving policyowners are assumed to die. Any survivors, in general practice, will be offered the death benefits as an endowment payment.

the company's assets as the valuation interest rate. The use of the above "10 times" rule of thumb is written into the statute and applied to the policy reserves of all companies so as to revalue them on an interest rate based on investment experience.

Change in Mortality Table

The effect of a change in mortality on individual policy reserves is not so predictable. Given the same rate of interest, a table with a lower inherent mortality will produce lower annual valuation premiums. However, the size of the reserve depends more upon the steepness of the mortality rate curve of the underlying mortality table than upon the actual mortality rates. This is illustrated in Table 12–5.

It can be seen from Table 12–5 that the 1958 CSO Table mortality rates are below those of the American Experience Table mortality rates at all points, but they rise more steeply at the higher ages. The annual valuation premiums on the 1958 CSO Table are lower, but the reserves for the first 25 years are larger under the 1958 CSO Table than under the American Experience Table.

Other Changes in Assumptions

In the section on level premium reserves above, the traditional assumptions of annual premiums paid at the beginning of the year and death claims paid at the end of the year were used for explanation. However, it was mentioned that other assumptions could be made. The mone-

TABLE 12–5. Comparison of Terminal Reserves per $1,000 Face Amount (straight life [male], Age 35)

	Annual Valuation Premiums
American Experience Table, 3 percent	$21.08
1958 CSO Table, 3 percent	16.29

	Rate of Mortality per 1,000 Lives		Terminal Reserves	
Years in Force	American Experience Table	1958 CSO Table	American Experience Table, 3 Percent	1958 CSO Table, 3 Percent
5	9.79	3.53	$ 68.16	$ 74.72
10	11.16	5.35	146.01	156.29
20	18.57	13.00	327.58	334.23
30	40.13	31.75	522.92	516.21
40	94.37	73.37	698.21	675.36
50	235.55	161.14	844.01	799.12
60	1,000.00	351.24	949.70	898.40
Age 96		400.56	1,000.00	910.79
Age 100				1,000.00

tary tables of valuation premiums, reserves, basic values, and nonforfeiture benefits published by the Society of Actuaries for the 1958 CSO Table were computed on two bases:

1. "Curtate" functions, which assume that premiums are paid annually and that death claims are paid at the end of the year; and
2. "Continuous" functions, which assume that premiums are paid continuously throughout the year and that death claims are also paid continuously as they occur.

Table 12–6 shows for selected years the difference in terminal reserves based on these assumptions. The difference may be explained by general reasoning. On the average, deaths occur approximately in the middle of the policy year. Under the assumptions involved in the "continuous" functions, the beneficiary not only receives the $1,000 approximately six months earlier, but the insured has paid only one half of a year's premium in the year of death. Because each "continuous" death claim is therefore "worth" somewhat more than $1,000, it follows that each "continuous" reserve must be somewhat larger than the corresponding "curtate" reserve.

OTHER RESERVES AND RELATED CONSIDERATIONS

Reserves also must be established for several additional types of coverages offered. Reserves that are merely "valuation single premiums" (that is, the present value of future benefits) are computed for all contracts on which no further premiums will be received. The principal examples of these are (1) single-premium life and endowment policies, (2) individual life annuities, (3) paid-up life and endowment policies, and (4) supplementary contracts issued to beneficiaries in lieu of a lump-sum payment.

Similarly, when a policyowner becomes disabled, "disabled life" reserves of the single-premium type are computed (for either waiver of premium alone, or the combination of waiver of premium and disability income). Single-premium reserves must be established on account of "payor" or "premium protection" benefits on juvenile and family policies when the applicant has died.

Reserves of the level-premium type are held during the premium-paying period for additional coverages such as (1) accidental death benefits, (2) waiver of premium, (3) disability income, (4) level term riders, and (5) increasing term riders.

TABLE 12–6. Comparison of Terminal Reserves per $1,000 Face Amount (straight life [male], age 35)

	Annual Valuation Premiums
Curtate	$17.67
Continuous	18.28

	Terminal Reserves	
Years in Force	Curtate	Continuous
5	$ 81.05	$ 82.81
10	167.90	171.53
15	259.12	264.74
20	352.54	360.17
25	445.78	455.44
30	535.77	547.38

The calculation of terminal reserves for decreasing term policies and riders frequently produces negative results. What this means is that the annual valuation premiums often are less than the value of the benefits in the early years. In such cases, no credit is taken for the fact that the present value of future premiums is in excess of the present value of future benefits. The negative terminal reserve is taken as zero, and the mean reserve becomes simply one half of the annual valuation premium.

Deficiency Reserves

The mortality experienced and the interest rates earned usually are more favorable than the conservative mortality and interest rates used for valuation. Therefore, some companies, particularly those selling non-participating insurance, may find themselves able to justify a gross annual premium lower than the annual premium required under the valuation standard they use. The gross premium, using realistic interest and mortality assumptions, can provide for commissions and other expenses as well as the expected mortality. In this situation, many states require that an additional "deficiency reserve" be set up immediately.

While the necessity for this reserve requirement can be debated, an argument for such reserves can be made. The usual prospective reserve (under either the level premium or the modified preliminary term methods) can be considered as the difference between the present value of future benefits and the present value of future annual valuation premiums.

If the gross premium is *less* than the annual valuation premium, the present value of future premiums is thus overstated according to the statutory standard and the reserve is, to the extent of the difference, understated. The "deficiency" is overcome by setting up a special reserve equal to the present value of the excess of the valuation premiums over the gross premiums.

This deficiency reserve requirement has caused a significant strain on the surpluses of many life insurance companies and was one of the major forces that led to the preparation and promulgation of both the 1941 and the 1958 CSO Mortality Tables as valuation standards. In each instance, the change permitted a reduction in valuation premiums to a more realistic level based on then current mortality experience.

Natural Reserves

The entire discussion above has been concerned with "statutory" reserves, that is, reserve liabilities computed in accordance with the standards of the various regulatory bodies. As has been mentioned, these standards are deliberately conservative, to ensure that sufficient assets are always on hand to meet a company's obligations to its policyowners.

Since the increase in reserve liabilities from one year to the next has a direct effect on the company's "earnings" for that year (see Chapter 69), the use of statutory reserve standards results in the emergence of annual "earnings" that are not in accordance with "generally accepted accounting principles."

One way of overcoming this difficulty involves the calculation of liabilities by using "natural reserves" rather than "statutory reserves." Under the natural reserve method, liabilities are computed on the basis of the mortality, interest, expense, and withdrawal assumptions used in computing the gross annual premium. However, the natural reserve premium, so computed, usually differs from the gross annual premium in that it does *not* contain any margin for profit.

Using these more realistic assumptions, the natural reserves are computed in a manner very much like the retrospective calculations shown in Table 12–3. Note that (1) the insurance in force would depend on withdrawal as well as mortality, (2) the "premiums received" should be net of expenses, and (3) the benefits paid would include cash values and other payments, in addition to death benefits.[6]

Cash Values and Reserves

Although the subject of cash values is considered in the next chapter, it should be mentioned here that consideration must be given to the level of cash values when determining the reserve liabilities. The *minimum* cash value prescribed by the regulatory authorities for a particular policy

---

[6] For a more detailed treatment of natural reserve computations, see J. B. Pharr, "The Natural Reserve Concept and Life Insurance Earnings," *Transactions of the Society of Actuaries,* Vol. XXIII (1971).

at a given duration will always be less than the minimum statutory reserve for the same policy and duration.

Many companies use a cash value schedule that, at least at the later durations, is in excess of the minimum cash values prescribed by statute. Since a cash value is a demand liability, the regulatory authorities require that the statutory reserve liability be not less than the cash value. Even when the natural reserve concept is being employed to determine the reserve liabilities, the natural reserve used for each policy should be at least equal to the cash value.

Company Reserves as a Measure of Solvency

In the light of the foregoing, it is suggested that the true financial health of a life insurance company cannot be determined merely by looking at the annual report prepared for the regulatory authorities.[7] From an actuarial point of view, the basic test of a company's solvency is whether or not it has sufficient sound assets to equal its liabilities under a "gross premium" reserve calculation. Such a calculation would be made prospectively, based on (1) an estimated mortality table closely equivalent to the individual company's experience; (2) realistic interest and expense assumptions, both for the present and for the foreseeable future; and (3) the fact that future premiums received will be the *gross* premiums less the anticipated expenses.

This is a complex calculation; and in practice, it is rarely made. The *minimum* valuation standards of the various regulating bodies are intended to produce aggregate reserves in excess of a gross premium valuation through the use of: (1) mortality tables with some margin for extra mortality, and (2) a maximum interest rate less than the yield expected to be received by the company over the long term on its investments. Since January 1, 1966, the minimum standard for new policies in most states has been the Commissioners Reserve Valuation Method, using the 1958 CSO Table and (usually) 3.5 percent interest (3 percent in New York).

Valuation of liabilities using the natural reserve concept generally will produce aggregate reserves closer to, but somewhat in excess of, those obtained by a gross premium valuation.

SUMMARY

In summary, then, it can be said that the policy and other insurance reserves are a measure, in the aggregate, of the liability of the company with respect to its contractual future guarantees. Allowance is made for expected future premiums. Valuation standards are set by the various regulatory authorities on bases which are intended to be conservative within a wide range of conditions. Since (1) no account is taken of the company's mortality or expense level, (2) the statutory requirement is the same for nonparticipating as for participating insurance, and (3) some companies use the highest permissible interest rate and a modi-

---

[7] See Chapter 69, "Company Financial Statements."

fied reserve system while others do not, the margin of conservatism differs widely between companies according to these circumstances.

In addition to the reserves for the basic policy benefits, reserves are also established on account of the many supplemental coverages which are attached to or arise out of the contract provisions.

SELECTED REFERENCES

Huebner, S. S., and Black, Kenneth, Jr. *Life Insurance.* 8th ed. New York: Appleton-Century-Crofts, Inc., 1972.

Jordan, C. W. *Life Contingencies.* 2d ed. Chicago: Society of Actuaries, 1967.

Mehr, Robert I. *Life Insurance: Theory and Practice.* Austin, Texas: Business Publications, Inc., 1970.

McGill, Dan M. *Life Insurance.* Rev. ed. Homewood, Ill.: Richard D. Irwin, Inc., 1967.

Pharr, J. B. "The Natural Reserve Concept and Life Insurance Earnings," *Transactions of the Society of Actuaries,* Vol. 23 (1971).

13

Nonforfeiture Values and Policy Loans

By CHARLES F. B. RICHARDSON

LIFE INSURANCE on the level premium basis is quite unlike most other forms of insurance because the risk of death increases rapidly with age, and because the premium remains level over an extended period of time. Under a level premium life insurance policy the premium in the early years is more than is necessary to cover mortality costs; and in the later years, it is less than is necessary to cover mortality costs. The excess of the premiums in the early years is accumulated to provide sufficient assets to offset the deficiency in the premiums in the later years. The so-called "nonforfeiture provisions" define the equity to which the policyowner is entitled in the event the policy is terminated other than by death. Nonforfeiture values are available in various forms, as may be elected by the policyowner.

HISTORICAL DEVELOPMENT OF NONFORFEITURE LEGISLATION

In the early days of life insurance in this country, a policy contained no provision for the payment of an amount representative of the insured's equity on termination of the policy prior to maturity, although in practice many companies voluntarily granted cash values or other forms of benefit upon termination of the policy. However, such values were usually allowed only if applied for soon after default in payment of the premium.

The first nonforfeiture law was enacted in Massachusetts in 1861. It required companies operating in that state to provide for extended term insurance for the period determined by application of 80 percent of the reserve on the policy computed on the Combined Mortality Table at 4 percent. The requirement that this law apply to all companies operating in the state is perhaps the first instance of extraterritorial regulation in this country. The law was changed in 1877 to apply only to domestic companies. Note that the law did not require a guaranteed cash value, but simply a continuation of coverage for a specified period. The law was defective in that the 20 percent deduction from the reserve applied to the reserve less any indebtedness, so that the deduction varied with the amount of indebtedness. Also, the amount of coverage continued was the full face amount, whereas the coverage should have been reduced by the amount of indebtedness. If the insured died during the term period, the company could deduct from the face amount the unpaid premiums accumulated at 6 percent interest. In 1900 the law was further amended to require guaranteed cash values, the forerunner of similar requirements in other states following the Armstrong Investigation.

New York did not enact a nonforfeiture law until 1879. It required a nonforfeiture benefit, upon demand within six months, in the form of either reduced paid-up insurance or extended term insurance. The amount of the benefit was obtained by applying the reserve according to the American Experience Table at 4.5 percent to purchase the coverage at the "published rates" of the company. Under such an arrangement the benefits could be reduced substantially by using excessive premium rates. It is understood that the requirement that benefits be requested within six months after lapse was strictly enforced. The law was later amended to require that the value of the benefit granted be at least two thirds of the reserve; but by modern standards, these were still inadequate benefits, especially at the longer policy durations.

During the period from 1879 to 1906, competition gradually forced more liberal attitudes on the part of the companies. Many other states enacted legislation similar in principle to the New York law; but prior to 1906, in most states, there was still no statutory requirement for guaranteed cash values. In practice, however, many companies allowed cash values; and some of them, around the turn of the century, began including guaranteed cash values in the policy.

In 1906, following the famous Armstrong Investigation in New York, there were enacted laws which remained substantially unchanged for nearly 40 years. These laws varied somewhat in the several states, but typically they contained several basic provisions. The laws required that the policy show the reserve basis, and a minimum basis was prescribed in the law. After payment of premiums for three years, the policy was required to guarantee a cash value equal to the reserve, less a deduction not exceeding $25 per $1,000 of face amount. Further, the policyowner could elect to take an equivalent value in the form of reduced paid-up or extended term insurance. Tables of these guaranteed values had to be shown in the policy. Although only one of the alternative options was required, nearly all companies included both in the policy; and in the great majority of cases, extended term was the automatic option if no election was made.

These laws applied to policies issued in each of the states. However, in 1940, New York amended its statute to require compliance by *all* companies operating in New York, rather than by domestic companies only, another example of extraterritorial supervision.

CONCEPTS UNDERLYING CURRENT NONFORFEITURE VALUE PRACTICES

In 1939, in order to conduct a study of nonforfeiture provisions, the National Association of Insurance Commissioners appointed a committee which rendered its report in 1941. This report, made after a thorough, professional study by a most competent committee headed by Alfred N. Guertin, recommended far-reaching changes in the existing laws. These changes were enacted by most states around 1948. To understand the so-called "Standard Nonforfeiture Law" which resulted from this study, it is necessary to consider some of the defects of the laws enacted in 1906 and in subsequent years.

The amount a company can afford to pay in cash upon termination of a policy must take account of a large number of factors. First, the expenses incurred in the first policy year, including compensation of the agent and manager, medical fees, and the expense of policy issue, are much higher than the provision for expenses, called "loading," contained in the first year's premium. These excess expenses are, in fact, amortized over a period of years from the excess of the loading and other margins in renewal premiums over the renewal expenses, and the company has to make an immediate investment from its surplus to put a new policy on its books.

Second, the cash value bears no necessary relationship to the reserve. The mortality assumed in the reserve basis, which must contain safety margins, is designed to be reasonably conservative and ignores the effect of selection on the mortality during the early policy years. The actual fund on hand, arising from premium income less expenses less cost of benefits (generally called the "asset share"), determines the cash values that can be allowed, and is computed with realistic provisions for mortality and other factors. The mortality provided for is entirely different from that involved in the legal reserve basis.

Third, guaranteed cash values are available upon demand, irrespective of financial conditions. Experience has proved that surrender rates are much higher in periods of economic depression than in prosperous times. It is possible that the company might have to sell assets in a depressed market to meet a high demand for cash values, although this is unlikely because the cash inflow of an established company generally exceeds the cash outflow by a substantial amount. However, the payment of cash values does reduce the amount of funds the company can invest, and the company may be deprived of favorable investment opportunities that may exist under depressed economic conditions. The existence of cash values available on demand also requires the company to keep a certain portion of its assets in liquid form, with consequent reduction in yield, the cost of which may properly be charged against those who surrender their policies. (See related analysis in subsequent "Policy Loans" section of this chapter.)

The rationale of the minimum legal requirements for nonforfeiture values was stated as follows in the Guertin Committee report:

It is fundamental in business relationships that contracts, other than insurance, which are terminated prior to their normal termination date, shall involve no loss to the party to the contract who is willing to continue the contract, and the party effecting discontinuance shall bear whatever loss is involved as a result of the termination of the transaction. It is stated elsewhere in this report that, in the case of life insurance, full forfeiture upon lapse is repugnant to the public interest and that it should be the policy of the state to establish a basis whereby the purchaser may recover in some form the unabsorbed part of the payments already made. However, it cannot be regarded as proper public policy to insist that the party to the contract who is willing to continue shall be made to suffer loss through the inability or lack of desire of another to continue his contract.

Equity, therefore, would appear to demand, as a general principle, that an insurance company transacting any type of insurance, as one contracting party, shall be left in as favorable a position following the termination of a policy by a policyholder as it was prior thereto, and equity does not demand that the seceding policyholder shall be in as favorable a position after termination as he was prior thereto.[1]

The technical process used by the actuary to determine the level of cash values is known as an asset share calculation. This is an a priori calculation involving forecasting of actual expected experience as to mortality, interest, expenses, and lapse rates, quite independent of statutory limitations or requirements. Stated in oversimplified terms, the policy is credited with premiums expected to be paid each year, less expected expenses as incurred, less the expected cost of mortality on a modern table, less anticipated dividends, and the balance is accumulated at an interest rate assumed to be realistic for the long term. Lapse rates also are frequently taken into account, any profit or loss arising from the difference between the asset share and the cash value being credited to or charged against the fund each year. From this accumulation, certain charges must be made for the items discussed above and also for a reasonable contribution to the surplus funds of the company. This last item is necessary because each new policyowner receives the protection of the surplus funds existing in the company when he enters the insured group, and therefore should leave a modest contribution to such funds when he terminates.

The Standard Nonforfeiture Law, passed about 1948 in most states, resulted from the recommendations in the Guertin Committee report. In brief, the major changes in this law, enacted to correct defects in the earlier statutes, were as follows:

1. The basis for determining the minimum nonforfeiture values was changed to take account of the high first-year expenses and of the fact that such expenses vary quite substantially by plan and age of issue. It also took account of the fact that these expenses are amortized over renewal policy years. The old law used a constant deduction from the reserve of $25 per $1,000 of insurance, irrespective of plan, age, or duration, and produced cash values that were too low in some areas and too high

---

[1] National Association of Insurance Commissioners, *Reports and Statements on Nonforfeiture Benefits and Related Matters* (Chicago: Actuarial Society of America and American Institute of Actuaries, 1942), pp. 43–44.

A number of actuaries support "a rival theory that asserts that the company, which must mean the continuing policyholders, must accept some dollar responsibility for having sold policies which those others were unwilling or unable to keep in force." (See "Lecture to Society of Actuaries on Project Two," presented by E. J. Moorhead, F.S.A., on May 15 and June 1, 1972. Text to appear in *Transactions of the Society of Actuaries,* Vol. 24.)

in others. Moreover, the maximum permissible deduction did not decline in the later policy years, as would have been proper.

2. The formula for determining the minimum value was established on a basis independent of the reserve basis used by the company. Under the old laws a company using a weak reserve basis (e.g., the minimum reserves permitted by law) had lower minimum statutory cash values than a company using a strong reserve basis. The minimum values also were independent of whether the company used preliminary term or net level reserves.

3. The new law required that reduced paid-up or extended insurance values be granted at any duration if the formula produces a value, whereas the old law did not require such values until the end of the third policy year. The result is that nonforfeiture values are now required in the second year in many cases, and in the first year for some plans and ages.

4. Cash values are not required until premiums have been paid for three years. However, in practice, cash values are generally allowed by the companies at whatever duration the law requires that paid-up or extended insurance values be granted.

5. In computing minimum extended term insurance values equivalent to the cash value, the new law recognized the higher mortality experienced on such coverage.

It is important to realize that the underlying requirements for reserves, which determine the company's liability for future benefits, are *aggregate* requirements and need not bear a fixed relationship to nonforfeiture values. These latter values should be based upon realistic assumptions so chosen that they result in equitable values as between *individual* policyowners who elect to terminate their policies and those who continue their coverage. The laws prior to the Standard Nonforfeiture Law did not recognize this important distinction.

NONFORFEITURE VALUES (OPTIONS)

The three types of nonforfeiture values required by statute will now be examined in some detail, covering the more important characteristics of each of the nonforfeiture options.

Cash Surrender Values

The mathematical process used to determine the minimum cash values under the Standard Nonforfeiture Law involves a process similar in principle to that involved in computing reserves, a subject treated in Chapter 12. Net level premium reserves are computed by deducting the present value of future net premiums from the present value of estimated future claims. In order to take account of the large first-year expenses relative to the loading in the first year's premium, the adjusted premium method provided in the standard nonforfeiture legislation makes allowance for a specified amount of excess first-year expenses in determining statutory *minimum* cash values. This is done by employing an adjusted premium sufficient to amortize the specified excess first-year expenses over the premium-paying period of the policy. The *minimum* cash value is found by deducting the present value of the adjusted premiums from the present value of expected future claims, on the basis of mortality and interest rates prescribed in the law.

Many companies allow cash values higher than the legal minimum. This can be done either (1) by using a rate of excess first-year expenses lower than the maximum allowed by law, or (2) by amortizing the excess first-year expenses over a period shorter than the premium-paying period of the policy. (Many companies amortize these expenses over 10 or 20 years.) Frequently, both these methods are combined to provide values larger than the legal minimum. In defining the basis of the cash values guaranteed in the policy, it is a common practice to refer in the policy to nonforfeiture factors, which are net premiums increased by amounts necessary to amortize the excess first-year expenses.

The level of cash values a company can afford to grant depends on many factors, including premium rates, dividends, expense rates, and many other items of a technical nature.

After the bank holiday and the government moratorium on the payment of cash values and policy loans in the financial crisis of 1933, most state laws were amended to permit the company to defer payment of cash values for three or six months. The Standard Nonforfeiture Law makes such a provision mandatory rather than permissive, and the period is six months, although companies rarely invoke this "delay clause."

Extended Term Insurance

As mentioned earlier, extended term insurance was the first type of nonforfeiture benefit used in the United States. The net cash value is applied as a single premium to purchase term insurance for the face amount of the policy, plus any dividend additions, less any indebtedness, for as long a period as the available cash value will purchase. When this provision becomes effective, any supplementary benefits, such as disability benefits, accidental death benefits, and term riders are cancelled. If the policyowner desires to resume payment of premiums while extended term is in effect, the company may require evidence of insurability, although in practice such evidence is generally not required if there is a long period of unexpired term remaining.

Some people do not understand why, under the extended term provision, the *amount* of coverage must be reduced by the amount of indebtedness rather than the period of time. An example should explain the reason. Suppose that a person in very poor health has a policy for $10,000 which has a loan value of $6,000. If he takes the maximum loan and later dies, the net sum payable is $4,000. Suppose, however, that he takes the $6,000 loan, and then exercises the extended insurance option. If the extended term coverage were for the full face amount, he would, in effect, obtain total coverage of $16,000 by exercising the option (but he would be covered for a shorter period of time). It is quite clear that this would subject the insurance company to a severe degree of antiselection and would be a most unsound procedure.

In the case of an endowment policy, the cash value, after a few years, is more than sufficient to purchase term insurance to the maturity date. Under these circumstances the balance of the cash value is used to purchase a pure endowment, payable only if the insured survives to the maturity date.

Before the enactment of the standard nonforfeiture laws in the late 1940s, the laws of most states required that the term insurance be purchased on the basis of the net single premium on the company's reserve basis. The Guertin Committee studied the mortality under extended term insurance and found it to be substantially higher than that under premium-paying policies. In connection with extended term calculations, therefore, the Standard Nonforfeiture Law permits the use of a special mortality table reflecting higher mortality than that under the mortality table used in reserve calculations.

Reduced Paid-Up Insurance

The reduced paid-up option provides that the cash value be applied as a net single premium to purchase a fully paid-up policy for a reduced amount payable at the same time as the original policy. If there is a policy loan, some policies provide that only the net cash value is applied and that the loan is repaid at the time the option is selected. Others provide that the gross cash value be used to purchase a larger amount of paid-up insurance and that the policy loan be continued.

The cash value of the reduced paid-up policy is the reserve for a paid-up policy for the reduced face amount and therefore increases from year to year.

In the case of limited-payment life and endowment policies, the amount of paid-up insurance bears roughly the same proportion to the original face amount as the number of premiums paid bears to the number payable. For example, under a 20-payment life policy the reduced paid-up insurance in the 15th year would be roughly three fourths of the original face amount. On straight life policies issued at the younger ages, the amount of paid-up insurance is generally greater than the amount of premiums paid. However, this is not true for the higher issue ages, because a larger part of the premium has been used to cover the cost of insurance in the early years of the contract.

When the original policy is participating, the reduced paid-up policy nearly always continues to be participating. On the other hand, extended term insurance is almost always nonparticipating, because any dividends that might be paid would be very small and not worth the administrative expense of handling.

In the absence of an election by the policyowner, and in the absence of the automatic premium loan provision, most standard policies issued today provide that extended term insurance is the automatic option that goes into effect in the event of a default in premium payments. Under substandard insurance, the reduced paid-up policy option is generally provided.

RELATED VALUES

Policy loans and automatic premium loans are features of the policy which arise out of the statutory cash value provisions. Although they are not, technically speaking, nonforfeiture options, they are important policy provisions which should logically be considered in conjunction with the options.

Policy Loans

State insurance laws require that long-term level premium policies provide for loans upon demand (subject only to the statutory provisions for deferral up to six months) up to the amount secured by the cash value of the policy, subject to interest at a guaranteed rate. This requirement came into existence during the legislative activity in the various states following the Armstrong Investigation, although some companies did allow policy loans prior to that time.

The maximum rate of interest the company may charge on policy loans varies in the several states from 5 percent in arrears to 6 percent in advance, the latter rate being equivalent to 6.38 percent in arrears. The laws of a few states prescribe no maximum interest rate on policy loans. Prior to 1939, the rate generally charged was 6 percent, but in that year the New York law was changed to provide a maximum rate of 5 percent in arrears on new policies, and this applied to both domestic and out-of-state companies. Many authorities consider that even 6 percent is not an excessive rate, for the following reasons:

1. The rate is guaranteed for the life of the policy, which could extend for a period as long as 50 years or more.
2. A policy loan is available upon demand, irrespective of economic conditions, and the loan cannot be called by the company.
3. Policy loans typically are of small average amounts, in most companies only a few hundred dollars; and the expense of administration is high, generally from .5 percent to 1 percent, depending on the average size of loan. Therefore, a gross rate of 5 percent becomes nearer 4 percent net of expenses. There have been many occasions in the past when the companies could invest funds at a substantially higher rate after investment expenses.
4. These loans are repayable in whole or in part at any time. In practice, however, the majority of policy loans are not repaid prior to surrender, maturity, or death, at which time they are deducted from the proceeds or cash value payable.
5. When market interest rates are higher than the rate charged on policy loans, the policyowner can borrow his equity and reinvest it at a higher rate elsewhere. This creates a cash drain upon the company and reduces the amount of money available for investing upon favor-

able terms. In this sense the borrowing policyowner gains an advantage at the expense of those who do not borrow. The lower the guaranteed rate, the more likely it becomes that such a situation will occur.

Frequently, market conditions are such that loans can be obtained at a lower rate of interest by borrowing from a bank on security of the policy. There are, however, several disadvantages in making such loans. Some banks are not interested in making small loans. They may change the rate of interest or call the loan. They may not allow partial repayment of small amounts, as the insurance company will permit. The procedure for negotiating the loan is more complicated and generally takes more time than the simple procedure involved in dealing with the insurance company. However, the use of life insurance contracts as collateral for bank loans is a common practice.

During the credit squeeze of 1969 and 1970 in which basic interest rates rose to levels unheard of for 100 years, the demands for policy loans, obtainable at 5 percent in a money market in which yields of 9 percent to 10 percent were common, put a severe financial strain on the companies. In the case of some mature companies, the increase in assets was less than the increase in policy loans, which meant that assets had to be sold in an adverse market to meet the heavy negative cash flow caused by the enormous demand for policy loans. During this period there was great pressure for a reform of the New York law and, indeed, for a substantial change in the approach underlying the state laws governing the interest rate on policy loans. Massachusetts increased its rate from 5 percent to 6 percent and New York remains the only state with a 5 percent rate. Many observers have concluded that in this kind of situation borrowing policyowners, in effect, are subsidized by those who do not borrow. One way to correct this situation would be the establishment, by law, of a flexible interest rate varying with some definable recognized market rate of interest. Another possibility might be an adjustment in the dividend to reflect the amount of policy loan, but this is of dubious legality and in any event would not cure the problem of nonparticipating policies.

Automatic Premium Loans

Many policies contain an automatic premium loan provision under which, if a premium is not paid within the grace period, it is automatically advanced as a loan, provided the cash value is sufficient to cover the premium. Subsequent unpaid premiums are similarly advanced until the cash value is exhausted. The laws of Montana and Rhode Island require the inclusion of such a provision, which must be effective unless the policyowner elects another option.

Usually, this provision is not an automatic option but must be elected by the policyowner either at the time the policy is issued or at a later date.

While premiums are being advanced under this provision, all other provisions of the policy remain in effect, and no evidence of insurability is required if the policyowner elects to resume payment of premiums.

Dividends continue to be paid, and any supplementary benefits such as waiver of premium, double indemnity, or term insurance riders (which terminate when extended term insurance or reduced paid-up insurance becomes effective) remain in force.

The main advantage of the provision is that it prevents inadvertent lapse of the policy, which sometimes occurs if the policyowner is away from home or ill, or is short of funds when the premium notice arrives. The disadvantage is that once the policyowner starts to use the provision, he may get out of the habit of paying premiums in cash, with the result that the policy may eventually terminate when the cash value becomes exhausted.

If the automatic premium loan provision is in operation instead of the extended term insurance provision, the period of coverage is generally somewhat longer, although the net amount payable on death gradually decreases because of the increasing loan. In the later policy years, particularly on participating policies where dividends are used to reduce premiums, extended term is likely to give a much shorter period of coverage than automatic premium loan. The chief advantage of the automatic premium loan provision lies in the fact that insurability is preserved and full coverage can be restored at any time.

On substandard policies, the extended term insurance provision is generally not available, particularly if the rating is high. The election of the automatic loan provision in such cases gives the policyowner more substantial immediate coverage upon default in payment of premiums than would be provided by the reduced paid-up insurance provision which would otherwise become effective.

A few companies have attempted to overcome the disadvantage of this provision by limiting the operation of automatic premium loans to two successive years, or a limited number of premiums, after which the extended term benefit becomes effective unless the premium is paid in cash. In the latter case, the automatic loan provision would again become effective in the event of a subsequent default.

SELECTED REFERENCES

Fassel, Elgin G.   "New Standard Valuation and Nonforfeiture Laws," *C.L.U. Journal,* Vol. 1 (September 1947), p. 407.

Hoskins, J. E.   "Asset Shares and Their Relation to Nonforfeiture Values," *Transactions of the Actuarial Society of America,* Vol. 40 (1939), p. 379.

National Association of Insurance Commissioners.   *Reports and Statements on Nonforfeiture Benefits and Related Matters.* Chicago: Actuarial Society of America and American Institute of Actuaries, 1942.

Richardson, Charles F. B.   "Guaranteed Cash Surrender Values under Modern Conditions," *Transactions of the Actuarial Society of America,* Vol. 39 (1938), p. 237.

Shepherd, B. E.   "Natural Reserves," *Transactions of the Actuarial Society of America,* Vol. XLI (1940), p. 463.

Townsend, Frederick S.   "Term Insurance and Minimum Cash Values," *Transactions of the Society of Actuaries,* Vol. 15, Part 1 (1963), pp. 465–77.

Wood, Glenn L. and Williams, C. Arthur, Jr.   "High Cash Value Life Insurance Policies and Unfair Discrimination," *Journal of Risk and Insurance*, Vol. 31, No. 4 (1964), p. 577. Discussion, Vol. 33, No. 1 (1966), pp. 125, 132.

Wood, Glenn L. "Life Insurance Policy Loans: The Emergency Fund Concept," *Journal of Risk and Insurance*, Vol. 31, No. 3 (1964), p. 411. Discussion, Vol. 33, No. 2 (1966), pp. 317, 322, 325.

14

Surplus and Dividends

By ROBERT T. JACKSON

APPORTIONMENT of policyowner dividends is one of the most important functions of life insurance companies writing participating business. That policyowner dividends are of immense significance to policyowners may be seen from the fact that dividends amounting to $3.7 billion were paid in the United States during 1971. Management decisions with respect to dividend determination must take into account stability of company operations, equity among policyowners, and the influence of dividends on a company's competitive position.

Definitions

Several definitions will be helpful, if not essential, to an understanding of policyowner dividends. First, a policy providing for payment of dividends is called a participating policy; a policy which does not provide for payment of dividends is a nonparticipating policy. A mutual company is owned entirely by its policyowners and normally writes only participating policies; in fact, in some states, mutual companies are prohibited by statute (with minor exceptions) from writing nonparticipating policies. A stock company is owned by its shareholders and generally writes primarily nonparticipating policies, although many stock companies offer participating policies as well.

Nature of Policyowner Dividends

A dividend is a refund of that portion of the premium paid that is in excess of the amount necessary for current benefit payments, expenses, and reserves required to cover future policy guarantees. Just how the dividend arises perhaps can be most easily seen by contrasting premium calculations for a nonparticipating policy with those for a participating policy.

In a stock company, in return for providing capital, shareholders hope to make a profit. Therefore, a nonparticipating premium for a group of policyowners in a stock company is calculated to provide as closely as possible the exact costs of the benefit to be provided, plus a margin for profit. If experience under nonparticipating insurance is adverse—for example, if death rates are higher than allowed for in the premium calculation—the shareholders bear the loss; if experience is favorable, the shareholders profit.

Calculation of a premium for a participating policy can be considered as proceeding in the same manner—calculation of the premium to provide, as closely as possible, the exact costs of the benefit to be provided—but instead of adding a small amount for profit, there is a substantial addition to provide a margin of safety. This addition will provide the basis for the dividend scale at time of issue. However, because actual profits from which to pay dividends are not level, the dividend scale normally will also be nonlevel. With the substantial margins built into the participating premium, adverse experience can be met by lowering the initial scale of dividends, and favorable experience will result in an increase in the scale.

The calculation of a premium for a life insurance policy obviously must cover the costs of paying death claims and the costs of doing business. In addition, for a contract providing coverage for a number of years, provision must be made for the higher costs of mortality in later years. Thus, the level premium calculation for longer term contracts includes sums of money not immediately needed for payment of claims or expenses, which the insurer will invest at interest. This interest income offsets some of the charges required for mortality and expense, and substantially reduces the premium that would otherwise be required. For a participating policy, an interest income assumption that is relatively conservative compared to what reasonably can be anticipated is included in the premium calculation. Conservative assumptions concerning mortality costs and expense costs also may be included in the premium calculation. Briefly then, the insurer has three sources from which funds to pay dividends can arise: (1) mortality savings; (2) investment margins, primarily interest; and (3) expense savings.[1] Of course, it is not necessary that each of these sources be positive, but only that the net of all three be positive.

It is important to realize that an individual dividend exists solely as a portion of the earnings of the company as a whole. The insurer invests the money received from all policyowners and it pays its expenses and claims from moneys received from all policyowners. No individual policyowner wants actual mortality results in his individual case charged to his policy; the whole purpose of buying insurance is to avoid the self-insurance that would imply. Further, the company funds are invested in all sorts of enterprises providing different rates of return and it would be extremely unfair, even if it were possible, to try to allocate to the individual policyowner the gains from the investment in which his particular funds may have been made. Finally, no policyowner would want the costs of han-

---

[1] By mortality and expense "savings" is meant the difference between the mortality and expense allowed in calculating the premium and that actually experienced by the company; the investment margin arises from investment earnings greater than those already assumed in the premium calculation.

dling his policy to depend solely on the qualifications of a person assigned to administer that single policy.

DETERMINATION OF DIVISIBLE SURPLUS

In fact, then, the company, consisting of all policyowners as a group, earns the funds which are allocated as dividends—and the individual policy contributes only as a part of the company, not as a unit in and of itself. That being the case, the dividend process begins with determination of the total company funds available for distribution as dividends. From all income (premiums and interest earnings less disbursements in the form of benefit payments and expenses) the company first must set aside any additional funds required to carry out future policy guarantees, referred to as the increase in reserves. Next, it is both desirable and necessary to set aside funds to allow for future unexpected fluctuations (funds available for adverse mortality experience or economic losses as in a recession). Such funds are called contingency or surplus funds. The remaining funds will be available for dividend distribution to the policyowners as a group.

It is in the determination of the dividend fund—the total amount to be distributed—that the difference between participating policies written by mutual and stock companies is to be found. In a mutual company, once requirements for reserves and contingency or surplus funds are determined, the entire remainder is available for dividend distribution. In a stock company, however, the determination of the dividend fund is not nearly so clear-cut. The laws of Canada and of a relatively small number of the states require separation of accounts between nonparticipating and participating business; the accounting is much as if there were two companies existing side by side—a nonparticipating company and a participating company with separate reserves and surpluses. In addition, Canada and some of the states requiring a separation of accounts also have a limitation on the amount of the profit for participating business that may be transferred to shareholders.[2] In states where no separation of accounts is required or where there is no limitation of shareholders' profits from participating business, the dividend fund is whatever amount the directors allocate, with no necessary or predetermined relationship to profits arising from participating business.

On the other hand, in states where a separation of accounts and a limitation on profits is mandated by statute, the dividend fund is determined much as in a mutual company, since the dividend fund will be the amount left in the participating account after setting aside reserves and contingency or surplus funds—the sole difference being that first there will have been a withdrawal from the fund for shareholder profits, up to the prescribed limit.

---

[2] The reader interested in more information about statutory limitations on stock companies writing participating business will find the subject thoroughly covered in Chapter 7 of Joseph M. Belth's *Participating Life Insurance Sold by Stock Companies*, published for the S. S. Huebner Foundation for Insurance Education, University of Pennsylvania (Homewood, Ill.: Richard D. Irwin, Inc., 1965).

INDIVIDUAL DIVIDENDS

Once the dividend fund has been determined, the next step is distribution to individual policyowners. The whole theory of equitable dividend distribution is based on providing a return to each similar group of policyowners (referred to as a policyowner "class," a term which has peculiar legal significance in life insurance law) that shall be as closely as possible in proportion to its contribution to the general funds available for distribution. A dividend class would be defined by some or all of the following common characteristics: the same type of coverage, the same year of issue, the same age of issue, the same number of premium payments made, and the same attained age.

In general, it can be said that the more care taken in identifying the classes with distinct differences, the more equitable the dividend scale that can be devised.

Three-Factor Method[3]

As has been indicated earlier, the primary sources of dividend moneys arise from favorable mortality and investment experience and from expense savings. It is evident, therefore, that dividend distribution is concerned with returning to the various classes of policyowners their interest in these gains in relation to the contributions of each class. The dividend scale attempts to return such gains in relation to the underlying pattern of experience of the company.

Mortality Element. As mentioned earlier, the premium calculation for a participating policy is normally based on a fairly conservative mortality table. The difference between these conservative rates and the actual experience of the company (smoothed for what appear to be random fluctuations) provides the mortality portion of the dividend. Obviously, the amount available for dividends from mortality will vary with the underwriting practices of the company—companies with strict underwriting standards having substantially larger amounts available than companies with less stringent underwriting practices. Until the early 1960s, dramatic improvements in mortality in this country provided ever increasing margins for dividends. In the last decade such improvements have virtually disappeared so that increasing margins from this source can no longer be counted on.

Investment Element. Earlier it was pointed out that the calculation of premiums includes the assumption of a specific return on investments. Actual investment earnings (if any) in excess of those used in the calculation of the premium determine the portion of dividend arising from this source. Investment income will be composed of interest earnings and capital gains and losses. These capital fluctuations may be included over a period of years in dividend payments. However, unless abnormally

---

[3] Much of the material in this section appeared originally in a paper presented by the chapter's author to the Society of Actuaries. See Robert T. Jackson, "Some Observations on Ordinary Dividends," *Transactions of the Society of Actuaries,* Vol. XI (1959). These materials are included in this chapter with the permission of the Society of Actuaries.

large, they are frequently handled directly in the surplus account, thus not affecting annual dividend payments. The larger the reserve under the policy, the greater will be the effect on dividends from investments.

Expense Element. The loading portion of the dividend arises from the difference between the expenses allowed for in the calculation of the premium (called the "loading") and those actually incurred by the company. Since actual expenses are not level, a considerable degree of smoothing is necessary in determining this portion of the dividend. The heaviest portion of the expenses are incurred in the first year, including the bulk of marketing expense, major expenses in underwriting, and the establishment of all records necessary for future handling of the policyowner account. Since the expense charge in the first premium does not cover anything like the actual expenses incurred (hence the lower nonforfeiture values in early years) such initial expenses are amortized over a number of years in calculating the portion of dividend arising from expense margins.

The Three-Factor Formula

The classic three-factor formula for dividend distribution is

$$D = (_{n-1}V + \pi)(i' - i) + (L - e)(1 + i') + (q - q')(1 - _nV),$$

where $_{n-1}V$ and $_nV$ represent the reserve of the preceding and current year, π the net premium, i' and i, respectively, the dividend interest rate and the interest rate originally assumed in the premium calculation, L the loading, e actual expenses as contained in the dividend formula, and q and q', respectively, the mortality rate allowed for in the premium calculation and the dividend mortality rate representative of the companies' actual experience.

Translated from the mathematical symbols, the dividend D equals the initial reserve $(_{n-1}V + \pi)$ times interest earned in excess of that required to maintain reserves $(i' - i)$ plus the excess of charges for expenses contained in the premium over expenses incurred $(L - e)$ multiplied by interest thereon $(1 + i')$ and plus the excess of mortality charged over that experienced $(q - q')$ times the actual amount at risk, the face amount less the reserve $(1 - _nV)$.

It is important to recognize, if only because the rationale underlying this formula appears so simple, that while in many companies it may provide the detailed method for dividend calculation, the total dividends thus produced must equal the dividend fund available for distribution, after recognition of other factors—contribution to surplus and contingency funds, and capital gains or losses, for example. Thus, the actual use of the formula is the last step in the dividend calculation. There also are many variations introduced to take care of special situations, and some companies use entirely different bases for dividend calculation.

Terminal Dividends

In addition to annual dividend payments, a large number of companies now provide for a terminal dividend payable when the policy terminates after a given period of years. Typically, the earliest a terminal dividend would be payable would be between 10 and 20 years after a policy has been in force, and it would be payable regardless of the method of termination—that is, whether as a result of surrender, a death claim, or maturity of the policy. However, a number of companies do not pay a termination dividend under all these conditions; for example, some pay no terminal dividend on death.

In the early policy years, the annual dividend paid normally will use up all the company's earnings on that particular policy class. At longer durations, however, policies begin to contribute to the general surplus and contingency funds. A terminal dividend then may be paid on the theory that surplus and contingency funds contributed by the terminating class of policies should be returned to their owners, being no longer required for their protection against catastrophe.

Statutory Requirements

By far the most comprehensive law governing dividends is that of New York State (Section 216 of the New York Insurance Law). The following provisions apply to policies of companies domiciled in New York:

1. Dividends must be distributed "annually and not otherwise."
2. Special and terminal dividends may be paid only with the approval of the superintendent of insurance.
3. Optional methods of using dividends must be offered—for term and annuity policies, those are in cash and to reduce premiums; on other plans, paid-up additions and accumulation of dividends at interest must be available as well.
4. The sale by mutual companies of nonparticipating policies, with minor exceptions, is prohibited and, as mentioned earlier, provisions designed to protect participating policyowners of nonparticipating companies are included.

Some of these provisions also are made applicable to policies issued in New York by out-of-state companies. These include the annual dividend requirement, the limitations on stock companies writing participating policies, and the requirement that policies issued by a mutual company, with minor exceptions, be participating. In addition to these direct requirements imposed on out-of-state companies, a separate section of the New York law (Section 42) requires substantial compliance by out-of-state companies with any portion of the insurance law applicable to domestic companies, wherever determined by the superintendent of insurance "reasonably necessary to protect the interests of the people of this state."

No other state has such comprehensive requirements regarding dividends. In fact, a dozen states have no specific legislation on the subject at all. Of those states with legislation concerning dividends, the most common requirement is that of annual distribution, although in many states no distribution is required before the end of the third policy year and in others, none before the fifth. Four states (Illinois, Maryland, Massachusetts, and Missouri) require the same four dividend options on most policies as does New York.

The dividend provisions of New York law have great influence throughout the country, partly because there is little dividend legislation elsewhere, but more importantly because 60 percent of all individual life insurance in force in the United States is with companies either domiciled in New York or doing business there. Thus, most companies, for obvious reasons, have made their entire dividend operation conform to New York requirements, rather than using a different system in other states.

Practical Considerations

A number of practical considerations influence the nature of a company's dividend scale. Included among these considerations are the following:

1. The total of the individual dividends must be approximately equal to the total available divisible surplus determined in advance.
2. The dividend scale must be as satisfactory as possible to existing policyowners. After a preliminary set of acceptable dividends are found which meet the first criterion, they must be examined in relation to the present scale. Whenever there has been a change in emphasis in the dividend structure (e.g., a decrease in the expense refund at the same time as an increase in interest allowed), the dividends resulting from the new formula must be checked against those actually paid under the existing formula. Policyowner satisfaction is, after all, a primary aim of all dividend schedules and on the whole this is best attained by the most equitable distribution possible. However, the existing schedule usually has conditioned policyowners to a relatively narrow range of dividends, probably increasing slightly from year to year. A serious reduction in dividends due solely to a more equitable assessment of expenses, for example, might well result in lapse of existing business and prolonged and expensive correspondence in the attempt to justify the change. As a practical matter such a change in emphasis normally must be accomplished by a series of adjustments in the dividend scale.
3. The net cost position of the company under the tentative scale must be checked against those of its chief competitors. Substantial departures from the net cost patterns of companies in similar financial positions may result in dissatisfaction among the agency force and a flow of business to those policies particularly favored in competition by the new scale.
4. There are limits on the reliability of available data for use as a basis for allocating costs, mortality, and income by group. For example, a small company can produce reliable mortality data only in broad groupings. It must, therefore, rely on the mortality statistics of the life insurance business generally, modifying them to its own situation. Even the largest company, however, will find it impossible (even if it is desirable) to get reliable and usable statistics on all possible refinements of mortality classes including age; underwriting class (standard, substandard and preferred risk); sex; race; occupation;

habitat; family history; habits; social, economic and family status; as well as the type and size of policy.
5. The administrative cost of operation of the proposed scale must be considered. Obviously, the pursuit of greater theoretical equity can be justified only when the results are significant enough to warrant the expense involved. Even with the largest computers, the number of dividend classes that can be handled economically is limited. Also, the expense involved in a change in scale is substantial enough to militate against frequent insignificant changes in the dividend scale.
6. The dividend scale adopted must represent the trend of the company's experience over a period of years, not merely the results of a single dividend year.
7. Simplicity is an important, though not overriding, objective of any dividend scale. Ordinarily, a simple scale will be easier to change to meet varying conditions and it almost certainly will be easier to explain to the inquiring policyowner who wishes to know the methods by which his dividend was determined. Refinements introduced in pursuit of more equitable distribution may, however, run counter to this objective.

DIVIDEND OPTIONS

Most policies contain four separate options under which the policy dividends may be made available to policyowners. In five states, these four options are prescribed by statute for most policies:

1. Dividends may be received in *cash.*
2. Dividends may be used to *reduce premiums* as they become due.
3. Dividends may be left with the company to *accumulate at interest.* The rate of interest which will be credited to the dividend fund is that determined by the board of directors, although most policies also contain a minimum rate guarantee.
4. Dividends may be used to purchase at net rates small amounts of single-premium insurance of the same kind as the basic policy. This is referred to as the *paid-up insurance* option.

Because the interest on dividends left to accumulate is taxable, whereas there is no tax on the increases in values of single-premium insurance, the latter option is more attractive, at least to those policyowners in high tax brackets. Furthermore, under the paid-up insurance option, the additional insurance is purchased at net rates (providing only for mortality and interest with no addition for expenses) and no evidence of insurability is required.

In addition to the preceding four rather standard options, a number of other dividend options may be provided in some policies. The entire dividend may be used to buy one-year *term insurance* at some prescribed rate. This option has been available in certain policies of some companies for a great many years. Its greatest disadvantage is that, since the probability of death increases sharply with increasing age, the amount of insurance purchased by the dividend decreases rapidly as the policy-owner grows older.

A more popular option in recent years has been to purchase with the dividend an amount of one-year term insurance equal to the cash value of the policy, with the balance of the dividend accumulating at interest. Under this method, known as the *fifth dividend option*, the amount of insurance protection increases for a good many years as the cash value of the policy increases and the dividend fund created by the accumulation of the balance of the dividends creates a reservoir from which the increasing costs of the term insurance can be withdrawn in later years. Nevertheless, this option eventually will result in decreasing amounts of insurance if the policy is kept in force long enough.

As a variation of the fifth dividend option, the balance of the dividend, after taking out the amount necessary to purchase one-year term insurance equal to the cash value, may be applied toward the purchase of small amounts of single-premium paid-up insurance. This avoids the tax on interest income, but in the later years the accumulated amount of single-premium paid-up permanent insurance must be reduced annually in order to provide term insurance.

Most policies contain valuable provisions that permit the use of accumulated dividends when sufficient to change the original policy, at net premium rates, to a paid-up policy of the same kind. A second clause may provide that when the value of the policy plus any dividends credited thereto equals the face, the policy will be matured as an endowment at the request of the policyowner. This latter clause actually provides no more benefit than can be achieved through surrender of the policy.

HEALTH INSURANCE DIVIDENDS

All the principles that apply to calculations of individual life insurance dividends apply equally to individual health insurance.[4] The sources of earnings for payment of dividends in individual health insurance are interest earnings and expense savings, just as in life insurance, and favorable morbidity experience (in lieu of mortality). In fact, however, there is a much less formalized approach to the payment of health insurance dividends than for life insurance dividends.

There is relatively little statutory restraint and the elaborate options available for life insurance dividends rarely are found in health insurance. Furthermore, the calculation of health insurance dividends is usually simplified—often a flat percentage of premiums paid, the percentage varying over a period of years with the actual experience of the company.

Perhaps health insurance dividends have been simplified compared with life insurance dividends because there are greater fluctuations in morbidity experience and the amount of health insurance premium on an individual life normally is smaller than that for life insurance. Therefore, the care and expense associated with the calculation of life insurance

---

[4] Group life and health insurance dividends are discussed in Chapter 29.

dividends does not seem justified for the determination of health insurance dividends.

SELECTED REFERENCES

Huebner, S. S. and Black, Kenneth, Jr. "Surplus and Its Distribution," *Life Insurance*, Ch. 27. 8th ed. New York: Appleton-Century-Crofts, 1972.

Jackson, Robert T. "Some Observations on Ordinary Dividends," *Transactions of the Society of Actuaries*, Vol. XI (1959), pp. 764–811.

Jordan, Robert H. "An Analysis of Contributions to Surplus," *Transactions of the Society of Actuaries*, Vol. XXI (1969), pp. 81–99, 307–14.

Maclean, Joseph B. and Marshall, Edward W. *Distribution of Surplus*. Actuarial Study No. 6. Chicago: Actuarial Society of America, 1937.

McGill, Dan M. *Life Insurance*. Rev. ed. Homewood, Ill.: Richard D. Irwin, Inc., 1967.

Mehr, Robert I. *Life Insurance: Theory and Practice*. Austin, Texas: Business Publications, Inc., 1970.

15

Risk Selection and Substandard Risks

By GAYLORD L. PAINE

RISK "APPRAISAL," RISK "SELECTION," OR "UNDERWRITING" all are terms describing the process by which a life insurer maintains insurance cost equity among its insureds. Life insurance is a socio-economic device for equitably sharing the economic loss resulting from death. The insurer seeks to charge each individual the premium that mirrors the risk of death to which he is exposed. This process of selection is basically a pricing operation.

Pricing by age, plan of insurance, and sex derive from the mortality tables on which the premium structure is based. The appraisal process is designed to refine this basic pricing structure schedule. Those concerned in the process are called "underwriters" though a more meaningful term would be "risk pricing analysts."

SELECTION OBJECTIVES

Antiselection

Why should further refinements than age and sex be required to satisfy proper equity? Because, under a system which leaves the choice of amount and plan to the individual, there is a human tendency to transfer to a life insurance company risk that is excessive when related to the cost of coverage provided. This tendency to transfer excessive risk is known as self-selection or antiselection. The effect of antiselection is well illustrated by the purchasers of annuities. Their ability to select against the insurers long since required adopting separate annuitants' mortality tables which reflect the greater longevity of the annuitant purchaser than that shown by the life insurer purchaser. Buyers of term insurance also have demonstrated this ability to engage in self-selection. Higher mortality experienced on term conversions is another example of the operation of antiselection.

Standard; Substandard; Unacceptable Risks

The great majority of risks submitted to an insurer fall within a normal pricing range. The risk of death to which this majority is exposed is termed "standard" and the premiums charged are known as "standard premiums." At the other extreme is a small minority on which the risk of early death is so great that no reasonable charge can be assessed to cover the hazard. Such risks are termed "uninsurable" and the insurer "declines" to accept them. Between these extremes are applicants whose demonstrable risk of death is greater than the normal or standard but still not sufficiently great to result in a declination. Protection against the death hazard for this group of applicants requires a price higher than the normal or standard charge. Somewhat unfortunately, because of semantic implications, this group of risks has been termed "substandard" and the premiums charged are known as "substandard." Applicants falling into this group are charged extra premiums of varying amounts dependent upon the hazards shown to exist. Actually, the extra premium charged is in reality a normal or standard premium for that particular risk.

To illustrate, a steeplejack obviously presents a greater risk than a housewife. The steeplejack would be expected, in the interest of equity, to pay a higher premium than the housewife for the risk to which he is exposed. The price he pays is called "substandard" to distinguish it from the normal premium, but he and other steeplejacks are paying a premium which in reality is "standard" for their particular class of risk. "Modified premium risk" would be a more apropos description of an applicant who may be insured on a basis other than standard.

Generally speaking, out of 100 applicants for insurance, 90 to 92 will prove insurable at normal or standard premium rates, 5 to 8 will be insurable on some modified premium basis, and 2 to 4 will be uninsurable. The development of substandard, or extra premium, or modified risk selection is relatively modern in concept. Refinements and changes in the process continue as statistical and clinical experience unfolds.

Individual Company Objectives

The appraisal or pricing of risks will differ from company to company, depending upon the objectives and philosophies of various companies, particularly with respect to cost of insurance and the particular market that is sought. Any underwriting department must continually walk a tightrope. Its selection procedures must be designed to permit acceptance of the large majority of risks at standard rates reflecting a reasonable mortality loss; yet equity demands that it impose modified premiums for risks not meeting standard norms. If selection is too severe, mortality costs may be cut but agents will lose a part of their market to competitors. If selection is too lax, the eventual mortality cost to future policyowners will be high and a shrinking market, particularly among normal risks, will result. Competitive factors therefore play an important part in the appraisal pricing objectives of the individual company.

Social Objectives

It is clearly in the public interest for the life insurance business to offer coverage to as high a proportion of the general public as possible. Hence, the ratio of uninsurable lives must be cut to the lowest percentage possible, and coverage on some modified premium basis be offered to risks involving high mortality.

FACTORS OF SELECTION

Mortality Classes

It should be clear from the discussion thus far that the majority risk—the normal standard—constitutes one large class. It would be possible, of course, to fragment this large class into segments and thus further refine the pricing procedure. Social and economic considerations suggest this to be undesirable and unnecessary, although some companies in theory offer so-called "preferred" risks special premium rates lower than the normal "standard" premium.

The more necessary refinements in appraisal of risks appear in the so-called substandard or extra premium class area. Since the cost of mortality is higher, it is imperative that reasonable equity be maintained by fragmentation into several classes. The number and premium structures for such varying mortality classes will differ from company to company. Obviously the narrower and more numerous the classifications, the more difficult the appraisal procedure in pinpointing pricing differentials.

Many factors affect mortality. The consideration of these factors, many of which are interrelated, determines whether the applicant is standard, substandard, or uninsurable. If a modified premium is indicated, these considerations determine the specific classification within the substandard range. These factors have been the object of considerable statistical research and the results of these studies widely published among underwriting and actuarial circles.

Age

Most companies grant life insurance to individuals from birth through age 75. Occasionally insurance is accepted by some companies at higher ages than 75, provided that proper need for the insurance can be shown and underwriting standards can be met. As previous chapters have suggested, the typical mortality curve commences at a high level for the first few months immediately following birth. It then rapidly falls and remains at low levels during the preteens and teens. There is a gradual upward sloping of the mortality curve during the 20s and 30s. Following age 40, the mortality slope increases steeply.

It should thus be apparent that underwriting selection during the few months following birth must be relatively cautious, due to the possibility of congenital birth defects which could affect mortality immediately. In the case of insurance on the lives of children, experience has shown that larger amounts of insurance must be screened carefully to avoid the possibility of speculation. A child is not an income producer and there is no substantial economic loss involved upon the death of a child.

Sound underwriting selection also imposes restrictions on juvenile insurance. The breadwinner must carry on his own life at least twice the amount of insurance proposed to be carried on the child. If there are siblings, they, too, must carry amounts similar to that proposed on the current juvenile applicant. The singling out of one child in a family for insurance raises the danger signal of possible speculation.

At the other end of the mortality curve, i.e., from the fourth decade of life, the degenerative diseases begin to evidence themselves. As a consequence, the selection of lives at older ages requires careful scrutiny and underwriting requirements are more numerous.

Sex

Although females show a lower mortality than males of the same age, underwriting departments must watch carefully for evidence of speculation on the lives of women.

An essential precaution in the underwriting of married women is to ascertain that the husband carries a commensurate amount of insurance on his own life. In the more distant past, insurance on married women was severely limited, but the market for life insurance on women, both married and single, has grown appreciably during the last decade, and many of the severe limitations originally suggested for the underwriting of female risks have long since been lifted.

Family History

It has been said with considerable truth that the best way to ensure a long life is to choose one's parents carefully. That longevity is a function of inheritance is clear from statistical evidence. Where family history shows a long-lived parentage, some credits in evaluating an impaired risk may be given. Conversely, the presence of cardiovascular deaths under age 60 among parents or siblings represents a decided debit, particularly when the applicant shows some current impairment such as overweight or hypertension. Indeed, when multiple deaths at age 50 or under have occurred within a family, many companies will classify the applicant as a ratable risk even if he himself shows no impairment.

Diabetes is also inheritable, and careful selection in multiple cases of diabetes in a family will necessitate blood and urine sugar tests.

Build (Height and Weight)

More statistical evidence relating to the effect of build on mortality has been amassed within the insurance industry than on any other underwriting factor. The most recent study was that completed on "Build and Blood Pressure" in 1959. Mr. Edward Lew has listed four major conclusions of this study:

1. Moderate underweight, once considered an impairment, is a most desirable condition in mortality consideration.

2. The relative mortality of overweight men has changed but little over many years except that the relative mortality of tall overweight men is somewhat lower than it used to be.
3. The pattern of overweight mortality among women is different than that of men and more favorable.
4. Much higher mortality is to be expected where overweight is combined with elevated blood pressure and other impairments. Thus, mortality is more than the simple sum of the excess mortality for each separate impairment.

The old saw that one's waistline measures his lifeline has been proven rather conclusively. Every insurer makes use of some form of build table, which for varying heights and weights shows the expected mortality and also the percentage variation from the normal weight for a given height. Lives not more than 30 percent underweight nor more than 25 percent overweight are generally considered at standard rates. Beyond these limits, extra premiums are usually assessed. Mortality credit may be given to an overweight for a good family history and for favorable chest and abdominal measurements. An additional mortality debit, however, is applied when overweight is associated with a poor family history or poor build measurements.

Medical History and Impairments

Every application for insurance contains statements by the applicant as to past illness and disease. The importance of the illness, the length of time disabled, and the consequences of the sickness are elements in determining the cost of mortality. Insurers develop histories of serious illnesses in detail to determine the effect upon future mortality, and will often require substantiation through detailed records from attending physicians.

Certain diseases such as ulcer, malignancy, and asthma may be recurrent in nature. Others, such as rheumatic fever and high blood pressure, may impair the function of vital organs and body systems. Some illnesses, such as diabetes and thyroid disease, result from malfunctioning of vital organs and glands.

Particularly important is the element of good faith on the part of the applicant in carefully detailing past personal medical history. Most of the unfortunate situations involving misrepresentation on the part of the applicant are concerned with this area of personal history because of its major impact in establishing the correct pricing for the insurance sought.

Certain applicants for life insurance are required to submit to a medical examination. These examinations may be necessary because of the amount of insurance, age of the applicant, or a history of some serious impairment or disease. The examination may be completed by a physician or in certain cases by medical technicians. Examinations by technicians—a rather recent development—are known as paramedical examinations.

The purpose of such examinations is to reveal any impairment which may exist currently. In the traditional form of physician's exam, the doctor directly checks the heart, oral and nasal cavities, sight and hearing, and the respiratory, genito-urinary, endocrine and musculoskeletal systems. In the more recent paramedical form, a fragmented blood test substitutes as a check for abnormalities of organs, systems, and glands. In both types of exam, urine analyses, blood pressure and pulse readings are made.

For larger amounts of insurance, special examinations are required, such as electrocardiograms, X rays, and special blood or urine tests.

Where an impairment is found, the case must be "priced" to mirror the mortality associated with that impairment. Probably the most common impairments found on examination are those involving the cardiovascular system. Most frequently the impairment is that of elevated blood pressure.

Hypertension is a symptom of cardiovascular disease. Since cardiovascular or heart disease is the greatest single cause of death in North America, its importance cannot be overstated. Organic heart murmurs, irregular pulse, abnormal EKG patterns,. and certain abnormalities of blood chemistry in the cholesterol and triglyceride area also are important in identifying and pricing what has come to be known as the "coronary profile."

Among abnormal urinary findings of import are those evidencing sugar —frequently an indicator of a prediabetic or diabetic condition. If by additional blood studies such impairment is shown to exist, there is a definite extra mortality requiring careful selective pricing or possible refusal.

Occupation and Avocation

Two decades ago, occupation was a primary factor in selection. With the advent of automation, industrial safety programs, and improved working conditions, the impact of occupation on mortality has decreased. Relatively few occupations today are listed by insurers as requiring an extra premium.

Certain occupations with a high accident hazard, such as steel erection, power-line maintenance, explosive handling, and diving, are associated with a greater than normal mortality. A second major group of occupations shows an additional mortality because of exposure to health hazards such as dust, poison, and radiation.

A third group of occupations is characterized by excess mortality because of environment. Unskilled laborers as a class will show an extra mortality, partially because of the accident hazard but also because of health factors associated with a lower living standard. The ready access to alcohol probably explains the excess mortality shown by bartenders and others concerned with the direct handling of alcoholic beverages.

Social, educational, medical, and industrial progress has lessened the impact of occupation on mortality but greater leisure time has brought with it a multitude of avocations which require pricing for the added mortality concerned. Readily apparent are the additional accidental death hazards associated with sky diving, mountain climbing, scuba diving, and racing of all types—auto, hydroplane, snowmobile, and motorcycle.

Aviation

The aviation underwriting factor contains elements that might be included under occupation and hazardous avocation. It is listed separately because of the large numbers of people involved and the appreciable amount of statistical information on mortality results.

Military aviation is associated with extra mortality both for pilots and crew members. Differences in mortality are linked to type of plane flown, hours of experience, and age. In combat situations statistical information and underwriting action will be subject to drastic change.

Experience with respect to civilian aviation shows standard mortality for commercial passenger plane pilots and crew members as well as for professional pilots of business-owned planes. Crop dusting, test or experimental flying, aerial surveying and mapping, charter and cargo carriers, stunt flying, and instruction show extra mortality and require extra premiums.

As an avocation, private piloting requires careful selection and obtainment of precise information as to hours of experience and annual hours flown. Pilot age, experience, and annual flying time are factors which affect mortality experience. Student pilots, young pilots, pilots with little experience, and pilots who fly generally in excess of 200 hours a year must be considered for extra premium treatment.

Military Service

Armed conflict produces excess mortality not envisioned by normal mortality tables. Even in peacetime a higher than normal accidental death rate occurs within the armed forces.

Selection practices have differed among companies. During World War II, war riders, which excluded coverage for death resulting from war, were rather universally required for members of the military and for applicants who might conceivably be subject to military service in the future. During the Korean conflict, some companies required riders for members of the military, while other companies attempted to hedge against the war hazard by limiting the amount of coverage granted to military personnel. In the Vietnam conflict, most insurers accepted members of the military for limited amounts of insurance provided the applicant had no orders for overseas duty or was not associated with combat groups which showed a particularly high mortality, such as the Marines, Special Forces, and helicopter units.

The desire for death protection by members of the military naturally will be high during a period of armed conflict and tend to diminish when the danger of possible combat death terminates as a result of peace or discharge from the armed services. This self-selection creates a rather poor persistency pattern, contributing to limitations on the amount of insurance granted by most insurers to military personnel even in times of peace.

Foreign Residence

Short travel trips to foreign countries by citizens of North America generally present no problem. Examples of exceptions include exploration trips or safaris into unsettled and uncivilized areas, and travel into regions where a state of armed conflict exists.

Residence for appreciable periods in foreign areas presents a somewhat different picture. In the temperate zones of Europe, Australia, and New

Zealand there is no problem since climate, public health facilities, and mortality follow patterns similar to those of North America. However, unsettled political conditions such as have existed in Asia and the Middle East may create a pricing problem.

In the subtropical and tropical areas of the world, particularly outside the larger cities, the factors of heat, humidity, sanitation, and lack of medical facilities may be so unfavorable as to require substandard premiums since excess mortality can result.

Recent Immigration

There exist in the world many mortality variations. The mortality experience among the general population of Asia, Africa, and South America is much poorer than that experienced in the United States, Canada, or Europe. Recent immigrants, particularly from the underdeveloped countries of the world, present selection problems. Readjustment to life in a new and strange country may result in emotional difficulties. Little can be determined fully as to past medical history since records are not easily available.

Insurers require a minimum period of residence, usually one year, and require documentary evidence that permanency of residence is both intended and possible before considering an application for insurance. Even then, some restrictions on plan and the amount of insurance are generally enforced.

Use of Alcohol and Drugs

The selection factor of use of alcohol and drugs perhaps should be entitled "misuse." The underwriter recognizes that alcohol, when used in excess, results in extra mortality. Extra mortality may come from physical effects such as deterioration of vital organs, from psychiatric effects which lead to violence and suicide, or from accidental effects so clear in the drinking-and-driving and drinking-and-piloting patterns of fatality. Where a pattern of frequent intoxication exists, i.e., six times a year or more, the mortality is two to three times that of normal. Those treated for alcoholism will be subject to heavy to moderately heavy extra premiums for several years following their cure because experience has shown the tendency to revert to old habits. Alcoholism or the misuse of alcohol is a disease and is so treated in the selection of risks.

Historically, drug use was an important but rather rare underwriting factor. Selection was concerned with the use of addictive drugs such as heroin, opium, morphine, and codeine. It was clear that their illegal criminal use involved unacceptable mortality. It was also clear that any cure was a long process and often ineffective. Today the selection problem is not so much concerned with the "hard" drugs—although their abuse has greatly expanded—but with the so-called hallucinogens such as LSD and DMT, and others which appear to involve a psychic dependence, if indeed not traditional addiction. The psychic-dependent drugs include marijuana, the amphetamines such as benzedrene and dexedrine, and the barbiturates. The use of these "soft" drugs has expanded rapidly within the younger segment of the population. There remains a serious question as to the eventual effects of these drugs on physical and mental well-being and consequently on mortality.

Some insurers attempt to distinguish between casual experimental use and steady use of drugs. The selection process generally should err on the conservative side if it is to avoid possible future high mortality costs to the insuring public.

Driving Record

"Only cardiovascular diseases and cancer exceed accidents as a cause of death in the United States. For males aged 15–24, motor vehicle crashes cause over 40 percent of deaths." So reads a portion of a report to the National Bureau of Economic Research.

In the selection of risks, life insurers are concerned with rejecting or properly rating poor drivers. Statistical evidence pinpoints the positive correlation between a poor driving record and fatal accidents. Many insurers specifically question the applicant as to recent motor vehicle violations and accidents. Obtaining motor vehicle records where violations and accidents are suspected is a fairly routine selection practice.

The frequency and severity of such violations and accidents are elements considered in the determination of substandard premiums to be charged and in the refusal or rating of accidental death benefits. A long record of violations involving speeding, reckless driving, and driving under the influence of alcohol or drugs properly may be grounds for refusal of the risk.

Departure from Social Mores

Environment as it pertains to the pricing of mortality risks may be defined as "all of the surrounding conditions and influences that affect the development and life of each individual." We live as individuals but we also live as a human community which for its own protection and survival sets rules of conduct. These rules may and do change over periods of time. They may take the form of legislation or of custom.

The individual acting in defiance of laws and customs accepted by society departs from social mores. Murder, theft, dishonesty, adultery, and homosexual activities, among many others, represent departures from social mores. Violent criminal acts clearly suggest the reasons for an increased mortality over the norm. Other social aberrations also may affect mortality unfavorably. Often these aberrations involve psychiatric difficulties associated with an unstable personality. Among individuals with social aberrations the incidence of violent death and suicide is high.

The underwriter does not seek to judge the morality of these departures in social mores; he seeks only to measure in a reasonable manner the effects on mortality and to provide the equity essential to life insurance pricing.

Financial Considerations

As early as the 18th century, legislation was passed in England to prevent the making of any life insurance contract where the owner-beneficiary had no clearly determinable interest in the life being insured. The presence of a true, valid and determinable economic interest in the life of another is termed "insurable interest." It is a legal prerequisite to any contract of insurance. This "insurable interest" concept as it has evolved through years of legislation, regulation and court decisions may be briefly summarized as follows:

1. Insurable interest need be demonstrated only at the commencement of a life insurance contract. Subsequent extinction of the interest does not void the contract.
2. Any person has unlimited insurable interest in his own life and may purchase any amount of life insurance that an insurer will issue to him naming such beneficiary as he may choose.
3. No person may insure the life of another unless he would suffer a specific and determinable economic loss on the death of the insured. Immediate relationship by blood or marriage is considered automatically to create such insurable interest. Hence husbands and wives, parents and children, have an insurable interest in each other's lives. More distant relationships do not create such interest automatically.
4. Creditors would have insurable interest in the lives of their debtors, and those engaged in financial "marriages" such as partners, employers, and employees would have an insurable interest in each other's lives. But in these cases the amount of insurance involved must bear a reasonable and direct relationship to the specific financial arrangements such as debt owed, salary paid, value of services rendered, value of stock, or partnership interest.

While legislation, regulation and court decisions require the existence of an insurable interest at the inception of a life insurance contract, further refinement of the concept is required through the selection process to avoid the excess mortality which has traditionally resulted from "overinsurance." It is essential that the insurer exercise some constraint by adopting some standards to measure insurable interest in both personal and nonpersonal or "business insurance" sales. The development and application of such standards form the process of "financial underwriting."

Income is the measure of financial ability to purchase food, clothing, shelter, insurance and all other necessities, and the luxuries of life. Income, therefore, must bear some reasonable relationship to the amount of and premium for the life insurance to be carried on any life. This is so not only because that income is necessary to continue premium payments but because the loss of that income through death, retirement, or disability is an important measure of the economic value of the life.

Many rules of thumb have been devised to measure this relationship between income and the total amount of personal insurance which may be issued. The capitalization of 75 percent of one's income assumed to be received over the applicant's economic lifetime is one method. Another suggests that the total annual premiums, based on an ordinary life contract for the attained age, should not exceed 20 percent of gross income.

Under either method, it is clear that at younger ages a greater ratio of life insurance to income is permissible than at the older ages.

Where insurance is purchased by a second party on another's life, the principle of specific indemnity against a precise economic loss resultant from death is followed. Corporate key-man insurance must bear a reasonable relationship to the gross salary paid the insured. The general rule of thumb is five to seven times the gross salary. Credit-debtor insurance would be acceptable only for the specific amount of the debt involved.

THE TOOLS OF SELECTION

Information relating to the previous listed factors of selection is secured through sources which may be termed "tools of selection." Acquisition of information involves a cost to the insurer. That cost must be measured against the savings in mortality to determine its effectiveness. Hence, while many tools of selection are available, their use may be varied depending upon the size of the case submitted.

The larger the case, the more tools used and the more searching the selective process. Larger cases have more individual effects upon mortality costs. Moreover, from a social viewpoint, the insurer must be careful that excess mortality which might be attributable to purchasers of large amounts of insurance is not being subsidized by the less affluent segments of the insurance buying public.

Application

The application for insurance identifies the proposed insured, his age, marital status, residence, and occupation. Also shown is the amount and plan of insurance sought and the relationship of the beneficiary to the applicant. Information concerning foreign travel and residence, aviation activities, exposure to hazardous avocations, and military service also is provided. Application forms of many companies ask questions covering driving records. Life insurance coverage already in existence is summarized as well as any previous difficulties in obtaining insurance from other insurers.

Special Questionnaires. Where further clarification is needed, most insurers furnish special questionnaires. The agent who is knowledgeable of his company's selection practices will obtain such questionnaires as addenda to the normal application. Special questionnaires provide additional information as to finances, foreign residence, military service, occupation, aviation, and avocation. The initial acquisition of precise information in the application and any suitable special questionnaires expedites underwriting processing and issue.

Evidence of Physical Insurability. Evidence of physical insurability may be nonmedical, medical, or paramedical. An examination by a physician or medical technician is required only under certain circumstances. In about 60 percent of insurance applications, physical evidence of insurability is submitted on a nonmedical basis. Here, the agent acts in lieu of a physician or medical technician. He asks the proposed insured questions concerning his past medical history, his family history, and his build; he also questions the proposed insured as to treatment undergone for any physical impairment or disease. Questions also are asked concerning possible symptoms of any impairment or disease, including alcoholism or drug misuse.

Although individual company rules differ, nonmedicals generally are acceptable evidence of physical insurability for amounts of insurance up to $30,000 at age 30 and under, and for somewhat lesser amounts up to age 40 or 45. The use of nonmedical has expanded rapidly since its introduction in the 1920s.

Clearly the agent who seeks to establish the physical insurability of his client has a major responsibility. He must be conscientious in his questioning and meticulous in detailing the answers. Medical histories and impairments, clearly and adequately detailed by an agent, will make the selection process easy, rapid, and efficient. Inadequate, untruthful, and careless completions lead to frustrating delays, searches for additional information, and poor public relations.

As has been previously suggested, older applicants, applicants for large amounts, and applicants whose medical histories suggest the necessity for further detailing and study, are subject to the more searching examinations made by a physician. The paramedical examination currently is being utilized in those areas where appropriate facilities exist, and generally for amounts of insurance beyond nonmedical limits and up to $100,000 or $150,000.

Agents' Reports

Most insurers require that specific information about a proposed insured be submitted by the writing agent. Such agents' reports give information as to applicant's income, his net worth, the background and purpose of the sale, and the length of time the agent has known the prospect. Professional merchandising of life insurance today requires the agent to seek out detailed information on the financial position of a client to determine properly his insurance needs. Such information from the agent is also an invaluable aid in the selection process.

Consumer Investigative Reports

Traditionally, consumer investigative reports have been called "inspection reports." These are written communications bearing on a proposed insured's general reputation, mode of living, health, finances, and exposure to abnormal hazards. The information is derived through personal interviews with friends, neighbors, associates, and often with the proposed insured himself. Reports generally are completed by nationwide organizations which have been engaged in this type of reporting for many years. A few insurers employ their own consumer reporting agencies.

CIR's usually are not obtained for smaller amounts of insurance. Each insurer has rules as to the size of applications which require this type of independent investigation. Legislation rightly requires that proposed insureds be fully advised when applications are made for which such consumer reports may be obtained. Should adverse action be taken by the insurer as a result of such a CIR, the proposed insured is given the opportunity to correct any information he can show was incorrect.

Inspection or consumer reports are a protective device for the buying public against adverse mortality costs which might be forced upon them by purchasers acting other than in good faith or who may be engaged in criminal activities.

Attending Physicians' Statements

Information from physicians who have attended the proposed insured is essential in some cases and discretionary in others. Where there has been a history of illness or impairment serious enough to consider rating or refusing the risk, statements from the applicant's physician are necessary. For large amounts of insurance, the history of even a routine checkup may require an attending physician's statement.

These medical summaries are an important selection tool. They give a clearer picture of symptomology and treatment, and permit sounder judgment as to the relative seriousness of the impairment. The information in such statements is privileged in nature and is given in confidence to the medical directors of the insuring company.

Medical Information Bureau

The Medical Information Bureau makes possible an exchange of pertinent underwriting information among life insurance companies. A major purpose is to help guard the interests of existing policyowners against concealment or fraud by new applicants. The information chiefly concerns medical facts, both favorable and unfavorable, about a small percentage of applicants for life insurance. The use of this information is strictly limited by the Bureau. There is no indication of the action that was taken by any insurer nor is the amount of insurance issued given.

M.I.B. information may be used only as an alert signal. Every member company is required to make its own independent underwriting investigation. Insurance cannot be denied nor an extra premium charged on the basis of M.I.B. information. Since the underwriting practices of member companies are not identical, it should be clear that one company may accept a risk which another company has either rated or rejected.

Thorough precautions are taken to see that M.I.B. information is kept in a confidential manner. All reports are made in code form, and full responsibility must be assumed both by the company and its medical director for the reporting and care of the information.

PRICING SYSTEMS FOR EXTRA MORTALITY

Excess mortality may be described in several ways. It can be expressed as the number of extra deaths which occur each year per 1,000 lives. This may be termed *extra numerical mortality.*

Mortality experienced which is higher than average also can be expressed as a percentage of the normal or standard which is represented by 100 percent. If at age 40 the standard mortality (100 percent) envisions

4 deaths per 1,000 lives, and a group of 1,000 lives age 40 experiences 6 deaths within the year, that group can be said to have a mortality of 150 percent. If a group experiences 8 deaths, its mortality is 200 percent, and so forth. This may be termed *extra percentage mortality.*

Several different methods have been designed to price mortality costs associated with risks classified other than standard. Any one insurer uses several of these pricing systems to reflect the cost of excess mortality in the premium charged.

Patterns of Mortality

The choice of a particular method of modifying the standard premium is dependent upon the pattern of mortality anticipated for the particular hazard involved. Three patterns of mortality are outlined below.

A Constant Extra Numerical Mortality That Remains the Same Each Year without Respect to Age. Specific examples of a constant extra mortality type would be certain piloting and accident hazards. If statistical evidence has shown an incidence of 10 extra deaths each year for each 1,000 crop dusters, then it is clear that excess mortality can be expected on a constant basis each year.

A High Initial Extra Mortality, Either Numerical or Percentage, Which Rapidly Decreases until Normal Mortality Is Anticipated after the Passage of a Very Few Years. Certain surgical operative procedures evidence a high initial mortality pattern for a period of several years following surgery.

An Increasing Extra Percentage Mortality Associated with Aging. An increasing extra percentage mortality pattern is demonstrated by such impairments as overweight, elevated blood pressure, and diabetes. At younger ages the extra deaths per 1,000 impaired lives may not represent a great percentage variation from the norm, but with increasing age the percentage of extra deaths per thousand slowly increases. Such a pattern might be considered analogous to the compounding of interest.

Substandard Pricing Methods

Permanent Flat Extra Premiums. A permanent flat extra premium is usually constant regardless of the age of the life insured. It is expressed as a fixed charge of so many dollars per $1,000 of insured amount. Examples of occupations charged permanent extra premiums are:

Bartenders	$ 5.00 per $1,000
Tower erectors	$ 3.50 per $1,000
Crop dusting pilots	$10.00 per $1,000

Generally the flat extra premium is used to price excess numerical mortality which involves a rather constant number of extra deaths each year. It is payable for the life of the contract unless reduced or removed upon change in or termination of the hazard.

Temporary Flat Extra Premiums. Temporary flat extra premiums are identical to those described above except that the insurer specifies at the outset of the insurance contract the precise number of years such extras will be charged. At the end of the specified period, the premiums for the contract are reduced to standard. The following is an example of a schedule of extra premiums that might be applied to persons undergoing major surgery:

Time Elapsed since Surgery	Extra Premium per $1,000	No. of Years Charged
Within one year	$7.50	4
1 to 2 years	7.50	3
2 to 3 years	7.50	2
3 to 4 years	7.50	1
4 years and over	None (standard)	

Temporary extras are used to price those risks, such as applicants recovering from surgery, in which the mortality pattern is anticipated as being high initially and falling rapidly to normal.

Multiple Table Extra Premiums. The multiple table pricing system, which takes several different forms, is the one most generally used for impaired risks. For each age and plan, a number of premium rates are established. The standard risk which is assumed to have a 100 percent mortality pays the normal or standard premium. Risks which are deemed to have a mortality of 150 percent, or 50 percent above normal, pay a higher premium. Risks with mortality deemed to exceed 150 percent pay a still higher premium.

These multiple tables may provide rates for assumed mortality percentages of 500 or 1000 or even higher. The tables any one insurer establishes may be numerous and narrow in mortality range or few and very broad in range. A typical table of mortality classes would be:

Designation	Average Mortality Assumed	Mortality Range
Table 1 or A	125%	120%–139%
Table 2 or B	150%	140%–165%
Table 3 or C	175%	166%–189%
Table 4 or D	200%	190%–215%
Table 5 or E	225%	216%–239%
Table 6 or F	250%	240%–265%

Such tables are intended to cover patterns of mortality which show, as do most impairments, an increasing extra percentage mortality associated with aging. The standard premium structure serves as the base for these multiple tables and standard reserves and cash values are generally used.

As was indicated, the amount of extra premium for any classification at a given age will vary by plan. For example, a person aged 35, classified as a 200 percent mortality risk, might pay an extra premium of $6.90 per $1,000 for ordinary life insurance. On a 20-year endowment, in contrast, he would pay but $3.05 extra per $1,000. The lower extra premium results because the exposure to excess mortality is considerably shortened on the endowment and because the actual amount at risk reduces so sharply.

Rate-Up in Age. While rate-up in age is the oldest system for pricing impaired risks, it is not used extensively today. It lacks to some degree the preciseness of classification of the methods previously described. But like the multiple table method, age rate-up was designed to cover constant or increasing percentage variations from standard mortality.

Dependent upon the classification, a risk could be rated up in age by one year, two years, five years, or more. This system provides the larger cash values which are linked to the older age, but removal or reduction in ratings at a subsequent date creates difficulty.

Lien System. The lien system presents a reverse twist to the charge for extra mortality. It provides that the risk will pay a standard premium for the age and plan involved but it reduces the amount of insurance protection granted for that premium. For example, at age 35, the standard premium for $1,000 coverage would provide $650 coverage during the first policy year to an applicant classified as a 175 percent mortality risk. The initial lien of $350 is gradually reduced each year until the full face amount of $1,000 is finally reached.

This method, also known as *graded death benefit*, generally is used only in the area of money purchase pension plans where, under the pension formula, the premium for a participant cannot be varied. More universal use of this method is considered rather undesirable since a beneficiary could misunderstand the payment of a lesser death benefit than the contract might appear to provide.

SIGNIFICANCE

Selection of risks is an essential exercise in pricing the hazard of death. It involves judgments based upon mortality experience gleaned from many sources—actuarial, clinical, and governmental. Pricing decisions sometimes must be empirical in nature. Experimentation is necessary when there is no past experience.

Underwriting is intriguing because it involves all the life patterns of people—social, environmental, and physical. Risk selection, with its demands for equity, and its needs for clear communication and understanding between the sales force and the buying public, is a challenging area of operation within the life insurance business.

SELECTED REFERENCES

Association of Life Insurance Medical Directors of America. *Transactions of the Association of Life Insurance Medical Directors of America.* Vols. I–LIV (1928–1971). Boston.

Cohen, Sidney. *The Drug Dilemma.* New York: McGraw-Hill Book Co., 1969.

Dublin, Louis I. *Factbook on Man from Birth to Death.* 2d ed. New York: Macmillan & Co., 1965.

Home Office Life Underwriters Association. *Proceedings of the Home Office Life Underwriters Association.* Vols. I-LII (1930–1971). New York. (Volumes X, XX, XXX, XL, and L contain 10-year indexes of subject matter.)

Institute of Home Office Underwriters. *Proceedings of the Institute of Home Office Underwriters.* Nashville, Tenn. Published annually.

Pedoe, Arthur. *Life Insurance, Annuities and Pensions.* 2d ed. Toronto: University of Toronto Press,1970.

Shepherd, Pearce, and Webster, Andrew C. *Selection of Risks.* Chicago: Society of Actuaries, 1957.

Society of Actuaries. *Build and Blood Pressure Study.* Chicago, 1959.

————. *Reports of Mortality and Morbidity Experience.* Chicago. Published annually since 1950.

16

Contract Cost and Benefit Comparisons

By E. J. MOORHEAD

IN LIFE INSURANCE as in other human institutions the results achieved by various companies differ materially. Whether due to judgment, determination, or fortune, some companies succeed in providing life insurance at lower cost than others do. This chapter discusses the procedures and the pitfalls involved in comparing policies as to price and benefits.

No entirely satisfactory method for making such comparisons is known. This is partly because the sheer quantity of differences among policies defies efforts to take them all adequately into account in the comparison process. Another reason is that each of the features of a life insurance policy has a utility, hence a value, that differs according to the circumstances of the policyowner. For example, liberal settlement options or a change of plan provision may be unimportant to one purchaser but of substantial significance to another.

Nevertheless a rational and illuminating analysis of cost versus benefit is generally agreed to be feasible. The question is which of the numerous processes that have been suggested most deserves to be employed.

It is important to realize that there are two distinct purposes for which price comparisons may be made, and that the most suitable techniques in these two situations are not necessarily identical. One purpose is that of a prospective buyer examining the alternatives available to him at a particular time, for a particular policy and amount. The other is that of an analyst attempting to compare performance over the range of policies offered by a number of companies. In the latter case refinement of method and of mathematics is appropriate. But for the individual buyer a simple system whose arithmetic is readily comprehensible is to be preferred *provided it has been shown that the simple system ranks the policies that are being compared in essentially the same order as does a more comprehensive system.*

211

WAYS IN WHICH CONTRACTS DIFFER

Participating and Nonparticipating Contracts

A prospective life insurance buyer may purchase a participating contract, the ultimate price of which depends upon future experience of the issuing company; or he may buy a nonparticipating policy in which the price is certain, subject only to the ability of the issuing company to perform as promised. Can these two types be compared satisfactorily with each other?

Yes, they can, subject to two important limitations. The first is that the published dividend scale at issue date of the participating policy be recognized for what it is. (This subject is examined later in this chapter.) The other is that allowance be made for the increased cost that a full guarantee almost inevitably entails.

In a business transaction in which payments are spread over a period, the purchaser should contemplate that he is likely to encounter a higher offered price if a relatively low ceiling is placed upon the largest amount he can be required to pay than if that ceiling is so high that it is unlikely to be touched even if the seller's experience turns out adversely. In short, an attractive guarantee of *maximum* cost tends to raise *probable* price. A nonparticipating life insurance policy gives the seller no option of subsequently increasing the price; a participating policy offered at a considerably higher premium rate gives the seller much leeway in this respect. For this reason the buyer of a nonparticipating policy must expect that at the date of purchase, the price offered him will be higher than is shown by the current dividend scale applicable to a similar participating policy. Only he can decide whether the lower initial outlay coupled with complete guarantee are worth the odds that he will pay more in the long run.

Benefits Other Than Death Benefits

If the only life insurance payout were on death or endowment maturity, the comparison problem would be much simpler than it is. But life and endowment policies feature cash values, patterns of which differ considerably among companies and within companies. Also, in a participating policy various dividend options are offered; some companies pay higher interest rates on dividends left to accumulate than others, and some offer dividend additions at more attractive prices. Also differences exist in grace period, reinstatement, policy change, disability, settlement, and other provisions.

As a practical matter, mathematical comparisons must generally be limited to examining the relationship among premiums, cash values, and dividends. The numerous other differences must perforce be given intuitive weight, except to the extent that the cost of a supplementary coverage such as the accidental death benefit can be identified.

Even in the limited area thus defined, judgment must enter into the analysis. For example, a policy with relatively large early cash values is not necessarily worth extra cost to a particular buyer, since he may have no intention of using those values.

COMPARING NEW CONTRACTS
THAT ARE SIMILAR

Current Dividend Scales and Dividend Histories

A key part of the information normally available for comparison of participating policies is a set of figures properly called a *dividend illustration*, and often inadvisedly called a dividend projection. Effective comparison is impossible without a clear understanding of (*a*) what a dividend illustration is, and (*b*) the significance thereof with respect to years that lie ahead.

A dividend illustration is not an estimate. It is not what the company hopes to pay in future years nor what the company believes it will pay. Nor is it what the company has paid in past years. A dividend illustration normally has no element of the future, nor of the past, in it. It depicts what the company is paying today, adjusted only to reflect structural differences between policies already in force and those now being offered. Even if a company has already decided to change its dividend scale upward or downward in the near future, it should not—in some jurisdictions is not even permitted to—reflect this knowledge in its dividend illustrations.

This being the case, what use is the dividend illustration to a prospective buyer, whose only concern is about the future? The answer is that it is of no use for distinguishing among companies whose costs shown by then current dividend scales are quite close to each other. But if the difference measured by current dividend scales is large or moderately large, experience shows that such a gap is rather unlikely to be wiped out in the relatively near future by dividend scale changes.

From this conclusion two others follow. Elaborate comparison methods are not worthwhile because of the imponderability of policy dividends. As has been said, if one must guess at the diameter of a circle it is pointless to compute the circumference from that guess to five decimal places.

The second conclusion is that illustrative dividends that will not become payable until many years into the future should not enter into cost comparisons. It appears reasonable to make calculations for as many as 20 policy years but no more, and this only if the calculation process results in giving low weight to the later part of those 20 years.

For established companies, dividend histories (i.e., dividends actually paid during the past 10 or 20 years) are available for use as an alternative to current illustrations. Some feel these are preferable on the grounds that they represent reality rather than supposition. However, except as a supplementary analysis for purposes of confirmation, the use of dividend histories is not desirable. A dividend history attributes too much significance to the accomplishments of the company 10, 15, 20 years ago. Much change for better or for worse may have occurred in so long a period. If current illustrations have been properly calculated—which generally is the case and which can be approximately verified if doubt exists—they offer an up-to-date portrayal of the company's dividend-paying ability.

Traditional Method of Cost Comparison— Description and Criticisms

The traditional method of cost comparison, widely used for many years and generally applied over a 20-year (or, less often, a 10-year) period, is extremely simple in concept and in application. Considering a pair of competing policies, the traditional method undertakes to answer two questions which a prospective purchaser may express thus:

① Using current dividend scales (or histories), which of these policies calls for the smaller net outlay on my part?

To calculate this it is customarily assumed that policy dividends are paid in cash each year, not left to accumulate or used to purchase additions. The premiums for the period are added together, the dividends are added together and subtracted from the sum of the premiums. A common expression for the result is *net payments.*

② If I surrender each of these policies at the end of the period, what are the comparative results?

The cash value, including any terminal dividend by the company's current scale (or history), is subtracted from the *net payments,* producing a figure often called the *net cost.*

Quite frequently the net cost by this process turns out to be negative. It has been common to label this negative figure a "profit" or "gain."

For almost as long as it has been used, this traditional method has been branded as unsuitable for comparison purposes. (These last three words are important; justifiable criticism arises only if the method is used to help decide which of two life insurance companies appears to offer the more attractive purchase.) The criticism is irrefutable. It is true beyond dispute that this method gives undue competitive advantage to a company whose dividend scale is relatively steep, or whose cash value at the end of the period, with or without a terminal dividend, is unusually large.

The reason the traditional method fails the test of reliability when used to compare policies is that it treats dollars paid by policyowner or company as of equal value regardless of when payable. The fact is that a dollar paid at the twentieth year, for example, has a value only about a quarter of the value of a dollar paid at the beginning of the first year. This difference is due partly to interest, and partly to the decreasing number of policies that remain in force as the years go by.

Another objection sometimes made to the traditional method is that it usually considers just two situations, each of which is unlikely to occur, i.e., that the purchaser keeps his policy for exactly 10 years or 20 years and then surrenders it. This objection has less validity than appears at first sight, because the tenth and twentieth year cash values, far from being arbitrary, are representative of the pattern of values at other times of possible surrender.

Survival of the traditional method for many years in the face of legitimate objections is largely attributable to the widely held belief that any more reliable index would be unacceptably difficult to calculate, to verify, and to understand.

Methods of Cost Comparison Proposed in Response to Criticisms

Numerous papers and at least one full-length book have been written by critics of the traditional method advocating some other system for comparison. Descriptions of many of these alternatives and their sources are set forth in the *Report of the Joint Special Committee on Life Insurance Costs* published in 1970.

Every one of these methods has something to recommend it. Every one may reasonably be rated superior to the traditional method except in simplicity. The question that had to be faced sooner or later was whether the simplicity of the traditional method is sufficiently attractive to justify its shortcomings. This task fell to the Joint Special Committee as will now be recounted.

Industry Study: The Interest-Adjusted Method

At the annual meeting of the Institute of Life Insurance in December 1968, its Chairman, John S. Pillsbury, Jr., addressed himself to the cost analysis question in these words:

There is a growing demand that something be done by somebody to clarify the question of cost of life insurance.

. . . From the standpoint of public relations, I am persuaded that if the realities of the life insurance process preclude a formula answer, then we must learn to communicate clearly why this is so in a manner that will be understood and accepted. If, on the other hand, there is an answer—at least a better one than we have produced thus far—and I for one believe that there must be—then we had better put the most capable minds in our business to work promptly and creatively on this problem.[1]

Soon afterwards three company associations—the Institute of Life Insurance, the American Life Convention, and the Life Insurance Association of America—formed the Joint Special Committee on Life Insurance Costs. The committee accepted the following as its assignment: "to devise a defensible and reasonably simple method of price appraisal for consumer use; or, if this goal is unattainable, to devise an acceptable explanation why this cannot be done."

The committee *Report* published in May 1970 expressed its members' recognition that no completely satisfactory method has been advanced or is likely to be. But the committee decided that a practical improvement over the traditional method is achievable. "The largest question," said the *Report*, "that has occupied us through our meetings and supplementary correspondence has been how far to go in introducing refinements." The essence of the committee's conclusions is contained on page 21 of its *Report*, reproduced in the quoted paragraphs that follow. This expresses preference for and describes a process called the interest-adjusted method.

---

[1] This statement referred particularly to an address made two months previously by Senator Philip A. Hart, cited at the end of this chapter.

Our Committee has concluded that the method called in this report the Interest-Adjusted Method is the most suitable of all those of which we have knowledge. Our principal reasons for this opinion are:

(1) It takes time of payment into account.
(2) Of all the methods that take time of payment into account it is the easiest to understand.
(3) It is possible to use this method without having recourse to advanced mathematics.   *e a s y*
(4) It does not suggest a degree of accuracy that is beyond that justified by the circumstances.
(5) It is sufficiently similar to the Traditional Method so that transition could be accomplished with minimum confusion.

The steps required to apply the Interest-Adjusted Method to a policy with level annual premiums are as follows:

1. Select the period over which the analysis is to be made. In practice, standardization using ten and twenty years is desirable. For periods shorter than ten years an index offers no advantage over what can be learned from direct inspection of the figures for individual years. Comparisons for periods longer than twenty years have, as already stated, too little significance to be advisable.

2. Select the interest rate to be used. Although it must be recognized that an interest rate that is appropriate for one individual may be inappropriate for another, a reasonable choice for general use is a rate close to the after-tax rate readily obtainable over a period of years on accounts in savings institutions.
   Currently a rate of 4% per year seems generally suitable. At first sight this seems low, but not so when it is realized that the selected rate must be reasonable for savings made gradually over a considerable period. This is quite different from the rate that applies at a particular time such as the day or month when the policy is issued.

3. Accumulate the annual dividends, if any, at interest to the end of the selected period, and add to them the cash value (and terminal dividend, if any) available at the end of the period.

4. Divide the result of Step 3 by an interest factor that converts it into a level annual amount accruing over the selected period. If the period is 20 years and the interest rate is 4%, this factor is 30.969, or, with sufficient accuracy, 31.

5. Subtract the result of Step 4 from the annual premium.[2] This is the Interest-Adjusted Cost. Divide by the number of thousands of the amount of insurance to arrive at the Interest-Adjusted Cost per thousand.

It may be noted that the traditional method is just a special case of the interest-adjusted method when the interest rate employed is zero percent. It is also important to notice that when results for numerous companies are compared using the interest-adjusted method many of the companies occupy about the same rank in the list by either that or the traditional method, but positions of some companies are changed considerably. This is demonstrated by the comparison in Table 16–1 of results among poli-

---

[2] This is the procedure when the premium is level throughout the period of analysis. If the premium is not level, an equivalent level premium is determined by accumulating the premiums at interest to the end of the period and dividing the result by the factor stated in Step 4.

TABLE 16–1. Comparative Results by Traditional and Interest-Adjusted Methods for Ten Policies

Policy	Net Cost per $1,000, Traditional Method		Index per $1,000 by Interest-Adjusted Method (4%)	
	Net Cost	Rank	Index	Rank
A	$—3.43	1	$4.77	5
B	—3.17	2	4.76	4
C	—3.05	3	4.58	2
D	—2.92	4	4.87	6
E	—2.78	5	5.12	9
F	—2.49	6	4.74	3
G	—2.24	7	4.21	1
H	—2.22	8	5.60	10
I	—1.19	9	5.01	7
J	—1.18	10	5.06	8

cies issued by ten selected companies. These figures are per $1,000 for 20 years using a participating straight life policy of $25,000 amount, issued at male age 35.

The figures for the policies labeled A and I deserve special attention. By the traditional method, A appears to offer far and away the most attractive net cost. Policy I appears to be practically the least attractive. And the difference between these two (A and I) is indicated to be $2.24 per thousand per year, which is not trivial at all.

But the interest-adjusted method moves policy A down to fifth position and policy I up to seventh position, and indicates an annual difference between them of only 24¢ per thousand which clearly is too small to be a matter of concern.

TABLE 16–2. Data on Two of the Policies Exhibited in Table 16–1

	Policy A	Policy I
Premium	$ 23.03	$ 18.33
Premium less dividend:		
First year	21.89	17.43
Second year	21.47	17.41
Fifth year	20.19	16.59
Tenth year	18.01	15.10
Twentieth year	11.88	11.81
Twentieth year cash value	413.32	321.00

Table 16–2 contrasts the premiums, premiums less dividends, and 20th year cash values for policy A and policy I. The reason for the difference in ranking shown in Table 16–1 is that the traditional method and the interest-adjusted method give materially different appraisals of the extent to which the larger twentieth year value of policy A offsets the smaller net payments under policy I.

A few critics of the interest-adjusted method have erroneously said that the cost index it produces includes the interest that the purchaser is assumed to forgo by purchasing life insurance. The index contains no such element, as can readily be seen by applying the method to a bank account that pays exactly 4 percent interest.

If one deposits $10 a year at 4 percent interest compounded annually, the amount at the end of 20 years will be $309.69. In applying the interest-adjusted method one may think of the $10 a year as comparable to an annual premium, and the $309.69 as the corresponding twentieth year cash value.

The arithmetic of the five-step interest-adjusted method would then be as follows:

Step 1	Analysis period	20 years
Step 2	Interest rate used	4 percent
Step 3	Twentieth year value	$309.69
Step 4	Divide by 30.969	$10
Step 5	"Premium" less result of Step 4	Zero

This shows that the index contains no interest element at all, because otherwise the result of Step 5 would have been a positive amount.

Rationale of Comparison Methods
Other Than the Traditional Method

The interest-adjusted method does not add interest into the cost index; it uses interest as a measure of the differences in value of dollars paid by the policyowner or by the company at different times. For this reason some have said the method might better have been named the time-adjusted method, or the interest-weighted method.

The use of interest to differentiate payments in terms of their respective dates is common practice in commercial arithmetic. But in the case of life insurance premiums and benefits, time has a second significance that is not so frequently encountered in other financial transactions. This second one concerns the size of the probability that any particular payment will ever be made.

For example, consider the fifteenth year dividend illustrated for a particular policy. Its value is affected by the fact that its date of payment is fifteen years away. But also to be considered is that it will never be paid at all if, as is quite likely, the policy terminates by surrender, lapse, or death before the fifteenth year.

Several of the methods that have been suggested take this second feature into account. Prominent among such methods are those developed by Professor Joseph M. Belth, particularly the level price method and the benefits-premiums method or retention method.

Checklist of Factors Requiring Attention

Cost comparison is desirable and a prudent step for a life insurance purchaser to take. But it is important that he not become so engrossed in the results produced by any particular method that he fails to pay attention to the following considerations:

1. A cost index does not by itself constitute adequate comparison. It is not a sufficient substitute for examining the premiums charged and the detailed year-by-year pattern of cash values and dividends.

②The usual cost indices do not reflect differences in policy features and supplementary benefits that may be of material significance.

③Every known method of comparison has limitations which must be recognized and respected.

④The necessity for basing the comparison on current scale dividends—which are nearly certain to differ from those that will be paid—is an important limitation.

⑤Quoting from the final two sentences of the committee *Report:* "The purchase of a policy commands not only the dollar benefits stated in the policy but also, and most importantly, the services of the agent and the company that issues it. These services are of tremendous value to the policyholder; differences in the quality of these services are far more important than moderate differences in apparent cost."

COMPARING NEW CONTRACTS
THAT ARE DISSIMILAR

Term and Permanent Contracts

Thus far we have been discussing comparisons among policies that are of the same type—straight life policies, for example. When it comes to cost comparisons among policies not of the same type the mathematics may be different. But more vital than the arithmetic is recognition that policies of different types are designed to take care of different needs. A purchaser should give higher priority to fitting the policy to his circumstances than to finding the least costly type.

The choice between term insurance and straight life depends substantially upon considerations other than cost comparisons. Often the need is for a mixture of the two rather than a choice between them. When the needed amount and period of insurance have been determined as best they can be, the choice of policy plan hinges largely upon the extent to which the policyowner has the capacity and the desire to prepay future insurance costs. Yearly renewable term insurance involves no prepayment at all; single-payment life involves complete prepayment; and there are many choices between these extremes. To the extent, however, that cost comparison between term insurance and straight life is needed or sought, the procedure set forth many years ago by the distinguished actuary, M. Albert Linton, is available.

The Linton process compares the situations of two hypothetical life insurance purchasers, A and B. A purchases a straight life policy, pays premiums for, say, 20 years, applies dividends to reduce premiums and takes the cash value at the end of the period. B incurs each year the same dollar outlay as A, but B purchases decreasing term insurance and places the remainder of his outlay in an outside investment fund. The amount of term insurance each year is determined so that if B dies in that year, the sum of the life insurance death benefit and the investment fund will match the death benefit of A's straight life policy.

Thus we know how much B will deposit each year in his investment fund, i.e., A's straight life outlay less B's term insurance outlay. It then can be calculated what net rate of interest B must earn on his investment

A Term vs
whole life
(reduced to
term)

fund in order that his accumulated fund at the end of the period shall equal the cash value of A's policy.[3]

The result of this calculation is greatly influenced by the size of the term insurance cost that is used. The interpretation of the result hinges upon several considerations, including the size of the income tax to which B should be considered liable each year on the earnings of his outside fund (see Chapter 4).

Endowment and Whole Life Contracts

Comparison of endowment and whole life contracts may be made by any of several methods[4] used for comparing two whole life contracts. The interest-adjusted method produces trustworthy results if the endowment period is sufficiently long—say, 30 years or more—so that the differences between amounts at risk on the respective contracts are not too extreme. Otherwise the standard mortality cost method, a refinement of the interest-adjusted method described by J. Stanley Hill may be used.[5]

The traditional method should not be used. It almost invariably signals the higher premium policy as the more attractive of the two regardless of the true situation.

Participating and Nonparticipating Contracts

As already stated, comparisons between participating and nonparticipating policies are of limited validity because the conditions involved are different. But they can be made using the interest-adjusted method, or other methods except the traditional method.[6] The traditional method severely distorts the comparison because the patterns of payments by policy year differ so greatly.

On the other hand, illustrations offering nonparticipating life insurance have been known to distort the picture in the opposite direction by showing the traditional method results in conjunction with a supposed investment at compound interest of the difference between the participating and the nonparticipating premium. This is not a valid method of comparing the two because the traditional method is predicated upon a zero interest rate.

Collateral Contract Features

Policies of some companies provide supplementary benefits, such as disability premium waiver, or extra benefit if death is by accidental means, without charging an identifiable extra premium. It is necessary to take these into account in any comparison but this may not easily be done on a fair basis.

---

[3] This process is described and analyzed in the paper by Joseph M. Belth, "The Rate of Return on the Savings Element in Cash-Value Life Insurance," *Journal of Risk and Insurance,* Vol. xxxv, No. 4 (December 1968), p. 569.

[4] A list of methods with descriptions is contained in the *Report of the Joint Special Committee on Life Insurance Costs.*

[5] Society of Actuaries, *Transactions of the Society of Actuaries,* Vol. XXIII (1971), p. 289.

[6] A list of methods with descriptions is contained in the *Report of the Joint Special Committee on Life Insurance Costs.*

Difficulty arises because the provisions of those benefits may not be similar in the two companies concerned. Also an automatic benefit involves different rating considerations because it does not separate those who would have qualified for it from those who would not if it had been available separately.

Another of the comparison problems that arise is between companies that use age nearest birthday and those that use age last birthday for determining the premiums, dividends, and cash values. Any particular prospective purchaser should use the age that applies to him even though it differs between the companies. Analysts not concerned with individual situations would use the mean of adjacent ages for one of the policies, but should be careful not to do this if the policy is limited payment, e.g., life paid up at age 65.

COMPARING NEW CONTRACTS
WITH CONTRACTS IN FORCE

Nature of the Problem

A need for comparison of a new policy with one already in force arises when the policyowner is considering discontinuing a contract he already has and buying a new one. This is called a replacement, and is generally assumed to be contrary to the best interests of the policyowner.[7] In fact, recommending it usually earns the stigmatic sobriquet "twisting." It is widely, but erroneously, believed that state laws forbid replacement. What they forbid is the misrepresentation or incomplete comparison that occurs in many suggestions for replacement.

An array of warnings of those contemplating replacement is extensively used. One version of this list reads as follows:

1. The new policy is likely to be at a higher premium rate based upon the insured's then attained age.
2. Replacement of an old policy by a new one means that the policyowner must pay initial costs of writing the insurance a second time.
3. Existing policies often have more favorable provisions than new policies in such areas as settlement options and disability benefits.
4. Contestable and suicide provisions begin afresh in a new policy.

Disadvantages

In considering this list it should be noted that the significance of the first, and also of the second, is subject to the result of testing the arithmetic of any particular contemplated replacement. The third was important years ago but now is close to being obsolete. The fourth is of concern to rather a small proportion of policyowners.

Unquestionably, many replacements are inimical to the insured. These are likely to have been made because the policyowner believed he could invest the amount of his cash value more rewardingly than leaving it in

---

[7] As a deterrent or to help pay the duplication of acquisition costs, companies frequently pay reduced commissions on policies that replace existing insurance in the same company. But few, if any, apply this restriction to replacements of policies of other companies.

the hands of the insurance company, or because he wished to be rid of a policy loan, or because he was misled by a misguided or unscrupulous advisor.

But there are situations in which replacement of an old policy by a new may benefit the policyowner. One such case is that of moving from a relatively high-cost life insurance company to one with relatively low cost. Another may be to replace a policy for a large amount that was issued before the era of grading premiums by size. Another candidate for replacement analysis would be an old nonparticipating policy issued on a rate basis considerably more conservative than is available today. A fourth may involve some unusual legal situation, probably concerned with taxation or ownership.

Since it cannot be taken for granted that replacement is a mistake, it is necessary to have some method for making an arithmetical comparison. One reasonably helpful procedure is to make a series of comparisons, the first over a two-year period, the second over five years, the third over ten years. In each case the situation if the present policy is continued is compared with that in which a new policy, arbitrarily assumed to be for a face amount equal to the difference between the amount of the present policy and its cash value, is purchased.

A worksheet to accomplish this comparison might be somewhat as follows:

	Result after 2 Years	Result after 5 Years	Result after 10 Years
I. If Present Policy Is Retained			
1. Cash value, end of period			
2. Dividends during period	___	___	___
3. Total (1 + 2)			
4. Less outlay ($... per year)	___	___	___
5. Item 3 less Item 4	═══	═══	═══
II. If Policy Is Replaced			
1. Present cash value of present policy			
2. New policy, cash value, end of period			
3. New policy, dividends during period	___	___	___
4. Total (1 + 2 + 3)			
5. Less outlay ($... per year)	___	___	___
6. Item 4 less Item 5	═══	═══	═══

A comparison made in this fashion is not valid if the analysis period is long because no interest is taken into account. Often, however, the contrast is sufficiently great to make the merit of retaining or replacing obvious.

Regulation

Belief that improper replacement of existing insurance has recently become a more serious problem has caused numerous states to introduce or strengthen laws and administrative regulations designed to cope with the problem.

These laws and regulations do not prohibit replacements. They aim to make sure that the policyowner receives complete and accurate information about the disadvantages as well as the advantages of the replacement. They call for written and signed recommendations so that the responsibility for the proposal can readily be fixed. They require that the agent writing the new policy notify his company that replacement is contemplated. And they may require his company to notify the company whose policy is to be replaced.

CONCLUSION

One of the consumer's rights that is receiving more and more attention is the right to exercise intelligent choice among available products. Helping life insurance customers to enjoy that right is necessary but is not easily accomplished. Such help entails a willingness to furnish reliable comparative data whether or not many people are likely to take advantage of it. More and more useful information about policy costs and provisions and about life company performance is being made available by publishing houses and companies. The buying public should be made more aware of its existence.

An experienced buyer contemplating the purchase of a substantial amount of insurance may well be interested in checking company operating performance, as distinct from the cost position discussed throughout this chapter. This point was made by Alfred N. Guertin, F.S.A., in 1958:[8]

. . . . . how does the policyholder seek to find the company likely to produce the best net cost in the future? It seems to this writer that the answer lies in the fundamental operations of the company. If the firm already has an accumulated surplus which is at least average for the business in relation to its reserves, if the net return on its investments is higher than average, if its mortality experience compares favorably with that of its competitors, and if it is economically managed, he has reasonable assurance of good results. . . . . (T)he best asset of any company is its management; and when you buy management, you seldom lose.

The problem is how to put this excellent advice to practical use. From published sources it is difficult to compare expenses satisfactorily, and it is nearly impossible to compare mortality experiences. The ratio of surplus to reserves is potentially misleading without thoroughly informed interpretation. Even investment yield comparisons are beset with pitfalls. The complexity of life insurance operations is a challenge to the business which, with the aid of independent evaluators, has a responsibility to furnish usable data for appraisal purposes.

SELECTED REFERENCES

A. M. Best Company. *Best's Flitcraft Compend.* Morristown, N.J. Published annually.

---

[8] Alfred N. Guertin, "Price Competition in the Life Insurance Business," *The Journal of Insurance,* Vol. XXV, No. 1 (July 1958), p. 1.

_____. *Best's Insurance Reports* (*Life-Health*). Morristown, N.J. Published annually.

Belth, Joseph M. *Life Insurance: A Consumer's Handbook.* Bloomington, Ind.: Indiana University Press, 1973.

_____. "A Note on the Interest-Adjusted Method," *CLU Journal*, Vol. XXV, No. 4 (October 1971), p. 74.

_____. "The Rate of Return on the Savings Element in Cash-Value Life Insurance," *Journal of Risk and Insurance.* Vol. XXXV, No. 4 (December 1968), p. 569.

_____. "The Relationship between Benefits and Premiums in Life Insurance," *Journal of Risk and Insurance.* Vol. XXXVI, No. 1 (March 1969), p. 19.

_____. *The Retail Price Structure in American Life Insurance.* Bloomington, Ind.: Bureau of Business Research, Graduate School of Business, Indiana University, 1966.

Guertin, Alfred N. "Price Competition in the Life Insurance Business," *The Journal of Insurance.* Vol. XXV, No. 1 (July 1958), p. 1.

Hart, The Hon. Philip A. "Life Insurance—The Consumer Perspective," *Proceedings of the Legal Section, American Life Convention* (October 1968), p. 252.

Moorhead, E. J. "Comparing the Cost of Life Insurance Benefits," *CLU Journal*, Vol. XXV, No. 1 (January 1971).

Moorhead, E. J., and Belth, Joseph M. "A Practical Improvement on the Traditional Method of Comparing Net Costs of Participating Life Insurance Policies," *Journal of Risk and Insurance.* Vol. XXXII, No. 4 (December 1965), p. 639.

National Underwriter Company. *Cost Facts on Life Insurance.* Cincinnati, Ohio, 1969.

_____. *Cost Facts on Life Insurance—Interest-Adjusted Method.* Cincinnati, Ohio, 1970.

_____. *Life Rates and Data.* Published annually.

Report of the Joint Special Committee on Life Insurance Costs. 1970. Available from Institute of Life Insurance, New York.

Schwarzschild, Stuart. "Rates of Return on the Investment Differentials between Life Insurance Policies," *Journal of Risk and Insurance,* Vol. XXXV, No. 4 (December 1968), p. 583.

Society of Actuaries. "Individual Life Insurance," *Transactions of the Society of Actuaries,* Vol. XIV, Part II. Discussions (1962), pp. D353–56.

_____. "Life Insurance Net Cost Comparison," *Transactions of the Society of Actuaries,* Vol. XXI, Part II. Discussions (1969), pp. D185–218.

_____. "Net Cost Comparisons," *Transactions of the Society of Actuaries,* Vol. XXII, Part II. Discussions (1970), p. D701.

_____. "Premiums and Dividends for Ordinary Insurance," *Transactions of the Society of Actuaries,* Vol. XX, Part II. Discussions (1968), pp. D266–74.

part III

Variable Life Insurance, Variable Annuities, and Mutual Funds

THE INSTITUTION of life insurance has assumed a leadership role in providing broadened financial services to its customers. Particularly noteworthy have been new equity-based products and services to meet the need of individuals in their personal financial planning, and of businesses and professional bodies in their arrangements for retirement, profit sharing, and other such needs. Part III discusses three types of equity-based products now available or soon to be offered by a growing number of life insurance companies and life underwriters.

These products have evolved in response to a number of market forces including rising discretionary income levels, heightened awareness of the need to protect purchasing power in the face of inflation, and greater consumer awareness of alternative forms of personal savings and investment.

17

Variable Life Insurance

By HARRY WALKER and JEROME S. GOLDEN

ONE OF THE MOST important changes in the investment climate and habits of American institutions and private investors over the past two decades has been the coming of age of equities as popular investment media. The increasing affluence and sophistication of consumers and the broadened acceptance of equities by institutional and private investors are economic facts of life today.

Variable life insurance (VLI) is a new product being developed in the insurance business, designed to combine the traditional protection and savings functions of life insurance with the growth potential associated with equities, particularly common stock. As defined in this chapter, variable life insurance is that form of life insurance contract under which the benefits, payable upon death or surrender, and/or the premiums vary with the investment performance of the assets derived from the sale of those contracts. As such, VLI must be distinguished from life insurance contracts with benefits dependent on some index as, for example, the Consumer Price Index (CPI). The experience of 1969, in which the cost of living as measured by the CPI rose by more than 6 percent while at the same time there was a bearish stock market, dramatizes this difference. Variable life insurance, so defined, would not provide a guarantee of an increase in benefits corresponding to an increase in the cost of living, as would an index contract tied to the CPI.

DEVELOPMENT IN OTHER COUNTRIES

Although a relatively new concept in the United States, variable life insurance has been sold for a number of years in Europe and, more recently, in Canada. Variable life insurance was first introduced in the Netherlands in the mid-1950s by the insurance company DeWaerdye, Ltd. The "Dutch" design of a VLI contract has premiums, death benefits, and cash values expressed in units with the value of the unit reflecting the investment performance of a fund invested in common stocks. Thus, both the premiums and benefits are variable. Endowment-type plans constitute most of such variable life insurance in force. Since 1966, nearly all Dutch companies have entered the variable life market, although until recently VLI accounted for only about 1 percent of insurance in force in Holland. This lack of sales success is due partly to the sales commission basis for variable life insurance which provides lower initial commissions than for conventional life insurance contracts. In addition, DeWaerdye was the only company offering VLI before 1966, and only lately has the Dutch public shown an interest in common stock investments.

Different forms of variable or equity-linked life insurance were developed in the United Kingdom in the early 1960s. Under one popular fixed-premium plan, a specified portion of each premium is invested in the shares of a "unit trust" (comparable to a mutual fund in the United States), and the remainder provides for expenses and decreasing term coverage. The death benefit equals (*a*) the value of the shares held plus (*b*) the sum of the remaining premiums. In addition, a minimum death benefit guarantee of all or a percentage of the total premiums payable over the intended term is usually provided. The benefit at maturity is the value of the shares held, less a deduction for a potential tax liability on capital appreciation reflected in the value of the shares.

A second common plan in the United Kingdom is the endowment assurance policy. Under this plan, as each premium is paid, an amount equal to (*a*) the basic sum assured, divided by (*b*) the premium payment period of the policy, is deemed to purchase shares of a unit trust. Dividend income earned on these shares is retained by the insurer and only capital gains (losses) are reflected in share values. The death benefit is the basic sum assured plus any appreciation (depreciation) in the shares, while the maturity benefit is simply the value of the shares. A guaranteed minimum death benefit equal to the basic sum assured is common. Other funding media used by British companies in connection with equity-linked life insurance include separate accounts maintained by insurance companies and, more recently, property bond or real estate funds.

Equity-linked insurance in the United Kingdom has enjoyed considerable success in the past few years. Approximately 25 percent of new life business in 1969 was equity-linked, and today more than 90 companies offer some form of variable life insurance. A great deal of the success of variable life in the United Kingdom can be attributed to the liberal tax allowance granted on life insurance premiums (as high as 40 percent for personal income tax purposes). It is possible, therefore, that under a plan providing for the purchase of unit trust (mutual fund type) shares plus decreasing term insurance, the tax benefit may be greater than the mortality and expense costs of the plan, thus providing "free" insurance coverage.

The early development of variable life insurance in Canada was largely influenced by the British. In 1967, a combination life insurance-equity investment contract was first introduced into Canada by a British company. In recent years, the development of variable contracts has been swift and, in many ways, different from that in the United Kingdom. Among various Canadian plans are:

1. A conventional participating contract with dividends used to purchase units in the insurance company's separate account, which would be invested primarily in equities.
2. A participating contract where a specified portion of the basic policy reserve is invested in the separate account and the dividends, dependent on the performance of both the general and separate investment accounts, are applied to purchase paid-up fixed dollar insurance (positive or negative).
3. A form of equity endowment with certain guaranteed minimum death benefits and maturity benefits.
4. A nonparticipating contract with the initial face amount guaranteed, where a specified portion of the basic policy reserve is invested in the separate account and the investment increments are applied to purchase paid-up insurance (positive or negative) having the same portion of the reserve invested in the separate account as the basic contract.
5. A participating contract with the initial face amount guaranteed where all or a specified portion of the basic policy reserve is invested in the separate account, and the dividends, dependent on the performance of both the general and separate investment accounts, are applied to purchase paid-up variable insurance (positive or negative).

Today, there are over 30 insurance companies in Canada offering some form of variable insurance. Several Canadian insurance companies have indicated that variable life sales account for about 15 to 30 percent of new business production.

EARLY DEVELOPMENT IN THE UNITED STATES

Because of the still unresolved questions of state and federal regulation, the general pattern in the life insurance business in the United States has been in the marketing of cost-of-living and index plans, rather than variable or equity-linked life insurance. Under some of the cost-of-living plans the policyowner bears the inflation risk. One such plan is the one-year term cost-of-living rider where additional term insurance, reflecting increases in the Consumer Price Index, is issued automatically each year on the anniversary date of the contract. An added annual premium, as specified in the contract, is payable for this extra insurance. There also are plans where the insurance company assumes the inflation risk (but on a limited basis only) and charges for the additional cost-of-living benefits through higher gross premiums or lower dividends. An example is a fixed-premium whole life contract, under which the death benefit varies with the CPI, subject to a maximum death benefit equal to twice the initial face amount.

The disadvantage in the above approaches is, of course, the relatively high cost of coverage. Variable life insurance, under the proper design, can serve as a viable alternative by providing the guarantees of a minimum death benefit and the possibility of increased benefits if the separate account, invested in equities, experiences a favorable investment return.

CONTRACT DESIGN

Except for a few special situations linked with corporate pension plans, variable life insurance has not been marketed in the United States as of early 1973. The analysis in this chapter reflects design and operational aspects as perceived at this stage of the development of VLI.

Alternative Approaches

A number of alternative contract designs have been suggested. Growing interest has been shown toward those with the following characteristics:

Fixed premium. Many insurance authorities believe that a fixed premium is necessary for the successful marketing of VLI in the United States. Some U.S. companies, however, may offer the fully variable "Dutch" design.

Guaranteed minimum death benefit. Most insurance experts consider it essential that a VLI contract include a guarantee that the death benefit in any year will never be less than the initial face amount.

One contract. Most of the discussion within U.S. life insurance has indicated a preference for a single integrated VLI contract, which is not manifestly separable into its protection and investment elements. This is in contrast to some of the contracts being offered in Canada and the United Kingdom.

Even within this limited framework there are many ways of reflecting investment performance in the contract benefits. The essential feature of all of these designs, however, can be summarized as follows:

As in the case of fixed-benefit life insurance (FBLI), the calculation of the premium rate, tabular reserves, and tabular cash values will require the use of an assumed rate of return on investment. The death benefit will vary to reflect, actuarially, the extent to which the net actual return in the separate account is above or below the assumed rate. The net actual return in the separate account will reflect dividend and other investment income earned, plus capital appreciation of stocks held less capital depreciation, and less any deductions for taxes, investment expenses, and contingencies. The death benefit may increase or decrease, but in no event will it be reduced below the initial face amount.

The best way to demonstrate differences in various designs is to show how the death benefit and reserve under different contract designs would have varied assuming several periods of historical investment performance. Table 17–1 presents illustrative death benefits and reserves under three proposed whole life contract designs, assuming that a contract with an initial death benefit of $1,000 was issued to a standard male age 35 in July of 1925 and 1945. The investment performance assumed in the illustrations was based on Standard and Poor's 500 Stock Price Index with dividends reinvested, with a deduction at the annual rate of 1 percent for investment expenses and contingencies, and with no deduction for taxes. Net level premium reserves, based on the 1958 CSO mortality table and

TABLE 17–1. Illustrative* Death Benefits and Reserves under Three Proposed Variable Whole Life Insurance Contract Designs (male issue age 35, $1,000 initial death benefit)

End of July	Death Benefits			Reserves†			Attained Age
	Contract A	Contract B	Contract C	Contract A	Contract B	Contract C	
			Issued End of July 1925				
1926....	$ 1,151	$1,151	$1,007	$ 16	$ 16	$ 17	36
1931....	1,282	841‡	974‡	116	76	80	41
1936....	1,553	1,352	1,126	269	234	233	46
1941....	1,076	901‡	948‡	281	236	234	51
1946....	1,992	1,664	1,405	702	587	589	56
1951....	2,714	2,118	1,815	1,206	941	969	61
1956....	6,311	4,446	3,881	3,368	2,373	2,553	66
1961....	8,384	5,294	5,097	5,164	3,261	3,704	71
1966....	10,088	5,758	6,105	6,957	3,971	4,778	76
1970....	9,183	4,860	5,564	6,825	3,612	4,556	80
			Issued End of July 1945				
1946....	$ 1,224	$1,224	$1,010	$ 18	$ 18	$ 18	36
1951....	1,669	1,484	1,110	151	134	136	41
1956....	3,881	2,680	1,679	673	465	492	46
1961....	5,155	2,835	2,061	1,348	741	820	51
1966....	6,201	2,877	2,397	2,187	1,014	1,170	56
1970....	5,645	2,343	2,205	2,406	999	1,188	60

* Investment Basis—Standard and Poor's 500 Stock Price Index, dividends reinvested, annual deduction of 1 percent for investment expenses and contingencies, no deduction for taxes.
† Reserve Basis—1958 CSO Mortality Table and 3 percent interest.
‡ Minimum death benefit of $1,000 would be payable.
Source: Data provided by the New York Life Insurance Company.

a 3 percent assumed net investment return rate, were assumed for each design.

Contract A is the fully variable "Dutch" design under which death benefits *and* premiums vary proportionately. Thus, increases in benefits will be accompanied by increases in the amount of premiums to be paid. Contract B is a fixed-premium VLI design under which the reserves per $1,000 of death benefit are exactly the same as the reserves per $1,000 for a corresponding fixed benefit contract.[1] Contract C is also a fixed-premium design which, in effect, uses the excess of the net actual investment return over the assumed rate to purchase paid-up variable life insurance (positive or negative). This feature assures that, regardless of past investment performance, the death benefit at any time will never be reduced below its then current level so long as the net rate of return in the separate account is thereafter at least equal to the assumed rate of return.

These are not the only designs possible but they are included to show illustrative patterns of death benefits and reserves. It may be noted that

[1] This contract design, commonly referred to as the New York Life design, was described in a paper presented to the Society of Actuaries in November of 1969 by Messrs. Fraser, Miller and Sternhell of the New York Life Insurance Company.

a design productive of higher reserves is likely to produce higher cash values.

Special Contract Provisions

In addition to a contract provision describing how the investment performance will be reflected in the variable death benefits, there will be other contract provisions designed specifically for VLI.

Under most VLI designs, the investment performance in the separate account also will be reflected in cash surrender values. While there will be a floor on the death benefit, it is unlikely that there will be guarantees as to the amount of cash value available during the insured's lifetime. The additional cost for this latter guarantee would be substantial since the insurance company would be exposed to the likelihood that policyowners (excluding, of course, those in very bad health) would demand the minimum guaranteed cash value in times of declining market values, when the assets of the separate account would not be sufficient to meet such a demand.

The reduced paid-up and extended term insurance nonforfeiture options may be offered on either a fixed or variable basis. Although there has been some debate as to whether any minimum death benefit will be guaranteed under these options if offered on a variable basis, it is questionable whether it is possible to do so at a reasonable cost.

While the inclusion of a policy loan provision in a fixed-benefit life insurance contract is a desirable feature, the inclusion of such a policy loan provision in a variable life insurance contract poses many problems. Several alternative approaches have been suggested. Under one approach, the value of the loan would reflect the investment experience of the separate account. This type of provision, however, would enable the policyowner to "play the market" so that repayment of the loan under certain circumstances might be less than the original amount borrowed. Another approach would involve a fixed-interest rate loan in which the cash value of the variable contract is the collateral. Since the amount of cash value of the contract might be variable, there would have to be limits on the ratio of the value of the outstanding loan to the cash value, and the insurer necessarily would retain the right either to call the loan or convert the VLI contract to a fixed-benefit contract. It should be noted that the National Association of Insurance Commissioners (NAIC) Model Variable Contract Law and Regulation, described later in the chapter, does not require a policy loan provision.

In lieu of a policy loan provision it is feasible to include a partial withdrawal or surrender provision, in which the amount of insurance coverage is reduced, with or without a reduction in the amount of premium. Repayment under this type of provision would be subject to evidence of insurability because the increase in death benefit would be larger than the cash amount repaid. This type of provision enables the insured to obtain funds without surrendering all his insurance coverage.

The NAIC model regulation requires that VLI policies include provisions for a grace period and reinstatement, recognizing in the model provisions the variable nature of the contract. The provision for a grace period would permit the insurer to reflect the actual date of payment in determining the benefits under the contract. In practice, however, most insurers probably would include a grace provision similar to those in fixed-benefit contracts and would not reflect the actual date of premium payment in determining benefits. The amount required to reinstate specified in the model provision reflects the variable nature of the contract and would be the greater of (a) all overdue premiums and the payment of any other indebtedness, with interest at a maximum of 6 percent compounded annually; or (b) 110 percent of the increase in the cash surrender value resulting from reinstatement.

In general, contract provisions under proposed variable contracts are reasonably consistent with existing fixed-benefit life insurance provisions modified, where necessary, to reflect the variable nature of the contracts.

GROSS PREMIUMS

Many factors must be considered by the insurer in setting gross premium rates for a variable life insurance contract. Different considerations are involved, of course, for VLI issued on a nonparticipating basis as compared to VLI issued on a participating basis. The distinction between participating and nonparticipating VLI relates only to expense and mortality experience, since the investment experience in any event will be reflected in contract benefits. Under both types, however, the following factors must be considered:

Assumed Rate of Return. The choice of an assumed rate of return has an important effect not only on the level of death benefits but on the level of gross premiums. A lower assumed rate of return for a particular contract design enhances the possibility of increases in death benefits and lessens the possibility of decreases in death benefits, while increasing the level of premiums. Typical rates mentioned have been 3 percent and 3½ percent.

Asset Charge. The insurer will make a charge against the assets to cover investment management fees, expense and mortality risks, and contingencies. The level of the charge will affect the level of the benefits provided, and will be considered in setting gross premiums.

Mortality. There is little reason to think that the mortality experience should be any different for VLI than for fixed-benefit life insurance. Consideration must be given, however, to the potential for increased death benefits, particularly for substandard risks.

Expenses. Expenses are a most difficult area in which to make predictions. The reflection of investment performance in death benefits and cash values, the additional notification procedures and reports, and the more involved accounting methods require a highly developed, integrated data processing system from the start. Substantial education and training expenses will be incurred. The commission and sales related expenses obviously will depend upon the compensation structure, discussed more fully in a later section.

Persistency. There has been some thought that persistency may not be as good under variable benefit products as under comparable fixed-benefit products, with stock market performance being a significant factor. The inclusion of a minimum death benefit guarantee and of a partial surrender or withdrawal provision may help to alleviate some of the potential problems in this area.

Cost of the Minimum Death Benefit. The cost of guaranteeing the minimum death benefit depends to a great extent on the contract design, the investment strategy of the separate account and, naturally, on the behavior of the stock market. The determination of the risk premium for this benefit is generally based on a method of simulating future stock market performance, using as a basis the past history of market trends. Literally thousands of possible patterns of fluctuation in the stock market over the lifetime of the insured may be considered. The risk premium will be charged as part of the gross premium, as a reduction in dividends, or as part of the asset charge.

Generally, the gross premiums for a nonparticipating VLI contract, with a minimum death benefit equal to the initial face amount, would be expected to be higher than those for a corresponding fixed-benefit contract for the same face amount. This relationship is not unreasonable, since a VLI contract with a minimum death benefit guarantee will provide death benefits which are never less than those of the fixed-benefit contract, and may be higher. On the other hand, premiums for a participating VLI contract may be about the same or only slightly higher than those for a participating fixed-benefit contract for the same face amount. Again, death benefits under participating VLI will be at least as great as those under the fixed-benefit contract, and possibly higher, although dividends may be lower in the absence of an interest component in the dividend formula.

UNDERWRITING AND ADMINISTRATIVE ASPECTS

In designing underwriting rules for variable life insurance, the insurer must consider the potential for increased death benefits under the VLI designs. Rules used for fixed-benefit life insurance may not be completely applicable, especially in the area of underwriting substandard risks. Under some designs, where large increases in death benefits in the early years are possible with favorable investment performance, the underwriter may need to reflect that possibility in underwriting impairments where the increased risk is in the early contract years. The questions of setting retention limits and in designing reinsurance arrangements must be studied carefully in connection with variable life.

The administration of a variable life contract is more complex than that for a fixed-benefit contract. The following is a partial list of the administrative functions and the impact of the variable features on such functions:

Accounting. Variable life insurance operations will involve the maintenance of two investment accounts—the company's general account and a separate account. There probably will be a continuous flow of transactions between the two accounts. For example, gross premiums under a VLI contract could be credited to the general account, and thus net premiums would have to be transferred from the general to the separate account.

Reporting to Policyowners. The NAIC model regulation requires that policyowners be mailed annually after the first year a statement of the dollar amount of their death benefit as of a date not more than four months previous to the mailing. In addition, the insurer is required to send the policyowner a statement of the investments held in the separate account.

Payment of Claims. The payment of death benefits may involve additional calculations for VLI depending upon how often the death benefit is varied. It is expected that death benefits under most designs would vary at least annually, with some designs having death benefits which may vary as often as daily. Cash values probably would vary daily to reflect the most current market values in order to avoid investment antiselection against the insurer.

Reinstatements and Changes. As indicated earlier, the reinstatement provision for VLI has been modified to reflect the variable nature of the contract. Contract changes involving variable life insurance will likewise reflect the variable features. An unresolved question is whether companies entering the VLI market will make changes from existing fixed benefit to variable life insurance on a basis that involves no new acquisition costs to the policyowners and no greater compensation to the agent than if the original policy were not changed.

STATE AND FEDERAL REGULATION

There are three legal and regulatory areas requiring special attention before variable life insurance can be marketed satisfactorily on a broad basis in the United States: (1) the overriding question of regulation under the federal securities laws must be resolved, (2) most state insurance laws will require amendment, and (3) changes may be needed in the life insurance company federal income tax law.

The federal securities laws in question are the Securities Act of 1933, the Securities Exchange Act of 1934, and the Investment Company Act of 1940. Among other things, the 1933 act requires that securities offered or sold in interstate commerce or through the mails be registered with the Securities and Exchange Commission (SEC), and that prospectuses be provided; the 1934 act requires the registration of salesmen selling unlisted securities and regulates their sales practices; and the 1940 act regulates investment companies and governs the sales load on securities issued by them. The life insurance business has filed a petition with the SEC urging the SEC to decide not to assert jurisdiction over a defined class of variable life insurance contracts so designed that it is clear that their basic and predominant purpose is to provide protection against death. These contracts would have the following characteristics:

1. The contract must provide lifetime insurance coverage. This would exclude endowment contracts.

2. The contract must guarantee that the death benefit payable at any time will never be less than the initial death benefit, no matter how adverse the investment experience of the separate account.
3. The death benefit in any contract year must be no less than a stated multiple of the gross premium payable in that year by a person who meets standard underwriting requirements. This would avoid the issuance of policies with a very short premium paying period, where the investment element might be considered the predominant element of the contract. It would also preclude artificially high premiums with a built-in element intended solely for investment.
4. The entire contract must be subject to regulation under the state insurance laws, including any required approvals by the state insurance commissioners.

The industry petition to the SEC states that a variable life insurance contract satisfying these conditions should not be subjected to the federal securities laws. The investment element of such a contract (i.e., the reserves and cash values), it is argued, is incidental and subordinate to the death benefit element and should be viewed only as a by-product of the level premium method of charging for coverage against the risk of death which increases with advancing age.

Public hearings dealing with these matters were held by the SEC over a two-month period from April to June 1972. Many witnesses testified and a record of over 2,300 pages of testimony and hundreds of pages of exhibits and other data were developed. On January 31, 1973, the Commission announced its determination on the regulation of variable life insurance that satisfies the conditions described above, as follows:[2]

(1) The investment character of variable life contracts would make them securities so that any public offering of the type of contracts contemplated in the hearings would have to be registered under the Securities Act (1933 Act).

(2) People selling these variable life contracts generally would have to register as broker/dealers under the Securities Exchange Act (1934 Act).

(3) The separate account of a company engaged in issuing and selling these variable life contracts would fall under the definition of an investment company under the Investment Company Act (1940 Act). However, the Commission determined to exempt by rule such accounts from the elaborate regulatory requirements of the Act in deference to state regulation of insurance and because of complex administrative problems that would arise in providing the substantial exemptions from the Act that would be necessary to make feasible operations of these accounts.

(4) An insurance company or other entity providing investment advice incidental to the issuance of variable life contracts would be an investment adviser under the Investment Advisers Act. However, the Commission determined to exempt by rule from the Act insurance companies or affiliated companies acting as advisers to these accounts essentially for the reasons cited in adopting the Investment Company Act exemption.

---

[2] See Appendix H for full text of Commission's release on policy on variable life insurance policies.

As of this writing, no companies are offering variable life insurance that would be affected by this ruling and, thus, it is difficult to assess the impact of the Commission's rules on VLI.[3] Most insurance executives, however, reacted to the SEC regulation with cautious optimism.

In December of 1969, the National Association of Insurance Commissioners approved a Model Variable Contract Law encompassing variable life insurance and amended the Model Variable Contract Regulation so as to include provisions regulating variable life insurance. Among other points, the model law and model regulation for variable contracts require that grace period, reinstatement and nonforfeiture provisions be included in variable life contracts, with such provisions appropriately modified to recognize the differences between variable and fixed-benefit contracts. Also, the method of calculating cash values in a variable life contract is to be made consistent with the procedures defined in the standard nonforfeiture laws. Moreover, the model regulation requires that a contract be so designed that expense and mortality results will not affect adversely the dollar amount of variable benefits or values under the contract.

As of May 1972, over 20 states had passed legislation which would authorize the sale of variable life insurance. In addition, the statutory and/or regulatory authority in some other jurisdictions appears broad enough to encompass the issuance of variable life insurance. The existence of the model law and model regulation, it is hoped, will result in a good degree of uniformity among the various jurisdictions.

The federal income tax aspects of variable life insurance have great significance both for the individual policyowner and for the insurance company. For the policyowner, under current law, the death benefits under fixed-benefit life insurance are excluded from the gross income of the beneficiary. It is felt that this, as well as other provisions of the law regarding taxation at the policyowner level, will apply to variable life policyowners. As far as income taxation at the insurance company level is concerned the picture is less clear. The Life Insurance Company Income Tax Act of 1959 and the amendments thereto were written at a time when there was no thought of variable life insurance being issued in this country. Careful attention must be given to possible changes in the law that may be necessary to assure reasonable tax treatment with respect to variable life insurance.

OUTLOOK

With respect to consumers, the appeal of variable life insurance, especially with a guaranteed minimum death benefit, should be fairly widespread. It should attract those insurance buyers who desire a life insurance contract with death benefits responsive to changes in the market value of equities.

---

[3] In 1972, the Aetna Variable Life Insurance Company began selling VLI to certain tax-qualified group pension plans. Since the offerings were not made to individual purchasers, there was no requirement as to registration under the Securities Act.

Advocates of VLI believe that companies which successfully market variable life insurance would increase the percentage of permanent insurance in relation to term coverages, minimize policy loan problems, and improve their recruiting and retention of agents. Some observers take the contrary view and observe that VLI can present many difficulties. For example, the net investment return in excess of the assumed rate of return in a variable contract will not be available to meet other contingencies and, in the case of a stock company, to increase stockholders' equity. Also the developmental costs will be substantial and the administrative costs may be greater than those for fixed-benefit insurance. Furthermore, acquainting the agent as well as the prospective buyer with the new product will be a major undertaking and will require a considerable investment in human and financial resources.

There is also the important question of the transfer of capital invested primarily in bonds and mortgages into equities. It is expected, however, that the introduction of VLI would in all likelihood have only a minor effect on the company's cash flow for many years and that the company would have ample opportunity to adjust its investment policy to the new situation. The amounts available for investment arising from fixed-benefit life insurance would be reduced somewhat in the early years of operation. The results will vary from company to company, depending upon the present distribution of fixed-benefit life insurance, the expected rate of growth of that business, and the anticipated rate of growth of variable life insurance.

A variable life insurance contract with fixed premiums and with a floor on the death benefit essentially will include the features of fixed-benefit life insurance except for a guarantee of the amount of cash value, and will at the same time give the policyowner an opportunity to participate in the growth of the economy by having assets supporting reserves under his contract invested in equities. It should appeal to the buyer of life insurance who wants the guarantees as to death benefit inherent in fixed-benefit life insurance and who is willing to forgo the guarantee of a stated cash value for the possibility of enhanced death benefits and cash values if investment experience is favorable. In time, variable life insurance may comprise a significant portion of the life insurance business sold in the United States.

SELECTED REFERENCES

Bragg, John M. and Stonecipher, David A.   "Life Insurance Based on the Consumer Price Index," *Transactions of the Society of Actuaries,* Vol. 22, No. 64 (1970).

Fraser, J. C., Miller, W. N., and Sternhell, C. M.   "Analysis of Basic Actuarial Theory for Fixed Premium Variable Benefit Life Insurance," *Transactions of the Society of Actuaries,* Vol. 21, No. 61 (1969).

Miller, Walter N.   "Variable Life Insurance Product Design," *The Journal of Risk and Insurance,* Vol. 38, No. 4 (December 1971).

Rosenbloom, Samuel.   "DeWaerdye Experience to Date," *Proceedings of the Conference of Actuaries in Public Practice,* Vol. 19 (1969–1970), pp. 317–21.

Sibigtroth, Joseph C. "The New York Life Approach to Variable Life Insurance," *Transactions XIXth International Congress of Actuaries* (1972).

Turner, Samuel H. "Equity-based Life Insurance in the United Kingdom," *Transactions of the Society of Actuaries*, Vol. 23, No. 67 (1971).

University of Pennsylvania, Wharton School of Finance and Commerce. *Variable Life Insurance: Current Issues and Developments*. Philadelphia, Pa., 1971.

Walker, H. "Some Reflections on the Development of Variable Life Insurance in the United States," *Transactions XIXth International Congress of Actuaries* (1972).

————. "Variable Life Insurance," *Transactions of the Society of Actuaries*, Vol. 22, Nos. 62A and 62B (1970), pp. D143–90.

18

Variable Annuities—
Principles and Practices

By PAUL A. CAMPBELL

THE DEVELOPMENT of variable annuities in the United States has been one of the more dramatic evolutions experienced in the insurance business. Insurance companies have committed substantial financial resources in developing variable annuity products, complying with federal and state regulation, and developing marketing skills. As a result of these efforts, the variable annuity has emerged as a unique insurance product and a valuable component of financial planning.

This chapter will describe how variable annuities meet needs for financial security, how the product development has been affected by philosophical and regulatory climates, and the role variable annuities can play in consumer service and corporate growth.

NATURE OF VARIABLE ANNUITIES

For many decades, the traditional concept of retirement security reflected the desire for an adequate income at retirement, in relation to salary earned during the working lifetime. Pension planning aimed at a level of income which, with social security benefits, might produce a retirement income of about 50 percent of annual earnings related to the level of earnings just prior to retirement.

Personal savings as well as insurance programs tended to be aimed at fixed retirement income or guaranteed settlement options, at levels geared to current spending patterns. The insurance business thrived on its unquestioned ability, through strict investment and reserve regulations, to guarantee levels of income.

Beginning in the early 1950s, more and more pension planners recognized that planning in terms of fixed-dollar levels alone might not be sufficient, and great significance was accorded the factor of inflation. Historical Consumer Price Index statistics demonstrate the erosion of the purchasing power of fixed-dollar pension benefits:

Year	Consumer Price Index	Purchasing Power
1940	48.4	1.00
1945	62.7	.77
1950	83.8	.58
1955	92.3	.52
1960	103.1	.47
1965	109.9	.44
1966	113.1	.43
1967	116.3	42
1968	121.2	.40
1969	127.7	.38
1970	135.3	.36

Today the phenomenon of inflation generally has been accepted. Methods of government financing, taxation, and subsidization; the implications of defense, poverty, and space programs; and private developments in areas of cost-plus contracts and wage agreements—all suggest that some amount of inflation probably will continue for the foreseeable future and have an impact on the savings and retirement plans of individuals.

Variable Annuity Concept

Variable annuities offer a fresh approach to retirement planning. They provide for the investment of contributions in a segregated portfolio of equity securities. Here they accumulate during the annuitant's working years and are subsequently used to purchase a lifetime income at a designated retirement date. Both the cash values and the retirement income purchased with the proceeds reflect the performance of the invested funds, rising or falling as the market values of the funds' securities increase or decrease.

The basis underlying the variable annuity concept is the historical long-range relationship between the cost of living and the investment performance of diversified portfolios of common stocks. Although short-term patterns reveal dissimilar and sometimes even opposite movements, the overall trend supports the conclusion that equity investments offer at least a partial answer to the inflation problem. Figure 18–1 illustrates the historical relationship.

Early Variable Annuity Plans

Detailed studies, over many historical time periods, were conducted by variable annuity pioneers to demonstrate the comparative purchasing power of annuities invested entirely in equities, entirely in fixed dollars, and in a balanced program. The most widely circulated report was prepared by Teachers Insurance and Annuity Association which showed equity investments to be more effective than fixed-dollar programs in maintaining purchasing power, but subject to downside risks even in periods of rising prices. It concluded that a balanced program, partially in fixed income and partially in equity investments offers the best possibility of income that is both free from wild fluctuations and protected from serious erosion by inflation.

The College Retirement Equities Fund (CREF), commonly regarded as the first variable annuity in the United States, was established in 1952 as a structural companion to Teachers Insurance and Annuity Association (TIAA). The combination is referred to as TIAA-CREF. One of the most prominent characteristics of the CREF plan is its success in meeting its objectives. Accumulation unit values have increased fourfold in the first 20 years, and annuity unit values have more than tripled in that period.

FIGURE 18–1.   Comparison of Industrial Stock Prices and the Cost of Living, 1900–70

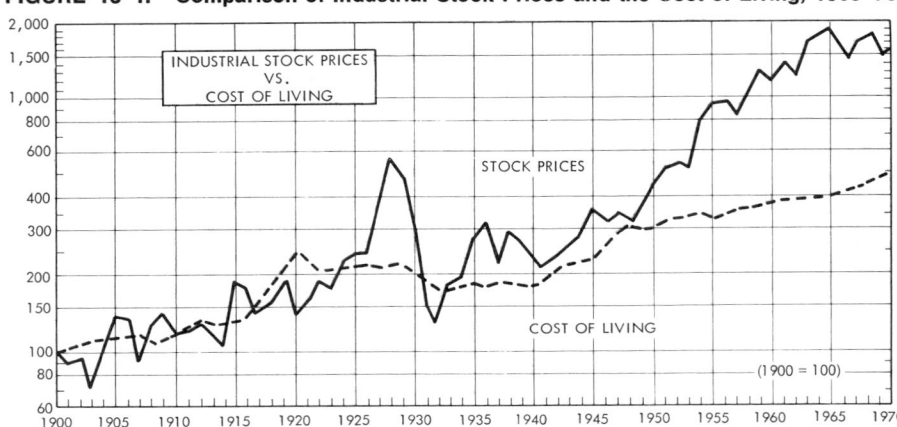

Sources: Chart, Wiesenberger Financial Services; data, Dow-Jones Industrial Stock Average; Consumer Price Index, compiled by Bureau of Labor Statistics, U.S. Department of Labor.

It is also important to recognize the significant role, both historical and current, played by noninsured, trusteed variable annuities. While insurance companies were prevented until the early 1960s from selling variable annuities, due to jurisdictional disputes with the Securities and Exchange Commission, many large firms established equity pension plans on a trusteed basis. The Long Island Lighting Company was one of the first, and the current list of major firms includes a significant number of major corporations.

The scope of the variable annuity has broadened greatly since its pioneers first advanced it as a means of enhancing retirement security. The concept of the variable annuity as an investment and tax-deferred device, as well as an inflation hedge, has become increasingly popular.

The investment annuity is an interesting departure from the variable annuity plans described above. Introduced by the First Investment Annuity Company (FIAC), this program provides flexibility in the choice of investment vehicles—annuitants retain control of the selection of investments throughout the lifetime of the contract—but not the simplicity of the insured variable annuity. The investment function is separated from the lifetime guarantees, which are purchased from the insurance company. In actual practice, FIAC underwrites a series of one-year term fixed annuities, renewing annually for life.

TYPES OF VARIABLE ANNUITIES

The variable annuity is a retirement planning vehicle that provides an annuitant with lifetime income payments which vary in relation to the performance of an equity portfolio. Premiums are invested in the equity fund by the insurance company; cash values, death benefits, and annuity payments reflect the investment performance of the fund.

Two characteristics are combined to make the variable annuity a unique and valuable financial tool—an income guaranteed for life and unlimited investment potential. Hence, a variable annuity often will be more attractive than a fixed annuity, particularly where a floor of benefits already exists. It may be more attractive than a bank account or mutual fund withdrawal plan since it is impossible to outlive the income.

Individual and Group Variable Annuities

The similarities between individual and group variable annuities generally outweigh the differences. Because of administrative and regulatory requirements, most policyowners, even employees under group plans, must be handled on an individual basis; exceptions are plans providing for unallocated deposits, and this discussion will not dwell on them. Hence, administrative procedures are quite similar, as are costs of administration. Guarantees are often identical. The sales process is often individualized and strictly controlled for both group and individual plans, so differences in distribution costs are not as pronounced as with other insurance products.

The major characteristic which sets many group variable annuities apart is their ability to escape federal securities regulation; these are generally qualified variable annuities, discussed later in the chapter. With the exception of an occasional reference to differences enjoyed by such plans, the remainder of the discussion will assume strong similarities between group and individual forms and consider them together.

There are three types of variable annuity contracts: a single-premium *immediate* variable annuity, a single-premium *deferred* variable annuity, and a *periodic-payment* variable annuity.

Single-Premium Immediate Variable Annuity

The simplest form of variable annuity is the single-premium immediate plan. After deductions for sales and administrative expenses, the net deposit is applied to a table of annuity purchase rates to determine an initial level of annuity benefits. Often referred to as conversion rates, they employ assumptions of mortality and assumed investment return (AIR) to provide for an annuity benefit in the same manner as fixed annuity benefits are determined. The assumed investment return, often 3½ or 4 percent, is a form of advancement by the insurance company of a portion of the net return it anticipates on the reserve; it is a rate of interest which, if exactly matched by net investment return, will produce a level annuity. The mortality assumption reflects the insurer's acceptance of the risk that annuitants may be subject to mortality rates lower than those assumed; its effect, too, is to make benefit levels higher than they might be without such pooling and transfer of risks, and its role is identical to that of its fixed-dollar counterpart.

After the first one or two payments, the similarity to a fixed annuity becomes less. Income payments fluctuate in relation to the investment performance of the equity fund (common stocks) where the net premium has been placed. The result is that, unlike the level of payments under a fixed annuity, the income varies up and down reflecting the actual performance of the fund.

The variable annuity payments are based on the investment performance of the fund (dividends and capital gains) adjusted for the following factors: (1) a charge against the fund for investment management services; (2) a deduction for the insurer's assumption of mortality and expense risks; and (3) a reduction for assumed investment return (AIR) credited in advance by the insurer. If, for example, the equity fund were to earn an investment return of 10 percent, and management fees were one half of 1 percent and charges for guarantees 1 percent, and an AIR of 3½ percent had been used in deriving conversion rates, the annuity benefit level would grow by approximately 5 percent (10 percent minus one half of 1 percent minus 1 percent minus 3½ percent), for that period.[1] The new amount serves as the "base" for the next period, and benefits generally change monthly.

In practice, the initial annuity benefit is usually converted to a number of annuity units, based upon the current value of such units. The insurance company then guarantees the payment of that quantity of units each month for the lifetime of the annuitant. If, for example, a single premium of $100,000 buys an initial monthly benefit of $650 and units at that time are worth $10, the amount of each monthly payment is equal to 65 units ($650 divided by $10), multiplied by the current value of one annuity unit.

Annuity units thus represent participation in the equity fund, varying according to net investment return (after adjustment for management fees, guarantees, and advanced investment). They also can be thought of as units of reserves for future payments; the insurer guarantees to pay that number of units for life.

The single-premium variable annuity thus provides a monthly benefit for life, the level of which fluctuates in relation to equity performance. In other words, it provides a guaranteed number of units of annuity benefit for life, the current value of which determines each monthly benefit.

Single-Premium Deferred Variable Annuity

The single-premium deferred variable annuity is a related product providing lifetime varying benefits after a specified period of accumulation.

---

[1] The exact formula in general use is

$$\frac{1 + (.10 - .005 - .01)}{1.035} = \frac{1.085}{1.035} = 1.0483$$

If the net investment increment after deductions for investment management and guarantees equals AIR, the variable annuity is a level annuity. Regardless of investment trends from year to year, benefits will continue to increase as long as net return exceeds the AIR.

After deductions for sales and administrative expenses, the net payment is invested in the equity fund, creating an account which grows or declines in accordance with net investment performance (dividends and capital gains) of the fund.

Variations in the policyowner account values are based on gross investment performance, adjusted for (1) a charge against fund assets for investment management and (2) a deduction for mortality and expense guarantees. These adjustments normally are identical to those made in the annuity period (described above) and do not include a deduction for nominal investment since none has been assumed during the accumulation period.

At retirement, the accumulation account value is applied to purchase "annuity units" in order to establish the benefit level (monthly payment). The benefit pattern described above for the single-premium immediate annuity then becomes operative.

For example, assume that a man age 55 deposits $100,000 in a single-premium deferred variable annuity, creating an initial account after loadings of $95,000. If net investment performance in each of the next 10 years is 7½ percent (9 percent minus ½ of 1 percent management, minus 1 percent for guarantees), his account value at age 65 would equal nearly $200,000. If a monthly annuity purchase rate of $6.50 per thousand dollars is applied to that account, his initial annuity benefit would be $1,300. Furthermore, if annuity units are worth $13 at that point, the insurance company would guarantee to pay him 100 units each month ($1,300 divided by $13) for his lifetime. The amount of each payment would depend upon the value of an annuity unit on that payment date.

In practice, the policyowner's net deposit is also converted into "shares" or units, the number of which depends upon the deposit and the current unit value. Accumulation unit values vary with investment performance, as adjusted for management and guarantees, and the policyowner's cash value or account value at any time is equal to the number of units he has received, multiplied by the current unit value. He then establishes a retirement benefit based upon the value of his account at retirement, which is converted into a guaranteed number of "annuity units."[2]

Periodic-Payment Variable Annuity

Periodic-payment variable annuities can be envisioned as a series of single-premium deferred plans, conveniently merged into one contract. Each payment, frequently made in accordance with a plan for level installments, contributes to an accumulating account that fluctuates in relation to net investment performance in the same way as the single-premium deferred plan. At an agreed retirement date, the value of the accumulation units is converted into a monthly annuity payment (annuity units) that also varies up and down depending upon investment performance.

---

[2] While the concept of "units" or "shares" initially may seem confusing or cumbersome, it definitely facilitates administration and account procedures. In addition, the "unit" concept is used in connection with mutual funds and is generally understood by the investing public.

From the standpoint of "shares" purchased, each payment buys a number of accumulation units which varies with the current value and the amount of the deposit. Each additional purchase adds to the aggregate number of units in the policyowner's account; the value of the account at any point is equal to the total number of units multiplied by the current value of one unit. At retirement the account value is ascertained, an initial benefit level determined, and a guaranteed number of annuity units calculated.

TABLE 18–1.   Illustration of Periodic-Payment Variable Annuity Account Growth

Date	Unit Value	Deposit	Units Credited	Total Units	Account Value
1/73	10.00	$10,000	1,000	1,000	$10,000
1/74	11.00	10,000	910	1,910	21,010
1/75	12.00	10,000	833	2,743	32,916
1/76	13.00	10,000	770	3,513	45,669
1/77	14.00	10,000	714	4,227	59,178
1/78	Purchase of Monthly Benefit			4,227	$63,405
	Initial Monthly Benefit at $6.50				$ 412
	Guaranteed Annuity Units at $10			41.20	

As an example, assume that a man age 60 deposits $10,000 after loadings in each of the next five years. Table 18–1 shows how his account grows and how monthly benefits are ultimately created at age 65:

GUARANTEES: CONSUMER PROTECTION AND SERVICE

Guarantees provided by most variable annuities include:

1. No increase in sales and administrative fees over initial levels, even if expenses increase. This is most appropriate in the periodic payment plan, where deposits made several years after inception are accorded treatment provided initially. In contrast, a voluntary mutual fund savings program could present difficulties to the long-term saver if fees were increased; no such guarantees exist.
2. Charges for investment management and guarantees will not increase. (A few companies reserve the right to increase these charges to a stipulated maximum level.)
3. Emerging mortality experience, no matter how adverse, will not affect either the purchase rates to be applied or the guarantee of benefits for life—a mortality guarantee.

Some group variable annuities limit the term of guarantees, with respect to future deposits, to periods of about five years, reserving the right to revise contracts for new deposits after that point. Accordingly, charges for guarantees under such plans are substantially lower.

Guarantees of mortality and expenses are an attractive feature which other investment vehicles cannot offer. Further, benefits varying solely from investment performance are more easily understood by policyowners.

Consumer protection provided by variable annuities, as a result of joint regulation by state and federal jurisdictions, is quite extensive. Solvency requirements for insurance companies, established by state insurance departments, are combined with disclosure and sales presentation requirements, as well as customer account rules established by the SEC. While such broad regulation does not extend to specific investment practices, it is comprehensive enough to establish a comfortable environment for the variable annuity policyowner.

A related feature, resulting from explicit regulation by the SEC of variable annuity policyowner administration, is the quality of *consumer service*. Premiums received by the insurance company must be processed on the day they arrive in the home office, confirmation statements follow every transaction affecting the customer's account, sales procedures are established and policed, and surrender rights are judiciously observed with refunds mailed in a minimum of seven days.

VARIABLE ANNUITY CONTRACT PROVISIONS

The variable annuity contract generally parallels the fixed annuity contract in language and format.[3] It contains an insuring clause, data regarding the insured and the beneficiary, a description of considerations and benefits, general definitions, nonforfeiture provisions, settlement options, general provisions (assignment, proof of age, incontestibility, misstatement of age), and tables of purchase rates for specified annuity options.

In addition, the vocabulary for variable annuity contracts encompasses their particular features. New terms, adopted to avoid undue confusion, refer to stipulated payments, annuity and accumulation units, net investment factors, and initial and subsequent benefit amounts. A number of these usually are defined at the beginning of the policy form.

A number of new contract characteristics have emerged:

1. A boldface statement on the front page indicates the variable nature of benefits and lack of guarantees.
2. Stipulated payments do not buy specified amounts of deferred income; they buy units and establish an account.
3. A sizable range exists for discretionary deposits above or below the stipulated level.
4. Sales loadings and administrative fees are fully described.
5. The right is reserved, under extreme emergency market conditions, to delay payment of withdrawal values.

Standard contracts also provide for withdrawal and death benefits. Generally, a policyowner terminating payments has the following options: right to receive his account value (less surrender charge) within seven

---

[3] Individual fixed-dollar annuities are discussed in Chapter 7, and group deferred annuities are covered in Chapter 39.

days, right to leave the account in inactive status for later payment of monthly income, and right to convert part or all to fixed-dollar benefits. The 1940 Investment Company Act provides a further right to some variable annuity policyowners. Called a "free look" provision, the law allows policyowners terminating within 45 days to recapture all charges for sales and administrative expenses, in addition to the value of their accounts.

Upon death prior to commencement of benefits, the value of the policyowner's account is payable to his beneficiary. Many variable annuities contain a minimum death benefit, often supported by a minimal charge equal to his account value or gross premiums paid by him, whichever is larger.

VARIABLE ANNUITY REGULATORY ENVIRONMENT

Federal Regulation

The Securities and Exchange Commission administers a number of federal acts related to the issuance, sale, and administration of securities. Those applied to variable annuities are the Securities Act of 1933, the Securities Exchange Act of 1934, and the Investment Company Act of 1940. These acts are referred to as 1933, 1934 and 1940 acts, and under them, respectively, the SEC regulates the variable annuity as a security, the selling entity as a broker-dealer, and the investment vehicle (usually a separate account) as an investment company. Variable annuities cannot be sold, in most instances, without prior and continuing compliance with strict regulation under all three acts. (Certain qualified plans are exempt from SEC regulation; these are discussed below.)

The Securities Act of 1933 has a twofold purpose: complete disclosure to the purchaser of the nature of the security, and prevention of fraud in the sale of securities. Important facts to be shown the prospective buyer include levels of charges, treatment of payments, investment objectives, rights of the policyowner, and financial information about the issuing company.

The 1933 act requires registration of securities before they are offered for public sale; a basic part of this filing is the prospectus which must be delivered to all prospective buyers at or before the time the security is marketed. Only after the SEC has reviewed and "cleared" the registration filing may a variable annuity be sold. This procedure often accounts for delays of six months or more in mounting a marketing effort.

The Securities Act of 1934 seeks to establish and maintain fair and honest securities markets. The provisions aim at equitable treatment of purchasers, establishment of financial criteria for obtaining a securities dealership, and guidelines for fair sales practices.

Under the 1934 act, the entity selected to market the variable annuity—the insurance company or a subsidiary sales company—must be registered as a broker-dealer with the SEC and comply with rigid rules established by either the SEC or the National Association of Securities Dealers (NASD), a private compliance association authorized under an act of

Congress. Both compliance routes require that associated persons pass an examination demonstrating their knowledge of the securities business; this encompasses all salesmen, field supervisors, advertising personnel, and investment managers. In addition, both organizations establish and police selling guidelines and customer administrative procedures.

The *Investment Company Act of 1940* seeks to protect public interest through registration and regulation of investment companies. The separate account used for most variable annuities is deemed to be such an investment company.

The act regulates investment company management and operation, establishing ground rules concerning securities' owners, maximum sales charges, periodic financial reports, and investment management of contributions. Insurance companies must file a lengthy registration form—independent of the 1933 act filing—describing the product, the company, and its management. This statement, too, must be cleared before variable annuities can be marketed. Aside from the sheer volume of paperwork and lengthy delays, the more pervasive effects of the law relate to pricing rigidity and product inflexibility.

Exemptions from SEC jurisdiction have been granted from time to time, some by the Commission itself, others by legislation. Early exemptions from the 1933 and 1940 acts were provided to qualified, noncontributory group plans under Rules 3(c)3 and 156 of the two acts. More recently, Rule 6(e)1 was adopted, allowing broader exemptions to qualified corporate and HR-10 plans, contributory as well as noncontributory.

The 1970 Investment Company Amendments Act took the largest step by exempting separate accounts used exclusively to fund qualified and HR-10 plans from the 1940 act, and corporate qualified plans from the 1933 and 1934 acts; monies must be invested in a nonregistered separate account. This amendment has led many insurers to establish "pure" separate accounts and to seek ways of marketing variable annuities on a nonregistered basis.

Regulation by State Insurance Departments

State regulation of insurance products has survived a number of challenges, including a Supreme Court decision which resulted in a temporary period of implied federal jurisdiction over insurance. The McCarran Act, which recognizes state regulation to be in the public interest, has also served to commit variable annuities to state regulation. Since the Supreme Court, in ruling that variable annuities are securities, did not conclude that they are *not* insurance, variable annuity insurers remain subject to regulation by the states as well.

Control over the operations of insurance companies is exercised by licensing requirements in each state. In addition, companies must obtain a variable annuity license before marketing variable annuities in each state. Requirements for approval relate to history and financial status, management ability, and regulatory conditions in the company's home state.

State insurance departments also control the design of variable annuity contracts, mortality and investment return assumptions, periodic reports, and licensing of agents to sell variable annuities. While the early years of variable annuity development were complicated by wide diversity of regulatory provisions among the states, recent years have seen the adoption of model laws and regulations by most jurisdictions.

In almost every state, variable annuities are exempt from treatment as securities. In those few states where state securities laws apply to variable annuities, contracts must be filed with the state securities department as well as the insurance department.

Impact of Regulation on Variable Annuity Operations

The most obvious characteristic of all this regulation is duplication in licensing, registration, examinations, fees, and reports. It gives insurance companies limited flexibility for development and marketing of contracts. It creates a huge development cost and long delays before effective marketing can begin.

It also forces salesmen to be careful not to mislead prospective buyers, requires prompt and equitable handling of policyowner transactions by the insurer, and leads variable annuity companies to pursue the equity investment business with diligence and care.

Corporate Structure and Management of Variable Annuities

Because of unique investment characteristics and broad regulatory powers given the SEC, the variable annuity creates the need for a thoughtfully conceived corporate vehicle to distribute the product.

One approach has been to establish a subsidiary variable annuity company, which is registered with the SEC. While this may create corporate barriers to federal intervention in "insurance" matters, it also creates delays and additional financial prerequisites in gaining state approval of the operation. Another technique is the establishment of a subsidiary sales company; this eliminates the need to register the life insurance company under federal laws as the selling entity for variable annuities.

In spite of some concern over SEC involvement in the traditional insurance business, insurance companies tend to favor the "in-house" approach over the subsidiary route.

Role of Segregated Accounts

Separate accounts have played an important part in the evolution of variable annuities. Investment limitations on insurance company general assets prevent substantial placements in equities with direct reflection on their performance in individual accounts.

The concept grew out of the group pension business, where life insurers had become intrigued with the investment flexibility and direct allocation possibilities of segregated accounts. Recognizing major opposition to legal establishment of separate accounts from mutual funds concerned about individual investors and pension trust accounts, they first introduced legislation limiting the concept to qualified plans covering at least 25 employees on a noncontributory basis. Extension of the concept to variable annuities and then individual purchasers followed.

Pricing Aspects of Variable Annuities

In accordance with the Investment Company Act of 1940, an insurer may deduct from variable annuity payments specified *charges for sales and administrative expenses.* Securities and Exchange Commission regulations restrict sales charges to the equivalent of a level 9 percent but will allow administration charges in addition to that level.

Competition, as well as regulatory agencies, has affected levels of charges adopted for sales and administration loadings. While a handful of companies assess a first-year loading substantially higher than 9 percent, most companies use level or "slightly heaped" patterns, and totals of sales and administrative charges seldom exceed the equivalent of a level 9 percent.

While the SEC restricts variations in pricing that would be deemed discriminatory, such as those favoring a large group sponsor over a smaller one, a number of pricing variations are permitted. Group plans involving lower distribution costs often have lower deductions for sales fees. Single payments under both group and individual contracts usually are charged lower amounts as the size of the deposit increases, and dollars transferred to variable annuity plans from other contracts held with the same insurance company often may be done at a reduced or no load under exemptions permitted by the SEC.

A number of companies, recognizing the closer relationship of administration expenses to transactions and routine procedures, deduct a flat dollar fee from the account each year or upon issue of the policy. Such fees usually are obtained by the cancellation of an appropriate number of units from each variable annuity account and often are felt to constitute a more equitable means of assessing the charge.

Variable annuity contracts normally guarantee that policyowner accounts and monthly income payments will not be affected by excessive levels of sales or administration expenses, or by variations in actual mortality from assumed levels. To support these contractual guarantees, insurers establish a contingency fund maintained by specified deductions from the assets in the equity fund. The charges are assessed each time the fund and its units are revalued, taking the form of deductions in investment performance. The annual equivalent of these periodic deductions from each account ranges from less than ½ of 1 percent to over 1 percent of principal in variable annuities issued today; the average is about 1 percent.

A third type of charge is a deduction for *investment management fees* assessed by the insurance company or, in some instances, by a subsidiary management company. Charges against principal for variable annuities marketed today range from about ¼ of 1 percent to over ½ of 1 percent, the average being about ⅓ of 1 percent. They, too, take the form of periodic deductions in investment performance and together with charges for guarantees usually constitute the difference between "gross" investment growth and "net" growth credited to customers.

The *purchase rates* applied at retirement are a part of the pricing structure and bear mention here. Occasionally, such purchase rates will not be as attractive as those for comparable fixed-dollar products issued by the same company for two reasons:

1. Since the insurer agrees to pass on to the annuitant all excess interest over the nominally assumed rate, it cannot apply such excess investment earnings toward mortality or expense losses, as it can do under fixed contracts. Hence, the mortality assumption is often slightly more conservative.
2. Variable annuity plans frequently assume a lower investment return (AIR) than fixed-dollar plans in order to increase the probability that benefit levels will keep pace with inflation. The higher the AIR, the higher investment performance must be for benefits to increase.

Installation and Administration of Variable Annuities

The variable annuity creates administrative challenges which require more effort and expense than the fixed annuity. The combination of insurance and investment features in one plan, under joint regulatory jurisdiction, requires the design of new policy forms and the establishment of more complicated administrative procedures.

A major component of this expanded environment is education. Employees involved in development and management of the product require a whole new orientation to the securities and compliance area created by the variable annuity. In practical terms, it is generally more efficient to set aside a division to handle all home office aspects of the product until a general feeling of comfort is achieved; then perhaps it is feasible to merge administrative functions with their fixed-dollar counterparts.

Policyowners must be educated, too. Possible variations in account values and income payments must be clearly understood by both individual purchasers and group sponsors. Of crucial importance is their understanding that no floor is guaranteed and that benefits can fall as well as rise. The prospectus can be a valuable component of educational tools, providing it is used properly and is accompanied by knowledgeable explanations.

Regardless of whether the variable annuity plan is group or individual, *individual records* must be maintained. Normally installed in a data processing system for equity products, such records contain detailed policyowner information, payment histories, numbers of units credited, and pertinent information about annuity options elected. A master file normally is processed daily so that contributions can be applied to buy units at that day's price. Similarly, there must be relatively rapid access to the file, as well as ability to effect reductions or withdrawals, in order to comply with rigid federal requirements. In short, the administrative process is a complicated, tedious, and expensive one compared to fixed-dollar plans, and the expenses accordingly are higher.

Policyowners periodically receive reports about the investment fund, as well as individual statements of account values. Such reports must be distributed at least annually, and confirmation statements must be mailed in connection with each transaction (deposit, reduction, administrative fee) which affects the participant's account.

Annuitants require particular attention; if lost in the shuffle of mechanized impersonality, they could be overwhelmed by the variations in benefit amounts. Therefore, each benefit payment is generally accompanied by an explanation of how it was determined, the number of annuity units it represents, and the current value of an annuity unit.

POTENTIAL VARIABLE ANNUITY MARKETS

In a number of marketing situations, variable annuities offer unique opportunities to provide for retirement income having a built-in hedge against inflation. The applications include personal savings and retirement programs, tax-deferred annuities, programs established by self-employed persons under HR-10, certain associations of HR-10 entities, and group variable annuity plans established by corporations.

Individual variable annuities can be attractive supplements to government and corporate retirement programs. Using life insurance proceeds or accumulations under personal savings programs, individuals may purchase immediate or deferred single-premium variable annuities. Dollars maturing under pension trust side funds and profit-sharing proceeds also may be applied where the buyer's objective is immediate or deferred lifetime income.

Individual savings programs occasionally may suggest the use of periodic-payment variable annuities. Although they generally are more expensive than mutual funds, they contain valuable guarantees of future mortality and expense charges and often provide some tax deferral.

Personal objectives are crucial to proper use of variable annuities; if income or "asset liquidation" goals are secondary to accumulation or conservation of assets, other forms of investment, such as mutual funds, may be preferable. In addition, there is a need in individual savings programs to insure the existence of a "floor" of fixed-dollar income.

Tax-deferred variable annuities can be sold on either a group or an individual basis. Section 403(b) of the Internal Revenue Code allows certain employers to provide annuity contracts with "before tax" dollars for their employees. Known as 501(c)3 organizations from the section where they are enumerated, they include religious, charitable, and educational institutions. Contracts must be owned by the employer, and salary deductions are limited to a level approximating 20 percent of earnings.

The group tax-deferred annuity has been the major cause of entry by insurers into the variable annuity field; market thrusts have been most successfully directed toward school teachers, hospitals, and nonprofit organizations.

HR-10 variable annuities, sold on an individual basis under the Keogh Act, have met some marketing success, although other accumulation approaches such as mutual funds have produced stiff competition.[4] Many client situations provide ideal applications of variable annuities; proximity to retirement, lack of other insurance coverage, and interest in mortality guarantees are a few.

The HR-10 market is a dual one; a second major source of demand exists among associations and franchises. Large associations of doctors, accountants, lawyers, and national or regional franchise groups of self-

---

[4] HR-10 plans are discussed in Chapter 36.

employed individuals show strong market potential. Demand arises from the tax-deferral characteristics of HR-10 plans, as well as the opportunity to supplement personal savings with equity investments.

Group variable annuities for corporate pension and welfare plans have evolved from a series of approaches aimed at providing "dollar security" in pensions for retirees. In assessing various alternatives, it is important to recognize the dual risk of pension planning: From the employee's point of view, benefits may fail to keep pace with the cost of living; from the employer's standpoint, commitments based on future earnings levels or plans passing the fruits of favorable investment performance to employees raise serious cost implications. The attractiveness of one approach versus another often depends on the point of view.

The final-pay plan was an early attempt to correlate retirement security with the cost of living. Retirement income, expressed as a percentage of earned income, is based upon earnings in the last working years. While they have been a major step toward retirement security, they obligate employers to unforeseen levels of benefits and generally provide no solution to the post-retirement inflation problem.

Cost-of-living plans, which provide for adjustments according to variations in a specified price index, have been fairly successful in meeting both employer and employee objectives. The U.S. Department of Labor Consumer Price Index is the most popular base, although combinations of wage and price indicators have been intriguing alternatives from the viewpoint of employees. The simplest application consists of post-retirement adjustments when the index exceeds a certain percentage of a chosen base period level. More complex arrangements provide for adjustments to accrued pension benefits to reflect cost of living changes since they were earned. The cost-of-living annuity offers a more budgetable cost pattern to the employer than under final-pay plans and lessens the risk to the retiree. However, cost-of-living plans cannot claim the open-end investment potential for plan participants inherent in equity-linked variable annuities.

Variable annuities not only provide potential protection from inflationary influences, but offer possible performance surpassing that of index-linked annuities. The risk to the participant is obvious, but the greater negative influence has been the employer's reaction to passing favorable investment return on to employees instead of being able to use it to reduce costs. Nevertheless, group variable annuities have proliferated, especially among contributory pension and profit sharing plans, thrift plans, and maturity funding programs. As mentioned above, they have been quite popular in trusteed, noninsured plans. Points of marketing emphasis for insured plans include (1) flexibility of guarantees and contribution levels, (2) ability to combine fixed and variable benefits, and (3) participation by employees in equity performance.

In the majority of variable annuity plans, the amount of periodic contributions is established by a contribution formula (subject to IRS limitations). An interesting variation is the "target benefit" plan; a "nominal" retirement income, based on anticipated earnings, is funded with excess investment return allocated to participants in the form of adjusted benefits instead of reducing employer costs.

THE SIGNIFICANCE OF
VARIABLE ANNUITIES

To the Consumer

If the consumer definitely contemplates future use of personal savings for retirement income, the variable annuity provides growth potential from equity investments, valuable guarantees of mortality and expense assumptions, and in many instances tax advantages. When combined with a floor of fixed-dollar income, it offers financial security as well as growth potential.

To the Life Underwriter

The characteristics making variable annuities attractive to consumers also benefit the insurance agent. Given the ability to recognize appropriate client objectives and to market a product in an understandable and fair manner, the agent is in the position of adding a valuable financial planning tool to his portfolio of products. The variable annuity places him one step closer to offering complete financial services to his client. In addition, because it occasionally leads to substantial purchases to meet client objectives, the variable annuity offers new opportunities for compensation. Of course, the agent must establish his competency by thorough study and successful completion of still more examinations than the life insurance business requires.

To the Company

The initial impact of variable annuity development and distribution can be disturbing to the company. Development expenses, delays in gaining regulatory approval of full distribution, and the need for new and complex administrative procedures usually are encountered in initial stages of the product's development. Nevertheless, the long-run picture for variable annuities is bright enough to overcome many misgivings. The provision of investment opportunities and potential retirement security to the American public, and the potential of profits from this enterprise, combine to create positive corporate attitudes about variable annuities.

Insurance companies undertaking development of variable annuities have as attainable rewards increased income, increased assets, increased competitiveness through complete financial service, and participation in reclamation by the insurance industry of a significant share of savings dollars.

SELECTED REFERENCES

Biggs, John H. "Alternatives in Variable Annuity Benefit Design," *Transactions of the Society of Actuaries*, Vol. 21 (1969), p. 495.

Campbell, Paul A. *The Variable Annuity*. Hartford, Conn.: Connecticut General Life Insurance Company, 1969.

Life Office Management Association. *Considerations in the Design of Accounting Systems and Controls for the Variable Annuity Insurance Product*. New York, 1969.

McClelland, H. F. "Tax Aspects of the Variable Annuity," *National Tax Journal*, Vol. 15, No. 2 (June 1962), p. 125.

Walker, Harry. "Actuarial Aspects of State Regulation of Individual Variable Annuities," *Transactions of the Society of Actuaries*, Vol. 20 (1968), p. 437.

Yates, H. Powell. "Equity Products—A Legal Appraisal," *C.L.U. Journal*, Vol. 25 (January 1971), p. 51.

19

Mutual Funds—
Principles and Practices

By JOHN J. PLUMB

IN THE DECADE of the 1940s, most Americans were interested in financial plans wherein the principal objectives were estate creation, and conservation and protection of their capital. There was relatively little interest in growth of capital with its attendant risk taking. Vivid memories of the great depression of the 1930s still lingered throughout the 1940s, resulting in a strong desire for the "guarantees" of fixed-dollar investments. The life insurance underwriter satisfied this public desire through life insurance contracts which created an immediate estate, provided guaranteed cash values, and guaranteed retirement income that could not be outlived.

During the 1950s and 1960s, certain developments took place which tended to increase public desire to consider equity investments as well as guaranteed fixed-dollar investments. The most significant developments were (1) the securities business experienced several bull markets; (2) people became more concerned over the eroding effect of persistent inflation on fixed-dollar investments and payments; (3) activities of some financial planners stimulated increased interest in the concept of a reasonable balance between fixed-dollar and equity-dollar investments; and (4) more Americans indicated a desire to participate in the economic growth of the country. These developments contributed substantially to the rapid and impressive growth of the mutual fund industry.

During the 1960s, an increasing number of life insurance companies decided to broaden their financial services by making the mutual fund product available to their life underwriters. They took this action in the belief that one sales representative could take care of a client's insurance needs and also recommend mutual fund shares in the overall financial plan. Also, they took the position that life insurance and mutual funds are complementary and not competitive with each other because the two products are designed to serve different needs in the estate plan. Whether the results expected by those insurance companies will be achieved will depend in part on the desire of their dually licensed representatives to acquire the level of knowledge and skills in both products that will be needed to do the professional job their clients will expect of them.

Growth of the Mutual Fund Industry

While the first mutual fund companies were formed in 1924, significant growth of the industry did not take place until after 1940. Assets of mutual fund companies in 1940, the year when the Investment Company Act was passed by Congress, were $447,959,000, and by the end of 1971 they had climbed to $58,159,800,000—representing approximately 92 percent of all investment company assets. In the same period, the number of shareholder accounts grew from 296,057 to approximately 11,000,000.

While there are several types of investment companies defined in the law (open-end, closed-end, face amount certificate, and unit investment trusts), the type that most people have in mind when they refer to investment companies is the "open-end" type, which is popularly known as a mutual fund company. Investment companies are organized under the Investment Company Act of 1940, and under this Act both open-end and closed-end investment companies come under the classification of "management" companies, as distinguished from face amount certificate companies and unit investment trusts.

Definition and Purpose of a Mutual Fund Company

A mutual fund company is defined as a corporation or trust whose sole business is investing its shareholders' money in securities of other companies, generally in common stocks or a combination of stocks and bonds. It invests its money for investment purposes only and does not intend to exercise control of other corporations. It invests its money in the hope of achieving the investment objective specifically stated in the fund's prospectus. Its basic purpose is to provide an investment vehicle whereby individual investors with similar needs and financial goals may pool their money to obtain continuous professional management of invested risk capital, diversification of investments, and convenience in handling administrative, tax, and other aspects of investments. In effect, a mutual fund is one large account owned by many investors who share its income and expenses, and its profits or losses, in proportion to their interests. Ordinarily, investment in a mutual fund is considered a long-term investment.

Unlike a closed-end investment company which has a relatively fixed capitalization and does not stand ready to redeem its own shares, an open-end investment company, or a mutual fund as we shall refer to it in this chapter, sells its shares continuously and stands ready to redeem the individual investor's proportional interest in the fund at a price based on the market value of the securities held in the fund company's portfolio. The redemption price may be more or less than the original cost of the investment, depending on the market value of the portfolio's securities at the time of redemption.

Like any other corporation, the mutual fund company issues shares of its own stock. Each share represents the same proportional interest as any other share in the fund's portfolio of securities. Income from the account, after deduction of the corporation's expenses, is received by the shareholder in the form of periodic dividends. Any net profits realized from the sale of portfolio securities are likewise distributed to the shareholders as capital gains distributions.

CLASSIFICATION OF MUTUAL FUND COMPANIES BY INVESTMENT OBJECTIVE

Mutual fund companies have varying investment objectives, and their programs of investing seek to obtain securities portfolios in keeping with such objectives.[1] With the large number of mutual fund companies doing business, the investor can choose the mutual fund company which is best suited to his needs, objectives, and financial circumstances. He can find mutual funds which invest in the type of securities in which he wishes to participate, be they blue-chip common stocks, speculative common stocks, high-grade preferred stocks, speculative preferred stocks, high-grade bonds, speculative bonds, or a balance between stocks and bonds.

Classification of mutual funds by investment objective is difficult because many mutual funds have both primary and secondary objectives. It is generally accepted that there are three primary objectives from which an investor will seek at least one. These primary objectives are (1) growth, (2) income, and (3) conservation of principal.

1. *Growth*—Growth funds usually are diversified common stock funds that invest substantially all of their assets in common stocks. It is virtually impossible to establish a general category of growth funds. For example, some growth funds say they seek "long-term growth of capital," while others say their primary objective is "long-term growth of capital and of income." There is considerable variance in the objectives and investment policies of growth funds. Moreover, there are differences in the aggressiveness of investment policies and the stress placed on the quality of the securities comprising the portfolio. Growth funds have varying degrees of risk ranging from the more conservative and "middle of the road" funds investing in basic, stable industries to the highly speculative funds investing in new and unseasoned companies and using investment techniques involving a high degree of risk.

Within the family of long-term growth funds, the investor will find "specialty funds" that specialize in the securities of a single industry or allied industries, or of companies located in a specific geographical area of the United States.

2. *Income*—The investor will find a number of "income funds" whose investment policies will indicate wide differences. With "income funds" the primary objective is usually stated as one seeking a "higher than average" current income return consistent with stability of capital. However, with many "income funds" the secondary objectives have a significant influence on investment policies, as evidenced by the fund whose prospectus states "growth of income and capital is an important secondary consideration."

---

[1] The Investment Company Act of 1940 requires that mutual fund companies state their investment objective and investment policies in their registration statement and prospectus. Under this law, the stated objective and investment policies cannot be changed without prior shareholder approval.

3. *Conservation of principal*—Funds with the primary objective of conservation of principal are usually "balanced" funds or "bond" funds. A "balanced" fund is one which achieves "balance" by investing both in senior securities such as bonds and preferred stocks and in common stocks. Because a "balanced" fund will never be invested 100 percent either in equities or fixed-income securities, it is regarded as a more conservative type fund.

A "bond" fund is a mutual fund that invests exclusively in bonds. However, it must be pointed out that not all "bond" funds invest in high-grade bonds. Some indicate in their prospectus that their policy will be to invest in medium-grade and low-priced bonds.

It can be stated that generally the mutual fund whose objective is stability of capital or conservation of principal will place primary emphasis on investments that are least likely to be affected by changing economic conditions.

ORGANIZATION AND STRUCTURE OF A MUTUAL FUND COMPANY

The operation of a typical mutual fund company involves four fundamental elements: (1) The mutual fund company, (2) the investment advisor or management company, (3) the fund custodian, and (4) the fund's national distributor or underwriter.

The Mutual Fund Company

A mutual fund is organized like any other corporation. It has directors (or trustees) elected annually (or at other periods) by the shareholders, and they are responsible for electing the fund's officers, administering the fund's operations, carrying out its stated objectives, and conducting the company's affairs in a manner desired by the shareholders. Federal law requires that the fund management must account to the shareholders, in the form of a report, at least once every six months.

In many cases, officers and directors of the fund company also are officers and directors of the investment advisor. However, the Investment Company Act of 1940 requires that not more than 60 percent of a fund's board of directors shall be comprised of "interested" persons associated with the investment advisor or the national distributor. Thus, the law makes sure that independent, outside directors serve on the board.

The Investment Advisor (or Management Company)

Successful investment management requires the full-time attention and skills of many people. To advise the fund's directors, a mutual fund either will have its own employees or will employ the services of an investment management company. If an investment management company is used, the fund's directors or shareholders approve a contract with the management company to perform required services which not only include responsibility for the selection and supervision of the investments in the portfolio, but also complete corporate administration of the fund. In many cases, the investment advisor also assumes certain expenses such as the cost of providing offices, statistical and research information, clerical assistance, and salaries and fees of the officers and directors of the fund who are not officers and directors of the investment advisor. The contract must be approved by the shareholders, or by a majority of the directors (including a majority of the independent "outside" directors) or by both groups. Ordinarily, the contract is for one year. The services of the investment advisor are paid for by the fund, typically at a rate based on a percentage of the fund's total net assets. The fee is usually one half of 1 percent of the average daily total net assets for the year up to a specified size, with provisions for a decreasing fee as assets grow above stated amounts. When the total of the management fee and the expenses actually paid by the fund itself exceeds 1 percent of the daily net assets for the year, the management contract often states that the management fee will be reduced so that the total charged to the shareholders will not exceed 1 percent. The fund's prospectus describes in detail the basis on which the management fee is calculated.

The Custodian

The second contract usually entered into by a fund is a contract with a national bank or trust company which serves as custodian of the fund's securities and cash. In addition to acting in a safekeeping capacity, the custodian bank typically performs a number of other services such as (1) disbursing income dividends and capital gains distributions to shareholders, (2) serving as transfer agent of the fund, (3) receiving investor payments and investing those payments in shares of the fund, (4) paying for securities purchased by the fund and receiving payment for securities sold by the fund, (5) mailing proxy forms and periodic reports, (6) daily pricing, and (7) other bookkeeping type functions.

The custodian's services do not include any participation in the management of the fund or the selection or supervision of its investments.

The National Distributor (or Underwriter)

A mutual fund is continuously offering new shares to investors. To market its shares to the public, the fund enters into a third contract with a national distributor or underwriter. Except in the case of "no load" funds that offer shares at net asset value with no sales charge and seek customers through newspapers, magazines, and direct mail, the fund company does not sell directly either to the public or to dealers. It sells shares to the distributor to fill orders placed with the distributor. In practice, the distributor only purchases shares from the fund after specific orders have been received for them. The distributor purchases the shares from the fund at the prevailing net asset value per share, and, in turn, the distributor, through its dealers or direct salesmen, or both, resells the shares to the public at the full offering price (net asset value plus a sales charge). The distributor pays a portion of the sales charge to the dealer or direct salesman and retains the balance to pay for all costs of distribution.

Often, the company employed as investment advisor also acts as national distributor, but two separate contracts are involved.

HOW MUTUAL FUNDS ARE PURCHASED AND ACCUMULATED

The investor who decides to use mutual funds as an investment vehicle has several ways in which to purchase mutual fund shares. Before discussing the various choices available to him, it is important first to understand the method used in pricing mutual fund shares.

Bid Price and Asked Price

The *bid price* of a fund share represents the mutual fund's actual net asset value. When an investor redeems his holdings, he usually is entitled to receive the net asset value per share without additional charges or commissions, and the redemption value may be more or less than his original cost depending on the value of the securities in the fund's portfolio at the time of redemption. The net asset value per share is computed by (1) determining the value of the fund's investments at current market value, adding cash on hand and any other assets; (2) subtracting all liabilities; and (3) dividing the total net assets by the number of fund shares outstanding.

The *asked price* (or public offering price) is determined by the fund company. As previously explained, a mutual fund offers its shares to the public through its distributor at a specified price, and agrees to redeem such shares at a specified price. Both of these specified prices are based on the current net asset value per share, and are based on a formula stated in the fund's prospectus.

The asked price is the current net asset value per share plus an acquisition or sales charge, if any. It is the price a purchaser must pay for shares. The difference between the bid price and the asked price represents the sales charge per share. When expressed in percentage terms, the sales charge is a percentage of the offering or asked price.

The net asset value per share (bid price) is computed daily, and many newspapers publish both the current bid and asked price. The asked price quoted is based on the maximum sales charge being used by the particular fund.

Three Ways to Purchase Mutual Fund Shares

Mutual fund shares may be purchased in three ways:

1. Single or lump-sum cash purchase.
2. Continuous purchases for cash either on a periodic basis or on a piecemeal basis.
3. Reinvestment of income dividends and capital gains distributions in additional shares.

Single or Lump-Sum Cash Purchase. A single or lump-sum cash purchase is made under an account called "regular account." A single purchase is made at one time, and the lump sum invested stays in the fund until the investor decides to redeem his holdings. Usually, any income dividends payable are paid in cash, and any capital gain distributions may be taken in cash or reinvested in additional shares.

Continuous Purchases for Cash, Either on a Periodic Basis or on a Piecemeal Basis. An investor may accumulate shares by continuing to purchase shares for cash, either on a periodic basis, or on a piecemeal basis. This method involves the open account, the voluntary accumulation plan, or the contractual plan.

The *open account* is much like the single lump-sum cash purchase. An open-account holder makes an initial purchase and then may make additional purchases, not necessarily of equal amounts, whenever he decides to invest more money in mutual fund shares. A large number of funds use this "open account" designation and allow reinvestment privileges for those who become "open account" holders.

There are two types of periodic purchase plans—voluntary and contractual. Under a *voluntary accumulation plan,* the investor indicates his intention to make periodic payments over an indefinite period of time. The voluntary plan starts with an application stating the amount of the initial purchase, usually $100, $250, or $500, and an indication of the amount to be invested periodically thereafter, either monthly, quarterly, or some other stated interval. There usually is a minimum of $25 required for the periodic payment. Each payment made is subject to the level sales charge, as distinguished from the periodic plan called the "contractual plan" where a higher sales charge is made in the first or early years than in the later years.

Under a voluntary plan, each purchase is an entity in itself, and there is no specified duration of the plan. It lasts as long as the purchaser wishes to continue making further payments. While the purpose of such programs is to get the investor in the habit of making periodic purchases, there is no built-in compulsion to do so. The purchaser can skip or stop payments any time he desires, without penalty. The voluntary plan combines the advantage of periodic investing over a long period with the level sales charge arrangement of the "regular account." With many funds, the voluntary accumulation plan is used as an "open account" by investors who, instead of making fixed payments on specific future dates, prefer to make irregular additions at varying times, thus obtaining maximum flexibility in contrast to the contractual plan.

Voluntary accumulation plans generally make available an automatic dividend and capital gain distribution reinvestment privilege.

The *contractual plan* is a formalized periodic payment plan wherein the investor commits himself to make investments of a stated dollar amount at regular intervals (usually monthly) for a fixed number of years, usually 10 or 15 years. By charging a substantial part of the total sales commission on the entire span of the plan in the front end of the plan, the plan holder is discouraged from discontinuing payments in the early years. The Investment Company Act of 1940 limits sales charges on contractual plans to a maximum of 9 percent of the total investments made over the life of the plan, but it allows on contractual plans a deduction for sales charges of up to 50 percent of the first year's investments, or, as provided by the Investment Company Amendments Act of 1970, up to 64 percent of the total investments made in the first four years. After the first year on a 50 percent plan, or four years on a 64 percent plan, a considerably reduced sales charge applies so that at the end of the contractual period, the total sales charge paid would not exceed 9 percent of the total investments made during the plan period. The larger sales charges in the early years explain why contractual plans have been called "front-end" plans. A contractual plan holder can terminate his plan at any time, as he is not under any legal obligation to continue to make payments.

The Investment Company Amendments Act of 1970 includes some new provisions concerning contractual plan mutual funds. The new provisions respond to SEC's concern over the traditional front-end loading of contractual plans and the consequent financial loss to the short-term investor.

The 1970 Act provides a purchaser of a contractual plan for mutual funds two separate refund rights. Under the first right, a 45-day right of refund, the purchaser is entitled to receive all of the sales and other charges he has paid plus the value of his account, within 45 days of the mailing to him of a notice of that right. Such notice must be mailed to him within 60 days after issuance of his plan certificate. Under the second right, until the expiration of 18 months after the issuance of the plan certificate, the purchaser of a 50 percent front-end plan is entitled to the value of his account plus a refund of that portion of the sales load paid on the plan which exceeds 15 percent of his gross payments. The 1970 Act also permits plan sponsors, as an alternative to charging the typical front-end load, to elect to charge a "spread load" not exceeding 20 percent of any payment, or an average of not more than 16 percent of the first 48 months' payments or their equivalent. Plans sold subject to "spread load" would not receive the 18-month refund right.

Contractual plans have been attractive to many people. They provide a compulsion to save, usually contain a partial liquidation privilege which allows withdrawal of a stated percentage of the net asset value of the account and later reinvestment of that withdrawn amount back into the plan at current net asset value without a sales charge, and usually provide an opportunity to add life insurance to complete the program in the event of the investor's premature death.

Reinvestment of Income Dividends and Capital Gains Distributions in Additional Shares. Another method of acquiring shares is for the investor to authorize the mutual fund company to reinvest all income dividends and capital gain distributions in additional fund shares. This is tantamount to an outright purchase of shares.

SPECIAL FEATURES AND SERVICES

In addition to offering participation in a continuously supervised mutual fund investment account, mutual fund companies also offer certain special services and devices which are convenient or economical for their shareholders. While the limited scope of this chapter does not make it possible to explain all of them, a few require brief treatment.

Quantity Discounts

On purchases of substantial amounts, most funds charge a lower sales charge, i.e., the effective public offering price may be lower than the published price. Practically all funds reduce the percentage of the sales charge as the amounts involved increase. The reduction usually starts with investments of $10,000 or $15,000, and becomes greater as the investment is larger depending on the "break points" used by the particular fund.

With many funds, it is not necessary to invest at one time the entire amount required to qualify for the quantity discount. The quantity discount is often available to investors who sign a "letter of intention," which states that the aggregate purchases made within a period of 13 months will total a certain sum. The initial and all subsequent purchases within the 13-month period are made at the price applicable to the total intended investment. If the investor does not make the full intended purchase, he is required to pay in cash the difference in sales charge, or shares held by the fund in escrow will be sold to the extent necessary to make up the difference.

Right of Accumulation

There is another method of reducing sales charges on substantial fund holdings. This privilege is called "right of accumulation," and there is no time limit on this right as there is with a "letter of intention." The right to a lower sales charge exists whenever a new purchase, combined with either the original cost or the current worth of existing holdings (depending on the requirements of the particular fund), exceeds a "break point" set forth in the prospectus, i.e., the point at which the sales charge decreases.

Redemption Privilege

The redemption privilege is a feature that distinguishes mutual funds from other types of investments. It means that on any business day the shareholder may redeem all or any part of his shares for cash at the then net asset value of the shares being redeemed. The redemption price is normally the net asset value per share next determined after receipt of the request. The net asset value may be more or less than the investor's original cost, depending on the market value of the securities in the company's portfolio at the time of redemption. Fund owners can usually redeem their shares without charge, although some funds actually levy a small redemption charge.

The Investment Company Act of 1940 requires that payment for any redeemable security must be made within seven days after its tender, except during periods when the New York Stock Exchange may be closed, its trading restricted, or emergency conditions exist.

Exchange or Conversion Privilege

If an investor's objective or needs change, and a different type of fund would be more appropriate than the one he already owns, it would benefit the investor if he could transfer from one fund to another without paying a second sales charge.

Many sponsors of mutual funds have a number of different mutual funds under their management. These are called "families" of mutual funds, i.e., separate funds with separate investment objectives ranging from conservative to the highly speculative type. These sponsors generally permit shareholders in one of the funds to transfer their holdings to another fund in the "family" at a nominal bookkeeping cost, and without the customary sales charge. For tax purposes, the exchange is not a tax-free exchange since it is considered as a sale of shares of one fund and a new purchase of shares in another fund.

Reinvestments of Income Dividends and Capital Gains Distributions

The typical mutual fund makes payments to shareholders in two distinct forms—dividends from net investment income consisting of dividends and interest paid to the fund on securities in the fund's portfolio, and capital gains distributions representing the net realized profits from the sale of securities once held in the fund's portfolio.

Mutual funds distribute substantially all the dividends and interest they receive from their investments after deducting operating expenses. The effect of the tax law, which will be explained later, usually results in fund companies paying out 100 percent of their net investment income. Payments may be made quarterly, semi-annually, or annually depending on the policy of the particular fund.

Mutual fund companies will, at various times, sell securities at a profit or loss. If the realized profits in a given fiscal period exceed realized losses, and if the securities have been held for more than six months, there is a "net realized long-term gain." The majority of mutual fund companies currently follow a policy of paying out their capital gains to shareholders in the form of capital gains distributions. Such capital gains distributions cannot be made more frequently than annually.

The moment an income dividend or capital gains distribution is paid to the shareholder, the per share net asset value of the mutual fund company's stock automatically declines by the same amount.

One of the most significant and valuable privileges afforded mutual fund shareholders is the opportunity to reinvest income dividends and capital gains distributions to acquire additional shares rather than accepting them in cash. Some funds reinvest at the regular offering price which includes the regular sales charge, while others allow reinvestments at the current net asset value per share, i.e., without a sales charge. Many funds provide for automatic reinvestment unless the shareholder requests otherwise.

The compounding of share ownership through reinvestment of income dividends and capital gains distributions is a certain method of increasing the shareholder's number of shares and thereby giving him a greater opportunity for possible growth of his investment account.

Regular Withdrawal Plans

The growing use of fund shares as sources of income for current needs or retirement income has caused fund companies to provide a special service under which an owner's holdings are liquidated (redeemed) on a prearranged schedule. This "withdrawal plan" (also called level payment plan, check-a-month plan, or periodic remittance plan) provides an investor with a specific sum of money at monthly or quarterly intervals. The amount specified by the investor usually is an amount exceeding the investment income alone, and the investor may increase or decrease his withdrawal at any time, or terminate the plan. To start a withdrawal plan, many funds require that the shares in the shareholder's account have a worth of at least $10,000.

If an investor who has $10,000 in his account decides to take out $50 a month (usually 6 percent of the principal on an annual basis represents the basic rate used in most withdrawal plans), to the extent that income dividends and capital gains distributions are insufficient to make the required payments, the fund automatically uses up capital by redeeming the number of shares necessary to make up the difference.

A withdrawal plan is not an annuity, as there is no guarantee that capital will last for a lifetime. There is no mortality factor. The investor maintains ownership and control over his investment, with the right to redeem large sums or liquidate completely.

Custodial Accounts under the Keogh Act

When the Self-Employed Individuals Tax Retirement Act of 1962 provided tax-saving features and made possible the so-called Keogh (HR-10) plans, most fund companies added another special service relating to retirement funds for self-employed persons and their employees.

The self-employed person who wishes to invest his contributions in mutual fund shares needs only to have an established plan and a custodial account. Many fund sponsors have set up bank custodial accounts for this purpose, and they usually provide forms which may be used, upon advice of counsel, in preparing individual retirement plans. Some sponsors have arrangements for "split-funded" Keogh plans which combine mutual fund shares and life insurance.

Prototype Corporate Retirement Plans

Corporate investors in mutual fund shares now have available prototype corporate pension and profit-sharing plans which have been approved by the Internal Revenue Service. The model prototype plan is a retirement plan preapproved as to form, and so set up as to be easily understood by corporations and easily installed. Corporations can adopt these plans without extensive legal procedures, red tape, and long delays.

MUTUAL FUNDS AND INCOME TAXES

Mutual Fund Companies

Most mutual fund companies are not taxed like ordinary business corporations. A special tax law relieves a mutual fund company of tax liability if it meets certain requirements. While there are several requirements to obtain special tax treatment, two shall be mentioned that are of special significance. A mutual fund is not subject to federal income tax on its income provided it agrees irrevocably (1) to be registered as a "regulated investment company" under the Investment Company Act of 1940; and (2) to distribute to its shareholders as taxable dividends for any taxable year at least 90 percent of its net investment income from dividends, interest, and short-term capital gains. There is an additional requirement that at least 90 percent of the fund's gross income for any taxable year must come from dividends, interest, and gains from securities.

By qualifying as a "regulated investment company" under Subchapter M of the Internal Revenue Code, mutual fund companies serve as conduits for passing on to their shareholders whatever dividends and interest they receive, and whatever net capital gains they realize on their portfolio securities. Generally, "regulated investment companies" distribute 100 percent of each year's net investment income and any net realized capital gains. If a fund elects to retain its earnings and not qualify as a "regulated investment company," it will be taxed in the same manner as any other corporation. Moreover, if it qualifies as a "regulated investment company" but does not distribute 100 percent of its net realized capital gains and net investment income to its shareholders, it must pay the regular corporate taxes on whatever amount is undistributed.

The Shareholder's Tax Liability on Income Dividends and Net Realized Capital Gains

Mutual fund shareholders must pay income taxes on their dividends and capital gains distributions. Thus, the shareholder includes these items in his income tax return.

Income dividends received are taxable to individuals at rates applicable to ordinary income. They qualify for the $100 exclusion for individuals, and the 85 percent deduction allowed corporations on dividends received from other domestic corporations. However, if the investment income of a mutual fund company consists of less than 75 percent dividend income from American corporations, the fund shareholder must make an apportionment of the dividends he receives that year as between qualifying dividends and nonqualifying dividends. Nonqualifying dividends include that portion of the dividend income received from the fund which represents income received by the fund from interest income and dividends from foreign sources.

For federal income tax purposes, the net realized capital gain paid to shareholders is treated by the shareholder as a long-term capital gain, and this is true regardless of how long the shareholder has held his mutual fund shares. However, if an investor sells his mutual fund shares within six months of purchase, he is subject to short-term capital gain or loss treatment, depending on his experience.

Income dividends and capital gains not received in cash but reinvested in additional shares must be reported year by year by the shareholder on his income tax return. When a shareholder redeems his shares, he realizes a gain or loss for tax purposes, just as he would if he bought and sold an individual security.

In the early part of each year, the mutual fund company sends to its shareholders copies of information returns it supplies to the IRS. This notice shows the total of all dividends and distributions followed by separate figures for qualifying and nonqualifying dividends and net realized capital gains distributed.

HOW MUTUAL FUND COMPANIES ARE REGULATED

While there is no way to protect the mutual fund investor against the results of poor management, he is protected legally by a wide variety of federal and state laws, rules and regulations, and self-regulatory bodies. The most important of the laws affecting mutual fund companies are:

1. The Federal Securities Act of 1933.
2. The Federal Securities Exchange Act of 1934.
3. The Federal Investment Company Act of 1940, and the Federal Investment Company Amendments Act of 1970.
4. The individual state laws which govern the sale of securities and the activities of the brokers and dealers within the state. These laws often are referred to as "blue sky" laws.

In addition to specific laws, mutual funds must comply with the Statement of Policy of the Securities and Exchange Commission. The federal laws are administered by the SEC.

The Federal Securities Act of 1933

This act deals with *new issues* of securities. The basic requirement of the Act is that the company must furnish full, fair, and accurate information with respect to financial and other corporate matters so that the prospective purchaser has the necessary facts on which to judge the security properly.

Because a mutual fund is continuously offering new shares to the public, it is subject to the registration and prospectus requirements of this Act. The items in the registration statement of most interest to the buyer must be printed in a prospectus. Mutual fund shares cannot be offered legally to investors unless preceded by, or accompanied by, a prospectus which has been filed with the Securities and Exchange Commission. The SEC does not pass on the investment merits of any security registered with it, nor does it guarantee the accuracy or adequacy of the disclosures in the registration statement or prospectus.

The Federal Securities Exchange Act of 1934

This act deals with *securities already issued and in the hands of investors*. It provides for regulation by the SEC of stock exchanges, over-the-counter markets, brokers, and dealers. It requires brokers and dealers to register with the SEC. Through an amendment enacted in 1938 (Maloney Act), the Act made possible the creation of the National Association of Securities Dealers, Inc. (NASD), the self-regulating arm of the over-the-counter business. The NASD supervises the sale of shares of the vast majority of mutual fund companies.

The Investment Company Act of 1940

This act is the principal legislation directly affecting the operations of mutual fund companies. The basic intent of the Act is to provide for the registration and regulation of investment companies and investment advisors. The Act was designed to make certain that the investor was given adequate and full information concerning the company and its investment program, and that the activities of mutual fund companies are based on the "public interest." It provides that major changes in the company's business policy must be approved by shareholders. Also the fund's contracts with investment advisors and distributors must be approved yearly by shareholders, or a majority of the independent outside directors.

On December 14, 1970, the Act was amended for the first time since its original enactment in 1940. The principal changes established by the amendment dealt with standards for management fees and sales charges, including sales charges in periodic payment "contractual plans."

State Laws

The state "blue sky" laws involve a wide variety of provisions, but, in general, they give protection to any purchaser of a mutual fund share who has been given inaccurate or incomplete information, or has been hurt as a result of an improper or unfair practice.

The Securities and Exchange Commission
Statement of Policy

On August 1, 1950, the Securities and Exchange Commission issued a "Statement of Policy" as a guide against violations of the statutory requirements in federal laws. It is not a law, but a set of rules which have the force of law. Its purpose is to advise mutual fund companies and their distributors, as well as dealers and salesmen, as to the types of advertising and sales literature which meet the law's requirements with respect to fair, proper, and accurate statements.

FINANCIAL PLANNING AND MUTUAL FUNDS

Mutual fund shares are used in the financial planning of individuals, business organizations, and institutions.

Mutual Funds in Programming Personal Needs

Proper and complete financial planning requires that the financial plan fit the individual's requirements and be integrated with all other assets. It should recognize such factors as age, family responsibilities, objectives, income requirements, degree of risk the investor can take, tax consequences, and so forth. Professional financial planners agree that before a person starts a program of capital accumulation through mutual fund shares, he should have a sufficient cash reserve for unforeseen emergencies and short-term needs, and adequate life insurance for protection of his family. He must also have at least a minimum retirement income plan so as to be assured of adequate protection against living too long. After taking care of those basic and essential needs, he then is in a position to add mutual fund investments to round out his program. By having both fixed-dollar and equity-dollar vehicles, he will have a possible hedge against both inflation and deflation.

In personal financial planning, mutual fund investments often have been used for retirement purposes, and for accumulating money to pay for the high costs of a college education. The equity dollar inflation hedge is not certain, but may provide for retired people some relief from the decline in the purchasing power of the dollar. In planning for the college education of their children, many parents have considered mutual funds an ideal vehicle for accumulating the needed money, especially when the mutual fund purchase is accompanied by a purchase of life insurance to cover the possibility of death prior to completion of the mutual fund plan.

Mutual Funds in Estate Planning

While mutual funds can play a role in the process of accumulating an estate, they also can be important in terms of estate conservation and distribution. The following represent some typical ways in which mutual funds have been used in estate plans:

1. To provide liquidity, to pay estate taxes, and to support the deceased's family in cases where the amount of life insurance was either not adequate or where the estate owner was uninsurable and could not qualify for life insurance. The executor's task of meeting the cash demands on the estate is eased if he finds large shareholdings of mutual funds among the assets of the estate.

2. To fund trusts. The built-in management, diversification, and economical and convenient administration of mutual funds can ease the trustee's task and simplify his duties. Mutual fund shares have been used in living trusts, reversionary trusts, trusts set up for minors, and in charitable trusts.

3. To ease the family's burden with respect to investment responsibilities. If the estate has assets other than life insurance, many estate owners, realizing that the members of their family have limited experience in investment matters, have arranged for a substantial portion of the assets to be left in the form of fund shares which provide continuous professional management and convenience in bookkeeping, accounting, and tax procedures.

Mutual Funds and Business Organizations

In various ways, business organizations (especially small or medium sized companies) have become investors in mutual fund shares. Mutual fund investments have been made in pension plans (often split funded with life insurance), profit sharing plans, thrift plans, executive deferred compensation plans for key personnel, corporate reserves established for depreciation or retirement of long-term debt, and payroll deduction programs. The trend toward use of mutual funds in employee benefit programs is due to the desire on the part of employees to balance fixed-dollar benefits with some possible protection against the effects of continued inflation.

Mutual Funds and Institutions

Schools and colleges, hospitals, churches, foundations, labor unions, and fraternal organizations are among the largest shareholders of mutual fund companies. This is because many institutions do not have among their personnel or trustees, persons qualified to manage an institutional investment account successfully. Even for those who have the qualifications, time pressures and other responsibilities make the job more difficult.

SALES OF MUTUAL FUNDS
BY LIFE UNDERWRITERS

In recent years there has been increasing recognition of the fact that life insurance and mutual fund investments are closely related and are complementary, not competitive. Financial planners have become increasingly aware that many of their life insurance clients who have fixed-dollar benefits in social security, life insurance cash values, and a fixed-amount pension plan, want to consider equity investments to balance out their overall long-term financial plan. These same clients have expressed concern about continued inflation, and are seeking ways to obtain growth to offset the decline in the purchasing power of the dollar.

Currently, most dually licensed life insurance representatives are providing balance by offering mutual fund shares principally in connection with combination funding wherein the individual investor's outlay is allocated between life insurance and mutual funds. This split-funded technique, using both mutual funds and life insurance, also is being applied in connection with executive deferred compensation plans for selected key personnel, Keogh plans, and corporate pension plans. Furthermore, it is becoming more evident that the dual salesman is becoming more and more aware of the great potential for selling mutual fund shares to people who are uninsurable, to people who are in the higher age brackets and have decided to purchase equity investments (usually in anticipation of retirement) rather than purchase additional life insurance, and to beneficiaries of death claims and matured endowments who have decided not to leave the proceeds with the life insurance company under the settlement options.

SELECTED REFERENCES

Casey, William J.   *Mutual Funds Desk Book.* Rev. ed. New York: Institute for Business Planning, Inc., 1969.

Cohen, Jerome B., and Hanson, Arthur W.   *Personal Finance: Principles and Case Problems.* 4th ed. Homewood, Ill.: Richard D. Irwin, Inc., 1972.

Graham, Bernard.   *A Life Underwriter's Guide to Equity Investment.* Lynbrook, N.Y.: Farnsworth Publishing Co., Inc., 1968.

Investment Companies.   1972 ed. New York: Wiesenberger Services, Inc.

Jacobs, Raymond H.   *Securities.* Vol. 2, 2d ed. Washington, D.C.: Kalb, Voorhis and Co., 1967.

part IV

Individual
Health Insurance

Protection against the economic consequences of sickness and injury is of growing significance to individuals and their families. Loss of income through disability and the costs of medical care have become increasingly heavy financial burdens that, for most people, can be shifted in large part to insurance organizations.

In addition to government and group health insurance programs, millions of Americans are being protected from economic loss through coverage under a wide variety of individual health insurance contracts. Part IV describes the forms of individual health insurance that have been created to provide for disability income needs and medical expenses, and considers important legal concepts, costs and pricing aspects, and the process of risk selection.

20

Individual Disability
Income Insurance

By BROOKS CHANDLER

INDIVIDUAL DISABILITY INCOME INSURANCE provides cash benefits to replace earnings lost during periods of incapacity due to injury or illness. As American life has become increasingly urbanized and money oriented, the need for protection against loss of income has assumed greater importance and has met with growing recognition at all economic levels.

Awareness of this need has resulted not only in rapid growth of group plans, particularly those providing benefits during disabilities of long duration, but also in increased pressure for expansion of government programs such as the compulsory state cash sickness plans for shorter disabilities and the federal social security system providing income during long-term disabilities. Although this growth in group coverages and coverage under government plans has limited the market for individual disability income insurance to some extent, particularly among lower income people, the percentage of gainfully employed persons with adequate income protection remains relatively small. In recent years, to encourage purchase of more adequate coverage, insurers have offered higher benefits for longer periods under more liberal conditions, and the volume of coverage has grown significantly.

The need for income when the family's head is disabled, equally as important as the requirement to provide income for family needs in the case of premature death, also has met with growing acceptance on the part of life insurance counselors and others engaged in personal financial planning. Increasingly, in connection with the arrangement of life insurance programs, the need for disability insurance is identified and appropriate coverage fitted to the requirements of the individual. This has provided a powerful stimulus to the purchase of individual disability insurance by persons with higher incomes.

Individual disability income insurance also is used for various business purposes. These include provision of income to cover continued overhead expenses of professionals and individuals in certain other occupations while they are disabled, replacement of income to a business organization when key personnel are disabled, and provision of funds for purchase of the business interest of a disabled partner or stockholder-executive.

While the needs for disability income insurance parallel those for life insurance, the contingency insured against is more difficult to define, and considerations which must be weighed in determining the existence of disability can be highly subjective. As a result, policy drafting, underwriting of applicants, and administration of benefit payments are quite different.

History and Development

Arrangements to provide various forms of aid to the ill and injured seem to have been present in even the most primitive societies. In the more recent past, associations such as the guilds which flourished in Europe during the Middle Ages and the British Friendly Societies which grew up during the 16th century, provided some limited benefits to disabled members. While life, fire, and marine insurance developed much earlier, disability insurance with any of the essential characteristics of the present form did not appear until the 19th century.

The earliest insuring organizations to offer benefits for death and other losses due to accidental injuries were formed to protect travelers on the new and then highly hazardous railroads. The first company in the United States was the Franklin Health Assurance Company of Massachusetts, organized in 1850, and the first to be notably successful was The Travelers Insurance Company of Hartford. Other companies were organized during the ensuing years, including the first fraternals, and coverage was extended to include certain selected sicknesses in addition to accidents. Many of the restrictions in earlier contracts were eliminated, but growth was slow until after 1890.

In the period from 1890 to the mid 1920s the first substantial growth in accident and sickness insurance occurred as casualty insurance companies entered the disability business (primarily to provide accident benefits), and major life insurance companies began offering disability insurance under individual policies and by means of riders issued in connection with life insurance policies. During this period supplementary benefits, such as a "principal sum" payable for accidental death and dismemberment, an increase in the benefit amount during hospital confinement, and payments for surgeon's fees, were first offered in connection with individual disability policies. Lifetime benefits were provided for accident disability, and sickness benefits were extended to cover all types of illnesses. Noncancellable contracts were introduced during this period and met with increasingly wider acceptance after 1915.

With the advent of the depression in the late twenties and early thirties, the disability insurance business suffered severe setbacks and losses. The imbalance produced by reduced income in relation to outstanding benefits resulted in overinsurance. The situation was aggravated by a combination of overly liberal benefit provisions and excessive indemnities.

Following the sharp reversals of the depression, the thirties were typically a period of retrenchment, with many companies withdrawing from the disability field and others offering only restricted contracts. By the late thirties, several adjustments had been made and confidence was rebuilding in the disability field. When World War II ended, disability insurance had undergone substantial liberalization although it retained certain protective features to prevent recurrence of the problems of the depression. The reentry of many life companies into the disability market heightened competition. Many of the overly restrictive features of the policies were eliminated or modified during this period.

A major development of the late sixties and early seventies has been the underwriting of disability insurance for substandard risks. Formerly insurance for impaired individuals was available only with exclusion riders (discussed later in this chapter). Today policies providing full coverage on impaired lives are being offered successfully by many insurers at premium rates reflecting the degree of impairment.

Extent of Coverage

More than 58 million persons have some form of disability income protection. Included in this total, in addition to those insured under individual disability policies, are people covered by group disability coverage, formal sick-leave programs, union-administered plans and federal mutual benefit associations. Approximately 17 million people are protected by disability income policies on an individual policy basis.[1] These policies largely cover wage earners, although some coverage is provided for housewives and students. The growth of disability income coverage is shown in Table 20–1.

BASIC PROVISIONS

Insuring Agreement and Definition of Disability

The insuring clause gives the general definition of the coverage provided by the contract. It identifies the parties to the contract and states that insurance is provided for loss subject to all provisions, conditions, and exclusions of the policy. A sample insuring clause covering accident and sickness reads:

The ABC Insurance Company hereby insures the person named as the Insured, subject to the exceptions and other provisions herein contained, against loss covered by this policy commencing while it is in force and resulting from (1) accidental bodily injuries occurring while this policy is in force, hereinafter referred to as injuries; or (2) sickness or disease which is first manifested while this policy is in force, hereinafter referred to as sickness.

Preexisting conditions are excluded, subject to a statutory time limit, either in the insuring clause as above or through an appropriate definition of "injury" or "sickness" appearing elsewhere in the policy. A probationary period is included in some policies. It is usually applicable to

---

[1] Health Insurance Institute, *Source Book of Health Insurance Data, 1971–72.* New York, 1972.

TABLE 20–1.   Number of Persons with Disability Income Protection by Type of Program in the United States (000 omitted)

End of Year	All Programs	Insurance Companies			Formal Paid Sick-Leave Plans	Other
		All Insurance Companies	Group Policies	Individual Policies		
1946	26,229	14,369	7,135	8,684	8,400	3,460
1950	37,793	25,993	15,104	13,067	8,900	2,900
1955	39,513	29,813	19,171	13,642	8,500	1,200
1960	42,436	31,836	20,970	14,298	9,500	1,100
1961	43,055	32,055	21,186	14,301	9,900	1,100
1962	44,902	33,602	22,313	14,854	10,200	1,100

Short-term Disability Income Protection

End of Year	All Programs	All Insurance Companies	Group Policies	Individual Policies	Formal Paid Sick-Leave Plans	Other
1963	43,927	31,927	22,669	12,902	10,900	1,100
1964	44,751	32,751	23,177	13,280	10,900	1,100
1965	46,347	33,547	24,615	12,559	11,700	1,100
1966	49,372	35,772	26,322	13,264	12,500	1,100
1967	51,230	36,830	27,632	13,004	13,300	1,100
1968	54,955	40,055	30,777	13,879	13,800	1,100
1969	57,004	40,404	30,865	13,807	15,500	1,100
1970	57,595	40,595	31,498	13,639	15,900	1,100

Long-term Disability Income Protection

End of Year	All Programs	All Insurance Companies	Group Policies	Individual Policies	Formal Paid Sick-Leave Plans	Other
1963	3,029	3,029	749	2,280	—	—
1964	3,420	3,420	1,257	2,163	—	—
1965	4,457	4,457	1,903	2,554	—	—
1966	5,002	5,002	2,376	2,626	—	—
1967	6,682	6,682	3,827	2,855	—	—
1968	7,718	7,718	4,710	3,008	—	—
1969	9,076	9,076	5,715	3,361	—	—
1970	10,740	10,740	7,176	3,564	—	—

Note. Data in the category "Insurance companies" refer to the net total of people protected, i.e., duplication among persons with more than one insurance policy has been eliminated. However, for years prior to 1963, any duplication resulting from the combination of numbers covered for short-term and long-term protection has not been eliminated. The category "Formal Paid Sick-Leave Plans" refers to people with formal paid sick-leave plans but without insurance company coverage. The category "Other" includes union-administered plans and the Federal Mutual Benefit Association.

Source: Health Insurance Council.

sickness benefits, and requires that a loss occur more than 30 days after the policy date. This restriction has been removed from most new policies.

Total Disability.   The definition of total disability, which is important in determining the liability of the insurer, is subject to variation. Early disability provisions of life insurance contracts and disability insurance policies provided for payment of lifetime benefits if the individual was unable to perform the duties of "his occupation." This led to abuse by insureds claiming total disability where they were unable to perform all duties of their occupation but where their earning power was not substantially impaired. In 1929 the National Convention of Insurance Commissioners prohibited use of this definition in life insurance, and health insurance policies thereafter generally provided for a limited period of "his occupation" followed by a definition defining total disability as "inability to perform the duties of any gainful occupation." A further modification of the gainful occupation definition resulted in addition of a phrase such as, "for which he is reasonably fitted by education, training, and experience."

The trend in recent years has been toward liberalization of the period for which the "his occupation" definition is applicable. For the professions, currently the typical period is for 5 or 10 years, or to age 65. Shorter "his occupation" periods are offered applicants in occupational classes other than the professions.

Confining and Nonconfining Disability. Some policies distinguish between confining and nonconfining disability when the cause is sickness. House confinement restrictions usually provide for the payment of benefits as long as the insured is confined to his house and regularly treated by a doctor. If the disability continues but the insured is no longer house confined, benefits generally reduce to one half and the benefit period is reduced to 26 weeks or some other nominal period of time.

While confining sickness provisions are still found in some contracts, they are no longer popular. This is due to the restrictive nature of the contract and misunderstanding of the actual benefits provided. In many instances the claimant would be prevented from receiving benefits under the house confining provisions even though he was not able to return to work. Further, the courts have liberalized the meaning of "confining," and it is no longer clear-cut as to those facts which truly distinguish between confining and nonconfining disability.

Partial Disability. Many contracts include partial disability benefits or offer the coverage as an option. The benefit is usually equal to 50 percent of the total disability benefit for a limited period of time, such as three to six months. Originally covering only partial disability due to accidents, the benefit is now available for partial disability for sickness immediately following compensable total disability due to sickness, particularly in long-term contracts.

Partial disability often is defined as "the inability of the insured to perform one or more of the important duties of his occupation." This benefit is not particularly appropriate for employees (as differentiated from the self-employed) who normally return to full salary at the time of their return to work even though partially disabled. It is much more meaningful when applied to a self-employed individual who is dependent on his ability to perform all of his functions as they would relate to his earnings.

Elimination Period and Payment Duration

The elimination period is that period of time at the inception of disability during which no benefits are payable. Elimination periods generally range from one week to one year, although in some exceptional situations a longer period such as two years may be provided where the insured person has adequate income protection for that length of time. The current trend is toward elimination periods of 30 days or longer.

As the length of the elimination period increases, the cost of the benefit subsequently payable reduces, making it possible for many individuals to secure protection against extended disability that otherwise would not be within their means. It should be recognized, however, that the longer the elimination period, the more difficult it may be to secure adequate proof of accident or illness.

The elimination period also serves to avert some instances of over-insurance. It allows recognition of the insured's economic circumstances and needs without duplication through the programming of replacement income to supplement salary continuation programs, social security disability benefits, state cash sickness benefits, and group insurance short-term benefits.

Under certain circumstances the elimination period may be used as an underwriting tool. An elimination period longer than that applied for may be used as an alternative to an extra premium rating, or to a rider excluding coverage for an existing condition likely to result in short-term disabilities.

The payment duration or benefit period of a policy will range from six months, to age 65, or even for the lifetime of the insured in the event of accident. Policies now may be purchased which provide lifetime benefits for sickness which totally disables the policyowner prior to attainment of a specified age, usually age 50. Early noncancellable disability contracts and disability insurance provisions in connection with life insurance policies provided benefits for the entire duration of disability. These were the types of contracts under which severe losses were incurred during the depression years and, as a result, contracts issued for a number of years thereafter usually provided for shorter benefit periods.

The vast majority of disabilities are of relatively short duration. Thus, policies with a short payment duration offer complete protection for most disabilities. However, they do not protect adequately against the infrequent long-term disability which is the most damaging economically. The length of the benefit period has a significant effect on the cost of the coverage, with the cost increasing as the benefit period lengthens.

A waiver-of-premium benefit is included in most modern individual disability income policies. Originally, this benefit provision was phrased so as to allow premiums to be waived during the benefit period following a qualification period of three or six months, or the elimination period, whichever was longer. The recent trend is to waive premiums throughout total disability, rather than during the benefit period only, and to return premiums paid during the qualification period.

Benefit Amounts

The amount of an applicant's earned income is the primary determinant in evaluating the amount of disability income benefits for which he qualifies. Net worth and unearned income are becoming of increasing concern; most companies consider these additional factors in connection with contracts providing larger benefits and where there may be less incentive for an individual to return to work.

Each insurer establishes an "issue limit" which is the maximum amount of disability income protection it will provide for an individual, and a "participation limit" which is the maximum total amount of coverage a person may have from all sources. It should be kept in mind that disability income benefits under a policy for which premiums are paid by the individual policyowner are tax free. Therefore, benefits generally should be limited to 40 to 75 percent of earned income. Each company has its own formula for determining the percentage of a person's earned income which it will insure, usually grading down the percentage as earned income increases. Company issue and participation limits vary widely, and some companies today will issue and participate to $3,000 or more of monthly benefits.

OTHER PROVISIONS

Overinsurance Provisions

An important consideration in underwriting disability income insurance is avoiding issuance of a policy which will provide benefits equivalent to too high a percentage of the insured's income—or even exceed his after-tax income. The Uniform Individual Accident and Sickness Policy Provision Law (discussed in Chapter 22) includes the three optional provisions described in the following paragraphs. These provisions may be utilized to reduce the possibility of overinsurance. However, it should be noted that competition has tended to restrict their use.

The *relation of earnings to insurance* provision (the average-earnings clause) is allowed only in noncancellable or guaranteed renewable disability income policies. It provides that if the insurance held by the insured under all policies exceeds his average earnings during the two years prior to the beginning of disability, the company will pay only such portion of the amount of benefit due as the amount of such earnings bears to the total benefit. The insurer in this circumstance is required to refund the premium for any excess insurance for a period limited to two years preceding the disability.

The *insurance with other insurers* provision allows a pro rata reduction in the disability benefit if the insured has other policies and has not so notified the insurer prior to the onset of disability. The insured will be paid pro rata benefits in proportion to the amount of insurance with the insurer as it relates to the total amount of insurance under all policies. This provision is not applicable to guaranteed renewable or noncancellable contracts.

The *other insurance with this insurer* provision permits two approaches for limiting the amount of like insurance granted to a single insured by the same insurer. The first alternative authorizes the use of a provision which contains a maximum aggregate indemnity for a particular type of coverage, voids any indemnity in excess of such maximum, and requires that the premium for the voided indemnity be returned. The other alternative is the use of a provision which limits coverage to one like policy with the same insurer. If there is more than one like policy, the insured may choose which policy will be kept in force and all premiums will be refunded on the other policy or policies.

Exclusions

Individual disability income policies customarily have contained certain exclusions which specify conditions not covered by the policy. These exclusions have eliminated from coverage disabilities resulting from war or act of war, self-inflicted injury, and disabilities incurred while acting as a pilot or crew member of an aircraft. The trend in recent years has been toward liberalization or elimination of exclusions and many contracts today exclude only losses caused by war or any act of war.

Guaranteed Insurability Provisions

The use of guaranteed insurability provisions in disability income policies has become increasingly popular. Under these provisions an insured is given the opportunity to purchase additional insurance in specified amounts at certain predetermined times. These provisions may be on an absolute basis with no further underwriting or insurability requirements to be met, or on a conditional basis where there is no need to reestablish insurability with regard to health but the additional insurance may be subject to financial underwriting.

SPECIAL FORMS

Waiver of Premium Disability Income Benefits under Life Policies

Provisions for waiver of premiums during an insured's disability are offered in connection with virtually all individual whole life insurance policies. Some companies include waiver of premium automatically for applicants qualifying on the basis of age or other factors as a basic policy provision, and include the cost in the premium. Where the waiver-of-premium benefit is optional, the majority of applicants elect the benefit. Underwriting is more liberal than would be necessary if a cash benefit were provided during disability.

Many life insurance companies also offer disability income cash benefits in connection with individual life insurance policies by means of an optional rider for which an extra premium is charged. The rider provides the payment of a monthly indemnity for total disability which begins prior to the rider termination age, usually age 55 or 60. The benefit amount is most commonly $10 monthly for each $1,000 of face amount.

Benefit payments for total disability are paid after an elimination period, six months being most commonly utilized. There rarely is any choice of elimination periods and no distinction is made between accident and sickness. Benefits usually are payable to age 65, with the further provision that the life insurance will mature as an endowment at age 65, if the insured is still totally disabled. There normally are no optional benefits such as partial disability, or provision for nondisabling injuries under life disability riders.

Rather strict underwriting controls are imposed for life insurance disability income riders. The maximum issue limit for a typical company would be $500 per month subject to a maximum participation limit of $1,200 per month or 50 to 60 percent of the insured's average monthly earned income, whichever is less.

Life companies rarely issue the benefit with term insurance contracts and seldom make it available to an applicant who is rated for physical or medical reasons. At extra premiums, the benefit may be issued to applicants in occupations for which ratings are necessary.

Franchise Disability Insurance

Individual disability policies are sold to employees of employers, members of trade and professional associations and their employees, and to members of unions, through franchise arrangements. These policies may be underwritten utilizing group insurance practices subject to preestablished participation levels and issue limits, or individual underwriting practices may be applied where individual selection of benefits is available. Normally, the insurer agrees to renew each individual contract without modification unless simultaneously discontinuing or modifying policies for all persons in the group.

Nonoccupational Coverage

Nonoccupational coverage, common in group insurance but relatively rare in individual insurance, excludes loss resulting from accident or sickness arising out of employment. It is often used to supplement workmen's compensation.

Mortgage Protection

Disability income policies are used to provide benefits to continue mortgage payments in the event of total disability. Such contracts are usually written for a moderate benefit period, or a benefit period which reduces as mortgage payments are made. Often these plans are written through savings and loan associations in conjunction with loans.

Industrial Disability Insurance

Industrial disability insurance is characterized by low benefit amounts with premiums collected monthly by the agent. The policies usually provide that the insurer may decline to renew at any anniversary date, and sometimes cancel during the policy term, while remaining liable for full payment of existing claims.

Health Care Supplements

A number of optional health care supplements may be offered in connection with individual disability policies. Frequently the supplements provide a daily hospital benefit in a fixed amount while hospitalized, surgical indemnities based on a schedule of surgical procedures, and a physician's fee benefit paying specified indemnities for doctor's visits while totally disabled.

Modified Premium Plans

In recent years modified premium plans have become more common. These plans vary from company to company but usually are of two general types. The first is "step-rate" and requires low initial premiums which increase periodically, usually every 5 or 10 years, either to a predetermined age or throughout the life of the contract. The other type, the "modified level premium," provides for a low initial premium which increases only once, either at the end of a specified period or at a predetermined age, to a level premium which is slightly lower than the attained age level premium which would be paid for the coverage by a new applicant.

Both types of modified premium plans are designed to provide young applicants with the capability of purchasing a quality disability insurance product at an affordable cost. The plans often are available on a noncancellable basis.

UNDERWRITING

Underwriting Standard Risks

The purpose of disability income insurance is to replace, for an insured person who is totally disabled, a sufficient portion of his earned income to enable him to maintain a reasonable standard of living. The applicant for coverage must be an acceptable physical risk and the benefit should not be sufficiently large to serve as an incentive to malinger, or deliberately refrain from engaging in productive activity. A disabled person with substantial net worth or unearned income may not have the same incentive to return to work as would a person relying entirely on earned income.

In individual disability income insurance, the underwriting, or selection of risks, involves the evaluation of the same elements of insurability as in life insurance, namely, medical history and present physical conditions, as well as nonmedical factors such as age, occupation, morals, habits, and financial status. However, these factors will vary in degree from the effect they would have in life underwriting. The significant differences arise from the nature of the risk insured and the fact that in most cases benefits are payable to the insured rather than to a third party.

Antiselection can be exercised more effectively by applicants for disability insurance than by applicants for life insurance. This occurs where the insurance may consciously be sought by individuals who have known impairments or whose probability of disability is much higher than the norm. The prevention of antiselection is an important objective of the underwriting process.

As noted previously, a major difference in disability underwriting is the subjective nature of the risk, the event causing loss and amount payable being considerably more difficult to define and prove on the basis of objective factors. Disability is a relative concept rather than an absolute concept such as the fact of death which satisfies the requirements for payment made under a life insurance contract. In life insurance there is generally a desire on the part of the insured to remain alive, whereas in disability insurance, even though a person may not wish to become disabled, once benefits become payable there may be a tendency to extend the qualification for continued payments as long as possible.

Underwriting Substandard Risks

Several techniques are utilized to offer insurance to the person who does not measure up to the qualifications of a standard applicant. The elimination period may serve as a tool to cope with certain minor types of impairment by utilizing long elimination periods. In other circumstances the risk may be made acceptable by utilizing a waiver or impairment rider which excludes coverage of a specifically named disease or condition. This offers the insurer the capability to provide protection against all other hazards which may be experienced under the contract and yet provide protection for the company against the known circumstance. It should be noted, of course, that the insured is left without protection for the most likely cause of disability. Normally, policies issued with impairment riders do not involve extra premiums.

Another technique for offering disability protection to a substandard risk is the utilization of a full coverage contract subject to an increased premium. The amount of the increase, therefore, reflects the additional hazard incurred by the company due to known medical history. The broad use of substandard extra premium underwriting is relatively new in the disability income field but has become increasingly prevalent in recent years.[2]

RENEWAL PROVISIONS

Disability income insurance policies contain a variety of renewal provisions. The extent of use of the various types of renewal provisions has fluctuated through the years, but currently follows more closely the practice of life insurance where a policy may be kept in force at the insured's option by the timely payment of the premium.

There are essentially three basic types of renewal provisions in use in individual disability income contracts presently being issued.

Cancellable Contracts

Renewal provisions used in cancellable (or "commercial") contracts, comparable to those used in the earliest forms of health insurance contracts, provide for renewal of the contract at the option of the insurer. The insurer would have the right not only to refuse renewal at the time any renewal premium was due, but also to terminate the policy at any other time on written notice as provided in the contract, refunding the pro rata unearned premium. The use of cancellable renewal provisions has become less common, and those contracts which continue to utilize this provision often specify that the insurer's right to terminate can be exercised only as of a premium due date.

Some states now prohibit cancellation by the insurer between premium due dates, or limit the right of cancellation to a short period of time after issue. The Uniform Policy Provisions Law provides that the insurer must give at least five days' written notice of cancellation.

Guaranteed Renewable with the Right of the Insurer to Change Premiums by Class

A second type of renewal provision guarantees renewal subject to timely payment of premiums until a specified contract termination age,

---

[2] See Chapter 24 for further discussion of the treatment of substandard risks in individual health insurance.

with the insurer retaining the right to adjust premiums for any underwriting class, but not on an individual contract. Class may be defined by age, sex, occupation, or other broad category. The guaranteed renewable provision may be used only in policies in which the insured has the right to continue the contract in force until at least age 50, or, in the case of a contract issued after age 44, for at least five years from the date of issue.

The use of the adjustable premium guaranteed renewable provision had its beginnings in hospitalization insurance, where the average claim results would be subject to increase not only through an increase in claim frequency but also through change in price level of services and facilities. This has been carried over into the disability field by insurers who do not wish to incur the ultimate risk of noncancellable underwriting and have used this provision as a protective feature.

Noncancellable Policies

A noncancellable policy specifies that the insured has the right to continue the policy in force up to a specified age by timely payment of the premium shown. The insurer does not have the right to change premiums or to refuse to renew the policy prior to the limiting age.

A less liberal contract utilizing the noncancellable provision was the aggregate type which specified an aggregate amount payable under the policy for all disabilities on a cumulative basis from the date of issue of the policy. The aggregate policy has been supplanted by a contract specifying a maximum benefit for each disability. Almost all noncancellable insurance is issued today on this basis, and a marked trend has been indicated in growth of this type of product.

ADMINISTRATION OF BENEFIT PAYMENTS

The administration of benefit payments is the process of obtaining relevant facts regarding an accident or sickness, determining the amount of benefits payable to the insured under the terms of the contract, and paying those benefits.

The Uniform Policy Provisions Law requires use of provisions specifying the basis on which notice of claim is to be given by the insured, claim forms are to be furnished, proofs of loss are to be required, and payments are to be made. A majority of claims are paid promptly on the basis of the proof of loss form. Some claims will require corroboration through further personal investigation by the insurer's staff or independent agencies, additional medical information and employment records.

Policies which have been in force for less than three years are checked carefully to be certain that there was no misrepresentation in the application, or evidence of a preexisting condition which is not covered under the contract. The company under these conditions may rescind the contract, revise the contract, or deny the claim. Preexisting conditions and misrepresentations are subject to the "time limit on certain defenses" provision of the Uniform Policy Provisions Law, which removes the defenses available to the company after three years or any lesser period stated in the policy.

With the advent of higher benefits for disability income policies and the availability of policies providing lifetime accident and long-term sickness benefits, rehabilitation is being utilized more by insurance companies. This is the process of restoring a disabled individual to productive work. Benefits usually are continued when the insured is employed on a trial basis as a part of a rehabilitation program. Even where no benefits for rehabilitation are included in the policy, insurers may pay for a rehabilitation program where the net effect is to reduce liability through an earlier return to productive work.

The payment of claims is affected by the same subjective elements of disability that enter into underwriting. The problems involved in substantiating the extent of disability will vary with the character and attitude of the individual, as well as being influenced by economic conditions and by other external factors such as workmen's compensation benefits or liability judgments.

Because of the subjective elements inherent in disability insurance, in a few instances differences may exist between the insured and the company which will result in a compromise settlement or legal contest.

RECENT DEVELOPMENTS

Business Overhead Insurance

During the late 1950s a special application of disability insurance was developed and special policies were devised to allow professional men or businessmen to insure their office overhead expenses in the event of disability. This product became more sophisticated during the 1960s and is now an important part of the portfolio of most companies. Overhead expenses generally are defined as regular expenses incurred in the conduct of the insured's business but excluding (1) his own compensation and the compensation of any person hired to perform his duties, (2) the cost of capital goods, (3) payment on the principal of an indebtedness, or (4) expenses for which the insured was not regularly and customarily liable prior to his disability. These contracts usually are for a short benefit period, i.e., one or two years, with a short elimination period. The benefit is the amount of overhead expense incurred up to a limit specified in the contract.

Business Interest Purchase

In the last decade many companies have experimented with the use of disability insurance to fund buy-out agreements between partners and among stockholders in small closely held corporations, in the same manner that life insurance is used to fund buy-outs upon the death of a principal. Numerous problems have been encountered, primary among them being the aspect of overinsurance when a benefit large enough to fund purchase of an individual's business interest is superimposed upon regular issue and participation limits. Other problems include those of defining total disability and establishing a "trigger point" for the buy-out. Several companies have found reasonably workable solutions to these and other problems, and are marketing business buy-out disability insurance.[3]

Cash Value and Return of Premium Provisions

Policies including provisions for cash surrender values, or for return to the insured of a portion of premiums paid at specified times under described circumstances, have been offered by an increasing number of companies during recent years. There has been considerable controversy over the desirability of these provisions and the attitudes of regulatory authorities are not firmly fixed, varying considerably among states.[4] One of the arguments against these features is that they may serve to deter the insured from claiming the income replacement benefits during disability which the policy was designed primarily to provide. New York Insurance Department regulations specifically prohibit use of policy provisions which provide for a return of premium or cash value benefit.

Policies with cash value provisions usually provide for payment of a specified cash sum upon surrender of the policy or the death of the policy-owner after the third policy year, or if the policy matures, at a predetermined date such as attainment of age 65 by the insured. The cash value is frequently the total premium paid reduced by any claim payments.

The most widely offered return of premium provisions are added by rider at additional cost and provide for return of all premiums paid during 10-year periods in the absence of claims, or for a return of part of the premium if claim costs do not exceed a stated percentage of premiums.

A few companies have marketed these policies with considerable success. Additional companies, including some of the larger writers of individual disability insurance, are expected to enter this field and more widespread public acceptance is to be anticipated.

Inflation Benefit

Several companies offer so-called inflation benefits designed to increase payments from time to time during lengthy disabilities so as to offset the declining purchasing power represented by the original dollar benefit amount. Normally, the benefit is increased periodically by a specified percentage determined as a fixed amount or reflecting the movement of a recognized price index. In either event, the increase may be subject to a cumulative maximum. Because of the general concern with the effects of inflation, these benefits have stimulated considerable interest; but few of the larger insurers have included coverage of this type in their portfolios.

SELECTED REFERENCES

Dickerson, O. D. *Health Insurance*. Rev. ed. Homewood, Ill.: Richard D. Irwin, Inc., 1963.

---

[3] For a discussion of income protection for business continuation, see Chapter 47.

[4] See the Report of the Industry Advisory Committee on Accident and Health Insurance with Cash Surrender of Other Nonforfeiture Value Benefits to the N.A.I.C. (C-1), Accident and Health Protection Subcommittee, Minutes of the 1971–72 Annual Meeting of the National Association of Insurance Commissioners, June 14–17, 1971.

Faulkner, Edwin J. *Health Insurance.* New York: McGraw-Hill Book Co., 1960.

Health Insurance Association of America. *Principles of Individual Health Insurance.* New York, 1968.

Society of Actuaries. *Health Insurance Provided through Individual Policies* (Edwin L. Bartleson, principal contributor). Chicago, 1968.

21

Individual Medical Expense Insurance

By JOHN S. THOMPSON, JR.

THE EARLIEST FORMS of individual health insurance provided for cash payment benefits to persons disabled by accidents or sickness. For several years, however, disability income insurance has been overshadowed by the growing importance of·insurance covering the expenses incurred for medical treatment of injury and sickness. Insurance on losses in this category, which may be referred to as "medical expense insurance," is designed primarily for coverage on some or all of the following kinds of expense:

1. Hospital charges for room and board, general duty nursing care, and other hospital services and supplies;
2. Fees for medical care or treatment by physicians, surgeons, and private duty nurses; and
3. Expenses incurred for other necessary medical and health care services and supplies, including dental care, nursing home care, medicines, and prosthetic appliances.

Although it is possible to describe insurable medical expenses in only three classes, modern-day medical practice has become so complex that each of these three classes is extremely broad. It is not surprising, then, that the various forms of medical expense insurance that have been developed in recent years differ widely with respect to the types of medical expenses that they cover and in their basic underwriting characteristics.

Medical expense insurance has developed on both an individual and a group basis. This chapter is concerned only with individual medical expense insurance.

Development

The earliest form of hospital coverage, introduced prior to 1910, was generally issued as an adjunct to disability income insurance and provided for a 50 or 100 percent increase in the monthly disability benefit during hospital confinement. The payment of the increased benefit was generally

TABLE 21–1.   Number of People with Medical Expense Protection under Individual Policies of Insurance Companies (000 omitted)

End of Year	Hospital Expense Insurance	Surgical Expense Insurance	Regular Medical Expense Insurance
1940	1,200	850	—
1950	17,296	13,718	2,714
1960	30,187	23,012	7,997
1965	37,372	29,239	11,013
1970	43,480	30,128	14,212

Source: Health Insurance Institute.

limited to a rather short initial period of confinement, such as 60 or 90 days. Since this form of hospital coverage was a "fixed benefit" payable without regard to the medical expenses of the insured, and since it was an adjunct of a disability policy, it could be regarded as a form of disability income benefit rather than an insurance for medical expenses.

It was not until the depression years of the 1930s that medical expense insurance was first developed as a kind of insurance distinctly different from disability income insurance. Since that time, this new form of insurance has shown vigorous growth in both group and individual forms. The growth in individual medical expense insurance is indicated by the data in Table 21–1, which show the rapid increase in the number of persons covered under the three important forms of individual medical expense policies over the past 30 years.

The increasing importance of medical expense insurance stems from improvements in coverage and the great advances that have been achieved in medical science. The improving quality of medical care has led to a preoccupation among the insuring public with all matters relating to health care. More importantly, the increasingly complex nature of medical care has resulted in substantial increases in the cost of such care. Consequently, the increasing utilization of medical facilities and their increasing cost have made it highly desirable for the insuring public to have a financing mechanism to assist them in the orderly budgeting of medical expenses. Medical expense insurance has been found to be eminently suited to fill this need.

FORMS OF MEDICAL EXPENSE INSURANCE

Medical expense policies, as currently written, may be put into two broad categories. The first of these is the so-called "basic coverages," under which benefits for hospital confinement begin with the first day of hospital confinement, and surgical coverages with the first dollar of professional fees for a surgical procedure. Typically, these basic coverages are subject either to a very small deductible or to no deductible. Benefits under basic coverages contain limitations on each element of medical expense, and thus are said to be on the "allocated" basis.

The second category of medical expense policies is that of "major medical" coverage. Major medical policies do not cover the first dollar of expense. Instead, they are designed to protect against the infrequent but financially catastrophic loss that occurs when sickness or injury requires a long period of hospital confinement or costly surgical or medical treatment. To accomplish this result, benefits under major medical policies are subject to a "deductible," in order to eliminate small losses for which administration costs are high and for which most families can budget. Also, benefits under a major medical expense coverage are not on the allocated basis, except to a very limited extent. Instead, a broad class of expenses is covered—subject to a deductible provision—with a "coinsurance" or percentage-participation-sharing of the risk, and usually with a single maximum benefit applicable to total benefits for each accident or each period of sickness.

Hospital Expense Benefit

The benefits payable under the hospital expense benefit are of two kinds: (1) the daily hospital expense benefit, and (2) the miscellaneous hospital expense benefit.

The purpose of the daily benefit is to pay for hospital charges for room, board, general nursing care, and other routine services covered by the hospital's per diem charge. The benefit generally is equal to hospital charges for such care up to the stated dollar daily hospital benefit limit, and subject to a limit on the number of days of hospital confinement for which the benefit is payable for each injury or each period of sickness. The limit on the compensable period of confinement for each period of hospitalization at first generally was a relatively short period, such as 30 days. Today, however, much higher limits, such as 365 days, are common.

In recognition of the use of "intensive care" units in most general hospitals, and the higher cost associated with such care, some basic hospital expense policies provide for additional benefits during the period that the insured is necessarily confined in an intensive care unit.

The miscellaneous expense benefit covers charges for hospital services and supplies not within the scope of the hospital's per diem charge. The use of the operating room, laboratory services, anesthetics, and drugs are examples of the types of hospital services and supplies that would be covered by the miscellaneous expense benefit, provided they are necessary for treatment and prescribed by the attending physician. As in the case of the daily hospital benefit, individual policies almost always specify an overall or maximum dollar limit on the miscellaneous expense benefit payable for each period of hospital confinement. The maximum benefit may be expressed as a multiple of the daily hospital benefit, such as 10 or 20 times the daily benefit, or a fixed amount may be specified as the maximum. Certain variations of this approach have been used. For instance, in some policies the maximum benefit has been graded by period of confinement, with a relatively low limit, such as five times the daily hospital benefit, for confinements of short duration, increasing to higher limits, such as 20 times the daily benefit, for confinements persisting for longer periods, such as 60 days or more.

Individual policies generally are so drafted that the hospital expense benefit is payable only if the patient is confined to the hospital as an inpatient. In some cases, a minimum period of confinement, such as 24 hours, is a further condition to receipt of benefits. These conditions may prevent use of the hospital for minor diagnostic treatment where there is no real sickness or injury and for outpatient services in general.

Some policies provide an "emergency accident benefit" which covers the cost of emergency treatment in a hospital as an outpatient within 24 or 48 hours after the time of the accident causing the injury. The maximum emergency accident benefit is usually two or three times the daily hospital benefit of the policy. One argument against providing the emergency accident benefit is that the average benefit payment is small and consequently the insurer's claim administration expense is relatively large in relation to the amount of benefit paid. On the other hand, a benefit of this kind is sound if it tends to reduce the number of hospital confinements in those cases where the insured can be treated as an outpatient.

It has become quite common to write individual hospital expense policies to provide for a small deductible, such as $25 or $50, to be applied to the sum of benefits otherwise payable for each illness or each accident. A deductible, even a relatively small one, enables the insurer to increase the benefits provided by each dollar of premium. This is accomplished by eliminating entirely the claims involving only a small amount of expense that would be covered in the absence of the deductible; claim rates and claim administration expense are thereby reduced.

Surgical Expense Benefit

The surgical expense benefit pays for surgical procedures, subject to a schedule of limits on the benefit payable for each type of operation. Limits vary with the nature of the operation and are intended to bear a close relationship to the average fee charged by doctors for the listed operations in the areas where the covered persons reside. For example, in a schedule providing a maximum benefit of $350, $20 may be the limit specified for correcting the fracture of a finger, $200 for an appendectomy, $250 for removal of a gall bladder, and $300 for removal of a kidney.

It is naturally impracticable to name or even to anticipate all of the many surgical operations that may be performed. Consequently, surgical schedules list only those operations which occur most frequently. The policy generally states that the maximum benefit for any unlisted operation shall be determined on a basis consistent with the limits in the schedule for comparable operations, subject to the overall schedule maximum.

The maximum surgical expense benefit for a surgical procedure generally is intended to apply to the total professional fees involved, including those of any assistant surgeon, and to the expense of postoperative care. Coverage for the cost of anesthetics and their administration has been handled in a variety of ways. In some cases, policies provide for a specific allowance for this item. It has been more generally covered, however, in the miscellaneous hospital expense benefit, even though in most hospitals it is not regarded as a hospital charge but is billed separately by a professional anesthetist. Another benefit sometimes found in surgical expense coverage provides for the cost of treatment of tumors by X ray or radium. This benefit may be provided by the surgical schedule or, alternatively, may be covered in a separate schedule.

In-Hospital Medical Expense Benefit

The term "medical expense benefit" is sometimes used in a narrow sense in health insurance to refer to coverage of charges by doctors for services other than those in connection with surgical procedures or post-operative care. (This coverage also is called "regular medical benefit" and "doctor fee" benefit.) In the field of individual medical expense insurance, coverage of doctor fees of this kind generally is found only in major medical policies and policies covering accidental injuries on a blanket basis. In basic coverages, benefits for doctor fees generally are provided only for such fees incurred during a period of hospital confinement and then only if no surgery is performed. A benefit of this type frequently is referred to as the "in-hospital medical expense benefit." A provision for this benefit recognizes that even if no surgery is performed during a period of hospital confinement, a patient normally requires professional medical services, so that it is reasonable to provide insurance coverage for doctors' fees in such cases. The amount of benefit provided for such fees typically is equal to the doctor's actual charges for professional services but no more than a specified limit, such as $5 for each day of confinement, subject to a limit on the number of days for which the benefit is payable.

Nursing Expense Benefit

Some policies provide a benefit for in-hospital nursing care required in connection with the treatment of injury or sickness. Such a benefit, like the hospital expense benefit and the in-hospital medical benefit, is subject to limitations on the daily rate of benefit and the maximum period for which it is payable. Typically, the coverage is written to provide only for care by a private duty registered nurse other than a member of the insured's immediate family.

Coverage for nursing fees generally is included in blanket accident and major medical expense policies, since the intent in these forms is to cover the broadest possible range of medical expenses. The nursing fees benefit also has been written with the basic coverages, but its use as a part of basic hospital and surgical policies has been relatively uncommon.

Extended Care Benefit

A recent development of considerable interest is the "extended care" benefit, which is designed to cover the expense incurred as a result of confinement in an extended care facility (i.e., a skilled nursing home). Interest in this form of coverage has stemmed from the increasing importance of nursing homes in comprehensive medical care.

An important factor in the growing interest in extended care coverage has been the increasing cost of medical care, especially the cost of hospital care. This has led to the development of new forms of medical facilities, such as extended care facilities that are appropriate for ambulatory patients and others who do not require the elaborate and costly care normally associated with general hospitals.

As currently written, the extended care benefit generally is coupled with coverage for hospital confinement and is so written that confinement in an extended care facility is covered only where such confinement follows a period of hospital confinement. The amount of benefit for confinement in an extended care facility generally is defined in much the same way as the hospital daily benefit. Under this approach, the amount of benefit is equal to actual charges for confinement in the nursing home but no more than a specified amount, such as $10, for each day of confinement, subject to a limit on the number of days for which the benefit is payable.

Hospital Indemnity Benefit

The hospital indemnity benefit is a separate approach that provides for a fixed benefit based on the period of hospital confinement, without regard to actual hospital charges. The benefit generally is defined as a specified daily hospital benefit payable for each day of confinement, subject to a limit on the period of compensable hospitalization; alternatively, the specified benefit may be a weekly or a monthly rate. It will be seen that the hospital indemnity benefit is comparable to the "hospital expense" benefit, except that the latter benefit is based primarily on actual hospital charges, while the hospital indemnity benefit is based solely on the period of hospital confinement.

Hospital indemnity benefits have been written for many years, but until recently hospital coverage on the "expense incurred" basis has been of far greater importance. During recent years, however, there has been a rather marked increase in the importance of the hospital indemnity type of coverage as compared to regular hospital coverage on the "expense incurred" basis. Perhaps the most important reason for this is the very rapid increase in the cost of medical care, which has made the underwriting of medical expense coverages, especially hospital expense insurance of the traditional type, extremely difficult. The newer forms of hospital indemnity coverage have overcome this problem by making benefits independent of hospital charges.

A second factor in the development of hospital indemnity coverage was the introduction of Medicare in 1966. This federal program for persons over 65 has required underwriters to develop new forms of coverage for such persons. The hospital indemnity type of benefit has been one of several answers to this general underwriting problem.

A third factor in the development of the hospital indemnity approach has been its simplicity, which has reduced the cost of administration and enhanced the marketability of this form of coverage.

Major Medical Expense Insurance

The major medical expense benefit was developed in the early 1950s, largely as a result of an increasing realization that basic coverages often pay the cost of minor injuries or sickness (which, in many instances, the insured could have met without the use of insurance) but are inadequate in paying the very large bills that may result from serious accident or prolonged sickness. Also, basic coverages emphasize hospital care and thus may encourage unnecessary utilization. Major medical was developed to meet the need for protection against a broad range of catastrophic medical expenses, whether incurred in or out of the hospital. Some of the earlier major medical policies were limited to expenses incurred in the hospital, a form of coverage which is sometimes referred to as major hospital expense. While major hospital expense coverages are still issued, most major medical expense policies do not require hospital confinement in order that the insured may qualify for benefit.

The major medical expense benefit usually is subject to a deductible, typically $500 or more. This means that no benefit is payable until covered medical expenses for the accident or sickness have exceeded the deductible amount. There may be a limit on the period of time, such as 90 days, during which expenses must be incurred in order that the deductible may be satisfied. In most individual major medical policies, the benefit is based on the expenses incurred because of a single accident or illness, and is limited to expenses incurred during a stated period, such as two years following the date of the accident or the inception of the sickness. After the stated period has elapsed, the deductible must again be satisfied before further benefits are payable.

The "each illness" approach to the definition of covered expenses requires that where two or more separate illnesses occur during a benefit period, expenses incurred in connection with each of these illnesses be segregated. The occasional claim administration problems encountered under the "each illness" approach have been avoided by combining all eligible expenses incurred in each calendar year or policy year, without regard to the cause underlying each item of expense. Under this approach the benefit is based on the amount by which total eligible expenses incurred during the year, whether a policy year or a calendar year, exceed the deductible amount. Most individual major medical policies are based on the "each illness" approach; the "calendar year" or "policy year" deductible is found principally in group major medical insurance.

The deductible amount eliminates from coverage those injuries and sicknesses which require only relatively minor medical treatment and for which medical expenses can generally be easily budgeted without hardship. As a result of the application of the deductible amount, claim frequencies are reduced, and the average benefit per claim is increased. Both the reduction in claim frequencies and the increase in the average benefit tend to reduce the cost of claim settlement in relation to benefit payments. Consequently, use of a deductible tends to increase the proportion of the premium that may be devoted to policy benefits. In addition to the reduction in expense rates, the application of a deductible amount tends to eliminate duplication with basic coverages.

Major medical policies usually provide for coinsurance or percentage-participation on the part of the insured. This is accomplished by providing that benefits will be a percentage, such as 75 or 80 percent, of the amount by which eligible expenses exceed the deductible. This provision gives the insured a financial interest in medical expenses incurred on his behalf, so that he will tend to avoid seeking unnecessary or unduly expensive medical care.

A practice that has developed in recent years in the drafting of major medical coverages is to provide for "inside limits," which are intended to impose reasonable limitations on certain covered expenses. They also serve to increase the insured's participation in the cost of his own medical care, when the cost of treatment exceeds the inside limit. The most common of these inside limits is a limit on the daily rate charged by the hospital for room, board, and general nursing services. Limitations on professional fees for surgery also are becoming quite common through the use of surgical schedules. These inside limits may be viewed as setting an upper limit that may not be exceeded if charges for medical services are to be "reasonable." Coverages like major medical, providing benefits for a broad range of eligible medical expenses, invariably require that expenses be "reasonable" and "customary." Accordingly, it is quite logical that the policy define "reasonable" in terms of an upper limit.

The total benefits payable under a major medical policy usually may not exceed a maximum benefit which may be $10,000, $20,000, or even more. A maximum benefit may apply to all benefits payable during each benefit period and to the aggregate benefits payable under the policy for all benefit periods combined resulting from the same or related causes. Under calendar-year deductible plans, the maximum benefit applies to the sum of all benefits payable under the policy during the calendar year, without regard to the cause of individual claims.

Comprehensive Medical Expense Insurance

Comprehensive medical expense insurance combines in one policy the benefits of basic hospital-surgical coverages and those of major medical coverages. This form of insurance is much like major medical insurance, but with a very low deductible, such as $50. In some forms, basic hospital, or hospital and surgical charges are covered in full without a deductible or, in some cases, without coinsurance or percentage-participation on the part of the insured. Comprehensive medical expense insurance has been written most widely under group contracts, but a considerable amount of experimentation with this form of coverage under individual policies also has been undertaken.

CHARACTERISTICS OF MEDICAL EXPENSE POLICIES

Renewability and Term

Medical expense insurance, unlike disability income insurance, can be written without regard to whether or not the persons to be insured are engaged in gainful employment. Furthermore, the need for medical care coverage not only continues throughout life but, in fact, actually increases with advancing age. Consequently, it had become quite common, until the advent of Medicare, to write medical expense policies to provide for lifetime coverage. Also, before Medicare, some companies had experimented with the issue of medical expense insurance at ages over normal retirement age.

The introduction of Medicare, with its virtually universal coverage at attained ages over 65, has resulted in several changes in underwriting practices. In the first place, lifetime coverage is no longer written except for policies of the hospital indemnity type. Where regular medical expense coverage is written on the "expense incurred" basis, coverage can be continued beyond age 65 only with a reduction in benefits for claims incurred after age 65 to avoid duplication with the benefits of Medicare. Also, medical expense coverage is no longer issued over age 65 except for policies that are appropriately integrated with the benefits of Medicare to avoid undue duplication of benefits. It is of interest, however, that over 50 percent of persons covered by the Medicare program have some type of private health insurance protection as well.

In addition to the term for which the policy is written, the conditions governing renewal of the policy are an important characteristic of individual health insurance policies. The earliest forms of individual medical expense insurance generally were written on the basis that the company had the right to cancel the policy at any time or to refuse renewal on any policy anniversary or any renewal date. Conservatism in this regard primarily was due to problems inherent in the forecasting of the net cost of insurance, which, in the case of medical expense insurance, is subject to many forces leading to rather rapid changes in such net cost, including highly unpredictable inflationary factors.

Cancellation of medical expense policies on an individual basis frequently results in loss of insurance coverage at a time when it is needed most. This undesirable effect of the "cancellable" type of policy led to the development of a new form of renewal provision for individual medical expense policies during the early 1950s. Under this new form, the so-called "guaranteed renewable" provision, the insurer guarantees renewal for a fixed term or to a fixed age, generally age 65 or for life, but retains the right to change the applicable table or rates. When premium rates are changed under guaranteed renewable policies, all policies within each class of business must be treated consistently, in order that discriminatory treatment of individual policyowners may be avoided.

While guaranteed renewable insurance was originally introduced, and continues to be used, primarily for medical expense insurance, it has been adopted for other types of insurance, such as personal disability insurance.

Probationary Period

Some individual medical expense policies provide that benefits will not be paid for expenses arising from sickness commencing during the first 30 days (or other specified period) following the policy date. The purpose of this "probationary period" is to minimize the number of borderline cases where it is difficult to establish the date of commencement of the sickness. It also serves as a deterrent to persons who are aware of a medical impairment and seek insurance coverage on losses which are practically certain. In addition to this form of probationary period, which is found in individual health insurance policies of all forms, the benefits payable under a medical expense policy with respect to specifically named surgical procedures may be subject to a longer probationary period, such as six months. Disorders subject to these special probationary periods are generally of the type for which treatment may be deferred at the insured's election. "Elective" or "postponable" procedures may occur, for instance, in the case of herniotomy or tonsillectomy.

Definition of Hospital

Since a substantial proportion of benefits under medical expense policies depends on confinement in a "hospital" as an inpatient, it is essential that both the insured and the insurer agree to the meaning of "hospital." This is accomplished by including a definition of the word "hospital" in the policy. One such definition is as follows:

Hospital means an institution operated for the care and treatment of sickness and injuries and having facilities for diagnosis, twenty-four hour nursing service, and, except in the case of a hospital primarily concerned with the treatment of chronic diseases, major surgery. The term "hospital" does not include an establishment that is, other than incidentally, a place for rest, a place for custodial care, a place for the aged, a place for drug addicts, a place for alcoholics, a nursing home, or a hotel.

While shorter definitions are frequently used, it is clear that an objective definition of "hospital" will avoid many troublesome questions that might otherwise arise.

Successive Periods of Hospitalization

Since benefits under hospital expense coverages are payable only during a fixed maximum period of hospital confinement, it is necessary to describe in the policy how the maximum benefit period applies in the event of two or more separate periods of confinement. This is accomplished by specifying that successive periods of confinement, resulting from the same or related causes, will be considered to be a single confinement unless separated by a specified period of recovery.

Exclusions

It has been customary, in writing medical expense policies, to exclude from coverage claims arising from intentionally self-inflicted injuries, air travel except as a passenger, and losses resulting from war. These exclusions are common to practically all forms of individual health insurance. In addition, losses for which compensation is payable under any workmen's compensation or occupational disease act or law are sometimes excluded, although this type of exclusion is not used universally in individual health insurance. There also are certain exclusions unique to individual medical expense policies. Some of the more important of these special exclusions are the following:

Governmentally Operated Hospitals. The exclusion of governmentally operated hospitals applies to services and facilities provided by a hospital owned or operated by the United States government for the treatment of members or ex-members of the armed forces. This exclusion is desirable because such services are available without charge to persons entitled to them.

Cosmetic Surgery. It is apparent that cosmetic surgery is "elective" and generally is not required as a result of injury or sickness. Correction of congenital anomaly in infants and surgery required as a result of injury normally would be covered.

Expenses Not Associated with Injury or Sickness. Eyeglasses and hearing aids or their prescription or fitting generally are not covered under major medical policies or other policies that cover the cost of medical services not supplied by a hospital. Likewise, dentures and dentistry usually are not covered, except to the extent that they may be required as a result of injury within a stated period following the date of the accident causing the injury.

Maternity. In theory, the expense incurred in connection with a maternity confinement does not constitute an insurable hazard, and so generally is excluded from coverage, especially in the case of major medical and comprehensive forms. Maternity benefits, however, are very popular and add greatly to the salability of hospital expense insurance. Consequently, it is quite common to provide maternity benefits in basic hospital expense policies, subject, however, to considerably lower limits than those that apply to hospital confinements generally. Furthermore, maternity benefits generally are subject to a special probationary period of, say, ten months, and the additional requirement that both husband and wife be covered at the inception of pregnancy. These special conditions applicable to the maternity benefit tend to limit the severe adverse selection against the insurer that otherwise would occur.

These exclusions are consistent with the basic principle that health insurance policies should cover only actual losses and only those losses that result directly from injury or sickness.

RISK SELECTION

The selection of risks for medical expense insurance involves much the same considerations as those that affect the underwriting of applicants for other forms of personal life and health insurance. Benefits under health insurance policies, however, including medical expense coverages, are not subject to the same objective determination as those of life insurance, but instead to some degree are subject to election by the insured. The nature of the risk assumed under health insurance coverages leads to adverse selection against the insurer. In some cases a person who knows, or suspects, that he may require medical treatment in the future may attempt to purchase medical expense insurance in order to defray the cost of the probable future treatment. This form of adverse selection may involve fraudulent concealment on the application or may be accomplished because of ignorance of basic insurance principles.

One of the principal defenses against the form of adverse selection that is encountered in applicants who are in poor health, in addition to the "probationary" period, is the so-called "preexistence" exclusion. This exclusion generally is accomplished in the insuring clause by stating that the policy covers only injuries occurring or sickness contracted and commencing after the policy date. It also may be accomplished by a specific exclusion stating that the policy does not cover any injuries occurring or sickness contracted prior to the policy date. In either case the effect is the same.

The subjective nature of medical expense insurance, which makes the use of the "probationary" period and the preexistence exclusion so important, also requires careful consideration of the overinsurance hazard. An important factor in all forms of personal life and health insurance, overinsurance is of special importance in medical expense insurance since, as noted above, an applicant may know of an impending need for medical treatment and so may be able actually to realize a profit from a period of hospital confinement or other medical treatment, unless the underwriter exercises appropriate precautions. There are two types of defenses against the overinsurance hazard. The basic method is to require disclosure in the application of all medical expense insurance owned by the applicant. Thus, any insurance issued can be so limited that overinsurance is avoided. Alternatively, the coverage issued can be so integrated with other coverage that duplication of coverage is avoided.

SUMMARY

The growth of medical expense insurance and its rapid development as an important means of financing health care attest to the present importance of this line as a full-fledged partner of individual life and disability income insurance. This growth has been achieved during a period when medical science and practice have been undergoing many important changes, and in competition with other systems for financing health care.

Dramatic results have been accomplished both in the volume of medical expense coverage distributed and in the expansion of the scope of coverage under modern forms of insurance. These accomplishments have been due to a willingness to experiment with new coverages and to a continuous search for improved methods of providing personal insurance. Advances are now being made in the area of coverage for dental care and confinement in extended care facilities. With continuing efforts in these, and other, directions, medical expense insurance will achieve even more important objectives in financing the health care needs of the nation.

Prior to 1967, medical expense insurance was provided solely by life and casualty insurance companies and service indemnity companies. With the introduction of Medicare in 1967, however, a substantial part of medical care insurance on persons over 65 was assumed by the federal government under social security; in 1972, the program was extended to certain younger disabled beneficiaries. Congress is considering similar proposals that would extend the federal government's role in health care, and its financing, much beyond its present position under Medicare. While these proposals range from full socialization of virtually all medical care to reforms of the existing system, there are certain concepts that are common to all—first, that the present system for delivery of health care is imperfect and requires major reforms; second, that adequate medical care is a basic right that should be made available to every citizen. Extensive study by Congress is likely before final action is taken on these proposals. However, it may be anticipated that existing mechanisms for financing health care will continue to contribute to maintenance of the nation's health care.

SELECTED REFERENCES

Dickerson, O. D. *Health Insurance*. Rev. ed. Homewood, Ill.: Richard D. Irwin, Inc., 1963.

Faulkner, Edwin J. *Health Insurance*. New York: McGraw-Hill Book Co., Inc., 1960.

Phillips, James T. "Some Considerations in the Development of an Individual Accident and Sickness Program," *Transactions of the Society of Actuaries,* Vol. VI (1954), p. 350.

Society of Actuaries. *Health Insurance Provided through Individual Policies* (Edwin L. Bartleson, principal contributor). Chicago, 1968.

22

Legal Concepts and Contract Provisions

By RICHARD P. COOLEY

A DISTINGUISHING feature of health insurance is its diversity of contract forms. This diversity results from several factors which include, among others, the variety of physical human risks that are properly the subject of health insurance and the circumstances under which such risks can produce loss. The risks anticipated within the scope of coverage may be broadly defined, or limited to risks anticipated in one given circumstance or undertaking, or defined so as to fall at some point between these two extremes.

Unlike certain forms of casualty or fire insurance, there are no standard forms prescribed by statute or by bureaus or associations. Each form of health contract, although subject to certain minimum policy provision requirements, is essentially an original document drafted by or at the direction of the insurer.

Health insurance is underwritten by life insurance companies, specialty or monoline health insurance companies, and by casualty companies. The health insurance operation of life companies and casualty companies is often vastly different, reflecting the manner in which the company conducts its other lines of business. Similarly, the specialty or monoline companies have yet other methods of operation.

All these variables are reflected in the contract of insurance and the type and scope of the application for such insurance, as well as the insurer's attitude toward common problems of operation. This chapter is concerned with the general legal problems involved and the more significant policy provisions of individual and family insurance contracts issued by private insurers.

Contract Principles Applicable

The mutual exchange of promises between the insurer and the insured is represented by the terms and conditions of the contract of health insurance as delivered by the insurer to the insured. As such it is a legal document subject to the usual law of contracts, except as modified in the case of insurance contracts generally.

The health insurance contract, other than the newly developing cash value disability contract, is an aleatory contract in that the promise of the insurer is conditioned upon the occurrence of some future fortuitous event which may or may not occur. The insured must sustain accidental bodily injury or suffer a sickness which produces a loss for which benefits are afforded before the promises of the insurer result in payment of a benefit. The cash value disability contract contains promises pertaining to cash values which are not necessarily contingent upon the occurrence of some future fortuitous event.

For there to exist a binding and effective agreement between the parties, the usual elements pertinent to an enforceable contract must have been satisfied. That is, there must have been a meeting of the minds between competent parties, based on an offer and an acceptance, supported by a good and sufficient consideration and effected for a legal purpose.

FORMATION OF CONTRACT

The signed application of the applicant for insurance is the cornerstone of the insured-insurer relationship and constitutes the "offer" of the "offer and acceptance" element of a valid contract. With relatively few exceptions, a written application is required in the underwriting of health insurance. The exceptions relate primarily to "ticket" policies, such as vacation or trip policies, which are issued directly by an authorized agent for a limited term, not to exceed 180 days and are not renewable, as well as enrollment programs where the solicitation is through mass media advertising.

The scope and detail of the application will vary according to the kind and extent of insurance being applied for as well as the extent of the guarantee of renewability set forth within the terms of the contract. An application for accident only insurance with limited right of renewability may be substantially abbreviated when compared to an application for accident and sickness insurance written on a noncancellable and guaranteed renewable basis wherein the insured is guaranteed the right of continuance at a guaranteed premium until a stated age, date, or event. In the latter instance, there is no future opportunity for the insurer to reevaluate or re-underwrite except in the event of lapsation for nonpayment of premium and a request for reinstatement of such contract.

The application will seek to identify the applicant with certainty through name, social security number, date and place of birth, and a physical description which will permit distinguishing the applicant from another person of like name. It will also seek information as to the applicant's occupation and duties if the premium for the insurance is predicated on a risk classification. It will seek to establish an insurance history through disclosure of health insurance or life insurance currently in force, together with information pertaining to the declination, postponement, or ratings applied to other applications for insurance. Finally, the insurer will seek to establish a health history through specific disease and general health questions. The questions in the application generally are classed as being either of a factual or opinion type. As to the latter type, the insurer can only require that the applicant respond to the best of his knowledge and belief.

Since the application is the cornerstone of the insured-insurer relationship, it is important that the application be completed fully and accurately and that its questions be sufficiently precise to make clear to the applicant the scope of the information that the insurer deems to be material. Improper or incomplete disclosure of requested information may lead to declination of the application, declination of a claim, or to an action to rescind the contract. In recognition of the importance of the application, some states now require that a notice form be attached to the face of the policy which advises the insured to review the application and immediately advise the insurer of any errors or omissions, because otherwise the insurance may not be in force in the event of a claim. Other states require the agent or both the agent and the applicant to certify, in a separate document, that the responses to the interrogatories have been properly recorded and are correct.

The offer, as made manifest by the application, is forwarded to the insurer for underwriting action. This most frequently is done at the home office or a regional office of the insurer. The extent of underwriting will correspond to the kind and extent of the insurance applied for. The decision to accept or reject may be based solely on the application, or the insurer may elect to seek additional information through a consumer reporting agency, or through examination by a medical practitioner. The Federal Fair Credit Reporting Act (Public Law 91–508) requires that an applicant be advised that a consumer report may be requested, if such be the case, and the scope of the investigation which may be requested. In the event an application is declined or the coverage applied for is rated or restricted because of information contained in the consumer report, the applicant must be so advised and furnished the name and address of the consumer reporting agency.

If the risk is accepted by the underwriter, the insurance laws generally require that a copy of the application be attached to and form a part of the contract of health insurance as issued, particularly where the application is expressed as an element of the consideration for the contract. If the application is not attached, the insurer will be precluded from using any misstatement within the application as a basis for denying a claim or rescinding or voiding the contract within the time permitted in the "time limit on certain defenses" or "incontestable" provisions of the contract. This concept is not designed to protect the fraudulent; rather, it affords the insured the opportunity to review the application and be fully informed as to the representations which form the basis of the insurer's acceptance of the offer. It also serves as a deterrent to the applicant as well as the agent recording incorrect or inaccurate responses to the questions.

The tender of the application and the first premium, or a required part thereof, is the offer on the part of the applicant. The issuance of the contract as applied for is an acceptance by the insurer of the applicant's offer. If the insurer, in accordance with its underwriting standards, cannot issue the contract as applied for but elects to counteroffer by proffering a modified plan incorporating reduced benefits, increased elimination or waiting periods, physical impairment riders, or special class rating, such counteroffer may be accepted or rejected by the applicant.

In conjunction with the application and in consideration of payment in advance of the premium with the application, a "conditional coverage receipt" is customarily issued. This receipt guarantees the applicant, if he is acceptable as a standard risk on the date of the application or on the date of completion of the insurer's standard underwriting requirements, that the insurance will become effective as of such later date notwithstanding a subsequent change in health prior to actual delivery of the contract.

The drafting of a conditional coverage receipt requires the utmost care to declare clearly the intention of the insurer if it wishes to avoid interim insurance irrespective of the applicant's acceptability from an underwriting standpoint. The conditional coverage receipt has been the subject of frequent and extensive judicial interpretations which are worthy of review and evaluation.[1]

POLICY CONTRACT

Face or Filing Back

The face or filing back of the contract serves as a focal point for various insurance department and statutory requirements.

The precautionary notice to the insured to review the application already has been mentioned. The *10-day right to examine policy* is now required in a substantial number of states. This notice gives the insured the option of returning the policy within 10 days from the date of receipt and securing a refund of all premium paid. Upon such surrender, the contract is void from the beginning. This notice may be printed on the face or filing back, or affixed as a sticker or notice. Other examples among states include a fraud or misrepresentation notice that must be affixed to the face or filing back; a large caption or notice, in contrasting ink color, if the policy is renewable subject to the consent of the insurer; and a notice if the contract affords benefits for hospital confinement but does not include confinement in a psychiatric hospital as a covered expense.

If an insurer uses a brief description of the policy, such must appear on the face or filing back of the policy. The use of a brief description generally is not required; however, where required it can be in the form of a notice or sticker.

With respect to *limited policies*, the *Third Official Guide* of the National Association of Insurance Commissioners requires that the insurer print diagonally across the face of the policy in 18-point outline type the words, "This is a Limited Policy—Read it Carefully." These words may be modified to reflect the kind of coverage afforded. The Guide defines a limited contract as one that contains unusual exclusions, limitations,

---

[1] Charles H. Stamm, III, "Conditional Receipts, A Status Report," *Proceedings of Association of Life Insurance Counsel*, Vol. 21 (1970), p. 303.

reductions, or conditions of such a restrictive nature that the payment of benefits under such policy is limited in frequency or in amount.

Insuring Clause

A critical paragraph of every insurance contract is the insuring clause. Such clause (*a*) identifies the insurer and the insured, thereby fulfilling one of the common-law requisites of a contract that the identity of the contracting parties be definite; (*b*) states that insurance is provided as to loss; (*c*) requires that such loss result from a stated cause of accident or sickness, and defines what constitutes an accident or sickness within the contemplation of the insurer; (*d*) specifies the extent to which loss is to be compensated through the use of words such as "to the extent hereinafter provided"; and (*e*) states that the promise of benefits is subject to all the provisions, conditions, and exclusions of the policy. Frequently, unusual or exceptional limitations applicable to the coverage will be set forth in the insuring clause and are necessary in fulfillment of the requirements of a limited number of states.

While the insuring clause incorporating the definition of what constitutes an accident or sickness continues to be used, there is a growing tendency to extract such definitions from the insuring clause and set them forth in a separate "definitions" paragraph. This procedure permits the setting forth of all pertinent definitions within a single area or provision and substantially simplifies the insuring clause.

Consideration Clause

One of the essentials of a contract is that there be good and sufficient consideration. This clause establishes (*a*) the application, and (*b*) the payment of premium, as the elements of consideration on which the contract is premised. In addition, this clause frequently will state the commencement date of insurance as well as the duration of the initial term for which the contract is issued. Thus, this clause fulfills the Uniform Individual Accident and Sickness Policy Provision Law requirements that the entire money and other consideration for issuance be stated therein, and that the time at which the insurance takes effect and terminates also be expressed therein. The consideration clause may be set forth as a separate paragraph or included as a part of the renewability clause. If the latter approach is used, such provision is frequently captioned "issuance and renewal."

Renewability Clause

The terms and conditions of renewability are set forth in detail in the renewability clause and a number of states, either through statute or regulation, require that this clause appear on the face or first page of the policy.

The terms of renewability encompass a broad spectrum ranging from the ticket policy forms which are issued for a specified term and are not renewable, to those which are "noncancellable and guaranteed renewable" (as defined by the National Association of Insurance Commissioners and adopted in a number of states) to a specified age, date or event, or even for life.[2] In between are forms which are renewable subject to the consent of the insurer. Such right of nonrenewal may be exercised by the insurer upon any renewal date or, as limited by a number of states, upon each anniversary of the policy or effective date. A number of states now require 30 days' notice of nonrenewal and limit such right to an anniversary of the policy or the last reinstatement of the policy as well as limiting the right to certain specified events or conditions. In one state the notice of nonrenewal may be as long as two years if the policy has been in force seven or more years. The insurer may modify the right of nonrenewal so that it will not refuse to consent to the renewal of the policy solely on the basis of deterioration of physical or mental health.

Also, there is the franchise type of renewability which guarantees the right of renewal during the continuation of a given status such as being employed on a full-time basis by a given employer or being a member in good standing of a named association, up to a stated age limit. However, the insurer reserves the right to terminate all such policies issued to employees of a given employer or members of a given association upon giving a specified period of notice (usually 30 days, except a limited number of states require 60 days). This latter type of renewability precludes individual nonrenewal by the insurer so long as the insured's status fulfills the specified requirements.

Payment of Premiums

A number of insurers, particularly those issuing noncancellable or guaranteed renewable forms of insurance, include a separate paragraph which spells out instructions as to the payment of premium and defines the due dates for payment of premiums.

Eligibility, Additional Family
Members, and Termination

The health insurance family policy, frequently employed in the writing of hospital or major medical insurance, will customarily include separate paragraphs that define those members of the family who are eligible for coverage (generally defined in the Uniform Policy Provisions Law)

---

[2] The terms "noncancellable" or "noncancellable and guaranteed renewable" may be used only in a policy which the insured has the right to continue in force by the timely payment of premiums set forth in the policy (1) until at least age 50, or (2) in the case of a policy issued after age 44, for at least five years from its date of issue, during which period the insurer has no right to make unilaterally any change in any provision of the policy while the policy is in force.

Except as provided above, the term "guaranteed renewable" may be used only in a policy which the insured has the right to continue in force by the timely payment of premiums (1) until at least age 50, or (2) in the case of a policy issued after age 44, for at least five years from its date of issue, during which period the insurer has no right to make unilaterally any change in any provision of the policy while the policy is in force, except that the insurer may make changes in premium rates by classes.

The foregoing limitation on use of the term "noncancellable" shall also apply to any synonymous term such as "not cancellable" and the limitation on use of the term "guaranteed renewable" shall apply to any synonymous term such as "guaranteed continuable." *Proceedings of the National Association of Insurance Commissioners,* Vol. I (1960), p. 153 et seq.

under the policy and the specific conditions under which new family members may be added. In addition, it may specify the conditions pertaining to the termination of insurance with respect to the spouse and children who may be insured thereunder. Customarily, coverage of the spouse will terminate upon attainment of the limiting age or in the event of a legal separation, divorce, or annulment of marriage. Coverage of children customarily will terminate upon marriage or upon attainment of the limiting age. Continuation of coverage of children over age 19 is conditioned on dependency as required under the Uniform Policy Provisions Law and, where dependency exists, a child may continue as a covered family member, usually to age 23. Upon death of the insured, most family policies provide that the surviving spouse (if covered under the contract) shall become the insured.

A substantial number of states, through legislative enactment, now preclude the termination of insurance for a dependent child who is mentally or physically incapable of earning his own living on the date specified for termination of insurance on account of age, if proof of such incapacity is furnished to the insurer within a specified period, usually 31 days. Upon receipt of such proof, coverage of the child may continue during the continuance of disability and while the policy remains in force, subject to the payment of the appropriate premium.

Benefit Clause

The paragraph or paragraphs describing the various benefits afforded by the policy and the circumstances under which they become payable customarily follow the definitional paragraph if set forth separately or, if not set forth separately, following the renewability clause.

Generally, a sickness benefit will require that the loss commence while the policy is in force. However, losses resulting from accident cannot be so limited if the renewability of the policy is of a kind which gives the right to the insurer to interrupt the continuity (nonrenewal or cancellation) of insurance or if the insurance is issued for a specified term only. In these situations, most insurance departments require that coverage be afforded if the loss occurs subsequent to termination of the policy if the accident producing the loss occurs while the insurance is in force. This extension, in the case of total disability benefits, may be limited to a loss commencing within 20 days after the date of accident, or, in the event of accidental death or dismemberment, may be limited to a loss which occurs within 90 days after the date of accident.

If an exception or reduction applies only to a particular benefit of the policy, a statement of such exception or reduction must be included with the benefit provision to which it applies. However, if the exception or reduction applies generally, or to two or more of the benefit provisions, it normally will be set forth in a separately captioned provision such as "exceptions," "exclusions" or "exceptions and reductions."

The contract structure may anticipate that the benefits provided form either a part of a *package policy* or parts of a *schedule policy*. The package policy anticipates that the issued contract will be inclusive of all the benefit provisions. There may be variations with respect to the benefit amounts, duration, waiting periods or similar items. These are customarily tailored to the needs of the insured.

The schedule policy, however, anticipates that the applicant may select only certain of the benefits as being the coverage desired. This concept requires that the policy include a schedule format which can be completed so as clearly to declare those benefits which are covered and those which are not covered. This latter concept permits the inclusion of a number of benefit concepts within a given policy form and facilitates selection of the benefits desired by the applicant. One jurisdiction requires that not only must the schedule be clearly definitive of the in-force coverages, but also that the inoperative benefit provisions be overstamped with words such as "not covered."

Exceptions and Reductions

Exceptions and reductions provisions are found in policies for several reasons, including the avoidance of costs involved in duplicating benefits, the control of potential catastrophic losses, and the elimination of areas not considered insurable or not insurable for reasonable costs. As social programs such as workmen's compensation, Medicare, Medicaid, veteran care, and the like expand, private insurance seeks to avoid duplicating the benefits of such programs. This conserves premium dollars that otherwise would be wasted through direct duplication of benefits.

Exclusions that seek to avoid catastrophic loss, as may result from declared or undeclared war, continue to be necessary to protect the financial integrity of the insurer. Exclusions in individual policies applicable to aircraft travel are much less restrictive today than formerly; however, exclusions which are operative while the insured is piloting or serving as a member of the crew of an aircraft, whether private or commercial, continue to be widely used. If desired, this exclusion can be eliminated from the contracts of some insurers upon the payment of the appropriate additional premium for the undertaking of such risk.

While foreign travel generally is not excluded, extended stays or foreign residence may result in the reduction or cessation of benefits, particularly those relating to income replacement during periods of disability. The necessity of such exclusion results from the difficulty in securing satisfactory proof of continuing disability. However, the need or lack of need of such exclusion or reduction may be reflective of the facilities which the insurer has for the ongoing evaluation of foreign claims.

Current events dictate the need of exclusionary controls in insurance contracts. The frequency of riots as well as the extensive use of drugs or narcotics may cause some insurers to use exclusions controlling losses resulting from such occurrences.

Preexisting Conditions

The insuring clause or the separate definitional paragraph will define what constitutes a covered accident or a covered sickness. Customarily, only an accident occurring or sickness "contracted and commencing" or "first manifesting itself" after the effective date of the policy and while the insurance is in force, will be considered for policy benefits. However, the effective date of insurance as to sickness may be delayed 15 or 30 days after the policy date. Since the definition excludes accidents occurring or sickness manifested prior to the effective date, it is not necessary expressly to exclude preexisting conditions; but it is not unusual for an insurer to exclude such conditions, in reinforcement of the definitional limitations, subject to the "time limit on certain defenses" provision.

UNIFORM POLICY PROVISIONS

The provisions generally governing the operation of the individual health insurance contract are now prescribed in the Uniform Individual Accident and Sickness Policy Provisions Law.[3] The law was developed in 1950 as a model law by the National Association of Insurance Commissioners and subsequently enacted or adopted in the 50 states, the District of Columbia, Puerto Rico, and the Virgin Islands. Commonly referred to as the Uniform Policy Provisions Law, it includes 12 required provisions and 11 optional provisions.

Prior to the enactment or adoption of the Uniform Policy Provisions Law, many states had enacted the Standard Provisions Law of 1912 which was developed and sponsored by the National Convention of Insurance Commissioners (forerunner to the NAIC). The 1912 law was developed to achieve standardization of general provisions for the protection of the insuring public, and to overcome the tendency of some insurers to utilize unduly restrictive or technical controls that frequently resulted in the declination of justified claims on a technical basis.

A number of the required and optional provisions of the Uniform Policy Provisions Law are substantially the same as those included in the Standard Provisions Law. However, unlike the Standard Provisions Law, the Uniform Policy Provisions Law is an "in substance" law which does not require that the provisions appear in the contract in the same form and context as set forth in the law. The insurer may modify the language of the provision so that it better fits the requirements of the contract, so long as the new wording is not less favorable to the insured and is approved by the insurance commissioner. In addition to permitting the adaptation of the policy provisions to new developments in health insurance, it also permits the insurer to effect liberalizations for the benefit of its insureds. There were two entirely new provisions in the Uniform Policy Provisions Law relating to time limit on certain defenses and grace period which are of substantial benefit to the insured.

While not required to use the exact statutory wording of each provision, the insurer generally is required to follow the sequence of the provisions except for appropriate integration with another provision or omission by reason of inapplicability.

Required Statutory Provisions

The *entire contract and changes* provision states that the "policy, including the endorsements and attached papers, if any, constitutes the

---

[3] See Appendix I.

entire contract." This precludes, generally, the utilization of extraneous papers or parole evidence as a means of modifying or extending the terms and conditions of the contract. It also states that no change in the contract can be effected until approved by an executive officer of the insurer and evidenced by an approval endorsed on or attached to the contract. In addition, the provision declares a precise limitation on the agent's authority to change or waive any of the provisions of the contract.

Many insurers modify the first sentence of this provision to read, "This Policy, including the application of the insured (copy of which is attached hereto and made a part hereof), endorsements and the attached papers, if any, constitutes the entire contract of insurance." Through this means the insurer can reinforce the consideration clause where the application is expressed as an element of consideration, and thus substantially reduces any question as to the insurer's reliance on the disclosures of the application while at the same time providing protection to the insured.

The *time limit on certain defenses* provision is divided into paragraphs (*a*) and (*b*). There are two versions of paragraph (*a*). The first, in order of appearance in the Uniform Policy Provisions Law, is used in contracts which are renewable at the option of the insurer, and the second in contracts which meet the definitional requirements to be guaranteed renewable or noncancellable and guaranteed renewable as specified by the NAIC and enacted into the laws of several states. If the second version is applicable, then the caption "incontestable" may be used.

The primary purpose of paragraph (*a*) is to specify a time limit after which the insurer may not challenge the contract on the basis of material nondisclosure or misstatements in the application. In the first version of paragraph (*a*), fraudulent misstatements are exempt from the operation of the time limit. While the fraudulent misstatement phrase is omitted from the second version, the time limit is extended by excluding therefrom all periods during which the insured is disabled. As a result of the difficulties inherent in proving fraud, it is probable that the second version of paragraph (*a*) affords a more positive value to the insurer by the possible enlargement of the period of time during which the insurer can assert material nondisclosure.

Paragraph (*b*) precludes the insurer from denying a claim on the basis of preexistence after expiration of the stated time limit, unless such condition has been excluded by name or specific description.

In a family form of insurance, both paragraphs (*a*) and (*b*) may be modified so that the expressed time limit runs from the date a family member becomes covered under the policy. This is important where eligible family members are added, subject to underwriting, at a date subsequent to initial issuance of the contract.

While the time limit in the model law, for both paragraphs (*a*) and (*b*), is three years, this has been reduced to two years in a substantial number of states and two years is the period most commonly used by insurers.

The *grace period* provision under the Uniform Policy Provisions Law specifies a grace period of 7 to 31 days, depending on the mode of premium payment or the term of insurance. A number of states now require a standard grace period of 31 days regardless of the mode or term. The coverage of the policy remains in full force and effect throughout the grace period whether or not the renewal premium is in fact paid. This is true even though the insured has given notice of intention not to renew, since it is possible that the insured can change his mind during the grace period and effect payment of the premium. From the legal standpoint there would be no consideration supporting the waiver of this valuable right by the insured. Some insurers utilize the optional unpaid premium provision as authority for making a premium deduction from a claim settlement due to loss occurring during the grace period. However, the payment of premium cannot be a condition precedent to the payment of the claim.

While the model law grace period provision makes reference to the optional cancellation provision, which permits an insurer to terminate coverage within a paid term upon the giving of timely notice, such provision has either been repealed, modified, or omitted from the law as enacted in a number of states.

The grace period or period of extended insurance can be avoided if the insurer gives adequate notice of its intention not to renew a policy which is renewable subject to the consent of the insurer. While the model law establishes a 5-day notice requirement, this has been changed to 30 days in a number of states.

The _reinstatement_ provision affords the insured an opportunity to request reinstatement of his contract in the event it lapses for non-payment of the required premium prior to expiration of the grace period. Reinstatement may be accomplished without the necessity of an application by acceptance of the premium by the insurer or by an agent authorized to accept the premium. However, if the insurer requires a reinstatement application and issues a conditional receipt for the premium tendered therewith, the policy will be reinstated only upon approval of the application or, lacking such approval, upon the 45th day following the date of the conditional receipt unless the insurer has given prior notice of disapproval.

The reinstatement application affords the insurer the opportunity to re-underwrite the application in its entirety and may, as a condition to its acceptance, impose limitations of the same kinds as may be imposed at the time of initial underwriting. The reinstatement provision also affirms that the reinstated policy does not afford coverage as to accidents occurring or sickness commencing during the period of lapsation since coverage is afforded only for accidents occurring after the date of reinstatement or such sickness as begins more than 10 days after such date. In all other respects the insured and the insurer shall have the same rights as those existing prior to the due date of the defaulted premium.

As to policies which are renewable subject to the consent of the insurer, the reinstatement provision limits the collection of arrearage premium to 60 days. However, this limitation does not apply to guaranteed renewable or noncancellable policies by reason of the reserve requirements applicable to such forms.

The entire contract, time limit on certain defenses, or incontestable and reinstatement provisions are silent as to the status of the reinstatement application. Section 5 of the Uniform Policy Provisions Law strongly implies that the reinstatement application need not be made a part of the policy upon reinstatement, and sets forth a procedure for furnishing the insured or a beneficiary a copy of the reinstatement application upon request. Failure to furnish a copy of the application within 15 days of the receipt of such request precludes the insurer from introducing the application as evidence in any action or proceeding based upon or involving such policy or its reinstatement.

The majority view holds that the time limit on certain defenses or incontestable provisions run anew from the date of reinstatement.[4]

The *notice of claim* provision states that the insured must give written notice to the insurer within 20 days after the occurrence or commencement of any loss covered by the policy or as soon thereafter as reasonably possible. What constitutes a reasonable period of time will vary substantially under changing fact circumstances. There are some indications in the judicial decisions that there must be proof of prejudice to the insurer through, or as a result of, the failure to give timely notice. This provision also provides for successive notices, each six months, as to a continuing loss which results from disability if the indemnity for loss of time may be payable for at least two years.

The *claim forms* provision requires the insurer to furnish forms for the submission of proof of loss by the claimant within 15 days following receipt of notice of claim. Failure of the insurer to provide the forms within the time limit permits the claimant the option of submitting proof in a form of his choosing so long as it fulfills the requirements of this provision as to written proof covering the occurrence, the character and the extent of the loss for which claim is made.

The *proof of loss* provision requires that written proof be submitted within 90 days after the date of loss or, in the event of a continuing loss for which periodic payment is provided, within 90 days after the termination of a period for which the insurer is liable. Failure to furnish the required proof will not, within itself, invalidate or reduce a claim if submitted within a reasonable time, up to one year, upon a showing that it was not reasonably possible to furnish proof within the time limit. The one-year period is extended for an indefinite period in the event of legal incapacity.

The *time of payment of claim* provision specifies that the insurer is obligated to pay benefits immediately upon receipt of due proof of loss, except for loss for which periodic payment is promised; then payment is to be made periodically, with the interval between payments not exceeding one month. In a limited number of jurisdictions, punitive damages may be recovered in the event of unwarranted delay in meeting the payment obligation imposed under this provision.

---

[4] K. B. Wilson, "Health Insurance Litigation; The 1950 Policy Provisions," *Proceedings of the Association of Life Insurance Counsel,* Vol. 19 (1968), pp 424–25.

The *payment of claims* provision states, as to any death benefit, that payment will be made to designated beneficiaries or, in the absence of such designation, to the estate of the insured. In some states the insurer, in the absence of any other designation, may stipulate that the proceeds shall be payable to the parents, spouse, or children of the insured. Such language facilitates the payment of death proceeds and avoids, in many instances, the cost of estate administration and the delays incident thereto.

This provision contains two optional paragraphs which may be used to facilitate payment. If any indemnity, not exceeding $1,000, is payable to the estate of the insured, an insured or beneficiary who is a minor or otherwise not competent to give a valid release, the insurer may pay such amount to any relative by blood, or connection by marriage to the insured or beneficiary who is deemed equitably entitled thereto. In addition, the insurer, in the absence of any direction to the contrary from the insured, may pay hospital, nursing, medical, or surgical services directly to the provider of such service even though an assignment of benefits has not been executed by the insured. An insurer may, on occasion, utilize this provision where it necessarily has made commitments as to benefits which become due and payable as the result of medical care or treatment of the insured.

The *physical examinations and autopsy* provision affords the insurer the opportunity to examine the person of the insured during the pendency of a claim under the contract. This provision is frequently extended in family forms of insurance to afford the insurer a like opportunity as to any family member covered under the contract. The provision, in the event of death, also provides the right of autopsy where not forbidden by law. A limited number of states prohibit the making of an autopsy at the request of an insurer.

The *legal actions* provision states that no action at law or in equity shall be brought to recover on the policy prior to the expiration of 60 days after written proof of loss, and that no such action shall be brought after the expiration of three years after the time written proof of loss is required.

It is well to note that the second of the two specified time periods may vary according to the statutes of a given state. Several states require express modification of this provision to delete the specified three-year period and the substitution, by rubber stamp or modification rider, of the period of years set forth in the applicable statute of such state.

The last of the 12 required provisions is that titled *change of beneficiary*. This provision reserves to the insured, in the absence of an irrevocable beneficiary designation, the right to change the beneficiary, surrender the contract or make any other change therein without the consent of the beneficiary or beneficiaries. Many insurers will combine an assignment provision with that of the change of beneficiary since the language pertaining to both is substantially similar. The permitting of irrevocable designations of beneficiaries is at the insurer's option, and therefore this language may be included or omitted. Generally, this clause is omitted.

If an irrevocable designation is desired by the insured, it is frequently accomplished through means of an absolute assignment of the death benefit which can be modified subsequently only with the consent of the assignee.

Optional Statutory Provisions

The *change of occupation* provision is of particular importance in accident insurance affording loss of life, limb, or sight and/or loss of time benefits. It sets forth the rights and obligations of the insurer, as well as those of the insured, in the event the insured changes or engages in a more hazardous or less hazardous occupation. It is important to note that any action undertaken pursuant to this provision must be premised on the occupational classification manual and premium rates last filed with the state insurance regulatory authority where such filing is required or, if filing is not required, the classification system and premium rates last made effective by the insurer in the given state prior to the occurrence of the loss or prior to the date of proof of change in occupation.

The *misstatement of age* provision as prescribed in the model law is frequently modified to accommodate contingencies which may exist in a given policy. If the policy affords coverage to family members, the provision may be modified so that the limitations expressed therein are equally applicable to each family member. If the rating structure anticipates an age limit for issue purposes, or the termination language of the contract anticipates discontinuance at a stated age and the policy is either issued or continued beyond such stated age, then the provision is modified so that the insurer's liability is limited to the refund of premium paid since issuance or since the date the policy would have terminated had the correct age been stated.

The next four optional statutory provisions pertain to duplication of benefits. Such duplication can involve overinsurance, which may encourage profiteering, unnecessary utilization of the insurance coverages, or unwarranted extension of periods of disability.

The *other insurance in this insurer* provision is primarily utilized in nonunderwritten forms of insurance where there is no opportunity to review the insurer's records as to other insurance. This concept primarily encompasses ticket forms of insurance as well as similar forms issued directly by machine or by an agent in an over-the-counter transaction. The concept permits a dollar limitation on amounts of insurance in force, or limits recovery to the benefits afforded under one policy as elected by the insured, his beneficiary or his estate.

Two provisions relate to *insurance with other insurers*. They are substantially similar except the first concerns itself with benefits afforded on a provision-of-service basis (for example, prepaid plans and Blue Cross) or expense-incurred basis, while the second relates to benefits provided on other-than-an-expense-incurred basis (for example, loss of income and other indemnity benefits). At the time the model law was developed, most hospital, surgical, or medical expense coverage, as well as loss of income insurance, was written on forms which were renewable subject to the consent of the insurer. The insurer, upon learning of substantial other insurance, might elect not to renew. However, most such coverages currently are written on forms which are guaranteed renewable. Thus, the initial insurer is precluded from terminating the policy or taking any unilateral underwriting action regardless of how much coverage subsequently might be secured. Notice of later acquired coverage to the initial insurer prior to the occurrence or commencement of loss would preclude the operation of the provision, thereby defeating its purpose.[5]

The *relation of earnings to insurance* provision may be used only in guaranteed renewable or noncancellable and guaranteed renewable forms. This provision is concerned with overinsurance for loss of time and permits the reduction of loss-of-time benefits only. The measure of liability is premised on the greater of the current monthly earnings at the time of commencement of disability, or the average monthly earnings during the two years prior to the commencement of disability.

A problem for the insurer in the operation of this provision is that the benefit level is based on 100 percent of earnings, as determined above, without any consideration being given to the tax impact on earnings or the fact that the loss-of-time benefits are not considered as earned income for federal income tax purposes. Unfortunately, because this provision is not required, it has become a point of competitive comparison which works to the disadvantage of the insurer who seeks protection against the subsequent acquisition of loss-of-time coverages. The industry is attempting to resolve the duplication of benefits problem in individual insurance, but no substantial progress has been made to date.[6]

The *unpaid premium* provision permits the insurer to deduct from a claim settlement any premium then due or payable or covered by any note or written order. As stated previously, this provision is sometimes used to effect payment of premium where loss occurs during the grace period.

The *cancellation* provision, which permits termination of insurance during a period for which premium has been paid, is now prohibited by a number of states. In such states, the provision has been deleted, by legislative action, as an optional provision, or has been restricted substantially so that it can be utilized only during a limited period of time such as six months following the date of issue.

While the optional provisions include those titled *illegal occupations* and *intoxicants and narcotics*, these have had only limited use. In recent years, however, there has been an increasing incidence of use of the latter provision.

The optional provision entitled *conformity with state statutes* is widely used. The provision, in effect, amends any provision of the contract which is in conflict with applicable statutes so as to conform the contract to the minimum requirements thereof. Its use frequently avoids the neces-

[5] H. Powell Yates, "Health Overinsurance: Myth or Menace," *Proceedings of the Association of Life Insurance Counsel,* Vol. 18 (1964), pp. 735–63.

[6] National Association of Insurance Commissioners, "Seventh Status Report on Overinsurance," *Proceedings of the National Association of Insurance Commissioners,* Vol. I (1964), p. 95. Enacted or adopted by regulation in Delaware (with modifications), Nevada, New Hampshire, North Dakota, and Wyoming.

sity of developing special state riders for the purpose of amending and conforming the contract to the laws of a given state. If the deviation is such as to affect the rights or notice of rights of the insured, the regulatory officials frequently require specific modification notwithstanding the use of such provision.

NATURE OF THE CONTRACT UPON RENEWAL

The status of an individual health insurance contract upon renewal has been the subject of extensive litigation. Some of the older decisions, which indicate each renewal is a new contract, reflect the distinctive influences of the origin and development of health insurance as a casualty form primarily underwritten by casualty insurers. Historically, casualty forms are not continuous and do not contain language providing for renewal from term to term. Rather, the form is that of successive contracts, each affording insurance for a stated period of time, whether the contract is endorsed to continue for a subsequent period or is continued through the issuance of a new contract. However, as health insurance has evolved from a casualty-oriented form to one more closely allied to life insurance and widely issued by life insurers, the courts generally are recognizing the substantial distinctions between health insurance and the various casualty forms.

As a general rule, where the renewal of the insurance is effected pursuant to a provision of the policy which so permits, the renewal is not a new contract but rather is considered as a continuation or extension of the original contract.[7] Whether the contract is renewable will be determined largely from the intent of the parties as evidenced by the language of the contract.[8] Where the renewal is a continuation of the original contract, all conditions and provisions may remain essentially the same except for the time of expiration.

There are distinct advantages to the insured as well as the insurer where the renewal of the policy is considered as a continuing or extended contract. From the standpoint of the insured, the legislatively prescribed "time limit on certain defenses" provision, with its beneficial results after two or three years, would never come into being if the contract ran anew from each renewal. Likewise, sickness first manifesting itself or injuries occurring in one term would be a preexisting disease or physical condition in a succeeding term, and thereby be excluded under the usual definitional concepts. Probationary periods would not be fulfilled nor would accumulation benefits mature.

From the insurer's standpoint, the state law controlling the contract would remain that of the state of initial delivery and would not need to be modified to accommodate changes in the law of such state subsequent to the date of issue. If considered as a new contract, the laws of the state at the point of renewal would control and would subject the policy to

---

[7] 43 Am. Jur. 2d, Sec. 379.
[8] 44 C.J.S. § 283.a. See also 17 Couch on Insurance 2d. Sec. 68:39.

modifications required as the result of change in the laws as effective at the time of renewal.

In the overall view, the continuation or extension concept is that which permits health insurance to fulfill its real and intended purpose of affording protection to an insured on an ongoing basis on and after its original effective date and while the insured continues to make timely premium payments.

SELECTED REFERENCES

Dickerson, O. D. *Health Insurance*. Rev. ed. Homewood, Ill.: Richard D. Irwin, Inc., 1963.

International Claim Association. *Life and Health Insurance Law*. Rochester, N.Y.: The Lawyers Cooperative Publishing Co., 1971.

Society of Actuaries. *Health Insurance Provided through Individual Policies* (Edwin L. Bartleson, principal contributor). Chicago, 1968.

23

Premiums and Reserves

By T. H. KIRKPATRICK

INDIVIDUAL health insurance policies cover a variety of risks, each involving different probabilities of loss. To determine premiums and reserves for these policies, it is first necessary to consider the nature of these probabilities and to evaluate them. This is not a simple task. Usually, it is assumed that future results will follow past experience. From existing data, an experience table is developed. This table is constructed in such a way that the underlying probabilities are expressed in a form that simplifies the calculations. Some of the several ways of constructing these tables and calculating premiums and reserves will be explained in this chapter.[1]

There are two types of premiums, *net* and *gross*. Net premiums take into account claims costs only. Gross premiums also include expenses and margins for contingencies and for dividends or profit.[2]

Reserves are of two general types, *active life* and *disabled life*. Active life reserves are like life insurance reserves. Disabled life reserves are of two types—those for benefits already accrued on the valuation date and those for future unaccrued benefits. The accrued liability will be exactly determined when the claims are reported and processed. Any type of estimate of this reserve can be easily compared with the exact amount and the method of estimating it refined to give better values for the future. On the other hand, reserves for unaccrued benefits involve the probabilities inherent in the risk. Theoretically, these reserves are determined from mathematical formulas which include these probabilities. Any other determination is an approximation and justifiable by its simplicity and practical results.

Active life reserves arise when part of the early premiums must be set aside and accumulated to meet later costs. If premiums can be freely changed or the policy canceled or not renewed by the insurer, the only liability is the unearned premium. More frequently, however, individual

---

[1] Many of the underlying principles developed in Chapter 10 on "Probability, Mortality, and Money Concepts," by Charles M. Sternhell and Walter Shur, are equally applicable in health insurance.

[2] Premium and reserve concepts in individual life insurance are covered in Chapters 11 and 12, respectively.

health insurance policies are issued as long-term contracts with level premiums. For the benefits provided, claims costs generally increase with attained age. This results in premiums and reserves which are similar in theory to those of life insurance policies, and the same principles and techniques may be used to determine them.

NET PREMIUMS

Progressing from the simplest to the most difficult formula, net premiums and reserves can be determined as follows:

1. If the benefit provides a fixed payment in the event of loss within the period of coverage, and the probability of loss is the same for all policyowners, irrespective of age or other characteristics, then the net premium is calculated by multiplying the amount payable by the probability. At any time, the only liabilities are the unearned premiums and unpaid claims. Air-trip insurance, for example, falls into this category.

2. If the annual claims cost varies with a single factor, such as age, it is necessary to analyze the experience and determine the probability of claim for each attained age. If premiums are to be on a one-year term basis, they are determined by multiplying the probability of loss for each age by the amount payable. There is a different premium for each age. It is not necessary to accumulate any part of the premium from age to age. This arrangement would apply if health insurance were sold on a yearly renewable term basis.

3. When the risk increases with age, the use of level premiums gives rise to active life reserves. The theory is the same as that for life insurance. A level premium and its resulting reserve can be calculated, using the same methods as for life insurance, by simply replacing the annual mortality cost with the annual claims cost. Most health insurance policies currently issued fall into this category, or the extension described in the next paragraph.

4. For loss-of-time benefits and occasionally for hospital and major medical benefits, additional flexibility is desired so that premiums for different elimination periods and benefit periods can be calculated from the same table. The experience table must then be constructed to show the number disabled for each day during the entire benefit period. For example, for 100,000 lives exposed at age X, the experience table would show those disabled for each day of disability. This arrangement of data is known as a *continuance table*.[3] The results for age 35 are somewhat as shown in Table 23–1.

If the claims follow Table 23–1, then, of 100,000 lives, at age 35, exposed for one year, 4,954 will be disabled for a continuous period of at least 32 days due to a disability commencing during the year. Some of these will recover or die on the 33rd day, so that only 4,731 will be disabled for at least 33 days.

---

[3] The question of whether the term "continuance table" should be limited to those already disabled is unsettled. Perhaps there are two types of continuance tables—an exposure continuance table and a claims continuance table.

TABLE 23–1.   Continuance Table at Age 35 Showing Number Disabled at Stated Durations (per 100,000 lives exposed)

Day	Number Disabled	Day	Number Disabled	Day	Number Disabled
1	32,900	31	5,192	757	137
2	31,380	32	4,954	758	136
3	29,540	33	4,731	759	135
4	27,490	34	4,521	760	134
etc.		etc.		etc. ....

Similar figures are obtained from the experience for other ages. In practice, quinquennial age groups are used. A complete table will show for each quinquennial age group the number disabled for each day of disability for which benefits are provided.

The annual claims cost for each age is calculated by discounting the amount payable for each day of disablement for the benefit period. This can best be explained by considering the following example:

The net level premium is required for a loss-of-time policy issued at age 35, guaranteed continuable at age 65, as follows:

Amount: $100 monthly ($100 × 12 ÷ 365 = $3.29 per day)
Elimination Period: 30 days
Maximum Benefit Period: Two years for any one disability
Assumed Interest: 3 percent
Mortality: 1958 CSO Table

First, it is necessary to choose an experience table. For this example, the continuance table described above will be used. From this table, it is possible to calculate the probabilities of disablement for each of the days of the benefit period.

The next step is to determine the *annual claims cost* for each year of age. This is done by discounting at interest the amount payable for each day of disablement after the elimination period for the benefit period. Since the continuance table shows only those who have survived and continue to be disabled, i.e., recoveries and deaths having been deducted, mortality has already been taken into consideration. Thus, the experience table shows that of 100,000 lives exposed at age 35, 5,192 will be disabled for a continuous period of at least 31 days. This period represents the first day of coverage after the end of the elimination period. The probability of disability for this period at age 35 can be shown as $\frac{5,192}{100,000}$. The amount payable for this day of disablement then would be $3.29 (the daily amount of coverage) $\times \frac{5,192}{100,000}$. This amount is discounted at the assumed rate of interest for 31 days to obtain the present value at the date of commencement of disability. Therefore, the present value of the benefit payable for the 31st day is $\frac{5,192}{100,000} \times \$3.29 \times \left(\frac{1}{1 \times i}\right)^{31/365}$, where i is the assumed interest rate. Similarly, the present value of the benefit payable for the 32nd day is $\frac{4,954}{100,000} \times \$3.29 \times \left(\frac{1}{1+i}\right)^{32/365}$, and so on, with the present value of the benefit payable for the 760th day (the last day of the maximum benefit period) being $\frac{134}{100,000} \times \$3.29 \times \left(\frac{1}{1+i}\right)^{760/365}$. The sum of these amounts is the annual claims cost for year-of-age 35.[4]

This summation technique to obtain the annual claims cost is an important concept in the calculation of health insurance premiums. The most important point in this discussion for the nonactuarial reader is an understanding of the nature of the process which is used to determine the premium rather than a knowledge of the specific actuarial formula used in calculating the premium.

The annual claims cost for all ages from 35 to 64, inclusive, are similarly determined. The level premiums and active life reserves can now be calculated, using the same methods as for life insurance. It is assumed that all claims commence in the middle of the policy year, and that the annual claims cost is discounted at interest and mortality to determine the present value of future benefits. To determine the level annual premium, the present value of future benefits (the single premium for the policy) is divided by the life annuity for the premium-paying period.[5]

Where the annual claims cost can be directly obtained without the necessity of using a continuance table, net premiums and reserves are obtained by simply discounting at interest and mortality the annual claims cost.

Waiver-of-premium benefits are frequently provided. The premiums for them are calculated as if they were loss-of-time benefits of an amount equal to the net premium, plus the expenses to be incurred while premiums are being waived.

RESERVES

Active Life Reserve

When a policy is issued with level premiums, *the present value of future net premiums is equal to the present value of future benefits.* When

---

[4] The actuarial formula which shows the annual claims cost for year of age 35 is as follows:

$$S_{35} = \$3.29 \left\{ \frac{5,192}{100,000} v^{31/365} + \frac{4,954}{100,000} v^{32/365} + \cdots + \frac{134}{100,000} v^{760/365} \right\}$$

$$v = \frac{1}{1+i}, \text{ the interest discount factor}$$

This S formula simply adds together the present value of the benefits expected to be payable for the various days of disablement.

[5] The actuarial formulas at age 35 are as follows:

a) The single premium is $A_{35:30} = \sum_{t=0}^{29} S_{35+t} \dfrac{D_{35+t+1/2}}{D_{35}}$.

b) The net level annual premium is $P_{35:30} = \dfrac{A_{35:30}}{\ddot{a}_{35:30}}$,

where D_x is the usual life insurance present value factor $v^x l_x$.

the annual claims cost increases with attained age, then, after the date of issue, *the present value of future benefits is greater than the present value of future net premiums. The difference is the active life reserve.* Consider two people now aged 45. One bought a policy 10 years ago; the other purchases his policy today. Both have the same future benefits. The only difference is that one will continue to pay the age-35 premium and the other the higher age-45 premium. Equality is established by the reserve which is equal to the present value of the difference between the net premiums. This is the 10th-year terminal reserve on a policy issued at age 35.[6] As for life insurance, alternative formulas are also available for the calculation of active life reserves.

To calculate the total active life reserve on the valuation date, the reserve factors are applied against the business in force by plan, year of issue, and age. The following practical problems, however, arise in this connection:

1. Preliminary term is frequently used for as long as a two-year period.

2. The active life reserve is determined directly by using midterminal reserves plus 50 percent of a modal net premium.

3. There is a large number of plans of insurance arising from different elimination and benefit periods. Furthermore, a wide variety of supplementary benefits is either provided by rider or built into the policy. Premiums vary by occupation class. A single valuation table is used for all classes. On account of this complexity, approximate methods are frequently used.

Historically, health insurance was developed as a casualty coverage. The insurance departments established a pattern of requiring a reserve at least equal to the unearned gross premium. For noncancellable and guaranteed renewable policies, the aggregate active life reserve far exceeds the unearned gross premiums. However, for cancellable policies or those which will terminate in a year or less, a reserve of the gross unearned premium is required.

Disabled Life Reserve

A *disabled life reserve* arises whenever a claim is incurred and the amount payable in the future depends upon future contingencies. For example, under a loss-of-time policy, a claim is considered as incurred when disability commences. Future amounts payable are dependent upon the continuance of total disability. *The disabled life reserve is the present value of the remaining benefits which the claimant may expect to be paid on his claim.* Contrariwise, if the amount is fixed as soon as the claim is incurred, disabled life reserves do not arise. The accidental death benefit is an example of the latter.

For each claim, the amount of the reserve depends upon the duration of disability already completed. It is therefore necessary to determine on the valuation date the distribution of disabled lives by duration of disability

---

[6] The actuarial formula is as follows:

$$_tV_{x\,:\,\overline{y-x}|} = (P_{x+t\,:\,\overline{y-x-t}|} - P_{x\,:\,\overline{y-x}|})\ddot{a}_{x+t\,:\,\overline{y-x-t}|}$$

where y is the age to which the policy can be continued.

before applying the appropriate type of actuarial formula. This can be done in either of two ways:

1. *Analysis of Open Claims.* The distribution of claims on the valuation date is determined directly from the actual claims open on the valuation date. They are sorted by duration of disability. The present value of future benefits is obtained by the summation method in the same way as was done in determining premiums, except that the starting point for each claim is the duration of disability as of the valuation date. For example, if the claimant had already been disabled six months, the summation process would start with those then disabled as represented by the experience table, and future benefits would be discounted to this starting point.

2. *Continuance Table.* If claims follow the continuance table, as assumed, then the distribution on the valuation date of claims by duration of disability can be determined. It is assumed that disabilities commence uniformly on each day during each year of age, 1/365 of the total for each day. The number remaining disabled on the valuation date is obtained by multiplying the number for each day of the benefit period by the appropriate probability that disability will continue to the valuation date. The result is the expected number disabled for one day, two days, three days, and so forth, up to the maximum period of disability for which benefits are payable. The present value of expected future benefits for each duration is calculated by the summation formula already explained. The total of the expected number disabled for each day, multiplied by the appropriate present value factor, gives the *total disabled life reserve.*

Other Claims Reserves

Reserve for Unreported Claims. On the valuation date, there are unreported claims. If time permits, calculation of the claims reserves can be held in abeyance until most of these claims are reported. If not, the lag in claims experienced in the previous year or two is analyzed to determine the amounts involved. These claims consist of amounts already accrued on the valuation date and unaccrued future benefits. Usually, simple factors are developed from experience and applied to the premiums in force or, in the case of unaccrued future benefits, to the disabled life reserve. The amounts can be affected by miscellaneous factors such as an epidemic just before the valuation date, irregularity in mail deliveries, or the manner in which the days of the week fall at the valuation date. Normally, the reserves have margins which are sufficient to cover these variations.

Reserve for Claims in Course of Settlement. Usually, the company keeps the books open until all claims are processed and paid up to the valuation date. It only takes a day or two to do this. If this is not done, there is a liability for the amount involved.

Reserve for Accrued Benefits Not Yet Due. For both reported and unreported claims, there are accrued benefits not yet due. For example, a monthly disability income payment is expected to be due 15 days after the valuation date. One half of a month's payment has already accrued.

The amounts involved are quite small, and a simple estimate arrived at by reviewing the company's business by type of coverage will indicate the appropriate amount.

Reserve for Resisted Claims. Claims resisted are usually set up as a liability for some fraction, perhaps 100 percent, of the amount resisted.

Reserve for Future Contingent Payments. Reserves for future contingent payments result from policy provisions which give rise to future liabilities under a variety of circumstances. Usually, they provide that even if a policy lapses, a claim may still occur—for example, as a result of the right of reinstatement without evidence of insurability. Typically, the amounts involved are small, and the liability is determined as a matter of judgment and experience. An important exception is where maternity claims are payable if pregnancy commences while the policy is in force. In this case, either (1) nine months' premiums for maternity benefits are carried as a premium reserve, or (2) nine months' maternity payments are carried as a claims reserve.

Deficiency Reserve

Individual health insurance policies are subject to relatively high·lapse rates. After a block of business has been in force for some time, say 20 years, antiselection develops as the result of lapsation. The few remaining policies in force experience a claims rate substantially higher than expected. If it is found that for the claims level now reached, the present value of future benefits, less the active life reserve, exceeds the present value of future gross premiums, less future expenses, then a *deficiency reserve* of this amount should be established. The present values include interest, mortality, and lapse factors. Otherwise expressed, future gross premiums, plus the active life reserve, should be sufficient to pay future claims and expenses. Any deficiency should be set up as a reserve.

Practical Considerations

Certain practical considerations are involved in the determination of premiums and reserves for other than loss-of-time benefits.

1. Hospital Benefits. It is helpful to construct experience tables, with the benefits broken down into (a) daily hospital benefits, (b) hospital extras, and (c) maternity benefits. Separate tables are prepared for males, females, and children. Where several benefit periods are to be used, annual claims costs for each may be determined from existing experience, or a continuance table may be constructed. Annual claims costs for maternity benefits decrease with attained age. Usually, however, the benefits are relatively small, and when combined with others in the policy, positive reserves are produced.

2. Surgical Benefits. The experience table for surgical benefits is constructed from experience on the same surgical schedule. Separate tables may be used for males, females, and children. A table of frequencies for the various surgical procedures can be developed. These frequencies can be used to evaluate the cost of a variety of surgical schedules.

3. Major Medical Benefits. The main problems in determining net premiums and reserves for major medical coverages are the diversity of benefit structures being offered by insurers and the effect of inflation on claims cost. The diversity of benefits makes it difficult to obtain data which accurately reflect the claim costs to be expected on a specific policy. Breaking the major medical contract down into its component coverages for pricing purposes is helpful in this respect. Care must be exercised to assure that the data gathered on the components are representative of the groups expected to be insured under the new contract. Even if these data are available, however, they may be rendered obsolete for future use by the recent spectacular increase in the cost of medical care. Since it is important that active life reserves and future premiums be adequate to fund all future claims, some provision for the secular trend usually will be incorporated into the underlying tables.

VERIFICATION OF CLAIMS ASSUMPTIONS

The assumption has been made that the claims cost for any policy follows an experience table. Premiums and reserves can therefore be mathematically determined. In practice, this is frequently not the case. Accordingly, the experience for various blocks of business must be kept under continuous scrutiny; and from time to time, adjustments are made in the experience tables so that they will in fact represent future results. Methods used for this purpose include loss ratios, actual to expected claims costs, and new experience tables.

Loss Ratios

A loss ratio is simply the *ratio of claims to premiums.* Usually, it is calculated on an incurred basis. It is easily prepared. It can be used to locate blocks of business requiring more detailed analyses. The important age factor is, however, obscured. Loss ratios on recently issued policies are usually very low. These ratios alone can be misleading and must be supplemented with other methods.

Actual to Expected

From experience tables the expected claims costs are calculated with extensive breakdowns by plan, age, occupational class, and so forth. These are compared with the actual amounts paid. Alternatively, the number of claims and the recovery rates, actual to expected, can be determined. The results are reliable. They are quite feasible with electronic equipment. All subgroups of a company's business can be monitored by this method.

New Experience Tables

Another approach requires a complete analysis of the actual experience and the development of new experience tables. It requires a large amount of data to obtain significant results on which complete experience tables can be constructed. It takes time to accumulate the data, which is a serious limitation. It is sometimes only practical to develop new experience tables from intercompany experience. Once new tables have been constructed, net premiums and reserves can be recalculated. New tables are usually required to justify a change in the valuation standard.

GROSS PREMIUMS FOR
NONCANCELLABLE POLICIES

Gross premiums must be *adequate, consistent, equitable, and salable.* *Adequacy* is obtained by basing premiums on a sound forecast of future results; *consistency,* by applying the theoretical formulas uniformly; *equity,* by basing premiums on realistic claims costs and with practical limits on expenses; and *salability,* by balancing the final gross premiums ᵗto a level which makes them competitive.

Premium scales usually show premiums for each plan by age at issue, sex, and occupational class. Occasionally, a residence factor is also included. In the calculation of gross premiums, any number of factors can be considered. Only the most important ones, however, are included in the agent's rate manual.

Basic Elements Affecting Premiums

The basic elements affecting gross premiums for health insurance policies are (1) claims, (2) expenses, (3) termination rates, and (4) interest and mortality.

Claims. In practice, it is quite difficult to find experience tables which forecast future claims costs. Claims rates change. Past experience does not necessarily represent future expectations. The characteristics of the policy for which premiums are being calculated usually differ from those reflected in the existing table. Frequently, only a single table exists, whereas theoretically a whole family of tables is required. A good deal of judgment is required in deciding on the table to be used. The future financial risk should be considered, and what future action can be taken if future claims are underestimated. In any event, a table must be decided upon so that the mathematical calculations can be made.

Expenses. Expenses generally follow the same pattern as applies to life insurance policies. In general, first-year costs exceed first-year income. The resulting first-year deficit is amortized from renewal premiums. Both direct and indirect expenses are analyzed and classified on a per policy and percentage-of-premium basis. They are divided between first-year and renewal expenses. To check this analysis, these charges are applied to a block of policies—for example, the expected sales for a year—and the results compared with the total expenses expected to be incurred on these policies.

Termination Rate. Lapses of individual health insurance policies are usually about 150 percent of those for life insurance policies. For noncancellable loss-of-time policies, lapse rates decrease rapidly with duration. Hospital, surgical, and major medical policies characteristically have about the same first-year lapse rates as loss-of-time policies, but renewal lapse rates tend to be substantially higher. A realistic table showing lapse rates by duration is constructed from the experience of in-force policies. Alternatively, the table can show the rates at which policies are continued, i.e., persistency rates.

Interest and Mortality. The effect of interest and mortality assumptions is minimal for health insurance benefits. Reserves are relatively small as compared with those for life policies. Usually, an interest rate from 2½ to 3½ percent is used. Mortality can be based on the 1958 CSO Table.

Methods of Calculation

Having decided upon the claims cost, expenses, termination rates, interest, and mortality to be used, gross premiums can be calculated using either a *Cammack-Jenkins type of formula* or the *Hoskins asset share method*. The former emerges from the basic relationship that the present value of gross premiums should equal the present value of all future claims and expenses. Interest, mortality, and persistency are included in the present value factors. The asset share method develops a fund supported by an assumed premium from which claims and expenses are paid as incurred. The balance of the fund at the end of some period, say 20 years, should be an amount sufficient to ensure that future claims on the few remaining insureds will be met. This amount is not less than the active life reserve for the 20th year on the policies remaining in force. The assumed premium is adjusted to the true gross premium so that this balance is achieved.

The asset share method is also quite valuable in testing variations in assumptions. Upper and lower limit results can be tested. Contingency or other miscellaneous factors can be inserted into the premium calculation and their results measured.

Theoretical gross premiums have to be reviewed to make sure they are salable. If not, the factors entering into the calculations must be reviewed. Expenses may have to be reduced. For example, many companies pay a lower first-year commission on hospital business as compared with loss-of-time policies. Lapse assumptions will change with the quality of the business written. Claims costs are related to underwriting standards.

SUBSTANDARD PREMIUMS

Because of the subjective nature of total disability, it is doubtful if substandard loss-of-time insurance can be generally issued. However, for certain impairments and for other benefits the extra risk is measurable, and substandard insurance is possible. The practice generally followed is to set up substandard classes on the basis of extra premiums of, say, 125 percent, 135 percent, and so forth, up to the highest class of, say, 200 percent of the standard premium. Impaired risks are assigned to these classes on a "best judgment" basis. Experience statistics have not yet emerged. Ultimately, each substandard class will develop its own experience table, and premiums and reserves can be based on them.

PRACTICAL PROBLEMS IN RATE MAKING

Lack of Experience Data

There is a very limited amount of published experience data. What is available may be useful for reserves but not for premiums. Experience will vary between companies even for the same policies. An experience table of some kind is essential, and the following are some sources:

1. *Papers and Committee Reports of the Society of Actuaries.* Group insurance experience from papers and reports of the Society of Actuaries can be adapted to measure the risk under individual insurance policies.

2. *Blue Cross/Blue Shield Experience.* Blue Cross/Blue Shield data are seldom available directly, but are occasionally analyzed and published by individuals.

3. *Published Studies Sponsored and Financed by Organizations Interested in the Subject.* The Health Information Foundation is a sponsor of experience studies. The cost of medical care for the aged is an example of a subject studied.

4. *Government Statistics—Federal, State, and Provincial.*

5. *Suppliers of Medical Care.* Both doctors and hospitals publish statistics which are sometimes helpful.

6. *Casualty Insurance Company Statistics.* Casualty insurance company statistical data cover automobile accident rates, workmen's compensation claims rates, and the like.

Statistics obtained from such sources as above always should be carefully interpreted and analyzed to determine if they are suitable to evaluate the benefits being contemplated. Where a company has sufficient data of its own for statistical credibility, they should be preferred to any of the above sources.

Adaptation of Table to Specific Policy

Even after statistics are located, it is necessary to modify them to make them applicable. Are they up to date? Will the lives insured be better or poorer risks? What will be the degree of selection against the company? Are claims to be handled more or less strictly than the experience? The result is that the existing data are frequently adjusted before being used in the experience table on which the premiums are to be based.

Practical Limits on Expenses

A low-cost policy can only carry a relatively small per policy expense. Where the risk can be carried by the policyowner in his budget, a relatively high percentage of premiums must be returned in claims. Accordingly, it is necessary to check that the expenses are within the practical limits which the policyowner is willing to pay. If not, the method of selling and administering the policy must be changed so that the expenses will meet this requirement. This may be done in a variety of ways—for example, through mass marketing and simplified underwriting, policy issuance, and record keeping.

Conservative versus Realistic Assumptions

In the calculation of premiums, assumptions must be made regarding future claims costs, future expenses, and future persistency rates. The most likely results can be assumed, or conservative assumptions can be chosen. In the first case, margins must be included to absorb adverse fluctuations and to provide for profit or additions to surplus, whereas the use of conservative assumptions implies that such margins are already present.

Secular Trends

The recent substantial increase in the cost of medical care has given rise to serious problems in rate making. If past experience is to be used as a guide, it would seem clear that this cost inflation should continue for the foreseeable future. Consequently, if gross premiums are to be adequate, some provision for inflation must be included. Where guaranteed premiums are involved, these likely would produce premiums so high as to prove not salable. As a result, most insurers now issue medical coverage on a guaranteed renewable or cancellable basis and project inflation only into the near future, say five years, with claim costs assumed level thereafter. Such plans must be observed carefully as experience unfolds to ensure that premium changes be made before large losses develop.

While the problem is most acute with claim costs on medical coverages, the same phenomenon, on a lesser scale, has developed with expense rates. Changes in public attitude toward loss-of-time insurance and the effect of government actions should be watched carefully to observe their effect on disability income claim costs. The solution to these problems would be similar to that outlined above.

Provision for Catastrophes

It is necessary to consider the financial results of catastrophic changes in the level of claims. What would be the amount of the loss to the insurer if there were a persistent increase in claims rates due to inflation, a general change in the attitude of the public toward early retirement, or wholesale lapsation of policies? Fortunately, even such adverse changes can be kept within permissible loss limits, largely due to the fact that through lapsation the company's risk continuously decreases and the lower renewal expense rates permit a substantial increase in claims rates before a group of existing policies becomes unprofitable. The premium guarantees, of course, have an important effect on the whole problem. Model calculations can be made with various assumptions as to the volume of sales, lapses, and claims rates, and in this way the limits of financial loss for any policy can be estimated and catastrophic hazards evaluated.

Completion of Premium Schedules

The amount of work involved in calculating a complete set of gross premiums is very great. Time can be saved by only calculating premiums for pivotal ages. Other ages are obtained by interpolation. Minor differences in plans are approximately calculated. Premiums are first obtained for the most important occupational class, and a simple formula is used to obtain premiums for other classes.

REGULATION

The regulation of health insurance is under the jurisdiction of the state insurance departments. Many states have adopted the NAIC minimum reserve standards as recommended in the 1964 Report of the Industry Advisory Committee on Reserves for Health Insurance Policies.[7] Thirty-six states require the filing of premiums, and a few also require approval before use. Elaborate filing requirements, including supporting statistics, are required by these approval states.

SELECTED REFERENCES

Barnhart, E. Paul. "Revised Tables for Major Medical Benefits," *Transactions of the Society of Actuaries,* Vol. 21 (1969), Part 1, p. 21.

————. "Some New Tables for Major Medical and Disability Benefits," *Transactions of the Society of Actuaries,* Vol. 13 (1961), Part 1, p. 497.

Bartleson, Edwin L., and Olsen, James J. "Reserves for Individual Hospital and Surgical Expense Insurance," *Transactions of the Society of Actuaries,* Vol. 9 (1957), pp. 334 and 404.

Bragg, John M. "Health Insurance Claim Reserves and Liabilities," *Transactions of the Society of Actuaries,* Vol. 16 (1964), p. 17.

Dorn, Lowell M. "New York Life Morbidity Experience under Individual and Family Major Medical Policies," *Transactions of the Society of Actuaries,* Vol. 15, No. 42 (1963), p. 275.

Hoskins, J. E. "A New Method of Computing Non-Participating Premiums," *Transactions of the Actuarial Society of America,* Vol. 30 (1929), p. 140.

Jenkins, Wilmer A. "Non-Participating Premiums Considering Withdrawals," *Record of the American Institute of Actuaries,* Vol. 21 (1932), p. 8.

Miller, Morton D. "Gross Premiums for Individual and Family Major Medical Expense Insurance," *Transactions of the Society of Actuaries,* Vol. 7 (1955), p. 1.

Society of Actuaries. *Health Insurance Provided through Individual Policies.* (Edwin L. Bartleson, principal contributor.) 2d ed. Chicago, 1968.

Society of Actuaries. *Reports of Mortality and Morbidity Experience,* p. 70. Chicago. Published annually.

---

[7] *1957 Proceedings of the National Association of Insurance Commissioners* (Chicago), Vol. II, p. 319.

24

Risk Selection and
Substandard Risks

By JOHN C. ANGLE and
JOHN J. McCUISTION

AN UNDERWRITER'S risk selection duties have a kinship to those of such diverse entities as university admission officials, the educational testing services, bank loan committees, licensing and professional examining boards of every sort, and personnel officers. All these individuals, committees, boards and organizations examine and classify applicants by closely following a set of "admission" standards. A favorable decision by the admitting official commits his organization to a financial, educational, or professional obligation on behalf of the newly admitted applicant. The admission standards seek to make certain that those who are admitted have the relevant knowledge, ability or financial resources required by the organization.

An analogous process takes place during the selection of health insurance risks, with the home office underwriter in the role of admitting official. His various duties in examining, selecting, and classifying risks are of paramount importance to the sound functioning of the insurance enterprise. By virtue of his assignment, the home office underwriter is a skeptic, a doubter, and a questioner. His inquisitiveness leads him to probe each application until the facts are known. Then, and only then, does he judge the degree of risk presented by each applicant and the nature of any preexisting conditions.

NATURE OF HEALTH INSURANCE UNDERWRITING

Health insurance underwriting may well be more of an art than its life insurance counterpart because of the subjective nature of disability, the number of rating factors (some authors have counted up to 15), and the lack of meaningful single or multivariate statistical analyses of rating factors. Health itself is frequently the end result of the individual's personal living habits and his sense of responsibility for his own health. Thus the underwriter must look for evidence that each applicant is interested in robust health and acts accordingly.

333

Not all health insurance necessarily entails individual risk selection. Under the now predominant group form of health insurance, all actively at work employees who elect group coverage are automatically insured under a uniform plan of benefits. Only employees who are tardy in enrolling are required to establish their insurability. In contrast to these characteristics of group insureds, individual applicants together do not form a well-defined, homogeneous, or essentially healthy group. They have complete individual freedom to apply for any plan or amount of health insurance without being bound by the decisions of other applicants. Because of the resulting vast differences in individual risks, insurers offering individual health insurance in a free, competitive insurance market must assess the risk presented by each applicant for insurance.

The process of risk selection culminates in a decision which assigns each applicant to a risk class. A risk class can be said to consist of a set of insured persons who face substantially similar risks of injury and sickness. The largest risk class is called the standard class, and the expected levels of benefit payments in other risk classes are defined as multiples, such as 200 percent, of the benefit payment levels of the standard class. The classes entailing greater risk are called substandard classes, to signify perhaps that they include insureds whose state of health is below that of the standard class. The standard class for health insurance contains at least 80 percent of all applicants, a percentage that may reach 90 percent of all applicants under favorable circumstances.

The neat, precise assignment of applicants to "classes" with premiums carefully varied in proportion to the degree of risk is an appealing concept. Unfortunately no single-variate model can be an accurate guide to the much more complex outcomes of selecting individual health insurance risks. One source of complexity is that more premium is scarcely a sufficient response to serious antiselection by applicants who need medical attention, have a chronic spinal ailment, or have a yen for skydiving. These people present such a degree of antiselection as to be insurable on an equitable footing with other insureds only with coverage eliminated for the preexisting impairment or hazardous avocation. This frequent need to offer modified coverage adds "standard rates but with an impairment exclusion rider" to the list of underwriting outcomes.

The relative number of unfavorable risk selection decisions will be influenced strongly by the insurer's marketing strategy and its implementation. The strategy, in effect, defines the pool of prospects from which the applicants will be drawn, and depends upon the quality of the company's agency force. Generally, the highest declination rates will be found in "mass-marketing" sales where applications are solicited by newspaper ads or computer-prepared mailings. This is particularly true if the amount and nature of the risk being insured are significant.

The likelihood of injury or sickness is so closely associated with age, sex, and occupation that these three items are almost always variables in an insurer's table of premium rates. Thus, the risk classification will reflect all other underwriting characteristics that are not explicit variables in the premium rate tables.

SELECTION OUTCOMES

Approximately 80 percent of all applicants for individual health insurance are generally accepted as standard risks.[1] This percentage is substantially below the 91 percent of applicants accepted as standard risks for individual life insurance.[2] The differing results can be ascribed to those aspects of health that significantly increase the disability and medical expense risk while generally being without consequence in life insurance risk selection.

In listing risk selection factors of consequence only to health insurers, one would include temperament, those chronic diseases that may frequently disable but are rarely fatal, medical conditions likely to receive surgical correction once health insurance is obtained, the neurosis that may lead a patient from physician to physician, and hazardous avocations. These are but a few of the factors that can indicate declination or extra-risk classification of a health insurance applicant who simultaneously may be able to purchase standard life insurance.[3]

Table 24–1 compares the pattern of selection outcomes for individual life insurance with those for individual health insurance. Health insurers decline or classify applicants as substandard risks twice as frequently as would be true of the selection outcomes typical of individual life insurance risk selection.

SUBSTANDARD RISKS

Impairment Exclusion Riders

Note that in Table 24–1, 8 of every 100 health insurance applicants are insured with an impairment exclusion rider. This form of rider has no counterpart in life insurance. Perhaps this is because life insurance would not be issued if an immediate claim were likely. Yet the immediate likelihood of claim is seen daily in health risk selection. In particular, one sees situations where the applicant at his option can seek medical treatment for an existing impairment or chronic condition so as to make frequent or prolonged disability quite likely.

As examples, inguinal hernia or appendicitis, of little significance in life insurance risk selection, poses the probability of almost certain health insurance claims. When newly insured, the man with the hernia will soon ask a surgeon to repair his hernia by surgically closing the weak point in the wall of his abdomen. The sufferer of appendicitis will almost inevitably be the subject of an appendectomy. There is no sound prac-

---

[1] See, for example, remarks of J. Henry Smith and John F. Ryan, *Transactions of the Society of Actuaries,* Vol. 13 (1961), pp. D427–32.

[2] See 1971 *Life Insurance Fact Book* (New York: Institute of Life Insurance, 1971), p. 94.

[3] Some economic underwriting factors are of greater significance in health insurance than life insurance, such as the relationship of insurance benefits to earned income and the potential for overinsurance.

TABLE 24–1.   **Illustrative Selection Action Taken on 100 Individual Life and Health Insurance Applications**

	Life Insurance (percent)	Health Insurance (percent)
Accepted as standard risks	91	80
Substandard; accepted with:		
Impairment exclusion rider	–	8
Extra premium	6	6
Declined	3	6
Total	100	100

Source: Institute of Life Insurance, *Life Insurance Fact Book,* 1970, p. 93; authors' own estimates for health insurance, but see *Transactions of the Society of Actuaries,* Vol. 13 (1961), pp. D427–32.

tical way to insure against certain loss. The only workable response is to offer insurance subject to a limiting endorsement, to be specifically consented to by the applicant, which "riders out" coverage for the one specific condition, such as hernia or appendicitis, that impairs the applicant's health. Except for the elimination of benefits for the medical condition described in the impairment exclusion rider, the ridered policy will provide full coverage for all other covered sicknesses or injuries.

A policy containing an impairment exclusion rider usually will be issued at standard premium rates. Occasionally, the applicant's condition may complicate the effects of other illnesses and accordingly require both an impairment exclusion rider and an extra premium. Impairment exclusion riders remain the principal means of offering substandard medical expense insurance, particularly when elective surgery or unusual amounts of medical care seem likely. On the other hand, full benefit disability coverage to an increasing extent is issued subject to appropriate extra premiums or with an extended elimination period.

Extra Premiums

In the years 1950 to 1955, a number of life insurers entered the individual health insurance business. These insurers often assigned health insurance risk selection to men whose entire experience had been in life insurance underwriting. While these men sought advice from individuals seasoned in home office health underwriting, they inevitably brought a life insurance orientation to their assignment. One reaction of many of these life insurers was that it should be possible more frequently to offer substandard risks full health insurance coverage at suitable extra premiums to avoid the need for impairment exclusion riders which were said to be vague in intent. Some individual health insurers already were providing full coverage at extra premiums for overweight applicants. One leading casualty insurer was experimenting extensively with ratings for elevated blood pressure. Nonetheless certain life insurers, including several active in reinsurance, deserve credit for laying a solid groundwork for substandard risk evaluation. In the years since 1955, extra premium ratings for a broad range of impairments have become widely accepted by almost all individual health insurers, especially for disability income insurance.

The usual approach to extra premium ratings corresponds to the numerical rating technique of life insurance risk selection.[4] It consists of the assignment of debits for build, for blood pressure, and for each other impairment. The sum of all debits determines the substandard risk class as well as the extra premium rating, which is expressed as a part of the standard premium. As is true in life insurance, extra premiums may be assessed only for a temporary period of years or may be permanent additions for the entire premium-paying period.

A substandard applicant offered full coverage at an extra premium cannot at his request receive instead a standard premium policy to be issued with an impairment exclusion rider. However, denying a choice of rated or ridered coverage poses no practical problems, since full coverage offers are more readily accepted by the public than are policies containing an impairment exclusion. On the other hand, substandard class offers are less likely to be accepted by applicants if the extra premium exceeds 100 percent of the standard premium. The resulting lower rate in the number of placements increases the likelihood of antiselection. For this reason, some insurers decline all applicants whose impairments require more than a 100 percent extra premium. Other insurers find they can place some policies with ratings of up to 300 percent of the standard premium but hold to lower limits of issue for highly substandard cases.

Overweight and elevated blood pressure are the two impairments most frequently insured on an extra premium basis. Because of the importance of build and blood pressure, these two aspects of risk selection will be treated at greater length in a later section. Next in importance are issues that insure applicants with stomach disorders, ulcers, abnormal urinary findings, functional heart murmurs, and asthma. While there have been worthy experiments, no insurer has successfully insured those who have a medical history of coronary artery disease or who have an organic heart murmur.

Modification of Coverage

One health insurance authority recalls reviewing an impairment underwriting manual to see how many impairments he could insure at standard rates, and without an impairment exclusion rider, by issuing disability coverage with at least a 30-day elimination period.[5] After going through the list in this specific situation, he decided that 25 percent of all exclusion riders would not be needed for disability coverage issued with a 60-day elimination period and that almost half could be dispensed with under 90-day elimination period disability coverage.

A concrete illustration of this technique might be an applicant who has a medical history of occasional but mild attacks of asthma. Such an appli-

---

[4] See Chapter 15 for a discussion of numerical rating systems used in life insurance.

[5] J. M. Wickman, *Evaluating the Health Insurance Risk* (Cincinnati, Ohio: National Underwriter Company, 1965).

cant necessarily would be a substandard risk when applying for seven-day elimination period disability coverage due to the likelihood that he would have frequent short disabilities. On the other hand, he could be accepted as a standard risk for disability coverage with a 30- or 60-day elimination period. As a practical matter, underwriters frequently offer disability coverage and occasionally major medical coverage at standard rates by issuing longer elimination periods or larger deductible amounts than requested by the applicant.

Evaluating Experience

One would like to say that continuing and detailed statistical analyses are made for each impairment with subdivisions by degree of impairment in order to refine the techniques of insuring substandard risks. As a practical matter, the candid answer is that insurers have found it possible only to calculate loss ratios for four or five aggregations of substandard risks. Generally, the resulting loss ratios have been equivalent to those seen for standard risks, though everyone wishes that the exposure were large enough to permit a more detailed statistical analysis.

RISK SELECTION FACTORS

Applicant's Health

The state of the applicant's health is by definition the most important factor in risk selection for individual health insurance. The evaluation of health begins with a review of the applicant's personal medical history. Acute episodes of illness or infection are without significance unless they are likely to recur or have left a residual impairment of the patient. Of considerable consequence in risk selection is any history of a chronic physical or emotional illness. The prevalence of chronic conditions likely to be encountered in health insurance underwriting is shown by the 1965–1967 National Health Survey.[6] This survey indicated that 22 million noninstitutionalized members of the civilian population were suffering from a chronic condition that limited or completely curtailed their participation in any major work activity.

After the evaluation of personal medical history, interest next turns to findings reflecting the applicant's present medical condition and indications of his susceptibility to future sickness or accident. Here significant indications of health or impairment may be indicated by the applicant's build, pulse, blood pressure, electrocardiophic abnormalities, urinalysis, environment, type of work, and family history. Obviously each applicant, medically speaking, presents a unique and complex amalgam of medical history, build and circulatory readings, habits, and socioeconomic and

---

[6] Data obtained from household interviews by the National Center for Health Statistics and published biennially: United States Department of Health, Education and Welfare, Health Services and Mental Health Administration, *Chronic Conditions and Limitations of Activity and Mobility, United States, July 1965–June 1967* (Washington, D.C.: U.S. Government Printing Office, 1971).

environmental factors which make his case different from any other. The unique combination of selection factors presented by each applicant make it unlikely that health insurance underwriting will ever become a mechanical process that can be entrusted to a computer.

History of Acute Illness. Episodes of acute illness from which recovery has been prompt do not affect insurability. This is true for illnesses such as flu, pneumonia, common fractures of the bone, and routine appendectomies.

But not all acute episodes of illness can be ignored. A victim of rheumatic fever is left with lifelong residuals that increase his vulnerability to other diseases. The same is true of one who injures his back or spine, suffers a concussion of the brain, or has tuberculosis. A patient with recently arrested tuberculosis must watch for possible recurrence and understand that he may be laid flat by an upper respiratory infection that would not affect another person who had not had tuberculosis.

When an acute episode of certain illnesses has occurred recently, insurers have found it prudent to delay insurance for at least six months. During this period, it can be seen if the disease has left any residuals and if there is any recurrence. This rule in practice can be illustrated by a patient who recently had two bouts of cystitis. Following the customary rule, he would be asked to wait six months before he could be offered insurance with a temporary extra premium; if he lived three years without a recurrence of the cystitis, he would become a standard risk.

Chronic Conditions. Chronic health conditions tend to be progressive in nature and are significant factors in risk selection. This is because they may limit the patient's capacity for work and require him to seek medical treatment more often than a standard risk. Some of the most frequently encountered chronic conditions that affect insurability and increase the likelihood of disability are arthritis, rheumatism, impairments of the back or spine, obesity, other disorders of the musculoskeletal apparatus, vision or hearing impairments, neoplasms, hypertension, and the cardiovascular-renal diseases.

Arthritis and rheumatism, though of minor significance for life insurance underwriting, are painful diseases that can make it difficult for a manual worker to continue more than limited work activity. In serious forms, arthritis and rheumatism can also curtail the activity of a white-collar worker.

Impairments of the back or spine almost always mean a substantially heightened risk for health insurance. Any applicant who currently or recently has been disabled by a back or spinal condition is not insurable, nor is an applicant with a marked spinal curvature. On the borderline, but essentially substandard, are applicants who have "chronic back trouble," an unoperated herniated disk with "low back syndrome," spondylolisthesis, or mild curvature of the spine. Back and spinal conditions frequently involve the nervous system and usually are more serious when arthritis is present.

Chronic coronary artery disease and other heart and circulatory diseases usually are progressive in nature. Recurrences are to be expected and these conditions will complicate the medical effects of other diseases. The hypertensive or heart patient presents an abnormal surgical risk that routinely must be met by elaborate medical preparations when a surgical procedure is necessary. One attack of coronary artery disease raises a suspicion of arteriosclerosis, a condition which ultimately gives rise to many other chronic and disabling conditions. As time passes following the patient's last heart attack, his prognosis improves and he can be placed in a class with a reduced rating.

The selection of applicants with cancers or neoplasms depends on the grade and location of the neoplasm. Only mild concern need be given applicants who have skin cancers or an epithelioma surgically removed. These applicants can be considered standard risks two years after the surgery. Other victims of malignant cancer are usually uninsurable.

A medical history of chronic illness may be significant in underwriting the hazard of accidental injury. Conditions that predispose one to more frequent injury include uncontrolled epilepsy, nervous conditions, partial paralysis, or other impairments affecting muscle coordination, spells of vertigo, and impaired vision or hearing. It also can be expected that the convalescence and recovery time of those injured in accidents will be extended if the victim is overweight, diabetic, or has a nervous condition.

Blood Pressure. The predisposition of U.S. males to coronary occlusion was shown by a two-year American Heart Association study of 10,000 male manufacturing and office workers in Chicago.[7] Thirty percent were found to be "high risk candidates" for a heart attack. These 30 percent suffered from two or more of the factors known to increase the risk of heart attack: cigarette smoking, high blood pressure, high cholesterol levels of the blood, overweight, diabetes, and abnormal electrocardiograms. Ten percent had three or more risk factors which means, according to the Framingham, Massachusetts study,[8] a risk of heart attack 10 times that of a normal person.

Systolic and diastolic blood pressure readings are routinely obtained on about 20 percent of all applicants, a variable depending upon the insurer's nonmedical underwriting rules. Blood pressure readings are also obtained from family or attending physicians of those with a history of hypertension. The readings are converted to underwriting debits or to a substandard class using blood pressure tables which give ratings based on age, systolic pressure and diastolic pressure.

The American Heart Association studies buttress the long-standing position of insurers and their medical directors that the risk of heart attack is greatly increased when both overweight and high blood pressure are present. Accordingly, whenever any one of the risk factors associated with heart attacks is uncovered, the applicant's medical record receives careful scrutiny to make sure that none of the other risk factors are also present.

---

[7] *New York Times,* March 22, 1970, p. 68.

[8] William B. Kannel, M.D., and Tavia Gordon (eds.), *The Framingham Study* (Washington, D.C.: U.S. Government Printing Office, 1970).

Build. The applicant is always asked: "What is your height and weight?" His answers are easily verified when necessary by a medical examiner. The question speaks to the significance of obesity in risk selection. The overweight person is more apt to develop diabetes, to become afflicted with cardiovascular-renal disease, is a greater surgical risk, and is accident-prone. Overweight people recover more slowly from illness.

The underwriting debits or risk classification for height and weight have been reduced to a "build" table. A health insurance build table tabulates the ranges of weight that correspond to each standard, substandard, or uninsurable risk classification for every one inch of normal adult height.

Occupation

Disability benefit costs vary from occupation to occupation in proportion to the hazard seemingly implicit in each career, profession or line of work. Actually it is believed that the variation seemingly due to occupation reflects at least four distinct influences. These are (1) the risk of on-the-job injury and of occupational disease, (2) the promptness with which the duties of an occupation permit one recuperating from non-occupational injury or sickness to return to work, (3) the sporadic nature of employment in some occupations, and (4) the socioeconomic characteristics of those who pursue each occupation.

The first influence is the most obvious one. The variations in occupational injury and sickness are frequently studied by workmen's compensation insurers and government agencies concerned about job safety. Inside clerical occupations are shown to be the safest, while logging, crop-dusting, and underground mining are among the most hazardous vocations.

The second element, the occupational variations in the period of recuperation from nonjob-related injury or sickness, is shown repeatedly by claim studies and claim-settlement guidelines.[9] A fracture at the neck of the femur or thigh bone normally will disable a clerical worker for no more than 16 weeks while light manual and heavy manual workers will be disabled 26 and 39 weeks, respectively. Pneumonia will disable a heavy manual worker twice as long as a clerical worker. For the opposite effect, consider a surgeon kept from his operating table by a minor hand injury or a lecturer silenced by an attack of acute laryngitis.

The permanence, stability, and regularity of employment give rise to the third risk element measured by occupation. In those occupations where work is sporadic or seasonal in nature, disability coverage can provide an invitation to malingering when work is scarce. More frequent, extended disabilities are apt to be experienced during the off-season.

The fourth element, socioeconomic influence, is perhaps the most difficult to demonstrate. Yet public health studies repeatedly show that such socioeconomic variables as income, education, living conditions, and

---

[9] See Wickman, *Evaluating the Health Insurance Risk.*

neighborhood are significantly correlated to illness rates and to the use of medical care. To the extent that members of any socioeconomic class or level favor certain occupations, occupation becomes an indirect indicator of the variations in sickness rates or in the use of medical care services that are known to be due to socioeconomic factors.

Insurers most commonly divide all occupations into five rating classes. These five typically are referred to as AAA, AA, A, B, and C and owe their origin to work done by a committee of the former Health and Accident Underwriters Conference.[10]

Class AAA: Includes most professions, as well as supervisory, clerical, and office jobs that have relatively light manual duties and no environmental accident or sickness hazards.

Class AA: Includes occupations with more risk of occupational injury than "office" occupations. Class AA also includes jobs where common illnesses or accidents are likely to result in longer absences from work than typical of Class AAA occupations.

Class A: Includes occupations where work involves considerable amounts of manual labor or requires use of light machinery entailing some risk of occupational injury. Class A occupations should be under favorable working conditions and not involve use of heavy machinery or exposure to dust, extreme temperatures, high voltage, or harmful chemicals.

Class B: Includes occupations in which work consists of strenuous manual labor or involves use of heavy machinery that presents a danger of serious occupational injury and of prolonged disability.

Class C: Includes unusually hazardous occupations. Because of the poor persistency of policies issued to Class C risks and the high premiums required, not all insurers will insure Class C occupations.

Applicants who have two jobs will be classified according to the more hazardous of the two occupations. There are only a few occupations, such as some logging, mining work, or crop-dusting, that are not insurable.

Occasionally an applicant's avocations or sports activities will increase materially the health insurance risk. Skydiving, motorcycle racing and stock car racing are examples of hazardous avocations. Even skiing can, in some instances, increase materially the risk of disability. Where avocation materially increases the risk, it is customary to attach a rider excluding loss caused by participation in the excluded activity.

Recent competition for disability income sales has led to a liberalization of the definition of disability used in insuring AAA and AA occupations. The "his-occupation" definition of disability which once applied only to the first three years of disability has been extended by many insurers to apply to the first 10 years of disability and in a few instances to

---

[10] Health and Accident Underwriters Conference, *The Occupational Classification Report* (Chicago, 1953).

apply for all years of disability to age 65. A minority view is that it may not be wise to insure a status—an occupation—rather than the event of disability; the best interest of the insured and insurer alike would seem to lie in retaining all incentives for rehabilitation and return to useful work. Nevertheless, these recent liberalizations in benefit language increase the importance of evaluating occupation in risk selection.

Habits

Out of concern over the health of the American people and about how best to provide medical care in this country has come a better understanding of the role of the individual with respect to his health. Venereal disease, alcoholism, drug addiction, lung cancer, and even heart disease are closely related to poor individual health habits.

The disease of alcoholism illustrates the importance of habits in risk selection. At least one of every 20 Americans over the age of 18 is an alcoholic. Unarrested alcoholism breaks down the essential functions of the body and leads to prolonged disability and ultimately death. Over half of all highway fatalities involve alcohol as do a remarkable number of other accidents.

Alcoholism presents difficulties of detection because the alcoholic is among the last to identify himself as such, and because his drinking habits may be hidden by his friends, family, and employer. Alcoholism is a recurrent disease and as a practical matter alcoholics are insurable only after clear evidence of a successful rehabilitation.

Like the alcoholic, the drug-using applicant also presents a significant accident and sickness hazard. He cannot be considered a standard risk for any form of health insurance.

Portion of Income Insurable

Disability income insurance seeks to replace a portion of income lost during disability. Hence it is fundamental to determine the applicant's earned income that would be put in jeopardy by disability, and the portion of income safely insurable without encouraging malingering or removing financial incentive for the insured to undertake rehabilitation.

Since the purpose of disability insurance is to replace income lost because of disability, only that income earned by working is insurable. Income from investments and other sources that is unaffected during disability is not insurable and is excluded in calculating an applicant's earned income.

Insurers usually will issue sufficient monthly disability income benefits to insure, with other coverage, one half or more of an applicant's earned income. The 50 percent rule takes suitable account of these three considerations:

1. Only after-tax income is insurable. Disability income insurance premiums paid by the insured are not tax deductible under current U.S. income tax law regulations. By the same token, disability income benefits are not taxable. This means that only an applicant's after-federal-income-tax-earned-income is insurable.

2. The nearly universal coverage of the Social Security Act makes any worker with a long-term total and permanent disability eligible to receive the primary social security benefit. Social security benefits must be recognized and counted as other disability coverage.

3. Given the subjective nature of disability, insurers consider it wise never to insure benefits which, together with OASDI benefits, exceed more than 80 to 90 percent of an insured's after-tax earnings. This leaves a reasonable co-payment of any loss to the insured and leaves unimpaired the financial incentive for return to work. It also recognizes that some expenses, such as those for clothing and transportation, vanish from the budget of one who is disabled.

Also of significance in risk selection are disability income benefits payable under state cash disability benefit plans, wage payments under employer sick leave plans, and group disability benefits.[11]

Insurers usually have an upper limit on the amount of monthly disability benefits they will issue to any individual. These limits range from $1,500 to $3,000 a month for class AAA occupations and typically are $600 a month for class B and C occupations. Since a $1,500 limit permits insurance of 50 percent of a $3,000 a month earned income, limits above $1,500 have been posted only by a handful of insurers who specialize in insuring highly paid executives and professionals. Lower limits for more hazardous occupations essentially reflect the lower average amounts sold and the limited demand for amounts in excess of these limits. ˙

A few insurers offer special use monthly disability benefits in amounts beyond the limits of issue for benefits payable directly to an insured under a personal contract. Special uses include keyman policies with benefits payable to a corporation, insurance to fund a buy-and-sell agreement, and overhead expense policies which pay business expenses during the first two years of disability.

At one time insurers were unwilling to issue more than $1,000 of monthly disability benefits, but were willing to participate in providing up to $1,500 of monthly benefits that might be issued or in force with all insurers. This distinction between issue and participation limits has virtually vanished as the availability of satisfactory reinsurance facilities have allowed primary carriers to issue all amounts of coverage desired by applicants.

Moral Hazard

The ethical foundations of insurance have been described as including scrupulous honesty, a belief in work, pride in accomplishment, a desire to preserve what we have, a willingness to obey the law, and acceptance of individual accountability for one's own actions.[12] It is maintained that insurance is successful in any stratum of society where the standards of

---

[11] California, Hawaii, New Jersey, New York, Rhode Island, and Puerto Rico have laws compelling employers to purchase and provide 26-week temporary disability benefits. Maximum weekly benefits range from $75 in New York to $105 in California.

[12] John D. Long, *Ethics, Morality and Insurance* (Bloomington, Ind.: Bureau of Business Research, Indiana University, 1971).

conduct correspond to these ethical standards. However, the necessary conditions for a workable contract of insurance cannot be said to exist for individuals who fail to honor such ethical conduct.

Over the years underwriters have described those few applicants who were unwilling to honor the prevailing ethical code as presenting a moral hazard. These persons who were declined as presenting a moral hazard might be found to make materially misleading statements, withhold pertinent information, engage in illegal activities, purchase more insurance than needed, associate with men of questionable integrity, or "cut corners." In such situations there simply is no operable basis for insurance, no premium rate high enough to offset the risk presented by those who would file false or exaggerated claims.

SOURCES OF INFORMATION

Application

In 8 out of 10 cases nonmedical underwriting rules apply, and the application is the principal source of individual health underwriting information. As a result, field underwriters have an obligation to obtain complete answers to all questions on the application, thus providing the home office underwriter with a word portrait of the applicant.

Typically, the applicant is asked when he was last attended by a physician, the nature and duration of any illness, and if he has fully recovered. The name and address of the attending physician seen by the applicant is always recorded along with the name of his family physician. A personal medical history covers at least illnesses or injuries suffered during the last five years. Specific questions seek indication of any disease of the heart, lungs, kidneys, high or low blood pressure, rheumatism, or other disease with risk selection significance.

The occupation and duties of the applicant are recorded along with mention of any other insurance owned by the applicant and whether he has ever had an application for insurance declined, postponed, or cancelled; or if he has been offered a modified policy by another insurance company.

Attending Physician's Statement

An attending physician's statement is sought from a physician seen by an applicant, and it is more useful than a medical examination in describing chronic diseases or impairments. This is because the applicant's personal physician has a more intimate knowledge of his medical history and better clinical records than can be obtained from any other source. For example, attending physicians' statements on "routine checkups" are particularly enlightening. Sometimes applicants report actual medical treatment as a "physical checkup," perhaps because they do not know their exact illness or do not understand the doctor's medical terms well enough to relate the diagnosis. In any case, attending physician's statements are most helpful in understanding the medical nature of an applicant's ailments.

Any applicant disclosing medical treatment is asked to grant the attending physician permission to disclose the otherwise privileged details about the illness. The physician's statement itself will describe the medical nature of any illness and treatment, its significance, and the prognosis. Most insurers use uniform attending physicians' blanks designed by the American Medical Association in cooperation with the Health Insurance Council.

Medical Examination

While four fifths of all health insurance applications are underwritten solely on the basis of the applicant's answers on the application blank, medical examinations are obtained when more information is needed or application is made for relatively large benefits. Medical examinations provide a verification of the applicant's personal medical history, and give an assessment of his current health through such findings as pulse rate, blood pressure, and urinalysis.

It is a routine practice to request a medical examination of an applicant for larger amounts of noncancellable disability income insurance. Insurers commonly require medical examinations when the amount of monthly indemnity exceeds $350 or the applicant is over age 45, though some require an examination for any amount of long-term disability income insurance.

Rising medical examination fees and a shortage of available physicians in family or general practice have created a need for an alternative to medical examinations. This need is met increasingly by medical screening centers. These centers are staffed by technicians and offer an abbreviated examination that includes a recording of medical history, height, weight, girth, blood pressure, pulse, and a chemical analysis of urine. They also offer a comprehensive technological screening that includes phonocardiogram, electrocardiogram and blood tests.

Other Sources of Information

Insurers generally order an inspection report when application is made for more than $300 of monthly disability income or when answers on the application blank raise doubts about the applicant's environment, the nature of his work or habits. The Fair Credit Reporting Act of 1970 requires advance notice to any person who will be the subject of an inspection report and supplementary advice if unfavorable action is taken based on the contents of the inspection report. These notices have not proved burdensome to insurers and for many merely formalize a common practice of telling all applicants that they might be the subject of an investigation to determine their insurability. Typically, inspection reports concern an applicant's finances, health, general reputation, driving record, habits, and moral conduct. The reports compile the impressions of friends, neighbors and business associates, and items drawn from newspaper articles, court records, and police reports.

The record of claims filed by previously insured applicants can be an invaluable source of information. The details of previous claims illuminate the applicant's medical history, reveal his attitude toward health insurance and indicate any tendency to malinger. The validity of claims information often makes it possible to act with a great degree of confidence in insuring those who already are policyowners.

One should not overlook the role of the agent both as a source of information and as a field underwriter in the most literal sense. He meets the applicant face-to-face and often sees his home environment and place of employment. Experienced agents become skilled judges of the insurability of the prospects they meet. The agent who avoids soliciting those who present a moral hazard or are apt to abuse their insurance, builds both a sound agency and a reputation for full disclosure that inevitably clears the way for prompt action on all applicants that he can recommend unreservedly for insurance.

SELECTED REFERENCES

Long, John D. *Ethics, Mortality and Insurance*. Bloomington, Ind.: Bureau of Business Research, Indiana University, 1971.

MacDonald, Roy A. *The Underwriting of Substandard Accident and Health Insurance*. Cincinnati, Ohio: National Underwriter Company, 1951.

Society of Actuaries. *Health Insurance Provided through Individual Policies*, Ch. 4, "Underwriting." (Edwin L. Bartleson, principal contributor.) Chicago, 1968.

Tilton, Earle B. and Yochem, Donald E. *A Guide to Health Insurance Underwriting*. Indianapolis, Ind.: Research and Review Service of America, Inc., 1961.

Wickman, J. M. *Evaluating the Health Insurance Risk*. Cincinnati, Ohio: National Underwriter Company, 1965.

part V

Group Life and
Health Insurance

THE GROUP METHOD of providing insurance coverage for death, disability, and retirement has proven to be a highly significant force in evolving financial security. Typically, group life and health insurance is a major part of employee benefit plans. It has grown immensely since its introduction in the United States early in the 20th century and is of increasing significance throughout the world.

Part V is concerned with group concepts, coverages, contracts, and company practices. These chapters are devoted to life, disability income, and medical expense insurance coverages. The group technique as applied to pensions and other forms of deferred compensation is presented in Part VI.

25

Fundamental Characteristics of Group Insurance

By DAVIS W. GREGG

GROUP INSURANCE, a major component of employee benefit plans, provides an insurance technique of considerable economic, social, and political significance. A substantial and increasing part of the labor force has protection under group insurance, and an increasing proportion of all other persons in the United States is insured by some form of dependents' coverage, senior citizen coverage and the like. Growth of the group business over the years suggests that ultimately the number of persons insured might be almost as great as under social insurance.

Group insurance usually is distinguished from other forms of personal insurance (as contrasted with property insurance) in two ways. It customarily is differentiated as a separate field from individual insurance and social insurance, the distinctions being based primarily upon the social philosophy and methodology underlying each of the three types.[1] Then,

---

[1] Social insurance is generally considered to have several basic characteristics that distinguish it from private insurance. One authoritative textbook (John G. Turnbull, C. Arthur Williams, Jr., and Earl F. Cheit, *Economic and Social Security* [3d ed.; New York: The Ronald Press Co., 1968], p. 23) indicates that social insurance differs from the most common forms of private insurance in four important respects:

"1) Participation is compulsory (with a few exceptions) for all eligible persons. Otherwise some individuals would elect not to be covered and the policy objective of a floor of protection for all members of a defined group would be thwarted.

"2) The benefits are prescribed by law. There are no contracts, and it is possible (but highly improbable) that Congress will rescind the benefits in the future. Periodic changes in the benefit structure are very likely through changes in the law.

"3) The system redistributes income in addition to providing protection through a pooling arrangement. The lower-income groups, the insureds with many dependents, and the participants who were elderly when the system was inaugurated receive more benefits for their contributions than most other participants. If this were not true, it would be impossible to achieve the public policy objective of a floor of protection for all participants, since some insureds would be unable to afford adequate protection. Old-age benefits during the early years of the system would also be limited. The

too, on the basis of state regulation and the operational practices of private insurance, group insurance is always distinguished from "ordinary" insurance and "industrial" insurance.[2] Group life insurance may be further divided into group term life insurance and group permanent life insurance. The group technique was initiated in the former context, and this type of group life insurance still represents by far the largest segment.

Within the context of the mechanism applicable to personal risks, as contrasted to property risks, group insurance has a broad connotation. It includes not only group life insurance and group health insurance but also the directly related area of pensions.

Group life and health insurance, the field with which this chapter is concerned, is somewhat difficult to delineate precisely. Group life includes forms such as group *term* life insurance and group *permanent* life insurance, the distinction essentially relating to benefit structure and price. Based upon the nature of the relationships of insurer-insured-beneficiary, most group life insurance may be labeled as employer-employee, union-member, creditor-debtor, and dependent coverage.

Group health insurance may be classified in a variety of ways. The principal categories are group *disability income* insurance and group *medical expense* insurance, the distinction resting mainly upon the type of loss with which the insurance is concerned. Group health insurance is labeled in several other ways that can only be clarified by definition and analysis to follow.

Group and Individual Contrasted

When group insurance is contrasted with individual insurance, a number of unique characteristics are evident. First, and probably foremost, is the group selection of risks as contrasted to individual selection. With few exceptions, group insurance is issued without medical examination or other evidence of individual insurability.

Another characteristic of group insurance is the coverage of a number of persons under a single contract. Interestingly, the persons insured are not actually parties to the contract, since legally the contract is between the insurer and the group policyholder, most commonly an employer.

---

benefits are not equitable in the private insurance sense, but they are not meant to be. Other standards of performance have been deemed more important. In short, the system stresses 'social adequacy' rather than 'individual equity.'

"The contribution rates are scheduled, but Congress may and has revised the schedule periodically. Consequently, bankruptcy is impossible as long as the government has an effective taxing power, although it is conceivable that the taxes may become unbearable. An individual's contribution may vary yearly even though the tax rate remains fixed, for the base (annual income) upon which the tax is levied may fluctuate from year to year. These fluctuations may have little or no effect on the benefits.

"4) The government system is a monopolistic system. However, public pressure forces a continual reassessment of benefits and contribution rates."

[2] Increasingly, ordinary and industrial tend to be grouped together as individual insurance, thus making the logical distinction between group and individual. See Davis W. Gregg, "Is Life Insurance Really Ordinary?", *The Journal of the American Society of Chartered Life Underwriters,* Vol. XVII, No. 3 (Summer, 1963), pp. 197–202.

A third characteristic of group insurance is that it is essentially low-cost, mass protection. A number of economies of large volume operation are obtained through mass distribution and mass administration methods.

Another special feature of group insurance lies in the fact that premiums usually are subject to experience rating. Except for small groups, the actual experience of an individual group may figure heavily in the determination of dividends or premium rate adjustments. Generally speaking, the larger the group, the greater the significance attached to its own claims and expenses in any policy year.

Group insurance contracts, as a rule, are of a continuing nature, in that the contract and the plan may last long beyond the lifetime, or membership in the plan, of any one individual. New persons are added to the group from time to time and others terminate their coverage. However, it is relatively rare for group coverage to be discontinued by an employer, since normally it is part of his overall employee benefit plan. It is less rare for group plans to be changed from one insurer to another.

TYPES OF GROUP LIFE AND HEALTH INSURANCE

Clear and definitive classification of the types of group life and health insurance is difficult. Yet, brief and reasonably descriptive definitions of the more significant forms seems desirable.

Group Life Insurance

Fundamentally, all forms of group life insurance are concerned with the payment of a benefit upon the death of the person insured.

a) Group term—One-year renewable term life insurance issued under a group contract to employers, creditors, unions, associations, and other eligible entities.

b) Group permanent—Life insurance under a group contract that provides for some form of accumulation of permanent or cash value units. Group paid-up, and level premium group permanent used in pension funding, have been the most common forms.

c) Group accidental death—A form of life insurance payable upon death as a consequence of accidental bodily injury. (Most often this insurance is written as "group accidental death and dismemberment" coverage and, strangely, is usually classified as a form of group health insurance. Since the accidental death part of the coverage represents more than 90 percent of the benefit payments, it is here classified as a special form of group life insurance.)

Group life insurance may be further classified by the nature of the group insured as employer group life, association group life, federal employees group life, and servicemen's group life, among others. So-called "wholesale life insurance" has many characteristics of group life, yet it provides individual insurance policies with some individual underwriting characteristics. "Survivors' benefit group life" is an increasingly popular form of coverage that pays an annuity to the insured's surviving spouse or children upon his death.

Group Health Insurance

Group health insurance is concerned with the provision of benefits for the loss of earning power due to disability, or for medical expenses due to illness, injury, or preventive care.

a) Group disability income–Insurance under a group contract to reimburse for the loss of income resulting from disability caused by sickness or accident. Short-term disability income insurance is characterized by benefit payments for periods up to 26 or 52 weeks. Long-term disability income insurance is concerned with benefit payments for periods substantially greater than one year, often until age 65, and most often with a 26- or 52-week waiting period before payments start.

b) Group medical expense–Insurance under a group contract (private insurance company, Blue Cross/Blue Shield, or prepaid group practice) to provide cash or service benefits for medical services of physicians, surgeons, dentists, nurses, hospitals, and for drugs, appliances, and other medical and allied goods and services. The various types of medical expense coverage include hospital expense insurance, surgical expense insurance, physician's visits insurance (often called "in-hospital medical expense" or "comprehensive medical expense" insurance), diagnostic X-ray and laboratory insurance, supplemental accident insurance, supplemental major medical and comprehensive major medical expense insurance, dental expense insurance, vision care expense insurance, radiology expense insurance, extended care facility expense insurance, home health care expense insurance, and prescription drug expense insurance. The government program of Medicare might also be classified as group medical expense insurance.

Other types of group health insurance, classified essentially by the nature of the group insured or by the nature of the insurer or provider of services, will be analyzed subsequently. So-called "franchise health insurance" has certain characteristics of group health insurance but essentially is individual health insurance protection provided to groups of persons in the same occupation or profession or to groups who cannot be written on a regular group basis under a single master policy (e.g., groups of less than ten employees).

BASIC FEATURES

Group insurance appears quite complex when one considers the variety and types of groups, sizes of groups, underwriting rules, premium plans and funding methods. Actually, however, there are certain features of group insurance which have a high degree of universality and which may be looked upon as embodying the fundamentals of this insurance technique.

Eligible Groups

State insurance laws and company underwriting practices are the two major forces determining the types of groups eligible for group insurance. The laws, variable among the states, describe the kinds of groups eligible. Insurer underwriting practices vary among the group-writing companies and may be more restrictive than any applicable statutory rules. Within the existing legal and underwriting framework, risks eligible for group insurance may be classified as individual employer groups, multiple-employer groups, labor union groups, creditor-debtor groups, and miscellaneous groups.

Individual Employer Groups. By far the most important type of eligible group, from the standpoint of number of group contracts, number of persons insured and amount of insurance in force, is the individual employer group. The employer may be a sole proprietorship, a partnership, or a corporation. The interpretation of "employees" is quite broad and includes, in addition to those normally thought of as employees of a firm, additional persons such as (1) proprietors and partners under group policies covering their employees; (2) employees of subsidiaries, affiliates, and associated firms; (3) retired employees; and sometimes, (4), independent contractors whose businesses are controlled by the master policyholder through contract or otherwise.

Multiple-Employer Groups. The multiple-employer group category includes negotiated trusteeships and voluntary trade associations. Typically, negotiated trusteeships are formed as an outgrowth of collective bargaining between a union and the employers of union members, in the same or related industry, and the group contract is issued to the trustees of the health and welfare fund. The Labor Management Relations Act of 1947 (the Taft-Hartley Act) applies where the employees are engaged in activities which affect interstate or foreign commerce and prohibits an employer from paying funds directly to a labor union even for the purpose of paying premiums for group insurance. Under the usual Taft-Hartley trust, contributions by the employer are made at a fixed rate and these monies, together with investment income, are used to purchase group insurance, provide for the expenses incurred by the trustees and the central administrative office, and to lay aside reserve and surplus funds.

Voluntary trade association groups are comprised of employers in the same industry or commercial enterprise (e.g., automobile dealers, retail grocers, manufacturers) with the association sponsoring a voluntary plan of group insurance under which the employees of member firms may be insured. The group contract is generally issued to a trustee but also may be issued directly to the association if there is no legal impediment.

Labor Union Groups. In labor union groups the coverage is provided union members under a contract issued directly to the union. The premium may come directly from the union's funds or jointly from those funds and members' insurance contributions.

Creditor-Debtor Groups. A creditor-debtor arrangement provides group life and group disability income insurance for debtors through a group contract issued to the creditor. Typically, the group insurance is provided through commercial banks, finance companies, small-loan companies, credit unions and retailers, with references to debts such as time payment purchases, charge accounts, personal loans and other forms of consumer debt. If the borrower dies (or is disabled), benefits are paid to the lender to cancel the insured part of the debt (or to relieve the debtor of the need to make his periodic payments while disabled).

Miscellaneous Groups. A great variety of groups beyond the foregoing classifications are covered by group insurance where permitted by state insurance laws and by group insurer underwriting practices. Among such miscellaneous groups are associations of public and private employees; professional associations of teachers, lawyers, physicians and dentists; fraternal society members; college alumni groups; savings account depositors; veterans organizations; religious groups; and many others. Significant group insurance plans that might fall in this category, even though more logically they may be considered employer-employee groups, are the United States government group life insurance plans covering federal employees ($39.7 billion at the close of 1970) and servicemen ($51.3 billion at the close of 1970). These are by far the largest group insurance plans in the world written by private insurers, and the risk is shared by some 600 companies through reinsurance arrangements.

Size Specifications

A fundamental issue in group insurance pertains to the number of persons needed to constitute a "group." Again, the issue is resolved by state insurance laws and company underwriting practices. There are rather well-defined—although changing—size specifications relating to the minimum number of persons and the minimum proportion of the entire group covered. These size and participation requirements also vary by type of coverage, that is, by the various forms of group life insurance and group health insurance.

Minimum Number. Group life insurance was the first form of group insurance written and, at the outset, the generally accepted minimum was 100 lives. Accumulated experience in group underwriting has resulted in the progressive reduction of the number considered to constitute a group until today, depending upon the state, the insurer, the type of group, and the type of group insurance, it might be as small as two or three persons. The most common requirement in group life and health insurance (by law and by underwriting practice) is ten persons, although often there is a lower minimum or no minimum for group health.

There are two basic reasons for requiring a minimum number of persons under group insurance; namely, (1) to reduce individual selection against the insurer, and (2) to spread the expense, thus lowering the rate of expense per insured person. A minimum of, say, 10 or 25 persons gives the insurer some protection against the insurance being taken primarily for the purpose of covering one or more individuals with incipient losses and claims. The larger the group, the less likely it is that the decision to insure the group will be determined by the impaired health of one or more lives, and also the less likely it is to contain an undue proportion of impaired lives. Any theoretical exactness in determining a safe minimum number is not possible. In any case, it should be recognized that no magic inheres in the number selected as the minimum, such as 10 or 25.

From a practical standpoint, however, the very important element in determining minimum group size is that of expenses. One of the cost advantages of group insurance lies in the substantial risk-handling economies attained through the group method. Since there are certain initial and continuing "per case" expenses which must be met regardless of the size of the group, it is obvious that the smaller the case the greater the rate of expense on a per-person or per-unit-of-insurance basis.

Minimum Proportion of Group. The extent to which the members within a given group participate in the group insurance plan is significant for the same reasons as is the minimum size of the group, namely, the avoidance of adverse selection against the insurer and the reduction of expenses per unit. As a result, every effort is made to secure a high percentage of participation initially and to keep the participation high in subsequent years.

In noncontributory plans, that is, where the participants make no payment toward the cost of the group insurance, it is typically required that all eligible persons must be insured. In the case of contributory plans, that is, where the premium is paid at least in part by the plan participants, it is typically required that at least 75 percent of the eligible persons must elect to take the insurance. The very practical reason for permitting somewhat less than 100 percent participation in the case of contributory plans is that some eligible participants may refuse to contribute.

The minimum participation requirement is important also from a personnel relations viewpoint. A group insurance plan with only a small proportion of all eligible employees enrolled, even if sound from an insurance standpoint, obviously would not be performing its proper function as an employee welfare plan. Keeping at least three fourths of the employees under the plan assures its value to the employer from this standpoint.

Benefit Schedules

Group insurance benefit schedules are based upon some plan designed to preclude individual selection either by the insured persons (usually employees) or by the party arranging the plan (usually the employer). Some sort of predetermined schedule or plan of benefits is required in every group insurance situation.

Important factors usually considered in the selection of a benefit schedule are (1) the needs of the employees, (2) the employees' ability to pay if the plan is contributory, and (3) the overall cost of the plan. The interrelationship of these factors has, over the years, resulted in the development of benefit schedules related essentially to earnings, to position or occupational classifications, or to the simple plan of a flat benefit amount for everyone covered. There are rare instances where group life insurance plans relate the amount of benefit to length of service. Finally, there are benefit schedules which are a combination of two or more of any of these basic types.

The most widely used benefit schedule is that which bases the amount of insurance (except for group medical expense insurance) on the employee's earnings. An illustration of a simple scale of group life and disability income insurance benefits is as follows:

Weekly Earnings	Life Insurance	Disability Income Insurance
Weekly earnings less than $100	$ 5,000	$ 50 per week
Weekly earnings $100 but less than $140	7,500	75 per week
Weekly earnings $140 but less than $200	10,000	100 per week
Weekly earnings $200 and over	12,500	140 per week

The plan may be based on any common earnings unit, e.g., annual, monthly, weekly, or hourly rates of pay, the governing factor usually being the payroll setup of the employer. As a rule, only the base pay is considered in determining an employee's earnings classification for insurance, and bonuses and overtime pay are excluded.

The position schedule provides varying amounts of insurance for employees depending upon their employment positions. For example, the employees might be classified as officers (defined), department heads (defined), salesmen and foremen, and all other employees. In any event, a uniform amount of insurance is provided within each classification, and different amounts are provided as between each classification. A typical position schedule, again for group life and disability income insurance, might appear as follows:

Position	Life Insurance	Disability Income Insurance
President, vice presidents, secretary, treasurer ..	$25,000	$150 per week
Department heads	20,000	125 per week
Salesmen and foremen	10,000	100 per week
All other employees	5,000	80 per week

In group health insurance, disability income benefits are almost always related directly to earnings and, in order to avoid malingering (the tendency of the insured to feign illness in order to receive insurance benefits rather than his wages), the benefit amount normally does not exceed about two thirds of average wages. Benefits under group medical expense insurance typically are fairly uniform for all persons covered, but with occasional differences between employees covered under collective bargaining agreements and salaried employees.

Financing

A group insurance plan may be financed on either a noncontributory basis with the employer paying the entire cost, or on a contributory basis with the employees sharing the cost with the employer. In some few cases, where not prohibited by law, participants may pay the entire cost.

In the history of group insurance there have been several trends and countertrends in financing. When group insurance began six decades ago, the noncontributory plan was the most popular. Within a period of about five years after World War I there developed a trend away from employer-pay-all plans. Not only was most new group insurance written on the contributory basis, but many of the old plans were switched to this basis. Several factors caused this shift, including the popularization of the payroll deduction idea in World War I, the business recession of the early 1930s, and the subsequent development of group health insurance benefits in the 1930s with a consequent need for employee contributions to share the cost of additional benefits.

During World War II a reverse trend became evident, and a majority of the new plans and many old ones were put on a noncontributory basis. Probably the most important reason for the change was the wage stabilization policy of the federal government that froze money wages but permitted group insurance as an extra employment benefit. Too, the fact that group insurance premiums paid by the employer usually are deductible as a business expense under the federal income tax law, and normally are not treated thereunder as income to the employee, no doubt encouraged many companies to absorb all the costs of group insurance and make these benefits available on a nontaxable basis to their employees. Still another factor of special importance has been the inclusion of group insurance as a negotiated welfare benefit under collective bargaining agreements. Through a trustee arrangement, management usually pays the entire cost for the employee and part of the cost for dependent coverage.

A number of advantages are claimed for the noncontributory, employer-pay-all basis for premium financing, including the following:

1. *Simplicity of administration.* The insurance records of individual employees under a noncontributory plan are somewhat simpler and, since no payroll deduction procedures are necessary, the employer obviously has fewer accounting operations to perform.
2. *Economy of installation and administration.* Since all employees are covered, it is not necessary for the insurance company and the employer to go to the expense of soliciting plan membership among individual employees. The continuing expense of soliciting new employees and getting waiver forms from nonsubscribing employees is avoided as well as certain other routine administration costs.
3. *Tax advantages.* Employer premium costs normally are deductible as an ordinary business expense for federal income tax purposes, whereas employee contributions are not deductible for personal income tax purposes except for group health insurance where contributions are partially deductible as medical expenses. Furthermore, the employer's contributions usually are not taxable to the employees for federal income tax purposes except for group life in excess of $50,000.
4. *All employees insured.* All eligible employees who have completed the probationary period and are actively at work have the full amount of insurance. This gives the plan maximum participation and minimizes adverse selection. It avoids problems for the employer which might

occur under a contributory plan when an eligible employee did not elect to take the insurance or dropped out of a plan without his dependents' knowledge. Also, there is less likelihood of clerical errors affecting the coverage of an individual.

5. *More control of plan.* Under a noncontributory plan the employer has more control over changes in coverage and benefits. In the absence of collective bargaining, unilateral action is feasible where employees are not sharing the cost of the plan.

The principal advantages claimed for the contributory plan of financing group insurance benefits are the following:

1. *Makes possible larger benefits.* For a given money outlay by the employer, a more liberal group plan is available if the employees also contribute. The employer may not be able to afford the entire cost of a plan, and unless the employees contribute, no plan can be installed. In other cases, employee contributions may permit additional types of insurance coverages or higher amounts of existing coverages.

2. *Greater employee interest and appreciation.* It is argued that employees generally have more interest in group insurance plans to which they are making some direct contribution. Also, because of their greater awareness of the plan, they presumably are more appreciative of its values.

3. *More effective use of employer's contributions.* It is argued that a contributory plan permits the employer to channel his insurance funds to the more needful and more important employees. In other words, the employees who refuse to participate in a contributory plan are most often the younger single females, who have few insurance needs, and among whom employee turnover is greatest. Therefore, the employer's funds are used more effectively in sharing the cost of benefits for the employees who have greater needs and also who are most likely to make a career of their jobs.

4. *Employees have more control.* From the standpoint of the employees, the contributory plan affords them a greater voice in the benefits provided. The employer is more likely to respect the opinions of the employees and is less likely to discontinue the plan altogether.

Available evidence indicates that well over 50 percent of all group life insurance in force is on a contributory basis. An even higher proportion of group health insurance benefits is on the contributory plan. There is some evidence that there is a trend toward providing group insurance benefits on a noncontributory basis, but most of this force seems to come through collectively bargained plans.

GROUP SELECTION

As mentioned earlier, perhaps the most important of the fundamental characteristics of the group technique is that of group selection, the effect of which is to provide life and health insurance coverage on an individual without any inquiry as to the quality of the individual risk and the likelihood of an early loss and claim. This unique element has been an important factor in the rapid extension of group life and health insurance to a majority of our population.

Group insurance companies usually adopt selection standards or underwriting rules which are broad enough to allow acceptance of a large majority of insurable groups at standard premium rates. For certain types of groups, such as those engaged in particularly hazardous industries, the mortality and morbidity rates are consistently higher than for standard groups, and they are classified, therefore, as substandard risks and charged a higher premium rate. In rare situations, a risk may be rejected entirely because the mortality and/or morbidity risk is so great, or unpredictable, that insurance is not practicable.

Within each classification of insurable risks, that is, within the standard class and within each of the several substandard classes, the chance of loss is never exactly the same for all risks or groups. In other words, within each class there are relatively "good" risks and relatively "poor" risks. Every insurance company is anxious to establish underwriting rules which will result in its getting at least an average proportion of good risks. If such a goal is attained, the average mortality and morbidity cost will be lower, and the company may be able to offer insurance at a lower net cost.[3]

The underwriting rules of any group insurance company, then, may be considered to rest logically on three basic objectives: (1) to obtain the proper balance between mass and homogeneity of risks to afford predictability of future results; (2) to establish standards which will permit acceptance of the large majority of groups at standard premium rates; and (3) to secure the largest possible proportion of the average and better than average risks within each classification. The rules which the various companies adopt to reach these objectives are based on experience, research, intuition, and judgment. It is doubtful that the underwriting rules of any two companies are exactly the same.

Theory of Group Selection

Group selection is not concerned with the conditions of health, morals or habits of any particular individual in the group.[4] Instead, group selection is aimed at obtaining a group of persons or, what is even more important, an aggregation of such groups of persons, that will yield a certain predictable rate of mortality or morbidity. If a sufficient mass of risk units (groups of persons in this case) is obtained, and if these risk units are reasonably homogeneous in nature, then advantage can be taken of the predictability of the death and disability perils. There is no conceivable reason why the adoption of the group as the unit of selection is not theoretically sound so long as a proper degree of mass and homogeneity of risk

---

[3] From a practical standpoint, experience rating in group insurance means that the larger groups tend to pay their way whether their results are better or worse than average. Thus, their experience does not contribute to the pooled risks to any significant extent.

[4] Individual risk selection is used at times in group insurance cases, but this does not detract from the theoretical premises of the group concept.

units is obtained. To assure that the risk units (groups) obtained will be satisfactorily homogeneous, the insurer must determine that certain essential features are either inherent in the nature of the group itself or may be successfully applied in a positive way to avoid adverse selection by entire groups or a large proportion of the individuals within a given group. In the following paragraphs the more important theoretical underwriting principles of group insurance are introduced.

Insurance Incidental to Group. One of the first elements looked for in the underwriting of group insurance pertains to the inherent nature of the group of persons seeking insurance. If the group is based upon some natural, preexisting relationship, and if it represents a group of individuals bound together by some strong community of interest other than the opportunity to obtain low cost insurance, then a group selection plan may be feasible.

Should the group be organized mainly for the purpose of obtaining group insurance, there is a possibility of selection against the insurer. With no common interest other than the desire for life and health insurance coverage, the poorer risks presumably would tend to seek and retain membership in the group, and the healthier persons presumably would tend to be indifferent to joining the group or continuing their membership. Thus, for a plan to be workable, it is desirable that the insurance be only a secondary or unessential feature motivating the formation and existence of the group.

Flow of Persons through the Group. A steady flow of persons through the group is another feature generally essential to sound group underwriting. If there is a stream of new entrants into the group representing the addition of young, healthy lives, and a flow out of the group by the aged and impaired lives, the obvious result is to keep the insurability of the group constantly "sweetened" and the rates of mortality and morbidity more or less stable. This is especially important in those groups where the employer may be unwilling to assume the full burden of any increases in cost resulting from increasing ages of employees in the group, since in this situation the younger employees would tend to drop out of the plan if they were asked to pay for the increased cost.

Automatic Determination of Benefits. The amount of benefits on individual persons should be determined in some automatic manner which precludes individual selection by either the employer or employees. Should employees have the option to take various amounts of insurance on their own volition, the unhealthy persons probably would tend to insure heavily and the healthy ones would not. If the employer had complete control in determining the amount of insurance on individual persons, there would be considerable chance for him to select against the insurer for the benefit of individual employees. Selection by either the employer or employee would serve to increase the cost of the plan and probably would result in its failure.

Minimum Proportion of Group. Another essential element in sound group underwriting is the requirement that all or substantially all eligible persons in a given group be covered by insurance. It is only by covering a large proportion of a given group that an insurer gains a positive safeguard against an undue proportion of substandard lives. Of course, it is likely that permitting less than 100 percent coverage in contributory groups introduces some degree of adverse selection. Counteracting this, however, is the fact that an insurer's overall spread of risk is increased, since many employers buy insurance on the contributory plan who would not do so if they had to bear the entire cost. Also, a powerful force at work is the reduction of expenses per individual and per unit of insurance where a high proportion of the group is insured.

Sharing of Cost. Except in unusual circumstances, a group insurance plan on a member-pay-all basis, especially in group life insurance where mortality rates climb sharply with age, possesses the seeds of its own destruction. Some plan of averaging individual premiums is desirable to avoid the increasing premiums for older persons for both life insurance and health insurance. Under member-pay-all coverage, the younger members help to pay for the older members. As they become aware of this, the younger members may tend to leave the group to purchase insurance at less cost elsewhere, thus aggravating the situation by raising average premiums still further. Eventually, if the aged and impaired lives should become the predominating members of the group, the scheme is almost inevitably doomed to failure because of the necessarily large premium charges.

Simplicity and Efficiency of Administration. If members contribute to the cost of group insurance, it is highly desirable that there be some simple, automatic method for them to pay their share, such as, for example, a payroll deduction plan. If the members' contributions are collected in this fashion, it is easier to keep participation at a high level than if each person must take the initiative to remit his contribution. There are many other details in the administration of a group insurance plan which, if left entirely to the employees to handle with the insurer, would be unwieldy and expensive and probably have serious effects on participation. Where administration is handled by an employer or some other central administrative unit, it often is possible to integrate the activities into other administrative functions to the extent that simplicity and efficiency are attained.

Departures from Group Selection Theory

The foregoing analysis of group selection emphasizes theoretical guideposts. From the very beginning of group insurance, there have been variations from these theoretical requirements where permitted by law and where an insurer has been willing to experiment. Examples include providing insurance coverage for retired persons and writing group insurance on associations established essentially for insurance purposes. Some experiments have been highly successful and others less successful.

In the last decade, particularly, there have been many extensions of the group insurance principle, both "vertically" and "horizontally." Vertical extension has been characterized by increasing amounts of insurance on the lives of individual persons, whereas horizontal extension has been characterized by an ever widening variety of groups. The result has been a substantial broadening of group insurance services to the public.

GROWTH AND SIGNIFICANCE

Scope of Group Coverages

A substantial majority of the population of the United States is insured under or protected by some form of group life and health insurance. The labor force is widely insured including governmental employees and servicemen. Dependents of working people are the beneficiaries of group life insurance and generally are directly insured under group medical expense benefits.

Quantitative data are summarized below with respect to current dimensions of group insurance as well as historical trends. Consolidated data on group life and group health generally are not available, so each will be presented separately.

Group Life Insurance. Starting with $403,000 of group life in force at the close of 1911, the amount of insurance has grown to $581 billion at the close of 1971, as shown in Table 25–1. There were three master policies and 427 certificates in 1911, and by 1971 the number had grown to 310,000 master policies and 81.5 million certificates.

TABLE 25–1.   Group Life Insurance in Force in the United States, 1911–71

Year	No. of Master Policies	Number of Certificates	Amount
1911	3	427	403,000
1915	300	120,000	100,000,000
1920	6,000	1,600,000	1,570,000,000
1925	12,000	3,200,000	4,247,000,000
1930	19,000	5,800,000	9,801,000,000
1935	18,000	6,400,000	10,208,000,000
1940	23,000	8,800,000	14,938,000,000
1945	31,000	11,500,000	22,172,000,000
1950	56,000	19,288,000	47,793,000,000
1955	89,000	31,640,000	101,300,000,000
1960	169,000	43,507,000	175,434,000,000
1965	233,000	60,657,000	306,113,000,000
1971	310,000	79,145,000	545,092,000,000
1970	303,000	81,548,000	581,434,000,000

Sources: Figures for 1911 obtained directly from Equitable Life Assurance Society of the United States. Other figures from Institute of Life Insurance *1972 Fact Book.* Figures exclude creditor life insurance.

The amount of life insurance under the average group life certificate exceeds the average size individual ordinary policy. Table 25–2 shows the comparative size of the average group certificate, ordinary policy, and industrial policy at ten-year intervals from 1920. In 1971 the average size group life certificate (excluding creditor group) provided $7,130 of life insurance as compared to $6,450 under ordinary and $520 under industrial. The rapid relative growth in the size of the group certificate reflects,

TABLE 25–2.   Average Size Group Certificate and Average Ordinary and Industrial Policy in Force in the United States, 1920–71

Year	Group	Ordinary	Industrial
1920	$ 960	$1,990	$150
1930	1,700	2,460	210
1940	1,700	2,130	240
1950	2,480	2,320	310
1960	4,030	3,590	390
1970	6,890	6,100	500
1971	7,130	6,450	520

Sources: Institute of Life Insurance and *Spectator Yearbook*. Figures exclude credit life insurance.

among other things, growth related to increased earnings of wage and salary workers during a long inflationary period since most commonly group life benefit schedules are related to earnings. The trend toward larger amounts of group insurance on the lives of higher-paid employees and executives also is a factor in relative growth of group.

Evidence of the growth of group life insurance as compared to ordinary and industrial is shown in Table 25–3. Note that in 1971, group represented 41 percent, or two fifths, of all life insurance in force in the United States as compared to a negligible 4 percent of the total in 1920. In this fifty-one-year period the ordinary share of the total has decreased from 79 to 56 percent and the industrial share has gone down from 17 to 3 percent.

TABLE 25–3.   Comparative Growth of Group, Ordinary, and Industrial Life Insurance in Force in the United States, 1920–71 (000,000 omitted)

Year	Group	Percent of Total	Ordinary	Percent of Total	Industrial	Percent of Total	Total	Total Percent
1920	$ 1,570	4	$ 32,018	79	$ 6,948	17	$ 40,536	100
1930	9,801	9	78,576	74	17,963	17	106,340	100
1940	14,938	13	79,346	69	20,866	18	115,150	100
1950	47,793	21	149,071	65	33,415	14	230,279	100
1960	175,434	32	340,268	61	39,563	7	555,265	100
1970	545,092	41	731,097	56	38,644	3	1,314,833	100
1971	581,434	41	789,167	56	39,202	3	1,409,803	100

Source: Institute of Life Insurance. Figures exclude credit life insurance.

Group Health Insurance.   A striking measure of the scope and growth of health insurance, group and individual, in the United States relates to the premiums paid as a percentage of total disposable personal income. In 1940, the premiums of insurance companies and subscription income of Blue Cross, Blue Shield, and other hospital-medical plans totaled $318 million, or four tenths of one percent of disposable personal income. By 1970, premiums and subscription income had increased to $17.3 billion and equaled 2.7 percent of disposable personal income.

TABLE 25–4. Number and Proportion of Population with Health Insurance

Type of Service	All Ages		Under Age 65		Aged 65 and over	
	Number (in thousands)	Percent of Civilian Population	Number (in thousands)	Percent of Civilian Population	Number (in thousands)	Percent of Civilian Population
Hospital care	162,989	80.3	152,567	83.5	10,422	51.3
Physicians' services:						
Surgical services	157,670	77.7	147,618	80.8	10,052	49.4
In-hospital visits	145,589	71.7	137,229	75.1	8,360	41.1
X-ray and laboratory examinations	142,441	70.2	134,839	73.8	7,602	37.4
Office and home visits ..	91,581	45.1	87,625	48.0	3,956	19.5
Dental care	12,210	6.0	12,079	6.6	131	.6
Prescribed drugs (out-of-hospital)	100,966	49.7	97,736	53.5	3,230	15.9
Private-duty nursing	100,235	49.4	97,017	53.1	3,218	15.8
Visiting-nurse service	106,882	52.6	103,064	56.4	3,818	18.8
Nursing-home care	32,392	16.0	27,371	15.0	5,021	24.7
HIAA estimates:						
Hospital care	181,624	89.4	170,214	93.2	11,410	56.1
Surgical services	167,850	82.7	158,406	86.7	9,444	46.4

Source: *Social Security Bulletin*, February, 1972, p. 4.

Table 25–4 summarizes the number of persons with some form of health insurance coverage at the close of 1970, showing the totals for all ages and also distinguishing the under- and over-age-65 groups. It is striking to note from the estimates of the Health Insurance Association of America that 89.4 percent of the population had hospital care coverage and 93.2 percent of those under 65 were so covered.

Table 25–5 shows the number of persons with health insurance protection, by type of protection, and including disability income coverage, for the period 1940–70. The trend in numbers of persons covered is sharply upward during this period. At the end of 1970, about 181 million persons were covered with some form of private hospital expense insurance, 169 million with surgical expense coverage, 145 million with "regular medical expense" (or nonsurgical physicians' visits) insurance, 78 million with major medical expense protection, 57 million with short-term disability income coverage, and 11 million with long-term disability insurance protection.

A comprehensive summary of private health insurance enrollment at the end of 1970 by type of plan and type of medical expense coverage is shown in Table 25–6. The percentage distribution of enrollment in private health insurance is shown in Table 25–7. The role of the group insurance approach is particularly evident from these data and especially so for certain types of health insurance coverage. Group enrollment in Blue Cross/Blue Shield plans is not separated in these tables but it is of major significance.

TABLE 25–5. Number of Persons with Private Health Insurance Protection by Type of Coverage in the United States (000 omitted)

End of Year	Hospital Expense	Surgical Expense	Regular Medical Expense	Major Medical Expense	Disability Income	
					Short-Term	Long-Term
1940	12,312	5,350	3,000	—	N.A.	N.A.
1945	32,068	12,890	4,713	—	N.A.	N.A.
1950	76,639	54,156	21,589	—	37,793	*
1955	105,452	88,856	54,935	5,241	39,513	*
1960	130,007	117,304	86,889	27,448	42,436	*
1961	134,417	122,951	93,466	34,138	43,055	*
1962	139,176	126,900	97,404	38,250	44,902	*
1963	144,575	131,954	102,302	42,441	43,927	3,029
1964	148,338	135,433	107,686	47,001	44,751	3,420
1965	153,133	140,462	111,696	51,946	46,347	4,457
1966	158,022	144,715	116,462	56,742	49,372	5,002
1967	162,853	150,396	122,570	62,226	51,230	6,682
1968	169,497	155,725	129,105	66,861	54,955	7,718
1969:						
Under 65	164,383	153,304	127,227	70,410	57,004	9,076
65 and over	10,838	8,840	7,703	1,882	—	—
Total	175,221	162,144	134,930	72,292	57,004	9,076
1970:						
Under 65	170,147	159,538	136,882	76,164	57,595	10,740
65 and over	11,364	9,423	8,412	2,053	—	—
Total	181,511	168,961	145,294	78,217	57,595	10,740

Note. The data refer to the net total of people protected, *i.e.,* duplication among persons protected by more than one kind of insuring organization or more than one insurance company policy providing the same type of coverage has been eliminated. The "Hospital expense," "Surgical expense," and "Regular medical expense" categories represent coverage provided by insurance companies, Blue Cross, Blue Shield and medical society-approved plans, and independent plans. The "Major medical expense" category represents insurance companies only. The "Disability income" category represents insurance companies, formal paid sick leave plans, and coverage through employee organizations.

* Included in "Short-term," with the possibility of some duplication of disability income coverage for these years.

N.A. — Not available.

Source: Health Insurance Council.

Forces Underlying Growth

Multiple forces of an economic, social, and political nature underlie the remarkable growth of group insurance over its first six decades. By the beginning of the 20th century our society was becoming increasingly industrialized and urbanized. This led to a greatly magnified interdependence of workers, with increasing insecurity of their positions. Adding to the workers' insecurity was the changing pattern of family life. Traditional family obligations to care for the old and the sick were weakening early in the 20th century. Also, there was growing dissatisfaction with the nature of public measures for the relief of the ill, the old, and the destitute.

These general trends set the stage for the development of group insurance. Other factors, more specific in nature, have been significant to its growth.

TABLE 25-6. Number of Persons Enrolled in Private Health Insurance Plans, by Type of Plan and Type of Medical Expense Coverage, December 31, 1970 (in thousands)

Type of Plan	Hospital Care	Physicians' Services				Dental Care	Pre-scribed Drugs (out-of-hospital)	Private-Duty Nursing	Visiting-Nurse Service	Nursing-Home Care	Vision Care
		Surgical Services	In-Hospital Visits	X-ray and Laboratory Examinations	Office and Home Visits						
Total gross enrollment	209,787	193,903	159,897	151,956	96,002	12,210	105,885	105,118	112,073	32,989	[1]
Blue Cross-Blue Shield	75,464	69,110	64,728	49,864	19,509	275	25,627	23,707	29,964	22,934	238
Blue Cross	72,942	3,874	3,508	[1]	1,168	[1]	[1]	[1]	[1]	[1]	[1]
Blue Shield	2,522	65,236	61,220	[1]	18,341	[1]	[1]	[1]	[1]	[1]	[1]
Insurance companies	126,192	114,261	85,437	91,660	67,361	6,685	75,437	75,199	75,199	7,915	[1]
Group policies	82,712	84,133	71,225	83,666	60,012	6,627	70,396	69,150	69,150	4,582	[1]
Individual policies	43,480	30,128	14,212	7,994	7,349	58	5,041	6,049	6,049	3,333	[1]
Independent Plans	8,131	10,532	9,732	10,432	9,132	5,250	4,821	6,212	6,910	2,140	7,537
Community	2,900	4,900	4,900	4,800	4,800	500	2,100	3,700	4,300	340	4,730
Employer-employee-union	5,200	5,500	4,700	5,500	4,200	1,700	2,700	2,500	2,600	1,800	2,690
Private group clinic	31	132	132	132	132	50	21	12	10	—	117
Dental service corporation	—	—	—	—	—	3,000	—	—	—	—	—
Net number of different persons covered, as estimated by:											
Office of Research and Statistics	162,989	157,670	145,589	142,441	91,581	12,210	100,966	100,235	106,882	32,392	[1]
Percent of civilian population[2]	80.3	77.7	71.7	70.2	45.1	6.0	49.7	49.4	52.6	16.0	[1]
HIAA	181,624	167,850	144,575	[1]	[1]	[1]	[1]	[1]	[1]	[1]	[1]
Percent of civilian population[2]	89.4	82.7	71.2	[1]	[1]	[1]	[1]	[1]	[1]	[1]	[1]
Gross enrollment as percent of different persons covered, as estimated by:											
Office of Research and Statistics	128.7	123.0	109.8	106.7	104.8	100.0	104.9	104.9	104.9	101.8	[1]
HIAA	115.5	115.5	110.6	[1]	[1]	[1]	[1]	[1]	[1]	[1]	[1]

[1] Data not available.
[2] Based on Bureau of the Census estimate of 203,046,000 as of January 1, 1971.
Source: Social Security Bulletin, February 1972, p. 4.

TABLE 25-7. Percentage Distribution of Persons Enrolled in Private Health Insurance Plans among Insurers, December 31, 1970

| Age Group and Type of Plan | Hospital Care | Physicians' services | | | | Dental Care | Pre-scribed Drugs (out-of-hospital) | Private-Duty Nursing | Visiting-Nurse Service | Nursing-Home Care |
		Surgical Services	In-Hospital Visits	X-ray and Laboratory Examinations	Office and Home Visits					
Total, all ages	100.0	100.0	100.0	100.0	100.0	100.0	100.0	100.0	100.0	100.0
Blue Cross-Blue Shield	36.0	35.7	40.5	32.8	20.3	2.2	24.2	22.6	26.7	69.5
Insurance companies	60.1	58.9	53.4	60.3	70.2	54.8	71.2	71.5	67.1	24.0
Group policies	39.4	43.4	44.5	55.0	62.5	54.3	66.4	65.8	61.7	13.9
Individual policies	20.7	15.5	8.9	5.3	7.7	.5	4.8	5.7	5.4	10.1
Independent plans	3.9	5.4	6.1	6.9	9.5	43.0	4.6	5.9	6.2	6.5
Under age 65, total	100.0	100.0	100.0	100.0	100.0	100.0	100.0	100.0	100.0	100.0
Blue Cross-Blue Shield	35.1	34.4	39.1	31.5	19.4	2.3	23.9	22.2	26.2	65.2
Insurance companies	61.0	60.2	54.8	61.7	71.2	54.5	71.7	72.0	67.8	28.0
Group policies	40.9	44.8	46.0	56.4	63.5	54.0	66.9	66.2	62.3	16.0
Individual policies	20.1	15.4	8.8	5.3	7.7	.5	4.8	5.8	5.5	12.0
Independent plans	3.9	5.4	6.1	6.8	9.4	43.2	4.4	5.8	6.0	6.8
Aged 65 and over, total	100.0	100.0	100.0	100.0	100.0	100.0	100.0	100.0	100.0	100.0
Blue Cross-Blue Shield	49.7	58.6	62.7	58.1	42.5	1.5	34.6	33.5	41.5	93.2
Insurance companies	46.4	36.0	30.8	34.2	46.2	79.4	56.4	56.5	47.6	2.2
Group policies	15.9	18.7	20.3	30.6	39.9	79.4	52.6	51.9	43.8	2.2
Individual policies	30.5	17.3	10.5	3.6	6.3	—	3.8	4.6	3.8	—
Independent plans	3.9	5.4	6.5	7.7	11.3	19.1	9.0	10.0	10.9	4.6

Source: *Social Security Bulletin,* February, 1972, p. 7.

Most employers made the decision to install group insurance plans because they were convinced that it would make employment conditions more attractive or lead to greater productivity by their employees, or both. Management decisions, by and large, have a rational base, and firms would not assume the continuing expense of group insurance if they did not believe the group plan would have a beneficial effect for the firm.

Organized labor has had a very active interest in obtaining group insurance benefits through collective bargaining. Court decisions holding group insurance to be a bargainable issue obviously accelerated the development along these lines. Further, imaginative efforts have been made by many unions, working with or without the assistance of insurers and employee benefit specialists, to design new forms of noncash compensation in the areas of need related to retirement, death, disability, medical costs, and the like.

It would appear that the great majority of employees covered by group insurance recognize and appreciate the protection it gives to their families and to themselves. Certainly this is true of the more mature employees with dependents. This appreciation, in turn, redounds to the benefit of the employer in improved employee morale and better satisfied and more loyal employees. There seems little doubt that the morale, and thus the productivity, of workers is improved if they are relieved of the anxieties concerning some of the consequences of death, disability, and medical care costs. In the case of union-negotiated benefits, the satisfaction of the union member with the financial security provided is similarly meaningful.

It is also claimed that a well-organized plan of welfare benefits for employees tends to reduce turnover of labor. Certainly the competitive nature of the labor market in most industries makes group insurance benefits a factor in attracting and holding labor on all levels of skill and responsibility. It should be added, however, that with the increasing universality of group insurance, pensions, and other benefits available to employees, the leverage of one company or one industry in this respect tends to diminish.

In most employer-employee relationships there is concern on the part of the employer for the welfare of his employees and their dependents. A formal plan of benefits in the event of premature death, disability, and retirement is a rational and businesslike approach to meeting the needs of the employee and his dependents. The group technique has proven highly valuable in providing benefits efficiently and in rational cost planning and projection.

Inflation also has been a factor in the growth of group insurance. As wages and prices have gone up, the need for protection has increased. Where benefit schedules are related to earnings, the escalation effect has been automatic. With the sharply increasing costs of medical care, there has been a substantial growth in group health insurance benefit schedules and premium costs.

Additional growth factors worthy of note include the wage freezes imposed by the federal government during World War II during which fringe benefits were vastly expanded, the development of new applications of the group principle such as creditor group insurance, the inauguration of private coverage for federal employees and servicemen under the aegis of the federal government, and the tax-deductible status of employer contributions for group insurance.

These factors, plus the inherent strengths of the group mechanism and the efficacy of group marketing techniques, have created the situation where group insurance almost has become a perquisite of employment; either it is required as part of a collective bargaining agreement or an employer feels that he must provide it in order to get and hold employees even if he sees no other merit in it.

Significance

The expansion in the kinds of group insurance and in the magnitude of benefits provided under group insurance has greatly broadened the ability of private insurance to provide security against premature death, disability and old age. Further, the group mechanism has permitted very efficient expansion of private insurance. It should be recognized, of course, that group insurance, like social insurance, provides security on a mass basis and cannot consider individual needs and desires to the extent that is possible where life and health insurance is provided on an individual basis. It seems obvious that the group technique has permitted the expansion of life and health insurance benefits to most members of our society, and this, in turn, has helped the private insurance institution to provide insurance service that might otherwise have been provided within the government framework.

SELECTED REFERENCES

Black, Kenneth, Jr. *Group Annuities.* Philadelphia: University of Pennsylvania Press, 1955.

Eilers, Robert D. and Crowe, Robert M. *Group Insurance Handbook.* Homewood, Ill.: Richard D. Irwin, Inc., 1965.

Gregg, Davis W. *Group Life Insurance.* 3d ed. Homewood, Ill.: Richard D. Irwin, Inc., 1962.

Ilse, Louise Wolters. *Group Insurance and Employee Retirement Plans.* Englewood Cliffs, N.J.: Prentice-Hall, Inc., 1953.

Pickrell, Jesse F. *Group Health Insurance.* Homewood, Ill.: Richard D. Irwin, Inc., 1961.

26

Group Life Insurance

By WILLIAM G. WILLIAMS

THE BASIC KINDS of individual life insurance are generally available under group life insurance policies. Group life policies may be written, with or without medical examination, on any standard form of life insurance, such as: whole life, limited payment life, regular term, decreasing and extended term, or even endowment and retirement income insurance. However, in actual practice, the principal types of group life insurance being marketed to eligible entities are as follows:

1. Group term life insurance is one-year renewable term insurance. In its most common form, this coverage is issued to a policyholder who is an employer for purposes of protecting his employees. It is also issued to unions, trusts, associations, and other entities. Coverage may be extended to cover the insured's spouse and eligible children where permitted by statute.
2. Group creditor life insurance is also one-year renewable term insurance. It is issued on the lives of installment borrowers or purchasers, and covers outstanding loans made by a creditor firm which is both policyholder and beneficiary.
3. Group paid-up life insurance is a combination of annually increasing, single-premium, permanent whole life insurance with cash values and decreasing one-year renewable term insurance.
4. Group ordinary life insurance is optional level-premium, group permanent insurance that is normally issued on a whole life, life paid-up at 65, ten-pay life, or retirement income at age 65 basis. As a result of a recent Internal Revenue Service tax ruling, the form that group ordinary will take in the future is in question.
5. Group survivor income benefit insurance is similar to one-year renewable term insurance (no cash, loan, or paid-up values) but it provides a monthly income benefit to eligible survivors rather than a specified lump sum.

GROUP TERM LIFE INSURANCE

The tremendous growth and popularity of group life insurance have undoubtedly been due to its ability to provide employers, unions, trustees, associations and certain creditors with needed low-cost "death benefits" for the protection of their employees, members or debtors. This low cost has resulted from the use of one-year renewable term insurance, which by its very nature does not require the reserve element found in level-premium life insurance.

The term premium only has to be sufficient to provide protection during the current policy year (i.e., the costs of the currently expected level of claims and expenses plus a reasonable margin for profit and contingencies). At the end of each policy year the average rate is recalculated on the basis of one-year term rates and the distribution by age of the insurance then in force. The actual renewal premium depends in part on the calculated rate and in part on the accumulated experience of the group. Theoretically, the very nature of the group tends to result in developing a continuing level premium cost because of the addition of young lives and the termination of old lives. Thus, turnover, experience credits and the tendency of an employer to assume any increasing cost offsets the increases an insured would have to pay on contributory plans due to the step-rate nature of group term life insurance.

Realistically, group term life insurance should be viewed as a type of insurance which has limited guarantees of permanence and few "living benefits," since it has no cash values. The principal attribute of group term life insurance is low-cost protection in the event of death or disability plus a conversion privilege.

Employee Coverage

An employer, in establishing a plan of group term life insurance, is concerned primarily with providing in a uniform, impartial and preannounced manner for the temporary replacement of an employee's earnings in the event of his death during the course of his employment.

The actual death benefit in force on any insured employee is shown by a schedule of benefits included in the employer's group life policy. Since benefits typically are based on the "extension-of-pay" concept, the schedule of benefits often has been keyed to income and replaces the loss of one, one-and-a-half, two, or even more years of earnings, subject to the maximum limits permitted by state law and the insurer's underwriting rules.

The persistency of employee coverage is fully dependent upon the employer-policyholder continuing the insurance in force. Since premiums may be terminated for reasons beyond an employee's control, group life insurance policies contain various provisions designed to continue his insurance under certain conditions beyond the date premiums are terminated. In addition, the policy permits an employee, upon termination of his group insurance coverage, to convert part or all of his insurance into an individual life insurance policy. These and other provisions are designed to prevent an insured employee from being deprived of his insurance protection through termination of his insurance at a time when he may need it most.

Provisions for Continuing Protection. The usual provisions for continuing protection under a group term life insurance policy are as follows:

1. *Conversion Privilege.* If all or part of an employee's insurance ceases because of termination of employment, membership in the classification(s) eligible for coverage under the group policy or attainment of a specified age or retirement, he may convert it to an individual policy without disability or supplemental benefits. He must apply to the company in writing within 31 days of termination and pay the premium for his attained age, type of insurance, and class of risk; however, he need not show medical evidence of insurability. It is important to note that in New York and West Virginia the converted policy may be preceded by term insurance for one year.

A more restricted conversion privilege may be provided for an insured employee if the master group policy is terminated or is amended so as to terminate the insurance in force on his particular classification. Usually, such an employee must have been insured for at least five years under the policy. The maximum amount which may be converted is normally $2,000 and will be less if the employee becomes eligible for group life insurance under another policy issued or reinstated within 31 days after the termination of the old group policy.

2. *Thirty-One-Day Continuation of Protection.* The death benefit is payable as a claim against the group policy when an employee dies within 31 days after termination of employment or termination of the group policy. Thus, the life insurance protection which an individual is entitled to convert is continued for a period of 31 days following termination of premium payments for his group life insurance.

This provision gives a terminated employee an additional 31 days of protection while debating the pros and cons of his conversion privilege or awaiting coverage under the group life plan of a new employer.

3. *Continuation of Insurance.* During temporary interruptions of continuous, active, full-time employment (such as an employee being laid off or granted a leave of absence), the employer can elect to continue the employee's group term life insurance in force for a limited period (e.g., three months) on a basis that precludes antiselection. The extension can always be increased by mutual agreement between the employer and the insurance company. Upon the expiration of the continuation period, premium payments are discontinued and the employee's insurance is terminated. However, the insurance is still extended for 31 days after the termination of insurance, as is the right to exercise the conversion privilege within this 31-day period.

4. *Waiver-of-Premium Provision.* On occasion, premium payments are discontinued on an employee whose active employment has terminated due to total disability. Disabled employees frequently are unable to convert their insurance for financial reasons. In order to furnish a proper safeguard to the rights of such employees, a waiver-of-premium provision has become standard issue on group life insurance policies. Under a typical provision the insurance will remain in force if (1) the employee is under age 60 at the date of commencement of his total disability, (2) his total disability commences while he is covered, (3) the total disability is continuous until the date of death, and (4) proof of total and continuous dis-

ability is presented to the insurance company at least once every 12 months.

If the waiver-of-premium benefits are terminated due to recovery, and the employee is eligible for insurance under the group policy, he again would become insured on a premium-paying basis. If the disability terminates and the employee is not eligible for insurance under the group policy, he becomes entitled to the rights and benefits under the conversion privilege.

The waiver-of-premium provision is actually one of three basic types of disability benefit provisions which have been used in connection with group life insurance plans. The second, the maturity value benefit, provides for the payment of the face amount of an employee's group term life insurance in a lump sum, or, more often, in monthly installments when an employee becomes totally and permanently disabled prior to attaining a maximum age, usually age 60. If the disabled employee recovers and again becomes eligible, the usual practice is to reduce the face amount of his insurance by any payments made while he was disabled. The extended death benefit, a third type of disability provision, provides for the payment of group life insurance death claims incurred within one year after termination of employment. It requires that the insured employee be continuously and totally disabled from the date of termination of employment and that death occur before attainment of a maximum age (usually age 65).

5. *Reduction Formula.* The employee is confronted with the fact that upon attaining a specified age (e.g., 65) or retirement, his group term life insurance may be eliminated, and the high costs of conversion may be beyond his means. Fortunately, due to general business practices, collective bargaining and employer concern, more and more employers are continuing reduced amounts of group term life insurance in force on older or retired employees under various types of reduction formulas. Among the formulas sometimes used is a 50 percent reduction at age 65 or a graded percentage amount which decreases each year after attaining age 65 until a minimum percentage is reached; for example, 10 percent per year until 50 percent of the amount in force immediately prior to age 65 is attained.

As the group ages, employers become understandably concerned about the ever increasing costs and may consider funding for retired employees through the use of group paid-up, group ordinary or a separate "side fund" which is accumulated to pay premiums at retirement.

Beneficiary and Settlement Options. An employee insured under group life insurance may name and change his beneficiary as desired. The face amount of insurance must be for the benefit of persons other than the employer and it is recommended that the payment be directed to a named beneficiary rather than the employee's estate. Much delay and expense associated with the probate estate is eliminated as are other expenses.

If at the death of the insured employee there is no named beneficiary, or if such named beneficiary does not survive the insured employee, the proceeds, subject to certain limits, may be payable at the *insurer's option* to any one or more of the following surviving relatives of the employee: wife, husband, mother, father, child or children, or to the executor or administrator of the deceased covered person. If any beneficiary is a minor or physically, mentally or otherwise incapable of giving a valid release for any payment due, the insurer is able to take positive action under a so-called "facility of payment" clause, subject to certain limits.

The insured employee, or, if he is deceased, his beneficiary, may elect that all or part of the face amount be paid on an installment certain basis, rather than in a lump sum. The installments are paid according to the procedures and table set forth in the group policy. Subject to stated option rules, an insurer generally will offer optional modes of settlement based upon life contingencies. But the basis is seldom mentioned or guaranteed in the contract, and insurance company practices at the time of death govern.

In the programming of an employee's life insurance, it is usually recommended that group life insurance proceeds be utilized as a "clean-up" fund to pay outstanding bills and funeral expenses, and create an emergency fund for unforeseen cash needs, thus freeing permanent life insurance for long-range needs under more flexible and guaranteed settlement options.

Assignment. Group life insurance may be assigned if the policy and state law both permit. However, not all states and policies permit assignment.

Dependent Coverage

Dependents group life insurance would seem to be a logical extension of the group insurance concept, but its development and growth have been relatively slow for the following reasons: (1) Some states do not permit its issuance; (2) Benefit levels, because of statutory limitations, are very modest; (3) It usually is not contained in collective bargaining agreements; (4) The coverage generally is not available to small groups; and (5) Ordinarily, only dependents of employees who are themselves insured for group life insurance are eligible for this coverage. Also there has been opposition to dependents' coverage as an unnecessary and undesirable substitute for individual coverage.

A typical schedule of benefits might provide the dependent spouse with insurance equal to 50 percent of the employee's coverage but not more than $1,000 or $2,000. Typical benefits for dependent children would be graded from $100 between ages 14 days and six months, and $1,000 between 5 and 19 years.

The death benefit normally is automatically payable in one lump sum to the insured employee or, in the event of the prior death of the employee, either to the employee's estate or, at the option of the insurer, to one of certain specified classes of "order of preference" beneficiaries.

The usual provisions for continuing protection for the employee under the group policy are extended to the covered dependents of the insured employee; however, certain differences exist. For example, the conversion privilege is usually provided only for the dependent spouse but a few states also require that the privilege be made available to insured dependent children. Waiver-of-premium or other disability benefits are rarely provided.

Since the proceeds are automatically payable to the employee, no beneficiary designation is necessary, assignment is not permitted, and settlement options ordinarily are not made available.

Advantages and Limitations of Group Term Life Insurance

While facts and figures are impressive, the individual employer or employee is mainly interested in knowing the answers to the question: "What does group life insurance have to offer to me?"

Advantages to the Employer. An employer may be convinced that all or most of the following advantages are applicable to his situation when he recalls the known inadequacy, and growing cost, of the earlier system of "passing-the-hat" among the fellow workers of the deceased employee in an attempt to tide over the surviving dependents in an immediate emergency.

1. It discharges the obligation of the employer in a uniform, preannounced and businesslike manner.
2. The coverage is competitively desirable, almost necessary, inasmuch as most employers offer this protection.
3. Employee morale and productivity are enhanced by offering this element of security.
4. The protection is an aid to attaining good public and employer-employee relations because it prevents an employee's family from being abruptly cut off without funds.
5. Its presence has helped to delay further government intervention into areas of private business.

Advantages to the Employee. It is readily apparent that group term life insurance fits advantageously into an employee's pattern of living.

1. It adds a layer of low-cost protection to personal savings, individual life insurance, and social security benefits.
2. Broad underwriting standards provide coverage for those who might be uninsurable.
3. It provides peace of mind by relieving the anxieties and consequences of possible premature death.
4. If employees are contributing toward the cost, the premiums are automatically withheld from earnings, thus reducing the hazard of lapse.
5. The employer's contributions are not reportable as taxable income to the insured employee for federal income tax purposes unless the total amount of group insurance at risk from all sources exceeds $50,000, and then only the contributions applicable to any amounts in excess of $50,000 are subject to possible taxation in accordance with the regulations.
6. The conversion privilege enables a terminated employee to convert his life insurance to an individual policy without having to pass a medical examination.

7. The death proceeds can be earmarked for "clean up" and emergency fund purposes, thus freeing the employee's individual life insurance for programming under guaranteed and favorable settlement options.

Limitations. Despite its many advantages, group term life insurance was never intended to supplant the need for a well-planned life insurance estate and an analysis of the financial problems of the individual. It has limitations which are of concern to the employers and employees involved.

Specifically, the employee has no assurance that his employer will continue the group policy in force from one year to the next, unless, of course, he happens to be a sole proprietor, partner, or company officer who has a voice in the renewability of the contract. The employer-policyholder and the insurer are the parties who control this all-important renewability, and this lack of any permanent guarantee emphasizes the temporary nature of this coverage. In actual practice these plans are seldom discontinued, but business failures can and do occur, and the conversion privilege upon termination of a group life policy may be of limited value to the employees because of the cost involved.

Another limitation is quite evident when individual employees change employers, because group term life insurance does not possess "portability." Only about one out of every hundred terminating employees exercises the conversion privilege. "Hope springs eternal" and it must be assumed that most transitory employees expect to be insured for the same or a higher face amount with their new employer. Many employees forget that this temporary form of insurance provides "protection only," often for inadequate limits, and let it obscure the need for permanent individual life insurance and the valuable services of a professional life underwriter.

GROUP CREDITOR LIFE INSURANCE

The financial burden of unpaid consumer debts is vitally real to the family of the deceased debtor. Since it is a financial loss attendant to the basic hazard of death, it is a proper subject for the use of life insurance. The idea for credit life insurance dates back to the early days of life insurance; and individual contracts long have been used as credit security and mortgage protection policies have been designed specifically to retire indebtedness.

Eligible Creditors, Loans, and Purchases

Group creditor life insurance, which is a specialized form of group term, owes its development and growth to its popularity with lending institutions and the ever increasing expansion of consumer credit. Today's eligible creditors generally include commercial banks, savings and loan associations, trust companies, sales finance companies, department stores, dealers, retail vendors, small loan companies, credit unions, colleges and universities, credit card companies, and mutual funds. State laws show considerable variation with respect to eligible creditors, as do insurance companies.

The eligible creditor-policyholder may wish to insure types of indebtedness involving unsecured personal loans or certain types of secured personal loans. These loans may involve motor vehicles, farm equipment, appliances, mobile homes, home modernization, crops, seed and livestock, educational loan plans, revolving credit (including bank line of credit), furniture, credit card charges, real estate mortgages, or the purchase of securities where permitted by state law.

Creditor Modifications of Conventional Term Plan

Many modifications have been introduced in adapting the conventional group term plan to fit the creditor-debtor relationship.

Contract Provisions. There is usually some degree of an employer-employee relationship in conventional group term life insurance, but creditor group life insurance is concerned only with a creditor-debtor relationship. For example, the group (debtors) may be the borrowers of a bank (creditor), with the group policy issued to the creditor; or the group may have purchased goods under conditional sales contracts from a vendor, with the group policy issued to the vendor. The uniqueness of a group creditor life policy is apparent in the contract's insuring clause, as the creditor is both the policyholder and the beneficiary. This clause also provides that the creditor must apply the death benefit toward the discharge of the debtor's indebtedness. Thus, such conventional group term life provisions as a conversion privilege, designation of a beneficiary, disability benefits, settlement options, and facility of payment are inappropriate.

Another unusual aspect is the declining amount of insurance on the life of each insured debtor. Fluctuations generally occur on a monthly basis when the debtor reduces the amount of his indebtedness by making his installment repayment. A proper insurable interest is maintained at all times, since the amount of insurance at any time is usually the amount necessary to pay the debtor's indebtedness, subject to the maximum amount stated in the group policy. This aggregate amount of insurance, which is in force on the life of the debtor, may not exceed the policy maximum regardless of the total amount of his debts.

Only one person can be insured with respect to any one indebtedness, but since co-signers often are involved in credit transactions, the creditor is given the right to select which debtor shall be insured.

Since practically all insurers forego the calculation of actual age data in favor of the promulgated initial premium rate, the misstatement-of-age clause has little or no application to group creditor life insurance. Also, the incontestable clause has little applicability because the facts provided by the creditor are readily verifiable by the insurer, and seldom does the insurer require any evidence of insurability from the individual debtors. Because of the length of the loan repayment period and the amount at risk, a suicide clause normally is found only in a group creditor policy covering mortgage loans.

The group policy may be terminated for nonpayment of premium, for failure to maintain a minimum volume of insurance, or for failure to obtain a minimum number of new debtors each policy year (e.g., 100). An individual debtor's insurance is terminated if (1) the group policy is terminated, (2) the indebtedness is discharged, (3) the indebtedness is transferred to another creditor, or (4) the debtor fails to make installment repayments when due. In some instances the creditor and insurer may agree to cover loans in default for a period of time (e.g., up to six months).

Most insurers issue a certificate of insurance to the individual debtors, although this usually is done only in those states where it is required by law or regulation. Actually, this document is called a "statement of insurance" and explains the nature of the insurance protection provided, the conditions under which the coverage terminates, and the refund formula which must be used in case the indebtedness is repaid prior to its scheduled maturity date.

Premium Rates. Group creditor life premium rates originally were intended to be based upon the ages of the lives insured, like conventional group term plans. However, due to the impracticality of obtaining age data and maintaining age records, an initial premium rate based upon the volume of indebtedness to be insured under the group policy is determined. The most common premium payment method is to base the premium payable on the amount of insurance outstanding on each monthly premium due date.

Underwriting. Since the creditor underwrites the debtors, adverse selection is always a matter of serious concern to the insurer. In addition, most creditor group life plans are debtor-pay-all, and a proper spread of risk is endangered when the consumer credit department does not aggressively sell the extra charge required for insurance protection on the life of the debtor, or does not make the taking of insurance a condition for the debtor obtaining the loan in states where such a requirement is not prohibited. This matter of marginal participation especially has become an acute problem under group creditor mortgage plans.

Regulation. Group creditor life insurance, unlike conventional group term, is influenced by indirect regulatory sources as well as by direct statutory regulation. For example, indirect regulatory sources may involve, at the federal level, the Comptroller of the Currency; and at the state level, the state banking departments, state interest and usury laws, and conditional sales acts. Various states have promulgated maximum rates, and no form of group life insurance is more stringently regulated by the states than group creditor life insurance.

GROUP PAID-UP

Most group life insurance after retirement is continued, subject to a reduction formula, under the employer's group term policy on a "pay-as-you-go" basis, because of the favorable income tax situation and the cost when compared with other funding methods. However, the potential deferred high cost of current funding, employee dissatisfaction with the cost of conversion, and the absence of permanent insurance policy values, has interested employers in finding ways to fund or reduce their accruing liabilities. An answer to these concerns is found in group paid-up.

Group paid-up life insurance is a combination of accumulating units of single-premium whole life insurance with correspondingly decreasing units of group term life insurance. The paid-up insurance and term insurance combined are at all times equal to the total amount of insurance protection to which the employee is entitled in accordance with the schedule of insurance in the employer's group policy. Thus, the policy combines the permanence and cash values of whole life insurance with the protection and low-cost features of conventional group term life insurance.

Allocation of Cost and Treatment of Cash Values

Because of present IRS regulations and rulings, the paid-up portion of the premium is employee-pay-all, and the term portion is employer-pay-all. While there is no statutory limitation on the amount of employee contribution for group paid-up, the most common contribution rate is $1.30 per month per $1,000 of total insurance, and, in some plans, contribution rates have been graded by age at entry to enable the older entrants to accumulate more paid-up insurance. The employer's cost for the first year of a group paid-up plan is close to that for a noncontributory group term plan which provides the same initial coverage, because at the outset the amount of paid-up insurance purchased by each employee is small. However, after the plan has been in force for some years, the effect of the paid-up insurance accumulated by the employees' contributions materially reduces the remaining amount of term coverage and, therefore, decreases the employer's overall cost.

Since a steady accumulation of employee-purchased paid-up insurance is essential to a successful plan, cash surrender values are not available before termination of employment. If cash values were available at any time, the plan would suffer from poor participation, discontinuous coverage, reinstatement problems, and high administrative costs. If cash values were available, employees would tend to place an unwarranted reliance on them in times of emergency with the particular danger of mass surrenders during periods of economic recession. Upon termination of his employment within five years, the employee may surrender his policy and receive at least his own contributions; if he surrenders after five years, he receives his contributions at interest, or the reserve, whichever is greater. The employee also may continue his paid-up insurance in force or surrender it and receive the cash value. Generally, if the employee's accumulated paid-up insurance is less than $250, his paid-up insurance will automatically terminate and he will receive its cash surrender value.

Provisions for Continuing Protection

The term portion of the coverage is treated as regular group term for purposes of conversion, disability, and continuation during a hiatus in employment.

A paid-up plan makes possible the funding of benefits for future retirees over their active working life. However, it should be remembered that the funding is done with the employees' money. The amount of paid-up values at retirement will be determined by such factors as the age of entry into the plan, the age of retirement, the amount of employee contributions, and the premium rate charged for the paid-up insurance. A special problem of sufficiency of paid-up benefits at retirement is created when employees enter the plan after age 45; most employers continue sufficient group term after retirement to keep the total protection on such employees at the desired level. As a general rule it is provided that term insurance will cease automatically in the event the employee surrenders his paid-up insurance for cash.

Advantages and Limitations

An analysis of group paid-up suggests a number of *advantages* including the following:

1. Group paid-up answers one of the traditional objections to conventional contributory group term insurance wherein an employee terminating after long years of participation in the plan has nothing to show for his contributions. Under group paid-up, his contributions are changed in part from an expense to an investment, and the "money back" feature means that he does not have to "die to win."
2. Group paid-up provides a practical solution to the problem of providing life insurance for retired employees at a realistic cost to management. The employee is assured that a minimum amount of life insurance will be fully paid for and under his control at his retirement. The employer is relieved of much of the financial burden of providing continued term insurance on retired employees.
3. At conversion, the employee pays the attained-age premium rates only on the discontinued term insurance portion of his total insurance. Since he has prepaid part of his insurance costs through his paid-up contributions, the overall effect is to reduce considerably the outlay required to continue his total amount of insurance.
4. Group paid-up affords the opportunity to purchase permanent insurance at lower cost and with higher cash values and paid-up amounts than are generally available when purchasing life insurance under individual policies.
5. Employees are more willing to contribute to a paid-up plan than a conventional group term plan.

Several *limitations* of group paid-up as compared to conventional group term may be indicated:

1. There is greater expense of administration since the accounting for individual equities and experience rating refunds obviously is more expensive to the employer and the carrier.
2. Group paid-up is available to fewer types of groups since most insurers will write it only for employer-employee groups with low turnover and strong central administration facilities.
3. Group paid-up provides less than total insurance protection for a given premium outlay.
4. The sale and service of the plan, particularly to large employers, are likely to center around cost projections, explanations of single-premium insurance, actuarial reserves, mortality and interest margins, and so forth. Thus, the direct attention of an actuary is required instead of occasional actuarial advice.

GROUP ORDINARY LIFE INSURANCE

Group ordinary life insurance usually is provided under a rider attached to a conventional group term life insurance policy, which enables an eligible employee to have all or a portion of his scheduled group term life insurance coverage changed to one or more forms of permanent life insurance. This elective permanent life insurance is generally offered in the conventionally available forms, including whole life, life paid-up at 65 (when offered at issue ages under 56), 10-pay life (when offered at issue ages over 55), or retirement income at age 65. The election usually can be made at issue (entry into the plan) and on any premium due date, subject to a minimum election amount; and the amount of group term life insurance in force is automatically reduced by the amount of permanent insurance elected. Thus, only the composition of insurance coverages is different, as the total amount of protection usually remains unchanged.

Tax Aspects

In 1950, the IRS established the position that premiums paid by an employer for permanent life insurance on the lives of his employees are taxable income to the employee if the employee has nonforfeitable rights in the coverage. As a result, the sale of conventional group permanent plans on a nonqualified basis has been almost nonexistent.

Group ordinary came into use in 1966 when revisions to Section 79 of the Internal Revenue Code were published. These regulations permitted an employer to make contributions toward the cost of permanent insurance for employees without such contributions being considered as taxable income to the employees, providing (1) the group policy set out the portion of the premium properly allocable to term insurance, (2) the employer's contribution did not exceed the portion properly allocable to term insurance, and (3) each employee covered under the plan was eligible for such optional permanent insurance. Vague wording in the regulations resulted in differences of opinion within the insurance business as to the correct basis on which to compute the premium for the group term insurance and its tax status. Most insurers developed a level premium (employer's premium) which was allocable to group term life insurance, but was based in part on the group term coverage and in part on the so-called pure-insurance protection (or amount at risk) provided in the permanent coverage. Other insurers developed a premium allocable to group term (employer's premium) which was based on the attained ages of the employees, stood on its own as to expense charges, loadings, dividends, and the like, and included no permanent insurance costs or risk elements.

In 1971, the long-expected revenue ruling amplifying Section 79 of the Internal Revenue Code was issued. The effect of Revenue Ruling 71-360 is to disqualify under Section 79 any program of group term life coverage providing permanent insurance which bases the employer's premium in part on the net amount at risk (or cost of pure insurance protection). This ruling further stated that each portion of the coverage (i.e., the group term and the permanent) must stand on its own as to expense charges, loadings, dividends, and so forth, and the employer cannot pay any part of the permanent insurance costs, including any part of those expense factors which properly must be allocated between the two types of coverage.[1] If Revenue Ruling 71-360 is not modified, most group ordinary will have to be revised to conform with the second premium computation method described above.

Provisions for Continuing Protection

Most group ordinary policies contain provisions for continuing protection which are similar to group paid-up, but certain differences are worth noting. Under the conversion privilege, the employee is allowed to convert his term insurance on the basis of his original entry age into the plan or his attained age. Also, waiver of premium is provided under both the term and permanent insurance. Finally, the cash values under many group ordinary policies are available upon termination of eligibility, termination of the group policy, or termination of employment.

Advantages and Limitations

Group ordinary has a special appeal to both the employer and the employee because it builds policy values, enables the employee to purchase permanent insurance on a guaranteed issue basis, provides a choice of an original age or an attained age conversion privilege, and minimizes the problem of continuing costly group term life insurance on retired employees. It also appeals to both agents and insurers because it involves the sale of familiar permanent life insurance coverages, provides a constant flow of new permanent insurance prospects, and commission scales encourage the agent to begin developing group business.

The limitations of group ordinary include the uncertainty resulting from Revenue Ruling 71-360, unavailability of cash values compared to ordinary insurance, lack of the group paid-up "money back" guarantee (i.e., return of contributions or cash values, whichever is the greater), and its higher marketing cost.

GROUP SURVIVOR INCOME BENEFIT INSURANCE

Group life and health insurance and pension plans have made substantial progress toward protecting the employee and his family against the perils of death, accidents, illnesses, and old age. Yet, a serious gap usually exists in this protection due to the unavailability of adequate continuing income for dependents who cannot sustain themselves or who would forfeit social security benefits by returning to work. There is a need for a group insurance benefit to provide monthly income over an extended period of time for the family of a deceased employee, to relate to the employee's final salary and to his family's requirements, and to take into consideration social security and other benefits. Such a product is group survivor income benefit insurance (SIBI).

---

[1] This provision also has implications for group paid-up life where the employer's contribution pays the expense for both the term and paid-up elements.

Survivor income benefit insurance is not a new concept, but it is now being shifted out of its traditional role as an ancillary benefit under a pension plan and is being written as a group insurance product. It is generally written to supplement group term life insurance, social security survivor benefits, death benefits under pension plans, personal insurance, and savings and investments. It is unlike group term life insurance in two important respects. First, the benefit is payable only if a qualified survivor exists and only for as long as one exists (i.e., both the fact of a claim and a maximum payment are subject to the contingency that there be a qualified survivor). Second, there is no lump-sum death benefit, as the benefit is always paid in equal monthly installments. Since the benefit is contingent upon the existence of a qualified survivor, some insurers view this coverage as being a marriage of features found in group term life insurance with those found in a reversionary annuity[2] or an annuity with contingencies.

Coverage and Benefits

SIBI provides a monthly income benefit to the qualified survivors of an insured employee. Normally included in this category are a surviving spouse and unmarried dependent children. Some insurers also will permit a designated beneficiary to be a qualified survivor, subject to a specified certain period only.

The amount of the monthly income benefit may be a fixed percentage of an employee's basic monthly earnings (exclusive of overtime pay, bonuses, commissions, and the like), a flat amount for all employees regardless of monthly salaries, or a specified amount based on job classifications. Under a typical plan, the spouse benefit may be 25 percent of the insured employee's monthly earnings, while the child's (or children's) benefit may be 15 percent, subject to a family maximum of 40 percent. The spouse benefit usually terminates on the 62d birthday of the spouse, or at death or remarriage, if earlier. Children's benefits are payable until the youngest unmarried child reaches age 19 or when there is no longer a living unmarried child. Usually, social security benefits would be payable in addition and this factor is taken into consideration in designing the plan. Benefit "certain periods" of 2, 5, or 10 years, to the spouse's age 65, or for life, are quite common, and some insurers even offer a "dowry benefit" (e.g., a lump-sum benefit payable upon remarriage of the spouse) to encourage prompt reporting of remarriage.

Provisions for Continuing Protection

Those insurers who are marketing this coverage as group life insurance include a conversion privilege (e.g., the amount of life insurance eligible to be converted is the commuted value of the survivor income benefit in

---

[2] A reversionary annuity is one under which payments depend upon the existence of a particular status (e.g., eligible survivors) after the failure of another status (e.g., death of insured employee).

force on the date of conversion) and a waiver-of-premium provision. The reversionary annuity advocates include a waiver-of-premium provision in their plans but usually do not offer a conversion privilege. Under either marketing approach, the 31-day continuation of protection and the continuation of insurance provisions as previously discussed are provided, and the insured employee's coverage terminates when he no longer has a qualified survivor, retires, or attains a specified age (e.g., 65 or 70).

Assignment

Some insurers include the privilege of assigning all incidents of ownership to the surviving spouse or any eligible dependent children, while other insurers do not permit assignments.

Advantages and Limitations

SIBI offers a fail-safe method of providing for some continuing living expenses for the surviving spouse and children. The circle of monthly income protection is complete when long-term disability income insurance, which provides "living death" benefits, also is in force.

The limitations associated with SIBI include the statutory life maximums for the group life advocates and possible estate tax problems for the reversionary annuity proponents. The complexities of administration also constitute a problem not present in group life coverages.

GROUP ACCIDENTAL DEATH AND DISMEMBERMENT INSURANCE

Many group life insurance plans are accompanied by an accidental death and dismemberment insurance (AD&D) benefit with the principal sum corresponding to the amount of group life insurance. This coverage provides the "double indemnity" feature, which is quite common in individual insurance, as well as defined dismemberment benefits. For example, the full principal sum for which the employee is insured is payable if the employee dies as the result of an accident. For loss of a hand by severance at or above the wrist, or the loss of a foot by severance at or about the ankle, or for irrecoverable loss of sight of an eye, only one half of the principal sum is payable. For the loss of more than one of the members in any one accident, the full principal sum is payable. Multiple benefits are payable as a result of any one accident, but not in excess of the principal sum.

This coverage can be, and usually is, "24-hour coverage" (i.e., like group life insurance, both occupational and nonoccupational), or it can be only nonoccupational.

Provisions for Continuing Protection

A conversion privilege normally is not available under this coverage but like group life insurance it may be continued for employees not actively at work because of temporary layoffs, strikes, or approved leaves of absence. Generally, it is not assignable and ceases upon the retirement of the employee.

Limitations

Unlike all the forms of group life insurance, group AD&D insurance contracts contain certain exclusions. An example would be refusal to pay for (1) suicide at any time; (2) disease or bodily or mental infirmity, or medical or surgical treatment thereof; (3) ptomaines, or any infection other than an infection occurring simultaneously with and through an accidental cut or wound; (4) war; and (5) travel or flight in any kind of aircraft as a pilot, student pilot, or as an officer or member of the crew.

VOLUNTARY ACCIDENTAL DEATH AND DISMEMBERMENT INSURANCE

The dramatic but infrequent occurrence of an accidental death and the comparatively low premium required to provide significant amounts of AD&D insurance led to the development of voluntary AD&D insurance as a separate coverage.

It is interesting to note that insurers offer this 24-hour coverage without two of the major safeguards against adverse selection, and that the absence of these safeguards is not counterbalanced by individually underwriting each participant. First, a voluntary AD&D plan is offered without the usual 75 percent participation requirement, where permitted by statute. Second, the employee may elect the amount of his principal sum, usually in $5,000 or $10,000 units, subject to a minimum (e.g., $10,000) and a maximum amount (e.g., $100,000) where permitted by statute. A $100,000 maximum is not unusual and, for larger groups, higher maximums have been provided (e.g., $250,000).

Insurers utilize attractive sales literature, which emphasizes the high death benefits and low cost, to attain good participation in the usual employee-pay-all voluntary AD&D plan. Participation may be as low as 30 to 50 percent; however, good marketing usually results in an enrollment of 75 percent or better. Experience has shown that the nature of the benefit (payment in the event of accidental death) does not influence the prudent person to take risks other than those which he might assume in the absence of insurance.

In some states it is possible to offer voluntary AD&D not only to the employee but to his spouse and children. Benefits for the spouse and the children often are expressed as a percentage of the employee's amount. For example, the voluntary AD&D benefit for the wife may be 50 percent of the employee's *principal sum* and the amount for each child might be 10 percent, subject to a minimum of $2,000.

The provisions for continuing protection are similar to regular group accidental death and dismemberment insurance.

Limitations

While the exceptions found in voluntary AD&D plans tend to parallel those found in regular group AD&D plans, some exceptions are not found in the more traditional form. For example, aviation activities are excluded except as a fare-paying passenger on a regularly scheduled airline. Furthermore, the insurer shall not be liable for an amount in excess of a cumulative aggregate limit of liability applicable to all persons dying as a result of one occurrence. If the benefits payable under the policy (i.e., the principal sum) exceed the aggregate limit of liability, the insurer shall pay for each insured the proportion of his benefits that the aggregate limit represents when compared with the total amount of coverage on all deceased persons. For example, if the policy provides an aggregate limit of liability of $1,000,000 and the total amount of coverage for all employees killed in a single occurrence is $1,250,000, 80 percent of each employee's principal sum would be paid. Finally, unlike other coverage, voluntary AD&D may be increased or decreased only on a policy anniversary date.

Related Factors

Most insurers of this coverage have secured reinsurance treaties in order to protect their book of business. Facultative treaties are used, for example, in case of an unusual hazard. If a policyholder chartered a plane to transport a large number of employees to a sales conference, the insurer might reinsure 100 percent of this temporary risk to protect the prime treaty against what could be a catastrophic loss.

Another variation of voluntary AD&D insurance is travel accident or business trip coverage which is usually limited to "losses while traveling for the employer on business" and to defined conveyances.

FEDERAL EMPLOYEES' GROUP LIFE INSURANCE PLAN

A significant impetus was provided group life insurance when in 1954 the federal government decided to establish a plan of group life and AD&D insurance for civilian employees of the federal government. At the end of 1970, the volume in force was $39.7 billion, making FEGLI the largest group life insurance case in the world. More than 360 life insurance companies are participating as reinsurers of the plan which is administered by the Metropolitan Life Insurance Company.

Benefit Structure and Amounts

Life insurance benefits for active employees are graded by salary brackets with amounts equaling one year's compensation rounded to the next higher $1,000, plus $2,000, with a minimum benefit of $10,000 and a maximum of $45,000. In addition, employees are eligible for optional insurance in the amount of $10,000. At retirement or upon attainment of age 65, whichever occurs later, benefits begin reducing at a monthly rate of 2 percent to an ultimate minimum of 25 percent of the amount of insurance in force immediately prior to retirement. Life insurance benefits (i.e., regular and optional) are supplemented by identical amounts of AD&D, except that no AD&D coverage is provided for retired employees.

Eligibility and Enrollment

Eligibility is extended to all active, full-time civilian federal employees except noncitizens employed at locations outside the United States, and part-time, seasonal, and intermittent employees. Retired employees who meet a minimum number of years of service and other requirements are also eligible for coverage.

Each eligible employee is automatically insured immediately upon becoming eligible for regular insurance, and for optional insurance if he elects it, unless he has given written notice of his desire to "elect out" of the plan for one or both insurance coverages. An employee cannot have optional insurance without having regular insurance. Such an election may later be rescinded by an employee, but only prior to his 50th birthday and not less than one year after the effective date of his prior written notice. Furthermore, the employee then will be admitted to the plan only if he furnishes at his own expense satisfactory evidence of insurability.

Cost

Since a complete census of participants by age and salary for the purpose of determining accurate premium rates would have been a formidable and time-consuming task, the government and insurance business conferees agreed that an empirical rate, based upon a study of large existing groups with similar characteristics, should be used initially. As of September 1971, for the regular insurance, active employees are currently contributing at the bi-weekly rate of $.275 per $1,000 of insurance, or about $.60 per month, and the government contributes at half this rate. For the optional insurance, the employees pay all of the premium, which is calculated at bi-weekly rates which vary by age from $.13 per $1,000 at ages below 35 to $1.90 per $1,000 at age 60 and over. The regular insurance premiums cease at retirement but the optional insurance premiums cease on the later of (1) retirement, and (2) the 65th birthday.

Insurers

The Metropolitan Life Insurance Company serves as the primary insurer and administrator of FEGLI. A reinsurer qualifies for participation if (1) it is licensed by a state or the District of Columbia to transact life and AD&D insurance, and (2) on the December 31 next preceding its election to participate it has some group life insurance in force. Reinsurance is allocated by formula and the formula favors the smaller companies. All reinsurers are kept fully informed about all developments by the Metropolitan and are supplied with copies of financial statements, statistical data, and pertinent correspondence. The Metropolitan participates in the plan on the same basis as any reinsurer (share allocated by formula), except that it is reimbursed for administrative expenses.

Provisions for Continuing Protection

The usual group life conversion privilege is available to a terminating employee and he may purchase his individual policy from any company that has applied to the Civil Service Commission and has been granted conversion authority. In order that no "converting" company will be exposed to an unduly burdensome share of the excess mortality which might develop under converted policies, a conversion pool, which includes all converting insurers, has been established to share the deficits and credits of the conversion operation. The conversion pool is operated by the Metropolitan, and it is also the custodian of all pool account funds. As of May 31, 1971, there were 101 pool members (insurers eligible to issue conversions).

The regular insurance and optional insurance are continued while an employee is on sick leave or annual leave with pay. Generally, both are continued free for up to 12 months if the employee should go on leave without pay. Unless an employee is granted military leave with pay, insurance does not continue while an employee is on active military duty.

The regular life insurance, subject to the reduction formula, is continued free on retirement but the employee must pay for the optional insurance until age 65 if he retires before that age. When the employee is both 65 and retired, the optional life insurance also is free.

All other provisions for continuing protection are quite similar to those previously discussed for group term life insurance.

SERVICEMEN'S GROUP LIFE INSURANCE PLAN

The law authorizing the Servicemen's Group Life Insurance (SGLI) program was enacted September 29, 1965. This group term life program is administered by the Office of Servicemen's Group Life Insurance and supervised by the Veterans Administration.

Eligibility and Enrollment

Basic coverage is provided for all commissioned, warrant, or enlisted members of the Army, Navy, Marine Corps, Air Force, or Coast Guard, and commissioned officers of the Environmental Science Services Administration and the Public Health Service who are on active duty. Reservist coverage is provided for all commissioned, warrant, or enlisted members of the Army, Navy, Marine Corps, Air Force, or Coast Guard Reserves, the Reserve Corps of the Public Health Service, the Army National Guard and Air National Guard, and members, cadets and midshipmen of the Reserve Officers Training Corps (ROTC) while engaged in authorized training duty.

Basic coverage and reservist coverage are automatically provided (i.e., the full amount provided under the law) unless the member elects in writing to be insured for a lesser amount, or not to be insured at all.

Benefit Structure and Amounts

The amount of insurance under the group policy is a flat amount of $15,000 unless a member files written notice of election to be insured for $10,000, $5,000, or not to be insured. If a member elects a lesser amount of coverage or not to be insured, he or she may subsequently cancel such election and, subject to evidence of insurability and certain other service requirements, may file an application to increase coverage or become insured for one of the permissible amounts.

The $15,000 maximum applies in all cases even if the member should be eligible for both basic coverage and reservist coverage. For example, basic coverage continues for 120 days after separation from active duty and during this same period the member could be eligible for reservist coverage. However, the total maximum permissible coverage is $15,000.

Cost

Premiums for this insurance, including its cost of administration, are deducted from servicemen's and reservists' pay and remitted by each uniformed service to the Veterans Administration, which in turn remits them to the primary insurer. The individual serviceman's premium for basic coverage, subject to change in accordance with the actual experience, was initially set at 20 cents per month per $1,000 of insurance and has not been changed since inception. Since reservists are covered only while engaged in authorized training duty, the premium for this reservist coverage is much lower; initially it has been set at 12 cents per year per $1,000 of insurance (reservist coverage became effective June 25, 1970).

Insurers

The primary insurer of SGLI is The Prudential Insurance Company of America. The plan is reinsured on a formula basis with over 560 reinsurers.

Provisions for Continuing Protection

The basic coverage is convertible to individual life insurance effective on the 121st day following separation from service. This privilege has been liberalized to permit a serviceman totally disabled at separation to convert beyond the 120-day limit, but not later than one year following separation if he continues to be totally disabled. The coverage during the 120-day period, and for continued total disability up to one year from the date of discharge, is free.

Under reservist coverage, there is generally no conversion privilege. However, if a reservist while covered is rendered uninsurable at standard rates, the insurance continues free for 90 days and he may convert to an individual policy on the 91st day.

All reinsurers are acting as converters, and an additional 25 companies are participating as converters only. When converters are unwilling to insure an applicant at standard premium rates, for health or other reasons, the extra cost of substandard conversions is shared by the converters and the SGLI Fund through a pool arrangement.

The federal employees and the servicemen's group life insurance programs are both excellent examples of government and private business working together.

SELECTED REFERENCES

Eilers, Robert D., and Crowe, Robert M. (eds.)   *Group Insurance Handbook.* Homewood, Ill.: Richard D. Irwin, Inc., 1965.

Gregg, Davis W.   *Group Life Insurance.* 3d ed. Homewood, Ill.: Richard D. Irwin, Inc., 1962.

27

Group Disability
Income Insurance

By MORTON D. MILLER

SINCE MOST INDIVIDUALS and their families rely almost exclusively upon current earnings for their maintenance, any contingency which may cut off the current flow of earnings presents a serious economic problem. Three major contingencies common to all are retirement, premature death, and disability. No one can escape all three.

Retirement is relatively predictable and since it comes at the end of a working career there is usually time to provide for it. While the occurrence of death is generally unpredictable, the economic loss resulting therefrom has received attention through the widespread provision of individual and group life insurance and other death benefits. The onset of a disabling illness or accident is also unpredictable, and even more likely to occur during a person's normal working career than death. Disability for an extended period may cause even more economic hardship to a worker's family than his death, because his own living expenses continue during his disability as well as those of his family, and he also may have additional costs of medical treatment and rehabilitation.

NATURE AND DEVELOPMENT

Group disability income insurance is designed to provide partial replacement of earnings lost during disability caused by accident or sickness. A weekly or monthly payment is provided, and is generally determined by the worker's normal rate of pay. Payments start after a fixed minimum period of absence from work and continue during disability up to a fixed maximum time limit. Policies with maximum benefit durations of up to two years are generally considered short term while those with longer durations are called long term. Most short-term policies have a benefit duration limit of 10, 13, or 26 weeks although some may provide benefits up to one or two years. Long-term policies may provide for payment of benefits until attainment of age 65 and, in some instances, lifetime benefits are payable when disability results from an accident.

Like group life insurance, this form of protection for employees was developed to meet financial needs arising as the nation shifted from an agrarian to an industrial economy. Protection of earnings against the hazards of illness or injury, as well as old age and death, became more and more important as this transition progressed. In Europe, workers had attempted to meet this need through the formation of guilds or fraternal societies. In America, so-called "establishment funds," providing small cash payments in the event of sickness or accident, made their first appearance during the 1800s. Toward the end of the 19th century, increasing concern for injured employees led to the strengthening of the employer liability laws, and many employers turned to the insurance companies for protection against adverse judgments in accident cases. For this purpose, workmen's collective insurance was introduced around 1896 in the form of a rider to employers' liability policies. Such riders covered accidents (sometimes both occupational and nonoccupational), but left unsolved the problem of disability of the worker through illness.

This problem was given serious consideration in the Montgomery Ward and Company negotiations that led to the introduction of group life insurance in 1911. Montgomery Ward met the problem by an arrangement with a casualty insurance company for a more comprehensive workmen's collective policy providing benefits for sickness as well as accidents. Many industrial firms followed that example. About 1915, however, a few insurance companies began to experiment with an idea borrowed from group life insurance, and group disability income insurance, much as we know it today, came on the scene. Around 1919, group disability income insurance became widely available from a number of insurance companies. Thereafter the market for workmen's collective insurance quickly declined as workmen's compensation laws gained momentum and the group-writing companies promoted group disability income policies.

Statistics on the growth of group disability income insurance are not available for the period before the mid-1930s, although by that time the coverage was well established. Table 27–1 gives an idea of the growth since then. The importance of this form of insurance also may be measured by benefits paid. The total of such payments in the United States in 1971 approximated $1,289 million.

The strong growth of group disability income insurance since 1940 is due to many of the forces affecting group life and to some related particularly to the disability area. Wage controls during World War II and shortly thereafter resulted in increased employee and employer interest in employee benefits, recognizing that these were an important element of total compensation. Labor agreements often contained disability wage continuance provisions, many of which were implemented by group short-term disability income policies. This accounts for much of the growth shown in Table 27–1 after 1940. In addition, the enactment of compulsory disability benefit laws in California, New Jersey, and New York during the period 1946 to 1950 gave important further impetus to the adoption of insured plans.

The increase in premiums and in volume of insurance in force has been greatly influenced by the increase in wages and by inflation, inasmuch as

TABLE 27–1.   Group Disability Income Insurance in the United States, 1935–71

Year	Number of Policies	Percent Increase	Number of Persons Covered	Percent Increase	Premiums	Percent Increase
1935	6,200	—	2,000,000	—	$ 26,000,000°	—
1940	13,300	114	3,840,000	92	48,000,000°	85
1945	23,059	73	5,928,000	54	125,000,000°	160
1950	175,780	662	15,104,000	155	272,300,000	118
1955	226,920	29	19,171,000	27	510,000,000	87
1960	281,180	24	20,970,000	9	707,000,000	39
1965	403,680	44	26,518,000	26	934,000,000	32
1970	458,050	13	38,674,000	46	1,744,000,000	87
1971	512,760	12	40,377,000	4	1,959,000,000	12

° Includes premium for accidental death and dismemberment protection.
Source: Health Insurance Association of America.

the benefit amounts are usually related to earnings. Also important is the fact that group disability income insurance can be, and often is, sold on an employee-pay-all basis.

The increase in number of policies over the years was affected importantly by a progressive reduction in size of groups acceptable for insurance, a trend which was influenced enormously by the various state compulsory disability benefit laws. Many companies undertook to insure the smallest groups subject to these laws, even though the minimum size requirement for a group generally called for 25 or more eligible employees.

Even in those states which have not adopted compulsory disability insurance laws, insurance companies gradually have reduced the minimum size of a group they will insure for short-term disability income benefits. Today an employer of 10 persons is considered large enough by most companies, and some carriers will accept smaller groups.

Especially noteworthy is the clearly discernible increased interest in group long-term disability coverage, as indicated in Table 27–2. This coverage provides important protection for the serious economic consequences resulting from a disability that extends beyond the limits of a short-term plan. For many years insurance companies were hesitant to underwrite long-term disabilities on a group basis because they remembered all too clearly the disastrous disability experience of the depression years. Further, the companies anticipated difficulty in administering such benefits. However, their participation in developing this group coverage has now passed beyond the experimental stage of the early 1960s. Recognition of the gap between cessation of short-term disability benefits and the beginning of retirement income, and the current general willingness of insurers to provide this coverage, are reasons to believe that this form of insurance will expand rapidly in the years ahead.

Credit insurance is a specialized form of group disability coverage written in connection with loan or credit transactions. Developed after World War II, it was offered initially on an individual policy basis. In the early 1960s, insurers began writing these benefits under a group policy and most credit disability income insurance is now offered in this manner.

TABLE 27-2.   Group Disability Income Insurance in the United States by Type of Program, 1963-71

| Year | Number of Persons Covered | | | |
	Short-Term Disability Income Protection°	Percent Increase	Long-Term Disability Income Protection	Percent Increase
1963	22,669,000	—	749,000	—
1964	23,177,000	2.2	1,257,000	67.8
1965	24,615,000	6.2	1,903,000	51.4
1966	26,322,000	6.9	2,376,000	24.9
1967	27,632,000	5.0	3,827,000	61.1
1968	30,777,000	11.4	4,710,000	23.1
1969	30,865,000	0.3	5,715,000	21.3
1970	31,498,000	2.1	7,176,000	25.6
1971	32,168,000	2.1	8,209,000	14.4

° Excludes those who also have long-term disability income protection.
Source: Health Insurance Institute.

Group credit disability income insurance usually is written as an addition to group credit life insurance and is generally available to those institutions lending money to be repaid on an installment basis or providing for the financing of goods or services to be paid for in installments. Few creditors provide disability coverage alone, although some may offer it in connection with home mortgage loans.

Data concerning group credit disability income insurance are available only since 1967. Table 27-3 shows the growth of this coverage since then. Payments to creditors under group credit disability coverage were $63.7 million in 1970 and $65.9 million in 1971.

TABLE 27-3.   Group Credit Disability Income Insurance in the United States, 1967-71

Year	Number of Policies	Percent Increase	Number of Persons Covered	Percent Increase	Premiums	Percent Increase
1967	7,650		5,768,000		$100,600,000	
1968	9,230	20.7	6,483,000	12.4	118,000,000	17.3
1969	9,700	5.1	6,326,000	—2.4	126,500,000	7.2
1970	13,280	36.9	6,851,000	8.3	153,700,000	21.5
1971	12,855	—3.2	7,325,000	6.9	175,215,000	14.0

Source: Health Insurance Association of America.

SHORT-TERM DISABILITY INCOME

Definition of Disability

While the actual language used varies from one insurance company to another, a typical short-term disability income policy defines the contingencies against which the employee is insured in the following terms: "If the employee shall become wholly and continuously disabled as a result of *nonoccupational* accidental bodily injuries or *nonoccupational* sickness, and thereby be prevented from performing any and every duty pertaining to his employment, the company will pay . . ." Partial disability is not covered; the test of disability lies in the phrase "prevented from performing any and every duty pertaining to his employment." In actual practice the question of eligibility for the benefit hinges on the question of whether the individual can perform his usual duties. Occasionally a more restricted phraseology is used, in terms of whether the individual can engage in *any* employment for compensation, which would exclude a case where the employee cannot do his usual work but can engage in some light occupation. In practice, however, most companies administer this form of insurance on the basis of whether the person is prevented from engaging in *his* actual work.

The determination of whether the person is unable to work usually rests on certification by a physician. Policies generally stipulate that benefits are not payable for a period of absence from work unless the employee is under the care of a physician during that absence. In practice, a statement as to the nature and severity of disability is required from the physician.

Although a strict reading of the insuring clause of the usual group disability policy would seem to rule out payments for absences from work because of pregnancy or childbirth, it is customary to treat such absences as if they are caused by sickness. However, as indicated later, special provisions are included regarding the amount or duration of payment. Where the policyholder so desires, however, the policy may be written explicitly to exclude payments in case of maternity.[1]

Duration of Benefits

Prior to commencement of benefits in case of sickness, there almost invariably is an initial waiting period, which occasionally is three, but more often seven, days. In isolated cases, some other period such as five work days may be used, while in others a relatively long period such as 14 or 30 days is specified because salary continuance or other temporary provision has been made for the initial part of the absence. Accident coverage either has the same waiting period as for sickness, or may have no waiting period in recognition of the fact that disabilities resulting from accidents (which account for only one eighth of all disability) are seldom within the control of the employee to the extent that they may be for sickness.

The federal income tax laws have had some minor influence on waiting period provisions. Prior to 1954, employer's salary continuance payments were taxable but insured disability income benefits were not. In that year, changes were made in the tax law to bring about equality of treatment for the two types of arrangement. The exclusion from gross income was limited to $100 a week and applicable to other salary continuance or disability income benefits received by an employee while absent from work on account of personal injuries or sickness. Amounts received for the first

---

[1] At this writing, whether or not the exclusion of or restrictions as to maternity benefits are discriminatory is under consideration by the courts.

seven calendar days of absence due to sickness did not qualify for the exclusion unless the employee was hospitalized for one or more days during the course of his illness. The seven-day waiting period did not apply if the disability was due to personal injury. Some group policies were written with corresponding waiting periods.

Further revisions were made in the tax law in 1964, and the law now provides that with respect to the portion of the benefit payment arising from employer contributions:

1. No exclusion is allowed for salary continuance or insured disability income payments for the first 30 calendar days of a period of absence from work on account of disability if the payments are in excess of 75 percent of the employee's regular weekly rate of wages.
2. If the weekly rate of sick pay is not more than 75 percent of the employee's regular weekly rate and if he is hospitalized at least one day at any time during his period of absence on account of personal injuries or sickness, then disability payments received for the first 30 days of the period of absence are excludable in an amount not to exceed a weekly rate of $75. But, if the claimant is not hospitalized, sick pay will not be excludable for the first 7 days of disability even when caused by personal injury, and the $75 maximum weekly sick pay exclusion will apply to the remainder of the first 30-day period, that is, from the 8th day through the 30th day of disability.
3. In any event, payments received after the expiration of the 30-day disability waiting period remain excludable in an amount not to exceed a weekly rate of $100.

When the employee contributes to the cost of the insurance, the portion of the benefits paid for by him is excludable from taxable income.

These provisions are so complicated as to discourage their direct incorporation into group disability income plans, although, in a few instances, plans have undertaken to do so. More commonly, the benefits are written without reference to the law. In the event of disability, the employee is later advised of the appropriate amount of his disability benefits to be treated as income for tax purposes.

The significance of the waiting period can be shown easily from the statistics on disability experience in Table 27–4 which bring out the frequency and the extent of disability to be expected among 1,000 male employees during one year of exposure. Column (1) represents the number per thousand, or the annual frequency, of those who in a year become disabled for t days or more and column (2) is the total number of days of disability after the tth day of disability to be expected from those remaining disabled for longer than t days.

Thus, over a one-year period among a group of 1,000 male employees, 196 disabilities can be expected which will result in a total of 6,476 days of disability. The table shows that 46 (196 minus 150), or about 23 percent of the total number of disabilities, do not last as long as eight days and would be excluded by a seven-day waiting period. Correspondingly, 1,264 days of disability (6,476 minus 5,212), or approximately 20 percent of the expected total number of days, would be excluded. A waiting period of 21

TABLE 27–4. **Annual Disability Experience (per 1,000 male employees)**

Duration of Disability t (in days)	(1) Number Disabled at beginning of Duration t	(2) Number of Days of Disability on and after Duration t
1	196	6,476
2	193	6,279
3	189	6,086
4	183	5,898
5	176	5,715
6	168	5,539
7	159	5,371
8	150	5,212
14	97	4,457
15	92	4,360
21	67	3,876
22	65	3,809
28	51	3,458
29	49	3,407
35	41	3,134

Source: Morton D. Miller, "Group Weekly Indemnity Continuation Table Study," *Transactions of Society of Actuaries*, Vol. 3 (1951), pp. 31–67.

days would eliminate from claim 131 (about 67 percent) of the disabilities and 2,667 (41 percent) of the days of disability.

Waiting periods serve the useful function of reducing the cost of the insurance, because they eliminate claims for a great many trivial disabilities for which the earnings loss is small, and omit payment for only a few days in the longer disabilities. This saves not only claims dollars but, of equal importance, the disproportionate expense of handling many very small claims. Another important function of the waiting period is to minimize the tendency for the insurance to encourage unwarranted absence from work, as will be discussed later in this chapter.

Once payments begin under a disability income policy, they continue as long as the employee remains unable to work, or until the end of the maximum period of benefits specified in the policy. This period varies from one plan to another, but commonly runs for 13 or 26 weeks. Most earlier plans used a 13-week limit; but in recent times, particularly where the specifications are set by union bargaining, the 26-week limit has become more frequent. A significant trend toward even longer benefit periods exists. Benefits negotiated in some industries now provide for payments as long as 52 and 104 weeks. Almost universally, the limit is the same for accident and sickness.

In most policies the maximum period of payment relates to each separate disability; therefore, a full maximum payment may be made more than once for a particular person. In some instances, however, policies are written with a cumulative maximum disability limit. For example, there may be no more than 26 weeks' benefits allowed during any one 12-month period, regardless of the number of causes of absence. This type of limit appears in policies written to conform to the minimum requirements of some of the state compulsory disability insurance laws. Also, this form of limit was common some years ago as a special provision applicable to older employees, such as those over age 60, but it is not widely used for that purpose today.

A subsequent period of disability raises the question of whether benefits should be renewed at once with previous payments charged against the maximum period, or whether a new waiting period should be required with a new maximum benefit period available. A typical solution is to provide that successive periods of disability will be considered as the same period if separated by less than two weeks of active employment, unless the second disability can be shown to be due to unrelated causes.

Except in cases where the policy excludes coverage of maternity absences entirely, the duration of benefits with respect to pregnancies and childbirth is usually six weeks. Although a rarity, a longer or shorter period may be used if the policyowner so desires. In some policies, it is provided that on cessation of work because of pregnancy, the maximum benefit computed for the specified period is payable in a lump sum.

Amount of Benefits

The insurance is intended as partial replacement of earnings lost because of disability and, however the amount of benefit may be determined, the relationship of the benefit to normal earnings (excluding overtime, bonuses, and other special compensation) is an important underwriting consideration. The benefit amount is often expressed as a fixed percentage of the employee's pay, subject to some maximum and possibly to some minimum amount. The benefit as a percentage of normal earnings does not often exceed 66⅔ percent and is seldom less than 50 percent.

In other cases the amount of insurance is given in a schedule of salary groupings. For example, a schedule like the following might be used:

Normal Weekly Earnings	*Weekly Benefit*
Less than $70	$ 40
$70 but less than $90	55
$90 but less than $110	65
$110 but less than $130	75
$130 but less than $150	85
$150 and over	100

The amount of insurance occasionally is determined according to the title or occupational classification of the employee, but this does not necessarily maintain a proper relationship between the amount of benefit and normal earnings. It is also difficult to arrive at occupational groups that are precise, definite, and properly differentiated.

Where the specifications for insurance are set by union bargaining, the amount of weekly benefit is often the same for all persons covered under the policy. This type of plan is satisfactory where wage rates are fairly homogeneous, but it is usually carefully underwritten to be sure that the amount provided bears a satisfactory relationship to the extremes of pay reported in the group. Usually a special clause is included so that the benefit payable will not exceed some fixed percentage, such as 66⅔ percent, of the employee's normal earnings.

Amounts of weekly benefit usually do not exceed $100 a week, although some plans in recent years have gone beyond that figure. In general, for federal income tax and other reasons, short-term disability income policies are not used to provide high benefit amounts for the higher paid personnel of an employer, even though a few experimental policies have been issued for this purpose. Benefits greater than $100 weekly for higher paid employees frequently are provided through formal or informal salary continuance plans.

It is usual to provide that the amount of insurance will change automatically when the employee's pay or insurance classification changes, except that if the employee is not then actively at work, any increase in the insurance is not effective until he returns.

Exclusions and Limitations

Although short-term disability income benefits are usually limited to nonoccupational causes of disability, in some instances where the state workmen's compensation law is thought to be inadequate, the group policy may provide supplementary occupational benefits, as described in the next section.

Otherwise, limitations on benefits under group policies are remarkably few. Unlike many policies issued to individuals, group policies usually do not exclude disability having a cause predating the insurance, except in some instances of very small groups. Furthermore, group policies usually do not exclude many of the causes (such as alcoholism, drug addiction, or nervous and mental diseases) that are often excluded in other forms of health insurance. The breadth of coverage so obtained in group insurance is one of its valuable assets; simplified claims administration and better policyholder relationships are the result.

Occupational Supplement

As indicated above, most short-term disability income policies limit protection to nonoccupational causes of disability. This results in coverage generally complementary to but not duplicative of workmen's compensation. In practice, the determination of whether a disability had a nonoccupational or an occupational cause usually hinges on whether workmen's compensation benefits are payable. In some instances, however (for example, where workmen's compensation payments are relatively low), the group policy may be written to cover all causes, omitting the word "nonoccupational" from the insuring clause. In such policies the amount payable in the event of an occupational accident is usually the amount by which the nonoccupational benefit exceeds the workmen's compensation payment so that the combination of workmen's compensation and group payments is properly related to earnings.

Termination of Coverage

Most short-term group disability policies technically are terminable by the insurer on any policy anniversary date, although this action is rarely taken. In addition, as with other forms of group insurance, it is usually stipulated that the policy may be terminated by the insurance company on any premium due date, generally once a month, when the number covered drops below some stated minimum or percentage (usually 75 percent) of those eligible. The employer usually can terminate the policy on any premium due date and, except as provided in the 31-day grace provision for payment of premium, the policy will terminate on default of payment of premium.

The nature of the insurance is reflected in the fact that the policy provision dealing with the termination of the insurance of individuals when they cease work is somewhat stricter than that used for group life insurance. Protection generally is not continued following termination of active work, and certainly not for any extended period of time. This is consistent with the basic purpose of the insurance, since when wages have ceased because of termination of employment, there can be no income loss resulting from a subsequent disability. Experience has shown that disability insurance, if continued during periods of layoff, leave of absence, or following termination of the employment relationship, is likely to be used as a form of unemployment compensation. Claims are prolonged beyond their normal or proper duration and claims are submitted for conditions that normally would not be disabling, or for spurious or exaggerated causes.

Cost Control Procedures

Broadly speaking, the usual principles of group insurance underwriting are applied as a means of controlling the cost of group disability income insurance. There is no individual screening of risks, but reliance on the average health composition of a group produces a sound insurance venture when premiums are properly computed.

There are, however, some features of group underwriting which take on special emphasis in this form of protection. One of these is that, in general, it is desirable to guard against unstable industries and those where employment is erratic or seasonal. Caution is necessary in insuring groups with periodic unemployment and shutdowns. In the latter category are school teaching and such seasonal industries as food canning, summer amusements, and resort operations. Whenever significant layoffs or interruptions in employment are to be expected, experience has shown that the insurance comes to be used as a kind of unemployment benefit. Feigned or imaginary illnesses, or those which the employee disregards in regular employment, become the causes of lengthy disability claims when unemployment is prevalent. Malingering is always a hazard, and it is exaggerated when those insured lose their source of livelihood. For seasonal industries, it is sometimes provided that protection ceases—and even benefit payments for those disabled cease—when the regular period of employment comes to an end, to be resumed when the regular period of employment starts up again.

Careful attention must be given to the waiting period, which is an important tool in controlling cost. Particularly where employment is irregular, a longer waiting period for sickness may help to obtain satisfactory results. Also, in irregular and unstable employment, it is important to limit the coverage to those who are employed for a substantial minimum period, such as six months, in order to exclude the seasonal and temporary employees.

Experience has shown that providing disability income benefits without at least a one- or two-day waiting period can lead to an unduly high absence rate.

There has been experimentation with retroactive payments upon completion of the waiting period. For example, a policy might provide that when the employee reached the fourth day of illness, payments would begin retroactive to the first day. In general, this type of provision has proved unwise—the temptation to malinger to get the bonus payment at the end of the waiting period was so strong that poor results were obtained. This type of provision is seldom used today unless benefits are supplemental to workmen's compensation, in which case retroactive payment may be made in order to parallel the workmen's compensation provisions.

An important safeguard against undue frequency of claims is a proper relationship between the amount of the disability benefit and the employee's normal wages. If the benefit approaches normal "take-home" pay, the employee has little incentive to maintain steady employment. Furthermore, the benefit should be related not to his gross earnings but, instead, to what will become his *net income after taxes,* and the favorable position accorded weekly disability benefits under the income tax laws should also be recognized.

As a practical matter, the benefit formula must be constructed in terms of gross earnings. Consequently, it becomes necessary, in order to approximate after-tax earnings, to use a benefit percentage in the formula that might otherwise seem low, such as 50 percent or 60 percent of gross pay (excluding overtime, bonus payments and such), and even less in some instances. It is difficult to maintain this underwriting principle where union bargaining establishes a uniform weekly benefit regardless of wages. Experience during poor economic times, however, has demonstrated conclusively the wisdom of maintaining a moderate relationship between benefits and normal wages.

Plans with long maximum benefit periods must be underwritten with caution where employment conditions are irregular or unstable. In all cases, however, the trend to longer durations of up to one or two years necessitates that disability income payments from other sources be taken into account. Social security is the principal source of such other income, but workmen's compensation, veterans' pensions, disability income provisions under employer pension and group life plans, and individual disability income policies, constitute other sources of income. Except for workmen's compensation, these other sources of income generally are subject to a longer waiting period, such as the six-month waiting period for social security, and therefore usually are not taken into account under short-term plans which provide benefit payments of 26 weeks or less. For plans which pay benefits for longer periods, however, the different benefits should be integrated so that the total payment from all sources is not too attractive when related to normal earnings.

Cooperation by the employer-policyholder is a most important element of cost control throughout. It is particularly important in claims administration for group disability income insurance, however. While the establishment and continuation of a claim depend upon the physician's certification of the disability, it has been demonstrated conclusively over the years that the employer's attitude toward absences significantly influences the frequency and duration of claim payments. Lax employment practices and the lack of employer follow-up of employees with minor disabilities can seriously impair the control of group disability income costs.

The employer will be most interested in assuming an active role in plan administration when he shares in the financing. His resultant stake in the dividends and premium refunds payable under the policy in the event of good experience bring about a cooperative and helpful attitude. For this reason, many insurance companies decline to accept cases in which the employees pay the whole premium.

The need for employer cooperation extends well beyond his disability income program. There is a growing awareness among employers of the importance of a total health insurance approach—one which considers together not only loss of earnings, but also employee protection against the cost of hospital and medical services for the treatment necessary to cure or prevent disability. In the process, employers are beginning to recognize that the cost of effective preventive programs, which bring to light and place potential disability claimants under early treatment, may be more than offset by the resultant savings under their disability plans. This is particularly true for those with alcoholic habits or mental and nervous conditions. Also, the trend to more extended benefit periods under short-term plans emphasizes the importance of rehabilitative programs.

LONG-TERM DISABILITY INCOME

Definition of Disability

In defining the contingencies covered, long-term disability income policies often make a distinction between disability which prevents the pursuit of the person's usual occupation and disability which results in the inability to perform any work for compensation. Thus, one frequently used provision defines disability with respect to an initial period, such as two years, as the inability of the employee to perform "any and every duty pertaining to *his occupation*." If disability continues beyond the two-year initial period, further payments are then conditioned on the more stringent test that the disability must be of sufficient severity to prevent the claimant from engaging in *any* employment whatsoever. In this way, if a claimant recovers sufficiently to be able to do some work, he may be expected to accept a job in any occupation that he is capable of performing. Otherwise, his payments would terminate.

Unlike short-term disability policies, most long-term policies provide coverage for both nonoccupational and on-the-job accidents and sicknesses, supplementing workmen's compensation insurance in the latter case.

Long-term income policies usually do not provide maternity benefits, however.

Duration of Benefits

Long-term disability income benefits normally start after short-term benefits or uninsured wage or salary continuance payments cease. Sometimes they precede or may supplement disability income payments under pension plans.

In order to integrate benefits with such plans, the long-term disability income policy usually has a long waiting period, at least equal to the benefit period under the short-term benefit plan (or earnings continuance plan); a six-month period is common in such instances. Even where the long-term plan is the only disability benefit, it is likely to have a substantial waiting period, such as 30 or 90 days.

There is a wide variation in the maximum duration of benefits. Some policies have a maximum period as short as two years; some provide benefits until the individual reaches normal retirement age; and a few have a lifetime benefit, at least for accidents. Durations of five years, 10 years and to age 65 are the most common. Some plans may vary the duration for different classes of employees, such as by providing a longer maximum duration for those with more years of employment.

Choices among these possibilities depend upon the other provisions which the employer may make for disability protection (e.g., under a retirement plan) and are sometimes influenced by a collective bargaining agreement. Costs, the nature and duration of employment, and the patterns in the particular industry are other factors that must be considered.

Amount of Benefits

Under group long-term disability income policies, the benefit amount, usually payable monthly rather than weekly, is determined in accordance with the same principles as were outlined for short-term disability income policies. But some additional considerations enter the picture. One of them is that this form of benefit has been provided extensively for higher paid employees and, therefore, the maximum amount often is considerably higher than for temporary benefits. Many plans have a maximum benefit of $1,000 or $1,500 a month, and some provide amounts as high as $3,000 a month.

However, care is taken to assure that the monthly benefit amount is significantly less than the individual could earn (net after taxes) if he were working. This means the benefit should not be much greater than 60 percent of normal gross earnings, and preferably no more than 70 percent of net earnings. Such a limitation takes on added importance in connection with long-term benefits because of the larger benefit amounts involved, especially for those with higher incomes whose taxes reduce their gross incomes substantially. Table 27–5 illustrates the relationship to net earnings of a long-term disability benefit at the level of 60 percent of gross income.

A further important consideration is the extent to which the claimant may be entitled to other disability income. Account must be taken of work-

TABLE 27–5. Relationship of Long-Term Disability Benefit to Net Earnings

Monthly Gross Income	Net Earnings°		60 Percent of Gross Income	Ratio of 60 Percent of Gross Income to Net Earnings	
	Single	Married†		Single	Married†
$ 400	$ 356	$ 377	$ 240	0.67	0.64
800	681	717	480	0.70	0.67
1,200	982	1,047	720	0.73	0.69
2,000	1,521	1,681	1,200	0.79	0.71

° Gross income less estimated 1970 federal income tax without adjustment for surtax.
† Family assumed to consist of employee, wife, and one child under age 18, filing a joint tax return.

men's compensation, social security, veterans' pensions, employer's pension plan disability benefits, and individually purchased disability income policies. For long-term benefits, the large amounts and extended durations of payment require "integration" with these other benefits in order to avoid making the total of the disability payments from all sources overly attractive as compared with normal earnings. The usual procedure is to provide that benefits from other sources will serve to reduce the long-term benefits otherwise payable under the group policy.

Long-term disability plans frequently include a supplemental benefit during the employee's period of disability in an amount sufficient to provide for the continuing accrual of benefits under a companion retirement income plan. This benefit, usually referred to as a "pension accrual benefit," may provide for a supplemental payment to the pension plan on behalf of the disabled employee. Alternatively, the long-term disability policy may provide payments commencing at normal retirement date, if the employee is still disabled, in an amount sufficient to provide the difference between the employee's actual retirement benefit and what his retirement benefit would have been had he not become disabled.

Some modifications of the usual long-term disability benefits, still somewhat experimental, attempt to recognize that along with other fixed income amounts, the monthly income tends to become increasingly inadequate as price and wage levels rise over the years. One procedure is to ignore any increases in social security benefits (which would otherwise be subtracted from plan benefits) after the long-term payments commence. A more direct method is to adjust the monthly income amount periodically in accordance with changes in the consumer price index. Adjustments are usually limited to, say, 3 percent in any one year, and it is usually provided that the benefit will not be reduced below the original benefit amount because of the changes in the index.

Many insurers include in their long-term plans a rehabilitation provision to permit a trial work period, such as one year, during which benefits are continued but reduced by some amount, perhaps 50 percent of the employee's earnings from rehabilitative employment. The disabled employee who is anxious, but not yet confident of his ability, is encouraged to return to active employment. If the trial work period indicates he is not yet capable of working, his long-term benefit period will not be terminated by reason of accepting employment and he will not have to resatisfy the waiting period.

Integration with Social Security

Social security benefits currently are available without age restrictions for all insured workers. The disability need not be permanent, but need only prevent the worker from engaging in any substantial gainful employment and be expected to last for at least 12 months. In this case, the worker qualifies for benefits which become payable after a six-month waiting period.

Social security benefits are based on the average of the individual's monthly earnings which become subject to social security taxes. During 1971, social security monthly benefit awards to disabled workers averaged about $152, with a corresponding maximum family benefit award of about $235. Benefits were increased 20 percent in 1972, so that the maximum monthly benefit in 1972, effective September 1, for an individual worker can be as much as $331 and for a family (including the worker) as much as $579.

Since the social security program covers essentially the entire work force and during disability replaces a substantial portion of current income, particularly for workers earning less than $750 monthly, it cannot be ignored in designing and administering long-term disability plans. Thus, the long-term disability benefits payable generally are offset by the amount of benefits payable under the social security program.

In order to encourage the employee to apply promptly for such benefits, it is common to provide that the long-term benefit automatically will be reduced by an estimated social security benefit until proof of the actual amount is established. For lower-paid employees, the operation of the social security offset may result in a very small long-term payment, or no payment at all. In order to avoid this situation, some plans exclude from eligibility employees earning less than a minimum amount, such as $750 per month. Other plans which include all employees regardless of earnings may provide a minimum long-term disability benefit, such as $25 per month, or may require no employee contribution on the first $650 of monthly earnings.

Exclusions and Limitations

Limitations on long-term disability benefits under group policies are remarkably few. Except for smaller groups, group policies usually do not exclude causes of disability which predate the effective date of the insurance. Also, unlike short-term policies which normally are limited to non-occupational causes of disability, long-term disability policies almost always provide coverage for occupational causes because the long-term benefit level is often substantially greater than workmen's compensation. The policy is written in such a manner as to make the long-term benefits supplemental to workmen's compensation; the amount of the long-term payment is reduced (through the integration provision) by the amount of workmen's compensation benefit payable. Group policies ordinarily include coverage for disabilities due to alcoholism, drug addiction, or nervous and mental diseases. It is customary, however, for long-term policies to exclude disability from self-inflicted injuries, an act of war, or participating in or committing a felony.

Termination of Coverage

Most long-term disability policies permit the insurer to terminate the policy on any anniversary date, though this provision is seldom employed. As in the case with other forms of group insurance, the insurer may terminate the policy on any premium due date when the number of covered employees drops below a specified minimum, such as 25, or the percentage of those insured is less than a stated amount, usually 75 percent of the number eligible. The employer usually can terminate the policy on any premium due date and, of course, except as provided in the 31-day grace provision for payment of premium, the policy will terminate on default of payment of premium.

As is the case with short-term disability coverage, and for the same reasons, an employee's long-term disability insurance coverage ordinarily terminates upon cessation of active employment.

STATE STATUTORY DISABILITY INCOME PLANS

Compulsory nonoccupational disability income laws were passed more than 20 years ago by four states—Rhode Island, California, New Jersey and New York—and until more recent enactments in Puerto Rico and Hawaii, these were the only states with this type of law.

The Rhode Island law, effective in 1942, provided specified weekly benefits in case of nonoccupational disability for the employees of all employers subject to the law, with continuing funding provided through a payroll tax on employees. The philosophy of this legislation is akin to unemployment insurance; it is, in fact, part of the unemployment insurance statute, and its funding was aided substantially when, in 1946, the Knowland amendment to the unemployment compensation provision of the Social Security Act of 1935 permitted states to recapture employee contributions (taxes that had been levied in earlier years) from the federal unemployment system. For Rhode Island, the funds transferred to the state fund amounted to $28 million. The state disability fund is the sole provider of benefits. There is no opportunity for employers to substitute equal or better benefits through private insured plans as a means of complying with the law.

In 1946, California adopted a law which, although similar to the one in Rhode Island, differed in one important respect by permitting employers to establish private insured or self-insured plans as an alternative to automatic coverage under the state fund. For private plans to be accepted, however, they must provide benefits more liberal in some respect than those of the state fund, be acceptable to a majority of the employees, and not result in a substantial selection of risks adverse to the state fund. The adverse selection requirement limited the use of private plans and, when tests involving distributions of employees by age, sex, and earnings were imposed in 1963, the effect was virtually to eliminate private plans.

The New Jersey law, effective January 1, 1949, was similar to the law in California but with an important innovation; the state fund set its charge for each group on the basis of its own experience, which avoids the need for a protective "adverse selection" provision and so permits competition by private plans. About 40 percent of New Jersey employees are covered by private plans.

The laws of Rhode Island, California, and New Jersey are part of the unemployment compensation statutes and their state funds use as a source of revenue a tax on wages. Rhode Island and California levy the tax only on employees, while New Jersey taxes both the employee and employer and accomplishes the experience rating by varying the employer tax rate according to his experience as indicated by the amount of benefits paid to his employees. Under the California and New Jersey laws, employers were automatically included under the state fund unless specific arrangements were made to comply with the law in some other manner.

The New York law, which became effective in 1950, is part of the workmen's compensation statute and has a correspondingly different philosophy. Weekly benefits of a certain standard are required, but there is no automatic provision; subject employers must take positive action to self-insure or insure the required benefits, either with an insurance company or the state fund. The state fund operates as an insurance company, determining and charging premiums and paying taxes on its premiums, just as an insurance company does.

After passage of the New York law, a period of almost 20 years elapsed before similar laws became effective in July 1969 in Puerto Rico, and in January 1970 in Hawaii.

As in California and New Jersey, the Puerto Rico law provides benefits through a state fund but permits private plans to be established. Benefits provided through the state fund are financed by a payroll tax shared by employees and employers. Since premium rates for private plans recognize the effect on claim costs of such factors as age, sex, and wage composition, it would be expected, in the absence of any controls, that the low-risk/low-cost groups would choose to be insured under a private plan. Hence, to minimize such adverse selection against the state fund, assessments will be charged to private plans which are deemed to be "select groups" as determined by the age, sex, and wage composition of the group. It is still too early to observe how this system will work in practice.

The state of Hawaii differs from the other states with disability benefit laws in that it sponsors no competing plan. Subject employers can comply only by insuring the benefits with an authorized insurer, or by self-insurance. To assure that coverage will be available for all employers, however, the law requires each authorized insurer to participate in a "pool" for the purpose of spreading among all insurers the risk attendant to insuring employer applicants who must comply with the law but cannot secure insurance through ordinary methods. As in Puerto Rico, not enough experience has been gained to permit an evaluation of this arrangement.

In establishing a group plan under one of these laws it is necessary to conform to legal specifications regarding benefits and policy provisions, and to comply with regulations concerning special reports and filing requirements. For this purpose, special benefit provisions and policy and reporting forms are needed.

GROUP CREDITOR DISABILITY INSURANCE

Unlike other forms of group disability insurance, group creditor disability insurance provides for the payment of benefits to a creditor rather than to the person covered. Benefits are payable for disabilities which begin while the debtor is insured, provided he remains continuously disabled for a specified period. The specified period, sometimes referred to as the qualification period, is usually 14 or 30 days. Benefits may be retroactive to the first day of disability (the first day of the qualification period), or, when not retroactive, are payable only for continuous disability after the qualification period.

The 30-day nonretroactive waiting period is more common in plans written for banks and sales finance companies. These institutions generally make credit transactions for larger amounts to persons whose income levels can be expected to absorb one monthly installment repayment despite a disability. Companies licensed under a small loans or similar act prefer a 14-day qualification period with retroactive benefits.

Determination and Duration of Benefits

Benefits are determined as of the due date of the debtor's monthly installment by one of two methods. The first, referred to as the *monthly installment method,* pays benefits equal to the debtor's full monthly payment if he completes the qualification period and continues to be totally disabled to the monthly premium due date. Since nothing is paid under this method unless the debtor is disabled on the installment due date, the second approach, the *pro rata payment method,* is preferred despite its necessitating some additional administrative detail.

Under the pro rata method, if the debtor qualifies and is disabled thereafter, one-thirtieth of the monthly installment is paid for each day of continuous disability. Thus, so long as the debtor qualifies, some benefit is paid whether or not he is disabled on the payment due date.

Disability benefits continue under either method while the insured debtor remains totally disabled but not beyond the scheduled maturity of the indebtedness. The maximum period of indebtedness covered is normally five years but recently longer coverage has been offered in recognition of the installment period common to home improvement loans and loans made for the purchase of mobile homes. The more usual periods of coverage for these plans are 84 and 96 months but some extend for 10 years or longer. Insurers who offer plans for longer than five years are doing so cautiously, however, because of the uncertainties present in underwriting a plan which, in effect, provides long-term disability income and is coupled with the short qualification periods typical of group credit disability coverage.

Exclusions and Limitations

A credit disability policy normally contains a preexisting condition clause to control possible adverse selection by individual borrowers. Benefits are excluded for disability resulting from a condition which manifested itself within a stated period, normally six months, immediately preceding the date the debtor became insured. As a rule, this exclusion is modified to allow benefits for such disabilities on account of the condition six months after the debtor has become insured. Hence, the exclusion is often called the "six and six" provision. Some policies provide for a 12 months' exclusion and there have been experiments with a shorter three months' exclusion. However, with a "three and three" provision, a person with a chronic illness could obtain disability coverage by refraining from treatment for only three months. Such a short time has been opposed by some as likely to be ineffective and to prove quite costly especially when the benefits under the plan are payable for an extended period.

While credit disability policies may require that the debtor be actively at work at the time his loan is taken out, this provision is not frequently used. It is felt that the creditor ordinarily will insist upon the debtor being gainfully employed before credit is extended.

Since social security and other forms of retirement income are not interrupted by periods of disability, the same need for disability coverage does not exist among those age 65 and over. Hence, it is common practice to limit credit disability coverage to debtors who have not yet attained age 65. Therefore, it is not surprising to discover that in 1969 only $800,000 was paid on behalf of debtors over age 65 out of the total $56.5 million in group creditor disability benefits that year.

Two methods are used to achieve this age limitation. The first and more frequently used is to restrict eligibility to those who have not attained age 65 at the time the debt is incurred. The second method is to require that the debt mature before the debtor attains age 66.

Disabilities caused by pregnancy and, normally, those resulting from acts of war are excluded from benefit payment. Some states will not permit group creditor disability insurance on those whose incomes will not be interrupted by disability. The main impact of this restriction is to exclude members of the armed forces. Unlike short-term disability income benefits, group creditor disability benefits are payable for both occupational and nonoccupational disabilities since installment payments must continue in either event.

The amount of the monthly disability indemnity is determined by the amount and number of repayment installments to be made by the borrower. The credit disability policy usually stipulates that the monthly disability benefit shall not exceed a maximum amount.

The policy also limits the aggregate of the disability payments that may become payable in respect to a disabled debtor's original indebtedness. The maximum insurance on an individual loan typically depends upon the ultimate loan volume to be expected from the case as a whole. (It is reasonable to anticipate that the loan volume eventually will level off depending upon the size of the lending institution and the amount of business it anticipates from its installment loan activities.)

The maximum insured amount would not necessarily restrict a vendor or a lender in making loans for a larger amount. However, the insurer's liability would be limited to the maximum amount in the event the debtor became disabled. In such case, the amount of the monthly insured payment would be determined in one of two ways, depending upon how premiums were charged. If, under the terms of the group policy, the coverage was paid for by means of a single premium that was due at the time the indebtedness was incurred and was calculated to be sufficient to cover the loan in its entirety, the monthly disability indemnity would be prorated. On the other hand, if premiums were payable monthly on the outstanding balance of the loan, the insurer would indemnify the full monthly installment during the disability until the maximum insured amount was reached. For example, a $10,000 loan which is insured for half that amount and was to be repaid in monthly installments of $200, would be indemnified at the rate of $100 per month extending over the full duration of the loan when the single-premium basis is used. If, instead, premiums relate to monthly outstanding balances, disability indemnity would be at the rate of $200 a month but would cease when payments totaled $5,000. In the latter circumstances, premiums would continue to be due and payable during the disability.

As with other group insurance contracts, participation must be maintained at a level such that significant adverse selection is avoided. Thus, some plans are written to include all eligible debtors for coverage. In such instances there would be no specific extra charge above the financing charges made by the creditor for the insurance. Where the cost of insurance is borne by the debtor, the coverage is optional and participation by eligible debtors must be maintained at a 75 percent level. In the event participation falls below 75 percent, the insurer reserves the right to require evidence of insurability and to accept or reject an individual debtor.

SELECTED REFERENCES

Dickerson, O. D. *Health Insurance.* 3d ed. Homewood, Ill.: Richard D. Irwin, Inc., 1968.

Faulkner, Edwin J. *Health Insurance.* New York: McGraw-Hill Book Co., Inc., 1960.

Gingery, Stanley W. "Extensions of Creditor Group Coverages," *Group Insurance Handbook* (eds. Robert D. Eilers and Robert M. Crowe), Chap. 35. Homewood, Ill.: Richard D. Irwin, Inc., 1965.

Ilse, Louise Wolters. *Group Insurance and Employee Retirement Plans,* pp. 145, 159–89. Englewood Cliffs, N.J.: Prentice-Hall, Inc., 1953.

Kedzie, D. P. *Consumer Credit Insurance.* Homewood, Ill.: Richard D. Irwin, Inc., 1957.

McCahan, David (ed.). *Accident and Sickness Insurance.* Philadelphia, Pa.: University of Pennsylvania Press, 1954.

National Association of Insurance Commissioners. *Study on Credit Life and Credit Accident and Health Insurance.* New York, 1957.

————. *Background Study of the Regulation of Credit Life and Disability Insurance.* Milwaukee, Wis., 1970.

Pickrell, J. F. *Group Health Insurance.* Homewood, Ill.: Richard D. Irwin, Inc., 1961.

28

Group Medical Expense Insurance

By CHARLES P. HALL, JR.

THE EXPRESSION "group medical expense insurance" is self-defining, in the broad sense. There are, however, many variations which are encompassed under this general heading. Not only are there different types of groups, but the coverage ranges from protection against the costs of one or several specific conditions and forms of treatment, to broad comprehensive benefits that pertain to almost every known disease and mode of treatment. Several distinct types of organizations provide the protection, and the benefits may be provided in cash or in kind.

NATURE AND DEVELOPMENT

Medical expense insurance may be provided through the mechanism of group insurance or individual insurance, but it has been dominated for years by the group approach, and that will be the focus of this chapter.

Origins

Although the historical purist could point to earlier examples, for practical purposes group medical expense insurance had its origins with private insurance companies early in the 20th century. It was preceded by group life insurance and disability income insurance, often appearing as a rider to the latter type contract. Unlike life insurance benefits, medical expense coverage was not considered to be a particularly desirable product by most insurers. Very little was sold, since many companies were skeptical as to the "insurability" of medical expenses. The devastating experience with early disability income benefits during the economic depression of the 1930s tended to strengthen those doubts.

The real impetus to the growth of medical expense insurance came from two entirely new sources—hospital service associations and medical service associations. The hospital plans had their genesis in the Baylor University Hospital Plan, founded in 1929. The main objective of this and other early hospital service association plans was, and still is in some areas, to facilitate the hospitals' collection of bills and to protect their solvency. More recently, the emphasis on consumerism which began in the late 1960s has changed this posture. These plans multiplied and prospered during the next decade, while progressing from single hospital plans through communitywide plans to statewide plans. At an early stage, the American Hospital Association (AHA) approved these plans in principle and began to promote their establishment and to set standards. Through a series of developments, all closely allied to the AHA, the separate Blue Cross Association finally emerged as the national coordinating agency. At the present time, there are about 75 Blue Cross plans in operation in the United States and Puerto Rico.

Medical service associations, in the form of county medical society plans, started in the Pacific Northwest in the 1920s, but Blue Shield as we know it today began much later, with the statewide California Physicians' Service in 1939. These plans, designed to cover physicians' fees, originally focused primarily on surgical benefits, though nearly all medical expenses have since been encompassed. As might be anticipated, the American Medical Association was intimately involved with early developments in this area, helping to found the predecessor to the current national coordinating body, the National Association of Blue Shield Plans (NABSP). As happened with the Blue Cross Association, the NABSP is now an independent organization, though close ties remain with organized medicine. At the end of 1972 there were 72 Blue Shield Member Plans in the United States and Puerto Rico.

Most Blue Cross and Blue Shield plans are organized under special enabling legislation which recognizes them as nonprofit organizations and exempts them from state insurance premium taxes. Some variety exists among Blue Shield plans, with a few organized as stock or mutual insurance companies sponsored by the medical profession and several others being directly affiliated with Blue Cross. In most areas, the two organizations have close working relationships.

It should be noted briefly that both hospital and medical service associations historically have been dominated, insofar as organizational control is concerned, by the providers they served. In some states this was required by the terms of the special enabling legislation creating the associations, but in all other areas it was, until recently, an unvarying custom.

Spurred by runaway inflation in health care costs and charges of conflict of interest on the part of hospital trustees and physicians on Blue Cross and Blue Shield boards, the wave of consumerism which has swept the nation in recent years has led to significant changes in the composition of many governing boards. It now seems inevitable that "consumer representatives," variously defined, will soon become a majority on most hospital and medical service association boards.

Growth and Competition

By 1940, it had become apparent that despite earlier reservations on the part of private insurance companies, medical expense benefits could be underwritten successfully. An era of intense competition and explosive growth ensued.

Thereafter, the rate of expansion slowed, though the increase in absolute numbers insured was still impressive. More importantly, the breadth of coverage continued to expand significantly, and special attention began to focus on "problem" segments of the population, including the elderly and the poor. It was during this later period that third parties—both private insurers and the Blues—came to realize that they were not only in competition with each other, but also with the federal government. Ironically, as the private sector became more successful in terms of covering a large proportion of the population, the more intense became the pressure for government intervention. This was caused not only by the obvious disparity in the circumstances of the insured and uninsured (often uninsurable) segments of the citizenry, but it was also accentuated by the soaring costs of health care, which consistently outstripped all other elements in the consumer price index.

Merging Philosophies

Indemnity versus Service Benefits—The Third Party View. During the three decades of competition after 1940, many significant changes took place in the medical expense insurance field. Originally, and predictably, the private insurance companies followed their historical insurance pattern of providing "indemnity" benefits and establishing premiums on a basic philosophy of "individual equity." Premiums, it was felt, should reflect, as much as possible, the true actuarial value of the risk presented by each insured group. Contracts were strictly between the insurer and employer of the group, with cash benefits payable directly to the covered persons after they had already paid the provider(s).

The Blues, in their early successes, insisted on differentiating themselves from insurance companies, emphasizing that they were nonprofit prepayment plans. Blue Cross, in particular, viewed itself as a quasi-public organization with a distinctive "social responsibility." It popularized both the concept of "service benefits" and "community rating." Basic hospitalization benefits, for example, were described in terms of days rather than dollars. This was possible because of the unique relationship the hospital and medical service associations had with providers. Not only did a contract exist with "subscribers" (rather than insureds), but the Blues also contracted directly with hospitals and physicians to establish agreed upon levels of cost for covered benefits.

In effect, benefits were promised to subscribers in terms of services, while reimbursement for hospitals and physicians was a matter of contract between the appropriate Blue Cross or Blue Shield unit and the provider. In the usual instance, the subscriber would not receive nor pay any cash—the provider would simply be paid directly by the Blue Cross or Blue Shield plan. The patient normally would be billed only for miscellaneous, uncovered charges, such as for telephone calls or the use of television. In exchange for this direct, and, presumably, prompt payment and the fact that in any given geographical area the single Blue Cross unit usually encompassed a very significant proportion of the total insured population, concessions often were granted in the Blue Cross-provider cost contract which in effect gave Blue Cross a distinct cost advantage compared to private insurance companies as well as noninsured, full-paying patients. This discount has been a recurring source of controversy, and a final court determination of its legality is still pending.

Indemnity versus Service Benefits—The Consumer View. From the consumer's viewpoint, the "indemnity" and "service" benefit approaches had some significant differences. With private insurers, the insurance contract was a two-party arrangement, with the company agreeing only to pay specified dollar amounts to the insured upon the occurrence of certain events. The doctor-patient relationship was entirely separate. Hence, there was never any assurance that the insurance benefit would completely cover the hospital or doctor bill, and the hospital or physician was free to charge a self-determined fee which might have no relationship to the available insurance benefit. The patient was legally obligated to pay the difference.

Under Blue Cross, the contractual relationship between the carrier and the hospital assured that the contracted amount would be accepted by participating hospitals as full payment, thus permitting the outright promise of "days of coverage." Blue Shield plans modified the "service benefit" approach to a degree. Undoubtedly influenced by their historical practice of using a "sliding fee scale" based on the patients' income, contracting physicians introduced the concept of income limits on the service benefits. That is, they would contract with Blue Shield to accept a given schedule of benefits as full payment for services provided to patients with incomes below a stated limit. At the same time, they reserved the right to increase fees for individuals whose incomes exceeded the prescribed limit. Thus, Blue Shield offered both service and indemnity benefits frequently combining the concept in a single contract.

First Dollar versus Major Medical. Closely allied to the Blues' early philosophy of service benefits was the concept of providing "first dollar coverage." Since the Blues were the early pace- and pattern-setters in the field, most hospital and surgical coverages followed this philosophy. The first real break with this tradition came with the introduction of the "major medical" insurance concept by private insurers around 1950. This development was, at least in part, an attempt to control rising premium costs, since, at least in percentage terms, a disproportionate element of administrative costs is involved in the settling of small claims. The Blues are not affected as much by the administrative cost problem because of their direct contractual relationship with the purveyors of care. More important, perhaps, major medical contracts stressed the traditional aim of insurance to provide for catastrophic losses while permitting the individual to bear the minor or "sniffle" costs on his own.

The immediate popularity of major medical coverage attests to the desire of many employers and employee groups to take advantage of the trade-off which offered high limits for a modest deductible. On the other hand, a philosophical struggle still rages over the relative merits of encouraging early treatment and prevention through first-dollar benefits versus the alleged impact on "overutilization" which results from initial deductible provisions. In the final analysis, the decision must rest on economic considerations and individual group preference.

Over the years, some of the distinctions between cash indemnity and service benefits have become blurred. With the introduction of major medical policies around 1950 and the subsequent appearance of the very broad "comprehensive major medical" policies, private insurers came up with a tool that enabled them to offer a reasonable proxy for service benefits even without separate provider contracts. Since these policies promised a very broad range of benefits with relatively few internal limits and high maximum dollar benefits, they often, from the patients' point of view, were equivalent to service benefits. The analogy is even more complete in the large number of cases where the insured signs an "assignment of benefits" agreement which provides for direct payment to the provider. In these cases, it might be argued that the indemnity concept, in a strict sense, is replaced by the reimbursement (of the provider) concept, since the insured never receives any cash payment, nor does he make one—except to the extent required by deductible and/or coinsurance provisions in the contract. It should be noted that many Blue Cross plans also have made reimbursement benefits available to their subscribers, even though the bulk of their contracts are still issued on the basis of service benefits.

Contractual Cost Controls. Blue Shield, in recent years, has moved rapidly in the direction of providing coverage on a "usual, customary and reasonable" (UCR) basis, with approximately one third of those enrolled under insured programs now protected on this basis. The usual and customary approach was originally introduced by private insurers as a cost-controlling element in major medical policies. Now, Blue Shield makes acceptance of the UCR approach a condition for membership of physicians in some areas.

Rates. An additional accommodation of originally divergent philosophies is exemplified in the area of rates. In keeping with belief in its social role, Blue Cross originally held to the concept of community rating—a single rate based on the composite experience of an entire community. Predictably, this attracted the poorer risks. The more desirable risks could obtain much lower premiums for similar benefits from insurance companies, and, naturally, many of them exercised this option. The result, of course, was a vicious cycle which forced Blue Cross to progressively more disproportionate rate hikes as the good risks left and only the less desirable ones remained. The once commanding enrollment lead of Blue Cross rapidly disappeared. Inevitably, competitive pressures forced the Blues to accept the concept of experience rating, at least for most group insurance business. Had they not done so, it is unlikely that they could have survived as a viable competitive force in the field. They still tend to favor a community rating approach for their individual contracts, however.

Prepaid Group Practice

The group practice concept represents an alternative approach to the organization and delivery of medical care. When combined with a prepayment mechanism, it is alleged to offer significant advantages in terms of cost control by furnishing incentive for providers to keep their patients well. It is also claimed that better quality care is likely to result because of a greater likelihood for "peer review" to take place in a group practice setting. Considerable evidence exists to support these claims, but it is hardly conclusive, both because of the rather limited segment of the population with experience in existing plans and because of the difficulty of measuring the quality of medical care. A common feature in these plans is that the membership charge is based on an annual "capitation," and participating physicians generally are paid by salary or some basis other than the traditional "fee-for-service." This is not, however, a necessary condition. They also tend to be identified with broad or "comprehensive" coverage.

The sudden wave of interest in prepaid group practice plans can be attributed to a number of factors, including a widespread conviction that only a drastic change in the organization and delivery of health services will enable us as a nation to provide high-quality health care for all our citizens, and an almost desperate hope that this kind of organization will somehow put a brake on spiraling costs.

Slow growth of these plans over the years can be attributed to many factors, including the following: opposition from organized medicine, tempered somewhat in recent years as the result of a favorable court decision; geographic limitations, resulting from small size and the absence of any coordinating relationships, such as those afforded hospital and medical service associations through the Blue Cross Association and the National Association of Blue Shield Plans; the apparent reluctance of many citizens to join a plan under which they think they will forfeit the right to develop a close doctor-patient relationship (not necessarily true); and the many difficulties involved in establishing a viable group practice prepayment plan, including raising the necessary start-up capital and finding a compatible group of physicians with an appropriate mix of professional specialties.

With the aid of strong backing by organized labor, as well as mounting general discontent with the existing structure of medical care delivery in the United States, these plans have grown significantly in the last few years, though they still represent only a very small part of the total. Their discussion here is important because many feel that they represent the "wave of the future." Existing federal legislation already provides modest financial incentives for the formation of these groups, and most pending legislative proposals for a scheme of national health insurance provide direct or indirect subsidy and encouragement to the formation of group practice plans.[1] It is worth noting that both the Blues and private insurers are exploring various ways in which they effectively can become the financing mechanism for comprehensive group practice plans.

Only time will tell whether all the rhetoric has been justified. The success of the Kaiser Permanente Plans, the largest and most often cited of the group practice plans now in operation, will not be easy to duplicate. The most severe test will occur as the concept is extended to encompass more diverse groups in society. To date, their membership has been dominated by middle-class wage earners and their families.

EVOLVING GROUP CONCEPTS

Most changes in the origin, composition, and size of groups insured under group medical expense insurance contracts since the coverage was

---

[1] The currently popular euphemism is HMO—Health Maintenance Organization.

first introduced have been evolutionary rather than revolutionary. The most common type of group has always been the employees of a single employer, but members of a labor union and employees of two or more employers in the same industry or an association of employers have become increasingly important in recent years. The insurance laws of most states define the types and sizes of groups which may be insured, and the definitions, in general, do not vary significantly from those covering other group life and health insurance.

The first group medical expense insurance contracts were designed strictly to provide benefits for the worker himself. Very soon, however, the logical extension of coverage for dependents became commonplace. Today it is almost universal. This is an area in which group medical expense insurance differs significantly from several other forms of group insurance which usually cover only the employee. Dependent coverage is always broad enough to encompass dependent spouses and children; occasionally a broader classification of dependents might be covered, such as dependent parents. Only in very unusual circumstances would coverage be provided for dependents alone. Dependent children are usually covered automatically to age 18 or 19, but this often is extended to age 23 or more, provided the child is enrolled as a full-time student in a college or university, and further extended for children incapable of self-support.

Many state insurance laws define the minimum legal size of a group for insurance purposes, with the most common limit being not less than 10. Some states do not prescribe a minimum, and others have specified a different number. In the early stages of development, the limit was frequently higher—if not by law, then by company underwriting practice. As actuarial experience and expertise were accumulated, the cost advantages of group insurance both in the form of lower premiums and the wider application of experience rating became more generally available.

As with all other forms of group insurance, medical expense coverage can be offered on either a contributory or noncontributory basis. Often, the decision rests on the result of collective bargaining negotiations. A fairly common arrangement is for the employer to pay the full cost of the coverage for the primary insured (employee), with the worker paying all or part of the surcharge for dependent coverage.

Provisions for continuation of group medical expense coverage upon termination of employment or termination of the master contract are similar to those found in other forms of group insurance. Usually, assurance is provided of convertibility to individual coverage, but premiums are not guaranteed. Generally, if benefits are being collected at the time of termination, they will continue until the spell of illness is completed or the benefits are exhausted. Special provisions relating to pregnancy are designed to exclude coverage for women already pregnant when they enter the group, but to extend coverage to women already pregnant when they leave the group.

BASIC MEDICAL EXPENSE COVERAGES

There are at least three types of basic group medical expense benefits: hospital, surgical, and medical. Some might wish to add an "other" category to deal with such recent developments as dental care, vision care, prescription drugs, and miscellaneous other benefits. Any discussion of the generic contracts, however, is largely of historical interest, and can therefore be brief. Most groups today either provide a combination of the basic types plus a supplementary major medical contract, or they operate under a single "comprehensive major medical" arrangement. Furthermore, nearly all of the major health insurance proposals currently before Congress call for "comprehensive" coverage.

Group Hospital Expense Insurance

Blue Cross traditionally describes its hospital benefits in terms of a specified number of days of coverage, usually for semiprivate accommodations in member hospitals. For Blue Cross and its subscribers, then, the major concerns were variations in utilization and hospital days exceeding the maximum covered, respectively.

Private insurers use a variety of benefit patterns, including: (a) a flat dollar benefit per day of confinement (under this pattern, the benefit normally is set at a level so it will be certain not to exceed the actual charge; maximum benefits are then described in terms of days of coverage or dollars); (b) payment of actual charges up to a specified maximum (a popular selection); (c) definition of benefits in terms of the actual hospital charge for a certain classification of room—usually semiprivate—without respect to dollar amounts. (Here, of course, the benefit is equivalent, for the patient, to a service benefit, and the maximum coverage is defined in terms of days, as with Blue Cross.)

Insurance companies and their insureds face slightly different risks than their Blue Cross counterparts, depending on which underwriting approach is utilized. For the insured under (a) or (b), there is the danger that actual hospital charges will exceed the insurance benefit, thus providing less than complete protection; for the company, there is the danger that the maximum stated benefit also becomes the minimum, as well as the same potential variation in utilization faced by Blue Cross. Under (c), the insured is in the same position as the Blue Cross subscriber, concerned only that his length of stay may exceed the covered days; the insurer, on the other hand, is exposed to a serious risk of changing hospital prices, since it is not protected, like Blue Cross, by a contract with the hospitals.

The basic benefit under almost all hospital expense insurance is for the daily room and board charge, which includes general duty nursing. Typically, other hospital services, including laboratory and X rays, drugs and the like, are dealt with separately. Blue Cross provides these benefits on a service basis too, occasionally with some exclusions or coinsurance (percentage participation) requirement. Insurance companies tend to limit their dollar exposure for these supplementary services to a multiple of their daily indemnity (e.g., 20 times the daily room and board limit) or a dollar maximum. Some plans have no limit on these benefits. Benefit amounts offered under hospital insurance contracts have grown substantially over the years, reflecting both inflationary costs and an expanding demand for full coverage.

Special internal limits usually are included in the contracts of both Blue Cross and insurance companies on maternity benefits under hospital insurance contracts. The extent of the limitation will vary among groups, depending, in part, upon the age composition and desires of the work force involved. Nearly all plans impose at least a nine-month waiting period on maternity benefits, and nearly all private carriers provide an extended benefit. Both types of carriers also impose clear limitations on their liability for the cost of private room accommodations.

Historically, a number of exclusions from coverage have been common with the Blues, including confinement for alcoholism, drug addiction, and nervous and mental disorders, to name a few. Confinement for diagnostic purposes and outpatient treatment are other important examples of past and continuing exclusions.

Group Surgical Expense Insurance

Hospitalization coverage was already extant when the first benefits for professional services began to evolve. It is not surprising, therefore, that coverage for surgery appeared first. It was a natural; it appeared to meet nearly all the requirements for an "insurable risk." Surgical procedures are clearly controlled by the physician rather than the patient, their use can be pinpointed in terms of time and place, and, by limiting coverage to procedures performed in hospitals and excluding such elective items as cosmetic surgery, insurers felt they had a fairly safe offering. Nevertheless, they usually defined (limited) benefits by means of a schedule which named specific reimbursement maximums for named procedures. The apparent simplicity, however, was deceptive.

While Blue Shield generally subscribed to the same service benefit philosophy espoused by Blue Cross, it was far more difficult to negotiate fixed-fee contracts with hundreds of physicians than with a few hospitals, especially when physicians had for years been accustomed to the "Robin Hood philosophy" of a sliding fee scale based on the patient's income. As stated earlier, Blue Shield was frequently unable to provide full service benefits to all subscribers, instead offering plans with "income limits" which allowed physicians to charge patients with incomes above a stated level the difference between the Blue Shield reimbursement and their usual fee. Originally, however, a surgical fee schedule was used by Blue Shield and private insurers. Where Blue Shield was able to negotiate full service benefits, the subscribers never saw the schedule—it was simply between Blue Shield and the participating physicians.

Insurance companies often developed their own surgical schedules, which have generally become identified in terms of the maximum fee they allow, e.g., a $200 schedule or a $300 schedule. Blue Shield at one point developed a Professional Services Index (PSI) as a basis for controlling costs. More recently, both the Blues and private carriers have been working on indexes which will serve a number of purposes, including help in determining the level of usual, customary, and reasonable (UCR) charges. Medical societies, too, have played an active role over the years in developing relative value schedules for surgical and other medical procedures. A relative value schedule (RVS) differs from a fee schedule in that it merely shows the value of one procedure in relation to another, rather than a relative dollar amount. Though the American Medical Association has never shown much inclination to become directly involved, a number of states, notably California, have acted, as have several specialty medical groups. The California RVS first appeared in 1956 and has gone through a number of revisions, most recently in 1969. It has been the most widely accepted RVS and, at times, has taken on national significance, as when it became something of a standard under the huge Federal Employees Health Benefits Plan—the largest group contract in the country. The RVS approach, when compared to the early surgical schedules, is more flexible in that it

TABLE 28–1. Schedule of Surgical Procedures (selected examples)*

Operation	*Unit Value*
Integumentary System	
Wounds of face, ears, eyelids, nose or lips, recent, simple	
repair of 1 to 2½ inches	1.250
Excision of cyst, fibroadenoma or other benign tumor	6.250
Musculoskeletal System	
Fractures	
Radius, distal end, closed manipulative reduction	5.000
Cardiovascular System	
Triple valve procedure, replacement, or repair, or both	100.000
Digestive System	
Tonsillectomy (age 12 or over)	6.000
Appendectomy	11.905
Hemorrhoidectomy, external, complete	6.000
Cholecystectomy	18.125
Herniotomy (age 5 or over)	11.250
Female Genital System	
Biopsy or local excision of lesion of cervix	0.750
Total hysterectomy	20.000
Dilation and curettage	5.000

* The maximum payments for these procedures are expressed in Unit Values. To determine the dollar maximum for any procedure, multiply the Unit Value applicable to that procedure by the Conversion Factor—in this case 18. The maximum benefit under the schedule is $1,800.

permits the use of varying "conversion factors" to reflect such things as regional differences in cost and different levels of professional expertise, e.g., as between a board certified surgeon and one who is not so qualified. Many group insurance surgical schedules today use a relative value type approach. Table 28–1 shows some sample values for selected operations under a current schedule offered by a leading insurance company with a conversion factor of 18 and a maximum benefit of $1,800.[2] The dramatic rise in surgeons' fees in recent years has been largely responsible for the increase in schedule benefits. An $1,800 schedule was unheard of a few years ago.

---

[2] A conversion factor of 18 means that the basic unit is $18. To determine the maximum allowable fee for a given procedure, multiply its relative value by $18.

A number of insurers as well as most Blue Shield plans now offer surgical benefits without specific schedules, instead limiting reimbursement to "usual and customary" or "usual, customary, and reasonable" charges.

As under hospital expense coverage, surgical policies usually set forth prescribed limits for obstetrical benefits. Blue Shield may also impose a waiting period for certain other common surgical procedures to minimize overt "adverse selection" by insureds.

Other Medical Expense Charges

The next logical development after surgical benefits was to provide protection for other professional medical charges. At first, benefits under Blue Shield and insurance company plans were limited to physicians' services provided in the hospital, but gradually the benefits were extended to cover office and, sometimes, home visits. As a separate package of benefits, this sometimes-called "medical expense" insurance never really closed the gap with hospital and surgical insurance, and most of these benefits are paid under major medical or comprehensive policies, as discussed below.

Other Group Health Insurance Benefits

A variety of disparate coverages has evolved in recent years. One of the more important is dental coverage. Though sometimes included in comprehensive group contracts, significant growth has taken place in the form of dental service associations. These prepayment arrangements tend to emphasize the importance of preventive therapy relating to oral hygiene.

The clamor for comprehensive protection also has led to many other developments, such as coverage for prescription drugs, vision care, extended care-facility coverage, home health care services, and so on. Few of these, however, are available as separate entities. Most are part of the broader comprehensive coverages discussed below.

In closing the discussion of the basic coverages, it should be noted that a common exclusion under all these plans applies to services provided under mandated government programs (e.g., workmen's compensation) or in government operated facilities (e.g., state mental hospitals or Veterans Administration hospitals).

BROAD MEDICAL EXPENSE COVERAGES

Integration or packaging of medical expense insurance benefits has existed to some extent since medical insurance began. As noted above, even the basic hospital expense policy packaged certain "hospital extras" along with protection against hospital room and board charges. As soon as Blue Shield plans began to offer nonsurgical, inhospital medical benefits, they were incorporated into the basic Blue Shield contract, as have been other more recent extensions of coverage. Blue Cross and Blue Shield plans have worked together for most of their history, often sharing both office facilities and staff. In many areas these organizations are virtually synonymous in the public eye, because they nearly always offer joint contracts to group insureds. Less common, perhaps, but certainly not rare, are examples in which private insurance companies have been paired with either Blue Cross or Blue Shield. And while separate hospital, surgical, and medical contracts are still available—and often purchased—for individual coverage, as a practical matter they have long since been available in single integrated packages for the group insurance market. A number of factors promoted the integration of group insurance benefits, but perhaps the greatest impetus was the result of product innovation.

Major Medical Expense Insurance

Until the introduction of major medical expense insurance coverage about 1950, the integration of basic medical coverages could only be described as superficial. While the scope of benefits available had been broadened significantly by that time, the emphasis had been on first-dollar coverage, with the upper limits of protection largely oriented toward acute, short-term protection. Furthermore, many groups had not availed themselves of all the many benefits offered.

Under major medical policies, several new concepts were introduced. The coverage was designed to deal with catastrophic situations, not minor problems or routine care. Maximum benefits were quite high initially, and, spurred by inflation, they have ballooned, so that now $25,000 limits are commonplace and substantially higher limits are not unusual.

Major medical was designed to be offered as a separate coverage or as an "umbrella" of protection over one or more basic policies. In the first instance, an initial deductible would be applied before any benefits became payable. In the second case, when added above some basic coverage, a "corridor deductible"—some specified out-of-pocket payment by the insured—was imposed after the basic benefits were exhausted but before the major medical coverage would begin. These relationships are presented visually in Figure 28–1 (B) and (C) on p. 426. Here, the type of benefits is indicated on the horizontal axis, the amount is plotted vertically, and the degree of reimbursement is indicated by shading. Figure 28–1 (A) illustrates a basic plan.

Deductibles came in many different forms. They could be uniform for all insureds or variable based on income. In some cases they varied depending upon the type of service received (hospital or medical) or the nature of the problem (accident or illness). They were available on a per illness, per family, or per calendar year basis. A large number of combinations was available.

Another concept common to most major medical contracts was the requirement that the insured participate in the loss which exceeded the deductible. This "percentage participation" or "coinsurance" generally ranged from 20 percent to 25 percent, though it went higher for some benefits (frequently, out-of-hospital psychiatric treatment). Beginning in the early 1960s some companies offered to drop the coinsurance requirement after losses exceeded some specified amount (e.g., $1,000).

Probably the most significant innovation of major medical was its "blanket" approach to medical expense protection. No longer was the insured required to incur his expenses in the "proper combination." He no longer had to be wise enough to guess whether his illness would require hospitalization, surgery, or both. With relatively few exclusions and only modest internal limits (e.g., semiprivate hospital room), the policy indemnified for all medical costs up to the policy limit.

The major medical approach caught on very rapidly. For the first few years, the Blues had no comparable coverage, and it became commonplace to find a private insurer group major medical policy superimposed on a basic Blue Cross/Blue Shield package. Before long, however, the Blues responded with "extended benefit" arrangements of their own. They tended to follow the private insurer models rather closely, incorporating both deductible and percentage participation arrangements. Restrictions in the special enabling acts of the Blues produced difficulties for the plans in achieving the same degree of integration provided by insurance companies. Blue Cross was forced to limit its extended benefits to the hospital area, while Blue Shield could deal only with the medical-surgical area. This occasionally left some gaps in the coverage available, though if combined, they were more or less comparable with insurance company plans. Most of the initial difficulties now have been overcome. Predictably, Blue Cross ordinarily described the maximum protection afforded under extended benefit contracts in terms of days (e.g., 730 days) rather than dollars.

Comprehensive Medical Expense Insurance

The next major development came quickly in the form of "comprehensive major medical" or "comprehensive medical expense" insurance. This coverage put into a single contractual package the whole spectrum of medical expense insurance benefits from the basic coverages through major medical. In doing so, it had available for use some interesting combinations of deductible and percentage participation provisions. See Figure 28–1 (D) and (E) on the following page.

The National Association of Blue Shield Plans considers comprehensive coverage so important that, as of June 1, 1970, the availability of the Blue Shield Comprehensive Contract, developed primarily to serve national accounts, became effective as a membership standard in the NABSP.

Patterns of Integration

Much group medical expense insurance coverage has been "tailor-made" as the result of negotiations among employers, employees (through their unions), and insurers. Certain large employers and industrial unions have been pattern setters and innovators. The Big Three automakers and the United Automobile Workers Union, for example, set a major precedent a few years ago by negotiating comprehensive outpatient psychiatric benefits. At the same time, it is often mistakenly assumed that the benefits provided under such large and widely publicized contracts are generally held by most other groups. This has not been the case. The majority of the nation's employees work for small- or medium-size companies.

The general trend of benefit integration, even in more modest group plans, however, can be traced. Nearly all started by combining basic hospital and surgical coverage, and most added some medical benefits, though not all provided broad coverage in this latter area. The next step usually

FIGURE 28–1.   Group Medical Expense Insurance Plan Approaches

A. BASIC PLAN

Hospital Charges	Surgery	Other Medical Expenses

E–1 MODIFIED COMPREHENSIVE PLAN – ALTERNATE 1

Hospital Charges	Surgery	Other Medical Expenses

B. MAJOR MEDICAL SUPERIMPOSED ON BASIC PLAN

Hospital Charges	Surgery	Other Medical Expenses

E–2 MODIFIED COMPREHENSIVE PLAN – ALTERNATE 2

Hospital Charges	Surgery	Other Medical Expenses

C. MAJOR MEDICAL SUPERIMPOSED ON
    HOSPITAL PLAN ONLY

Hospital Charges	Surgery	Other Medical Expenses

E–3 MODIFIED COMPREHENSIVE PLAN – ALTERNATE 3

Hospital Charges	Surgery	Other Medical Expenses

D. PURE COMPREHENSIVE PLAN

Hospital Charges	Surgery	Other Medical Expenses

E–4 MODIFIED COMPREHENSIVE PLAN–ALTERNATE 4
     (GENERAL ELECTRIC)

Hospital Charges	Surgery and Diagnostic X–Ray	Other Medical Expenses

REIMBURSEMENT RATIO

100%	85%	75–80%	0%

Source: Towers, Perrin, Forster & Crosby, Inc.

was a progression to an overriding major medical policy, often followed by the unifying step of purchasing a single comprehensive policy.

Regardless of whether accomplished with a series of interlocking policies or a single comprehensive package, the trend over the years has clearly been to provide broader and more extensive protection. The specifics, however, vary widely. In any given situation, only a limited number of dollars is available and, depending on such factors as the age and income distribution of the group, its geographical location, and the priorities of the bargaining parties, the marginal dollar may be allocated in different situations to dental benefits, vision care benefits, a longer maximum hospital stay, or, perhaps, to increases in take-home pay or pension benefits.

FIGURE 28–1. *(continued)*

EXPLANATION

A. *Basic Plan.* The shaded area of this chart represents that portion of all medical expenses covered by a typical basic hospital-surgical-medical or Blue Cross-Blue Shield program. Recent studies indicate that approximately 50 percent of a family's average medical expenses are covered by a typical basic plan of hospital-surgical and inhospital medical benefits. Thus, the shaded area in this chart covers approximately 50 percent of the total area.

B. *Major Medical Superimposed on Basic Plan.* The superimposition of a major medical plan on the present basic plan is by far the most common method of providing catastrophe coverage.

C. *Major Medical Superimposed on Hospital Plan Only.* The premium saved by eliminating the basic *surgical—other medical* (*inhospital*) plan frequently is sufficient to cover the greater part or all of the premium necessary to provide an adequate major medical program. While this approach has not become popular, it has the theoretical advantage of eliminating those coverages which are open to the most abuse and which pay many small "budgetable" claims.

D. *"Pure" Comprehensive Plan.* In this approach, the deductible and the coinsurance percentage are applied to all expenses (hospital-surgical—other medical). A more salable version of this approach in which no deductible is applied to hospital charges incorporates essentially all of the advantages of the "pure" approach without appreciably increasing the cost of the plan.

E. *"Modified" Comprehensive Plans.* The following approaches entail certain compromises which have or could be used to ease the change from the traditional basic plan approach to the comprehensive approach utilizing coinsurance and deductibles:

(E-1) *Alternate 1.* This approach eliminates the deductible for hospital charges and pays 100 percent of such charges up to a certain limit; otherwise it is the same as the "pure" approach.

(E-2) *Alternate 2.* This approach eliminates the deductible for both hospital and surgical (inhospital) and pays 100 percent of such charges up to a certain limit.

(E-3) *Alternate 3.* In this approach the deductible is applied to all expenses incurred. The plan then pays 100 percent of hospital charges in excess of the deductible up to a certain limit. Variations of this approach could include a "100 percent zone" schedule for surgery and/or a "100 percent zone" for out-of-hospital medical expenses.

(E-4) *Alternate 4.* This approach was first used by General Electric and now has been adopted by a small number of other companies. An "across the board" deductible is applied to all types of expenses incurred and an additional deductible applied to medical expenses other than hospital, surgical, and diagnostic X ray. The plan pays, in excess of the deductible, 100 percent of hospital and surgical expenses up to certain limits.

The Blue Cross Association provides a useful summary of the major benefits offered by its member plans, broken down according to what is available in the "most widely held group certificates" and the "most comprehensive group certificates." Table 28–2 shows this information for 1971. In addition to the benefits shown in the table, a number of plans offer others, including the following: blood and plasma, transfusion service, coverage in intensive care units, student coverage, private duty nursing, prosthetic appliances and durable equipment, home care, organ transplants, outpatient and out-of-hospital diagnostic, outpatient psychiatric, and kidney dialysis. Extended, major medical, or master medical coverage

TABLE 28–2.   Blue Cross Benefits in 1971 (number of plans providing stated benefits under two categories of group certificates)*

Type of Benefit	Most Widely Held Group Certificate	Most Comprehensive Group Certificates
Seventy or more hospital days	67	75
X-ray examinations (other than inhospital diagnostic or outpatient accident or surgery)	64	66
Laboratory services (other than inhospital diagnostic or outpatient accident or surgery)	73	73
Alcoholism in general hospitals: regular benefits	28	32
Limited days of benefits only	28	27
Maternity (normal delivery)	75	75
Coverage of inhospital drugs (full coverage)	72	74
Nervous/mental conditions	72	72
Coverage of drug addiction	54	57
Anesthesia coverage	60	71
Tuberculosis in general hospitals	61	65
Radiation therapy	29	34
Physical therapy (full coverage)	58	72
Oxygen therapy	62	75

° This tabular presentation is illustrative—it does not fully describe all the variations which exist, nor does it list all the types of benefit available.
Source: Blue Cross Association, January, 1972.

is offered by 55 U.S. plans, and 13 have a dread disease endorsement covering from 9 to 11 illnesses.

Table 28–3 shows a listing of the basic benefits required under the Blue Shield comprehensive contract which is now a membership standard. They are provided on the basis of usual, customary, and reasonable charges, defined as follows:

Usual.   The most consistent charge by an individual physician or provider of service to patients for a given service.

Customary.   A fee is customary when it is within the range of usual charges for a given service billed by most physicians or providers of service with similar training and experience within a given area.

Reasonable.   When it meets the usual and customary criteria, or it may be reasonable if in the opinion of an appropriate medical review committee it merits special consideration based on complexity of treatment of the particular case.

The above definitions provide for flexibility based on locality, skill and complexity, but Blue Shield makes the determination. This may help control costs.

A brief example of insurance company comprehensive group medical expense coverage is exhibited in Table 28–4. Also, refer again to Figure 28–1 (D) and (E). With several hundred companies in the market, so many variations exist that it is dangerous to characterize any single example as "typical," although many similarities exist. It would be common, for example, to have an internal limit with reference to hospital room and

TABLE 28–3. Types of Benefits Provided under Blue Shield Comprehensive Contract

1.	Surgical service: Assistant surgeon Human organ transplants.	°11.	Out-of-hospital diagnostic X-ray, laboratory and pathological services.
2.	Anesthesia service.	12.	Physical therapy.
3.	Radiation therapy services.	°13.	Home, office, and outpatient visits.
4.	Diagnostic X-ray.	14.	Newborn care.
5.	Laboratory and pathology.	°15.	Annual physical examination.
°6.	Inhospital medical care (excluding surgery and maternity).	16.	Psychiatric care.
		17.	Inhalation therapy.
°7.	Inhospital medical care (TB, mental, drug addiction, alcoholism).	°18.	Ambulance service.
		°19.	Prosthetic appliances and orthopedic braces.
°8.	Maternity care.	°20.	Rental or purchase of durable medical equipment.
°9.	Outpatient emergency care.		
°10.	Consultations.		

° These benefits all provide for some degree of flexibility in the amount of coverage provided or allow various options and/or exclusions.

Source: National Association of Blue Shield Plans, June 8, 1971.

TABLE 28–4. Illustrative Group Comprehensive Medical Expense Insurance Plan (brief description of plan)

Benefits:

A. Amount: After an initial calendar year deductible of $50, the company shall pay an amount of benefits equal to:
   1. With respect to charges made by a hospital for a period of confinement
      a) with respect to the first $1,000
         (i) 100 percent of covered charges, excluding charges for private room and board
         (ii) 80 percent of covered charges for private room and board;
      b) with respect to all other covered charges during such confinement: 80 percent.
   2. With respect to all other covered charges: 80 percent.
   Subject to an overall maximum amount of benefit per insured person of $15,000.
B. Reinstatement: In the amount of not more than $1,000 is automatic without evidence of insurability on any January 1; reinstatement of the full maximum benefit is possible upon submission of evidence of insurability.

Covered Charges:

A. Charges by a legally constituted and operated hospital for room and board and other services.
B. Charges made for diagnosis, treatment, and surgery by a physician legally licensed to practice medicine and surgery.
C. Charges made by a registered nurse for private duty nursing service.
D. Charges for the following: local ambulance service, equipment, medication, appliances, X-ray services, laboratory tests, the use of radium and radioactive isotopes, oxygen, iron lung, physiotherapy.
E. Charges made by a Doctor of Dental Surgery for the performance of oral surgery consisting of cutting procedures for the treatment of diseases or injury of the jaw or extraction of impacted teeth, provided that such oral surgery is performed during a period of hospital confinement.
   In no event will payment be made for charges in excess of the regular and customary charges for the services, supplies and treatment furnished.

board charges. In some cases, surgical schedules may be included, often based on a relative value approach. Special provisions are almost always available for maternity benefits and the complications of pregnancy. Riders broadening the dental coverage or extending benefits for confinement in extended care facilities or for home health care are becoming more common. Varying combinations of deductibles and coinsurance provisions are also common.

Critics and others who are unfamiliar with insurance contract language regularly fail to recognize how broad much of this coverage has become. The insuring clauses often are virtually all encompassing, and in the absence of specific exclusions, unnamed services, supplies, and treatments often are covered.

PROSPECTIVE FUTURE DEVELOPMENTS

Throughout the history of group medical expense insurance many challenges and problems have been faced and policies have been developed to deal with them. A complete enumeration of these issues would serve no useful purpose, but briefly tracing the history of three of the most persistent problem areas may be instructive as to future developments. These areas deal with the persons covered, the breadth and extent of coverage, and costs. Clearly, there is considerable overlap.

Persons Covered

The early efforts in the area of group medical expense insurance were directed almost solely toward the provision of protection for members of the active labor force, with attention focused especially on the employees of a single employer. Through successive developments, needs were recognized and techniques developed to cover dependents and to offer group insurance to smaller and more diverse groups. Great pressure developed during the 1950s and 1960s to cover the elderly. Though considerable progress was made in a relatively short time, the efforts of the private sector were belated and ultimately were deemed inadequate. The resulting Medicare legislation was enacted in 1965 and implemented in 1966.

By then the challenge to the insurance industry was clear: Find a way to provide essentially universal protection for those under age 65 or face the development of additional government-run or government-mandated programs. By the start of the 1970s the portion of the under 65 population with some medical expense insurance was approaching 90 percent, but the existence of remaining uninsured pockets—especially among the poor and in rural areas—continued to defy solution.

Breadth and Extent of Coverage

Much of the early emphasis of group medical expense insurance was directed toward protecting the solvency of hospitals and, later, reducing the "bad debt" experience of physicians. With the then existent level of medical technology, the only real concern was with protection for institutionalized care. This also reflected the belief that only by relying on the institutional controls concomitant with actual hospitalization could medical expense insurance be properly and safely underwritten.

With the startling advances in medical technology which have taken place over the past several decades, it has become possible through drug therapy and sophisticated outpatient procedures to deal with many conditions which formerly required hospitalization. Thus, pressures emerged which called for the broadening of coverage to encompass a much wider range of benefits. Again, the lesson of Medicare was clear: Merely providing some protection for a large percentage of the population is not enough. That coverage must be sufficiently comprehensive to furnish meaningful protection for a wide range of services and conditions over fairly large periods of time and/or dollar amounts. Insurers responded quickly by expanding even further the scope of benefits offered. This has been particularly true in the group insurance field.

Costs

The technical availability of broad benefits is rather meaningless unless the cost of those benefits is kept low enough to make them practically available. Cost concerns have been with medical expense insurers ever since the coverage was first offered, but, beginning in the 1950s and especially since the mid-1960s, the prices of health care services have been accelerating at a pace much above that of the overall consumer price index. Again, the Medicare experience emphasizes that if it is felt that people cannot afford to purchase available health insurance benefits, the government will step in and use the tax mechanism to finance the benefits. In light of this, it is perhaps ironic that Medicare itself is thought to be a major factor in the inordinate price increases of the past few years.

Response to the cost problem over the years has taken many forms, encompassing direct contracts with providers, fee schedules, relative value schedules, coinsurance and deductible clauses, promotion of peer and utilization review committees, coordination of benefits provisions, preadmission testing, prospective rate review, and other techniques. Also, costs of administering the insurance itself have been reduced—especially in the group insurance field—by refining underwriting and claims procedures, introducing electronic data processing, direct claim procedures, and so on.

Nevertheless, costs continue to spiral, and it is increasingly evident that insurers alone can do little to alter the trend. It is, after all, the basic prices of the services themselves, as well as utilization rates, that really determine the total cost of care. Many now feel that only a restructuring of the medical care system itself—both the organization and delivery of services—can do the job. Insurers can play a key role, of course, in such a restructuring if it is to come.

Cooperation

At the present time, Congress is flooded with a spate of proposals for some kind of national health insurance plan. The Nixon administration has submitted the "National Health Insurance Partnership Act of 1971," and private insurance companies have developed a "Healthcare" proposal.

Both of these bills, as well as several others, call for a "cooperative federalism" which involves extensive cooperation between government and the private sector. The emphasis in most of these proposals is strongly on the group insurance technique as the vehicle for dealing with the problems. Government would be responsible primarily for setting standards of coverage and providing, under certain circumstances, financial support. Industry would be responsible for handling the actual insurance functions. As a corollary to the financing mechanism, nearly all major proposals provide strong incentives for changing the health care system.

While medical expense insurance, particularly the group segment, has had many notable achievements in its relatively brief history, its future, at least in its present form, is uncertain. With most experts now predicting the passage of some form of national health insurance legislation within the next one to five years, the challenge is clear. Unless the major problems which have been identified are satisfactorily solved, private health insurance as we know it today will be changed drastically. The only alternatives to the successful implementation of "cooperative federalism" in this field seem to be either a totally government-financed health program or a fully socialized system of medical care. In either case, private health insurance could only survive as a relatively small shadow of its present self, relegated to an administrative role or a role of providing nothing more than elective supplementary coverage to ever-expanding government benefits.

The resiliency of private insurance has often been tested in the past, but never more severely than today. The future of the entire health insurance industry virtually is hanging in the balance, with many of the critical variables beyond its immediate control. With a combination of strong, imaginative leadership and a large measure of good fortune, the future may still be bright.

SELECTED REFERENCES

Blue Cross and Blue Shield Fact Book. Chicago, Ill.: Blue Cross Association and National Association of Blue Shield Plans. Published annually.

Dickerson, O. D. *Health Insurance.* 3d ed. Homewood, Ill.: Richard D. Irwin, Inc., 1968.

Eilers, R. D. *Regulation of Blue Cross and Blue Shield Plans.* Homewood, Ill.: Richard D. Irwin, Inc., 1963.

Eilers, R. D., and Crowe, R. M. (eds.). *Group Insurance Handbook.* Homewood, Ill.: Richard D. Irwin, Inc., 1965.

Follmann, J. F., Jr. *Medical Care and Health Insurance.* Homewood, Ill.: Richard D. Irwin, Inc., 1963.

Hedinger, F. R. "The Social Role of Blue Cross," *Inquiry,* Vol. 5, No. 16.2 (June 1968), p. 3.

Myers, Robert J. *Medicare.* Homewood, Ill.: Richard D. Irwin, Inc., 1970.

Somers, Herman M., and Somers, Anne R. *Doctors, Patients, and Health Insurance.* Washington, D.C.: The Brookings Institution, 1961.

————. *Medicare and the Hospitals: Issues and Prospects.* Washington, D.C.: The Brookings Institution, 1967.

Source Book of Health Insurance Data. New York: Health Insurance Institute. Published annually.

29

Group Underwriting and Reinsurance

By GORDON W. THOMAS

THE MOST SIGNIFICANT CHARACTERISTIC of group insurance underwriting is that typically there is no evaluation of the insurability of individual lives. If a large group of persons is insured without any opportunity for individuals within the group to select against the insurer, their loss experience will be predictable and will approximate the experience of similar groups not insured. Since few groups are large enough to provide wholly predictable experience on their own, group insurers seek to insure enough groups so that the accumulated lives will provide predictability. The process by which they select and rate these groups is called "underwriting" or "risk selection."

GROUP UNDERWRITING

Group underwriting involves appraising a risk, deciding the conditions of its acceptability, and establishing a rating basis. The underwriting takes place both initially when the case is considered for insurance and subsequently upon renewal, usually annually. Statutory and nonstatutory factors are involved.

Statutory Requirements

An important consideration in the underwriting of a group risk is its conformance with the statutes and the interpretive regulations of the various states. In states where there are such laws, they usually establish the minimum number of individuals necessary to constitute a group, the eligibility of insureds, and the types of groups which are permissible. They sometimes are concerned with policy provisions, minimum rates, maximum amounts of coverage, and other procedural requirements intended to assure the soundness and fairness of group insurance plans. Although there is considerable variation from state to state in the application of these requirements, most have the practical effect of imposing underwriting considerations which a prudent insurer normally would consider if they were not otherwise present.

Insurance Incidental to the Group. The group to be insured must be bound together by a common relationship where there are strong interests other than that of obtaining insurance. Usually the state law will list the types of groups permitted, such as employer-employee, union-member, debtor-creditor, trade association, and the like. In general, groups formed primarily for the purpose of obtaining insurance are not eligible groups within existing statutes.

Minimum Number. The most common number of persons required by statute for group life and health insurance is ten. Often there is a lower minimum or no minimum for group health. Some states have no statutory requirement regarding size.

Percentage of Enrollment. In order for the insurance company to obtain a proper spread of risk, there must be a high percentage of enrollment. The standard legal requirements normally call for an enrollment of at least 75 percent of those eligible for the plan if a contributory plan, and 100 percent if noncontributory. Practical underwriting considerations would require similar enrollment percentages, and in instances where only a small number of individuals are eligible on a contributory basis, an even higher percentage might be required.

Nondiscriminatory Classifications. The classes of employees to be insured must be established in a nondiscriminatory fashion usually determined by conditions pertaining to employment (i.e., length of service, earnings, and job functions), membership, debtor relationship, or equivalent basis depending upon the type of group to be insured. Besides being a legal requirement, good underwriting judgment would also require nondiscriminatory classification of eligible individuals to avoid possible antiselection against the plan.

Amounts Precluding Selection. To protect against possible adverse selection by individuals against the plan, statutory regulations and sound underwriting procedure require that amounts of insurance be determined by a plan which precludes such selection. Typically, the amount of insurance is related to the individual's earnings, job classification, length of service, or age. The insured person may not select his own individual amount of insurance.

Maximum Amounts. Although a majority of states place no limitation upon the maximum amount of group life insurance that may be issued, the other states have some form of limitation. The most common limitation provides that the amount of group term life insurance may not exceed $20,000 unless 150 percent of the employee's annual compensation exceeds $20,000, in which event the maximum amount shall not exceed $40,000 or 150 percent of his annual compensation, whichever is less.

Nonstatutory Underwriting Factors: Characteristics of Acceptable Groups

In addition to statutory underwriting requirements there are a number of additional underwriting considerations and practices that are reviewed by the underwriter prior to both acceptance of the risk and determination of rates to be applied.

Administrative Control and Cooperation. The success of the group insurance plan depends heavily upon the cooperation of the group policyholder and his willingness and ability to provide administrative assistance and control. Included in the range of administrative activities assumed by the policyholder are promotion and enrollment of the plan, collection of individual contributions, and record keeping. In many instances the policyholder is also responsible for self-billing of premium, certification of eligibility of the insured individual, and claim administration. The degree of involvement varies, but the essential ingredient of cooperation and assistance is needed to develop the efficiencies and low expenses associated with successful group plans. Poor administrative practices on the part of the policyholder or lax claim and personnel procedures can adversely affect the financial experience of the group.

Policyholder Sharing of Cost. A successful group plan requires involvement of the policyholder not only in the administration of the plan but also in its cost. Without a significant contribution from the group policyholder, the cost to the individual insured might be beyond the financial means of many, and most plans undoubtedly would suffer from poor enrollment and possible adverse financial experience. Because of the direct correlation between age and the cost of group life insurance, this factor actually has been incorporated into the NAIC group life model bill. However, it is not a requirement under group health regulation.

High Expectation of Persistency. Although most group plans are reunderwritten each year, the cost of underwriting a new plan is highest in its initial year with the result that some of these costs are amortized over more than one year. In addition, there is the likelihood of adverse experience in any one year which may be recovered in subsequent years as well as being provided for prospectively through reserves. Therefore, when reviewing a new risk, the underwriter looks for a group that shows permanency and one where there is a high expectation of persistency so that the insurer will not be abandoned with a financial loss.

Flow of Persons through Group. Neither a static group nor a highly volatile group is desirable. There must be new entrants into the plan with a normal or average amount of turnover of insured individuals to maintain the health of the plan itself. Either extreme of too high or low a flow can lead to increased claim costs. It is sometimes possible to control flow within a group by tightening the eligibility provisions.

Size of Group. The extent of fluctuation in experience tends to decrease as the number of employees increases. For smaller groups, the underwriter is more likely to use manual rate structures, while for larger groups, where experience is more predictable, he is more willing to rely on prior experience as an indicator of the appropriate rate structure. Also, as a case increases in size, its expenses normally decrease as a percentage of total premiums.

Composition of Group. Age, sex, and income are influencing factors in the mortality and morbidity experience of a group. As one might expect, mortality is higher for older age groups; but it is also higher for males than for females, and the newer mortality tables reflect expected variations. The number and proportion of females have an effect upon the expected frequency and duration of disability inasmuch as their morbidity factor is higher than males. Income level also can be an important factor in influencing the cost of medical services, although its significance may be fading.

Industry. The type of industry, the nature of working conditions and the health hazards associated with the industry may lead to increased mortality of the group through either normal or accidental means and to a higher incidence and increased duration of nonoccupational disability. The additional risk inherent in such endeavors as mining, quarrying, cement and gypsum manufacturing, logging, tanneries, foundries, laundries, taxi companies, and others of a similar nature can affect experience under all forms of group coverage and must be considered in establishing rates.

Environment and Geographic Area. The location and surroundings of the individuals making up the group can affect the risk. The working and living conditions and the availability of adequate health care in certain inner city or rural areas can give rise to higher than normal rates of disability or mortality within the group. Charges for various medical services and supplies will vary by geographic area and should be considered in establishing rates for medical insurance coverages.

Economic Conditions. The nature of the economy and its likely impact upon the stability of the group to be underwritten is a factor to be evaluated. Reductions in the number of insured individuals because of layoff or termination, inability of the employer to pay required premiums, or other instability resulting from economic conditions should be anticipated in determining acceptability of the group, the premium structure, and other necessary protection if the group is accepted.

Transferred Business. When insurance coverage is transferred from another carrier, the underwriter must pay particular attention to the claims experience with the prior carrier. Often it will give him a more reliable basis for estimating future claims—especially for larger groups. Depending upon the size of the group and the underwriting practices of the insuring carrier, the underwriter will want to know the prior carrier's benefit and rate structure, the premium and claim history during the past two or three years, the nature of any rate increase being requested, and the persistency history of prior carriers. Acceptance of the risk will depend upon expected persistency of the group and the ability to establish an adequate rating structure.

Plan Design

Eligibility. The eligibility requirements of a group insurance plan will vary to some extent by the type of group insured. For employer plans—the most common type—the standard requirements restrict participation in the plan to permanent, full-time employees (and their dependents, if covered) who have been continuously employed over a predetermined probationary period. The length of the period will vary and will usually range from one month to three months. If turnover is high, it may be desirable to establish a probationary period sufficient to screen out the transient employees. Proper eligibility provisions will protect the plan against adverse selection by either the group policyholder or the individual participant. Individuals need not participate under a contributory plan, but those eligible are normally given a period of 31 days after their eligibility date in which to apply. Persons who do not apply within the eligibility period, but do so at a subsequent date, typically are required to furnish evidence of individual insurability at their own expense. One exception to this rule would be during "nonmedical campaigns" which are run periodically to encourage participation. During these campaigns all persons who have passed the probationary period may enroll without proving insurability.

Actively at Work. In order to be eligible for participation in the plan, the employee usually must be actively at work on the effective date of his coverage, and his eligible dependents must be performing their normal functions, i.e., performing the duties of a housewife, attending school, and the like. This provides some assurance of the health of the individuals insured. The actively-at-work requirement may be waived initially in some situations, usually involving larger groups where the underwriter has some assurance that the rating structure established will be adequate to cover the increased mortality and morbidity that can be expected.

Benefit Levels. In order for a plan to be underwritten successfully, it must include a realistic schedule of benefits in relation to the nature and type of group to be insured. Benefit levels should not be excessively high so as to be uninsurable or encourage unnecessary overutilization, nor should they be unreasonably low resulting in poor participation. The structuring of relative benefit levels among the classes within an individual group is important for the same reasons.

Contract Provisions. An important aspect of program design is the inclusion of sound contract provisions. For example, the inclusion of a coordination-of-benefits provision may reduce expected claim costs under health insurance programs by avoiding unnecessary duplication of benefit payments. Exclusion of preexisting conditions under certain types of coverage may protect against antiselection. Provisions covering termination of coverage in the event of layoff, leave of absence, strike, or illness can have a material effect upon the experience of the plan and should be carefully considered by the underwriter. Frequently, when plans are transferred from one carrier to another, the underwriter is asked to provide continuity of coverage. Of necessity, he should review the previous carrier's contract to know the effect of their extended benefit provisions on expected claim payout under the plan he will underwrite, and also to avoid unreasonable contract or benefit provisions which the previous carrier may have included inadvisably under its contract. Considerable additional unexpected liability can result from a failure to review carefully the benefit provisions of the prior carrier.

Underwriting Variations by Type of Policyholder

For the most part, the basic underwriting considerations that have already been reviewed would apply to the standard employer group. Additional considerations are called for in less standard situations such as seasonal employee groups, public employee groups, groups with retired employees, small groups, union groups, multiple employer groups, and professional association groups.

Seasonal Employees. Groups with seasonal employment such as vacation resorts, canneries, contractors, and race tracks generally do not offer the continuous employment necessary to assure stability. Often the administration is complex and costly. Extreme care must be exercised in underwriting any type of disability income or medical expense insurance programs for groups of this type.

Public Employee Groups. Underwriting groups of individuals employed by a government or political subdivision presents unique considerations. Before such an entity can purchase group insurance for its employees, there must be enabling legislation passed by the state legislature. The underwriter must then verify that the governmental unit has the legal right to use its funds to purchase group insurance under the terms of the policy, make salary deductions and contract for the policy. Higher ages and low participation may lead to adverse experience. Insuring and rating problems associated with policemen, firemen, and hospital employees may be significant. Persistency of the group is also a major concern, as the policyholder often must put the program out to bid annually or whenever a change in rates is requested. The group often is then required by law to accept the low bid. Further, a change in political parties may bring about a change in insurers.

Groups Including Retired Employees. Continuation of insurance on retired lives can be expected to cause a substantial increase in the cost of a group insurance program. This increased cost may not be apparent initially, but as the number of retirees grows in proportion to the actively employed group, and as the ages of the retirees increase, costs will tend to rise sharply over a period of years.

Most plans which continue group life insurance benefits on retired employees usually will specify a reduction in the amount provided after retirement. Usually the amount is a percentage of the amount in force immediately prior to retirement, but it can be a uniform amount for all retired persons.

Because of the introduction of Medicare benefits for retired persons age 65 and over, the need to continue medical benefits under the group plan is somewhat limited. Most plans either terminate the group medical expense benefits or substitute a coverage that coordinates and integrates the benefits with those provided under Medicare.

Small Groups. Special plans have been devised for small groups such as 3–24 or 10–49 lives. These plans sometimes are standardized packages of life, disability income, and medical expense insurance, and frequently are not marketed or underwritten in the normal fashion. Policy forms and administrative procedures usually are streamlined to minimize expenses, with little or no deviation from the standard package permitted. Small substandard groups known to present special problems (such as taxi companies) are often declined. Inspection reports are commonly used to verify the legitimacy of the group insured and employment status. Evidence of insurability may be required on groups which have a low number of employees, usually less than 10 or 15, or which request relatively high amounts of group life or long-term disability insurance. In some instances, short-form health questionnaires or even medical examinations may be required. Rejection of the individual applicant or the entire group case may result from such a review. Normally, at least 85 percent of the eligible group must participate if fewer than 15 lives are eligible, otherwise the standard 75 percent usually will apply.

Taft-Hartley Trusts. The Labor Management Relations Act of 1947 (Taft-Hartley Act) applies where employees are engaged in activities which affect interstate or foreign commerce and requires the establishment of a trust fund which must be administered jointly with equal representation by union and management trustees. Payments are made by employers as a result of collective bargaining solely for the purpose of providing welfare benefits to employees who are union members and their families. Such funds typically are established in those industries or trades where it is common for the union member to move from one employer to another such as, for example, building trades, hotels and restaurants, and trucking. In addition to observing the general underwriting principles which apply to most groups, the underwriter is concerned particularly with the stability of the group, the adequacy of its financing and administration of the program. Copies of the bargaining agreement, trust instrument, constitution and bylaws of the union and any authorizing resolutions pertaining to the plan should be reviewed. The method of contribution and premium payment must be established with assurance as to the adequacy of available funds to pay premiums when due.

Careful attention must be paid to eligibility. Eligibility typically is based upon a minimum number of hours worked during a prior period, and it is possible that the member will not be actively at work on the effective date of his insurance or his coverage will continue for an extended period beyond his termination from employment. For example, a fund might require that a member work a minimum of 300 hours in the prior quarter to qualify for coverage during the current quarter. It is also necessary for the underwriter to be particularly careful of the eligibility provisions to assure premium adequacy. Premium contributions for each hour worked by both eligible and noneligible members should be sufficient to cover members who have satisfied eligibility requirements. In addition, these contributions build up reserves (1) to meet unusual contingencies such as heavy layoffs, (2) to provide for any increases in premium payments because of poor experience which may be needed before an increase in contributions can be renegotiated with employers, and (3) to provide for the necessary costs of plan administration.

Usually the underwriter will require a minimum of at least 100 eligible members, if not more, before he will accept a Taft-Hartley Trust. Also, he will need some assurance that the trust, through its own facilities or through use of a third-party administrator, will be able properly to administer the plan. Because any request for increased premiums may result in the plan being put up for bids by other insurers, the underwriter will often require establishment of a claim fluctuation reserve under the policy to protect the company from being left with a deficit at the end of the policy year or in the event of policy termination.

Union Groups. There are a number of instances where a union will make arrangements to insure its members without any employer participation. Usually insurance costs are paid from contributions by the union member with limited participation by the union from its treasury. Union groups must be given careful scrutiny as to probable stability. Renewal premium increases are usually difficult to negotiate because each individual member must be sold the increase if adequate participation is to be maintained. Union plans should make provision for a reasonable waiting period and mandatory participation of eligible members should be a condition of the plan. Care should be exercised that there is an influx of new members and there is proper control over insurance on inactive members. Because of the difficulty of properly underwriting union groups, coverage frequently is limited to life insurance only.

Trade Associations. Group insurance may be written legally in all states for employees of employers who are members of a trade association. The general underwriting principles applicable to employee-employer groups apply to trade association underwriting but additional conditions are necessary to keep the better groups from being lured away into their own employer plans. The underwriter also wants to be assured that the association—which can be national, state, regional or local in scope—is a strong, stable, closely knit organization whose leaders are willing to promote strongly the success of the group program. It is important to review the trust agreements involved and to make certain that the laws of the state in which the policy is to be issued are followed. If the group is a national association, the underwriter must be concerned with the special legal requirements of such states as Ohio, Texas, New Jersey, and Wisconsin. For example, separate trusts must be established in Ohio and Texas if members in those states are to be covered.

It is very important that the trade association determine the interest of its members in the group insurance program through use of a carefully drawn survey questionnaire or in some other manner. Further, steps to secure and maintain an adequate enrollment for an ongoing proper spread of risk is vital. Normally, interest in participation will be strongest among smaller employer members where the possibility of adverse selection is greatest. Care must be exercised to minimize selection through proper design of the plans to be offered. The employer should make a substantial contribution toward the cost for his employees. The plan should establish satisfactory eligibility requirements, and after the initial enrollment period, it should limit new entry dates only to specified periods. A minimum initial enrollment usually will require at least 100 insured employees or 10 percent of the total employees eligible, whichever is greater, with an enrollment of a substantially higher number, perhaps 500 or more, by the first policy anniversary. Premium rates should be lower than individual members could obtain independently in order to make the plan attractive and assure participation. Typically, the underwriter will require that life insurance be included in the plan to provide stability, and in some instances, the nature of the association will preclude disability income or medical expense coverages. The association should be strong financially with central facilities to assure proper promotion and administration of the plan, collection of premiums from members and subsequent payment to the insurance company.

Multiple-Employer Trusts. Of recent significance has been the strong growth of multiple-employer trusts under state laws permitting two or more employers in the same industry to establish a trust. These plans, which may be established within broad industry classifications such as manufacturing, transportation, wholesale and retail trade, and construction, generally do not have the strong central cohesiveness of trade association groups and often are administered by third-party administrators not connected with the industry itself. Employers are solicited by persons connected with the insurer or the administrator and they are usually compensated through payment of commissions or fees.

Because of the nature of these plans, the underwriter must be concerned particularly with the soundness and the cost of plan administration, the financial stability of the program, and possible adverse selection. The underwriting rules applicable to small employer-employee groups must be observed with exclusion of noneligible employers and use of evidence of insurability or medical requirements similar to small group requirements.

Professional Associations. Typically, a professional association is formed by a group of individuals bound together by a common interest for purposes other than obtaining insurance. To be eligible for insurance, an association normally must have been in existence for some number of years. Doctors, lawyers, accountants, engineers, and others who comprise professional associations usually are interested in relatively large amounts of life and disability income insurance. It is difficult to obtain a sufficiently high enrollment to provide adequate selection of risks, and the underwriter must take protective measures, usually requiring evidence of insurability with the right to reject applicants in poor health or otherwise limit benefits for impaired lives. Benefit schedules are often graduated on a decreasing basis by age brackets, or if held constant, it is not uncommon for the rate structure to be graduated upward as age increases. Typically, coverage will terminate upon attainment of age 65 in either event. The underwriter must be assured that sound administrative facilities exist for promotion and enrollment of the plan with proper procedures for premium and claim administration since he cannot look to the association for coordination and handling of these activities. Usually, administration of professional associations is handled by a third-party administrator or by the insurance carrier.

UNDERWRITING VARIATIONS BY COVERAGE

Up to this point, the general underwriting principles that apply to most group insurance business and some of the underwriting considerations applicable to special types of groups have been reviewed. It is appropriate here to consider the major coverage areas of life, disability income, and medical expense to point out certain important underwriting practices.

Group Life Insurance

Term Coverage. Yearly renewable term coverage insuring the employee during his period of employment is the most common form of group life insurance. A minimum amount of $1,000–$2,000 usually is required, while the maximum amount, subject to statutory regulations and company practices, must be reasonable in relation to the total volume of life insurance for the entire group. It is desirable to have a reasonably balanced schedule which does not provide a disproportionate amount of the total coverage on a few lives. This is best accomplished under an earnings schedule where benefit amounts may be a multiple of earnings, such as one or two times. In some cases, the number of individuals who will be eligible under each benefit class within the schedule is a significant consideration.

Many states limit the maximum amount of group life insurance on a single life but other states have no limit. Where the maximum amount may be well in excess of $100,000, even under a well-balanced schedule, evidence of insurability often will be required, and higher rate classifications will be applied to the poorer risks. In some instances, the underwriter may require a medical examination or preclude coverage for excess amounts over what would be considered a normal maximum.

Permanent and Paid-Up Life Insurance. Because of the long-range aspects of permanent and paid-up forms of group life insurance and the higher costs of administration, additional underwriting considerations normally are involved. A higher minimum number of eligible employees is required, usually 50 to 100 lives, although some companies will write the coverage with as few as 10 lives. Greater stability, both with respect to persistency and as to employee turnover, is of importance. A longer probationary period before the employee becomes eligible for permanent or paid-up coverage normally is required.

Survivor Income Benefit Insurance. A relatively recent introduction to markets in this country, although quite common in countries elsewhere, is the concept of survivor income benefit insurance (SIBI). A guaranteed monthly income is paid upon the death of the insured employee, usually to a predetermined beneficiary, normally the spouse and/or children, for a guaranteed period of time as long as the beneficiaries satisfy the requirements of an eligible survivor. SIBI plans are written both as a form of group life insurance and as a group reversionary annuity. Many states view SIBI as a reversionary annuity because it involves long pay-out periods and the cessation of benefits if there is no eligible surviving dependent. In these states it is not subject to the statutory limitations on group life insurance amounts or to life insurance premium taxes. The underwriter must be concerned, however, with the total amount of combined coverage for which the employee may be eligible under both his basic group life and SIBI plans. A minimum of 50 to 100 insured employees often is required for this coverage.

Disability Income Plans

Short-Term Disability. In analyzing the short-term disability income risk, the underwriter is concerned particularly with those factors relating to the type of industry or risk, working conditions, characteristics of the work force, environmental conditions, seasonal or part-time elements, and the probability of layoff. All of these factors bear upon the likelihood of absenteeism and expected morbidity experience of the risk.

If satisfied with the acceptability of the risk, the underwriter then can focus his attention on plan design and those elements which influence claim frequency and duration. Two of the more important considerations are (1) eligibility, and (2) relationship of benefits to earnings. A soundly conceived eligibility provision can minimize turnover and exclude part-time or seasonal employees, assuring coverage for those employees deemed to be relatively permanent. A plan with a benefit that bears a high percentage relationship to earnings, usually 70 percent or higher, may provide a benefit which is too close to take-home pay. It could serve to encourage employees to feign or extend disabilities. An additional provision of importance in controlling the frequency of claims is the waiting period for commencement of benefits. A plan which has a very short waiting period, usually less than seven days prior to commencement of benefits for illness, typically will encourage a higher frequency of claims, as there may be little to discourage the employee in taking a few days off.

Long-Term Disability. Long-term disability income coverage is characterized by low claim frequency and high potential liability. Claim levels differ with variations in economic factors and the personnel policies of the employer. Due to the still somewhat experimental nature of the coverage, the underwriter lacks a reliable basis for estimating claim cost; therefore, he often is cautious in his approach to long-term disability coverage. He must be more selective in the risks accepted than he is for short-term disability risks. Added safeguards against antiselection by the policyholder are necessary. Many companies limit eligibility to salaried groups only, due to the unfavorable experience for hourly groups during a recessionary period when heavy layoffs or terminations occur.

A longer probationary period, usually six months or more, is required before individual coverage becomes effective. Also, the actively-at-work provision may require that the employee be on the job for an extended number of days without illness or injury before his coverage becomes effective. Preexisting exclusion conditions and evidence of insurability requirements are more common to smaller groups. However, in many cases they are applied effectively on large groups to classes with high amounts of indemnity. Plan design is an extremely important underwriting consideration, and benefits usually commence at the conclusion of short-term disability or salary continuance programs. Shorter duration waiting periods, i.e., three months or less, resulting in higher claim frequencies, are avoided. Waiting periods of six months or longer after commencement of disability assure the legitimacy of the claim and provide a sound underwriting basis. Recent experience has shown that a conservative definition of disability is a desirable factor (i.e., that the insured person be unable to perform any occupation for which he is trained by education or experience, rather than that the individual is unable to perform his own job).

Disability benefits usually are related to a percentage (50–60 percent) of salary after integration with other social security, group, or employer-paid benefits to which the employee may be entitled. Benefits must be integrated into the overall employee insurance and pension program, and proper precautions must be included to discourage employer exploitation of and selection against the plan (i.e., using the plan for early retirement or pension benefits). The great potential liability per individual requires extreme care in setting the maximum benefit amount. The size of the case and economic conditions also will limit the maximum benefits. Some large cases will provide benefits as high as $3,000 per month. Benefits may be payable to age 65 for disability due to illness, and lifetime benefits for disability due to accident. Morbidity statistics now being developed indicate a relatively high incidence of claim frequency with a relatively lower rate of expected recovery during economic downturns.

Medical Expense Plans

A matter of significance in underwriting group medical expense plans has been the ability of the underwriter to anticipate and reflect the rapid escalation of medical care costs which in recent years have been further accelerated by the introduction of Medicare and Medicaid programs. In the face of continuing competitive pressures, it has been most difficult for the underwriter to build sufficient margins into new and renewal rates in order to offset emerging upward trends in claim costs. Particular caution must be exercised by the underwriter when underwriting open-end semiprivate and "reasonable and customary" type medical care plans where the upward cost trend is likely to be reflected immediately in increased benefit payments. Increased costs also are reflected in dollar limit plans, but to a lesser, more predictable extent. Caution also is necessary in underwriting transferred business of any type, as transfers typically result from efforts by the prior carrier to increase rates due to adverse medical experience. To a limited extent, when possible, the underwriter makes use of protective features such as claim fluctuation reserves and retroactive premium adjustment provisions as a hedge against inadequate rating structures. Excessive or unnecessary utilization of medical services and other program abuses have added to the inflation of claim costs.

Protective safeguards such as front-end deductibles, percentage participation or co-payment clauses, and coordination of benefit provisions can serve to reduce the overutilization of benefits. Introduction of benefit provisions which encourage the use of alternative, less expensive but equally adequate, means of providing medical care also can help to dampen the rise in medical costs. The addition of outpatient medical and diagnostic benefits, recognition of preadmission testing programs, and recognition of ambulatory surgical facilities are provisions of this type. The ability to underwrite group medical expense plans successfully requires careful review of all facets of the case likely to affect experience, but in the final analysis, it may in the future be dependent upon the effective control of medical care costs and a restructuring of the basis for providing medical care.

Several new types of medical expense coverage, including plans for dental and vision care, extended care, home care, and prescription drug expense service, have been introduced. There are unique concerns related to benefit design and plan provisions for these coverages. Experience to date has been relatively limited but as additional morbidity experience becomes available, it is expected that underwriting principles and practices will emerge.

Group Creditor Life and Disability Insurance

Group creditor insurance is based upon a creditor-debtor relationship providing protection to individuals who become indebted under a contract or other agreement that requires the debt obligation to be repaid, typically in installments. Group creditor life and disability insurance protects both the creditor and the debtor against financial loss occasioned by death or disability by providing for payment of all or a portion of the outstanding indebtedness or monthly payment due. Although most of the underwriting principles previously outlined have general application to group creditor insurance, the nature of the risk is sufficiently different from employer-employee type business to warrant specialized underwriting attention.

Group creditor life and disability insurance is subject to considerable regulation. Several considerations common to this kind of insurance, and often required by law, are also sound from an underwriting standpoint.

1. The maximum amount of insurance which may be written on any one debtor is usually limited to $5,000 or $10,000 for installment loans and up to $20,000 for mortgage loans where the latter are permitted by statute.
2. The maximum amount of insurance or indemnity paid may not exceed the debtor's indebtedness.
3. The maximum repayment period usually is limited to 5 years for installment loans, and to no more than 25 years for mortgage loans.
4. Often the minimum number of new eligible debtors per year is 100.
5. Where the cost is paid by the creditor, 100 percent of the eligible debtors must be enrolled. Where the debtor pays all or part of the cost, at least 75 percent of the eligible debtors must be enrolled.
6. The maximum rate that may be charged is subject to statutory regulation.
7. Payment of dividends to the creditor policyholder may be limited by statute.

The underwriter will want to review the financial background of the creditor, the type of loan made and credit instrument used. He then must be satisfied there is a favorable loan portfolio and that the classes of indebtedness to be insured are eligible according to the insurer's underwriting standards. For example, certain types of commercial loans, balloon notes, indirect loans, purchase agreements for hearing aids, fuel oil or 30-60-90-day charge accounts may not be eligible for coverage and would be excluded. The presence of significant volumes of home modernization, heavy equipment, trailer, revolving credit, prime collateral, FHA Title I, education, or agricultural loans may produce significantly higher risk characteristics requiring proper safeguards. The total amount of outstanding indebtedness must provide sufficient spread of risk to underwrite properly the risk on a group basis. Typically, on a relatively small volume of total indebtedness, the maximum permitted will be substantially less than allowed by statute. The permissible maximum normally will increase on a graduated basis subject to statutory limitations as the total volume of eligible indebtedness increases. The duration of loan that will be covered for group creditor life or disability insurance also will be related to the total volume of indebtedness to be insured.

Other common underwriting safeguards relate to age restrictions where borrowers age 65 and over, if insured, may be required to submit evidence of insurability. Certain classes of loan may require relatively lower age limits. The underwriter also may recommend an evidence of insurability requirement for loans involving high amounts of coverage for cases where less than 75 percent enrollment is expected, or where a specific class of loans is involved. For example, evidence of insurability may be required on all mortgage and educational loans issued.

For loans involving creditor disability insurance, the plan of insurance to be written is an important consideration. Frequently, the underwriter may require that creditor life coverage must be written in conjunction with the creditor disability insurance. Normally, preexisting conditions, disabilities resulting from pregnancy, and disabilities during which the insured is not under the care of a physician will be excluded.

GROUP REINSURANCE

Reinsurance is a method by which an insurer, by means of a contract, relieves itself of a share of the liability it has assumed contractually, in order to level peak liabilities (risks which the insurer has insured for amounts in excess of the normal amount of liability it will assume on a risk) or to distribute the risk.

Reinsurance falls into one of two forms—"pro rata" or "excess." Under the pro rata form, the reinsurer receives a proportion of the original premium (less commission and other agreed upon expenses) and pays the same proportion of loss. Excess of loss reinsurance, as the name implies, pays only that part of a loss that exceeds a predetermined amount to be retained by the insurer.

The main purposes for which the reinsurance technique is used in group insurance are for protection from catastrophic losses, for sharing of a portion of normal risks of group insuring, and for sharing of business for nonrisk reasons.

Catastrophic Accident Risk

With the high amounts of group life and accidental death and dismemberment coverage being written today, insurers may wish to minimize the loss that would occur if several insured employees are involved in a single accident. Such a situation could arise because of a concentration of risk in connection with one firm (such as several of a company's executives traveling together in the same airplane). Or, it could occur because of a large exposure resulting from an unusual loss situation that affected several firms merely through chance. The combination of high amounts of insurance per individual plus several such individuals being involved in a single accident could have a substantial adverse effect on a company's current operating results. Reinsurance can reduce the impact of this event.

Usually group life and accidental death and dismemberment benefits are reinsured together. A typical arrangement might involve reinsurer liability for all or a portion of any loss above a minimum amount when several (e.g., three or more) individuals die in the same accident. The reinsurer may use maximum limits and coinsurance provisions on its share of the risk. The reinsurance agreement (often called a "treaty") ordinarily is of a broad nature that does not involve the reinsurer in any underwriting decisions or specific group cases. This type of reinsurance usually is provided by a carrier that specializes in reinsurance activity rather than being procured from other group insurance carriers.

Sharing Portion of Normal Risk

Companies whose total amount of group insurance business is small, particularly new companies and companies that are entering the group field, may wish to avoid taking the full risk involved in typical group cases. By reinsuring large portions of their group cases, these insurers can build the volume of group business that they control while at the same time diminishing the possibility of unfavorable financial consequences. Without the aid of the reinsurance technique, the strain on a company's surplus because of group claims, personnel costs, administrative expenses, and reserve establishment might be heavy.

This type of reinsurance may be used for all group insurance lines or for only specific lines, such as those that have the greatest experience fluctuation possibilities. Even those insurers with substantial experience in the group field and a sizable group business volume may wish to reinsure certain lines such as long-term disability benefits, or high amounts of life insurance or accidental death and dismemberment coverage. The latter two benefits usually are reinsured above some specific amount (such as $50,000) on any one life.

The usual method of reinsuring medical expense lines is the pro rata technique. Each reinsurer accepts a certain percentage such as 60 or 75 percent of a risk. If 60 percent of a benefit is reinsured, the ceding company pays 60 percent of the gross premium (less a specified percentage for expense allowances, including commissions) to the reinsurer. In return, the reinsurer assumes 60 percent of the claims. Usually, the reinsurer does not require claims settlement details but makes its payment to the ceding company on the basis of the latter's total claims payments each month. However, the reinsurer has the right to ask for details concerning the claims.

Long-term disability coverage is one of the group insurance lines frequently reinsured because of the very high potential liability associated with that type benefit. Normally, the risk is ceded on a quota share basis (e.g., 50–50), or amounts above some maximum monthly indemnity per insured individual, such as $300, are reinsured. This type of reinsurance usually is written by companies that specialize in the reinsurance business.

Sharing Business for Nonrisk Reasons

Group insurance companies also may reinsure a portion of any case for nonrisk reasons, that is, for example, for reasons of business relationships of the policyholder. Reinsuring for purposes of sharing business normally involves carriers operating primarily in the group business rather than in the reinsurance business. As a general rule, the policyholder's desire to apportion his group business among several insurers is the basis for this use of reinsurance.

Another example of this type of reinsurance is that of an American insurer not licensed to do business in Canada negotiating a reciprocal reinsurance agreement with a Canadian insurer not licensed to do business in the United States. In such a case both insurers can protect their domestic business and yet offer coverage and service to subsidiaries in the reciprocal country, such as, for example, a parent corporation domiciled in the United States with a Canadian subsidiary.

The Treaty

The reinsurance agreement, known as a treaty, is made between the ceding and receiving insurers. It may be executed each time a special case is ceded. This would be the case for a situation of sharing business for nonrisk reasons. But more often the treaty is a standing general agreement whose terms govern all the reinsurance transactions between the ceding company and the reinsurer.

There are two basic types of reinsurance treaties that are used in connection with group insurance: (1) automatic quota share reinsurance treaties, which are designed to protect insurers against aggregate losses (on all group cases) in excess of amounts which companies can handle financially or which would cause undesirable variations in surplus; and (2) facultative quota share treaties, which transfer part of the risk on specific group cases.

Automatic quota share treaties provide for the reinsurer to share a fixed percentage of each claim and to receive the same percentage of premium, less an allowance for premium taxes, commissions and expenses. The automatic quota share treaty is used only when the reinsurer has satisfied itself that the issuing company has knowledgeable underwriting personnel who are writing group business within rules known to and accepted by the reinsurer.

Facultative quota share treaties usually provide for the accepting company (the reinsurer) to underwrite and rate the ceding company's risk. The accepting company either accepts the requested reinsurance percentage of the risk (the usual maximum that can be reinsured is 75 percent), based on its underwriting and rate, or declines to reinsure any part of the risk. For all practical purposes, the reinsurer is required to accept the initial underwriting performed and the rates established by the insurer if he wishes to participate in the risk.

Two methods of handling dividends (or retrospective premium adjustments) are used under group reinsurance treaties: the "New York Method" and the "Hartford Method." Under the New York Method, the reinsurer introduces administration and acquisition expense charges made by the ceding company into its own dividend formula in place of similar charges normally made, and adds charges for commissions paid, sales overhead, federal income tax, risk, and profit. These latter charges are not made by the ceding company for the reinsurer's share of the risk. The resulting dividend is then paid to the principal insurer, which adds it to its own dividend—similarly determined—and pays the combined dividend to the policyholder, noting the respective parts.

With the Hartford Method, the reinsurer is charged for a fixed percent of the dividend (e.g., 50 percent) determined by the ceding company as if there were no reinsurance. The Hartford Method binds the reinsurer to the risk and profit charges, sales overhead charges, and federal income tax charges of the principal insurer. In essence, the Hartford Method binds the reinsurer to the retention charges of the ceding company, whereas the New York Method does not.

Reinsurance treaties do not have to be filed with state insurance departments. The treaties are essentially "gentlemen's agreements" which may be terminated on short notice, are renegotiable periodically (e.g., from year to year), and require good faith and fair dealing between the parties.

SELECTED REFERENCES

Archibald, J. C. "Underwriting Group Life Insurance," *Group Insurance Handbook* (eds. Robert D. Eilers and Robert M. Crowe), ch. 10. Homewood, Ill.: Richard D. Irwin, Inc., 1964.

Chandler, Brooks. "Underwriting Group Disability Insurance Coverage," *Group Insurance Handbook* (eds. Robert D. Eilers and Robert M. Crowe), ch. 21. Homewood, Ill.: Richard D. Irwin, Inc., 1964.

Cody, Donald D. "Underwriting Group Medical Expense Coverage," *Group Insurance Handbook* (eds. Robert D. Eilers and Robert M. Crowe), ch. 19. Homewood, Ill.: Richard D. Irwin, Inc., 1964.

Green, Edward A. "Underwriting, Reinsurance and Claim Adjustment—Group Contracts," *Accident and Sickness Insurance* (ed. David McCahan), ch. X. Philadelphia: University of Pennsylvania Press, 1954.

30

Legal Concepts and Taxation

By WILLIAM H. RABEL

Two HIGHLY SIGNIFICANT dimensions of group insurance relate to legal concepts and taxation. The regulatory framework within which group insurance functions has many features common to other forms of insurance but also many distinct characteristics. The very nature of the group master contract and certificate establishes legal and regulatory dimensions different from individual life and health insurance. The taxation features of group insurance from the standpoint of the policyholder and the certificate holder are unique and meaningful.

REGULATION

Regulation of the business of insurance traditionally has been left to the states. For a brief period in 1944 and 1945, this matter was questioned after the Supreme Court reversed a precedent of long standing[1] and held that insurance is commerce.[2] The impact of this decision was to make all insurers who were involved in interstate operations subject to the commerce clause of the U.S. Constitution which expressly provides that interstate commerce may be regulated by the federal government, and which impliedly limits the power of states to tax and regulate interstate commerce. In 1945, however, Congress indicated its belief that state regulation of insurance is in the public interest by passing the McCarran Act. Under the McCarran Act, Congress provided that the federal antitrust statutes are applicable only to boycott, coercion, or intimidation, and, with respect to other antitrust limitations, only to the extent not regulated by the states.

Insurance regulation has among its basic goals: (1) financial soundness of insurers and (2) fairness, equity, and reasonableness in the treat-

---

[1] *Paul* v. *Virginia*, 8 Wall 168 (U.S.) (1868).
[2] *United States* v. *South-Eastern Underwriters Association*, 322 (U.S.) 533 (1944).

ment of consumers. Group insurance regulation can accomplish these goals and still be less stringent than individual insurance regulation for several reasons. One is the level of sophistication of the parties to the group contract. Frequently the group buyer is highly knowledgeable and he may make use of well-qualified specialists.

Another reason is the relative simplicity of group insurance ratemaking. Most group products are based on one-year coverage and the actuarial calculations are not as difficult to follow as those associated with individual products which usually make long-term guarantees. Furthermore, the costs of coverage are more readily apparent to the policyholder—particularly on large cases. A third reason (partly attributable to the foregoing reasons) is that the level of competition is quite high in the group area; competition has proven to be a prime regulator.

A final important reason for less stringent regulation is that flexibility is of great importance for the effective design of group insurance plans. It seems unlikely that group insurance would have achieved its position as a vital force in our security plans today if it had to conform to a set pattern as carefully as do individual products.

State Insurance Departments

Insurance regulation may be carried out by a state's courts, its legislature or its department of insurance.[3] Courts exercise their role primarily by interpreting laws passed by the legislature. Legislatures may enact laws, but are not involved in enforcing them. The most active bodies involved in insurance regulation are the state departments of insurance. Among their duties are (1) making rules and regulations, (2) suggesting laws to the legislatures, (3) licensing insurers and agents, (4) controlling the financial conditions of insurers through examinations and other means, (5) controlling policy forms and rates, and (6) controlling marketing methods.

State insurance departments operate under the direction of a commissioner, director, or superintendent of insurance who may be elected or appointed. All state insurance commissioners are members of the National Association of Insurance Commissioners which meets periodically and maintains standing committees to investigate matters of general interest. This cooperative effort has led to a much higher degree of regulatory uniformity among the states than would otherwise have been possible. Perhaps the most important product of this effort has been the model laws and regulations that the NAIC has adopted and which frequently have become the prototype across the country. Standardization of reporting forms and methods of operation, and cooperation in the examination of insurance companies have saved the insurance business untold millions of dollars which in turn has lowered the cost of insurance to the consumer. Although the NAIC has no control over state courts, legislatures, or insurance commissioners, the quality of its work has been such that its recommendations always receive careful consideration.

---

[3] Traditionally, the life insurance business has done an excellent job of self-regulation, a topic not dealt with in this chapter.

Regulatory Jurisdiction

Group insurance regulation by the states is so heterogeneous that the question of which state law governs a particular contract can be very important. State laws strongly influence the design of group benefits and contractual provisions, and they may even determine whether a group can be underwritten and under what conditions. Furthermore, it is important that a multistate plan be uniformly regulated regardless of the residence of its participants.

A large majority of the states recognize that the law of the state wherein the contract is delivered should govern. However, there may be a question about where delivery actually took place. The Joint Group Insurance Committee of the American Life Convention and the Life Insurance Association of America recommended in 1960 that delivery be construed to take place in the state (1) where the group policyholder is incorporated, or, if the policyholder is a trust, where the trust is created, or, if the policyholder is an association, where the articles of association are settled; (2) where the policyholder's executive or principal office is located; (3) where the greatest number of plan participants is located; and (4) if the policyholder is a trust, where an employer or labor union party to the trust is located. Clearly these conditions could arise in two or more states, thereby raising a question within the rules as to where the situs of the contract would be. Under these circumstances the insurer will choose as the state of delivery the one believed to provide the most flexibility.

Group Life Insurance Regulation

Group term life insurance regulation in most states is based on the National Association of Insurance Commissioners 1956 model bill (although wide variations in acceptance and design of certain provisions exist among the states).[4] Regulation by the State of New York (whose law is based on the NAIC model bill, but differs in several important respects) is of great significance because it attempts to apply some of its rulings on an extraterritorial basis.

Group term life insurance regulation may be divided into four broad areas, namely: (1) the definition of eligible groups; (2) limitations on the amount of coverage available to each insured; (3) premiums, reserves, and dividends; and (4) standard contractual provisions. The first three areas will be covered here, while a separate section will be devoted to contractual provisions.

Various forms of group life insurance are also sold on a permanent basis, as may be survivor income benefit insurance (SIBI). Permanent coverages generally are subject to the same requirements as group term, except for requirements concerning limitations on amount, actuarial aspects of the products, and policy provisions relating to nonforfeiture values. These areas generally conform to the requirements for legal reserve life insurance policies.[5] The extent to which SIBI is subject to group

---

[4] The NAIC group life insurance model bill is found in Appendix K.
[5] See Davis W. Gregg, *Group Life Insurance* (Homewood, Ill.: Richard D. Irwin, Inc., 1962), pp. 117–18, for a discussion of actuarial matters.

term life insurance regulation depends upon whether a particular state treats it as life insurance or a reversionary annuity. Where it is treated like life insurance, term life regulations generally apply except for actuarial matters. Therefore, except for the reservations given above, the following analysis generally applies to all forms of group life insurance.

Eligible Groups. There is little uniformity among the states as to the types of groups which are considered eligible for group life insurance. The NAIC model bill allows employers, unions, multiple-employer trusts, and creditors to establish group plans, but most states recognize other groups as well.[6] The nature of the groups that generally are recognized has been discussed in Chapter 25.

It is important to emphasize that eligible groups must meet certain requirements before group life insurance can actually be written. With the exception of a creditor group, all group life coverages permitted by the NAIC model bill are for the benefit of employed persons or retirees. In other words, only active and retired employees (and their eligible dependents in some states, although not included in the model bill) may be covered. In Colorado, Louisiana, and New York, directors of a corporation may be insured as employees. In most other states having statutory provisions, individuals who are directors may be covered if they also are bona fide employees of the firm. Similar treatment is accorded individual proprietors and partners; they must demonstrate that they are engaged in the conduct of the firm's business.

Another important requirement holds that only group creditor life may be financed wholly by the insured. Under all other coverages, there must be a third party sharing the burden of the premiums. If the insured is required to contribute part of the premium, he has the option of electing out of the plan. The law states that groups using contributory financing cannot be underwritten unless 75 percent of those eligible elect to participate. Noncontributory plans (where the employer pays all premiums) must cover all eligible persons.

Still another type of requirement, dealing with participation, states that eligible groups must contain a minimum number of lives. The number required varies by the type of group covered, but for employer groups the most common number is 10. The expanded use of multiple-employer trusts among small employers has greatly reduced the significance of the requirement of a minimum number of lives pertaining to employer groups.

A final requirement relates to employee-centered coverages and holds that benefits must be based on some plan precluding individual selection. This requirement is not applied to group creditor life because benefits are related to the amount of the debt owed. To the extent that a debtor can select the amount of his debt, selection of benefits within amounts permissible under the law and the contract cannot be put beyond his control.

Benefit Limitations. Although 31 states place no limitation on the amount of group term life insurance that may be issued to an individual,

---

[6] The following states have no statutory definition of eligible groups: Alabama, Connecticut, Minnesota, Mississippi, Missouri, North Dakota, Oregon, Rhode Island, and Tennessee.

the remaining jurisdictions set some kind of limit in employee-centered cases. Only three adhere strictly to the so-called 20/40 rule under which group life insurance on an individual may not exceed $40,000 under any circumstances and may exceed $20,000 only to the extent that 150 percent of the insured's salary exceeds $20,000. It is important to note that benefit limitations have been widely circumvented by selecting a situs with favorable limits or by attaching term riders of individual insurance to the group policy, or by the use of group permanent insurance continuing nonforfeiture rights.

Creditor group life insurance benefits are related to the amount of the debt, and only 16 states place no limit on the amount of insurance that may be issued. Benefits are limited in 3 states to $5,000, in 16 states to $10,000, and in 16 states to amounts ranging from $12,500 to $40,000.

Premiums, Experience Rating, and Reserves. The subjects of premiums, experience rating, and reserves are covered in Chapter 31, so only a brief overview is needed at this point. Three states, including New York, require that the first-year premium on a group term life insurance case be at least as great as the premium calculated according to procedures and assumptions set forth in the state insurance code. New York also limits by regulation the contributions employees may make toward their group life insurance.

Group insurance policyholders may receive dividends or premium adjustments which will reflect the experience of all group cases a company may write, and perhaps the experience of the particular group as well. The extent to which a group's own experience will be reflected in its dividend depends upon the credibility the group has attained, which in turn will vary with the group's size and the length of time the insurance has been with the carrier. New York and 18 other states require that any premium refunds in excess of an employer's contributions be returned to employees or applied to their benefit. Generally, they are used in one of three ways: (1) to reduce further contributions, (2) to increase benefits by amending the policy, or (3) to pay for other coverage (such as health), or to fund other programs.

Group term life insurance policies will develop a policy reserve which is equal to the pro rata cost of the unexpired period of coverage for which premium has been received or is due. Most states require that the reserve valuation be based on the Commissioners Standard Group or Commissioners Standard Ordinary mortality tables and a 3 percent interest rate. However, individual companies generally have some flexibility in choosing an exact method for calculating policy reserves. In addition to policy reserves, life insurance companies maintain reserves for unpaid claims and contingencies.

Group Health Insurance Regulation

The NAIC has not adopted a model health insurance law, but one has been proposed by the Health Insurance Association of America. The HIAA model group accident and sickness bill contains fewer regulatory provisions than the NAIC's model group life insurance bill and, therefore, provides less direction to the states (see Appendix N). Perhaps this is one reason why group health insurance regulation is more heterogeneous (and less stringent in many states) than is group life insurance regulation. Another reason would be, of course, that group health insurance services are much more diverse than group life insurance services.

Unlike group life insurance regulation, group health insurance regulation does not limit benefits available to any individual or regulate first-year premiums except that insurers may not quote less than their filed minimums on group health coverages. However, it defines eligible groups and (as will be discussed in another section) it specifies certain standard policy provisions. The HIAA model bill allows employers, unions, and multiemployer trusts to purchase group health insurance. In addition, any group to which a group life contract may have been issued, or any group deemed eligible by the state insurance commissioner, may purchase it. There is a requirement in the bill that classes of insureds be carefully defined in such a way as to preclude individual selection. Unlike all employee-centered group life plans, group health insurance plans may be financed solely by the contributions of employees.

Well over half of the states have adopted at least a skeletal definition of eligible groups such as the HIAA definition. In the jurisdictions where no regulation has been adopted, an insurer may underwrite any type of group health coverage it deems feasible. Of course, in most states the company is still required to file forms and rates with the insurance department and comply with the general regulations governing insurance company operations.

Other Group Insurance Regulation

Other types of regulation also influence group insurance. At least 33 states have adopted laws regulating both individual and group credit life and health insurance. Several states have adopted the NAIC Code of Ethical Practices with respect to the insuring of the benefits of union and union management welfare and pension funds. Finally, several states have enacted laws calling for disclosure concerning employee benefit plans.

At the federal level, the Fair Credit Reporting Act, the Welfare and Pension Plan Disclosure Act, the Fair Labor Standards Act, and the Civil Rights Act of 1964 all have an impact on group insurance.

MASTER CONTRACT AND CERTIFICATE[7]

As with other life insurance company products, group contracts and riders must be filed with the state in which the contract is to be delivered. It is widespread practice for the states to require the filing of group certificates. These materials are checked to ensure that they substantially conform with a state's standard provisions.

The NAIC model bill has been particularly influential in standardizing group life insurance provisions among the states. However, the HIAA

---

[7] A sample policy is found in Appendix L, and it will be helpful to refer to specific policy provisions as they are discussed in the text. A sample certificate booklet is found in Appendix M.

model group accident and sickness bill offers few guidelines for policy provisions and the scant standardization that exists is primarily the result of other forces. Neither group life nor health regulation is all encompassing, and many features of group contracts and certificates have resulted from industry practices and the desires of contracting parties.

To an ever-increasing extent, practitioners in the group insurance field think of group life and health insurance as a package. This section will be oriented in that way, and it is especially appropriate in view of the many areas of commonality between group life and health insurance contracts. Therefore, it may be presumed that the following discussion refers to both group life and health insurance unless the context indicates otherwise.

Formation, Amendment, and Termination of the Contract

Insuring Agreements. The obligations of the insurer and the contractual relationship between the parties of a group insurance contract are found in the contract's insuring agreements. There the insurer agrees to pay specified benefits to insureds or their beneficiaries upon the occurrence of certain specified contingencies. Exclusions found in the policy may narrow the insurer's obligation, and it may also be modified by endorsements or "riders." As consideration for the insurer's promise, the policyholder-applicant submits the application and the first premium.

One unusual feature of group insurance contracts is that the policy does not insure the policyholder as an entity. Instead, the insured persons are third parties, usually employees, while the policyholder is usually an employer or a trust. In the case of group life, a fourth party, the beneficiary, also enters the picture.

The law is well settled that the insured and his beneficiaries are not parties to the group insurance contract, although they may enforce it according to its terms.[8] Rather, the contract is between the insurer and the policyholder with the latter acting for itself or as an agent for the insureds for purposes of procuring and administering the policy.[9]

State laws generally require that group policies contain a provision stating that the application (and any individual applications submitted by insureds, if required) and the policy constitute the entire contract. The group certificate (or other statement of benefits) which is given to plan participants as evidence of their insurance is not part of the contract. Furthermore, no agent may waive any provision, and no change in the policy shall be valid unless it is signed by an officer of the insurer. Finally, any contractual provision required by law will be read into the policy whether or not it is located there.

---

[8] *Magee* v. *Equitable Life Assurance Society*, 62 N.D. 614, 44 N. W. 518, 85 A.L.R. 1457; *Alsup* v. *Travelers Insurance Co.*, 196 Tenn. 346, 268 S. W. 2d 90; *Rivers* v. *State Capital Life Insurance Co.*, 245 N. C. 461, 96 S. E. 2d 431, 68 A.L.R. 2d 205.

[9] *Boseman* v. *Connecticut General Life Insurance Co.*, 110 A.L.R. 732, 57 S.Ct. 686.

Application and Effective Date of Coverage. When compared with applications for individual insurance, the group application is quite brief. Among the items requested on the typical application will be general information such as the name and address of the policyholder, the legal form that the business takes (proprietorship, partnership, or corporation), and the names of any subsidiaries or affiliates that are to be included under or excluded from the policy. Financing arrangements, in which the applicant indicates the desired premium payment period and whether the plan is contributory or noncontributory, also are provided. Features of the plan are stated, such as eligible persons, the probationary period and date of eligibility, and the general schedule of benefits. Sometimes the application also calls for information about previous group insurance, maximum contributions required of employees, and the agent or broker who will receive commissions under the policy.

Usually included in the application are statements reminding the policyholder that (1) 75 percent of eligible insureds must participate before contributory plans go into effect, (2) the plan must (in certain states) have a minimum number of insureds, and (3) insureds must be actively at work for their coverage to take effect. Upon signing the application and paying the first premium, the applicant is issued a conditional receipt which has the effect of starting coverage on that date if the application is accepted by the company.

The application which is attached to the policy usually is very brief because most of the information included in the preliminary application actually will be incorporated into the body of the policy. Generally, only the name and address of the policyholder and a statement that the group policy is approved and terms accepted are included in the signed application.

Amendment or Termination of the Policy. Policyholders may amend or terminate a policy at any time. Should a policyholder wish to terminate a policy, he may do so by giving the insurer 31 days' advance written notice. If the policy runs past the premium due date, it will be cancelled on the date that written notice is received by the insurer or at the end of the 31-day grace period. The policyholder is liable for premiums on coverage that extends into the grace period. Most policies require that participation by insured lives meet the minimum number and proportion standards called for in the state law or company underwriting requirements. Upon termination of the master policy, the coverage on all insureds ceases.

Even though a policy may be amended or terminated, an insured may not be deprived of rights which have already attached under the policy. Therefore, if the insured has qualified for benefits in some form, he will continue to receive them.

Policyholder's Provisions

Premiums and Participation. Group insurance premiums usually are paid monthly, but they may be paid quarterly, semiannually, or annually. First-year premiums are computed according to rates specified in the policy (and according to law, for companies operating in some states), but the assumptions on which rates are computed usually may be changed at any premium due date after the premium rate in use has been in effect for 12 months. Also, rate changes generally may be made when changes in the plan are made.

Group plans generally provide that policyholders will participate in the favorable mortality, investment, or expense experience of the company, and payments (called dividends by mutual companies and refunds or premium rate adjustments by stock companies) are made to policyholders on each policy anniversary.

Contributions by insureds for term coverage usually are limited to 60 cents per $1,000 per month or some similar figure. Usually the employer receives all dividends, but several states limit the employer to the amount of the employer's contributions; all dividends in excess of policyholder contributions must be used by the policyholder to benefit insureds.

Grace Period.   All group contracts contain a grace period provision under which the policyholder may pay the premium as late as 31 days after it is due without the policy lapsing. Although insurers sustain a loss of interest and incur extra expenses when premium payments are late, no extra charge is made when the privilege is exercised. The policyholder, however, remains liable for the premium on coverage provided during the grace period.

Policyholder Report and Audit.   Both insurers and policyholders are required to maintain certain records. A typical master policy provides that the insurance company shall keep records of essential information relating to each employee's insurance, and that the policyholder periodically shall inform the insurer of changes and additions such as information about new employees becoming insured, changes in amounts of insurance and terminations of coverage. Larger cases may involve more self-administration by the policyholder, in which case the insurer would be given detailed information about the employees covered under the plan at less frequent intervals, typically annually. Monthly summaries for premium purposes would still be submitted. Irrespective of the type of administration involved, an employee will not be denied benefits if the policyholder fails to include his name on the rolls. Conversely, an insured's coverage does not continue because the policyholder fails to remove his name from the rolls after coverage is supposed to cease.

Another requirement generally found in the master policy holds that "the employer's payroll and such other records as have a bearing on insurance shall be open for inspection by the insurance company at any reasonable time." This provision is one of the important ways the insurer protects itself against dishonesty by the minority of firms having unscrupulous management.

Assignment of the Master Policy.   Group insurance plans generally consist of one-year coverage, so most of them do not develop the reserves that are associated with individual contracts. However, a group policy may develop a substantial experience credit in one year which would be lost if the policy did not persist. If a firm were to change ownership or corporate form, the group contract would be terminated because one of the contracting parties no longer existed. A new contract would have to be issued at standard rates, albeit to the same group, and the experience credit would be lost. This dilemma could be resolved if the contract were assigned to the new owner. General legal practice provides that all contracts may be assigned unless their provisions specifically prohibit such action. Some group contracts are silent on the subject, but those that cover it hold that (1) no assignment is binding on the insurer until a written copy is filed in the home office, and (2) the insurance company assumes no responsibility for the validity of any assignment.

Insured's Provisions

Group Certificate. The prevailing view is that the group certificate is merely evidence of insurance rather than a contract between the insurer and the insured or the policyholder and the insured. Group certificates summarize the information in the master contract that relates to the insured and place it in a form that he can easily understand. The face of nearly every group certificate contains a statement to the effect that, "All benefits described herein are governed by and are subject in every respect to the group policy, which alone constitutes the agreement under which payments are made." This statement is usually considered sufficient to inform the insured that he must look to the master contract as the ultimate source of information about his coverage. There are, however, several recent cases which hold that the certificate language controls if different from the master contract.

Many companies are now combining the group certificate with the announcement booklet that is used to inform employees about group insurance plans when they are being installed.

Inception of Coverage. It was noted in the section on regulation that eligible employees are defined in group insurance laws. All eligible employees are not covered automatically, however, and to be covered, group policies usually require that employees comply with one or more of the following requirements.[10]

A. *Actively at Work.* An employee must be actively at work on the date he becomes eligible for his initial coverage or at the time he becomes eligible for any subsequent increases in benefits. This requirement gives the insurer some protection against adverse selection, particularly from small groups where insurance might be purchased specifically for one or more employees who are seriously ill.

B. *Probationary Period.* Employees who join a firm after its group coverage is in effect must satisfy a probationary period, generally from one to three months, before their coverage attaches. The probationary period serves three important purposes. It reduces administrative expenses

---

[10] Dependents must comply with substantially the same requirements. Children generally are not covered after a certain age, typically 18, unless in college and then age 22. A substantial number of states, through legislative enactment, now preclude the termination of insurance for a dependent child who is mentally or physically incapable of earning his own living on the date specified for termination of insurance on account of age, if proof of such incapacity is furnished to the insurer within a specified period, usually 31 days. Upon receipt of such proof, coverage of the child may continue during the continuance of disability and while the policy remains in force, subject to the payment of the appropriate premium.

by excluding new employees until they have proved some minimum attachment (or permanency) to their employment. Second, it seems likely that workers who move from job to job are also poorer risks on the average than those who are more permanent in their attachment to a particular firm. Thus, the probationary period may improve a plan's experience. Finally, the probationary period helps exclude those persons who secretly know that they are ill and join a firm merely for the purpose of obtaining insurance.

The length of the probationary period varies with the nature of the risk, but it rarely exceeds 12 months. As a rule, noncontributory plans employ longer probationary periods than contributory plans because the employer (who pays the entire cost) wishes to allocate his contributions to those employees who seem more permanent.

C. Eligibility Period and Evidence of Insurability. After the probationary period has been satisfied, the employee has 31 days to enroll in the plan. Should he fail to do so, he must submit evidence of insurability if he enrolls at a later date. This provision protects the insurer against the adverse selection that would certainly occur if enrollment without evidence of insurability could take place at any time. Evidence of insurability is also required if an insured drops out of the plan and wishes to reenroll, as well as in the event of a request for reinstatement of the maximum. Further, it may be required if an individual exercises his group insurance conversion privilege and then later wishes to reenter the same group plan while his converted policy remains in force.

In order to maintain high participation in a plan covering a large group, so-called medical waiver campaigns or reenrollment periods are sometimes conducted during which the medical examination and other evidences of insurability are waived. Various conditions usually are established when these campaigns are waged in order to prevent adverse selection against the insurer.

Assignment by the Insured. Until recently it was customary for insurance companies to discourage and even prohibit the assignment of group life insurance by insured employees. Most requests for assignment were motivated by an insured's desire to remove benefits from his estate in order to avoid estate taxes. However, many authorities doubted that all incidents of ownership could be assigned, so the hopes for estate tax benefits were deemed to be ephemeral at best. Furthermore, the insurance companies and employers had a strong desire to see benefits paid to the insured's dependents, and the likelihood of this happening increased if assignment were prohibited. In the face of an increasing number of requests for assignment, and in reaction to tax rulings, the insurance companies have begun to permit and even encourage assignment. Most states have enacted statutes permitting assignment in the absence of a policy provision to the contrary.

Conversion Privilege

A. Group Life Insurance. Insureds under a group life policy may convert their term insurance to an individual policy of permanent insurance under certain well-defined conditions. If an individual terminates his employment or moves into a class of ineligible employees, he is entitled to convert all or part of his group coverage within 31 days without showing evidence of insurability. The converted policy may take any of the forms customarily issued by the insurer at the age and amount applied for, with the exception of term insurance and certain features such as disability income and accidental death and dismemberment.[11] The insured's premium is computed at the insurer's then customary rate applicable to the form of policy, the insured's attained age, and the class of risk into which he falls. Thus, although the insured is not required to show evidence of insurability, he may be classified as substandard for reasons other than health (for example, his job classification).

Master contracts may be terminated by the policyholder or the insurer, or the master contract may continue but with coverage terminated on one or more classes of insureds. Those persons who are affected by these changes may convert their coverage to individual policies under the same general conditions as persons whose employment is terminated. However, additional requirements are imposed which limit the value of the privilege. First, the master contract must have been in force for five years. Some insurers give credit for previous coverage if it was replaced by the current policy. Second, the amount of coverage is limited to the lesser of $2,000 or the amount of insurance coverage terminated less any replacement coverage for which the insured may become eligible within the following 31 days. The purpose of these requirements is to protect the insurer against adverse selection.

It is worth noting that, except in a few states where it is required by law, group creditor life insurance does not contain a conversion privilege.

B. *Group Health Insurance.* The laws of some states, including New York, require that a conversion privilege providing certain minimum benefits be inserted in group health contracts delivered in the state. Benefits under conversion privileges are not uniform, and are frequently limited to basic hospital and surgical coverage. Coverage is not available to retired persons who are eligible for Medicare. Dependent coverage may be converted, but frequently family coverage is not available at conversion and each individual must acquire his own policy. Should the certificate holder die, his dependents may convert their insurance.

Group health insurance may be converted within 31 days, but only if the insured was covered continuously for three months. The premium for the conversion is that which is applicable to the policy form, the age and the class of risk to which the insured belongs. Overinsurance is guarded against in underwriting conversions and the individual policy usually contains a nonduplication of benefits provision.

Continuance of Policy Benefit after Termination of Coverage

A. *Group Life Insurance.* An employee who dies within 31 days after the termination of his coverage will be protected under his group life insurance even though he has not exercised his conversion privilege. The

---

[11] New York requires that the insured be able to purchase a one-year, single-premium term insurance contract before selecting a permanent policy.

amount of protection afforded under the extended death benefit is the maximum amount the insured was eligible to convert.

B. Group Health Insurance. Benefits under a group medical expense policy are extended for as long as one year if the insured was disabled at the time insurance terminated. The insured must remain continuously disabled, or the privilege will lapse. Extended benefits are identical to those under the group policy.[12]

Claim Provisions

Claim Procedures. Group life insurance policies do not require that the company be notified of a claim within any prescribed period. Some group health insurance contracts may require notice within a fixed period (New York specifies 20 days) unless it can be proved that it was not reasonably possible to give notice.

Claims are usually paid promptly after a written proof of loss is submitted on forms provided by the company. In the case of group life insurance, a certified death certificate also usually is required. Supporting bills and statements by attending physicians usually are required on health insurance claims.

Contest of Claims. State laws typically require that all statements in a group insurance application be treated as representations, not warranties. The legal significance of this position is that in order successfully to contest the coverage, the insurer must prove that the statement is both (1) false and (2) important in underwriting the coverage. Under the doctrine of warranties, the insurer would be required only to prove that the statement is false in order to have the contract rescinded or claims denied.

Group life insurance contracts contain an incontestable clause that prevents the company from contesting the policy "after two years from the date of issue." Also, "the life insurance of any insured person shall be incontestable after such insurance has been in force for two years during such person's lifetime." Due to the limited information found in a typical group life insurance application, the policy incontestable clause is of less significance than the comparable provision in an individual insurance policy. Furthermore, the portion of the clause relating to insurance on an individual life has applicability only when a plan participant makes statements concerning his insurability—a small minority of cases.

Misstatement of Age. Where an insured's age has been misstated under a group life insurance policy, the amount of his benefits will remain unchanged and the employer's premium will be adjusted. One exception to this rule would be the case where benefits are related to age. The misstatement of age provision in group life insurance obviously is much more liberal for the insured who understates his age than the provision found in individual policies which requires the benefits to be changed to the amount the premiums would have purchased at the insured's true age.

Beneficiaries. All the conventional beneficiary designations associated with individual life insurance also are found in group life. For example,

---

[12] The NAIC has adopted model rules on discontinuance and replacement of group coverage. See Appendix P.

one or more primary beneficiaries may be named, with their interests to pass to subsequent or contingent beneficiaries under various sets of circumstances. Certain designations, such as the naming of the policyholder (in most states), are forbidden; others, such as "my unmarried children," are discouraged because they are ambiguous; still another, the naming of the insured's estate, is discouraged because it may result in delays and a waste of benefits on litigation expenses.

Beneficiary designations are usually revocable. If there are multiple beneficiaries, each is assumed to have an equal interest in the absence of any directions to the contrary. Also, unless the insured specifies otherwise, the interest of a beneficiary terminates if he predeceases the insured, and such interest is divided among surviving beneficiaries. If no named beneficiary survives the insured, or if none has been named, the benefits will be distributed according to the *successive beneficiary* clause in the contract. In the absence of this clause, benefits would be paid to the insured's estate; however, under the clause the insurer may, at its option, pay the benefits to a member of the insured's immediate family such as his spouse, parents, or children. Furthermore, a *facility of payment clause* usually is included under which the insurer may distribute up to $500 of the proceeds to anyone who has incurred burial expenses on behalf of the insured. In the event that the beneficiary is a minor, or other person incapable of giving a valid release, the insurer is sometimes empowered to "make payment of the amount payable to such beneficiary at a rate not exceeding $50 (or other designated amount) per month to any relative by blood or connection by marriage of such beneficiary, or to any person or institution appearing to it to have assumed the custody and principal support of such beneficiary."

Settlement Options.   Only a small minority of group life insurance benefits are paid through settlement options despite the advantages that may be associated with such an arrangement. (Among the possible advantages are freedom from investment worries, creditor protection and possibly the use of an option based upon life contingencies.) Some companies do not offer annuities based upon life contingencies, but all offer "installment time" and "installment amount" options. Of course, all funds held under settlement options are credited with interest at a minimum guaranteed rate. However, contrary to the practice under individual policies, the terms of the option, including life contingencies, if any, are set at the time the option is selected, not when the group policy goes into effect. Either the insured during his lifetime, or the beneficiary after the insured's death, may select a settlement option. Insurance companies generally reserve the right to refuse to place sums of $1,000 or less under settlement options, or to make installment payments for less than specified amounts (such as $20).

Preexisting Conditions.   Disability income, major medical, and comprehensive medical expense policies usually contain a provision which excludes from coverage for a given period of time any medical condition that existed at the time the insurance took effect. (Such a clause generally has not been necessary on basic medical expense policies.) Periods of 3, 6, 9, and 12 months are common, but periods longer than 12 months usually are avoided for fear they might engender ill will among employees.

Various phrases have been used in defining preexisting conditions and the area is not completely settled. One common definition considers such a condition to be one for which the individual received medical treatment, diagnosis, consultation, or prescribed drugs during the 90 days preceding the effective date of his coverage. Total or partial waiver of these conditions is not unusual in business changing from one carrier to another or in substantial size cases.

Examination and Autopsy. Group health insurance policies provide that the insurance company shall have the right to examine a claimant when and as often as it may reasonably require while a claim is pending. In states where it is not prohibited by law, the company also reserves the right to make an autopsy if a claimant dies.

Providers of Group Health Services. Under the HIAA model bill, the policyholder may request a clause providing that the insurer, at its option, may make payments directly to the purveyors of medical services. Of course, the policy may not limit the insured's free choice of medical services. In addition to being a convenience for the insured, this provision ensures that benefits will be used for the purpose for which they were intended. Further, and very important from the insured's viewpoint, if such a provision is not included in his policy, many hospitals require an admission deposit.

Nonduplication of Benefits. Adverse selection probably is a greater cause for worry in the writing of long-term disability income insurance than in any other line written by life and health insurance companies. Underwriters of this coverage take scrupulous care to see that benefits bear a reasonable relationship to the insured's earnings. As an extra precaution, it is general practice for policies to provide that income from some or all other sources will be considered when determining benefits.

If the plan is underwritten carefully, income seldom will appear from sources not anticipated in the plan design. Should this happen, however, the policy may deal with the situation in one of two ways. Under the direct offset method, disability income benefits are reduced by $1 for each dollar of income from a collateral source. Another method is to ignore other income until the combined benefits reached a predetermined proportion (such as 60 percent) of the claimant's regular earnings.

The precept that an insured should not receive insurance benefits in excess of his loss has for centuries been regarded as fundamental to insurance theory. Prior to the early 60s, many major medical plans contained a nonduplication of benefits clause which attempted to prorate benefits between carriers where overlapping group coverages existed. In the early 60s, steps were taken to refine this principle for a broader segment of medical care insurance written, and eliminated inequities inherent in the prorating approach. An all-industry committee with representatives from the ALC, HIAA, ICA and LIAA[13] formulated a Model Group Anti-Duplication Provision that established priorities for payment by each

---

[13] American Life Convention, Health Insurance Association of America, International Claim Association, and Life Insurance Association of America. The first and the last named organizations were merged in 1973 into the American Life Insurance Association (ALIA).

carrier insuring a claimant. Under the provision, an insured may not receive benefits in excess of his actual covered expenses; therefore, he cannot make a profit from his disability.

All policies not containing the model provision are considered to be primary coverage, and a policy containing the provision will pay (within the policy limits) the difference between the primary coverage and total covered expenses as defined in the contract. If more than one contract contains the Model Provision, the order of benefit determination is established as follows: (1) coverage other than as a dependent shall be primary to coverage as a dependent, (2) coverage as a dependent of a male shall be primary to coverage as a dependent of a female, and (3) where (1) and (2) do not establish an order of coverage, the plan which has covered the claimant the longest shall be primary. Several other sources of indemnity, such as awards in liability suits and individual health policies are not included in the provision; nevertheless, it represents a giant step in the right direction.

TAXATION

Group insurers are taxed at both the state and federal levels. The states levy a tax on insurance companies, typically 2 percent of premiums. Federal taxation may have implications for the policyholder, the insured and (under life insurance policies) the beneficiary. Federal income, estate, and gift taxes, as well as similar state taxes, all may have an impact on group insurance.

Group Term Life Insurance

In General. For federal income tax purposes, an employer's plan is not one of group term life insurance unless it provides protection for at least 10 full-time employees at some time during the calendar year. A plan which provides protection for fewer than 10 full-time employees for an entire calendar year may nevertheless qualify if, in general, the plan provides protection for all full-time employees and the amount of protection for such employees is computed either as a uniform percentage of salary or on the basis of coverage brackets established by the insurer such that no bracket exceeds 2½ times the next lower bracket and the lowest bracket is at least 10 percent of the highest bracket. In an under-10-life plan, evidence of insurability may be a factor affecting either an employee's eligibility or the amount of coverage afforded him, but only if such eligibility is determined *solely* on the basis of a medical questionnaire completed by the employee (i.e., no medical examination may be required).[14]

Taxation of Premiums. Premiums paid by an employer on behalf of his employees are tax deductible if (1) when added to all other employer compensation, they represent reasonable compensation for services actually rendered, (2) they are ordinary and necessary business expenses, and (3) the employer is not directly or indirectly a beneficiary of the

---

[14] The regulations under Section 79 of the Internal Revenue Code [1.79–1(d)] contain additional specific rules, definitions, and exceptions which somewhat enlarge the general framework considered in this paragraph.

insurance.[15] Where an insured is also a stockholder, it must be made clear that the premium is compensation for services actually rendered as an employee and not a dividend. While premiums for sole proprietors or partners are not deductible, premiums for their employees may be deductible.

Premiums for "group term life insurance" are generally not taxable to employees. However, the *cost* of such coverage is taxable to an employee to the extent that such coverage exceeds the lesser of $50,000 or the maximum amount of such coverage permitted under the laws of the state where the employer has its principal place of business, plus the amount (if any) paid by employees for the purchase of such coverage.[16] When an employee is covered in excess of this limit for any part of his taxable year, he must include in his gross income the cost of such excess coverage computed from Table 30–1 less the amount (if any) he paid towards the pur-

TABLE 30–1.   Uniform Premiums for $1,000
of Group Term Insurance
Protection

Age Bracket	Monthly Cost per $1,000 of Insurance
Under 30	$0.08
30 to 34	0.10
35 to 39	0.14
40 to 44	0.23
45 to 49	0.40
50 to 54	0.68
55 to 59	1.10
60 to 64	1.63

chase of any part of his coverage. However, the cost of group term life insurance in excess of the foregoing limit is not taxable to the insured who has terminated his employment and who either has reached the retirement age with respect to his employer or is disabled. Likewise, no part of the cost of any amount of group term life insurance is taxable to an employee if his employer is directly or indirectly the beneficiary. However, it should be noted that laws in many states prohibit such an arrangement.

The spouse and children of employees may be covered under group term life insurance provided by the employer without tax consequence to employees if the amount of such coverage is merely incidental. Under the Treasury Regulations, any such coverage in excess of $2,000 is deemed not to be merely incidental, and the entire cost thereof for any part of the employee's taxable year must be computed from Table 30–1 and included in the employee's gross income.[17]

Taxation of Benefits.   For federal tax purposes, group term life in-

---

[15] IRC 162(*a*); IRC 264(*a*)(1).
[16] IRC 79(a); Reg. 1.79–1(b)(1)(i); Rev. Rul. 69–423, 1969–2 C.B. 12.
[17] Reg. 1.61–2(d)(2)(ii)(b).

surance proceeds are treated in the same manner as proceeds from other forms of life insurance. Generally, life insurance death proceeds paid in a lump sum are exempt from income taxes. When benefits are taken under the interest option, or under an installment option (whether or not based on life contingencies), any payments or parts of payments that are attributable to interest will be taxed as ordinary income to the beneficiary. An important exception to this rule is the exclusion of up to $1,000 of such interest annually if it constitutes part of installment payments of life insurance proceeds to the decedent's surviving spouse.

If at the time of his death the insured employee possesses any incidents of ownership in group term life insurance provided by his employer, or if the proceeds thereof are payable to or for the benefit of his estate, the proceeds will be included in his gross estate for federal estate tax purposes.[18] If permitted by applicable state law and the terms of the group contract, the employee may, by absolute assignment, divest himself of all incidents of ownership in the coverage provided by his employer, including the right of conversion (if any) exercisable upon his termination of employment. In most states, such assignments are expressly authorized by law.

Permanent Forms of Group Life Insurance

Death proceeds paid under the various permanent forms of group life insurance receive the same tax treatment as proceeds paid under a group term life policy (see above). Unlike term policies, however, permanent policies develop a cash value and there are income tax implications if a policy is surrendered. Group and individual policies receive identical income tax treatment at surrender by the insured. The excess, if any, of cash values over premiums directly or indirectly paid by the insured are taxed to him as ordinary income.

A final topic, the tax treatment accorded premiums, is more involved and has had a strong influence on the three forms that permanent life insurance has taken. Therefore, the taxation of premiums will be the topic for the remainder of this discussion.

Level Premium Group Permanent Life Insurance. Level premium group permanent represents perhaps the most natural form of permanent group life insurance. However, as far back as 1950 the federal income tax treatment of this coverage has severely limited its use for the group life insurance market (although it is sometimes used to fund pension trusts). In that year, a Treasury Department Ruling[19] required employees to include as taxable income any employer contributions toward the cost of permanent insurance. Although this ruling has recently been declared obsolete, it served as a clear statement that such premiums will be taxed to the employee. Treasury Regulations now make it clear that the protection afforded by a policy of permanent insurance does not constitute term insurance, that the benefits of Section 79 of the Internal Revenue Code are not available where such coverage is provided by an insured's

---

[18] IRC 2042(2); IRC 2042(1).
[19] Mimeograph 6477, 1950–1 C.B. 16.

employer, and that premiums paid by the insured's employer for such coverage will constitute an item of gross income to the insured employee.[20]

The employee will not be taxed if group permanent coverage is fully forfeitable upon termination of employment. However, it appears that any form of guarantee, even at retirement, would create a tax liability for him. Thus, level premium group permanent has important weaknesses, and the need for permanent protection usually can be satisfied more effectively by another form of coverage.

Group Paid-Up Life Insurance. Under this combination plan, employees purchase units of paid-up permanent insurance and employers purchase units of decreasing term insurance. The cost of the group term life insurance will not be taxed to the employees (up to the previously mentioned limit) so long as the policy specifies the portion of the premium which is allocable to the group term life insurance, and no part of the premium allocable to paid-up permanent insurance is paid by the employer. If employer contributions are used to purchase paid-up units, the tax advantages accorded the purchase of group term insurance are lost. Furthermore, under Revenue Ruling 71–360, each element of coverage must be supported by its own expense factor. It is common practice for paid-up increments to be purchased at net rates. Therefore, at least in the early years, the expenses for paid-up policies must be borne by the term insurance premium. It now appears that all tax advantages of the group term life insurance element will be lost if insurers continue to follow this procedure.

Although employer contributions for the group term life insurance element usually are deductible as an ordinary and necessary business expense and are not taxed to the employee (within $50,000 or lower state law limits), the employee's contributions must be made with after-tax dollars and are not deductible by him.

Group Ordinary Life Insurance. Group ordinary life insurance provides both group term life insurance protection and permanent insurance protection. Under recently promulgated income tax regulations[21] if such insurance protection is made available by an employer, the group term life insurance element will receive favorable tax treatment if (1) the policy specifies the portion of the premium which is allocated to the group term life insurance element, and (2) the policy expressly provides that no part of the premium which is not so allocated (i.e., no part of the premium for permanent insurance coverage) is to be paid by the employer. Even if these policy requirements are met, the entire amount of the employer's premium will be included in the employee's gross income if the employer pays more than the amount specified by the policy as allocable to the group term life insurance element and such payment in fact exceeds the amount properly allocable to the group term life insurance element. However, where these policy requirements are met, if the employer pays only the amount specified in the policy as allocable to the group term life insurance element and such amount in fact exceeds the amount properly allocable to the group term life insurance element, only the amount

---

[20] Reg. 1.61–1(d)(2)(ii) and 1.79–1(b)(1)(i).
[21] Reg. 1.79–1(b)(1)(ii).

paid by the employer in excess of the properly allocable amount will be included in the employee's gross income.[22]

Group Health Insurance

Taxation of Premiums. All premiums, when added to all other employer compensation, are deductible by the employer if they represent reasonable compensation for services actually rendered. Furthermore, under Section 106 of the Internal Revenue Code, they are not taxable to the employee. If the employee pays a health insurance premium and is reimbursed by his employer, this reimbursement will not be treated as part of his gross income.[23]

If a person itemizes his deductions when computing his federal income tax, he may claim a certain amount of group (or individual) medical and dental insurance premiums as deductions. The amount of the deduction allowed under the Internal Revenue Code varies with the amount of premiums and other medical expenses that are incurred during the year.

Taxation of Benefits. Health insurance benefits (both medical expense and income replacement) that are attributable to premiums paid by an employee are exempt from taxes.[24]

Medical care benefits paid to an individual or his dependents, which are attributable to premiums paid by his employer, are excluded from gross income to the extent that they do not exceed expenses actually incurred.[25] This rule applies regardless of whether the plan is group or individual. However, if medical expenses were deducted in a prior year and the insured is indemnified in the current year for such expenses, the indemnification benefits must be treated as ordinary income to the extent a deduction was allowed in the prior year. Dismemberment benefits under accidental death and dismemberment coverage also are excluded from taxable income.

To the extent that they are financed by the employer, long- and short-term disability income benefits are subject to the sick pay exclusion in the Internal Revenue Code.[26] If weekly benefits exceed 75 percent of the regular weekly pay rate, the employee will be taxed on all benefits received during the first 30 days. From the 31st day forward, benefits up to $100 per week will be excludable from his gross income.

If weekly benefits paid during the first 30 days of disability are less than 75 percent of the employee's regular weekly pay rate, he may exclude up to $75 per week for the first 30 days of disability. A seven-day waiting period is required before this exclusion takes effect if the employee is not hospitalized; if he is hospitalized for at least one day during the period of absence from work, the waiting period does not apply. After 30 days, the employee insured may exclude benefits received up to $100 a week.

---

[22] With respect to policies in existence on December 21, 1972, in this latter situation, the excess amount paid by the employer need not be included in the employee's gross income for taxable years beginning before January 1, 1973.

[23] See Rev. Rul. 61–146, 1961–2 C.B. 25.

[24] IRC 104(*a*)(3).

[25] IRC 105(*b*).

[26] IRC 105(*d*).

SELECTED REFERENCES

Dickerson, O. D. *Health Insurance.* 3d ed. Homewood, Ill.: Richard D. Irwin, Inc., 1965.

Eilers, Robert D. and Crowe, Robert M. *Group Insurance Handbook.* Home-Wood, Ill.: Richard D. Irwin, Inc., 1965.

Gregg, Davis W. *Group Life Insurance.* 3d ed. Homewood, Ill.: Richard D. Irwin, Inc., 1962.

Pickrell, Jesse F. *Group Health Insurance.* Homewood, Ill.: Richard D. Irwin, Inc., 1961.

31

Group Premiums, Experience Rating, and Reserves

By DONALD D. CODY and HERBERT J. BOOTHROYD

THE ORGANIZATION of an insurance company, the conduct of its business, and its methods of pricing are similar to those in industry generally. Because of differences in nomenclature and the intangible nature of the insurance product, this similarity has not generally been recognized. As a result, pricing of the group insurance product has had an air of mystery which has hampered public understanding of the methods of determining initial premiums, renewal premiums, retrospective rate credits, and dividends. The whole concept of insurance pricing should be considered in the same perspective as pricing in production and service industries that produce, distribute, or service tangible products.

The Group Insurance Product

Group insurance provides death benefits, disability income benefits, medical expense benefits, and dental expense benefits to groups of employees. These benefits, along with pensions, are recognized as fringe benefit additions to the wages of employees and employers purchase them with the same care as they make other expenditures. Employers choose their carriers on the basis of quality of the product, level of pricing, and ability to perform long-range service functions.

Because group insurance is part of the fabric of personnel relationships, the design of the group product is concerned not only with pricing and design of benefits but also with a complex of human relationships. For instance, carriers are concerned with the relationships of the employer with his employees, including bargaining with his unions. Carriers usually deal with the employer through an agent, a broker, or an actuarial consultant. The employer and the employees are involved with doctors, hospitals, and other providers of medical care in the sensitive areas of quality of care and fee making.

Because of this complex of relationships, group product design not only involves the selection and pricing of benefits which are familiar topics in connection with individual policies, but also includes a system design encompassing procedures at the sale and installation of a group case as well as month-to-month activities during the continuance of the case. Each group case differs from other group cases in greater or lesser degree.

General Theory of Pricing in Group Insurance

The pricing of group insurance is important in a highly competitive market. Since there is no practical limit on the capacity of insurance companies to provide service and risk assumption facilities, the group market is essentially a buyer's market. Pricing is important both at time of sale and at time of each renewal, for many group cases face competitive bids at each renewal as employers seek to obtain better pricing or more extensive service.

Group insurance premiums, adjusted for net investment income earned on group funds and for retrospective rate credits or dividends, must be large enough in the aggregate for the whole group line to cover incurred claims, commissions and other expenses, taxes, risk charge, and profit. Claims constitute the cost of material in a general business sense. The expenses and taxes are similar to the corresponding items in general business. The risk charge recognizes the insurance risk on each policy—a charge sufficient in the aggregate for the whole group insurance line over a period of years to cover unanticipated losses on high-claim cases. The risk charge, as a percentage of premium, is greater on small cases than on large cases. The profit charge finances the expansion of the insurance company, provides for growth of contingency reserves, and, in stock companies, also compensates the owners for use of their capital. The formulation of risk and profit charges varies from company to company.

Most group insurance is on the one-year term basis. For group paid-up life insurance and group permanent insurance, however, premiums also must provide for the development of actuarial reserves for the future payment of benefits.

The following pages describe the determination of initial premiums, renewal premiums, and dividends, together with an explanation of experience rating and reserves. At the end of the chapter an arithmetic illustration is given on a representative case.

INITIAL PREMIUM RATES

Group Life Insurance

The initial premium rates for group life insurance for all companies licensed in New York are based on a minimum standard promulgated by the New York State Insurance Department for use in the first policy year. Companies licensed in New York must recognize this minimum standard extraterritorially in all states. The mortality basis of these rates is the 1960 Commissioners Standard Group Table (CSG), developed from intercompany group experience with an aggregate of nearly 60 million years of lives exposed. The net premium rates are loaded for expenses by a formula which broadly recognizes the level of expense by size of case. The rates vary by 35 percent between the largest and smallest cases, and rates for females are 60 percent of those for males. Table 31–1 shows these rates at decennial ages for males.

TABLE 31–1. Commissioners Standard Group (CSG) Monthly Life Rates (per $1,000) (illustrated for decennial ages only)

Age	Male	Female
20	$0.23	$0.14
30	0.27	0.16
40	0.45	0.27
50	1.06	0.64
60	2.51	1.51
70	5.81	3.49
80	12.83	7.70

Adjustments: (1) To the aggregate premium determined from the above rates, $0.20 per $1,000 is added, with a maximum of $8 per group. (2) The aggregate premium determined by (1) is reduced by the following percentage reductions, shown only for selected premium sizes:

Aggregate Monthly Premium Before Reduction	*Percentage Expense Reduction (Percent)*
Under $ 200	0
$ 350 – 400	5
600 – 650	10
1,000 – 1,200	15
2,500 – 3,000	20
6,000 – 7,500	25
20,000 – 27,000	30
80,000 and over	35

The states of Maine, Ohio, and Pennsylvania also have a minimum standard applicable just to groups within these states; Pennsylvania additionally allows a lower premium based on reasonable assumptions as to probable interest, mortality, and expense factors in a particular group.

Companies not licensed in New York State usually use somewhat lower rates outside of Maine, Ohio, and Pennsylvania, but the majority of large companies are licensed in New York, so that most new cases are issued with CSG rates. These companies usually rerate these cases at renewal somewhat below CSG rates.

The costs of the waiver of premium on disabled lives and of the conversion privilege are included in these rates. Conversions produce very strong adverse selection against the company. The loss from this excess mortality on conversions is reflected in the experience of the individual business. However, since it is actually the cost of an additional benefit under the group insurance coverage, it is charged against the group business. The individual (ordinary) department assesses against the group department a charge per $1,000 of insurance converted.[1]

While the rate of mortality on converted policies is high, the magnitude of the problem is not great because only a small proportion of those eligible actually convert their insurance.

While some distinction should be made among groups of persons where there is an obvious and estimable difference in hazard or chance of loss, the number of substandard classifications because of industry or occupation has been kept to a minimum in group life insurance, especially when compared to the number of classifications in coverages such as workmen's compensation.

Group Health Coverages

Initial premium rates are determined by each company independently, although most companies rely upon intercompany experience compiled by the Society of Actuaries for the more common forms of coverage. Other useful data are often obtained from organizations such as the American Hospital Association, the American Dental Association, the Department of Health, Education and Welfare, and the Bureau of Labor Statistics' Consumer Price Index. The results are then updated for trends and adjusted to reflect the effect on claims costs of the difference in a company's operations from reported composite intercompany studies. A loading for expenses and risk margin is then added and checked for reasonableness. Rates for an entirely new coverage, or a new feature in existing coverage, are made on a judgment basis. Data from other fields may be used if available, but much of the rate depends upon actuarial judgment until experience data are available.

Accidental Death and Dismemberment Insurance. In the long run, the average loss ratios for accidental death and dismemberment coverage are relatively stable and tend to decrease slowly with the reducing occupational accident hazards. In some industries with serious accident hazards, higher premiums are used where benefits are paid for both occupational and nonoccupational losses. The typical monthly premium is about 5 cents per $1,000 for nonoccupational coverage, or for nonoccupational and occupational coverage in industries without accident hazard. In industries with the greatest accident hazard, the premium can run three to five times this level where there is occupational coverage.

Short-Term Disability Income. A typical monthly premium rate on an all-male group for a benefit period of 26 weeks, with benefits starting on the first day in the case of accident and on the eighth day in the case of sickness, is about 70 cents per $10 weekly indemnity prior to the application of any expense reduction factors. Rates depend on the percentage of

---

[1] The assessment varies by company. At present, many companies charge $65 per $1,000, although others charge amounts such as $75 or a schedule which increases by age at conversion.

females, age distribution and the presence of maternity benefits. Claims levels on this coverage on small groups run about 70 percent of premiums on the average and higher on large groups. The claims levels, however, vary considerably from group to group reflecting different economic status, stability of employment and personnel practices.

Long-Term Disability Income. Premiums for long-term disability income insurance are based partially on group intercompany experience developed by the Society of Actuaries, and partly on a company's own experience. Experience under disability features of individual life insurance policies and personal disability income policies also is utilized, particularly for disability termination rates after three or four years of disablement, where group data are sparse.

Claim rates for this type of coverage will vary considerably with economic conditions, and also can be expected to vary from year to year even more than life insurance claims on particular cases. Premium rates depend upon distribution of benefits by age and sex. Primary and dependent disability benefits payable by social security after six months are usually an offset against the group benefit. An estimate of these amounts is required to determine the group premium.

Medical Expense Insurance. Claims and hence premium rates for broad medical coverage (major medical or hospital coverages providing semiprivate room and board charges without a dollar-per-day maximum and large amounts of extras) have been increasing annually by 8 to 15 percent. Claims under policies providing scheduled hospital and surgical benefits are not affected by increases in the price of all of the medical care services, but increases in utilization and upgrading of the quality of services results in premium increases of 4 to 8 percent annually.

It should be noted that where broad coverage is provided through basic scheduled benefits plus superimposed major medical, the superimposed portion receives most of the impact of cost increases. As a result, the superimposed portion of premiums increases 20 to 35 percent annually; however, the total premium for basic and superimposed plans of benefit increases by 8 to 15 percent.

Premium rates for hospital insurance are made up of a rate per dollar of room and board charges covered and a rate for extra charges. Premium rates for surgeons' and doctors' fees depend on the dollar amounts provided by the schedule of benefits (where full semiprivate hospital charges or unscheduled benefits for surgeons' and doctors' fees are provided, premium rates are based on the anticipated level of charges). These rates are then adjusted for the variation in claim risk by age and sex, with patterns similar to disability income coverages; the rates for maternity benefits are adjusted separately and decrease by age. These rates are also adjusted for variations by geographical area; this is caused by significantly different levels of utilization and hospital pricing in various parts of the United States.

Major medical expense rate making is a great deal more complicated. Experience data are in sufficient detail to permit the reflection of various pertinent cost factors by class characteristics, such as the following:

1. Deductible and coinsurance factors, and variations in benefit design and coverage.
2. Geographical area. In addition to the variances in rate of benefit utilization also applicable to scheduled benefits, major medical rates must reflect the wide variances by area in levels of hospital charges and doctors' and surgeons' fees. Adjustments for both differences produce claim costs 75 percent higher in the most expensive areas than costs in the least expensive areas.
3. Income of the employee. Claim costs on high-income employees are 100 percent higher than on low-income employees.
4. Age and sex. Costs at age 65 are three and a half times costs at age 20; female costs exceed male costs by 15 to 50 percent; maternity costs decrease by age. These adjustments are similar to those made for scheduled benefits described above.

Premiums for liberal medical care benefits may amount to as much as $50 a month or more for each employee with a family.

Dental Care. Group dental care insurance is a relatively new, but increasingly popular, form of coverage. Claim estimates for premium purposes are based upon the experience of a number of pioneering service plans and labor-management trustee plans, and upon data compiled by the American Dental Association. Costs of procedures in local areas have been compiled by county and state dental societies.

Benefits may be expressed in either a scheduled or unscheduled comprehensive form. The schedule lists maximum payments for specified procedures. The comprehensive approach pays a percentage, such as 80 percent, of reasonable and customary charges incurred after an annual deductible, such as $50 per person or $150 per family, subject to a maximum benefit payable per year. Special benefit provisions are required for elective procedures, such as bridgework and gold inlays.

In addition to benefit design, premiums are dependent upon several factors, such as geographical area (range of 1.6 to 1), percentage of females (range of 1.15 to 1), age distribution (range of 1.3 to 1), and income level (range 1.8 to 1). These differences reflect differences in utilization and dental fee patterns.

The effect of the existence of insurance on utilization and charges is not yet clear. In some cases, claims are highest in the first year of the plan, perhaps due to people seeking treatment previously deferred because of family finances. In other cases, utilization increases after the first year, perhaps because the initial fear of seeing a dentist gradually dissipates. The inflationary trend in charges made by dentists has been lower than that previously indicated for medical care.

Recognition of Expenses by Size of Case

Group health insurance premiums at issue are subject to adjustment by size of aggregate premium which broadly reflects the decreasing percentage of premium required for expenses as the case grows in size. Adjustments can range from discounts of up to 20 percent for the largest cases to additional charges of up to 15 percent for small cases with modest coverage per life.

Extended Rate Guarantees

Premiums traditionally have been guaranteed for 12 months, with the right reserved to change at annual intervals. Some companies have recently offered two- and three-year guarantees of rates, typically on cases of less than 50 or 100 lives.

The same principles of rate making apply, with the following additional factors to be considered:

1. The risk of change in claim trend factors extends further into the future, and such projections require more margins for error.
2. The risk of change in the nature of the group—size of group, average age, female percentage—is increased, and requires additional margin.
3. The risk of early lapse is decreased, and requires less margin.
4. The expense of processing renewals and dividends, if any, is incurred less often, and reduces expense charges.

Some companies offer a plan which guarantees only a rate basis by individual covered, thus lowering the initial cost. Premium rates are set for each individual reflecting age and sex, and expense factors vary as the number in the group varies. The initial cost difference for a group of 10 employees is as much as 8 percent for a two-year and 12 percent for a three-year guarantee. For groups which expect to be stable or to grow, the ultimate cost advantage is substantial.

EXPERIENCE RATING

Group insurance coverages are experience rated with respect to claims and cost accounted with respect to expenses. The experience rating and cost accounting are required for two purposes: determining dividends, or retrospective rate credits in the case of stock companies; and determining renewal rates or prospective rates. This approach is not solely at the option of the insurance company but is required by the demands of a competitive market.

In the absence of such experience rating and cost accounting, individual companies could restrict themselves to specific geographical areas and to classes of policyholders which are known to have low levels of claims and low expenses. However, most insurance companies operate in a wide geographical area, offering their product essentially to all employed groups. Operation over such a broad spectrum of policyholders necessitates experience rating so as to meet the competition of specialty companies and self-insurance.

Also, group insurance is usually offered without individual evidence of insurability, and there are wide variations in claims characteristics from group to group. Large employers with good claims experience naturally seek carriers with experience rating, so that their costs will reflect their better claims experience. Conversely, those with bad experience would seek out companies without experience rating.

The question arises as to how Blue Cross/Blue Shield associations in many areas operate without experience rating in this competitive market. Essentially a franchise operation in a particular area, they have no competition by any other carrier operating in the same manner. Blue Cross/Blue Shield associations contract with doctors and hospitals; charges are made in accordance with cost determination formulas, giving cost advantages not available to the general population, including the part of the population insured by insurance companies. In many of the states, Blue Cross/Blue Shield plans are not subject to state premium taxes, which add at least 2 percent to premiums.

The price advantages, together with the predilection of many people to the guaranteed full-payment benefits offered by some plans, permits Blue Cross/Blue Shield to operate successfully in a wide segment of the medical expense market without experience rating. However, in many areas, Blue Cross/Blue Shield associations have adopted experience rating for sizable employers for the same reasons that insurance companies experience rate.

Factors in Experience Rating

Expenses. Careful cost accounting is applied in expense determination which recognizes the various costs incurred at issue and during the continuance of the policy. Results usually are translated into formula charges, some of which are independent of the size of the case, while others depend upon number of employees, amount of premiums, number and type of claims, and level of commissions. For very large cases or unusual services, cost accounting records may be used directly for expense charges. In determining both initial and renewal premium rates, the variations of these expenses are reflected by differences of as much as 35 percent between the largest and the smallest cases. In computing dividends, a more refined formulation of these expenses is made.

Claims Costs. Claims costs may reflect the average level of claims in the whole class of policyholders for each type of group insurance, the actual claims on each case, or a blend of both. The claims of small policyholders will vary considerably from year to year in each case because of random fluctuations; little, if any, attention is paid to actual claims under the case in such instances.

In cases with several thousand lives, claims vary less widely as a percentage of premium from year to year, and a high degree of recognition is given to the group's own experience. In fact, in very large cases the claims charge used by most companies is the group's actual claims incurred, without any recognition of average claims in the class of cases. Between the smallest and largest cases, there is a blend, as illustrated below. Of course, a fundamental criterion for all formulas is that the aggregate of claims charges realized must be equal to the aggregate of actual claims incurred for each year over all groups.

Experience Rating Formulas

The formulas for experience rating of claims to be charged to a particular group take a number of forms, but those in most general use fall into two categories.

Type 1—Risk-Averaging Formula. The risk-averaging type of formula calculates the claims charge as a weighted average of (1) actual claims on the case, and (2) average claims on the class of cases.[2]

In determination of dividends or retrospective rate credits, the formula is applied to the experience of the policy year, and the credibility factor might be as shown in Table 31–2. Thus, in a group with 600 lives, seven tenths of the claims portion of its life insurance dividend calculation would be determined by its own claims experience. It should be noted that the annual premium earned also is related on an experience basis, so that the average claims level reflects past experience as well.

TABLE 31–2. Illustrative Credibility Factors for Group Insurance Dividends by Size of Group

Size of Group (Lives)	Life Insurance	Medical Care and Short-Term Disability Insurance
100	0.0	0.2
200	0.2	0.5
300	0.3	0.8
600	0.7	1.0
1,000	1.0	1.0

The same type of formula may be used to determine renewal rates, except that the values of actual incurred claims and annual premiums earned reflect experience over a longer period of time than one year, the experience for the latest year usually being weighted more heavily than for prior years. Claims for past years must be adjusted to reflect typical trends in claims levels. Premiums for past years must be adjusted to a level constant with present rates. Similarly, the credibility factor reflects the number of life-years of exposure in past years. The credibility factor

---

[2] The risk-averaging formula for determining the claims charge can be expressed as follows:

$$K = y\,C + (1 - y)\,kP,$$

where, for each coverage on each case,

K = Claims charge
C = Actual incurred claims
P = Annual premium earned
k = Average ratio of claims to premiums on class of coverage
y = Credibility factor varying by coverage and dependent on volume of exposure, as measured by number of lives or amount of premium (larger factor for larger numbers of lives or larger premium)

usually is lower in renewal rate determinations than in dividend determinations (because policyholders prefer relative stability in rate levels and expect dividends to adjust for unusual fluctuations), and typically might be as shown in Table 31–3.

TABLE 31–3. Credibility Factors for Group Insurance Renewal Rating (by size of group and length of period insured)

Size of Group (Lives)	Life Insurance		Medical Care and Short-Term Disability Insurance	
	One Year	Five Years	One Year	Three Years
100	0.00	0.25	0.20	0.40
500	0.25	0.60	0.75	0.80

The credibility factors actually used vary among carriers. One carrier might use higher credibility, but would require larger margins for fluctuation in its premiums in order to minimize the number of cases where the claims charge exceeded the available premium.

Type 2—Risk-Charge Formula. The risk-charge type of formula, used only in connection with dividends or retrospective rate credits, utilizes an additional risk charge, the amount of which depends upon the type of coverage and, as a percentage of premium, varies inversely with the size of the case.[3] The additional risk charge is realized only on those cases where actual claims are less than premiums earned after provision for expenses, commissions, taxes, normal risk charge, and profit. Hence, the level of the risk charge on each case must be adjusted so that the aggregate over all cases on which the risk charge is so realized is equal to the aggregate excess of claims incurred over premiums (adjusted for expenses, commissions, taxes, normal risk charge, and profit) on all other cases.

Note that where credibility is 100 percent, Type 1 and Type 2 are identical, and the risk charge in Type 2 plus the premium margin becomes identical with the premium margin required for Type 1.

It is usual for all coverages under a group policy to be experience-rated together, and for premiums for all coverages to be treated as a combined premium so as to obtain more stability from offsetting random variations in the various coverages. The larger the premium, the lower is the risk charge made by the insurance company as a percentage of pre-

---

[3] For the risk-charge formula, the determination of the claims charge K is in this form:

$$K = C + R$$

where
C = Actual insured claims
R = Additional risk charge

mium, in recognition of the greater stability which accompanies larger numbers of lives and coverages. The employer thus enjoys a lower cost from the combination of coverages.

Treatment of High Limits

Amounts at risk may be very large under all forms of group insurance, but particularly on group life, accidental death, and disability income coverages. Also, wide variability in group claims may be experienced from year to year. Where the occurrence of claims for such high amounts could bring about a serious deficiency in the group's experience, special methods are used in determining the claims charges in the dividend formula. These methods fall into the following four general classifications.

Additional Risk-Averaging Method.   Heavier emphasis on the average claims costs in the class of insurance may be used in claims charges. For instance, a 1,000-life case, which normally would have full-experience rating (i.e., no emphasis on the average level of claims) might have a 70 percent weighting of average claims in the class of case where the ratio of maximum amount of insurance to average amount of insurance is high (say, eight to one).

Extra Contingency Reserve Method.   Contingency reserves may be built up out of dividend margins, and the high levels of claims, as they occur, are charged against the contingency reserve. The contingency reserves are then built up again to the desired level.

Excess Amounts Pooling Method.   The insurer may designate a limit on the amount of insurance which normally is available per person with full-experience rating. Amounts in excess of this limit will then have no experience rating. Claims charges for these amounts may be based only on the ages of the individuals covered, or they may reflect appropriate standard and substandard ratings as determined by nonmedical, or in some cases, medical evidence. A particular company may use one, two, or even all three of these methods. For example, for a particular size case, one company might pool all individual amounts over $50,000, with those amounts in excess of $100,000 requiring nonmedical evidence and those in excess of $250,000 reserving the right to require medical evidence.

Loss Limit Method.   The loss limit is the ceiling on incurred claims to be charged against the risk in a given policy period. Typically, it is expressed as a percentage of the initial annual premium, and usually is selected by negotiation. Thus, in a case with an annual premium of $50,000, a loss limit of 120 percent might be selected. Claims in excess of $60.000, therefore, would not be charged to the experience of the case. An additional risk charge is made for this "stop loss" provision. It declines as the percentage amount of the limit increases. Furthermore, large groups will have a smaller charge percentagewise because their experience is more stable.

Renewal Rating of Group Insurance

As has been noted, experience rating has application in the determination of premium rates on renewal as well as in the determination of dividend and retrospective rate credits at the end of each policy year.

On a particular case, it is easy, by cost accounting methods, to determine the portion of the premium rate needed for expenses, commissions, taxes, risk charge, and profit charge. The more important problem is to determine the portion needed to cover the claims charge for the coming year.

As indicated in the discussion of experience-rating factors, the claims charge (Type 1) is determined by a blend of average experience on the class and actual experience on the case. In the smaller cases, where random fluctuations are most likely, greater emphasis is put upon the experience of the entire class and, in the larger cases, more and more emphasis is put upon the actual experience of the cases. On life insurance, accidental death and dismemberment insurance, and long-term disability income insurance, greater emphasis is put upon class experience for a case of a particular size than is true for medical expense insurance and short-term disability income insurance, where chance fluctuations of experience are likely to be smaller.

Because of the trend in medical care costs, the expected claims for the coming year are calculated on the basis of the experience-rated claims plus a trend factor of the size indicated in the earlier discussion of medical expense cost trends. In addition, on the more fully experience-rated cases companies add a margin on the order of 5 to 10 percent of expected claims to take care of unusual random fluctuations in the claims. This fluctuation factor is necessary because medical care costs in particular areas move in unusual jumps; for instance, hospitals are more likely to increase their charges every other year rather than every year. There also can be sudden changes in the pattern of utilization of facilities on particular cases; for instance, a large layoff could change the average age and other characteristics of the case.

In the event that the actual claims charge is lower than the expected claims charge provided for by projecting the experience of the previous year with the use of trend and fluctuation factors, the insurance company reflects the excess premium in a dividend or retrospective rate credit.

However well informed policyholders may be with respect to rising medical care costs, it seems difficult for them to appreciate the need for insurance companies to keep premiums in line with increasing costs and include a margin. This has led to high lapse rates as employers move from one carrier to another as the rates are increased. These lapses have also increased the cost of conducting the group insurance business, because with each lapse the costs of reselling and reinstalling the group case fall upon group policyholders generally.

Rating of Transfer Cases

Since group insurance is experience rated, carriers usually take account of experience with the previous carrier in their underwriting of a prospective case which is in the market for transfer of carriers. The theory of setting rates for such a case is identical with that for determining renewal rates; however, there are often practical problems in interpreting another carrier's data and assuring comparability. Evaluating previous experience is a very important underwriting safeguard in health insurance coverages, especially medical expense coverage, because an unwary carrier would otherwise accumulate an undue proportion of high claims cases at inadequate rates.

Dividends and Retrospective Rate Credits

Mutual life insurance companies return as dividends the excess of premium and investment income over the sum of incurred claims charges, expense charges (including amortization of acquisition expense charges), commissions, taxes, risk charges, and profit charges. Increases in actuarial reserves also enter the determination in the case of group life insurance with paid-up amounts and group permanent life insurance.

Retrospective rate credits paid by stock companies are similar to dividends paid by mutual companies; in this section the term "dividends" will be used to cover both mutual life insurance company dividends and stock company retrospective rate credits.

It is important to emphasize that in determining dividends, the insurance company looks back over the preceding year; whereas in determining renewal premiums, it looks forward to the next year.

Company dividend formulas establish equity among policyholders and, together with the system of renewal rerating, are aimed at the development of surplus on each class of case in accordance with a general fiscal plan. The claims charges used in dividend calculations are based on the same concepts previously referred to in the discussion of renewal premium rates, but in many companies the credibility factor used is somewhat larger in dividends than in renewal rating. Determination of the expense charges is considerably more precise in dividends than in renewal premium rates.

Dividend formulas usually also carry forward any deficiency resulting where the claim and expense charges in a particular year, despite the averaging, are higher than the premium collected. Such deficiency is then recovered gradually in the following years as margins thus become available.

Premium rates on smaller classes (under 50 or 100 lives) usually are without dividend margins. Because dividends would reflect only class experience, rather than that of the particular case, competition makes lower premium rates more attractive than dividend possibilities. Hence, dividends usually are paid only on larger cases.

GROUP RESERVES

An insurer must compute group insurance reserves for two purposes, namely, valuation of liabilities for the annual statement, and determination of incurred claims for experience rating of individual cases.

Reserves for Annual Statements

An accurate estimate of total reserve liabilities as of December 31 must be made by each group insurer every year in the completion of the National Association of Insurance Commissioners (NAIC) annual statement blank. Considerable care is necessary in the preparation of this estimate, because the statement blank requires subdivision of the reserve liabilities into separate components recognizing the specific situations that actually gave rise to the reserve liabilities. There are four broad categories of reserves in the annual statement: premium reserves, claim reserves, dividend reserves, and contingency reserves.

Premium Reserves. Premium reserves reflect the fact that certain premium payments in the insurer's hands must be held as reserves insofar as they are for coverage not yet extended.

Unearned Premium Reserves. At any point in time, the proportion of the policy period that remains is equal to the proportion of the premium that is unearned. As an example, consider a monthly premium due and paid on December 15 for the period extending to January 15. On December 31, the insurer is logically required to hold half of the monthly premium as an unearned premium reserve liability because only half of the paid-for coverage actually has been provided.

Premiums Paid in Advance. Policyholders may elect to pay premiums in advance because they will be discounted by the insurer at an agreed upon rate of interest. Of course, the discounted value of such premiums as of December 31 must be included in this liability, since none of the coverage for which they were paid has been provided.

Claim Reserves. Claim reserves are necessitated because some of the claims actually incurred during the calendar year are not paid in full at the close of the year. The six subcategories required of claims for which reserves must be established are:

1. Claims approved and due but not yet paid.
2. Claims in course of settlement.
3. Claims incurred (and ultimately payable) but not yet reported.
4. Deferred maternity and other extended claim liabilities.
5. Amounts not yet due on open claims.
6. Approved disability claims under group life insurance.

Dividend Reserves. Dividends paid on group policies are commonly based on policy years which do not coincide with the calendar year. Thus, on December 31 most policyholders are part way through the policy years for which they ultimately will earn a dividend. That portion of total estimated future dividends that in fact have been earned prior to the calendar year-end must be maintained as a reserve liability of the insurer.

Contingency Reserves. Group insurers often allocate additional amounts of their surplus, not to cover specific identifiable liabilities but to protect against insufficiency of funds in unusual loss situations, such as a catastrophic accident or epidemic. Such contingency reserves in effect cover the responsibility of the insurance company to protect the entire body of policyholders from the consequences of its lack of funds as a result of such contingencies. While premium and claim reserves are liabilities on the balance sheet of the insurer, contingency reserves are allocations of surplus.

Reserves for Experience Rating

The second important type of reserve computation deals not with an entire block of group insurance policies, but with the experience rating of claims for single group policyholders. At this point it is important to discuss the distinction between paid claims and incurred claims during the period of coverage. While paid claims reflect the actual cash payments for policyholder claims during a period of time, this usually is not a valid representation of the true claims cost under the insurance coverage for the period. It is likely that some losses incurred during the period still are payable and would remain so even if premium payments were to cease, while other claims actually paid during the period were incurred in a prior period. The lag between paid and incurred is particularly significant under health insurance.

Since it generally is not practical to wait until all claims have run their course and thus accurately identify their current incurral dates, estimates of claim reserves are used to convert an accurate paid claims amount into an estimated incurred claims amount. The formula used is as follows:[4]

Paid claims during period + claim reserve at end of period —
claim reserve at beginning of period = Incurred claims

It is important to note that there is no claim reserve at the beginning of the first policy year of any group insurance contract. Therefore, in the initial experience-rating period, the incurred claims are equal to paid claims plus the claim reserve at the end of the initial period. Thus, incurred losses, and, therefore, claims charged, often substantially exceed paid claims in the first year.

It is difficult for some policyholders to understand the claims reserve, but it is analogous to accrual accounting in the policyholder's own business; he does not know his true income and profit picture for the year, nor how to adjust his product prices for the future, until his cash figures have been adjusted for incurred items such as bills yet to be paid, sales yet to be collected, and taxes due but unpaid.

The only reserves normally applicable to the experience-rating situation are the six subcategories of claims reserves listed in the above discussion of annual statement liabilities. It is not necessary, however, to subdivide the total claims reserve in such detail for experience rating.

For practical purposes, the reserve required for a large number of similar policies is determined and related to the total annual premium or, alternatively, to claims. This relationship is then considered applicable to each policy of the same type when determining incurred claims for ex-

---

[4] The logic of this conversion formula can be seen readily in terms of the text above. Adding the end-of-period reserve accounts for those claims truly incurred but not yet paid, while subtracting the beginning-of-period reserve, prevents charging for that portion of paid claims that were incurred in prior periods. This correction yields the best available estimate of the true losses for the period and is the one commonly used in the experience rating claim charge formulas outlined in the preceding section.

TABLE 31-4.   Typical Claims Reserves as a Percentage of Annual Premium

Type of Coverage	Percentage of Annual Premium
Life insurance*	12
Short-term disability income	18
Basic medical care without maternity	15
Deferred maternity	75
Supplementary major medical	50
Comprehensive major medical	30

* Life insurance claims reserves would also include reserves for known claims under waiver of premium provisions.

perience rating. Typical claims reserve requirements expressed as a percentage of annual premium are displayed in Table 31-4.

There is considerable variation among carriers in the amount of reserves held per dollar of premium because of differences in specific types of coverage, procedures for reporting and paying claims, and accounting methods. For example, some carriers may hold the accounts open for two weeks or one month after the end of the period and classify claims paid during this time as paid during the preceding period. Such a carrier properly would need a lower reserve. The appearance would be that this carrier had set up smaller liabilities to the advantage of the policyholder; however, the fact would be that a similar offsetting amount had been added to paid claims, so that the formula produced an equivalent incurred claims result. Thus, no conclusions may be drawn as to relative reserve levels of carriers unless full specifics on these items are known and adjustments made for the difference.

OTHER GROUP RATING AND RESERVE CONCEPTS

Funding of Life Insurance for Retired Employees

The cost of continuing life insurance on retired employees can become quite sizable relative to the cost of life insurance on active lives, especially where large amounts are continued. Occasionally, employers provide for funding of retired life costs during the active life service of each employee. There are three procedures in general use.

The first procedure is very similar to that used in pension plans. Under this system an entry age normal cost for providing the life insurance after retirement is determined, taking some age such as 45 as the entry age. At the time the funding is introduced, a past-service liability is determined and is funded over a period of 10 years or more, as in pensions. The reserves are used to pay one-year term premiums on the retired lives. For tax reasons, the reserves must be dedicated to this use so that the employer can never recover them. The income tax situation for these reserves was clarified in 1969 so that employer payments are a deductible business expense in the year paid, and interest on those reserves is not income to the employer.

The second procedure is to provide that amounts otherwise payable as dividends be accumulated in a special reserve, which will be drawn upon later to level out premium costs as the number of retired lives increases. This procedure is used in some large group life plans including the Federal Employees Group Life Insurance Plan.

The third procedure is the use of group paid-up life insurance or group permanent life insurance, as described in Chapter 26.

Minimum Premium Plans

State premium taxes on group life and group health premiums vary from 1.7 percent to as much as 4 percent, averaging somewhat over 2 percent. On large cases, where retentions can be as low as 5 to 6 percent, the net premium tax charge becomes as much as 35 percent or more of retention.[5] Under these circumstances, employers give serious consideration to self-insurance.

During 1962, a number of companies in the group insurance business introduced in a minimum premium plan for health insurance which does not change in any manner the risk of the insurance company and reduces premium taxes to about 10 percent of their level under a normal group insurance arrangement. When dealing with a large employer with retention of, say, 5 percent, the insurance company can make an arrangement whereby it becomes liable for claims only after the aggregate claims payments during the period (e.g., policy year or each month) have risen to the level of, say, 90 percent of the premium normally charged. Prior to this "trigger point," claims are the responsibility of the employer's plan and are paid from his funds. Claims administration under the plan can be carried out either by the policyholder or the insurance company.

In this example, to cover the risk, the insurance company need charge only 10 percent of its normal premium. Out of this 10 percent, the insurance company covers the drafts written for claims incurred after the "trigger point" is reached; reimburses itself for its expenses, commissions, taxes, risk charge, and profit; and sets up whatever increase in normal claims reserves is needed. The insurance company remains liable for the manner in which the employer settles claims throughout the policy year and for the guarantee of continued claims payments to the employees as provided under the contract, even after the termination of the contract by the employer.

These plans primarily are applicable to the large employer because the premium tax savings are significant and the plan is fully experience rated. A disadvantage of the plan is that it does not operate too well with group life insurance, especially where some employees have sizable amounts of life insurance. Claims on life insurance can vary considerably from year to year, and the availability of settlement options may be a problem. Waivers of premium claims and conversions also add complications.

The legal and premium tax status of these plans is not too well established. They have been ruled unacceptable in several states. California and Michigan subject employer plan claim payments to premium taxes.

---

[5] Retention may be defined as the residual amount of the gross premium retained by the insurance company over and above incurred claims and premium refunds (whatever the form).

Other states may later attempt to assess premium taxes. However, in 1971, the Attorney General in New York ruled that employer plan payments were not subject to New York premium taxes.

Modified Premium—Dividend Plans

It has been noted that initial and renewal premiums must include a margin for fluctuations in claims experience and charges for the insurance company's risk-bearing service. Several variations have been developed to minimize such margins and risk charges. These variations generally are applicable only to group health coverages and only on cases covering 1,000 or more lives with fully credible experience.

1. *Cost Plus.* The policyholder agrees to pay for claims actually incurred up to a stated maximum, plus a predetermined percentage of retention for the cost of plan administration and a small profit margin. In its purest form, this is simply self-insurance with the purchase of administrative and claims services from an insurance company. No insurance risk is borne by the insurance company.

2. *Stop-Loss.* The policyholder pays a specific charge, either as a premium or as a dividend charge, for a provision that losses exceeding a predetermined amount or a percentage of a predetermined base will not be charged against the experience of the case. This provision may be added to either a conventional group premium case or to a cost plus arrangement.

3. *Retrospective Premium.* The policyholder pays an advance premium set at one level with a contractual agreement to pay up to a specified higher level at the end of the policy year if the incurred claims plus retention exceed the advance premium. This plan essentially provides for the margins for fluctuation to be payable only if required in retrospect.

4. *Administrative Services Agreement.* Under this plan, the insurance company provides claim and other administrative services for the employer's self-insured plan. There is no insurance; the carrier merely provides a service function. (This is the way in which insurance companies and Blue Cross/Blue Shield associations handle Medicare for the government.) Under this plan, it is not necessary that benefits comply with insurance law, nor is there an insurance certificate. The employer, therefore, need commit funds only as claims arise and are actually paid. It is believed quite likely that in many states this new plan will not be subject to state premium taxes.

All of these plans suffer the disadvantages of great potential for misunderstanding and uncertainties as to the attitudes of regulatory authorities. Care must be taken to assure that the policyholder appreciates what services and risk protections are being given up in return for anticipated advantages, and what possible problems could arise with respect to regulation and taxation.

ILLUSTRATIVE CALCULATIONS

In elaboration of the principles outlined in the preceding initial rating and experience rating sections of the chapter, Figures 31–1, 31–2, 31–3, and 31–4 are presented to demonstrate, in a general way, how manual rate and dividend calculations are actually performed for a typical insured group. Space limitations have required the simplification of the presentation to a considerable extent, but the general approach and format should be considered realistic and typical.

No attempt is made to describe the derivation of the many so-called factors which are presented as "given" in the examples. These factors are developed by complex actuarial techniques alluded to earlier in the chapter. While the factors are not identical to those in use by any single group insurance company, they are close to those employed by many carriers.

The illustrations are based on a hypothetical group of 250 employees, of whom 175 have at least one eligible dependent, covered for the following plan of benefits:

Life Insurance: $12,500 for each employee.
Health Insurance: Comprehensive medical plan with $50 deductible,
    80–20 coinsurance, $25,000 maximum, no maternity benefits.

The employer has provided data on the employees as to their age, sex, income, location of employment, and dependency status.

FIGURE 31–1.   Group Life Insurance Rate Calculation—CSG Basis

Age	Employees		Volume (000)		Unadjusted Rate		Unadjusted Cost
Males							
30	50	×	12.5	×	$0.27	=	$ 168.75
40	60	×	12.5	×	0.45	=	337.50
50	50	×	12.5	×	1.06	=	662.50
60	40	×	12.5	×	2.51	=	1,255.00
							$2,423.75
Females							
30	20	×	12.5	×	$0.16	=	$ 40.00
40	15	×	12.5	×	0.27	=	50.63
50	10	×	12.5	×	0.64	=	80.00
60	5	×	12.5	×	1.51	=	94.38
							$265.01

Male Cost $2,423.75
Female Cost .... +265.01
Lesser of $0.20 per $1,000 and $8 .... +   8.00

Total Cost before Expense Reduction $2,696.76

Expense Reduction (Table 31–1): 20 percent
$1.00 − 0.20 = 0.80$
$\$2,696.76 \times 0.80 = \$2,157.41 = $ Adjusted Monthly Premium

$$\frac{\text{Adjusted Premium}}{\text{Total Volume (000)}} = \frac{\$2,157.41}{3,125} = \$0.69 = \text{Monthly Rate per Thousand}$$

FIGURE 31–2.   Development of Census Factors for Medical Rate

Census Age Factor

Age	Males	Females	Total	Individual Age Factor	Product
30	50	20	70	.70	49.00
40	60	15	75	.90	67.50
50	50	10	60	1.30	78.00
60	40	5	45	2.00	90.00
	200	50	250		284.50

Census Age Factor $= 284.50 \div 250 = 1.14$

Census Age-Sex Factor

Female percent $= 50 \div 250 = 0.20$

Census Age-Sex Factor $=$ Age Factor $+$ [Constant $\times$ Female percent]
$= 1.14 + [0.32 \times 0.20] = 1.20$

Census Spouse Factor

Census Spouse Factor $=$ Age Factor $+$ Constant
$= 1.14 + 0.32 = 1.46$

Census Income Factor

Income	Employees	Individual Income Factor	Product
$10,000	200	1.00	200
$15,000	40	1.50	60
$20,000	10	2.00	20
	250		280

Census Income Factor $= 280 \div 250 = 1.12$

Census Area Factor

	Employees	Individual Area Factor	Product
Chicago, Ill.	200	1.20	240
Greenville, S.C.	50	0.70	35
	250		275

Census Area Factor $= 275 \div 250 = 1.10$

FIGURE 31–3. Rate Calculation for Comprehensive Medical Plan

		Male Employee	*Child(ren)*
1.	Starting Rate ($100 deductible, 80–20 coinsurance, $5,000 max.)	$10.00	$ 7.50
2.	Adjustment for $50 deductible	+ 1.00	+ 1.40
		$11.00	$ 8.90
3.	Adjustment for $25,000 maximum	+ .35	+ .20
		$11.35	$ 9.10
4.	Adjustment for Location	× 1.10	× 1.10
		$12.49	$10.01
5.	Adjustment for Income	× 1.12	× 1.12
6.	Adjusted Table Rates	$13.99	$11.21

Employee Rate Adjusted for Age & Sex: $13.99 × Age-Sex Factor (1.20) = $16.79
Spouse Rate = $13.99 × Spouse Factor (1.46) = $20.43
Child(ren) Rate = $11.21

Composite rate for spouse and/or one or more child(ren) of one employee:
  Spouse Rate × .95 + Child(ren) Rate × .70 = $27.26
   Expense Discount Based on Size of Group: 12 percent
   Expense Adjustment Factor: 1.00 − 0.12 = 0.88

   Final adjusted rates:
     Employee: $16.79 × .88 = $14.78
     Composite Dependent: $27.26 × .88 = $23.99

        Total Monthly Premium

   Employee Life: $0.69 × 3,125(000) = $2,156.25
   Employee Medical: $14.78 × 250 = $3,695.00
   Dependent Medical: $23.99 × 175 = $4,198.25

   Note that in the majority of group insurance programs, the employer pays the cost of most or all of the employee life and medical premiums while the dependent medical premium is often paid for substantially by the employee.

FIGURE 31–4.   Sample Dividend Calculation

		Life	*Medical*	*Total*
1.	Premium	$25,000	$100,000	$125,000
2.	Paid Claims	12,500	90,000	102,500
3.	Beginning Claim Reserve	2,700	26,000	28,700
4.	End Claim Reserve	3,000	30,000	33,000
5.	Incurred Claims: (2) − (3) + (4)	12,800	94,000	106,800
6.	Expected Claims	16,500	85,000	101,500
7.	Credibility	.25	.65	—
8.	Charge for Claims:			
	(7) × (5) + [1.00 − (7)] × (6)	$15,575	$ 90,850	$106,425
9.	Expense Charges			
	a) Commissions	$ 1,000	$ 4,000	$ 5,000
	b) Taxes	625	2,500	3,125
	c) Other Administration and			
	Risk Charges	1,200	8,000	9,200
	d) Less Interest on Reserves	− 100	− 1,250	− 1,350
	e) Total	$ 2,725	$ 13,250	$ 15,975
10.	Dividend Earned: (1) − (8) − (9e)	$ 6,700	−$ 4,100	$ 2,600
11.	Less Deficit Carried Forward			
	from Prior Period	—	—	$ 2,000
12.	Deficit to Be Carried Forward:			
	(10 Total) − (11), if less than 0			$ 0
13.	Dividend Payable:			
	(10 Total) − (11), if greater than 0			$ 600

An approach similar to the one demonstrated in this dividend calculation would be employed to estimate the appropriate level of renewal premium. However, in the latter case, the desired dividend margin becomes the starting point with expected claims and expenses added to develop the required premium. In addition, since the renewal calculation is prospective rather than retrospective in nature, care must be taken to assure that actual and expected claims, as well as expenses, are appropriately adjusted to reflect anticipated inflation.

SELECTED REFERENCES

Eilers, Robert D., and Crowe, Robert M. (eds.). *Group Insurance Handbook.* Homewood, Ill.: Richard D. Irwin, Inc., 1965.

Gregg, Davis W. *Group Life Insurance.* 3d ed. Homewood, Ill.: Richard D. Irwin, Inc., 1962.

Jackson, Paul H. "Experience Rating," *Transactions of the Society of Actuaries,* Vol. V (1953), p. 239.

————. "Self-Insurance and Group Insurance," *Journal of the American Society of Chartered Life Underwriters,* Vol. XVI, No. 4 (Fall 1962), p. 300.

Keffer, Ralph. "An Experience Rating Formula," *Transactions of the Actuarial Society of America,* Vol. XXX (1929), p. 130.

MacIntyre, Duncan M. *Voluntary Health Insurance and Rate Making.* Ithaca, N.Y.: Cornell University Press, 1962.

Pickrell, J. F. *Group Health Insurance.* Homewood, Ill.: Richard D. Irwin, Inc., 1961.

32

Group Insurance Marketing

By JAMES B. JACOBSON

THE BUSINESS of providing employee benefits has achieved impressive stature. A survey by the Chamber of Commerce of the United States, covering 1,115 reporting employers, estimates that 1969 employee benefit costs, excluding payments for time not worked such as vacations, holidays, rest periods, and so forth, amounted to 13 percent of total wages and salaries paid by employers.[1] This was equivalent to 7 percent of the Gross National Product.

Group insurance marketing reflects the vitality of the group insurance field. The number of insurance companies and other professionals, well supplied with variations, alternatives, and new approaches, is abundant. The demand from a growing number of knowledgeable group buyers for new, improved, or more efficient group insurance products and services is strong. Success in group marketing has come to those who have responded most intelligently to the needs of the marketplace, have best identified and served new markets, and have developed the necessary team of expert specialists needed for effective operation.

NATURE OF THE GROUP MARKET

Importance and Growth

Group insurance continues to expand its relative importance within the insurance business. While the term nature of most group insurance does not build insurance company assets like more permanent forms of coverage, group insurance is assuming a larger proportion of total insurance in force. At the end of 1971, $581 billion of group life insurance (excluding credit life) represented 40 percent of all life insurance in force with legal reserve life companies. This exceeded a tenfold growth since 1950, when group life insurance in force was about $48 billion and 20 per-

---

[1] Chamber of Commerce of the United States, *Employee Benefits 1969* (Washington, D.C., 1970), p. 30.

cent of all legal reserve life insurance in force.[2] Group credit life insurance, which increased 2340 percent since 1950 to $74 billion at the end of 1970, is almost 85 percent of total credit life insurance in force.[3] The over $8 billion of annual group health premiums represented 71 percent of total health insurance premiums written by insurance companies in 1970. Annual group health premiums in 1950 were less than one twelfth of this figure, and were then slightly less than one half of the total health premiums paid to insurance companies.[4]

The impressive growth of group insurance has come from intensive cultivation of the market and from expansion of the market itself, enhanced by general economic expansion and population growth, a general inflationary trend, and a continuing increase in the demand for security. Widespread interest in group marketing as a means of increasing consumer marketing economies also has contributed to the growth of group insurance.

Group marketing as an insurance distribution system possesses some significant advantages. Since the risk is spread by group exposure, underwriting usually can be liberalized and acceptance by the insurer is thus greater. Also, insurance company unit expenses are reduced, resulting in lower cost. Sponsorship of group insurance by an employer tends to give the individuals insured an assurance that their coverage has been reviewed by professionals and that the benefits and costs are proper. The extension of these advantages to employer groups with as low as two employees and to groups of individuals outside the usual employer-employee relationship has broadened the group insurance market considerably.

Although it is a rare employer of ten or more employees who does not now have some form of group insurance coverage, and although the issue of national health insurance clouds the group health area, continued growth of the group market is assured. Not only will the economic and social factors mentioned previously continue to influence the growth of group insurance favorably, but the general consumer trend toward purchases through mass distribution is increasing the availability of insurance coverages to more and more consumer groups in many unique ways. In addition, vertical market penetration will continue as more intensive cultivation of the small employer market of two or more employees is made. New product development will continue to meet the needs of the insuring public, as consideration is given to such areas as group property and casualty insurance, group equity products, and group legal services. Also, market penetration of such existing relatively new products as survivor income benefits, long-term disability coverage, dental benefits, vision care and prescription drugs will increase. In addition, increasing attention will be given to worldwide markets. Although foreign marketing to date by United States group insurance companies has been limited,

---

[2] Institute of Life Insurance, *Life Insurance Fact Book* (New York, 1972), p. 24.
[3] *Ibid.*, p. 33.
[4] Health Insurance Institute, *Source Book of Health Insurance Data* (New York, 1971), pp. 40–42.

in the past few years most major carriers have entered into cooperative reinsurance arrangements with foreign insurers, and this market can be expected to expand.

Characteristics

Because of its complex and flexible nature, group insurance marketing is highly specialized. While the majority of small cases is developed by agents, most group insurance premium is developed through brokers and consultants who specialize in or have departments for group insurance, assisted by group insurance specialists. The group insurance buyer is more sophisticated than the typical buyer of individual insurance, and the larger group buyers have risk managers who are knowledgeable in the group insurance area. Competition is keen, and the group buyer not only buys through competitive bidding but continuously reviews his program from a comparative cost and benefit standpoint. Thus, benefit plan changes are frequent and often involve transfer of coverage among insurers and brokers. Continuous client service by brokers and insurance companies is essential, and technical competence and an appreciation of specific client objectives are paramount.

Group insurance marketing is strongly influenced by regulatory factors at both the state and federal level. In the area of taxation, the expansion of group insurance has been strongly aided by favorable income tax treatment of group life proceeds and employer contributions for group insurance. On the other hand, state taxation of insurance premiums has prompted some large employers to explore alternate methods for financing employee benefit plans and has limited certain areas of the group insurance market. Most states define eligible groups, regulate premium rates, and require approval of contract forms. Regulations vary from state to state, and group insurance products and marketing techniques must be adjusted to comply with the laws and regulations pertaining to the situs of each group contract. In addition, many states limit the maximum group life insurance benefit that can be provided.

Marketing limitations at the federal level have resulted from inclusion of disability coverage under social security and from Medicare legislation providing health benefits for persons age 65 and over. The expected passage of federal legislation providing for a national health insurance program will have a major impact on the entire health insurance market. Whether this effect will expand or contract private group health insurance will depend upon the exact nature of the legislation.[5]

Description of the Market

The group insurance market can be divided into various segments based on the types of groups insured.

Individual Employers. The largest segment of the group insurance market by far is individual employers providing coverage for their employees. Although the group insurance policy is issued to the employer, the type and level of benefits for hourly employees are determined by

---

[5] See Chapter 50 for a discussion of the implications of national health insurance.

collective bargaining in many instances. Most insurance companies writing group insurance concentrate the bulk of their group insurance activities in this market. Insurance company agency forces obtain nearly all of their group business in this segment, principally with employers having less than 100 employees.

Joint Employer-Union Groups. Group policies issued to trusts insuring members of one or more labor unions employed by one or more employers for benefits arising from collective bargaining represent an important segment of the group insurance marketplace in terms of insurance in force. This type of group is permitted by most state statutes, and the trust arrangement is provided for under the Labor Management Relations Act of 1941. The group policy is issued to the trustees of the trust, who are comprised equally of management and labor representatives. Broker and consultant specialists are particularly important in this market segment.

Associations of Employers. A small but important segment of the group market is employer-provided coverage through trade associations or trusts involving employers in the same industry, who have common business problems and interests. Most states allow group contracts to be issued to multiple-employer trade associations or trusts involving employers in the same industry. Some states allow contracts for multiple employers in different industries. A few insurance carriers are sponsoring widespread multiple-industry employer trusts that provide group insurance benefits for groups with as few as two employees.

Associations of Individuals. Depending upon state regulation, associations of individuals such as professional, fraternal, alumni, or community service groups are growing markets for group insurance. Statutory restrictions affecting group insurance in many states necessitate the use of wholesale or franchise policy forms for these types of groups. Specialty products, such as accident insurance or plans paying a fixed amount for each day a person is hospitalized, are common in this market.

Customer Groups. Reflecting the increasing trend toward mass marketing, such groups as savings depositors, credit card holders of banks and savings and loan associations, and customers of oil companies, department stores and utility companies, constitute a growing market for group insurance. Wholesale, franchise, or individual policy forms are necessary in many states because of statutory restrictions. This market segment does not include installment debtors of creditors, who are considered a separate category.

Labor Unions. While most state statutes allow issuance of group policies to labor unions, federal law prohibits an employer engaged in interstate commerce from making group insurance contributions directly to a union. Since group insurance financing for a labor union group thus must come directly from union members or the union treasury, group marketing directly to labor unions is not significant. Benefits purchased under such plans are not a result of collective bargaining.

Creditors. Group life and disability coverages covering installment debtors of creditor institutions such as banks, finance companies, credit unions, and retail vendors represent a significant portion of the group market. At the end of 1970, group credit life insurance amounted to nearly

12 percent of all group life insurance in force.[6] The rapid growth of consumer credit has been responsible for the expansion of this market. Some insurance companies have specialized in this field; others have not pursued it.

Comparative Size. Table 32–1 indicates the relative size of group life in force by type of insured group.

TABLE 32–1.   **Group Life Insurance in Force by Type of Insured Group— 1968 (excludes dependent coverage, group credit life, Federal Employees' Group Life and Servicemen's Group Life)**

	Master Policies		Insurance in Force	
Type of Group	Number	Percent of Total	Amount (000,000 omitted)	Percent of Total
Related to employment or occupation				
Employer-employee	239,820	87.5%	$298,481	83.9%
Union and joint employer-union	5,060	1.9	22,447	6.3
Professional society	670	.2	7,669	2.2
Employee association ...	1,690	.6	10,840	3.0
Other	1,550	.6	4,978	1.4
Total	248,790	90.8	344,415	96.8
Not related to employment or occupation				
Fraternal society	50	*	241	.1
Savings or investment group	23,890	8.7	8,421	2.4
Other	1,260	.5	2,486	.7
Total	25,200	9.2	11,148	3.2
Total all groups	273,990	100.0%	$355,563	100.0%

* Less than 0.05%.
Source: Institute of Life Insurance.

THE MARKETING SYSTEM

The group insurance marketing system includes a number of basic components. The group buyer is of prime importance, and the relative significance of the other components varies among market segments and type and size of cases.

Group Buyer

The entire marketing process focuses on the group buyer, who may be an employer, a group of trustees, a union, a creditor, an association, or other contract entity. In the case of an employer, the individual who makes the buying decision depends mainly on the employer's size. For other than large employers (e.g., employers with under 500 employees),

---

[6] Institute of Life Insurance, *Life Insurance Fact Book* (New York, 1971), p. 33.

he generally is a key executive, often the chief executive. For large employers, the buying decision is often made by a risk or employee benefit manager or executive responsible for this area, although final ratification by higher authority frequently is necessary.

A risk manager for a large corporation usually is knowledgeable in group insurance and frequently supervises a large employee benefit department. In performing his functions, he determines the feasibility of self-insurance, partial insurance with large deductibles, and full insurance as solutions to various coverage needs. Thus, group insurance buying may involve more than choosing among insurance coverages and carriers; it also may mean choosing between insurance and partial or full absorption of some risks. Recently, growing concern with costs and tight money has increased employer interest in alternative devices to minimize group insurance premium taxes and claim reserves. A few large employers have self-insured their group health programs and purchased administrative but not risk-bearing services from insurance carriers, although as yet there is no trend in this direction.

Brokers and Consultants

Almost all large group buyers retain a broker or consultant to provide professional advice on group insurance. The broker or consultant advises in such areas as plan design, administration and claim procedures, employee communications, financial considerations, and regulatory requirements, and represents the client in selecting and dealing with insurance carriers. The primary (although not always sharp) distinction between a broker and a consultant is that the former generally is compensated by commissions paid by the insurance carrier and charged against the financial experience of the group policy, while the latter generally is compensated directly by the group buyer on a fee basis. This component of the group marketing system can be divided broadly into the following two types.

Small General Lines Brokers. The small general lines broker usually is not specialized in the group insurance area. While brokers of this type usually have long-standing relationships with their commercial property and liability accounts, many do not handle their clients' employee benefit programs. This may be due to their lack of expertise in the group insurance area or fear that adverse group health claim settlements may jeopardize the property and liability insurance relationship with their clients. Where such a broker handles a client's employee benefit program, he usually depends heavily on the expertise of the insurer's group representative. Small general lines brokers increasingly are becoming involved in group insurance to enhance their income and prevent larger group brokers from making inroads on their clients.

Group Insurance Brokers and Consultants. The major portion of group insurance premiums is handled by specialty brokers or consultants, or large brokerage or consulting firms with specialized group departments. The client relationship established by these brokers and consultants through their specialized group insurance knowledge gives them tremendous advantages over nonspecialized brokers, and accounts for their dominant position. Often their staff members are former insurance company group representatives. Many of these firms also handle general lines of insurance and have national and international operations.

Insurance Company Agents

Agency representatives of insurance companies are an important component of the group insurance market, particularly with employer groups of under 100 employees. An agent's general group marketing role is similar to that of the small general lines broker—his group client contacts come through his primary nongroup insurance activities, and he frequently needs sales and technical assistance from insurance company group representatives. While most agents do not possess extensive group technical knowledge, some agents specialize in or write a large amount of group insurance and require less assistance from company group representatives.

The potential commission income from group sales offers an agent incentive to develop this market, as do the potential by-product sales of individual insurance to the employees covered under the group plan. While there has been some agent opposition to group insurance on the grounds that it reduces the agents' individual insurance market, this attiude has lessened significantly. In some instances, an agent's own company does not market group insurance and a group representative from another company often motivates such an agent to place group business with the group representative's company.

In addition to functioning as the agent for the sale of a master group contract to a group client, an insurance company agent sometimes engages in enrollment activity on a case where another agent or broker has sold the master contract. These cases are typically employer associations, where enrollment of individual employer units is best handled on a direct, personal contact basis by sales personnel. Agents acting in such a capacity are usually paid an enrollment commission. Some large brokerage firms also perform this function.

Group Insurance Administrators

Another component of the group insurance marketing system is the professional group administrator, a third party, who is found largely in the trust fund area involving both association and labor-management negotiated plans. His function normally is to handle the administration of established plans on a fee basis. This usually involves premium collection and remittance to the insurance company, handling additions and terminations under the plan, making claim or annuity payments, and fund accounting. While an administrator usually does not function as a broker or consultant, some perform these functions as well.

Group Representatives

The group representative is a group insurance specialist responsible for selling his insurance company's group products and servicing in-force group clients (these functions are split in some companies). His sales activity normally is conducted through his company's agents and through brokers and consultants whom he motivates to place group business with his company. He usually is salaried and receives a productivity bonus, although some group representatives are salaried only.

The group representative's sales activities include developing group prospects through brokers, consultants and agents; securing necessary underwriting data; assisting in plan design; preparing group proposals; presenting proposals to prospects and brokers; and, after the plan is sold, assisting in enrolling the eligible individuals. His service activities include installing administrative procedures for new group cases, keeping in-force clients informed of developments affecting their group insurance, advising on plan modernization, assisting in administrative problems, assisting in periodic group plan financial reviews, and preventing the loss of in-force clients.

It can be seen that some of the functions of the group representative, agent, broker and consultant overlap. The exact nature of their roles with a particular group client is determined by the client, and depends upon the relative expertise and relationships of the individuals involved. The knowledgeable group representative will attempt to develop successful relationships with agents, brokers and consultants by offering them meaningful suggestions; information on trends, legislation, and competitive devices; and by providing prompt and accurate service on their cases.

Direct Marketing

Nearly all group buyers purchase coverage through an intermediary broker, consultant, or agent. Occasionally, a buyer will approach one or more insurance carriers on a direct basis. Where this occurs, the buyer usually has a knowledgeable group insurance staff which, in effect, performs the usual functions of an intermediary. Where a new case is closed through direct marketing of this type, a minimum commission charge usually is made by the insurance carrier.

Marketing by Mail and Other Mass Media

Marketing by mail is generally used for marketing mass coverages such as hospital indemnity, accident coverage, and term life insurance to customer groups and associations of individuals. After the master sale is made to the sponsoring organization, enrollment of individuals is made through direct mail and mass media such as newspapers, magazines, radio, and television. Enrollments per solicitation of one or two percent of those eligible are typical. Insurance carriers often test the market on a pilot basis before attempting to enroll the entire eligible group.

GROUP INSURANCE COMPENSATION

As previously noted, group insurance compensation to agents and brokers normally is in the form of commission payments from the insurance carrier, while consultants are compensated through fees paid directly by the group policyholder. Commissions are by far the most prevalent form of compensation.

Commission Levels

Compared to individual insurance policies, commissions for the sale of group term insurance are much lower as a percentage of premium. This is due to the size of the premiums, the marketing system and the competition involved.

Although it usually takes considerable time and effort to sell group coverages, the dollar amount of premium produced from a sale normally is much greater than the premium on an individual policy. In addition, a salaried group representative usually aids the agent or broker in much of the sales, service and technical activity on the group case. The use of lower commission scales for group insurance also has been influenced by the highly competitive climate of the group marketplace and the greater degree of continuing service required. The group buyer is more aware than his individual counterpart that the cost of his program is affected by the level of commissions. Under most group policies covering 100 or more employees, the group policyholder is aware of the amount of commissions being paid, since such disclosure is required by the Federal Welfare and Pension Plans Disclosure Act (Public Law 85–836). Thus, the group buyer is better able to measure the continuing service provided by the agent or broker against the commissions being paid, and the buyer will change agents or brokers if he is not satisfied. The continuous right of the group policyholder to designate the agent or broker is recognized by most group insurance carriers.

Types of Commissions

There are two basic types of commission schedules for group term insurance. The standard, or *regular* scale, uses a higher first-year scale coupled with a lower scale for renewal years. The *level* commission scale uses the same scale for both the first and renewal years. The two scales are designed to provide the same amount of commission over a ten-year period for a given amount of premium. Except for certain classes of business, agents and brokers often are able to choose either scale for new group business. Insurance company rules often require the level scale to be paid on cases transferred from another insurance company and on certain types of cases where a higher than normal chance of lapse may be anticipated.

Commissions under each of the schedules normally are broken into selling commissions and service commissions. Selling commissions generally are set at a low level. The service commission component usually is paid to the broker or agent after the first year only if he continues to provide services on the group case satisfactory to the client and to the insurance carrier. In actual practice, service commissions usually are discontinued only if the agent or broker terminates his relationship with the case or if the client specifically requests that a change be made.

Group insurance commissions are not uniform among all insurance companies, and there is a wide range among carriers on some types of groups or some size cases. The major group carriers, however, tend to be fairly uniform on the larger cases. Under the *regular* scale, a typical first-year commission is 20 percent of the first $5,000 of annual case premium, 15 percent of the next $5,000, 12.5 percent of the next $10,000, and 10 percent of the next $10,000, graded down to .1 percent. Typical renewals in the second through tenth policy years provide 5 percent of the first $1,000 of annual case premium, 3 percent of the next $4,000, and 1.5 percent of the next $5,000, graded down to .1 percent.

A representative *level* ten-year schedule pays each year 6.50 percent of the first $1,000 of annual case premium, 4.70 percent of the next $4,000, 2.85 percent of the next $5,000, 2.60 percent of the next $10,000, and 2.35 percent of the next $10,000, graded down to .1 percent.

Some carriers will continue to pay commissions beyond the normal ten-year period provided the agent or broker continues to perform service satisfactory to the policyholder and carrier.

Small Case Commissions

Since total premiums for a case of less than 25 employees are small and the agent or broker is expected to require less group representative sales and service assistance, commission scales usually are higher than those used for larger groups.

Group Permanent Commissions

Generally, group life insurance plans which have cash values compete in a market where individual policies are solicited. Commissions for group permanent insurance, therefore, combine the commission practices of both group term life and individual life insurance, and scales higher than regular group term commissions usually are used. An illustrative regular scale for level premium group permanent whole life insurance might grade downward, starting with the first $5,000 of annual premium, from 40 percent in the first year and from 4.25 percent in the second through tenth years.

THE SALES PROCESS

Factors Motivating the Group Insurance Purchase

Group insurance has become more than a "fringe benefit." Today, employee benefits are considered a part of overall compensation. Most employees, especially those belonging to unions, expect a wide range of benefits with heavy employer financing. The employer normally does not decide *if* benefits should be provided; he determines (often jointly with one or more unions) the *extent* of the benefits and how he will provide them. In order to attract and retain good employees, the group buyer finds it important to maintain a competitive employee benefit program by periodically increasing benefits or adding new coverages.

In addition, the term nature of group insurance, the expense outlay involved, and the intense competition in the group marketplace result in considerable switching of carriers by group buyers, particularly by small and medium size employers. Such switching can be triggered by many causes, including poor service, an increase in premium rates, and higher-than-projected administrative expenses of the insurer.

Steps Leading to the Group Insurance Purchase

The sales process can start in a variety of ways: group representative motivation of an agent, broker, or client; prospecting by an agent or broker; contacting of an agent, broker, or insurance company by a prospective group buyer; collective bargaining; and legislation affecting employee benefits. Initial development frequently takes a long period. As early as possible in the sales process, the person soliciting should determine that he has a bona fide group prospect and should attempt to work with a person who can make or at least strongly influence the buying decision. The necessary underwriting data on which to evaluate the risk and prepare the group proposal then should be obtained. The data include employee information, such as age, sex, salary, location, and dependent status; occupational information; and, if there is a group insurance plan in force, benefit details, rate history, and claim experience.

Except for very small cases, where an agent or general broker is involved the group representative usually will be brought in at an early stage and will influence the plan design. Where a group broker is involved, the group representative may not become involved until after the broker has secured the data and has developed a fairly rigid set of plan specifications on which insurance carriers are to base their quotations. In either case, the request for a group proposal and accompanying data will be given to the group representative. An agent sometimes and a broker almost always will deal with a number of insurance companies on a particular case. Risk evaluation and rate calculation will be done either in the insurance carrier's field group office or home office, depending upon the nature and size of the case and the general practice of the insurance company. For very small groups, some insurers provide computer-prepared proposals. The variety of benefits may be more limited in such cases.

After the proposal is prepared, the group representative often will accompany the agent or broker to make the presentation to the prospect. This frequently does not occur where a group broker or consultant is involved, since many of them prefer to make a comparative analysis of the bids and make their own presentation to the group buyer. In such instances, the group representative will make his proposal presentation to the broker or consultant. Before a final decision is made as to selection of a carrier, it is not uncommon, particularly on the larger cases, for alternate quotations to be requested and for further negotiation with one or more insurance carriers to take place.

Selection of a carrier is made by the group buyer with the assistance of his broker or consultant. Where an insurance company agent is involved, he usually is competing for the sale with other brokers and agents unless he is acting as the client's sole broker. This is also true for some small general brokers. Group brokers and consultants, on the other hand, usually act as the client's sole representative in the selection of a carrier.

Selection of a carrier is based on a variety of factors, both objective and subjective. These include projections of net cost; initial premium rates; plan provisions; sales, administration, and claim facilities; compliance with plan specifications; and the general reputation, expertise, and credibility of the insurer. Intelligent selection requires an evaluation of variations, which can be significant, in expertise and service among carriers.

After the Purchase

After the plan of benefits and carrier have been selected, a number of postsales steps must be undertaken to put the plan into operation. While the nature of these steps varies among segments of the group market, the basic principles generally are the same.

In the typical employer-employee group, the first step is the *enrollment* of eligible employees. Because most plans involve some employee contribution and because group underwriting usually requires a 75 percent enrollment, the planning and execution of this step are vital. The key to a successful enrollment is the employer's support in using key supervisory employees in the enrollment process and in permitting employee enrollment meetings during working hours. The insurance carrier normally prepares the solicitation material (including announcement letters, booklets, enrollment cards, and waiver cards), and makes group representatives available to conduct enrollment meetings. The agent or broker also plays an important role in this step.

Following the enrollment, the insurance carrier completes the *issue* work for the case. This involves calculation of final rates based upon the enrollment and issuance of the master contract, employee certificates, premium billing and claim forms, and appropriate administrative and claim processing instructions.

The third step is the *installation* of the case, in which the group representative, usually accompanied by the agent or broker, meets with the appropriate personnel in the policyholder's office to review and sign the master contract, deliver the administration and claim manuals and forms, and explain all administrative procedures. This step is essential to the future operation of the group program. The policyholder must collect employee contributions, report changes, remit premiums, and enroll and often prepare certificates for new employees. While some large policyholders pay claims on insurance company drafts, the majority certify claim eligibility and forward claims to the carrier for payment.

Following installation, the group representative makes periodic *service calls* on the policyholder to assist in the continued orderly operation of the plan. In many insurance companies the group representative uses a service report form as a guide in reviewing key aspects of the plan's operation. After the call, the completed report is submitted to the home office for review. Periodic service calls are important in maintaining good client rapport and providing opportunities for new business through plan modernization or added coverages.

An important part of service call activity is *conservation* of the policyholder against switching to another insurance carrier. Since switching is most frequently the result of a rate increase, it is important for the group representative to keep the policyholder informed of cost trends throughout the policy year. If a rate increase is necessary, the group representative should contact the policyholder as far in advance as possible to explain and document the factors necessitating the increase. Conservation activity is very important in maintaining good case persistency.

INSURANCE COMPANY ORGANIZATIONAL STRUCTURE

General Considerations

The nature and size of an insurance company's group organization are influenced by many factors. Foremost are the company's overall objectives and marketing policy, as well as the nature and size of the agency force and the relationship of the group operation to it. Some companies market group insurance primarily through their own agency force, some concentrate on brokers, and others operate in both areas. Group structure and size also are dependent on the potential group markets the company is attempting to penetrate. For example, a carrier may target primarily on the small employer market, or alternatively on a specialty market, such as direct mail or credit life insurance. A company selling to a diverse market, widespread geographically, will structure differently than one specializing in one geographic area or product. A company's group structure also is dependent on the size and complexity of its group operation.

Home Office

While group insurance organizational structures vary widely, the functions of a typical large group operation of a major insurance carrier, excluding pensions, can be divided logically into at least three broad areas: (1) marketing, (2) actuarial and technical services, and (3) administration and claims. These functions are illustrated in Figure 32–1.

Some operations can be handled properly in more than one functional area or in a different area than shown. For example, policyholder service might be supervised in the administration area, and underwriting and dividend calculations for routine and small cases might be handled in the administration area following guidelines established by the actuarial area.

A large group insurance operation lends itself to a fully integrated structure, as illustrated in Figure 32–1. The highly technical nature of group marketing requires the services of many specialists for successful operation. These specialists must keep in mind at all times the overall objectives of the organization if they are to function effectively as a well-knit team.

Field

Marketing. While no two group field organizations are identical, the group field marketing structures for most carriers are similar. The basic field unit is the group office, which usually is located in a major city and is responsible for group insurance sales, and usually service of in-force

FIGURE 32–1.   Company Group Insurance Department Functional Organization

GROUP INSURANCE DEPARTMENT		
Marketing	Actuarial and Technical Services	Administration and Claims
1. Supervision of group field staff.	1. New and renewal case underwriting.	1. Policy issue and amendment.
2. Supervision and review of policyholder service.	2. Premium rate determination.	2. Booklet and certificate preparation.
3. Large case relations.	3. Dividend or experience refund determination.	3. Premium and commission accounting.
4. Specialized broker and consultant relations.	4. Valuation and annual statement preparation.	°4. Claim payment.
5. Agency relations.	5. Contract development and filing.	°5. Claim analysis and control.
°6. Advertising and sales promotion.	6. Product development.	°6. Computer systems.
7. Product development.	7. Planning, objectives and evaluation.	7. Product development.
8. Planning, objectives and evaluation.		8. Planning, objectives and evaluation.

° Frequently these functions may be assigned to a separate department as part of a company-wide function.

group cases, in a specific geographic area. The office is managed by a group manager who is in charge of one or more group representatives, depending upon the volume of business handled. It is not unusual for group managers of smaller companies or offices to be the only group representative in the office. The group offices of companies whose group operations are an adjunct to their agency operations are frequently a part of their agency offices. The group manager normally reports to a regional manager of group marketing who is located in a regional or home office. The regional manager has a number of group managers under his supervision, and usually reports to the group marketing vice president.

Other. Most group companies with widespread operations have field group claim pay points. A group claim pay point may be located in a group office, with claims paid by a separate claim staff. Many field claim offices are apart from group offices but located in the same cities. Insurance company group claim representatives, who visit large policyholders to assist with claim questions and procedures and who maintain contacts with local medical practitioners, sometimes work from field claim offices.

Some large companies have regional administration offices apart from their home offices, where home office administration, claim and technical functions, including group insurance, are handled for a given geographic area.

ENTERING THE GROUP MARKET

Reasons for Entry

Only 7 of the 100 leading life insurance companies (by total business in force) operating in the United States had not actively entered the group life insurance market by the end of 1970. Smaller carriers, however, will continue to consider whether or not to enter the group insurance field actively. Reasons for entering the group field include the following:

1. To provide additional earnings and prestige for the company's agency force through direct group commissions and by-product sales of individual insurance.
2. To provide a facility to enable the company and its agents to adjust better to the trend toward mass marketing.
3. To provide group facilities for the company's agents so they will not take group prospects to other insurance companies.
4. To contribute further to the profit or surplus of the company.
5. To maintain or increase the growth and prestige of the company and its position in the business.
6. To fulfill further the insurance business's social responsibility to the insuring public.

Problems to Be Considered

Basic factors an insurance company should consider prior to entering the group market include anticipated expenses and financial results, organizational considerations, and agent relations.

The investment needed to begin a group operation, particularly if the market is to be pursued aggressively, is substantial. The specialized nature of group insurance will require the acquisition of a trained staff for both home office and field operations, mainly from outside the company. The rapid expansion of group insurance has resulted in a tight labor market for qualified group personnel. Before marketing can begin, heavy expenses will be incurred in developing products and establishing actuarial, administrative, claim and marketing procedures. A carrier also must prepare and file policy and certificate forms with the insurance departments of the states in which it will operate.

Consideration must be given to the organization of the group operation and how it will be integrated into the company's overall structure. This will depend upon the company's motives for entering the group market and the nature and anticipated scale of its group operation.

Agent reaction to entering the group business should be weighed. Although group insurance will provide additional earnings potential, some agents perceive group insurance as reducing their individual markets. Also, the dominant position of brokers in group marketing may cause agent morale problems.

In addition to the foregoing considerations, there are a number of marketing problems to be faced. In which major marketing segments can the company compete most successfully? Which geographic markets should be entered? As a new group company without an established group reputation, how can it successfully compete for business? Should the company charge rates lower than its competition? This practice is especially dangerous for health insurance, considering the rapidly rising trend of medical care costs. Assuming its group marketing is not to be confined to its agency force, how will the company get business from brokers? Brokerage relations must be established, unless the company previously has developed such relations through other lines of business. If the company's agents are to participate aggressively in group marketing, will the company's new group field force be able to handle this demand? These questions must be answered satisfactorily if the newly entering group company is to be successful.

SELECTED REFERENCES

Chamber of Commerce of the United States. *Employee Benefits 1969*. Washington, D.C., 1970.

Deric, Arthur J. (ed.). *The Total Approach to Employee Benefits*. New York: American Management Association, 1967.

Eilers, Robert D., and Crowe, Robert M. *Group Insurance Handbook*. Homewood, Ill.: Richard D. Irwin, Inc., 1965.

Gregg, Davis W. *Group Life Insurance*. 3d ed. Homewood, Ill.: Richard D. Irwin, Inc., 1962.

Health Insurance Institute. *Source Book of Health Insurance Data, 1971–72*. New York.

Institute of Life Insurance. *Life Insurance Fact Book, 1972*. New York.

Milliman, Wendell. *Is Group Insurance for You?* New York: North American Reassurance Co., 1958.

Pickrell, Jesse F. *Group Health Insurance*. Rev. ed. Homewood, Ill.: Richard D. Irwin, Inc., 1961.

part VI

<hr>

Pensions and Other Qualified Deferred Compensation Plans

PRIVATE PENSIONS have existed in a formal sense for about a century, providing retirement and other benefits for employees in the private and public sectors of society. Immense growth has occurred in the past half century and now some 50 million persons are participants. Major changes in laws and regulations have occurred in recent years to encourage and to strengthen this important segment of economic security.

Part VI is concerned with a thorough analysis of the theoretical and practical aspects of private pensions and other qualified deferred compensation plans.

33

Nature and Development of Private Pensions

By JOSEPH J. MELONE

MAN IS CONSTANTLY seeking means by which to enhance his economic security. One cause of economic insecurity is the probable reduction of an individual's earning power at an advanced age. In this country, this risk is met through one or more of the following means: personal savings (including individual insurance and annuities), private pensions, and government-sponsored programs. The rather dramatic growth of private pensions in the past two decades has focused considerable interest on this form of income maintenance. The purpose of this chapter is to outline briefly the nature of the economic problem of old age, the rationale of the private pension movement, the reasons for the growth of these plans, and the broad characteristics of current private pension programs.

ECONOMIC PROBLEM OF OLD AGE

Increasing Longevity

The fact that life expectancy has been increasing is well recognized. However, that this increase in longevity is a recent and quite dramatic development is often not appreciated. Within the last 60 years the life expectancy at birth has increased from 47 years to approximately 70 years. This result has been achieved in spite of the limited gains in life expectancy in the last decade. The rates of mortality at the earlier ages are now so low that further improvements in mortality at these ages would have little impact on further extensions of the average length of life. If additional improvements in longevity are to be realized, reductions in mortality at the older ages are required. This impediment to further extensions in life expectancy may be overcome if medical advances result from the current concentration of research in the areas of the chronic and degenerative diseases.

One effect of the improvements in longevity in the 20th century has been an absolute and relative increase in the population of persons aged

65 and over. In 1900, there were approximately 3 million persons aged 65 and over, whereas there were about 18 million aged persons in 1963. By 1980, persons aged 65 and over are expected to number about 24.5 million. The proportion of the United States population aged 65 and over is currently about 9 percent, whereas the proportion of the population in these age brackets in 1900 was about 4 percent. It is estimated that aged persons will constitute about 10 percent of the population by 1980. The problem of old-age economic security, therefore, is of concern to an increasing number and percentage of the United States population.

Nature of Risk of Excessive Longevity

It seems rather paradoxical to speak of the *risk* of excessive longevity. Good health and long life are considered by most people to be desirable rather than unfavorable contingencies. The concern in this discussion is, of course, restricted to the economic risk associated with longevity. Longevity is a source of economic insecurity in that an individual may outlive his financial capacity to maintain himself and his dependents.

The assumption is often made that the financial needs of an individual decrease after retirement. To some extent, this assumption is valid. The retired individual generally has no dependent children, and a home and its furnishings generally have been acquired by retirement age. However, the actual aggregate reduction in the financial needs of a person upon retirement has probably been overstated. Social pressures discourage any drastic change in one's standard of living. Furthermore, urbanization and its corollary, apartment living, minimize the prospect of retired parents moving in with their children. It is questionable, therefore, whether one should assume any significant decrease in basic financial needs upon retirement, at least for individuals in the low- and middle-income categories.

The extent to which an aged person will have the financial capacity to meet self-maintenance costs and those of dependents depends upon his employment opportunities and the prior provisions made to meet this contingency.

Employment Opportunities

The proportion of persons 65 and over with some income from active employment is currently about 20 percent, and this percentage has been declining steadily in recent years. To catalog all of the many factors which account for the reduction in the percentage of the aged in the labor force is an impossible task. A large number of older workers voluntarily retire from the labor force. If one has the necessary financial resources, he may wish to withdraw from active employment and live out his remaining years at a more leisurely pace. Others find it necessary for reasons of health to withdraw from the labor force at an advanced age. The aging process takes its toll, and many individuals are physically unable to operate at the level of efficiency attainable at the younger ages. Disabilities at the older ages tend to be more frequent and of longer duration.

Voluntary retirement and the physical inability to continue employment are undoubtedly important reasons for the decrease in the percentage of older persons participating in the labor force. However, these are probably not the most important factors affecting employment opportunities for the aged. The effects of industrialization and the development of the federal Old-Age, Survivors, and Disability Insurance program (OASDI), private pensions, and other employee benefit programs probably have had a more significant impact on this problem.

The rapid pace and dynamic evolution of industrial employments operate to the disadvantage of older persons. Automation and the mass-production assembly lines put a premium on physical dexterity and mental alertness. Employers generally are of the opinion, justifiable or not, that the younger workers are better suited to the demands of industrial employment. In an agricultural economy the able-bodied older person could continue to work, at least on a part-time basis.

The OASDI program and private pension plans, although created to alleviate the risk of excessive longevity, have aggravated the problem, in that these programs have tended to institutionalize age 65 as the normal retirement age. Also, some employers may hesitate to hire older workers on the assumption that these employees would increase pension and other employee benefit plan costs. It is difficult to generalize as to the impact of the older worker on employee benefit plan costs. Nevertheless, it must be recognized that an employer's attitude toward the hiring of older workers may be influenced by the assumption, justified or not, that fringe benefit costs will be adversely affected.

Capacity to Save

If employment opportunities for the aged are decreasing and financial needs are still substantial at advanced ages, the need for savings becomes quite apparent. There is relatively little information available on the extent of savings among the aged. What little data are available clearly indicate that assets, other than the equity in a home, of persons age 65 and over are relatively small.

However, the value of homeownership for the economic security of the aged should not be underestimated. Studies indicate that a substantial proportion of the homes owned by the aged are clear of any mortgage. Homeownership reduces the income needs of the aged insofar as normal maintenance costs, and taxes are less than the amount of rent required for comparable housing accommodations. It has been estimated that the maintenance costs for an unencumbered home are about one third to 40 percent less than the costs of renting comparable facilities. Furthermore, there is the possibility that the home can be used in part as an income-producing asset.

Also, in any evaluation of the economic status of the aged, resources available in time of need from both the immediate and extended family (i.e., children away from home and relatives) cannot be ignored. However, it does appear reasonable to conclude that the accumulated savings alone of many aged persons are not adequate to provide even a subsistence level of income for their remaining years.

There have been many forces at work which have restricted the growth of savings among the aged. Advertising, installment credit, and the media of mass communications encourage individuals to set their sights on a constantly increasing standard of living. This competition from consumption goods for current income dollars results in a lower priority being placed on the need for accumulating savings for old age. Also, the high levels of federal income tax rates reduce an income earner's capacity to save. In recent decades, inflation has presented one of the most important threats to the adequacy of savings programs. For employed persons, increases in the cost of living may be offset, in part or in whole, by increases in current earnings. That possibility does not exist for most aged persons. Therefore, these latter individuals are faced with the alternatives of accepting a lower standard of living or more rapidly liquidating their accumulated savings. Lastly, one must recognize that changing economic conditions may appreciably affect one's savings program. A severe depression may impair employment and earnings opportunities, and thereby necessitate the use of past savings to meet current living costs. The depression of the 1930s undoubtedly adversely affected the economic position of many of the current aged persons in our country. However, for those just entering upon their retirement years, the financial impact of the depression on their savings position was probably negligible. A substantial proportion of their working years covered the prosperous period beginning in the early 1940s. If this period of prosperity continues, the economic position of future aged persons may be considerably improved in comparison to the current group of individuals aged 65 and over.

RATIONALE OF PRIVATE PENSIONS

Early industrial pension plans were viewed as gratuities or rewards to employees for long and loyal service to the employer. These plans were largely discretionary, and management usually took the attitude that employees had no contractual rights to benefits under the plan. Continuation of the pension plan was dependent upon prevailing competitive conditions and management policy. Furthermore, management often reserved the right to terminate benefit payments to pensioners for misconduct on the part of the beneficiary or for any other reasons justifying such action in the views of the employer.

Several reasons have been suggested as to why these early plans were established. Some firms that had been established for a long period of years were increasingly faced with the problem of aged employees. These workers were often maintained on the payroll, and jobs suited to their capabilities had to be found. Also, in certain industries, notably railroads and utilities, the carelessness or inefficiencies of aged workers increased the probabilities of accidental injury to other employees and members of the public. Thus, pensions served as a logical method of removing superannuated employees from the payroll in a socially desirable manner. The adoption of a pension plan undoubtedly enhanced the reputation of the company in the community, as well as increasing the morale of the workers and the capacity of the employer to attract the more able employees. It has also been suggested that some employers established pension plans as a means of reducing strikes and to discourage the growth of unions.

To the extent that benefit payments could be discontinued at the discretion of the employer, a pension plan could have been used as a weapon against union activity. This possibility, plus the paternalistic nature of early pension programs, largely accounts for the resistance of union leaders at the time to industrial pensions.

All of the above reasons explaining the growth of early pensions might be best categorized by a single concept, i.e., *business expediency*. Business expediency, by the very nature of the concept, implies that the establishment of a plan is a management prerogative and that the primary motivation for the creation of such plans was the economic benefit, direct or indirect, that accrued to the employer. But as the economy became more and more industrialized and pension plans became more prevalent, there was increasing interest in the view that employers had a moral obligation to provide for the economic security of retired workers. This point of view was expressed as early as 1912 by Lee Welling Squier, as follows: "From the standpoint of the whole system of social economy, no employer has a right to engage men in any occupation that exhausts the individual's industrial life in 10, 20 or 40 years; and then leave the remnant floating on society at large as a derelict at sea."[1] This rationale of private pensions has come to be known as the *human depreciation concept* and was the point of view taken by the United Mine Workers of America in their 1946 drive to establish a welfare fund:

The United Mine Workers of America has assumed the position over the years that the cost of caring for the human equity in the coal industry is inherently as valid as the cost of the replacement of mining machinery, or the cost of paying taxes, or the cost of paying interest indebtedness, or any other factor incident to the production of a ton of coal for consumers' bins. . . . [The agreement establishing the Welfare Fund] recognized in principle the fact that the industry owed an obligation to those employees, and the coal miners could no longer be used up, crippled beyond repair and turned out to live or die subject to the charity of the community or the minimum contributions of the state.[2]

This analogy between human labor and industrial machines was also made in the report of the President's "fact-finding" board in the 1949 steelworkers' labor dispute in support of its conclusion that management had a responsibility to provide for the security of its workers: "We think that all industry, in the absence of adequate Government programs, owes an obligation to workers to provide for maintenance of the human body in the form of medical and similar benefits and full depreciation in the form of old-age retirement—in the same way as it does now for plant and machinery."[3] The report continues as follows: "What does that mean in terms of steelworkers? It should mean the use of earnings to insure against

[1] Lee Welling Squier, *Old Age Dependency in the United States* (New York: Macmillan Co., 1912), p. 272.

[2] United Mine Workers of America Welfare and Retirement Fund, *Pensions for Coal Miners* (Washington, D.C., n.d.), p. 4.

[3] Steel Industry Board, *Report to the President of the United States on the Labor Dispute in the Basic Steel Industry* (Washington, D.C.: U.S. Government Printing Office, September 10, 1949), p. 55.

the full depreciation of the human body—say at age 65—in the form of a pension or retirement allowance."[4]

The validity of the human depreciation concept of private pensions has been challenged by many pension experts. The process of aging is physiological and is not attributable to the employment relationship. Admittedly, the hazards of certain occupations undoubtedly shorten the life span of the employees involved. In those instances the employer can logically be held responsible only for the increase in the rate of aging due to the hazards of the occupation. More importantly, the analogy between men and machines is inherently unsound. A machine is an asset owned by the employer, and depreciation is merely an accounting technique for allocating the costs of equipment to various accounting periods. Employees, on the other hand, are free agents and sell their services to employers for a specified wage rate. An employee, unlike a machine, is free to move from one employer to another. The differences between men and machines are so great that one must question the value of the analogy as a basis for a rationale of private pensions.

In recent years a view of private pensions that has achieved broader acceptance is the *deferred wage concept*. This concept views a pension benefit as part of a wage package which is composed of cash wages and other employee fringe benefits. The deferred wage concept has particular appeal with reference to negotiated pension plans. The assumption is made that labor and management negotiators think in terms of total labor costs. Therefore, if labor negotiates a pension benefit, the amount of funds available for increases in cash wages are reduced accordingly. This theory of private pensions was expressed as early as 1913:

> In order to get a full understanding of old-age and service pensions, they should be considered as a part of the real wages of a workman. There is a tendency to speak of these pensions as being paid by the company, or, in cases where the employee contributes a portion, as being paid partly by the employer and partly by the employee. In a certain sense, of course, this may be correct, but it leads to confusion. A pension system considered as part of the real wages of an employee is really paid by the employee, not perhaps in money, but in the forgoing of an increase in wages which he might obtain except for the establishment of a pension system.[5]

The deferred wage concept has also been challenged on several grounds. First, it is noted that some employers who pay the prevailing cash wage rate for the particular industry also provide a pension benefit. Thus, it can be argued that in these cases the pension benefit is offered in addition to, rather than in lieu of, a cash wage increase. Second, the deferred wage concept ignores the possible argument that the employer is willing to accept a lower profit margin in order to provide a pension plan for employees. Third, it is sometimes argued that if pension benefits are a form of wage, then terminating employees should be entitled to the part of the retirement benefit that has been earned to the date of termination.

---

[4] *Ibid.*, p. 65.

[5] Albert deRoode, "Pensions as Wages," *American Economic Review*, Vol. III, No. 2 (June 1913), p. 287.

In practice, one finds that only a small proportion of the plans provide for the full and immediate vesting of all benefits. However, it can be argued that the deferred wage concept does not necessarily require the full and immediate vesting of benefits. Proponents of this concept view the pension benefit as a wage, the receipt of which is conditioned upon the employee remaining in the service of the employer for a specified number of years. This view of the pension benefit is similar, conceptually, to the pure endowment, the consideration of the employee being the reduction in cash wages accepted in lieu of the pension benefit.

In spite of the appeal of the deferred wage theory, it is questionable whether the private pension movement can be explained solely in terms of this concept. Indeed, there is probably no one rationale or theory that fully explains the "reason for being" of private pensions. This conclusion is not surprising in view of the fact that these plans are *private*, and the demands or reasons that gave rise to one plan may be quite different in the case of another plan.

DEVELOPMENT OF INDUSTRIAL PENSION PLANS

The beginnings of industrial pension plans in the United States date back to the establishment of the American Express Company plan in 1875.[6] The second formal plan was established in 1880 by the Baltimore & Ohio Railroad Company. During the next half century, approximately 400 plans were established. These early pension plans were generally found in the railroad, banking, and public utility fields. The development of pensions in the manufacturing industries was somewhat slower, due largely to the fact that most manufacturing companies were still relatively young and therefore not confronted with the superannuation problems of the railroads and public utilities.

Insurance companies entered the pension business with the issuance of the first group annuity contract by the Metropolitan Life Insurance Company on December 25, 1921. The second contract was issued by the Metropolitan in 1924 to an employer who already had a retirement plan on a "pay as you go" basis. In 1924 the Equitable Life Assurance Society announced its intention of offering a group pension service, thus becoming the second company to enter the field.

The rate of growth of private pensions was retarded by the depression of the 30s. However, the data indicate that insured pension plans continued to grow during the decade of the 30s both as to number of plans and as to persons covered.

The bulk of the growth in private pension plans has occurred since 1940. Two developments during the Second World War had a significant impact on the expansion of pension programs. First, the high rates (approximately 82 percent) of normal and excess profits taxes imposed on corporations encouraged some firms to establish plans. Since the employ-

---

[6] Murray Webb Latimer, *Industrial Pension Systems* (New York: Industrial Relations Counselors, Inc., 1932), p. 21.

er's contributions to a *qualified* pension plan are deductible for federal income tax purposes, a portion of the plan's liabilities could be funded with 18-cent dollars. Furthermore, the employer's contributions to a pension fund do not constitute taxable income to the employee in the year in which contributions are made. The pension benefits derived from employer contributions are taxed when received by the employee. However, the employee is expected to be in a lower tax bracket when retirement benefits are received.

The second wartime development which helped to stimulate the growth of pensions was the creation of a wage stabilization program as part of a general price control scheme. Employers, in competing for labor, therefore, could not offer the inducement of higher wages. Under these conditions, union leaders found it difficult to prove to their membership the merits of unionism. Therefore, the War Labor Board, in 1944–45, attempted to relieve the pressure from management and labor for higher wage rates by permitting the establishment of fringe benefit programs, including pensions. This policy further stimulated the growth of pension plans during this period.

From 1945 to 1949 the rate of growth of new plans fell off markedly. During this postwar period, employee interest centered upon cash wage increases in an attempt to recover the lost ground suffered during the period of wage stabilization. In the latter part of the decade of the 40s, union leaders began once again expressing an interest in the negotiation of pension programs. The renewal of interest in pensions was probably due to two factors. First, there was increasing antagonism on the part of the public against what were viewed by many persons as excessive union demands for cash wage increases. The negotiation of fringe benefits was one way of possibly reducing pressures from this quarter. Second, some union leaders argued that social security benefits were inadequate, and a supplement in the form of private pension benefits was considered to be necessary. Also, certain labor officials believed that the negotiation of employer-supported pensions would weaken the resistance of the latter toward liberalizations of social security benefit levels. Thus, pension demands became a central issue in the labor negotiations in the coal, automobile, and steel industries in the late 40s. Although unions had negotiated pension benefits prior to this period, it was not until the late 40s that a major segment of labor made a concerted effort to bargain for private pensions.

Labor's drive for pension benefits was facilitated by a National Labor Relations Board ruling in 1948 that employers had a legal obligation to bargain over the terms of pension plans. Until that time, there was some question as to whether employee benefit programs fell within the traditional subject areas for collective bargaining, i.e., wages, hours, and other conditions of employment. The issue was resolved when the National Labor Relations Board held that pension benefits constitute wages, and the provisions of these plans affected conditions of employment. Upon appeal, the court upheld the NLRB decision, although it questioned the assumption that such benefits are wages. The result of these decisions was that an employer cannot install or terminate or alter the terms of a pension plan covering organized workers without the approval of the authorized bargaining agent for those employees. Furthermore, management has this obligation regardless of whether the plan is contributory or noncontributory, voluntary or compulsory, and regardless of whether the plan was established before or after the certification of the bargaining unit.

Labor was quick to respond to these decisions, and the 1950s were marked by union demands for the establishment of new pension plans, liberalization of existing plans, and the supplanting of employer-sponsored programs with negotiated plans. Undoubtedly, labor's interest in private pensions has been an important factor in the tremendous growth in plans since 1949.

CURRENT SCOPE OF PRIVATE PENSIONS

Coverage of Plans

At the end of 1971, some 50 million persons were estimated to be participants in major private and public pension and retirement programs, other than social security, in the United States. Thus, about one half of all workers in commerce and industry, and three fourths of all government civilian personnel are members of retirement programs other than OASDI. Since plans have been established by most large employers, the future extension of private pension coverage depends largely on the extent to which programs are started by smaller employers. The fact that many smaller employers do not have pension plans is understandable. The costs of a pension program are fairly substantial; and many small firms are unable, or at least hesitant, to assume a financial obligation of such magnitude. Also, there is probably less pressure on small employers to establish pension plans. The employees of these firms are often not represented by a union, and this source of pressure to establish plans is nonexistent. Even if the employees are organized, the high rates of turnover among employees or the economic condition of the employers or the industry may reduce the prospects for negotiating a retirement benefit. Furthermore, small employers do not seem to have the personnel problem of larger firms, that is, the need to match the employee benefit programs being offered by competing firms.

However, small employers must compete with the large firms for qualified employees; and as pensions become more common, it may be increasingly necessary for small firms to provide pension benefits. Also, the problem of establishing pension plans in industries characterized by small employers and high rates of employee turnover has been partially met by the recent growth of multiemployer pension plans. A multiemployer pension plan is a plan that covers the employees of two or more financially unrelated employers. Pension contributions are payable into one common fund, and benefits are payable to all employees from the pooled assets of the fund. Employees are free to transfer from one participating employer to another without loss of earned pension credits. These plans generally require uniform contribution rates and uniform benefit provisions. Although there are a few nonnegotiated multiemployer plans in operation, these plans have been established almost exclusively as a result of collective bargaining. These plans cover more than six million employees and have been growing at about double the rate of increase for single employer plan coverage during the last decade.

Another factor which probably to some extent discouraged the establishment of pension plans by small employers has been the unfavorable federal income tax treatment, prior to 1962, accorded plans established by sole proprietorships and partnerships. A sole proprietorship or a partnership can deduct for federal income tax purposes the contributions to a qualified pension plan made on behalf of employees. But no tax deduction was permitted for contributions under those plans made on behalf of the sole proprietors or partners. The Keogh Act, passed by Congress in 1962, amended the Internal Revenue Code to permit tax deductions for contributions made to pension plans on behalf of sole proprietors and partners. In order to be entitled to these deductions, the plan must meet the requirements set forth in the 1962 amendment. There are limitations on the amount of deductions for contributions made on behalf of the self-employed owners, and the Act requires that all employees who have a specified number of years' service with the firm must be included in the plan.[7] There is growing interest in the establishment of professional corporations by doctors, lawyers, and other professionals, where the principal motivations for the corporate form of organization is to obtain the tax advantages of qualified plans for the employee-owner without the deduction limitations imposed by the Keogh Act.

It is difficult to determine to what extent these developments will encourage the growth of pension plans among smaller employers.

Benefit Levels

The amount of the retirement income benefit has an important bearing on the value of pension programs in meeting the risk of excessive longevity. There are, as one would expect, considerable variations in the level of retirement benefits provided by different plans. Pension benefit formulas are often related to an employee's compensation and/or years of service, although flat benefit amounts are also used, particularly under multiemployer plans. For example, a plan may provide that an employee is entitled to a retirement benefit of 1 percent of annual compensation for each year of service. If an employee was covered under this plan for 30 years and had an average annual salary of $10,000, his retirement benefit would be $3,000 a year. The early negotiated plans provided a flat benefit (e.g., $100 per month) less any social security benefits received by the retired worker. Therefore, any increase in social security benefits reduced employer's cost of providing private pensions. The union leaders hoped that plans of this type would reduce employers' resistance to the liberalization of social security benefits. In recent years, labor has favored benefit formulas related to compensation or a monthly retirement benefit (e.g., $4.00) per year of service, without any offset of an employee's social security benefits.

---

[7] See Chapter 36 for further analysis of pension and profit sharing plans for self-employed individuals.

What constitutes an ideal or adequate benefit level for private pensions is a subjective concept. It has been suggested that a reasonable objective would be to provide the employee, through private pensions and social security, a retirement income equal to about 50 percent of his average annual earnings during his last 5 to 10 years of employment. Although there are some plans which meet this objective, many plans provide benefits at levels short of this goal.

Pension plans often provide benefits in addition to a normal retirement benefit. For example, a plan may permit retirement at an age earlier than the normal retirement age. The early retirement benefit amount is almost always less than the normal pension. The benefit formula often defines the benefit as the actuarial equivalent of the normal pension benefit. Also, it may be necessary to terminate an employee's services before normal retirement age because he is permanently and totally disabled. A disabled employee may be eligible for early retirement if this benefit is available under the plan. Some plans provide a disability benefit separate and distinct from any provision for early retirement.

A pension plan may also provide either a preretirement or a postretirement death benefit, or both. Pension plans in the United States generally do not provide a death benefit, with the exception of those plans funded by individual life insurance policies or group permanent insurance contracts. There is a trend, especially among larger plans, to provide survivor provisions.

Lastly, a withdrawal or vested benefit may be provided to employees under a pension plan. The nature of vested benefits is discussed more fully in the following section.

Security of Benefits

The possibility that employees currently covered under private pension plans may never receive any benefits under those plans is one of the most important issues involved in private pension planning. If the employee does not receive the benefits promised under the plan, then the pension program has added little to the old-age economic security of the employee. Indeed, under such circumstances, the pension plan has had a negative effect on the employee's economic security. If an employee assumed that this source of income would be available at retirement, he would have less incentive to make other provisions for his old age during his working years.

For what reasons might an employee not receive the retirement benefit promised under the plan? First, pension plans usually require that the employee be a certain age, usually 65, and perform a fairly long period of continuous service for the employer in order to be entitled to a pension. In some plans, if the employee leaves the firm before the eligibility requirements are met, all rights to pension benefits are forfeited. Therefore, many employees currently covered under pension plans may never receive retirement benefits under those plans.

However, the great majority of plans provide vested benefits. A vested benefit is that portion of a participant's benefit the entitlement to which is not contingent upon continuation of employment. Since an employee is always entitled to the return of his own contributions upon termination of employment, the term "vesting" refers to benefits derived solely from employer contributions.

The absence of vesting provisions in some plans is of increasing concern to many management, labor, and governmental officials, and others interested in the private pension movement. Several bills have been introduced in Congress that would require all qualified plans to provide full vested benefits after a specified period of service (e.g., 10 years).

It can be argued that vesting should not be provided if a pension plan is viewed as a reward for long and loyal service to a particular employer. On the other hand, if one views pension benefits as a form of deferred compensation, the argument for a vesting provision becomes more persuasive. If vested benefits are provided, the cost of the pension plan will increase. Furthermore, rates of turnover vary greatly from industry to industry and among firms within an industry, and therefore the impact of a vesting provision on pension costs will vary significantly to match this diversity. There are implications other than cost adding to the complexity of the issue of vested benefits. The pension student should give some thought to the broad social and economic ramifications of vested pension benefits from the standpoint of management, labor, and society.

Another reason why employees may never realize the benefits promised under these plans is the fact that some pension plans are not adequately financed. If the plans are not properly financed, benefit payments may be reduced or terminated entirely at some future date, thereby impairing the old-age economic security programs of many participants. This problem is particularly significant in pension plans, since eligibility for benefit payments is earned over a considerable period of time. An employee may find that after many years of service for an employer, retirement benefits have been decreased or eliminated. It is difficult for that employee, at that point, to make adequate financial provision for his old age. The employer should be aware of the responsibility assumed in establishing a pension program, and provision should be made to finance the plan adequately.

In a recent study by the Pension Research Council of about 1000 plans covering about 4.5 million participants, it was concluded that a high degree of benefit security had been achieved by a vast majority of the plans included in the study. For example, assets were sufficient, on the average, to cover 94.4 percent of all accrued benefits under plans whose effective funding periods were 15 years or more.

In spite of these findings, there is considerable pressure in some quarters for legislation requiring minimum funding standards for all qualified plans. There have also been several proposals for the establishment of a pension plan reinsurance scheme (similar to the concept of insuring bank deposits through the Federal Deposit Insurance Corporation) to protect participants under terminated plans from loss of accrued benefits.

Funding Plan Benefits

The first financial decision to be made in pension planning is to determine whether benefits are to be funded or whether the plan is to be financed on a "pay as you go" basis. The tax advantages of funded plans that meet the requirements established by the Internal Revenue Service for *qualification* of pension plans have all but made the "pay as you go" plan obsolete. Having chosen one of these alternatives, the broad *financing policy* of the plan has been established. Assuming that agreement is reached on a financing policy of funding benefits, then several decisions under the general heading of *funding policy* must be made.

The first decision that must be made is the choice of a funding agency. A *funding agency* is an organization or individual that provides facilities for the accumulation or administration of assets to be used for the payment of benefits under a pension plan. Funding agencies include life insurance companies, corporate fiduciaries, and individuals acting as trustees. These funding agencies have several different contracts or instruments through which pension benefits are funded. Insured pension plans, for example, may be funded through individual policies, deferred group annuities, deposit administration group annuities, and so forth. These various contracts are referred to as funding instruments. A *funding instrument* is an agreement or contract governing the conditions under which assets are accumulated or administered by a funding agency for the payment of benefits under a pension plan. Funding instruments include contracts with life insurance companies, and trust agreements with corporate fiduciaries or individuals acting as trustees.

An *insured plan*, then, is a pension plan for which the funding agency is a life insurance company; all contributions are paid directly or indirectly to the insurer, which pays all benefits to individual participants. A *trust fund plan* is a plan for which the funding agency is a corporate fiduciary or individual(s) acting as trustee(s); the responsibilities of the funding agency for investment of funds, and for any other functions, are generally provided for in a trust agreement. A *combination plan* is an arrangement under which two funding agencies are used, with a portion of the contributions placed in a trust fund and the balance paid to an insurance company as contributions under a group annuity contract or as premiums on individual annuity contracts and life insurance policies. The entire pension for each participant is sometimes paid by the insurance company, with transfers from the trust fund being made as required.

Of the nearly 34 million persons currently covered under private pension plans (excluding private pensions for public employees), about 24 million are covered under trust fund plans. These plans hold an estimated $96 billion of the total of $136 billion held in all private pension funds.

The trustee under a trust fund plan is usually a corporate trustee, although individuals often act as trustees of funds, particularly among multiemployer plans. The duties and functions of the trustees vary considerably among plans, i.e., from mere custodian of securities to full investment authority. In any case the responsibility of the trustee never extends beyond the prudent investment of trust assets. In other words, the trustee is never responsible for the adequacy or inadequacy of trust assets to meet the liabilities under the plan. The adequacy of the fund is the sole responsibility of the employer. Admittedly, the employer will usually seek advice from a consulting actuary in determining the amount of funds that should be set aside to meet the obligations arising under the plan. But the trustee is in no way responsible if these estimates prove to be erroneous or if the employer fails to make the necessary contributions.

Considerable variations in insurance company plans also exist because of the variety of pension products offered by insurers. Insurance companies offer a full spectrum of funding instruments varying from individual policies to an immediate participation contract and an associated separate account with equity investments. Thus, it can be seen that the pension client has a broad choice of insurance company pension products. The nature and the advantages and disadvantages of each funding instrument will be discussed at length in the following chapters. It will be seen that the spectrum of group annuity contracts offers varying degrees of flexibility to the employer. It should be recognized, however, that the increased flexibility to the employer is made possible only by the relinquishment of certain guarantees by the insurance company. In other words, the greater the flexibility of the plan, the greater the responsibility that rests with the employer as to the adequacy of the fund to provide the benefits promised under the plan.

PENSION PLAN DISCLOSURE LAWS

Federal Welfare and Pension Plans Disclosure Act

The Federal Welfare and Pension Plans Disclosure Act applies to private pension plans covering more than 25 persons. The law requires the administrator of the plan to file a description of the plan with the United States Department of Labor. The required information includes a description of the plan and the type of administration; the schedule of benefits; the names and addresses of any trustees; copies of the plan, bargaining agreement, trust agreement, or other instrument; financing arrangements; and procedures for processing claims for benefits.

Plans covering 100 or more participants are also required to file an annual financial report. This report requires information such as the amount of employer and employee contributions; the amount of benefits paid; a statement of the amount of specified types of assets; a statement of liabilities, receipts, and disbursements; and a detailed statement of the salaries, fees, and commissions charged to the plan, to whom paid, in what amount, and for what purposes. Specific data are required depending upon whether the plan is unfunded, insured, or trusteed, including, in the latter case, the type and basis of funding, actuarial assumptions used, and the amount of current and past service liabilities.

The plan administrator is required to make available to plan participants and beneficiaries copies of the plan description and the latest annual report in the principal office of the plan. This information must also be made available upon the written request of a plan participant or beneficiary by mailing such documents to the last known address of the person making such request. Also, two copies of the plan description and the annual report must be filed with the United States Department of Labor.

The Act requires that anyone handling funds or other property of an employee benefit plan must be bonded. The bonding requirement does not apply if benefits are payable solely from the general assets of a union or an employer. Penalties are imposed for any willful violation of any provision of the law or conviction for theft or embezzlement from an employee benefit plan.

State Disclosure Acts

Five states presently have welfare and pension plan disclosure laws. These states, and the years in which these laws were enacted, are Washington (1955), New York (1956), Massachusetts (1957), Wisconsin (1957), and California (1970).

The scope of coverage and the information required under the state statutes is generally less extensive than under the federal disclosure act. Regulation under the state statutes is more comprehensive than under the federal act to the extent that the state authorities in New York, Washington, and Wisconsin must examine each plan at least once during a specified period—for example, three or five years. Under the federal law an investigation is permitted only upon complaint or if the Secretary of Labor suspects a violation of the Act.

ACCOUNTING FOR PENSION COSTS

There are a variety of acceptable actuarial cost methods, thus permitting employers considerable flexibility in determining the amounts of annual contributions and the rate at which past service liabilities are to be funded, if at all. For purposes of financial statement accounting, most employers treated actual contributions or annuity premium payments made during the year as the firm's pension cost for that period, i.e., a cash accounting approach. With the flexibility available in calculating contributions, it is not surprising that the accounting for the cost of pension plans has varied widely among companies and has sometimes resulted in wide year-to-year fluctuations in the provisions for pension costs of a single company.

This wide variation in accounting practice has been of concern to the accounting profession for several years, particularly in view of the increasing magnitude of pension costs relative to a firm's financial position and operating results. After many years of research and study, the Accounting Principles Board of the American Institute of Certified Public Accountants issued, in November 1966, *Opinion 8*, to clarify the principles regarding accounting for the cost of pension plans.

Opinion 8 specifies that accounting for pension cost should not be discretionary, and provision for pension cost should be made annually on a consistent and systematic basis, whether or not contributions were actually made during the particular accounting period. Thus, pension costs are to be recognized on an accrual basis rather than a cash accounting basis.

Opinion 8 does not alter in any way an employer's legal obligation to covered employees as specified in the plan agreement and related legal documents. Employers generally limit their legal obligation by specifying that pensions shall be payable only to the extent of the assets in the pension fund. Nor does this recommended accounting procedure alter IRS rules regarding deductibility of pension contributions, which continue to be based on actual contribution payments.

The *Opinion* applies to unfunded plans as well as to insured plans and trust fund plans; to defined contribution plans as well as to defined benefit plans. *Opinion 8* has a rather dramatic impact on plans utilizing the cash disbursement (pay-as-you-go) or terminal funding approaches, in that annual pension costs calculated in line with the requirements of the *Opinion* are likely to differ significantly from actual benefit or contribution payments. Thus, the relatively few plans utilizing the current disbursement or terminal funding approach are likely to adopt advance funding as a result of *Opinion 8*.

SELECTED REFERENCES

Griffin, Frank L., Jr., and Trowbridge, Charles L. *Status of Funding under Private Pension Plans*. Pension Research Council, Wharton School of Finance and Commerce, University of Pennsylvania. Homewood, Ill.: Richard D. Irwin, Inc., 1969.

McGill, Dan M. *Fundamentals of Private Pensions*. 2d ed. Pension Research Council, Wharton School of Finance and Commerce, University of Pennsylvania. Homewood, Ill.: Richard D. Irwin, Inc., 1964.

————. *Guaranty Fund for Private Pension Obligations*. Pension Research Council, Wharton School of Finance and Commerce, University of Pennsylvania. Homewood, Ill.: Richard D. Irwin, Inc., 1970.

Marples, William F. *Actuarial Aspects of Pension Security*. Pension Research Council, Wharton School of Finance and Commerce, University of Pennsylvania. Homewood, Ill.: Richard D. Irwin, Inc., 1965.

Melone, Joseph J. *Collectively Bargained Multi-Employer Pension Plans*. Pension Research Council, Wharton School of Finance and Commerce, University of Pennsylvania. Homewood, Ill.: Richard D. Irwin, Inc., 1963.

Melone, Joseph J., and Allen, Everett T., Jr. *Pension Planning: Pensions, Profit Sharing, and Other Deferred Compensation Plans*. Rev. ed. Homewood, Ill.: Richard D. Irwin, Inc., 1972.

34

Pension Plan Design and Funding Considerations

By EVERETT T. ALLEN, JR.

AN EMPLOYER who is adopting a qualified pension plan must make a number of decisions as to the basic features to be included in the plan. In addition, he must be concerned with the actuarial assumptions and cost method used to determine estimated plan liabilities and the incidence of contributions. This chapter first reviews the major design features of a pension plan; the last portion deals with actuarial cost considerations.[1]

BASIC PLAN FEATURES

In designing a pension plan, the employer's objectives as to benefit and cost levels are of paramount importance. With these objectives in mind, the employer must determine the class of employees to be covered; when and under what conditions these employees will be eligible for participation; what benefits they will receive upon retirement, death, disability, or severance of employment; how and when these benefits will be paid; and whether or not employees will contribute toward the cost of these benefits.

Plan design should also take into account the employer's existing employee benefit program (to avoid unnecessary duplication or overlapping of benefits), as well as the demands of any collective bargaining unit and the patterns established by competing business organizations. The requirements of federal tax law are also important since, if the employer wishes to obtain the favorable tax benefits that flow from having a "qualified" plan, it is necessary that the plan be designed in a manner such that it does not discriminate in any way (i.e., in benefits, contributions, or coverage) in favor of officers, stockholders, supervisors, or highly compensated employees—often called the *prohibited* group of employees.

---

[1] For treatment in greater depth of pension plan design and funding considerations, see Joseph J. Melone and Everett T. Allen, Jr., *Pension Planning: Pensions, Profit Sharing, and Other Deferred Compensation Plans*, Chapters 2 and 3. Rev. ed. (Homewood, Ill.: Richard D. Irwin, Inc., 1972).

The first portion of this chapter deals with design considerations of *qualified pension* plans established by *corporate* employers. This material also applies, except as noted, to qualified pension plans adopted by Subchapter S corporations and by professional associations or corporations that possess sufficient corporate characteristics to qualify as corporations under federal tax law.

Eligibility Requirements

In the generally accepted sense, eligibility requirements are those conditions an employee must meet in order to become a participant in the plan. There are two broad types of eligibility requirements—those which defer an employee's participation until some stipulated conditions are met, and those which exclude an employee from participation on a permanent basis (or, at least, until the employee has had some change in his employment status). Those eligibility requirements which defer participation are often included for administrative cost considerations (e.g., the cost of creating and maintaining records for employees who are not likely to remain employed). Those eligibility requirements which permanently exclude employees are generally dictated by the employer's objectives, by bargaining agreements or, as is very often the case, by cost considerations.

Requirements of the Internal Revenue Code are an extremely important consideration in the establishment of eligibility provisions. The Code requires that (1) at least 70 percent of all employees be covered; or (2) in a plan requiring employee contributions at least 80 percent of all eligible employees be covered, provided that at least 70 percent of all employees are eligible for coverage. Employees with less than the years of service specified by the plan (not to exceed five years) and part-time and seasonal workers may be excluded in determining "all employees." In lieu of the foregoing, the law also permits eligibility to be determined by special classifications of employees if such classifications do not discriminate in favor of officers, stockholders, supervisors, or highly compensated employees.

The most common eligibility requirements are discussed below.

Years of Service. A years-of-service requirement is frequently found in contributory pension plans or in plans funded with an allocated funding instrument. Typically, this requirement will range from one to three years and in some cases up to as much as five years. It should be noted that the Internal Revenue Service generally will not permit the years-of-service requirement to exceed five years and, often, will require that this period be less than five years in order to prevent discrimination in a specific plan.

It is possible to employ a dual-service requirement which establishes a longer service period for individuals who become employees after the effective date of the plan. This will be acceptable if employees in the prohibited group can, at the time the plan is established, meet the more stringent requirements set for future employees. Also, it should be noted that under federal tax law, any employee of a newly incorporated firm who was formerly a partner or proprietor of the predecessor business organization may measure service only from the date of incorporation.

A minimum service requirement for initial eligibility is rarely found in negotiated plans; however, these plans frequently require that an employee, to be eligible for retirement benefits, must have completed some minimum period of service, such as 10 or 15 years, by the normal retirement age specified in the plan.

Minimum Age. Again, a minimum age is typically found in contributory plans or in plans funded with allocated funding instruments. The age usually employed is 25 or 30 years, and it should be noted that the Internal Revenue Service generally will not permit the minimum age to be greater than 30. Also, as with the years-of-service requirement, a higher minimum age may be required for future employees provided that employees in the prohibited group can satisfy this higher requirement at the time the plan is established.

Maximum Age. The maximum age provision is the type of eligibility requirement that permanently excludes individuals from participation. As a result, its use is generally dictated by cost considerations. Most plans include a maximum age provision and a typical provision would exclude individuals over some age such as 55, 60, or 65.

The selection of an appropriate maximum age is difficult since the employees excluded may be the very reason that the employer is considering the adoption of a pension plan. Just what should be done will vary from case to case, keeping in mind the employer's objectives, the actual cost problems involved, and the actuarial cost method and the funding instrument being employed for the plan. Many plans are established with a high maximum age for employees on the effective date but with a lower maximum age for future employees. Another approach is to exclude employees who are hired after some maximum age, thus including older employees with long service at the time the plan is established, while at the same time excluding those with short service. Another approach is to include older employees at the time the plan is established, but to use a staggered schedule of normal retirement ages so as to give the maximum period possible for accumulating the necessary funds (as well as reducing the actual cost of providing a given amount of benefit). In any event, where employees are excluded from the plan because of the maximum age provision, the employer often provides some benefit for them on an informal pay-as-you-go basis.

Earnings Requirements. Some plans require that an employee, to be eligible to participate, must be earning in excess of some stipulated amount. The amount frequently used for this purpose is the social security taxable wage base. When this approach is followed, the plan must meet specific requirements of the Internal Revenue Code that deal with plans that are integrated with social security benefits. These plans are discussed at greater length later in this chapter.

Employment Classification. It is possible for plans to be established for only those employees who work in a specific plant, or at a specific location, or in a specific occupation. These classifications are not used too frequently (except for negotiated plans) and, when used, must not produce discrimination in favor of the prohibited group of employees.

Another form of employment classification that is used more frequently is that which limits coverage to salaried employees only. At one time, it was quite common to use such a requirement; however, it has become increasingly more difficult to qualify plans with this limitation. As a general rule, if the salaried employees are all earning more than the hourly employees, the plan will not be acceptable to the Internal Revenue Service. Acceptability of such a plan increases, however, when hourly employees earn substantially the same as some of the salaried employees. Also, the acceptability of a salaried-only plan is increased when a separate plan is in effect for hourly employees as, for example, under a union-negotiated plan. However, it is still necessary to show that the hourly employees are provided with contributions or benefits which are comparable to those being provided the salaried employees.

Retirement Ages

Normal Retirement Age. The normal retirement age in most plans is 65. Occasionally, an earlier age such as 60 will be chosen as the normal retirement age although, to a great extent, this practice has been confined to public, quasi-public, and charitable institutions, along with a few industries where an employee's working career is shorter because of occupational considerations. It should be noted, however, that there has been a growing interest (both with management and employees) in retiring earlier than age 65, frequently by means of some form of subsidized early retirement benefit.

A "floating normal retirement age" is sometimes used in negotiated plans. Under this type of arrangement the employee has the right to retire with full benefits upon attaining some minimum age, usually 65; however, the employer does not have the right to retire the employee until he attains some maximum age, usually 68. In the interim, the employee has the right to retire with full benefits credited to his actual retirement.

A staggered normal retirement schedule is sometimes used for older employees when the plan is established. A typical schedule would state that anyone over age 55 would retire at the end of 10 years or, if earlier, at age 70. Such a schedule should develop lower pension costs since the amount needed to provide a given amount of pension will decrease as the employee's normal retirement age increases. Also, the employer is able to spread the cost of an older employee's pension over a longer period of time. From the employee's viewpoint, such a schedule also might give him the opportunity to accumulate additional benefits. Finally, both employer and employee are given adequate time in which to plan for retirement.

Early Retirement Age. Most plans provide that an employee may choose early retirement on a reduced pension, although a few plans limit this feature to cases of total and permanent disability. Typically, the employee must have attained some age, such as 55, and must have completed some service or participation period, such as 10 years.

The benefit at early retirement is usually reduced from what would have been payable at normal retirement. This is because the employee's full benefits will not have accrued by his early retirement date, and also the benefit will be paid over a longer period of time. Thus, an actuarial reduction factor is usually applied to the value of the employee's accrued benefit in order to determine his early retirement benefit. Some plans do not require a full actuarial reduction at early retirement and may not even provide for any reduction at all—particularly if the employee has completed a substantial period of service. For example, some plans might provide for the full accrued benefit to be payable at early retirement, without any actuarial reduction if the employee has attained age 60 and has completed at least 30 years of service.

Late Retirement Age. Most plans also allow an employee to defer his retirement, usually with employer consent. The benefit payable at late retirement may be the same as would have been payable had the employee retired on his normal retirement date, or the benefit may be an increased actuarial equivalent. It is even possible to provide that an employee may accrue additional pension credit between his normal and late retirement dates. However, if the pension plan is to accomplish its real purpose, the election of late retirement should not be made too attractive to employees. Accordingly, it is generally preferable that the benefit at late retirement be the same as would have been payable at normal retirement.

Retirement Benefits

Many employers feel that a plan should be designed so as to provide a higher-paid career employee with an income after retirement which, together with primary social security benefits, will be about 45 percent to 50 percent of his earnings just before retirement. For lower-paid employees, the percentage would generally be set at a higher level, perhaps as much as 65 percent or 70 percent.

Basically, there are two types of benefit formulas for the employer to consider. The first type is called the *defined contribution* or *money purchase formula*. Under this type of formula, contribution rates are fixed and an employee's benefit will depend upon such factors as the amount of the contributions made and investment earnings, and the employee's age, sex, and normal retirement age. The second type is called the *defined benefit* or *annuity purchase* formula. Here, a definite benefit is established for each employee, and contributions are determined to be whatever is necessary to produce the desired benefit results. Defined benefit formulas are far more popular than defined contribution formulas and, in themselves, may be subdivided into several different classifications.[2]

Determination of Earnings. Since the amount of benefit under most formulas is based on an employee's compensation, it is important, before discussing specific formulas, to have a clear idea of the different consid-

---

[2] It has been said that a third type of benefit formula is emerging—one where the employee's benefit will vary, depending upon the performance of the common stock market or changes in the cost-of-living index. Actually, this is not so, since variable benefit plans involve either a defined contribution or a defined benefit formula. These plans are discussed in Chapter 18.

erations involved in selecting the compensation base to which the formula will be applied.

Normally, only basic compensation will be considered for benefit purposes. Thus, bonuses, overtime pay, and other forms of extraordinary compensation are not included. As a matter of fact, the inclusion of bonuses could result in a plan that discriminates in favor of the prohibited group. On the other hand, if the plan is integrated with social security benefits, the Internal Revenue Service may require that "total" compensation (including overtime pay) be used unless it can be demonstrated that a more restrictive definition of compensation does not result in prohibited discrimination.

Another aspect of the problem of earnings is the question of whether plan benefits should be based on the average of the employee's earnings over the entire period of his participation or an average of his earnings during some shorter period of time which is nearer his normal retirement age. The advantage of a "final-pay" plan is that it relates an employee's benefits to his earnings and his standard of living during a period just preceding his retirement. As a result, his benefits tend to keep pace with any inflationary or deflationary trends. Moreover, a final-pay plan is more responsive to meeting employer objectives as to benefit levels than is a plan basing benefits on the employee's career pay. However, a final-pay plan is usually more expensive than one which bases benefits on career earnings. It could also create problems under certain funding instruments if additional benefits for an employee must be paid for over a short time before he retires. Many employers therefore feel it best to use a career average earnings plan and to make periodic adjustments in the formula when economic trends justify such an action.

Defined Contribution Formulas. As previously noted, defined contribution formulas do not provide a fixed benefit for employees. Instead, the rate of contribution is fixed, usually as a percentage of the employee's earnings, and this contribution is applied (together with the employee's contribution under a contributory plan) to buy whatever pension benefit can be purchased. Since the cost of the given amount of benefit varies by age, sex, and normal retirement age, the benefits for any employee will depend upon these factors.

Defined contribution plans are often contributory. In this case, the employer's contribution either matches or is a multiple of the employee's contribution.

A defined contribution formula is employed primarily by nonprofit organizations where there is often a need, because of cost considerations, to be able to predict future plan liabilities with some degree of certainty. It is used to some extent in plans adopted by professional associations or corporations, and, because of the limitations on deductions that apply to shareholders of Subchapter S corporations, it is expected that defined contribution formulas will become more widely used in plans adopted by such organizations. Otherwise, this formula has had little popularity because of several inherent limitations. The first of these is that an employee who joins the plan at an older age will have only a short period of time in which to accumulate funds, with the result that his benefit will often be inadequate. Younger employees, who have a much longer time to accumulate funds, will receive proportionately larger benefits. Also, the sex of the employee will influence the amount of benefit received. This lack of certainty with respect to benefits to be provided could prove to be unsatisfactory from the viewpoint of employee relations. Finally, the variations in benefits among employees make it difficult, if not impossible, to design a formula that provides adequate benefit levels that are uniformly responsive to employer objectives.

Defined Benefit Formulas. Generally speaking, there are four basic types of defined benefit formulas. The first of these is the *flat amount* formula which treats all employees alike, regardless of service, age, or earnings. A typical benefit might be $100 or $150 a month. The flat amount formula, since it is considered to produce inequitable results, is seldom used by itself. On occasion, though, it is used in conjunction with some other type of formula. For example, a plan may provide for each covered employee a flat benefit of $75 a month, plus a percentage of his earnings in excess of the current social security taxable wage base.

The second type of formula is the *flat percentage of earnings* formula. This type of formula is used frequently today, particularly in plans which cover salaried or clerical employees. Some percentage of earnings, usually ranging from 20 percent to 40 percent, is selected as the measure of the pension benefit. It may be used with either career average or final average earnings, although it is most frequently used in final-pay plans. This type of formula does not take an employee's service into account except in those plans which require that an employee must have completed some minimum period of service by normal retirement date, and which provide for a proportionately reduced benefit if the employee's service is less than the required number of years.

The third type of formula is the *flat amount per year of service* formula. This type of formula is frequently found in negotiated plans and provides a flat dollar amount for each year of service accumulated by the employee, such as $5 or $6 a month per each year of service.

The fourth type of formula is the *percentage of earnings per year of service* formula. This type of formula is used a great deal since it is considered by many practitioners to provide the most equitable results. Under this type of formula, an employee receives a benefit credit equal to a percentage of his earnings for each year that he is a participant under the plan. This benefit is called his future service or current service benefit. A typical percentage might be 1 percent or 1¼ percent. The formula may be used with career-average or final-pay plans. Many plans also include a past service benefit for employees who enter the plan on its effective date. If the future service benefit is based on career pay, the past service benefit is usually based on earnings at the time the plan is put into effect and a lower percentage is applied for purposes of determining the past service benefit. Where the plan bases benefits on final pay, usually no distinction is made between past and future service benefits.

Variable Benefit Formulas. Variable benefit plans are designed to protect an employee against the effects of inflation. They take either of two general forms: (*a*) the benefit varies to reflect changes in the value of a specific portfolio of common stocks and similar investments, or (*b*) the benefit varies to reflect changes in a recognized cost of living index such as that published by the Bureau of Labor Statistics. In either case, the plan tends to adjust the retired employee's benefits to keep his purchasing power on a relatively level basis.

Integrated Formulas. For most individuals, retirement income will be derived from both social security benefits and private pension plans. Since the employer bears part of the cost of social security benefits, it is only logical that he might wish to recognize these benefits in the benefit formulas of his plan. Thus, it is not uncommon for an employer to establish his retirement plan on a basis that excludes employees who are earning less than the social security taxable wage base. An alternative and more prevalent approach is to provide a higher level of benefits for earnings above this taxable wage base than is provided for earnings below this amount. While at first glance such a plan would appear to discriminate in favor of the prohibited group, federal tax law expressly permits this type of plan provided the benefit formula *integrates* with social security benefits. The basic concept of integration is that the benefits of the employer's plan must be dovetailed with social security benefits in such a manner that employees earning over the taxable wage base will not receive combined benefits under the two programs which are proportionately greater than the benefits for employees earning less than this amount. The Internal Revenue Service has published detailed rulings which set forth the maximum percentages that might apply in the plan benefit formula. These percentages vary, depending upon the type of formula employed, the earnings base to which it is applied, and whether or not other benefits such as pre- and post-retirement death benefits are included in the plan. These rulings also limit the benefit that might be payable in the event of early retirement or disability, and provide for an adjustment in the allowable percentages in plans where employees make contributions.

Minimum and Maximum Benefits. Closely related to the choice of an adequate benefit formula is the question of whether or not a provision for a minimum or maximum pension should be included in the plan. A minimum pension provision is generally a desirable feature in any pension plan since the benefit formula could, in some circumstances, produce a very small amount of benefit as it applies to certain employees. A frequently used minimum is $20 a month.

The use of a maximum pension provision can be important in limiting the cost of a pension plan and, in some cases, it may be necessary if discrimination in favor of the prohibited group of employees is to be avoided. The general trend, however, appears to be away from the inclusion of a maximum pension provision. When included, there are several ways to establish such a limitation. The most common method involves the use of the maximum dollar amount of pension such as $1500 a month. Another method is to specify that earnings in excess of some amount such as $25,000 a year will not be considered for benefit purposes. Still another method is to limit the total years of credited service that will be counted for benefit purposes.

Death Benefits

A death benefit provided by employer contributions is an optional benefit under pension plans; however, a great many plans include such a benefit. Broadly speaking, such a death benefit may take either of two forms—life insurance under some form of individual policy or group life insurance contract, or a cash distribution from plan assets. Death benefits may also be classified as being payable in the event of death either before or after retirement.

Death benefits provided under a pension plan are subject to the requirements of the IRS that they be "incidental." Under a defined benefit plan, the incidental test is satisfied if the benefit does not exceed 100 times the expected monthly pension or, if greater, the reserve for the pension benefit. If a defined contribution plan includes life insurance benefits, the test is satisfied if: (1) the aggregate of the premiums paid for the participant's life insurance is less than 50 percent of the contributions allocated to him at any particular time; and (2) the plan requires the trustee to: (a) convert the value of the life insurance contract at or before retirement into cash; (b) provide periodic income so that no portion of such value may be used to continue life insurance protection beyond retirement; or (c) distribute the contract to the participant.

The preretirement death benefit of an individual policy fully insured plan is usually 100 times the expected monthly pension or the reserve for this benefit, if greater. (If retirement annuity contracts are employed, the death benefit is equal to the premiums paid for the coverage or the cash value of the contract, whichever is greater.) In individual policy combination plans, the death benefit is usually 100 times the expected monthly pension although, within the incidental test of the Internal Revenue Service, different schedules of death benefits are possible.

Group pension and trust fund plans occasionally provide for some lump-sum cash death benefit paid out of employer contributions. There has also been increasing interest in the inclusion of spouse benefits in such plans. Such a benefit usually takes the form of a life annuity payable to the employee's spouse. The amount of the benefit may be that amount which can be provided by part or all of the reserve accumulated for the employees' pension benefit or, as is more commonly the case, the amount may be all or a percentage of the employee's accrued pension. The benefit may be payable for a period that is for less than the spouse's lifetime and it may be subject to termination in the event of remarriage.

Death benefits are often provided in the event of death after retirement. Frequently, in an individual policy plan, the basic or normal form for the payment of benefits provides that these payments will be made for a guaranteed period of at least 5 or 10 years and, thereafter, for the remaining life of the employee. On occasion (usually under trust fund or group pension plans), post-retirement spouse benefits are provided. Apart from the death benefit included in the normal form, it is also possible to provide some amount of death benefit under various optional forms of payment which the employee might elect by taking a reduction in his normal retirement benefit.

Disabilty Benefits

An increasingly popular form of employee benefit is a provision for some continued income in the event of total and permanent disability. While this benefit is often provided by means of separate insurance contracts, a number of employers provide disability benefits in conjunction with their retirement plans. The treatment of disability varies a great deal. In some plans, the employee is provided with full and immediate vesting —a meaningful provision only if the plan also provides for the vested benefit to be immediately available in the form of cash, either in a lump sum or in installments. Other plans treat disability as early retirement if the employee has completed some minimum period of service or participation in the plan and has attained some minimum age.

Some group pension and trust fund plans provide for a separate and distinct benefit in the event of total and permanent disability. The benefit is usually a specified dollar amount, a specified percentage of earnings, or an amount equal to the employee's accrued or projected pension credit (with or without actuarial reduction). Often, the disability benefit is integrated with benefits available from governmental programs such as workmen's compensation or social security. Frequently, the plan will provide that the disability benefit will terminate when the employee reaches normal retirement age, at which time his accrued normal pension benefit will be payable.

Severance of Employment Benefits

The rights of an employee to the benefits attributable to his employer's contributions under a pension plan in the event of his termination of employment prior to retirement has been a subject of considerable discussion in recent years. The Internal Revenue Code does not specifically require vesting as a condition for favorable tax qualification of a pension plan.[3] Notwithstanding, there has been a noticeable trend in recent years for the IRS to require some degree of vesting if a plan is to qualify, particularly in the case of plans for small employers. Quite apart from the attitude of the IRS, it is quite possible that legislation will be passed in the near future that requires vesting after an employee has completed some minimum service requirement.

If vesting is to be included in the plan, there are two basic questions involved. The first of these is how much of a benefit will be provided and the second relates to the manner in which the benefit will be made available to the terminated employee.

As to the first question, a plan might provide for full and immediate vesting, or it might stipulate that an employee has no rights until he has attained some minimum age and/or has completed some minimum period of service or participation, at which time his accrued benefits will become fully vested. A common provision is a graded vesting schedule which provides that an employee is entitled to an increasing portion of his accrued benefit as his length of service and plan participation increases.

---

[3] The IRS, however, will generally require vesting, and at a relatively rapid rate, in connection with qualified profit sharing plans.

As to the second question, the vested benefit is generally made available either in the form of a cash payment (or its equivalent) or as a deferred benefit. To some extent the form of the vested benefit is influenced by the funding instrument employed to provide plan benefits. In individual policy plans, the form of vesting is usually cash or its equivalent. In group pension or trust fund plans, however, the benefit is frequently available only in the form of a deferred benefit commencing at the employee's normal retirement date.

Employee Contributions

While the trend is clearly in the direction of noncontributory plans, a number of plans still require that employees share in the cost of providing plan benefits. Arguments advanced in favor of contributory plans include the following:

1. If employees contribute, it will mean a smaller employer contribution to provide the same overall benefit.
2. If the employer does not want to use employee contributions to reduce his own contribution, the overall plan benefits will be larger.
3. Regular deductions from earnings will continually remind the employees that the employer is assuming a large share of providing plan benefits.
4. Employees are encouraged to save and, in the process, solve a portion of their own retirement problems.

The proponents of the noncontributory plan hold that the contributory plan has the following disadvantages:

1. Employer contributions represent dollars which have not been taxed. On the other hand, dollars received by the employee as earnings, which are then contributed under the plan, are dollars which have been taxed to the employee.
2. Deductions can be a source of constant irritation to employees.
3. The employer might be forced to increase salaries in order to compensate for the additional deductions.
4. The number of participants required for a qualified plan (or by an insurer under certain funding instruments) might not enroll. Some employees might refuse to participate, in which case the employer will still have a problem on his hands when such an employee reaches retirement age.
5. Additional records must be kept by the employer, thereby increasing administrative work and costs.
6. The portion of any death benefit attributable to employee contributions will be included in the employee's gross estate for federal estate tax purposes.

If the employer decides that employees should make contributions, his next decision will be the amount of contribution. Generally, employee contributions are related to current earnings. If the plan includes a formula that is integrated with social security benefits, the contribution rate should reflect the different levels of benefits as to earnings under and over the compensation breakpoint used in the plan. It is also necessary in a contributory plan to include some provision with respect to the right of the employee to suspend or discontinue his contributions.

If an employee fails to join when eligible, but joins at a later date, he usually incurs some sort of penalty, such as a forfeiture of past service and any future service benefits that might have accrued from the time he could have begun participation.

General Plan Provisions

The preceding portion of this chapter has dealt with major plan provisions. There are a number of other provisions that are a part of any plan and that relate generally to the rights and duties of the interested parties.

An essential plan provision is one which gives the employer the unilateral right to amend or terminate the program at any time. However, any plan amendment may not reduce benefits related to contributions made prior to the amendment, deprive any employee of his accrued vested interest, or permit the employer to recover any funds previously contributed to the plan. The termination-of-plan clause makes provision for the distribution of plan assets in the event of this contingency. In allocated funding instruments, the assets, in effect, have already been allocated, and very little need be done in this regard. Under an unallocated funding instrument, the assets are usually allocated on the basis of some order of priorities or on some proportionate basis. The priority order basis usually gives employees who are in a retirement status the first priority, with the priorities descending in terms of those who are eligible for retirement, those who are fully vested and finally, all other employees. It is also necessary to include a provision in the plan which limits the benefits payable to certain employees in the event of early plan termination (within the first ten years). The employees affected by this provision are the 25 highest paid employees when the plan was established whose annual benefit from employer contributions will exceed $1500. The limitation is that, if the plan is terminated within ten years after its effective date, the benefits payable to the employee or his beneficiary cannot exceed those purchasable by the greater of (*a*) $20,000 or (*b*) 20 percent of the employee's annual compensation up to $50,000 multiplied by the number of years since the effective date of the plan.

Other provisions in the plan relate to: (1) the naming and changing of beneficiaries; (2) a facility of payment clause to permit payments to be made to someone other than the payee if the payee is in any way incompetent to receive proceeds; (3) the trustee provisions which relate to the resignation or removal of the trustee and the appointment of a successor, the payment of the trustee's expenses, the powers and duties of the trustee, the administrative responsibilities and authority of the trustee, and the like; (4) the small benefit provision which permits the payment of an employee's benefit in a lump sum if it would provide a benefit of less than some amount such as $40 a year; (5) a leave of absence provision that provides for the contingency of an employee being absent due to authorized or military leave and what effect this might have on his benefit accruals; (6) the governing law provision which establishes the state whose laws will control in the interpretation of the plan; (7) the spendthrift provision which prohibits the alienation, assignment, pledge, or encumbrance of plan benefits; and (8) a provision which states that the plan does not give the employee the right to be retained in the employ of the employer, nor any legal or equitable rights against the employer.

ACTUARIAL COST CONSIDERATIONS

Estimated Cost versus Ultimate Cost of Plan

If an employer wishes to set aside funds in advance of the retirement date of employees, he must have some idea of the cost of the benefit in order to determine the amount of periodic contributions required under the plan. An employee is normally entitled to a pension benefit only after attainment of age 65, or some specified normal retirement age, and after a specified number of years of service with the employer. Thus, it is clear that not all current employees of the firm will be entitled to benefits under the plan. Indeed, one can argue that the *ultimate* cost of a pension plan cannot be determined until the last annuitant dies and all benefit payments terminate under the plan. The ultimate cost of the plan would then be the total benefits paid to all covered employees plus the expenses of operating the plan, less investment income earned on the accumulated assets in the pension fund. However, no business firm would ever establish a pension plan if the cost of the plan were indeterminate until the plan is terminated at some date in the distant future. The obvious solution lies in the fact that although the specific ultimate cost is unknown, actuaries are able to estimate with reasonable accuracy the ultimate cost of the plan. Assumptions must be made regarding the factors that affect the ultimate cost. In subsequent years, adjustments in the estimated cost of the plan may be required based on comparisons between the actual experience under the plan and the expected experience.

Cost Assumptions

A logical approach in considering the factors affecting the costs of a pension plan might be to relate these factors to the formula for determining the ultimate cost of the plan, i.e., benefits paid plus expenses less investment earnings.

Benefits Paid. The amount of pension benefits paid under a plan depends on several factors. The first factor is the number of retired workers who will receive benefits under the plan. The number of workers who will be eligible for benefits will depend in turn on three other factors: (1) mortality rates among covered employees; (2) rates and duration of disabilities among covered employees; and (3) rates of layoff and voluntary termination of employment. Mortality, disability, and turnover would prevent many workers from reaching retirement age, and thereby reduce the cost of the plan. If death and disability benefits are provided under the plan, then the costs of these benefits must be added to the cost of the normal retirement benefit. Likewise, the turnover assumption to be used depends on whether the plan provides a vested benefit and, if so, the liberality of the vesting provision.

The second factor affecting the amount of benefits paid under the plan is the length of time that retired workers receive their pension benefits. The length of the benefit period in turn depends on the age at which employees retire and the longevity of retired workers. In estimating the cost of pension benefits, then, one must make an assumption as to a normal retirement age. The higher the normal retirement age, the lower will be the cost of the plan. An assumption must then be made regarding mortality among retired lives in order to estimate the length of the benefit period. If the plan promises that benefits will be paid for a period certain, then this factor must be taken into account in the mortality assumption.

The last factor affecting the total amount of pension benefits paid under the plan is the amount of monthly pension paid to each retired worker. Even if one assumes a given benefit formula, there may still be a need for projections regarding the probable level of benefits that employees will receive under the plan. For example, if the benefit formula calls for a pension benefit related to compensation, cost estimates might include an assumption regarding expected future increases in the salaries of covered employees. More specifically, if a plan provides a pension benefit of 1 percent of salary per year of service, increases in salary will increase benefit levels and therefore increase costs under the plan. The same conclusion applies regardless of whether the benefit formula calls for a benefit related to career average earnings or to final average earnings.

Expenses.   The expenses of administering the pension plan must be added to the amount of benefits paid in arriving at the ultimate costs of the plan. The expense assumption used should reflect the type of administration, the particular funding instrument involved, and any other factors in a particular case that might affect the rate of expenses (e.g., single employer versus multiemployer arrangement, insured versus trust fund plan, the type of insured funding instrument used, or corporate versus natural person trustees in the case of a trust fund plan).

Investment Income.   The investment income earned on the accumulated assets in the pension fund reduces the ultimate cost of the plan. The tax-deferred accumulation of investment income under qualified plans adds significantly to the cost-reducing effect of this factor. The yield assumption used should take into account the size of the fund, the anticipated investment policy of the trustees or insurance company, current and projected long-term rates of return, and any other factors that might affect the future pattern of earnings of the fund.

Choice of Assumptions

There are two additional points that should be made regarding the *choice* of assumptions in calculations of estimated pension costs.

First, the flexibility available to the employer in choosing a particular set of actuarial assumptions depends in large part on the funding instrument involved. The greatest flexibility is available under trust fund plans. Practically the same degree of flexibility in choice of cost assumptions is available to the employer under deposit administration and immediate participation guarantee contracts issued by life insurance companies. The individual policy, group permanent and group deferred annuity instruments offer the employer the least flexibility in cost assumptions, since the insurance company establishes the assumptions to be used in setting the premium rates for these contracts.

Second, the choice of a particular set of assumptions normally does not alter the ultimate cost of the plan. The actual experience that will be realized under the plan is not affected by the estimates of the actuary. This conclusion does not apply fully in the case of plans funded with individual policies. In this case, there is a certain degree of pooling of experience among the entire class of business which affects the dividends paid. In the case of group plans, experience rating will produce a long-run ultimate cost fairly similar to that resulting under deposit administration or trust fund plans. However, even in the case of group permanent and group deferred annuities, there is an element of pooling which might produce long-term ultimate costs which are slightly different from, say, a trust fund or immediate participation guaranteed plan. It must be remembered, however, that the greater the freedom of choice of actuarial assumptions, the less significant will be the guarantees that the insurer can offer, and therefore the greater the responsibility imposed on the employer for the adequacy of the pension fund.

Actuarial Cost Methods

Techniques that are used to measure the accrual of costs and liabilities of pension plans are referred to as *actuarial cost methods*. Even after an estimate is made of the ultimate cost of a pension plan, some actuarial technique is still needed to determine how the cost of the plan will be allocated over future years.

Although actuarial cost methods are used to calculate the amount of annual contributions required under the plan, the concept of allocating pension costs can be separated from the funding policy or the pattern of contribution payments to the pension fund followed by the employer. Once an employer promises his employees a given pension benefit, liabilities begin accruing under the plan, regardless of whether the employer makes contributions to the pension fund. Actuarial cost methods are used to value these plan liabilities. Therefore, there is a difference between costing and funding techniques.

Possibly the point can be made more clear by considering a somewhat analogous situation in a nonpension situation. There is general agreement that good accounting practice requires a firm to charge against operating income an amount reflecting depreciation of plant and equipment. Of course, the plant and equipment depreciates whether or not the firm charges annual amounts of depreciation as costs of operation. Furthermore, even if the firm did make annual charges for depreciation, these charges need not (and generally are not) related to any funding or financing policy of the firm to set aside funds or establish a sinking fund to replace the depreciated plant and equipment. The depreciation costing problem, and the replacement financing problem are, therefore, two different and distinct problems. Likewise, the determination of pension costs and the decisions of the employer regarding the rate at which contributions are made to the pension fund are two separate matters. However, it is important to note that, in practice, an employer's contribution pattern generally follows the pattern of costs developed through the use of one of the actuarial cost methods.

Choice of Actuarial Cost Method. Various actuarial cost methods will produce different annual contribution levels. But the choice of a particular actuarial cost method will not affect the ultimate cost of the plan, except to the extent that the varying patterns of contributions can produce varying amounts of assets and, therefore, investment income. An increase in investment income will decrease the ultimate cost of the plan.

If the choice of actuarial cost method has little effect on the ultimate cost of a pension plan, what factors determine which method will be used in calculating the amount and incidence of pension contributions? The basic considerations are (1) the benefit formula specified in the plan, (2) the funding instrument used, and (3) the degree of flexibility in annual contribution requirements desired by the employer. All three factors are not equally important in every case. For example, an employer may have chosen a deposit administration contract or a trust fund arrangement because of a strong desire for flexibility in his annual contribution commitment. In that case, the benefit formula specified under the plan has little bearing on the choice of actuarial cost method used. However, although any actuarial cost method can be used in the case of a deposit administration or trust fund plan, the desire for flexibility in annual contributions probably would lead the actuary to use, for reasons which will be made clear later, a projected benefit method with a supplemental liability. On the other hand, if the employer had adopted a fully insured plan using individual or group permanent contracts, a projected benefit cost method without supplemental liability probably would be used, and the accrued benefit cost method would be used under a plan providing a unit benefit that is funded through a group deferred annuity instrument. Therefore, the employer has little flexibility in the choice of actuarial cost method under insured allocated funding instruments, and considerable flexibility in the case of unallocated funding instruments.

Accrued Benefit Cost Method. Under the accrued benefit cost method the cost of each unit of benefit is associated with the year in which the benefit is credited. This method is best adapted to those plans that provide a unit benefit type of formula, e.g., a percentage of each year's compensation, or a specified dollar amount for each year of credited service. Under these benefit formulas, a precisely determinable unit of benefit is associated with each year of a participant's credited service.

Assume, for example, that a plan provides a benefit of one percent of compensation per year of service. If a covered employee, age 35, earned $6000 of annual compensation, he would receive credit for $60 of annual pension benefit starting at age 65. The cost of this benefit would be the single-premium sum required to purchase a nonrefund deferred annuity of $60 a year beginning at age 65. The cost of the benefit credited each year will vary with the age of the employee and the amount of benefit credited. The annual contribution required for the plan as a whole is determined by adding the single-premium sums required to purchase the benefits credited during the year for all participants. Thus, it can be seen why some people refer to the accrued benefit cost method as the single-premium method of funding.

At the inception of the plan, there undoubtedly will be some accumulated credits for past service. Under the accrued benefit method there is some flexibility in funding the past service (supplemental) liability. However, if a group deferred annuity contract is used, the insurer normally requires that the past service liability of an employee be funded by his retirement date. Thus, the employer's total annual contribution will be composed of the cost for the benefits credited during that year plus the supplemental costs for the portion of the supplemental liability funded during that year.

Projected Benefit Cost Method without Supplemental Liability. Rather than costing the benefits credited during a specific year, one can project the total benefits that will be credited by retirement date and spread these costs evenly over some future period. A logical future period over which costs can be spread is from the attained age of the employee at the time he becomes eligible for participation in the plan to his expected date of retirement or the normal retirement age under the plan.

For example, assume that a plan provides a benefit of $200 a month beginning at age 65 and after a minimum of 10 years' service. If the employee is 35 years old when he enters the plan, the employer can set aside equal installments for each of the next 30 years to accumulate the single premium amount needed to provide $200 a month income at age 65. At the inception of the plan, an employee may receive benefit credits for prior years of service. These benefits would be added to projected future service benefits to be credited by retirement age and the cost of total benefits would be spread evenly over the years from the attained age of the employee at the inception of the plan to his retirement age. Thus, this method makes no separation between the funding of past service and future service credits. This is the method used when individual policies are used to fund the plan. The approach used here also explains why this method has sometimes been referred to as the "attained-age level premium" method of funding.

Projected Benefit Cost Method with Supplemental Liability. Another cost method is similar to the previous method, except that the period over which the cost of projected benefits is spread begins with the age of the employee in the first year for which he receives credited service. For an employee who becomes eligible for participation in the plan after the inception date of the plan, there is no difference between the annual costs generated under both cost methods. However, the two methods will not produce similar annual costs for an employee who receives credit for past service prior to the inception date of the plan. Using the example given in the previous section, assume that the employee entitled to a pension of $200 a month is age 35 at the inception of the plan and already has 5 years of credited past service. The employer would be required under this latter cost method to make annual contributions for current service based on the assumption that he had 35 years rather than 30 years over which to fund the benefit. Since the period over which benefits are to be funded is longer, these annual contributions will be less. However, since the projected benefit of $200 a month is identical in both situations, the lower annual contributions will be inadequate to provide the full benefit, thereby creating a supplemental liability. Obviously, this method cannot be used under an individual policy plan. However, this method can be used for the auxiliary fund under a combination plan or under deposit administration and trust fund plans.

The projected benefit method with supplemental liability offers the employer considerable flexibility in annual contributions. Each year the employer may pay interest only or fund a portion of the supplemental liability, in addition to the normal costs under the plan. Since this method is used with unallocated funding instruments, there is no requirement that the supplemental liability pertaining to a particular employee be funded by his retirement date. This method is sometimes referred to as "entry-age normal" method of funding.

Aggregate Cost Methods. The aggregate cost methods are quite similar to the individual projected benefit cost methods discussed above. The distinguishing characteristic of the aggregate level cost methods is that the normal cost accruals are calculated for the plan as a whole without identifying any part of such cost accruals with the projected benefits of specific individuals. The cost accruals can be expressed as a percentage of compensation or as a specific dollar amount. Like their individual cost method counterparts, the aggregate methods can be used with and without a supplemental liability.

The following list of the various actuarial cost methods indicates the corresponding names under older terminology and the funding instruments normally employing each method:

New Terminology	*Old Terminology*	*Funding Instrument Normally Associated with Each Method*
Accrued benefit method	Single-premium; unit cost or unit credit methods	Group deferred annuity, unallocated funding instrument
Projected benefit methods individual level cost		
with supplemental liability	Entry age normal method	Unallocated funding instruments and auxiliary fund
without supplemental liability	Attained age level premium method	Individual policies and group permanent contracts
Aggregate level cost methods		
with supplemental liability	Entry age normal with frozen initial liability, aggregate method with frozen initial liability	Unallocated funding instruments
without supplemental liability	Attained age normal method or aggregate method	Unallocated funding instruments

SELECTED REFERENCES

McGill, Dan M. *Fundamentals of Private Pensions.* 2d ed. Pension Research Council, Wharton School of Finance and Commerce, University of Pennsylvania. Homewood, Ill.: Richard D. Irwin, Inc., 1964.

Marples, William F. *Actuarial Aspects of Pension Security.* Pension Research Council, Wharton School of Finance and Commerce, University of Pennsylvania. Homewood, Ill.: Richard D. Irwin, Inc., 1965.

Melone, Joseph J. *Collectively Bargained Multi-Employer Pension Plans.* Pension Research Council, Wharton School of Finance and Commerce, University of Pennsylvania. Homewood, Ill.: Richard D. Irwin, Inc., 1963.

Melone, Joseph J., and Allen, Everett T., Jr. *Pension Planning: Pensions, Profit Sharing, and Other Deferred Compensation Plans.* Rev. ed. Homewood, Ill.: Richard D. Irwin, Inc., 1972.

35

Profit Sharing and Thrift Savings Plans

By JAMES B. ZISCHKE

PROFIT SHARING and thrift savings plans are widely used vehicles by which business enterprise provides significant employee benefits. Most often these plans accompany private pension plans as introduced in the two previous chapters. The analysis in this chapter will provide in essence a comparison of profit sharing and pension plans. Further, this chapter is concerned only with plans for common-law employees since self-employed individual plans are discussed in the following chapter.

PROFIT SHARING PLANS

The term profit sharing, broadly speaking, embraces any program under which profits of a business enterprise are shared with its employees. Thus, the term includes so-called "cash" plans under which the employees' share of the profits is paid to them currently as a wage supplement (and taxed on top of their other income), as well as various types of programs under which amounts credited to employees are paid incrementally over a period of time or accumulated for later distribution.

When used in the context of employee deferred compensation plans, however, the term profit sharing customarily refers only to qualified profit sharing plans under which the employer's contributions are deposited in a trust fund and accumulated for subsequent payment to participating employees.

Qualified profit sharing plans (or as they are sometimes called, "deferred profit sharing" or "profit sharing trust" plans) are closely related to qualified pension plans in terms of their tax treatment and requirements for qualification under the Internal Revenue Code.

Both pension and profit sharing plans afford essentially the same tax advantages to employers and employees, namely:

1. Under both types of plans an employer's contributions (within prescribed limits) are currently deductible.

2. There are no taxes (except in the case of unrelated business income) on any investment earnings or gains attributable to funds held under either type of plan (i.e., there is a full before-tax compounding of any investment increments).

3. Participating employees under either a pension or a profit sharing plan are not (with minor exceptions) taxed currently on amounts contributed to the plan or credited for their benefit, but rather, pay tax only when they receive distributions from the program (at which time, depending on the circumstances and nature of the distribution, the amounts paid out may receive favored tax treatment).

To be eligible for these tax advantages, both pension and profit sharing plans must meet nearly identical requirements for qualification under the Internal Revenue Code and Regulations. Both types of plans must be written, separately funded programs, established by an employer for the exclusive benefit of his employees (and communicated to them); and they must be intended to be permanent (with provisions preventing reversion to the employer of any contributed funds). In order to qualify, both pension and profit sharing plans must also meet prescribed mathematical tests with respect to employee coverage (the minimum being, generally, coverage of at least 70 percent of those full-time employees who have completed at least 5 years of service), or it must be demonstrated that coverage does not discriminate in favor of so-called prohibited group employees (i.e., employees who are either highly paid, officers, shareholders, or supervisors). In addition, it must be shown that neither benefits nor contributions discriminate in favor of the prohibited group employees.

Differences between Pension and Profit Sharing Plans

Despite similarities in tax treatment and in requirements for qualification, there are numerous differences between pension and profit sharing plans. The basic difference is one of emphasis.

Pension plans, as the name implies, are and must be established for the primary purpose of providing systematically for the payment of benefits to employees after their retirement. Pension plans may provide incidental death benefits, as well as disability retirement benefits and vested benefits upon severance of employment; but they may not provide any benefits not customarily related to pensions, such as layoff or illness benefits, nor may they provide for any distributions of employer contributed funds prior to a participant's separation from service. Furthermore, contributions to a pension plan must not be dependent on profits.

On the other hand, while a profit sharing plan may have as its primary objective the accumulation of funds for employee retirement, this is rarely, if ever, the plan's sole benefit objective. Within the purview of the Income Tax Regulations, the term profit sharing includes any qualified plan of deferred compensation which is supported by an employer's contributions out of either current or accumulated earnings or profits and which provides for accumulating the funds contributed in a trust for distribution to participating employees after either a fixed number of years, upon attainment of a stated age, or upon prior occurrence of some specified event such as layoff, illness, disability, retirement, death, or severance of employment.

In short, pension plans are essentially retirement benefit vehicles whereas profit sharing plans are essentially vehicles for accumulating funds that may be used for a variety of employee benefit purposes. This difference in emphasis, in turn, leads to a number of differences in the operational structure and benefit potential of the two types of programs, as well as various differences in their technical treatment under the Income Tax Regulations. The key differences in each of these areas can be illustrated by comparing the characteristic provisions included in typical profit sharing plans with their pension plan counterparts.

Eligibility Provisions. Pension plans, in order to hold down costs, typically require anywhere from a 3- to 5-year period of service and often attainment of a minimum age (such as age 25 or 30) before an employee is eligible for coverage; or they may limit benefits to those employees who have completed a qualifying period of service, such as 10 or 15 years and, possibly, have attained a minimum age (such as 40). Plan coverage is often not afforded to employees who have reached a maximum age (usually somewhere between 50 and 60) at date of hire, in order to avoid the relatively higher costs entailed in providing pension benefits for older employees.

Under the typical profit sharing plan, on the other hand, cost is not a function of either the number or age of covered employees. If more employees are covered, it simply means a proportionate reduction in the amount initially allocated to each participant from the employer's profit sharing contribution for a year. Consequently, requirements for employee participation usually are more liberal under profit sharing plans. While there are exceptions, the majority of profit sharing plans require a service-eligibility period of less than three years; and one year is probably average. Minimum or maximum age restrictions on eligibility are rare.

Employer Contribution Requirements. Under a qualified pension plan, an employer must contribute over a period of years the amount necessary to fund that portion of the promised benefit not otherwise provided from employee contributions (or, in the case of a money purchase pension plan, the employer must contribute each year the fixed amount or percent of salary specified by the plan). An employer's pension plan contributions are thus required contributions, although their amount and incidence from year to year may be varied to some extent under most plans other than money purchase pension plans.

Under a profit sharing plan, however, there is no requirement as to the amount which an employer must contribute each year. The Regulations simply provide that contributions to a profit sharing plan must not be made at such time or in such amounts as to produce discrimination in favor of prohibited group employees; and, to the extent that an employer has profits, he must make more than a single or occasional contribution to the plan. Beyond these general requirements, an employer is completely free to establish any criteria he wishes for determining the amount he will contribute to a profit sharing plan. Thus, an employer may establish a definite formula for contributions (such as 10 percent of pretax profits);

or he may simply determine on a year-to-year basis the amount or percent of profits to be contributed; or he may set up a target formula for predetermining normal yearly contributions, but then reserve the right to increase or decrease the amount to be contributed depending on business circumstances.

This flexibility in determining employer contributions is one of the main differences between pension and profit sharing plans. The fact that a profit sharing plan does not require any fixed commitment to make contributions unless an employer has profits is often cited as one of the great advantages of profit sharing; and certainly in many planning situations, particularly in newer companies or where earnings tend to fluctuate widely, it can be an overriding consideration in choosing between the establishment of a profit sharing plan as against a pension program. On the other hand, this "advantage" can have obvious disadvantages in situations where providing a particular level of benefits is important, since there is no advance assurance as to what profits or profit sharing contributions may be.

Another important difference between pension and profit sharing plans, as regards employer contributions, lies in the area of deduction limitations. The deduction for employer contributions to a profit sharing plan is limited in any year to an amount which does not exceed 15 percent of the aggregate compensation paid or accrued to participating employees during that year. If contributions in a year are less than this 15 percent figure, the deficiency may be carried over and made up in a subsequent year (subject, however, to a secondary limitation that any "make-up" contributions, together with regular contributions, cannot exceed for deduction purposes in a single year more than 30 percent of covered payroll).

The net effect of this limitation on profit sharing contribution deductions is to limit benefits under a profit sharing plan to such amount as can be provided by employer contributions not exceeding an average of 15 percent of covered payroll.

There is, in essence, no similar percent of payroll limitation on deductions that can be taken for pension plan contributions. If the cost of providing a desired level of pension benefits is, say, 30 percent of payroll, then that amount may be contributed and deducted each year. Thus, in any situation where the desired level of deferred compensation benefits entails employer contributions in excess of 15 percent of payroll, profit sharing plans may be at a disadvantage as compared to pension programs.

Allocation Formulas. Under standard defined benefit pension plans (i.e., plans which contain a formula for predetermining an employee's retirement benefit), employer contributions are either currently or eventually "allocated" to participating employees in accordance with the cost of providing their pension benefit credits (including any credits for service prior to the plan's inception). However, standard pension plans do not contain allocation formulas, as such.

Profit sharing plans, on the other hand, are required to have a definite formula for allocating employer contributions each year among the trust accounts of participating employees. Typically, such allocations are made in proportion to the participating employee's compensation for the period covered by the contribution. However, other factors such as years of service may be introduced into the formula (for example, one unit or share per $100 of compensation, plus one unit or share per year of service). Under thrift savings profit sharing plans (as described later) allocations typically are made in proportion to the employees' contributions.

Whatever allocation formula is used under a profit sharing plan, however, it must not discriminate in favor of prohibited group employees. For this purpose, the test is basically whether higher-paid employee groups receive greater allocations under the formula as a percent of current compensation than do the lower-paid employee groups. If they do, the IRS will normally not approve the formula.

This testing for profit sharing discrimination on the basis of relative allocations as a percent of salary produces one of the important differences between standard pension plans and profit sharing plans. Under the standard defined benefit pension plan, costs attributable in any year to a particular employee will depend not only on the benefit formula, but also usually on the employee's age and, often, on his period of past or expected service. Furthermore, pension plan benefits (and consequent contributions) may be related to an employee's highest average compensation over a limited period (such as three or five years), rather than to current compensation levels each year. Consequently, it is not unusual for an acceptable nondiscriminatory pension formula to produce employer contributions on account of older or longer-service employees (who are often higher paid) that, as a percent of current compensation, are far greater than those currently being made for younger or shorter-service employees (who are often lower paid). Such "discrimination" in terms of contributions is permissible under standard pension plans, whereas it is not possible under regular profit sharing allocation formulas.

This possible advantage in favor of standard defined benefit pension plans may be further extended in many situations under the rules relating to integration of private qualified plans with social security. Under profit sharing plans (as well as money purchase pension plans) these rules permit "special" allocations or contributions to be made each year for the benefit of higher-paid employees, provided the amount is not more than 7 percent of their current compensation in excess of the current wage base for social security tax purposes. Under standard pension plans, however, the integration rules are based on benefits, rather than on contributions or allocations; and the benefit, in turn, may be related to the amount by which an employee's highest 5-year average compensation exceeds the maximum wage base for social security benefit purposes in the year in which he attains age 65. The resultant benefit, when related back to employer contributions required to fund the benefit, in effect, can compound the "permissible discrimination" in favor of older and higher-paid employees in terms of allowable contributions as a percent of their compensation, as compared to allowable allocations to them under integrated profit sharing or money purchase pension plans.[1]

---

[1] The comparative effects of integration under profit sharing or money purchase pension plans versus standard pension plans can be illustrated hypothetically by the contributions that could result in the case of two example employees, each earning

Retirement Benefits. Benefit formulas under standard pension plans, as already noted, can be related to an employee's total period of service (including past service) as well as to current or highest average levels of compensation. Thus, meaningful retirement benefits can be provided employees from the very commencement of a pension plan.

Retirement benefits under a profit sharing plan, however, are a function of the amount accumulated in an employee's trust account at his retirement. This, in turn, depends on the length of time the employee has participated in the plan, and the amount that has been allocated to his trust account from employer contributions, forfeitures, and investment earnings and gains. In terms of producing what might be called a satisfactory level of retirement benefits, 20 or more years of profit sharing plan participation may be required. For example: assuming a 4 percent per year rate of salary increase, and a profit sharing plan producing allocations averaging 10 percent of salary and investment earnings of 6 percent annually, the resultant accumulation at age 65, after 20 years' participation, might produce a life pension of around 27 percent of final 10-year-average salary (or 23 percent of final salary).

Thus, for the employee who is older at the time a profit sharing plan is initiated, potential retirement benefits may be relatively low. On the other hand, for the employee who is relatively young at the time he enters the plan, retirement benefits could be substantial (under the plan used as an example in the preceding paragraph, an employee entering at age 30 could expect the equivalent of a pension of 56 percent of final 10-year-average salary or 47 percent of final salary).

It should also be noted that profit sharing plans do not provide automatically for payment of lifetime retirement benefits, as do typical pension plans. If the plan provides (as many do) for distributing profit sharing

---

$50,000 annually, but one of whom is age 35 and the other age 50 at the time a plan is instituted. Under an integrated standard pension plan providing a preretirement death benefit at least equal to the accumulated value of the employees' accounts, the benefit formula might typically call for an annual pension beginning at age 65 equal to 30 percent of the employees' annual earnings in excess of $6,000. Thus, each of the two example employees under such a plan nominally would be entitled to a pension of $13,200 annually at age 65 (i.e., $50,000 − $6,000 × 30% = $13,200). However, assuming the employer funds these benefits on the basis of level annual deposits to retirement, the net annual contribution over a 30-year period to provide the $13,200 pension for the 35-year-old might approximate $2,070 per year, while the contribution to provide the same pension over a 15-year period for the 50-year-old would approximate $6,370 annually. On the other hand, if the two example employees were covered under a profit sharing or money purchase pension plan, with a similar $6,000 integration level, the maximum permissible annual integrated contribution would be the same for each employee, namely, $3,080 per year (i.e., $50,000 − $6,000 × 7% = $3,080), which, comparatively speaking, would represent approximately a 50 percent contribution increase for the 35-year-old, but an over 50 percent decrease for the 50-year-old.

In short, where the planning objective is to favor the younger employees or to treat all employees alike in terms of relative employer contributions for their benefits, the profit sharing (or money purchase) approach usually will provide the best solution. However, where the objective is to produce a higher rate of employer contributions for older, and particularly older higher-paid, employees (or where the objective is equivalent final benefits for all), a standard pension approach may provide the most satisfactory solution.

accounts in installments over a fixed period (say, ten years) following retirement, it is likely that a substantial number of retired participants will outlive their "pensions."

To obviate this problem, most well-designed profit sharing plans provide that part or all of an employee's accumulated account may be used at retirement (or sometimes currently) to purchase a nontransferable fixed or variable annuity for him, under which an insurance company guarantees the retirement payments for life (with such survivor or term certain benefit provisions as the employee may have elected). Such annuity purchase options can offer special tax advantages at retirement, since the annuity payments are taxed only as received (and any survivor benefit may be exempt from federal estate taxes). Further, distribution of an annuity contract, as part payment of a total distribution of a terminating employee's account, does not destroy the long-term capital gain, special-income-averaging treatment for the remainder of the distribution. This is extremely valuable in situations where optimum tax results can be achieved from "splitting" a profit sharing accumulation into two parts for tax purposes, one of which is taxed currently on a favored basis (but is not thereafter exempt from federal estate taxes), and the other (the annuity) is taxed on a spread basis over future years (and remains exempt from federal estate tax).[2]

Death Benefits. The typical industrial pension plan does not provide benefits (or provides only limited benefits) in event of death before retirement (this normally being considered the function of group insurance). Death benefits, however, may be provided by a pension plan (and often are in "white collar" and smaller company plans), so long as they are "incidental." For this purpose, a death benefit under a standard defined benefit pension is considered "incidental" if the total amount provided either through life insurance or otherwise does not exceed 100 times the employee's expected pension (or the cash reserve being held for his pension benefit, if greater).

Profit sharing plans, on the other hand, normally provide a death benefit of the full amount accumulated in a deceased employee's account. This means that during the early years of an employee's participation, the normal death benefit is relatively small; whereas, during the later years, depending on the success of the plan, it may be substantial.

---

[2] An example of such a situation would be a retiring employee with a $100,000 profit sharing account who has sufficient available deductions in the year of retirement to offset the taxes on a total distribution of $50,000, but thereafter expects to have deductions and exemptions which would offset only $5,000 of taxable income per year. If such an employee took $50,000 of his $100,000 in a "lump sum" and the remainder in the form of a nontransferable annuity starting the next year and returning not more than $5,000 per year, he would, in effect, avoid all taxes on the distribution. On the other hand, if the employee takes his full $100,000 in a lump sum in the year of retirement, at least $50,000 will be subject to tax under the total distribution rules (a tax of somewhere between $6,000 and $9,000, depending on the employee's filing status); or, if he takes installment distributions of, say, $10,000 from his account each year, he might escape tax on the first year's payment, but thereafter at least $5,000 of each distribution would be taxable as ordinary income (resulting in possible total taxes over the period of the distribution of somewhere between $9,000 and $13,000).

The amount of the "normal" death benefit under profit sharing is thus often in inverse proportion to an employee's actual needs, being small when he is younger with a growing family, and large when he is older and with lessened family responsibilities. This factor has led a number of profit sharing plans to include life insurance death benefits in the program, either through provision for automatically applying a portion of each participant's account to the purchase of a life insurance policy for the benefit of his account, or giving the employee an option to have part of his account invested in such a policy. This latter optional approach to the purchase of insurance (which unfortunately has received too little attention) is particularly appropriate in plans where only a portion of the employees need or can benefit from increased death benefit protection.

There are no limitations on the amount of an employee's profit sharing account which may be applied to purchase retirement income or endowment insurance. Neither are there limitations on the amount that may be used to provide regular ordinary life insurance coverage if funds allocated to the account for less than two years are not used to pay premiums. Where employer contributed amounts which have been allocated to an employee's account for less than two years can be used to pay premiums on ordinary life insurance coverage, however, IRS rulings limit the aggregate amount that may be so applied to not more than 50 percent of the aggregate allocations to the employee's account from company contributions and forfeitures.

Where life insurance benefits are provided under a profit sharing plan, they are treated for tax purposes in the same manner as life insurance under a pension plan, namely, the net term premium value of the pure insurance coverage provided from employer contributions is considered currently taxable income (however, the amount reported becomes a nontaxable credit against the taxable portion of any subsequent benefits distributed from the policy); the amount of pure insurance coverage is nontaxable to a beneficiary upon distribution; and the entire proceeds of the policy may qualify for exemption from federal estate tax. This means that profit sharing plans can, in effect, permit employees to buy needed coverage with what amounts to practically before-tax dollars and, at the same time, keep the entire amount of the insurance proceeds out of their taxable estates.

Severance Benefits. While various provisions for severance or vested benefits in event of early termination of employment are included in the majority of pension plans, they tend, primarily for cost reasons, to be limited to employees who have completed some qualifying period of service (often ten years or more) and frequently to employees who have also reached a stated age (such as 45 or 50). Under a pension plan, forfeitures accruing by reason of employee terminations prior to their being fully vested cannot be used directly to increase benefits of other employees and, in effect, serve to reduce costs of the pension plan to the employer.

The situation in profit sharing, on the other hand, is the reverse of that in pensions. Under the typical plan, costs are not related to benefits provided, and forfeitures may be used to increase the benefits of other employees. Thus, while some profit sharing plans provide for full and immediate vesting of employees' accounts, the majority of plans contain provisions for forfeiture of part or all of an employee's account in event of early termination of employment, with these forfeitures then being reallocated, usually in the same manner as contributions or in proportion to account balances, to increase the benefits of remaining employees.

There is a potential for a tontine effect in profit sharing forfeiture reallocation provisions. Where vesting is delayed and there is heavy employee turnover, a handful of longer-service employees can end up with the bulk of the trust funds in their accounts. The IRS has recognized this possibility and the fact that in most cases the longer-service employees tend to be those in the higher-paid or supervisory categories. Consequently, there has been a tendency in recent years to require relatively rapid vesting formulas in any profit sharing plan which includes prohibited group employees, with full vesting after 10 years' service or participation (and incremental 10 percent per year partial vesting) being a rule of thumb. Furthermore, in such situations, the IRS normally will not approve forfeiture reallocation formulas based on relative account balances, since such formulas can favor longer-service, higher-paid employees who have the largest accounts.

Other Benefit Provisions. A major difference between pension and profit sharing plans is the ability of the latter to provide benefit distributions prior to an employee's separation from service.

Under pension plans, unless an employee terminates early (or unless the plan is terminated) his benefits and his share of employer contributions are tied up until retirement.

Under a profit sharing plan, distributions for specified purposes, such as financial hardship or need for funds to educate children, can be made prior to termination of employment. Or the plan may provide that an employee can withdraw portions (or even all) of his accumulated funds after a period of time, such as five or ten years (shorter periods are possible, so long as funds available for withdrawal have been in the plan at least two years). Profit sharing funds can also be used to provide health insurance or to reimburse medical expenses, although this is rarely done since in most situations it is simpler and less costly taxwise if done outside the plan (i.e., premiums or reimbursement for such coverage is taxable income, if paid by the plan, but nontaxable if paid directly by the employer).

Profit sharing plans can even be set up on a basis which gives an employee the choice of taking part or all of his allocations as a taxable cash bonus or of having them deferred on a noncurrently-taxable basis. In order for the deferred portion of such combinations to qualify, however, at least one half of the participants in the deferred plan must come from the lower-paid two thirds of those eligible.

This benefit flexibility of profit sharing plans is a distinct advantage where the objective of a program is intermediate term deferred compensation, more immediate employee appeal, or provision for a wide range of benefit possibilities.

Investment of Plan Funds

There are no specific limitations on investments which may be made with the funds of either a pension or profit sharing plan, except the self-dealing restrictions contained in the prohibited transaction rules of Section 503(b) of the Code and the general exclusive-benefit-of-employees requirement that cost of investments not exceed fair market value and that investments provide a fair rate of return and be consistent with the purposes of the plan.

In general, profit sharing plans and pension plans can be, and often are, invested in a similar manner or in similar investment media. Thus, funds of either type of plan may be invested in a broad range of securities, including mutual funds; used to purchase real property or mortgages; or invested in various types of insurance company contracts including variable annuity and separate account contracts.

Investments of a profit sharing plan must be valued at least annually on the basis of their fair market value, and the accounts of participants adjusted in accordance with such valuation as well as in accordance with their share of any investment earnings, gains, and losses of the trust fund. This means that employees' profit sharing accounts, and resultant benefits, may fluctuate in value if the underlying investments are subject to fluctuation in current market price. In order to minimize such fluctuations (and the potential problem of employees retiring at a low point in the market), some profit sharing plans invest part or all of their funds in annuity contracts or in insurance company deposit administration contracts which guarantee principal; or they may provide options under which employees, particularly those close to retirement, may elect to have their accounts so invested.

Profit sharing plans may also make two types of special investments which normally are not made by pension plans. The first of these is investment in the employer's own securities, even though they may not be dividend paying, if the plan is designed as a stock bonus plan or if part of its purpose is to encourage stock ownership by employees. The second type is key man insurance. Such an investment is normally made in situations where one or several key men are largely responsible for continuing corporate profitability. In these situations, the trust takes out a life insurance policy on the life of the key man, with the proceeds payable to the trust in event of his death. If the key man continues to live, the participants under the trust will absorb the cost of the life insurance but presumably have as an offset the continuance of a high level of profit sharing contributions. In event of the key man's death, however, the insurance proceeds will be payable to the trust and compensate for the decrease in profit sharing contributions and resultant benefits that may ensue. A variation of this type of investment is sometimes used where a key man is also a stockholder or where one of the objectives of the profit sharing trust is to accumulate sufficient funds so that employees may eventually buy part or all of the business through their profit sharing accounts. In these cases, the key man insurance covers the life of the stockholder and, in event of his death, makes funds available to the trust which can be used to purchase part or all of the deceased stockholder's shares.

Combination Pension-Profit Sharing Programs

Any comparative discussion of pension and profit sharing plans leads inevitably to the question of which type of plan is better. The answer, of course, depends on a particular company's situation and objectives. While a particular set of circumstances may dictate one type of plan as against the other, there are numerous cases where the answer is not clear-cut in favor of either type of plan and both may offer advantages. In such cases, a correlated program, based on a combination of a pension plan and profit sharing plan may provide the most satisfactory solution.

Such combination programs may take various forms, including combinations which emphasize the profit sharing plan as a supplement to a base pension plan and combinations under which the pension plan provides only career retirement benefits, while the profit sharing plan is geared primarily to provide for other benefit contingencies, such as layoff, early termination, and supplementary death and disability coverage.

While the combination approach has become increasingly popular in recent years, it is subject to special deduction limitations under the Internal Revenue Code which can restrict its operation in certain situations. Section 404(a)(7) of the Code provides an overriding limitation of 25 percent of compensation on the aggregate deduction that may be taken in any year for contributions to combination pension-profit sharing programs (under a carry-over provision, this limit may be increased to 30 percent of compensation in years after the first year). This limitation has the dual effect of limiting overall benefits under combination programs to those that can be provided by a contribution of 25 percent of aggregate compensation of participants (30 percent in cases where the carry-over provisions are utilized), and of limiting the deductions in any year for the profit sharing portion of the program to the difference between this limit and the amount contributed to the pension plan (which, in turn, may limit somewhat a profit sharing plan's flexibility to make large contributions in some years and small or no contributions in others).

In most cases, these Section 404(a)(7) limitations are sufficiently broad as to pose no problem for combination programs. However, they are a potential trap and should be carefully considered when either planning a combination program or initiating new pension or profit sharing plans in situations where there is already an existing plan of the other type.

THRIFT SAVINGS PLANS

Despite their growing popularity, thrift savings plans (or as they are sometimes called, "investment savings plans") are not recognized as such under Section 401(a) of the Internal Revenue Code. Technically speaking, a tax-favored thrift or investment savings plan must be formulated as either a pension, profit sharing, or stock bonus plan (or be a part of such a plan), which meets the applicable qualification requirements of the Code and Regulations.

While any contributory qualified plan can, in a sense, be classified as a thrift plan, the true thrift savings plan which has emerged in recent years has the following general characteristics:

1. The plan has been established either separately, or in conjunction with a regular pension or profit sharing plan, for the purpose of encouraging thrift or investment savings on the part of employees.

2. Participation in the plan normally is voluntary on the part of eligible employees (although it can be mandatory).
3. Contributions to the plan by participating employees are made through payroll withholding (or sometimes, also, by direct deposit) and accumulated in separate nonforfeitable trust accounts for their benefit; and, in most plans, the employee has at least some choice with respect to how his contributions will be invested by the trustee.
4. If employer contributions are also made under the plan, their allocation is normally related, at least in part, to the amount contributed by employees.

Standard Thrift Savings Plans

Standard thrift savings plans normally are established as separate plans and involve at least a minimum employer contribution, which may be related to amounts contributed by employees, or determined, partially or wholly, in relation to profits.

Under standard plans, prescribed rates are set forth for employee required contributions ("required contributions" being classified as any contributions which result in an employee's receiving a greater share of employer contributions). The prescribed rate may be a set amount, such as 5 percent of pay. More often, it is based on an optional scale, with a prescribed minimum amount, such as 2 percent of pay, and a set maximum amount (which usually cannot exceed 6 percent of pay, unless it can be demonstrated that a higher rate will not exclude lower-paid employees from full plan benefits by reason of their not being able to afford maximum contributions).

In addition to "required contributions," standard thrift plans may permit additional voluntary contributions by participating employees ("voluntary contributions" being contributions that do not result in an entitlement to any greater share of amounts contributed by the employer). Under present IRS rulings, such voluntary contributions may not exceed an amount equal to 10 percent of the aggregate compensation paid an employee during the period of his plan participation.

A variety of allocation formulas are in use under standard plans for determining the employee's share of amounts contributed by the employer. Where the amount contributed is a matching proportion of the employees' required contributions (such as 50 cents on the dollar), allocation is normally made in accordance with the contribution rate. If employer contributions are based on profits, allocation is normally made in proportion to the amount contributed by each employee.

In many plans, the contribution and/or allocation formula escalates in accordance with service or participation (for example, 25 cents on the dollar the first year; 50 cents the next two years; and $1.00 per $1.00 after four or more years).

The great majority of standard thrift savings plans are designed to qualify as profit sharing plans, and their benefit and other provisions normally follow a profit sharing format. Eligibility provisions are generally very liberal; and vesting, if not immediate, is usually rapid. Forfeitures may be reallocated to increase benefits; however, under many fixed rate plans, forfeitures are used to reduce the employer's matching contributions. Employees are normally given the right to suspend participation at any time. Changes in elected contribution rates (where the plan provides a choice of rates) are usually permitted at fixed intervals, and most plans allow participants to make partial or full withdrawals from their accounts after a set period of participation or in event of financial hardship.

Satellite or Voluntary Thrift Savings Plans

Satellite or voluntary thrift savings plans are basically arrangements under which provisions for voluntary employee contributions are "tacked-on" to a regular pension or profit sharing plan. No employer contributions, as such, are made with respect to the savings plan; and participating employees are simply given the opportunity to make voluntary contributions (usually up to the prescribed 10 percent of pay maximum) to their own separate trust accounts. Rules respecting suspension of contribution, changes in elected rates, and withdrawals normally follow the same pattern as standard plans.

Investment Provisions

Under some thrift savings plans, all contributions are pooled in a single trust fund (or with an existing pension or profit sharing trust fund) for investment purposes, and employees' thrift accounts simply are credited with their proportionate share of any investment earnings, gains, or losses.

The majority of plans, however, give the employee various choices with respect to investment of his own contributions, and often with respect to any employer contribution for his benefit. The usual range involves a choice between an equity fund, a balanced investment fund, some type of fixed dollar investment account, and often an employer stock fund. The investment vehicle for the equity and balanced funds may be a separately invested trust fund. However, most plans utilize either existing mutual funds, a bank pooled trust fund, or an insurance company separate account arrangement. Fixed dollar choices similarly may utilize a separate trust; or an existing fixed income fund of a mutual fund, bank, or insurance company (including insurance company deposit administration contracts); or they simply may provide for investment in a savings account. Either fixed or variable annuities are often included among the investment options offered. Employees are usually given an opportunity at periodic intervals to change their investment election and perhaps switch past investments from one medium to another.

Advantages of Thrift Savings Plans

There is no tax advantage, as such, with respect to an employee's own contributions to a thrift savings plan (since they must come out of after-tax dollars). However, such plans afford the other tax advantages of qualified plans, namely, the opportunity to compound any investment increments on a before-tax basis and no current taxability of any employer contributions.

The main appeal of thrift savings plans from an employee's standpoint, however, is generally not their tax-favored treatment (although this can be an important advantage over a period of time), but rather the opportunity they afford for systematic investment of small amounts through weekly or monthly payroll deductions on a comparatively low-cost basis. An employee attempting to set up a systematic investment program on his own may find himself paying out 10 percent or even more of his periodic investment in brokerage charges or mutual fund commissions; whereas under most thrift profit sharing plans, these costs can be substantially reduced through pooled investment purchases (or even eliminated, where the employer is paying the costs of investment administration).

From an employer's standpoint, thrift savings plans represent a low-cost (or no-cost) benefit vehicle that over a period of time can result in employees accumulating substantial amounts to supplement their benefits under other programs, such as a pension plan. In turn, this can relieve pressure on the employer to increase benefits under these other programs. Employers have also found that thrift savings plans can have wide employee appeal; and the same employees who would balk at or resent forced contributions to a pension plan will flock to join an investment savings plan that may actually cost the employer less money.

Longer range, however, the most important advantage to be derived from the growing spread of thrift savings plans may be the fact that these plans can afford an opportunity for millions of workers to become, for the first time, investors in the U.S. economy, with a growing personal stake in the free enterprise system.

SELECTED REFERENCES

Bankers Trust Company. *1972 Study of Employee Savings and Thrift Plans.* New York, 1972.

Commerce Clearing House, Inc. *Pension Plan Guide.* Multivolume loose-leaf service. Chicago, n.d.

Metzger, B. L. *Profit Sharing in Perspective.* 2d ed. Evanston, Ill.: Profit Sharing Research Foundation, 1966.

Prentice-Hall, Inc. *Pension and Profit Sharing.* Multivolume loose-leaf service. Englewood Cliffs, N.J., n.d.

Spencer, Charles D. & Associates, Inc. *Spencer's Retirement Plan Services.* Multivolume loose-leaf service. Chicago, n.d.

Zischke, James B. "Tax and Business Considerations in Setting up Profit Sharing Plans," *Tax Ideas.* Englewood Cliffs, N.J.: Prentice-Hall, Inc., 1970.

36

Pensions and Profit Sharing for the Self-Employed

By THAXTER P. SPENCER

ATTEMPTS by the self-employed to obtain for themselves the benefits of qualified pension and profit sharing plans fall into two separate patterns, each of which has left a lasting mark on employee benefit planning. One was the development of amendments to the Internal Revenue Code extending to the self-employed benefits previously available only to common-law employees. A decade of effort to amend the Code culminated in the Self-Employed Individuals Tax Retirement Act of 1962, the results of which are the subject of this chapter. The other was an attempt by self-employed individuals to adopt forms of organization which would enable them to be treated as common-law employees for tax purposes, thereby enabling them to participate directly in qualified plans without changes to the Internal Revenue Code. This latter activity produced the variety of professional corporation statutes which are now generally in effect throughout the United States. Material dealing with professional corporations will be found in Chapter 48.

The Self-Employed Individuals Tax Retirement Act of 1962 amended the Internal Revenue Code by creating a new and restricted category of qualified plans for the self-employed. This was accomplished by treating for eligibility purposes a proprietor as his own employee and a partner as the employee of his partnership (but not of himself). Simple though this concept may seem, it has been encrusted with complex requirements and restrictions largely designed to assure the Congress and the Treasury that the participation of the self-employed would neither cause excessive loss of tax revenue nor result in unreasonable benefits for these participants. The qualification restrictions described below that are imposed upon plans covering the self-employed are in addition to the Code requirements which must be met by qualified plans that do not include the self-employed.[1] These restrictions take the form both of provisions which

---

[1] Hereafter for ease of reference these plans somewhat inaccurately are called "corporate plans."

562

must be set forth in the plan itself and of limitations upon the participation and benefits available to self-employed individuals, primarily owner-employees. In addition to these restrictions, the law introduced a new concept which requires the extension of plan benefits to eligible employees in any other unincorporated business "controlled" by a participating owner-employee (see "Definitions" below).

NATURE OF PLANS

Choice of Funding Methods and Vehicles

The Act authorizes four types of plan design: the trust arrangement, annuity plan, custodial account, and bond purchase plan.

Trust. A formal trust arrangement is similar to trusts in corporate plans, except for the general requirement that a bank must be used as a trustee. However, individual trustees are permitted when a trust invests in annuity, endowment, and life insurance contracts of a life insurance company *exclusively* to fund the benefits prescribed by the trust. Even in these circumstances the use of individual trustees is subject to three conditions.

1. The life insurance company must supply annually certain information about trust transactions.
2. The trust itself must provide for the substitution of a bank as trustee if the district director of Internal Revenue requires.
3. All proceeds under each contract must be payable directly to the employee or his beneficiary.

Despite the requirement that a bank be appointed trustee in certain circumstances, the plan may give power to persons other than the bank to control investments.

Annuity Plan. An annuity plan (without an intervening trust) is one pursuant to which the employer purchases nontransferable annuities (which may include incidental life insurance protection) on the several participants. For purposes of qualification, annuity plans include the purchase of face amount certificates.[2] In those plans where the participant is the owner of the contract or certificate he must agree not to deal with it in a manner inconsistent with the terms of the plan.

Custodial Account. A relatively new type of qualified plan involves a custodial account in which the custodian must be a bank and in which investments are either in mutual funds or in annuity, endowment, or life insurance contracts.[3] The advantages of this arrangement are limited, since the custodial services required by the Regulations are so extensive that significant savings over the conventional trust arrangement are largely eliminated.

---

[2] A face amount certificate defined in Section 2(a)(15) of the Investment Company Act of 1940 is a security which represents an obligation by its issuer to pay an amount or amounts at determinable dates more than 24 months after issue.

[3] It has come to the writer's attention that the national office of the IRS has approved at least one master plan funded by insurance policies in combination with a custodial account invested in mutual funds.

Bond Purchase Plans. Special nontransferable U.S. government bonds purchased in the name of a participant comply with all of the requirements of the Act. While these bonds require negligible administration and eliminate the need for a trust or plan document, they have certain disadvantages. They are nonredeemable except for disability or death prior to age 59½, and thus a bond holder terminating employment at an earlier age cannot realize cash even though he could have done so (with or without penalties) if the plan had used other forms of investment. No tax is payable by the participant until redemption of the bond, at which time a tax at ordinary income rates is payable on the proceeds in excess of that portion of the cost of the bond for which no tax deduction had previously been taken.

Subject to the limitations and exceptions already indicated for the various types of plan, benefits under self-employed plans may be funded through any type of investment which is permissible in corporate plans.

Definitions

Because the Act introduced concepts new to conventional pension and profit sharing plans, the following terms are necessary to any understanding of plans covering the self-employed.

Self-employed person is defined as an individual who owns an interest (capital or profit or both) in an unincorporated trade or business and who receives earned income from personal services rendered to it. Although not conclusive, it generally is true that a person who can treat his compensation as earnings from self-employment for social security purposes can participate in a qualified plan covering the self-employed. However, this does not apply to certain common-law employees who qualify for self-employment treatment under social security as, for example, ministers and members of religious orders. The final determination of who is self-employed depends upon all of the facts.

Owner-employee is defined as a self-employed person who (a) owns the entire interest in an unincorporated trade or business; or, (b) in the case of a partnership, owns more than 10 percent of *either* the capital interest *or* the profit interest. In the absence of written provisions, the profit interest of a partner is generally determined in the same manner as his distributive share of net taxable income, and in the case of capital, his share on liquidation of the partnership or his withdrawal—whichever interest is the greater.

Partner-employee. Since there is no formal term in the Act to describe self-employed individuals who are not owner-employees, they are referred to as "partner-employees" in this chapter. These are self-employed individuals who own 10 percent or less of both the capital interest and the profit interest of the partnership.

Controlled Business. An owner-employee might evade the limitations of the law by fragmenting his activities into several business entities for which he would establish separate plans in order to pyramid his participation while excluding as many employees as possible by shifting their employment. To prevent this, the Act introduced the concept of the controlled business. If an owner-employee in one business owns—alone or with one or more owner-employees—a 50 percent or greater interest in one or more other unincorporated trades or businesses, the latter are deemed to be controlled by such owner-employee, and plan coverage must be provided on a comparable basis for the eligible employees of all of the businesses. For example, assume an owner-employee in an unincorporated business participates in a plan established by that business. If he controls another unincorporated business there must be a comparable plan for the employees of both businesses. Such plans then are viewed as one plan for purposes of applying the maximum contribution limitations for owner-employees.

Contributions and Deductions

Basis of Contributions. For the self-employed, plan contributions must be based upon net earned income from self-employment, and for common-law employees, contributions are based upon compensation. Contributions for each self-employed individual are paid from his distributive share of the partnership net earnings after deductions for expenses, including deductions for partnership contributions to qualified plan benefits for common-law employees. The compensation used for determining contributions to be made for common-law employees may be either total compensation (including bonuses, overtime, and other irregular payments), or it may be basic compensation (excluding irregular payments), in which case there must be a reduction in the earned income base for the self-employed. This reduction is determined by calculating the percentage of the common-law employee total compensation which is represented by irregular payments, and then providing a corresponding reduction in net earned income.

Contribution and Deduction Limits. There is no dollar limit on contributions which may be made for nonowner-employees, since any limit is subject to the same rules that apply to corporate plans. With respect to contributions for owner-employees, the Act provides an automatic maximum of the lesser of 10 percent of current earned income or $2500. Although designed to put a maximum on amounts which could be taken by high income owner-employees, this automatic limitation has become a means of using the nondiscrimination requirements of the Code to minimize the contribution levels for nonowner-employees. While one may question whether this result should have been inevitable, it is now well accepted that the owner-employee may determine the percentage of his earned income which is represented by his maximum permitted contribution, and he then may use a similar percentage to determine contributions to be made for nonowner-employees. Ironically, this means that going up from an earned income level of $25,000, the higher the earned income of the owner-employee, the lower the dollar contribution for the nonowner-employees.

Full tax deductions are permitted for contributions on behalf of common-law employees, and up to the maximum limit for contributions for owner-employees. In the case of partner-employees, however, although there is no limit on contributions, they are deductible only to the lesser of 10 percent of earned income or $2500. While it might appear impractical to make contributions in excess of the deductible limits, such an arrangement can be attractive for the partner-employee, since these amounts even though not tax deductible will accumulate under the terms of the plan without current income tax until such time as they are distributed.

Where contributions are based upon the three-year average rule, there is one further exception to the deductibility of contributions for owner-employees, in that the full contribution computed on the three-year average cannot be deducted in any year in which the owner-employee's earned income falls below the three-year average. Thus, if he is entitled on the basis of the three-year average to make a contribution of $1000 under a 10 percent money-purchase plan, and if his earned income in some year should fall to $8000, the maximum deduction available would be $800 even though he is permitted to continue the contribution of $1000 to the plan.

Cost of Life Insurance Protection. The treatment under the Act of the cost of life insurance protection, the pure one-year term insurance, or so-called "PS-58" costs, presents certain complications. In a level premium contract each premium pays in part for pure protection (the amount at risk), and in part for cash value. Since amounts paid for the cost of insurance do not produce retirement benefits, they are not deemed to be contributions to the plan and may be contributed in addition to the maximum permitted plan contributions. Thus, if an owner-employee is entitled to contribute $2500 for his benefits, and if the one-year term insurance cost at policy issue is $300, a plan policy may be purchased with a premium of $2800. However, the annual pure term costs are a function of the age of the insured and the amount at risk. If these costs decrease sufficiently in future years there will be an automatic excess contribution. This problem is intensified for policies issued at older ages. For this reason, the amount of premium for owner-employees must be kept sufficiently low to prevent an excess contribution in any years when insurance costs decrease to the point where an excess contribution could occur.

For example, assume an owner-employee is age 45 with earned income to permit a $2500 contribution. A gross premium of $2822 on a retirement income policy includes a term insurance cost of $322 which is not considered a contribution to the plan. In the second year, the insurance cost for this policy is $331; thus $2822 less $331 produces a contribution of $2491, which is within acceptable limits. However, in the 18th policy year the insurance cost has decreased to $300, which would have the effect of producing a contribution in excess of $2500.

To avoid the occurrence of this technical excess contribution, there are at least two solutions. The simplest is to change the dividend option so that dividends will be applied to reduce premiums commencing in the year when the excess contribution would first occur. A less satisfactory and more complicated solution is to ascertain the lowest amount of term cost attributable to any year of the policy and add this amount to the permitted contribution ($2500 in the example) in order to establish the proper insurance premium.

Contributions of Property. The Regulations are very strict in forbidding, on behalf of an owner-employee, contributions of property other than money. There had been some hope that this requirement would be relaxed in the case of an insurance policy; however, it is quite clear that existing insurance policies on owner-employees cannot be transferred to plans covering them.

Required Employee Contributions. Although it is possible for a plan to require contributions by participants toward their own retirement benefits, such a provision may be unwise. The law provides that all partner-employees or common-law employees meeting the eligibility requirements of the plan actually must participate if the plan is to qualify. Hence, a refusal by one eligible individual to make a required contribution will preclude qualification of the plan.

Voluntary Employee Contributions. Voluntary contributions are permissible except that they can be made by owner-employees only if there is a nonowner-employee participating in the plan who has the right to make voluntary contributions (the nonowner-employee does not actually have to make contributions if he elects not to do so). The maximum voluntary contribution from any participant is 10 percent of his earned income or compensation, as the case may be. However, an owner-employee is not permitted to contribute a greater percentage than is permitted for other participants, and his voluntary contributions may not exceed $2500. Furthermore, after March 5, 1972, he may not withdraw any of his voluntary contributions prior to attaining age 59½ or disability. Plans which permit such withdrawals must be appropriately amended no later than the end of the first taxable year beginning after March 5, 1972.

Excess Contributions

Definition. An excess contribution is that portion of a contribution made by an owner-employee which exceeds the maximum permissible contribution on his behalf. The concept of excess contributions applies only to owner-employees, since the contribution limitations for partner-employees and common-law employees are similar to those contained in corporate plans. The Code and Regulations are detailed and narrow in their approach to the handling of excess contributions.

Treatment. The handling of excess contributions depends upon whether they are willful or nonwillful. They generally are nonwillful if made through misunderstanding, and not to inflate contributions or deductions. If discovered, the excesses plus any increment should be returned to the owner-employee. If determined by the IRS to exist, the law requires that they plus any increment be returned within six months after notification to the plan, and that the gross income of the owner-employee be increased by the net income attributable to the excess amount for each year in which there was an excess contribution. If the excess amounts are returned later than six months following notification, the increment on the total contribution must be included in the gross income of the owner-employee. However, in lieu of being returned, the excess amounts may be applied against either the following year's contribution or against voluntary contributions if permitted.

Where an excess contribution is deemed to have been made willfully, there must be a complete distribution to the owner-employee of his *entire* interest in the plan, including all increments. The plan then becomes disqualified with respect to the owner-employee for the taxable year in which the willful excess contribution was made and for the next five succeeding years during which no contribution may be made to the plan for the benefit of the owner-employee. In addition, such a distribution is subject to the penalty tax on premature distributions (see below).

Three-Year Average Rule for Insurance. In a fully insured plan using level premium contracts, potential fluctuations in the income of self-employed persons would require constant adjustments in policy face amounts. In order to avoid this problem the Act specifically makes provision for plans funded solely by annuity or insurance contracts. For such plans, a contribution, i.e., premium, will not be deemed excessive as long as it does not exceed the average *contribution* which could have been made for the insured, determined over each of the three years immediately prior to the purchase of the contract (or the number of years he has been in business if less). This does not permit the averaging of earned income for these years, but requires a determination of what would have been the permissible contributions and then requires an averaging of these amounts.

The use of the three-year average, while it avoids the danger of excess contribution in years when the owner-employee's earned income falls, has at least three disadvantages. First, it is detrimental to an owner-employee whose earned income is rising steadily. Second, it does not preserve the full deduction for the premium in those years when the owner-employee's actual earned income falls below that necessary to support the premium. Finally, in applying the $2500 maximum contribution limitation the pure term cost of insurance must be included in the $2500 maximum. It is not, however, included in determining the 10 percent limitation until the amount contributed becomes subject to the ceiling limit of $2500.

Plan Design

Because almost all of the requirements imposed by the Act pertain to plans in which there is an owner-employee participant, in the following discussion of plan design requirements it is assumed that there will be one or more participating owner-employees. If there is to be no owner-employee participant, a plan will be governed (with minor exceptions) by the same qualification rules which govern the plans of corporate employers.

Coverage Requirements. Eligibility requirements may specify any period of aggregate employment not in excess of three years, but must include all full-time employees (other than owner-employees) who have completed that period of service (part-time employees may be included if the employer wishes). As in corporate plans, a full-time employee is a person whose customary employment is for more than 20 hours a week or for more than five months in a calendar year. No minimum or maximum age requirement may be used. If an owner-employee with less than three years of service is to participate at the inception of the plan, the service requirement for other employees correspondingly must be reduced. However, a professional individual is usually regarded as being in the continuous practice of his profession even though he may relocate his practice, acquire a completely different clientele and employ a totally different group of employees.

Waiver of Participation. An owner-employee who does not wish to be covered by a plan may waive participation (he is deemed to have done so if a contribution is not made on his behalf). However, once a plan is established, he must contribute his share of contributions for the common-law participants. All eligible partner-employees and common-law employees must be covered if the plan is to qualify.

Entry Date. If a common entry date is to be used, the maximum service requirement of three years requires that eligibility be so defined that every employee joining the plan will have no more than three years of service on his initial entry date. For example, an acceptable eligibility provision would be participation on the entry date following two years of employment, since there could be 11 months and 29 days between the entry date of the plan and the third anniversary of a participant's employment.

Shared Employees. Where the services of an employee are shared by different employers under an agreement which governs the employee's compensation (for example, a medical clinic that is not operated as a partnership), the total time worked by an employee for all employers in the group is a measure of whether the employee is a full-time employee. Where one of the employers establishes a plan, the contribution required from that employer is based upon the portion of the employee's compensation which that employer pays.

Prior Service. The eligibility requirement may be satisfied by counting years of service with a former employer if the plan permits. However, no contributions on account of past service may be made for any self-employed individual. If the owner-employee includes for himself service with a former employer he must allow partner-employees and common-law employees to count any prior service to any prior employer no matter how remote in time.

Vesting. Unlike corporate plans, the contributions or benefits arising from contributions for both the partner-employee and the common-law employees must be nonforfeitable at the time the contributions are made.

Benefit Formula. Except for the maximum limits on contributions for the owner-employee, the benefit formula may be designed in the same way as for corporate plans, i.e., fixed benefit, money purchase or profit sharing.[4] Money purchase and profit sharing are preferred in most cases, since the Act is couched in terms of contributions rather than benefits, and in profit sharing plans the formula may specify that the percentage of compensation to be contributed for nonowner-employees for each year will be the minimum amount which will produce the maximum contribution for the owner-employee. However, the Regulations specifically forbid the reduction of an employee's compensation at or about the time the plan is adopted, even though such a reduction is authorized by Revenue Ruling for corporate plans.

---

[4] There must be a definite formula for allocations to a profit sharing plan.

Integration with Social Security. The rules applicable to the integration of corporate plans with social security do not apply to plans covering owner-employees. Plans for the self-employed will be integrated only if not more than one third of the total employer contributions under the plan is made for owner-employees. If this requirement can be met, the plan may be integrated under special rules which take into consideration only the amount of social security taxes paid by the employer. As a practical matter, unless there is a reasonably large number of participating nonowner-employees, social security integration is unavailable.

Limitations on Form and Methods of Payment

Loans and Assignments. A loan, an assignment, or an agreement by an owner-employee to assign any portion of his interest in a plan is deemed to be a distribution to him in the amount of the values involved. Any repayment of such a loan is a contribution to the plan in addition to any other contributions being made for the current year.

Retirement. Each plan must establish a normal retirement date for the commencement of benefit payments. However, regardless of the provisions of the plan, no distributions may be made for an owner-employee except for death or disability prior to his age 59½. Distributions may not commence later than his age 70½, regardless of whether or not he retires. Should he continue in employment beyond age 70½, he may continue to make deductible contributions, but each contribution made thereafter must be applied to a payout arrangement which will produce an added increment to the retirement benefits which he is receiving.

Method of Payment. A plan must provide for one of five methods of payout, and appropriate provisions to control these methods must be contained in every plan which covers a self-employed individual so that every participant will receive payment in accordance with one of the following:

1. Lump sum.
2. Over the life of the participant.
3. Over the joint lives and the survivor life of the participant and his spouse.
4. Over a period certain not extending beyond the life expectancy of the participant.
5. Over a period certain not extending beyond the joint lives and survivor life expectancy of the participant and his spouse.

Furthermore, the amount to be distributed each year must at least equal the amount obtained by dividing the participant's entire interest by his applicable expectancy, although lesser amounts may be distributed as long as the aggregate amounts actually distributed by the end of any year are at least equal to the aggregate of the minimum amounts required to have been distributed by that time. In spite of the foregoing, a nontransferable annuity may be distributed at any time.

Termination of Employment. There is no limitation restricting the way in which benefits on termination of employment may be paid to nonowner-employees, except that when payment occurs it must be consistent with the methods of payment described above. For the owner-employee, no values in his account may be paid to him prior to his attainment of age 59½ except for reasons of complete disability or death, and the payment of such values is subject to a premature distribution penalty.[5] In view of the seeming inconsistency between the provision of the law prohibiting such premature distribution and another provision providing for a penalty if such a premature distribution is made, the question has been raised as to whether it is permissible for an owner-employee to take early distribution as long as he suffers the penalties provided by the law. The IRS has ruled that the penalty provisions are not intended as a substitute for the nondistribution requirement and that the penalty was intended only to cover situations where the distribution is made in error.

Premature Distributions. A premature distribution to an owner-employee subjects him to two separate penalties:

1. A penalty tax against the deductible amounts contributed on his behalf while he was an owner-employee. If the amount is less than $2500, he is taxed on it at the rate of 110 percent of the normal tax increase on account of the inclusion of this amount in his gross income in the year of distribution. If the amount received is $2500 or more, the tax is computed by spreading the amount received over the year of receipt and the four prior years, and then taking 110 percent of the aggregate tax increase.

2. Where a premature distribution has been made, no contributions may be made on behalf of the owner-employee for any of the five succeeding taxable years.

Death. There are no specific provisions covering the method of payment at the death of a nonowner-employee except that it must be consistent with the general requirements for corporate plans. Upon the death of an owner-employee or his surviving spouse during the time when benefits are still due, the law requires that distribution must be completed within five years of the death; or, if the amount due is not to be paid out by that time, it must be applied to purchase an immediate annuity for the beneficiary either for life or for a term not greater than the life expectancy of the beneficiary.

Prohibited Transactions

If a plan includes an owner-employee, the rules with respect to prohibited transactions are considerably stronger than those applicable to corporate plans. The prohibited transactions relating to the owner-employee include the making directly or indirectly by the plan of any loan whatever to an owner-employee or a member of his family, the paying of any compensation to him for services rendered to the plan, the making available of services on a preferential basis, or the acquisition from him or selling to him of any kind of plan property.

Taxation

Although not within the scope of this chapter, it may be noted that the taxation of benefits for the self-employed is substantially different from

---

[5] This also includes his voluntary contributions (see "Voluntary Employee Contributions," *supra*).

the taxation of benefits for common-law employees. Among the principal differences in the taxation of the self-employed are the following:

1. The long-term capital gain treatment for lump-sum distributions is not available to the self-employed individual or to his beneficiary.[6]
2. The $5000 death benefit income tax exclusion is not available for beneficiaries.
3. The cost of pure insurance protection cannot be used as part of the cost basis.
4. Neither the estate tax exclusion under Code Section 2039(c) nor the gift tax advantage under Code Section 2517 is available.

Discontinuance of Contributions and Disposition of Plan Assets

One of the continuing problems which has never been fully explored is the disposition of assets when a plan terminates or an employer goes out of business either by reason of incorporation or because of his cessation of all business activity. There are few authoritative answers, but adherence to certain principles should give some measure of protection as well as administrative simplification.

Cessation of Business Activity. Because the Act prohibits distribution of contributions or benefits to an owner-employee prior to his attainment of age 59½, the choices for the handling of his interest upon the termination of business or plan are limited. However, these include:

1. Freezing the plan while maintaining the trust or custodial account, if any, and making distribution of assets in the time and manner required by the plan. This means keeping track of handling what may be small amounts with the resulting continuation of trustees' fees and other costs.

2. Converting plan values to nontransferable annuities which can be assigned to the participant with subsequent termination of the plan.

3. Converting values to the special series of U.S. government bonds.

4. Paying the values to the owner-employee subject to the tax on premature distributions. The IRS has ruled that the payment of the penalty tax is not an alternative to keeping the values within the plan, and has stated that the plan must contain a specific provision against early distribution. In spite of this, it is difficult to understand how an owner-employee could be hurt by committing a breach of plan and paying the penalty tax, other than through his inability to participate in another plan for the self-employed for five years.[7]

5. Transferring the assets to another qualified plan subject to all of the restrictions which are required with respect to owner-employees. Such a transfer may present some technical complications, but the key to a nontaxable transfer is avoidance of constructive receipt.

Incorporation of Business. Increasingly, professionals with self-employed plans are seeking incorporation under state professional corpora-

---

[6] A five-year averaging arrangement may be used for an owner-employee who has been in the plan for five years provided that he is age 59½, dies, or becomes disabled.

[7] At least one IRS district has attempted to prevent such an owner-employee from participating in a corporate plan following his incorporation.

tion laws. This activity poses questions which are beyond the scope of this chapter and to which the answers depend upon the particular facts. However, the alternatives outlined above give some guidance, with the added comment that if self-employed assets are transferred to a corporate plan, or if a self-employed plan is amended to a corporate plan, it is necessary to segregate the assets attributable to owner-employees within the new plan and to assure that the plan itself contains all of the provisions which will continue the transferred assets subject to the self-employed requirements.

CONTINUING SIGNIFICANCE OF PLANS FOR THE SELF-EMPLOYED

Since the advent of professional corporations, pension and profit-sharing opportunities available for the self-employed have received less attention. While such an attitude may be justified in the eyes of professionals who follow the route of incorporation, the fact remains that the choice to obtain qualified benefits under self-employed plans cannot be ignored, since in a number of instances these may be the only qualified benefits available. There are many situations in which the economic advantages to incorporation cannot justify a change from the partnership or proprietorship form of organization. Many professionals who feel that the retention of the traditional professional status associated with the proprietorship or partnership form of organization is more important than the advantages of incorporation. In some states the ability to incorporate is not extended to all of the professions, and, of course, professional incorporation is not available to the nonprofessional proprietor or partner who must still look to the Self-Employed Individual Retirement Act for his benefits.

In addition to the foregoing, it is important not to overlook the freedom from restrictions which exists in plans for the self-employed where there is no owner-employee participation. This situation can arise either where a plan provides that an owner-employee cannot participate, or in those many situations where the partnership interests are such that there is no partner owning more than 10 percent of the partnership interests. Here, the ability to establish a plan closely resembling a corporate plan without the necessity of attempting incorporation makes a plan for the self-employed decidedly worthwhile.

SELECTED REFERENCES

Goodman, Isidore. "HR-10 Tax Questions," speech delivered at a meeting of the Southern Maryland Dental Society at the University of Maryland, April 8, 1968. Published in Commerce Clearing House *Pension Plan Guide* and Prentice-Hall *Pension and Profit-Sharing.*

————. "The Mounting Volume of HR-10 Plans," speech delivered before the San Francisco Chapter of the Western Pension Conference, September 28, 1967. Published in Commerce Clearing House *Pension Plan Guide* and Prentice-Hall *Pension and Profit-Sharing.*

Questions and Answers on Retirement Plans for the Self-Employed. Publication No. 560. Washington, D.C.: Government Printing Office, October 1970.

Ray, George E. "Retirement Plans for the Self-Employed; The Treasury's New Promise to Professionals," *Notre Dame Lawyer,* Vol. 46, No. 3 (Spring 1971), p. 461.

Retirement Plans for Self-Employed Individuals. Publication No. 560. Washington, D.C.: Government Printing Office, October 1970.

Rustigan, Edward C. "Retirement Plans for the Self-Employed," *Taxes,* December 1968, p. 763.

37

Tax Deferred Annuities

By CHARLES C. HINCKLEY

TAX EXEMPT EMPLOYERS have no tax incentive for establishing qualified retirement plans. Historically, many of them have not had adequate funds to provide benefits to retired workers. As a result, Congress provided a special tax deferred pension vehicle for employees of certain nonprofit educational, charitable, and religious organizations.[1] In addition to the extraordinary income, estate and gift tax benefits afforded employees under this law, there is an unusual amount of latitude and informality allowed in selecting participants and establishing benefits under such plans.

Benefits Available

Contributions up to an amount labeled the "exclusion allowance" can be applied to the purchase of an annuity by an eligible employer. Ownership of this annuity can be given to an employee. Neither the amount of premium paid nor value of the annuity is reported as income. When payment is received under the annuity, the payment is reported as ordinary income, but this generally is after retirement when the employee will be in a lower tax bracket because of:

1. lower income;
2. the double exemption allowed taxpayers over 65 (four exemptions if both employee and his wife are over 65);
3. the increased deduction allowed for medical expenses after 65; and
4. the tax preferred nature of much retirement income (e.g., social security is not reportable).

Also available are a valuable estate tax exclusion, exemption of the first $5,000 of death payments from federal income taxes if paid to a named beneficiary, and an exemption from the gift tax.

Although these benefits are similar to the benefits available under tax qualified plans, generally there are no requirements of nondiscrimination

---

[1] Internal Revenue Code Section 403(b), tax shelter for employees of organizations described in IRC Section 501(c)(3).

or formal plans or trusts. It should be noted that tax deferred annuity benefits are available to employees receiving nonforfeitable interests in retirement contracts, and employees may own the policies and be entitled to all the rights of ownership. These benefits may be made available to an employee without additional expense to the employer if the employee is willing to have a portion of his future salary diverted to tax deferred annuity premiums.

ELIGIBLE EMPLOYERS

Internal Revenue Code Description

The Internal Revenue Code description of employers eligible to make this benefit available includes nonprofit corporations, community chests, funds and foundations organized and operated exclusively for religious, charitable, scientific, literacy, or educational purposes; for testing for the public safety; or for the prevention of cruelty to children or animals.

Three further requirements are contained in the Code: (a) No part of the organization's net earnings may inure to the benefit of any private shareholder or individual; (b) No substantial part of the group's activities may be for political purposes, carrying on propaganda or attempting to influence legislation; and (c) The organization must not aid the campaign of any candidate for public office.

In addition, the Code specifically includes public schools in its definition of employers qualified to purchase tax deferred annuities for its employees.

Regulations

Internal Revenue Regulations elaborate on the description of Section 501(c)(3) by defining "charitable" and giving examples of educational organizations. The term "charitable" is held to include relief of the poor and distressed, or of the underprivileged; advancement of religion; advancement of education and science; erection or maintenance of public buildings, monuments, or works; lessening the burdens of government; and promoting social welfare.

Educational organizations include primary and secondary schools; colleges; professional or trade schools; organizations whose activities consist of presenting public discussion groups, forums, panels, lectures or similar programs; correspondence schools; museums; zoos; planetariums; symphony orchestras; and other similar organizations.

IRC Regulations made it clear that people occupying elective or appointive offices for public schools are not employees performing services for educational institutions unless they are offices to which an individual is elected or appointed only if he has received training or is experienced in the field of education.

Determining Tax Exempt Status

Practically speaking, how does one ascertain whether an organization comes within these Code requirements? In many cases, little effort is required to uncover the information needed. Generally, the administrative officer of the organization will know whether the organization is a Section 501(c)(3) organization tax exempt under Section 501(a).

If the information is not available from the organization's treasurer, secretary, lawyer, or accountant, it can be obtained from either the District Director of Internal Revenue or the Commissioner of Internal Revenue. The information will be on file with the local District Director for organizations gaining tax exempt status after November 3, 1958. Information concerning organizations gaining tax exempt status before that date can be obtained from the Commissioner in Washington. In any case, a Letter of Determination, stating that the employer in question is an approved employer, can be obtained by the employer from the IRS.

Employees of Government Institutions Other than Public Schools

Some municipal, state, and federal organizations other than public schools seem to come within the definition of Section 501(c)(3), i.e., hospitals, museums, libraries, and zoos. Amendment of the Code to include public school teachers seems to have compounded the misunderstanding regarding employees of other government institutions coming within the description of Section 501(c)(3). Since the problem is that these organizations are not tax exempt under Section 501(c), the logical procedure is to seek exemption even though they are already tax exempt. This procedure was followed by some public schools prior to the Code amendment.

Revenue Rulings lay down the circumstances under which the IRS will and will not approve applications for exemption. If the organization is "an integral part of a state or municipal government, provisions of 501(c)(3) would not be applicable . . .," and an exemption under Section 501(a) will not be granted. If the organization is an autonomous unit, exemption will be granted even though funds are received from some government unit. Therefore, employees of a separately organized school, college, or hospital may be eligible to receive tax deferred annuities.

ELIGIBLE EMPLOYEES

It is important to understand that only individuals working as employees, as opposed to independent contractors, can receive tax deferred annuities. The Code, Regulations, Rulings, and Congressional committee reports shed no direct light on the question: Who is an employee for the purposes of tax deferred annuities?

This may not seem to present much of a problem. However, the question often arises in cases of doctors who are working for hospitals as radiologists, pathologists, and the like. Not only are their working conditions and methods of remuneration somewhat unlike what is found in a normal employer-employee relationship, but they sometimes are reluctant to admit to an employer-employee relationship for professional reasons. An employer-employee relationship suggests a degree of control by the employer which the medical profession is reluctant to tolerate for fear that such control may constitute an impediment between doctors and their patients.

The key to resolving this conflict is in determining whether a hospital can possess a sufficient degree of control over a doctor to make him an employee for federal tax purposes without offending the medical profession's canons of ethics. Selected judicial language and several private letter rulings indicate that a doctor can be an employee within the meaning of the Internal Revenue Code without offending professional standards.

Social security coverage as an employee will be helpful evidence. It would seem untenable for the IRS to treat an individual as an employee for social security purposes without recognizing the same status for purposes of tax deferred annuities.

CONTRACTS

Both guaranteed annuities and variable annuities qualify. Also, an endowment contract providing only incidental life insurance protection may be purchased to fund this tax benefit. Life insurance protection is considered incidental if the death benefit provided by the contract does not exceed 100 times the monthly life income. Use of contracts with incidental life insurance entails special income tax treatment which will be discussed later.

A relatively recent development is the investment annuity which allows the employee to direct the investment of the annual contributions that must be accumulated to provide his annuity. This is practical in cases of large deposits. As part of the investment, the employee may direct the purchase of a whole life policy, provided the test of "incidental" insurance is met.

Annuity and endowment contracts issued subsequent to December 31, 1962, must be nontransferable except to the issuing company. This is only a slight impediment to the flexibility of the plan.

The annuity need not be purchased initially by the contributing employer. It might have been purchased initially by a previous employer or the employee himself.

TAX DEFERMENT AND EXCLUSION ALLOWANCE FORMULA

Definition of Benefit

The primary tax benefit is a present exclusion from an employee's gross income of amounts contributed by a qualified employer for the purchase of an annuity contract in which the employee has a nonforfeitable interest. Reporting of the income is deferred until the employee receives payments under the contract. The amount which can be deferred is limited by an exclusion allowance established in the Code.

Exclusion Allowance Formula

Basically, the exclusion allowance is equal to 20 percent of reportable earnings from the qualified employer multiplied by the number of years of past service and reduced by the amount equal to previously contributed tax-free annuity premiums and other qualified plan contributions for this employee. For example:

```
Available to compensate employee........  $12,000
                                          ×   .20
                                          ───────
                                           $2,400
Service  ...............................  ×    4
                                          ───────
                                           $9,600
Less previous contributions .............  −   $0
                                          ───────
Exclusion allowance ....................   $9,600
```

Includable Compensation

The basic factor in the formula is labeled includable compensation. As a general rule this can be defined as taxable income from a qualified employer for the tax year. Notice, it is taxable income; therefore, it does not include tax deferred annuity contributions or contributions to a qualified plan made during the tax year or other period under consideration.

There are two exceptions to the general rule. First, although an annuity premium that exceeds the exclusion allowance is partially reportable as ordinary income currently, the reportable excess cannot be considered includable compensation. Second, by Code definition, includable compensation includes sick pay although sick pay may be excluded from income.

If a tax deferred annuity is being purchased under an arrangement for a salary reduction, includable compensation decreases by the amount of the annual contributions since income received in the form of contributions to a tax deferred annuity is not taxable income. An employee with no past service can divert one sixth of the total amount available from his pay to the tax deferred annuity. For example:

$$\frac{\$12.000}{6} = \$2,000$$

```
Available to compensate employee .......  $12,000
Less annuity ...........................  −2,000
                                          ───────
Includable compensation ...............   $10,000
                                          ×  .20
                                          ───────
                                           $2,000
Service  ...............................  ×    1
                                          ───────
                                           $2,000
Less previous contributions .............  −   $0
                                          ───────
Exclusion allowance ....................   $2,000
```

For a part-time employee, includable compensation is compensation earned over the most recent period of employment which is the equivalent of one year of full-time service. It is not the current annual salary rate multiplied by the number of calendar years that constitute the equivalent of one year of full-time service; rather, it is the collection of income over the period of time which is the equivalent of one year of full-time service. For example, if a teacher taught three hours for each of four semesters in a school where nine hours for two semesters was considered full time, and followed this six hours of teaching for two semesters, the income for the total six semesters would be added together to determine the includable compensation. This minimizes the effect of a higher salary rate during the latter portion of the period under consideration.

Years of Service

The 20 percent limitation would be unfair to employees who worked many years for these organizations before this advantage was available, and who could not realize any substantial benefit in the years remaining before retirement. Recognizing this, Congress added a years-of-service factor to the exclusion allowance formula. The amount equal to 20 percent of includable compensation is multiplied by the number of years of past service.

For a part-time employee, the years-of-service factor equals one until his part-time employment adds up to the equivalent of one full-time year. Thereafter, it is expressed in terms of its exact full-time equivalent. For example, an employee working 50 percent of what is considered normal full-time employment for 3 years is considered to have one and one-half years of service. The norm is what is considered full-time employment in the job under consideration, not what portion of the individual's productive time is devoted to the job.

Adjustments for Contributions to Tax-Free Retirement Plan in Previous Years

The Regulations create a substantial problem in determining the impact of the final factor in the exclusion allowance formula—the reduction for amounts previously contributed by the employer for annuity contracts and excludable from gross income. Whatever the total of such previous contributions may be, it must be subtracted from the amount previously arrived at by multiplying includable compensation by 20 percent and then by years of service in order to arrive at the exclusion allowance.

One might assume that Congress intended this reduction to include only prior contributions which would have been includable in gross income, but for Section 403(b). However, it appears that the IRS is attempting to construe this to include not only contributions to retirement plans under Section 403(b), but also to all qualified plans under Section 401–404 of the Code.

Aside from the legal question involved and the potential serious curtailment of benefits under Section 403(b), there is the practical problem of determining the value of benefits under plans that do not call for specific contributions or segregation of contributions into individual accounts. This is a particular problem in determining exclusion allowances for public school teachers, because retirement systems for public school teachers are fairly uniform in providing for benefits based on years of service and income with some form of unallocated funding that is not related to the individuals in the system.

The Regulations concerning unallocated funding (of qualified plans) furnish helpful guidelines for complying with the IRS interpretation of the law. The approach used in the Regulations is to develop an annual valuation for use in the exclusion allowance formula by applying actuarial factors to the benefits contemplated from the retirement system. Of course, this takes no cognizance of the fact that the taxpayer may never realize benefits in many cases. Also, in the majority of cases the final exclusion allowance probably will be generous enough to allow substantial contributions to a nonforfeitable tax deferred annuity plan if the employee has some past service.

Practical Considerations

In most cases, budgetary constraints will limit the amount employers will be able to afford for retirement plans. In cases where employees are making money available by cash salary reductions for the purchase of tax deferred annuity contracts, the employee generally will have a specific dollar amount in mind for retirement savings. In these situations, a determination of whether the amount available comes within an individual's exclusion allowance can be made by calculating the exclusion allowance based on the reduced salary available.

Caution should be exercised, however, because it is possible that a contribution may be within the exclusion allowance during a number of beginning years but be in excess later. For this reason, calculation of a hypothetical exclusion allowance for the years of retirement, similar to the calculation for the current year, will reveal whether all presently contemplated contributions will receive the tax shelter.

A commonly accepted formula for arriving at an acceptable level deposit to contemplated retirement is:

$$X = \frac{.2T}{(.2T) + P} = A$$

$X =$ maximum acceptable level annual premium
$T =$ total years of service at contemplated retirement date
$P =$ number of premiums until retirement
$A =$ total current salary (before reduction for annuity)

Example: An employee, age 45, with 4 years' service to date would like to divert the maximum amount to annuity from \$20,000 of current salary until age 65.

$$X = \frac{.2 \times 24}{(.2 \times 24) + 20} \times \$20,000 = \$3,871$$

Of course, most employees contemplate salary increases over the years. Such salary increases will increase the exclusion allowance and have a multiplier effect because the past service factor is applied to present includable compensation. Likewise, a decrease in salary may have a reverse effect on the current contribution, but there is no provision for reflecting a decrease to previously gained tax deferral.

ADDITIONAL INCOME, ESTATE, AND GIFT TAX BENEFITS

In addition to the income tax deferment benefit just discussed, the following federal tax advantages are available for retirement plans established by some Section 501(c)(3) organizations:

1. Exclusion from income of the first $5,000 of death benefit payable to a named beneficiary of the employee.
2. Exclusion from the employee's gross estate.
3. Exclusion from gift tax upon designating an irrevocable beneficiary.

These are the same tax benefits as under qualified corporate plans. An added benefit under corporate qualified plans is long-term capital gain treatment of lump-sum distributions. The only tax relief available for bunching caused by lump-sum distributions under a tax deferred annuity is relief under the income-averaging provisions of the Code.

There are three important exceptions to eligibility for the additional benefits labeled (1), (2), and (3) above. These exceptions are private foundations of a charitable, religious, or educational nature; correspondence schools; and, in the opinion of many, public schools. The technical reason for ineligibility is the Code requirement that in order to qualify for these additional benefits, taxpayers must be employees of organizations which not only are described in Section 501(c)(3) but also are exempt under Section 501(a), and come within the more limited description found in Section 170(b)(1)(A)(ii) or (vi) or be a religious organization. In the case of public school employees, it is theorized that the exclusion from these extra benefits results from not meeting the eligibility requirement of exemption under Section 501(a).[2]

Sections 170(b)(1)(A)(ii) and (vi) contain the following description: (1) A religious organization, or (2) an educational organization that normally maintains a regular faculty and curriculum and normally has a regularly enrolled body of students in attendance at the place where educational activities are regularly carried on, or (3) an organization normally receiving a substantial part of its support from the United States or any political subdivision thereof or from direct or indirect contributions from the public.

$5,000 Income Exclusion

The $5,000 income exclusion allows a widow (or other named beneficiary of death proceeds) to receive a death benefit of up to $5,000 income-tax free from a tax deferred annuity plan. Payment of up to $5,000, that would have been reportable as ordinary income if the annuitant had lived and taken the payments under the contract, are thus received income-tax free.[3]

---

[2] For a contrary opinion, see Charles C. Hinckley, "The Direct Impact of the Tax Reform Act of 1969," *C.L.U. Journal*, Vol. 34, No. 3 (July, 1970), p. 15. See also *Estate of Johnson*, 56 T.C. No. 74, Docket No. 6306–69 (8–9–71).

[3] I.R.C. Sec. 101(b)(2)(B)(iii).

Estate Tax Exclusion

The estate tax exclusion safeguards the estate from additional tax as a result of owning tax deferred annuities if they are payable to a beneficiary other than an annuitant's estate.[4]

Gift Tax Exclusion

The gift tax exclusion prevents attachment of a gift tax if the owner of a tax deferred annuity makes an irrevocable election benefiting a survivor annuitant. In the absence of this exclusion, such an election would result in a taxable gift.[5]

Tax Deferred Appreciation

Reserves held by insurance companies for tax deferred annuities receive a tax advantage under Code sections treating the income taxation of insurance companies. Typically this advantage is reflected in dividends apportioned to these contracts in a mutual company.[6]

Where a participating company issues the tax deferred annuity and dividends will be paid, the employee should choose his dividend option with care. If he receives his dividend in cash, an amount equal to that dividend should be included in his taxable income. If he elects to have the dividends accumulate at interest, the interest will be taxable to him in the year it is credited to his account and the accumulation also might be considered taxable income in the year of the increase in accumulations. His most prudent approach is to elect a dividend option of paid-up additions.

THE PROBLEMS OF FUNDING; SALARY REDUCTIONS

The problem of financing the purchase must be considered. Although the employee is given a nonforfeitable right to the annuity contract, it must be purchased by the employer. This purchase must be made with funds to which the employee has no claim, actual or constructive, before premium payment.

There does not seem to be any problem involved in a situation in which the employer is furnishing the retirement plan in addition to current salary, or where the original employment agreement provides for the payment of a certain amount of cash supplemented with payments to a tax-deferred annuity plan. The problem arises in situations in which the employer is not in a position to provide the premium contributions and they are made available by the employee agreeing to a reduction in cash salary for future services.

Adherence to general principles of law pertaining to constructive receipt will avoid potential problems. The annuity contract should be pur-

---

[4] I.R.C. Sec. 2039(c)(3).
[5] I.R.C. Sec. 2517(a)(3).
[6] I.R.C. Sec. 805(d).

chased with funds the employee cannot claim as cash. A salary reduction transaction should consist of an agreement to accept reduced cash for future services supplemented by premiums for an annuity contract owned by the employee. This should include a relinquishment of any right to receive this compensation except in the form of additional value in the annuity contract.

The IRS has established the requirement that the employee must not be permitted to make more than one agreement during any taxable year. However, this does not negate the possibility of terminating the entire agreement with respect to amounts not yet earned. The essential points are that the agreement be made before the services are performed and that the employee relinquish his right to the amount of the premium except in the form agreed upon.

INCOME TAXATION UPON RECEIPT UNDER A TAX DEFERRED ANNUITY

Annuity without Incidental Life Insurance

When proceeds are received from a tax deferred annuity, the employee (or other recipient) must report the payments as ordinary income unless there were contributions to the contract in excess of his exclusion allowance. Contributions in excess of the exclusion allowance and other contributions which were not excluded from income in previous years (e.g., employee contributions in a contributory plan) are considered a return of investment in the contract and received income tax free. Also, named beneficiaries of death proceeds are allowed to receive up to $5,000 income tax free.

The treatment of policy loans is provided for in Revenue Ruling 67–258.[7] In it the IRS states that any receipt under the contract, even in the form of a loan, is a taxable event.

Annuity with Incidental Life Insurance

In addition to receipt of retirement benefits, several other potential taxable events are present when using a contract with incidental life insurance.

Life insurance protection must be valued and the value reported as ordinary income during the years prior to the time the cash value exceeds the initial face amount of the contract. The value is determined by applying one-year term values to the difference between the contract cash value and the face amount. This element is present until the contract cash values exceed the initial face amount. These values are the same as those used in conjunction with qualified pension and profit sharing plans and also applicable to split dollar transactions (the so-called "P.S.-58 cost"). When the policy matures the amount reported as cost of insurance is recovered as "basis," i.e., tax free.

Death proceeds in excess of contract cash values are free of federal income tax. Amounts equal to the cash value are reportable as ordinary

---

[7] C.B. 1967–2, 68.

income as received, except for the $5,000 that passes to named beneficiaries income-tax free and an amount equal to the accumulated cost of insurance which also is recovered tax free.

TERMINAL RETIREMENT FUNDING

Frequently, organizations of the nature qualified to provide retirement plans under Section 403(b) find themselves in the position of *ex post facto* retirement planning. Therefore, it should be kept in mind that these retirement plans can be provided in addition to salary—and in substantial amounts if an employee has long years of service. This should not be forgotten in the enthusiasm about salary reduction possibilities. Also, it is entirely possible to provide an annuity for an employee who is retired. The basis for his exclusion allowance formula is his includable compensation for the last year of work.

TERMINATION OF EMPLOYMENT

A frequent question concerns what happens if an employee wishes to quit, change employers, or terminate participation in the retirement plan. The answer is very simple. First, the premiums can be continued with after-tax dollars. Second, the new employer can continue the premium payments. Third, the employee can elect a paid-up contract. Fourth, the employee can surrender the contract for any cash value, with the attendant reporting of income.

Tax deferred annuities offer a great deal more flexibility than qualified plans. There is a certain degree of portability in that the employee may take his annuity from one qualified employer to another without any loss of rights or values. Although the new employer can continue to pay the premiums for the tax-deferred annuity, a new exclusion allowance must be calculated. This new exclusion allowance will have to be based on the years of service with the new employer only. This can have the effect of greatly reducing the exclusion allowance from that which was available under the old employer. As was pointed out above, if the employee terminates his employment with a qualified employer and begins to work with a nonqualified employer, he may continue to pay the annuity premiums with after-tax dollars. Additionally, many companies offer a "stop and go" provision which permits the employee temporarily to withdraw from the tax deferred annuity plan while on a sabbatical or for other reasons.

CONCLUSION

The basic principles of tax-deferred annuities can be reiterated in a few brief statements. Tax deferred annuities are designed to furnish employees of certain educational, charitable and religious organizations with a tax preferred pension vehicle without the formalities of a qualified pension plan. The primary benefit is a tax deferment, and the medium to be used is an annuity. An employer can make this benefit available to all employees or selected employees. If the employer is not in a position to make this benefit available in addition to present salary, the employee may request a diversion of a portion of his unearned future salary to the purchase of tax-deferred annuities. The amount that is eligible for the tax benefit is limited by the exclusion allowance formula.

SELECTED REFERENCES

Hinckley, Charles C., and Rotgin, Philip N. "Annuities for Employees of Section 501(c)(3) Organizations and Public Schools," *Tax Ideas—Transaction Tax Guide*. Englewood Cliffs, N.J.: Prentice-Hall, Inc., 1967. Updated periodically.

Tarver, Norman H. *The Sales Manual on Tax Sheltered Annuities*. Rev. ed. Indianapolis, Ind.: Research and Review Service of America, Inc., 1967.

38

Funding Instruments—
Individual Policy and
Combination Plans

By VERNE J. ARENDS

A PENSION PLAN, the major fringe benefit of most working Americans, can be funded in at least a dozen different ways. All funding media have a basic aim: to accrue the necessary money to enable payment of the benefits promised by the plan. The individual policy is particularly suited for small groups of about 50 or fewer initial participants. If the number is nine or less, there usually is no other suitable funding medium. Use of individual policies enables an employer to insure its pension plan in whole or in part, with or without equity investment exposure, and with the help and advice of life insurance companies through their many thousands of knowledgeable field and home office personnel.

An advantage of individual policy pension plans is their simplicity of operation. Furthermore, individual policy plans may be particularly compatible with personal insurance of the employee and business insurance of the employer. They also provide, along with basic retirement benefits, additional benefits in event of disability, death, termination of employment, and plan termination.

INDIVIDUAL POLICIES

Changes since the 1940s in certain group media and the creation and improvement of new types of insured group coverage for pension purposes, such as group permanent and deposit administration plans, have moved the individual policy plan into a relatively smaller area of acceptability. Nevertheless, the overall growth of individual policy pension plans has been great. At the end of 1940 there were 440 plans in being in this country. By the end of 1948 the number had increased to 16,440. By 1970 the total exceeded 170,000. In the future, individual policy plans will be of continuing importance. Most of the approximately 30 million workers not yet covered by private pension plans are employed by employers with a relatively small number of employees.

Most large and medium-sized corporations already have adopted and are funding pension plans (or deferred profit sharing plans providing pension benefits) through the use of group media such as deposit administration, group annuity, group permanent or self-administered arrangements. There are, however, multi-thousands of small corporations, incorporated professional practices, partnerships, and proprietorships for which the individual policy plan is ideally suited. These smaller businesses offer opportunities for beneficial financial planning through the medium of qualified plans, including the estate and income tax advantages accruing to the owner-operators, their employees, and their families.

Nature of Individual Policies

Individual endowment, annuity, and whole life policies used to fund pension plans usually are the same kinds of policies that an individual purchases for himself. Thus, virtually all of the policy rights and privileges available to an individual purchaser are contained in pension plan policies and are available for use by the policyowner for the benefit of plan participants and their beneficiaries.

Premiums are based on assumptions made with respect to mortality of the insured persons, interest to be earned on invested policy reserves, and the cost of selling and administering the policy contract. Part of the premium paid for participating policies typically is returned to the premium payer as a dividend, when experience shows a cost less than that conservatively assumed for participating insurance. Depending on the type of plan, dividends are used to reduce the current cost of the plan to the employer or to increase benefits to the plan participants.

Individual policies have cash surrender and loan values. Subject to plan provisions and Treasury Department regulations, the values may be used to pay the premium for policies owned by the plan if an employer encounters temporary financial difficulties. Otherwise, such difficulties may prevent the employer from making a required annual contribution to the trust. Under such conditions, the premium may be borrowed on a pro rata basis for that year and subsequently paid back when the required contributions are resumed and additional contributions can be made by the employer. Policy loan provisions also enable the trust to take advantage of temporary investment opportunities offering more favorable yields without replacement of the policy as a permanent funding instrument.

If an employer finds it necessary to terminate a pension plan, the individual policies can be readily transferred to the respective employees. The employees then may maintain them on a premium-paying basis for their personal benefit. Or, they may change the type of coverage to a lower cost plan, subject to the rules of the insurer. Also, if an employee wishes, he may take paid-up insurance or surrender his policy to the insurance company for its cash value to be paid in one sum or under one of the settlement options described in the policy.

Individual policies in a pension plan require service similar to those owned by individuals. Deaths, retirements, salary changes, employment terminations, changes in dependency situations, and other developments call for professional counsel. The trustee or employer generally looks to the insurance agent for help and guidance. To keep service work at a minimum and to permit prompt and efficient handling, maintenance by all concerned of clear and complete records from the start is imperative.

Types of Policies

Contracts *containing a protection element* run the gamut from pure term policies having no cash value through the whole life policy that contains a blend of term insurance and cash values, to the retirement income and retirement endowment policies that emphasize cash values. Each of the following examples assumes that the face amount payable in event of death before retirement is $10,000.

Term. The term policy is pure insurance and contains no cash value. The total $10,000 is payable at death whether it occurs one day after issue or a day before retirement. It is used mostly in profit sharing plans and in money purchase pension plans when the respective participants have the right under the trust or plan to direct the earmarked investment of funds credited to their accounts.

Retirement Income/Endowment. Premium rates for the retirement income/endowment policy are deliberately constructed to produce large cash values during the early years of the contract. That process results in a cash value equal to the face of the policy ($10,000) by the time the participant gets within five to seven years of his retirement age. Therefore, the amount at risk, or pure protection element, reduces sharply through the life of the contract. If the insured dies just after the policy is issued, virtually all of the $10,000 payable would arise from the protection element except for an amount approximately equal to the initial premium paid. However, if death occurs the day before he retires, not only would there be no pure protection element in the benefit payment but the cash value comprising the benefit payable would approximate $16,000 instead of the face amount of $10,000. This policy is used in fully insured plans and is purchased on the basis of a $1,000 face amount policy for each $10 of promised monthly pension.

Whole Life. Whenever death occurs, the $10,000 payable in the example will have pure protection and cash value as components to make up the total. However, unlike the retirement income policy, the whole life policy will never pay more than its face even if death occurs at age 64. At that point there would still be a blend of both pure protection, or amount at risk, and cash value in the proceeds. Accordingly, the annual premium for a whole life policy of $10,000 will be substantially less than that for a retirement income policy of like face amount.

Whole life policies issued in connection with pension and profit sharing plans contain a provision usually not found in whole life policies sold to individuals. In order to carry out the purpose of the combination plan, the cost of changing the whole life policy to an annuity policy at a later date is guaranteed in the policy when issued. It is possible, therefore, to make reasonable assumptions about the amount of money to be accumulated for the subsequent change of policy.

Individual policies *without a life insurance protection element* used in employee benefit plans include level premium retirement annuity contracts, flexible premium retirement annuity contracts, and variable annuity contracts. Although these contracts do not contain a life insurance element, they do provide a death benefit. The retirement annuity policies usually provide a return of premiums paid or the guaranteed cash value, whichever is greater. The variable annuity provides an amount determined by the value of the accumulation units at the time of death, and generally this death benefit will be no less than the total of the premiums paid in. Under a variable annuity contract the available cash value at any time depends upon the investment experience of a separate equity account into which premiums or contributions for that contract have been invested.

When a level premium retirement annuity contract is used, additional policies are purchased each time application of the pension formula to the increased salary of a participant calls for another $10 of pension. Under the flexible premium retirement annuity contract, after the initial policy is purchased, no additional policies need thereafter be obtained. When the promised pension is increased under the formula because of a compensation change, the owner of the contract thereafter merely pays a larger premium on the initial contract instead of buying another new policy.

The individual policies just described may be used as the sole funding product for pension and profit sharing plans—and they often are used as such in small cases. However, they also may be used effectively as a part of the package in partially insured plans. It is popular today to handle the pension fund on a balanced investment basis, some of the contribution being placed in guaranteed or fixed dollars and part in equity or variable dollars. Flexibility of individual policies and the funding instruments designed for their use enables employers to satisfy their wishes in this respect whether the balance desired is 25 percent fixed and 75 percent equity, vice versa, or any combination in between.

COMBINATION PLANS

When individual policies and a related investment facility are used in tandem, the obvious result is a combination plan. In most cases a combination of fixed dollars in the form of the individual policy and equity dollars in the form of an auxiliary or policy change fund is involved. Money in the "side fund" portion of the tandem arrangement is most often used at retirement to change an individual life policy to a retirement annuity policy for pension payments.

The auxiliary or policy change fund is handled in one of three basic ways. Under a deposit agreement with the insurer, it is invested with its general portfolio. The general investment portfolio of most large insurers is conservatively invested with 90 to 95 percent of it in guaranteed or fixed dollar investments such as bonds and mortgages. State insurance laws limit the extent to which insurers may invest their general portfolio in equity or high risk ventures.

A recent development is the creation by life insurance companies of separate equity accounts. Side fund money in a combination plan may be paid into such an account. When cash is needed to change individual life policies to annuity contracts at retirement, portions of the respective account values are redeemed at the then market price and used for that purpose. As a third possibility, if the side fund is large enough, the trustee may either use its own judgment or, in conjunction with the employer, invest the money directly in stocks, bonds, real estate, and the like.

IMPORTANT CONSIDERATIONS

Trust Agreement

A standard legal document when individual policies are used in pension funding is the trust agreement. After an employer has made final decisions on the specifications involved in a plan—eligibility rules, type and amount of benefits, normal retirement age, and funding method—he arranges with his attorney to draft them into proper legal form. Validity of the arrangement for tax and other legal purposes is governed by state as well as federal law.

Preparation of a trust agreement requires legal ability, knowledge of all applicable federal and state laws, and an understanding of the relationship of legal aspects to the details of life insurance. The employer's attorney frequently will seek counsel and advice about the life insurance aspect of the arrangement from insurance company representatives. Home offices of insurance companies generally are willing and eager to review presumably final drafts of such documents and to offer suggestions. Many attorneys have found such reviews beneficial and helpful. Most insurance companies offer sample plan and trust agreements for guidance.

If an individually tailored trust is to be used, the parties must finalize the document, select the trustee, and execute the agreement. The completed agreement usually is submitted to the Internal Revenue Service for review and approval soon after the plan is installed. Detailed instruments for such submissions are available from district offices of the IRS throughout the 50 states.

A recent development has minimized some of the technical requirements regarding creation and approval of qualified plans. Under Treasury Department rules and regulations it now is possible for a certain class of sponsors to create so-called master or prototype trusts and to have them approved in advance at the Washington, D.C., office of the IRS. A similar procedure is applicable to plans for corporate employers, for businesses operated as partnerships, or for sole proprietorships. Both corporations and the self-employed have available a wide choice of approved master and prototype pension and profit sharing trusts sponsored and operated by insurance companies, banks, mutual funds, and trade associations. Prototype trusts are, in fact, IRS approved specimen trusts which, if used by an employer without change, will make it easier to obtain IRS approval of the specific arrangement.

An employer becomes a party to a master trust by signing a joinder or adoption agreement wherein he makes appropriate selections from available choices relating to eligibility rules, retirement age, amount of benefits, and so forth. Under a master trust, the sponsor has selected the trustee and the employer accepts that selection when he joins the master .plan. Under a prototype trust each employer selects and appoints his own trustee.

Some insurance companies, in an attempt to make it easier for the small employer to install and administer a pension plan or a profit sharing plan providing pension benefits, have used the IRS master plan approval system to create master pension plans which do not use a trust agreement or a trustee. The insurer is the creator, sponsor, and administrator of the plan. All contributions to the plan are applied as premiums or payments on one or more types of individual policies previously mentioned. The employer is not required to make day-by-day investment decisions. If he wants all contributions invested in equities, he joins a master plan which uses variable annuity contracts exclusively. If he wants all contributions to the plan put into fixed or guaranteed dollars, he joins a master plan which uses only retirement annuity and retirement income policies. For those who want a mix of fixed and variable dollars, master plans using life policies and variable annuity policies or a separate account in tandem are available. Many variations can be found on the employee benefit plan merchandising shelves of most insurance companies.

This relatively new master plan funding instrument has given new life to the individual policy as a tool in the pension field. It is an extremely effective answer to the needs of the small employer and serves well the self-employed with one or two common-law employees who want a qualified plan on an insured basis.

Effect of Investment Experience

The effect of investment gains or losses on pension plan benefits depends upon the pension design. For example, an employer may say he wants part of the contribution to the plan invested in equities to counter the anticipated inflationary trend. He expects gains from wisely made equity investments to enlarge pension payments to employees and thus, to some degree, take care of the rise in the cost of living. If that is his goal he should be advised to select a money purchase plan. A fixed benefit plan will not serve his purpose (although in such a plan the benefits can rise with salary increases and thus reflect the forces of inflation).

A money purchase plan ultimately produces a pension in an amount which can be purchased by a predetermined annual contribution. For example, an employer may agree to put into a pension plan each year an amount equal to 6 percent of each employee's compensation. Those contributions, plus any investment gain and less any investment loss, will be used at retirement to buy a pension for the participant.

On the other hand, under a fixed benefit or predetermined pension formula, the pension goal is first determined. That goal then governs the required employer contribution. For example, assume the pension goal is an amount of monthly income at retirement equal to 25 percent of the employee's compensation. Employer contributions are made pursuant to the assumptions used relative to mortality, investment experience, and the cost of handling the plan. Under this arrangement, investment gains or losses affect the amount of the employer's annual contribution. If investment gains exceed the assumption, the required contribution is reduced by such gain in the year they occur. If losses result in any year, the normal required contribution of the employer will be increased to the extent that the assumed earnings goal was not attained.

Under profit sharing plans the accounts of all plan participants will be adjusted to reflect investment experience, be it good, bad, or average. Thus, in all cases, the benefit for employees will be directly affected by the investment experience of the plan portfolio.

Effect of Employee Turnover

A relatively important item in the long-term cost of money purchase and fixed benefit pension plans is forfeitures, that is, the accumulated values held for participants who sever employment with only a partial vested interest in those values. The nonvested portion of such values usually will be applied to reduce the employer's required contribution to the plan. In profit sharing trusts, such forfeitures may inure to the benefit of continuing trust participants.

Employer's Options and Actions

A trust agreement incorporating pension plan terms drafted on a case-by-case basis is a useful and effective instrument when individual annuity and insurance policies are to be used as the investment medium in whole or in part. However, many small corporations, partnerships, and sole proprietors are turning to the use of IRS approved master and prototype trusts and plans established by insurance companies, banks, and trade associations. Such trusts and plans make it relatively easy to provide employee benefits. Because of the work already done by the sponsor of the trust or plan, the employer's legal fees generally are substantially less than for a tailor-made trust that the attorney must prepare "from scratch."

Least complicated of all seems to be the master pension plan without a trust or trustee. The use of individual conventional or variable annuity policies keeps the employer free of continuing investment decisions and reduces his administrative costs and duties. This arrangement might prove to be the best accepted instrument for pension plans in the 70s, particularly by the small businessman.

If an employer, after consideration of his specific needs and a review of the various funding media, decides that a pension trust using individual policies in whole or in part is the best solution to his problem, certain steps should be followed in setting up the plan. First, the employer should request his attorney to prepare a plan and trust agreement which, in legal language, expresses the employer's intentions. The agreement will include eligibility requirements for participation, age of retirement, amount of retirement benefits, vesting on employment termination, death benefits, and source of funds. An approved prototype trust or other specimen trust agreement may be used by the attorney as a guide. In the event a master trust or plan is to be used, the attorney should review it for suitability.

Then the employer, if a corporation, by proper action would adopt the plan and authorize the proper officers of the corporation to sign the trust agreement with the trustee or the joinder agreement. By similar action it would authorize payment of the initial contribution necessary to establish the plan. The trust or employer, acting in accordance with the terms of the trust agreement or plan, will apply to an insurance company for required policies on the life of each eligible participant.

Thereafter the trustee or employer will hold and administer the policies and the applicable funds in accordance with the terms of the trust agreement or plan. When an employee reaches normal retirement age, the party in control will direct the insurance company to pay the pension to the employee. If an employee dies before attainment of normal retirement age, the insurance company will be directed to pay the death benefits to the beneficiaries of the employee. Should an employee terminate employment before death or retirement occurs, proper distribution will be made of any vested interest the employee might have in the policy and funds being held for his benefit.

INDIVIDUAL POLICIES FOR NONQUALIFIED PLANS

All preceding material relates to IRS qualified funding instruments using individual policies as the sole or main ingredient. This chapter should not end without recognizing the versatility of the individual policy used in a simplified manner to fund pensions for employees on a selective basis without IRS plan approval. Under this arrangement, employer contributions are deductible as made, a major reason for the creation of many qualified plans. However, those contributions will be reportable for income tax purposes by the employee when made.

How does one overcome this obstacle in order to use an informal, nonqualified plan for selected employees? Actually, it is quite simple. Assume the employer cannot afford a pension plan for the group if eligibility rules required to qualify a plan were applied. He does have a retention concern with respect to one key person. If he directly raised that employee's salary $1,000 per year, the amount would be deductible by the employer but would be reportable by the employee. The employer determines that the tax impact on the latter would be $300. So a retirement annuity policy is applied for, with the employee as owner, requiring an annual premium of $700. As a result, the employer gives the employee a direct salary increase of $300 and deducts $1,000 as a business expense. The employee reports $1,000 of additional income and has the $300 in hand with which to pay the tax. He owns a pension policy costing $700 per year with no reduction in his take-home pay.

To insure that the annuity purchased under this arrangement is not dissipated before retirement, the employer could provide for a restrictive endorsement on the policy. Such an endorsement can require the consent of the employer before the employee may surrender or assign the policy or, at retirement, take settlement on any basis other than as a life annuity. An endorsement in those terms should not jeopardize the employer's deduction because it gives him no rights in the policy. He merely places a restraining hand on the exercise of rights given to the employee-owner by the terms of the contract. The restrictive endorsement on an individual policy is a useful device where nonqualified plans are concerned. It, too, should be considered as a possible arrangement in the unusual case.

SELECTED REFERENCES

Commerce Clearing House, Inc. *Pension Plan Guide*. Multivolume loose-leaf service. Chicago, n.d.

Employee Benefit Plan Review. Monthly magazine published by Charles D. Spencer and Associates, Chicago.

McGill, Dan M. *Fundamentals of Private Pensions*. 2d ed. Pension Research Council, Wharton School of Finance and Commerce, University of Pennsylvania. Homewood, Ill.: Richard D. Irwin, Inc., 1964.

Prentice-Hall, Inc. *Pension and Profit Sharing Service*. Multivolume loose-leaf service. New York, n.d.

39

Funding Instruments— Group Permanent and Group Deferred Annuity Contracts

By G. DAVID HURD

GROUP PERMANENT and group deferred annuity contracts are issued by an insurance company to an employer, or a retirement plan trustee, to furnish benefits for employees under retirement programs. These two funding instruments are based on "allocated" concepts. In "allocated" funding, money placed in the retirement plan is credited immediately to the account of a particular person covered by that plan. In unallocated funding, money placed in the retirement plan is deposited to an unallocated fund and no allocation of funds to a particular person occurs until some later point in time, such as when an annuity is purchased upon an employee's retirement. Although group permanent and group deferred annuity contracts are based on the allocated concept, the usage of unallocated funds as companions thereto is relatively common.

Compared to unallocated forms, allocated funding instruments are characterized by (1) a higher order of risk taking by the insurer, (2) stronger guarantees to the customer, and (3) greater security of benefits to covered employees. On the other hand, unallocated funding instruments generally feature a higher order of flexibility for (1) meeting plan costs, (2) investment of plan assets, and (3) design of benefit structure and features of the plan. The use of pure allocated instruments has not kept pace with unallocated and combination concepts during the last two decades. This trend, shown in Table 39-1, is a reflection of (1) employer efforts to spread plan costs over longer periods, thereby reducing annual outlay, (2) desire for investment of part of plan assets in common stock, and (3) benefit designs not compatible with allocated concepts.

TABLE 39–1.   Number of Insured Plans and Persons Covered under Certain Allocated and Unallocated Funding Instruments

Year	*Plans*			*Covered Persons*		
	Group Permanent	*Deferred Annuity*	*Unallocated Funding**	*Group Permanent*	*Deferred Annuity*	*Unallocated Funding**
1950	380	2,460	160	85,000	1,950,000	275,000
1970	6,360	10,280	15,020	285,000	1,955,000	6,525,000

* Deposit administration group annuity including immediate participation guarantee.
Source: Institute of Life Insurance, *1970 Life Insurance Fact Book*, p. 38; *1971 Life Insurance Fact Book*, p. 38.

GROUP PERMANENT CONTRACTS

Group permanent insurance tends to serve retirement plans that otherwise might be funded through individual policies (typically covering salaried workers), but are of sufficient size to benefit from the economies inherent in group products. The average individual policy plan in 1970 covered about 12 people,[1] and Table 39–1 indicates that the average group permanent plan covered about 45 people.[2]

Original Plans

Group permanent was introduced as the United States entered World War II. It was and is a relatively small part of the pension market (see Table 39–1).

In its early days, group permanent was utilized primarily in the form of a fully allocated product. In later years, the fully allocated version has been joined by another which makes strong use of both the allocated and unallocated concepts.

Group Permanent Retirement Income Contract

The group permanent retirement income contract, also known as "income endowment," "income to insured," and "fully insured," is a fully allocated product.

Basic Structure.   The coverage provides life insurance protection for an employee from his date of entry into the plan continuously to his retirement. The life insurance ceases at retirement and the pension begins. Typically, the coverage is built on a unit of 1,000/10—that is, $1,000 of life insurance and $10 of monthly pension. An employee upon entry into the retirement plan is furnished initial coverage according to the retirement plan's benefit formula. A benefit formula might be 30 percent of

---

[1] Institute of Life Insurance, *1971 Life Insurance Fact Book* (New York, 1971), p. 38.
[2] Straight arithmetic averages ignore size range, and the typical group permanent plan in effect in 1970 probably covered fewer than 45 persons.

average pay over the five years ending at age 60 with an age 65 normal retirement age. With an entry pay rate of $500 per month, the employee's initial pension expectancy is $150 of monthly pension. The 1,000/10 unit would call for $15,000 of insurance coupled to the $150 monthly pension expectancy. As the years roll along and the employee's pay changes, his coverage likewise adjusts by 30 percent of the pay change with a separate piece of coverage resulting from each pay increase—and each based on the 1,000/10 relationship. At age 60 the pay average would become finalized, and no further changes in coverage would occur in the remaining years to age 65.

The retirement plan provisions may be contained in the group permanent contract or may be in a separate plan document. A wide range of provisions is used to specify when an employee enters the plan, the benefit formula, the pay-averaging period, the normal retirement age, and so forth.

No-Evidence Limits. Because premium rates for life insurance are constructed on the expectation that certain average mortality results will be achieved, the insurer has a natural interest in the probable mortality of the individuals to be covered. If substantially greater deaths than expected should occur because of poor underwriting, financial loss and future noncompetitive pricing of products could be the result. In group permanent insurance, as in the more widespread group term insurance, the handling of this question differs from the techniques used in underwriting individual life insurance.

Group permanent contracts require the employee to be actively at work to gain coverage. All such persons are covered automatically for life insurance without any evidence whatsoever as to their state of health, habits, hobbies, and so forth, up to a certain "no-evidence" dollar limit.[3]

The no-evidence limit for a particular contract tends to rise as the number of employees covered and total volume of insurance increase. Whether the amounts of insurance are relatively uniform across the group of employees, or tend to be "piled up" on a few individuals, also is of interest. Other factors such as an inherent accident hazard (for example, test pilots) may be included in the determination of a no-evidence limit. No-evidence limits were quite conservative in the very early days of group permanent, but with good experience over many years, it is not uncommon today to see no-evidence limits of $30,000 on quite small plans, with substantially higher limits on larger plans. Employees eligible for coverage in excess of the no-evidence limits are required to submit evidence of insurability satisfactory to the insurer for that excess coverage. Whether or not they qualify has no bearing on their coverage up to the no-evidence limit.

The employers with experience-rated plans (see discussion below on experience rating) have a financial interest in the level of the no-evidence limit. Deaths for coverage below the no-evidence limit tend rather di-

---

[3] This limit is sometimes loosely referred to as a "nonmedical" limit; however, the latter implies the absence of a medical examination with the possibility of other requirements, whereas the former actually is a "no-evidence" limit.

rectly to decrease employer dividends, whereas deaths as to coverage above the no-evidence limit tend to be pooled across the entire block of group permanent business of the insurer.

Premiums and Guarantees. Each increment of coverage—the initial coverage and each segment of coverage resulting from pay changes—is paid for by guaranteed level annual premiums payable from the effective date of the increment of coverage until the normal retirement age. The level premium rate for a 1,000/10 unit pays for the $1,000 of insurance protection and builds guaranteed cash values which will be adequate at normal retirement age to furnish the $10 monthly pension expectancy. The total guarantee from the insurer to the customer is quite extensive; not only is there a ceiling cost guarantee on the package of future interest, mortality and expense levels as to monies already placed under the contract, but the same guarantee extends to all future premiums to be paid under the contract for the increments of coverage in existence on any date. Any change in rates is applicable only to increments of coverage which come into being subsequent to the rate change.

Premium rates are relatively low for coverage effective at young ages when there is a long period of time until retirement age to build the amount needed to furnish the pension, and are relatively high at older ages because the funding period is short. A separate premium rate is used (1) for every age at which coverage is effective, (2) for males and females because of important differences in life expectancy, and (3) for differing normal retirement ages.

The premiums may be wholly paid by the employer, or by the employer and the employees jointly, depending upon plan design. The premium for an individual ceases at the earliest of termination of employment, death, or normal retirement age.

Benefits before Retirement. Figure 39–1 is illustrative of group permanent retirement income coverage issued at age 30 with normal retirement at age 65. The $1,550 guaranteed value at age 65 is a typical value for the most common form of pension furnished—$10 monthly pension payable for life or 10 years, whichever is longer. Note that in the years

FIGURE 39–1. Illustration of Group Permanent Retirement Income Coverage Issued at Age 30 with Normal Retirement at Age 65

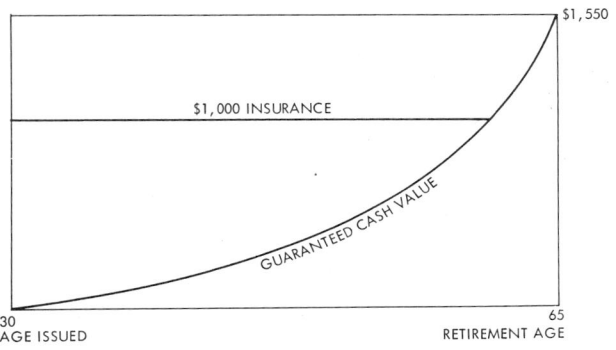

just before retirement, the guaranteed cash value exceeds the $1,000 basic death benefit. In this period the death benefit is the guaranteed cash value. If the employee leaves the plan prior to normal retirement age, the then existing guaranteed cash value is used according to plan provisions, in whole or in part, (1) to provide paid-up coverage providing death benefit before retirement and pension thereafter (in an amount smaller than if premiums had continued), or (2) to provide an immediate cash benefit, or (3) to reduce the employer's cost by paying part of the next premium due.

In cases of disability, the cash value may be used to provide an immediate income to the disabled employee; or sometimes the group policy contains a provision calling for continuation of full coverage with waiver of any further premiums if the employee is totally and permanently disabled. Occasionally the policy essentially treats total and permanent disability as a death with payment of the face amount of insurance to the disabled employee over a period of time.

Dividends.   The sum of guaranteed premiums for all increments of coverage for covered employees is the plan's gross cost to the employer (less any part paid by the employees). The gross cost is reduced by dividends, and any "nonvested values" (guaranteed cash values released upon a covered employee's termination of employment that are not used for his benefit). Dividends and nonvested values are used to pay part of the next gross premium due. Gross premiums are based on premium rates deliberately intended to be more than adequate under normal conditions—thus constructed from conservative assumptions as to future investment earnings, mortality experience, and expenses. To the degree that actual experience is better than that assumed in constructing premium rates, dividends result. Therefore, dividends are a return of gross premium not needed to provide insurance protection, build guaranteed cash values, pay expenses, and make pension payments.

Larger plans are experience rated in determining the dividend; smaller plans are pooled. Some insurance companies use the investment year basis for investment income in the experience rating process. Some group permanent coverage is written on a nonparticipating basis where premiums are set at levels that do not anticipate dividends or premium adjustments.

The experience rating process on larger plans follows a simple concept. Performed annually, the dividend is calculated as the excess of an experience fund for the group contract over the liabilities for that contract. The experience fund is computed recognizing all events from the inception of the plan to the date of calculation. The experience fund is the sum of (1) premiums received, and (2) actual investment income earned by the insurer on those premiums, less the sum of (3) expenses incurred by the insurer on that plan, and (4) all cash benefit payments made under the terms of the plan (retirement, death, termination of employment, and the like). The experience fund so computed may be increased or decreased by a mortality adjustment which has the temporary effect of partially replacing deviations in the actual mortality results from mortality results expected according to standard tables. The liabilities which are offset against the experience fund are the insurer's estimate of the amounts needed to make good on the long-term guarantees and benefits promised by the contract.

Figure 39–2 illustrates how dividends reduce gross premium outlay for one increment of coverage. Dividends generated by reserves during the retirement period would operate to reduce cost further.

FIGURE 39–2. Illustration of How Dividends Reduce Premiums on Group Permanent Retirement Income Coverage

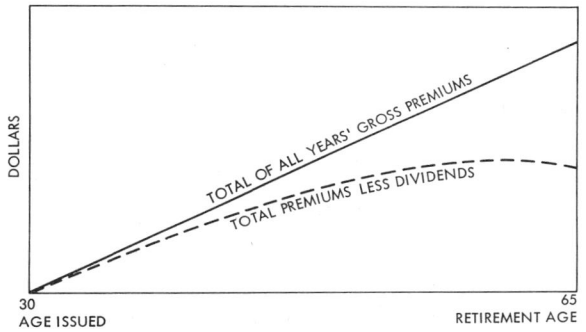

Funding Pattern—An Overview. For the group as a whole, there are two powerful elements pushing downward on net annual outlay to pay for the plan. One is dividends. In times of rising interest rates, such as during much of the period since the end of World War II, dividends can grow to substantial amounts in relation to annual premium. After a plan has been operating for a number of years, the accumulation of prior years' premiums generates total plan assets (guaranteed cash values plus reserves on pensions in the course of payment) that are quite large in relation to a single year's gross premium. Investment income in excess of that assumed in the construction of the premium rates has a powerful effect in increasing dividends.

The other factor is associated with the budgeting pattern. On the plan's effective date, the covered employees fall into a range of ages from old to young—with higher salaries, thus higher benefits, tending to fall at the older ages. For one benefit unit, the annual level premium starting from age 55 runs four to five times larger than the annual level premium starting from age 30. With the passage of time, as older employees retire and are replaced by younger employees, the funding pattern for the group as a whole would resemble that illustrated in Figure 39–3.

This suggests that the funding pattern tends to put relatively more of plan costs in the early plan years and less in the later years, and also furnishes a high order of benefit security to the employees. It also suggests that an employer could look forward to decreasing plan costs. All true.

FIGURE 39–3. Illustration of Funding Pattern for Group Permanent Plan in Which Older Employees Retire and Are Replaced by Younger Employees

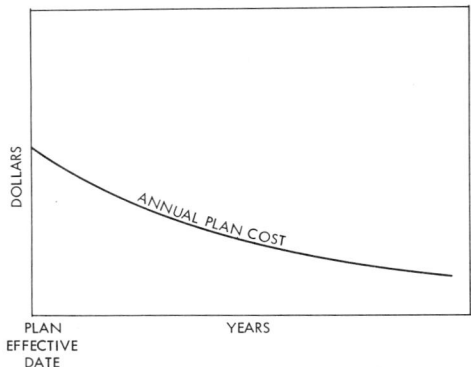

Adapted from C. L. Trowbridge's "Fundamentals of Pension Funding," *Transactions of the Society of Actuaries*, Vol. 4 (1952), pp. 17–43.

However, the counterforces since World War II of (1) rapidly rising salary levels, (2) rapidly expanding work forces, and (3) changes in plan design such as increasing the plan benefit formula and basing benefits on pay averages nearer retirement, have tended to lift the cost curve and result in higher levels of annual outlay. Initial plan costs, which had appeared manageable at first but were levered upward by these forces, caused many employers to search for relief from this cost onslaught. That relief was found in many ways:

1. *Example of a Modest Adjustment.* To blunt the sharp impact of high premium rates related to coverage starting a few years before retirement, some plans were amended to provide that level premiums are never for a period shorter than 10 years, so that, for example, on a pay change producing an increased benefit at age 60, the premium is paid from age 60 to 70 even though retirement occurs at age 65. The employee's benefit has not been fully purchased at retirement, but pension starts in the full amount at age 65. Spreading the premiums over a longer period substantially lowers annual outlay for that benefit.

2. *Example of a Substantial Structural Change.* When the plan is amended to increase the benefit formula, the benefits attributable to the formula change are funded through an unallocated vehicle, retaining the group permanent contract for the original benefit formula. The budgeting arrangement for the portion of benefits to be funded on an unallocated basis can spread costs over a longer period than the level premium individual allocation approach of group permanent.

3. *Complete Abandonment and Substitution of Some Entirely Different Vehicle.*

Although these adaptations and abandonments of the group permanent retirement income contract may have been generated in large part by the economic conditions that produced rising annual outlays to maintain a retirement plan, other important factors were closely interwoven. Following World War II, common stocks entered an essentially uninterrupted 20-year bull market. The investment returns available on common stocks in this period were significantly above those of fixed income instruments. No meaningful way exists to put group permanent retirement income contract assets into common stock. Because investment results serve to cut employer costs in these plans, strong interest in common stock investments was an important factor in the trend away from this and other fully allocated vehicles. The inherent benefit design was a further factor. Generous preretirement death benefits and after-retirement death benefits are simply part of the product. In many situations these were not desired. Even where death benefits were desired, a peculiarity in the income tax laws produced some current income tax to employees under this contract which was avoided if death benefits were provided in other ways, such as through group term life insurance.

In spite of the extremely strong guarantee package built into a group permanent retirement income contract, in spite of the high order of benefit security to employees, in spite of the assured, orderly budgeting pattern for the employer, this contract became less popular. In this environment, a different form of group permanent came on the scene and began to supplant the retirement income version.

Group Permanent Whole Life and Conversion Fund

Group permanent whole life and conversion fund is also known as group ordinary life and "side fund" or "auxiliary fund."

Basic Structure. The structure of a group permanent whole life plan is inherently the same as group permanent retirement income with one major difference. The guaranteed level premiums build guaranteed values equal to only a fraction of the values needed at retirement to furnish the promised pension. That fraction can be generalized as one fourth to one third though it varies for each benefit increment for each individual depending upon the age when funding of the benefit increment begins. However, some insurers arrange the premium structure so that the guaranteed cash value is always the same amount at age 65 regardless of issue age; for example, $300 per $1,000 of insurance. Thus, the level premiums for whole life insurance are substantially lower than for retirement income insurance. The balance of funds needed at an employee's retirement are built by deposits to an unallocated conversion fund which can accommodate a wide variety of budgeting arrangements for handling this portion of plan costs. Conceptually, the framework of this product is essentially the same as that of the group permanent retirement income contract combined with an unallocated fund.

The conversion fund device permits flexibility as to the *timing* of meeting plan costs. For reasons already discussed, this timing flexibility usually results in *slower* funding than for the group permanent retirement income plan. The conversion fund also permits the use of common stock investments.

The 1,000/10 relationship of life insurance to pension expectancy is not a necessity in this case because the whole life cash value does not provide the full pension. Many plans have used a 500/10, 750/10, or other relationship to meet an employer's specific plan design objectives. The majority of group permanent whole life plans probably use the 1,000/10. The lower the ratio, the less life insurance is provided, and more of the funding of pensions is done through the conversion fund.

The group whole life contract typically guarantees the annuity purchase rates at which whole life insurance can be converted into pension at retirement. This long-term guarantee attaches to each increment of life insurance as it comes into being—a promise of the insurer that may be made 40 years or more in advance. The guarantee attaches not just to the cash value of the whole life insurance but also to the additional amounts needed to convert each $1,000 of insurance to $10, $20, or $30 or more of pension (depending upon the insurance/pension ratio; for example, a 500/10 ratio requires conversion of each $1,000 of insurance into $20 of pension). Notice this approach does *not* guarantee that the employer's year-by-year funding is adequate to provide the promised pensions at retirement, as is true of group permanent income endowment.

If the employee leaves the plan prior to normal retirement age, the plan vesting provisions probably will be in terms of (1) pension credits earned to date of termination of employment, or (2) funds accumulated for the employee to that date. In either instance, to the degree this vesting cannot be fully provided for by the whole life cash values, the remainder is furnished from the conversion fund. Various options may be available to the terminating employee to take vested benefits in the form of paid-up life insurance and deferred pension or in cash (perhaps with the cash option restricted to the life insurance cash values). In some cases, vesting may be restricted by plan provision to the whole life values. Any nonvested whole life values are applied against the next insurance premium due; any nonvesting as to benefits supported by the conversion fund is reflected in the budgeting arrangement for the conversion fund for subsequent years.

Handling of disabled employees may follow any of the patterns described for group permanent retirement income contracts, or the plan simply may provide for an immediate start of the amount of pension the employee would have received at normal retirement date (which is possible under this coverage because the necessary amounts can be obtained from the conversion fund).

Investment of Plan Assets. The assets comprising the guaranteed values of whole life insurance are unequivocally promised by the insurer to individuals to meet the plan's benefits. These guaranteed assets are invested by the insurer in its general account, a mix of many kinds of investments, chiefly of the fixed income type. There is no necessity to invest the conversion fund in the insurer's general account, for it is not specifically promised to individual employees as are the whole life guaranteed cash values. Rather, the conversion fund supports the plan as a whole. Some or all of the conversion fund nevertheless may be invested in the insurer's general account. Or, it may be partially invested in the insurer's common stock separate account for retirement plans, or with another institution such as a bank's pooled fund for retirement plans or a mutual fund.

A Compromise Coverage. Group permanent whole life and conversion fund is a mix of allocated whole life and unallocated conversion fund. It is a mix of guaranteed benefit security to employees as to the whole life values, and nonguaranteed benefit security as to conversion fund assets. It is a mix of guaranteed maximum cost to the employer as to the level premium for whole life, and nonguaranteed cost as to funding needed for the conversion fund. It can be a mix as to budgeting arrangements for meeting plan costs—individual level premium on the whole life, and any of many other methods on the conversion fund. Typically, it is a mix as to investments, with some in fixed income assets and some in common stocks.

GROUP DEFERRED ANNUITIES

Classical Group Deferred Annuity

The group deferred annuity contract, which originated in the early 1920s or before, was the first group product used by insurance companies in the pension field. It is built on a durable concept that survives today, both in its original form and in variations on the original design.

Future Service. An allocated product, the classical group deferred annuity uses single premiums to purchase each year, for each employee covered under the plan, a fully paid-up annuity equal to the pension credit earned by the employee in that year. At retirement the ending pension is the sum of all these year-by-year "future service credits." Frequently a percentage of pay in the current year is the pension credit for the year under group deferred annuity contracts. In effect, the sum of the year-by-year future service pension credits is based on career average pay over the period of participation in the plan. The paid-up annuity is a "deferred" annuity, i.e., the pension begins at retirement age. This is a "defined benefit" approach; its antithesis is discussed later in this chapter.

The insurer's guarantees thus are quite extensive. At any point in time the paid-up annuities purchased to that date are fully guaranteed. In effect a package of interest, mortality, and expense guarantee exists for future indeterminate periods, which for the youngest covered employee covers all of his remaining period to retirement and entire life-span after retirement. Typically, the insurer retains the right to change premium rates after the fifth contract year for purchases made after the date of change, but the employer is not obligated to continue purchases, and can change insurers or funding instrument instead.

Past Service. On the effective date of the group deferred annuity contract, there usually are some covered employees who have meaningful amounts of prior service with the employer. Credit for this "past service" is almost never based on an actual average of pay over the period of prior service, but on the employee's pay level on the effective date of the plan (less frequently, it is based on an average of pay over a few years preceding the effective date). To correspond roughly with the career average theory for future service, these past service credits usually are based on a somewhat lower percentage of pay than that used for future service.

As already stated, paid-up annuities equal to the future service credits are purchased by single premiums as they are earned. What about the past service credits? The earliest approach was to compute the single-premium value of all past service benefits as if paid on the effective date of the plan, the employer then contributing premiums for this "past service liability" over a period of years. Each past service payment would be applied as a single premium (just as with future service credits) to buy a paid-up deferred annuity for the oldest employee until his past service credit is purchased, then similarly for the next oldest, and so on, until all past service credits eventually are paid. This "in order of age—oldest first" approach is aimed at being both equitable and practical. In the event of plan termination before the past service funding is complete, the oldest employees have had highest priority. In a typical ongoing plan, an employee's pension tends to be fully purchased by the time he retires, with yet-to-be-funded past service credits belonging to those who have not yet reached retirement age.

Unless the funding is progressing considerably faster than retirements occur, however, difficulties may arise. An employer might be funding at the outer edge of his financial capability. An employee might choose early retirement before his past service is funded. Several other employees closer to the usual retirement age already may be funded. The employer has no more money at the moment. What to do?

The common solution is not to get in this predicament. That is, past service credits are funded from inception by deposits to an unallocated fund (deposit administration type) and as an employee retires, whether early, normal or late, the past service pension is then purchased for the retiring employee by a single premium from the unallocated fund. This unallocated approach eliminates much of the timing problem of having used the past service payments for one individual when it is another who decides to retire. The product in this version is a mix of allocated future service and unallocated past service.

Benefit Formula. An example of the resulting defined benefit pension formula might be 1 percent of pay in each future service year, plus 0.75 percent of pay on the plan's effective date multiplied by total past service years. It is typical under a group deferred annuity with a defined benefit formula to provide no preretirement death benefit from employer contributions (employee contributions are returned to his beneficiary at death).

Strengths. The major strength, after the past service liability has been funded, is that covered employees have pension benefits earned to date on a fully paid basis. The employer is assured that this orderly budgeting arrangement is disposing of liabilities as they are created. The insurer guarantees the integrity of the purchased pensions. Funding of past service credits need not be on a rigid basis year by year, allowing flexibility in meeting this part of the plan costs.

Weaknesses. The principal disadvantage of group deferred annuity defined benefit plans is relative inflexibility. There are at least four inflexibilities of significance: (1) plan design limitation, (2) limited opportunity for common stock investment, (3) a rigid budgeting arrangement, (4) lack of ability to transfer assets to other funding agencies. The first is discussed below.

The pension benefit formula for practical purposes is limited to one that fixes in the current year the pension credit earned in the current year. Only on this basis can the necessary single premium for the current year's pension credit be determined and the necessary paid-up annuity purchased. Each year is a "closed book" as it occurs. This fact of life tends to limit group deferred annuities to a formula based on service and career average pay, or a flat dollar per year of service formula (e.g., $5 of monthly pension for each year of service without reference to pay level). Group deferred annuity contracts fit such formulas very well.

However, rapidly changing pay levels since the end of World War II have tended to put ever greater emphasis on final-pay formulas. An existing group deferred annuity plan can adapt to a change in its pension formula from career to final-average pay by continuing to fund the original career average formula through the group deferred annuity contract, and by funding the expected excess of pension at retirement date on the final-pay basis over the career average pension through an unallocated fund (deposit administration type). This particular mix of allocated and unallocated funding has a conceptual cousin in the previously discussed group permanent whole life and conversion fund. An employer introducing a new plan on a final-average pay base is unlikely to choose such a mix.

Another example of an awkward fit is the pension formula that is not service related, such as one in which the pension equals 30 percent of pay for employees with more than 15 years of service.

A third example is the offset formula, such as 2 percent of pay for each year of service inclusive of the initial primary social security amount the employee receives at retirement. The amount of pension attributable to each year of service is not known until retirement occurs and the social security amount becomes determinable.

In those plans which stay with career average salary service formulas and under which the original past service credits have been fully purchased, an unallocated fund still may be brought into being from time to time. This may be appropriate because pay levels in general have advanced upward to the extent that credits earned many years earlier are relatively low and resulting pensions will fall short of adequacy. The employer may amend the plan to base all prior years' credits on current pay levels. This approach is not equivalent to a final-average formula, since future credits would be based on each year's pay. But in this instance, one stroke of the pen has very substantially increased prior credits; the difference between the credits previously purchased and their amounts on the amended basis must be funded. Usually an unallocated fund is brought into play to fund over a period of years this newly created "past service liability."

Another example is a plan amendment changing the automatic form of pension from a lifetime-only pension to a lifetime pension with, say, five years of payments guaranteed in case of early death. More money is required to convert the previously purchased paid-up annuities from the old no-death-benefit basis to the new. An unallocated fund may be resorted to, and once again a liability has been created as to the death benefit addition to credits earned prior to the plan amendment.

Trend. In consequence of the complexities noted above, the trend has been for group deferred annuity plans to convert fully to one or another of the unallocated funding vehicles available in the marketplace. Encouraging that trend has been the desire of some employers and unions for at least partial common stock investment of plan assets. Because of the insurer's guarantee of the integrity of paid-up annuities, the assets backing up pension credits purchased under a group deferred annuity contract are in the insurer's general account which is invested primarily in fixed income instruments. (A major exception to this statement will be discussed below.)

The various temporary and semipermanent unallocated funds that may operate in conjunction with a group deferred annuity offer some opportunity for common stock investment. But frequently, an employer or union wants a significant portion of plan assets in common stock, and the conversion to an unallocated vehicle is undertaken to accomplish that goal.

Countertrend. Group deferred annuity contracts accommodate variable annuities quite nicely.[4] If a significant portion of the credits are purchased on a variable annuity basis, a career-average salary service formula may be able to keep pace with economic trends and pay levels. This assumes a long-term correlation between such economic trends and common stock performance.

A plan using group deferred annuities, say, 50 percent of credits on the classical fixed-income basis and 50 percent on a variable-annuity basis, provides a hedge against the chance that a career-average pay base otherwise may become out of date. Good common stock performance will increase the pension credits earned in prior years. Poor performance will decrease them. Such allocated contracts mixing fixed income and common stock investments have been available since the early 1960s.

Money Purchase Plans

Thoroughly embedded in the retirement plan field for many years, "money purchase" plans in recent years have been identified as "defined contribution" plans. Money purchase or defined contribution plans are those in which the contribution or premium is defined by the retirement plan (for example, the contribution made for an employee is 10 percent of his pay) and the benefit is whatever that defined contribution produces.

A group deferred annuity contract is highly compatible with a defined contribution plan. The contribution is made in stipulated amounts, is applied at the premium rates in the contract, and results in however much paid-up deferred annuity that relationship produces. The eventual pension benefit is the sum of the credits purchased year by year.

Teachers Insurance and Annuity Association—College Retirement Equities Fund (TIAA-CREF), one of the most famous plans in the coun-

---

[4] See Chapter 18 for a discussion of variable annuity concepts.

try, uses this vehicle for college teacher plans. As the name suggests, part of the defined contribution may go into a variable annuity.

The introduction of a variable annuity element into a defined contribution plan has exactly the same philosophical thrust as under a defined benefit career-average pay plan. If the defined contribution is 10 percent of pay, the contribution for an employee over his period of participation in the plan will have been 10 percent of his career-average pay over that period. Economic changes can erode credits from contributions based on pay of many years ago, unless some update mechanism is used. Common stock investment is an attempt at an automatic update.[5]

There is probably a good deal more of the "deferred wage" notion inherent in a defined contribution plan (whether the defined contribution is dependent upon profits, or the amount of employee contributions, or is a fixed commitment by the employer) than in a defined benefit plan. For this reason, defined contribution plans have tended to feature earlier vesting and provide preretirement death and termination of employment benefits equal to the accumulated defined contributions plus investment income. Thus, group deferred annuities used for defined contribution plans have tended to be "full refund" at death rather than the "no refund" (as to employer contributions) form typical of defined benefit plans.

Benefits for employees disabled before retirement can easily be included in such "full refund" plans by simply using the accumulated cash for this purpose. In contrast, disability benefits cannot be easily included in the typical "no refund" deferred annuity commonly used for defined benefit plans. In the "no refund" concept, if the employee dies before retirement, his annuity values are used to support annuities for those who live (the premiums have been discounted for expected deaths before retirement).

It is in this field of defined contribution or money purchase group deferred annuities that some extremely interesting variants on the classical group deferred annuity have evolved.

Funding for the Individual Employee

Defined Benefit Plans. The future service element, assuming the employee receives no pay increases, produces a constant pension credit year after year. For example, a 1 percent of pay formula on a $10,000 salary results each year in $100 of pension credit for that year. Assume that this condition continues from entry into the plan at, say, age 25 until retirement at age 65. Each year for four decades a $100 credit is earned and is purchased by a single premium in that year producing a final pension of $4,000 per year. The annual credits are level. The annual single premiums are not. The single premium is the amount needed today to provide the pension at retirement. The premium is assumed to accumulate at some rate of investment return to age 65, recognizing expenses, and allowing

---

[5] Note that a variable annuity within a defined *benefit* plan of the type discussed earlier has the effect of converting the plan to a defined *contribution* basis. The defined benefit requires a particular amount of premium. Once the premium is paid, the benefit attached to it fluctuates up and down depending on common stock results and loses its original definition. In effect, the defined benefit serves only to define the premium, and thereafter operation is like a defined contribution plan.

for the fact that some employees will die before retirement and their premiums can be used to help provide for those who live. The premium at age 25 for $100 of pension to begin at age 65 is about 3 percent less than the premium at age 26, and about 75 percent less than the premium at age 64.

FIGURE 39–4.   Illustration of Level Pension Benefit Credits under a Defined Benefit Plan

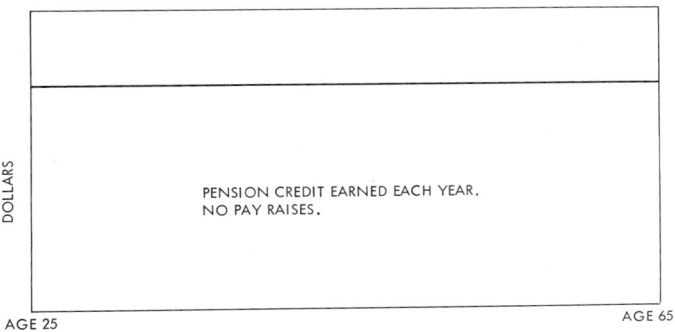

Illustrations of the credits and premiums for one employee's future service are shown in Figures 39–4 and 39–5. This single-premium funding pattern is known as step-rate or unit-credit funding.

Defined Contribution Plans. Figures 39–6 and 39–7 illustrate credits and premiums for defined contribution plans.

FIGURE 39–5.   Illustration of Single-Premium Contributions under a Defined Benefit Plan

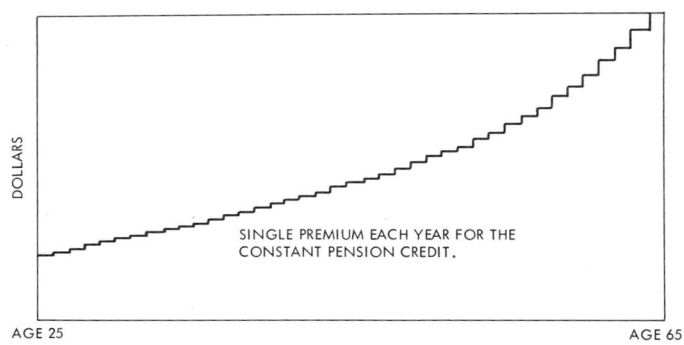

Past Service. Past service credits (credits for service before the effective date of the plan) can accompany both defined benefit and defined contribution plans. The funding is likely to be on a unallocated basis in the preretirement period, payments being made by the employer over a period of years, with allocation occurring in the single-premium purchase of an immediate annuity equal to the past service credits at the employee's date of retirement.

Costs.   In the classical group deferred annuity, the single premiums are a guaranteed gross cost (defined benefit plans). The sum for all employees is reduced by dividends reflecting better-than-anticipated investment income, mortality, and expense experience. The unallocated fund

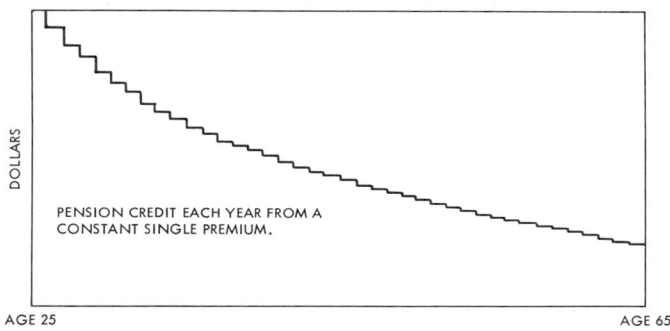

FIGURE 39–6.   **Illustration of Pension Credits for Each Year from a Constant Single Premium under a Defined Contribution Plan**

for past service operates like the deposit administration approach discussed in the next chapter. The experience rating calculation of dividends follows the same general process described earlier for group permanent retirement income contracts.

Gross cost is also reduced by reserves released on annuities cancelled when employees who are not fully vested terminate employment. A trou-

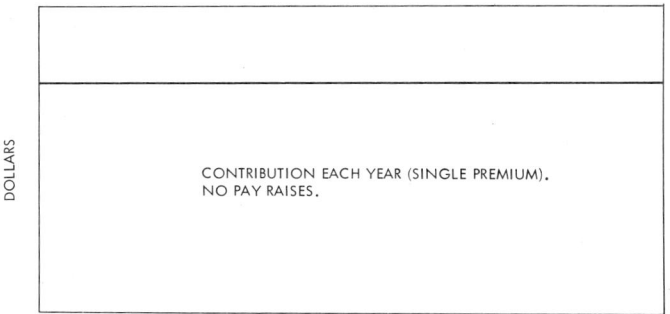

FIGURE 39–7.   **Illustration of Single-Premium Level Contributions under a Defined Contribution Plan**

blesome problem arises in this connection. As mentioned earlier, the single premiums, and thus gross cost, have already been discounted in the expectation that some employees will die before retirement and the reserves of their annuities can be used to support the annuities of those who live. Terminating employees may range from those in excellent health to those who are on death's doorstep. In theory, for those who will not survive to retirement age the reserve released on termination of employment should *not* be directly applied against the next premium due, but instead be indirectly handled through the dividend calculation as a death. The obvious difficulty is that no one really knows on the date of an employee's termination of employment whether he will or will not survive until retirement, and the decision has to be made then and there on which way to handle his nonvested reserves. Several marginally satisfactory techniques are used to resolve the problem. One is to get the health information on the employee and make a judgment on expected longevity. The larger the dollar amount involved, the more health information is desired. Another is to credit directly an arbitrary percentage (say, 95 percent) of all nonvested reserves below a certain dollar amount without resort to health information.

In defined contribution plans, dividends conceptually should increase the employees' benefits. Under the classical deferred annuity, however, they sometimes are used to reduce costs because of the complexities in allocating the total dividend among the employees. In defined contribution pension plans, reserves released by nonvested terminations of employment must, under Internal Revenue Service rules, be used to reduce gross cost.

Funding Pattern—An Overview. The step-rate funding approach for future service credits for one employee under a defined benefit plan obviously results in a steadily increasing cost for him (Figure 39–5). For the group of employees as a whole, however, this is not true. Older employees leave the high end of the staircase by reason of retirement and death and are replaced by younger employees at the low end. Dividends further tend to reduce annual outlay. In times of stable pay rates, future service costs in a mature group of employees would tend to decrease because of dividends. Past service costs are amortized over a period of time, and once paid in full, annual outlay for them ceases.

Total annual outlays to fund future service and past service would tend to decrease over the years. Pushing in the direction of increasing premium outlays, however, are the dynamic factors of (1) wage inflation, (2) increasing numbers of employees covered, and (3) plan amendments improving benefits.

Variations of the Group Deferred Annuity

During the past 10 to 15 years a number of products have emerged which can be lumped under the label of "accumulation" products. They start from the concepts inherent in the classical group deferred annuity. These "accumulation" products are aimed at the defined contribution or money purchase type of plan. The "accumulation" label comes from the defined contribution approach of "accumulating" contributions in an account for an employee to provide as much pension or lump-sum benefit for him as those contributions plus investment income will furnish.

The first modifications dispensed with the actual purchase of deferred annuities on receipt of each premium, and instead featured the deposit of the premium less an expense factor in an account of the employee, the guarantee of the interest rates at which the employee's account would accumulate, and the guarantee of the rates at which the accumulated account could purchase an annuity at retirement. This allows dividends simply to be added to the individual employee's account as they occur.

The second step was to compute dividends using the investment year method.

The next step was to purchase the annuities, at retirement, at rates which were constructed on realistic rather than conservative assumptions, thus eliminating dividends after retirement and maximizing the monthly pension starting at retirement. (In some cases conservative rates were used and dividends added to the guaranteed pension.)

The advent of separate accounts allowed part or all of the pre-retirement accounts to be invested in common stocks and accounted for on a market value basis. The introduction of variable annuities for the payout of pensions in the retirement period came shortly after separate accounts evolved. Also coming into play was direct rating, or the elimination of dividends in the preretirement period by crediting investment income and expense results directly to the employee accounts.

Techniques were developed to account for the portion of the employee's values invested in the insurer's general account on something akin to "market value," so that his entire account was valued realistically in terms of the then current investment marketplace.

The resulting product allows accumulating monies for individual employees in fixed income and common stock investments with benefits being in the form of lump-sum cash or fixed and variable annuities. Expenses and total investment productivity—good or bad—are reflected directly to the employee's account. This type of plan is highly suited to the changeable investment climate of the early 1970s. It is also a considerable distance down the evolutionary trail from its ancestor, the classical group deferred annuity.

SELECTED REFERENCES

Alvord, Morgan H. "Insured Pension Plans in the United States and Canada," *Transactions XVth International Congress of Actuaries*, Vol. 1 (1957), p. 187.

Bronson, Dorrance C. "Pension Plans—Provisions for Termination of Plan," *Transactions of the Society of Actuaries*, Vol. 8 (1955), p. 225.

Darnton, John M. "Are Pension Plans Facing Runaway Costs?" *Proceedings: Conference of Actuaries in Public Practice*, Vol. 16 (1966–67), p. 396.

McGill, Dan M. *Fulfilling Pension Expectations.* Pension Research Council, Wharton School of Finance and Commerce, University of Pennsylvania. Homewood, Ill.: Richard D. Irwin, Inc., 1962.

————. *Fundamentals of Private Pensions.* 2d ed. Pension Research Council, Wharton School of Finance and Commerce, University of Pennsylvania. Homewood, Ill.: Richard D. Irwin, Inc., 1964.

Siegel, Conrad M. "Group Annuity Ill-Health Terminations," *Transactions of the Society of Actuaries*, Vol. 11 (1959), p. 114.

40

Funding Instruments—
Deposit Administration
Contracts and
Separate Accounts

By DOUGLAS B. HUNTER*

DEPOSIT ADMINISTRATION pension plans generally are considered to have been originated about 1929. Significant interest in this type of plan did not develop, however, until the end of World War II. This interest was due largely to a growing desire on the part of larger employers for more flexibility in the funding of pensions, to a need for a type of plan that was more suitable for the pension agreements negotiated with labor unions, and to meet the growing competition of trustee funding.

A group contract is usually issued directly to an employer in connection with deposit administration plans, although in some instances a trustee is the holder of the contract. Deposits are made periodically to a fund, or funds, established under the contract. This fund is maintained for active employees, and no part of it is allocated to a particular employee until an annuity is provided for him. This usually is done upon retirement by charging against the unallocated fund an amount sufficient to provide an immediate annuity for the retiring employee. Except when employee contributions are involved, it is not necessary for the insurance company to maintain any individual records until an annuity is provided.

The amount of the employer's periodic deposits is calculated by an actuary based on the actuarial cost method chosen or approved by the employer. Either the insurance company or a consulting actuary acts in this capacity. The actuary's calculation of the deposits needed to provide

---

* The author wishes to acknowledge that the basic outline of this chapter was prepared by Morgan H. Alvord for the second edition of the *Life and Health Insurance Handbook,* and is used for the third edition with his consent.

the benefits of the plan, as well as his determination of the financial status of the plan, is based on assumptions as to future investment returns, mortality, expenses, retirement age, employee turnover, salary trends, and annuity purchase rates. The employer furnishes the actuary with statistical data with respect to his employees, usually is consulted as to the assumptions used, and assumes responsibility for the adequacy of the fund.

PLAN SPECIFICATIONS

Eligibility

Since funds are not allocated to individual employees prior to retirement, the need to exclude short-service employees, which is a characteristic of a deferred annuity contract, is not present to the same degree in this type of contract. Hence, all employees potentially eligible for benefits typically may be covered by the plan, or relatively short waiting periods, such as six months or one year of service, may be used.

Employee Contributions

While the majority of plans are on an "employer pay all" basis, some plans require employees to pay part of the costs through their own contributions. Because of employee participation, a plan of this kind differs from a noncontributory plan in certain important respects. Records are kept of individual employee contributions. Withdrawal and death benefits may be paid from the deposit administration fund. Restrictions as to eligibility similar to those under a group deferred annuity plan usually are imposed. A separate fund is often maintained for the employees' contributions, and deferred annuities sometimes are purchased with these contributions as made.

Retirement Age

A normal retirement age is established, but since no annuities need be purchased until actual retirement, there is significant flexibility in determining benefits for early and late retirements. To the extent permitted by the Internal Revenue Service, adjustment for early retirement may be more liberal than that produced by using actuarial equivalents. With respect to retirement after the normal retirement age, it is common to have benefits accrue for service to actual retirement, especially in union-negotiated plans.

Cost estimates may be based upon an assumption as to the expected average retirement age of the entire group of employees. It was common in the 1960s, for example, to assume a retirement age beyond normal retirement age when there was no compulsory retirement; however, with the current emphasis on liberalized early retirement benefits, there is a trend toward assuming a retirement age earlier than normal retirement.

Pension Benefits

A flexible pension benefit provision may be adopted, since no annuities are purchased while the employees are in active employment. Rather than basing benefits upon average earnings, it is common to base them upon "final" earnings.[1] In estimating costs, an assumed salary scale is introduced, adding little to the complexities of valuations and calculation of normal costs, and improving accuracy of projections.

Other kinds of pension benefits which may be funded without difficulty under this type of contract include amounts based on earnings only; pensions depending solely upon years of service; minimum benefits which are independent of the basic formula; pension benefits which are geared to social security benefits; pension benefits which vary with a cost-of-living index or, by means of a separate account, with the investment result of funds invested in common stocks; benefits payable to a dependent spouse or orphans; and disability benefits.

Withdrawal Benefits

Under a contributory pension plan an employee is permitted to withdraw his contributions under certain conditions, such as termination of employment. If cash refunds are paid to an employee from a deposit administration fund, there is usually a charge against the fund of 3 to 5 percent. In certain cases, however, this charge may be avoided if the administrator makes the payment from funds which otherwise would have been paid to the deposit administration fund. The insurance company then receives only the net amount.

Usually there is a provision for vesting accrued pension benefits, in whole or in part, if an employee terminates employment after a certain age and number of years of service. Under a deposit administration plan, the vested pension usually remains as an obligation of the plan on a basis similar to that of the accrued benefits of the active employees, with no purchase of an annuity until annuity payments are to begin. Occasionally, the vested annuity may be purchased in full for the withdrawing employee at the time of withdrawal.

Death Benefits

Death benefits before retirement arising from employee contributions are administered in a manner similar to withdrawal benefits. An employer may desire, however, to include a modest death benefit in his pension plan which is not based upon employee contributions and which is incidental to the other benefits. When this is done, the actuary includes an allowance for this benefit in his cost estimates of the size of the annual deposit.

After retirement, various types of death benefits usually are available in the form of optional annuities, such as joint and survivor annuities, and annuities with payments guaranteed for a certain period and life thereafter. While similar options are available under group deferred annuity contracts, they may be provided under a deposit administration contract with less restrictions. For example, the requirements of advance notice

---

[1] In order to avoid possible discrimination and difficulty with the IRS, it is usual to establish final earnings as the average of the last 5 or 10 years' earnings prior to retirement age.

of election of an option could be modified or eliminated if the purchase price of the annuity is appropriately increased to allow for antiselection.

Disability Benefits

When a disability retirement benefit is included in a pension program, the risk is generally assumed by the employer. The disability payments usually are made either directly by the employer or from a deposit administration fund. If such a fund is used, the insurance company or consulting actuary generally makes recommendations as to the amount of additional deposit which the employer should make. While the final determination of whether an employee qualifies for disability benefits is the responsibility of the employer or administrator of the plan, many employers find it of considerable value to use the facilities of the insurance company for advice.

Discontinuance Provisions

When deposits are discontinued, the retirement benefits already being paid are unaffected, since such benefits are provided by single-premium immediate annuities purchased from the fund at the time an employee retires. To the extent that vested deferred annuities have been purchased, the benefits provided by these annuities are similarly unaffected by a discontinuance of deposits.

If deposits are discontinued and the pension plan is continued under some other arrangement, the contract usually may be continued without further deposits. As employees retire, their annuities are purchased from the deposit administration fund until it is exhausted.

Most contracts provide that on discontinuance of deposits and of the pension plan, the deposit administration fund must be distributed among the active employees by the purchase of fully vested deferred annuities. This distribution may be made in several different ways, provided they are mutually satisfactory to the employer and the insurance company. Under Internal Revenue regulations, the method must be stipulated in the plan. Any appropriate method of allocating the fund to individual employees will be approved by the insurance company if it can be administered reasonably and does not involve selection through placing undue weight upon the healthy lives. One method, which is frequently made an automatic provision, is to apply the fund as far as it will go in the purchase of accrued benefits in full, starting with those nearest normal retirement age. Another method is to allocate the fund among active lives on some basis proportionate to accrued or prospective benefits. A variation is first to purchase accrued benefits in full for employees who qualify for vested benefits under the plan and then to use up any remaining portion of the fund in one of the two preceding ways. The requirement for distribution of the deposit administration fund stems, at least in part, from IRS requirements applicable to a qualified pension plan when terminated.

If a pension plan is continued in some other way, the employer may wish to transfer the deposit administration fund to the new funding agency. Almost all insurance companies will permit such a "cash-out" under some circumstances, although the conditions vary greatly among companies. This will be discussed in more detail below.

UNDERWRITING AND CONTRACTUAL PROVISIONS

Contract Holder

In offering to issue a contract, the insurance company considers various factors. The plan presumably should be permanent. The employer should be one whose earning power is sufficient to support his pension program, and his facilities to administer the plan should be adequate. Associations of employers and political subdivisions are carefully screened to see whether they have the legal right to enter into a contract of this nature and can meet the other important qualifications.

Minimums and Maximums

Originally, requirements as to minimum number of lives and deposits were quite high. During the last few years, however, competition and more experience with this type of contract have resulted in a sharp decrease in these minimums. The minimum number of lives permitted under a contract has been reduced during recent years to 10 or even lower by some insurance companies. Minimum annual deposit requirements have also been decreased to $10,000 or less.

Great flexibility is permitted in the size and the timing of the deposits that may be made. Most insurance companies require that the amounts paid must be on a reasonable basis although a great degree of flexibility is permitted in the actuarial assumptions and methods used in determining these amounts. Companies wish to avoid the possibility of receiving greatly increased deposits during periods when investment earnings are falling rapidly, and thus generally impose restrictions as to the size of the deposits they will accept in any one year. While these maximums vary considerably with different companies, most of them usually will accept much larger deposits on special request.

Inclusion of Plan Specifications

In some cases the specifications of the plan, such as eligibility, retirement age benefits, and the like, are included in the contract. In many instances, the employer may wish to keep the specifications out of the contract and operate the plan under provisions in a formal document outside the contract. Subject to proper safeguards as to future changes in the provisions, a contract may be written in this manner. When this is done, the contract, of course, becomes a simpler document.

Contributory Plans

While the majority of deposit administration plans are on a noncontributory (i.e., "employer pay all") basis, there are some plans where the employees also make contributions. Under this type, the insurance company requires that the fund always be sufficient to return the employees' contributions with whatever interest is guaranteed. A common provision is to require that the deposit administration fund always be at least 105 percent of the employees' contributions with guaranteed interest. The additional 5 percent provides a margin for any charges made upon cash payments from the fund.

When there are employee contributions, the contract usually has one of the three following provisions: (1) The contributions, when made, are applied to purchase deferred annuities; (2) the employee and employer contributions are applied to purchase deferred annuities at the time when the annuities vest, in accordance with the provisions of the plan; (3) the employee contributions are maintained in a separate employee fund, or in the overall fund, and are withdrawn from the active life fund at the time of retirement to provide immediate annuities.

Deposit Administration Fund

A deposit administration fund[2] is maintained under the contract on an unallocated basis for the active employees. This fund always must be kept in excess of the amount needed to purchase annuities as employees retire, in accordance with the requirements of the plan. Sufficient amounts are transferred from this fund when an employee retires and, sometimes, when his accrued pension becomes vested, to purchase the benefits to which he is entitled. A modification of this during the early years of a plan is to provide for the gradual purchase of annuities until sufficient funds have been built up to purchase fully the annuities at retirement.

The principal of the fund is guaranteed, as well as a minimum interest rate. The annuity rates applicable to current contributions withdrawn in the future also are guaranteed. Since the interest and premium rates in effect when the contributions are made are guaranteed, it is necessary to require that withdrawals be made on a first-in, first-out basis, i.e., contributions are transferred in the order in which they are received.

Guarantees

Deposit administration plans are similar in many ways to uninsured trusteed arrangements, but the insured plans contain important guarantees which are not available under wholly uninsured funding instruments. The most important are:

1. The principal of the fund is guaranteed, regardless of the investment experience of the insurance company.
2. When a contribution is made, a minimum interest rate is guaranteed, usually on a basis where the rates are graduated downward periodically, until the contribution is transferred from the deposit administration fund. In most contracts, this minimum guaranteed rate may be changed with respect to contributions made five years or more after

---

[2] Also referred to as "deposit fund," "deposit account," "active life fund," and "purchase payment fund."

the effective date of the contract. Investment earnings in excess of the minimum become available through the experience-rating procedures of the insurance company.

3. At the time a contribution is made, the annuity purchase rates which may be used when it is later withdrawn to purchase an annuity are guaranteed, usually on a basis where the rates are graduated upward periodically, until the contribution is withdrawn from the fund. Generally, these guaranteed annuity rates may be changed with respect to contributions made five years or more after the effective date of the contract.

4. Since annuities are purchased when employees retire or, in some cases, when the annuities become vested, the pensions, after purchase, are guaranteed for life regardless of the future of the plan.

Discontinuance of Contributions

The principal ways in which contributions may be discontinued are: (1) By the employer upon appropriate notice; (2) by the insurance company under one of the following circumstances: (a) if the number covered under the plan falls below some minimum, such as 10; (b) if the insurance company desires to exercise its rights to modify certain terms of the contract and the employer does not agree; or (c) if any deposits are due and are not paid within the grace period.

When contributions are discontinued, the deposit administration fund may be distributed among the active employees by the purchase of paid-up deferred annuities on a basis where there is no selection because of health considerations (described in more detail in the plan specifications section of this chapter).

If the pension plan is continued through some other funding agency, the employer may wish to transfer the fund to that new agency. Practices of insurance companies vary greatly in this respect, although none of them will permit the transfer of any annuities already being paid to retired employees. Most of them are willing to make a decision with respect to the transfer of funds at the time of discontinuance in the light of the circumstances of each individual case. Some insurers include in their contracts a clause allowing the employer the option to transfer the deposit administration fund to another funding agency.

When a transfer of funds is permitted, the general practice is to allow a cash-out of the deposit administration fund, less a percentage which usually does not exceed 5 percent. Such a cash-out may be spread equally over a period of 10 years. Any unpaid balance in the fund will usually continue to be credited with interest at the guaranteed rate. In recent years an alternative is frequently offered whereby a lump-sum payment is made without any right to spread. In this case the amount paid is modified to reflect the market value of the securities in which the fund is invested.

EXPERIENCE RATING

Whether a contract is issued by a stock or a mutual life insurance company, it is usually experience rated. Any rate credits or dividends resulting from this process are credited to the deposit administration fund and reduce the amount of deposits needed.

While there are differences in detail, the basic principles usually followed by insurance companies in experience rating are essentially the same. The experience fund of each case is credited with the deposits received and the interest rate allowed by the company to this class of contract. Since the assets arising from these contracts are commingled with the insurer's total assets, this interest rate represents the share of such contracts in the insurer's net interest earnings. The experience is then charged with the benefits paid and expenses incurred. The difference between the income and the charges is the experience rating fund.

Next, the "liabilities" of the deposit administration plan are determined. They consist of the actuarial and contingency reserves. The actuarial reserves are principally the liability of the insurance company because of the deposit administration fund and the reserves needed to pay any annuities already purchased for the employees. The contingency reserves are primarily a protection against possible, but not assumed, future developments which could result in larger payments on the part of the insurance company than anticipated. Any excess of the experience rating fund over the "liabilities" of the deposit administration plan is available as rate credits or dividends.

A relatively recent development has been the pooling of smaller contracts for experience rating or dividend purposes. Under this concept, a group of contracts is combined, and the same process described earlier is applied to the combined experience. Rate credits or dividends are then allocated to individual cases in proportion to reserves held or some other similar basis. This provides a means of reducing the need for contingency reserves and hence making the rate credits or dividends arise more quickly. It also means that mortality gains or losses will be spread among all the participating contracts.

IMMEDIATE PARTICIPATION GUARANTEE

An immediate participation guarantee contract[3] is a form of deposit administration contract. As in the case of the latter, a fund is established, and deposits are made by the employer upon the advice of an actuary. The employer assumes responsibility for the adequacy of the fund to provide the benefits of the plan.

There are certain essential differences, however, between the normal type of deposit administration contract and an immediate participation one. Under the latter, there is usually no guarantee of a minimum rate of interest on the fund. Instead, interest at a rate on a basis described in the contract, generally closely related to the insurance company's net rate earned on its assets, is credited to the fund each year. In some instances, guarantees of interest are made for a relatively short period, such as five years. Expenses incurred are similarly charged. When an employee retires,

---

[3] Sometimes referred to as a "pension administration" or "direct-rated deposit administration" contract.

an annuity normally is not purchased.[4] Instead, the annuity payments are made directly out of the fund. In order to assure retired employees that their pensions will be paid as long as they live, these contracts contain a clause to the effect that if the fund should decrease to an amount just sufficient to purchase annuities at the rates specified in the contract for the retired employees, the fund shall be applied immediately for this purpose, and the "immediate participation" feature eliminated.

From the preceding, it is evident that there is no need to experience rate this type of contract in the usual manner, since the experience is immediately and automatically reflected each year through the procedures described. It is from this that the name "immediate participation guarantee" was derived. It is general practice to offer this form of contract primarily to larger sized groups for which it is the insured counterpart of the self-insured plan. During recent years most larger contracts have been written on this basis, and its use is being extended to smaller groups, in some cases down to $50,000 of annual contributions.

A modification of this form of contract is to establish an IPG contract for the active life fund, with interest credited directly to the fund and expenses charged as incurred. At retirement, annuities are purchased on the basis of guaranteed rates, and this portion of the contract is then treated separately. It can be on an experience-rated basis or on a guaranteed-cost basis.

SUPPLEMENTARY DEPOSIT ADMINISTRATION

A deposit administration plan can be used very effectively in supplementing another pension plan. Under one arrangement, the basic plan provides for the current benefits and there is a deposit administration facility for past service benefits. Such an arrangement gives more flexibility in funding the past service benefits. The initial deposits can be based on anticipated employee turnover and less conservative interest and mortality assumptions, since the employer assumes responsibility for the adequacy of the fund. It is not necessary under this arrangement to allocate any of the deposits until an employee actually retires. In the event of discontinuance of contributions, the fund is available to be distributed on some pro rata basis among all the active employees. Under the normal group deferred annuity, all the premiums paid for past service usually have already been allocated on a "nearest to retirement age" basis.

As an offset to these advantages, the use of a supplementary deposit administration plan for past service benefits with a basic group deferred annuity for future service puts the plan on a hybrid basis, with only part of the benefits fully guaranteed. As in all pension planning, there is no one right way. The employer should select the funding basis which most nearly meets his individual requirements and desires.

---

[4] Some insurance companies purchase annuities at the beginning of each year and then make adjustments at the end of the year, so that the effect is the same as if the annuities had not been purchased.

Where there is a basic group deferred annuity plan with pensions based upon a definite formula, such as a certain percentage of each year's earnings during the employee's participation, a minimum pension benefit (which might be related to final pay, social security benefits, or other elements difficult to predict) may readily be supplied through a supplementary deposit administration plan. Since the need of providing for an additional pension to meet a minimum for any particular employee is difficult to predict, the flexibility of deposit administration funding is an excellent way of meeting this situation.

A problem in most pension plans is to be able to retire some employees earlier than on the normal retirement date. Since an employee who retires early usually will not accrue his full benefits, a further actuarial reduction in his expected pension because of his early retirement often results in an inadequate income. A supplementary deposit administration plan provides a practical way of accumulating sufficient funds to allow larger pensions at early retirement than the actuarial equivalent.

It is desired under some pension plans to provide substantial death benefits through individual life insurance. This may be done by an arrangement of such nature that when an employee retires, his ordinary life insurance under the individual policy pension trust or under a group permanent contract is converted to an annuity, with an additional annuity of sufficient amount being purchased from a supplementary deposit administration fund.

SEPARATE ACCOUNTS

A separate account[5] is a facility under which an employer may arrange with a life insurance company for the investment of pension funds arising from its own payments in an account operated separately from the general funds of the insurance company, on a basis which gives the employer the direct benefit of the investment experience of that account. Thus the income and gains or losses, realized or unrealized, from the assets in the account are credited to or charged against the account without regard to the other income, gains, or losses of the insurance company. The insurance company is not a trustee in such an arrangement. Both fixed and variable annuities may be provided. Plans qualified under the Internal Revenue Code are substantially exempt from Securities and Exchange Commission regulation.

The first separate account facilities underwritten by a U.S. life insurance company generally are considered to have been put into effect in 1961. This facility was the result of an increasing desire on the part of employers to invest a portion of their pension funds in equities. Before separate accounts could be offered generally, revisions in the federal tax laws were needed, permissive legislation had to be obtained from many states, and a decision from the SEC had to be secured exempting this medium of funding from much of its regulations. These barriers were removed, and life insurance companies have contracts available for almost every pension funding need.

---

[5] Also referred to as "segregated assets" and "flexible funding."

A separate account facility is usually a part of a group deposit administration contract. The contract provides that the employer may allocate a portion of the pension plan contributions made under the contract to a separate investment account maintained by the insurance company with respect to this portion of its assets. Except under variable annuity plans, employee contributions normally are not allocated to such account. The contributions not allocated to the separate account usually are allocated to a conventional deposit administration or immediate participation fund, with the principal and, in the case of conventional deposit administration, interest return guaranteed. Under the conventional deposit administration form, at the time of retirement, sufficient amounts are withdrawn from this fund or the separate account to provide the annuity payments to which the employees are entitled under the pension plan. Under the immediate participation form, sufficient funds are maintained in this fund to guarantee the annuities. In the case of variable annuity plans, the appropriate funds are retained in the separate account or transferred to the variable annuity separate account.

Several types of separate accounts are available. Under all of them the insurance company has the responsibility of deciding on the investments, and the only guarantee with respect to investment results is that the contributions allocated to the account will participate in its experience. An important type of this account is a pooled account. Each employer shares in the investment results in proportion to the size of its interest in the pooled account. The assets of this account usually are invested primarily in common stocks, although the insurance company has some flexibility for other types of investment. Some companies offer several kinds of pooled accounts, so that an employer may select the type of investment he desires. Currently, these accounts are mainly for mortgages, bonds, and real estate. In addition there are different common stock accounts to reflect different investment policies. Where the annual payments into the account are large, some companies have individual separate accounts available in lieu of the pooled ones.

SPLIT FUNDING

Split funding is an arrangement under which one portion of the funding of a pension plan is on an insured basis and the other portion is on a trusteed basis. While the individual or group contracts that generally are issued for pension plans may be used for the insured portion, a great many of the pension plans on a split funding basis, particularly the larger ones, are funded through a combination deposit administration contract and a trust fund. The contract may be issued either directly to the employer or to the trust. In this latter event the contract becomes, in a sense, an asset of the trust.

Split funding is frequently used when an employer wishes to invest a portion of its pension funds in equities in a trust fund and still retain the other features of an insured plan. This may be accomplished in combination with a deposit administration plan. The balance of the deposits is paid to the deposit administration fund where it is commingled with the insurance company's assets for investment purposes. These investments are almost wholly of the fixed-dollar type.

Employers frequently desire to retain as many of the guarantees of an insured plan as possible. Split funding meets this need, since all the pension payments may be on a fully guaranteed basis. The principal of the funds invested in the deposit administration contract is guaranteed, and a minimum interest rate on these funds also may be guaranteed.

A more recent development of split funding is the use of the insurance company primarily as an investment vehicle. Under this concept the contract normally would be issued to the trust and would be treated as an asset of the trust. The plan would be administered by the trust and benefits paid from the trust. While the deposit administration contract would provide for the purchase of annuities on an optional basis, no such purchase would be required and no guarantee would be made to the retired employees. Contributions would be made to the contract in accordance with the investment plan of the trust and funds would be withdrawn, when needed, to pay benefits. This type of contract can start out providing only investment services, with the other services provided by the insurance company added from time to time as desired.

ACCUMULATOR

Another recent development is the use of a deposit administration contract with a separate account to provide for the accumulation until retirement of individually allocated employee and employer funds together with investment appreciation, with the option at that time by the employee to take the cash value in a lump sum or use it to purchase an annuity, either on a fixed or variable basis or both. This form of contract can be used for a money purchase pension plan, a thrift or savings plan, a voluntary employee contribution plan added to a conventional pension plan, or a profit sharing plan. Expenses charged are deducted from the contributions before they are allocated to the deposit administration fund or the separate account. The employer frequently will pay the expense charges.

The employer or, in some instances, each employee designates what portion of a particular contribution should be allocated to the deposit administration fund and which portion to the separate account. A record is maintained for each employee of the contributions made by him and by the employer on his behalf. The portion allocated to the deposit administration fund is credited with a stated rate of interest. The portion allocated to the separate account is credited with the investment experience of that separate account. At retirement, the amount standing to the credit of the employee is available to purchase an annuity or to be paid out in cash. At termination of employment or death before retirement the value of the accumulated employee contributions plus any vested portion of the employer contributions is available in cash or may be used to purchase an annuity.

The interest rate applied to the deposit administration fund is usually determined each year by the insurance company and reflects the net interest earned by the insurance company on the funds paid into this contract. The separate account used for this type of contract usually is a pooled separate account invested primarily in common stocks, but can be other types of separate accounts. The allocation of funds between the deposit administration fund and the separate account can be decided either by the employer for all his employees or individually by each employee. The annuity purchase rate available at retirement normally is based upon the rates in effect at that time.

SELECTED REFERENCES

Commerce Clearing House. *Pension and Profit Sharing Service*. Chicago, Ill. Looseleaf service.

Hicks, Ernest L. *Accounting for the Cost of Pension Plans*. New York: American Institute of Certified Public Accountants, Inc., 1965.

McGill, Dan M. *Fundamentals of Private Pensions*. 2d ed. Pension Research Council, Wharton School of Finance and Commerce, University of Pennsylvania. Homewood, Ill.: Richard D. Irwin, Inc., 1964.

Melone, Joseph J. and Allen, Everett T., Jr. *Pension Planning*. Rev. ed. Homewood, Ill.: Richard D. Irwin, Inc., 1972.

Prentice-Hall. *Pension and Profit Sharing Service*. Englewood Cliffs, N.J.: Looseleaf service.

41

Funding Instruments—
Trust Fund Plans

By PAUL H. JACKSON

Trust funds are widely used for the funding of private pension plans. Under this arrangement, contributions made by an employer or his employees are deposited in a trust fund which is normally held by a bank or trust company, either as a corporate trustee or as a custodian acting on behalf of individual trustees. In either case the bank invests the funds and pays the benefits to those entitled under the plan. Usually, there is one document setting forth details as to the benefits provided by the program, and a separate trust agreement between the employer and a corporate trustee or individual trustees specifying the various financial and investment responsibilities.

The trust fund mechanism is one of the earliest approaches to pension funding, and descriptions of it in extensive detail are found in actuarial literature 80 years ago. The first primitive pension arrangements consisted of vague benefits paid directly by the employer. Subsequently the benefits became more specific and detailed so that they could be communicated to the worker in more specific terms, and the employers who were conscious of the financial obligations involved sought a means to discharge that obligation during the working lifetime of the beneficiaries of the plan. The clear-cut statement of benefit details has evolved into the plan document. The desire to prefund has led to the creation of a trust in order to segregate the pension plan assets from the employer's general assets and to place the plan assets beyond the reach of the employer's creditors. With more and more employers adopting such programs, various rules and regulations have been imposed under the Internal Revenue Code, the income tax regulations, IRS rulings (published and private), securities laws, labor laws, disclosure laws, and other legislative enactments, most of which apply to both trust fund plans and insured plans.

The trust fund has been a highly popular funding method for pension plans. The number of participants covered under trust fund plans and the amount of assets developed under trust fund programs are roughly double the corresponding figure for insured pension plans as shown in Table 41–1.

TABLE 41-1. Assets of All Private Pension Funds, 1961–1971 (book value, in billions of dollars)

	1961	1962	1963	1964	1965	1966	1967	1968	1969	1970	1971
Insured pension reserves (statement value)	$20.2	$21.6	$23.2	$25.2	$27.3	$29.4	$32.0	$35.0	$37.9	$41.2	$46.4ʳ
Separate accounts, included above	—	†	†	.1	.3	.6	1.2	2.2	3.5	4.9	7.1ʳ
Noninsured pension funds*	37.5	41.9	46.6	52.4	59.2	66.2	74.2	83.1	90.6	97.0	106.4
Total	$57.8	$63.5	$69.9	$77.7	$86.5	$95.6	$106.3	$118.0	$128.5	$138.2	$152.8
Percent noninsured	64.9	66.0	66.7	67.4	68.4	69.2	69.8	70.4	70.5	70.2	69.6

Note: Figures may not add to totals due to rounding.
* Includes funds of corporations, nonprofit organizations and multiemployer and union plans.
† Less than $50 million.
ʳ Revised.
Source: S.E.C. Release No. 2599, June 28, 1972, "Private Noninsured Pension Funds 1971."

NATURE OF THE TRUST AGREEMENT

The trust agreement establishes a trust fund, gives it a name, designates the trustee, and sets forth the various duties and responsibilities of the trustee under the instrument. By becoming a party to the trust agreement, the trustee agrees to perform the specified duties such as accepting contributions, investing, managing, and administering in trust the assets pursuant to the terms of the trust agreement. Often the trust agreement is separate and apart from the document setting forth the benefits to be provided under the plan, and the trustee usually has no particular administrative responsibilities under the plan other than the payment of benefits from the fund. The amount of benefit, the form of payment, the time of payment, and the recipient are furnished to the trustee by the plan's administrative committee or the employer's benefit department.

Investment of the Trust Fund

One of the most important provisions in the trust agreement instructs the trustee to invest and reinvest the principal, interest, and dividend income of the trust funds. Typically, the instructions are to invest them in securities or property, whether real or personal, including bonds, mortgages, trust and participation certificates, common stocks (listed or over the counter), preferred stock, and the like. In a number of cases, the trustee is given the specific right to invest the trust funds in pooled or commingled funds of corporate trustees, or in insurance or annuity policies. Most pension trust agreements provide that the trustee is not restricted to securities or property that may meet standards required by the local law applicable to trust investments.

Since the employer is the creator of the trust and one of the two parties to the agreement, he can impose whatever restrictions he desires on the trustee's investment activities. Examples of typical restrictions on the trustee's investments would be:

1. Restriction to a specific percentage invested in common stock.
2. Prohibition of investing the funds in any notes, property, or capital stock of the employer.
3. Limitation of investments to those that would meet the requirements for the investment of insurance company funds.
4. Maximum percentage that could be invested in the securities of a single issuer.
5. Limitation of common stock investments to those that are listed on specific exchanges, such as the New York Stock Exchange, the American Stock Exchange, and other exchanges, as opposed to securities traded over the counter.
6. Restrictions on the amount to be invested in common stock as may be set by the retirement committee from time to time.
7. Prohibition of the investment of any of the funds in puts and calls, options, futures, commodities, and the like.
8. Reservation by the employer's investment committee to approve (or reject) each investment proposed by the trustee.

Powers of the Trustee

The trust agreement, in imposing on the trustee certain duties, extends to him in general the power to take any steps that may be necessary to carry out the purposes of the trust. While these powers vary from case to case, some of the typical powers are the right to purchase property or to sell it, the power to exercise any ownership rights relating to securities held by the fund, the power to borrow or lend in the name of the trust, to employ counsel, to acquire and in some cases manage real estate, to purchase insurance or annuity contracts, to execute documents, and to settle claims and debts. In some instances, the trustee is also given authority to employ investment counsel, actuaries, consultants, and the like, as may seem desirable from time to time, and a representative of the corporate trustee may serve on a designated retirement committee established by the employer or otherwise assist in the management of the plan.

Payments from the Trust

In the usual situation, the trustee is directed by a retirement committee or by the sponsoring employer to pay benefits to specific participants or beneficiaries. In most instances, the trustee is not charged with the responsibility of ascertaining the correct amount of benefit under the plan or, for that matter, whether the particular individual designated by the employer or by the retirement committee is entitled to the benefit. In fact, the trust agreement typically directs the trustee to rely on such advice as he receives and simply to draw the checks and see that they are mailed on a prompt and efficient basis. Compensation for the trustee is usually paid directly by the employer, but such trustee fees may constitute a charge on the fund in the case of failure of the employer to pay. The trustee is also authorized to pay any taxes that might be levied on the fund assets or income. Compensation for the services of individual trustees, accountants, legal counsel, actuaries, or consultants may be paid from the fund itself or may be paid directly by the employer sponsoring the program (the latter would appear to be the more prevalent approach, but payment from the fund is not uncommon).

Record Keeping

The trust agreement usually imposes on the trustee the responsibilities to keep accurate records as to the amount of benefit payments made to each beneficiary, the monies received from the employer or employees in the form of contributions to the plan, the investments bought and sold by the fund, and the dividend and interest income received by the fund. In the usual situation, an annual statement covering these items is sent to the sponsoring employer, and there is a provision for audit. The records required of the trustee usually relate to the financial transactions of the trust itself as opposed to the record keeping that might be required for the plan, such as the amount of credited service, accrued benefits, average earnings, and so forth.

Essentially, the trustee maintains his records on an initial cost basis, generally referred to as "book value," i.e., the specific securities the trustee has purchased will be carried on the books at a value equal to the funds applied for their purchase so that the trustee can account for the proper use of all the funds with which he has been entrusted. This accounting system quite naturally requires that upon the sale of a security, any excess of the proceeds over the book value must be recorded as an addition to book value, usually called a realized capital gain, in order that the trustee be held accountable for the appropriate additional amount of funds. This traditional method of accounting for the application of trust assets and the determination on an inventory basis that the assets of the trust are actually on hand, coupled with an annual statement from the trustee listing the book value, has led to the practice of many years' standing of using such book value figures as representing the amount of assets in the fund for the determination of any required contributions in actuarial valuations and for the sufficiency of the funds to cover accrued pensions and the related funding position for the plan.

Miscellaneous Provisions

The trust agreement usually contains a provision offering immunity to the trustee or protection and indemnification of the trustee in case of unfortunate investments, failure to purchase insurance, reliance on benefit certifications, and so forth. In the usual case, the trustee would not be liable for misconduct except in cases of gross negligence on the part of the trustee or conduct which violates the so-called "prudent man" rule. The trust agreement also frequently contains a provision for the removal of the trustee or for his resignation, and for the possibility of transfer of the funds to a successor trustee or other financial institution. The trust agreement sometimes states that the adoption of the plan and the trust agreement does not create a right to employment on the part of any individual. The agreement may specifically provide that any liability of the trustee will be discharged by the payment of benefit and may extend to the trustee the right to get a receipt for any expenditures. Finally, the agreement might state that the participants' interests are not subject to alienation, anticipation, assignment, or the claims of creditors.

Amendment and Termination

By its very nature, a trust agreement is not expected to continue forever, and further, there are numerous unpredictable events that can bring about the termination or modification of the trust. Accordingly, provision for amendment of the agreement or for its termination is always included.

Since all of the types of events that might result in termination of the trust cannot be foreseen at the time of its inception, this particular provision is usually found to be silent on the specific facts that would trigger termination. In recent years, the majority of trust terminations have been due to the merger of one company with another or the replacement of one plan by another. The merger of two companies and their respective pension plans into a single trust and pension plan raises some very complex questions as to the rights of the individuals in the separate groups. For example, the merger of two companies, one having a fully funded plan and the second having a plan with more generous benefits that is largely unfunded, might result in the adoption of the more generous plan of benefits and the merger of all assets to cover those benefits so that the interests of the employees of one of the companies in the fund may be seriously diluted in the process. Some corporate trustees under such circumstances have felt that their trusteeship of the funds imposes on them the general obligation to protect the interests of the employees covered under the plan, even though the trust agreement may not impose that specific obligation on them.

PLAN DOCUMENT

The benefit provisions in a trusteed pension plan are usually set forth in a "plan document" that is separate and apart from the agreement of trust itself. This plan document is sometimes printed in booklet form and given to the participating employees, or, in the case of union-negotiated programs, the plan document may be included as part of the labor agreement in the form of a separate agreement on pension benefits.

General Rules

One of the basic matters that must be spelled out in the plan document is exactly who is entitled to benefits from the plan. Usually there is a statement with respect to the classes of employees to be covered under the program. For example, in most plans part-time employees, casual workers, and temporary employees would be excluded. In most cases, this section of the plan document would also set forth the rules on credited service and the effect of any breaks in service. Where benefits are related to pay as well as service, the types of pay that would be counted for pension credits must be defined, and it is usual to exclude overtime, commissions, bonus payments, and other nonregular compensation.[1] The plan document also would define the normal retirement age, any mandatory retirement age, and the age and/or service requirements for early retirement, disability retirement, death benefits, or vested rights.

Benefit Formula

The plan document must give the rule or the formula for determining the amount of benefit available upon retirement at normal retirement age. These benefits can be a flat monthly amount such as $50 (usually reduced pro rata for short service, say, less than 15 years), a flat monthly benefit unit for each year of service such as $7.50 monthly, a flat

---

[1] Revenue Ruling 71–446 requires that for plans with benefits integrated with social security, compensation must either be all pay subject to social security tax or it must be shown that the exclusion of certain forms of pay such as overtime cannot result in discrimination in favor of highly compensated employees. The practice under some municipal plans of basing pensions on the final year's pay including overtime has been found to encourage the older worker actively to seek work as a substitute for other younger employees in his department in order that he may accumulate unusually large amounts of overtime pay for the specific purpose of adding to his pension.

percentage of pay such as 30 percent (again reduced pro rata for service short of 15 years), or a percentage of pay such as 1¼ percent for each year of service. Pay can be defined as average compensation over the employee's entire career, or average compensation during the final 5 or 10 years of service.

In case of retirement after normal retirement age, the plan document must specify whether service credits continue or whether the career average or final average pay is to include the pay received after normal retirement age. Most commonly, the pension is frozen as of normal retirement date and there would be no increase in benefit by reason of later retirement.

Early Retirement

Benefits available at early retirement are usually expressed in terms of the regular benefit accrued to the date of retirement (i.e., the benefit determined by the benefit formula as though normal retirement age had been attained), with reduction to actuarial equivalent for the earlier age at commencement or with reduction by some formula, such as ¼ percent per month short of normal retirement age. In a growing number of plans, full benefits are provided at early retirement and sometimes there are additional "social security make-up" benefits paid to age 65 or earlier commencement of full social security.

Disability Retirement

Some plans make no special provision for employees whose employment is terminated by disability and such employees would be entitled only to whatever benefits are specifically provided for voluntary terminations or early retirements. Many plans make special provision for the employee who is totally and permanently disabled after five or ten years of service, and in a separate benefit section provide for the payment of full normal retirement benefits based on service and pay to date of disability, or projected to normal retirement age, without any reduction for earlier inception of benefit payment. The definition of disability is subject to tailor-making to fit the particular circumstances.

Death after Retirement

Almost all trusteed pension plans permit the election by the employee of various options providing for reduced benefits to the employee with a continuation after his death to a surviving beneficiary. In recent years there has been some trend toward special spouses' options that do not require full actuarial reduction in order to encourage their election by retiring employees. In a few cases the election is made the automatic form of benefit so that the employee who does not want the spouse's option has to sign a form rejecting it. Usually the election must be made three or six months prior to retirement or evidence of good health may be required.

Death before Retirement

Trust fund pension plans occasionally provide widows' pensions in case of death before retirement.[2] And, of course, under contributory plans a return of contributions with interest is customary. Widows' pensions are determined either as the amount that would have been paid if the employee had retired early and had elected a 50 percent joint and survivor option, or as a flat percentage such as a 30 percent or 40 percent of the pension accrued by the employee based on the normal retirement benefit formula and service and earnings up to the date of death.

Vested Rights

The employee terminating employment after meeting certain age and service requirements may be given a deferred benefit to commence at normal retirement age in an amount determined by the normal retirement benefit formula based on age and service to date of termination. Even where unreduced benefits are available at early retirement, the vested rights are usually deferred to normal retirement age. In some instances, graded vesting is employed where only a part of the accrued benefit is vested at the earliest service point with a year-by-year increase to 100 percent vesting after some longer period of service.

Adjustments to Benefits after Retirement

If any recurring adjustments are to be made in the benefits payable after retirement, the form of adjustment must be stated in the plan document. Such adjustments might take the form of a variable income based on the investment performance of the fund, an increase in pension benefit related to increases in the cost-of-living index, an increase in pension based on increase in pay rates for the job last held, or an increase in benefits based on increases in the standard of living. Most commonly, adjustments in pensions already being paid are made on a one-shot basis in order to compensate for a specific inflationary period, and this type of adjustment would require separate amendment to the plan document.

Plan Termination

The pension plan document usually contains a section setting forth the conditions under which the plan can be terminated or amended, and in case of termination of the plan, how the balance in the fund is to be distributed. Usually assets in the fund are allocated first to retired persons, including surviving beneficiaries with benefits payable under options, and disability pensioners. If the assets are insufficient to provide the full amount of benefit to this first group, provision would be made for a pro rata reduction of each individual's benefit with all other employees receiving no benefit whatever. If assets are sufficient to provide the full benefit to the first priority class, a second class, usually consisting of those who had already met age and service requirements for normal

---

[2] With the advent of equal opportunity regulations, widows' pensions are being extended to dependent widowers as well. Alternatively, a few plans have been able to demonstrate a comparable cost as between male employees' pensions with widows' pension and female employees' pensions without, by reason of the differential in mortality rates by sex.

retirement or early retirement, would be considered in the aggregate, again with pro rata reduction if insufficient funds are available. It is customary in such provisions to take care of the oldest employees first on the grounds that they are least able to protect themselves or to take steps to recover from any loss in pension benefit.[3]

Past Service

At the inception of a pension plan or at the time of an increase in plan benefits, it is customary to extend benefit credits to service rendered prior to the date of the plan or the amendment. In this way more adequate benefits can be provided for those workers nearing retirement age than would be possible if each individual's foregone wages or share of the cost were merely placed in a bank account for him. Of course, as plan improvements are extended backward to cover all past service, the funding progress made by the plan is set back to that extent so that in case of termination of the plan, assets would run out at an earlier point in the process of allocation to priority classes.

Labor Agreement

Where pension plans are the subject of negotiations between an employer and a union, the labor agreement usually will make provision for the establishment of the plan and incorporate the current plan document describing the benefits being agreed upon. In addition, the labor agreement also may impose on the employer a requirement to provide information on the financial operation of the plan to the union on a regular basis; occasionally, annual actuarial reports are required. The labor agreement also may set minimum objectives for the financing of the plan either in general terms with a requirement that the plan be maintained on an actuarially sound basis, or in specific detail by requiring contributions to be made in accordance with a particular funding method and amortization period for past service liabilities. The labor agreement usually specifies the effect of retirement on the employee's status and his seniority, and may impose on the employer a requirement for the deduction of union dues from the pension itself.

The typical labor agreement will give the employer the right to select either a corporate trustee or an insurance company for the funding of the plan. In some instances, the labor agreement may require the employer to hire actuaries to determine required contributions and certify as to their payment on an annual basis, and might even set forth the minimum qualifications which such actuaries must possess. Finally, the labor agreement may get into the details for the administration of the plan, such as union

---

[3] One common problem is that the termination section of the plan document is written when the plan is started and subsequent amendments made to early retirement or to the requirements for vested rights are frequently not paralleled by concurrent appropriate amendments of the plan termination section, so that some individuals who have terminated with vested rights to deferred pensions may end up in the last priority class in case of plan termination. See Carl H. Fischer, *Vesting and Termination Provisions in Private Pension Plans* (American Enterprise Institute for Public Policy Research, 1970). (Library of Congress Catalog No. 71–1411429.)

representation on a retirement committee or central board of administration, grievance procedures, and the like.

ACTUARIAL ASPECTS

The selection of the trust fund as the financing method automatically carries with it the necessity to obtain actuarial assistance in the management of the pension fund. Unlike an insured program, there is no "premium" automatically due by its terms and thus an actuary must be employed to take the employee data and the benefits under the plan and develop a long-range plan for funding those benefits. Currently the employer is permitted to deduct up to 5 percent of compensation, or, alternatively, the normal cost of the plan plus 10 percent of the unfunded past service liability. Minimum deductions are set at interest on unfunded past service liability plus the normal cost of the plan.

Funding Methods[4]

A wide variety of financing patterns have been developed for trust fund plans. The most common are the entry age normal cost method, the unit credit method, the aggregate cost method, and the frozen initial liability method. Essentially, the entry age normal cost method develops for each employee a level dollar contribution, or level percent of pay, from entry age to retirement age, which will be sufficient to fund his anticipated benefit. Under the unit credit method, the required current service contribution is simply the cost of the pension accruing in each year; as individuals approach retirement age, the required contribution per dollar of pension accrual tends to increase because the likelihood of their actually reaching retirement is greater and there is a shorter time the contribution can earn interest. Under the aggregate cost method, the present value of all prospective benefits is determined. To the extent that such benefit liability exceeds the assets, the balance is spread over all anticipated future payroll (for the present closed group of workers) as a uniform percentage of payroll. The frozen initial liability method is a special combination of the entry age normal method and the aggregate cost method where the initial past service liability is determined under the entry age normal method with that dollar amount being considered to be equivalent to an employer I.O.U. in the pension fund, and with funding from that point on proceeding as under the aggregate cost method.

While the selection of a funding method can be a complicated matter, with many ramifications, in the final analysis the particular funding method chosen merely determines the incidence of cost required to support a particular plan of benefits. Since any one of a number of funding methods may be appropriate, the choice is usually left to the actuary although, in the case of large employers, the actuaries may merely present a series of alternatives together with recommendations with the choice

---

[4] For a further discussion of pension funding considerations and actuarial cost methods, see Chapter 34.

being made by the employer or by agreement between the employer and the union. In any case, the trust fund financing method does not carry with it any specific funding method as would be the case, say, under an individual policy pension trust plan or a group deferred annuity program.

Actuarial Valuation

The process of determining the benefit liabilities and contribution requirements for a trust fund pension plan is called "actuarial valuation" and in the United States is customarily conducted annually. Triennial or quinquennial valuation is customary in England, and valuation at least every three years is required by statute in Canada. For the actuarial valuation, the employer must supply data for the individuals covered under the plan, giving age, sex, rate of pay where benefits are pay-related, and date of hire. The employer also must provide data for analysis of mortality, disability, and compensation experience of the firm. At the same time, the trustee supplies certain financial figures as to the book value and market value of trust fund assets and the rate of interest earned, assets bought and sold, and so forth, during the plan year just ended. With this basic data the actuary must then conduct the plan valuation, and in doing so must make certain basic assumptions as to the anticipated future rates of mortality, disability, interest, separation from service, retirement, salary increases, and the like. In certain of these areas the actuary is likely to be given a free hand—namely, mortality, disability, and separation. In the case of the interest rate assumed, the actuary normally will select an appropriate rate after discussion with the employer and trustee, but there are situations where the employer decides on the rate of interest after consulting with his own financial staff and the trustee or investment counsel. After the development of a set of actuarial assumptions which in the actuary's judgment are appropriate for the particular group of employees and the particular plan of benefits, the calculation of actuarial liabilities, unfunded liabilities, and the required contributions is then made. Usually the actuary presents the appropriate figures in a report to the employer and, in certain circumstances, certifies the appropriate funding progress to a union or a governmental body.

Valuation of Assets

In the development of pension costs under a trusteed retirement plan, the future contributions to be made by the employer, along with the interest earned on the initial assets, are intended to make up the difference between the pension liabilities and the assets on hand. Accordingly, the selection of an appropriate value for the assets is most important since any variation in the asset value would be translated into a decrease or increase in required contributions for the current year. For many years it was customary for actuaries to use the book value of assets as reported by trustees. In recent years, however, with significant amounts of trust fund assets being invested in common stocks having a market value that is occasionally well in excess of the book value, the selection of an appropriate asset value closer to market value has been either suggested or required by IRS, the Defense Contract Audit Agency, and the accounting profession. While the actuary is not usually responsible for, or consulted with, in connection with the selection of individual investments, the placing of a value on the trust assets so directly affects the required contribution that the actuary must be satisfied that an appropriate value has been set on the assets.[5]

Measurement of Investment Performance

The actuary, in the course of his analysis of the trust fund financial transactions, will of necessity conduct certain studies relating to the rate of investment growth of the trust fund in order to test from time to time the interest rate assumed for actuarial valuation. Fairly rough measures of investment performance generally will suffice for the determination of an appropriate interest rate for actuarial valuation. In recent years more refined studies have been suggested as a means of measuring the performance of the trustee or investment counselor and such studies may be conducted by the actuary, by an investment broker, or by a corporate trustee.[6] While such studies are primarily intended to help the plan sponsor in the selection of an investment advisor, they are also of value to the actuaries in assessing the likely course of future costs and the extent to which the interest assumption is appropriate.

RESPONSIBILITY

The Actuary

Actuaries who are members of the Society of Actuaries, the Conference of Actuaries in Public Practice, or the American Academy of Actuaries are bound by the guides to professional conduct of those various organizations. Such guides require that the member must "bear in mind that the actuary acts as an expert when he gives actuarial advice" and instruct the individual actuary to "give such advice only when he is qualified to do so." The actuary is required "to exercise his best judgment to ensure that any calculations or recommendations made by him or under his direction are based on sufficient and reliable data, that any assumptions made are adequate and appropriate, and that the methods employed are consistent with the sound principles established by precedent or common usage within the profession." Where an actuary is required to prepare a study which deviates from standard practice, his report must include "an

---

[5] One widely recognized pension expert has noted, "Certainly actuarial soundness is not independent of the investments of the pension fund. In fact, these investments are more tangibly important than are the actuary and his techniques; the fund is really the essence of the matter. I believe it is distinctly a responsibility of the consulting actuary to satisfy himself on the character of the assets." D. C. Bronson, *Concepts of Actuarial Soundness in Pension Plans* (Homewood, Ill.: Richard D. Irwin, Inc., 1957), p. 109.

[6] The Bank Administration Institute has recently published a compendium of the procedures considered appropriate for measuring investment performance and offers computer programs for member institutions as well. Cohen, Dean, Durand, Fama, Fischer, Lorie, and Shapiro, *Measuring the Investment Performance of Pension Funds for the Purpose of Inter-Fund Comparison* (Park Ridge, Ill.: Bank Administration Institute, 1968).

appropriate and explicit qualification of his findings." While the actuary is thus charged by his professional associates with the responsibility for conscientious and careful work, he usually is not in a position to insist that any recommended sums actually be deposited into the trust fund or even that the calculations be based on the specific assumptions he recommends.

In the day-to-day operation of the plan, the actuary may have the more mundane responsibility of certifying as to the benefits payable to individual pensioners, the cost of joint and survivor options, and the determination of various figures needed for personal income or estate taxes.

The Employer

In the typical situation of a trust fund pension plan covering the employees of a single employer, the basic records as to date of employment, rates of pay, date of birth, sex, dates of commencement and cessation of any leave of absence, lay-off, furlough, and so forth, are the responsibility of the employer, who must maintain sufficient internal records to supply the information necessary for the effective administration of the plan. In addition, the plan when adopted must be filed with the IRS for qualification. While the employer would usually rely on the services of legal counsel and perhaps the services of a consulting actuary for this purpose, basically the responsibility is his to see that such steps are taken to qualify the program in order to avoid the tax penalties associated with nonqualified plans.

The provisions of the Welfare and Pension Plans Disclosure Act impose certain obligations on the employer to file descriptions of the plan and, in his capacity as administrator, to file annual financial reports for the plan. In doing so the employer may make use of the services of legal counsel, actuary, and trustee. Where the employer wishes to deduct his contribution to a trusteed pension plan as a necessary and reasonable business expense, he has the responsibility of seeing that certain tax forms are filed to support the deduction. Proposed legislation regarding the administration of pension funds and requirements as to vesting, funding, and reinsurance would expand the areas of employer responsibility considerably.

The trust fund mechanism is primarily a method for accounting for certain funds and for assuring their safekeeping and their profitable investment. The funding mechanism itself, however, does not carry with it automatic actuarial, legal, and investment services as is the case with insured plans, but rather the employer must select an actuary, legal counsel, and investment advisor, and then has the responsibility of tracking the performance of each of these experts and replacing them where appropriate. Finally, within the framework of any legal requirements or specific provisions in the labor contract, the employer must decide upon the particular funding method, rate of amortization of unfunded past service, and actuarial assumptions.

The Union

Where trust fund pension plans are negotiated, the union responsibility extends to the establishment of reasonable grievance procedures so that any dissatisfied beneficiaries may have a ready avenue for complaint, and to establish such an audit on the actual operations of the program so as to assure that the program agreed upon is actually being carried out in accordance with the terms of the labor agreement. Further, the union clearly has the responsibility of continuing to sample the opinions of its members as to their benefit needs and the problem areas under the plan. In some instances, unions have felt it was necessary to consider the alternative funding methods and to specify a particular funding method in a labor agreement. There are some unions that would maintain they have a responsibility to their members to see that the actuarial assumptions being used are, in fact, reasonable and justified by the facts, and that the actuary for the plan be reasonably independent of the employer and in general agreement with the financing procedures adopted. Finally, some unions have considered it their responsibility to see that the trust funds are not only productively invested but that a reasonable spread of the investments has been allocated to socially desirable projects rather than merely to maximize investment returns.

Multiemployer Plans

The trust fund mechanism also has served as the funding instrument for pension plans set up by agreement between a number of employers in a given industry or area and a labor union. In such cases, the labor agreement usually calls for setting up a board of trustees,[7] and this board takes on many of the employer responsibilities noted previously. The board must arrange for the collection of appropriate employer records from the individual employers involved, for the qualification of the plan, the disclosure and tax forms, selection of actuary, consultant, legal counsel, corporate trustee, investment advisor, and so forth. In practice, the administration by a board of trustees tends to be dominated by the labor union representative, first, because of continuity of service of the union trustee and, second, because the union may represent a large number of employees whereas any single employer may have only a limited financial stake.

A good many multiemployer funds are set up on a basis where both the level of benefits and the level of employer contributions are specified in the labor agreement itself. Under such plans it is necessary to determine the set of actuarial assumptions that will permit the specified benefits to be supported by the specific contribution level and then test such assumptions very carefully against continuing experience. Usually it is impractical to reduce the level of benefits if it becomes obvious that they cannot be supported. The most common solution is to agree in negotiations to greater employer contributions to maintain fund solvency.

CURRENT PROBLEM AREAS

A good many of the problems facing trust fund pension plans are com-

---

[7] These "trustees" are individual persons and should not be confused with the corporate trustee responsible for investment or holding of the fund under agreement of trust. Usually there is an equal number of such individuals chosen by the union and by the employers with a "tie-breaking" trustee agreed to by both parties. Sometimes the public is represented in this tie-breaking role.

mon to pension plans generally, including insured plans. Viewed from the standpoint of trust fund plans, however, the problems may present a different aspect. Perhaps the most pressing current problem is that of inflation and its effect on the adequacy of pension benefits. Funded pension plans in France, for example, have had such a discouraging history that the French have developed a very special financing mechanism, the "repartition system," under which employers and employees agree to pay a certain percentage of wages for pensions, which amounts are then split up among the currently retired individuals. Similarly, the assets of funded pensions in Germany have stood still in several past periods while inflation drove up the need for income to such incredible levels that many of the German workers would prefer to have a pension that is not backed by assets in a separate fund but rather by the earning power of their former employer. The opposite side of this problem is the effect of a sharp drop in the market value of assets. In the long run, it might be observed that if inflation is not kept under control, any funds set aside in investments to cover pension liabilities may diminish in value to such an extent that any funding, whether through a trust or an insured program, may be meaningless.

A second problem area for trusteed retirement plans lies in the varying use of some of the benefit provisions. It is widely recognized that the incidence of disability is not independent of the economic cycle. Accordingly, many employers have expressed concern about the disability pension, the definition of disability that is employed, and the effective administration of the provision. Controls have been set up to reduce or avoid a drain on fund assets during an economic depression when the market values of the assets may be temporarily depressed and the benefit outgo for disability might otherwise rise to unrealistic levels. The trend in trust fund plans toward providing far more generous early retirement benefits at the option of the employee raises the question of whether the assets should be invested in securities that could be cashed in at times when early retirements are likely to increase.

A third problem area for trust fund plans is that much of the flexibility in financing that was formerly permitted and accepted as an advantage of trust funding has been lost through laws, rules, and regulations. Examples are the IRS minimum and maximum contribution regulations, accounting *Opinion No. 8*, the armed services procurement regulations applicable to pension reimbursement for government contractors, and the potential federal law and regulation currently under consideration.

A final specific problem area is that interest rates have currently reached an all-time high leading to the use of higher interest assumptions in plan valuations. To some extent this may lead employers to the adoption of benefits that are higher than they can eventually support if interest levels gradually drop back to a more historic norm and actuarial assumptions must be revised downward.

SIGNIFICANCE

A private pension plan is essentially a social tool for pooling the interests of a group of employees so as to provide reasonable benefits for those who are too old or ill to work. The trust fund mechanism exemplifies this pooling of interest because usually there is no separate account balance for each individual employee. All employee interests are spelled out in the plan document while the assets backing those interests are represented by a specific set of securities owned by the fund which are not naturally divisible. Because of this pooling feature, the pension plan serves a purpose different than a series of individual bank accounts and, accordingly, should be judged on how well it serves that different purpose. While this pooling of interest and unallocated funding is natural to the trust fund plan, and to those insured approaches such as deposit administration pension contracts that have been developed to match certain trust fund characteristics, it clearly runs counter to the concept of individual equity as characterized by individual policy pension trust programs or by group deferred annuity plans. Under such latter programs, recognition of past service may be limited in order to provide full funding for current service accruals. On the other hand, under the trust fund program the treatment accorded the aged and the disabled may be more generous but at a loss-of-benefit security for the young, active employees.

The trust fund plan, by its very nature, does not offer the same guarantee of benefit delivery as the purchase of an individual annuity policy. The pooling of assets will in the final analysis support a certain level of benefits which can only be estimated in advance. While the trust fund plan can only pay benefits to the extent assets are sufficient, an insured plan can, in fact, provide a guarantee that a specific dollar benefit will be paid to a specific individual (as long as the insurance company remains solvent). The value of such a guarantee decreases sharply with the prevalence of inflation. Moreover, the necessity for an insurance organization to cover the anticipated potential cost of any such guarantee leads in general to the provision of lower current benefits per dollar of plan contribution so that the present older workers really end up paying for the guarantee by getting smaller benefits.

The popularity of the trust fund as a funding instrument for private pensions derives primarily from its simplicity and flexibility. The trust fund concept is straightforward and easily understood. The trustee receives certain monies and must account for their application in the purchase of securities which are then physically held in the fund so that at any point in time the assets of the trust can be accurately inventoried without recourse to any of the complex formulas that have been developed by insurance companies to determine dividends, new money interest, and the like. Further, any charges made against the fund are clearly visible. Unions have favored the trust fund vehicle, partly because of this straightforward accounting for the fund and their feeling that any money put in the fund must eventually go to their members. Similarly, the larger employers have favored the trust fund medium because the segregation of specific investments means that the fund can be shifted to another trustee or even transferred to an insurance company without penalty.

Both unions and employers have found the flexibility in benefit design available under a trust fund plan to be most helpful. This flexibility means that the employer can gear administrative requirements to his own internal accounting practices and benefit design to employee needs. A union can negotiate for benefits on the basis of perceived need of the union members without regard to various underwriting rules, requirements for actuarial equivalence, medical examinations, advance notice, and so forth, that might be required under an insured arrangement.

On balance, the trust fund mechanism has been an efficient means of investing funds and paying benefits. The greatest area of use has been the large employer fund and the union negotiated plan. At plan termination, or sometime thereafter, it is frequently found desirable to apply the assets under an insured arrangement to provide the final guarantees. For the going plan, however, the mechanism is highly efficient and will continue to be a popular financing medium.

SELECTED REFERENCES

American Enterprise Institute for Public Policy Research. *Private Pensions and the Public Interest.* Washington, D.C., 1970.

American Federation of Labor and Congress of Industrial Organizations. *Pension Plans under Collective Bargaining.* Publication #132. Washington, D.C., 1964.

Bronson, Dorrance C. *Concepts of Actuarial Soundness in Pension Plans.* Pension Research Council, Wharton School of Finance and Commerce, University of Pennsylvania. Homewood, Ill.: Richard D. Irwin, Inc., 1957.

Bureau of National Affairs, Inc. *Pensions and Profit Sharing.* Washington, D.C., 1964.

Griffin, Frank L., Jr., and Trowbridge, Charles L. *Status of Funding under Private Pension Plans.* Pension Research Council, Wharton School of Finance and Commerce, University of Pennsylvania. Homewood, Ill.: Richard D. Irwin, Inc., 1969.

Hamilton, James A., and Bronson, Dorrance C. *Pensions.* New York: McGraw-Hill Book Co., Inc., 1958.

Houseman, Raymond F., and Riggs, Arthur J. "Some Thoughts on the Drafting of Individually Designed Self-Insured Pension Plans," The *Proceedings of the Conference of Actuaries in Public Practice,* Volume XXI, 1971–1972.

Latimer, Murray Webb. *Industrial Pension Systems.* New York: J. J. Little & Ives Company, 1932.

McGill, Dan M. *Fundamentals of Private Pensions.* Pension Research Council, Wharton School of Finance and Commerce, University of Pennsylvania. Homewood, Ill.: Richard D. Irwin, Inc., 1955.

part VII

⠿⠿⠿

Business Uses of Life and Health Insurance

AN INCREASINGLY significant and creative use of life and health insurance is in solving problems of business and professional organizations. The principal asset of most organizations is people. They are subject to premature death, disability and retirement. These events can bring about major changes in organizations from the standpoints of earnings and ownership. Part VII addresses the problems and opportunities associated with such changes, with particular emphasis on the needs of small and medium sized businesses and professional corporations.

Other *Handbook* chapters of related interest are those focusing on benefits for employees. Part V is devoted to the subject of group insurance and Part VI provides comprehensive coverage of pensions and other qualified deferred compensation plans.

42

Key Man Protection

By J. CARLTON SMITH

THE NATURE OF KEY MAN LIFE INSURANCE

A Form of Business Insurance

Key man life insurance is insurance purchased by a business firm on the life of an owner or employee whose services contribute substantially to the success of the business. The key man may be thought of as a valuable asset that is insured by his firm—in the same way that a building is insured against physical damage.

The basic motive which prompts a business firm to purchase key man life insurance is the desire to protect itself against the monetary loss which would result from the key man's premature death. All key man insurance rests on this foundation of the value to the firm of the key man's services.

Because of the purpose for which it is owned, key man life insurance is a type of business insurance. Business insurance, of course, also is used to fund buy-and-sell agreements in sole proprietorships, partnerships, and close corporations. Of these two, key man insurance is used more widely because of its applicability to publicly owned corporations in addition to closely held businesses. It is employed even by publicly owned corporations where a ready market for the stock may make a buy-and-sell agreement unnecessary.

The Human Factor in Business Success

The conclusion that the human factor is vitally important to success in business is inescapable. Studies have been made which indicate that incompetent management is the chief cause of business failure. Profits are to a large degree the result of the contributions of key men who possess the managerial skills and the experience to direct the efficient use of the material resources of the business.

Not only are human life values indispensable to the profitable ultilization of property values, but life values are more vulnerable to loss. The danger of a business experiencing a serious loss by reason of the death of a key man is much greater than the danger of a serious fire loss. Moreover, the average fire will cause only partial destruction of the property, while the death of a key man produces a total loss for the firm. The plant destroyed by fire can be rebuilt, but the key man lost through death may have possessed skills and abilities which will be difficult, if not impossible, to find in a successor.

In the same manner that property values almost universally are protected by insurance from the many hazards to which they are exposed, the business firm should protect the human assets, which are often of even greater importance.

Factors That Make a Key Man

There are a number of factors that make a person a key man for life insurance purposes. Three of these factors deserve special emphasis.

1. Skill and Knowledge. In many business firms, there is one man whose technical knowledge, experience, or particular skill make him the most valuable asset of the firm and make him almost indispensable to the successful operation of the business. A key man may be a gifted executive, a research chemist who has developed new products for the firm, an extremely capable sales manager, or a highly efficient production man. In each case, the key man possesses skill and knowledge related to the firm's affairs which could be acquired by a successor only after considerable time.

2. A Source of Business. Often the key man of a firm is a valuable source of business. He has close personal contacts with substantial buyers of the goods or services produced by the firm. Business which comes to a firm because of personal ties with a key man can very quickly go elsewhere in the event of the key man's death. Such ties break easily, and normally cannot be kept intact by the key man's successor.

3. A Source of Firm Credit. In many businesses, some one man is the chief source and strength of the firm's credit. In some cases, he is a wealthy individual, either an active or an inactive part owner of the firm, who stands ready at all times to supply needed funds. Even more frequently, such a key man is indirectly an important source of credit from banks or others because of his integrity, the size of his personal fortune, or his managerial ability.

SERVICES OF KEY MAN LIFE INSURANCE

Provides Indemnity in Case of Loss

The most effective method of offsetting the financial loss resulting from the death of a key man is to arrange for the payment of adequate life insurance proceeds to the business at the time of his death. The insurance proceeds will idemnify the business for the loss, at least in part, just as the firm would be indemnified by insurance in the case of property loss from fire, burglary, explosion, or robbery. When death strikes one of the leaders of a firm, the receipt by the business of a sizable amount of life insurance proceeds to compensate for at least a portion of the loss may be of the utmost importance to the profitable continuance of the business.

The indemnity provided by key man insurance places the firm in a better position to finance the replacement of the key man. In order to induce a man of equal experience to leave his present employer, it usually will be necessary to offer him either a substantial increase in salary or retirement benefits greater than those he now enjoys.

Accumulates a Business Emergency Fund

Permanent life insurance on the lives of active business owners and key executives provides a safe, convenient, and simple method for the gradual accumulation of a substantial emergency fund in the cash and loan values of the policies. Such insurance provides the business firm with considerable financial independence. Regardless of any stringency in general credit conditions, the firm may go to the life insurance policy and without publicity obtain the emergency funds needed by borrowing the required portion of the cash value. Furthermore, the rate of interest will never be higher than that fixed in the policy, regardless of conditions in the money market.

Many benefits are inherent in the use of permanent life insurance for purposes of accumulating a business emergency fund.

1. For the business firm, as for the individual, a plan is needed that will make the accumulation of a savings or emergency fund automatic and incidental. All business firms disburse funds on a regularly recurring basis to meet various expenses. The cash value life insurance plan involves similar periodic payments, hardly distinguishable from those made to meet expenses except that they flow into an accumulation fund to meet emergencies. Moreover, the cash value life insurance plan adds some degree of compulsion to the accumulation of the business savings fund.

2. The savings fund accumulated under the life insurance plan is invested automatically with the other funds of the life insurance company, and represents a cross section of the company's assets. Broad diversification is thus obtained. Furthermore, since the insurance plan of accumulation provides a highly specialized staff to invest the fund, the business managers are free to devote their undivided attention to the problems of operating their business.

3. The problem of "changing values" is a serious one in any plan for the accumulation of a business savings fund. Invested in normal channels, such a fund tends to reach its lowest value to the business just at the time it is needed most—in a period of financial stringency. But under the life insurance plan, values are *guaranteed in advance*. Thus, the firm is assured that the emergency fund will continue to grow even during an economic downturn.

4. To make certain that the savings fund will not be invaded for current needs, the business savings plan should provide for segregation of the funds from the regular business assets. If the fund is accumulated in cash or in other liquid form, management may be tempted to use the fund in some current business project. Under the life insurance plan, the accumulations are held by the insurance company and kept entirely apart from the firm's other assets. Though available at any time, the insurance cash value is removed sufficiently from the normal business assets so that it

generally is not looked upon as a fund available for routine business operations.

Strengthens the Credit of the Firm

Credit is the lifeblood of business. A company whose credit is dependent upon the reputation, energy, and ability of a key man may suffer a tremendous shock upon his untimely death. In such circumstances, creditors normally press for payment, and debtors have a tendency to delay payment of their obligations. Many firms have been forced into dissolution or receivership because of their inability to obtain adequate operating capital during the critical months following the death of a key man. Whether or not a business will fail in these circumstances may well hinge on the presence or absence of insurance on the key man's life, payable to the firm.

Key man insurance may have the effect of strengthening a firm's credit position, resulting in a greater volume of credit or better credit terms. There are three basic reasons why key man insurance may provide this stronger credit position.

1. Indemnity for the Loss of the Human Element. The indemnity function of insurance on the life of the key man strengthens the credit of the firm in case of the key man's death as well as during his lifetime. Lending institutions will usually renew and extend loans from time to time as long as the business is making money. But capital is timid and runs for safety at the first sign of trouble.

If the firm owns insurance on the life of the business owner or key man, at his death a large amount of cash automatically becomes available to the firm. The firm can liquidate the bank and other loans, and finance operations out of this cash fund until experience under the new management restores confidence in the business. Creditors are assured that their claims will be paid, and with this assurance are usually in no hurry for payment.

2. Evidence of Character and Stability. The maintenance of life insurance by the firm indicates character of management, and in the case of cash value insurance, it indicates the willingness and ability to save. It also indicates that the firm recognizes its responsibilities to creditors, and is evidence of the good health of the key man. Key man insurance adds stability to the business, since provisions for the insurance on the lives of the key personnel add a financial safety factor.

3. Provides Supporting Collateral for Loans. There are two basic types of loans. The first type, the collateral loan, is one secured by stocks or bonds or other evidences of wealth that are quickly marketable. The lender places his chief reliance upon his ability to sell the pledged collateral if that should become necessary to protect the loan.

The second type, the unsecured loan, is one which requires the lender to depend primarily upon the capacity of the business to produce earnings with which to pay principal and interest. Creditors must be assured that the key men of the firm will live to produce these earnings, or that the firm will be indemnified in case of the death of any one of these key management men.

If fire insurance is necessary to safeguard property values used as security for collateral loans, life insurance should likewise be employed to safeguard the human values which justify the granting of loans secured only by the general credit of the firm. Through life insurance the firm is able to capitalize these human life values of the business upon which general creditors depend so largely.

Provides a Means of Funding a Deferred Compensation Arrangement for the Key Man

Another related service of key man life insurance is that it may be combined with a deferred compensation plan for a key employee. The firm needs key man life insurance to indemnify itself for loss in event of the key man's death during his working years. It also may need a deferred compensation plan as an added inducement to a valued key man who otherwise may be receptive to offers from competing concerns. A combination key man deferred compensation plan may be adopted and funded with a single life insurance policy which performs the function both of indemnity to the firm in the event of death and of retirement income for the employee in the event of survival. Such a plan does not necessarily provide any benefits to the key man's family in the event of death during his working years, although such benefits can be provided through appropriate modifications of the plan.

KEY MAN LIFE INSURANCE ARRANGEMENTS

The Policy Provisions

Life insurance bought solely for key man indemnification is arranged more simply than other business insurance plans. No agreement between the key man and the firm is necessary, and no special contract is required. The key man is merely the subject of the insurance.

1. *The Applicant.* It is the practice of most companies to suggest that the firm apply for the insurance. The application is signed, for the firm as applicant, by an officer other than the insured. The key man also will be asked to sign to affirm the personal data appearing on the application and to acknowledge his willingness to be insured.

If a corporation is the applicant, most authorities suggest that a resolution be passed by the board of directors authorizing the purchase of the key man insurance. It is advisable for the resolution to state the purpose of the life insurance, i.e., to indemnify the corporation partially for the loss it will suffer in the event of the key man's death. The adoption of a resolution may avoid complications and lawsuits, and some life companies require that a copy accompany the application for life insurance.

2. *Payment of Premiums.* The premiums for key man life insurance are in all cases paid by the firm. This appears to be the logical arrangement in view of the fact that the insurance is bought for the sole benefit of the firm.

3. *Ownership of the Policy.* The firm is always the owner of pure key man life insurance. The insurance company will be informed that the firm

is to be the owner of the policy either by notation in the application or by separate notification. The insurance company will include a clause in the policy providing that all incidents of ownership are vested in the firm.

4. *Beneficiary Designation.* Since key man life insurance is bought primarily for the purpose of indemnifying the firm for at least a portion of the financial loss that will be sustained by the firm upon the key man's death, the firm in all cases should be named the beneficiary to receive the death proceeds.

5. *Type of Policy.* The type of policy used for key man insurance purposes should be the best suited to the needs and premium-paying ability of the firm. Perhaps the best-suited policy in the typical case is straight life, with its ideal balance between the protection and savings elements. A higher premium policy can be used where there is need for a more rapidly accumulating business reserve fund than straight life will provide, as, for example, a policy that will be paid up at retirement age. In some cases, the premium outlay the firm can afford may dictate the use of term insurance. Of course, where term insurance is used, there will be no emergency fund created during the lifetime of the key man.

6. *Waiver of Premium.* The key man insurance policy may include a waiver-of-premium provision, which would relieve the firm of premium payments during the total and presumably permanent disability of a key man, thereby freeing the dollars previously used for premiums. This would enable the firm to continue the salary of the disabled key man without adversely affecting its cash flow position.

If a key man should become disabled, it would be to the firm's advantage in most cases to retain the policy on his life. If the key man should recover, the firm would be assured of protection even if he had lost his insurability. If the key man's impaired health should dictate an early retirement, the firm could use the policy for the purpose of deferred compensation. If the disability should hasten the key man's death, the policy proceeds would indemnify the firm for the loss sustained.

Use of Existing Life Insurance

The transfer for value of an existing policy to the firm for the purpose of serving as key man life insurance may give rise to serious income tax disadvantages. If the key man is not a partner, shareholder, or officer of the firm to which the policy was transferred, the death proceeds, less the cost of purchasing the contract and any premiums paid thereafter, may be taxed as ordinary income. Such adverse tax treatment does not apply to a partnership where the insured key man is a partner, nor to a corporation where the insured key man is a shareholder or officer.[1]

Even in the absence of adverse tax treatment, perhaps in relatively few cases is it advisable to use existing life insurance. Only in rare instances will the key man be likely to own life insurance which he no longer needs as personal insurance. Typically, men tend to maintain the level of their life insurance at its highest peak and to buy additional amounts as they

---

[1] Internal Revenue Code, Sec. 101(a)(2)(B).

grow older. In most key man cases, protection in favor of the firm will take the form of newly purchased life insurance.

Disposition of the Policy if the Key Man Leaves the Firm

When the key man leaves the firm, a question may arise as to whether the firm has the legal right to continue to pay premiums during his lifetime and to receive the proceeds upon his death. The majority of judicial decisions support the general rule that a policy which is valid when issued remains valid despite later termination of the policyowner's insurable interest.

Although a firm may have the right to maintain insurance on the life of a former key man, there appears to be little justification for doing so. The basic need for the insurance for indemnification no longer exists. Therefore, it is best under most circumstances for the firm to sell the policy to the former key man, to be continued by him as personal insurance. If the key man does not wish to buy the policy, the firm may surrender it to the life insurance company. Whether sold to the former key man or surrendered to the insurance company, the cash value and the future premiums will be freed to buy key man insurance on the former key man's successor, or on the lives of other key men.

Insurable Interest

It is important in key man insurance to determine whether the business firm has an insurable interest in the key man's life at the time application for insurance is made. This is perhaps the primary legal question associated with key man insurance.

The United States Supreme Court, in an important case,[2] upheld the validity of a policy purchased on the life of the president of a corporation for the purpose of indemnifying the corporation for the loss of earning power that would occur upon the president's death. Other court decisions have held that a business can have an insurable interest in (1) a substantial stockholder or director,[3] (2) an active manager,[4] and (3) a secretary or treasurer.[5] Although insurable interest rules vary among the states, most legal authorities agree that any firm (corporate or noncorporate) has an insurable interest in any person actively associated with the firm whose continued life would be of financial benefit to the business.

Valuation of a Key Man for Insurance Purposes

Because of the intangible nature of the human life value, many view the accurate evaluation of a key man's services to the firm as an almost unsolvable problem. It is true that there is no blanket formula for the appraisal of human life values, but it is equally true that no one formula

---

[2] *United States* v. *Supplee-Biddle Hardware Company,* 265 US 189.
[3] *Keckley* v. *Conshocton Glass Company,* 86 Ohio St. 213, 99 NE 299.
[4] *Wurzberg* v. *New York Life Insurance Company,* 140 Tenn. 59, 203 SW 332.
[5] *Reilly* v. *Penn Mutual Life Insurance Company,* 201 Iowa 555, 207 NW 583.

exists in the field of property appraisals. As Dr. S. S. Huebner points out: "Expert appraisers of property values often are able to reach only fair approximations. . . . Many instances are on record where two or more groups of expert appraisers, working independently and at the same time on the appraisal of a given property, have reached conclusions that varied from 20 to 30 percent."[6]

Many examples of the difficulty of accurately valuing property can be cited. Five expert appraisals of the value of the Empire State Building would almost certainly produce five different valuations. What could be more inexact than the valuation of a producing oil well, in the face of the impossibility of knowing how long it will produce and at what rate? The conclusion is forced upon us that the valuation of all property is at best an intelligent estimate. This truth is no more or less applicable to human life valuation than to the appraisal of tangible property.

In key man life insurance cases, valuation involves primarily the value of human services. Methods of appraising the life value for family insurance purposes are equally applicable to the appraisal of the value of a key man to his firm.[7] The value of a key man may be appraised by determining the principal sum which would be lost to the firm following his death. For example, assume that a key man, aged 50, has at least 10 years of active service ahead of him, and the firm estimates that its loss of earnings would be $30,000 annually after his death. Over the 10-year period, the firm would lose $300,000 if the key man should die tomorrow. We need to determine the amount of insurance which would produce an income to the firm of $2,500 a month ($30,000 annually) for 10 years. It is a simple matter to find the answer by consulting settlement option tables in a rate book or policy.

Estimating the share of the firm's annual earnings attributable to the key man involves a careful analysis of the value of his services. If the key man is engaged in some project for the firm, the loss resulting from the abandonment of the project upon his death may be a measure of his value to the firm. If the key man's death will result in the loss of the clientele he attracts to the firm, his value may be measured by the amount of the estimated loss of such trade.

One commonly used approach to valuation takes the tangible value of the business, assumes an investment return on that tangible value, say 5 percent, deducts that amount from the average profits after taxes, capitalizes the difference by a multiple of 5 or 6, and treats the resulting figure as the earning power derived from the application of management skills to tangible assets. This figure is then divided among the key men according to their estimated contribution to the profitability of the business, and the resulting figure is the amount for which their lives are underwritten.

Another measure of the value of a key man is the "replacement cost" either of training a successor or of inducing an experienced employee engaged in the same work to leave his present firm. If a successor is to be

---

[6] S. S. Huebner, *The Economics of Life Insurance* (3d ed.; New York: Appleton-Century-Crofts, Inc., 1959), p. 59.

[7] *Ibid.*, pp. 47–48.

trained, there will necessarily be a loss attributable to the less skillful performance of the duties involved. If a replacement is to be employed, it will be necessary to offer a higher salary or other costly inducement for him to leave his present employer.

From a practical standpoint, the factor of greatest importance is the acquisition without undue delay of a reasonable amount of insurance protection against the premature death of the key man. It is far better for a firm to hedge even partially against this potential loss than to delay indefinitely in search of an exact and scientific measure of the key man's value. In practice, the amount of coverage will usually be established by the owners in a more or less arbitrary fashion. In many cases, the amount of key man insurance will be determined by the amount of premium outlay the firm feels it can afford on a permanent basis, even if the protection is admittedly only a fraction of the key man's value to the firm.

Whatever approach is employed in arriving at the valuation of the key man's services for life insurance purposes, it should be remembered that there is some maximum amount of coverage which the insurance company will issue on a given key man's life for the specific purpose of indemnifying the firm for the loss caused by his death. It is the duty of the home office underwriter to see that the amount of life insurance bears a reasonable relationship to the value of the key man to the firm. The typical limit for this purpose appears to be an amount equal to about five times the key man's annual earnings as a rule of thumb, with provision for issuing somewhat more in particular cases. The rationale of this limit appears to be that it is presumed that in most cases a replacement for the deceased key man can be found and completely trained within a five-year period.

TAXATION OF KEY MAN LIFE INSURANCE

Federal Income Tax

Deductibility of Premiums. Key man life insurance premiums are not deductible as a business expense. The Internal Revenue Code provides that no deduction is allowed for "premiums paid on any life insurance policy covering the life of any officer or employee, or any person financially interested in any trade or business carried on by the taxpayer, when the taxpayer is directly or indirectly a beneficiary under the policy."[8]

Increase in Cash Values. A large number of business firms carry substantial life insurance cash values on their balance sheets.[9] It is usual accounting practice to write up each year the increase during the current year in cash values of company-owned life insurance. Such increases in cash values, including those on key man life insurance, are not subject to federal income taxation.

Suppose the key man leaves the firm, and the firm wishes to surrender the policy to the life insurance company for its cash value. There is a

---

[8] Internal Revenue Code, Sec. 264(*a*)(1).

[9] Todd Planning and Service Company, *Corporations Owning Substantial Amounts of Business Insurance* (Chicago: National Underwriter Co., 1970).

monetary gain if the cash surrender value received exceeds the aggregate net premiums and other consideration paid.[10] The gain is taxable as ordinary income.[11] If a loss results from the surrender of a policy, it is normally looked upon as the cost of insurance protection and is not deductible.

Taxability of Proceeds. Life insurance proceeds received by a firm upon the death of a key man generally are not subject to federal income taxation. The Internal Revenue Code provides that ". . . gross income does not include amounts received . . . under a life insurance contract, if such amounts are paid by reason of the death of the insured."[12] This rule applies to sole proprietors, partnerships, and corporations as beneficiaries.[13] An exception to the rule exists if the beneficiary is not an exempt transferee of a policy transferred for value as is indicated above in the discussion of "Use of Existing Life Insurance."

Accumulated Earnings Tax. The Internal Revenue Code provides for a penalty tax, called the accumulated earnings tax, on corporate income unreasonably accumulated.[14] In general, the tax is levied whenever the corporation allows earnings in excess of $100,000 to accumulate in reserves and corporate surplus beyond the reasonable needs of the business. Corporations may engage in this practice in order to avoid distribution of income and so reduce the individual income tax liability of stockholders.

The loss to the corporation that can occur as a result of the death of a key man is well recognized, and the purchase of life insurance to offset that loss is clearly a purpose within "the reasonable needs of the business." The opinion in the celebrated Emeloid[15] case included the famous query, "What corporate purpose could be considered more essential than key man insurance?" The decision went on to say, "The business that insures its buildings and machinery and automobiles from every possible hazard can hardly be expected to exercise less care in protecting itself against the loss of two of its most vital assets—managerial skill and experience."

The purchase of key man life insurance by a corporation should not invite the accumulated earnings tax if there is a genuine need for the protection and if the type of policy is appropriate and the amount of insurance is reasonable in light of the insured's value to the firm. The type of policy generally should be in keeping with the indemnification objective. The underwriting practices of insurance companies ordinarily will prevent the issue of an excessive amount of insurance on a key man's life.

Despite the substantial amounts of key man life insurance owned by corporations, there have been no rulings or court cases involving the relationship between corporation-owned key man life insurance and the accumulated earnings tax since the passage of the 1954 Internal Revenue Code.

---

[10] Internal Revenue Code, Sec. 72(*e*).

[11] *Avery* v. *Commissioner,* 111 F.(2d) 19.

[12] Internal Revenue Code, Sec. 101(*a*) (1).

[13] Regulation 1.101–1(a); *United States* v. *Supplee-Biddle Hardware Company,* 265 US 189.

[14] Internal Revenue Code, Secs. 531–37.

[15] *The Emeloid Co., Inc.* v. *Commissioner,* 189 F.(2d) 230, CA-3, 1951.

Federal Estate Tax

Taxation of Key Man Insurance Proceeds. Life insurance proceeds are included in the estate of the insured for federal estate tax purposes (1) if they are payable to or for the benefit of his estate; or (2) if payable to others, he possessed any incidents of ownership in the policy on the date of his death.[16]

In key man life insurance, the firm ordinarily possesses all incidents of ownership and is the beneficiary. The proceeds are not paid to the key man's estate, nor does he possess any incidents of ownership in the policy on the date of his death. The proceeds therefore are not includable in the key man's estate.

Effect of Insurance on Value of Key Man's Stock. A key man in a corporation is often a stockholder as well. A question arises as to whether the life insurance proceeds received by the corporation after the key man's death increase the value of his stock for purposes of determining his federal estate tax liability. The cases which have considered the problem seem uniform in holding that life insurance proceeds paid to a corporation under a key man policy are corporation assets to be considered in valuing the corporation's stock included in the insured key man's estate.[17] It may therefore be concluded that in the absence of offsetting factors, the receipt by the corporation of key man life insurance proceeds will increase the value of the key man's stock for estate tax purposes.

A factor which may partially or wholly offset the effect of the life insurance proceeds on the value of the key man's stock is the loss the corporation sustains because of the key man's death. If, for example, the amount of key man proceeds is $100,000 and it can be shown to the satisfaction of the tax authorities that the corporation sustained a loss of $100,000 as a result of the key man's death, the value of the key man's stock should not be increased by virtue of the existence of key man insurance on his life. It has been held, however, that the loss sustained by the corporation must be adequately proved by the key man's estate in order to support a reduction in the value of the stock for estate tax purposes.[18] The adoption of a resolution by the board of directors authorizing the purchase and the payment of premiums, and stating the purposes for which the insurance is being purchased, is perhaps the most acceptable evidence in establishing the fact of loss to the firm upon the death of a key man.

It should be noted that where the key man is a sole stockholder, he will be deemed to have an incident of ownership in the corporate-owned key man life insurance policy by virtue of his 100 percent stock ownership.[19] However, where the life insurance proceeds themselves are includable in

---

[16] Internal Revenue Code, Sec. 2042.

[17] *Estate of W. A. Blair*, 4 BTA 959; *Estate of Edward Doerken*, 46 BTA 809; *In re Reed's Estate*, 243 NY 199, 153 NE 47; *In re Patton's Will*, 227 Wis. 407, 278 NW 866.

[18] *Estate of Scherer*, BTA Memo., 10–25–40.

[19] Reg. Sec. 20.2042(1)(c)(2).

the insured's estate, such proceeds should not also be used to increase the estate tax value of the insured's stock in the corporation.[20]

Preoccupation with the effect of the life insurance proceeds on the value of the key man's stock for estate tax purposes should not be permitted to obscure the fact that the key man's estate will enjoy a gain through the possession of stock in a corporation which has received life insurance proceeds as a tax-free addition to surplus. If the tax authorities refuse to recognize the loss to the corporation of the key man's services as an offsetting factor, the gain is merely diminished, but not eliminated.

KEY MAN HEALTH INSURANCE

The Need

The total and permanent disability of a key man can result in as serious a loss to the business as that occasioned by the death of a key man. In either case, the services of the key man are permanently lost to the firm. Moreover, the incidence of the risk of total and permanent disability during the years of active employment is greater than that of death. The conclusion is inescapable that the need of business firms for this type of protection is great. Despite this fact, key man health insurance has not been widely employed up to the present. This may be due, in part, to the fact that business uses of health insurance are a relatively recent development, and in part to the limitations which are presently inherent in the use of health insurance for key man indemnification purposes.

Purpose of Key Man Health Insurance

The purpose of pure key man insurance, either life or health, is to indemnify the business for the loss caused by the premature cessation of the key man's services. This discussion will treat the use of health insurance as a means of indemnifying the firm for the loss occasioned by the total and permanent disability of a key man. The uses of health insurance to provide fringe benefits for key men and other employees will not be discussed, as they are treated elsewhere in this *Handbook*.

Indemnification for Loss through Life Insurance

Assuming that the key man's disability is destined to be truly total and permanent, the measure of the loss of his services to the firm is the same as that resulting from his death. Any life insurance which the firm owns on the key man's life may be retained for the purpose of ultimately reimbursing the business for a portion of this loss, but the recovery through that method may be long deferred because of the key man's continued life. If such life insurance bears the disability waiver-of-premium rider, the firm will enjoy some measure of immediate indemnity through being excused from paying further premiums. Other than this small indemnity, however, the recovery by the firm through life insurance of at least a

---

[20] *Cockrill* v. *O'Hara,* 302 F.Supp. 1365 (1969).

substantial portion of the loss caused by the key man's disability may be long delayed.

Indemnity for Loss through Health Insurance

A more immediate and continuing indemnification for the loss caused by the total and permanent disability of a key man is available through the medium of health insurance, subject to the limitations which are discussed below. A business may arrange for the indemnification of at least a portion of that loss through the purchase of a disability income policy on the key man's life. The business will own, pay the premiums on, and be the beneficiary of the policy. The premiums are not deductible by the firm on the ground that the premiums are expenses paid to acquire tax-exempt income.[21] The disability income, regardless of amount, is wholly tax-exempt to the firm.[22]

Indemnity through Health Insurance—an Example

In the discussion earlier in this chapter of the valuation of a key man's services for life insurance purposes, an example was used in which it was assumed that the key man is aged 50 and that the loss to the firm will be $30,000 annually in the event of his premature death. Assuming further that the key man's salary is $24,000 annually, this example may be employed to illustrate the use of health insurance as a means of partially indemnifying the firm for the loss (equal to that caused by death) of the key man's services because of his total and permanent disability. It will not be possible to provide for total indemnification for the $30,000 annual loss, as health insurers commonly limit rather strictly the amount of disability income coverage which can be purchased. Such limitations are essential to protect the insurer, but they vary widely among companies. A typical limitation on coverage may be approximately 50 percent of the monthly earnings from the insured's occupation. In our example, the key man earns $2,000 a month, and $1,000 a month in disability benefits will be the limit of purchase permitted by the 50 percent limitation. The purchase by the firm of a disability income to age 60 or 65 policy on the key man's life will therefore provide for the indemnification of $12,000 of the $30,000 annual loss assumed. While not indemnifying the firm for the loss of the key man's services, the receipt of $12,000 a year will help cushion the effect upon the firm of the loss of the key man's services. Coupled with the money freed by virtue of the waiver of premium feature taking effect on the key man life insurance, the cushioning effect is maximized.

The Indemnity Motive—Practical Limitations

Provision by a business for indemnification in the event of the disability of a key man is not as feasible as is the provision for indemnification in the

---

[21] Internal Revenue Code, Sec. 265(1); Rev. Rul. 66–262, 1966–2 CB 105.

[22] Internal Revenue Code, Sec. 104(a)(3); Rev. Rul. 66–262, supra; *Castner Garage, Ltd.*, 43 BTA 1.

event of death. It has been seen that key man life insurance provides for indemnification only on a deferred basis, as the ultimate death of the key man must be awaited. Health insurance also has its limitations as a means of indemnification of the loss caused by disability.

1. *Limitation of Coverage.* It has been seen in the example given above that the amount of disability income coverage obtainable normally will be somewhat less than the amount of the loss sustained each year by the firm. In any case where the annual loss to the firm because of the key man's disability is as high as or higher than the key man's salary, it usually will not be practicable to provide for more than 40 to 70 percent indemnification of loss.

2. *Effect upon Key Man's Personal Coverage.* The purchase of disability income insurance by the firm on the key man's life may materially limit the key man's ability to obtain disability income protection for the benefit of himself and his family. There is a very real limit to the amount of disability income coverage which any given key man's salary income will sustain. If the firm owns the maximum limit for indemnity purposes, the key man may be unable to purchase any additional amount as personal coverage.

3. *Reluctance of Firm to Retain Benefits if Key Man Not Covered.* Perhaps a majority of business managers would be reluctant to receive disability income payments for the indemnification of the firm while at the same time the key man and his family were suffering extreme financial hardship as a result of the disability. If, under these circumstances, the firm pays over to the key man the payments it receives from the insurance company, there has been no indemnification of the firm for the loss of the key man's services.

The Indemnity Motive—Conclusions

The limitations of health insurance for key man purposes seriously restrict its broad use, but do not prevent its feasibility in the proper sets of circumstances. As to the limitation on coverage, surely a 40 to 70 percent indemnification goes a long way toward softening the blow to the firm of suddenly losing the services of a valued key man. The second and third limitations discussed above lose their effects in cases where the key man will have an adequate income in the event of disability provided by personal savings or a salary continuance plan, or both. There may be relatively few such cases, and this appears to be the area which most greatly restricts the use of health insurance for key man indemnification purposes. The limitations of key man health insurance are real and vital, and they should be given careful consideration in planning for key man indemnification purposes.

Key Man Disability Indemnification—Conclusions

It has been seen that neither key man life insurance nor key man health insurance provides for total and immediate indemnification to a firm for the loss caused by the total and permanent disability of a valued key man. The indemnification through life insurance must await the key man's death, while that through health insurance is only partial because of limits of coverage.

Perhaps the ideal means available to a firm of providing for something approaching total indemnification for the loss of a key man's services because of disability is through the use of a combination of key man life insurance and key man health insurance. Key man health insurance provides a means (subject to the limitations discussed above) of recovering from 40 to 70 percent of the annual loss on a continuing basis until the key man dies or reaches retirement age. Key man life insurance may be continued on the key man's life (without the necessity of paying premiums if the waiver-of-premium provision is included) so as ultimately to provide for the recovery of the remainder of the loss. Thus the combined use of key man life insurance and key man health insurance accomplishes an end which cannot be achieved by the use of either coverage standing alone.

SELECTED REFERENCES

Dickerson, O. D. *Health Insurance*. Rev. ed. Homewood, Ill.: Richard D. Irwin, Inc., 1968.

Dornfeld, Kivie. "Taxation Affecting Health Insurance," *Journal of the American Society of Chartered Life Underwriters*, Vol. XVIII, No. 4 (Fall 1964), pp. 359–74.

Harmelin, William, and Osler, Robert W. *Business Uses of Health Insurance*. Bryn Mawr, Pa.: American College of Life Underwriters, 1969.

Huebner, S. S. *The Economics of Life Insurance*. 3d ed. New York: Appleton-Century-Crofts, Inc., 1959.

McCaffrey, C. B. "Some Practical Uses of Life Insurance in Modern Business," *Journal of the American Society of Chartered Life Underwriters*, Vol. XIII, No. 4 (Fall 1959), pp. 370–81.

National Underwriter Company. *The Diamond Life Bulletins Service: Business Insurance Volume*. Cincinnati. Loose-leaf Service.

————. *Selling Business Health Insurance*. Cincinnati, 1961.

Research and Review Service of America, Inc. *Advanced Underwriting and Estate Planning Service*, Vol. II. Indianapolis. Loose-leaf Service.

Smith, J. Carlton. *Key Man Uses of Life Insurance*. Bryn Mawr, Pa.: American College of Life Underwriters, 1964.

Wolfe, Don M. "Business Uses of Health Insurance," *Weekly News Review Digest*, April 1, 1961, pp. 1–6.

43

Nonqualified Deferred Compensation Plans

By CHARLES B. McCAFFREY

DEFERRED COMPENSATION arrangements are, and will continue to be, an important part of the executive compensation package. Among the factors contributing to this result are progressive income tax rates and the requirement of accounting on an annual basis for tax purposes. It is quite apparent that an individual with high earnings bunched within a relatively few years bears a heavier income tax burden than another with the same aggregate income spread over a longer period.

Inflation is another factor to be considered. Salary increases designed to compensate for the declining value of the dollar tend to push taxpayers into higher brackets and are thus somewhat self-defeating.

It is worth noting at this point that the current 50 percent maximum tax on earned income[1] can prove quite illusory to anyone who has, in addition, investment income. The reason for this is that the unearned income is taxed at the rates that would be in effect if there were no limitation on the tax on earned income. The increased earned income pushes the unearned income into higher brackets. While this seemingly only increases the tax on the investment income, realistically the effect is to push the rate of tax on the earned income well beyond the supposed 50 percent figure.

Nature of Deferred Compensation

Deferred compensation, as the term implies, embraces those arrangements under which services performed in the present are compensated for in the future. It is normally expected that through these devices payment will be made to the employee at a time when his tax bracket will be much lower.

The most widely used of all these arrangements are the so-called "qualified plans" under Section 401–404 of the Internal Revenue Code. But the broad base coverage and nondiscriminatory requirements of these plans make them inappropriate when the object is to benefit a few selected high-

---

[1] I.R.C., Sec. 1348.

salaried executives. Many employers with well-established pension or profit sharing plans desire to offer additional benefits to a limited number of executives whose need for and ability to demand deferment exceeds that of the general rank and file personnel. Consequently, many such corporate employers and their executives eventually turn to some form of the "nonqualified plan" of deferred compensation. In this way they hope to meet more fully their desire to reduce the tax burdens on the executive and to assure him an adequate income for his inactive years.

CONTRACTS AND PROVISIONS

A study of deferred pay contracts, as they are being written today, will reveal a wide variety of provisions. But as in automobiles and apparel, there is a prevailing unmistakable style.

Ordinarily, the employer agrees with one or more employees to pay a stipulated sum, for a fixed period or for life, commencing at retirement. The contract frequently provides benefits for the widow or other designated beneficiary in the event of the employee's prior death. Currently, the trend is toward including some form of disability benefits. The benefits are usually payable in cash, but may be in stock or a combination of both cash and stock.

Most agreements contain contingencies of varying degrees of substance. The great majority provide for future consulting services and ordinarily prohibit competitive activities. In some, the future payments are made contingent upon the employee's remaining with his employer until retirement or other agreed upon termination. Others will make the payout dependent on the future financial status of the employer or on the outside income of the employee.

It is important to distinguish at this point between a contract which agrees to defer to the future what the employee could have had today, and one offering additional future benefits to certain key executives on a selective basis. In other words, there is a considerable difference between being offered additional income on a deferred basis and electing to defer what is, in a sense, one's own income. The relative bargaining strengths would, of course, differ depending upon the nature of each case. Consequently, the number and substance of the contingencies written into the contract will vary accordingly. It can be concluded that the reason for such forfeiture clauses is not solely dependent on tax considerations. They can have a considerable effect on employer-employee relationships. The additional compensation type of deferment (as contrasted with the reduction type) can offer executive retention insurance, and act as a financial lure to attract executive personnel of other companies. No progressive employer today can afford to overlook the practical value of this type of inducement in obtaining and retaining top calibre management. The importance of these varying contingencies, from a tax point of view, will now be considered.

INCOME TAX CONSIDERATIONS

Assume that for each year an employee performs prior to retirement or other termination, his employer agrees to pay him or his designated beneficiary—in addition to any other current compensation—the sum of $10,000 in annual installments commencing on the first day of the year following said retirement or other termination. Assume further that there are no "ands," "ifs," or "buts" to this contract but that it is completely nonforfeitable insofar as the employee or his beneficiary is concerned. Query: On what legal basis, if any, will the employee be taxed currently on the sums promised for the future?

Constructive Receipt

To be taxed currently under the well-established doctrine of constructive receipt, the income in question must be credited to, or set aside for, the taxpayer without "any substantial limitation or restriction" as to the time or manner of payment and must be available to him "so that it can be drawn at any time." Except in situations where the deferment is contractually arranged after the compensation has been earned and is due, the employee must have a present, unfettered right to the income in order for the doctrine to apply.

A most interesting case in point is *Hyland* v. *Commissioner*.[2] The taxpayer was president and 85 percent owner of a personal service corporation. He kept his books and filed his income tax returns on the cash receipts and calendar year basis. The corporation was awarded two Navy contracts with respect to which the taxpayer performed valuable services during 1942 without any contract as to his compensation until December 23, 1942. On that date the directors voted to pay him $40,000 for his services which was to cover the period from February 1, 1942 to January 31, 1943 (the corporation's fiscal year). On March 6, 1943, the $40,000 was paid to him. Since it was admitted that $34,166.66 of this sum was for services rendered in 1942, the main issue was whether that amount should be taxed in the year of actual receipt or in the earlier year under the doctrine of "constructive receipt."

The tax court decided on the merits that the sum in question was not constructively received by the taxpayer in 1942. This decision was affirmed on appeal.

"There is nothing," said the higher court, "aside from his stock ownership, to indicate that he could have obtained any of the money at any time before the whole of it was paid to him on March 6, 1943."

It is contended "that he had unrestricted control of this sum because all he had to do to receive it was to draw a check for this amount. No doubt it is true that the taxpayer by reason of his very large stock ownership, could have effectively directed the various agents having charge of the corporation's bookkeeping and financial affairs to take action to make available to him the necessary cash and to draw a check in his favor for the amount claimed by him for the 1942 services. But he did not do so . . . The argument that the rule of constructive receipt becomes applicable with the mere possession of such power, without any indication of an intent to exercise it, proves too much. It would mean that in every close corporation the corporate earnings are immediately constructively received by the controlling stockholder provided their withdrawal would not make the corporation insolvent. But the law ordinarily treats a corporation and its con-

---

[2] Court of Appeals of the United States, Second Circuit, 175 F.2d 422 (1949).

trolling stockholder as separate juristic persons, and they are separately taxable." In invoking the doctrine of constructive receipt, it must be proved that the requirements of the Regulations have been satisfied. Such proof is not made "merely by showing that he owns more than 50% of the corporation's outstanding stock. Accordingly, the taxes for the year in suit should be imposed as they would be if the (taxpayer) were not the corporation's controlling stockholder."

Two things are worth noting in this case:

1. The executive-employee was controlling stockholder of the employer-corporation;
2. There were no express contingencies in regard to the payment of the compensation due him for past services rendered.

If a majority stockholder is not in constructive receipt of a nonforfeitable right to monies due him for past services, *a fortiori*, an executive who owns no stock at all or who, at most, is a minority holder, would certainly not be.

Since, by its very nature, a deferred compensation arrangement of the type under discussion precludes sums being "drawn at any time" by the employee, it can be concluded that the doctrine of constructive receipt has no application at all in the type of case under discussion. This conclusion would be valid regardless of whether the employee's rights under the contract are forfeitable or not.

Economic Benefit

If an executive, under the proposed arrangement, is to be taxed prior to his actual receipt of the cash payment, it would have to be under the "economic benefit" doctrine. This doctrine embodies the "payment in kind" or "cash equivalent" principle. It has been applied successfully in cases involving delivery to an employee of commercial annuities, rent-free properties below their fair market value, and the like.

For example, in the Brodie[3] case an executive received a nonassignable annuity contract in payment of his share of a bonus. The contract provided for the payment of an annuity to begin at age 70 and for death benefits payable to the employee's designated beneficiaries. The employee never had the opportunity to choose between cash and the annuity, consequently the doctrine of "constructive receipt" could not have been invoked successfully. Nevertheless, the employee was taxed on the full cost of the annuity. The Court found that the payment was for his (the employee's) benefit—and the contract so purchased was issued in the name of the annuitant and was delivered to him and was part of the plan for his additional renumeration.

Likewise, in the Morse[4] case, the result was the same on somewhat similar facts. There the Chrysler Corporation had a key employee too old to participate in the firm's regular pension plan. Prior to his retirement date, the corporation purchased a single-premium annuity policy for the purpose of providing some retirement benefits. The ownership and all

---

[3] *Renton K. Brodie,* 1 T.C. 275 (1942).
[4] *Eliot C. Morse,* 17 T.C. 1244 (1952).

rights under the policy were vested in the Chrysler Corporation. When the employee retired two years later, the corporation transferred all rights in the policy to him. At the same time, the policy was endorsed with a provision making it nonassignable and prohibiting commutation, anticipation, or encumbrance. In other words, the employee had no right to any cash surrender value. He was only entitled to the annuity payment each year. Nevertheless, the Court held that the entire value of the policy constituted income to the employee in the year in which it was delivered to him.

Bare Promise versus Commercial Annuity

It is important to note that both of the above cases are concerned with commercial annuities purchased from an insurance company and transferred to the employee. We are no longer dealing with a mere promise by an employer to make future payments to an employee, but have shifted the obligation to an institution engaged in the business of making such promises. Therein lies the difference and it is sufficient to justify the taxing of the economic value to the employee. On the other hand, there has been no case holding that a mere contractual right to future payments of compensation, whether forfeitable or nonforfeitable, is of sufficient tangible benefit to constitute the realization of income by a cash-basis taxpayer. In fact, in the relatively few instances in which this question has arisen, the authorities have taken the opposite view. The distinction seems to turn on the difference between a commercial annuity contract purchased from an insurance company, and a promise of payment made by an employer to an employee. In the first instance there is income without receipt, in the second there is not. Why? Is there really any substantial difference between a commercial annuity contract and a promise of a large, unquestionably solvent corporation? Assuming, for the sake of discussion, there is little or no difference between the two, how many employers are large and unquestionably solvent? Most are not. Ninety percent of corporations employ less than 50 people. The annual corporate death rate is another significant factor. Would it be administratively practical to make tax consequences depend on the size and solvency of the individual employer-obligor? In this light, it seems to make sense to continue the distinction between insurance company contracts and promises made by other employers.

Cash and Accrual Accounting

There is another and more important reason for maintaining the position that a mere right to future payment is not equivalent to cash receipt. To hold otherwise would be to upset the well-established basic difference between cash and accrual accounting. For example, "A," a physician, performs surgery on "B" in November. "A" bills "B" in December. "B" pays "A" in January of the following year. Since there is a promise to pay express or implied, running from "B" to "A" for the services rendered, in what year should "A," a cash-basis taxpayer, report the particular fee as income? Suppose "B's" employer, a "large and unquestionably solvent" corporation, agreed with "A" to pay all of "B's" surgical expenses, should the result be any different? Of course not. In either case "A" would report the fee as income in the year in which he actually received it. This has to be the result unless the IRS is prepared to force "A" and others like him onto the accrual basis of accounting. Up to now there has been no indication from the IRS that it is contemplating any such move.

Rights Vested or Contingent

It should be noted that up to this point, the discussion has concerned a vested contractual right to payment sometime in the future. No mention has been made of contingencies. If a vested contractual right has been held nontaxable currently, it would seem all the more remote that a contingent right would be deemed taxable. Consequently, a good many executive deferred compensation contracts are written in such a manner as to make the deferred payment forfeitable if a breach of certain conditions should occur. This is as good a point as any to recall the distinction between an employee agreeing to perform services for deferred income in lieu of current cash as contrasted with an employer offering an additional deferred benefit in the nature of an informal, nonqualified pension for one or more key employees on a selective basis. In the one case it is the employee's own money in a sense; in the other it is the employer's. Obviously, whatever forfeiture provisions are contemplated can be made much stronger in the one case than in the other. It would depend, for the most part, on the relative bargaining positions of the contracting parties. Naturally there are those who will accept supplementary deferred income on a contingent basis, who would not consider deferring on the same basis what they might have had in cash currently. It is simply an application of the old "bird in the hand worth two in the bush," or "take the cash and let the credit go" philosophy. Yet the current style in drafting deferred compensation contracts is to include contingencies of varying degrees of substance.

Some of the typical forfeiture provisions are as follows:

1. A requirement that the employee continue in service for a specified period. Whatever value, if any, such a provision might have would disappear completely as soon as the employee had worked the required period.
2. A typical provision requires that the employee refrain from competition after retirement. One might ask who would be inclined to compete at age 65 or 70 and, if so, with what company? Furthermore, such a contingency, if too broad as to time and place, may be deemed an invalid restraint and thus unenforceable. On the other hand, if the covenant is too narrow, the courts may ignore it as having no substance.
3. Another feature frequently found in deferred compensation agreements is the requirement that the retired employee be available in a consulting capacity. It would seem that if any substance is to be attached to such a contingency, the provision should state clearly the nature and frequency of the consulting service required.
4. In some cases conditions are inserted which make payments dependent upon other earned income of the employee or upon the amount of net

income before taxes of the employer. The former, since entirely under the control of the employee, ought to have considerably less substantive effect than the latter. At the very least, the latter provision should tend to depress the value of the economic benefit upon which the tax might possibly be imposed.

To summarize, the current practice in regard to deferred compensation contracts is to insert one or more contingencies. Presumably, the prevailing belief is that such arrangements, from a tax point of view, will thereby be strengthened.

FUNDING THE DEFERRED COMPENSATION AGREEMENT

Technically speaking, the term "funded" in the deferred compensation area refers to amounts set aside for the benefit of an employee and placed beyond the employer's control. Such a fund is usually placed in trust or in an escrow account and is completely segregated from the employer's general assets.

At first glance this would appear to be the ideal arrangement. The Code specifically provides that contributions to this type of segregated fund are deductible by the employer to the extent that the employee's rights in the fund are *nonforfeitable*.[5] Unfortunately, if the employee's rights are nonforfeitable, he will be taxed currently on the employer's contributions.[6] This latter result is enough in itself to preclude the use of a fully vested nonforfeitable trust or escrow arrangement.

The next step suggests making the employee's rights to the segregated fund *forfeitable*. Although the employer would have to forgo a current income tax deduction on the contributions, the employee will not be taxed until the amounts become vested or are paid to him. The problem with this arrangement is that the employee's rights in the fund must at all times be subject to substantial forfeiture provisions.[7] Otherwise, the entire fund could become taxable to him or his beneficiary in one taxable year.

At this writing, there is a great deal of uncertainty as to just what type of forfeiture provisions will be acceptable by the IRS as being of a substantial nature. Because of the income tax uncertainties and disadvantages associated with plans funded outside the employer-firm, the great majority of nonqualified deferred compensation contracts are really not funded in the technical sense. The employee-participant must look to the unsecured promise of the employer to fulfill the latter's contractual obligations.

Intra-Company Funding

Nevertheless, some type of funding process strongly suggests itself. The firm has a liability to meet in the future. To ignore it for the present would be equivalent to overstating current profits. Sound business practice

---

[5] Sec. 404(a)(5).
[6] Sec. 402(b).
[7] I.R.C., Sec. 83.

would require a sinking fund in which annual deposits are made sufficient to produce the sum necessary to meet the obligation when it becomes due.[8] Such a fund would remain within the firm. The firm would own it. The employee would be given no rights in it whatsoever. Since the employee has no interest in the fund, since he cannot, at any time, compel a distribution from it, the fund should in no way alter or disturb the tax status of the proposed agreement. Of course, the employer-firm cannot deduct the annual deposits to the fund, but, instead, will deduct the payments made from it to the employee at a later date. The employee will then be taxed as he receives the payments.

Use of Life Insurance

Funding can be in the form of cash, securities, annuities, or life insurance. Since, under many deferred compensation plans, the employer-firm will be assuming obligations that may be accelerated in the event of death or disability, insurance on the lives of the employees involved would appear to be the most appropriate funding instrument. The type of policy to be used would depend upon the individual circumstances in each case. A nonparticipating endowment or a participating endowment on a net basis usually can be made to fit in very well. A straight life policy may be used if the emphasis is to be on protection. For the average deferred compensation case, however, the paid-up-at-65 whole life contract on a gross basis seems to offer the greatest flexibility. The dividend each year can be used to purchase paid-up additions, thus increasing the build-up of cash values, so that the aggregate amounts available at age 65 will be sufficient to fund the entire pay-out.

COST CONSIDERATIONS

Where a deferred compensation plan is funded by life insurance, the following facts should be clearly understood. The required annual premium deposit consists of two things:

1. A capital transfer (cash into policy cash values). This part of the transaction can be likened to a transfer of corporate surplus funds into a savings account, government bonds, or some other type of fixed-dollar investment. It should be noted that the interest earnings on the fund are currently free of federal income tax.
2. An expense (the charge for the insurance element).

Neither segment of the premium deposit is a deductible item. Obviously, there could be no more expectation of deducting the capital transfer portion than of deducting a deposit to a bank account. As for the expense portion, it is not deductible because it is not considered a true expense of operating the business. In fact, there is a specific provision in the Code

---

[8] An approach that has proved quite successful in a number of cases involves funding for the "cost" of the promised payout. In a 50 percent tax bracket corporation this would mean establishing a fund equal to one half of the deferred compensation benefit.

prohibiting the deduction of premiums on business-owned life insurance.[9]

What It Costs the Corporation

Another question frequently arises in regard to deductibility and deferred compensation. Ordinarily couched in the form of an objection by the employer (apart from whether life insurance is considered or not), it runs somewhat as follows: "If we pay the executive $10,000 in cash this year, it only costs $5,000 (deductible expense).[10] If we set $10,000 aside for him, it takes $20,000 to do it (nondeductible item—$10,000 tax). Therefore, it costs us $15,000 more to defer it than to pay it."

A simple way to get a true picture of the situation is to isolate a segment of the firm's operating income before taxes, say, $100,000. Then, look at the effect on surplus under three separate sets of circumstances: (1) The $10,000 is not paid to the executive at all, (2) it is paid to him currently, (3) it is deferred until later.

Not Paid	Paid Currently	Deferred
$100,000 Gross income	$100,000 Gross income	$100,000 Gross income
	10,000 Bonus (deductible)	
50,000 Income tax		50,000 Income tax
	$ 90,000 Income before corporate tax	$ 50,000 Net after tax
		10,000 Fund for deferred payout (nondeductible)
	45,000 Income tax	
$ 50,000 Net for surplus	$ 45,000 Net for surplus	$ 40,000 Net for surplus

When the ultimate effect on corporate surplus is considered, the above figures clearly confirm the employer's initial statement, namely, that it costs the firm $5,000 to pay the executive $10,000 currently (a difference of $50,000 and $45,000 to surplus).

But what of the employer's conclusion that it costs $15,000 more to defer and set aside the $10,000? This is obviously false. The difference in effect on surplus between paying the executive and setting aside the deferred amount is only $5,000. Besides, the firm still has the use of the $10,000. If so desired, it could invest it in stocks, in bonds, in key man life insurance, or in the business enterprise itself. In fact, the $10,000 could well be carried currently as a part of surplus, thus putting surplus in the same position, for the time being, as if the firm had not paid the executive. If the annual deferred amount is invested in life insurance, the surplus account would be reduced by only the early-year cost of the protection element.

If the $10,000 is invested each year in life insurance, does that preclude the possibility of the aggregate deposits being used in the business if

---

[9] "No deduction shall be allowed for premiums paid on any life insurance policy covering the life of any officer or employee, or of any person financially interested in any trade or business carried on by the taxpayer, when the taxpayer is directly or indirectly a beneficiary under such policy." Internal Revenue Code, Sec. 264(*a*)(1).

[10] Assuming 50 percent federal corporate income tax bracket.

needed? Not at all. The cash value is available and readily acceptable at any time as collateral security for a nonrecourse loan. The issuing company itself will lend up to 6 percent, which constitutes an interest ceiling for borrowing purposes. It must also be remembered that if and when the cash values are being used in the business, the insurance company is crediting the borrowed amount with interest. Many companies, though guaranteeing 2½ percent, are crediting in excess of 4 percent currently. So, in determining the effective cost of borrowing the cash values for business purposes, the fact that the 6 percent interest charge is deductible under present law (assuming a valid business purpose) and that the 4 percent credited is currently free of income tax cannot be overlooked. Balancing each other, it is more like a 3 percent effective cost against a 4 percent credit.

Employee Benefits

Assume that it has been agreed to make certain payments to the employee executive and/or his family commencing with his retirement, death, or disability. With multiple-purpose key man life insurance as the funding instrument, the procedure, in brief, would be as follows:

Death Benefit. Though the executive is willing to defer certain amounts until retirement, he desires that his wife or other designated beneficiary collect every dollar he defers in the event he does not live to do so himself. In the type of case described, this is invariably a basic minimum demand. Naturally, he will be pleased to accept a greater death benefit but ordinarily will not insist on it. This factor becomes of the greatest importance in gaining acceptance by the employer of the insured plan. A glance at Table 43–1 will reveal why.

This illustration compares the benefits, to a corporation in the 50 percent bracket, of an unfunded plan with a plan funded by life insurance. The figures are based on a life fully paid at 65 participating policy issued on a male at age 50 with a gross annual premium of $10,000. The dividends are being used to purchase additional amounts of paid-up insurance. The figures, except for those which appear in parentheses and which will be referred to later, are self-explanatory. The advantages of the insured plan appear evident over the entire period of the deferred arrangement. The point to be noted and stressed is the tax-free benefit which will accrue to the corporation in the event of the employee's death prior to retirement. Line 7 shows the difference between the total net outlay under the insured plan (line 5) and the death proceeds (line 6), and may be considered free key man indemnity. The term "free" is used in the sense that although this amount accrues to the benefit of the corporation, it was actually the insured's deferred income which paid for it. True, the benefit decreases each year until finally, as the employee approaches retirement, there is nothing left. But this is as it should be and is in keeping with the generally accepted principle of indemnity. There is no point in a firm being indemnified for the loss of a *retired* key man.

Observe that in the early years of the contract, this indemnity is quite substantial. The firm may agree to pay a portion of it, which, when added to the total amount deferred, would constitute a minimum death benefit.

TABLE 43-1. Funded versus Unfunded Deferred Compensation Plan—A Cost Comparison*

	If Death Occurs at Age							
	50	55	60	65	70	75	80	85
1. Net costs to corporation of payments to executive and/or beneficiary (50% tax bracket)	$ 5,000	$ 25,000	$ 50,000	$ 75,000	$ 75,000	$ 75,000	$ 75,000	$ 75,000
2. Reduced by tax-free offset of paid-up dividends under insured funded plan					8,742	17,902	27,419	37,198
3. Reduced net cost	$ 5,000	$ 25,000	$ 50,000	$ 75,000	$ 66,258	$ 57,098	$ 47,581	$ 37,802
4. Total insurance deposits	10,000	50,000	100,000	150,000 C.V.(151,804)	150,000	150,000	150,000	150,000
5. Total net outlay under insured funded plan (line 3 + line 4)	15,000	75,000	150,000	225,000	216,258	207,098	197,581	187,802
6. Total recovery under insured funded plan	161,214	169,275	181,043	195,875	195,875 (209,095)	195,875 (222,959)	195,875 (237,791)	195,875 (250,234)
7. Excess or deficit of insurance proceeds over total outlay under insured funded plan	+146,214	+95,275	+31,043	−29,125	−20,383 (−15,905)	−11,223 (−2,041)	+1,706 (+12,791)	+8,073 (+25,234)
8. Advantages of insured plan over unfunded plan (compare line 1 with line 7)	151,214	119,275	81,043	45,875	54,617 (59,095)	63,777 (72,959)	73,294 (87,791)	83,073 (100,234)

* The illustrative dividend results shown herein are based on the dividend scale in use currently. They are not a guarantee, promise, or estimate of future results, which necessarily will depend on future experience.

Such an amount might be measured by one or two years' base salary. To agree to pay the executive the full amount, however, particularly as it stands for the earlier years, might be objectionable on two grounds.

1. The amount, being quite large, could possibly be deemed an unreasonable payment for such relatively short service, and consequently not deductible.
2. Such an arrangement ties the policy itself too closely to the deferred contract. It might just possibly destroy the deferred tax treatment.

Retirement Benefit. When the executive reaches retirement age (herein assumed to be age 65), the corporation has several choices in regard to the use of the life insurance policy:

1. It may take the then cash value in cash or place it under one of the optional modes of settlement. In our example the estimated combined value at age 65 is $151,804, which is greater than the aggregate premium deposits of $150,000.

   The type of option selected will ordinarily depend upon the nature of the agreed-upon payout with the executive. It may be for 10 years or 15 years, as in the instant case. If a life income is desired, the particular policy used in the illustration will produce an income of approximately $800 per month, with a minimum guarantee of the return of the full cash value. Again, it should be stressed that it is the corporation which receives these monies from the insurance company, and it is the corporation which expenses them out to the executive. In effect, the corporation is the annuitant and will receive back its total deposits free of income tax, with only the interest element being taxable income under the annuity principle.

   The executive, of course, will report the full amounts received by him. His net after taxes during the retirement payout should be compared with what he would retain currently on the same amount when added to his other income. In many cases the deferment will more than double the effectiveness of his savings for retirement.
2. Since at age 65 the suggested policy of insurance is fully paid up, the corporation may elect to keep it in force and ultimately collect the paid-up face value of $195,875 (see Table 43–1, line 6, ages 65 on). Meanwhile, the payout to the executive would be made out of current operating income. It should be noted that this particular policy continues to participate in dividends even though no further premium payments are required. The total paid-up dividends are shown in five-year intervals on line 2. These amounts are received free of income tax by the corporation and can be used each year to offset the payout to the executive. Observe that under this procedure the maximum cost or deficit to the corporation is $29,125 (line 7, age 65). This can only occur if the executive dies at age 65. If he dies earlier, the corporation's outlay is reduced by the saving in premium payments and by the greater excess of death proceeds over the total premium deposits; if he dies later, the outlay is reduced by the paid-up dividend.

3. The third choice is much the same as number two, with this difference:
The corporation, instead of taking the paid-up dividends in cash, continues to use them to purchase paid-up additions. Under this arrangement the amount of the death benefit continues to increase, as indicated by the figures within the parentheses on line 6. Of course, the
paid-up dividend setoff is postponed until the executive dies; so in determining the excess or deficit of insurance proceeds over the total corporate outlay (line 7), the total net outlay figure of $225,000, unreduced
by the paid-up dividends, is the proper one. To use the reduced
amounts of the later years for this purpose would be to count the paid-
up dividend twice. Again, line 8 shows the overall advantage to the
corporation of the insured plan over an unfunded arrangement.

Disability Benefits. For a relatively small additional amount,[11] a
waiver-of-premium provision can be inserted in the policy. Should the
insured become disabled within the terms of this provision, the premium
will be waived by the issuing company. The corporate owner then will be
relieved of the necessity of making the annual premium deposit, and still
the cash values in the policy will continue to grow and to enhance the
surplus position. This amount comes into the corporation on a tax-free
basis. Again assuming a 50 percent tax bracket, the sum is equivalent to
$20,000 of operating income. In fact, the corporation could expense out
$20,000 per year to the disabled executive at no cost to it at all. Again
isolating $100,000 of operating income and comparing the effect on sur-
plus between no disability arrangement at all and the proposed insured
plan utilizing the waiver-of-premium provision, the results would be as
follows.

No Disability Benefit	*$20,000 Annual Disability Benefit*		
$100,000 Gross income	$100,000 Gross income	+	$10,000 — Tax-free in-crease in cash value
0 No disability benefit	—20,000 Disability pay-out (de-ductible)		
$100,000 Income before corporate tax	$ 80,000 Income before corporate tax		
—50,000 Income tax	—40,000 Income tax		
$ 50,000 Net to surplus	$ 40,000	+	$10,000 = $50,000 Net to surplus

Of course, it is not necessary for the corporation to go to the full extent
of $20,000 a year. Very often the disability benefit agreement is limited to
the amount the employee can receive tax free under a salary continuance
plan.[12] The point to be kept in mind is that if the disability payout is less

---

[11] The additional premium for the waiver provision would be approximately $250
annually. Some companies write a waiver provision which extends to age 65 on a life
paid-up-at-65 contract. This would fit in nicely with the proposed deferred compensation arrangement.

[12] Internal Revenue Code, Sec. 105(d).

than twice the annual increase in the cash value, the corporation will realize a profit. In other words, the waiver-of-premium provision affords considerable flexibility.

SUMMARY

The selective or nonqualified plans of deferred compensation offer an attractive means of providing additional benefits for executives and other key personnel. In addition to the inherent tax advantages, there usually will be sound business reasons for the use of such plans. They may be used to help retain the executive's services to retirement, to supplement the limited benefits of a qualified pension or profit sharing plan, to serve as an attractive lure in obtaining top personnel, and to increase the financial security of the executive at retirement.

Very often, in these arrangements, some type of funding is desirable. Life insurance and annuity contracts can be used appropriately for funding in a great many cases, especially in those situations requiring cash commitments at the time of death or disability.

SELECTED REFERENCES

Batchelder, Joseph E., III.   "Executive Compensation after the Tax Reform Act of 1969," *Taxes,* Vol. 48, No. 11 (November 1970).

Lynch, William B.   "Insurance with Restricted Trusts," *Taxes,* Vol. 49, No. 5 (May 1971), p. 302.

Moore, Russell F. (ed.)   *Compensating Executive Worth.* New York: American Management Association, 1968.

Smyers, John D., and Feinberg, Paul H.   "A Catalogue of Deferred Compensation Plans—After the Storm," *Practical Lawyer,* Vol. 16, No. 5 (May 1970).

Washington, G. T., and Rothschild, V. H., II.   *Compensating the Corporate Executive.* 3d ed. New York: Ronald Press, 1962.

44

Split-Dollar Plans

By WILLIAM B. LYNCH

SPLIT-DOLLAR insurance is a form of insurance co-ownership and is used primarily as a means for one party to help another carry the life insurance protection he needs. The policy must be of a permanent insurance type because the "split" generally divides the cash value from the pure protection element. Usually, one party pays a portion of each premium equal to the annual increase in cash value, and the other party, usually the insured, pays the balance. At the death of the insured, the noninsured party receives a portion of the proceeds equal to the cash value, and the balance of the proceeds is payable to the insured's designated beneficiary. The result is that the insured obtains insurance protection at very little cost to himself, the principal premium share being borne by the party helping him.

Background

Split-dollar insurance has been in use for a considerable time, at least since the 1930s. Now considered primarily an employee benefit plan, it probably began as a simple arrangement between a father and his son. For many years, it was hampered by its uncertain tax status. That changed with the issuance of two diverse revenue rulings nine years apart—one in 1955 and the other in 1964. Both rulings dealt with employer-employee split-dollar plans. The older ruling still applies to all policies purchased under split-dollar arrangements, or policies modified to split-dollar on or before November 13, 1964. It stated that split-dollar plans resemble loans without interest, and held that the forbearance of interest is not a taxable event. Consequently, the employee would not be taxed on the value of the benefits provided him by the other party.

The later ruling (Revenue Ruling 64–328, 1964–2 CB 11) applies to all policies purchased under or modified to split-dollar plans after November 13, 1964, and so is of much greater current interest.[1] According to this ruling, split-dollar plans are not essentially interest-free loans but are, instead, plans intended to provide an economic benefit for employees.

---

[1] See Appendix Q for the full text of the 1964 revenue ruling.

The ruling also held that the employee should be taxed on the value of the benefit received. Each year, the taxable value is determined by multiplying the government's P.S.-58 one-year term rate at the insured's attained age by the amount of the proceeds which would be payable to the insured's beneficiary, less any actual contribution by him. Both rulings agreed that the proceeds, on death, would be received income-tax free by both parties.

Typically, the split-dollar plan is arranged between an insured and his employer; therefore, the rest of this discussion refers to the party providing the premium assistance as the "employer." Bear in mind, however, that any party can share premiums with another. The plan is not limited to situations involving an employment relationship.

HOW SPLIT-DOLLAR WORKS

Basic Patterns

With the usual level-premium insurance plans, the face amount is level. At any given point in time, the face amount consists of two parts: the cash value or reserve, and the amount at risk. With split-dollar plans the employer is entitled to the cash value, or at least enough of it to equal its share of premium payments. As a direct result, the insured's protection tends to decline as the cash value goes up. This is clearly shown in Table 44–1. In the tenth year of the plan, for example, the insured's protection has fallen from $98,874 to $79,954. At that point, the employer's share of the proceeds would be $20,046 because the total death benefit remains level at $100,000. By age 65, the insured's protection would have fallen to $55,312.

To counteract this, many participating policies permit a portion of the dividends to be used to purchase one-year term insurance. This term insurance increases in amount each year, keeping exact pace with the cash value of the basic policy, and is payable to the insured's beneficiary. As a result, the protection for the employee's family is kept level from the year in which the first dividend is available until the year in which the dividend is insufficient to purchase one-year term insurance equal to the full cash value of the contract. One major company projects that this point would be reached when the insured attains age 65 for a male aged 40 at issuance of his policy, using early dividend balances to reduce premiums. That would be the last year in which the protection for the insured would be level. From then on, it would decline at an ever steeper rate. This plan is shown in Table 44–2. Had early dividend balances been accumulated for later use, the same company would project a final level year at age 68. Many nonparticipating policies achieve much the same leveling result by building an increasing term insurance feature into the basic policy.

Notice, in Table 44–1, that in the first year the employer pays $1,126 toward the premium. The second year the employer pays $2,346, then $2,367 the third year, and so on. These amounts paid by the employer are equal to the increase in the cash surrender value of the policy for the year. The insured pays the balance of the premium each year. By the eleventh

TABLE 44–1. Split-Dollar Insurance Ledger Illustration Using Dividends to Reduce Premiums* (age 40, $100,000 straight life, gross annual premium $2,783)

Start of Policy Year	Net Premium Deposit°	Premium Division		Death Benefit	
		By Employer	By Insured	To Employer	To Family
1	$2,783	$ 1,126	$ 1,657	$ 1,126	$98,874
2	2,563	2,346	217	3,472	96,528
3	2,492	2,367	125	5,839	94,161
4	2,423	1,985	438	7,824	92,176
5	2,357	2,002	355	9,826	90,174
6	2,294	2,019	275	11,845	88,155
7	2,233	2,033	200	13,878	86,122
8	2,176	2,045	131	15,923	84,077
9	2,122	2,057	65	17,980	82,020
10	2,072	2,066	6	20,046	79,954
11	2,024	2,024		22,070	77,930
12	1,961	1,961		24,031	75,969
13	1,901	1,901		25,932	74,068
14	1,845	1,845		27,777	72,223
15	1,791	1,791		29,568	70,432
16	1,738	1,738		31,306	68,694
17	1,686	1,686		32,992	67,008
18	1,634	1,634		34,626	65,374
19	1,583	1,583		36,209	63,791
20	1,531	1,531		37,740	62,260
20-year total	$41,209	$37,740	$3,469		
Age 65	1,298	1,298		44,688	55,312

° The dividends, and consequent net premium deposit shown, are not guaranteed.

year, the annual cash value increase is greater than the net premium, so the insured pays no more, yet his protection continues. His annual cost to age 65 would average about $1.80 per $1,000 of protection. It should be borne in mind, however, that the policy dividends are not guaranteed. Were they to change from those illustrated, the insured's costs would correspondingly change.

In Table 44–2, some of the dividends are used to buy the annual term insurance, with the result that the net premium stays relatively high and always exceeds the cash value increases. The insured never quite gets away from paying a portion of the premium. Nevertheless, he would obtain his $100,000 of level protection at an average annual cost to age 65 of less than $3.25 per $1,000.

Pattern Variations

The plans illustrated in Tables 44–1 and 44–2 use straight life, probably the most commonly used policy form but certainly not the only one available. Any permanent policy can be used, and the parties should use the type best suited to their purposes.

For example, split-dollar for employee benefit plans is often best funded with a policy paid up by age 65. This plan can provide the insured with

TABLE 44-2. Split-Dollar Insurance Ledger Illustration Using Dividends to Purchase One-Year Term Insurance and Reduce Premiums* (age 40, $100,000 straight life, gross annual premium $2,783)

Start of Policy Year	Net Premium Deposit*	Premium Division		Death Benefit*	
		By Employer	By Insured	To Employer	To Family
1	$ 2,783	$ 1,126	$ 1,657	$ 1,126	$ 98,874
2	2,577	2,346	231	3,472	100,000
3	2,517	2,367	150	5,839	100,000
4	2,459	1,985	474	7,824	100,000
5	2,407	2,002	405	9,826	100,000
6	2,359	2,019	340	11,845	100,000
7	2,315	2,033	282	13,878	100,000
8	2,279	2,045	234	15,923	100,000
9	2,249	2,057	192	17,980	100,000
10	2,226	2,066	160	20,046	100,000
11	2,210	2,073	137	22,119	100,000
12	2,183	2,079	104	24,198	100,000
13	2,164	2,083	81	26,281	100,000
14	2,155	2,083	72	28,364	100,000
15	2,154	2,083	71	30,447	100,000
16	2,161	2,079	82	32,526	100,000
17	2,177	2,075	102	34,601	100,000
18	2,203	2,066	137	36,667	100,000
19	2,239	2,057	182	38,724	100,000
20	2,286	2,045	241	40,769	100,000
20-year total	$46,103	$40,769	$5,334		
Age 65	2,760	1,949	811	50,725	100,000

* The dividends are not guaranteed, and there is consequently no guarantee of the net premium shown nor of the one-year term insurance reflected in the death benefits shown. The one-year term rates illustrated are not guaranteed.

nonterminating level protection equal to the face of the policy less the amount paid by the employer toward the premiums for the rest of his life after retirement at age 65. If the policy is participating, any dividends that are paid may compensate the employer for this continued use of its funds. Observe, however, that although the employee may have no premiums to pay on policies purchased after November 13, 1964, he may have a heavy tax burden. For example, by age 70 he would have $48.06 of taxable income for each $1,000 of protection; by age 80, $111.04 per $1,000. For that reason, for employees whose potential postretirement income is likely to be substantial, such plans often provide that the employee may purchase the entire policy from his employer at retirement.

Various kinds of term insurance riders may be attached to the basic policy, either to give some key man protection to the employer (in which case the employer pays the extra cost of the rider) or to give the insured some optional additional protection (in which case he pays the extra cost). The advantage is, of course, that the term insurance purchased as a rider is usually much less expensive than term insurance purchased alone.

Aside from variations in the policies themselves, there are many ways to split the premiums and even the proceeds. Tables 44-1 and 44-2 follow the classic pattern. The contracts illustrated in those tables are high early cash value policies. When the earliest split-dollar plans were written, such policies were not available. Often the policies showed no cash values at all in the first year or so, requiring the insured alone to bear the full early premiums. The high early cash value policies were designed to alleviate this problem, and Table 44–1 shows the result: The insured would pay but $1,657 out of a total first-year premium of $2,783. Despite this, however, and despite the low overall cost to the insured, he often has difficulty paying his share of the first premium.

Consequently, many split-dollar plans have been designed which permit the insured to spread his share of the premiums over some selected number of years. For example, the insured in Table 44–1 might pay a level premium of $347 each year for ten years (in the illustration, the total employee contribution for the period shown is $3,469). The employer, in such case, would have to pay a larger portion of the first premium. Going a major step further, the insured might skip payments altogether. The employer would pay all premiums. Such noncontributory plans have become exceedingly popular in recent years.

It is often contended that because the employer in classic split-dollar plans always gets its share of the premiums back, the plan costs it nothing. This is obviously untrue. The employer's cost for supplying its share of the premium is measured by the value of the loss of use of its money. Since nearly all of the employer's share of the premiums under a conventional split-dollar plan can be obtained through policy loans at a guaranteed maximum loan rate of no more than 6 percent, it is obvious that the maximum cost to an employer would be 6 percent per annum on its share of the premiums. If, under the circumstances, an employer is allowed to deduct the interest, then its cost would be even lower. Still, why not make the plan truly costless to the employer? This can be done by dividing the proceeds at the time of the insured's death so that the employer receives not only an amount equal to its premium deposits (reduced by the amount already received as policy loans), but also an amount equal to its interest costs.

MAJOR SYSTEMS

Having decided on the plan pattern he wishes to apply, the underwriter must then choose one of the two major split-dollar systems. The basic mechanics of these systems are compared in Figure 44–1, and each possesses its own special advantages.

Collateral Assignment System

The collateral assignment system has an advantage in that it is easy to explain. The insured owns his own policy and puts it up as security for loans, just as he would at the bank. The only difference is that the loans carry no interest. This corresponds with everyone's conception of insurance in general and loans in particular. If the insured's employment terminates, and the plan with it, no policy repurchase is required—the

FIGURE 44–1. Comparison of Collateral Assignment and Endorsement Split-Dollar Systems

Item	Collateral Assignment	Endorsement System
Policy applicant	Insured*	Employer
Policyowner	Insured	Employer and Employee
Premium division . . .	All paid by insured, subject to receipt of loan from employer equal to: year's cash value increase; or average cash value increase over a stated number of years, e.g., 10 years; or entire premium	All paid by employer, subject to variations: Reimbursement from insured for excess of premiums over year's cash value increase Reimbursement from insured for one-year term cost No reimbursements from insured
Death benefits	All to insured's designee, subject to repayment of loan to employer	Split: Portion equal to employer's share of total premiums to employer; balance to insured's designee

* Where the insured is an out-of-state resident, underwriting can be simplified by designating the employer as applicant.

insured may simply pay off the loans if the insurance policy is to be continued by him.

The direct benefit of participating policy dividends goes to the insured as owner of the policy under the collateral assignment system. It is mechanically easy to remove the policy from his taxable estate by an absolute assignment (subject to the collateral assignment) to his wife or to someone else.

Because the collateral assignment system involves loans as a part of its basic mechanism, it lends itself well to an insured's averaging his share of the premiums, itself calling for a series of loans. The part of the loan attributable to the averaging should, however, be repaid in a reasonably short time, e.g., during the first ten policy years.

Endorsement System

The employer's retention of policy ownership and control under the endorsement system may be more appealing to stockholders—and stockholder reaction can be important in many cases. The absence of any actual loan to the employee may be an important factor, too, because some states have laws prohibiting or restricting loans by corporations to their officers. Furthermore, this absence of a loan may enhance the deduction of interest under Internal Revenue Code Section 264, if the plan is terminated and the insured later finances his premiums.

Split-dollar plans are often combined with other plans, such as selective deferred compensation or stock redemption plans. These combinations are much more easily carried out when the corporation, and not the insured, is the owner of the policy. A combination, in fact, may be one with a purely business purpose, e.g., plant expansion or equipment acquisitions.

As owner, the company would have direct access to the policy cash values for these purposes. Apart from convenience, this might help the corporation avoid assessment of the accumulated earnings tax under Internal Revenue Code Section 531. One test, incidentally, of whether that section applies to a corporation is the existence of outstanding loans to stockholding employees. As a practical matter, a noncontributory plan can be more easily established under the endorsement system.

PUTTING THE PLAN TOGETHER

With the pattern and the system tailored to their needs, the parties are ready to put the package together. One component will usually be a written agreement. Drafting this is the attorney's province. To assist him, many insurance companies have prepared sample forms covering a wide range of plans.

Under the collateral assignment system, the life insurance policy is applied for and owned by the insured. Premium notices are sent to him, and he designates the beneficiaries of his choice. Upon issuance of the policy, the insured assigns it to his employer as collateral security for loans to be advanced. An assignment form often used is the ABA-10 form adopted by the American Bankers Association. Banks and insurance companies usually have supplies of these or their own forms available.

The second step is the execution of the written plan agreement, describing the policy by number, amount, insurer, and ownership. The parties normally are the insured and the employer. They typically agree that as long as the insured remains employed, the employer will lend him each year, without interest, an amount equal to the lesser of the year's net premium or the cash value increase. These loans normally are repayable only at death, out of the policy proceeds, or on the earlier termination of employment, out of the policy cash values. Where dividends are used to reduce the premiums, the future annual net premiums will not be known when the plan is installed, nor will the insured or the employer be readily able to compute the annual loans in advance. Here the parties can prepare an open-end note and work sheet like that in Figure 44–2, with the underwriter providing the cash value information in column B. With such a form, the parties can fill in the information each year and endorse the addition.

The agreement usually has provisions for termination of the plan; for example, if the insured leaves his employment. In this event, the insured may be required within a fixed time to pay off the loan in full. The agreement should make it possible for him to do this through a policy loan. That may require either a release of the policy by the employer to the insured, or the employer must secure such a loan on his behalf before releasing the policy. If the insured does not repay the loan, the employer may surrender the policy to recover the premiums it has advanced.

Under the endorsement system the policy is applied for and owned by the employer, who receives the premium notices. The plan includes an endorsement which splits the ownership of the policy between the two parties. The employer owns all policy values except the right to designate

FIGURE 44–2.   Open-End Note and Work Sheet for Collateral Assignment Split-Dollar System (age 40, $100,000 straight life, gross annual premium $2,783)

The undersigned promises to pay to the order of _____ (Employer) _____ , on demand and without interest, the cumulative total of the amount shown in column C, below, opposite which he has placed his initials in column D, below. Such amounts so owed are secured by collateral assignment to said payee of Policy Number _____ issued by _____ (Insurance Company) _____ on the life of the undersigned.

In Year	(A) Net Premium per Premium Notice	(B) Guaranteed Cash Value Increase	(C) Enter Lesser of (A) or (B)	(D) Initials of Undersigned
1964	$2,783	$1,126	$1,126	____
65	____	2,346	____	____
66	____	2,367	____	____
67	____	1,985	____	____
68	____	2,002	____	____
1969	____	2,019	____	____
70	____	2,033	____	____
71	____	2,045	____	____
72	____	2,057	____	____
73	____	2,066	____	____
etc.	etc.	etc.	etc.	etc.

Dated _____ , 19____   _____
                                                                                 (Insured)

beneficiary of the proceeds in excess of its own interest. At the insured's death, the employer normally will receive an amount equal to its share of the premium payments or, if greater, an amount equal to the cash value. The insured's own beneficiary would receive the balance of the proceeds. It is this ownership endorsement which gives the system its name. The respective owners then designate a beneficiary for their portion of the proceeds. The employee has a direct ownership in a piece of the policy, and this kind of system is sometimes called a "split-ownership" plan.

Under the endorsement system used by some insurance companies, all ownership rights are in the employer. The beneficiary provision is divided into two parts. The employer is beneficiary under Part A for an amount of the proceeds equal to its premium contribution; the employee designates the Part B beneficiary to receive the balance of the proceeds. The policy is then "endorsed" to the effect that the Part B beneficiary can't be changed without the consent of the insured.

The second step is the execution of the written plan agreement. The parties typically agree that as long as the insured remains employed, the employer will pay all premiums as they become due. The insured then will reimburse the employer for his share of the premium. As indicated earlier, this may be the difference between the increase in cash value and the premium for the year, or any other amount which is mutually agreeable to the parties. The agreement permits the employee to name his own

FIGURE 44–3.   Work Sheet for Endorsement Split-Dollar System (age 40, $100,000 straight life, gross annual premium $2,783)

The amount computed each year for column *C*, below, is the amount payable by the insured to the employer each year, on or before the due date in such year, for the annual premium on the policy, all in accordance with the provisions of Section _____ of that certain split-dollar agreement dated _____ _____, 19_____, to which this work sheet is annexed.

In Year	(A) Net Premium per Premium Notice	(B) Guaranteed Cash Value Increase	(C) Enter Excess, if Any, of (A) over (B)
1964	$2,783	$1,126	$1,657
65	_____	2,346	_____
66	_____	2,367	_____
67	_____	1,985	_____
68	_____	2,002	_____
1969	_____	2,019	_____
70	_____	2,033	_____
71	_____	2,045	_____
72	_____	2,057	_____
73	_____	2,066	_____
etc.	etc.	etc.	etc.

beneficiaries for the part of the death benefits which exceeds the employer's interest. Just as with the collateral assignment system, the amount of future net premiums will be unknown where dividends are used to reduce them. If the plan is contributory, the premium division is easy for the parties to compute, if they use a work sheet as shown in Figure 44–3.

Provisions in the agreement for termination of the plan should include procedures for transferring ownership of the policy from the employer to the insured. This transfer is a sale and requires that the employer execute an absolute assignment or modification of ownership form. The purchase price is usually the employer's share of total premiums or the reserve of the policy. The insured may find it necessary to borrow against the policy to meet this price, and provision should be made in the agreement for that contingency.

TAXATION

Income Taxation

Reference already has been made to Revenue Ruling 64–328, the basic tax authority for split-dollar plans. When the Revenue Act of 1964 was first proposed to Congress, the Treasury Department suggested that legislation might be in order on the subject of split dollar. Committees of both houses of Congress, however, turned the question back to Treasury for further study and the "possibility of administrative action." Revenue Ruling 64–328 resulted.

After reviewing the findings of the old 1955 ruling, the new ruling concluded that it had incorrectly analyzed the substance of split-dollar arrangements. According to the new ruling, split-dollar plans are not plans for making interest-free loans but are, instead, plans for providing an economic benefit for employees. Its purpose and effect, said the ruling, is ". . . to provide an economic benefit to the employee represented by the amount of the annual premium cost that he should bear and of which he is relieved." In sum, the ruling provided that the value of the economic benefit (valued at one-year term premium rates for the protection provided at each attained age) would be taxed as income to the employee to the extent that value exceeds his premium contribution for the year. It agreed with the 1955 ruling, however, in stating that the proceeds on the employee's death would be tax free to each party receiving them.

The term premium rates specified by the ruling are shown in Table 44–3. These are commonly referred to as "P.S.-58 rates," after an old ruling of that number which was concerned with insured qualified plans. In 1966, a further ruling elaborated on these rates.[2] It held that lower rates than those shown in Table 44–3 could be used if the insurer actually charged lower rates on individual one-year term insurance available to all standard risks. An insurer's rates for term riders cannot be used.[3] In addition, the 1966 ruling explained that, if dividends or their values are distributed to the employee, he is to be taxed on the actual amount of the dividend in addition to the term rates. This would be true, for example, if the dividend is paid to him in cash, used to provide him with additional one-year term insurance, or allowed to accumulate at interest for his benefit. On the other hand, if the dividend buys paid-up additions which are themselves split like the basic policy, the employee would be taxed only on the value of the pure protection shown in Figure 44–3.

If the insured's contribution toward the premium exceeds the value of the benefit received, the excess may not be carried over to future years as an offset. For example, in Table 44–1, the term cost in year 1 is only $437.02 (i.e., $4.42 per $1,000), but the employee's excessive contribution ($1,219.98) cannot be carried into the second and later years.

While holding the employee to be taxable on the benefits received, the 1964 ruling also holds that the employer is not entitled to any deduction for its share of premiums. The ruling bases this conclusion on Internal Revenue Code Section 264, which prohibits a deduction when the taxpayer is a beneficiary under the policy. While that may have some merit relative to the part of the employer's premium attributable to its share of the policy, it seems unwarranted when applied to the employee's share. If the policy can be seen as split from the employee's point of view, the same should be true from the employer's side.

Certain nagging problems remain, the chief one concerning stockholding employees, especially those who control their closely held companies. Several private rulings issued under the old 1955 ruling held that it was not intended to apply to stockholders, without stating what does apply to them. The later published rulings include nothing which indicates that shareholder-employees would be treated differently from nonshareholders.

---

[2] Revenue Ruling 66–110, 1966–1 CB 12.
[3] Revenue Ruling 67–154, 1967–1 CB 11.

There seems to be one serious possibility: the penalty tax under Internal Revenue Code Section 531. This tax is levied on close corporations which accumulate rather than distribute their incomes in order to shelter those incomes from the high personal brackets of their stockholders. A good defense against this tax is a showing that the accumulations are for the reasonable needs of the business. In the matter of a stockholder's split dollar, however, just the contrary would be easier to prove. The reasonable needs of the business, however, are likely to include obtaining and keep-

TABLE 44–3.   Revenue Rulings 64–328 and 66–110 Uniform One-Year Term Premiums for $1,000 Life Insurance Protection (Table of P.S.-58 one-year term rates)

Age	Premium	Age	Premium	Age	Premium
15.	$1.27	40.	$4.42	65.	$31.51
16.	1.38	41.	4.73	66.	34.28
17.	1.48	42.	5.07	67.	37.31
18.	1.52	43.	5.44	68.	40.59
19.	1.56	44.	5.85	69.	44.17
20.	1.61	45.	6.30	70.	48.06
21.	1.67	46.	6.78	71.	52.29
22.	1.73	47.	7.32	72.	56.89
23.	1.79	48.	7.89	73.	61.89
24.	1.86	49.	8.53	74.	67.33
25.	1.93	50.	9.22	75.	73.23
26.	2.02	51.	9.97	76.	79.63
27.	2.11	52.	10.79	77.	86.57
28.	2.20	53.	11.69	78.	94.09
29.	2.31	54.	12.67	79.	102.23
30.	2.43	55.	13.74	80.	111.04
31.	2.57	56.	14.91	81.	120.57
32.	2.70	57.	16.18		
33.	2.86	58.	17.56		
34.	3.02	59.	19.08		
35.	3.21	60.	20.73		
36.	3.41	61.	22.53		
37.	3.63	62.	24.50		
38.	3.87	63.	26.63		
39.	4.14	64.	28.98		

ing skilled employees, so a plan with a "employee" label is likely safer than one with a "stockholder" label. To give the label substance, the plan should be extended to cover nonstockholding employees on a substantial basis. If broadening the base proves unpalatable, the corporation might effect maximum loans against the policies and invest the proceeds in the business, so using the accumulations for its needs.

Private plans—those between parties not in an employment relationship —are not subject to the ruling and ordinarily no taxable income is created by their establishment. Plans between fathers and sons and other family plans are quite common.

Estate Taxation

Life insurance proceeds will be included in the gross estate of the insured if payable to his estate, or if he possesses any incidents of ownership in the policy at the time of his death, exercisable either alone or in conjunction with any other person. It is easy enough to avoid these provisions if proper care is taken, but it is equally easy to assume that they have been avoided when they have not. The typical split-dollar plan would terminate, for example, upon termination of the insured's employment. If the plan is under the collateral assignment system, little danger exists because termination of the plan means only that the employer would no longer make loans and would recover its interest (which is secured by the policy values) from the insured.

Under the endorsement system, on the other hand, the employer owns the cash value portion and alone has the power to surrender the contract, so if employment terminates and the policy is surrendered, the right to designate beneficiaries ceases. The power to terminate the right to designate a beneficiary is an "incident of ownership." When the plan hopes to avoid the estate tax, of course, the person owning the beneficiary designation right would be someone other than the insured, perhaps his wife.[4] But her right would terminate on the insured's termination of employment and the surrender of the policy. That is, despite appearances, he may be held to have an incident of ownership evidenced by his power to defeat his wife's ownership interest in the policy. Therefore, if the estate tax is to be avoided under the endorsement system, the plan either should not terminate with the end of the insured's employment or should give his wife the right to convert the plan (i.e., buy the policy from the employer). This latter choice presents a serious dilemma, however. If she actually exercised the right, she would be a "transferee for value" with adverse tax results under Internal Revenue Code Section 101. If the insured was given the purchase right, hoping to avoid Section 101, that in itself might be an incident of ownership in the policy.

Gift Taxation

A split-dollar plan between an employer and an employee usually has no gift tax consequences. There may be a gift, however, if the employee assigns his rights to his wife. While no published ruling has said as much, it seems probable that the measure of this gift would be the same term rates given in Table 44–3, applied to the pure protection provided the

---

[4] Treasury Regulation Sec. 20.2042–1(d)(2) holds that an insured's ownership of all of the stock of a corporation which owns insurance on his life is, itself, sufficient grounds for inclusion of the full proceeds in his gross estate. This is based on the theory that the insured's sole control of the corporation gives him effective control of the insurance, and hence, incidents of ownership in the policy. It may be that, even though the risk portion is owned by the insured's wife, that portion may be taxed in his gross estate if he is the sole stockholder of the corporation. Revenue Ruling 71–463, 1971–42 IRB 25, had held the same principles would apply if the insured merely controlled the corporation, but that ruling has been revoked by the IRS.

employee regardless of reportable income for tax purposes which might be less if the employee contributed to the premiums.

In purely family split-dollar plans, as between a father and his son, the term rates are also the probable measure of the gift. On the other hand, these family arrangements should have no income tax consequences except when conducted between an income-producing trust and its beneficiary.

CASE EXAMPLES OF SPLIT-DOLLAR PLANS

Example 1. Pacific Data Processing is a small company with seven full-time employees. It wishes to install an employee life insurance program and is impressed with the fact that the company's premiums would be tax deductible under group insurance. At the insurance agent's suggestion, however, a split-dollar plan is installed wherein each insured contributes an amount equal to the annual term cost on his own policy through payroll deduction. The company is to pay the balance of the premiums. The plan is arranged so that Pacific Data Processing will not only receive a return of its premiums but interest as well. As a result, the company can provide its program at a zero cost and not merely a deductible cost.

Example 2. John Garmor and Henry Philips are the equal stockholders of Garmor-Philips, Inc. They are studying the possibility of a stock purchase agreement and conclude that, but for one thing, a cross-purchase plan would be better suited to their purposes than a stock redemption plan. That one thing is that Garmor-Philips, Inc., in a better cash position than the individuals, could fund more efficiently than they. But they now have a cross-purchase plan, with the funding borne by the company through split-dollar insurance. Each stockholder owns split-dollar protection on the other's life.

Example 3. Coast Girder Corporation is a sizable company with the usual pension plan and group benefits. Some years ago, it created a selective nonqualified deferred compensation plan for certain officers which provides for benefits only in the event an officer lives to retirement. The plan has been funded by annual deposits to individual securities investment accounts owned by the company for the benefit of each participating officer. These investments have been profitable, and the accounts have grown. The absence, nevertheless, of protection for an officer's account in the event of his death—future deposits and growth, and the estate tax payable—leads Coast Girder to adopt a split-dollar plan to provide the death benefit desired. A portion of the employer's deferred compensation plan contribution could be used, and the cash values would represent a part of the deferred compensation payments if the officer lived to retirement.

Example 4. Seven of the officers of Granite Rubber Company, Inc., have qualified stock options. These options run for five years. In the event of an officer's death, his estate may exercise his option to the same extent as he, for three months after his death. Recognizing that in the event of the death of any officer during the option period, the value of the option would be includable in the estate, and his family would want to have the cash to exercise his option, the company provides split-dollar insurance for each officer in an amount related to his own option program.

SELECTED REFERENCES

Diamond Life Bulletins. Cincinnati, Ohio: National Underwriter Company. Volume 5 of loose-leaf service.

Nolan, Stephen. "Split Dollar Applications," *C.L.U. Journal,* Vol. 18, No. 1 (Winter 1964), pp. 14–20.

Randall, Gerald J. *The Employer-Pay-All Split-Dollar Plan: A Unique Fringe Benefit Package.* Booklet No. A-274 for *Estate Planners Quarterly.* Lynbrook, N.Y.: Farnsworth Publishing Co., Inc., 1969.

Research and Review Service of America, Inc. *Advanced Underwriting Service,* Section 16-E. Indianapolis, Ind.

Thomas, James E. "Special Uses of Split Dollar," *C.L.U. Journal,* Vol. 22, No. 3 (July 1968), pp. 40–44.

45

Business Continuation—Unincorporated Business Interest

By ARTHUR J. WOJTA

THE MAJORITY of American business enterprises are operated in the unincorporated form. While business growth often leads to incorporation, the small business normally begins as a sole proprietorship or partnership. Such a business is created easily, often informally. It operates with a minimum of "red tape" and regulation. But this ease of creation and operation can lull a sole proprietor or partner into a false sense of security. The informal nature of the unincorporated business has its problems, too.

THE PROPRIETORSHIP

To put it simply, a proprietor is in business for himself. He is not an employee; he is the business owner. He may employ others as his business grows, but he employs them in a direct, personal way, rather than through the less direct partnership or corporate manner. His family and business roles necessarily become enmeshed.

A Family Business

The proprietor cannot effectively separate his personal from his business life. He is acting for his family in every business decision he makes. The family shares in the proprietor's gains to the extent his efforts create personal spending dollars. But the family is not always aware of the substantial risks being taken by and for every family member. The business creditors can destroy the family's financial security if the proprietor's business should fail.

While the proprietor can limit effectively the risk to his family by using good business judgment, the contingencies of good health and of life itself create special problems. If the proprietor is healthy and on the job, he can manage his family's investment effectively. But if the proprietor suffers a long-term medical disability, his control is usually lost.

The Disability Hazard

Statistics show that the risk of a temporary disability exceeds that of early death. A sole proprietorship should be protected against that hazard by the purchase of long-term disability income insurance. If the hazards of long-term disability are not reduced, the business often will fail for two reasons:

1. Many sole proprietorships have no surplus cash. Most of their assets are in the business, and of the nonliquid variety. The disabled proprietor usually will find it difficult to obtain bank credit if he suffers a long-term disability.
2. The business will have to generate a continuing income for the proprietor, and perhaps even additional funds for unusual medical expenses. The need to continue income to the business owner may foreclose the possibility of hiring a temporary replacement for him. The need to continue his family's income with business earnings generally will place a severe financial strain on the proprietorship.

In some cases business overhead expense insurance may be available for which premiums are deductible and benefits received are taxable for federal income tax purposes. This short-term disability policy protects the business for 18–24 months in most instances, and it can be a valuable addition to the personally owned disability income policy of the proprietor.

The Mature Proprietorship—A Crossroads

When the sole proprietor reaches his 50s, he will be forced to consider whether the business is to continue as a proprietorship or be terminated upon his retirement or death. Often the proprietor wants to see his business continue beyond the time when he will no longer be able to continue as its driving force. This may be possible if there is a son to groom as a replacement, or perhaps a key man who can buy the business.

The proprietor's potential successor may receive the business as a gift or bequest if he is a member of the proprietor's family. If not, the potential new business owner must devise a method to purchase the business at some future date. The original business owner may want to change the form of the business to a partnership or to a corporation so that his successor can join in the business ownership prior to the time full control is transferred. Before making a decision, all of the advantages and disadvantages of partnerships and corporations should be considered.

Sale to a Key Man

If a key employee agrees to purchase the proprietorship, a formal written buy-and-sell agreement is essential. The agreement should establish the purchase price and the time and terms of the sale. Death, disability, and retirement of the sole proprietor should be considered. The agreement usually directs the buyer to insure the seller's life.

Now the key man will have particular value to the proprietor in addition to his value as a key man in the business. Therefore, the proprietor may want to insure the life of the prospective key man purchaser.

Keeping the Business in the Family

If a family member, such as a son, is to assume control of the proprietorship, the father must decide whether to give or sell the business to him. The proprietor may want to see his son continue the business in the family name, but he also must provide for two other classes of family members:

1. His spouse, who will usually have a right to a fractional share of his assets, including the business, either as community property or as a statutory or common law dower right. How can the proprietor take care of his wife and still leave the proprietorship to a son who knows the business?
2. His other children, who cannot participate effectively in the business. How can the proprietor provide for all of his children and still have the business continue?

Insurance on the life of the proprietor can solve both of these problems. Life insurance can provide the spouse and other family members with cash rather than a portion of the business. The wife can agree to receive her share of the insurance proceeds as her marital or community share. The other children can receive their life insurance shares outright, or in trust.

Liquidating the Business

The mature sole proprietor may reach the crossroads of his business career and decide that there is no way the business can continue beyond his retirement, disability or death. If the business is of a personal service nature, such as a medical, dental or law practice, it is realistic to assume that the sole proprietor's family will be able to count on only an orderly liquidation of the business when one of these three contingencies occurs. The retired or disabled proprietor often can manage an orderly termination of his business. The executor of a deceased proprietor's estate should be selected to assure that liquidation losses are kept to a minimum. The sizable reductions in value of business assets that result from a forced "estate sale" are well known to all businessmen.

The proprietorship that eventually will terminate creates a need for sizable amounts of liquid assets outside of the business for a comfortable retirement as well as to pay transfer costs at death, and to maintain an adequate income standard for the surviving family. Insurance on the life of the proprietor can satisfy these needs. If there is a federal estate tax problem, the insurance often is owned by the proprietor's spouse or an irrevocable trust for his family so that the insurance proceeds will be available to provide liquidity without being subject to the estate tax.

Planning for the Sale of the Business at the Death of the Proprietor

If the key man or family member is to purchase the business of the proprietor when he dies, life insurance is commonly used to provide the buyer with the cash required to make an immediate transaction. The insurance is on the life of the proprietor, owned by the potential buyer. Permanent insurance normally is used so that substantial funds will be available to apply toward the purchase price in the event of the disability or retirement of the proprietor. The business owner may have to increase the salary of the key man in order to allow him to purchase the policy on the life of the proprietor. Such a salary increase would be deductible by the proprietor. The insurance premiums cannot be deducted by the key man for federal tax purposes, but the death proceeds will be received by him free of federal income taxation.

If the business is to be liquidated or sold by the executor on a "best effort" basis when the sole proprietor dies, his will should contain special provisions to facilitate the performance of the executor's duties. First, the executor should be allowed to maintain the business for a reasonable period of time, until a satisfactory buyer can be found. Without special authority an executor cannot continue a business without incurring personal liability for any business losses. Perhaps a family member can serve in the capacity of executor, but more often a corporate fiduciary is best able to arrange the sale of a business interest. Special attention also should be paid to the needs of minor children. If minor children are to share in the proceeds from the sale of the business, local law and court procedures should be considered. Special authority may be needed for the executor to continue the business whenever minor children are beneficiaries under the will.

The business that is to be continued for a period of time must be provided with liquid operating capital. The executor must be assured that there are sufficient funds to meet the demands of "timid" creditors and to hire key operating personnel. Taxes must be paid in cash, and the attorney for the estate wants his fee in cash, too. The cash provided by insurance on the proprietor's life can help maintain the business until it can be sold as a "going concern."

Without a will the administrator of a proprietor's estate often cannot proceed effectively with the continuation and orderly sale of the business. It may be difficult for the administrator to secure court authority to continue the business for a reasonable period of time. Because of the potential liability for continuing a business without specific authority, the proprietor always should have a will that considers this problem if the business is to be continued beyond the time needed for its liquidation. Otherwise, the administrator may have the duty to liquidate the business in an expeditious manner.

Establishing Value of the Business

One collateral benefit of a buy-sell agreement between a proprietor and his key man is its ability to establish value. If the following conditions are satisfied, the price established by the agreement will determine the value of the business for federal estate tax purposes:

1. A price must be established either by a formula or by agreement.
2. The proprietor's estate must be obligated to sell upon demand of the buyer.

3. The proprietor cannot dispose of the business during his lifetime without first offering it to the buyer at no more than the contract price.
4. The price must be fair and adequate when the agreement is made, i.e., an arm's length transaction.

Valuation of a business is an imprecise art at best, but it occupies an inordinate amount of time when the IRS and the executor of the proprietor's estate become involved in any valuation question. For purposes of planning, whenever the business is to be sold under the terms of a buy-sell agreement, advantage should be taken of the fact that the purchase price can establish the value of the business for estate tax purposes. Whenever a business is liquidated by the executor, the proceeds of the sale are readily ascertainable and the estate tax value can be established thereby if the alternate valuation date is elected by the executor and the sale takes place within six months of the date of death (the alternate valuation date). Problems arise if the business is bequeathed to a family member, or continued by the executor with the hope of a later sale. In each case, the executor likely will seek out a local expert to help establish the "fair market value" of the business.

Reporting Gain from Sale of the Proprietorship

The successful sole proprietor creates a substantial asset, but the sale of the proprietorship is not entirely a capital transaction that will be taxed at the more favorable capital gains rates. The operating assets and the goodwill attached to the business usually are capital assets subject to capital gains tax rates, but the sale of accounts receivable and certain inventory items may be taxed as ordinary income. The buyer and the seller should seek out expert advice concerning the allocation of the sales price between capital gains and ordinary income items. Often the overall price is finally determined after a close look at the overall tax impact on both the buyer and the seller. One of the advantages of the buy-sell agreement is the ability to control in advance the tax results of the sale. An executor trying to sell the business usually is not dealing from strength, and consequently may have to sacrifice some tax advantages.

Other Provisions in the Buy-Sell Agreement

Agreements to sell a proprietorship may vary, but after establishing the value of the business and the exact terms of the payment for the business at death, it is customary to consider the following:

1. A disability buy-out, including the definition of "disability."
2. A specified date for a retirement buy-out, and perhaps alternate provisions for the payment of the purchase price, often over a longer period of time.
3. Consent of the wife in community property states, and provision for the disposition of the wife's community interest if she predeceases her husband.
4. Disposition of the insurance on the life of the sole proprietor if the agreement is terminated, or if a retirement or disability buy-out occurs.

5. The means of paying any purchase price not funded by life insurance or other assets of the buyer, including the terms of the promissory note and the interest payable on the note.
6. Provision for simultaneous death of the buyer and seller, or the occurrence of their deaths within a specified period of time.
7. An agreement to amend the will of the seller directing his executor to consummate the sale as specified.
8. Provision for bankruptcy, business liquidation, and death of the buyer, as well as specific mention of any arrangements for mutually terminating the buy-sell agreement.

THE PARTNERSHIP

A partnership is defined as an association of two or more persons to carry on a business for profit. Often it is a proprietorship that has "grown up." Sometimes the proprietor has taken on a partner in order to acquire additional capital. Or perhaps the sole proprietor has taken his key employee into partnership to keep him from starting a competitive business. A third possibility, prevalent in the medical and law professions, is the desire of the sole practitioner to join with someone with similar expertise in order to provide better service to his clientele and more time with his family.

A Shared Responsibility

All general partners share authority for the operation of the partnership. A major drawback of the partnership method of operation is its similarity to the sole proprietorship—the general partners share unlimited liability for all business debts.

It is this idea of the partnership as an indivisible business unit that creates its strengths and weaknesses. While a partnership can function without a formal agreement, it functions best when all rights and duties of the partners are spelled out in writing. The ease with which a partnership can be created has a corresponding drawback in that the partnership can be just as easily dissolved if one member of the partnership should be unwilling or unable to continue in the business enterprise. While a minority shareholder in a corporation is often "locked in," any partner can terminate his relationship, and an entirely new partnership must be created if the business is to continue. Because of the intimate nature of the working relationships of the partners, one partner cannot sell out his interest to an outsider, or make a gift of it to a family member without the consent of the other partners. The remaining partners have a right to reject outsiders; they do not have to enter into a partnership with anyone they find undesirable. Instead, they can liquidate the interest of the withdrawing partner, and then form a new partnership.

Formalizing the Agreement

Because of the "delicate" nature of the partnership, it is especially important that a formal working agreement called the "articles of partnership" be drafted by legal counsel. A properly drafted agreement will include provisions for the withdrawal of a partner, the specific ownership shares, and the allocation of the operating responsibilities.

An alternative to a legal partnership is a "joint venture"; usually a specific short-term business operation. A "limited partnership" is another possibility. The limited partner is not involved in the daily operation of the business, and his risk is correspondingly limited to his investment in the business. Unlike the general partners, the limited partner does not risk all of his personal assets in the business operation. There must always be at least one general partner in any limited partnership. While limited partners are often found in the real estate investment business, most commercial and professional partnerships contain only general partners.

Federal Income Tax Aspects

A partnership is not a separate tax entity. The partnership is required to file an annual informational return, but (unlike the corporation) it pays no tax on retained earnings. The tax liability for the earnings of the partnership is passed on to the partners in their agreed shares. The unincorporated business owner, whether he is a proprietor or a partner, is not considered an employee. For this reason there are very few fringe benefits available to partners on a tax favored basis. Such benefits as group insurance, disability income, and accident and health plans can be provided by a partnership on a tax-deductible basis only for its employees, not for the partners who would have to include any partnership contributions to such plans on their behalf in their taxable incomes.[1]

Continuing the Partnership—A Matter of Planning

The withdrawal of any partner can dissolve the partnership arrangement effectively. Because one dissident partner thereby can disrupt the partnership by electing to withdraw, the articles of partnership usually provide for withdrawal of a partner by choice, or by reason of death, disability, or retirement. The intention of all those involved in the business operation is to assure that a withdrawing partner will disrupt the business routine as little as possible. A partner cannot dispose readily of his interest to outsiders, either by gift or by sale, since the remaining partners cannot be forced to accept an unwanted replacement for the withdrawing partner. Instead, they can choose to liquidate the partnership and reorganize without the dissenter. However, liquidation of the partnership can be extremely disruptive. This means that an arrangement to handle the disposition of a partner's interest has value to both the withdrawing partner and to the remaining partners.

Problems of Liquidation

When a partnership is dissolved, it must either be liquidated or reorganized. Liquidation is an elaborate, costly affair that is best avoided by proper planning. Liquidation requires that the remaining partner

---

[1] The "Self-Employed Individuals Retirement Act" described in Chapter 36 is one prominent exception.

or partners act as liquidating trustees, with a duty to wind up the partnership affairs and to terminate the business on a formal basis. A liquidating trustee is required to dissolve the business as quickly as possible, and he is responsible for all losses incurred if the business should be continued unnecessarily. He must sell the business assets for cash and collect the accounts receivable. He must pay the partnership debts and keep a strict accounting of all transactions. Finally, he must divide the net assets among the partners. This places a substantial burden on the remaining partners, and this fact gives the dissident partner some "leverage." He may be able to force the remaining partners to offer an unrealistic price for his interest if they wish to avoid the liquidation process.

So long as the business has value as a going concern to any other partner, the normal liquidation procedure should be avoided. Rather, the articles of partnership or a separate agreement should specify the rights of the remaining partners, or the partnership itself, to purchase the interest of the withdrawing partner. The agreement will cover withdrawal during lifetime, whether voluntary or by reason of disability or retirement. It will also provide for withdrawal upon the death of a partner.

Effects of the Death of a Partner

The death of a partner has a profound impact upon the rights and obligations of the surviving partners as well as the heirs of the deceased partner. In effect, death legally dissolves the partnership arrangement, but it is not terminated at that point. The partnership is terminated only upon completion of the winding up of the partnership affairs and the liquidation of the firm by the surviving partners in their role as liquidating trustees, or upon reorganization of the firm. If there is no agreement to purchase the interest of a deceased partner, the result of the death of a partner is that the authority of the surviving partners who act for that partnership is terminated, except to the limited extent required to wind up the business affairs of the partnership. This includes the completion of transactions already begun but not completed.

Alternatives to Liquidation at Death

The alternative to winding up and liquidation is to reorganize the partnership and continue the business after the death of a partner if the surviving partners and the heirs of the deceased partner can agree upon some workable arrangement. The possibility of taking in the heirs of the deceased partner as members of a new partnership arrangement may be subject to substantial legal and economic obstacles. Legally, the heirs may find that they cannot enter into a new partnership unless the estate is closed, a procedure which might involve a considerable amount of time. Frequently the rights of creditors or of minor heirs also will interfere with the formation of a new partnership. From the standpoint of the surviving partners, it is likely that the heirs will neither be capable nor personally compatible partners.

Another method of continuing the partnership as a business entity is to arrange for the heirs of the deceased partner to sell the business interest to an outsider. This may result in the old partners being forced to accept an unsuitable partner in order to continue the business without having to liquidate and then reorganize. The same problems with delays of the probate process may be encountered. The executor of the deceased partner's estate may not feel free to sell the partnership interest if he thinks the proceeds from liquidation would be greater.

A third possibility is to end all the interests of the surviving partners in the business, and to sell out the business to the heirs of the deceased partner. This assumes that the heirs are inclined to continue the business and have the cash to pay a fair price for the surviving partner's interests. The delays in the probate process and the possibilities of minor heirs being involved in guardianship arrangements make this a complicated procedure. Furthermore, the surviving partners then would find themselves with cash, but with no business of their own.

The most desirable solution, but also the solution that imposes the greatest financial burden on the surviving partners, is to have them purchase the interest of the heirs of the deceased partner. Again, estate probate delays may arise. Because all of the heirs must join in the sale, there may be pressure to bargain for a purchase price beyond a fair value. The surviving partners face the problem of raising enough money to purchase the deceased partner's interest, and financing may be difficult to arrange at that time. This is particularly true if the deceased partner had furnished a large portion of the management ability in the old partnership. There is also the surviving partners' fiduciary duties to consider. If the surviving partners try to purchase from the heirs, they are in the position of a trustee who seeks to purchase trust assets. Even though the purchase price is fair in all respects, it may be open to attack by a dissatisfied heir. Court approval probably will be required if there is a minor heir involved.

The Buy-Sell Agreement

Because it is generally in the best interest of both the surviving partners and the heirs of the deceased partner to have the business interest of the deceased partner purchased by the surviving partners, it is desirable to provide a binding buy-sell agreement in advance. Properly drawn, the agreement between the partners (or between the partners and the partnership) requires the estate of the deceased partner to sell his interest to the surviving partners (or the partnership). The agreement is legally enforceable by either party; the purchaser is usually entitled to specific performance of the agreement. It generally sets a fixed purchase price or provides for a definite formula for evaluating the worth of a deceased partner's interest. The written agreement eliminates uncertainties. The heirs cannot block the sale of the partnership interest, and the estate of the deceased partner must perform according to the terms of the agreement and sell the deceased's share within an agreed time after death. In order to provide certainty for the estate, the surviving partners, or the partnership itself, are also bound to purchase the deceased partner's share of the business.

Selecting the Buy-Out Method

There are two possible ways to arrange the buy-sell agreement. The remaining partners have a choice of purchasing the interest of a withdrawing or deceased partner, either on a personal basis, or through the partnership entity itself. If the remaining partners wish to preserve their same proportional interest in the business, the "entity" method of purchase is usually selected. Purchases by the entity are made in effect pro rata for the benefit of those continuing in the business. If the remaining partners do not wish to have their interests increased on a pro rata basis, some adjustment of the proportionate interests of the remaining partners may occur through the use of a "cross purchase" agreement among the partners in their individual capacities.

In summary, the "entity" arrangement involves a withdrawing partner and the partnership itself, and the "cross purchase" arrangement involves the withdrawing partner and the remaining individual partners.

Income Tax Treatment of Purchase and Sale of a Partnership Interest

For income tax purposes, the sale of a business interest may result in the receipt of both capital gain and ordinary income. To the extent the sale is for unrealized receivables and substantially appreciated inventory, it may result in ordinary income treatment to the seller. The portion of the sales price allocated to the partnership operating assets is generally subject to capital gain treatment. Payments for "goodwill" may be treated as capital assets subject to the more favorable capital gain rates, depending upon the manner of arranging the agreement. The entity method of buy-out may produce slightly different tax results than the cross-purchase method. As in a proprietorship buy-out, the allocation of the purchase price to capital and ordinary income assets may be an important part of the discussion surrounding the buy-sell agreement.

The provisions of the buy-sell agreement will affect the tax results of both the seller and the buyer. Therefore, if the buyers (surviving partners) are expected to have a higher tax rate than the seller, arranging the agreement to maximize their deductible costs may make it feasible to be more liberal in the purchase price than otherwise. Thus, it is important when negotiating the agreement to make projections for both parties.

Funding the Buy-Sell Agreement

A properly drafted business purchase agreement involving a partnership interest will contain substantially the same provisions covered in the sole proprietorship section of this chapter. Above all, it will specify a price and set the time and terms of the buy-out arrangement. Lifetime withdrawals from the partnership occurring because of dissension or long-term disability are difficult to fund completely in advance because of the uncertainty as to the time of need. However, a purchase to take place at retirement of a partner should establish one important goal. The partnership entity (or the remaining partners) will want to have at least a substantial portion of the buy-out funds available by the time the retirement date is reached. Ideally, the buy-out should be fully funded at that time. This means the accumulation of assets either within the partnership, or by the individual partners, on a systematic basis. Permanent life insurance is the ideal way to fund a business purchase agreement. The insurance can provide the funds needed for the immediate buy-out of a deceased partner's interest, when death occurs prematurely. Depending upon the cash values of the life insurance funding vehicle, a substantial portion of the funds needed for a retirement buy-out can be made available when needed. With permanent life insurance on each partner the agreement is funded, at least in part, from the day it is executed and the insurance placed in force.

The need to raise money out of personal resources or out of the assets of the partnership can be reduced or eliminated through the purchase of cash value life insurance. The need to raise money by borrowing at a moment's notice is reduced or eliminated. When a partner dies or withdraws from a partnership, lending institutions often are unwilling to grant a loan. Borrowed money must be paid back with after-tax dollars, plus interest. The need to pay the purchase price on an installment basis out of future earnings is reduced or eliminated when life insurance is used as a funding vehicle, depending upon which event creates the need for the buy-out.

If the partners decide to purchase a withdrawing partner's interest individually, each partner will own insurance on each of the others, in an amount at least required to cover the partnership interest he expects to purchase. This arrangement works out to best advantage when there are a limited number of partners. Where a large number of partners are involved, the operation can become cumbersome in operation, primarily because of the many policies that will be required. Because each partner applies for, owns and pays for the premium on a policy on the life of each other partner who is a party to the agreement, the numbers of policies increase rapidly as the partnership expands. If there are ten partners involved, each partner would own nine policies—one on the life of each other partner. Assuming all other things are equal, the multiplicity of policies required in a large partnership is one good reason for using the entity method of buy-out.

With the entity method, the partnership is established as the party obligated to purchase the interest of each withdrawing or deceased partner. The partnership insures each of the partners in an amount at least equal to the value of his interest. The partnership is the owner of the life insurance, and the beneficiary. It pays the premiums on each policy from general partnership assets. For accounting purposes, the premiums generally are prorated and charged to the respective accounts of the partners. In this way the insured indirectly contributes toward premiums on his own policy, and the purchase price for his interest may be increased on a systematic basis in order to take this fact into consideration.

The entity method of owning cash value life insurance necessarily increases the value of the partnership interest. However, the entity method is simple to arrange, and the number of insurance policies required to fund the entity method may be considerably less than the amount required for a cross-purchase arrangement. If the tendency for the entity method of funding a buy-out agreement to increase the value of each partnership interest over a period of time is a substantial objection, the agreement may be drawn specifically to exclude the value of the policy on the life of the deceased partner, or it may be preferable for the partners to consider the cross-purchase method.

Naturally, other objections to either the entity or cross-purchase method may arise, not related to the life insurance funding vehicle. Overall, the advantages of life insurance for funding a buy-sell agreement make it the most desirable funding medium. The problems incurred in attempting to fund the purchase of the interest of an uninsurable partner support this conclusion.

Other Considerations

For federal income tax purposes, the premiums paid on insurance used to fund a buy-sell agreemer .t are not deductible. Death proceeds ordinarily are received income tax free. This is a substantial advantage to the surviving partners. The heirs of the deceased partner must consider the income tax status of the payments made by the partnership or by the surviving partners. It may be possible that a portion of the purchase price will be ordinary income to the estate and the heirs.

Where estate taxes are a problem, the ability of the buy-sell agreement to establish a value for federal estate tax purposes is an important attribute to be considered. Essentially the same considerations discussed in the sole proprietorship section of this chapter will apply.

THE PROFESSIONAL

An important member of any business community is the professional involved in individual practice or in a professional partnership. For many years, professionals were unable to practice in corporate form, but now the legal barriers to incorporation have been eliminated in every state. In some cases a professional will find it financially desirable to incorporate. The many fringe benefits available to employees often are a major factor behind this decision.[2] But many other professionals will find it preferable to remain in the unincorporated form of doing business.

The professional's ability to generate substantial income usually results in a high standard of family living, and increases his need for life and disability insurance. He also can add to his accumulation of retirement dollars through the use of the "Self-Employed Individuals Tax Retirement Act."[3]

The professional has one major financial problem—the virtual inability to sell or will his practice to a family member. Except in rare cases, he must be satisfied with the liquidation of his business interest. If he is a partner, a buy-sell agreement among the partners is essential to guaran-

---

[2] For a discussion of professional corporations, see Chapter 48.

[3] Chapter 36 covers pensions and profit sharing for the self-employed.

tee the sale of his interest. The IRS now will allow the professional to allocate a portion of the purchase price for his business interest to goodwill, a capital asset. Payments for the professional's accounts receivable are deductible by the purchaser, and constitute ordinary income to the recipient. Life insurance is often used to fund the partnership buy-sell agreement between professionals.

In some cases, the professional partnership will purchase a building that will serve as the location of the professional practice. This is often arranged as a separate real estate partnership in order to ease the buy-out problems when death occurs. In that situation the practice will be purchased by the partnership entity or by the surviving professional partners, but the building partnership may continue unchanged. This would allow the widow to share in the rental income received from the surviving partners. In other instances, the deceased partner's interest in the real estate partnership is also sold at death, and the purchase obligation also may be funded with life insurance.

SELECTED REFERENCES

Aronsohn, Alan J. B. *Parnerships and Income Taxes*. Practicing Law Institute, 1966.

Dillavou, Essel R. *Principles of Business Law*. Englewood Cliffs, N.J.: Prentice-Hall, Inc., 1964.

Pennell, John S., and O'Byrne, John C. *Federal Income Taxation of Partners and Partnerships*. Philadelphia: The American Law Institute, 1971.

White, Edwin H. *Business Insurance*. Englewood Cliffs, N.J.: Prentice-Hall, Inc., 1963.

46

Business Continuation—
Corporate Business Interest

By STUART A. MONROE

THE CORPORATION, a popular form of business organization, is faced with a great variety of real and continuing risks. Like any business, it is subjected to all of the vicissitudes of the business cycle. Its continuing health is subjected to the whims of consumer demand for its products and services and the effectiveness of its management. Its material assets are subjected to fire, flood, and earthquake. Not the least important of the risks it faces is the potential destruction by disability or death of its principal owners. It is this latter risk with which this chapter will be concerned.

NATURE OF THE CORPORATION

A corporation is a separate, distinct, and legally recognized entity, created by law and usually existing for the purpose of engaging in business for profit. The original capital is normally furnished in the form of money (but occasionally consists of property or services). Those who make the capital contributions receive stock entitling them to share in the management and profits of the enterprise. The corporation is created by state law, generally through the filing of a "certificate of incorporation." This certificate will set forth the name of the corporation, the number and types of shares which can be issued, the number of directors, and the purpose for which organized, as well as the types of businesses in which it may engage.

If the stockholders are few in number, the corporation usually is referred to as a "close corporation." In a close corporation, the stockholders generally are active in the management and operation of the business as officers and employees. The stock is not listed on an exchange and has no ready market. It is this kind of corporation which is most likely to need insurance for business continuation purposes.

Unlike a partner in a partnership, a stockholder has limited liability; that is, he cannot lose more than he has invested in the corporation. A general partner, on the other hand, can be held liable for everything he owns (outside and inside the partnership). In a partnership, upon the death of a partner, there is a dissolution of the business. This is not the case in a corporation. Stockholders may die, but the corporation lives on. Thus, there is, in effect, perpetual life in the case of most business corporations. When a stockholder dies, the shares of stock he owns pass to his executor or administrator and then to the beneficiaries of his estate. During lifetime, they may be transferred by the owner to another by sale or by gift. The ease of transfer from one owner to another is a major reason why the corporate form of doing business is so popular. The owner of the stock may vote it; and if the interest represents a majority, then such owner may vote the stock so as to elect at least a majority of the board of directors and thereby, for all practical purposes, control the business.

In a closely held corporation, and as long as the business prospers, the livelihoods of the stockholders who are active in management are assured by salaries, bonuses, and, in some cases, dividends. Any excess earnings, if not distributed as dividends, are reflected in the increased value of the stock. The benefits from a stockholder's interest in a close corporation may be great to him, but they may not be to his family or to others who share in his estate. If a co-stockholder dies, the value of the surviving stockholders' shares may be greatly diminished by reason of the loss of their associate's peculiar talents and abilities.

The problem that death creates in a partnership can be seen rather easily. There is a dissolution at death, and the parties are faced with the liquidation imposed by law unless some alternative solution can be worked out. A buy-and-sell agreement is a logical solution. But a corporation does not "die" with the death of a stockholder—it has continuing life. However, there are very real problems caused by the death of a principal stockholder in a close corporation.

PROBLEMS CAUSED BY DEATH
OF PRINCIPAL STOCKHOLDER

Upon the death of a principal stockholder the *surviving stockholders* must either:

1. Continue the business with the decedent's family or other estate beneficiaries, who may not be familiar with the business nor be able to work in harmony with the surviving stockholders; or
2. Buy the decedent's stock, provided they can raise the necessary cash and are willing to outbid competitors; or
3. Continue the business with any outsiders to whom the decedent's estate may sell his stock; or
4. Sell their stock for whatever the decedent's estate or other purchasers will offer.

The situation is just as bad from the standpoint of the family or other estate beneficiaries of the deceased stockholder. They may:

1. Continue in business with the surviving stockholders; or
2. Buy the stock of the surviving stockholders, provided they have the necessary cash; or

3. Continue in the business with any outsiders to whom the stock of the survivors may be sold; or
4. Sell the decedent's stock for whatever the surviving stockholders or other purchasers will offer.

The problems extend even further, in that a basic conflict often exists between the surviving stockholders and the widow. The widow needs income to replace her husband's salary. There may not be sufficient other income-producing property. It may not be possible or desirable to pay dividends on the stock. What can she do? This phase of the problem can best be explored by analyzing the basic elements of a share of stock.

BASIC ELEMENTS OF A SHARE OF STOCK

With respect to a closely held corporation, a share of stock can be said to comprise four separate elements: (1) the right to work, (2) the right to receive dividends, (3) the right to vote, and (4) the right to sell. Generally, a share of stock carries with it no right to work and to receive a salary. But in the closely owned corporation, an owner frequently makes his investment in the business to secure the status of a salaried officer as well as to become a stockholder. His stock interest plus his ability, while alive, will usually give him the right to work. In regard to these basic elements, consider the situations of the minority stockholder, the majority stockholder, and the equal stockholder.

The Minority Stockholder Situation

First, a minority stockholder dies owning, for example, a one-third interest. What is the problem facing his widow? It is one of income. Her husband's salary terminates immediately upon death, and she seeks a source to replace that income. She asks the surviving stockholders to place her on the payroll, but is politely told there is no place for her. As time goes on, the need for income may become more pressing. She asks the survivors when they expect to pay a dividend. Their reply is that they have never paid one; furthermore, at present, there is the need to establish a better credit position and purchase new machinery. She now consults an attorney. He advises that the payment of a dividend in this instance is within the discretion of the board of directors and apparently the board feels the needs of the business do not warrant the declaration of a dividend. They can, in some instances, be compelled to declare a dividend, but these instances are exceedingly rare, costly, and time-consuming. While legal proceedings may be possible, it will be difficult for the widow to obtain dividend payments. Pursuit of the "right to receive dividends" is fruitless. Obviously, two of the benefits of a share of closely held stock are eliminated.

She attends a stockholders' meeting to vote her stock, but finds that a minority interest is readily outvoted. This right of the shareholder gives no relief.

Now, being somewhat desperate for income, she seeks to sell her stock and is advised that the best market would be the surviving stockholders. In discussing it with them, they ask her what she feels is a fair price for the stock. She indicates that her husband told her it was worth about $160 a share. Their response leaves no doubt where they stand. In their opinion, the husband's valuation was substantially out of line, and the best offer from them is $85 a share. The squeeze is now on. She is forced to sell on their terms.

The Majority Stockholder Situation

Now, consider the second situation—that involving a deceased majority stockholder. The widow has the same basic problem—loss of income. The husband's salary must be replaced. But in this case, through the right to vote and elect directors, the widow can, in effect, control the corporation. Through her voting control, members friendly and sympathetic to her view can be placed on the board of directors. Because the board controls the appointment of officers and payment of compensation, the widow can place herself on the payroll. However, the business may be one that requires competent management which only the surviving minority stockholder-officers can provide. By threats to leave or to set up a competing company, they can force their views upon the widow. Her position then becomes a weak one.

The Equal Stockholder Situation

A third situation develops when the surviving stockholder and the widow each own an equal interest (50 percent each). Neither person would be in control of the corporation. The basic conflict of interest would persist, but could not be resolved. This can be an extremely troublesome situation. Not infrequently, a deadlock results, which hurts both parties as well as the business itself.

The Situations Reversed

The implications of these three situations can be reversed. In the first one, the surviving and controlling stockholders dominated the widow. She was forced into a very unsatisfactory sale because of her need for income. Suppose that the widow had sufficient income from outside sources. With no need to sell hastily, she could become a considerable nuisance to the corporation as a minority stockholder. In time, the survivors might be very willing and anxious to buy her out and this time at a price more favorable to her than to them. Thus, in this kind of situation the surviving stockholders may be subjected to repeated harassment.

In the second situation, the widow was the controlling stockholder and, as such, can squeeze the surviving stockholder-officers. Unless they conform to the management views of the widow, their jobs can be in jeopardy.

Finally, we saw two equal stockholders battling. Sometimes the widow may occupy the dominant position and cause the most trouble. But it could be the surviving stockholder, who by manipulation forces the widow into a weak position, so that she is compelled to sell on his terms.

Importance of Situation Analysis

These situations are intended to suggest that each case should be analyzed to visualize the situation upon the death of the client, and particularly the effect his death could have upon the value of his interest in the business as a part of his estate and from his family's viewpoint. This is especially significant when the client is a primary motivating force in the business and when the business interest comprises the major portion of his wealth.

There must also be considered the effect that the death of one of the other principal stockholders could have upon the interest of the client during his lifetime, and the possible complications which may arise in conducting the affairs of the corporation due to dissatisfaction among the heirs of such stockholder. Unless adequate precautions are taken, it is almost impossible for a closely held corporation to escape serious pressures one way or another at the death of a major stockholder.

It is always desirable to take the long-range view to determine ways in which the values of a business may be preserved.

It is axiomatic that the prosperity of any business is dependent upon its management, and this is particularly true of a close corporation. Management can be most efficient and effective in the closely held corporation where it possesses voting control. It is almost always embarrassing for the survivors to have the family of the deceased as continuing stockholders. Such stockholders are seldom satisfied with the benefits received from the corporation after the death of their breadwinner when compared with the benefits they received during his lifetime. If a lag in profits occurs, they are apt to blame the management rather than recognizing that it might be due to unavoidable conditions, perhaps due to the death of the working stockholder.

Thus, it can be seen that in many cases the transmission of the stock interest to his family by a stock owner poses a problem not only to the family but to the surviving stockholders as well. A buy-and-sell agreement is a frequent solution to prevent distribution of stock interests into the hands of inactive or possibly unsympathetic individuals. The buy-and-sell agreement also provides the stockholder with a market assuring a fair price for his stock upon his death, and removes his family from the hazards, risks, and harassments of the business.

RETENTION OF STOCK INTEREST BY THE FAMILY

It should not be assumed that every situation calls for the sale of the stock interest in a closely held corporation upon the death of a stockholder. There will be situations where, because the business is a highly profitable one and the personal guidance of the stockholder is not completely vital, the stock interest may be retained for the family. In other cases, the retention of the stock interest will be desired because there are family members who work in the business or who eventually will come into the business.

The factors which will influence the decision to retain or sell the stock interest will usually be:

1. Are there sons or sons-in-law for whom it should be retained and preserved?

2. Is the stock interest a majority one? If the interest is a minority one, can the family get along with the surviving shareholders, or will it be at their mercy?
3. What are the future prospects of the industry and the particular business within that industry? In short, is it a good investment?
4. Is competent management available?

If the decision is to retain the stock interest within the family, certain problems of valuation and liquidity will be encountered.

Valuation of Stock Interest—If Retained

A basic problem is that of determining at what value the stock will be included in the gross estate of the decedent stockholder for federal estate tax purposes. Because a close corporation is one with very few stockholders, normally there is no market for the stock. The federal estate tax regulations require that the "fair market value" be ascertained. This has been defined as the price at which the stock would change hands between a willing buyer and a willing seller, neither being under any compulsion to buy or to sell, and both having reasonable knowledge of all relevant facts. But such definition does not help very much in practical situations. Artificial means must be employed to arrive at "fair market value."

Revenue Ruling 59–60 (1959–1 CB 237) must be considered in dealing with the valuation of stock of a closely held corporation since it contains the most current and comprehensive explanation of valuation. The ruling lists and discusses eight factors involved in valuing closely held corporation stock. These eight factors are:

1. *Company History and Nature of the Business.* The valuation of stock can be affected by the position the particular business occupies within its own industry, as well as by factors and events that have been present in the past but are unlikely to occur again in the future.
2. *General Outlook of the National Economy and of the Specific Industry.* It is important to look at the specific business within the framework of trends in the national economy and in the particular industry.
3. *The Company's Financial Position.* Balance sheet data for prior years must be prepared and studied to determine the company's growth or lack of it. A necessary step is the calculation of the stock's book value per share.
4. *Earning Capacity of the Business.* Frequently it has been said that the single most important element of valuation is the earning capacity of a company. Profit and loss statements for prior years (usually at least five) should be considered. In the closely held corporation, the net earnings available to common stockholders is the significant figure. This means net profit after income taxes and after the payment of dividends on preferred stock, if any. The earnings trend will be important.
5. *Dividend History and Dividend-Paying Capacity.* The capacity of the company to pay dividends is the true measure of this factor rather than the actual dividend record.
6. *Goodwill.* The presence or absence of that intangible value usually

called goodwill rests primarily upon the excess earning power of the business over what might be called a fair or reasonable return on the net tangible assets and services rendered by the stockholders.

7. *Sales of the Stock.* Any previous sales of the company stock should be taken into consideration. The price for a share of stock in such sales must be equated with the number of shares sold and whether the parties were dealing at arm's length.

8. *The Market Value of Stock of Comparable Companies Whose Stock Is Publicly Traded.* The essential factor in this element of valuation is that the stock to be used for comparison should be that of a corporation engaged in the same or similar line of business and that it be actively traded in a free public market as of the valuation date.

While these eight factors serve as guidelines in the valuation process, it must be recognized that there is no one prescribed method or "right" answer to the difficult problem of valuing the stock of a closely held corporation.

Estate Liquidity Problem Where
Stock Interest Is Retained

A decision to retain the stock creates not only the problem of valuation but also that of estate liquidity. The problem of valuation will remain uncertain, but the hardship of raising cash for estate costs has been somewhat alleviated by Section 303 of the Internal Revenue Code.

Section 303, in effect, provides that a corporation may make a partial redemption of its own stock from the estate of a deceased stockholder without the estate running the risk of having the purchase price declared a taxable dividend. However, certain stated conditions must be met.

The major condition is that the stock must constitute more than 35 percent of the gross estate of a deceased stockholder, or more than 50 percent of the taxable estate. If the decedent owned more than 75 percent of outstanding stock of each of two or more corporations, and these stock interests were included in the gross estate, they may be combined for the purposes of meeting the 35 or 50 percent rule.

The provision that Section 303 may be used when the value of the stock interest is more than 50 percent of the taxable estate makes it relatively easy to qualify when there is a surviving spouse and the maximum marital deduction is used. Since the taxable estate is the amount remaining after all the deductions, including the marital deduction and specific exemption, are subtracted from the gross estate, the 50 percent of "taxable estate" test is met more readily than might first appear.

The estate or other holder of stock that was included in the gross estate may take advantage of the provisions of Section 303 through a sale of stock to the corporation to the extent of the total of the federal and state death taxes, funeral expenses, and administration costs. Furthermore, the estate may redeem corporate stock under Section 303 even though it has other liquid assets to meet these costs. The estate need not be "tight" for cash.

Section 6166 of the Internal Revenue Code is also of interest in this connection. This law permits the estate owning an interest in a closely held business to pay that portion of the federal estate tax allocable to the business interest in installments over a period not to exceed 10 years. The major pertinent requirements of this section are as follows:

1.　Similar to Section 303, the value of the business interest included in the estate must exceed either 35 percent of the gross estate or 50 percent of the taxable estate. Two or more businesses can be combined to meet these requirements if the decedent held more than a 50 percent interest in each such business.

2.　When the business interest in the estate is stock in a close corporation, as opposed to an unincorporated business interest, there must have been 10 or fewer stockholders, or the decedent's stock interest must represent 20 percent or more of the voting stock.

3.　The installment payment privilege is available only for the portion of the total federal estate tax attributable to the inclusion of the business interest in the estate. The balance of the tax must be paid within the usual nine-month period after death.

4.　Four percent interest is charged on the unpaid balances.

State death taxes, administration expenses, and funeral costs, even though substantial in amount, cannot be paid by installments under Section 6166 but must be paid in full within the time limits applicable.

DISPOSING OF STOCK INTEREST
THROUGH FORMAL AGREEMENT

In many instances, the answers to the questions previously posed as influencing retention or sale will lead to a decision that the stock interest should not be retained for the family. When disposition of the stock is indicated, a market can be best established by use of a buy-and-sell agreement.

There are four basic kinds of buy-and-sell agreements:

1.　The purchaser is obligated to buy the stock, and the estate of the deceased stockholder is obligated to sell. This is frequently referred to as a mandatory agreement of purchase and sale.

2.　The purchaser has an option to purchase the stock of the deceased stockholder; and if exercised, the estate must sell.

3.　The estate of the deceased stockholder has an option to sell; and if exercised, the other party must buy.

4.　Neither of the parties is obligated to buy or to sell, but if a stockholder or the estate of a deceased stockholder desires to sell, the stock must first be offered to the other parties before it can be sold to a third party. This is sometimes referred to as a "first-offer" type of agreement.

The mandatory buy-and-sell agreement is the one most frequently used when stockholders desire to dispose of their holdings upon death. When the agreement is between the corporation and the stockholders, with the corporation as purchaser, it is usually referred to as a *stock redemption agreement*. If between the stockholders only, the buy-and-sell agreement is referred to as a *cross-purchase agreement*.

Whether the buy-and-sell agreement is one of stock redemption or cross-purchase, the mandatory type of agreement accomplishes the desired basic results: it provides a market for the stock interest in the event of death; it prevents outsiders from acquiring an interest in the business; it removes the family from the hazards and risks of the business; and it provides liquidity to pay estate costs and taxes.

Various court decisions support the conclusion that the price of the stock as established in the agreement will determine its value for federal estate tax purposes, if the following conditions are met:

1. The estate of the deceased stockholder is obligated to sell the stock.
2. The surviving stockholders or the corporation must either be obligated to buy or have the option to buy.
3. The price of the stock must either be fixed by the terms of the agreement or there must be a method stipulated in the agreement for determining the price.
4. The agreement must forbid each stockholder from disposing of his stock during lifetime without first offering it to the other parties to the agreement at a price not higher than the price to be paid in the event of death.
5. The agreement is the result of an arm's length transaction. It should be based on adequate consideration and not be a substitute for testamentary disposition. This means the parties must deal with each other as they would with strangers.

Parties

Not all of the stockholders need be included, whether the plan be stock redemption or cross-purchase. Perhaps only three out of five stockholders desire a buy-and-sell agreement for their stock interest. The three stockholders can be parties to a cross-purchase agreement among themselves, or a stock redemption plan can be entered into between these three stockholders and the corporation. Those stockholders desiring to participate will be parties to the agreement. If the plan is to be one of stock redemption, then the corporation, of course, must be a party to the agreement.

The services of a trustee may be desired in some situations. A chief reason for the use of a trustee is that an impartial person is made responsible to see that the terms and conditions of the agreement are carried out promptly and properly. The trustee, who can be either a disinterested individual or a corporate trustee, will be the beneficiary of the life insurance policies and have possession of the stock certificates. When a trustee is used, the trustee becomes a party to the agreement as well.

Stock Redemption versus Cross-Purchase

The fundamental differences between a stock redemption plan and a cross-purchase plan may be analyzed as to enforceability, funding, premium payment, transfer of policies, income tax status, beneficiary designation, and estate tax status.

Enforceability. The difference between stock redemption and cross-purchase with respect to enforceability centers on the power of a corporation to purchase its own stock. When the plan is stock redemption, a corporation, in most states, can purchase its own stock, provided it is done out of surplus and the interests of creditors are not jeopardized. If such a purchase cannot be made, then the agreement may be unenforceable. Where the agreement is cross-purchase, no such problem arises.

Funding the Agreement. The buy-and-sell agreement, by its very nature, creates an obligation in the corporation or the survivors to purchase the stock interest of the first stockholder to die. The manner in which this obligation is to be discharged becomes most important. Do they wish to discharge this obligation from accumulated cash reserves, which may not be available at the time needed? Do they wish to use promissory notes? Or do they want installment payments over a long period of time? Since the obligation may mature with unexpected suddenness, the problem of providing funds to purchase the interest of a deceased owner is most satisfactorily solved through the use of life insurance.

Impact of Premium Payments. Under a stock redemption plan, the corporation will own the life insurance, be the beneficiary, and pay the premiums. The premiums paid by the corporation are not deductible for income tax purposes, and the policy proceeds payable upon death are not includable in the corporation's gross income. The payment of premiums by the corporation has the effect of allocating the total amount of premiums among the stockholders according to their shareholdings. The larger, and often older, stockholder "pays" the major portion of the premiums, whereas the younger, and smaller, stockholder would "pay" very little. In a cross-purchase plan, these positions would be reversed. If the parties to a stock redemption plan feel that the impact of the premiums is inequitable, a solution might be worked out by including a portion of the proceeds of the life insurance policy on the deceased stockholder's life in the purchase price formula. This would, in effect, reimburse the estate for the premiums advanced.

Under a cross-purchase plan, the stockholders take out insurance on each others' lives and pay the premiums. For example, assume that a corporation valued at $100,000 is owned 60 percent by A, 25 percent by B, and 15 percent by C, and the survivors want a plan under which the proportionate ownership interests of the survivors to each other is maintained. The life insurance arrangements in this instance might be as shown in Table 46–1.

TABLE 46–1.   Illustrative Life Insurance Arrangement in a Cross-Purchase Plan for Close Corporation

Policy	Life	Amount of Insurance	Owner Beneficiary, Premium Payor
1.......	A	$37,500	B
2.......	A	22,500	C
3.......	B	20,000	A
4.......	B	5,000	C
5.......	C	10,588	A
6.......	C	4,412	B

The age and stock interest will determine the impact of the premium payments. If B and C are appreciably younger than A, it will be seen that they will pay far more in premiums than A. It can be argued that this is as it should be because the younger and smaller stockholders will benefit substantially should A die. Thus, they should bear the impact of the premiums on the life insurance required to acquire that ownership.

Transfer of Insurance Policies. Under a stock redemption plan, the life insurance policies are purchased and owned by the corporation, and only one policy may be required for each life. Under a cross-purchase plan, the number of policies required can be computed by multiplying the number of stockholders involved by one less than that number (if five stockholders, 5 times 4, or 20 policies would be needed).

Upon the death of a stockholder under a stock redemption plan, no transfer of a policy is necessary. The corporation owns the policies on the surviving stockholders' lives.

Under a cross-purchase plan with the policies owned by the stockholders on a criss-cross arrangement, upon the death of one of them, a transfer of each policy owned by the deceased stockholder on the survivors' lives to the survivors is necessary if the life insurance coverage is to remain the same and the policies are to integrate with the agreement. Each such transfer would constitute a "transfer for value" within the meaning of Section $101(a)(2)$ of the Internal Revenue Code. Under this section, transfers of life insurance policies may be made between partners, to a partnership, and to a corporation of which the insured is a stockholder or officer, without adverse tax consequences, but this is not so of transfers between stockholders. In respect to Section $101(a)(2)$, the stock redemption plan has an advantage over cross-purchase.

Income Tax Basis. Under a stock redemption plan, the purchase of stock of a deceased stockholder by the corporation generally has the effect of increasing the value of the stock of the surviving stockholders. The cost basis of the survivors' stock, for determining gain or loss upon a subsequent sale for income tax purposes, has not changed.

To illustrate, let us assume that A, B, and C each paid $10,000 for 100 shares of stock. Today the corporation has capital and surplus of $60,000 (capital $30,000 and surplus $30,000). Each of the 300 shares has its original cost basis of $100 and, if sold at today's book value, would bring a price of $200, or a long-term capital gain of $100 per share.

If this corporation, pursuant to a stock redemption plan, owns $20,000 of life insurance on A's life and he dies, the proceeds would be used by the corporation to acquire A's 100 shares at the agreement price of $200 per share. The capital and surplus would remain at $60,000. The insurance would increase the surplus to $50,000, but then $20,000 would be used to purchase A's stock. This would leave 200 shares of stock outstanding: 100 owned by B and 100 owned by C. But with the corporation still valued at $60,000, each share would be worth $300 book value. If B or C should then sell his stock at book value, he would have a long-term capital gain of $200 per share. For simplicity, policy cash values have been ignored.

It is important to note that A's estate would have no income tax problem at all. Property sold subsequent to death takes as its income tax basis the value used for estate tax purposes. The agreement price, $200, would control for federal estate tax purposes, and the income tax basis would be $200. Therefore, there is no gain on the transaction and no taxable income to the estate, despite the fact that A paid only $100 per share and never paid income tax on the increment.

Under a cross-purchase plan, the result is a different one for the survivors. They acquire an increased income tax basis for their stockholdings purchased from the deceased stockholder's estate. Using the same situation as above, B and C would each purchase 50 shares from A's estate at $200 per share (the agreement price). B and C now own 150 shares each. The newly acquired shares would have an income tax cost basis of $200 per share (the price they paid), and 100 shares (the original holdings) would have a basis of $100 per share. B and C have a total cost basis for their stock of $20,000 each. A subsequent sale of the stock at $200 per share (book value of $60,000 divided by 300 shares) would result in no gain on 50 shares and $100 capital gain per share on 100 shares, or a total gain of only $10,000.

Beneficiary Designation.   The beneficiary of the life insurance policies under a stock redemption plan will be the corporation because it has the obligation to purchase the stock interest. When it is desired under a stock redemption plan to use the services of a trustee, then, of course, the trustee will be the beneficiary of the insurance proceeds.

Different beneficiary designations have been used on cross-purchase plans, not always properly. In some instances the estate of the insured has been used. This designation should be avoided. The stock passes to the estate of the deceased stockholder, and if the insurance proceeds are also received by the estate, it would seem that the executor or administrator of the estate has control over both the stock and the proceeds. Creditors of the estate can attack the insurance proceeds.

In other situations, the designation of the deceased stockholder's wife or other family member is frequently motivated by a desire to obtain the optional modes of settlement for the beneficiary. Such a designation must be carefully worded and coordinated with the agreement, so that the estate will not be bypassed. Unless this precaution is taken, the following problems can result:

1. *Objections of Other Estate Beneficiaries.*   Assume that the beneficiary of the insurance is the wife and the stockholder leaves no will. If there are children and some or all of them are minors, there is a question as to the position of the minor children. They will take an interest in the estate the same as adult children, but they cannot consent to any transfers. It is most unlikely that the administrator will convey the stock to the surviving stockholders when payment for it goes directly to the widow—ignoring the interests of the children.

2. *Creditors of the Estate.*   If the estate does not possess sufficient cash or liquid assets to pay creditors or death taxes, can the stock be transferred to the surviving stockholders when payment, pursuant to the agreement, goes directly to the widow?

3. *Income Tax Base.*   The Legallet case (1 BTA 294) held that a surviv-

ing partner did not receive an increased cost basis when the proceeds of the life insurance policy were payable directly to the beneficiary of the deceased partner and were not received actually or constructively by the surviving partner. The same conclusion could be reached under a similar situation involving a stock interest in a corporation. However, the Mushro case (50 TC 43, 1968) is contrary to the Legallet case. It permitted the survivor to include the insurance proceeds (payable directly to the insured's personal beneficiary) in his cost basis for the stock since there was a legally binding agreement between the stockholders to apply the proceeds to the purchase of the stock. The Internal Revenue Service has issued a nonacquiescence to the Mushro case (IRB 1970–38, p. 5).

These problems can be avoided when availability of the settlement options is desired by providing that the proceeds payable to the named beneficiary be held at interest for a period of time during which the purchaser or trustee will have a right of withdrawal that can be exercised at the request of the executor or administrator of the deceased stockholder's estate. In most cases, such right will not have to be exercised, but it is available if a problem arises.

Naming the surviving stockholders as beneficiary is the most logical plan when the optional modes of settlement are not desired because those obligated to purchase the stock interest of a deceased stockholder receive the insurance proceeds. The contingent beneficiary should be the estate of the surviving stockholder.

The use of a trustee is often desired to assure performance pursuant to the terms of the agreement. Payment of the life insurance proceeds will then be made to the trustee in a single sum. The trustee disposes of the proceeds as directed by the agreement.

Estate Tax Status. When the agreement is negotiated in good faith and at arm's length, and is binding during the lifetime of the owner as well as at death, the price agreed upon will probably be controlling for estate tax purposes.

Special Family Situations

There are numerous closely held corporation situations where the stockholders are members of the immediate family. For example, a father, a son, and a son-in-law comprise the stockholders, and a buy-and-sell agreement is contemplated. The implications of Sections 302 and 318 of the Internal Revenue Code must be observed.

Should they adopt a stock redemption arrangement, then upon the father's death, the corporation will purchase the shares from his estate. Section 302 tells us that if this purchase completely terminates the estate's stock interest in the corporation or is "substantially disproportionate," capital gains treatment will be given to the transaction (to be substantially disproportionate, after the purchase, the estate must own less than 50 percent of outstanding voting stock, and the percentage of the total outstanding voting stock—owned directly or constructively—immediately after the redemption must be less than 80 percent of his percentage of such stock outstanding immediately before redemption). Thus, no income tax problems are encountered. However, if these tests are not met, then the purchase of the estate's stock may be considered a dividend distribution by the corporation and the purchase price taxed as ordinary income. The latter would be a most serious income tax burden.

The requirements of Section 302 seem simple enough—redeem *all* of the father's shares. But it is not so easy, because Section 318 invokes certain rules of attribution. This means that in certain instances, shares of stock in a corporation owned by one person are assumed to be owned by other members in his family unit, or vice versa. Also, stock ownership of estates, partnerships, corporations, or trusts is attributed to the estate beneficiaries, partners, stockholders, and trust beneficiaries, respectively, or vice versa. Therefore, in the above situation, if the son is a beneficiary of his father's estate, the estate will be deemed constructively to own the son's shares. Likewise, the son-in-law's stock will be deemed owned by his wife (the daughter) through family attribution and this, in turn, attributed to the father's estate if the daughter is a beneficiary. Thus, compliance with Section 302 becomes impossible, and we may have a dividend distribution with disastrous income tax consequences.

If a stock purchase arrangement is used in this situation, the income tax problem will not be involved. Sections 302 and 318 apply only to the purchase of its stock by a corporation.

Advantages of the Buy-and-Sell Agreement

The advantages of a buy-and-sell agreement funded through life insurance might be summarized as follows:

1. To the surviving stockholders:
    a) They become the sole owners of the business.
    b) Outside stock interests cannot interfere.
    c) The terms of the sale, such as price and payment, are fixed in advance.
    d) The cash to finance the purchase is provided automatically at the death of a stockholder by the life insurance.
2. To the family of the deceased stockholder:
    a) The family has an assured market for the stock at a fair price.
    b) The widow is free from business responsibility.
    c) The cash received in full for the stock interest is free from the hazards and risks of the business.
    d) Settlement of the estate can be made with dispatch because the cash received provides a fund from which estate costs and taxes can be paid.
    e) The value of the stock is fixed for estate tax purposes.
    f) Family dependency upon the fortunes of the business and its management is removed.

SELECTED REFERENCES

Appleman, John Alan (ed.). *Basic Estate Planning*, chaps. 4 and 5. Indianapolis, Ind.: Bobbs-Merrill Co., 1957.

McCabe, Thomas C.; Mitchell, William H.; and Plowden-Wardlaw, Thomas C. "Integrating Life Insurance with Business Planning," *Journal of the American Society of Chartered Life Underwriters*, Vol. 12, No. 2 (Spring 1958), p. 176.

Monroe, Stuart A. *Disability, Salary Continuation and the Corporation Buy-Sell Agreement*. 2d ed., Lynbrook, N.Y.: Farnsworth Publishing Co., Inc., 1971.

————. *How to Use Section 303 to Sell Business Insurance*. 2d ed. Lynbrook, N.Y.: Farnsworth Publishing Co., Inc., 1971.

Tremayne, Bertram W., Jr. "Estate Planning for the Man with a Business," *Washington University Law Quarterly*, 1955, No. 1, p. 40.

"The Use of Life Insurance to Fund Agreements Providing for Disposition of a Business Interest at Death," *Harvard Law Review*, Vol. 71 (1958), pp. 687–712.

White, Edwin H. *Business Insurance*. 3d ed. Englewood Cliffs, N.J.: Prentice-Hall, Inc., 1963.

47

Income Protection for
Business Continuation

By WILLIAM HARMELIN

THE PROLONGED DISABILITY of sole proprietors, active partners, or close corporation stockholders without adequate income protection usually results in the "economic death" of their businesses. When disability lasts long enough to destroy earning capacity, personal and business reserves are soon dissipated. Under these conditions, the individuals involved and their businesses face very serious economic problems.

It is common practice for sole proprietorships, partnerships, and close corporations to buy life insurance for the purpose of reducing the financial loss to a business and the threat to its continuance which are caused by the death of an owner or key employees. There has been an increasing awareness, however, of the need for similar insurance coverage to protect against the staggering financial losses which occur when these business people become disabled for long periods of time. A Certified Public Accountant wrote:

> The death or poor health of the owners or key men may seriously affect the business and its continued profitable operation. Planning for these human factors is often overlooked by many otherwise astute businessmen who have inventory costs, sales, expenses, and cost profit margins under finger tip control.
> The completely planned business enterprise gives to the one the same full and exacting attention as it does to the other. Moreover, the necessary planning to protect the business enterprise against human mishaps is relatively simple and will demand but little time at the planning level.[1]

These thoughts pinpoint the fact that business advisers are beginning to understand the meaning of the late and revered Dr. S. S. Huebner's third kind of economic death: the "living death." In this connection, Dr. Huebner has stated: "He who becomes a living death, totally and perma-

---

[1] N. R. Caine, "Health a Big Factor in Business," *New York World Telegram,* April 25, 1963.

nently, is just as dead economically as he who is actually dead. . . . The difference between the 'living death' under conditions of permanency and the 'actual death' is only six feet of sod. And if anything, the living death is the worst economically."[2]

Disabilities lasting at least 90 days and averaging over 5 years in duration are about two and a half times as frequent as death before age 65. Of 300 men aged 35, over 100 will be disabled for 90 days or more before reaching age 65, with an average disability period of 6½ years.[3]

This chapter will deal with the economic effect of serious disabilities of sole proprietors, active partners, and stockholder-employees on their businesses. Proposed solutions to the various problems created by such disabilities also will be discussed.

EFFECT OF DISABILITY ON A BUSINESS

Sole Proprietorship

Sole proprietorships represent about 70 percent of all business establishments. The sole proprietor is a man of many talents. In effect, he is the president, treasurer, purchasing agent, sales manager, and board of directors of the business—all rolled into one person.

The sole proprietor and the business are one and the same.[4] He makes his own decisions. He does not have to consult anyone. The business will prosper and grow in direct proportion to his know-how, personality, experience, reputation, judgment, and ability to work. Thus, the success of the business depends almost entirely on the owner's ability. If the business profits, he profits. If the business loses, he loses. He is personally liable for business debts even to the extent of his personal assets.

In most businesses, when the sole proprietor becomes seriously disabled, the business suffers. Businesses do not run by themselves. Sole proprietors recognize this fact, and while they are in good health, they rarely take vacations for extended periods of time. However, when a serious sickness or accident compels them to remain away from the business for an extended period of time, the economic effects on the sole proprietorship, as well as on their personal lives, are often disastrous.

The business may continue to function while the sole proprietor is disabled. However, unless it is a most unusual business, profits will drop because of the loss of the special skills and mature judgment of the sole proprietor. If the sole proprietor cannot work for a long enough period in a business which requires his personal services, the business will fail.

---

[2] Unpublished observation made in lecture and confirmed by the late Dr. S. S. Huebner, former President, American College of Life Underwriters, Bryn Mawr, Pennsylvania.

[3] "Report of the Committee on Disability and Double Indemnity," *Transactions of the Society of Actuaries*, Vol. 5, No. 2 (1953), p. 70.

[4] A large number of professional people are sole proprietors, including accountants, attorneys, dentists, doctors, veterinarians, architects, and the like. However, more and more professionals have been incorporating their practices as all states have enacted enabling legislation which makes incorporation possible.

Partnership

The general business partnership is a type of business organization that in part attempts to avoid the weaknesses of the sole proprietorship. Instead of one person carrying the full burden of risk of the business, two or more people pool their credit, labor, and skills to do a more effective job. Partners strengthen a business by complementing one another with added skills, ability, and capital.

When an active partner suffers a long-term disability, the business loses his services just as quickly and surely as if he were dead. The other partners are faced with a multiude of problems suggested by such questions as:

1. Can they make the business earn enough to continue the disabled partner's income?
2. Can they assume the disabled partner's former job responsibilities in addition to their own?
3. Can they continue to give the prompt service their customers demand?
4. Can they continue to meet production schedules?
5. Can they afford to hire a replacement for the disabled partner? If they can afford him, where can one be found?
6. If no replacement is found, how long can the other partner or partners continue to do the work of two men without the danger of becoming disabled themselves?

In the personal service or professional partnership, often used by accountants, architects, dentists, doctors, engineers, lawyers, and others, the physical assets of the partnership are usually very limited. The earnings of most professional partnerships depend primarily upon personal services, skill, and goodwill. In a professional partnership, the goodwill created by a partner will, to a large extent, diminish on that partner's total and permanent disability. But the other partners often feel morally obligated to distribute part of the partnership earnings to the disabled partner for a period of time. However, when it becomes apparent that the disability will be permanent, the normal reaction is to try to buy out the interest of the disabled partner. Typically, the other partner or partners will not continue to carry the burden of paying the disabled partner his salary for an unlimited period of time, with the resulting reduction in compensation for themselves. Accordingly, the need for a buy-and-sell agreement is obvious.

Close Corporation

Stockholder-employees are in a position which is similar to that of partners. The closely held corporation is frequently referred to as an "incorporated partnership." Unlike the partnership, however, the withdrawal or death of a stockholder does not terminate the corporation. The business will continue, but major problems may remain.

The serious disability of a close corporation stockholder-employee whose services are important to the success of the business often has a number of effects:

1. The ability, skill, and services of the stockholder are lost to the business. Sooner or later, the firm must face the question of discontinuing his salary or other compensation for his services. Yet the disabled stockholder and his family may not understand the need to pay a replacement. To them, the fact that the firm cannot afford the burden of double salaries is secondary compared to their need for funds.
2. The financial structure of the firm may be weakened. Suppliers who furnished goods on credit may become wary about future credit, banks may shorten credit lines, and other creditors may begin to be concerned and demand payment. Customers also may lose faith in the corporation's ability to meet its commitments.
3. The disabled stockholder's desires cannot parallel those of the active stockholders. The latter think of expansion and growth. The disabled stockholder wants to conserve capital to guarantee his own compensation without risk.
4. Although the disabled stockholder is unable to contribute to the business, he is entitled to his share of the profits. Also, in some firms, extra compensation to stockholder-employees over a fixed basic amount is related to gross income. If such an agreement is in effect, the disabled stockholder might continue to share in this extra compensation. Normally, the other stockholder or stockholders do everything in their power to keep payments to the disabled stockholder at a minimum because of his inability to contribute his efforts to the success of the company.

SOLUTIONS TO DISABILITY PROBLEMS
WITHOUT DISABILITY INCOME INSURANCE

The Sole Proprietorship

When a sole proprietor becomes disabled, a member of the proprietor's family often tries to take over and run the business. This is difficult in any sole proprietorship. It is impossible in a profession, unless the member of the family has been trained and is licensed in that profession.

Sometimes an effort is made to hire a competent employee to run the business. However, it is usually very difficult to find a suitable replacement for the sole proprietor. Even if this can be done, the salary payments to the replacement will reduce the income left for the sole proprietor and his family. Most sole proprietorships can earn only one good income, and if a large part of that money must go to pay a replacement, there is usually little left for the disabled sole proprietor and his family.

Sometimes the disability of a sole proprietor makes it necessary to sell the business or practice. Whenever any business is sold under pressure, the buyer has an advantage. Unless the sole proprietor has considerable reserves and/or a continuing income, he may be at the mercy of the purchaser and be forced to sell at a distress price.

The Partnership

When a partner becomes disabled, a member of his family sometimes tries to fill his place. This situation is even more difficult than in the case of the sole proprietorship. If the member of the disabled partner's family is not acceptable to the other partner or partners, they do not have to engage in a partnership with him. Only in rare instances is a family member both qualified to make a contribution to the business and acceptable to the other partner or partners.

It is sometimes possible for the partnership to hire a replacement for the disabled partner at a lower salary than he had been earning. This may be a temporary and partial solution to the problem, but it is almost never a permanent solution.

The partnership may continue the disabled partner's salary for a period of time, perhaps six months to one year. Then, if he is still disabled, the other partner or partners may wish to buy him out. The problems in this situation relate to whether the partnership can afford to pay the disabled partner for six months to a year with no services performed and whether the other partner or partners will have the money to buy him out. The other partner or partners might borrow the money, or they might pay for the disabled partner's interest in installments out of earnings and capital. Either approach presents problems, however. Then, too, there remains the basic question of the members of the firm agreeing on a fair price. Further, the disabled partner might refuse to sell his share of the business even though he has been disabled for six months to a year, because he hopes to recover.

Another possible solution would be to attempt to negotiate a change in the status of the disabled member from a general partner to a limited partner with no voice in the business affairs of the partnership.[5] Obviously, some financial consideration to the disabled partner would be involved in this approach.

However, without advance provision, liquidation of the partnership may be the only practical solution to the situation. Under such circumstances, it is unlikely that the partners will realize the full value of the business as a going concern. All partners usually sustain considerable financial loss in such a liquidation. Accounts receivable must be collected quickly, and some of the firm's debtors will not pay under these conditions. The firm's debts will have to be paid. It could become necessary to sell the firm's assets at sacrifice prices. Goodwill may be lost. If the other partner or partners go back into business, they probably must start all over again. Most of the problems of starting a new business may be encountered.

The Close Corporation

Possible solutions to the problems which arise in the close corporation when an active stockholder becomes totally disabled somewhat parallel those solutions described above for the partnership. If a member of the stockholder's family tries to take the place of the disabled stockholder, the likelihood of that person adequately filling the gap left by the loss of the services of the formerly active stockholder is remote. If buying the interest

---

[5] The danger to which some limited partnerships are subject, namely, that they may be considered associations taxable as corporations, should not arise merely by virtue of this step. See William Harmelin and Morris Friedman, *Disability Insurance in the Business Buy-out Agreement* (Rev. ed.: Indianapolis: Rough Notes Co., Inc., 1965), p. 68.

of the disabled stockholder seems to be the logical solution, then the questions of price, availability of funds to purchase the interest, and other such matters usually complicate the picture. It is rare that either the corporation or the other shareholders will have sufficient capital of their own to buy out the interest of a disabled stockholder without advance provision. From the point of view of the disabled stockholder, even if the funds can be supplied by the corporation or the other shareholders, his position is a difficult one. Unless the disabled party is in much better financial condition than the average small businessman, he would be compelled to accept a settlement after a period of time as a noncontributing stockholder-employee of the corporation. The disabled party would not have as much bargaining power after the disability occurs as he would have had under an agreement which had been executed while all parties were contributing their full share to the success of the business.

SOLUTIONS TO DISABILITY PROBLEMS WITH DISABILITY INCOME INSURANCE

The Sole Proprietorship

In most instances the disabled sole proprietor has two major financial problems, namely, to provide sufficient income to support his family and pay his medical expenses, and to provide for the cost of hiring and reimbursing a competent replacement who is capable of operating his business successfully. A disability income insurance policy will provide a guaranteed income to the disabled sole proprietor and his family. Individually owned major medical expense protection will enable him to meet the catastrophic medical expenses which are likely to accompany the disability. These insurance payments will enable him to use part or all of his normal income from the business to hire and pay the right replacement. With the business operating successfully under the direction of a competent replacement, there may be some income left over for the disabled sole proprietor.

When the disability is of long-term or permanent duration, major medical and disability income protection will afford the sole proprietor the necessary time to dispose of his business if he so desires. This will help to avoid a forced sale with the usual resulting loss. On the other hand, if he wishes to pass the business on to his son or some other relative, the payments from the insurance will enable him to hire a manager to run the business until his son or relative is ready to take over.

Although premiums for disability income insurance normally are not deductible as a business expense to the extent that benefits are payable to the sole proprietor,[6] benefit payments received from the insurance company generally are free of income tax.[7]

---

[6] Revenue Ruling 59–90, CB 1958–1, 88, and Revenue Ruling 55–331, CB 1955–1, 271, except premiums for a business overhead expense policy (Revenue Ruling 58–480, CB 1958–2, 62) and except that premiums paid for medical expense and specific reimbursement may be included in medical expenses. (Regulation 1.213–1(e)(1); Revenue Rulings 19, CB 1953–1, 59, 55–261, CB 1955–1, 307, and 55–331, CB 1955–1, 271.)

[7] Internal Revenue Code, Sec. 104 (a)(3); Regulation 1.101–1(d) except for bene-

An exception to the general rules pertaining to the taxation of disability income insurance exists where the insurance is intended to provide business overhead expense coverage. Premiums paid for such disability income policies are treated as a direct business expense for tax purposes, and the benefits received are considered as gross income.[8] Business overhead expense plans are designed to provide funds to pay rent, electricity, heat, water, laundry, repairs, depreciation, salaries for employees, and other fixed expenses which are normal and customary to the operation of a sole proprietorship or professional partnership. These plans do not permit the payment of an income to the disabled party. Most such plans pay benefits after 30 days of total disability. Monthly benefits can be purchased up to the average amount of monthly expense during the six months immediately preceding the disability. Plans are offered with benefits for 12 to 18 months.

The Partnership

Partnerships closely resemble sole proprietorships in the basic need for health insurance protection. The disabled partner needs income and funds with which to pay medical bills. The big difference is that when a partner is disabled, he becomes a financial drain on the business and his partner or partners. For this reason, a partnership buy-and-sell agreement, to be financed through disability income insurance, usually is needed.

Under the cross-purchase type of partnership buy-and-sell agreement, it has been well established that premiums paid by one partner for life insurance which he owns on the life of another partner do not constitute deductible business expenses for federal income tax purposes. Similarly, premiums paid by one partner for disability income insurance on another partner will not be deductible as business expenses.

If the partner paying the premiums is the owner and beneficiary of the disability income policy, he will receive tax-free funds with which to pay for part, if not all, of his obligation under a disability buy-out provision. This solution is not ideal because it does not provide a lump sum payment. However, it is one method of providing funds for the installment purchase of a business interest.

Under the entity type partnership buy-and-sell agreement, the partnership would be the purchaser of a disabled partner's interest. The disability income benefits would be used to pay the disabled partner for his partnership interest.

To the extent that payments by a partnership to a partner are not attributable to the retiring partner's interest in the assets of the partnership (other than unrealized receivables), they will be considered "guaranteed payments" (if the payment is determined without regard to in-

---

fits from a business overhead expense policy. (Revenue Ruling 55–264, CB 1955–1, 11).

[8] Premiums a business expense: Revenue Ruling 58–480, CB 1958–2, 62. Benefits includable as gross income: Revenue Ruling 55–264, CB 1955–1, 11. However, it must be stressed that a standard disability income policy does not qualify for the premium deduction even if intended as payment of business overhead expense: Revenue Ruling 58–480, CB 1958–2, 62.

come of the partnership) and will be deductible by the partnership[9] and taxable to the partner as ordinary income.[10] The Internal Revenue Service has ruled that amounts paid by a partnership to a partner who is absent from work due to sickness or accident cannot be excluded from the disabled partner's gross income under Section 105(*d*) of the Internal Revenue Code.[11] This principle has been adopted in the Income Tax Regulations respecting so-called "guaranteed payments" taxable to a partner as ordinary income. If the partnership is the owner and beneficiary of the disability income insurance on the partners, benefits received by the partnership and paid over to a partner will be taxed in full to the partner as guaranteed payments. Yet, if benefits are paid directly to the partner, they will be completely excludable from his gross income.[12] Of course, when taxed to a partner as guaranteed payments, such benefits are deducted in computing the partnership's net income which reduces the taxable distributive shares of the other partners.

For the most advantageous tax treatment to the disabled party, however, disability income benefits should not flow through the partnership but should be paid directly to the disabled partner.

Premiums paid for disability income insurance, whether paid by the partnership or by the partners individually, are considered nondeductible expenses under Section 262 of the Internal Revenue Code.[13]

Disability provisions in a partnership agreement may contemplate a specified period during which the disabled partner will receive disability income benefits. These will either be taxed to him (if paid by the partnership) or received tax-free (if received by him directly from the insurance company). Thereafter, payments would be made by the partnership in purchase of the disabled partner's interest.

If a shortage of funds makes it impractical to acquire the total interest of the disabled partner, the purchase of that part of his interest for which cash is available, combined with the suppression of the disabled partner's business voice to that of a limited partner, may satisfy the need.

The Close Corporation

The working stockholders of a close corporation are in a position which is very similar to that of partners. Their need for disability income and major medical expense insurance parallels the need of partners.

Where a corporate employer purchases health insurance on behalf of one or more employees, the premium cost is deductible by the corporation as a business expense under Section 162 of the Code if (1) the corporation is not a beneficiary under the policy; (2) the premiums are paid in consideration of personal services actually rendered by the employee; and

---

[9] See Sec. 1.736–1 of the Income Tax Regulations.

[10] If the payments are attributable to unrealized receivables or to goodwill not provided for in the partnership agreement, they will also be deductible by the partnership and taxable as ordinary income to the partner.

[11] See Revenue Ruling 56–326, CB 1956–2, p. 100.

[12] Sec. 104(*a*)(3) of the Code.

[13] See Revenue Ruling 58–90, *IRB* 1958–11, p. 12, which so treats such premiums paid by a sole proprietor.

(3) the total compensation paid to the employee, including the premiums, is not unreasonable compensation for the services rendered.[14]

The example given in the cited ruling stipulates that the employee is not a stockholder. In the opinion of many authorities,[15] however, if the foregoing tests are met, the premium cost is excludable from gross income of even the stockholder-employee, in accordance with the provisions of Section 106 of the Code.[16]

In the example described in Revenue Ruling 58–90, the employee had all the rights of ownership in the policy. Furthermore, the benefits under the policy comprised only income replacement payments. The benefits were found to be excludable from the employee's gross income to the extent permitted under the general rules relating to wage continuation plans.[17]

The Code, in both Section 106, relating to nontaxability to the employee of the employer's premium cost, and in Section 105, covering the limited nontaxability to the employee of his benefits, refers to "accident and health plans." The regulations make it clear that a plan may cover one or more employees, and that there may be different plans for different employees or classes of employees.

Regulation 1.105–5(a) provides this definition of a plan:

In general, an accident or health plan is an arrangement for the payment of amounts to employees in the event of personal injuries or sickness. A plan may cover one or more employees, and there may be different plans for different employees or classes of employees. An accident or health plan may be either insured or noninsured, and it is not necessary that the plan be in writing or that the employee's rights to benefits under the plan be enforceable. However, if the employee's rights are not enforceable, an amount will be deemed to be received under a plan only if on the date the employee became sick or injured, the employee was covered by a plan (or a program, policy or custom having the effect of a plan) providing for the payment of amounts to the employee in the event of personal injuries or sickness, and notice or knowledge of such plan was reasonably available to the employee.

Court decisions have made it clear that arbitrary payments to one or more employees do not constitute a plan. There must be clear and convincing proof that specific employees or classes of employees are covered under the plan.

In July 1967, the Tax Court decided the Larkin case.[18] Medical expenses had been paid for two officer-stockholders of the corporation for about five years. In two later years, limited amounts had been paid for a nonstockholder-employee. The Tax Court held that this was a plan for stockholders, not employees as such—and that all medical expenses paid by the corporation were dividends, taxable to the corporation and includable in the taxable income of the individuals. The case went to the

---

[14] See Revenue Ruling 58–90, *Internal Revenue Bulletin* 1958–11, p. 12.

[15] See Kivie Dornfeld, "Taxation Affecting Health Insurance," *Journal of the American Society of Chartered Life Underwriters*, Vol. XVII, No. 2 (Spring, 1963), pp. 120–22, for a discussion of this point.

[16] See Sec. 1.106–1 of the Income Tax Regulations.

[17] Sec. 105(d) of the Code.

[18] 48 TC 629, affirmed 394 F 2nd 494.

First Circuit Court of Appeals, which upheld the Tax Court, which laid down the following:

1. There must be a plan;
2. The plan must be for the benefit of employees; and
3. Most important, even if nonstockholders are included, benefits for them must be on some basis other than "incidentally and sporadically," as in the Larkin case.

In July 1968, the Tax Court in a memorandum decision decided that a medical expense reimbursement "plan" for a 50 percent shareholder and his family was "for employees." Only the president and the treasurer (each of whom owned outright or beneficially 50 percent of the stock) were covered. The "plan" was upheld; the corporation had an insured medical expense plan for all employees. Thus everyone, stockholder or not, had benefits. The fact that the stockholder-employees had better benefits did not disqualify the "plan," since such plans can be discriminatory.[19]

The cross-purchase arrangement in the close corporation is identical to that used in the partnership.

Under the stock redemption arrangement, premiums paid by the corporation will not be deductible, since the benefits under the policy will be payable to the corporation, becoming part of its general assets, whether or not intended to fund a plan of disability payments.

The disability benefits the corporation receives as owner and beneficiary of the policy on the disability of the insured employee, represent receipts flowing from nondeductible expenditures and as such are excludable from its gross income.[20]

Amounts paid by the corporation to the disabled stockholder on account of the purchase price of his stock will be nondeductible to the corporation and, to the extent of any gain realized, treated as a capital gain to the individual. Disability, unlike death, does not result in a stepped-up basis for the stock and the escape from taxation of the appreciation in its value.

In this instance, the corporation can apply the tax-free proceeds of the health insurance policy toward its obligation under the buy-out agreement.

If, in addition, the corporation were to make payments to the employee-stockholder under a wage continuation plan, the payments would be deductible by the corporation and tax-free to the employee to the extent permitted under such plans.

A CHECK LIST OF IMPORTANT POINTS TO BE COVERED IN THE DISABILITY BUY-AND-SELL PORTION OF A BUSINESS AGREEMENT

The following check list is intended to serve as a guide to important points to be covered in a disability buy-and-sell agreement.[21]

---

[19] *Bogene, Inc.*, 27 TCM 730.

[20] Internal Revenue Code Sec. 104(a)(3); Rev. Ruling 66–262.

[21] See Appendix R for sample agreement. Also see Harmelin and Friedman, *Disability Insurance in the Business Buy-Out Agreement.*

1. Definition of Disability

If the provisions of a specific insurance policy are used as a measure of disability, the acceptance within the terms of the buy-and-sell agreement of the insurance company's definition of what constitutes total disability will settle the matter.

2. Amount of Salary during Disability before Buy-Out

With respect to salary to be paid during disability, one agreement, for example, states: "Full salary plus bonuses for three months. Full salary less salary of replacement but not less than one-half salary, plus bonuses for additional nine months. After 12 months, 25 percent of salary plus bonuses for one year."

3. When Buy-Out Becomes Mandatory

Provision as to when buy-out becomes mandatory will vary with the nature of the business and the thinking of the parties to the agreement. If the business does not require the personal services of the partners or stockholders, a disability buy-out is not very important. However, if the business requires the personal services of the partners or stockholders, a disability buy-out provision is needed. Here is the provision of one such agreement: "If the said period of disability shall extend for a period of more than two (2) years, then and in that event the nondisabled stockholder shall purchase, and the disabled stockholder shall sell, the interest of the disabled stockholder for the purchase price specified in Article Second of this agreement upon the following terms and conditions."

4. Source of Funds for Buy-Out

If there is no guarantee of funds when the disability occurs, it may be difficult to fulfill the conditions of the agreement. Noncancellable disability income insurance or disability income coverage written with life insurance can provide all or a part of the funds on an installment basis when the disability occurs.

In recent years there has been growing interest in the problems related to funding a buy-out of a business interest in case of total disability. This has resulted in new disability products being designed for the purpose of funding disability buy-out agreements. One major life insurance company offers a guaranteed renewable disability income policy which pays a lump sum after two years of total and continuous disability. Such payments can be as much as 80 percent of the first $25,000 of the insured's business interest and 50 percent of the balance with a maximum benefit of $100,000.

Another major insurer will issue up to a maximum of $8,000 of monthly disability income payments to fund buy-and-sell agreements on an optionally renewable basis with benefits starting after one year of total disability. Under its rules, this insurer will consider disability benefits for 100 percent of the first $50,000 of business value and 50 percent of the excess for each stockholder or partner up to a maximum of $100,000.

At the time of this writing, one of the largest companies in the insurance field has begun to offer a life insurance product on a guaranteed cost basis which is intended to provide a lump sum for funding a disability buy-out. This contract is issued in amounts of $5,000 to $500,000 on the endowment-at-age-70 plan. After three years of total and permanent disability, the face amount of the contract becomes payable. This business buy-out contract is available only for business owners who are active in the operation of the business. Since the business buy-out contract is an endowment policy, the face amount is also payable upon death or upon reaching age 70.

5. Number of Installments to Effect the Buy-Out

The number of installments to effect the buy-out will often depend upon the relationship between the value established for the interest of the disabled party and the earnings of the business without the services of the disabled party. This decision should be given serious consideration by the principals with the guidance of their accountant and attorney.

6. Disposition of Business Life Insurance Policies on the Healthy and Disabled Partners When Disability Buy-Out Becomes Effective

With reference to the disposition of business life insurance policies on the healthy and disabled partners when disability buy-out becomes effective, one agreement, for example, provides: "As soon as practicable, the disabled partner shall transfer his partnership interest to the partnership in exchange for any life insurance policies owned by the partnership on the disabled partner's life and a series of negotiable promissory notes made by the partnership and the nondisabled partner to the disabled partner with interest at 5 percent per annum."

7. Provision for Contingency of Death during Period Disability Buy-Out Payments Are Being Made

With reference to the contingency of death during the period the disability buy-out payments are being made, one agreement, for example, covers this point as follows: "If selling partner dies before all notes are paid, purchasing partner receives insurance proceeds and pays balance due to legal representative of selling partner."

CONCLUSION

The weight of evidence is that the sole proprietorship, the partnership, the close corporation, and the active owners of such businesses add stability to their business and personal requirements by using an insured plan of disability income protection in the business continuation situation. Without insurance, the problems which result are often insurmountable.

While a number of favorable tax advantages have been outlined, the motivation for using insured income protection programs is not to take advantage of a tax situation, but rather to guarantee that when the problem arises, the money will be there.

The future for disability income protection for business continuation purposes is very bright.

SELECTED REFERENCES

Brown, Robert A., Jr. "The Role of Disability Income Insurance in the Business Continuation Plan," *Journal of the American Society of Chartered Life Underwriters,* Vol. VIII, No. 1 (Winter, 1953), pp. 50–57.

Dornfeld, Kivie. "Taxation Affecting Health Insurance," *Journal of the American Society of Chartered Life Underwriters,* Vol. XVII, No. 2 (Spring, 1963), pp. 116–30.

Harmelin, William, and Friedman, Morris. *Disability Insurance in the Business Buy-out Agreement.* Rev. ed. Indianapolis: Rough Notes Co., Inc., 1965.

Harmelin, William, and Osler, Robert W. *Business Uses of Health Insurance.* Bryn Mawr, Pa.: American College of Life Underwriters, 1960.

Osler, Robert W. *Disability Income Selling . . . Approach to Application.* Cincinnati, Ohio: Rough Notes Co., Inc., 1970.

48

Professional Corporations

By HERBERT CHASMAN

"PROFESSIONAL SERVICE ORGANIZATIONS organized and operated under the various state professional association or corporation statutes shall, generally, be treated as corporations for federal income tax purposes." This seemingly redundant statement was first issued by the Internal Revenue Service in August of 1969 as Technical Information Release No. 1019. Since then the IRS has formalized its position in Revenue Ruling 70–101. This was the catalyst for the phenomenal growth in popularity of the professional corporation to a point where they now number in the thousands and are found in every state.

A brief look into the history of events leading up to acceptance by the IRS of corporate tax treatment for professional corporations is a must in order to appreciate fully its significance.

IN THE BEGINNING

When this issue first arose in 1935 the positions of the IRS and the professionals were the reverse of what they would later become. This was because corporations were then more severely taxed than individuals. Thus, with an eye toward treating a maximum number of taxpayers as corporations for tax purposes, the IRS successfully established the "resemblance test" in the now famous Morrissey case.[1] Under the resemblance test, if a business organization, although not a corporation as a matter of state law, resembled a corporation in its operations, it would be treated as such for federal income tax purposes. A year later the IRS successfully applied this test to a medical clinic organized as a business trust in order to tax it as a corporation.[2]

Kintner Case

In the ensuing years, the growing popularity of the tax benefits available under qualified retirement plans and group life and health insurance

---

[1] *Morrissey v. Commissioner*, 296 U.S. 344 (1935).
[2] *Pelton v. Commissioner*, 82 F.2d 473 (7th Circuit, 1936).

plans, as well as the ever increasing ordinary income tax rates for individuals, resulted in some professionals voluntarily seeking corporate tax treatment. In 1954 the IRS decided to reverse its position and challenge the corporate tax treatment sought by a group of physicians in Montana who, relying on the resemblance test, had organized a common law association. They then filed their income tax return as a corporation and claimed a deduction for contributions to a qualified corporate retirement plan. The IRS was unsuccessful in its attempt to deny corporate tax treatment to the Kintner group[3] as it would be in every court case involving this issue thereafter.

State Law Governs

In the wake of its defeat in the Kintner case, the IRS seized on the fact that none of the states had laws expressly permitting professionals to practice in corporate form. New regulations were issued requiring the presence of a majority of enumerated corporate characteristics in order to be eligible for corporate tax treatment, with the determination to be based on the law of the state in which the professional practice was conducted.[4]

It was not long thereafter that the IRS apparently regretted elevating local law to a controlling position on this issue. Under the urging of various professional groups, state legislatures soon began to pass statutes enabling professionals to form corporations or associations that, by express provision, were to be treated as corporations. Although a handful of states were slow to act, all states now have some form of professional corporation or association law.

A Federal Question Once Again

In light of the onslaught of state professional corporation laws, the IRS once again revised its position by issuing amendments to its regulations.[5] These provided that for a professional practice to qualify for corporate tax treatment, the business entity must possess a majority of the corporate characteristics set out in the U.S. Treasury regulations. In making this determination, state law no longer would be a factor. The new regulations set out the test in such a way that it was virtually impossible for professionals who met the requirements for incorporation under the terms of any of the state laws, also to possess enough corporate characteristics to come within the definition of a corporation for federal income tax purposes.

Despite the 1965 Regulations, a host of professionals, on the advice of counsel that the position of the IRS would not be upheld in court, formed professional corporations under their applicable state laws. The IRS refused to give ground and rejected corporate tax treatment for these professionals. The IRS's position as set out in the 1965 Regulations was tested in the courts on 15 different occasions, and on each and every one of those occasions the federal district court involved ruled in favor of the taxpayer by holding, in effect, that the Regulations were invalid and unenforceable.

---

[3] *U.S.* v. *Kintner*, 216 F.2d 418 (9th Circuit, 1954).
[4] Reg. Sec. 301.7701–1(c) (1960).
[5] Reg. Sec. 301.7701–2(h) (1965).

Four of these decisions were appealed by the government and in each case the district court decision was affirmed.[6]

The IRS Agrees to Corporate Tax Treatment for Professionals

After finding itself in the unenviable position of having lost three court of appeals' decisions in three different circuits, the IRS finally relinquished its stand and agreed to treat professional corporations and associations under the same tax rules applicable to all other corporations.[7]

In applying the general rule of corporate taxation to a professional service organization, the IRS was quick to point out the need to be organized and *operated* as a corporation in order to be eligible for corporate tax treatment.[8] Thus, where a group of professionals incorporated under the terms of their state's professional corporation statute but failed to operate as a corporation, the tax court held that the group was not entitled to be treated as a corporation for tax purposes.[9] Thus, if the professionals ignore the existence of their corporation, so will the IRS. Evidence of operation as a corporation which will help to satisfy the IRS's requirement of substance as well as form include the following:

1. Election of a board of directors who meet regularly to decide how the corporation should be run.
2. Execution of all business transactions in the name of the corporation.
3. Execution of employment agreements that establish reasonable compensation.
4. Filing of annual income tax returns and withholding of income taxes on wages paid to *all* employees of the corporation.
5. Payment of social security taxes by the corporation and withholding taxes from the salaries of *all* corporate employees.
6. Having all records and billings of the corporation stress the corporation as the provider of services, rather than any of the individual practitioners.

TAX ADVANTAGES OF PROFESSIONAL CORPORATIONS

There are no *unique* tax advantages attached to practicing *a profession* in corporate form as opposed to partnership form. Rather, the tax advantages are those that pertain to any closely held business organized as a corporation instead of as a partnership. These tax advantages stem from two facts. The first of these facts is that a corporation is a tax-paying entity separate and apart from its stockholders. Thus, income accumulated in a corporation is taxable to the corporation, not to the stockholders. In con-

---

[6] *U.S.* v. *Empey,* U.S. Court of Appeals (10th Circuit, 1969); *U.S.* v. *O'Neill,* U.S. Court of Appeals (6th Circuit, 1969); *U.S.* v. *Kurzner,* U.S. Court of Appeals (5th Circuit, 1969); *U.S.* v. *Holder,* U.S. Court of Appeals (5th Circuit, 1969).

[7] TIR 1019 (8/8/69).

[8] Rev. Rul. 70–101, *Internal Revenue Bulletin* 1970–9, p. 13.

[9] *Roubik* v. *Commissioner,* 53 T.C. 365 (1969).

trast, a partnership is merely a conduit for income tax purposes. Income produced by a partnership must be reflected on the income tax returns of the partners, regardless of whether such income is distributed to the partners or accumulated in the partnership.

The second important fact is that an individual who works for a corporation on a regular basis is considered to be an employee of the corporation regardless of whether he is also a stockholder. The result is that a stockholder-employee is eligible to participate in all the tax-favored fringe benefit programs of the corporation to the same extent as any other employee. On the other hand, a partner is not classified as an employee of his partnership. The result is that a partner generally cannot participate on a tax-favored basis in the fringe benefit programs of his partnership. The advent of qualified self-employed retirement plans in 1962 has created an exception to this general rule. Under the Self-Employed Individuals Tax Retirement Act, a partner is given the classification of an owner-employee so that he may participate in the qualified retirement plan of his unincorporated business on a tax favored basis. However, it will be pointed out later in this chapter that the benefits available under the Self-Employed Individuals Tax Retirement Act generally are far less attractive than those available under a qualified retirement plan of a corporation.

Creation of a New Taxpayer

As a separate tax-paying entity, a corporation pays income tax at the rate of 22 percent on its first $25,000 of net income and 48 percent on any net income in excess of $25,000. Thus, if a group of professionals who have incorporated are in personal income tax brackets in excess of 22 percent (which will very likely be the case), tax leverage can be provided by allowing income of up to $25,000 per year to accumulate in the corporation subject to an income tax of only 22 percent.

Although there will be an income tax savings by allowing some income to accumulate and be taxed to the corporation rather than distributed and taxed to the practitioners, the practitioners will not benefit from this tax saving unless the accumulated after-tax income can be used by the corporation to meet future expenses and provide benefits for which the practitioners would otherwise have to pay from dollars that have been taxed to them in their much higher personal income tax brackets.

Provide Capital. The capital expenditures of a professional corporation typically are much lower than those of a business corporation. Nevertheless, amounts will have to be spent for furniture, technical equipment, office equipment, fixtures, and so forth. To the extent that these expenses are not paid for out of current income, they can be met with the "lightly taxed" dollars that have been left in the corporation rather than by after-tax capital contributions to the corporation by the practitioners.

Funding a Stock Redemption Plan. The professional corporation laws of most states provide that the stock of a deceased or withdrawing stockholder can be transferred only to another licensed practitioner. Furthermore, many state statutes provide that unless an express agreement to the contrary has been entered into during lifetime, the stock of a deceased shareholder in a professional corporation must be sold to the corporation for its book value. During the period of his association with a professional corporation, a practitioner will develop many close relationships with patients or clients. This "goodwill" is likely to inure to the benefit of the surviving members of the professional corporation as these patients or clients continue to use the facilities of the professional corporation after the practitioner is gone.

In order to provide some compensation for this "goodwill" factor, many professional corporations enter into buy-sell agreements calling for a purchase price in excess of book value for a practitioner's shares. The typical method of funding the agreement is through the purchase of life insurance. If the surviving stockholders are going to be the purchasers under a cross-purchase buy-sell agreement, then they will personally own and pay for life insurance on each others' lives. On the other hand, if the corporation is going to purchase the interest of a deceased stockholder under a stock redemption buy-sell agreement, then the corporation will be owner of and premium payor for life insurance on the life of each stockholder in order to fund the agreement. Under either plan the premium dollars used to purchase the life insurance will not be a deductible expense for income tax purposes. The significant difference is that under the cross-purchase plan, the premiums will be paid with dollars that have already been taxed to the professionals in their top personal income tax brackets of perhaps 50 percent; whereas, under the stock redemption plan, premiums will be paid with dollars that have already been taxed to the corporation in its income tax bracket which may be as low as 22 percent. Thus, by selecting the stock redemption plan, the professionals can take advantage of the tax leverage created by the fact that their corporation is a separate tax-paying entity.

Split-Dollar Life Insurance.[10] The lightly taxed dollars of a professional corporation can be used to provide personal life insurance protection, on an individual basis, for selected members of the corporation through a split-dollar plan. This will reduce or eliminate the need to provide one's own life insurance protection with dollars that are subject to personal income tax rates. A split-dollar plan can take any one of a number of forms. Generally speaking, it is an arrangement under which the corporation will pay all or a portion of the premiums for an individual cash value life insurance contract on the life of a selected employee. At the death of the insured-employee, the corporation will be reimbursed from the death proceeds in an amount equal to the sum it has paid in premiums. The remainder of the proceeds will be payable to the insured's designated beneficiary. In order to maintain the amount payable to the insured's beneficiary at approximately the face amount of the policy, dividends can be used to purchase one-year term insurance protection.

Under such a plan, an insured-professional receives an "economic benefit" from the corporation. It generally is measured by the term cost of the insurance protection provided the insured-professional's beneficiary each year, less any portion of the premium paid by the professional himself.

---

[10] For a more thorough discussion of split-dollar plans, see Chapter 44.

The value of this economic benefit is includable in the insured-professional's taxable income. However, this is a small price to pay for the benefit provided. Currently, the IRS takes the position that the portion of the premium paid by the corporation is not deductible because the corporation is a beneficiary under the terms of the policy. It is for this reason that the split-dollar plan is illustrated as a benefit that can be provided by the lightly taxed dollars accumulated in a professional corporation.

Nonqualified Deferred Compensation, the $5,000 Tax-Free Death Benefit and the 85 Percent Dividend Credit. Another use for the "lightly taxed" dollars of a professional corporation is to fund a nonqualified deferred compensation plan. If a professional man is in a personal income tax bracket that far exceeds the tax bracket of his corporation and he has more income than he currently needs, he may agree to defer receipt of a portion of his salary until he retires with the thought that he then will be in a much lower income tax bracket.

The stability of the professional corporation is an important factor in deciding whether or not to enter into a nonqualified deferred compensation plan. This is because the professional employee, in order successfully to defer income taxation, probably will have to be satisfied with the mere unsecured *promise* of the corporation to provide him with the future benefits that are anticipated under the terms of the agreement. The funding of the plan is done on an *informal* basis, with any amount set aside remaining the unencumbered assets of the corporation. The corporation can fund its future obligation by investing in life insurance contracts, one or more forms of equity products, or a combination of both. Where the corporation invests in stock of other domestic corporations, 85 percent of any dividends earned will be received tax free. Any death proceeds of life insurance used to fund the plan also will be received tax free by the corporation. In the event the professional employee should die prior to reaching retirement age, the plan can be so arranged that the first $5,000 of benefits paid to his designated beneficiary will be received by her free of income tax even though fully deductible by the corporation. This $5,000 tax-free death benefit is available only to an employee, not to a partner.

Since this is a nonqualified plan utilizing the after-tax dollars of the corporation, the corporation is free to pick and choose those of its employees upon whom it wishes to confer this benefit. This alternative to defer the personal receipt of taxable income until retirement, on an individual basis, is available to professionals only if they incorporate.

Tax Favored Employee Fringe Benefits

The relationship between a corporation and a shareholder also may be one of employer and employee. The same cannot be said of the relationship between a partnership and a partner, or a sole proprietorship and the proprietor. It is the much more attractive fringe benefits available to a practitioner in his role as an employee that is primarily responsible for the popularity of professional corporations.

Qualified Retirement Plans. Qualified retirement plans may be established by both unincorporated and incorporated professional practices.

However, where a sole practitioner or a partner owning more than a 10 percent interest in a partnership is a participant in the qualified retirement plan of an unincorporated business (HR-10 plan), the tax benefits and flexibility in plan provisions become severely limited in comparison with those available under a corporate qualified retirement plan. This is true even if the corporate qualified plan has as a participant a 100 percent shareholder of the corporation who also is a director and president of the corporation.

The basic income tax benefits of a qualified retirement plan, whether corporate or noncorporate, are three in number. First, employer contributions made to the plan are deductible. Second, appreciation in value of the assets in which the plan contributions are invested is not subject to income taxation during the period the assets are accumulated under the plan. Finally, a participant is not taxed on amounts contributed to the plan on his behalf; the incidence of income taxation is postponed until distributions are made from the plan to the participant or his beneficiary.

Figure 48–1 is a comparison of the flexibility of plan provisions and the degree to which the above enumerated tax benefits are available under the qualified retirement plans of a corporation and an unincorporated practice which has a sole practitioner or one or more partners having an interest in excess of 10 percent (owner-employees) as participants.

In a specific instance the importance of the distinctions made above between corporate and unincorporated qualified retirement plans will depend upon a number of factors such as the ability of the professionals to set aside substantial amounts of income in excess of $2,500, the number of nonowner-employees that would have to participate, the advisability of taking a lump-sum distribution of benefits, and the estate tax brackets of the professionals. On the whole, however, the conclusion is easily reached that from the standpoint of the professional man the corporate qualified retirement plan is the superior vehicle.

Group Term Life Insurance. If a professional practice is incorporated it may provide group term life insurance benefits on a tax favored basis to all its employees including its shareholder-employees. Premiums paid for group term life insurance by the corporation are a deductible business expense. Equally important, as much as $50,000 of death benefits from group term life insurance may be provided an employee with no part of the cost being includable in the employee's taxable income. Provision of group term life insurance protection in excess of $50,000 will result in additional taxable income to the covered employee. However, the amount to be included in the employee's gross income is calculated by use of favorable rate tables set out in the Treasury Regulations which make the additional coverage available at a reasonable cost.[11]

The death proceeds of group term life insurance, regardless of the amount, will be received by the employee's beneficiary free of income tax. It now appears that by a properly executed assignment to a third party (the insured-employee's spouse for example), the death proceeds of group

[11] Reg. Sec. 1.79–3.

FIGURE 48–1. Comparison of the Flexibility of Provisions of Corporate Qualified Plans and Unincorporated Qualified Plans (HR–10)

CORPORATE QUALIFIED PLANS	UNINCORPORATED QUALIFIED PLANS (HR-10 PLAN)

Coverage

Any nondiscriminatory classification, including a minimum and maximum age requirement and up to a five-years-of-service requirement, is possible.

All full-time employees with three years or more of service must be covered.

Maximum Deductible Contribution

No statutory percentage limitation on contributions to pension plan; 15% of compensation (excluding carryovers) limit on contributions to profit sharing plan; overall 25% of compensation limit to combination pension and profit sharing plans.

Limited to the lesser of $2,500 or 10% of earned income.

Vesting

Plan may provide any vesting schedule which does not discriminate in favor of the highly compensated employees.

All benefits must vest in all employees immediately.

Distribution of Benefits

Benefits may be payable without age restrictions at retirement, disability, death, discharge, or resignation. In addition, profit sharing distributions may be made during employment for limited emergencies.

Owner-employees may not receive benefits until age 59½ and must begin to receive them by age 70½. Disability or death are exceptions.

Taxation of Lump Sum Distribution of Benefits

Capital gains treatment available except for amount of distribution equal to employer contributions made in 1970 and thereafter. Latter sum taxed as ordinary income but may come under special seven-year averaging formula.

No capital gains treatment for owner-employee. Taxed as ordinary income under special five-year averaging formula.

Federal Estate Tax Treatment of Death Benefits

Death benefits attributable to employer contributions and payable to a beneficiary other than the shareholder-employee's estate are received free of estate tax.

Includable in owner-employee's gross estate.

Equity Funding

Plan may be funded in whole or in part with equities even though practitioners act as their own trustees.

To fund the plan with equities, in whole or in part, a bank must act as trustee or custodian.

Effect on Other Business Interests

Shareholder-employee may participate in plan of one corporation without regard to whether he has other corporate or noncorporate business interests with or without qualified plans.

Owner-employee may be required to establish a similar plan for other businesses in which he is also an owner-employee.

FIGURE 48–1 (continued)

CORPORATE QUALIFIED PLANS	UNINCORPORATED QUALIFIED PLANS (HR-10 PLAN)

Treatment of Term Cost of Life Insurance Protection

Includable in shareholder-employee's taxable income during participation in the plan but recoverable tax free when benefits are received at retirement.	Includable in owner-employee's taxable income during participation in the plan and not recoverable tax free out of retirement benefits.

Social Security Integration

Plan may be integrated with social security, either to restrict benefits to, or provide higher benefits for, persons whose compensation exceeds a stated social security compensation level.	Available only if less than one third of total deductible contributions are made on behalf of owner-employees. Even when available, integration is possible only to the extent of offsetting social security contributions against plan contributions made with respect to both partners and employees.

Prohibited Transactions

A shareholder-employee may borrow money from the plan at a reasonable interest rate and with adequate security, buy from and sell property to the plan for adequate consideration, and charge reasonable fees for services rendered.	An owner-employee may not borrow money from the plan, buy property from or sell property to the plan, or charge for services rendered to the plan.

term life insurance also may be excludable from the gross estate of the insured-employee for federal estate tax purposes.[12]

Even though a professional practice is not incorporated, it may provide group term life insurance benefits for its employees with tax deductible dollars. Such benefits can be provided by the practice for a sole practitioner or the partners of a partnership but only with after-tax dollars since they are not considered employees for this purpose.

Medical Expense Benefits. As an employee of his professional corporation, a practitioner may receive benefits for medical expenses incurred due to injuries or sickness under a medical expense plan maintained by the corporation. As long as the amounts received do not exceed the expenses incurred by the employee for the medical care of himself, his spouse, and dependents, nothing will be includable in his gross income.[13] These benefits, when paid by the corporation, are deductible from its gross income. Where the employee is named the beneficiary for a medical expense benefits insurance policy paid for by the corporation, the premiums will be fully deductible by the corporation and excludable from the gross income of the employee.[14]

Although an unincorporated professional practice may provide medical expense benefits for its employees on a tax-favored basis, a sole practi-

---

[12] Revenue Ruling 69–54, 1969–6 IRB 20.
[13] IRC Sec. 105(b).
[14] IRC Sec. 106; Reg. Sec. 1.106–1; Reg. Sec. 1.162–10(a).

tioner and the partners of a partnership are not considered to be employees for this purpose. However, an unincorporated practitioner, along with every other individual taxpayer, is entitled to a personal income tax deduction of up to $150 for the cost of medical expense insurance. He also may deduct the cost in excess of $150 for medical expense insurance as well as his other unreimbursed medical expenses, but only to the extent the total exceeds 3 percent of his adjusted gross income.

Salary Continuation Plans. A professional corporation can establish a salary continuation plan for a select class of employees, providing disability income payments on a tax-favored basis during periods of inability to work due to injury or sickness. Generally speaking, after a 30-day waiting period, the first $100 per week of such disability income will be received by the employee free of income tax. Such benefits, when paid by the corporation, will be fully deductible from its gross income. Where the plan is funded through the purchase of disability income insurance payable directly to the insured-employee, the premiums paid by the corporation will be deductible and not taxable as income to the covered employees.[15]

This tax benefit is not applicable to a sole practitioner or a partner, either of whom must purchase disability income protection using after-tax dollars. However, where disability income protection is purchased on a personal basis with after-tax dollars, any benefits received are fully excludable from the gross income of the disabled insured.

Marginal Efficiency of Profits

Figure 48–2 is an illustrative comparison demonstrating how incorporation can increase the marginal efficiency of the profits of a professional practice. It shows (1) the available current spendable income, and (2) the amount that may be set aside for retirement, when the same professional practice is organized first as a partnership and then as a corporation. Note that gross profits of the practice are the same in both instances ($180,000). The differences in tax treatment result in each incorporated practitioner being able to set aside for retirement an additional $3,500 annually, while at the same time increasing his net spendable income by $2,300 each year.

NONTAX ADVANTAGES OF PROFESSIONAL CORPORATIONS

Just as there are no unique tax advantages associated with incorporating a professional practice as compared with incorporating a closely held business, the nontax advantages also are generally the same in both instances. The significance of these nontax benefits varies directly with the size and complexity of the particular corporation.

Limited Liability

One reason for incorporating a business or profession is to limit the financial liability of an owner to his investment in the business or profes-

---

[15] *Supra,* footnote 13.

sion. It is true that in most states, liability for *contracts* entered into by a business or professional corporation is limited to the corporate assets and does not extend to the personal assets of the shareholder. On the other hand, where a business or a professional practice is organized as a partnership, liability for contracts entered into by the partnership can extend to the personal assets of all the partners where the partnership defaults on its obligation. The significance of this distinction is somewhat offset in most small closely held business or professional corporations by the fact that persons contracting with them also will often require the shareholders to obligate themselves personally as a condition of the contract.

Under most state professional corporation laws, the rules regarding limited liability for negligent acts committed by an employee of the corporation, including a shareholder-employee, are similar to those applicable to any closely held business corporation. Where a person, in his capacity as an employee of a corporation, commits a negligent or wrongful act he is always personally liable. In addition, liability extends to all the assets of the corporation. However, in most states no other employee, shareholder, or otherwise, will be personally liable unless the erring employee was under the direct supervision and control of another employee while rendering services on behalf of the corporation. In contrast, a negligent or wrongful act committed by an employee or partner of a partnership results in liability extending from the erring employee or partner to the partnership and to the personal assets of each partner.

This distinction is especially significant in the professional practice area where malpractice suits are so prevalent. Only by incorporating may a practitioner protect his personal assets from liability for the negligent acts of those of his associates over whom he has no direct control.

Centralized Management

Management of a corporation is vested in a board of directors elected by the shareholders. In turn, the board elects the officers of the corporation who run the business on a daily basis. Such a hierarchy does not apply to a partnership which, in general, is run by the partners themselves with each partner having an equal voice in making business decisions. The benefits of centralized management are virtually nonexistent in the small closely held corporation. However, where a relatively large medical clinic, law firm, or other professional partnership incorporates, the existence of a mechanism through which responsibility for the various affairs of the corporation can be delegated becomes a meaningful advantage of practice in corporate form.

Continuity of Life and Ease of Transferability

A partnership will be dissolved automatically by the retirement, death, or withdrawal of a partner, or by a change in its membership for any other reason. Although the business of the partnership may be continued by the remaining partners, the law requires that they go through the formality of forming a new partnership. On the other hand, a professional practice, once incorporated, can have perpetual life regardless of how often the interests of the shareholders are transferred. Most state statutes permit shares of a professional corporation to be transferred to the corpo-

FIGURE 48–2. Comparison of Professional Partnership and Professional Corporation with Respect to Available Current Spendable Income and Amount Set Aside for Retirement

Partnership Form*

Item	Each Partner	Total of All Partners
1. Earned income from partnership	$60,000	$180,000
2. HR-10 contribution deduction	$2,500	$7,500
3. Personal exemptions and standard deduction	$4,500	$13,500
4. Taxable income	$53,000	$159,000
5. Federal income tax	$18,600	$55,800
6. Net available after-tax income [1 − (2 + 5)]	$38,900	$116,700
7. Personal investment ($2,500 voluntary HR-10 contribution and $2,500 nonqualified investment)	$5,000	$15,000
8. Personal life insurance coverage ($50,000 permanent and $50,000 term)	$2,100	$6,300
9. Personal medical expense insurance and disability income insurance	$1,000	$3,000
10. Life insurance to fund partnership entity buy-and-sell agreement	$1,200	$3,600
11. Net current spendable income [6 − (7, 8, 9, 10)]	$29,600	$88,800
12. Total set aside for retirement annually (2 + 7)	$7,500	$22,500

Corporate Form*

Item	Corporation		Each Share-holder-Employee		Total of All Share-holder-Employees	
	Not de-ductible	Deductible	Taxable	Non-taxable	Taxable	Non-taxable
1. Gross profits of corporation	$180,000				—	—
2. Salary to shareholder-employees		($132,000)	$44,000		$132,000	
3. Contribution to qualified retirement plan (25% of salary)		($33,000)		$11,000		$33,000
4. Life insurance for shareholder-employee ($50,000 group term and $50,000 split-dollar)	$4,800	($1,200)	$300†	$1,700	$900†	$5,100
5. Medical expense insurance and disability insurance		($3,000)		$1,000		$3,000
6. Life insurance to fund stock redemption buy-and-sell agreement	$3,600			$1,200		$3,600
7. Other taxable income (unallocated)	$2,400		—		—	
8. Personal exemptions and standard deductions	—		($4,500)		($13,500)	
9. Total taxable income	$10,800		$39,800		$119,400	
10. Tax due		$2,400	$12,100		$36,300	
11. Net current spendable income (7 − 10 for corporation; 2 − 10 for shareholder-employees)		0	$31,900		$95,700	
12. Total set aside for retirement annually (3)			$11,000		$33,000	

* These illustrations assume there are three 45-year-old practitioners, each of whom is married and has two children. They all share equally in the profits of the practice. Further assume that they have no outside incomes.
† Includable in taxable income as economic benefit from split-dollar plan.

ration itself, or to another practitioner licensed in the state of incorporation.

The continuity-of-life feature of a professional corporation will be important to a group practice that experiences frequent turnover of members. The characteristic of continuity of life also facilitates the carrying out of the corporation's obligations under a nonqualified deferred compensation agreement entered into by a practitioner and the corporation.

An interest in a partnership is represented by contractual rights. Modification of a partnership interest requires the execution of a new contract spelling out any changes that are to be made. If a professional partnership incorporates, ownership rights will be represented by shares of stock. Ownership interests then can be rearranged by the simple expedient of transferring a certain number of shares of stock with such transfer having no effect on the existence of the corporation.

Furthermore, the sale of stock in a corporation, professional or otherwise, is a capital transaction generally eligible for capital gain tax treatment. Upon the sale or liquidation of an interest in a partnership, professional or otherwise, the purchase money must be apportioned among all the assets of the partnership that are sold. The share of the purchase price attributable to some of those assets, such as accounts receivable, may receive ordinary income tax treatment.

PROBLEM AREAS FOR
PROFESSIONAL CORPORATIONS

Now that the Treasury has agreed to classify a professional practice which has been incorporated under an appropriate state statute as a corporation for federal tax purposes, professional corporations will be subject to the myriad of Code provisions that attempt to protect against a corporation and its shareholders paying less than their "fair share" of income taxes.

One-Man Professional Corporation

As long as the applicable state statute permits a sole practitioner to incorporate, being a one-man professional corporation is not, in itself, a basis for denying corporate tax treatment. However, the sole practitioner should take every precaution to operate his corporation as a separate tax paying entity to avoid being classified as a "sham." If he is required to show a "business purpose" for incorporating, it may be a difficult task. The usual nontax reasons for incorporation, such as centralized management, continuity of life, and limited liability, have little or no significance to the one-man corporation. For this reason it is extremely important that a one-man corporation carry out all of the functions and formalities that generally are applicable to corporate entities. In order to enhance corporateness, it has been suggested that even if the state statute allows a one-man professional corporation to have a one-man board of directors, it may be desirable to have more than one director. Also, perhaps shares of stock should be held by one or more other professionals, even though they are not active in the corporation, in order to provide a possible purchaser for the principal shareholder's interest when he dies or retires.

Personal Holding Company Tax

A professional corporation, especially a one-man professional corporation, may find itself categorized by the IRS as a personal holding company. A corporation may be taxed as a personal holding company where more than one half of its stock is owned by five or fewer individuals, and 60 percent of its adjusted ordinary gross income comes within one of the categories designated as personal holding company income. In addition to regular corporate taxes, a personal holding company is taxed at the rate of 70 percent on its undistributed personal holding company income. A category of personal holding company income that might apply to a professional corporation is amounts received pursuant to personal service contracts under which the purchaser of the services has the right to designate the individual who is to perform the services and the designee is the actual or constructive owner of 25 percent or more of the outstanding stock of the corporation.

The personal holding company tax is no problem where there are five or more equal shareholders. Even if there are four or fewer shareholders, there will be no problem in those cases where the patient or client retains the professional corporation as such, and the corporation chooses the particular principal shareholder who will perform the services. In some instances, however, the patient or client may have a degree of control over the choice of the professional who will handle his problem. In the cases that have been litigated, the requirement of a "right to designate" has been narrowly construed to include only those situations where the right to select the individual who is to perform the services is contained in a written contract, or where the purchaser of the services may terminate the contract if a principal shareholder ceases to devote his efforts to the activities of the corporation. In the absence of a legally enforceable right to designate the person who is to perform the services, even where all the parties expect a certain individual will perform the services, such as in a one-man corporation, it has been held that the corporation did not come within the definition of a personal holding company.[16]

Even if the courts' interpretation of the "right to designate" is broadened to include oral understandings, it should be kept in mind that the personal holding company tax applies only to personal holding company income that is *not* distributed. Thus, the tax will not apply in any case where a professional corporation pays out all its personal holding company income in the year it is earned.

Reasonableness of Compensation

The unreasonable compensation provisions of the Internal Revenue Code are designed to prevent a corporation from turning a portion of its distributed earnings that should be taxed as a nondeductible dividend, into an ordinary and necessary business expense that will be deductible to the corporation. Thus, to the extent that compensation payments are unnecessary or unreasonable, they will be treated as constructive dividends

---

[16] S. O. *Claggett*, 44 T.C. 503 (1965). I.R.S. has acquiesed in this decision, 1966–2 *Cumulative Bulletin* 4.

and will not be deductible to the corporation. Since most of the earnings of a professional corporation can be attributed to the rendering of personal services by its employees, it may pay out most of its earnings in the form of compensation. However, where some of the earnings paid out in the form of salaries or other compensation to shareholder-employees are generated by nonshareholder-employees or by the investment of capital which represents an income producing factor in the corporation, a portion of the compensation paid to the shareholder-employees may be held to be a dividend because it is not a reasonable or necessary payment for services rendered. This may be a particularly vexing problem where goodwill is found to exist and a portion of earnings are attributable thereto.

Unfortunately, there is no way of accurately determining what is reasonable compensation. The nature of the services performed, the qualifications of the employee and the compensation which other corporations in the same profession and geographical area pay employees in comparable positions are all important factors that should be considered.

If provision is made *before* the fact, it is possible subsequently to reverse the tax consequences of dividend treatment for unreasonable compensation. This can be done by having the shareholder-employees enter into a legally binding contract with the corporation requiring that in the event the corporation is denied a deduction for any portion of the compensation paid to a shareholder-employee, he is legally obligated to repay such amount to the corporation in one or more subsequent years. Where the shareholder-employee is legally bound to make the repayment, he will be entitled to deduct the repayment from his taxable income for the year of reimbursement. There appears to be no limitation on when the shareholder-employee may repay such amount. Therefore, he should be free to choose one or more high income tax years in order to get the most benefit from the deduction.

Unreasonable Accumulation of Earnings Tax

Retention of earnings in the corporation may avoid an unreasonable compensation tax problem, but may give rise to an unreasonable accumulation of earnings tax problem. This is a special tax imposed on the unreasonably accumulated taxable income of a corporation in order to prevent the purposeful avoidance of the payment of income tax on dividends by stockholders. The penalty tax rate is 27½ percent on the first $100,000 of unreasonably accumulated taxable income and 38½ percent on any excess. The Code provides an accumulated earnings credit that permits a corporation to accumulate a minimum of $100,000 before it has to show that its accumulation is necessary for the reasonable needs of the business. It probably would be unusual for a professional corporation to require accumulations in excess of $100,000 for reasonable business purposes. Some examples of when the accumulation of earnings beyond $100,000 might be justifiable include plans to acquire real estate or anticipated investment in expensive equipment.

The existence of the accumulated earnings tax, together with the rules applicable to the payment of unreasonable compensation, make it evident that a professional corporation must give serious thought to financial planning if it is to minimize effectively the payment of income taxes.

A LOOK INTO THE FUTURE

There does not appear to be any new legislation on the horizon that would single out professional corporations for special tax treatment. On the other hand, many proposals have been set forth recently that would affect the nature and extent of fringe benefits that are available to employees of corporations and to employees, sole practitioners, and partners of unincorporated businesses and professions.

The central theme of most of these proposals is to equate the fringe benefits that are available to shareholder-employees, regular employees, sole practitioners, and partners. In the area of qualified retirement plans, one can expect the eventual tax benefits to fall somewhere between those now available to owner-employees under HR-10 plans and shareholder-employees under corporate qualified retirement plans. As to other tax-favored fringe benefits such as group insurance, medical expense insurance, and disability income coverage, it is hoped that sole practitioners and partners will be elevated to a position comparable with the shareholder-employee of a corporation. However, until these changes are brought about, the popularity of professional corporations should continue to expand.

SELECTED REFERENCES

Chasman, Herbert, and Rotgin, Philip. "What You Should Know about the Professional Corporation," *Estate Planners Quarterly*, Booklet No. 998 (June 1969).

Eaton, Berrien C., Jr. "Professional Corporations and Associations, Tax and State Law, Analysis, Procedures and Forms," *Business Organizations Service.* Vol. 17, 17A & 17B. Albany, N.Y.: Mathew Bender and Company, Inc., 1970.

————. "The 531 Penalty Tax and Subchapter 5: Applying Them to Professional Corporations," *Journal of Taxation*, Vol. 34, No. 3 (March 1971), pp. 143–44.

Georgetown Law Journal. "Professional Corporations: Analysis under the Tax Reform Act and Survey of State Statutes," Vol. 58, No. 3 (February 1970).

Gibbs, Lawrence B. "Getting out of a Professional Corporation: Preparing for the Forthcoming Problems," *Journal of Taxation*, Vol. 34, No. 3 (March 1971), pp. 134–39.

Ginsburg, Joseph. "What Are the Long-Term Qualified Plan Benefits to Professional Stockholders?" *Journal of Taxation*, Vol. 34, No. 3 (March 1971), p. 145.

Horsley, Walter H., and Dray, Mark S. "Compensating Officer-Stockholders of Professional Corporations: An Analysis," *Journal of Taxation*, Vol. 34, No. 3 (March 1971), pp. 146–49.

Jones, H. Bradley. "Is There a Dividend Requirement for Professional Corporations?" *Journal of Taxation*, Vol. 34, No. 3 (March 1971), pp. 139–40.

Milliken, Charles B., and Lloyd, Alex. "The Service Business: Partnership or Corporation," *Connecticut Bar Journal*, Vol. 43 (1969), pp. 259–318.

O'Neill, Albert C., Jr. "Professional Service Corporations: Coping with Operational Problems," *Journal of Taxation*, Vol. 30, No. 8 (August 1969).

Ray, George E. "Factors That Go into Decision of Whether to Operate as a

Professional Corporation," *Journal of Taxation,* Vol. 34, No. 3 (March 1971), pp. 130–33.

Taylor, Robert C.   "PHC Penalty Tax: Steps That Corporations of Professional Can Take to Sidestep It," *Journal of Taxation,* Vol. 34, No. 3 (March 1971), pp. 141–42.

Thies, Winthrop D.   "An Estate Planner's Approach to the Professional Corporation," *Trusts and Estates,* Vol. 109, No. 2 (February 1970), pp. 83–86 and 152–55; Vol. 109, No. 3 (March 1970) pp. 163–69 and 253–57; Vol. 109, No. 4 (April 1970), pp. 289–94 and 378–79.

Worthy, K. Martin.   "I.R.S. Chief Council Outlines What Lies Ahead for Professional Corporations," *Journal of Taxation,* Vol. 32, No. 2 (February 1970), pp. 88–93.

part VIII

Government Benefits— Protection and Retirement

GOVERNMENT benefit schemes to provide protection against the economic risks of death, disability, and retirement have grown immensely in the past four decades. Social security, Medicare, and military service-related benefits constitute the largest segment of security expenditures from the public sector, with the group insurance, private pension, and individual insurance segments representing the role of the private sector.

The three chapters in Part VIII summarize the nature and extent of social security benefits for retirement, disability, and survivorship; Medicare and other government health benefits; and servicemen's and veterans' benefits.

49

Social Security Benefits for Retirement, Disability, and Survivorship

By ROBERT J. MYERS

THE SOCIAL SECURITY program significantly affects the lives of the vast majority of the citizens of the United States. This program is commonly called "social security," although a more accurate title is "old-age, survivors, and disability insurance"—or OASDI. It was inaugurated by the Social Security Act of 1935 and has been amended from time to time. This description of the program is based on the law as amended in October 1972.

About 28 million persons received monthly benefits under the program in December 1972; about 96 million persons paid contributions (or taxes) in 1972. Many millions of other persons are also directly affected by the program in that they are potential beneficiaries in the event of the retirement, death, or disability of the covered workers.

The financial impact of the program can be seen from the fact that total benefit disbursements in 1972 amounted to $42 billion, while total contribution income was about $46 billion. The administrative expenses involved in collecting the contributions, maintaining the earnings records, and paying the benefits were about $850 million in 1972, or 1.8 percent of the contribution income. The assets of the trust funds of the OASDI system amounted to $43 billion at the end of 1972 and had earned interest income of about $2.2 billion in that year.

COVERAGE PROVISIONS OF OASDI SYSTEM

Virtually all gainfully employed persons are covered under the program (or could be covered by election). The major exceptions are most policemen with their own retirement systems, federal government employees under the civil service retirement system, low-income self-employed persons, and farm and domestic workers with irregular employment. Railroad workers have a separate system under the Railroad Retirement Act but are, in essence, covered under OASDI as a result of provisions for transfer of wage credits of employees with less than ten years of service and a financial interchange between the two systems.

Nonfarm Self-Employed

All nonfarm self-employed persons are covered—both nonprofessional, such as store owners, and professional, such as lawyers, physicians, and dentists, provided their net annual earnings are at least $400. Earnings are reported on the income tax return.

Farm Operators

Farmers are covered on the same general basis as other self-employed persons, except for a special simplified reporting option based on gross income for those with low net income.

Ministers

Ministers are covered on a compulsory basis, unless they opt out on the grounds that they are opposed, by reason of conscience or religious principles, to all public insurance which provides death, disability, or retirement benefits. Such election must, in general, be made within two years after coverage is first applicable. Their earnings are considered as self-employment income even if their compensation is in the form of a regular salary.

Employees of Nonfarm Private Employers

All employees in private industry and commerce are compulsorily covered, with no minimum restrictions as to amount of earnings or length of employment. Full-time life insurance agents are defined to be "employees" regardless of their common-law status.

Employees of Nonprofit Organizations

Coverage for employees of nonprofit organizations such as churches, private hospitals, and private schools is at the option of each employing unit but requires the concurring vote of the employee concerned. Once coverage is established, however, it is compulsory for new employees.

Employees of State and Local Governments

Employees of state and local governments can be covered at the option of the state and of the employing unit. Where there is an existing retirement system, a majority of the employees therein must vote in favor of coverage; however, policemen under an existing retirement system cannot be covered, except in a few specified states.

Employees of Federal Government

Virtually all federal civilian employees not under an existing retirement system and all members of the uniformed services are covered on a regular contributory basis.

Employees of Foreign Governments and International Agencies

American citizen employees of foreign governments and international governmental organizations who work in the United States are covered, on a compulsory basis, as self-employed persons since their employers cannot be compelled to pay the tax.

Farm Workers

Farm employment is covered if cash wages in a year from an employer amount to at least $150 or if there are 20 or more days of employment remunerated on a time basis.

Domestic Workers

Domestic servants are covered if cash wages are $50 or more in a quarter from a single employer.

Tips Received by Employees

Tips of $20 or more per month to employees are covered as wages and are reported through the employer (but only the employee contribution is paid).

Employment Abroad

The preceding discussion relates to employment in the United States (including American Samoa, Guam, Puerto Rico, and the Virgin Islands) and on American vessels and airplanes, and applies to United States citizens working abroad for American employers. Also, at the option of the American employer, United States citizens working for foreign subsidiaries of American companies may be included in the system.

Military Service Wage Credits

The "noncontributory" wage credits of $160 a month for military service after September 15, 1940, terminated at the end of 1956, when regular contributory coverage began. For military service after 1956, in essence, an additional $100 of wage credits is given for each month of service (as an allowance for remuneration in kind). The OASDI system is reimbursed for the additional cost of benefits paid with respect to the "noncontributory" credits.

OASDI INSURED STATUS CONDITIONS

There are three kinds of insured status: fully, currently, and disability. Fully insured status provides eligibility for all types of old-age and survivor benefits. Currently insured status gives eligibility for certain survivor benefits. Disability insured status is a partial requirement for the disability "freeze" and for disability monthly benefits. Insured status is defined in terms of quarters of coverage—either $50 of nonagricultural wages paid in a calendar quarter or $100 of self-employment income credited to that quarter. Self-employed individuals generally are credited with four quarters of coverage each year, as is the case for persons with the maximum amount of taxable wages in a year. Special rules similar to those for self-employed individuals apply to farm workers.

Fully insured status is achieved if the individual has at least as many quarters of coverage (acquired at any time) as the number of years elapsing after 1950 (or age 21, if later) and before the year of attainment of age 62 (for men attaining age 62 before 1975, a somewhat longer period is required, generally based on when age 65 was attained), with minimum and maximum requirements of 6 and 40 quarters of coverage, respectively. For example, persons who attain age 62 in 1975 are fully insured with 25 quarters of coverage (1974 minus 1950).

Currently insured status is achieved by having 6 quarters of coverage in the 13-quarter period ending with the quarter of death, attainment of age 62, or actual retirement.

Disability insured status is achieved by having 20 quarters of coverage in the 40-quarter period ending with the quarter of disablement, with a lower requirement for persons becoming disabled before age 31. Periods of total disability for individuals who have both fully insured status and disability insured status are excluded in measuring the elapsed period for any of the insured status categories (the "disability freeze" provision).

OASDI BENEFICIARY CATEGORIES

Old-Age Beneficiaries

Fully insured individuals are eligible for a full old-age benefit at age 65. The amount of this benefit is 100 percent of the primary insurance amount (defined later). The old-age benefit can be claimed between ages 62 and 65, with a reduction of 5/9 percent for each month below age 65 at time of retirement. Thus a person retiring at exact age 62 receives a 20 percent lifetime reduction, which closely approximates an "actuarial equivalent" basis.

Disability Benefits

An individual is eligible for a disability benefit of 100 percent of his primary insurance amount if he is permanently and totally disabled and has been so disabled for at least five months, and has fully and disability insured statuses. By total and permanent disability is meant inability to engage in any substantial gainful activity by reason of a medically determinable impairment that can be expected to continue for at least 12 months or to result in death. The waiting period of five consecutive months of disability is not a presumptive period which, if satisfied, would "prove" the existence of a qualifying permanent disability. The determinations of disability are made by state agencies (generally the vocational rehabilitation unit) with review by the Social Security Administration.

The determination of continuance of disability is made by the Social Security Administration. Individuals must, in general, undertake vocational rehabilitation training, during the first year of which benefits are paid regardless of earnings. With this exception, there is no permitted amount of earnings as there is for retired workers and for dependent and survivor beneficiaries (earnings test). Instead, a disability beneficiary might have small earnings and still continue to receive benefits as long as he is considered not able to engage in any substantial gainful activity. The disability benefits terminate at age 65, when the beneficiary goes on the old-age benefit roll.

Combined disability benefits and state workmen's compensation benefits cannot exceed the higher of 80 percent of average earnings in the highest five consecutive years, or his highest earnings rate in any year in the last six years, or his OASDI average monthly wage (as defined later).

Supplementary Benefits

If the retired or disabled individual has a wife (or dependent husband) aged 65 or over (regardless of her age, if she has in her care a child under age 18 or a child of any age who has been totally disabled since before age 22), an additional benefit of 50 percent of the primary insurance amount is payable. There is a similar benefit for each eligible child, including also children aged 18–21 who are in full-time school attendance (subject to the family maximum provisions). It is important to note that the mother's benefit is not payable if the only eligible children receiving benefits are students aged 18–21. A wife between age 62 and age 65 without an eligible child, or a dependent husband, can elect to receive benefits which are reduced 25/36 percent for each month under age 65 at time of claiming benefit, such reduction to continue during the joint lifetime of the couple. Thus, such a wife claiming benefits at exact age 62 has a 25 percent reduction—somewhat less than the approximately 30 percent needed on an "actuarial equivalent" basis. A larger reduction than for the worker is required because it applies only while the spouse is alive, rather than during the entire lifetime.

Survivor Benefits

Widow's benefits are payable at age 60, or at ages 50–59 if the widow is disabled, if the deceased husband was fully insured (including death after retirement). Parallel benefits are payable with respect to dependent widowers. This benefit is 100 percent of the primary insurance amount if first claimed at age 65 or over; the amount is 71½ percent at age 60 and 50 percent at age 50 (with proportionate amounts for intervening ages). However, the widow's benefit cannot exceed the benefit that the husband was receiving if he retired at ages 62–64 on a reduced amount.

When a fully insured worker dies, parents' benefits are payable (upon attainment of age 62) to parents who have been dependent upon such individual. The benefit is 82½ percent of the primary insurance amount if there is one parent, and 75 percent each if there are two parents.

When a fully or currently insured individual dies leaving an eligible child, benefits are payable to the children and the widowed mother in the same manner as for the children and wife of a retired worker. These child survivor benefits are also payable in respect to the death of an insured female worker, regardless of current dependency of the child at time of death. The benefits are 75 percent of the primary insurance amount for the widowed mother and 75 percent for each child, subject to the family maximum provision.

Lump-Sum Death Payments

In all cases of death of a fully or currently insured individual, a lump-sum death payment of three times the primary insurance amount (which will produce at least $253.50) is payable. This payment, however, may not exceed $255, the maximum amount available under the 1952 Act and not increased subsequently. The lump sum is payable in full to a surviving spouse but in other cases may not exceed the actual burial costs—a restriction of little impact in light of even minimal burial costs at present.

Special Age-72 Benefits

Certain persons aged 72 or over who are not fully insured and who attain age 72 before 1972 for men and 1970 for women (primarily persons who attained age 72 before 1968), can receive special flat-amount benefits of $58.00 per month. This benefit is not payable if the individual is receiving public assistance; it is reduced by the amount of any other governmental pension the individual receives.

General Benefit Provisions

No individual can receive the full amount of more than one type of monthly benefit. For instance, if a woman has an old-age benefit in her own right and a wife's or widow's benefit from her husband's earnings, then, in effect, only the larger of the two benefits may be received. Payments are made only after an individual files a claim, with retroactive payments of monthly benefits for as long as 12 months before filing. Certain restrictions on payment of benefits apply to persons convicted of crimes affecting the security of the nation.

OASDI BENEFIT AMOUNTS

The *primary insurance amount* (PIA), from which all benefits are determined, is based on the average wage of the insured individual.

Average Monthly Wage

The concept of *average monthly wage* (AMW) used in OASDI is, in essence, computed over the entire potential period of coverage, but with certain periods of low earnings disregarded. In general, the average is computed from the beginning of 1951 (or age 22, if later) to the beginning of the year of death, attainment of age 62 (but for men attaining age 62 before 1975, the end point is generally age 65), or disability, whichever is applicable. In computing this average, five calendar years may be dropped from consideration; further, years with high earnings beginning with the year of attainment of age 62 may be substituted for previous years with lower earnings.

For example, consider a person who attains age 62 in 1980 and who has had maximum covered wages in all years since 1950 ($3,600 in 1951–54, $4,200 in 1955–58, $4,800 in 1959–65, $6,600 in 1966–67, $7,800 in 1968–71,

$9,000 in 1972, $10,800 in 1973, and $12,000 thereafter, ignoring the effect of the automatic adjustment provisions, described later). Suppose that he retires at the beginning of 1982. His AMW is based on the average of his 24 "best years (1980 minus 1951, minus 5). These "best" years include eight at $12,000, one at $10,800, one at $9,000, four at $7,800, two at $6,600, seven at $4,800, and one at $4,200.

In addition, under the "disability freeze" provision, periods of disability may be eliminated; such disability must be of at least six months' duration, and the disabled worker must have both fully insured status and disability insured status. Also, the AMW may be computed back to the beginning of 1937 on the same basis as when computed back to 1951, if a larger benefit will result.

Benefit Formula

Before the 1958 amendments, definite benefit formulas were prescribed. For example, the 1954 Act benefit formula applicable to earnings after 1950 was 55 percent of the first $110 of AMW, plus 20 percent of the next $240 of AMW (reflecting the $4,200 earnings base). Under subsequent amendments, a considerably different procedure has been prescribed, with a benefit table giving the PIA for various ranges of AMW (e.g., in the legislation enacted in July 1972, where the AMW is $441–45, the PIA is $248.90). The benefit table also provides for conversion of benefits for those on the roll on the effective date of the legislation, and shows the maximum family benefit applicable for each PIA (e.g., $465.30 where the AMW is $441–45.

Actually, the benefit table is based on a definite formula and on definite minimum and maximum benefit provisions, so that in reality, these are built into the table. Certain approximations have been made because of the grouping involved in rounding the benefits.

The benefit formula underlying the present benefit table is 108.01 percent of the first $110 of AMW, plus 39.29 percent of the next $290 of AMW, plus 36.71 percent of the next $150 of AMW, plus 43.15 percent of the next $100 of AMW, plus 24 percent of the next $100 of AMW, plus 20 percent of the next $250 of AMW (except that in some cases, for AMW under $85, a slightly higher amount is payable so as to fit in with the minimum benefit). The minimum PIA, before reduction for early retirement of those workers claiming benefits before age 65, is $84.50 a month. A higher minimum PIA is payable to those with at least 22 years of coverage (defined as a year in which the worker had covered earnings equal to at least 25 percent of the earnings base); the amount is $8.50 per year of coverage in excess of 10 years up to a maximum of 30 years (i.e., $170 for 30 years of coverage).

The benefit table also provides for the determination of the PIA when it is more advantageous for the beneficiary to compute the AMW back to 1937 and to use the benefit computation method of the 1939 Act. Under these circumstances, Table 49–1 shows illustrative figures.

A delayed-retirement increment is paid to the worker who continues to work beyond age 65. This is at the rate of 1 percent of the PIA for each

TABLE 49–1.   **Primary Insurance Amounts Computed
under Method of 1939 Act**

Benefit Computed under Method of 1939 Act	Primary Insurance Amount
$10	$ 84.50
15	84.50
20	92.90
25	112.10
30	130.50
35	145.20
40	159.30
45°	174.80

° Maximum possible is $45.60 (which produces same PIA as $45.00).

year's delay (up to age 72), but it is not payable with respect to dependents or survivor benefits.

The legislation enacted in 1972 provided for automatic adjustment in the benefit formula (applicable both to future beneficiaries and to beneficiaries on the roll) for changes in the cost of living (as measured by the Consumer Price Index), recognizing only increases therein. Adjustments are to be made each January, beginning in 1975, but only when the CPI has risen at least 3 percent from the time when the last previous benefit increase occurred. The adjustments will not be made if Congress has already legislated a benefit increase in the preceding year. Each factor in the benefit formula is increased by the increase in the CPI. When the earnings base is increased (see later discussion), a factor of 20 percent applies to the new band of AMWs. The automatic-adjustment provision is not applicable to the special minimum benefit based on years of coverage.

Minimum and Maximum Family Benefits

The minimum family benefit for survivors (applicable only when there is one such survivor) is $84.50. The maximum family benefit is 150 percent of the PIA for AMWs up through $239; this proportion then increases for larger AMWs, reaching a maximum of 188 percent for AMWs of $432–36 and then decreasing to 175 percent for AMWs of $628 and over.

Table 49–2 shows illustrative monthly benefits for various categories, giving consideration to the applicable benefit proportions, the minimum and maximum benefit provisions, and the reductions for workers and wives claiming benefits before age 65.

OASDI EARNINGS TEST

Benefits for retired workers and their eligible dependents, for eligible dependents of disability beneficiaries, and for survivors are, in general, not paid when the beneficiary is engaged in substantial employment, nor are benefits paid to the eligible dependents of a retired worker who is

TABLE 49–2. Illustrative Monthly Benefits under OASDI System for Various Family Categories, Based on Earnings after 1950 (all figures rounded to nearest dollar)

Average Monthly Wage	Aged 65 Retirement° or Over at	Worker Retiring at Age 62	Worker Aged 65 or Over with						
			Wife Aged 65 or Over at Retirement†	Wife Aged 62 at Retirement	Wife and One Child°‡	Widow and One Child§	Widow and Two or More Children#	Widow Aged 60	Widow Aged 65 or Over
$76 or less	$ 85	$ 68	$127	$116	$127	$127	$127	$ 75	$ 85
100	109	87	163	150	163	163	163	78	109
200	154	124	232	212	232	232	232	111	154
300	193	155	290	266	317	290	317	138	193
400	233	187	350	321	426	350	426	167	233
500	270	216	405	371	495	405	495	193	270
600	310	248	465	426	548	465	548	222	310
700	343	274	514	471	599	514	599	245	343
800	365	292	547	501	638	547	638	261	365
900	385	308	577	529	673	577	673	275	385
1,000	405	324	607	556	708	607	708	289	405

° Also applies to disability beneficiary.
† Also applies to worker and dependent husband aged 65 or over, and to worker and one child.
‡ Also applies to worker and two children; or to worker, dependent husband aged 65 or over, and one child.
§ Also applies to two aged dependent parents or two children alone.
# Also applies to three or more children alone.

Note: Since the average monthly wage is computed over a period of many years, and since the earnings base has been increased many times, the highest level of AMW generally cannot be attained for many years.

engaged in substantial employment. Benefits are payable for all months in a year if the annual earnings from all types of employment (whether or not covered) are $2,100 or less. If earnings exceed $2,100, then $1 of benefits may be withheld for each $2 of such "excess earnings." In no event are benefits withheld for a month in which the individual has wages of $175 or less and does not render substantial self-employment services. Moreover, the earned income restriction is not applicable at all after the individual reaches age 72. The annual and monthly exempt amounts are adjusted in the same manner as the earnings base (as discussed later).

As an example of how the earnings test operates, consider a retired worker under age 72 with an eligible wife, whose monthly family benefit is $235. If he works only from March through December at $300 per month, then he will without question receive benefits for January and February. His benefits of $2,350 for the other ten months will be reduced by $450, since the excess of his earnings over $2,100 is $900. In actual practice, this individual might receive his benefits through October and then have them suspended, with a final accounting and adjustment after the end of the year.

Payments of OASDI Benefits Abroad

Benefits are not payable in the case of deported persons, whose rights are terminated until they are subsequently lawfully admitted. In the case of persons residing in certain countries where there is no reasonable assurance that checks can be delivered or cashed at full value, the benefits are withheld but can subsequently be paid if conditions change.

For aliens residing outside the United States who came on the roll after 1956, benefits are payable only if the insured worker has 40 or more quarters of coverage or has resided in the United States for 10 or more years, or if the country of which he is a citizen has a reciprocity treaty with the United States or has a general social insurance or pension system that will continue full benefits to United States citizens while outside of that foreign country.

OASDI FINANCING PROVISIONS

The benefits and administrative expenses are paid out of two separate trust funds. The old-age and survivor benefits come from the Old-Age and Survivors Insurance Trust Fund, while the monthly benefits for disabled workers and their dependents come from the Disability Insurance Trust Fund. A separate trust fund was established for the disability program when it was inaugurated so that any unfavorable experience of this program would not endanger the OASI portion of the system.

The income to these trust funds is derived from contributions (taxes) on covered workers and employers, and from interest earnings on investments. The total contribution income is divided so that, for 1970–72, an amount based on a combined employer-employee rate of 1.1 percent (and .825 percent for the self-employed) was allocated to the DI Trust Fund and the remainder goes to the OASI Trust Fund. For 1973–77, the employer-employee allocation rate is 1.1 percent, while for 1978–2010, it is 1.15 percent, and for 2011 and after it is 1.5 percent; the corresponding rates for the self-employed are .795 percent, .84 percent, and .895 percent.

Other than for a relatively small cash working balance, the trust funds are invested in interest-bearing debt obligations of the United States. These can be either marketable issues or special issues bearing an interest rate approximating the average market yield rate on all government obligations having at least four years to run until earliest maturity as of the issuance date of the special issue. In actual practice, the vast majority of the invested assets are in special issues.

The contribution or tax rates—past, present, and scheduled in the law for the future for the OASDI system—are shown in Table 49–3, along with the applicable maximum taxable and creditable earnings base. As a result of the legislation enacted in 1972, this base is to be automatically adjusted upward, in accordance with changes in earnings in covered employment, but only for years when benefits too are so adjusted.

TABLE 49–3. Past and Future Financing Provisions of OASDI System

Period	Maximum Earnings Base	Combined Employer-Employee Tax Rate	Self-Employed Tax Rate
1937–49	$ 3,000	2.00%	*
1950	3,000	3.00	*
1951–53	3,600	3.00	2.25 %
1954	3,600	4.00	3.00
1955–56	4,200	4.00	3.00
1957–58	4,200	4.50	3.375
1959	4,800	5.00	3.75
1960–61	4,800	6.00	4.50
1962	4,800	6.25	4.70
1963–65	4,800	7.25	5.40
1966	6,600	7.70	5.80
1967	6,600	7.80	5.90
1968	7,800	7.60	5.80
1969–70	7,800	8.40	6.30
1971	7,800	9.20	6.90
1972	9,000	9.20	7.00
1973	10,800	9.70	7.00
1974–77	12,000†	9.70	7.00
1978–2010	12,000†	9.60	7.00
2011 and after	12,000†	11.70	7.00

* Self-employed not covered in this period.
† Subject to automatic adjustment for 1975 and after (see text).
Note: See Table 49–4 for combined OASDI and hospital insurance tax rates.

In considering the financial impact and burden of the social security program (which is of significance in determining what role the private sector should and can play in providing economic security for the populace), it is necessary to consider also the payroll taxes that support the hospital insurance (HI) portion of the Medicare program, which is described in detail in Chapter 50. The combined tax rates and the maximum earnings bases applicable are shown in Table 49–4. It is noteworthy that the combined employer-employee tax rate is scheduled to rise to an ultimate level of 13.1 percent. There is some question as to whether the scheduled OASDI contribution rates will be sufficient to finance the program over the long range, since they have been developed under somewhat optimistic assumptions as to future conditions. If the nation continues to move toward a demographic condition of zero population growth, or if productivity does not increase as rapidly as it did in the past (or, in other words, if wages do not increase much more rapidly than prices), significantly higher tax rates will be needed than the schedule contained in the law.

TABLE 49–4.   Past and Future Financing Provisions of OASDI and HI Systems

Period	Maximum Earnings Base	Combined Employer- Employee Tax Rate	Self- Employed Tax Rate
1966*	$ 6,600	8.4%	6.15%
1967	6,600	8.8	6.40
1968	7,800	8.8	6.40
1969–70	7,800	9.6	6.90
1971	7,800	10.4	7.50
1972	9,000	10.4	7.50
1973	10,800	11.7	8.00
1974–77	12,000†	11.7	8.00
1978–80	12,000†	12.1	8.25
1981–85	12,000†	12.3	8.35
1986–2010	12,000†	12.5	8.45
2011 and after	12,000†	14.6	8.45

* HI taxes were first applicable in 1966.
† Subject to automatic adjustment for 1975 and after (see text).

Congress, in connection with the 1950 Act and subsequent amendments, has consistently enunciated the principle that the OASDI program should be self-supporting from the contributions of the covered workers and their employers, according to the intermediate cost estimates. Of course, it would be only by coincidence that an exact balance would be shown. Generally, there has been a small deficiency, under the intermediate cost estimate, between the level contribution rate needed to finance the benefits and the level contribution rate that is equivalent to the graded contribution rates in the law.

Although the financing of OASDI differs in certain respects from that of private pension plans, these differences are more of degree than type, except that the OASDI financing is based on the "open-group" concept (i.e., assuming that new entrants will always come into the plan—as the law generally requires) rather than the "closed-group" basis properly applicable to private plans. The graded contribution schedule is intended to finance the system fully without any need for government subsidy.

Finally, one of the most important points in connection with the sound financing of the OASDI system is that, over the years, there has been a strong cost-consciousness on the part of Congress and all others who have been concerned with the program.

BASIC PRINCIPLES OF OASDI SYSTEM

There are a number of what might be termed "basic principles" of OASDI and, even more broadly, basic principles of many social insurance systems. Among these are the following: (1) the benefits are based on presumptive need, (2) the benefits provide a floor of protection, (3) the benefits are related to earnings, (4) a balance between social adequacy and individual equity is present, and (5) the financing is on a self-supporting contributory basis.

Benefits Based on Presumptive Need

Certain categories of social risk are established by the law, and benefits are, in general, paid when these eventuate. Thus, for example, old-age benefits are not payable automatically upon attainment of a given age, such as 62, but rather only upon retirement. Likewise, benefits for surviving widows are not payable for their lifetime, but rather only while they have eligible children present or are aged 60 or over (or aged 50 or over and disabled), and only so long as they are not remarried and not gainfully employed with earnings above those noted earlier.

The retirement requirement is frequently misunderstood as being a kind of means or needs test (that is, a test of the individual's situation to make certain he needs the income to meet subsistence-level economic requirements). When considered in that light, some critics believe that the earnings test is unfair, in that only earned income is used as a criterion for paying benefits, while investment income is disregarded. This procedure, however, is essential if there is to be a system paying retirement benefits, and not a charity program based on individual needs as determined by social workers. The latter would be an inimical basis insofar as insurance companies and other savings organizations are concerned because individual and group thrift thereby would be discouraged. Furthermore, the elimination of the earnings test would be very costly, requiring an increase of about 0.7 percent in the combined employer-employee contribution rate. It would be questionable whether giving "retirement" benefits to fully employed persons would be the best use of this money (about $4 billion annually).

Floor-of-Protection Concept

It is generally agreed that OASDI benefits should provide only a minimum floor of protection against the various risks. There is, however, a great diversity of opinion as to how far apart the floor and the ceiling should be. At one extreme, there are those who believe that the floor should be very low or that there should be no OASDI program at all. At the other extreme, some believe that the floor should be high enough to provide a comfortable standard of living by itself, disregarding any economic security that individual or group methods might provide. These observers really believe that OASDI should be expanded to do the *entire* job for the vast majority of persons.

The middle group believes that the OASDI benefits should, along with other income and assets, be sufficient to yield a reasonably satisfactory minimum standard of living for the great majority of individuals. Then, any small residual group still in need should be taken care of by supplementary public assistance.

Earnings-Related Benefits

As a consequence of the floor-of-protection concept, it seems desirable from a social standpoint that benefits should be relatively larger for those with low earnings than for those with high earnings. Accordingly, the benefit formula under the OASDI system has always been heavily "weighted," so that a higher benefit rate applies to the lower portion of earnings than to the higher portion. Thus the higher income groups receive greater benefits, but there is the weighting in favor of low-income groups. Since contributions (or taxes) are likewise related to earnings—directly proportional, up to the maximum earnings base—there is some appeal to the public in the fact that the higher an individual's earnings (and likewise his taxes), the higher his benefits will be.

Individual Equity and Social Adequacy

Whenever a social security system involves contributions from the potential beneficiaries, the question of individual equity versus social adequacy arises. Individual equity means that the contributor receives benefit protection directly related to the amount of his contributions or, in other words, actuarially equivalent thereto. Social adequacy means that the benefits paid will provide for all contributors a certain standard of living. The two concepts are thus generally in direct conflict, and social security systems usually have a benefit basis falling somewhere between complete individual equity and complete social adequacy. The tendency is generally more toward social adequacy than individual equity, and this is the case with the OASDI system. If individual equity were to prevail when a system is started, the benefits paid would be relatively small, since they might be related solely to contributions paid or to service rendered after the effective date. Thus, many years would elapse before the system would begin to meet the purposes for which it was established.

Self-Supporting Contributory Financing

In brief, the principle of self-supporting contributory financing means that no general revenue appropriations will be needed to pay for the benefits (and the administrative expenses), except possibly in the case of special transitional benefits for certain closed groups. Available for such purposes under OASDI will be the contributions (taxes) from workers and employers and the interest earned on the trust funds resulting from the excess of income over outgo of the system (which, by law, must be invested only in United States government securities). Such interest does not represent "contributions" or "financial support" from either the general treasury or the general taxpayer, since the interest on these investments has to be paid, regardless of whether they are held by the trust funds or by private investors.

The basic financing principle for OASDI—adopted by Congress in 1950—is that the program should be completely self-supporting from contributions of workers and employers. Self-support can be achieved by any number of different contribution schedules—ranging, at one extreme, from a schedule higher in the early years than in the later ones (possibly sufficiently so as to produce a "fully funded reserve") to, at the other extreme, a schedule so slowly graded up that "pay as you go" financing would, in effect, result. The actual basis adopted for OASDI in the past was between "pay as you go" and "fully funded," but much nearer the former. However, the legislation enacted in 1972 shifted the basis completely to "pay as you go" with only a small contingency fund to be maintained (about one year's outgo in size).

In carrying out this principle, the employer and employee share the cost of OASDI equally. Self-employed individuals initially paid a tax rate for OASDI equal to 75 percent of the combined employer-employee rate (with a maximum rate of 7.0 percent)—a "political" and "practical" compromise between paying only the employee rate and paying the combined employer-employee rate. The 7 percent ceiling was reached in 1973 and will apply thereafter.

DEVELOPMENT OF OASDI SYSTEM

The original 1935 Act (effective in 1937) provided only for retirement benefits (with no supplements for dependents) and lump-sum death payments (in the nature of refunds of accumulated contributions) for workers in commerce and industry. The 1939 amendments broadened the program by including monthly survivor benefits and supplementary monthly benefits for retired workers with certain kinds of dependents. In addition, the size of the benefits payable in the early years of operation was increased, while benefits in the long-distant future for workers without dependents were decreased.

During the 1940s the legislative enactments related primarily to financing. Several times, the scheduled increase in the contribution rates was postponed, and the initial rate of 1 percent each from employer and employee was continued until 1950.

The 1950 amendments modified the system by a sizable extension of coverage to employments previously not included, by roughly doubling the size of the benefits (the average increase being about 77 percent) and by liberalizing the earnings test. The principal effects of the 1952 amendments were to raise the benefit level (by an average of about 14 percent) and to liberalize further the earnings test. The 1954 amendments extended coverage even further (to virtually all types of employment), again increased the benefit level (by an average of about 13 percent), further liberalized the earnings test, introduced the "disability freeze" provision, and increased the ultimate contribution rates.

The 1956 amendments extended coverage on a regular contributory basis to the armed forces, enlarged some beneficiary categories (by providing child's benefits beyond age 18 if disabled), lowered the minimum eligibility age for benefits for women from age 65 to age 62 (but with "actuarial" reductions for all except widows), added monthly disability benefits beginning at age 50, and provided an immediate increase in the tax rates (to support the disability benefits). The 1958 amendments increased benefits (by 7 percent across the board), liberalized the disability benefits by adding dependents' benefits, and strengthened the financing basis.

The 1960 amendments made disability benefits available regardless of age (i.e., eliminated the age 50 requirement) and improved the earnings test by making it more flexible (so that an individual could gradually ease off from full employment to retirement without losing money by working). The 1961 amendments lowered the minimum eligibility age for benefits for men from age 65 to age 62 (but with "actuarial" reductions as for women), raised the benefit rate for widows aged 62 or over, and increased the contribution schedule to meet these costs.

The 1965 amendments, which also added the Medicare program described in the next chapter, extended coverage to self-employed physicians, enlarged some beneficiary categories (reduced widow's benefits at age 60, child's benefits if in school at ages 18–21, and divorced wife's and widow's benefits if married for at least 20 years), added a coordination provision for DI and workmen's compensation benefits, updated the earnings test provisions, and increased benefit amounts (by 7 percent across the board). The financing provisions were also increased, by providing a $6,600 taxable earnings base and higher future tax rates (an ultimate combined employer-employee rate of 9.7 percent).

In 1966, legislation added special age-72 transitional benefits. The 1967 amendments provided for benefits (at a reduced rate) for disabled widows and dependent widowers at age 50 or after, provided survivor-benefit protection for insured women not currently employed at time of death, updated the earnings test provisions, and increased benefit amounts (by 13 percent across the board). The financing provisions were also increased, by providing a $7,800 taxable earnings base and higher future tax rates (an ultimate combined employer-employee rate of 10 percent).

The 1969 amendments increased benefit amounts across the board by 15 percent, but made no change in the financing provisions. The amendments made in 1971 increased benefit amounts across the board by 10 percent and changed the financing provisions (by providing a $9,000 taxable earnings base and increasing the ultimate combined employer-employee tax rate to 10.3 percent).

The legislation enacted in July 1972 increased benefit amounts across the board by 20 percent, raised the earnings base to $10,800 for 1973 and $12,000 for 1974 and after, and provided for automatic adjustment of benefits and the earnings base for changes in prices and wages, respectively.

Further significant legislation was enacted in October 1972. A special minimum primary benefit was provided for those with long and substantial coverage, amounting to $8.50 per year of coverage (defined as a year with earnings credits equal to at least one fourth of the maximum earnings base) in excess of 10 years, up to a maximum of 30 years (i.e., producing a maximum of $170). Benefit amounts and eligibility for men are to be computed in the more liberal way now applicable for women. A 1 percent increase in the primary benefit is given for each year of delay in retirement after age 65.

Widow's and widower's benefits under this 1972 legislation are at a rate equal to the insured worker's primary insurance amount if claimed at age 65 or after, with graded amounts ranging down to the present 71½ percent at age 60 for those first claiming benefits at ages 60–64, but in no case in excess of the benefit (if any) that the deceased worker had been receiving. Widower's benefits in nondisability cases are payable at age 60. Childhood disability benefits are payable if disability occurred at ages 18–21 (as well as before age 18). Child school-attendance benefits are payable until the end of the semester in which the twenty-second birthday occurs. Benefits are available for grandchildren who are full orphans.

The annual exempt amount in the earnings test was increased to $2,100, and the "$1 for $2" band extends without limit beyond $2,100. Further, it is to be subject to automatic adjustment after 1979.

The waiting period for disability benefits is reduced by one month. Blind persons are not required to have disability insured status to be eligible for disability benefits (but rather only fully insured status). The workmen's compensation offset against disability benefits is based on 80 percent of the highest earnings in any year in the last six years.

A simplified method of reporting earned income, similar to the present provisions for self-employed farmers, is made available to the non-farm self-employed. The $100 monthly gratuitous wage credits for military service now applicable for 1967 and after was made available for 1957–66.

This considerable expansion of the OASDI program requires higher contribution rates. The ultimate OASDI tax rate for employer and employee combined (for 2011 and after) would be increased to 11.7 percent, and the corresponding rate for OASDI and HI together would rise to 14.6 percent. The magnitude of these rates could well have serious implications for private-sector activities in the economic security field.

SELECTED REFERENCES

Bowen, Harbison, Lester, and Somers (ed.). *The American System of Social Insurance: Its Philosophy, Impact, and Future Development.* New York: McGraw-Hill Book Co., Inc., 1968.

Burns, Eveline M. *Social Security and Public Policy.* New York: McGraw-Hill Book Co., Inc., 1956.

Cohen, Wilbur J. *Retirement Policies under Social Security.* Berkeley: University of California Press, 1957.

Corson, John J., and McConnell, John W. *Economic Needs of Older People.* New York: Twentieth Century Fund, 1956.

Myers, Robert J. "Automatic Cost-of-Living Increases in Federal Benefit Plans," *Pension and Welfare Plans,* March 1970.

————. "Employee Social Insurance Contributions and Regressive Taxation," *Journal of Risk and Insurance,* Vol. XXXIV, No. 4 (December 1967).

————. "Financing Features of Social Security," *C.L.U. Journal,* Vol. XXII, No. 2 (April 1968).

————. "The Future of Social Security: Is It in Conflict with Private Pension Plans?" *Pension and Welfare News,* January 1970.

————. "The Role of Government in Providing Economic Security," *1970 C.L.U. Forum Report.* Bryn Mawr, Pa.: American Society of Chartered Life Underwriters, 1970.

————. *Social Insurance and Allied Government Programs.* Homewood, Ill.: Richard D. Irwin, Inc., 1965.

————. "Status of the Social Security Program in the Mid-Sixties and Its Possible Future Trends," *C.L.U. Journal,* Vol. II, No. 3 (Fall 1966).

United States Social Security Administration. "History of the Provisions of Old-Age, Survivors, Disability, and Health Insurance," *Social Security Bulletin,* Annual Statistical Supplement, 1970, p. 13.

United States Social Security Board. *Social Security in America.* Washington, D.C.: U.S. Government Printing Office, 1937.

Witte, Edwin E. *The Development of the Social Security Act.* Madison: University of Wisconsin Press, 1962.

————. *Social Security Perspectives.* Madison: University of Wisconsin Press, 1962.

50

Medicare and Other Government Health Benefits

By ROBERT J. MYERS

THE MEDICARE PROGRAM is coordinated with the cash-benefits portion of the social security program, discussed in Chapter 49. Medicare was the first major entry of the federal government into the area of financing or providing medical care for the general population. In 1972, great public interest was being expressed in the possibility of expansion of the federal government's role in the health care field.

This chapter is primarily concerned with the Medicare program as it was constituted at the end of 1972. The chapter concludes with brief summaries of other medical care and health benefit programs that are administered by governmental agencies.

The history of proposals that would introduce governmental action in the medical care and health benefits area in the United States is quite long. In the 1910s, a strenuous effort was made to have state programs of cash sickness and medical care benefits enacted, without success. Following World War I, this movement lessened as the advocates shifted toward a national program.

When the Social Security Act was being developed in 1934–35, strong efforts were made to include some form of medical care or health benefits, again unsuccessfully, except that extensive studies were made, and continuing studies authorized for the future. As a result, further efforts in this area were again made during the 1940s, once again without success, as the growing amount of private health insurance reduced both the necessity and the demand. In the 1950s and early 1960s, the efforts of the expansionists in the field of governmental medical care and health benefits shifted from coverage of the total population to that segment having the greatest medical needs and the lowest income—namely, persons aged 65 and over. Finally, after many legislative rebuffs and defeats, efforts in this direction were successful when the Medicare program was enacted in 1965, covering persons aged 65 and over. In 1972, it was extended to certain disabled beneficiaries under the social security program.

HOSPITAL INSURANCE UNDER MEDICARE

The Medicare program is divided into two separate parts—hospital insurance (HI), and supplementary medical insurance (SMI). The law designates these as Part A and Part B, respectively, and these terms are often used in public discussion of the program. This section discusses the various aspects of the HI program, while the next section deals with SMI.

Coverage and Eligibility

The HI program basically is a contributory social insurance program, providing hospitalization and related benefits on a "service" basis for insured persons aged 65 and over, and for disabled beneficiaries who have been on the roll for at least 2 years. HI for insured persons is financed completely by payroll taxes (or contributions) on covered workers and employers. The workers covered by the program are the same as those covered by the OASDI (cash benefits) program, except that railroad workers are covered under exactly the same conditions as all other workers (with the railroad retirement system collecting the contributions and transferring them over to the HI Trust Fund, after deducting its accompanying administrative expenses).

The HI benefits are available to all persons aged 65 or over who are receiving, or who upon retirement could receive, monthly cash benefits under OASDI or RR, and to all disabled beneficiaries who have been on the roll for at least 2 years. Such benefits are also available to noninsured persons who were over age 65 when the program began and to such persons attaining age 65 before 1968, with the cost for this group being met by general revenue taxation. The 1972 legislation established a voluntary HI program, quite similar to SMI (as described later), for persons who are not protected by the regular HI program. The entire cost is intended to be borne by the enrollee, and the initial premium rate for July 1973 through June 1974 is $33 per month.

It should be noted that the HI insured beneficiaries include not only the covered worker, but also such secondary beneficiaries as wives, dependent husbands, widows, dependent widowers, and, in some cases, dependent parents and children (in all cases with the minimum age requirement of 65). The disabled beneficiaries covered under HI include not only insured disabled workers, but also disabled widows and dependent widowers aged 50–64 and disabled children (of retired, disabled, and deceased insured workers) aged 18 or over. As a special "catastrophic" case, insured workers and their dependents, regardless of age, who have chronic kidney disease requiring dialysis or transplant, are considered for Medicare to be disability beneficiaries after three months of treatment (no 2-year requirement). Eligibility for noninsured persons, of course, is solely on an individual basis, depending upon attaining age 65 in the required period.

Benefits

The HI benefits follow the basic principle of providing hospital and posthospital services after certain cost-sharing amounts are paid by the beneficiary, rather than providing specified indemnity benefits and leaving the beneficiary to pay the difference between the charges made and the benefits payable. In this respect, HI is patterned more along the lines of Blue Cross benefits than those in the more usual insurance company plans. The providers of HI services are reimbursed after extensive auditing, on a cost basis.

Three separate types of HI benefits are provided—inpatient hospital services, posthospital skilled nursing facility services, and posthospital home health services. The intent is that the latter two benefits will serve to hold down, if not reduce, the amount of hospital benefits that would otherwise be incurred.

Inpatient hospital benefits are provided for the first 90 days in a spell of illness; in addition, each beneficiary has a lifetime reserve of 60 days that can be used at any time after the exhaustion of such 90 days. The term "spell of illness" is a technical one, defined as the period beginning on the first day of receipt of inpatient hospital benefits and terminating at the end of the 60-day period thereafter on which the beneficiary has not been an inpatient in a hospital or skilled nursing facility (SNF).

The inpatient hospital benefits include virtually all services provided in a hospital, except luxury items and the services of hospital-based physicians in the fields of radiology and pathology (whose services are covered under SMI).

The beneficiary must pay certain cost-sharing charges with respect to the inpatient hospital services. First, there is an initial deductible in each spell of illness, which was $40 from the beginning of the program in July 1966 through 1968, and was increased automatically thereafter in accordance with rises in hospital costs (being $72 in 1973). Second, there is a daily charge for each day of hospitalization from the 61st through the 90th, and then for each of the lifetime reserve days. This daily charge for the 61st through the 90th days is one fourth of the amount of the initial deductible; the daily charge for the lifetime reserve days is one half the amount of the initial deductible. Finally, there is a blood deductible, under which the beneficiary is required either to replace the first three pints of blood in a spell of illness or to pay the cost thereof.

The SNF benefits are available only after hospitalization of at least three days, and only for the purpose of furnishing necessary health care for the illness for which hospitalization was required—not for custodial or domiciliary care. The SNF benefits are available for a maximum of 100 days in a spell of illness. Cost-sharing is introduced after the 20th day, with the daily rate therefor being one eighth of the amount of the initial deductible for inpatient hospital care.

Home health services benefits are available after hospitalization (or after both hospitalization and SNF services). These benefits, in essence, consist of visiting nurse services, although on a somewhat amplified basis. A maximum of 100 home health services are provided within one year after the most recent discharge from a hospital or an SNF, and before the next spell of illness begins. There are no cost-sharing provisions for these benefits.

Financing

The HI program is basically financed from the payroll taxes (or contributions) paid by covered workers and employers. These taxes go into the HI Trust Fund, from which the benefits (reimbursements to the hospitals and other institutional providers of services) are paid. The administrative expenses of the program are also paid from this trust fund. The assets of the trust fund are invested in obligations of the federal government, and interest receipts help to meet the cost of the program. The benefit payments with respect to noninsured persons (and accompanying administrative expenses) are paid from the HI Trust Fund and are reimbursed by the General Fund of the Treasury (from general revenues).

As in OASDI, the employer and the employee pay equal contribution rates. However, unlike OASDI, the self-employed do not pay a higher rate than employees, but pay the same rate. The maximum annual earnings base on which taxes are levied is the same for HI as it is for OASDI (i.e., $9,000 in 1972, $10,800 in 1973, and $12,000 in 1974 and after—but subject to automatic adjustment related to changes in wages beginning with 1975).

In 1966, the combined employer-employee rate was 0.7 percent, and it rose to 1.0 percent in 1967 and 1.2 percent in 1968–72. This rate is 2.0 percent in 1973–77, with gradual increases thereafter to the ultimate level of 2.9 percent in 1986 and thereafter.

Administration

The administration of the HI program is carried out in a diverse, pluralistic fashion. The federal government is, of course, directly responsible for the collection of the taxes, the maintenance of the earnings and benefits records, and providing the funds for the payment of benefits. Each provider of HI services can elect to receive payments from, and be audited by, a fiscal intermediary approved by the federal government, rather than deal directly with it. The vast majority of the hospitals have selected the Blue Cross Association as fiscal intermediary, although some have chosen insurance companies, and a few deal directly with the federal government. A lesser proportion, but still a majority, of the ECF's and home health services agencies use Blue Cross as intermediary.

SUPPLEMENTARY MEDICAL INSURANCE UNDER MEDICARE

The second portion of the Medicare program is supplementary medical insurance (SMI), often referred to as Part B. This program is of a somewhat different nature than HI in that it is a voluntary program and is not financed by payroll taxes. Since coverage is available on an individual voluntary basis, SMI lacks one of the distinguishing features of a social insurance program—namely, compulsory coverage for the vast majority of the persons involved. Instead, SMI can more properly be termed a government subsidized individual insurance program.

Coverage and Eligibility

The SMI program provides indemnity-type benefits designed to meet part of the cost of physician and related services. Almost any individual in the country aged 65 or over, regardless of his status under the OASDI or railroad retirement programs, can choose whether or not he wishes to participate in the SMI program. Such action must be taken in the 7-month period centered around his 65th birthday (for those over age 65 when the program began, in the period before July 1966) or in annual enroll-ment periods. In the same way, the disabled beneficiaries who are covered by HI can elect SMI coverage. Individuals may drop out of the program and reenroll later, but such action can be taken only once.

Benefits

The SMI benefits apply primarily to physician services, although cer-tain other related services are also covered. The latter include ambulance services, rental or purchase of medical equipment (such as iron lungs and oxygen tanks), prosthetic devices, diagnostic tests, therapy services, limited chiropractor services, and home health services (limited to a maximum of 100 per calendar year). Not covered are routine physical examinations, inoculations, and dental services (other than for surgery related to the jaw or any facial bone).

Benefit reimbursement is based on the concept of reasonable charges (except for those services that are furnished by hospitals or home health agencies, where the reasonable-cost concept of HI applies). Reasonable charges are determined for each individual physician or other provider of services by considering his past customary charges and also the pre-vailing charges in the particular community (with a considerable lag, so that recognized reasonable charges are significantly below the current level). The prevailing-charges limit is further limited by the actual pre-vailing charge in July 1972 to June 1973 as increased by an economic index (reflecting general earnings levels and costs of operation). Thus, the prevailing charges basis has really been eliminated, and eventually all physicians in an area will be reimbursed by Medicare on the basis of a uniform fee schedule.

The beneficiary first has an annual deductible of $60 per calendar year. Then, for all recognized charges above $60, the beneficiary receives a benefit of 80 percent—or, in other words, must himself make a 20 percent cost-sharing payment. There are three exceptions to this general cost-sharing basis: for psychiatric services outside of a hospital, the cost-sharing proportion is 50 percent, and there is, in general, a maximum benefit of $250 per year; for pathology and radiology services in a hos-pital, there are no cost-sharing provisions; and for home health services, there is no coinsurance.

If a physician accepts the so-called assignment reimbursement basis, the benefit is paid directly to him, and under such circumstances he can-not charge the patient more than the cost-sharing amounts; in other words, in these cases, the physician must accept the government's determination of the reasonable charge as being the total charge. If the physician does not accept assignment in any particular case, the beneficiary receives the determined benefit amount, and he must settle with the physician for his full charges.

Financing

The SMI program is financed from premium rates charged to the enrollees and from matching amounts paid by the federal government from the General Fund of the Treasury; i.e., from general-revenue taxation. The law prescribes that the same premium rate shall be paid by all enrollees, regardless of age, except that persons enrolling later than the earliest period during which they could have enrolled must pay an increased premium rate (10 percent higher for each year of delay). In the past, the premium rate was determined on the basis that the enrollees and the government would share the cost equally. Beginning July 1973, this basis was changed, since the premium rate will be based on the enrollees aged 65 and over paying half their cost but with the limiting proviso that, in the future, any percentage increase in the rate cannot exceed the percentage general increase in the cash-benefits level under OASDI (if any) in the previous year. Thus, the government will pay more than half the cost of SMI—because the cost for the disabled is significantly larger than for the aged and because of the limitation on premium-rate increases relative to cash-benefit rises. The law also prescribes that the premium rate shall be determined on an actuarial basis, so that income therefrom along with the government contribution will be expected to meet the cost of the benefit payments and the related administrative expenses, on an incurred-cost basis.

The premium payments and the government contributions go into the SMI Trust Fund. From this fund are paid the benefits and administrative expenses of the program. The assets of the SMI Trust Fund are invested in obligations of the federal government, and the interest receipts help to meet the cost of the program.

The standard premium rate for the initial period (July 1966 through March 1968) was established at $3.00 per month. This rate was increased to $4.00 for April 1968 through June 1970, and then was $5.30 and $5.60 for the two succeeding 12-month periods. For the year beginning July 1972, the rate is $5.80, while for the next year it is $6.30.

In the actual experience, the computed premium rate was somewhat too low in each of the early periods (but especially so in the period July 1969 to June 1970) insofar as incurred costs were concerned, but the natural lag between the time costs are incurred and the time benefits are claimed enabled the program to operate successfully on a cash basis. The rates applicable after June 1970 have been somewhat more than adequate to meet the costs in this period; as a result, the significantly depleted cash condition of the SMI Trust Fund was improved.

Administration

As in the case of the HI program, the administration of SMI is accomplished in a diverse, pluralized fashion. The federal government is directly responsible for collection of the premiums, maintenance of the premium and benefit records, and providing the funds for the payment of benefits. Carriers are appointed by the federal government to be responsible for claims payments in various geographical areas—often in state units, although in some of the larger states, there is geographical subdivision into several areas. The carriers are about equally divided between insurance companies and Blue Shield or similar organizations.

MEDICAID PROGRAM

When Medicare was enacted in 1965, the same legislation contained medical care provisions of a public assistance nature applicable to younger persons as well as to those aged 65 and over. These provisions both amalgamated and extended similar provisions previously present. The formal name of this program is Medical Assistance, but it is popularly referred to as Medicaid or as Title XIX (of the Social Security Act). For persons aged 65 and over, Medicaid primarily supplements Medicare, just as Old-Age Assistance supplements OASDI.

Medicaid is a federal-state program with substantial federal financial participation. It is intended to provide medical assistance for certain categories of people who are medically needy—i.e., going beyond the class of persons who need public assistance payments to meet their current daily needs. The categories included are the four that can qualify for cash-assistance payments—the aged, the blind, the disabled, the families with dependent children—plus medically needy children under age 21 even though they do not meet the eligibility requirements for Aid to Families with Dependent Children.

The federal law contains only broad specifications as to medical costs which a state plan must cover in order to qualify for federal financial assistance. As a result, some states (such as California and New York) have very liberal and far-reaching protection, whereas other states do not.

The federal financial participation is of an open-end nature insofar as the amounts of medical expenditures for which matching will be made. The actual federal matching proportion varies inversely with the state average per capita income. A state whose average is the same as the national average receives federal reimbursement of 55 percent of its total expenditures. The minimum such ratio is 50 percent (applicable to most states with above average per capita incomes), and the maximum ratio is 83 percent (applicable to only one state).

The expenditures of the Medicaid program have been unusually high. As might be expected, there is much dissatisfaction with this program because of its cost and also because of the reduced or inadequate medical services provided thereunder and curtailed eligibility in some states. Some proposals currently under consideration are to eliminate the Medicaid program and replace it through giving regular health insurance policies to eligible medically needy persons.

MILITARY AND VETERANS' PROGRAMS

Traditionally, the armed forces have provided medical care (as well as other maintenance items) for their personnel and often for their dependents as well. This is done through military personnel who are qualified physicians and medical technicians and through a large network of hospitals and other medical institutions. It has often been said that this is an old, well-established form of socialized medicine in the United States, but here the argument divides as to whether or not this has produced good results (or the best possible results).

The dependents of those in active military service are at times furnished medical care in military installations, but more recently there has been a shift toward more formalized insurance provisions for dependents through a system (originally called Medicare) administered by several insuring organizations.

Members of the armed forces who are on retirement pay continue to receive medical care in the same manner as when they were on active duty. Other former members of the armed forces (veterans) receive full medical care in government installations operated by the Veterans Administration with respect to any service-connected cause of injury or disablement. Such veterans can also receive full medical care for other causes if they cannot afford to obtain it privately and if governmental medical facilities are available.

WORKMEN'S COMPENSATION PROGRAMS

Combined with the cash benefits payable under state workmen's compensation programs are medical-care benefits applicable to work-connected injury or disease. The same type of protection is also available to employees of the federal government under a law that provides them with workmen's compensation benefits (namely, the Federal Employees Compensation Act). Similar protection at the federal level is provided for the special group of workers covered under the Longshoremen's and Harbor Workers' Compensation Act. Railroad workers are not covered by workmen's compensation, but they can receive payment for medical costs in connection with work accidents by law suits under the Federal Employer's Liability Act (which is applicable only to railroads).

During the latter part of the 19th century, with the growth of industrialization in the United States, the problem of providing for industrial accident and disease had become so significant in numbers and so difficult of satisfactory solution under the historical common-law doctrine of employer liability that various groups began to try to evolve a more efficient and equitable technique for dealing with them. Investigating committees were established at both federal and state levels, and by many interested groups, to review and to study the effects of developments in Europe and to draft proposals for legislation for possible use in the United States.

The first attempts to deal with the problem uniformly at the state level were made between 1900 and 1910. By 1920, all but six states had adopted workmen's compensation legislation of some variety. At the present time, all states and the federal government have workmen's compensation statutes covering most of the industrial workers and, in some cases, other types of employees.

In general, the workmen's compensation statutes establish the principle that injury in the course of employment—and in most cases, this includes industrial disease—is compensable without regard to the question of fault. In effect, the doctrine holds that injuries under certain conditions and some occupational diseases are compensable by the employer, not because he is assumed to have basic responsibility for them, but because social policy has determined that industry, as one of its costs of operation, must assume such responsibility.

The basic theory underlying the law holds that, in return for assumption of responsibility for social or individual costs resulting from damage in the performance of assigned tasks in employment, the employer's liability for such costs should be limited. Thus, in effect, all workmen's compensation laws provide that, while compensation for injury shall be paid without regard to fault, the amount of the compensation so payable is fixed by law. Such compensation includes medical care costs, to a greater or lesser extent, depending upon the state; disability income for such period as may be required, up to some limit; rehabilitation benefits; and for certain specific injuries, such as dismemberment, specific lump-sum benefits. In most cases, the statues contain specific exclusions for self-inflicted injury and injury while intoxicated and, in some cases, provide for supplementary or elective liability coverage.

Typically, disabilities are classified into groups: total and partial, temporary and permanent. In most cases the benefits payable for all types of total disability are the same, as far as weekly benefits are concerned, but the maximum number of weeks over which payments can be made differs. The amounts payable in both cases are usually determined as some portion of weekly wages. Where disability is permanent and total, the procedure normally involves payment of a weekly indemnity for some specific period of weeks up to a maximum of some given amount, or, in some states, for life.

Partial disabilities may be temporary and may begin as a total disability. In these cases, the payments usually take two forms: first, replacement of the scheduled proportion of wages during the period of total disability; thereafter, a scheduled payment equal to some part of the full weekly indemnity for some given period of time—as, for example, 50 weeks. The theory here is that these payments will serve to make up some portion of the future wage loss resulting from the injury causing the disability.

The objective of workmen's compensation is to assist the injured worker in recovering so that he can return to work. There are two broad philosophies evident in the program as it exists in the several states. In all jurisdictions, the objective of workmen's compensation is to relieve the injured of the burden of medical expense and to replace some portion of the wage loss resulting from the disability while he continues unable to work. In some jurisdictions, an additional effort is made to restore the individual, in the sense of rehabilitating him for work after injury, albeit at a different job, in the industrial system. In a few cases, this attitude has developed to the point where rehabilitation, in fact, has become the chief purpose of the statute from the social viewpoint.

Because workmen's compensation is a state program, except for federal employees and certain others, one must look to state laws for any description of the coverage and benefits available. There are wide variations in the program in the various states.

With regard to coverage, the typical workmen's compensation law excludes agricultural and domestic workers. A few laws also exclude many nonhazardous occupations. Almost half of the laws exempt small employers, with the limit ranging from 1 to 14 employees (generally, 2 to 4).

The coverage, though required by law, is provided by a monopoly state fund in only a few of the states. In most others, it may be provided by private carriers; while in a few others, it may be provided competitively by either the state fund or a private carrier. In many of the jurisdictions, self-insurance is also permitted. The program for federal employees is financed by direct appropriations of Congress and administered by the Department of Labor.

There are wide variations in benefits available under the law. In some cases, medical care costs are paid without limit. In other states, only limited amounts are available for medical care costs. In all states, covered workers are provided with cash benefits usually amounting to about 66⅔ percent of weekly earnings, up to some limit (which is often relatively low).

TEMPORARY DISABILITY
INSURANCE PROGRAMS

Five states (California, Hawaii, New Jersey, New York, and Rhode Island) and Puerto Rico now have programs to protect against income losses due to temporary disability which is not work-connected. The railroad retirement system contains similar provisions, on a nationwide basis, for railroad workers. Strictly speaking, these programs do not provide health benefits generally, but rather cash income during illness, which may be used to meet health care costs.

These various TDI programs provide earnings-related benefits, usually after a waiting period of about one week. In all states but New York, and in the railroad system, the benefits are geared to somewhat the same basis as that used in the respective unemployment insurance programs. In New York, the benefit structure is wage-related, but it is administered through the workmen's compensation agency. Rhode Island has a monopolistic state plan, whereas in the other states, employers can elect to insure privately. Such opting out of a state-administered program has been rather successful in all the states where this is possible, except California, where it would appear that the state plan unfairly competed with private plans by charging inadequate rates for a period of time and thus drove many private plans out of the market.

All the programs except that in California pay only cash sickness benefits (including also maternity benefits in some plans). In California, however, there are additional benefits for persons who are hospitalized—namely, $12 per day for the first 20 days within a benefit period, as well as elimination of the waiting period for the regular cash benefits. Such additional hospitalization benefits by themselves, of course, do not go very far toward meeting hospital costs. But since the vast majority of the covered workers have other hospital insurance, these benefits can be a valuable supplement.

STATE AND LOCAL GOVERNMENT HEALTH PLANS

A wide variety of health services are provided by state and local governments. For one thing, the vast majority of long-term medical care (often of a custodial nature) for mental disorders is provided by state governments. The same is also true for tuberculosis, but this problem was of far greater importance in bygone days than it is currently.

Many state and local governments (particularly the latter in metropolitan areas) provide general medical care of needy persons in governmental hospitals and in their outpatient clinics. The extent and use of this type of inpatient hospital care has diminished somewhat in recent years due to the growth in private insurance and the inauguration of the Medicare and Medicaid programs. On the other hand, the use of outpatient departments and other governmental clinics has increased and is a primary source of medical care for many persons. A wide variety of school health programs exists, generally of a universal nature, rather than being based on need.

SELECTED REFERENCES

Follmann, J. F., Jr. *Medical Care and Health Insurance: A Study in Social Progress*. Homewood, Ill.: Richard D. Irwin, Inc., 1963.

Klarman, H. E. *The Economics of Health*. New York: Columbia University Press, 1965.

Myers, Robert J. *Medicare*. McCahan Foundation Book Series. Homewood, Ill.: Richard D. Irwin, Inc., 1970.

Osborn, Grant M. *Compulsory Temporary Disability Insurance in the United States*. Homewood, Ill.: Richard D. Irwin, Inc., 1958.

Somers, H. M. *Medicare and the Hospitals*. Washington, D.C.: The Brookings Institution, 1967.

U.S. Congress, House of Representatives, Committee on Ways and Means. *Analysis of Health Insurance Proposals Introduced in the 92nd Congress*. Washington, D.C., August 1971.

U.S. Department of Labor. *State Workmen's Compensation Laws*. Bulletin 161 (revised 1969). Washington, D.C.: Wage and Labor Standards Administration, 1969.

————. *Medical Care under Workmen's Compensation*. Bulletin 244. Washington, D.C.: Bureau of Labor Standards, 1962.

51

Servicemen's and Veterans' Benefits

By BARNIE E. ABELLE

IN JUNE 1971, the number of veterans in civilian life exceeded 28 million. Over 5 million of these veterans carried approximately $37.5 billion of government life insurance. Four million two hundred thousand members of the uniformed services on active duty (including 900,000 members of the Reserves, National Guard and ROTC in training) carried $49.7 billion of servicemen's group life insurance. The number of active compensation and pension benefit cases being administered by the Veterans Administration was 3.2 million. In addition, a number of other veterans' benefits were being made available. All persons involved in insuring human life values who wish to provide the highest level of professional service should be familiar with these benefits, as should those to whom these benefits are available.

Included in this review of servicemen's and veterans' benefits are the following: (1) government life insurance, (2) servicemen's group life insurance, (3) compensation and pension benefits, (4) orphans', wives', and widows' education benefits, (5) social security, and (6) other death benefits.[1] Excluded from this discussion are service-type benefits or payments in kind made on behalf of servicemen or veterans and resulting from disability.

GOVERNMENT LIFE INSURANCE

The United States government, through the Veterans Administration, *operates* five life insurance programs. No veteran can own more than $10,000 of government life insurance under any one or combination of these programs. In addition to operating five life insurance programs, the Veterans Administration *supervises* the Servicemen's Group Life Insur-

---

[1] Detailed information concerning any of the topics discussed in this review may be obtained from the nearest office of the Veterans Administration.

ance (SGLI) program. Members eligible for life insurance under this program may purchase up to $15,000 coverage.

Selected information concerning each of these life insurance programs is shown in Table 51–1. Note that the largest life insurance program operated by the United States government is the National Service Life Insurance (NSLI) program. Also of interest is the fact that among government operated programs, only Service Disabled Veterans Insurance (SDVI) is open to new issues. Inasmuch as the amount of new life insurance issued under the SDVI program is relatively small, total life insurance in force with the United States government is declining continuously.

Brief History

United States Government Life Insurance (USGLI) was issued on a participating basis beginning January 1, 1919, and was made available to individuals on active duty until NSLI was established on October 8, 1940. USGLI also was made available to veterans of World War I who had active service between October 6, 1917 and July 2, 1921. For these veterans, its availability continued until new sales of USGLI were terminated, effective April 25, 1951, by Public Law 23—The Servicemen's Indemnity and Insurance Acts of 1951. Plans of insurance include 5-year level premium term, ordinary life, 30-payment life, 20-payment life, 30-year endowment, 20-year endowment, endowment at age 62, and special endowment at age 96.

National Service Life Insurance "V" series was issued on a participating basis to individuals on active duty between October 8, 1940 and April 25, 1951. It also was made available to veterans of World War II who had active service between October 8, 1940, and September 2, 1945. New sales of NSLI "V" series also were terminated by Public Law 23 on April 25, 1951. Premiums, reserves, and life income settlement options for beneficiaries are based on the American Experience mortality table and a 3 percent interest assumption. If the policyowner elects a life income based upon the cash surrender value of his policy or the maturity of an endowment, the Annuity Table for 1949 is used. However, no distinction in annuity payments is made for differences in male and female longevity. Original plans of insurance include 5-year renewable and convertible term, ordinary life, 20-payment life, 30-payment life, endowment at age 60, endowment at age 65, and 20-year endowment.

In May 1965, a modified life plan was added to the six permanent plans then in use. The premium rate for this plan is level for life, but lower than that charged for ordinary life insurance. NSLI policyowners are eligible to convert their present insurance to modified life prior to insurance age 61. At age 65, the amount of modified life insurance in force is automatically reduced by one half. However, special ordinary life insurance can be purchased equal to the amount of the reduction. No medical evidence of insurability is required to qualify for this additional coverage. If the insured is totally disabled at age 65, the special ordinary life policy will be issued with premiums waived.

Public Law 23 provided that persons on active duty between April 25, 1951 and January 1, 1957, should receive $10,000 of free term life in-

TABLE 51-1. Government Insurance Programs

Program	Series	Beginning Date	Ending Date for New Issues	Issued to Whom	Partic-ipating	Number in Force Dec. 31, 1970 (1) Insureds (2) Policies		Insurance In Force Dec. 31, 1970 (in billions)
U.S. Govt. (USGLI)	K	Jan. 1, 1919	Apr. 25, 1951	Generally to veterans of World War I	yes	(1) (2)	165,503 191,233	$ .8
National Service (NSLI)	V	Oct. 8, 1940	Apr. 25, 1951	Generally to veterans of World War II	yes	(1) (2)	3,976,453 4,387,602	28.9
Veterans Special (VSLI)	RS or W	Apr. 25, 1951	Dec. 31, 1956	Generally to Korean veterans separated from service without a service-connected disability	no	(1) (2)	596,608 616,596	5.4
Service-Disabled (SDVI)	RH	Apr. 25, 1951	Open to new issues	To veterans separated from service with a service-connected disability	no	(1) (2)	103,157 105,311	.9
Veterans Reopened (VRI)	J, JR, JS	May 1, 1965	May 2, 1966	Generally to World War II and Korean veterans with service-connected or serious nonservice-connected disabilities	no	(1) (2)	192,171 193,395	1.3
Servicemen's Group (SGLI)		Sept. 29, 1965	Open to new issues	Members of the Uniformed Services on active duty	no	(1) (2)	3,239,000 3,239,000	48.5
		June 25, 1970	Open to new issues	Members of the Reserves, National Guard & ROTC in training	no	(1) (2)	944,000 944,000	1.2
Total (excluding SGLI)						(1) (2)	5,033,892 5,494,137	

surance. Since $10,000 was the maximum amount of government life insurance permitted, servicemen with either USGLI or NSLI in force when this gratuitous or servicemen's indemnity became available were allowed to terminate such coverage with the option to reinstate or repurchase upon application while on active duty or within 120 days after separation. Or, if he chose, the serviceman could elect to continue his USGLI or NSLI in force with a waiver of premium in effect on the actual cost of life insurance at risk. This waiver continued during service and for 120 days after separation. USGLI or NSLI maintained in force on any basis was deducted from the Servicemen's Indemnity otherwise available. Thus, the total death benefit available did not exceed $10,000. Servicemen separated after April 25, 1951, received gratuitous coverage for an additional 120 days, but not beyond December 31, 1956.

Veterans separated from service between April 25, 1951, and December 31, 1956, were eligible to apply within 120 days after separation and without evidence of insurability for Veterans Special Insurance. This coverage, designated "RS" series, was issued as 5-year renewable, nonconvertible, nonparticipating term insurance. Actuarial assumptions underlying "RS" insurance, as well as the various plans into which it could be converted effective January 1, 1959, are less liberal than actuarial assumptions underlying NSLI or USGLI issued prior to April 25, 1951. The amount of "RS" insurance available to a veteran was limited to $10,000 less any government life insurance in force at the time of application.

Veterans separated from service after April 25, 1951, and found uninsurable by the Veterans Administration as a result of a service-connected disability of a compensable type, are eligible to apply within one year of the determination of disability by the Veterans Administration for Service Disabled Veterans Insurance. This program, designated "RH" series, is available on any NSLI plan but on a nonparticipating basis only. Actuarial assumptions are less favorable to the policyowner than those used prior to April 25, 1951. The total amount of "RH" insurance plus any additional government life insurance carried by a veteran cannot exceed $10,000.

In 1964 Congress enacted legislation which provided for the limited reopening of NSLI for a period of one year beginning May 1, 1965. Eligibility was restricted to veterans with service-connected or nonservice-connected disabilities who had active service between October 8, 1940, and January 1, 1957. Called Veterans Reopened Insurance, this coverage is nonparticipating and was issued on permanent plans only. Three forms were made available. Insurance issued at the standard premium rate was prefixed by the letter "J." Rated insurance due to service-connected disabilities was prefixed "JR." Rated insurance due to nonservice-connected disabilities was prefixed "JS." Premium rates for this insurance depended upon the nature and severity of the disability. For those with only service-connected disabilities, the rates varied from standard to a maximum of three times standard. For those with serious nonservice-connected disabilities, the rates varied from two to three times standard to a maximum of $50 a month plus the standard rate per $1,000 of insurance.

Unlike other forms of government life insurance that carry no expense loading, the premium for Veterans Reopened Insurance includes an added policy administrative charge of $.42 per month. This charge may be changed periodically. Furthermore, the basic premium rates also are subject to change based upon actual experience in this program.

General Policy Provisions

Government life insurance contains no restrictions as to residence, travel, occupation, or military or naval service. All policies are incontestable from date of issue, reinstatement or conversion, except for fraud, nonpayment of premiums, or because the applicant was not a member of the military or naval forces of the United States. Policies are not assignable by the insured, nor can the insured divest himself of ownership. However, policies may be assigned in connection with a loan on the policy itself. Inasmuch as commercial life insurance policies are freely assignable and generally cannot be contested for fraud after the contestable period, they are more liberal than government life insurance policies in these two important areas.

A grace period of 31 days is allowed. If death occurs during the grace period, the amount payable is reduced by the amount of the monthly premium due.

Proceeds of government life insurance are exempt from all direct taxation. They also are exempt from claims of creditors of the insured or beneficiary. However, certain claims of the United States government are not subject to this exclusion. Proceeds are includable in the insured's estate for federal estate tax purposes.

Guaranteed Values

The five-year level premium term policies have no guaranteed values. Guaranteed values on permanent plans take three forms—cash, reduced paid-up insurance, and extended term insurance. Extended term insurance is the automatic option. If a permanent plan policy lapses after being in force at least three months, it is automatically extended as term insurance. If premiums were paid or waived at least 12 months before lapse, cash values, but not loan values, will be available.

Loan values are available on permanent plans up to 94 percent of the policy reserve after the policy has been in effect at least one year.

Reinstatement

Generally, permanent plans surrendered for cash or reduced paid-up insurance cannot be reinstated. USGLI and NSLI terminated between 1951 and 1957 to take advantage of the gratuitous indemnity available during those years was an exception to this general rule.

If application for reinstatement is made within six months from the date of lapse, a good health statement may be submitted. If application is made after six months, evidence of good health including a physical examination is required. Applicants 50 years of age or under whose coverage has not lapsed for more than one year are required to submit only a medical questionnaire in lieu of the results of a physical examination. Excluded from these good health requirements are lapsed permanent plan policies, if the remaining extended insurance protection at the time of application for reinstatement runs for five or more years, or on an endowment policy, to the end of the endowment period.

Term insurance may be reinstated within 5 years after lapse. Two monthly premiums must be paid—one for the month of lapse and one for the current month. If coverage lapses in the 59th or 60th month, application for reinstatement may be made within the following 5-year term period.

Lapsed permanent plan insurance can be reinstated at any time during the term for which it was originally written. Payment is required of all back premiums plus 4 percent interest from the date of lapse to the month of reinstatement. No interest is charged if reinstatement requirements are met within six months after the date of lapse.

A lapsed total disability income provision may be reinstated under the same conditions as the policy itself, except that health requirements are never waived.

Conversion and Change of Plans

Term insurance may be converted to one or more permanent plans. The entire amount of term insurance may be converted or any part of it, but no less than $1,000. Conversion may be made effective on the date the current premium on the term insurance becomes due, or on any previous premium due date including the date on which the term policy first became effective. If the converted policy is backdated, the insured must pay the value of the accumulated reserve plus the current premium. Conversion to whole life plans is allowed even if the insured is totally disabled. Conversion to an endowment plan while the insured is totally disabled is not allowed.

A permanent plan policy may be exchanged for another permanent plan policy of an equal or lesser amount, with the same effective date and based on the same age as the existing policy. If the change is to a plan with a higher reserve, the insured pays the difference between the reserve on the new plan and the reserve on the old plan. If the change is to a plan with a lower reserve, evidence of good health must be submitted.

Dividends

Virtually all policies issued since 1951 have been on a nonparticipating basis, so the importance of dividends to policyowners of government life insurance will continue to decline. However, dividends still are payable to policyowners of NSLI "V" series. In 1970, the amount paid as dividend on "V" policies was $254.5 million.

Dividends are paid on participating NSLI whether on a current premium-paying basis, held as paid-up insurance, or on the extended term nonforfeiture option. Dividends may be paid in cash; held as a credit, with interest, to prevent lapse (automatic option); applied to pay premiums in advance; used to reduce a loan or lien indebtedness against the policy; and, on permanent plans, placed on deposit at interest. If the latter option is selected, dividends on deposit are included in the net cash value of the policy for the purpose of purchasing extended or paid-up insurance.

Beneficiary Designations

Any person, firm, corporation, the insured's estate, or other legal entity may be named as beneficiary. These may be named individually or as a trustee. One or more principal beneficiaries and one or more contingent beneficiaries may be named. Beneficiary changes may be made at any time without the knowledge or consent of current beneficiaries. If no beneficiary is named, or if none is living at the time of the insured's death, payment will be made to the estate of the insured in one sum. If the beneficiary is a minor at the time the insurance becomes a claim, the proceeds will be payable to the legally appointed guardian for the benefit of the minor. An original beneficiary designation, but not a change of beneficiary, may be made by last will and testament.

Settlement Options

Four settlement options are available to NSLI policyowners. Selection or change of an option will not be valid until notice in writing is received by the Veterans Administration. Furthermore, selection or change cannot be made by last will and testament, except in connection with an original designation of beneficiary made in that manner. Note that unlike commercial insurance, the interest option is not available to government life insurance policyowners or their beneficiaries. The options are:

Option 1—In one sum (face amount less any indebtedness).

Option 2—In equal monthly installments of from 36 to 240, in multiples of 12 (36 equal monthly installments is the automatic option).

Option 3—In equal monthly installments for the lifetime of the first beneficiary, with 120 monthly installments guaranteed.

Option 4—Refund life income. This option is not available if settlement would result in fewer than 120 monthly installments.

Only the insured can select Option 1. If Option 1 is selected by the insured, the principal beneficiary may elect to receive the insurance proceeds under Options 2, 3, or 4. If the principal beneficiary dies before receiving all the installments due under Options 2, 3, or 4, the present value of the remaining unpaid guaranteed installments will be payable to the estate of the principal beneficiary to the exclusion of any contingent beneficiary. If the beneficiary selects Options 2, 3, or 4, the present value of any unpaid guaranteed installments may be taken in cash. Resumption of payments to the beneficiary under Options 3 or 4 will occur if the beneficiary survives the guaranteed period.

If the insured makes no selection or selects Options 2, 3, or 4 and the principal beneficiary and contingent beneficiary, if any, die before receiving all of the guaranteed installments, the present value of the remaining unpaid installments will be payable to the estate of the insured. Holding the estate of the insured open, or reopening the estate of the insured after it has been closed a number of years, can be avoided by naming an institution such as a hospital, university, or church as final contingent beneficiary.

If no option is selected, settlement will be made under Option 2 in 36 monthly installments. In this case, the beneficiary may elect to receive the proceeds under Option 3 or 4 or over a longer period under Option 2.

Options 2 and 4 are available to owners of policies surrendered for their cash value or because they have matured as endowments. Prior to January 1, 1971, Option 2 was available to owners of matured endowments, but no options were available to insureds surrendering policies for their cash values.

Disability Coverage

Waiver of premium in the event of total disability is included in NSLI policies without additional cost. A total disability income rider is available for an additional premium charge and subject to evidence of good health.

Total disability is defined as any impairment of mind or body which continuously makes it impossible for the insured to follow any substantially gainful occupation. Presumptive total disability results from the permanent loss of the use of both feet, or both hands, or of both eyes, or of one foot and one hand, or of one foot and one eye, or of one hand and one eye, or the total loss of hearing of both ears, or the organic loss of speech.

Eligibility for waiver of premium requires continuous total disability commencing before the insured's 65th birthday and continuing for at least six consecutive months. If the insured makes the appropriate claim to the Veterans Administration, waiver of premium will take effect on the first premium due date following the sixth consecutive month of total disability. However, if death occurs during the six-month period, and during this same period the policy has lapsed for nonpayment of premium, the insured's beneficiary may nevertheless be entitled to the proceeds of the policy.

Total disability income is paid from the seventh month of continuous total disability that commences either before age 60 or age 65. Payments continue as long as total disability continues. Disability income payble is either $5 monthly or $10 monthly per $1,000 insurance in force depending upon the applicable provision.

Three disability income provisions have been made available to NSLI policyowners—(1) $5, age 60 provision; (2) $10, age 60 provision; and (3) $10, age 65 provision. The first provision was available from August 1, 1946, to November 1, 1958; the second from November 1, 1958, to January 1, 1965. The third provision became effective January 1, 1965, and is still available provided application is made before the insured's 55th birthday. Policyowners with either the first or second provision may exchange them for the third provided the exchange occurs before the insured's 55th birthday. Exchange of the $5, age 60 provision requires evidence of good health. Exchange of the $10, age 60 provision does not require evidence of good health.

SERVICEMEN'S GROUP LIFE INSURANCE

Servicemen's Group Life Insurance (SGLI) is not government life insurance. However, it is supervised by the Veterans Administration.

Administration of the program is through a primary insurer licensed in all 50 states and the District of Columbia. There are approximately 600 private life insurance companies providing back-up reinsurance for the primary insurer. SGLI is available to all members of the uniformed services on active duty. Authorized by Public Law 89–214, approved in 1965, $10,000 of contributory group term life insurance was provided automatically on all eligible persons without evidence of insurability. Public Law 91–291, approved in 1970, increased the maximum insurance to $15,000. In addition, it extended coverage to all reservists, members of the National Guard, and ROTC members while engaged in authorized training duty. Affirmative action in writing must be taken if no insurance is desired under this program or if the eligible member would prefer to limit his coverage to $5,000 or $10,000. No other options are available.

Premiums paid by servicemen are designed to cover normal peacetime mortality costs and administration expenses. Additional costs attributable to the hazards of military service are paid by the federal government.

Insurance available under this program is in addition to USGLI, NSLI, or Federal Employees Group Life Insurance the eligible member may have or acquire.

The insured may designate any person or legal entity as beneficiary. In the absence of a designation, or in the event all designated beneficiaries predecease the insured, proceeds are payable in the following order of preference—(1) widow or widower, (2) child or children and descendents of deceased children by representation, (3) parents, (4) executor or administrator of the estate, and (5) next of kin under laws of the insured's state of domicile.

Proceeds are payable in one of two ways—lump sum or 36 equal monthly installments. If the insured selects a lump sum payment, the beneficiary may change the settlement option to 36 equal monthly installments. No change may be made by the beneficiary if the insured selects 36 equal monthly installments. If the insured makes no selection, the beneficiary is free to select either of the two settlement options.

Protection under SGLI continues without premium payment for 120 days following separation from service. If the veteran is totally disabled, protection continues for one year. During this period the veteran may convert an amount of group term life insurance not in excess of the amount in force while in service to an individual permanent policy without regard to his physical condition. Such conversion may be effected by applying, within the 120-day period following separation from the service, to any of the 600 approved companies for permanent coverage on any plan approved for conversions and then being written by the company.

COMPENSATION AND PENSION BENEFITS

The distinguishing characteristic of compensation benefits is that they are paid to veterans and/or their dependents as a result of *service-con-nected* disability or death. Such disability or death can be the result of either peacetime or wartime service. Compensation payments usually are made irrespective of the availability of outside income.

The distinguishing characteristic of pension benefits is that they are paid to veterans and/or their dependents as a result of disability or death that is *not service-connected*. Such disability or death benefits will be paid only if the veteran was in service during wartime or the Mexican Border period. No pension benefits are available to veterans of peacetime service or their dependents for nonservice-connected death or disability. Unlike compensation benefits, pension benefits are subject to outside income limitations.

Wartime service for pension benefits is defined to include the following periods:

Mexican Border Period—May 9, 1916, to April 5, 1917.

World War I—April 6, 1917, to November 11, 1918; extended to April 1, 1920, for those veterans who served in Russia; also extended through July 1, 1921, for those veterans who had at least one day of service before November 12, 1918, and who served after November 11, 1918, and before July 2, 1921.

World War II—December 7, 1941, to December 31, 1946.

Korean Conflict—June 27, 1950, to January 31, 1955.

Vietnam Era—August 4, 1964, to date to be determined.

Disability Compensation

Disability compensation is paid on behalf of veterans of either wartime or peacetime service with service-connected disabilities. Service-connected disabilities are rated by the Veterans Administration on a scale from 10 percent to 100 percent. In determining the appropriate rating, the Veterans Administration takes into consideration the average impairment of earning capacity in civilian occupations resulting from such disabilities. Compensation rates applied to disabilities incurred during peacetime are 80 percent of compensation rates applied to disabilities incurred during wartime. Veterans evaluated as 50 percent or more disabled are entitled to extra allowances for dependents consistent with the degree of disability. The wartime compensation rate in 1971 ranged from $25 monthly for a 10 percent disability rating to $450 monthly for a 100 percent disability rating. In specific cases this rate can be increased to $1,120 monthly. Additional amounts are allowed to qualifying veterans based on the number and type of dependents.

Disability Pension

To qualify for pension benefits, the veteran must have served during wartime and have a nonservice-connected permanent and total disability. Veterans 65 years of age or older are presumed to be permanently and totally disabled for disability pension purposes.

Two pension systems are in effect. All veterans placed on the pension rolls on or after July 1, 1960, receive pension benefits under the current pension system. Veterans on the pension rolls on June 30, 1960, receive pension benefits under the prior pension system. Veterans receiving benefits under the prior pension system may change to the current pension system. The major differences between the pension systems are reflected in the rate structure, income limitations and net worth features.

Under the current pension system the less income a veteran has, the higher will be his pension benefit. Conversely, the more income he has, the smaller his pension benefit. Benefit amounts also vary depending upon the number of the veteran's dependents. If the veteran's net worth is considered excessive, the disability pension may be discontinued.

Veterans receiving pension benefits are required to make an annual report of their income and the "corpus of their estate." Effective January 1, 1972, veterans who are 72 years of age or older are excused from making this required annual report if they have received pension benefits for at least two consecutive calendar years. However, they still are subject to the income and net worth limitations.

Monthly pension rates for veterans under the current pension system range from no monthly pension if annual income is more than $3,800 to a monthly pension of $150 if the veteran's annual income does not exceed $500 and, in addition, he has three or more dependents.

Death Compensation

The system of death compensation existing before January 1, 1957, has been largely replaced by Dependency and Indemnity Compensation (DIC). Generally, payments under DIC are higher than those available under the pre-1957 death compensation system. DIC payments are made to widows, children, and certain parents of servicemen who die on or after January 1, 1957, from (1) a disease or injury incurred or aggravated in line of duty while on active duty or active duty for training; or (2) an injury incurred or aggravated in line of duty while on inactive duty training; or (3) a disability otherwise compensable under laws administered by the Veterans Administration.

Widows, children, and parents who are on the rolls, or found to be eligible for death compensation by reason of a death occurring before January 1, 1957, may elect to receive DIC payments in lieu of death compensation. Once this decision is made, it cannot be reversed.

To be eligible for benefits, the widow must have lived continuously with the veteran from the time of marriage until the veteran's death, except where there was a separation procured by or due to the misconduct of the veteran without fault on the wife's part. Remarriage by a widow following the death of her veteran husband makes her ineligible for compensation benefits until the subsequent marriage is dissolved. A widow also may be ineligible for benefits if she lives with another man and holds herself out openly to the public as his wife.

The rate of DIC payments is based on the veteran's pay grade, and varies from $184 a month if the pay grade is E-1, to $469 a month if the pay grade is 0–10. This range of monthly payments for widows is increased by $22 monthly for each child. Additional payments may be made for aid and attendance for widows who are in a nursing home, helpless or blind, or so nearly helpless or blind as to need or require the regular aid and attendance of another person. Although generally benefits are for childern under age 18, special financial provisions are made for helpless children and children under 23 attending school.

DIC payments to parents vary according to the number of parents, the amount of their individual or combined total annual other income, and whether or not they live together. The income limitation for parents living together is $3,800; it is $2,600 each if they are living separately. Effective January 1, 1972, recipients who are 72 years of age or older are excused from making the required annual report of income and "corpus of estate," provided they have recived DIC for at least two consecutive calendar years. However, they still are subject to the income and net worth limitations.

Death Pension

A death pension is payable only to eligible widows and children of *wartime* veterans, and those of the Korean conflict, Vietnam era and Mexican Border period who have died of nonservice-connected causes; that is, causes not related to their service. All widows and children, except those of Spanish-American War veterans, who came on the pension rolls on or after July 1, 1960 will receive pension benefits under the current pension system. Eligibility requirements for the widow's benefit as well as conditions causing ineligibility are the same as those discussed under death compensation.

The benefit payable under the current pension system to widows and eligible children is affected by both income and net worth considerations. No pension is payable to those whose estates are so large that it is reasonable for them to look to the estate for maintenance. No payment is made to a widow with an annual income exceeding $2,600. A widow and one child lose all benefits if the annual income is more than $3,800. Monthly pension rates for a widow alone range from $17 to $87. With one child the range becomes $42 to $104. An amount equal to $17 is added for each additional child. Benefits also are available to children when there is no surviving widow.

Eligibility for benefits under the prior pension system in effect before July 1, 1960, required a service-incurred disability at the time of death for a World War II or Korean conflict veteran. Inasmuch as the current pension system applies to death from nonservice-connected causes, many dependents of deceased veterans not previously eligible under the prior pension system became eligible with the introduction of the current pension system on July 1, 1960.

In determining the annual income of a widow, every form of income she receives is taken into account, including social security. However, only 90 percent of commercial life insurance payments received are considered income in the calendar year of payment. This applies to income under any settlement option, even in those situations where the beneficiary has the right to elect a lump sum payment or to withdraw principal.

ORPHANS', WIVES', AND WIDOWS' EDUCATION BENEFITS

Educational benefits may be available to orphans, wives, and widows of veterans whose death or permanent and total disability is service-connected and occurred after the beginning of the Spanish-American

War on April 21, 1898. Eligibility generally applies to sons and daughters between 18 and 26. In some instances, handicapped children may begin a special vocational or restorative course as early as age 14.

The period of eligibility for educational assistance or special restorative training ends on an eligible child's 26th birthday, plus any period of time after his 18th birthday which was required to process his application. However, a number of exceptions apply to the general rule.

Marriage of a child is not a barrier to the educational assistance benefit if the child is otherwise eligible. A widow's remarriage terminates her entitlement until such time as her remarriage may be terminated.

An eligible person may receive up to 36 months of schooling, or the equivalent of 36 months if enrolled part-time. The aggregate entitlement to educational benefits under various laws administered by the Veterans Administration may not exceed 48 months.

Training may be taken in schools and colleges only. On-the-job training, on-the-farm training, vocational flight training and correspondence school training are prohibited. However, specialized vocational training that does not require high school background as a prerequisite is an exception if such training will fit the participant for a vocational goal. Benefits under this program are $175 a month, if enrolled full time; $128 a month, if enrolled three-quarters time; $81 a month, if enrolled half time; $81 for less than half time but more than quarter time; and $41 if enrolled one-quarter time or less. Individuals enrolled in cooperative courses—alternating classroom study and related experience on-the-job—receive $141 a month. This training may be taken only full time. Special restorative training may be provided to eligible persons unable to pursue an education because of some physical or mental disability. A monthly allowance of $125 is paid to persons taking this special training.

OTHER BENEFIT CONSIDERATIONS

Social Security

Military personnel make social security contributions on their base pay in the same manner as their civilian counterparts. Contributions by servicemen are matched by their employer, the United States government. In addition to base pay credits, gratuitous social security credits, generally amounting to $100 for each month of active duty after 1967, are included in a serviceman's total social security account. Prior to 1957, servicemen did not make social security contributions. Instead, between September 16, 1940 and December 31, 1956, veterans with at least 90 days' active service were entitled to a gratuitous social security wage credit of $160 for each month of this service.[2]

Other Death Benefits

A number of other benefits are available as a result of the death of veterans. Specific information on eligibility requirements for these benefits is available from the Veterans Administration.

---

[2] Additional information about social security benefits for servicemen or veterans may be obtained from the Social Security Administration.

A payment, not to exceed $250, towards a veteran's burial expenses can be claimed within two years after the veteran's permanent burial or cremation. A veteran may be eligible to receive an American flag to drape his casket, after which it may be given to his next of kin, or to a close friend or associate of the deceased. Burial is available to any deceased veteran of wartime or peacetime service whose last period of active service (other than for training) terminated honorably, by death or otherwise. Reservists who die while performing active duty for training also are eligible. Burial also is available to the eligible veteran's wife, husband, widow, widower, minor children, and, under certain conditions, to unmarried adult children. If an eligible veteran's spouse, minor child, or an eligible adult child dies before the veteran, the decedent may be buried in a national cemetery provided the veteran's written intention is to be buried with the decedent.

A headstone or grave marker is available for any deceased veteran of wartime or peacetime service whose last period of active service, other than for training, terminated honorably by death or otherwise. Reservists who die while performing active duty for training also are eligible. A memorial headstone or marker may be furnished on application of a close relative recognized as the next of kin to commemorate any member of the armed forces of the United States who dies in the service and whose remains are not recovered and identified or are buried at sea.

A sum equal to six months' pay of the deceased, including special incentive, hazard, and basic pay, but not allowances, may be paid to a veteran's spouse, child or children, or, if designated by the deceased, to parents, brothers, or sisters if the veteran's death occurred while he was on active duty, active duty for training, or inactive duty training. The gratuity also is payable if a service member or former service member dies of a service-connected cause within 120 days after discharge or release from active duty or active duty for training other than under dishonorable conditions. In the case of inactive duty training, the gratuity is payable if death occurred within 120 days and is the result of injury received during that training. Regardless of the monthly pay of the deceased, the death gratuity shall not be less than $800 nor more than $3,000.

Changes in Benefits

Laws applicable to benefits for servicemen, veterans, and their dependents change frequently. New benefits are introduced, and former benefits are modified. Many of the rules surrounding the availability of benefits are detailed and extensive. Consultation with the Veterans Administration should be sought if more detail about any of these benefits is desired.

SELECTED REFERENCES

Life Insurance Agency Management Association. *Veterans' Benefits.* 17th ed. Hartford. February, 1971.

Veterans Administration. *Government Life Insurance Programs.* Annual Report, Calendar Year 1970. Washington, D.C.: U.S. Government Printing Office, 1971.

————. *National Service Life Insurance.* VA Pamphlet 29–3 (V-H Policies). Rev. ed. Washington, D.C.: U.S. Government Printing Office, January, 1970.

————. *National Service Life Insurance.* VA Pamphlet 29–20 (RS-W Policies). Rev. ed. Washington, D.C.: U.S. Government Printing Office, January, 1970.

————. *National Service Life Insurance.* VA Pamphlet 29–9A (RH Policies). Rev. ed. Washington, D.C.: U.S. Government Printing Office, September, 1969.

————. *National Service Life Insurance.* VA Pamphlet 29–17 (J and JR Policies). Rev. ed. Washington, D.C.: U.S. Government Printing Office, June, 1970.

————. *Summary of Benefits for Veterans and Servicemen with Service Since January 31, 1955, and their Dependents.* VA Pamphlet 20–67–1. Rev. ed. Washington, D.C.: U.S. Government Printing Office, April, 1971.

————. *United States Government Life Insurance.* VA Pamphlet 29–1 (K Policies). Rev. ed. Washington, D.C.: U.S. Government Printing Office, July, 1970.

————. *Federal Benefits for Veterans and Dependents.* VA Fact Sheet IS-1. Washington, D.C.: U.S. Government Printing Office, March, 1971.

part *IX*

Planning Small and Large Estates

SOUND PLANNING with regard to the economic impact of death, disability, and retirement on family life and business interests is highly desirable. Life insurance and health insurance are valuable and highly creative instruments in this planning. The life underwriter typically is the initiator of the planning and, where the assets are of substance and the planning is complex, the attorney, the accountant, and the trust officer are important members of the team.

Part IX considers estates of all sizes, including those that suggest only the simple process of programming. Other chapters are concerned with highly complex instruments, laws, taxes, and procedures used in the most complex estate planning situations.

795

52

Concepts of Programming

By LELAND T. WAGGONER

PROGRAMMING IS to life and health insurance what diagnosis and prescription are to the field of medicine. In other words, it is the vehicle for carrying the product to the client. Just as a good doctor would not blindly prescribe a medicine or surgical procedure, a good life underwriter would not recommend a life or health insurance contract unsuited to his client's particular needs.

Programming Defined

Programming is the process used by a life and health underwriter to assist a client in measuring his desired financial goals and aspirations against his present assets, including life insurance, health insurance, and other investments. As a normal result, through life and health insurance, the underwriter is able to assist his client in solving financial problems and in reaching his financial goals.

In this chapter programming of both life insurance and health insurance will be considered concurrently. However, to keep the ideas clear, the two functions will be separated. In practice, the information obtained on the initial interview with the client would be sufficient to make recommendations in both areas.

Essentially, there are three basic programming problems facing every man and his family. All three problems involve loss of funds and/or income that must be replaced in the event of the three forms of economic death, that is, premature death, disability, or retirement. In addition, the living values of life insurance and other investments are brought into the picture.

Through the professional application of good programming techniques, the life underwriter evaluates each of the above hazards with the client and together they work out the solutions. The greater the client's understanding of his problems, the more eager he will be to solve them. Hence, the rule in programming is to have the program developed based on the client's ideas and not those of the life underwriter. This is achieved through proper fact finding. Here, the questions asked cause the client to think about the problem before the solution is recommended.

The approach is very much like that of an architect. He asks his client what he wants in the way of a house. He then draws up a working plan based on the client's ideas. The client and the architect discuss the plan, work out reasonable alternatives, and then decide on the final home to be built. The same concept is employed in professional programming. So, regardless of the details of a specific company's programming technique, the concept of fixing the problem, analyzing the problem, planning the solution, and recommending the solution are the same.

The question of the relationship of programming to estate planning is only a matter of degree. For the purposes of this chapter, it will be assumed that programming involves the measuring of financial goals, comparing them to a client's assets, and uncovering needs for new life insurance, health insurance, or other investments.

Estate planning includes in its application all the elements of programming and it adds estate conservation and distribution. Estate planning also includes the disposition of business interests and the use of pension and profit sharing plans and other devices for individuals to help them establish larger estates with tax-deferred dollars.

The purpose of this chapter is to analyze the financial problems of the client who is not primarily concerned with federal estate taxes and who will not have a need for trust agreements, business purchase agreements, or unusually complicated wills. It is significant to note that these persons make up the great majority of the insuring public. A recent study indicated that widows received, on the average, only $11,900 in lump-sum payments from all sources, including life insurance, settlements under employee retirement plans, Veterans Administration and social security funeral benefits, gifts from friends and co-workers, and the sale of possessions or business interests.[1] Life insurance accounted for 69 percent of the lump sum received. When personal and group insurance lump-sum and income payments are taken into account, it is likely that as much as 80 percent of the typical man's estate consists of life insurance. For such a man, the organization and planning of assets equal to as much as 80 percent of his estate is of significant importance, and it matters little whether the process is called "programming" or "estate planning."

Human Life Value Approach to Programming

The human life value concept, as developed by Dr. S. S. Huebner, has had a very significant influence on the theory of programming. Briefly, the human life value concept assumes that every person who performs a valuable economic service has a very real financial value, and that this value should be replaced by life insurance in the event of premature death. Thus, the man who insures a piece of property for its value in the event of loss should apply the same concept to his own economic value. If a man dies prematurely, his family will suffer a very real economic loss

---

[1] Loran E. Powell and Paul W. Thayer, *The Widow's Study: Preliminary Findings and Implications* (Hartford, Conn.: Life Insurance Agency Management Association, 1970).

which can be compensated for in some measure by the presence of life insurance.

The human life value of an individual may be determined by calculating the present value of that portion of his estimated future earned income that would be devoted to his family.[2]

Estate Creation, Conservation, and Distribution

Programming can be related to three principal functions. For most persons, the major function is *estate creation.* Most individuals are insured for only a relatively small part of their human life value. Consequently, the premature death of a husband typically results in serious financial problems for his widow and children. However, in the presence of accumulated wealth, the functions of *estate conservation* and *estate distribution* may become equally important, or even more so.

Estate distribution is important even though ·the individual's estate may be relatively small. In fact, from the standpoint of having a margin for error, the smaller the estate, the more important it is to make certain that the insurance proceeds and other assets go to the intended parties, and in the appropriate manner.

PROGRAMMING PROCESS

It is often helpful to consider programming as a *process.* When viewed in this way, programming becomes a series of related steps, all of which are designed to accomplish a given goal or goals. The goals of individuals will vary widely and change with the passing of time. Consequently, a reasonable degree of flexibility should be maintained in carrying out each step in the process. If some major step is omitted, or carried out in an inadequate manner without complete information, then the final program will not be realistic.

Most life insurance companies have developed a standardized programming process their life underwriters may follow in serving their clients. By introducing the new life underwriter to a "programming process," rather than vague guidelines, he has a definite procedure to follow and knows what to do and how to do it.

The following list of processes is by no means uniform. In fact, it seems reasonable to assume that no two companies suggest precisely the same processes or procedures to their life underwriters. However, the following list is reasonably typical:

1. Analyze all relevant factors.
2. Determine the goals of the client.
3. Compare present resources with those required to meet the client's goals.
4. Prepare a specific plan to meet the client's goals.
5. Provide for the creation, conservation, and distribution of the estate.

---

[2] The steps in calculating the human life value are discussed in Chapter 2.

Analyze Relevant Factors

Since a worthwhile program can only be based on the information supplied by the client, the life underwriter should seek to obtain all relevant information. This includes a detailed analysis of the client's present assets and liabilities, his family relationships, and his goals and aspirations.

It is important for the life underwriter to have some type of checklist to make certain that all assets and liabilities are taken into account. Most companies have prepared a confidential information form of some type. Typically, this will begin with questions to identify the client and his dependents, and give biographical data regarding each person. The length of the "confidential" varies from company to company. It may be a brief form, or it may be highly detailed. Figure 52–1 is an illustrative confidential programming survey form that includes the typical types and kinds of information needed.[3]

Determine the Goals of the Client

To a certain extent, the goals of the client are closely related to his needs. However, there is a tendency to think of his "goals" as what he would like to achieve financially for himself and his family, whereas "needs" are often considered the absolute necessities which must be provided for.

Goals of the client were partly analyzed when the "confidential" was completed. At this point, a closer look is taken of those goals. For example, has he set definite goals in all the areas in which they should be set? Are his goals realistic in the light of his present and probable future situation? Has he set conflicting goals for himself without realizing it?

The client may have given considerable thought previously to his goals, or this may be the first time that he actually has ever established clear-cut goals. The amount of discussion involved regarding each of the client's goals will depend partly upon how much previous thought he has given to them.

The statement is sometimes made that the most important aspect of goals is that they should be realistic. Naturally, what is realistic for one individual may not be realistic for another. In many instances, the client actually wants the life underwriter to guide him in determining what is a realistic goal.

If the life underwriter accepts the goals of the client without question, it can be argued that the resulting program may not be realistic and will not meet the needs of the individual and his dependents. On the other hand, if the life underwriter exerts too much influence, then the final program may represent the life underwriter's goals instead of those of his client. Perhaps the most common practice is for the life underwriter to help the person question whether or not his goals are realistic. Such questioning may motivate him to adopt more suitable goals; on the other hand, the individual may continue to insist that his goals are realistic. In either case the life underwriter generally prepares a program on

---

[3] Pages of survey form relating to information on business interests not shown.

FIGURE 52–1.   Illustrative Confidential Programming Survey and Analysis Form

CONFIDENTIAL INFORMATION

Client_____*John Smith*_____Age_*33*____Birth Date_____

Place of Birth_____Birth Evidence Available_____

Recommended By_____Field Underwriter_____

Residence Address_____Phone_____
zip code

Business Address_____Phone_____
zip code

Name of Firm_____Position_____

DEPENDENTS

NAME	RELATIONSHIP	BIRTH DATE	AGE	PLACE OF BIRTH	BIRTH EVID. AVAILABLE
wife *Jane*			*30*		
oldest child *Richard*	*son*		*5*		
Harry	*son*		*2*		

Were All Children Born of This Marriage?_*Yes*_ (If no, indicate by asterisk next to name)

MORTGAGE

Would Family Continue To Live in Present Home?_*Yes*____

Purchase Price of Home $_*35,000*___Amount & Type of Mortgage_*$28,000*_

Date of Mortgage_____Rate of Interest & Duration_____

Prepayment Clause_*Yes*_____Unpaid Balance $_*18,000*_

Monthly Payment $_*200*_____

     Includes Taxes   Yes ☒ No ☐
     Includes Insurance Yes ☒ No ☐

Liquidate Mortgage Yes ☒ No ☐   Provide Mortgage Payments Yes ☐ No ☐

1

whatever basis the client decides. From a psychological as well as practical standpoint, it is imperative that the program represent the client's goals, and not just the goals which the life underwriter considers important.

② Prepare a Specific Plan to Meet the Client's Goals

Programming typically involves a minimum of two interviews with the client. During the first interview, the life underwriter usually explains the type of service he renders, and, assuming the client is sufficiently in-

FIGURE 52–1 (continued)

FAMILY BUDGET *(after John's death)*

Estimate ①   Actual ②

Adequate Monthly Income .... $ _950_ $ _1,000_

Allocation of Income:

   Shelter (15%-25%) .... $ _150_ $ _120_
    Includes—Rent   Payment on House
          Taxes   Insurance
          Repairs

   House Operation (15%-20%*) .... $ _200_ $ _200_
    Includes—Heat   Water
          Gas & Elect. Laundry
          Telephone   House Help

   Food (25%-35%*) .... $ _150_ $ _250_

   Clothing (10%-15%*) .... $ _150_ $ _100_

   Personal & Miscellaneous (25%-35%*) .... $ _250_ $ _230_
    Includes—Transportation   Contributions
          Recreation   Other Insurance
          Medical & Dental Incidentals

   Income for Contingencies (10%*) .... $ _50_ $ _100_

Total Adequate Monthly Income Need .... $ _1,000_
(after Richard is age 18, reduce to $800 until Harry is age 18.)

Is There Any Guaranteed Income, Other Than Life Insurance,
To Provide Part of the Total Amount Needed? If so, What Is It?

   Social Security; personal savings

How Much Monthly Income Does This Provide? .... $ _400_

Balance To Be Provided .... $ _600_

Life Income for Wife (monthly) *(after Harry is age 18)* ... $ _600_

Other Guaranteed Income .... $ _400_

Balance To Be Provided .... $ _200_

*Percentage based on nationally known budget studies.

① *John's initial thoughts on needs of surviving family members.*
② *John's final thoughts on needs of surviving family members.*

2

terested, the life underwriter will complete the confidential information form. The information which the life underwriter obtains in the process of taking the confidential is used to prepare a program. The program is a specific plan, designed to enable the client to meet the goals which he wishes to achieve.

In preparing a specific plan, two of the most important decisions are the amount and type of life insurance to recommend. In determining the

FIGURE 52–1 (continued)

READJUSTMENT INCOME OR FUND

(Include Provision for Unexpired Leases, Moving Expenses, and/or Time To Sell Home)

Additional Monthly Income Required ....$ 200 for 24 Months

Additional Fund To Be Provided ....$ 4,800

EMERGENCY FUNDS

Amount Required ....$ 4,000

EDUCATIONAL FUNDS

	NAMES	Richard	Harry			
COLLEGE	IF YOU LIVE	8,000	8,000			
	IF YOU DIE	8,000	8,000			
OTHER (GRAD. SCHOOL, SPEC. TRNG.)	IF YOU LIVE					
	IF YOU DIE					

Do You Have a Definite Plan Now for Accumulation of Educational Funds?

If So, What Type of Plan? none

OTHER NEEDS

	NAME	DATE OF BIRTH	AMOUNT	HOW PAYABLE
PARENTS	none Dependency/Retirement Inc.		$	
CHILDREN	none		$	
RELATIVES	none		$	
BEQUESTS	none		$	
CHARITIES	none		$	

3

amount of life insurance to recommend, the life underwriter will often use a "planning calculator" which has been prepared by his company. It enables him to determine the amounts of life insurance needed to provide the various monthly income requirements through the use of settlement options.

In many companies a computer has been programmed to handle the calculations and the presentation material that goes back to the client.

FIGURE 52–1 (continued)

IMMEDIATE CASH DEMANDS

CURRENT OBLIGATIONS

First Month's Living Expenses ....$ *1,200*

Notes and Collateral Loans *(mortgage to be paid in* $ *18,000*
full)

    Monthly Payments ....$ *0*

    Final Payment Date_____

    Covered by Life Insurance?_____

Installment Obligations (Unpaid Balance) ....$ *0*

    Monthly Payments ....$ *0*

    Final Payment Date_____

    Covered by Life Insurance?_____

Life Insurance Loans (Details) ....$ *0*

_____

Any Other Liabilities (Details) ....$ *0*

_____

TOTAL ....$ *19,200*

FINAL EXPENSES

Amount Required To Pay Doctors, Nurses, Hospital, Funeral, etc. ....$ *1,000*

TAXES

Property (Next Installment) ....$ *200*

Federal Income Tax (Next Quarter) ....$ *500*

State Income Tax ....$ *100*

Federal Estate Tax* ....$ *0*

State Inheritance Taxes* ....$ *0*

TOTAL ....$ *800*

ADMINISTRATION EXPENSES

Amount Required for Executor's and Legal Fees, etc. ....$ *1,000*

TOTAL CASH DEMANDS ....$ *22,000*

*Determine from data on pages 6 and 7.

4

The life underwriter obtains the necessary information on the client's objectives and his assets. This is transferred to an input form for the insurance company's computer and sent to the home office. The home office computer then works up the plan for the client.

The advantages to this method are speed and accuracy of calculation and a uniform method of approach to solving the problems. This works best if terminal computers are available in an agency. The types and

FIGURE 52–1 (continued)

RETIREMENT FUNDS

Guaranteed Monthly Income Required at Age *65* .... $ *1,000*

Sources of Guaranteed Income, Other Than Life Insurance

Pension (at age *65*) .... $ *80*
(Obtain Descriptive Booklet or Current Statement)

Social Security .... $ *300*

Other (Give Source Below) .... $ *20*

_____ *savings* _____

TOTAL FROM OTHER SOURCES .... $ *400*

BALANCE TO BE PROVIDED .... $ *600*

Cash Demands .... $ *22,000*

Cash Funds (Emergencies, etc.) .... $ *20,000*

Wife's Continuing Life Income .... $ *65/mo.*

SOCIAL SECURITY

Do You Have Coverage? *yes* _____ Social Security Number_____

Are You Covered as Employee? *✓* _____ Or as Self-Employed?_____

Have You Had Continuous Coverage Since January 1, 1951? *no*

Have You Obtained Up-To-Date Statement of Your Account? *no*

Details_____

Social Security Card Signed ☒

MILITARY SERVICE

Did You Serve in the Armed Forces? *no* Dates_____

Serial No._____

Branch of Service_____Rank Attained_____

Will You Qualify for Military Pension? If Yes, Describe_____

Disability Payments, If Any_____Current Condition of Health_____

Current Military Status_____

EMPLOYEE BENEFITS

Group Life Insurance .... $ *12,000*

Pension Plan (Describe) *$80/mo. @ age 65*

Death Benefits Under Pension or Profit Sharing Plan .... $ *0*

Deferred Compensation Plan, Present Value .... $ *0*

Stock Option, Value .... $ *0*

Do You Have Contract?_____

Stock Purchase Plan, Value .... $ *0*

TOTAL DEATH BENEFITS .... $ *12,000*

Do You Have Booklet Explaining Benefits? *yes*

Are You Satisfied with Plan? *no*

Executive Responsible for Plan *Warren Jones – Personnel officer*
                              Name, title, address

5

degree of sophistication in computerized programming vary widely. They range from simply supplementing social security to planning complex estate situations.

④ **Program the Life Insurance**

In the case of "income needs," the benefits provided by policies of different companies and different policies issued by the same company

FIGURE 52–1 (continued)

TAX DATA

Computation of federal estate and state inheritance tax liabilities
requires complete and accurate information on your general estate.

LIFE INSURANCE

	OWNED BY		
	HUSBAND	WIFE	JOINTLY

Do You Own All of the Insurance on Your Life?

If No, Give Details *yes*

Total Owned on Your Life (Exclusive of Group)..... $ *45,000* $_____ $_____

How Are Dividends Used? *accumulated at interest*

Total Accumulated .... $ *1,000* $_____ $_____

Total Additional Insurance .... $ *0* $_____ $_____

Do You Own Any Insurance on the Lives of Your
Children, Business Associates or Other Persons?
If So, Indicate on Whom and Amounts.

Wife – $2,000

COMPANY DEATH BENEFITS

Group Life Insurance .... $ *12,000*

Return of Pension Plan Contributions *0*

Pension or Profit-Sharing Plan Death Benefits *0*

Value of Any Deferred Compensation Plan *0*

Stock Purchase Plan, Value *0*

Cash *0*

REAL ESTATE

Home, Net Value .... $_____ $_____ $ *23,000*

Summer Home, Net Market Value .... _____ _____ _____

Rental Property, Net Market Value .... _____ _____ _____

Other Real Estate, Net Market Value .... _____ _____ _____

BUSINESS INTEREST*

Sole Proprietorship, Value .... $_____ $_____ $_____

Close Corporation, Value .... _____ _____ _____

Partnership, Value .... _____ _____ _____

*See Pages 9 and 10.

Subtotal .... $ *58,000* $_____ $ *23,000*

6

---

are not necessarily identical; there may be substantial differences because the settlement options of some contracts are more liberal than others. For example, the life income options of National Service Life Insurance (NSLI) and United States Government Life Insurance (USGLI) and those of older policies generally should be used to provide life income benefits because the guaranteed income payments under the settlement option provisions usually are more favorable than recently issued policies.

FIGURE 52–1 (continued)

TRUST FUNDS

| | OWNED BY | |
| | HUSBAND | WIFE |

Currently in Effect .... $_____ $_____
Sources and Purpose_____

Rights in Trust_____

LIQUID ASSETS

STOCKS AND BONDS

		TOTAL	OWNED BY		
DESCRIPTION	PRICE	ANNUAL INCOME	HUSBAND	WIFE	JOINTLY
				(Give Current Values)	
			$_____	$_____	$_____

CASH IN BANK

	HUSBAND	WIFE	JOINTLY
Amount in Savings Account .... $	1,400	$_____	$_____
Amount in Checking Account	600	_____	_____
Other Accumulations	0	_____	_____

Do You Have a Plan of Regular Savings? If So,
Describe___none____

Are You Satisfied with Present Plan?__no____
Any Change Contemplated?__no____
Amount Saved Monthly $__varies__
Total Saved Last Year $__400__

MISCELLANEOUS PROPERTY

Household Effects .... $	5,000	$_____	$_____
Personal Effects (Jewelry, Furs, Boat, Stamp Collection)	2,000	_____	_____
Automobiles	3,000	_____	_____
Art Objects	0	_____	_____
Other (Mortgages or Notes Owned)	0	_____	_____

ESTATE INVENTORY, TOTAL VALUATION

Subtotal from page 6 .... $	58,000	$_____	$ 23,000
Grand Total .... $	70,000	$_____	$ 23,000

• • • • • • • •

Do Your Children Own Any Substantial Assets?__no____
Do You Have Any Independent Source of Income We Haven't Discussed? If So, Describe__no____

Personal Taxable Income Last Year $__15,000__ Personal Estimated Taxable Income This Year $__16,000__
Estimated Taxable Income Five Years Hence $__20,000____ Ten Years Hence $__25,000__
Does Wife Have Income from Employment? If So, Give Annual Amount $__none__ Temporary ☐
                                                                   Permanent ☐
Is There a Possibility Either You or Your Wife or Your Children Will Inherit Any Substantial Amount
of Property?__no____

7

Ⓢ Provide for the Creation, Conservation, and Distribution of the Estate

The major problem for the average client is estate creation. However, conservation and distribution should be considered regardless of the size of the estate. If the estate is very large, this may create a need for tax planning, trusts, and the other more advanced forms of estate planning. For the person of limited or average means, two key steps are (1)

FIGURE 52–1 (concluded)

DISPOSITION OF ESTATE ASSETS

Have You a Will? _no_ Does Wife Have a Will? _no_
Do You Have a Trust Under Your Will? If So, What Type of Trust and What Rights Will Widow Have?
_____

Is Guardian Provided? If So, Give Name_____
When Was Will Last Reviewed? _____
To Whom Are Assets Being Left? _____
_____

Do Wills Accomplish What You Now Have in Mind For Your Estate? _____
    Attorney's Name and Address _____
_____

If Assets Are To Be Distributed Through a Trust:
    Trust Company_____Address_____
    Trust Officer_____
If It Becomes Desirable To Use a Trust Company for Some or All of Your Estate Matters, Which
Would You Use? Give Name and Address _____
_____

Have You Made Any Gifts Requiring a Gift Tax Return? If So, To Whom Was Gift Made and What
Was Value? _none_____
Have You Taken Advantage of Marital Deduction Privileges As Outlined in the Internal Revenue
Code?_____
Is All Property Left To Wife Qualified for Marital Deduction? ___yes_____
Has Your Life Insurance Property Been Qualified for Deduction? ___yes_____

having his attorney prepare a will for both husband and wife, and (2) having his life underwriter arrange for the proper naming of beneficiaries and selection of settlement options in the life insurance policies.

ANALYSIS OF NEEDS

The basic financial needs of a family are often divided into two types—cash needs and income needs. Money for "cash" needs is not necessarily paid in a lump sum but may be held by the insurance company at interest until needed for any subsequent emergency, education of children, and the like. The following list gives an overview of the needs of most families with children.

Cash Needs	*Income Needs*
Final expenses	Readjustment income
Emergency	Dependency income
Mortgage	Life income for widow
Education	Retirement income

This list assumes that the husband has died. In the event the husband lives to retirement, the emphasis shifts to providing an adequate retirement income for the husband and wife.

Cash Needs

Final Expenses. A final expense fund is needed to meet obligations which are outstanding at the time of death, or which are caused by death itself. Examples are medical expenses, burial expenses, outstanding installment debts, taxes, and the cost of estate settlement. The amount needed to pay final expenses will vary considerably, but most authorities feel that $3,000 to $5,000 represents an absolute minimum. Of course, in the larger estates, liquid funds needed for estate or inheritance taxes would materially increase these figures.

Emergency Fund. The emergency fund is to provide for unexpected financial needs. While it is possible to estimate anticipated future expenses with some degree of accuracy, even the most careful planning may be jeopardized by one or two unforeseen expenses.

Many financial experts recommend that the emergency fund be approximately 25 percent of the family's annual earned income. Thus, if the client's annual earned income is $16,000, an emergency fund of $4,000 would be suggested.

Mortgage Fund. The purpose of the mortgage fund is to provide the money needed for the widow to pay off the remaining balance of the mortgage on the family home. In the absence of a mortgage fund, the amount of the monthly mortgage payments must be included in the income needs of the widow until such time as the mortgage payments have been completed.

Education Fund. The dramatic increase in the cost of securing a college education is common knowledge. The result is that these funds must be available when needed or else a college education may be financially impossible. The actual cost of a college education is difficult for many parents to comprehend—until their own children start college. The fact that these costs are increasing means that it is probably unrealistic to consider any figure less than $2,000 per year. If a high-tuition school is selected, then the annual cost can easily jump to $5,000 per year or more.

Income Needs

Readjustment Income. The purpose of the readjustment income is to provide temporarily the same income to the widow as was available before her husband died. This is usually provided for one or two years. The value of this arrangement is that it permits the widow to recover her emotional equilibrium, and to make her plans for the future without having to cope with financial worries at the same time.

The amount of the readjustment income, for any given program, will be larger than the amount the widow receives during the dependency period. Thus, a given program might provide $1,200 a month readjustment income for two years, and then decrease to $850 a month for the dependency period.

Dependency Period Income. The income during the dependency period is expected to provide the widow with a fixed income until the children reach a specified age. Most programs provide dependency incomes until the youngest child reaches age 18. If plans have been made for the children to attend college, then the education fund would provide for their needs until they complete college.

An alternative method is to provide dependency income until the youngest child reaches age 21 or 22, and reduce or eliminate the education fund.

Life Income for Widow. The life income for the widow starts at the end of the dependency period and continues for her lifetime. Typically, the amount of the life income will be considerably less than the income during the dependency period since the children are expected to be self-supporting. The usual practice is to start the life income when the youngest child reaches age 18. If the children plan to attend college, then hopefully this has been provided for by means of an education fund.

Since most children will receive some education beyond the high school level, some life underwriters continue the dependency period income until the youngest child reaches age 21 or 22. In the event that no education fund has been provided, this may enable the widow to pay for part of the cost of education beyond the high school level.

Retirement Income. Retirement income will begin when the husband reaches his designated retirement age, typically age 65. The amount of the retirement income is often expressed as a specific monthly income while both the husband and wife are alive, with a different figure being payable upon the death of either. Typically, the monthly income paid to the survivors is two thirds of the amount paid to both.

While specific retirement income policies are issued by most companies, the usual practice is to convert the cash values of permanent life insurance policies into an annuity by utilizing the life income option at the time of retirement. If the client feels that a certain amount of protection should be kept in force, then the reduced paid-up nonforfeiture option can be elected for one or more policies.

Preparation of Programming Chart

Assume that a family consists of a husband, age 33; wife, age 30; and two children, ages 2 and 5. The client wants a $4,000 final expense fund, a $4,000 emergency fund, an $18,000 mortgage fund, and a $16,000 education fund.

As far as income needs are concerned, he wants a readjustment income of $1,200 per month for two years, an income of $1,000 per month until the oldest child reaches age 18, and an income of $800 per month until the youngest child reaches age 18. He then wants his wife to receive a lifetime income of $600 per month.

Assuming that he lives, he wants to plan for a retirement income of $1,000 per month as long as he and his wife are alive, with a lifetime income of $650 payable to the survivor. He wants the retirement income to start when he is age 65, at which time his wife will be age 62.

In order to compare present resources with those required to accomplish the above objectives, a chart similar to Figure 52–2 may be prepared. This chart shows, in graphic form, the present resources of the individual as compared to the financial goals he has set. It helps the client to recognize the difference or discrepancy between what will be provided by his present assets, and the assets that are needed to enable him to reach his goals.

Social security benefits, if available, typically are shown first in preparing the chart. In theory, social security benefits should be calculated carefully. However, because of the frequent changes in legislation and the amount of time necessary to compute social security benefits, many life underwriters simply show a close approximation of the social security benefits which will be payable.

Social security benefits are shown at the bottom of the chart. It will be noted that social security benefits provide a level income until the oldest child reaches age 18; at that time, benefits are reduced, but continued until the youngest child reaches age 18. Social security benefits for students are available from age 18 to age 22 under certain conditions.[4]

Assuming that the children do not attend school past age 18, all social security benefits cease until the widow reaches age 62. (If the widow elects to do so, she can receive reduced benefits starting at age 60.) The period between the time that the youngest child reaches age 18 and the widow reaches age 62 is often referred to as the "blackout period," since no social security benefits of any type are payable. Consequently, this represents a period when the widow may have little or no income, unless specific provisions are made to provide an adequate income for her.

Starting at age 62, the widow receives a lifetime income. If the husband has lived to age 65, then the wife is eligible for retirement benefits as the wife of an insured worker. Later, if the husband predeceases the wife, the social security benefits to the widow are increased.

After the social security benefits have been charted, the value of the client's present life insurance and other assets are represented by the other shaded areas in Figure 52–2. They are sufficient to meet the $4,000 final expense fund, the $4,000 emergency fund, the $18,000 mortgage fund, the $16,000 education fund, and to provide a very small income to the widow from age 30 to age 62. In the event the insured lives to retirement, his present assets are sufficient to provide about one seventh of his retirement income needs.

The difference or discrepancy between the client's goals for himself and his family and what social security, his present life insurance, and other assets will provide, is the amount to be provided by new life insurance as indicated in Figure 52–2. If the client purchases the recommended amount of additional life insurance, all of his goals can and will be met. If the client is unable or unwilling to meet the necessary premium requirement, then some of the goals must be reduced or eliminated from the program.

HEALTH INSURANCE PROGRAMMING

Most of the basic concepts which apply to life insurance programming also apply to health insurance programming. In both, an attempt is made

---

[4] The latest information and schedule of benefits payable under social security can be obtained free of charge from the nearest office of the Social Security Administration.

FIGURE 52–2. Life Insurance Programming Chart

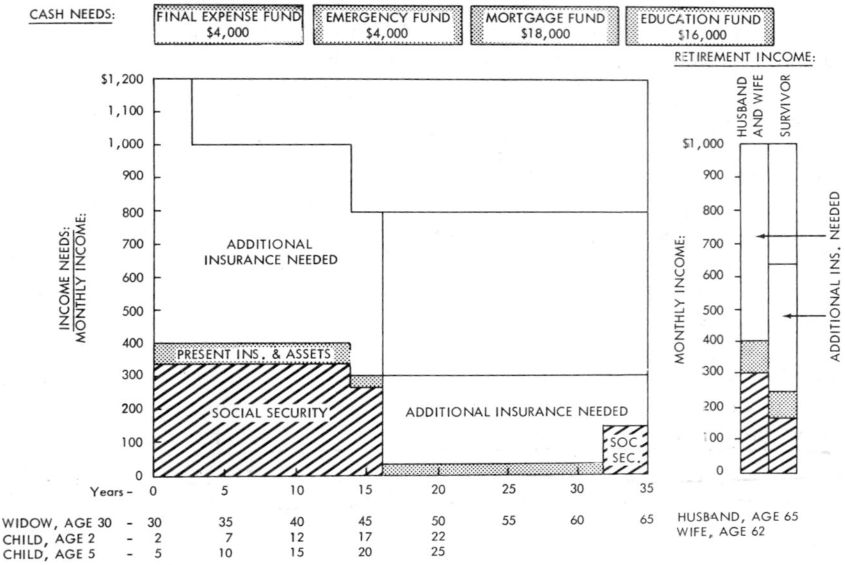

to determine the needs and goals of the client, to analyze how far his present assets and insurance will go, and to provide for the deficiency, if any, by additional insurance.

Preparation of a Health Insurance Programming Chart

In order to analyze the existing health insurance program of a client and illustrate the additional coverages needed to meet his goals, a programming chart is often prepared. The chart shown as Figure 52–3 illustrates that the client already has purchased hospitalization, surgical, and major medical coverages on a family basis. The income which he would like to receive in the event of disability is made up of four parts: a one-year salary continuation plan, social security disability income payments, present health insurance which pays a monthly income, and the additional insurance needed to meet his goals.

In order to keep the premium figure at a reasonable level, the program provides for benefits that are reduced considerably after 10 years. In Figure 52–3 the shaded area shows that the salary continuation plan provides $500 per month for the first six months of disability, and $200 per month for the next six months. Social security disability income benefits, which start after a waiting period of six months, are assumed to pay $200 per month as long as the client is disabled. These benefits are shown by the diagonally lined area in Figure 52–3. The client's present personally owned disability income insurance, shown in the crosshatched area, pays $100 per month for a maximum of 10 years after a one-year waiting period.

The additional insurance required to complete a program which will

FIGURE 52–3.   Health Insurance Programming Chart

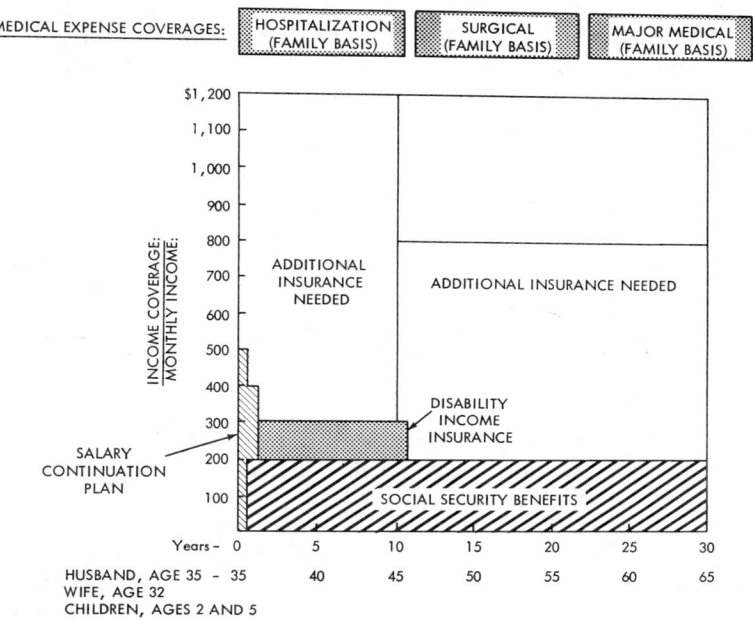

provide $1,200 per month for 10 years and $800 per month thereafter until age 65 is indicated in Figure 52–3. The additional amount required is $700 per month for six months, $800 per month for six months, $900 per month for 9 years, $500 per month for 1 year, and $600 per month for 19 years.

KEY CONCEPTS OF PROGRAMMING

Ability to Pay

In considering the client's ability to pay, it is only natural to think of a dollar sum, a percentage of income, or some other figure. However, his ability to pay may be determined, to some extent, by the value and importance he places on life and health insurance. The greater the importance which he places on family financial security, the larger the amount of premium he will be willing to pay.

Perhaps the major reason this concept is easily misunderstood is the ambiguity of the word "ability." If a client feels he absolutely must have a new Cadillac every year, this necessarily reduces his ability to pay in other areas. On the other hand, if the client feels he must maintain a certain level of financial security for himself and his family, his ability to pay for such needs will be significantly enhanced.

The programming approach often assumes that the client is able to meet the necessary premium requirements. If he is unwilling to pay the premium necessary for accomplishing the goals he has established for himself, the first assumption is that he is not being realistic as to his

financial goals. An attempt then should be made to have the client rede-
fine his goals so as to coincide with his ability to pay. In addition, an
attempt may be made to help him identify sources of income which he
is overlooking—such as dividends or interest on securities, or dividends
on existing life insurance policies.

Self-Disclosure

If the life underwriter attempts to complete a detailed "confidential"
before he has gained the respect and confidence of his client, one of two
results is likely. Either the client will refuse to give the information or,
more likely, he will give information which bears little relationship to
the actual facts. A program which is prepared on the basis of distorted
information will have inherent shortcomings and is not likely to motivate
the client, since he knows it is not based on facts.

Concept of Service

The programming approach generally involves the life underwriter in
providing a good deal of service to the client through the initial presentation and periodic reviews. The nature and amount of this service depends
to a large extent upon the motivation of the life underwriter to develop
a continuing relationship with his client. For a growing number of companies, the programming approach is part of the company's basic philosophy, and all life underwriters are expected to learn and use the programming approach and to provide the services that are a part of it.

As mentioned previously, the use of a programming approach generally
requires two or more interviews. It has been noted that during the first
interview, the life underwriter typically attempts to gain the confidence
and trust of the prospective client, to explain the nature of the programming service he is prepared to offer, and to identify all relevant factors in
the client's financial situation. He attempts to help the client verbalize the
short- and long-term goals which he has for himself and his family. If a
detailed analysis is to be made of the person's present life insurance, the
life underwriter picks up the present policies, together with any other relevant documents, such as wills, trusts, and a description of any retirement
plan.

The second interview consists of a review of the client's goals for himself and his family, consideration of the extent to which his present insurance and other assets will meet such goals, and determination of the additional life insurance which may be required to complete the program. An
attempt is made to convince the client to purchase insurance which will
permit him to attain all his goals. If this is not possible, then some type
of compromise plan will be presented.

Need for Program Review

From the client's point of view, an annual or at least a biennial review
of his program is essential. Not only do his needs change but his income
tends to increase, and his social security and employee benefits change.
Each change should be analyzed to determine if it requires a revision of
the program, and hence there are endless opportunities for sales and service for existing clientele.

Providing Monthly Income by Means of Settlement Options[5]

Most people think of life insurance in terms of a lump sum of money. In fact, it is probably not unusual for a client to ask an agent, "It's true that you've prepared a very logical plan, but what guarantee do I have that the plan actually will be put into effect after my death?" The answer is that the client may elect a combination of settlement options at the time the plan is put into effect that provides for the proceeds to be paid to his wife and children in the way he prefers.

Need for Flexibility

In the plan designed through programming, it is important that flexibility be allowed in the final setup of the plan. The well-intentioned fixed settlements of life insurance contracts through unchangeable settlement options can be devastating if the plan is not reviewed annually. In addition, future changes in circumstances, such as remarriage of the widow or her death, can change needs. A good rule is to provide for the needs through life and health insurance but give essential freedom in the manner of ultimate distribution.

PROGRAMMING IN THE FUTURE

Future developments in programming will be influenced by a number of factors. These include the extent to which there is a continued acceptance of programming by the public, the use of group life insurance coverages (many of which now provide monthly benefit payments for widows or children), and the degree to which social security benefits are expanded.

Changes in interest rates and investment opportunities will continue to have an influence on the use of settlement options, and the possible use of variable annuities for a significant portion of life insurance proceeds will be important in the future.

The programming of life insurance, already of major significance, probably will gain in popularity. The use of computerized programs likely will increase but the need for the knowledge and skill of the professional life insurance practitioner will, in an age of consumerism, be even more important for the insuring public.

SELECTED REFERENCES

Brosterman, Robert. *Complete Estate Planning Guide.* New York: McGraw-Hill Book Co., 1964.

Harris, Homer I. *Family Estate Planning Guide.* 2d ed. Rochester, N.Y.: Lawyers Cooperative Publishing Co., 1971.

McGill, Dan M. *Life Insurance.* Rev. ed. Homewood, Ill.: Richard D. Irwin, Inc., 1967.

Mehr, Robert I. *Life Insurance.* Austin, Texas: Business Publications, Inc., 1970.

---

[5] See Chapter 54 for a detailed discussion of settlement options.

53

Ownership Provisions and Beneficiary Designations

By PAUL L. WISE

OWNERSHIP PROVISIONS

A LIFE INSURANCE contract consists of a bundle of many rights and the person who can exercise those rights during the lifetime of the insured is the owner of the policy. Some of the most common rights are the right to designate the beneficiary who is to receive the death proceeds and to select settlement options for the proceeds; the right to make an absolute assignment or name another owner; the right to make policy loans or to assign the policy for collateral purposes; the right to surrender a policy and receive the cash surrender value; the right to receive proceeds at maturity of an endowment; the right to elect dividend options and receive dividends; and the right to select the nonforfeiture provisions to be operative upon nonpayment of premiums.

Third Party Ownership

The insured is usually the owner of the policy, but in many instances it is desired to place ownership in someone other than the insured. The use of ownership in a third party (the insured and the insurance company being the other two) is most widely used in business insurance cases and in certain estate planning situations. Such third party owner may be designated from the inception of the policy, or ownership may be transferred to him at some later time.

The vehicle for placing ownership in a third party depends on the practice of the particular insurance company. In many cases, an absolute assignment form is used. In other cases, owners are designated by making use of an "ownership clause" incorporated into the policy. Such clause resembles the absolute assignment in many respects, but it actually may be more limited in scope than the absolute assignment form. For example, the policy may refer to the rights exercisable by the "owner" of the policy. The policy may provide that the insured shall be the owner in the absence of a contrary provision. The application for the policy may request that the insured's wife or other third party be named as owner. A typical clause may be incorporated in the policy as follows:

Ownership—The insured is the owner of this policy unless otherwise provided in the application or by later transfer. Subject to the rights of any prior assignee, and unless the owner and the Company shall agree otherwise, all rights which are available while the insured is living are vested in the owner, and may be exercised by the owner without the consent of anyone else. Proceeds payable at the insured's death are payable to the beneficiary and not to the owner unless the owner is also named as the beneficiary.

If ownership is transferred after the policy is issued, and if company practice prescribes use of an ownership clause instead of an absolute assignment form, appropriate language is embodied in the policy or in the instrument of transfer. When an individual person is named as owner, an ownership clause offers more potential flexibility than the conventional form of assignment. Where company practice permits, it is useful when it is desired to name successive owners if the first owner dies before the insured. It is also useful to name an owner for a limited period of time, such as during minority, or until a specified date, or the occurrence of a specified event, with provisions for automatic transfer of ownership thereafter. However, company practices differ; many policies do not provide for an automatic change of ownership for any event other than the death of the owner.

Some policies may require physical endorsement of a transfer of ownership, while other policies may be transferred without an actual endorsement.

Naming of a contingent or successive owner is advantageous in some cases. Although it does not avoid death taxes in the estate of the owner, it enables the owner to avoid having the policy pass through his probate estate; and it is vital to the insurance company to know with whom it can deal after the death of the original owner.

In considering the inter vivos transfer of ownership by a third party owner, the problem that comes most immediately to mind is the common law requirement that one having an interest in a life insurance policy on another must have an insurable interest in the insured's life. The law of insurable interest as it relates to the naming of a beneficiary is fairly well settled. Almost without exception, an assignee or a transferee of ownership is not required to have an insurable interest, where the assignment or transfer is made in good faith.

Case Law

Cases involving successive transfers by third party owners of life insurance policies are scarce.[1] The Gray case illustrates the use of contingent or successive owners. The insured absolutely assigned a policy on

---

[1] *Gray* v. *Penn Mutual Life Insurance Co.,* 5 Ill. App. 2d 541, 126 N.E. 2d 409 (1955).

his life to his mother. Thereafter, she transferred ownership of the policy to herself under an ownership clause which read: "Edna A. Fonyo, while living, thereafter to Melvin A. Krauss, friend of the insured, while living, thereafter to the insured." The ownership clause provided that all rights of ownership in the policy were in the owners in the order specified. The mother died. Shortly thereafter, the insurance company made a policy loan to Krauss. Sometime later Krauss reassigned the policy to the insured, who on discovering the policy loan sought to have it set aside, on the theory that the attempted transfer to Krauss was an invalid testamentary disposition. The court said the transfer was not testamentary in character. The court cited with approval the Ellis case which involved a widow beneficiary who elected an interest option for herself, with a right of withdrawal and then directed that any proceeds at her death be paid to others.[2] The administrator of the estate attacked the arrangement, but the court held it was not a testamentary disposition.

Multiple Owners

Several persons may be designated as the owner, but generally the written joinder of all the owners is then required for the exercise of certain ownership rights. Because of this requirement, the gift of a policy to joint donees has been held to be a gift of a future interest and therefore not entitled to the $3,000 annual exclusion from gift taxes, since the right of any donee to enjoy the property depends upon the consent of others.[3] Similarly, premiums paid on a policy jointly owned by several donee-beneficiaries are also gifts of future interests because no one donee can act with respect to the property without the consent of the other owners.[4]

Companies cannot permit the "splitting" of all ownership rights, because the exercise of a right by one owner may affect the rights of another. For example, if one of several owners could individually make a loan against a portion of a policy, what would be the rights of each party upon a subsequent lapse? On the other hand, it might be possible (if there is no contrary provision) for one owner to assign his ownership rights without the consent of the other owners. However, in general, it is preferable to avoid multiple ownership and to have two or more policies issued, each separately owned.

Transfer of Ownership May Not Affect Death Benefits

It is important that the ownership clause of the policy be examined carefully to determine the contractual effect of a transfer. The owner may merely "stand in the shoes" of the insured. His rights may be limited to the rights which the insured himself might have exercised during his lifetime, and those rights may expire with the death of the insured. Since the insured himself could not have received the death benefit, the third

---

[2] *Mutual Benefit Life* v. *Ellis,* 125 F.2d 127 (2d Cir. 1942), cert. denied, 316 U.S. 665 (1942).

[3] *Nashville Trust Company* v. *Commissioner,* 2 CCH, TCM 922; Revenue Rule 55–408.

[4] *Skouras* v. *Commissioner,* 14 TC 523; 188 F.2d 831.

party owner likewise may not be automatically entitled to receive that death benefit. Accordingly, whenever ownership of a policy is transferred to someone other than the insured, it should also be determined whether a change of beneficiary to the owner should be made.

When someone other than the insured owns a policy and a third party is named as the beneficiary (e.g., where the husband transfers ownership in policies on his life to his wife who, in turn, names their children as beneficiary), at the husband's death it may be that the wife has made a taxable gift of the proceeds of the policy to the children. This is because the wife, as owner, had the right to name herself as beneficiary and did not do so; therefore, the wife may be considered to have made a gift to the children.

BENEFICIARY DESIGNATIONS

Life insurance policies issued today uniformly contain provisions permitting the designation of a beneficiary to receive the proceeds payable at the insured's death. There are additional provisions permitting the beneficiary to be changed and successively changed. All these provisions will usually be found under a heading such as "Beneficiary" or "Change of Beneficiary." Too frequently, just one beneficiary is named when a policy is issued, and the designation is not reviewed again for many years. This discussion will assume that the insured is the owner, except where the context clearly indicates otherwise.

Revocable and Irrevocable Beneficiaries

An insured normally reserves the right, on his sole signature, to designate and change the beneficiary. Such a beneficiary is said to be designated "revocably," and the modern rule prevailing in all but a few states is that such a beneficiary's interest is a mere expectancy. This being the case, the insured is allowed to exercise every right under the policy without the beneficiary's consent.

Where the right to change the beneficiary is not reserved, the designation of beneficiary is said to be "irrevocable." Here the beneficiary acquires a vested interest which the insured cannot change or defeat, except with the beneficiary's consent. There may be uncertainty as to the effect of an irrevocable beneficiary designation, in that, at one extreme, such beneficiary's interest may be limited merely to a requirement that his or her consent be obtained to effect a change of beneficiary but is not needed in order to exercise the other incidents of ownership. At the other extreme, the beneficiary may be regarded as actually possessing incidents of ownership jointly with the insured so as to require the beneficiary's consent before the insured may exercise any rights under the policy. This uncertainty may arise either because of the failure of a company to specify the rights that flow from an irrevocable beneficiary designation or because of different interpretations made by the courts. As a protection to the company, as well as to the other parties in interest, many companies specify the precise rights created by an irrevocable designation. Such a beneficiary clause may read as follows:

The insured hereunder having so requested, it is agreed and understood that the insured may not revoke and change the beneficiary designated under this policy during the beneficiary's lifetime without the written consent of the beneficiary so designated. While said policy remains payable to such beneficiary during the beneficiary's lifetime, the insured, without the written consent of such beneficiary, may not make loans on this policy, except for the sole purpose of paying a premium or premiums on this policy, or interest on any indebtedness on this policy, or both, and the insured may not exercise, without the written consent of such beneficiary, any other option, right, or privilege provided therein, including but not limited to the right to elect any of the nonforfeiture provisions thereof or the right to assign this policy. The insured and not the said beneficiary shall have the right to receive all amounts payable hereunder if this policy matures as an endowment.

Today the irrevocable beneficiary designation is in limited use. It is seen most frequently in agreements relating to separation and divorce, where provision for the maintenance of an insurance policy is included in the agreement, and where it is desired specifically to restrain the insured in the exercise of the various policy rights without actually transferring ownership to the beneficiary. Under the quoted form, if the irrevocable beneficiary predeceases the insured, the insured regains full control over the policy.

Primary and Contingent Beneficiaries

Consider this beneficiary designation: "Mary Doe, wife of the insured, if living at the death of the insured, otherwise to such of the lawful children of the insured as may be living at the death of the insured." Mary Doe is known as the "primary beneficiary"; the children, as "contingent beneficiaries." Two or more primary beneficiaries may be named to share the proceeds—for example, equally or all to the survivor—and contingent beneficiaries may be designated in the event that none of the primary beneficiaries survives the insured. Normally, it is considered good practice to designate a contingent beneficiary.

Most policies currently being issued provide that if all named beneficiaries die before the insured, the proceeds of the policy, at the insured's death, will then be paid to the insured's estate. Where the owner of the policy is someone other than the insured, however, it is usual to provide that if all named beneficiaries predecease the insured, the policy proceeds, at the insured's death, will be paid to the owner, or to the owner's estate.

Insurable Interest

The presence of insurable interest is required only at the inception of the policy and not upon a subsequent transfer of the policy or at maturity of the policy as a death claim.

For many years, there was doubt whether a policy, valid at its inception, could be payable to a beneficiary or an assignee who, at the death of the insured, had no "insurable interest" in the life of the insured. Broadly speaking, "insurable interest" arises either out of close family relationships or from substantial economic interest in the continued life of the person insured. In other words, there must be a reasonable ground to expect some benefit or advantage from the continuance of the insured's life. In more recent years, either by judicial decision or by statute, a person has been regarded as having an insurable interest in his own life. He may legally contract for insurance of which he is the owner and may generally name a beneficiary of his own choosing—even if the beneficiary has no insurable interest in the insured's life. However, if the policy is applied for and owned by someone other than the insured, the applicant-owner must have an insurable interest in the life of the insured.

Identity of the Beneficiary

The following are several of the more popular types of beneficiary designation:

The Insured's Estate.   The proceeds may be made payable to the executors or administrators of the insured and thereby added to the other probate assets of the estate. This arrangement is useful if the proceeds are intended to cover debts, funeral expenses, taxes, and expenses of administering the estate. However, such a designation may subject the proceeds to state inheritance taxes and increase the administration expenses of the estate. In addition, such a designation will subject the proceeds to claims of creditors of the estate. These results may be avoided in whole or in part by designating a named beneficiary such as the insured's wife to receive the proceeds.

Specifically Named Persons.   The most commonly used designation names the wife of the insured as primary beneficiary, with the children as contingent beneficiaries. The designation may read: "Mary Doe, wife of the insured, if living at the death of the insured, otherwise to such of John Doe and Susan Doe, children of the insured, equally, or to the survivor of them, at the death of the insured." It is customary to describe the beneficiary by reference to his relationship to the insured.

Class Designations.   It is sometimes desired to designate a group of persons without identifying the individual members of the group. This is known as a class designation. The designation of "lawful children of the insured" is a common example of such a class designation. The beneficiaries actually entitled to receive the proceeds at the death of the insured will be determined by the members of the class in existence at that time. Such a designation automatically includes members of the class who may be born after the date of the beneficiary designation and before the insured's death. Companies tend to limit the designation of this type of beneficiary to classes of people closely related to the insured, where the members of the class are easily identified.

When it is desired to name children as beneficiaries, the simplest and usually the safest way is to designate "children of the insured" as a class. If the children are designated by name as "John Doe and Susan Doe, children of the insured," then unnamed children or children born after the date of the beneficiary designation will be excluded. If this result is not desired, "children of the insured," or "children of the insured, including John Doe and Susan Doe," should be designated.

One word concerning adopted children: Adoption proceedings may require months or even years in some states. Until the proceedings are completed, such children would not be included in a class designation such as "children of the insured." To share in the proceeds before adoption proceedings have been completed, their names would have to be included specifically in the beneficiary designation.

In any class designation the company will usually require an exculpatory clause in the designation which permits the company, in determining the identity and the existence of the persons in the class, to rely upon an affidavit or other evidence satisfactory to it. For example, if "children" as a class are designated, the company may not know the names and addresses of all the children. Such a clause may read as follows:

The Company, in determining the existence, identity, ages or any other facts relating to any persons designated as beneficiary herein, either as a class or otherwise, may rely solely upon any affidavit or other evidence deemed satisfactory by the Company, and each and every payment made by the Company in reliance thereon shall, to the extent of such payment, be a valid discharge of the Company's obligation under this policy.

"Per Stirpes" or "Per Capita"?

"Per stirpes" and "per capita" are legal terms that describe alternative methods of distributing property to one's descendants. Which method of distribution was intended by a decedent is not always an easy question to answer.

To illustrate the problem, let us assume that an insured has in mind that the proceeds of his policy shall be paid to his children, John, William, and Mary, or to the survivor or surviving children of a deceased child. Suppose John and Mary die before the insured. John leaves four children surviving him. Mary has no children. How shall the proceeds of the policy be distributed at the insured's death? To answer this question requires a determination of the insured's intent when he spelled out the beneficiary designation.

"Per stirpes" means "by branches" of the family. A per stirpes distribution gives the share of the deceased child to his children. Accordingly, under a per stirpes distribution, William would take one half of the proceeds, and John's surviving children would divide the other half among them.

"Per capita," on the other hand, means "by heads." A per capita distribution will give one share of the proceeds to each beneficiary. On a per capita basis, William and each of John's four children would receive one fifth of the proceeds.

Per stirpes distributions are more popular. In any case, it is most important that the request for a beneficiary designation reflect the distribution desired by the insured, and that such distribution be clearly set forth in the actual beneficiary designation.

Business Organizations

An insured may name a corporation or a partnership as beneficiary in the same manner as he would an individual. The problems here are essentially the same as with the individually designated beneficiary. Where it is intended that the proceeds of a life insurance policy be received by a partnership, it is advisable to designate the partnership itself as a beneficiary to receive the proceeds rather than designating the individual partners by name to receive the proceeds on behalf of the partnership. Where the partnership itself is designated as beneficiary, additions or withdrawals of partners will present no problem as to the proper payee of the proceeds at the death of the insured. Such a designation might read: "Brown and Company, a partnership, or its assigns."

As for naming a corporation, the customary form is: "The XYZ Company, a Pennsylvania corporation, its successors or assigns." The use of the phrase "its successors or assigns" will cover a possible change in the corporate structure, such as a merger or consolidation occurring after the date of the beneficiary designation and before the death of the insured.

When naming a corporation as beneficiary, it is wise to check the exact corporate title. A corporation may be popularly known by one name, but its correct corporate title may be quite different. Moreover, several corporations may have similar names. This is particularly true in the case of charitable organizations, such as hospitals, churches, or homes for the ill or aged.

Trustees

The insured may wish to have the death proceeds paid to a trustee who will administer the fund for the beneficiaries of a trust. On policies for larger amounts, the use of trustees for lump sum settlements has been greatly on the increase with a corresponding diminution in arrangements for life companies to retain the proceeds under settlement options. The trust may be established by the insured either by agreement during his lifetime or at death under the terms of his will.

Where the life insurance trust agreement created during lifetime is used, a typical trustee beneficiary designation would read: "Henry Black and the XYZ Trust Company, as trustees, their successor or successors in trust, under trust agreement dated _____. . . ." The insured's wife is often named as an individual co-trustee. Additional language is frequently included in the beneficiary designation by the life insurance company, the effect of which is to relieve the life insurance company of any responsibility for the proper administration of the insurance proceeds once they are paid over to the trust.

Some insureds name the wife as primary beneficiary and the trustee as contingent beneficiary. The proceeds may be paid to the wife in one sum, or they may be retained or distributed for the wife's benefit under one or more of the optional modes of settlement discussed in the following chapter.

The trust arrangement should be carefully studied to be sure whether the trustees are merely to be named beneficiaries, or whether, as is often the case with an irrevocable trust, ownership of the policy should be transferred to the trustees.

The designation of trustees under the insured's will as beneficiary introduces complications which are avoided by a signed agreement executed during the lifetime of the insured. A trust created under a will can take no effect if the will fails to qualify for probate or if it should be declared invalid for any reason. There may be a question of the validity of such an arrangement under some state laws. There is a danger that the insured may change his will and forget to change the benficiary designation that ties into the will. A new will may name no trustee. Even if one is named, the insured may no longer desire the proceeds of the particular life insurance policy to be payable to the trustees under the will.

The will may create two or more trusts with different trustees, and a problem would be presented as to which trustee should receive the proceeds. In spite of these potential complications, the practice of the designation of testamentary trustees as beneficiaries has increased during recent years. Several states have passed laws which encourage the practice by specifically providing that proceeds payable to a testamentary trustee will not attract state inheritance taxes and will not be subject to the claims of creditors. An example of this type of law may be found in Section 13–3.3 of the New York Estates Powers and Trusts Law. Prior to these special laws, it was felt that proceeds payable to a testamentary trustee would be subject to claims of creditors and subject to state inheritance tax in the same manner as if the proceeds were payable to the insured's estate. The designation of trustees under the insured's will as beneficiaries should not be attempted without the advice of the insured's lawyer. The following is an example of one form for designation of a testamentary trustee:

The proceeds shall be paid to the trustees designated under the insured's will or their successor or successors in trust; but if the company receives written evidence satisfactory to it that:

1. The trustees for any reason fail to serve and no successor trustee was appointed; or
2. A will of the insured, which was admitted to probate, made no provision for trustees; or
3. A personal representative of the insured has been appointed in intestacy;

then, in any such event, the proceeds shall be paid to the executors or administrators of the insured; provided, however, that the company shall be fully discharged for any payment made to said trustees before receipt of written evidence satisfactory to it that said trustees are not entitled to payment under the provisions of this Designation; provided further, however, that if there is more than one trust established under the probated will of the insured, the proceeds shall be divided among such trusts in such proportion as shall be designated in writing to the Company by the executors of the insured, and the Company shall be fully discharged in making payment to such trustee or trustees in the proportions so designated.

Minor Beneficiaries

Under the common law, a minor under the age of 21 cannot give a valid release for receipt of life insurance proceeds. Many states have lowered the age at which a minor, or in some cases a married minor, attains majority. In many states there are statutes applying to the minor's rights to receive benefits which permit payment of a modest amount, such as $2,000 or $3,000, directly to a minor who has attained a specified age (such as 16 or 18) or to the probate judge or other official for the benefit of the minor. If one of these special statutes does not apply, it is necessary to have a guardian appointed to receive payment on behalf of the minor, with the attendant formality, expense, legal steps, and numerous restrictions as to who may be guardian and what he may do with and without specific court approval.

The problem is simplified by permitting the proceeds to be retained at interest by the company with the full right reserved for the minor's benefit to withdraw or to elect any other settlement option in the policy. The minor is named as beneficiary, but it is provided that if he is still a minor at the time for payment to him, a trustee, rather than a guardian, will receive the payments on behalf of the minor and may exercise the specified withdrawal privileges. The trustee is also empowered to select one or more of the installment options in the policy in lieu of the interest option. The trustee may be appointed under a separate formal trust agreement or, under the practice followed by some companies, may be named in the settlement agreement or beneficiary clause. There also may be provision for a successor trustee if the one first named fails to serve or ceases to serve. When there is no separate trust agreement, the settlement agreement itself may contain simple trust provisions to the effect that the trustee shall hold and expend the monies received from the life insurance company for the benefit of the minor until the age of majority and shall then pay him any unexpended funds. The extent to which these various procedures may be utilized will depend on company practice in each case.

How to Designate and Change Beneficiaries

The first beneficiary designation usually appears in the application for the policy. Requirements for subsequent change are given in the policy, with which compliance ordinarily is easy. Typically, the policy provides that the request for change shall be made in writing on a form satisfactory to the company, and each company supplies forms for this purpose. Most of the older policies require endorsement of the policy to effect a change of beneficiary, but the modern trend is to make the change effective after approval or recording of a form filed with the company without physically endorsing the policy.

There are instances where an insured desires to change the beneficiary but for some reason is unable to comply with all the prescribed formalities. For example, the policy may require its submission for endorsement of the change, but the present beneficiary may be wrongfully withholding possession from the insured. As another example, the insured may execute the forms, mail them to the insurance company, and then die before the company has completed its formalities. The majority rule applicable in such cases is that if the insured does all that he reasonably could be expected to do in order to indicate his intention to make the change, the change will be deemed to have been accomplished. Generally, a beneficiary change cannot be made by a will or a codicil to a will.

Ordinarily, a change in the relationship of the parties will not of itself affect an existing beneficiary designation. Suppose "Jane Doe, wife of the insured," is designated as beneficiary under her husband's policy and that Jane and her husband are divorced. Further suppose that the husband does not change the beneficiary. Unless the divorce decree or a specific statute in the particular state terminates a divorced wife's interest in the policy, Jane would be entitled to receive the proceeds upon the death of her ex-husband. Courts rule that the words "wife of the insured" are merely descriptive of the relationship and that the insured intends that the proceeds shall be paid to the named individual.

Simultaneous Death Clauses

An insured and his wife rarely die simultaneously, whether in a common accident or otherwise. However, the contingency should be considered. As mentioned previously a popular beneficiary arrangement may provide, in substance: "Jane Smith, wife of the insured, if living at the death of the insured, otherwise equally to such of the children of the insured as may be living at the death of the insured." Under such a designation, if the wife survives the insured for only a few moments, her estate will be entitled to payment of the proceeds. Accordingly, the proceeds will be exposed to probate expenses in her estate and possible claims of her creditors. In addition, the proceeds will pass in accordance with the terms of her will, or if she left no will, to her next of kin under the intestate laws of the state having jurisdiction. This result can be avoided by making all or a portion of the proceeds payable to the wife under the interest option subject to her full right of withdrawal, and naming children or other persons as contingent beneficiaries to receive any proceeds remaining with the company whether the wife dies before or after the insured. If the wife dies shortly after the insured, she presumably will not have expressed her right of withdrawal.

Another variation is to require that the wife survive the insured for a specified period, not to exceed six months. If the wife survives the specified period and then dies, the proceeds will become part of her estate, as in the case of the designation first described in the preceding paragraph. The wife is not protected against possible claims of her creditors, as she would be under the standard clauses incorporated in agreements using the interest option or other settlement options. Further, this second procedure may have disadvantageous estate tax results; in larger estates where qualification for the marital deduction will minimize federal estate taxes, the deduction is lost if a common disaster actually occurs, and if the wife dies after the insured's death and within the period specified.

It has been suggested that when proceeds are payable in one sum, the Uniform Simultaneous Death Act, which is in force in practically all states, takes care of the contingency of common accident or common disaster. This is not the case. That Act merely provides that if it cannot be determined whether the insured or the beneficiary died first, the insured will be presumed to have survived. Where the wife survived the insured by as little as a few minutes, the Uniform Simultaneous Death Act obviously does not apply. Also, provisions and concepts predicated on parties dying "as a result of a common disaster" are basically ambiguous and indefinite in meaning and effect, since one party may live for days, months, or even years and still die as a result of a common disaster.

If from an overall estate planning viewpoint it is vital that the proceeds qualify for marital deduction purposes in the event of death in a common disaster, the settlement agreement may incorporate a "reverse common disaster presumption." This expression refers to a provision that if the insured and his spouse, the primary beneficiary under the policy, die in such circumstances that it cannot be determined who died first, it will be presumed that the beneficiary survived the insured. The presumption created by this clause will be recognized for marital deduction purposes under the Internal Revenue Code.

State Creditor Exemption Statutes and Their Effect

Practically all states, by statute, place life insurance beyond the reach of creditors of the insured to some degree and under some circumstances. These statutes are known as "exemption statutes," and their provisions vary greatly. Under the most common type of statute the exemption applies if premiums are not paid in fraud of creditors and the policies are payable to or for the benefit of the wife, children, or other relatives dependent on the insured, even though the insured retains the right to change the beneficiary. Some statutes apply the exemption if the policy is payable to any beneficiary other than the insured's estate. In a few states the exemption is limited to some stated amount of proceeds or to proceeds purchased by a stated amount of annual premium.

Spendthrift Clauses and Their Use

Spendthrift clauses are concerned with creditors of the beneficiary, not creditors of the insured. There are a few states whose statutes automatically provide certain exemptions for life insurance proceeds from claims of the beneficiary's creditors. In a substantial number of states, though, by statute or by court decisions, the policyowner may use a so-called "spendthrift clause" if settlement options are specified for the beneficiary. Life insurance companies customarily include spendthrift clauses in agreements by which optional modes of settlement are elected. A typical clause reads as follows:

Unless otherwise provided in this settlement option agreement, no beneficiary may commute, anticipate, encumber, alienate, withdraw, or assign any portion of his share of the proceeds. To the extent permitted by law, no payments to a beneficiary will be subject to his debts, contracts, or engagements, nor may they be levied upon or attached.

In a very few states, such spendthrift clauses apparently are considered to be against the public policy of the state and will not be upheld.

Federal Tax Liens

State exemption statutes do not give full protection against creditors if the creditor is the United States government under a federal tax lien against the insured. In such instances, the government may reach the lifetime values, even though the taxpayer-insured may have designated his wife, child, or dependent relative as beneficiary. If a lien arises against the insured during his lifetime, and the insured then dies, the government can reach the proceeds to the extent of the cash value just prior to the day of death. If the beneficiary owes taxes, the government, after the insured's death, could reach the proceeds payable to the beneficiary under a lien arising against the beneficiary.

COLLATERAL ASSIGNMENTS

Life insurance contracts are freely assignable by the policyowner unless some limitation is placed in the policy. Life insurance companies routinely furnish assignment forms. By an assignment, the owner transfers his rights in the policy to the assignee. The extent to which these rights are transferred depends upon the provisions of the policy concerning assignments, the intention of the parties as expressed in the assignment form, and the circumstances surrounding the actual assignment.

Types of Assignments

Assignments are conventionally of two types: absolute and collateral. The absolute assignment normally is intended to give the assignee every right in the policy that the owner possessed before the assignment. When the transaction is completed, the prior owner will have no further interest in the policy. The phraseology of absolute assignments differs. In essence, it is stated that the policyowner transfers to the assignee all his rights, title, and interest in the policy. As was discussed in the first section of this chapter, some companies use an "ownership clause" to accomplish the assignment or transfer of ownership rights.

The collateral assignment, on the other hand, is a more limited type of transfer. It contemplates a security arrangement to protect the assignee who has made a loan, taking the policy as security for repayment. After the indebtedness is repaid, it is contemplated that the assignee will release his interest in the policy, i.e., that he will transfer back the rights transferred by the assignment. If the collateral assignment is still in force at the death of the insured, under usual procedure the assignee certifies to the insurance company the amount of indebtedness, including interest at that time, and receives that amount in a lump sum. Any excess proceeds are then payable to the named beneficiary in accordance with the beneficiary designation.

ABA Assignment Form

Even though the arrangement is one merely of security calling for a collateral assignment, many lenders insist on receiving a form called an "absolute assignment." This insistence probably stems from the practice of some life insurance companies of demanding joint signatures of the assignor and the assignee if the latter wishes to deal with the policy. Even the use of the absolute assignment form may not assure the assignee in every case that the company will deal with him alone. Despite the sweeping language, it may not spell out clearly the prematurity rights the assignee is intended to have. Too often the parties to the assignment fail to make their intentions plain in this respect. For example, should the assignee alone be permitted to surrender the policy for its cash value if such value is less than the obligation for which the policy was assigned?

Problems such as these led to the creation of a middle-ground form of assignment through the joint efforts of the Bank Management Commission of the American Bankers Association and representatives of the Association of Life Insurance Counsel. This form is shown as Figure 53–1. It states five specific rights that pass to the assignee and that may be exercised by the assignee alone. Included is the sole right to collect the proceeds at the death of the insured or on the date of the maturity of the policy, and the sole right to surrender the policy for its cash surrender value. Without impairing the right of the assignee to surrender the policy, certain rights are reserved to the insured. Included are the right to receive disability benefits that do not reduce the amount of insurance, and the right to designate and change the beneficiary. Also, the assignee promises not to surrender the policy without giving the insured notice of his intention to surrender. The assignee also promises that any amount received at death, maturity, or surrender which is in excess of existing liabilities will be paid to the persons otherwise entitled thereto under the policy. This so-called "ABA assignment form" is now in use by many banks, and is recommended by a substantial number of insurance companies. In fact, many companies have adopted it as their own standard form.

Notice of Assignment to the Insurance Company

To protect the assignee fully, notice must be given the life insurance company that the assignment has been made. If a company with no notice of assignment makes payment of the proceeds to another assignee or to a named beneficiary, it cannot be made to pay a second time. A typical policy provision concerning assignments is: "No assignment shall be binding upon the company until the original or a duplicate thereof is filed at its home office. The company assumes no obligation as to the effect, sufficiency, or validity of any assignment. All assignments shall be subject to any indebtedness to the company on this policy."

Need the Beneficiary Be Changed before Assignment of the Policy?

Some modern policies and some beneficiary forms provide, in effect, that "the rights of any revocable beneficiary will be subordinate to the rights of any assignee of record with the company, whether the assignment was made before or after the date of the beneficiary designation." When this provision appears, most banks will accept the assignment, and most life insurance companies will record the assignment without change of beneficiary. Unless there is clear-cut language in the policy that the beneficiary's interest is diminished by an assignment, or unless the assignment is to be made to the beneficiary named in the policy or the beneficiary joins in executing the assignment, the best practice is to change the beneficiary to the insured's (owner's) estate prior to making the assignment. Frequently, a second change of beneficiary is made, to be recorded im-

FIGURE 53–1.   ABA-10 Collateral Assignment Form

FORM APPROVED BY
BANK MANAGEMENT COMMISSION
AMERICAN BANKERS ASSOCIATION

FORM No. 10—LIFE INSURANCE ASSIGNMENT

ASSIGNMENT OF LIFE INSURANCE POLICY AS COLLATERAL

A.   *For Value Received* the undersigned hereby assign, transfer and set over to_____
_____of_____
_____ its successors and assigns, (herein called the "Assignee") Policy No._____issued by

(herein called the "Insurer") and any supplementary contracts issued in connection therewith (said policy and contracts being herein called the "Policy"), upon the life of_____
of_____and all claims, options, privileges, rights, title and interest therein and thereunder (except as provided in Paragraph C hereof), subject to all the terms and conditions of the Policy and to all superior liens, if any, which the Insurer may have against the Policy. The undersigned by this instrument jointly and severally agree and the Assignee by the acceptance of this assignment agrees to the conditions and provisions herein set forth.

B.   It is expressly agreed that, without detracting from the generality of the foregoing, the following specific rights are included in this assignment and pass by virtue hereof:
1. The sole right to collect from the Insurer the net proceeds of the Policy when it becomes a claim by death or maturity;
2. The sole right to surrender the Policy and receive the surrender value thereof at any time provided by the terms of the Policy and at such other times as the Insurer may allow;
3. The sole right to obtain one or more loans or advances on the Policy, either from the Insurer or, at any time, from other persons, and to pledge or assign the Policy as security for such loans or advances;
4. The sole right to collect and receive all distributions or shares of surplus, dividend deposits or additions to the Policy now or hereafter made or apportioned thereto, and to exercise any and all options contained in the Policy with respect thereto; provided, that unless and until the Assignee shall notify the Insurer in writing to the contrary, the distributions or shares of surplus, dividend deposits and additions shall continue on the plan in force at the time of this assignment; and
5. The sole right to exercise all nonforfeiture rights permitted by the terms of the Policy or allowed by the Insurer and to receive all benefits and advantages derived therefrom.

C.   It is expressly agreed that the following specific rights, so long as the Policy has not been surrendered, are reserved and excluded from this assignment and do not pass by virtue hereof:
1. The right to collect from the Insurer any disability benefit payable in cash that does not reduce the amount of insurance;
2. The right to designate and change the beneficiary; and
3. The right to elect any optional mode of settlement permitted by the Policy or allowed by the Insurer;
but the reservation of these rights shall in no way impair the right of the Assignee to surrender the Policy completely with all its incidents or impair any other right of the Assignee hereunder, and any designation or change of beneficiary or election of a mode of settlement shall be made subject to and to the rights of the Assignee hereunder.

D.   This assignment is made and the Policy is to be held as collateral security for any and all liabilities of the undersigned, or any of them, to the Assignee, either now existing or that may hereafter arise in the ordinary course of business between any of the undersigned and the Assignee (all of which liabilities secured or to become secured are herein called "Liabilities").

E.   The Assignee covenants and agrees with the undersigned as follows:
1. That any balance of sums received hereunder from the Insurer remaining after payment of the then existing Liabilities, matured or unmatured, shall be paid by the Assignee to the persons entitled thereto under the terms of the Policy had this assignment not been executed;
2. That the Assignee will not exercise either the right to surrender the Policy or (except for the purpose of paying premiums) the right to obtain policy loans from the Insurer, until there has been default in any of the Liabilities or a failure to pay any premium when due, nor until twenty days after the Assignee shall have mailed, by first-class mail, to the undersigned at the addresses last supplied in writing to the Assignee specifically referring to this assignment, notice of intention to exercise such right; and
3. That the Assignee will upon request forward without unreasonable delay to the Insurer the Policy for endorsement of any designation or change of beneficiary or any election of an optional mode of settlement.

F.   The Insurer is hereby authorized to recognize the Assignee's claims to right hereunder without investigating the reason for any action taken by the Assignee, or the validity or the amount of the Liabilities or the existence of any default therein, or the giving of any notice under Paragraph E (2) above or otherwise, or the application to be made by the Assignee of any amounts to be paid to the Assignee. The sole signature of the Assignee shall be sufficient for the exercise of any rights under the Policy assigned hereby and the sole receipt of the Assignee for any sums received shall be a full discharge and release therefor to the Insurer. Checks for all or any part of the sums payable under the Policy and assigned herein, shall be drawn to the exclusive order of the Assignee if, when, and in such amounts as may be, requested by the Assignee.

G.   The Assignee shall be under no obligation to pay any premium, or the principal of or interest on any loans or advances on the Policy whether or not obtained by the Assignee, or any other charges on the Policy, but any such amounts so paid by the Assignee from its own funds, shall become a part of the Liabilities hereby secured, shall be due immediately, and shall draw interest at a rate fixed by the Assignee from time to time not exceeding 6% per annum.

H.   The exercise of any right, option, privilege or power given herein to the Assignee shall be at the option of the Assignee, but (except as restricted by Paragraph E (2) above) the Assignee may exercise any such right, option, privilege or power without notice to, or assent by, or affecting the liability of, or releasing any interest hereby assigned by the undersigned, or any of them.

I.   The Assignee may release or release other security, may release any party primarily or secondarily liable for any of the Liabilities, may grant extensions, renewals or indulgences with respect to the Liabilities, or may apply to the Liabilities in such order as the Assignee shall determine, the proceeds of the Policy hereby assigned or any amount received on account of the Policy by the exercise of any right permitted under this assignment, without resorting or regard to other security.

J.   In the event of any conflict between the provisions of this assignment and provisions of the note or other evidence of any Liability, with respect to the Policy or rights of collateral security therein, the provisions of this assignment shall prevail.

K.   Each of the undersigned declares that no proceedings in bankruptcy are pending against him and that his property is not subject to any assignment for the benefit of creditors.

Signed and sealed this_____day of_____, 19____.

_____   _____(L.S.)
Witness   *Insured or Owner*

_____   _____
                                                                            Address

_____   _____(L.S.)
Witness   *Beneficiary*

                                                                       _____
                                                                            Address

mediately following the assignment, to reinstate the beneficiary designation. At least one company follows the procedure of incorporating requests for both changes of beneficiary in the assignment form itself.

If someone other than the assignee is designated as beneficiary at the time the assignment is made, and if this possibility and its effect are not covered in the policy or the beneficiary designation form, there is a question under the court decisions in several states whether the assignee or the named beneficiary will be entitled to payment of the proceeds when the insured dies. A different answer may be given in the case of an absolute assignment than in the case of a collateral assignment transaction.

As respects absolute assignments, one view interprets the assignment either as a change of beneficiary or as the destruction of the interest of the beneficiary. Under this view, the assignee is entitled to receive the proceeds of the policy when the insured dies. Under the opposite view, the policy specifies a definite procedure for changing the beneficiary, and this procedure must be followed. The theory in support of this view is that the named beneficiary would have received the proceeds at the insured's death had there been no assignment, and a mere change in ownership rights should not change this concept or this result. It is important to give the absolute assignee the rights of a beneficiary as well as ownership rights.

When the question has been litigated under a transaction in which an assignment was given as collateral security for money loaned, most courts have ruled that the rights of the assignee are superior to those of a revocable beneficiary. Since assignments are used so frequently in collateral security transactions, there are compelling business reasons for a rule of law that will give maximum protection to those who lend money with policy values as security. However, a few courts have ruled that the beneficiary cannot be deprived of his interest without his consent, unless a change of beneficiary is made exactly as provided in the policy.

Obviously, troublesome questions such as those just described can be avoided by a change of beneficiary prior to making the assignment when that procedure is indicated.

IMPORTANCE OF KEEPING CURRENT

A sufficient number of problems has been discussed in this chapter to indicate the need for careful study of all the facts when an insured considers the designation of a beneficiary or the transfer of ownership or the making of an assignment of his policy. Beneficiary designations become outmoded with the passage of time. Countless beneficiary designations and assignments now in existence may one day pose problems ranging from delay in payment of proceeds to exclusion of those whom the insured had intended should share as beneficiaries. Lawyers, life underwriters, trust officers, accountants, and people in home offices and field offices of life insurance companies can render a significant service by being on the alert to discover these problem areas and then calling them to the insured's attention either for correction of an existing transaction, or, if the transaction is not yet concluded, so that the necessary steps may be taken to avoid the problem.

SELECTED REFERENCES

Best's Settlement Options: The Programming Manual. Morristown, N.J. Annual editions.

Dibrell, Charles G., Jr. "Life Insurance Policies—Transfers by Third Party Owners," *The Forum,* Vol. IV, No. 1 (October 1968), p. 26.

Maclean, Joseph B. *Life Insurance.* 9th ed. New York: McGraw-Hill Book Co., Inc., 1962.

McGill, Dan M. (ed.). *The Beneficiary in Life Insurance.* Rev. ed. Homewood, Ill.: Richard D. Irwin, Inc., 1956.

54

Settlement Options

By LAWRENCE R. BROWN, JR.

THE SETTLEMENT OPTIONS contained in life insurance policies provide the policyowner and his beneficiaries with the means of obtaining a planned income arrangement on a guaranteed basis. They were developed by life insurance companies in response to the demands of the public for security of income, the need for which was brought into sharp focus by the depression of the 1930s, the enactment of the Social Security Act, and the development of government and private group insurance and pension programs.

The public's use of settlement options grew rapidly over the years to a peak in 1967 when $940 million of new life insurance proceeds were left under settlement options and over $1.1 billion in income payments were made by the companies out of proceeds already under option. Since 1967 there has been a slight decrease in the total amount of new life insurance proceeds left under settlement options. Several things have contributed to this decline, principally inflation and the high interest rates available.

SETTLEMENT OPTIONS DEFINED

Most individual life insurance policies specifically provide that the proceeds will be paid in a lump sum in the absence of some other written direction of the policyowner or beneficiary. However, those policies generally also offer four optional methods for settlement of the proceeds: (1) the interest option, (2) the fixed-amount option, (3) the fixed-period option, and (4) the life income option. Subject to individual company rules, these four "settlement options" may be used singly or in combination. Additional options often can be obtained by request, and some or all of the options may be obtainable in forms of policies other than individual life insurance policies, such as group life insurance and certain annuity contracts.

The Lump Sum Settlement

Although the lump-sum settlement of proceeds is not usually referred to as a "settlement option," in some life insurance policies it is in fact an optional method of settlement, since in those policies the proceeds are specifically payable in installments unless otherwise directed. In any event, the essential decision to be made with regard to life insurance proceeds is whether to have them paid to the beneficiary in a lump sum or under the settlement options. This decision ordinarily is the policyowner's to make, but it often confronts the beneficiary as well. If the proceeds are payable in a lump sum, the beneficiary usually can elect to receive payment under one or a combination of the settlement options.

In certain situations the lump-sum settlement may be appropriate. If the policyowner has already created a trust or creates a trust in his will to provide for his beneficiaries, ordinarily the proceeds should be payable in a lump sum to the trust. On the other hand, the policyowner may wish the beneficiary to have the cash for a given purpose or to expend as he or she deems best. However, since many policyowners automatically elect to have the proceeds paid to their beneficiaries in a lump sum, it is appropriate to mention here some of the disadvantages inherent in a lump-sum settlement:

1. It does not protect against the possibility that the beneficiary may survive the insured by only a short period of time, whether because of death due to a "common disaster" or otherwise. In that event, the proceeds will pass through the beneficiary's probate estate, incurring unnecessary probate costs and possibly being distributed under the beneficiary's will to persons other than those desired by the policyowner. In addition, the proceeds may be subjected to death taxes in the beneficiary's estate. It may well be that the particular insurance company will permit the inclusion in the lump-sum settlement of a "common disaster" or "delayed payment" clause to help solve this problem. However, such a clause should not be used unless its use is consistent with the policyowner's general estate plan.

2. It does not protect against creditors of the beneficiary. Such protection can usually be obtained by the policyowner by inserting a creditor-protection or "spendthrift" clause in the settlement option election executed before the insured's death. Usually, such a clause provides that the beneficiary cannot withdraw or assign the proceeds unless otherwise stipulated in the election and that proceeds shall be free of attachment by creditors to the extent permitted by law.

3. It may result in imposing unnecessary restrictions on the beneficiary's election of an income settlement plan. Although most companies allow the policyowner to elect income arrangements not specifically provided by the policy, they usually are not as liberal with elections by a beneficiary who has been designated to receive a lump-sum payment.

4. It may cause the beneficiary to lose interest on the proceeds between the date of the insured's death and the date on which payment is made or an income settlement plan is elected. Many policies do not provide for such interest, but some companies do allow interest for a limited period after date of death, the duration of the period varying among companies.

The above-mentioned disadvantages of the lump-sum settlement should be given due consideration in the determination of the manner in which the proceeds are to be paid.

The Interest Option

Under the interest option, proceeds are retained by the company and interest at a minimum guaranteed rate is paid to the beneficiary monthly, quarterly, semiannually, or annually. Many companies pay surplus, or excess, interest if any is earned above the minimum rate, either at the end of each year or in the same periodic manner as the basic guaranteed payments. An unlimited withdrawal right may be given the beneficiary, or withdrawals may be limited to a specified annual sum or to a total cumulative amount. The beneficiary also may be given the right to elect another settlement option or combination of options; or it may be directed that such a change occur automatically at some stated age or date, or on the happening of a specified event.

The Fixed-Period Option

The fixed-period option provides for proceeds to be paid in equal monthly (or less frequent) installments, liquidating principal with interest over a specified period of years, from one to as many as 25 or 30 years. The specified rate of payment per $1,000 of proceeds is based on a guaranteed interest factor, and any surplus interest declared may be paid at the end of each year or used to increase the next year's installments. Usually, the payee may be given the right to commute all remaining unpaid installments and withdraw in a lump sum; but because of the nature of this option, partial withdrawals are not generally permitted.

The Fixed-Amount Option

Under the fixed-amount option, proceeds are payable in regular installments of specified amount until principal and interest are exhausted. Basically similar to the fixed-period option, and usually based on the same guaranteed interest factor in a given policy, the fixed-amount option is much more flexible. Generally, the beneficiary may be given the right to withdraw principal or to elect other options as outlined above for the interest option. In addition, the level of installment payments may be varied to meet certain needs. For example, payments might be specified at the rate of $100 per month for two years, $75 per month for the next year, and $50 per month thereafter until proceeds and interest are exhausted. The effects of increases or decreases in total proceeds arising from surplus interest, dividends, or loans are quite different from those applying to the fixed-period option. Such factors will affect the length of time over which fixed-amount installments are payable, but not the amount of each installment.

The Life Income Options

The life income or annuity option provides orderly liquidation of proceeds with interest over the payee's entire lifetime. It is peculiar to life insurance companies, as no other financial institution provides a guarantee of income for life.

The amount of each periodic installment per $1,000 of proceeds is determined by the type of annuity selected, the rate of interest, the age of the payee when the income commences, and the sex of the payee. The four principal forms of life income options are outlined below. Not all policies contain these four types of life income options or all their variations; however, those not provided in the policy often may be secured by special request.

Life Income Option. The life income option provides that installments are payable as long as the payee lives, with no guarantee that total payments will equal the principal sum. Because there is no guarantee to return principal, this option provides the highest rate of life income. However, most people wish to avoid the risk of capital loss through early death of the life annuity payee because they have other relatives whom they wish to protect. For example, this form of pure life annuity income normally would not be used for a widow with young children, because it affords the children no protection in case of their mother's early death.

Refund Life Income Option. Under the refund life income option, payments are guaranteed as long as the payee lives, but if his or her death occurs before receiving an amount equal to the principal sum, the difference between total payments and the principal sum is paid to a second payee.

Life Income Option with Period Certain. Under a period certain option, payments are guaranteed for as long as the payee lives, but should death occur before payments have been made for a specified number of "years (or months) certain," installments may be continued to successive payees until the end of the certain period, or the commuted value of unpaid certain installments may be paid in cash or in some other specified manner. Usually, the certain period runs for 5, 10, 15, or 20 years, the most popular periods being 10 and 20 years.

Joint and Survivorship Life Income Option. A variation of the life income option provides an income for two lives, usually for the lifetime of the insured and his wife when the insured retires. Often the option also can be used for two beneficiaries, such as parents, upon the death of the insured. Under some plans, payments are continued in the same amount to the second payee. In others, at the death of one payee, instalments are reduced to three fourths, two thirds, or one half of the original amount for the second payee's remaining lifetime.

SPECIAL ARRANGEMENTS AND POLICIES

A wide variety of income payment patterns may be arranged by using the various options outlined above. For example, special educational settlement plans and family income or family maintenance options are sometimes offered. Many companies offer special policies payable directly in income, the construction of which is based on one or more of the standard options. Finally, most companies will permit the proceeds to be paid in any other manner mutually agreeable to the policyowner and the company.

USE OF SETTLEMENT OPTIONS

Experience has proved that many beneficiaries are unable to invest properly the funds received through life insurance. Of course, the capabilities and needs of each person's family vary, but settlement options are a vehicle by which each policyowner can provide a planned income arrangement to meet the basic needs of his family. Selecting the proper optional method of settlement is as important as properly disposing of property by a will. In neither case should an improvident beneficiary be given unlimited access to funds nor should the access to funds be so restricted as to impose a severe hardship on the beneficiary. Various uses of settlement options are discussed below from the standpoint of meeting the major family needs at the death of the breadwinner.

Cash Funds

There are at least three principal needs for having cash readily available: the immediate cash or cleanup fund, the mortgage cancellation fund, and the emergency fund. Though these needs might be accomplished through a lump-sum settlement, such an arrangement may not be appropriate for the reasons given earlier, except where the amount is small or where the beneficiary is an estate or a trust which will take care of those needs.

With these exceptions, where it is believed that the beneficiary may need to have cash available, the proceeds normally should be retained under one of the settlement options, and three general principles may be found helpful in setting up such cash funds.

First, a settlement option, normally the interest option with an unlimited right of withdrawal, should be used to avoid the disadvantages of an outright cash payment. In the event that the primary beneficiary survives the insured by only a short period of time, the proceeds will pass to or for the benefit of the secondary beneficiary under the contractual terms of the settlement option election, rather than be included in the probate estate. In addition, the proceeds are protected from the claims of the beneficiary's creditors by the spendthrift provision.

Second, whenever the interest (or other) option is used with an unlimited withdrawal right, the right to elect any other option in the policy at any time should be elected, to the extent that company rules permit. This right may preserve favorable income rates in the policy. Without it, a change of option requested by the beneficiary after the insured's death may be granted only on the basis of income rates in new policies being issued at that time. Such "then current" rates may be less favorable than those in older policies.

Third, beneficiaries for each fund should be chosen on the basis of the purpose of the particular fund.

Immediate Cash or Cleanup Fund. Most estates are modest and are composed largely of life insurance which essentially is the main source of liquid funds. It is important that liquid funds be available to satisfy the debts, funeral expenses, death taxes, and administration costs imposed against the insured's estate. Failure properly to provide ready cash for these estate obligations often results in the forced sale of estate assets at a fraction of their value.

Usually the wife is the primary heir of the estate, and will be most concerned that there be cash available for estate obligations. Therefore, it may be logical to have the life insurance proceeds payable to the wife under the interest option with an unlimited right of withdrawal and the right to elect other options. She then can withdraw such amount of the proceeds as and when necessary to meet the estate obligations and give the estate liquidity by purchasing assets from the estate or by making loans to the estate.

It is important to realize that the insured's estate should be designated contingent beneficiary, rather than minor children, because generally funds payable to minors must be paid to their legally appointed guardian who can only use those funds for the exclusive benefit of the minors. However, simply naming the estate contingent beneficiary is not enough to cover all contingencies. To the extent that the proceeds are not withdrawn by the wife they will be payable at her subsequent death to the insured's estate which may mean a costly reopening of that estate. This problem can be solved by including a "delayed payment" clause in the settlement plan, whereby the proceeds are left under the interest option to the wife if living, otherwise to the insured's children, with full right of withdrawal and right to elect options, but if the wife predeceases the insured or dies within a specified period after his death the proceeds are paid to the insured's estate.

Having the proceeds payable to a personal beneficiary, such as the wife, for estate obligations presumes that the beneficiary, in fact, will make those funds available to the estate to the extent of liquidity needs. For this reason, or because the insured may not wish to have a personal beneficiary responsible for the arrangement, he may have the proceeds payable directly to his estate or to a trust as primary beneficiary. Although making payment directly to the estate may seem logical since it is responsible for the obligations, such an arrangement has the disadvantage that any exemption from state death taxes that might apply to life insurance proceeds would be lost. If the disadvantage is relatively unimportant in a particular case, inquiry should be made to determine if the company will permit the proceeds to be paid to the estate under the interest option for a limited period and any balance at the end of the period to be paid to the wife or children. Choosing the alternative of making the proceeds payable to a life insurance trust may be attractive to the insured, since such an arrangement may result in saving state death taxes and administration expenses and it has the added advantage of affording protection against claims of creditors.

Mortgage Cancellation or Permanent Home Fund.   For most families home ownership is preferable to renting on a long-term basis. Therefore, a fund is often provided to cancel an existing mortgage or, alternatively, to help the widow buy a home for which the family has planned, even though the plan has not been carried out prior to the insured's death.

Where the insured holds title to the home in his own name, the mortgage cancellation fund may be paid to his estate. However, if the home is owned jointly, or if the wife is expected to purchase the home, such payment normally should be made to her under the interest option with the right to withdraw proceeds or elect other options. In most such cases, children would be logical contingent beneficiaries, but if they are minors, a trust for their benefit may be more appropriate. As previously mentioned, a guardian for the children may be required and, if such is the case, it may be difficult to obtain the court's approval to use the proceeds to cancel the mortgage.

Emergency Funds. Emergency funds can be provided in a number of ways. If a separate policy or a portion of the proceeds from a large policy is set up for this purpose, the interest option with the right to withdraw or to elect other options normally will prove satisfactory. Beneficiaries would be the wife, if living, otherwise the children.

In some cases, emergency funds can be provided by allowing withdrawal rights under a plan for providing family income which has been set up on the fixed-amount option. In such cases, the beneficiary should be warned that excessive use of the withdrawal privilege may sharply reduce or eliminate future income for her support in later life.

If desired, the right to withdraw can be limited under either plan, thus preventing premature dissipation of proceeds.

Regular Income for the Family

While income needs can be classified generally as readjustment, dependency period, social security gap, and the widow's life income, relating to separate periods in the economic life of a family, they also overlap in some respects. Thus, while discussed separately, these needs should be considered in relation to each other.

Readjustment Income. Often, it is deemed necessary or desirable to provide a larger amount of income to the widow during the first year or two after the insured's death than it is possible to provide on a permanent basis. The fixed-period option may be used to provide this extra income, but the fixed-amount option may be a better choice because it is more flexible. The latter will be found especially helpful where a step-down income is desired, or where the extra readjustment income is to come from a large policy allocated primarily to other income needs. Obviously, the interest option with right to withdraw proceeds or elect other options may also be used to provide readjustment income.

Dependency Period Income. The period of dependency for minor children commences at the insured's death, extends through the readjustment period, and continues until the children become self-supporting. Social security payments usually will cover a large part of this need until the children reach age 18 (age 22 if they are full-time students). For families in the middle or upper income brackets, however, this source may represent only a small portion of the total income required. Some of the need for dependency period income may be met by interest payable on life insurance proceeds retained for later use, such as educational funds or funds to be distributed subsequently under a life income option for the widow.

Generally, the fixed-amount option will provide the best arrangement because the income can be specified definitely and because this option is flexible. Provision can be made for partial withdrawal rights and settlement of proceeds remaining at the end of the dependency period under another option, such as one of the life income options.

Social Security Gap Fund. Since no social security benefits are payable between the youngest child's eighteenth birthday (twenty-second birthday if a full-time student) and the widow's age 62, the need for increased income from insurance during this period is obvious, even though total income needs may be less than during the dependency years. Sufficient proceeds to fill this gap under the fixed-amount or fixed-period option may be retained at interest until the youngest child is 18. Or proceeds held at interest until that time may be settled under one of the life income options with an appropriate period certain, depending on the age of the widow and other factors in the situation. Often the face amount of a family income or family maintenance policy will become payable at or after the time the gap begins, and logically can be settled under one of the installment or life income options at that time.

Widow's Life Income. While the need for an income which the widow cannot possibly outlive is recognized as basic, this does not necessarily mean that the life income option should be used for payments commencing at the death of the insured. Nor does the treatment of the widow's life income following the end of the dependency period indicate that this is the proper time for commencement of life income option payments. The determining factor will normally be the extent to which the policyowner wishes to preserve guaranteed values for children or other contingent beneficiaries. Obviously, other factors in choosing the life annuity option, and in choosing the certain period to be used in connection with it, are the characteristics and ages of the contingent beneficiaries to be protected.

Accordingly, it is common practice to hold sufficient proceeds under the interest option until the widow reaches age 50, 55, or older, or at least until the end of the dependency period, to provide the income she will need in later life. Additional proceeds are then settled under the fixed-period or fixed-amount option to supplement interest earned on the amount held for such later life income, thus bringing the dependency and gap period incomes up to the required levels.

There are exceptional cases where there may be no children or other members of the family the insured desires to protect, or where everyone except the widow has been adequately cared for from other funds. In such cases, the shortest possible certain period may be indicated in order to give the widow the largest possible annuity income. Here, settlement under the straight life annuity—without refund or guarantee return of principal—may be entirely logical, if such a plan is available from the company. However, such cases are rare, and most situations are better solved by the approach suggested in the preceding paragraph.

Income for Children

While the widow is living, all income typically is payable to her for the support of herself and the children, except in some large estates where it may be desirable to allocate some income directly to children as a means of reducing the overall income tax burden. In most cases, children become direct beneficiaries of life insurance only after both parents have died.

The income needs of minor children are not easily projected, and often settlement agreements that endeavor to carry out specific income patterns for them are very complicated. A more practical approach might be to retain each child's share under the interest option, with the right to withdraw all or any part of that share or to elect any settlement option in the policy. This plan is simple and flexible, but it alone does not provide the ideal solution because life insurance companies usually will not make payments directly to a minor due to the inability of a minor to give the company a valid release. If a minor is designated as the payee under a settlement option, unless state law permits otherwise, the companies will make payment only to a court-appointed guardian which can prove costly. To help alleviate this problem, some states have enacted laws which specifically permit a minor over a specified age, such as 18, to give a valid release for the payments. Ordinarily, such laws limit the amount which can be so paid in one year to a specific amount, such as $3,000.

Some companies permit naming an individual trustee in the policy or settlement option election to administer payments for specified minor beneficiaries. But merely naming a trustee without specifying his powers and duties may lead to litigation of the question whether a valid trust is created.

Educational Funds

It generally is recognized that life insurance is an excellent vehicle for accumulating funds to provide higher education for young people. Sometimes an endowment policy on the child's life is used for this purpose, but it is usually preferable to have the insurance issued on a parent's life. Normally, the father is insured but sometimes the circumstances indicate insurance on the mother's life.

Assuming the life insured is the father's, educational funds usually are payable to the wife as primary beneficiary. Most men prefer to allow their wives full discretion in handling these funds, often by settling proceeds under the interest option with right to withdraw principal and to elect other options. Special educational income provisions are not required in case the wife also dies before the child or children finish college, if each child's share is also retained at interest with right to withdraw or change options. The child's guardian or a named trustee may act on his behalf to withdraw funds as needed or to set up an appropriate income when he is ready for college.

Some parents, however, prefer to set up definite monthly income patterns for the child, both before and during college. These may be arranged in a variety of ways under the standard settlement options, or under the special educational settlement plans offered by most companies. For example, payments for college expenses can be set to commence at a definite time, or when requested by the child's mother—or his guardian or trustee if she is not living—or when evidence is furnished that the child has enrolled in a school of higher learning. Maintenance income may be made payable on a 12-month basis, or perhaps for 9 or 10 months in each college year if the child is expected to work during summer vacations. Tuition and other expenses falling due by semesters can be covered by special extra payments at the beginning of each semester and, if desired, a final "graduation gift" check can be arranged.

Whatever the general pattern, it is important to keep educational settlement provisions as simple and flexible as possible, and particularly to consider the channels through which such funds should be paid if both parents die before the child finishes college.

Special Purpose Funds

In addition to providing for basic family requirements, life insurance proceeds often are used to meet various special situations or secondary needs. For example, one might wish to provide for one or more aged relatives. If total life insurance protection is more than adequate for the immediate family, it is easy to allocate a portion of the proceeds to the older person. This portion might be settled under the interest option, with a limited or unlimited withdrawal privilege and, of course, the right to change to other options. Or it might be settled on the fixed-amount option or, depending upon age and condition of health, on the life income option with an appropriate period certain.

Another special purpose fund might provide for holiday, birthday, or anniversary gifts. Proceeds can be held on deposit, with interest payable annually at Christmas or at some other specified time. The fixed-amount option often is used to pay a stated sum each year on some such particular date, or the interest option may be used with a right to withdraw a limited sum of principal annually at the specified time.

Many people are interested in religious, charitable, or educational institutions and would like to make some provision for them through life insurance. Settlement options enter the charitable bequest picture primarily where it is desired to name a religious, charitable, or educational institution to receive whatever may remain after the death of all members of the insured's immediate family. This can readily be arranged by incorporating appropriate provisions into the income settlement agreements covering distribution of policy proceeds.

SOME GENERAL RULES

Election of Settlement Options

Usually, the owner of a life insurance policy may specify that proceeds be payable under one of the settlement options. In most cases the owner is the insured, but sometimes the owner is a person or entity other than the insured. Generally, where the insured owns the policy, he may elect settlement options for beneficiaries or for himself. In the latter case, the options usually may be applied either to the proceeds of a matured endowment policy or to the cash value of some other permanent contract. Company practices vary as to the extent to which an owner who is not the insured may utilize the settlement options.

After the insured's death the beneficiary of a lump-sum settlement normally may elect an income plan instead of taking the cash. Also, a beneficiary may be able to change an income plan set up before the death of the insured, if the income plan permits such changes to be made.

The extent to which trustees or business entities, as owners or beneficiaries of life insurance policies, can use the settlement options varies with the company and the circumstances. For example, the proceeds of business life insurance purchased to fund a buy-and-sell agreement often can be set up under settlement options, while at the same time giving the corporation or other purchaser of the deceased's business interest, as well as his estate, access to the proceeds until the buy-and-sell transaction is completed. Settlement options frequently are used in connection with life insurance purchased to fund pension and deferred compensation plans for employees.

Basic Company Rules for Using Options

As a rule, not less than $1,000 may be placed under a settlement option. A number of companies have raised this minimum to $2,000 in recent years. Often a minimum installment also is specified in the policy, such as a periodic installment of not less than $10 or $20 to each beneficiary. In addition to these limitations, the fixed-amount option usually contains an additional requirement that installments be not less than a specified minimum rate per $1,000 of initial proceeds, perhaps $5 or $6 per month per $1,000. This is to insure that all proceeds and interest will be paid out in a reasonable period of time.

Company rules also limit the length of time that proceeds will be retained under a settlement option. These apply primarily to the interest option, as liquidation of proceeds generally is automatic within a reasonable time under the installment and life income options. Most companies will retain proceeds at interest for the lifetime of the primary beneficiary or until the death of the survivor of joint primary beneficiaries. Some companies also will hold proceeds for the lifetime of a contingent beneficiary, but the majority will not. Frequently, a time limit of 30 years after the death of the insured is specified for proceeds held at interest for a contingent beneficiary. In a few cases, the time limit for a contingent beneficiary is expressed in terms of his or her age, usually between age 21 and age 35. Interest payments normally cannot be continued to a third beneficiary.

Requesting Settlement Agreements

Settlement agreements may be requested in the application for a new policy. However, in most cases, space is inadequate to describe properly what is wanted, and a separate memorandum is better. Obviously, in the case of a policy already in force, some kind of letter or memorandum is indicated.

Many companies have simplified this procedure by furnishing check lists or form letters for use by agents. An increasing number of companies have carried this one step further by furnishing settlement agreements in check list form. One copy of such a check list is returned to the insured for attachment to his policy, after being recorded and certified by the home office. Some companies still handle settlement option elections by means of individually drafted agreements and by physically endorsing the arrangement on the policy itself.

SELECTED REFERENCES

McGill, Dan M. *Life Insurance.* Rev. ed. Homewood, Ill.: Richard D. Irwin, Inc., 1967.

Settlement Options. New York: Flitcraft, Inc. Published annually.

55

Estate Planning Principles

By LAURENCE J. ACKERMAN

To ENDOW THE EXPRESSION "estate planning" with its fullest meaning calls for language so general and so broad that it borders on the vague and the trite. Yet we need some golden nail upon which to hang the seamless tapestry of estate planning. An estate plan is an arrangement for the devolution of one's assets. Estate planning is the process for the creation of this arrangement. The term has a range which encompasses the small estate handled perhaps by a simple will, as well as the large, intricate, complex estate with its army of vehicles of estate transfer.

Cautions Regarding Estate Planning

Three caveats are important at this point. Estate planning and tax planning are not synonymous terms. The latter is only a facet of the former. Its function is to minimize the tax burden involved in the disposition of the estate. Too often, the estate owner seems motivated more by hate than by love. His hatred for taxes outstrips his love for his family; he may permit tax considerations to dictate the disposition of his estate. To elevate tax savings to the supreme role—to display indifference to family needs—is, in essence, saying: "My money won't do my family much good when I die, but look how little tax I'll have to pay."

The second caution is to criticize the term "estate planning" as not the aptest of expressions. There is too much connotation in it of a singular devotion to a plan for the estate when the owner dies. But the estate planner is concerned usually with the wisest and most prudent use of his client's assets during his lifetime as well as after his death. Estate planning is a two-phase undertaking. It seeks to maximize, for the estate owner and his family, the security and enjoyment flowing from property ownership, both during lifetime and after death.

The third alert is the erroneous yet widespread belief that estate planning is the special privilege of the large estates. Both in lifetime and in testamentary planning, many common problems are found in the large and in the small estate. Frequently, the differences are only in degree and not in kind. It is the small estate owner who can least afford to neglect estate planning or to make an estate planning mistake. The failure or waste of a single asset in his estate could bring hardship both to him and to his family.

Estate Planning Not New

Estate planning is not a new art. It is one of the oldest of the arts, although it may be one of the newest of the professions. The privilege of disposing of one's property at time of death was permitted by the early Egyptians. The Code of Hammurabi made provision for both testate and intestate succession. Turning to one of our direct legal ancestors, the English legal complex, we see the modern trust evolving out of the "use" found in feudal times. The Statute of Wills came into being in 1540 in the time of Henry VIII. The rule against perpetuities appeared in 1685. The law against accumulations emerged in 1800. Forces were building up which called for counsel and advice in the disposition of one's property interests.

In America, it was the tax statutes of the 19th and 20th centuries which acted as the catalysts for the tremendous interest in estate planning. In the latter part of the 19th century, states enacted inheritance taxes. In 1913 the U.S. income tax law was passed. The U.S. estate tax statute came on the scene in 1915. The U.S. gift tax followed in 1932. In predictable manner, the rates of taxes accelerated rapidly over the intervening years. The net result was a rapid quickening of the interest in and need for estate planning.

FORCES OF ESTATE IMPAIRMENT

Viewing the vistas of today, we see many forces of impairment which tend to shrink estates, decrease their efficiency, and frustrate estate owners' objectives. First, there are the costs associated with death itself, such as last illness and funeral expenses. Then there are the current unpaid bills and the more substantial, longer range debts, such as the mortgage, installment contracts, and business obligations with claims against the personal assets. Probably there will be unpaid income and property taxes. There are the costs of estate transfer which include the administration expenses, state inheritance taxes, U.S. estate tax, and, in Canada, Canadian succession duties. These are obvious obstacles of impairment.

But there are more subtle elements of estate impairment. Our economic climate influences estates in a most profound and pervasive manner. The erosion in value of the dollar because of inflation compels constant reappraisal and rearrangement of the family estate plan. To ignore the direction of economic change is to impose a continual levy on one's capital. The failure of one's assets to provide persistent and expected income can destroy the most praiseworthy estate plan.

Instability of values can be another thief of estate assets. It might occur through improper management of a business asset, through the impact of changes in consumer preferences or obsolescence, or through improper management of the general estate assets after death.

An important force of impairment is lack of liquidity to pay the financial costs associated with death and to honor cash bequests. These may compel sacrifice of assets which have substantial income-producing power for the family.

Sometimes the improper use of vehicles of transfer can impair an estate. Lawyers and other estate planning advisers occasionally find that estate assets, under the legal documents in force, will pass to unintended beneficiaries. This may be accounted for by an old will which was not kept current with family change.

It is not unusual to find life insurance improperly arranged. A major function of the life insurance in the estate is to bridge the gap between the income potential of the other estate assets and the needs of the beneficiaries. The life insurance may have been programmed with little or no consideration of the adequacy of the other sources of estate income. The lack of coordination between the attorney planning the general estate and the life underwriter planning the life insurance estate is all too frequent, and may have disastrous results.

Sometimes the most ambitious and airtight estate plan is destroyed by prolonged and expensive disabilities. Not only is a person faced with a loss of income, but his problem is compounded by the financial involvements of the illness itself. Health insurance can assist in the completion of estate plans in the same manner as life insurance.

By no means to complete the full array of forces of estate impairment, but merely to offer one more illustration, the legal documents associated with the estate plan may have considerable impact. They may have a rigidity which materially penalizes the objects of the estate owner's bounty. Management "from the grave" has led to weird and tragic consequences.

ESTATE PLANNING PROCESS

Designing and fabricating an estate plan is almost always a custom-tailored effort. People differ so in their temperaments, in their sets of values, in their asset and liability statements, in their family responsibilities and relationships, that even though the material may be the same in many cases, the pattern and cut of the plan should probably always be different. The estate planner must have a viewpoint the opposite of Procrustes and not stretch or shorten his client's objectives to fit some preconceived arrangement.

The estate planning process, for purpose of analysis, can be broken up into six component parts. First, an adequate fact base must be fashioned. Once this is done, the forces of impairment which threaten the estate should be identified as a second step. Third, an estate plan should be formulated. Fourth, the proposed plan should be tested in a hypothetical framework. Fifth, the final plan should be implemented by the execution of the appropriate legal documents. Sixth, the plan should be subject to periodic review to test its adequacy in the crucible of time.

1. Getting the Facts

Facts are the lifeblood of any effective estate plan. Professionals in the field have struggled with this problem at length. As a result, there are numbers of lists, questionnaires, fact finders, and the like to aid in the fact-gathering operation.

No one doubts the value of adequate and exact facts. The real mark of the professional estate planner, however, is the ability to extract these facts from the estate owner. Simple and complex psychological theories have been concocted to explain the bashful silence of many estate owners when confronted with questions about their personal and financial lives. But the sad truth remains: Questionnaires are easy to assemble; full and accurate answers from the client, not so simple a task. The facts sought can be divided into five categories: (*a*) domicile, (*b*) family, (*c*) property, (*d*) current estate plans, and (*e*) estate owner's objectives.

Domicile is significant in the estate plan. It identifies the law which will govern the validity of the will and most of its provisions. With our nomadic civilization, tracking down domicile is not a mild task at times. There has been at least one reported case in which each of four states attempted to collect death taxes. Each claimed to be the domicile of the decedent.

Family facts are equally important. Needed is such elementary information as the full names and dates of birth of the estate owner, his wife, his children, his grandchildren, and any other intended beneficiaries. One must unearth such personal information as the character of the wife and her business acumen, the state of health of the estate owner and his beneficiaries, the amount of wealth now available to the wife and children, and the attitudes of individual family members toward each other.

Next comes the *property* profile of the estate owner. This must be exhaustive and detailed. A complete rundown of the person's assets and liabilities is essential. Some of the details which are required are cash in individual accounts and in various types of joint accounts, real estate owned separately and jointly, tangible personal property owned individually and jointly, securities owned individually and jointly, business interests, personal life insurance, employee benefits, social security rights, claims under wills and trusts, and rights in future interests. Shifting to the other side of the balance sheet, full information must be procured about the estate owner's obligations. Such items as debts, accrued taxes, mortgages, leases, installment contracts, and so forth must be explored. All of this sounds dreary, unromantic, and dull. To the experienced estate planner, this is often one of the most exciting and illuminating parts of the process. Few estate owners ever go through such a procedure with themselves. When they do it under the guidance of the estate planner, the estate owners are often surprised, amazed, chagrined, even angered, and sometimes delighted by what they see. It is during this phase of the estate planning activity that the seeds of sound planning ideas can be sown in the owner's mind.

What is the *current estate plan* of the owner? Every estate owner has a plan, whether developed consciously or accidentally. If, for example, a person should die intestate, i.e., without properly executing a will, the state will impose a straitjacket distribution plan for him. He will forfeit many privileges when he fails to execute a will. Briefly, he surrenders these significant privileges:

1. To dispose of his property as he wishes.
2. To name the beneficiaries of his assets.
3. To name an executor, i.e., the person or entity that will guide his estate through the probate process.
4. To nominate the guardian of his children.

5. To excuse his fiduciaries from the duty of furnishing a probate bond.
6. To designate the source for the payment of his taxes.
7. To make the most effective use of the marital deduction.
8. To denote the appropriate procedures for the disposition of his estate in the event of a common disaster.

These observations emphasize the pitfalls of dying intestate. Therefore, determining if a will exists is one of the first steps in estate planning. If there is a will, the estate planner should obtain copies of it and of any trusts that form a part of the estate owner's current plan.

The question of gifts should be investigated. If the estate owner has made gifts, then questions will be asked as to when the gifts were made, to whom, the nature and value of the assets, how made, and whether they were reported for gift tax purposes.

Finally, in the fact category, there is the very important *objectives* section. One must ascertain the estate owner's philosophy about the financial maintenance and security of his family. Some estate owners have a mortal fear of entrusting substantial sums of money to their widows and children. Others feel that such an experience is the only way to sound money management. Some heads of families feel that their children should receive comparatively little and should fight their way through life, as their fathers did. In some estate owners, there is a keen and deep sensitivity to societal obligations and a desire to return the bulk of their wealth to the community in the form of charitable bequests. Very frequently, the estate owner has not thought through these all-important questions. The estate planner then has to don the mantle of the devil's advocate and help to evoke a concrete, definitive philosophy from the estate owner.

In the traditional situation, the objectives will not be complicated. The typical individual probably will prefer to give specific items of property to certain persons or institutions, with the remainder to his wife and children.

Business interests almost always cause extended discussion between the estate planner and the estate owner. One reason is that business interests often comprise a substantial part of the estate. The estate owner may be the sole proprietor of a business, or the asset may be a share in a partnership, or stock ownership in a close corporation, or a combination of these. Many vital decisions must be made. A basic exploration revolves about the question: Will the estate owner's objective be served best through retention of the business interest in the family, or should it be sold? This often produces a crisis in the relationship between the estate owner and the estate planner. So many times, the coldly logical, analytical businessman becomes an impractical dreamer when it comes to the disposition of his business interest. The path to the right decision may be a hard and rocky one. Until the time of the testator's death, the business may be the mainspring of his economic and personal development. Once he dies, it becomes an investment of an estate, valuable only if it can produce an adequate level of income.

A stream of queries flows from the estate planner if the estate owner indicates a strong desire to retain the business interest. How dependent will the family be on the business for its support? Are there family members who can manage the enterprise? If not, are there key employees available for the managerial role? What potential rifts might develop between these key employees and the family after the estate owner's death? How stable have the business earnings been in the past, and what does the future look like? What capital contributions will be necessary to keep the profit stream running in its accustomed manner? If the decision is to sell, is there a logical purchaser? If so, where will the funds to buy come from? Discussion also must take place about the valuation of the business interest.

Only a few of the objectives have been mentioned. They portray some of the dimensions in this area of the estate planning procedure.

To obtain the facts, the estate planner must talk with the estate owner and probably with members of his family. It may be unwise to do this on a mass basis. Individual consultations may be preferable. Whoever is planning the estate (frequently the life underwriter) will want to consult with the estate owner's other estate planning advisors. It is noted later in this chapter that in addition to the life underwriter, the estate owner's accountant, attorney, and local banker, all can furnish important data. The planner should examine such instruments as income and gift tax returns, wills and trusts, life insurance policies, deeds, mortgages, business interest agreements, and any other legal documents pertinent to the task of estate planning. Even if no new illumination is cast on the problem, an examination of these documents should aid the estate planner in confirming the accuracy of the data furnished by the estate owner in their discussions.

2. Evaluating Estate Impairment Items

Once the facts have been amassed and arranged, the forces of estate impairment can be analyzed and estimated dollarwise. What guess can be made as to last illness and burial expenses? What measure can be placed on the debt structure of the decedent? What are the probable transfer costs, such as executor's commissions, attorney's fees, miscellaneous probate fees, state inheritance taxes, and federal estate taxes? What unpaid real estate and personal property taxes will there be? What unpaid federal income tax will remain at time of death? One might include in this estimate possible income tax deficiencies for prior years. Can the widow's and children's allowances be roughly computed? Aside from the information furnished by the estate owner, the planner will be aided by his experience and the various insurance and tax "services" in making his rough "guesstimates" of these costs. These estimates will furnish the cash requirements needed at time of death and will create additional background material for the preparation of the estate plan.

3. Designing the Plan

Step three is the design of the plan. As a fact gatherer, the estate planner played the role of an investigator. In appraising the forces of impairment, he displayed his knowledge of the probate process and the complexities of the tax laws. Now, new characteristics are called into play. The planner must show that he has creative skill and the ability to weld together the estate owner's variegated assets into a smooth, acceptable house of security. He must help the testator produce the liquidity necessary to discharge the estate obligations. He must produce a plan which can take the rest of the assets and move them in the direction of his client's wishes. The planner has a variety of vehicles of transfer to accomplish these objectives. Through trial and error and experimentation, he will finally bring forth the ultimate plan. Probably the estate owner has a current plan, and the new one may well be a rearrangement of the old plan.

It is not possible within the confines of this conceptual approach to estate planning to mention all or to dig deeply into any of the available vehicles of transfer As in the previous steps, a few will be mentioned for illustrative purposes.

The *will* is a key vehicle of transfer. A typical goal of an estate owner in the preparation of a will is to qualify just the right amount of property for the marital deduction. This is because overqualification can result in the payment of unnecessary estate taxes at the death of the surviving spouse. This goal is often accomplished by the creation of two trusts in the will. In one trust, all income will be paid to the wife during her lifetime. She is given full power of appointment, by the will, over the trust property. In default of the exercise of the power by the wife, the trust property will be paid to the children of the testator. This trust is drawn to qualify for the marital deduction. Thus, it is not taxed in the husband's estate for federal estate tax purposes. In the other trust, the income is payable to the wife for life. On her death the property will be paid to the children. The assets in this trust do not qualify for the marital deduction and are, therefore, taxable in the husband's estate. But they would not be a part of the wife's gross estate for federal estate tax purposes upon her subsequent death.

The use of the marital deduction has as its basic consideration the saving of taxes. But every tax saving has its price, be it in the form of loss of control of an asset (e.g., a gift), the compromise of one's objectives (e.g., the desire to cut the wife's income if she remarries), or possible deferred increase in transfer costs (e.g., in the wife's estate if the marital deduction is employed). Therefore, even as to the marital deduction the estate planner will weigh the current tax saving against the eventual price paid to obtain it.

The estate planner will also evaluate the choice of property which goes into the marital deduction trust. He may consider it wise for the husband to avoid using assets with strong potential for appreciation in value. A substantial increase in the value of the assets which are qualified for the marital deduction will produce a proportionate increase in taxes on the subsequent death of the wife. If the assets are not easily marketable, the wife's estate faces not only an increased transfer tax liability, but also an increased cash deficit to pay the tax. Contrariwise, it may be appropriate to use assets which will depreciate in value. These will have an opposite effect from the use of the appreciating assets in the estate of the wife. For example, insurance proceeds may be qualified for the marital deduction under some type of fixed or life income arrangement.

Another important vehicle of transfer is *life insurance*. It is the only practical plan which can guarantee that cash will be available at death to meet the financial costs of death. The use of life insurance to meet estate liabilities may prevent the forced sale of prime assets. This, in turn, will reduce the ultimate shrinkage in estate values and perhaps keep alive a source of income for the beneficiaries of the decedent. The presence of life insurance with a named beneficiary will in some states bring savings in state taxes. Probate and administration costs also will be saved. For these reasons, many planners point out that a dollar of insurance is far more valuable at death than a dollar in cash—as in a bank. It is difficult to conceive of an estate plan today which does not employ life insurance as a significant catalyst to its accomplishment. In the final analysis, insurance in the estate plan will be determined by the needs for liquidity, flexibility, tax minimization, investment, and the requirements of family income.

Trusts, both *inter vivos* and testamentary, are used as vehicles of transfer.[1] Sometimes, when there is the possibility of heavy cash requirements at death, or perhaps a need for broad discretion over income and principal, an *inter vivos* life insurance trust may be created.

When there is both an *inter vivos* trust and a testamentary trust, the planner may suggest that both be combined and administered as one. One way to do this is through a "pour-over" trust. Both trusts may well have the same distributive provisions, the same beneficiaries, the same trustee(s). The trustee of the testamentary trust will be authorized to turn over the assets, when received from the executor, to the trustee of the *inter vivos* trust. Local law governs the availability of this technique, and its use has increased substantially during the past few years.

There are a number of distinct advantages to the establishment of a living trust and the use of a pour-over device. A single living trust permits a consolidation of family assets. In turn, this should produce savings in administrative expenses plus an opportunity for the trustee to invest a substantial corpus and obtain the benefit of diversification of trust investments. A related advantage of the pour-over is the more simplified and convenient administration of assets under a single trust instrument. A third advantage is in the area of reduced estate administration expenses. Some expenses such as executor commissions and attorney fees are generally based on the value of the probate estate. The greater the value of the probate estate, the more these expenses will be. In addition, there are a myriad of court costs during the estate administration process. Revocable lifetime transfers represent nonprobate property and as such will not give rise to estate administration expenses. If life insurance is payable to the trustee of a revocable living trust, the proceeds may be available for the payment of death costs without increasing estate administration expenses. A fundamental advantage of the revocable living trust is that its terms and the identity of the beneficiaries may be kept secret. The provisions of a testamentary trust are matters of public record available for all to see. In a similar vein, there is, as a general rule, continued judicial supervision and accounting of the testamentary trustee. Most states which permit the use of a pour-over impose no such requirement on the trustee of a living trust. There is a choice of law because the trust may be established wherever

---

[1] For a discussion of trusts and their uses, see Chapter 56.

the local law is most favorable to the grantor's purposes. The living trust even gives lifetime benefits. It furnishes the grantor with a "dry run" test of the trust's provisions and the trustee. The grantor can change either prior to death, if actual operation does not live up to his expectations. Valuable custodianship may be provided when the grantor is too busy, traveling, ill or mentally incompetent, without the need and the risks of powers of attorney or the necessity of appointing a conservator.

The *gift* is another effective tool for estate planning. It has significance beyond transfer tax savings. It can be utilized to buy life insurance for liquidity purposes without increasing the estate tax liability. This is accomplished by having the donee lend money to, or purchase assets from, the estate. It can be used to serve specific desires the estate owner may have for his children. It might serve as a medium to continue control of a business interest within the family. In its use, there must always be a consideration of the price paid for the advantage—namely, loss of control of this asset.

Joint ownership with right of survivorship is often suggested as an effective vehicle of transfer. It has the advantage that upon the death of a co-owner, the share of the deceased automatically passes to the survivor and is no longer part of the deceased's estate for administration purposes. But for federal estate tax purposes the estate of the decedent is subject to tax for the full value of the entire property if the deceased furnished all of the money for the purchase. The survivor has to prove the extent of her contributions, if any. In addition, jointly owned property may be taxed in the husband's estate and later in the wife's estate. Joint ownership may result in an unwanted distribution of property. Assume that the wife survives, along with some children. The property passes to her as surviving joint tenant. She remarries. Husband No. 2 may then receive a substantial portion of the property left by the first husband. The latter would probably have preferred that his children receive the property. Instead, much of it could go to an "outsider."

Other examples of tools utilized in estate planning are *sprinkling trusts, private annuities, powers of appointment, and charitable foundations.* The uses of the latter device have been severely limited by the 1969 Tax Reform Act.

4. Testing the Plan

Once a complete plan has been agreed upon, step four is in order. This is to test the proposal. A few of the criteria employed can be mentioned. Does the plan seem to accomplish its objective? One way to assay this is to put the plan through a hypothetical administration and to test the resulting net income and its distribution. Have all of the assets been meshed together into a single workable plan? Finally, is the plan flexible enough to meet the test of today and the probable tests of tomorrow?

5. Executing Legal Documents

Step five introduces the necessity for concise and unambiguous draftsmanship by the attorney. He must see to the preparation of all the legal instruments necessary to carry out the plan.

6. Periodic Review

Finally, it must be remembered that family situations change, laws change, the tax structure goes through a periodic revolution, and economic forces run through cycles. This risk and this uncertainty produce a need for constant attention and perhaps occasional revision. Many estate planners review their clients' situation on an annual basis.

ADVANTAGES OF PLANNED ESTATE

There are many advantages to the planned estate. It enables an estate owner to preadminister his estate and gain an insight into its probable costs and its potential for the achievement of his objectives. A planned estate should ordinarily minimize transfer taxes. A planned estate should be superior to an unplanned one in the achievement of the estate owner's objectives for his family. A planned estate should bring greater peace of mind to the estate owner. A planned estate should give the estate owner greater freedom of financial action.

THE ESTATE PLANNING TEAM

The field of estate planning has led such a dynamic life during the past 25 years that it has engendered at least one major status conflict. This revolves about the question: Who should do estate planning? Some five groups claim this privilege but fortunately not to the exclusion of each other. These are the lawyers, the life underwriters, the trust officers, the accountants, and the investment counselors.

The lawyer may claim that the estate plan is essentially a legal transaction and therefore falls essentially within his jurisdiction. The life underwriter may contend that life insurance today is so vital a part of the estate plan that without his active participation, estate planning has little meaning for the typical estate owner. The trust officer may state that his vast practical experience in such matters stamps him as the person best fitted to serve the estate owner. The accountant may point to his intimate knowledge of his client's affairs and to his exhaustive experience and know-how in the field of taxation. The investment adviser offers his knowledge of investment media as a badge entitling him to participate in the estate planning process.

Estate planning today is so complex and subtle a process that it calls for teamwork. Each of these professional groups can play a role in the accomplishment of the estate owner's objectives without any necessary conflict. The life underwriter is frequently the initiator of the idea because, unlike the lawyer and accountant, his is a license to solicit business. He can supply a vehicle of transfer through life insurance. He is in a position to recommend the most effective settlement options. The lawyer will draft the legal instruments which will furnish the power for the execution of the estate plan. The accountant can be of help in supplying the intimate financial data necessary to the formulation of the estate plan. He is also the appropriate person to resolve the vital question of *value* for the closely held business interest. The trust officer can lend advice on the practicalities of the estate plan and can play a major role in the estate administration. If the estate is large enough, the investment adviser can be a vital person on the team.

In 1953 an article[2] was published, under the sponsorship of the National Conference of Lawyers and Life Insurance Companies, entitled "Some Guideposts for Cooperation between Lawyers and Life Insurance Representatives." This Conference was organized in 1951. Its membership comprised the membership of the Joint Committee on Practice of Law of the American Life Convention and the Life Insurance Association of America along with the American Bar Association's Standing Committee on Unauthorized Practice of the Law. The article, which was circulated widely, attempted to outline areas of activity in which lawyers, life underwriters, and home office counsel could cooperate in the complexity of estate planning. The Conference has handled complaints, has issued informative bulletins, and, most important of all, has served to keep the lines of communication and mutual discussion open between the life insurance industry and the organized Bar.

In the "Guideposts" article, it was agreed that the life underwriter may prepare a thorough analysis of the client's life insurance estate. He may advise on beneficiary changes; the use of optional modes of settlement; whether policies should be converted or paid up; the appropriate plan under which new insurance should be written; and the use of supplementary features, such as disability riders, accidental death benefits, term riders, and the like. Forms dealing with the disposition of insurance proceeds by the company, approved by home office counsel, may be provided by the life underwriter.

A life underwriter may, in discussing an insurance program with a prospect, refer to general subjects which it would be pertinent for the prospect's lawyer to consider in his advice to his client. Further, the life underwriter may develop for his prospect an overall estate plan, solely for the purpose of demonstrating the compelling necessity of putting his affairs in order and inducing the client to consult his lawyer.

The "Guideposts" article was most helpful in clarifying the role of the life underwriter in the estate planning process. It did not alter certain propositions found in the 1948 "National Statement of Principles of Cooperation between Life Underwriters and Lawyers." In substance, the unaltered principles are that a life underwriter may *not:*

1. Practice law; give legal advice; and prepare legal documents, such as wills, trust agreements, and business insurance agreements.
2. Dissuade a client from seeking the advice of legal counsel or attempt to divert legal business from one attorney to another.

---

[2] Harry S. Redeker, "Some Guideposts for Cooperation between Lawyers and Life Insurance Representatives," *Journal of the American Society of Chartered Life Underwriters,* Vol. 8, No. 1 (Winter 1953), pp. 86–99. *Editor's note:* The National Statement of Principles of Cooperation between Life Underwriters and Lawyers is presented in Appendix U. Appendix V is the Statement of Guiding Principles for Relationships between Life Underwriters and Trustmen.

3. Act as intermediary and furnish attorneys who will give cost-free legal advice to the underwriter's clients or prospects.
4. Share the attorney's fee or pay any part of his life insurance commission to an attorney or other person not a life underwriter.
5. Obtain legal opinions from an attorney and circularize them as selling documents.

Estate planning is a flourishing area of service to the American public. If reasonable freedom in the acquisition, conservation, and distribution of property can be maintained, then estate planning should always be a great challenge to superior minds engaged in the professions concerned.

SELECTED REFERENCES

Davis, Gene C. *Estate Planning, A Client's Handbook.* New York: Practicing Law Institute, 1971.

Estate Planners Quarterly, Lynbrook, N.Y.: Farnsworth Publishing Co.

Farr, James F. *An Estate Planner's Handbook.* 3d ed. Boston, Mass.: Little, Brown & Co., 1966.

MacNeill, Earl S. *Making the Most of Your Estate.* New York: Harper & Bros., 1957.

Shattuck, Mayo A., and Farr, James A. *Estate Planners Handbook.* 2d ed. Boston, Mass.: Little, Brown & Co., 1953.

Trachtman, Joseph. *Estate Planning.* New York: Practicing Law Institute, 1964.

Wormser, Rene A., *Guide to Estate Planning.* Englewood Cliffs, N.J.: Prentice-Hall, Inc., 1958.

Wren, Harold G. *Creative Estate Planning.* 2 vols. New York: Practicing Law Institute, 1971.

56

Trusts and Their Uses

By V. N. WOOLFOLK

TRUSTS were introduced into English common law shortly after the Norman Conquest, perhaps being modeled on earlier German or Roman law. Broadly stated, they were arrangements whereby one wishing to enjoy the fruits of property ownership could do so without also assuming the burdens of ownership. Much the same objective is applicable today for many trusts in common use by estate planners.

THE TRUST RELATIONSHIP

A trust is a fiduciary relationship where one person holds legal title to property with an obligation to keep or use it for the benefit of the equitable owner, usually another person. The one who causes the trust to come into existence is called the settlor, the grantor, the trustor, the creator, or, if the trust is created in a will, the testator. The trustee is the one who holds the property for the benefit of the other, called the beneficiary or the *cestui que trust.* The trustee may be a natural person or a corporation. The trust property to which the trustee has legal title may be any recognized property interest in any personal or real property or an enforceable contract right. The trust property is usually called the *corpus, res,* or principal of the trust.

The trustee must deal with the trust property honestly, putting the beneficiary's interest above his own. The grantor of the trust, therefore, must use care in selecting a responsible trustee—one in whom he has the utmost confidence. The relationship between the trustee and the beneficiary is also very close. The beneficiary also should have confidence in the integrity and fairness of the trustee and in his ability to treat different classes of trust beneficiaries impartially. If the beneficiary has no part in the selection of a trustee, the grantor should consider carefully this trustee-beneficiary relationship when selecting a trustee.

The trustee must follow closely the guiding instrument in administering the trust. If the trust instrument directs something to be done, the trustee has no choice; he must carry out the direction except in those rare cases where he would apply to the supervising court for relief. Modern trust instruments give the trustee wide discretion in investments, in day-to-day management, and even in the paying and withholding of income and principal. Naturally, the trustee chosen must be willing to accept the discretion given to him, and the grantor should be satisfied that he will use the discretion conscientiously and without fear of a later surcharge.

Even though there are at least three parties to a trust, they are not necessarily different legal entities. For example, the grantor of a trust also may be a trustee; a beneficiary may be one of the trustees; or the grantor may also be a beneficiary. At least two different legal entities are usually necessary for a valid trust.

TYPES OF TRUSTS

Trusts may be classified variously—by the formality of their creation, by the nature of the trust property, by the time of their creation, by their degree of permanency, by their duration, and by the nature of the trustee's duties, among others. Estate planners normally are concerned with express trusts—those created intentionally in writing. They may be testamentary trusts—those created in a will; or living or *inter vivos* trusts —those that come into operation during the grantor's lifetime. Among living trusts, those revocable and amendable during the grantor's lifetime are as important as those that cannot be so changed—irrevocable trusts.

Life Insurance Trusts

Life insurance trusts are extremely important in estate planning today because life insurance represents the largest single class of estate assets for many clients. It is imperative that these assets be handled in the estate so that the objects of the client's bounty get the most benefits out of them.

A personal life insurance trust is a trust designed to receive, hold, invest in, and/or administer proceeds of life insurance for the benefit of the policyowner's family or other beneficiary of the trust. It may be a living or a testamentary trust. In addition to the usual trust parties—the grantor or testator, the trustee, and the beneficiary—the insured and the policyowner also must be considered as essential parties. Again, the parties may not all be different, but it is essential to a proper understanding of a life insurance trust that the function of each party be understood.

The consideration of life insurance trusts in this chapter is limited to express living trusts for nonbusiness purposes,[1] the principal of which contains a significant amount of life insurance, the proceeds of such insurance, or similar proceeds paid as a result of an individual's death. Charitable trust beneficiaries are not considered.

Uses for Living Life Insurance Trusts

A policyowner has available to him a number of alternative dispositions for the death proceeds of life insurance. He can have them paid in a

---

[1] Testamentary life insurance trusts also are important in estate planning. For example, a father owning insurance on a son or daughter can provide in his will for this insurance to become a part of his residuary trust, using income or principal to pay subsequent premiums.

lump sum to a designated beneficiary, left with the insurance company under a settlement option, paid to the trustee of a living life insurance trust, or he can designate his estate as the beneficiary. In some states, the death proceeds also may be paid to a trustee named in the insured's will. Each alternative has its uses, but having the proceeds payable to the trustee of a living trust may solve certain estate planning problems better than any other available method.

Those choosing to have the death proceeds paid to the trustee of a living trust usually do so for management or tax reasons. Sometimes both reasons combine to dictate the use of a living insurance trust.

Direct payments to a person under a legal disability, such as a minor, can be a cumbersome and costly method of distribution. A trustee can be authorized to make payments for his benefit, avoiding the complications and cost of a guardianship. A trustee's investment powers often can be broader than those given to a guardian by law, and periodic accountings usually can be dispensed with. The grantor of a living trust has a choice of the law that will govern the administration of his trust. The law of his domicile at death usually governs the administration of a testamentary trust. A grantor has almost complete freedom in selecting his trustee; a testamentary trustee may have to meet certain statutory qualifications as to residence, relationship, and the like, before letters of trusteeship will be issued to him. In some states the court supervising a living trust is not the same court that supervises testamentary trusts. The rules for, and expenses of, accounting may favor the living over the testamentary trust. For example, testamentary trusts may require annual attorney fees for presentation of accounting to the probate judge, while living trusts need not.

The client may not wish his estate plan to be available for public inspection. A will is a public record, whereas a trust agreement is not normally made available to the general public, but it may be available to those concerned with the administration of the grantor's estate. Testamentary trusts usually must remain in domicile of probate, whereas living trusts may be portable.

Settlement options are contractual arrangements with the insurance company. The beneficiary and the insurance company stand in a creditor-debtor relationship. In its role as debtor, the insurance company will not make payments to the beneficiary in any manner other than that called for by the settlement agreement. However, the beneficiary may be given authority to make withdrawals or change the settlement option to take care of unforeseen contingencies. The trustee of a life insurance trust normally is given adequate authority to deal with unforeseen and unanticipated postdeath events, and he is able to do so without difficulty. Most well-drawn trust agreements also give the beneficiary a power of appointment, allowing him to adjust the ultimate disposition of the trust principal to take into account events occurring after the insured's death.

The client may have a number of policies from various companies in amounts ranging from $5,000 to $100,000 or more. Combining all these policies in an integrated settlement option plan may be difficult, if not impossible. If a trustee is made the beneficiary of all policies, all death proceeds can be administered under a single instrument to carry out a carefully integrated plan.

Money left with an insurance company becomes part of its investment funds. Each company's investment program is subject to state rules and regulations that often are directed toward fixed dollar investments, since the company's obligations are stated in dollar amounts. A grantor can give his trustee broad investment authority, allowing him to follow an investment program best suited to the individual beneficiary's needs. If the amount available is adequate, he can invest to provide for future growth, providing a possible hedge against inflation for the beneficiary.

All available tax saving devices can be incorporated in a trust arrangement except the $1,000 annual interest exclusion for the surviving spouse provided by the Internal Revenue Code for combination payments of interest and principal under a life insurance settlement option. A trustee also can provide tax exempt income by investing in municipal bonds. The trustee of a properly drawn living trust can qualify as a "named beneficiary" for any state inheritance and estate tax exemption as well as for receiving the tax exemption applicable to qualified employee death benefits under Section 2039(c) of the Internal Revenue Code. By careful drafting, a life insurance trust can be designed to save gift, income, and/or estate taxes. These tax saving possibilities are examined in connection with the following trust examples.

The Unfunded Life Insurance Trust

An unfunded life insurance trust is one having no significant principal except one or more life insurance policies, or the right to receive death benefits under such policies upon the death of the insured. Certain employee death benefits not provided by life insurance also may be payable to such a trust. Unfunded trusts are more common than funded life insurance trusts and therefore play a more significant role in estate planning. The right to receive these death benefits normally is sufficient trust principal for a valid trust either by statute or by court decision. In addition, most states recognize the validity of "pour overs" from the insured's will to such an unfunded trust.[2] The unfunded life insurance trust can then operate as a will substitute when this combination plan is used.

The Revocable Unfunded Life Insurance Trust

Most unfunded life insurance trusts provide no tax savings at all. Their primary objective is to serve as a will substitute to achieve one or more of the advantages previously discussed. The grantor-insured creates a trust, reserving all rights in the policy, and the right to amend or revoke the trust during his lifetime. Appendix W, Section I, gives a form for the administrative provisions of such a trust. There is no gift tax involved and the proceeds of the insurance are subject to federal estate tax in the usual way under the provisions of Sections 2036, 2038, and 2042 of the

---

[2] A "pour over" trust is designed to receive the insured's residuary estate, after the payment of taxes and administration expenses, as an addition to the principal. The trust then operates as a living trust without supervision by the probate court.

Internal Revenue Code. A revocable life insurance trust is frequently used if the insured has substantial and significant qualified employee benefits. If the benefits are payable to the trustee of a properly drawn trust, the federal estate tax exemption provided by Section 2039(c) will be available. Payment of the proceeds directly to a testamentary trustee may, or may not, provide such tax exemption. Payment of the proceeds to the employee's executor to be ultimately held in a testamentary trust certainly will not qualify them for this exemption.

In more modest estates, the estate plan may require all insurance to go to the wife if she survives. This would entitle the husband's estate to the full marital deduction. The second tax on the wife's estate is not likely to be significant because she will exhaust most of the capital to support herself and to educate the children. If she does not survive, the money will be required for the support and education of their minor children. To avoid the problems and expenses of guardianship, the insured may create a contingent life insurance trust. In this arrangement, the wife is named as primary beneficiary of the husband's insurance; the trustee of the trust is named as contingent beneficiary. The trust agreement is designed to provide support for the children until they reach majority. If the fund is small, which is normally the case, it may provide for the fund to be held intact until the youngest child finishes his or her education before it is distributed. In this event, the trustee probably will be given authority to use income and principal equally or unequally among the children in accordance with their individual needs, rather than being required to apply it equally.

Another useful type of revocable life insurance trust is one created by someone other than the insured. If a wife owns outright substantial amounts of insurance on her husband's life, the death proceeds may not be making the maximum contribution to their respective estate plans. Normally, the proceeds of the policies are made payable to her in a lump sum to avoid any possible gift tax at the time of her husband's death. Also, it probably is planned that she will make the proceeds available in some way for her husband's death costs. The wife may be completely unequipped to manage the proceeds, and she is under no legal obligation to use the proceeds to pay her husband's death costs. In addition, her subsequent remarriage may divert this property from the husband's children to her second spouse and to the children of her second marriage.

These problems can be solved by having the wife create a life insurance trust with the insurance she owns on her husband's life. She, of course, is the income beneficiary of the trust. To eliminate the possibility of the remaining property at her subsequent death passing to her second husband and their children, the terms of the trust make it irrevocable upon the death of the first to die of the insured-husband or the grantor-wife. The gift tax that would become payable at the death of the insured during the life of the grantor is avoided by allowing the grantor-wife to retain a power of appointment by will. All that is necessary to avoid the gift tax is a limited power—usually limiting the class to the insured-husband's children. A general power can be retained by the wife if desired, although it would permit appointment to a second spouse or their children. Either the policy, if the grantor predeceases the insured, or the proceeds of the policy, if the insured predeceases the grantor, is included in the grantor-wife's estate. This estate tax result is exactly the same as if she had retained the policies out of trust. The proceeds, with proper planning, need not be included in the insured-husband's estate on his prior death to any greater extent than without the trust. Since the trust becomes irrevocable upon the husband's death, the funds can be made available to assist in paying the husband's death costs by authorizing the trustee to purchase assets from his estate or to loan money to his estate. The income tax consequences to the grantor-wife during the period of her survivorship also would be the same as if she received the proceeds in a lump sum and similarly invested them. Capital gains realized in the trust as well as the income from the trust would be taxed to her.

The major problem in this arrangement is paying the premiums on the policies if the grantor-wife predeceases the insured-husband. This problem can be solved by including in the trust a policy on the wife's life that, when invested, can generate enough funds to carry the policy during the period of the insured's survivorship. If the wife has sufficient assets of her own, she also can leave these assets to the trust by her will to accomplish the same purpose. Another source of premium dollars would be the loan values of the life insurance itself. The earnings of the trust during the period of the insured's survivorship should not be taxed to him under the provisions of the revised Section 677 of the Internal Revenue Code since he was not the grantor of the trust. Section 677 concerns taxing the grantor of the trust for trust income used to pay premiums on life insurance on the grantor or grantor's spouse.

The Irrevocable Unfunded Life Insurance Trust

The estate planner may desire to get the proceeds of life insurance out of both the insured's and his spouse's estate. This may be completely or partially accomplished by creating an irrevocable unfunded life insurance trust with the policies. Sample administrative provisions of such a trust are shown in Appendix W, Section II.

It is important that the insured be the grantor of the trust if the proceeds are to be used for the support of his surviving spouse. If she were the grantor and reserved any income interest in the trust, the principal of the trust would be included in her estate under the provisions of Section 2036 of the Internal Revenue Code. Usually the creation of the irrevocable trust will constitute a gift of a "future interest." This can, over the years, become onerous to the grantor because it requires the filing of a gift tax return each quarter in which a premium is paid. Eventually some gift taxes may have to be paid when his lifetime exemption runs out. It is important that the trust beneficiary not pay the premiums, for by so doing she may have made a gift of a "future interest" to the trust remaindermen; but more importantly, she will become co-grantor of the trust and may have a portion of the trust principal included in her own taxable estate under the provisions of Section 2036 of the Internal Revenue Code.

If the insured continues to pay the premiums after the trust is established, the government no longer will contend that a pro rata share of the death proceeds should be included in his taxable estate as the value of the last three years' premiums paid in contemplation of death. Instead, only the dollar value of the three premiums may be includable as gifts made in contemplation of death.[3]

The irrevocable unfunded life insurance trust can be created by someone other than the insured, but this is not very common. As mentioned earlier, if the grantor retains the income from the trust, the principal of the trust will be included in his estate. Since the insurance will be in the grantor's estate in this event anyway, there is no need to give up the right to revoke or amend the trust. Creating an irrevocable trust in this situation may incur unnecessary gift taxes.

Sometimes, however, a wife may own substantial insurance on her husband's life that she acquired during the early years of marriage. The original purpose of the insurance was to support her if her husband died prematurely. If this purpose is no longer important because of the financial success of the husband or because the wife has inherited substantial property from her family, she could create an irrevocable unfunded trust with this insurance for the benefit of the children at little or no gift tax or estate tax cost.

Funded Life Insurance Trusts

Although unfunded life insurance trusts are used widely, it is sometimes desirable to create a trust having a significant principal in addition to the life insurance policies. This is usually done to save income or estate taxes.

Most funded life insurance trusts are irrevocable, but it sometimes happens that a revocable life insurance trust is funded. This usually occurs when a revocable life insurance trust is utilized to provide investment management after retirement. Many draftsmen of revocable life insurance trusts provide that they may be funded before the insured's death to provide for this eventuality. If the trust is revocable by the insured and funded by him, the trust income, including realized capital gains, is taxed to him during his lifetime. There are no gift tax consequences in funding such a trust and the funds, as well as the life insurance proceeds, are included in his estate.

The usual arrangement for a funded life insurance trust is for it to be irrevocable from the very beginning. If the trust is created by the insured, the trust income used to pay premiums on his own life or his spouse's life without the consent of an adverse party is taxable to the grantor. Prior to the Tax Reform Act of 1969 this would not have been the case as to premiums for policies on the life of the grantor's spouse. The gift tax consequences of such an arrangement are the same as for any other funded trust. The authority to use the trust income to pay life insurance premiums makes the income interest a "future interest" for gift tax purposes.

---

[3] Revenue Ruling 71–497. *Editor's note:* Payment of the premiums by the grantor/insured could cause the policy proceeds to be in the insured's estate as a gift in contemplation of death if he dies three or less years after the trust acquires ownership of the policy. *Detroit Bank & Trust Co.* v. *U.S.*, No. 71–1970 (6th Cir. 1972).

For tax purposes, the payment of premiums on life insurance by a trust is generally equivalent to the accumulation of trust income. The Tax Reform Act of 1969 amended the Internal Revenue Code to provide an unlimited throwback rule to distributions of all accumulated trust income, including realized capital gains. Normally a first-in, first-out rule applies on distributions of all trust income accumulated after December 31, 1969. Estate tax consequences of this trust arrangement are the same as for any other funded irrevocable trust. The fact that the grantor is taxed on the trust income under the provisions of Section 677(a)(3) should not require the inclusion of the trust principal in his estate under the retained life income theory of Section 2036. Because of the adverse income tax consequences to the grantor, this trust arrangement is fairly uncommon.

There are some substantial tax advantages in a funded irrevocable life insurance trust if it is created by someone other than the insured or insured's spouse. Perhaps the most common vehicle of this type is the short-term, or "Clifford," trust where income-producing property reverts to the grantor at the end of a term in excess of ten years or the lifetime of the trust beneficiary. The Tax Reform Act of 1969 cut down some of the benefits of these arrangements, so they are not as common or as useful as they once were. Accumulations of income in the trust are now subject to the unlimited throwback rules, and thus they are taxed to the trust beneficiary at the time they are distributed.

A popular type of short-term trust is one created by a grandfather with insurance on the father. Income from the trust property is used to pay premiums on a high reserve policy to be distributed to the grandchildren at the end of the trust term at the same time the income-producing property reverts to the grandfather. The children would then own a fully paid-up policy on their father's life, paid for with dollars taxed initially at the lower rates of the trust, but subject to the unlimited throwback rules. The application of the throwback rules in this instance may not require the payment of any additional tax because the grandchildren may not have much income from other sources during the trust accumulation years. If they had *no* other income, they would be entitled to a tax refund!

One inherent problem in all short-term trusts is the fact that, under the usual agreement, all capital gains realized in the trust are taxed to the grantor when realized, even though they are not distributed to him until the end of the trust term. The short-term trust arrangement was previously used (with the husband as the grantor and the wife the insured) for the benefit of the children to offset the loss of the marital deduction if the wife of a wealthy husband predeceased him. The amendment to Section 677(a)(3) eliminated the income tax savings of this device.

Another type of funded irrevocable trust provides no reversion to the grantor—a truly irrevocable trust. Income from the trust property is used to pay premiums on an insurance policy not on the life of the grantor or his spouse. The income so used is taxed to the trust, subject to the new unlimited throwback rules as to income and realized capital gains. The gift tax consequences on setting up such a trust would be the same as setting up any other irrevocable trust where the entire interest is a "future interest." Thus, the entire value of the income-producing property and policies placed in the trust is subject to the gift tax. The principal advantage of this arrangement is that it eliminates the problems for future premium payments that are inherent in the unfunded irrevocable trust. There is no need to file gift tax returns when future premiums are paid, since the gift is made only once, at the inception of the trust.

The estate tax advantage of the funded trust is further amplified by the value at death of the life insurance placed in the trust. The premiums may be paid with dollars subject to a lower tax bracket initially, but again the money accumulated in the trust by paying premiums will be subject to an income tax payable by the trust beneficiary when distributed in the future.

The fact that a trust is funded may show a living motive for the trust, eliminating or reducing the danger that the gift will be held to have been made in contemplation of death. In an unfunded irrevocable trust, the danger of the gift being held to have been made in contemplation of death is much greater because of the inherent testamentary nature of life insurance. Thus, a properly designed funded life insurance trust, under present law, may reduce or at least postpone somewhat the income tax burden on the premium dollar and keep the property funding the trust, as well as the insurance proceeds, out of the grantor's estate, the insured's estate, the insured's spouse's estate, and perhaps even out of the insured's children's estates. For example, a grandfather could create a funded trust containing insurance on his son's life. After the son's death, the trust income would be payable to his widow for life. When she died, the trust principal would be divided so that each of their children would receive income from one share. Upon that child's death, the trust would terminate as to that share, and the trust principal would be paid to that child's living issue. In addition, the trustee could be authorized to use the principal for any member of the family. Such a trust would not violate the common law rule against perpetuity if all grandchildren were alive when the trust was created. A modification in the dispositive scheme would have to be used if future grandchildren could reasonably be expected.

SUMMARY

Trusts, including life insurance trusts, should not be used in an estate plan unless there is an objective that can be achieved only with a trust. Versatile as the arrangement is, it is not the answer to all estate planning problems. Legal fees must be paid for the preparation of a trust, and a trustee fee usually must be paid.

There is every indication that the trend in New York toward having the proceeds of life insurance paid to trustees appointed under the insured's will is spreading to other states. Most of the advantages of living trusts are available under this arrangement, especially if there is no exposure to greater taxability and administration expenses. Where this procedure is not definitely established by statute, the revocable unfunded life insurance trust, as a will substitute, will become increasingly more popular.

Irrevocable unfunded life insurance trusts are currently enjoying a revival. The complications of paying future premiums interrupted their growth trend for some time, but they received new strength when the government recognized the possibility of getting noncontributory group insurance out of an employee's estate by assignment. If it can be removed from an employee's estate, why not also from his wife's estate as well?

Funded life insurance trusts have been mortally wounded by the Tax Reform Act of 1969. Other than the grandfather short-term trust, many of the tax reasons for creating funded life insurance trusts are gone. If, however, the estate plan calls for creating a funded irrevocable trust, the planner should consider carefully the possibility of increasing the tax leverage of the arrangement by including some life insurance in the trust principal.

SELECTED REFERENCES

Bush, J. S.; Lacovara, P. P.; and Schlesinger, E. S. (eds.). *The Best of Trusts and Estates—Estate Planning*, ch. 7. New York: Matthew Bender & Co., Inc., 1965.

Casner, A. James. *Estate Planning*. 3d ed. Boston: Little, Brown & Co., 1961. Supplement, current year.

Cox, Norwood. *The Role of Personal Life Insurance Trusts in the Estate Plan*. Springfield, Mass.: Massachusetts Mutual Life Insurance Co., 1962.

Guilfoyle, A. F., and Schachleiter, K. T. *Tax Facts on Life Insurance*. Cincinnati, Ohio: The National Underwriter Co., annual editions.

Research and Review Advanced Underwriting Service. *Living Gifts and Trusts*, Section 8. Indianapolis, Ind.: The Research and Review Service of America, Inc., loose-leaf service.

Schlesinger, E. S. "How to Use Insurance Trusts in Estate Planning," *J. K. Lasser's Estate Tax Techniques*, Vol. 1, p. 799. Loose-leaf service.

————. *Life Insurance Trusts*. Coral Gables, Fla.: University of Miami, 1967. First annual Institute of Estate Planning.

57

Income Taxation of Life and Health Insurance

By FRED J. DOPHEIDE

LIFE INSURANCE has received favorable tax treatment since 1916 when the federal income tax law first exempted life insurance death benefits from taxation. Although the laws concerning taxation of life insurance have changed since then, Congress has continued to recognize the social value and utility of sheltering life insurance from the erosion of the federal income tax.

It will be the purpose of this chapter to present the general rules of income taxation of life and health insurance and to discuss the tax consequences of certain specific life insurance arrangements. In examining specific arrangements, three interrelated questions will be given attention:

1. When are proceeds received at death or as living benefits subject to income taxation?
2. When are premiums a deductible item for income tax purposes?
3. When are premiums paid by an individual or entity taxable to the party receiving the economic benefit from such payment?

GENERAL RULES

Life Insurance Death Benefits

Lump-Sum Payments. Generally, life insurance death benefit payments payable by reason of death of the insured are excluded from the gross income of the beneficiary.[1] It matters not whether the beneficiary is an individual or an entity. In addition to death benefits payable under individual life insurance policies, the term "death benefit payments," for purposes of exclusion from income tax, includes death benefits payable under accident and health insurance contracts and workmen's compensation in-

---

[1] IRC, Sec. 101(*a*)(1).

surance[2] but does not include death benefits payable under an annuity contract.

Interest Option. When death proceeds are held by the insurer for future withdrawal or distribution and only interest on the proceeds is paid to the beneficiary, the full interest payment is taxable.[3]

Installment Options. For policies that matured by death before August 17, 1954, the proceeds distributed under policy settlement options are fully tax free even though each payment contains an interest element. The law changed in 1954. For policies maturing by death after August 16, 1954, that portion of each payment made under the fixed period, fixed amount, or life income installment options representing the principal of death proceeds, is received tax free but that portion representing interest is taxable. To calculate the taxable portion, the lump-sum death benefit that could have been received tax free is prorated over the payment period of the option and the portion of each payment representing principal is receivable tax-free. The remainder representing interest is reportable as ordinary income.[4] In this calculation the "payment period of the option" must be determined. Where the fixed period option is in operation, the payment period is the number of guaranteed annual installments; where the fixed amount option is in operation, it is the number of annual installments of a specified amount produced under the guaranteed interest rate in the policy; and, under the life income option, the payment period is the life expectancy of the beneficiary. (If the life income option has a refund or period certain feature, the present value of such feature must be subtracted from the lump-sum death proceeds before proration.) Life expectancy and valuation of refund features are determined by reference to mortality tables and interest rates of the insurer.[5]

Interest Exclusion. A surviving spouse may exclude from income up to $1,000 of interest payable under a settlement option but only where the option is installment in nature, i.e., where the payments are a true combination of both interest and principal.[6] Thus, if only interest is payable, as under the interest option, the exclusion is not available. Irrespective of the number of policies on the insured's life placed under installment options, the maximum exclusion available is $1,000.

Contingent Payees. Where the primary beneficiary dies before receiving all installments under the fixed period or fixed amount options, the contingent payee will be taxed in the same manner as was the primary beneficiary. That is, the contingent payee will exclude the same portion of each installment from income and include the same portion of each installment in income.[7] Where the primary beneficiary was receiving a life income settlement and dies during a period of guaranteed payments, the contingent payee in most instances receives the balance of period certain or refund payments tax free because it is wholly in lieu of the present

---

[2] Regs., Sec. 1.101–1.
[3] IRC, Sec. 101(c).
[4] IRC, Sec. 101(d)(1).
[5] Regs., Sec. 1.104–4(c) and (e).
[6] IRC, Sec. 101(d)(1)(b).
[7] Regs., Sec. 1.101–4(a).

value of such guarantee plus the present value of payments made to the first beneficiary, and is therefore entirely an "amount held by an insurer" paid at a date later than death.[8]

Life Insurance Living Benefits

Lump-Sum Payments. Where the owner of a life insurance contract receives the lifetime maturity proceeds or cash surrender value of the policy in a one-sum payment, he will be subject to ordinary income tax on the amount received in excess of his cost basis.[9] His cost basis is his investment in the contract which is the sum of premiums paid, less policy dividends actually received, less any policy loans,[10] less extra premiums paid for certain supplementary benefits such as waiver of premium and accidental death protection.[11]

Gain realized upon surrender or maturity of U.S. Government Life Insurance (World War I) or National Service Life Insurance (World War II) is exempt from tax.[12]

Where, upon maturity or surrender, the amount received is less than the cost basis, no loss is recognized. The difference represents the cost of pure insurance protection—a nondeductible expense.

Where the owner of a life insurance contract sells the policy to a third party, such a transaction is not considered a "sale or exchange" for income tax purposes. Thus the gain in such a transaction is taxed as ordinary income and not capital gain.[13] Any gain is taxable as ordinary income and is determined in the same way as upon surrender of the contract.

Interest Option. Where the policyowner leaves matured endowment proceeds or cash surrender values with the insurance company under the interest-only option, the interest earned will be taxable as ordinary income when received or credited to the payee.[14] In addition, at the time of maturity or surrender, if the values available to the policyowner exceed his cost basis, the gain will be taxed as ordinary income at this time even though he leaves these lifetime proceeds with the insurance company, *provided* he also reserves the right to withdraw the proceeds at any time.[15] This right of withdrawal places him in constructive receipt of the gain. To avoid constructive receipt and thereby postpone the tax on any gain, the policyowner must elect the interest option *before* maturity or surrender and give up the right to withdraw the proceeds.[16] In such case the person who ultimately receives the proceeds will bear the tax liability for the gain.

Installment Options. When the policyowner places maturity or cash surrender values under any of the installment options, the annuity provisions of the Internal Revenue Code apply.[17] Part of each installment

---

[8] Regs., Sec. 1.101–4(*d*)(3).
[9] IRC, Sec. 72(*e*).
[10] Regs., Sec. 1.72–6 (*a*)(1).
[11] Rev. Rul., 55–349, 155–1 Cum. Bull. 232.
[12] 38 USC Sec. 3101(*a*).
[13] *Commissioner* v. *Phillips,* 275 F 2d 33 (CA 4, 1960).
[14] IRC, Sec. 72 (*j*).
[15] Regs., Sec. 1.451–2; *Blum* v. *Higgins,* 150 F 2d 471 (CA 6, 1945).
[16] *Constance C. Frackelton,* 46 BTA 883, Acq. CB 1944, p. 10.
[17] IRC, Sec. 72(*a*).

payment is considered a return of principal and is not subject to tax. The percentage of each installment received tax free is found by dividing the investment in the contract by the expected total return.[18] The Code provides a "sixty-day rule" which affects the definition of "investment in the contract."[19] The rule has significance where, at the time of maturity or surrender, the lifetime proceeds exceed the owner's cost basis. The rule enables the policyowner to avoid immediate tax on the gain but as a result a larger percentage of the installment payments will be subject to tax. The rule works this way: If the policyowner elects the installment option no later than 60 days following the date of maturity or surrender of the policy, there will be no tax on the unrealized gain until installments begin and "investment in the contract" will be the aggregate of premiums paid less dividends, loans, and premiums for certain supplementary benefits.[20] If, on the other hand, the owner delays electing the installment option until beyond the 60-day period, he will be taxed on his total unrealized gain as of the time of maturity or surrender but his investment in the contract will be increased to the total maturity or surrender value, thus enlarging the tax-free portion of future installments. This will be accomplished, however, at the expense of exposing to taxation in one year the total gain on the contract.

Where the option selected is the life income option, the "investment in the contract" is reduced by the actuarial value of any refund or period certain feature.[21]

The expected total return under the fixed period option is determined by multiplying the fixed number of years or months by the amount of the guaranteed payment provided in the contract for such period.[22] Under the fixed amount option, it is determined by multiplying the fixed installment amount by the number of guaranteed installments.[23] Under the life income option, the expected return is determined by multiplying the periodic payment by the payee's life expectancy as determined by government tables.[24]

Once the taxable amount is determined under the installment options, it ordinarily does not change. Thus an annuitant-payee who lives beyond his life expectancy may recover tax free much more than his investment in the contract.

Contingent Payees.   Where the primary payee dies before receiving all installments under the fixed period or fixed amount options, the contingent payee will be taxed in the same manner as was the primary payee. That is, the contingent payee will exclude the same portion of each installment from income and include the same portion of each installment in income. Where, however, the primary payee was receiving a life income settlement and dies during a period of guaranteed payments, the

---

[18] IRC, Sec. 72(*b*).
[19] IRC, Sec. 72(*h*).
[20] See citations in footnotes 8 and 9, *supra*.
[21] IRC, Sec. 72(*c*).
[22] Regs., Sec. 1.72–5(*c*).
[23] Regs., Sec. 1.72–5(*d*).
[24] Regs., Sec. 1.72–5(*a*).

contingent payee will have no taxable income until the total amount he receives, when added to the amount which was received tax free by the primary payee, exceeds the investment in the contract.[25] Thereafter the full amount of each payment will be taxed as ordinary income.

Health Insurance Benefits

Disability Income Payments. Disability income insurance can be provided as a rider to a life insurance policy or through a separate contract. In either event, income payments on policies owned and paid for by the insured are received by the insured tax free.[26] Where payments are made to a policyowner other than the insured—for example, to a corporation which has purchased the disability income insurance as key man insurance —the benefits paid by the insurance company continue to be tax free.[27] A different situation arises, however, where disability income insurance is paid for by an employer to fund a salary continuation plan for employees and the benefits are paid by the insurance company directly to the individual employees. Upon receipt of disability income from such a policy, an employee must include in income amounts received during the first 30 days of continuous disability and amounts in excess of $100 per week thereafter.[28] However, where the sick pay provided is less than 75 percent of the employee's weekly rate of wages, this fully taxable period of 30 days is reduced to 7 days or eliminated entirely if such employee is hospitalized.[29] In this situation, the tax-exempt amount payable to such an employee during the first 30 days is limited to $75.

Medical Reimbursement. Benefits payable from hospital and surgical policies, major medical policies and other medical expense coverages whether individual or group, are exempt from income tax.[30] However, any benefits received must be used to reduce the amount of related medical expenses otherwise deductible for the year. In addition, to the extent that reimbursement is received for medical expenses taken as a tax deduction in a prior year, it will be taxable in the current year.

Income Tax Treatment of Premiums

Personal Life Insurance. The general rule with respect to the income tax treatment of life insurance premiums is that they are a personal expense and as such they are not deductible.[31] The rule applies whether the premium is paid by the insured, the beneficiary, or policyowner. Exceptions to the general rule exist in certain situations, based upon the use to which the life insurance is put. Examples include premiums paid by a business creditor for insurance purchased as collateral security for the debt, premiums paid for life insurance owned by a qualified charitable organization, premiums paid for life insurance by an ex-husband as part

[25] IRC, Sec. $72(e)(2)(A)$.
[26] IRC, Sec. $104(a)(3)$.
[27] *Castner Garage, Ltd.*, 43 BTA 1, acq. (1935).
[28] IRC, Sec. $105(d)$.
[29] See citation in footnote 27, *supra*.
[30] See citation in footnote 25, *supra*.
[31] Regs., Sec. $1.262-1(b)(1)$.

of an alimony decree, and premiums paid by a business for life insurance used to fund certain employee benefit plans.

Business Life Insurance.   Generally, premiums paid on business life insurance are not deductible. The Internal Revenue Code is explicit: "No deduction shall be allowed for . . . premiums paid on any life insurance policy covering the life of any officer or employee, or of any person financially interested in any trade or business carried on by the taxpayer, when the taxpayer is directly or indirectly a beneficiary under such policy."[32] Premiums on business life insurance have been characterized by the Internal Revenue Service as a capital investment and not a business expense even though the policy is term insurance.[33]

Personal Health Insurance.   Prior to 1967, the question of whether personal disability income premiums were a deductible medical expense led to considerable litigation. Eventually the Internal Revenue Code was amended to provide that for years beginning with 1967, premiums paid for personal disability income insurance are not deductible.[34] Included in the definition of disability income insurance are policies which pay a weekly income payment to the insured while hospitalized.[35]

Premiums paid for medical reimbursement insurance are deductible within certain limits. One half of these premiums is deductible from the first dollar but the maximum deduction is $150. The excess over $150, if any, is considered a medical care expense under the Code[36] and is deductible to the extent that it, along with other itemized medical care expenses, exceeds 3 percent of the taxpayer's adjusted gross income.

Business Health Insurance.   Where an employer pays premiums on a disability income policy on the life of an employee, and benefits are payable to the employer, no premium deduction is allowable[37] but the benefits are received tax free. This tax treatment is similar to key man life insurance owned by a business on a key employee.

Where, however, the employer pays premiums on disability income insurance with benefits paid directly to the employees under a salary continuation plan, such premiums are deductible by the employer and not taxable to the covered employee[38] provided such premium payments, when added to all other compensation paid the covered employees, do not exceed a reasonable allowance for personal services rendered.[39]

Premiums paid by an employer on a policy providing medical reimbursement to the employee are deductible to the employer and not taxable to the employee if they meet the test of reasonableness[40] and are part of a plan of employee benefits.[41]

---

[32] IRC, Sec. 264(*a*)(1.)
[33] O.D. 699 CB 3, 1261.
[34] IRC, Sec. 213(*e*)(1)(*C*).
[35] Rev. Rul., 68–451, 1968–2 Cum. Bull. 111.
[36] IRC, Sec. 213(*e*)(1).
[37] Rev. Rul., 66–262, 1966–2 Cum. Bull. 105.
[38] IRC, Secs. 105(*c*) and 106.
[39] IRC, Sec. 162(*a*)(1).
[40] See citation in footnote 38, *supra*.
[41] Regs., Sec. 1.162–10(*a*).

LIFE INSURANCE ARRANGEMENTS GIVING RISE TO TAX CONSEQUENCES

Transfer for Value

Perhaps the most prominent exception to the general rule that life insurance death proceeds are tax exempt is the transfer-for-value rule.[42] Where a policy which has been transferred by assignment or otherwise for a valuable consideration matures by reason of death, the transferee will be liable for income tax on the amount of death proceeds in excess of the actual value of the consideration paid for the contract plus the total of net premiums subsequently paid by the transferee.[43] This rule, which seems to be deeply grounded in public policy, is designed to prevent a tax-free windfall that might come about from speculation in life insurance policies. Life insurance enjoys an income tax favored position because of its unique economic function of protecting families and business interests that would profit more by the insured's continued life than by his death. Thus, one who buys life insurance policies for speculation with the hope of realizing a substantial monetary profit on the death of the insured will not enjoy the tax exemption.

However, Congress did recognize that certain transfers of life insurance for consideration are not motivated by a desire for profit but for valid personal or business reasons. Thus Congress included in the Code an exception to the transfer-for-value rule.[44] This exception provides that in the case of specified transfers for value, the death proceeds are income tax free. These transfers include transfers for value to the insured, to a partner of the insured, to a partnership in which the insured is a partner, and to a corporation in which the insured is a shareholder or an officer. The only other exception from the rule is one which excludes transfers in which the transferee's basis in the transferred policy is determined in whole or in part by reference to the transferor's basis. This excludes transfers in a tax-free exchange; for example, where one corporation transfers a corporate-owned key man policy to another corporation in a tax-free reorganization.

It is perhaps worthwhile to reflect on the conspicuous absence in the Code of other transfer situations which are not excepted and yet may be motivated by personal or business reasons which are equally as valid as those surrounding the exceptions enumerated in the Code. One can think of many family transfers that would not involve speculation but would be made for sound estate planning reasons. One glaring omission is the transfer of a policy from an insured who is a shareholder in a closely held corporation to a fellow shareholder. As in the transfer of a policy from a partner-insured to a fellow partner, there may be sound business reasons for such a transfer, yet the rule excepts the latter but not the former. Conscientious planners need to be especially mindful of these non-exceptions.

---

[42] IRC, Sec. 101(a)(2).
[43] Regs., Sec. 1.101–1(b).
[44] IRC, Sec. 101(a)(2).

The tax results of a transfer-for-value problem can be most onerous. Because of the aleatory nature of a life insurance contract, the amount exposed to ordinary income in one year can be substantial. Thus, careful attention must be paid to every transfer of a life insurance policy in order to avoid the tax pitfall of the transfer-for-value rule. Examples of transfers which are not uncommon but which violate the rule include the following:

1. A policyowner sells a policy on his life to a corporation in which he is an employee and/or member of the board of directors. (The insured must be a shareholder or officer.)
2. A and B own all the stock of a corporation and enter into a buy-sell agreement on a cross-purchase basis. Instead of buying new life insurance on each other's lives to fund the agreement, A and B each transfer to the other an existing policy on his life. (Co-shareholders are not exempt transferees.)
3. K, a key man, terminates employment with X Corporation. K wishes to obtain, as personal insurance, the key man policy owned by X on his life. To keep the proceeds out of K's estate, the corporation transfers the policy for value to his wife.

The above transactions are clearly transfers for value subject to tax. Other more subtle situations may bring the rule into play. In some instances, the parties may be unaware that a transfer is being made or unaware of the consideration involved.

For example, assume that corporate owners, A and B, enter into a cross-purchase buy-sell arrangement and elect to fund it with group life insurance—a procedure not normally recommended. A, on his group certificate, names B as beneficiary; and B, on his certificate, names A as beneficiary. A and B may not be consciously aware that they are transferring anything to each other, but the broad definition of "transfer for a valuable consideration" given in the Regulations seems to suggest that A and B are transferees for value:

> . . . a "transfer for a valuable consideration" is any absolute transfer for value of the right to receive all or a part of the proceeds of a life insurance policy. Thus, the creation, for value, of an enforceable contractual right to receive all or a part of the proceeds of a policy may constitute a transfer for a valuable consideration of the policy or an interest therein. . . .[45]

Thus it might be argued that A and B have transferred for consideration an interest in their group life insurance to each other. The consideration seems to consist of reciprocal promises to fund their business agreement with cross-beneficiary designations.

Another risky transfer is the absolute transfer of a policy from husband to wife under a divorce or separation agreement. Can it be said that the husband has made a gift of the policy to the wife? It seems more likely that there is consideration involved. Section 2516 of the Code states that agreements disposing of marital and property rights are deemed to be

---

[45] Regs., 1.101–1(*b*)(4).

made for "full and adequate consideration."[46] Thus, such transfers can lead to unfortunate tax results for the ex-wife upon the ex-husband's death. One answer might be for the wife to apply for a new policy on the life of the husband, the premiums on which the husband will be required to pay under the decree.

A policy which has been transferred for value can be cleansed of the taint by a subsequent transfer of the policy, for value or otherwise, to an exempt transferee; for example, the insured.[47] However, the transfer-for-value taint is not removed by a subsequent gift of the policy to a non-exempt transferee. Thus, where A, the insured, sells his $10,000 policy to S, his son, for $3,000 and S then gives the policy to his sister, D, the policy is still subject to the transfer-for-value rule. At the insured's death, the proceeds in excess of $3,000, plus premiums paid subsequent to the transfer to S, will be subject to ordinary income tax.[48]

Lack of Insurable Interest

The concept of insurable interest has had an influence on the taxation of life insurance proceeds. Lacking the requisite of insurable interest, life insurance has been viewed as a mere wagering contract entered into for profit. This was the view of the court in a case[49] where a corporation paid the premium on accidental death insurance on its truck drivers with the corporation named beneficiary of the death proceeds. When a driver was killed, the proceeds collected by the corporation were held to be profits subject to ordinary income tax. It was the view of the court that the truck driver was not a key man and that the corporation did not at any time have an insurable interest in his life. The decision reminds us that the question of insurable interest in a business insurance situation is one that continues to merit careful attention.

The Tax Court in an earlier case[50] went so far as to tax the proceeds of a key man policy where an insurable interest existed at the inception of the contract but presumably not when the policy matured as a death claim. On appeal, however, the Sixth Circuit Court reversed and held that the proceeds were not taxable for lack of an insurable interest. The court pointed out that local law required an insurable interest only at the time of inception of the contract. Except in Texas, the requirement of insurable interest only at inception is the general rule in life insurance situations.

Proceeds as Corporate Distributions

Business life insurance is occasionally arranged so that proceeds of policies which are owned and paid for by a corporation are paid to beneficiaries other than the corporation. Such nonparallel owner-beneficiary designations can raise complex problems, depending upon who the named beneficiary is. Where the beneficiaries are shareholders of the

---

[46] IRC, Sec. 2516.
[47] Regs., Sec. 1.101–1(b)(2) and (3).
[48] See citation in footnote 47, *supra*.
[49] *Atlantic Oil* v. *Patterson*, 331 F 2d 516 (CA.5, 1964).
[50] *Francis H. W. Ducros*, 272 F 2d 49 (CA 6, 1959).

corporation, they may contend that the proceeds paid directly to them by the life insurance company retain their tax-free character. The IRS has refused to accept this point of view, maintaining instead that such insurance proceeds are taxable as dividends because the result is the same as if the proceeds were received tax free as life insurance proceeds by the corporation and then distributed to the shareholders as a dividend. The IRS's position has the advantage of logic and this was acknowledged in at least one case.[51]

A collateral problem raised by unorthodox business insurance arrangements is taxability of the premiums. If a corporation pays premiums on business life insurance where shareholders are beneficiaries, or where shareholders are beneficiaries and owners of the life insurance, the premiums are taxable to the shareholders as dividends.[52]

Thus, in situations where a corporation owns and pays for life insurance to fund a buy-sell arrangement or to protect the corporation against the loss of a key man, the corporation and not the shareholders should be the beneficiary.

Creditor-Debtor Situations

Life insurance serves a valuable commercial function in the extension of credit. The security against death provided by a life insurance policy may mean the difference between a loan being granted or not. But what are the tax consequences of life insurance used in this setting?

Before examining the tax aspects, it might be helpful to keep in focus the gradations of life insurance arrangements possible where a creditor wishes life insurance security. Perhaps the simplest arrangement is for the insured-debtor to use an existing policy and simply name the creditor as beneficiary. Although this is the simplest method, it would hardly satisfy most creditors. The next possibility is to have the insured-debtor effect a collateral assignment of an existing policy to his creditor. The insured would still pay the premiums and the creditor would have limited rights in the policy which would terminate upon satisfaction of the debt. Conceivably, the creditor could pay the premiums in these instances, but practically it would only happen where the debtor was unable to do so. The next gradation would be a new policy on the insured-debtor owned by the creditor with the creditor named beneficiary. The creditor might or might not pay the premiums.

Deductibility of Premiums. Where the debtor owns the policy on his life and pays the premiums, it seems quite clear from the cases that the premiums are not deductible.[53] This is true even where the debtor is required to provide life insurance in order to obtain the loan. The same rule of nondeductibility applies where the debtor assigns his personally owned policy to the creditor as collateral security and the debtor continues to

---

[51] *Golden* v. *Commissioner*, 113 F 2d 590 (CA 3, 1940); Rev. Rul., 71–79, IRB 1971–7, 17.

[52] Rev. Rul., 59–184, 1959–1 Cum Bull. 65.

[53] *Glassner* v. *Commissioner*, 360 F 2d 33 (CA 3, 1966); *Klein* v. *Commissioner*, 84 F 2d 310 (CA 7, 1936).

pay the premiums. The courts have held that the insured, in paying premiums, is buying a benefit for himself because the purchase of the policy enables him to obtain a loan. In addition, his estate would benefit because the debt would be eliminated upon death. For these reasons, the premiums constitute personal nondeductible expenses.

Where the debtor owns the policy and collaterally assigns it to the creditor to secure the debt, and the creditor pays the premiums, deductibility of the premium payment may apply in special circumstances. The position of the IRS is that the premiums are deductible as a bad debt only if (1) the creditor has a right to reimbursement for premiums paid (a not unusual circumstance in business loans), and (2) such right is worthless in the taxable year in question.[54] Assuming that the policy involved was term insurance and that the debtor was insolvent, it would seem that the creditor would be entitled to a bad debt deduction for the amount of the debt including premiums paid. Further, if the creditor continued to pay premiums on the assigned policy, continuing premium payments would be deductible. The IRS litigated the question in insolvent debtor cases where the policies involved had cash surrender values, contending that the creditor had a right to reimbursement of premiums paid from the cash values, hence no premium deductibility. In these insolvent debtor cases, however, courts have been more liberal and have allowed the deduction, without regard to the creditor's ability to recover the premium out of the cash value of the policies.[55] The deduction has been allowed as an ordinary and necessary business expense with emphasis placed on the creditor's need to protect his collateral by keeping the policy in force. It is well to remember, however, that these taxpayer victories in favor of deductibility have occurred in situations where the debtor was insolvent.

In the situation where the creditor applies for, owns, and pays the premiums for a policy on the debtor's life, one can be more positive regarding the deductibility of the premiums. An old ruling of the IRS[56] granted a deduction to the creditor but limited it to the excess of premiums over cash surrender value; presumably that portion of the annual premium which exceeded the cash value increase for the year in question. A more recent Revenue Ruling[57] states that if the policies purchased and owned by the creditor are term life insurance policies with amounts of insurance that do not exceed the unpaid balance of the debt, then the creditor's premium payments are fully deductible as ordinary and necessary business expenses. Thus, in determining whether premiums paid for insurance on the life of a debtor to secure the debt are deductible, key questions concerning policy ownership, premium payor, amount and type of insurance need to be answered.

---

[54] IRS, GCM 14375, XIV–1 Cum. Bull. 52.

[55] *Commissioner* v. *Charleston National Bank*, 213 F 2d 45 (CA 4, 1954); *First National Bank and Trust Company of Tulsa* v. *Jones*, 143 F 2d 652 (CA 10, 1944).

[56] OD 38, 1 CB 104 (1919). Obsolete Ruling list, Rev. Rul., 68–575, IRB 1968–43, 31.

[57] Rev. Rul. 70–254, IRB 1970–21, 6. 1970 Cum. Bull. 31.

Death Proceeds. The proceeds of life insurance on the life of a debtor received by a creditor are not tax exempt as life insurance proceeds. They are received as a collection of the unpaid balance of the debt rather than "by death of the insured" as that language is used within the meaning of Section 101(*a*).[58] Proceeds received to the extent of the outstanding debt are tax free as a return of capital unless the creditor has previously taken a bad debt deduction, in which case the proceeds so received must be included in gross income.[59] Any premium amounts that have been deducted by the creditor and later recovered as proceeds must be reported as taxable income.[60] Any amounts of the proceeds representing interest on the debt are taxed as ordinary income to the creditor.[61] Should the creditor receive amounts in excess of the outstanding debt, premiums paid and other amounts owing to the creditor, it would seem that such "excess" proceeds would still not be tax exempt because of the important question of insurable interest. This might be the case in creditor-owned life insurance originally purchased and owned by the creditor as distinguished from collaterally assigned life insurance or even absolutely assigned life insurance where, in most states, the creditor's recovery of proceeds is limited to the amount of the debt plus the premiums paid, interest, and other expenses, with any excess deemed to be held by the creditor as a constructive trustee for the benefit of the named beneficiary or estate of the insured.

Charitable Contributions

Premiums paid on life insurance owned by a qualified charitable organization are deductible to the donor as a charitable contribution, subject to the charitable contributions limitations.[62] It is important that the charity be the owner of the policy and have the exclusive right to cash in the policy, borrow on it, or change the beneficiary.

One technique for achieving deductibility of life insurance premiums which is occasionally suggested is simply to name the charity irrevocable beneficiary of the policy proceeds. This technique is to be avoided because it is fraught with uncertainties. We know that the irrevocable beneficiary is given some ownership interest in the policy but the exact nature is frequently clouded, especially in the area of charitable giving. Perhaps more importantly, the Tax Reform Act of 1969 in broad language denies a charitable deduction for gifts to charities where less than the taxpayer's entire interest in the property is contributed.[63] The Act enumerates certain exceptions which do not seem to encompass partial gifts of life insurance.

---

[58] Albeit death is a prerequisite to the fund coming into existence. Regs., Sec. 1.101–1(*b*) (4); *Landfield Finance Co.* v. *U.S.*, 418 F 2d 172 (CA 7, 1969).

[59] *T. O. McCamant*, 32 TC 824.

[60] *St. Louis Refrigerating and Cold Storage Co.* v. *U.S.*, 162 F 2d 394 (CA 8, 1947).

[61] See citation in footnote 60, *supra.*

[62] IRC, Sec. 170; *Eppa Hunton IV*, 1 TC 821.

[63] IRC, Sec. 170(*f*)(3).

Separation and Divorce

Income tax consequences need to be considered carefully where life insurance is involved in separation agreements and divorce decrees. Whether premium payments are deductible, whether premiums constitute taxable income, and whether life insurance proceeds are taxable depends on the specific arrangements made.

Premium Payments. Premium payments by the husband or ex-husband on life insurance benefiting his wife or ex-wife are deductible by the husband under Section 215 of the Code and taxable to the wife or ex-wife under Section 71 of the Code:

1. Provided the premium payments are pursuant to a decree of divorce or separate maintenance or under a written separation agreement or are pursuant to a decree for support.[64] (Premiums paid in discharge of the obligation of child support are not deductible by the husband);[65] and

2. Provided the premium payments qualify as "periodic payments." Payments are deemed periodic under Section 71 of the Code if the amount to be paid is indefinite in the sense of being incapable of a mathematical determination, or if a definite sum is payable in even installments over a period of more than 10 years from the date of the agreement. (One writer has suggested that if a limited pay life policy is involved, then it must have remaining at least 10 annual premium payments);[66] and

3. Provided the wife is the absolute owner of the life insurance policy.[67] It is not enough that the settlement arrangement requires that the wife be named beneficiary even though she be named irrevocably. If the husband retains ownership rights in the policy, or if the policy rights will revert to the husband upon the wife's death or remarriage, the premiums paid are not deductible. Thus, for premiums to be deductible, the policy must be absolutely assigned to the wife or a new policy on the husband must be applied for and completely owned by her. Perhaps the best course is to have the wife pay the premiums on the policy owned by her. Periodic alimony payments (deductible to the husband and taxable to the wife) can be increased to provide the additional dollars for the wife to meet the necessary premiums.

Death Proceeds. Life insurance proceeds paid in the form of alimony are vulnerable to income tax. Section 101(e) of the Code and attendant Regulations[68] excepts alimony from the general rule that life insurance death proceeds are exempt from income tax. Whether or not life insurance

---

[64]Regs., Sec. 1.71–1(b)(1); Rev. Rul. 70–218, IRC, 1970–19, 7; 1970–1 Cum. Bull. 19.

[65] *Ashcraft* v. *Commissioner,* 252 F 2d 200 (CA7, 1958).

[66] George, "Disposition and Taxation of Life Insurance on Separation and Divorce, *C.L.U. Journal,* Vol. 23, No. 3 (October 1969).

[67] Rev. Rul. 70–218, IRB 1970 19, 7; 1970–1 Cum. Bull. 19.

[68] Regs., Sec. 1.101–5.

proceeds constitute alimony is determined by reference to Section 71 of the Code. That section provides that payments will be considered alimony if they are made pursuant to a court decree or separation agreement and are periodic and are being made in discharge of a legal obligation arising out of a marriage relationship.[69] Thus where a husband is required under a divorce decree to own and maintain a policy on his life as security for postdeath payments, and the payments are construed as periodic, the life insurance death proceeds paid in installments would be taxable as alimony to the divorced wife.

To avoid the impact of income tax on proceeds of life insurance in divorce and separation situations, the husband's policy should not be used to guarantee periodic alimony payments after his death. Absolute assignment of the policy to the wife would probably not avoid adverse tax consequences either because of the specter of the transfer-for-value problem discussed above. The safest course is for the wife to obtain a new policy on the husband owned by her with premiums paid by her from alimony payments.

Additional Compensation

Premium payments by an employer on an individual policy insuring the life of an employee, where the employee is the policyowner and the employer has no beneficial interest in the policy, may be deductible to the employer.

Such an arrangement is often referred to as an "informal pension plan" whereby an employer selects certain favored employees for this non-qualified fringe benefit. The employee applies for the policy and possesses all incidents of ownership. The employee names his own personal beneficiary for the death benefit and the employer pays the annual premium. Such payment, if considered additional compensation to the employee for services rendered, will be deductible under Section 162 of the Code as an ordinary and necessary business expense.[70] An important element in the success of this arrangement is the need for the payments to qualify as additional compensation and not as dividends should the employee also be a shareholder. It is also important that the total amount of compensation realized by the employee, including the premium payment, meet the test of reasonableness. Finally, the employer must not be a beneficiary of the policy either directly or indirectly.[71]

Such premium payments by the employer are taxable to the employee when paid. The question is often asked, why arrange such a plan; wouldn't it be equally effective if the employer simply increased the employee's salary by the amount of the premium and let the employee buy the life insurance with the increase in salary? It is true that the same tax result would follow but whether or not the effect would be equal is the question

---

[69] See citation in footnote 65, *supra*.

[70] *Twin City Tile and Marble Co.*, 32 F 2d 229 (CA 8, 1929); *Hubert Transfer and Storage*, 7 TCM 171; Regs., Sec. 1.61–2(d)(2)(ii)(a).

[71] IRC, Sec. 264 (a); Rev. Rul. 70–148, IRB 1970–14, 9; 1970–1 Cum. Bull. 60.

to ponder. The employer has an opportunity to place himself in a psychologically advantageous position by selecting one or more "key men" for the benefit "plan." The package of benefits embodied in a life insurance contract such as a substantial death benefit, disability features, and lifetime guaranteed retirement income may be much more appreciated by an employee, and especially by his family, than what might otherwise appear as a nominal salary increase.

Group Term Life Insurance

Where an employer pays premiums on group life insurance for the benefit of his employees, such premiums are deductible as an ordinary and necessary business expense.[72] Taxation to the employee for the cost of the group life insurance benefit provided is based on rates set forth in the Regulations.[73] Generally speaking, however, employer premium payments for the first $50,000 of group term life insurance death benefits are tax exempt to an employee.[74]

Split Dollar Life Insurance

An increasingly popular fringe benefit for selected employees is the split dollar life insurance plan. Under a typical split dollar arrangement, an employee and employer share or "split" the premium payments. Cash value type policies are almost universally used with the employer's share of annual premium being measured by each year's increase in cash value. The employee's share of each premium payment is generally the difference between each year's cash value increase and the amount of net premium due. The employer is named beneficiary to the extent of the cash value and the employee has the right to name his own beneficiary for the difference between the total death proceeds payable and the cash value.

Under such a plan, an employee receives a substantial amount of life insurance at a relatively low cost. The employer pays the major share of each premium (at some point in the life of the policy, the employer may be paying *all* the premium) and thus the providing of split dollar life insurance for an employee bestows an economic benefit on the employee.[75] The employee thus must include in his gross income each year the value of the economic benefit received which is measured by the government's P.S.-58 rates. The value of each year's economic benefit to the employee is determined by multiplying the applicable P.S.-58 rate at the employee's age by the amount of net death protection provided for him that year. The employee's part of the premium paid for that year (if any) may be subtracted from the total value of the economic benefit.

No deduction is available to the employer for contributions to a split dollar plan[76] because the employer is also a beneficiary under such policy within the meaning of Section 264(a)(1) of the Code.

---

[72] IRC, Sec. 162(a).
[73] Regs., Sec. 1.79–3(d)(2).
[74] IRC, Sec. 79(a).
[75] Rev. Rul. 64–328, 1964–2 Cum. Bull. 11.
[76] See citation in footnote 75, *supra.*

SUMMARY

Although death proceeds of life insurance enjoy shelter from the impact of federal income tax in the vast majority of instances, the very nature of life insurance as valuable property and its flexibility in solving human problems has led to its imaginative use in business and personal situations where careful planning is required to avoid income tax pitfalls. Thus, all proposed transfers of life insurance should be closely examined to avoid transfer for value problems; the requirement of insurable interest should be taken into account as a tax-oriented dimension of concern; the property arrangement of policy ownership and beneficiary designation should be given thorough consideration where premiums are paid with corporate dollars; and the disposition or use of life insurance in separation and divorce cases should be coupled with specialized guidance to assure favorable tax results.

The questions of life insurance premium deductibility and taxation are of special concern in insured-debtor situations, in charitable giving and in planning life insurance fringe benefits for selected employees. Again, in these complicated, yet common transactions, the desired tax results can be accomplished best through an awareness of the tax principles involved.

SELECTED REFERENCES

George, Albert, Jr. "Disposition and Taxation of Life Insurance on Separation and Divorce," *Journal of the American Society of Chartered Life Underwriters,* Vol. 23, (October 1969).

Redeker, Harry S. and Reid, Charles K., III. *Life Insurance Settlement Options.* Homewood, Ill.: Richard D. Irwin, 1964.

Simmons, Sherwin P. *Federal Taxation of Life Insurance.* Philadelphia, Pa.: American Law Institute and the American Bar Association, 1966.

White, Byron F. "Survey of Problems Involved in Ownership and Transfer of Life Insurance Policies," *California Western Law Review.* Vol. 2, (Spring 1966).

58

Estate and Gift Taxation of Life Insurance

By LEONARD L. SILVERSTEIN and GERALD H. SHERMAN

U.S. FEDERAL TAX LAWS historically have recognized the special social utility of life insurance. While other forms of property obviously serve social purposes, the scope of those purposes is normally limited by the physical and economic boundaries of a single item of property. The values of that item simply have limited leverage possibilities. Life insurance is, in a sense, a unique product in that it provides a means for escaping the restricted range of other forms of property. The magic of life insurance enables the entire wealth of the issuing company, as contrasted to economic values of a single person or single item of property, to be harnessed in a manner that provides catastrophe protection (in an economic sense) for that single person or similar small unit of persons. Life insurance, therefore, deserves the encouragement it sometimes receives from the tax laws.

The estate and gift tax provisions in our tax laws generally have followed the tendency of providing a reasonably fertile loam from which life insurance can grow and be utilized.

In developing a description of the place of life insurance in the estate and gift tax structure, the future prospects for life insurance vis à vis that structure will not be discussed in detail. However, the reader's attention is directed to the fact that the Internal Revenue Service is taking an increasingly critical view of the favorable tax treatment of life insurance, particularly when used in new forms and combinations, as those forms evolve in an expanding technological society.

FEDERAL ESTATE TAX

As a general rule, the federal estate tax applies to the value of property that is owned by the decedent at the time of his death and is passed on to heirs and other beneficiaries in connection with, or by reason of, death. Sometimes it also applies to the value of property which was transferred by the decedent to a beneficiary prior to death such as where the transfer took place in contemplation of death.

If such general rules applied literally to life insurance, the estate tax values of life insurance contracts which are owned by the insured at his death, or which were previously transferred by the insured "in contemplation of death," would be equal merely to the cash value of those contracts at death. However, the value of life insurance which is generally includable in the decedent-insured's gross estate in these instances is the face value of the policy, not merely its cash value. The criteria upon which it must be determined whether such face value is or is not includable in the gross estate are manifold. This chapter will examine such criteria and suggest ways in which to work with them.

Identity of Beneficiary

If an insurance policy is payable on death to the estate of the insured, normally through being made payable to the executor of that estate, the full face amount of the policy is includable in the insured's gross estate. This rule applies even if the insured does not own the policy at death and even if the policy is payable for the benefit of the estate only through indirection. For example, if a policy on the life of the insured is pledged as collateral security for a loan made by the insured during his life, so much of the proceeds as are equal to the loan balance outstanding at death will be deemed to be for the indirect benefit of the insured's estate and will be includable in his gross estate for federal estate tax purposes. The underlying theory is that the discharge of the debt with the insurance proceeds renders a general benefit to the insured's estate and to all takers thereunder.

Where the policy is payable on death to a person other than the insured's estate, susceptibility to the estate tax depends upon the ownership and other criteria discussed hereafter.

It should not be concluded that in no event is it advisable to structure insurance coverage so that it is payable to the insured's executor or to his estate. In cases where it is planned that the face amount of the policy is to be specifically includable in the insured's gross estate (as, for example, where it is intended that the face amount of the policy is to qualify for the marital deduction), it may be beneficial to provide for the disposition of such proceeds under the insured's will rather than directly under the policy. In such event, a policy provision making the proceeds payable to the insured's estate on death is an appropriate course of action.

Owner of Policy

If the insured owned the policy on his life, or, in the catchphrase of the statute, possessed any of the policy's "incidents of ownership," the face amount of the policy will be includable in his gross estate at death.[1] This is true irrespective of the identity of the policy's beneficiaries. Furthermore, the incidents of ownership in the policy need not be exer-

---

[1] But see the special rule for benefits payable under a qualified profit sharing or pension plan, discussed in Chapter 36.

cisable by the insured alone. Even if he shares possession of those incidents with another person, such as his wife or an institutional fiduciary (e.g., a bank), the full face amount of the proceeds will be subject to estate taxes in his estate.

Neither the manner of creation of the ownership nor the fact that, in a practical sense, it may not be possible to exercise such ownership is pertinent. The insured may have received the incidents of ownership through gift and may never have paid any of the premiums under the policy; nevertheless, the face amount of the proceeds is still includable in his gross estate. The insured may have purchased a flight insurance policy in an airport immediately before boarding a plane which crashes and may never in any real sense have had an opportunity to exercise such rights of ownership.[2] The proceeds, nevertheless, will be subject to the estate tax.

Definition of Ownership. "Incidents of ownership," although it is a phrase that appears in the Internal Revenue Code, is not defined in the Code. However, over the years various rights to, or powers over, all or a portion of a life insurance policy have become generally accepted as examples of incidents of ownership, possession of any one of which will taint the policy for the purposes we are considering. Such rights and powers as listed in the income tax regulations include:

a) The right to change the beneficiary;
b) The right to surrender or cancel the policy;
c) The right to assign the policy;
d) The power to revoke an assignment;
e) The power to pledge the policy for a loan; and
f) The right to obtain from the insurer a loan against the cash surrender value of the policy.

Incidents of ownership need not necessarily be possessed directly by the insured; indirect possession can be a sufficient basis upon which to charge the insured with ownership of the policy. For example, the IRS in its regulations has long taken the position that the insured possesses the necessary incidents of ownership if he is the sole stockholder of a corporation which has the power to change the beneficiary of a policy on his life.[3]

Ownership Transfer. The crucial importance of the ownership of the policy leads to an obvious conclusion. If it is desired that the face amount of the policy not be includable in the insured's gross estate on his death, either he should never have acquired incidents of ownership to the policy in the first instance, or, having acquired such ownership, he should transfer it by some means to a third person. If the problem is recognized at

---

[2] It is to be noted that an accidental death policy is treated as life insurance under the Internal Revenue Code.

[3] At the time of the preparation of this chapter, the IRS announced the issuance of proposed regulations which, if adopted, would alter its position. Under the new proposed regulations, a corporation's incidents of ownership would not be attributed to the insured unless he is a controlling stockholder, and then only to the extent the proceeds are not payable to the corporation or to a third person for a valid business purpose of the corporation, such as the satisfaction of a business debt.

the time of the issuance of the policy, it becomes a simple matter for the person who is chosen to own the policy (e.g., the insured's wife) to apply initially for its issuance and to become its first owner. In this fashion the insured never is tainted with the proscribed incidents.

However, where this protective step is not taken, the first problem to arise is the need to determine the best means of transferring ownership from the insured to a third person. A series of difficulties can be present in this situation. For example, it is usually not appropriate for the insured to sell the policy to a third person for the amount of its cash value. Detrimental income tax consequences (a description of which is beyond the scope of this chapter) can result through operation of the so-called "transfer-for-value" rule.[4] Although there are exceptions to the rule, in most cases the policy should be undertaken through gift or, at a minimum, through a part gift, part sale arrangement.

If the insured dies within three years after making the gift, a rebuttable presumption arises separate and apart from the basic incidents of ownership test that the transaction constitutes a gift in contemplation of death and that the full face amount of the policy is includable in the insured's estate. Although the mere fact that the insured makes a gift of a policy is not conclusive evidence that the gift is made in contemplation of death, the burden will be on the insured's estate to prove otherwise.

If the presumption of a death motive can be rebutted by proving a living motive, or if the insured does not die within three years of making the gift, no part of the proceeds should be includable in his taxable estate. Remaining are the basic questions respecting the estate tax implications for the new owner of the policy. For example, suppose that the insured has made a gift of the policy to his wife, who predeceases him. The cash value of that policy, or more specifically its interpolated terminal reserve value, will be includable in the wife's gross estate.

This result conceivably could be avoided by making the initial gift transfer to a trust for the benefit of the wife. In fact, such a trust arrangement is often used to avoid the possibility of estate tax in the event of the prior death of the wife. It also serves the purpose of avoiding a second tax which might otherwise be placed on the proceeds of the policy in the estate of the wife, should she survive the husband and later die in possession of most or all of the proceeds which were received under the policy on the prior death of the husband. This generation-skipping result is accomplished by making the wife's interest under the trust a lifetime interest, with the principal of the trust being payable upon the wife's death to other beneficiaries, e.g., the insured's children. In this fashion, we may effectively skip the wife's generation as a bearer of estate taxes that might otherwise attach to the value of the policy proceeds.

Relationship to Compensation Arrangements. The mere fact that there are many useful and advantageous forms through which life insurance is provided to employees as a means of added compensation does not mean that those forms necessarily avoid application of the incidents of ownership test. If an employer takes out and pays the premiums on a policy on the life of an employee, that employee will be deemed to possess incidents

---

4 "Transfer for value" is discussed in Chapter 57.

of ownership in the policy where he has the right, as is often the case, to name the beneficiary.

Two popular forms of such compensation are split dollar insurance and group term life coverage. In both situations it is normal for the employee to have the right to name the beneficiary. As is true for life insurance in general, one way of avoiding the tax consequences attendant upon possession of incidents of ownership is to make a donative transfer of the policy, i.e., of those incidents. However, when the employee's rights in the policy are derived from his employment relationship, special problems exist.

It is sometimes recommended that the employee's wife be made the owner of his interest in the split dollar policy. However, the IRS might argue that the employee's right to terminate employment and, thereby, to terminate the insurance coverage is an incident of ownership which in no event can be given up. Consequently, the transfer to the wife might be insufficient to accomplish the intended result. One possible way around this result is for a written split dollar agreement to be entered into that gives the wife the right to purchase the policy from the employer in the event of a termination of employment. Another approach may be to enter into a so-called collateral assignment split dollar plan under which the wife is designated owner of the policy from the start.

In contrast to the lack of reliable precedent upon which to judge this aspect of the split dollar situation, specific attention has been directed to the issue of the donative transfer of the employee's rights under a group term policy. The IRS states and the courts generally have concluded that, if local law and the policy itself permit the assignment of the policy and particularly of the employee's right to convert that policy upon termination of employment, the assignment is effective to remove the incidents of ownership from the employee's possession. However, where the employee retains the right of conversion, or local law or the policy itself does not permit the assignment of such right, the IRS will in no event recognize the severance from the employee of such incidents.

Although there is still some doubt under the law of a number of states respecting whether an interest in a group term life insurance policy can be assigned, many states have passed statutes expressly permitting such assignment. In any event, little tax detriment will result from the making of the assignment. At worst the policy will be deemed to be includable in the employee's gross estate—the result that would have clearly occurred if the assignment had not been attempted. Most companies will provide the insured with a form by which the assignment can be made. However, the companies normally will disclaim any assurances concerning the assignment's effectiveness under state law.[5]

Payor of Premiums

Prior to 1954, the identity of the payor of the premiums was, in a large majority of the cases, of crucial importance to the estate tax issue, even where the policy was not payable to the insured's estate and the insured

---

[5] See Chapter 36 for discussion of the special estate tax situations of benefits payable under qualified profit sharing and pension plans.

did not possess incidents of ownership in the policy. This so-called premium payment test was abolished by Congress in 1954 and the identity of the payor of the premiums was generally thought thereafter to be of no consequence for estate tax purposes.

However, in a situation involving the gift of a policy or the gift of one or more of the policy premiums, the IRS has taken the position that a form of premium payment test still may have some applicability. To illustrate, assume that the insured makes a gift to a third person, e.g., his wife, of the incidents of ownership in a policy and continues to pay the premiums. If the insured dies more than three years after the date of the gift, the IRS will contend that, although the full face amount of the policy is not subject to estate taxes (the three-year cutoff having eliminated "gift in contemplation of death" reasoning), the value of the premiums paid by the insured within the three-year period should be included in his estate.

If the gift of the policy occurs within the three-year base period, the estate tax consequences are, of course, more severe. The IRS has specifically stated that, where the decedent purchases a one-year term accidental death policy and designates his children as owners, the full face amount of the policy will be included in his estate, should he die during the term of its coverage. In such a situation, the insured not only has made a gift of the policy within three years of death, but he has paid all the premiums due on the policy within that period.

The IRS has not specifically stated what its position would be where the insured makes the gift of the policy within the three-year period but pays none or only a portion of the premiums due during that period. In such cases, it is not clear whether the amount includable in the insured's estate is something less than the full face amount of the policy.

Although the full significance to be attached to the insured's payment of premiums within the three-year measuring period is subject, at time of this writing, to some conjecture, it doubtless would be preferable as a matter of caution for someone other than the insured to pay the premiums due after the date of the gift. Alternatively, the payment of premiums by the insured more than three years after the gift of the policy can generate estate tax consequences no more serious than the inclusion in the insured's estate of the amount of the premiums paid by him during the three years preceding death. To illustrate, assume that the gift of the policy is made in year 1 and that the insured dies in year 5. Assume further that the grantee-owner of the policy paid the premiums in years 1, 2 and 3, and that the insured paid the premiums in years 4 and 5. The insured's gross estate for estate tax purposes will include the value of the premiums paid by him in years 4 and 5, the only premiums he paid during the three years preceding his death.

Relationship to Qualified Retirement Plans

If the insured is an employee who is covered under a qualified pension, profit sharing or annuity plan, any death benefits payable under such plan will be excludable from the insured's gross estate if they are payable to a beneficiary other than the insured's estate. This exclusionary rule holds true irrespective of the fact that the insured may possess one or more incidents of ownership in a life insurance policy purchased under the plan, as, for example, where the insured has the right to name the beneficiary.

The rule is intended to be applicable in the case of employer-paid compensatory death benefits. Therefore, the portion of the death benefit which is attributable to premium amounts contributed by the employee will not be excludable from the gross estate. In fact, this is a special kind of premium payment test.

The method of computing the portion of the death benefit which is attributable to employee payments is not totally clear. For example, are required employee payments, as contrasted to voluntary employee payments, to be treated as employer payments and, thus, not in reduction of the amount that qualifies for the estate tax exclusion? This question is particularly relevant where employers require employees to pay a portion of death benefit costs to offset P.S.-58 rate income measurements for income tax purposes. In such a situation, if the required employee payment is treated as an employer payment, the income tax saving does not entail any additional estate tax cost. However, if the required employee payment is not treated as an employer payment, it will cause a pro rata reduction in the estate tax exclusion. As a consequence, the income tax saving will be purchased at the cost of additional estate taxes.

This special rule applicable to death benefits which are payable under qualified plans is also applicable to death benefits which are payable under an annuity contract purchased for an employee by certain tax-exempt schools, churches, and other charitable institutions,[6] and to death benefits which are payable under the military retirement system.

FEDERAL GIFT TAX

The usual motivation for a noncharitable, donative transfer (of life insurance or any other property) is the love and affection of the donor for the donee. A favorable tax benefit is to be derived from the gift in that it removes the policy from the donor-insured's gross estate by relieving him of incidents of ownership in the policy. If this has been accomplished successfully, it normally will result in a transfer subject to the federal gift tax.

However, if the donor retains a reversionary interest in himself or his estate valued at more than 5 percent of the value of the policy, or retains the power to revest the economic benefit in himself or his estate, or to change the beneficiaries or their proportionate benefits, the gift is incomplete and no gift tax will be due. Alternatively, the purpose of removing the face amount of the policy from the insured's gross estate will not be served.

Taxable Value and Tax Rates

The value subject to gift tax upon the gift of a single-premium or other fully paid-up policy is the replacement cost of such policy, i.e., the cost of a single-premium policy at the insured's attained age which is necessary

---

[6] For a discussion of tax deferred annuities, see Chapter 37.

to replace the policy as of the date of the gift. Where premiums remain to be paid under the policy, the value that is subject to gift taxes is the interpolated terminal reserve plus the unearned portion of the premium for the current period, plus any dividends on deposit and less any loans outstanding.

It should be clear, therefore, that the transfer of an existing policy containing a substantial cash value can result in a gift tax liability. In most situations, except for any unearned premium, value is not assigned for gift tax purposes to the transfer of a term policy having no cash value. From this point of view, the term policy would be the most likely candidate for a gift, the primary purpose of which is the ultimate avoidance of estate taxes.

This distinction between types of policies, important as it is for a full understanding of the pertinent gift tax considerations, is of less concern than the distinction between the taxable value for gift tax purposes of a gift of a policy and the taxable value for estate tax purposes of that policy when it is included in the insured's gross estate.

The gift tax value will in no event exceed the cost of replacing the policy and is usually limited to the policy's interpolated terminal reserve. Of course, if future premiums are paid by the donor they will constitute additional future gifts which are subject to gift tax. In comparison, if incidents of ownership in the same policy remain with the insured, the policy will be includable in his gross estate and will be subject to estate tax at the substantially higher face amount value. This distinction between the gift and estate tax taxable values is doubtless the most crucial point of contrast in understanding the relationship between the taxes.

Another important feature in understanding the consequences of a gift of an insurance policy relates directly to the rate differentials between the gift and estate taxes. The gift tax rates are uniformly three quarters of the estate tax rates at the same dollar brackets. For example, the first $100,000 of net property value subject to estate taxes generates an estate tax of $20,700. The first $100,000 of net property value subject to gift taxes generates a gift tax of $15,525. Furthermore, the accelerated rate structures of both taxes come into play. Each dollar of gift, although it is subject to gift tax at the the lowest gift tax rate applicable to the donor, is removed from the donor's gross estate at the highest estate tax rate applicable to the estate.

For these reasons, the same dollar transferred as an *inter vivos* gift usually results in a lower gift tax than the amount of estate tax that would result if it were passed on as a testamentary transfer.

Annual and Lifetime Exclusions and Exemptions

Each calendar year a donor may transfer to each donee to whom he makes a gift that year up to $3,000 in value free of gift tax, provided that the gift represents a present interest in property as contrasted to a future interest. A direct gift of life insurance from A to B is clearly the transfer of a present interest.

However, where the insurance is placed in trust, the trust beneficiary usually will not have the current use and enjoyment of the policy benefits. For this reason, there will not be a gift of a present interest within the meaning of the statute. Alternatively, where the trust beneficiary is given the additional powers to cause the corpus of the trust to be invested in income-producing property and to invade the principal of the trust, it can reasonably be contended that a present interest has been created.[7] If so, not only should the initial transfer in trust qualify for the $3,000 annual exclusion, but any subsequent gifts of premiums also should qualify.

Above and beyond the cumulative total of all annual exclusions, each donor is permitted a $30,000 lifetime gift tax exemption. This lifetime exemption does not apply with respect to each donee as in the case of the annual exclusion, but applies to total taxable gifts by the donor after application of the annual exclusion.

To illustrate, if during a single year A, an unmarried individual, made a gift to B of a life insurance policy having a gift tax value of $5,000 and also made a $2,500 cash gift to C, he would have to use $2,000 of his lifetime exemption in order to avoid the payment of a gift tax. Of the cash gift to C, all would be exempt by virtue of the annual exclusion. Of the life insurance gift to B, $3,000 would be exempt by virtue of the annual exclusion, leaving $2,000 of the gift to "eat into" A's lifetime exemption. For all future years, A would have available a remaining lifetime exemption of $28,000. For each such future year A would have a new annual exclusion of $3,000 for gifts of a present interest to each donee.

Donor's Marital Status

The donor's marital status can have a substantial effect on the gift tax consequences. If the donor is married and is making a gift to a person other than his spouse, it may be possible to increase the effective size of the annual exclusion and the lifetime exemption from $3,000 to $6,000 and from $30,000 to $60,000, respectively. The Internal Revenue Code permits the spouse of the donor to join in the gift and to agree to the treatment of the gift as having been made one half by the donor and one half by the donor's spouse. Consequently, each half of the gift will qualify for a separate $3,000 annual exclusion and each spouse's independent $30,000 lifetime exemption also will be applied separately.

The split gift approach is, of course, feasible only where the donee is not the donor's spouse. Where a policy is gifted by the donor to his spouse, the gift, in most circumstances (if it does not reflect a terminable interest), will qualify for the gift tax marital deduction. One half of the gift so qualifying will not be subject to gift taxes.

The study of split gifts and the marital deduction is in itself a sizable undertaking. For purposes of this chapter, suffice it to say that, in any gift situation, the consequences of these concepts always should be carefully considered.[8]

---

[7] Where the income beneficiaries of the trust are children, it may be possible to qualify for the annual exclusion by means of a so-called Sec. 2503(c) gift-to-minors trust and avoid the necessity of utilizing the described powers.

[8] For additional reading, see Chapter 57, "Income Taxation of Life and Health Insurance"; Chapter 59, "Gifts of Life Insurance"; and Chapter 60, "Estate Planning— An Illustration."

Inadvertent Gift

Previously, in discussing ways in which the insured can give away incidents of ownership to the policy, consideration was given to a gift transfer to the insured's wife. However, in view of certain estate tax detriments which can result if the wife predeceases the insured, the possibility of a gift to a trust for the benefit of the wife was suggested. Now, a gift tax reason for avoiding a donative transfer of the policy directly to the wife should be considered.

If she has made a third person, such as a child, the beneficiary of the policy and her insured-husband predeceases her, the wife will find that, through inadvertence, she has made a taxable gift to her child of the face amount of the policy. Until the moment of the insured's death, the wife had the power to remove the child as beneficiary and name any person she wished, including herself. However, by voluntarily permitting the child to remain as the beneficiary until the moment of the husband's death, she has at that moment transferred all rights under the policy to the child. Here the measure of the gift, unlike the measure of a gift of a policy by the insured, is the full face amount of the proceeds. It is the postdeath value of the proceeds, rather than the predeath value of the policy, which is the subject of the gift.

Avoidance of this inadvertent gift result can be accomplished if the owner of the policy, in this case the wife, names herself as beneficiary. In that event, no gift can result upon the death of the insured.

SELECTED REFERENCES

Bowe, William J. *Estate Planning and Taxation,* Chartered Life Underwriter ed. Homewood, Ill.: Richard D. Irwin, Inc., 1972.

Casner, Andrew J. *Estate Planning.* Chap. 8. 3d ed. Boston, Mass.: Little, Brown Company, 1961.

Commerce Clearing House Editorial Staff. *Federal Estate and Gift Taxes Explained.* (Explains the law, court decisions, rulings, and estate and gift tax regulations.) Chicago, Ill.: Commerce Clearing House, Inc., 1971.

Kahn, Douglas A.; Colson, Earl M.; and Craven, George. *Federal Taxation of Estates, Gifts and Trusts.* Philadelphia, Pa.: American Law Institute/American Bar Association, 1970.

Mertens, Jacobs. *Law of Federal Gift and Estate Taxation,* Chap. 17. Chicago: Callaghan & Co., 1959. Revision by P. Zimet.

National Underwriter Company. *Tax Facts on Life Insurance.* Cincinnati, Ohio. Published annually.

Rabkin, Jacob, and Johnson, Mack H. *Federal Income, Gift and Estate Taxation.* Chap. 61. Albany, N.Y.: M. Bender & Co., 1972.

Research and Review Service of America, Inc. *Fundamentals of Federal Income, Estate and Gift Taxes,* with emphasis on life insurance. Indianapolis, Ind., 1972.

Taxation Affecting Life Insurance. Englewood Cliffs, N.J.: Prentice-Hall, Inc. Published annually by Special Publications Division.

59

Gifts of Life Insurance

By W. R. HUEY, JR.

THIS CHAPTER deals with the two major types of life insurance gifts, namely, the many uses and advantages of life insurance gifts to family members, and life insurance gifts to charity. The reader also may wish to refer to the preceding two chapters for a full discussion of the income, estate, and gift taxation of life insurance.

FAMILY GIFTS OF LIFE INSURANCE

Accumulating an estate takes all the skill, perseverance, and good judgment that a person can bring to bear over a period of years. Preserving that estate for future generations is a difficult matter as well. Outside forces, particularly death taxes, claim large handfuls of the estate as it passes from generation to generation. But much of this shrinkage can be avoided.

It is a sad paradox that so many men whose ingenuity built their wealth shrug off future estate shrinkage as inevitable. Proper planning today, while they live, will save thousands of dollars for their spouses, children, and grandchildren in the future. A most effective instrument for attaining these savings is the use of living gifts of life insurance. Such gifts also offer many nontax advantages as well.

Tax Savings Available

The federal gift tax rates aggregate only three quarters of the federal estate tax rates. However, the savings through the making of living gifts ordinarily are considerably greater than this 25 percent differential in rates. There are two reasons for this.

1. When part of the estate is given away during lifetime and part transferred at death, the estate benefits from two sets of exemptions: (*a*) those under the gift tax as to the part disposed of by way of living gift, and (*b*) those under the estate tax as to the part which passes at death; and

2. Under the progressive rates provided in both estate and gift tax laws, the property given away reduces the estate in the top brackets of the

estate tax, and is in turn taxed in the lower brackets for purposes of the gift tax.

As a result, it is often advantageous from a tax standpoint for an individual to make gifts of life insurance policies on his own life to other family members. In order for the proceeds of such policies to remain outside the donor's gross estate, certain rules must be met. The estate and gift taxation of life insurance is discussed in detail in Chapter 58. However, a brief summary of the more important rules follows:

Section 2042 of the Internal Revenue Code specifically deals with the estate tax treatment of life insurance.[1] The proceeds of a policy on an insured's life are included in the gross estate if they are receivable by:

1. The decedent's estate, either directly or indirectly; or

2. Named beneficiaries, if the decedent possessed any "incidents of ownership" in the policy at the time of his death.

Proceeds Payable to the Estate. Obviously, insurance payable *directly* to the estate presents no real problem for analytical purposes—the proceeds are always included in the insured-decedent's gross estate. The problem arises where the proceeds are receivable *indirectly* by the estate. This situation comes up where, for example, a policy is made payable to a trustee or other individual beneficiary (as distinguished from the estate or the executor or administrator). In such a case, the proceeds are still considered receivable by the estate and fully taxable if the beneficiary is under a legally binding obligation to use such proceeds to pay taxes, debts, or other estate obligations (such as funeral and burial expenses).

Proceeds Payable to Named Beneficiaries. The basic question in determining whether life insurance proceeds receivable by a named beneficiary will be included in the insured's gross estate is whether the insured has any "incidents of ownership" in a given policy.

It also should be noted that Section 2042 provides that the proceeds are includable in the decedent's gross estate if he retains these incidents of ownership "either alone or *in conjunction with any other person.*" For instance, if a beneficiary is irrevocably named, and his consent is required before the insured may exercise any incidents of ownership, the proceeds nonetheless will be included in the insured's gross estate; this is, of course, because the insured could exercise these ownership rights "in conjunction with some other person."

Some of the more important rights the insured may have in a policy which are considered incidents of ownership include the right to change the beneficiary, the right to surrender or pledge the policy, and the right to select or revoke a settlement option.

---

[1] There could be situations where life insurance proceeds, cash values, and/or premiums may be included in the gross estate under some other Code section including Section 2037, reversionary interest; Section 2035, transfers in contemplation of death; Sections 2036 and 2038, transfers with retained interests or powers. *Editor's note:* Recent court decisions have held that life insurance proceeds will be included in the insured's estate as a transfer in contemplation of death under Sec. 2035 if the insurance was owned by a third party for a period of three years or less prior to the insured's death. *Bel* v. *U.S.*, 29 AFTR 2d (5th Cir. 1971), cert. den., — U.S., —; *Detroit Bank & Trust Co.* v. *U. S.*, No. 71–1970 (6th Cir. 1972); *First National Bank of Ore.* v. *U. S.*, PH Paragraph 147, 705 (DC, Ore.).

Gift Taxation of Life Insurance. When an individual makes a gift of a life insurance policy, the value of the policy for gift tax purposes varies according to the type of policy involved. If the policy is a paid-up policy, the value is equal to its "replacement cost." On the other hand, if premiums remain to be paid on the policy, its value is its "interpolated terminal reserve value." These values usually approximate the policy's cash surrender value.

To illustrate the tax savings possible, assume a man with a taxable estate of $400,000. Let's assume he makes a gift of a $100,000 face amount life insurance policy he presently owns on his life to one of his children. Further assume the policy has a $30,000 value for gift tax purposes. The $100,000 of life insurance proceeds would have been taxed at the 32 percent level in his estate. However, assuming he is married and has not made any previous gifts, he and his wife would have a combined gift tax exemption of $60,000. In addition, each would have the $3,000 annual exclusion available. Thus, no gift tax would be payable and only $12,000 of each spouse's specific exemption would have to be used. Thus, $32,000 in federal estate taxes could be saved as a result of this gift.

Tax Advantages of Life Insurance Gift to Donee

As the subject matter of a gift, life insurance, when compared with other types of property, provides certain special tax advantages to the donee. For example, interest earnings on the cash value portion of a gift of permanent life insurance are not currently taxable to the owner-recipient of the policy.

In addition, the donee as beneficiary of the policy's face value at the death of the donor-insured will receive the proceeds free of federal income tax. If they are paid to the donee in the form of monthly income, that part of each monthly installment representing principal is income tax free, just as it is when the proceeds are paid in a lump sum. Furthermore, if the donee-beneficiary is the donor-insured's spouse, then the first $1,000 of interest received each year under the installment option will be income tax free.

Nontax Advantages of the Life Insurance Gift

In several respects, aside from all tax consideration, a gift of life insurance may be made more readily, more simply, and with less disturbance than a gift of ordinary estate property.

Avoids Disturbance to Business Interests. Certain gifts of property may be inadvisable because of business interests in the estate over which it is important for the estate owner to retain control during his lifetime. The life insurance gift involves no disturbance of or loss of control over such business properties.

No Reduction in Income. The life insurance portion of the estate does not ordinarily produce living income to the donor. As a result, the gift of life insurance property involves no reduction in the current income of the donor as is inevitably involved in the gift of an income-producing part of the general estate. However, before making the gift the insured should consider whether the life insurance might be needed in later years for his own retirement income purposes.

May Be Kept Confidential. The life insurance gift can be made a confidential transaction insofar as business associates, bankers, and various members of the family are concerned. There are no deeds or other papers to record, no transfers of business interests, and so on.

Gives Children Head Start on Insurance Program. As a young boy grows into manhood and takes on the responsibilities of marriage, parenthood, and a career, his need to protect his future earning ability for his family through life insurance becomes great. But with his limited income at this early point in his career, together with heavy current responsibilities, accumulating a sufficient amount of life insurance to do the job is no easy task.

To remedy this, many fathers purchase life insurance for their sons "one generation ahead," that is, while the sons are still in childhood. In this way they embark upon a gift program designed to give their sons a head start in obtaining the life insurance they will need later on. The attractively low premium rate established at the time such a gift of permanent insurance is made is guaranteed for life, so that when the son takes over the payments from his father later on, he does it at a substantial savings over the premium otherwise payable if he were to purchase new protection at his attained age.

This benefit is accompanied by the fact that the insurance protection can never be taken away from the son, even if he becomes uninsurable later in life. Thus, a life insurance gift purchased at an early age can be instrumental in averting economic tragedy if the son is later unable to obtain protection on his own.

No Investment Hazards. A gift of life insurance is free from the red tape accompanying certain other forms of giving. Because the accumulating savings are held by the life insurance company and return a guaranteed rate of interest, there is no need to set up elaborate safeguards to protect the gift from dissipation through normal investment hazards.

Dissipation Not Likely. The very nature of a life insurance gift discourages early dissipation by the recipient. If, for example, the recipient is also the insured on the policy, he knows that the protection he is afforded is of real value to others, as well as himself. He knows, too, that if he were to surrender the policy for its cash value, he would not be able to replace it if he suddenly became uninsurable. Realizing too, that it undoubtedly could not be replaced at the same premium rate, the recipient is strongly motivated to keep the gift intact.

Wedding Present. A wedding present of life insurance is one of the most thoughtful gifts that parents can make to a son or son-in-law. It can take many forms, from a payment of several advance premiums to an agreement to pay premiums annually, or share them, until the son is financially able to assume full control of his life insurance plan.

In addition, there are valuable collateral benefits available, such as a guaranteed insurability feature permitting the son to add to his life insurance estate at specified future dates without the need for a medical examination. A gift incorporating this feature can obviously be extremely valuable in protecting a young husband's future economic worth to his family.

Support to Dependent Parents. A son who uses a portion of his present income to help support dependent parents is justifiably concerned about their welfare if he should die before they do. His own death would create enough economic problems for his wife and children without saddling them with an obligation to provide income to parents whose needs continue undiminished.

A life insurance gift to the parents, a policy on the son's life, solves this problem. Under such a plan, the parents are the owners and beneficiaries of the policy, but the son pays the premiums. If he should die before his parents (or in-laws), replacement income is immediately assured them by the life insurance gift made earlier. It does not create a hardship for his own wife and children, as it does not come from the principal estate set up for their benefit. Consequently, a life insurance gift to the parents actually creates substantial peace of mind for two families.

College Fund: Policy on Child or Grandchild. Through life insurance, a parent or grandparent can give his children or grandchildren the priceless gift of a college education. An endowment policy on a child's or grandchild's life can create an educational fund large enough to cover part or all the college expenses when the child graduates from high school.

College Fund: Policy on Father's Life. A father can guarantee his child a college education, even if the father should die, by purchasing a life insurance policy on his life, and directing that the proceeds be used to fund the college education. If the father survives, the cash value of the policy could be borrowed to help fund the education. In either event, the child's education is better assured.

Direct Gifts

The gift of life insurance may be made either directly to the donee-beneficiary, or may be made in trust for the benefit of such beneficiary. The direct gift possesses advantages of simplicity and finality, but by no means is it entirely free from possible drawbacks. Discussed next are some of the problems that can arise when a *direct* gift of life insurance is made.

Gifts to Minors. Certain difficulties may arise where gifts of life insurance are made outright to a minor donee. As a general rule under the common law, persons below the age of 21 are minors and as such lack the legal capacity to enter into fully enforceable contracts. In addition, if a minor owns property, he may not manage and control such property himself. A legal guardian must be appointed for this purpose. However, many states have enacted statutes which have the effect of rendering a minor who has reached a specified age legally competent to contract for insurance and to exercise all rights in a policy as though the minor had reached the age of 21. In addition, such statutes enable a minor to give a valid release when policy proceeds are paid to him.

The statutes of one group of states lower the age at which a minor attains majority for all purposes. Most of these statutes lower the age of majority to 18, particularly in the case of females. A person's marital status often is the determining factor.

Some states have enacted statutes that authorize payment of insurance proceeds in certain specified amounts over specified periods of time to a minor where the minor is the beneficiary of a policy (usually for educational purposes) *on someone else's life.* Here again the effect is to give the minor legal competency to execute a valid release.

As will be seen, this problem often can be solved by gifts to minors in trust or, in some cases, gifts in custodianship.

Problem of Future Interests.   Where a restriction is placed on the donee's right to the use, possession, or enjoyment of the policy, the gift of the policy is one of a future interest and the donor will not be entitled to the annual gift tax exclusion. For example, where a policy designates one child as death beneficiary, but the incidents of ownership are assigned to all of the donor's children jointly so that the consent of all is required to exercise the policy rights, there is a gift of a future interest. Likewise, where the donor makes the donee irrevocable beneficiary of the policy, but such action does not give the donee acting alone the right to surrender or borrow against the policy, there is a gift of a future interest.

The Donee Can Surrender the Insurance.   Ordinarily, the absolute assignment of a policy places full ownership and control in the assignee; it must do so in order to constitute a present interest gift. Accordingly, the donee can, if he or she desires, surrender the policy, secure policy loans, or exercise other privileges under the contract. If personal needs should become acute, even though the condition is merely temporary, there is inevitably the danger that the policy values since they belong to the donee will be applied to personal use. Such action may defeat the objective of the insurance gift in many cases.

The Problem of Settlement Options.   Difficulties may be encountered in the effort to make a direct gift to the donee, and yet have the insurance proceeds paid under some elective settlement option in the policy.

Some companies will not permit the insured to designate a mode of settlement and then assign the policy. Furthermore, if the mode of settlement cannot be changed at the free will of the donee, the gift probably will be considered a gift of a future interest, and the annual gift tax exclusion will be lost. Of course, this difficulty might be overcome by making the assignment first and then having the assignee-beneficiary elect a settlement option. But even here there are difficulties. First, it is doubtful whether any protective "spendthrift trust" provision (under which the proceeds would be free from claims of the beneficiary's creditors) could be included. The addition of such a clause by the beneficiary himself after the assignment would amount to his creation of a spendthrift trust in his own favor, which is not ordinarily permitted. Second, if the donee is a minor, a legal guardian would have to be appointed to act under the supervision of the court in selecting a mode of settlement.

Where the subject matter of an outright gift is a policy of insurance on the life of a person other than the donee, the living value of the policy will be included in the gross estate of the donee, in the event of his decease prior to that of the insured. If it is a single-premium or paid-up policy, this value will be the cost, at the time of the donee's death, to replace the policy. If the policy calls for future premiums, the value will be the interpolated reserve plus any unearned portion of the premiums paid.

The mere fact that the then value of the policy will be included in the donee's gross estate in the event of his death prior to the insured, how-ever, is not a problem that should deter the making of such a gift. The tax advantages previously discussed usually outweigh any resultant tax liability in the estate of the donee if he dies first. In most instances, furthermore, the probability of this happening is small, for usually the donee is younger than the insured. In any event, care should be taken to avoid having the policy come back to the donor should the donee be the first to die.

Should the donee survive the insured and subsequently receive the policy proceeds, which is the more probable event, there is the problem of estate taxation brought about by the inclusion of the value of the un-expended portion of these proceeds in the donee's gross estate at his death. The tax liability thereby involved must be weighed against the benefits derived from making the gift.

The Gift of Insurance Policies in Trust

The principal difficulties of the direct and absolute transfer to the beneficiary can ordinarily be avoided by making the gift indirectly through the medium of an irrevocable trust. The procedure is simple. The donor prepares a trust agreement and then makes an irrevocable assign-ment of the insurance policies to the trustee named in this agreement, to be held by the trustee for the benefit of the donee-beneficiary of the trust.

The use of a trust in connection with the insurance gift may prove desirable and advantageous. Nontax advantages include:

1. A trust permits a variety of policies in different companies to be brought into one fund and distributed under a uniform plan.
2. A trust may permit the trustee to use the proceeds to purchase assets from the insured's estate to forestall liquidation of assets to meet death taxes and other charges.
3. The trustee may be vested with discretionary powers in exercising policy rights during the insured's lifetime not possible under a direct gift.
4. The trustee may apply the income to the use of a minor, without the interposition of a guardian.

Tax advantages in the use of a trust include:

1. If the trust is irrevocable and the trust instrument is properly drawn, insurance proceeds payable to the trust at the insured's death will not be included in the insured's gross estate.
2. The trust may be so arranged to eliminate tax in the estate of a bene-ficiary who predeceases the insured.

3. If the trust is funded and the insurance is not on the donor's life or the life of his spouse, the income of the trust used to pay premiums will be taxed to the trust, thereby saving income taxes in the donor's top bracket.[2]

However, the gift in trust is not without its minor problems. Most important is that the gift in trust is more complicated and requires more paper work than the direct gift.

Future Interests.   Where a gift is made to a trust, the donor is entitled to as many $3,000 annual exclusions as there are beneficiaries, if each beneficiary receives a gift of a present interest at least equal to this amount.

A single gift may consist of both present and future interests in combination. Again, a gift may consist in its entirety of a present or a future interest to the exclusion of the other. Therefore, where life insurance or annuities are involved, the gift must be considered both in its entirety and from the standpoint of rights in the policy itself, and premium payments.

Where the policies are transferred to a trustee who is given the exclusive right to exercise all the options and rights in the policies, and the use of dividends is left entirely to the discretion of the trustee, the gift is a future interest in its entirety. Under such an arrangement the beneficiaries receive no unconditional present right to income. Likewise, unless they survive the insured, they will never have a right to enjoy the corpus or the income therefrom.

If life insurance policies are given to an irrevocable trust but the beneficiaries cannot obtain the corpus except under certain contingencies that might never occur, or distribution is postponed until specified future dates, the gift is one of a future interest.

The problem of qualifying a gift of trust corpus as a gift of a present interest is the same whether the corpus consists of a life insurance policy or of other property. If the trust beneficiary under the trust terms can at any time effectively demand delivery to him of the trust corpus, he has the right presently to use, possess, and enjoy the corpus. If the beneficiary is a competent adult, there unquestionably is a present interest gift of the corpus under such circumstances.

Where the beneficiary of the trust is a minor, and he or his guardian is given the right at any time to demand the corpus, the appointment of a guardian may be necessary before the gift will qualify as a present interest.

Gifts under Section 2503(c).   Under Section 2503(c) of the Internal Revenue Code it is provided that a gift in trust for a minor is considered wholly a gift of a present interest (and therefore entitled to the annual exclusion) if all of the following requirements are met:

1. Both the property and the income therefrom *may* be expended by, or for the benefit of, the minor *before* he attains age 21;

---

[2] See Chapter 56, "Trusts and Their Uses."

2. Both the property and the income therefrom *will* pass to the child when he attains age 21, or before; and

3. Should the minor die before he attains age 21, the property and the income therefrom will then be payable to his estate or to his appointee under a general power of appointment.

Under a trust meeting these requirements, the trustee may be given wide discretion. For example, it may *permit* him to accumulate income and not pay it to the minor beneficiary until he reaches 21. However, the trust instrument may not *direct* the trustee to accumulate the income since this would violate requirement (1).

A trust that meets the requirements of Section 2503(c) can be useful where life insurance is involved. For example, consider the so-called "grandfather trust." A typical grandfather trust is one where a grandfather establishes an irrevocable trust for the benefit of one or more of his minor grandchildren. Further, the trustee is directed to purchase an insurance policy on the life of the children's father (the grandfather's own son). Premiums for such insurance come from trust income, or from annual contributions to the trust, made by the grandfather.

The Gift Tax Marital Deduction. If a husband gives property (or a property interest) in trust for his wife, and the trust instrument grants her all the income for life and a general power of appointment over the corpus, he is entitled to the gift tax marital deduction.

The property granted to the trust may comprise insurance policies on the settlor's life. However, the gift will not qualify for the marital deduction unless the wife is given either (*a*) all the trust income for life, plus a power to require surrender of the policies and acquisition of income-producing property in their stead; or (*b*) a power to terminate the trust and demand the policies at any time.

The advantages of qualifying for the marital deduction have to be weighed in each case against the wisdom of giving the spouse these powers.

Gifts of Life Insurance to Minors in Custodianship

Outright gifts to minors are uncomplicated and inexpensive, but they can cause problems because of the minor's legal disability to deal with the property until he reaches adulthood. The appointment of a guardian may obviate these problems, but a gift of life insurance under a guardianship arrangement may be expensive and entails a good deal of cumbersome red tape. A trust is another alternative, but requires more paper work than a custodianship.

A simpler solution is now available in the form of the so-called "gift in custodianship." This is a special statutory device now available in many states where gifts of life insurance are concerned.

The Custodianship. A custodianship may be compared to the trust and guardianship concepts, having characteristics of each. In a custodial arrangement, even though the custodian acts as a "manager" over the custodial property, the minor donee is the legal, as well as the equitable, owner. In a trust, on the other hand, the trustee is vested with legal title to the trust property, while the trust beneficiary is the equitable owner.

The donee under a custodianship arrangement may be any individual under age 21. The custodianship ends when the donee dies or attains age 21. In the latter event, the custodian delivers the property and any withheld income to the new adult. If the child should die before reaching age 21, the procedure is for the custodian to deliver the income and principal to the minor's estate, i.e., to his executor or administrator.

Custodial Property. The state laws uniformly permit gifts of money and securities. In addition, many states permit gifts of life insurance, or life insurance and annuities, in custodianship. (The term "life insurance," most likely, includes endowment policies; some states, however, specifically allow endowment gifts in custodianship.)

The Custodian. In some states, the donor may name as custodian *any* adult individual or trust company. Other states restrict the list of eligible individuals to the child's legal guardian, parents, grandparents, brothers, sisters, uncles, and aunts. It is not generally wise from an estate tax standpoint for the donor to be named as custodian, since the custodial property will be included in his gross estate if he should die during the custodianship. In this regard, the courts have held that where one transfers property to himself as custodian, he thereby has a right to terminate the arrangement, resulting in the inclusion of the property in his estate.

Manner of Making Gifts. The method of making custodial gifts is carefully spelled out in the statutes. The recommended language is found in the text of the 1966 Uniform Gifts to Minors Act revision, the relevant provision of which is reproduced below:

Section 2. [*Manner of Making Gift.*] (*a*) An adult person may, during his lifetime, make a gift of a security, a life insurance policy or annuity contract or money to a person who is a minor on the date of the gift:

* * *

(4) If the subject of the gift is a life insurance policy or annuity contract, by causing the ownership of the policy or contract to be registered with the issuing insurance company in the name of the donor, [another adult] [an adult member of the minor's family, a guardian of the minor] or a trust company, followed, in substance, by the words: "as custodian for ＿＿＿＿＿＿＿＿＿＿＿＿＿＿＿

(name of minor)

under the [name of enacting state] Uniform Gifts to Minors Act."

Gifts of Life Insurance. An increasing number of states are permitting gifts of life insurance in custodianship. Under these state laws, a gift of life insurance or an annuity contract must be on the life of the minor donee, or on the life of a member of his family—parents, grandparents, brothers, sisters, uncles, aunts. Where the minor is the insured, the designated beneficiary must generally be his estate; where a person other than the minor is the insured, the custodian is ordinarily named as the beneficiary.

With regard to gifts of life insurance in custodianship, the custodian (in his fiduciary capacity) has all incidents of ownership in the policy as if he were the owner, except with regard to the beneficiary designation limitations. The custodian may pay premiums on the policy out of custodial funds.

Payment of premiums from custodial funds must be distinguished from holding a policy in custodianship, with premiums paid from another source, e.g., from gifts made to the donor. Even though a particular state statute may permit *gifts* of life insurance in custodianship, it does not necessarily follow that the custodian may *invest* custodial funds in life insurance. The laws require the custodian to heed the so-called "prudent man" rule of investment. The reasonable income and capital preservation requirements of the prudent man rule ordinarily preclude investment in life insurance.

On the other hand, some states specifically allow life insurance as custodial property. Where investment in life insurance is authorized, the insurance generally must be on the life of the minor or for his benefit.

CHARITABLE GIFTS OF LIFE INSURANCE

Americans are charitably minded. Each year millions of individuals make contributions in support of churches, educational institutions, hospitals, public welfare agencies, and a multitude of similar organizations generically referred to as "charitable." Philanthropy is one of the ten largest industries in the United States. Contributions to charity each year for the past several years have exceeded $10 billion. Treasury Department statistics reveal that over 95 percent of the taxpayers who itemize their income tax returns claim a charitable deduction.

Charitable giving has developed an extremely broad base, with contributions coming from both the average citizen and from the very wealthy. But despite this benevolence, the financial problems of many of our religious, educational, and other charitable institutions have become pressing. These institutions face a paradox: Their endowments or donations pay less of their operating expenses; yet a rapidly increasing population requires continual expansion of their services. Many people are concerned about the financial plight facing so many charitable institutions. But this concern may be accompanied by frustration; the urge to make substantial charitable gifts is there, but many feel their resources will not permit it.

The gift of life insurance is one method of giving that provides the opportunity to do far more for a favorite charity than many donors might think possible.

Advantages of Life Insurance as a Charitable Gift

A life insurance policy on the life of a donor, and payable in whole or in part to a selected charity, represents one of the most attractive and flexible methods for making a charitable contribution. Here are some of the reasons why:

1. Life insurance enables a donor to make a substantial gift to a charity at death by making small contributions during his lifetime. For example,

an annual premium of $250 paid by a donor age 35 will purchase a policy for the benefit of a selected charity of almost $10,000. This amount will be paid to the charity whenever death occurs.

2. A life insurance gift is made without impairing other assets earmarked for the donor-insured's family. He makes his gift on the installment basis by paying an annual premium out of current income. His other assets are kept intact.

3. Payment is made to the selected charity promptly and in cash. This may not be the case when provision is made for a charitable bequest under the terms of a will; here payment necessarily is delayed. All estate liabilities must be met before the charitable bequest may be made. This period of delay can range from a few months to several years, depending upon the complexity of the estate settlement procedure. Payment of life insurance proceeds is not subject to probate and other delays. Consequently, the charity need not wait in line for a share of an estate that may take months or even years to settle.

4. The gift is not subject to attack by disgruntled heirs. Since life insurance proceeds paid to charity are not part of the insured-donor's probate estate, the payment cannot be contested by anyone. In fact, no one need know that the payment has been made since the proceeds are paid without publicity. Of course, publicity may be given if desired.

5. The charitable institution may make use of the life insurance company's investment facilities. By electing to leave the death proceeds with the company under one of the several attractive settlement options, the organization is entitled to the insurance company's management services at no cost. Thus, the charity is relieved of virtually all investment and reinvestment problems.

The accumulating cash value in the policy likewise grows at a guaranteed rate under the insurance company's expert investment supervision. This is an added benefit to a charity named owner of the policy.

Significant Tax Advantages

Aside from the fact that a donor is able to make a substantially larger contribution to charity through the use of life insurance than he might otherwise be able to make, he also gets an assist from the federal government in terms of various income, gift, and estate tax savings.

Income Tax. The premiums the donor pays are income tax deductible if the selected charity is named owner of the policy or is its irrevocable beneficiary. In the latter case care must be taken that under local law and the policy provisions, the insured has not retained the right to the cash surrender value of the policy. In general, deductible charitable contributions are limited to 50 percent of the taxpayer's adjusted gross income. Any excess in the current year may be deducted during the next five-year period under a "carry-over" provision. The gift may be made directly "to" or "for the use of" the charity, but in the latter case the annual income tax deduction will be limited to 20 percent of adjusted gross income.

Gift Tax. Gifts to charity are deductible in full for federal gift tax purposes. And, unlike the income tax situation, there is no percentage limitation on the amount of the gift tax deduction.

Estate Tax. Finally, the death proceeds of an insurance policy are paid to a charitable beneficiary without incurring any federal estate tax. And this is so both when a charity owns the policy and when it merely is named policy beneficiary.

These income, gift, and estate tax advantages become particularly meaningful when viewed in the light of specific situations.

Insurance Gift Made in Lieu of Current Cash Gifts

Consider a recent college graduate, age 30, who is in a position to make annual contributions of $200 a year to his alma mater. A life insurance policy, owned by and payable to the college would make these modest annual contributions far more meaningful. An endowment policy, or possibly a policy calling for premium payments for only a limited number of years, would fit this situation best, because the college would have a foreseeable date when it would receive the full value of the policy. And such a plan would be self-completing in case of a premature death.

A $200 annual premium would purchase a 20-year endowment policy of about $4,000. At the end of 20 years, or immediately upon death should it occur at any time, $4,000 would be paid the college. On the other hand, a $200 annual premium would purchase a 20-pay life policy with a face amount of over $6,500. This, then, would be the sum payable should this young man die. This policy at the end of 20 years would have an accumulated cash value of almost $3,600, and no further premiums would be due.

With the college owning the policy and controlling its cash value, the donor-insured could deduct his premium payments as charitable contributions. This deductible feature reduces the cost of the gift. For example, if this person is in a 25 percent income tax bracket, the after-deduction cost of the $200 annual premium gift would be only $150.

Charitable Bequest at Death

Many persons wish to make substantial charitable bequests at death and have implemented their intentions by making appropriate will provisions. A whole life insurance policy purchased in favor of a selected charity is an attractive alternative for achieving the same result.

Consider, for example, a leading lay person, age 50, who already has made provision in his will for a cash bequest of $10,000 to his church. With an annual premium deposit of only $500, this donor would create a potential gift of over $10,000 represented by the face amount of a whole life insurance policy owned by and payable to the church. At the insured's death, whenever it occurred, the cash gift would be made promptly, without disturbing other assets earmarked for the family. The church would receive the gift without waiting for the donor's estate to be probated. During the donor's lifetime the church would have the use of the policy cash values.

Here again, with the church owner of the policy, all premiums would be income tax deductible. The insurance proceeds would be paid free of both gift and estate taxes.

Existing Policy Given to a Charitable Institution

In the normal course of events, as one grows older there may be a decrease in the needs which the life insurance portion of one's estate is designed to protect. The children get their education, marry, and become financially independent. The mortgage on the home is paid off. In such a situation, a gift of an existing insurance policy to a selected charity would satisfy an individual's benevolent intentions.

Consider the case of a father, age 55, whose two children completed college a few years ago and are now self-supporting. The father had purchased a $10,000 insurance policy when he was age 30, which was intended to offset the cost of the children's college education in the event of the insured's premature death. This policy now has a present value (its approximate cash value) of about $3,500. If ownership of this policy is transferred to a charitable institution, the donor-insured would have an income tax deduction of $3,500 in the year of the transfer. For example, if he was in a 40 percent bracket, such a transfer would result in an increase in spendable income of $1,400, this being the savings in taxes otherwise payable had the charitable gift not been made. Of course, all premiums the donor-insured pays after transferring this policy also would be income tax deductible.

Group Support of a Charitable Institution

The success of most fund-raising drives generally depends upon the generosity and support rendered by the most prominent group of persons associated with the institution. Examples of such groups would be the directors of a hospital, the trustees and faculty of a university, and the governing laymen of a church or synagogue.

An attractive life insurance plan is available for such groups and would serve as inspiring evidence of support and dedication. A hospital, for example, may have a board of trustees numbering 25 people. In such a situation, a program could be implemented which would allow for the placement of permanent life insurance on each member's life on a so-called guaranteed issue basis; that is, without being required to submit to a medical examination. Such a program would permit all board members to participate in the program regardless of health considerations. It also could result in increasing the level of giving of some members of the group, as well as resulting in gifts from some who otherwise might not make a contribution. All policies issued under the plan would be owned by the hospital and therefore, once again, premiums paid by the members of the group would be income tax deductible.

Gift Combined with Additional Personal Life Insurance

A person may want to make a gift to charity and at the same time buy additional life insurance for the benefit of his family. Both objectives may be accomplished economically and with an income tax saving by splitting the proceeds of a policy between the charity and the family beneficiary.

This plan contemplates taking maximum advantage of the inherent flexibility of any permanent life insurance policy. The policy basically consists of two elements: a savings element represented by the policy's cash value, and a protection element. The protection element, sometimes referred to as the amount at risk, is the difference between the face amount of the policy and its cash value. Naturally, as the cash value increases, the protection element decreases. However, most insurance companies make available various riders and options which, when attached to the basic policy, will produce a level amount of insurance for the benefit of the family.

Consider how this basic characteristic of a permanent policy may be utilized in a plan mutually beneficial to the insured's family, and a selected charity. A permanent policy is purchased and the charity is given all rights in the cash value. The insured's wife, for example, is named beneficiary of the protection element, as well as any riders attached to the policy. The donor-insured pays the full premium. However, since the charity has full rights in the cash value, the insured-donor may take an income tax deduction for the annual cash value increase. At the same time, the family has the benefit of the pure protection portion of the policy, which, incidentally, "costs" less as part of a permanent policy than it would cost if purchased as a separate term insurance policy.

SELECTED REFERENCES

Bohner, Theodore J.   "Irrevocable Life Insurance Trusts to Pay Estate Settlement Costs," *C.L.U. Journal*, Vol. 25, No. 1 (January 1971).

Bowe, William J.   *Estate Planning and Taxation*, ch. 15. 3d ed. Homewood, Ill.: Richard D. Irwin, 1972.

Chasman, Herbert.   *Gifts to Minors in Trust and under Custodianship. Estate Planners Quarterly* Booklet No. 305, March 1971.

Ford, Curtis B.   "Intra-Family Gifts of Life Insurance," *C.L.U. Journal*, Vol. 22, No. 1 (January 1968).

Piro, Robert J.   "How to Cut Taxes by Giving Away Life Insurance," *The Practical Accountant*, Vol. 4, No. 3 (May/June 1971), pp. 16–23.

Rocco, Carolyn F.   "How to Handle Gifts of Life Insurance Outright or in Trust," *Successful Estate Planning Ideas and Methods*, paragraph 5503. Englewood Cliffs, N.J.: Prentice-Hall, Inc., 1969.

60

Estate Planning–
An Illustration

By LAWRENCE G. KNECHT

THE BASIC THEORY and principles which are involved in any and all estate planning cases have been set forth in a previous chapter. However, as so often happens in all technical fields, when the principles are applied in actual practice, somehow things go wrong because of a lack of ability to work them out in a live problem.

What this chapter will attempt, therefore, is to take a specific case and show, in step-by-step fashion, how the case proceeds in applying the principles from the very beginning until the close. The emphasis all the way through will be on *procedure* and *technique* rather than the specific facts of the particular case.

Many estate planners have found that the procedure of estate planning, which is commonly thought of as a single operation, is far more easily understood and handled if considered as being in *three* distinct steps, which are:

1. An analysis of the entire estate as it presently exists.
2. A simple enumeration of the problems, that is, those specific points in which the present estate plan fails to accomplish the owner's objectives.
3. The actual planning stage, where corrective procedures to eliminate or reduce these problems are studied, implemented, and tested.

ANALYSIS OF THE CASE— ESTABLISHING THE FACTS

General Observations

Before planning can start, a base point must first be established. Therefore, the estate owner's exact present situation must be ascertained. This includes all his present assets, his liabilities, his will (or no will, as the case may be), his life insurance under its present settlement provisions, his income and its specific sources and outgo, shown by definite categories, and all the rest of the picture. Obviously, not only the nature of the assets themselves must be ascertained, but also whether those assets are separate or community property, and in either case whether they are in the sole name of the estate owner or in the names of the estate owner and any other person or persons. If they are in more than one name, is there a right of survivorship? Whose money paid for them?

In addition to a complete statement of all assets and liabilities, including the precise way in which titles are held, there must also be available copies of any wills of the estate owner and his wife, trusts of which they are either grantors or beneficiaries, divorce decrees, support agreements, and all insurance policies. Furthermore, if the client owns an interest in a closely held business, copies of financial statements of the business for the last five years (including both balance sheets and operating statements) will be needed with a list of all shareholders and their relationships and a copy of any buy-sell agreement that may exist. Last, but not least, specific authority should be obtained to consult with the estate owner's attorney and insurance companies.

Data of the Illustrative Case

Family and Wills. The estate owner, Mr. White, is an active, equal partner in a successful two-man firm; he is 38 years old; his wife is 35 years of age; and they have three children—two daughters aged 12 and 10, and a boy aged 7, all in good health. They are residents of Ohio. Both the estate owner and his wife have wills but no trusts. His will, after providing for the payment of debts and funeral expenses, leaves his interest in the family residence and personal effects to his wife outright and provides that the balance of his estate is to go to his wife for life only and at her death to the children. The wife is named as executrix and, as such, is given specific power to continue his interest in the partnership; thereafter, she is given power as life tenant to continue to operate the partnership without liability for depreciation.

The wife's will leaves all her assets to her husband if he survives, but if not, then to the children. In both wills Mr. White's sister is designated as guardian of the person and property of minor children.

Inventory of Assets. Mr. White's assets and those of his wife are as follows:

Item	Mr. White's Assets	Wife's Assets	Joint and Survivor
Cash on hand and in bank	$ 4,000	$ 2,000	
Series "E" bonds (payable on death to wife)	2,000		
Series "E" bonds (joint with wife)			$5,000
Series "E" bonds (joint with children)			3,000
Mutual fund shares	7,500		
Home (tenancy in common)	21,000	21,000	
Real estate (parking lot in Erie, Pa.)	20,000		
Personal effects	6,000	9,000	
Partnership interest (book value)	88,700		
Life insurance	66,000		
$10,000 policy on wife's life, owned by husband (cash value)	800		
Totals	$216,000	$32,000	$8,000

His present liabilities consist of the following:

Current bills and accounts (personal)	$ 900
Accrued taxes on home	800
Accrued taxes on parking lot	600
Mortgage on home	8,000
Income tax (based upon one quarter of last year's return)	4,500
State income tax	200
	$15,000

Of the "E" bonds held jointly with his wife, she contributed 20 percent of the purchase price from funds she inherited from her mother.

Neither the estate owner nor his wife has made any gifts in the past that required the filing of a gift tax return.

Life Insurance. With regard to Mr. White's life insurance, it consists of three policies, the first being a $20,000 ordinary life contract purchased when Mr. White was age 24. His wife is the primary beneficiary and his parents are secondary beneficiaries. The proceeds are payable in a lump sum. The second ordinary life policy for $10,000 was taken out when Mr. White's first child was born. It, too, is payable in a lump sum to his wife but, alternatively, to his children. The third policy, which he purchased shortly after his second child was born, is a family income policy, having a present commuted value of $36,000. His wife is the primary beneficiary, and the children are the secondary beneficiaries. The policy is payable on income installment provisions of about $200 a month, and his wife has no right to commute or withdraw or change the secondary beneficiary; payment to the children is to be in a lump sum. He has maximum coverage under social security.

Income and Expenses. From the standpoint of his income, he draws $2,000 per month out of the partnership (plus extra amounts at times to pay income taxes). In addition to this, his parking lot pays annual rents of $3,000. From this, he must pay the real estate taxes of $600 but he has no maintenance expense, since the tenant under the lease is required to pay all such items. He receives around $300 per year as dividends on his mutual fund shares.

The wife will need $16,000 for the first year after his death, and then an income of $18,000 at least until the children are through college. He wants an $8,000 emergency fund and $12,000 for each child's education.

The Partnership. The partnership is in the plastics business, manufacturing various items of toys and sundry gadgets used in the premium business. The business started about six years ago, with the two present partners each contributing a nominal amount of capital. It has proved to be a very successful operation. The estate owner is the production man and knows how to figure costs, design dies, schedule production, and get the maximum efficiency out of the plant. The partner is the salesman of the organization, who has proved his ability to go into a competitive situation and walk away with orders in spite of competition.

The company has a reputation in the industry of turning out good jobs in a short time and at a low price. By and large, the relationship of the two partners is excellent, although the other partner is a free spender on his expense account. The two partners have an oral understanding that when one of them dies, the survivor will carry on the business with the family of the decedent. Both appreciate, however, that the survivor will have quite a load because neither of the partners' wives has any business experience. The estate owner, recognizing all this, has calculated that from his family's share of the income, his wife can hire (at $20,000) a man who can replace the estate owner in at least his nonmanagement duties; that she will also be able to reinvest ("plow back") about $10,000 of earnings a year which is necessary to maintain growth; and that after all this she will still be able to take out $22,000 per year to pay income taxes and use for family expenses.

The other partner, Mr. Lewis, is 42 years of age and in good health; he also draws $2,000 a month (plus) out of the business.

The firm, on an accrual basis for income tax, has earned over the past five years an average net of $90,000 per year. The accountant has advised the partners that if the company were incorporated, around $24,000 for each of them would be considered a reasonable allowance for salary. Over the last five years the average invested capital was about $112,000.

The present balance sheet indicated that their total assets are $208,400, with liabilities of $31,000, leaving a net worth of $177,400. However, if the business were liquidated, the net realizable value from the assets, after paying all liabilities, is estimated at $99,000. They lease the property in which they operate, but the rental is so favorable that the property could be sublet to other tenants for at least as much as they are paying.

Running the Hypothetical Probate

The Theory. With this factual background to start with, the next job is the analysis, i.e., to find out what would happen with reference to the total estate picture if Mr. White, the estate owner, were to die today without having made any changes of any kind. To do this, the procedure is that of a hypothetical probate following exactly the same steps that would be taken in running the estate through the process of administration. The factual summary plus the hypothetical probate combine to form the first step of the total procedure set out in Chapter 55 on estate planning principles.

There is a division of opinion as to how specific or general the analysis should be. In actual practice, some estate reports are very meticulous and detailed, whereas others are the roughest approximations of tax and other factors. The persons who favor the latter method usually argue that there is no real point in making the figures exact because the amount involved in the present estate will never actually be the exact amount when the estate becomes a reality, and that therefore spending time on details is wasteful. The argument on the other side is that if one follows the broad estimate theory, he will in most instances overlook some of the extremely important details, and in almost every instance will be unable to present to the estate owner any sort of accurate picture of the postprobate estate and the family income.

As between these two extremes, it would seem that the average analyst will be better off to do a thorough and meticulous job than to do the very rough estimate sort. Those who take the pains to do the job completely find that it is far more effective.

This chapter presents the form of detailed analysis on the theory that if one understands how it is done this way, he can readily shift over to a shorter form.

Inventory and Classification of Assets. The first step in analysis is to make an inventory and classification of the assets, listing all the items which will be involved in the estate and at the same time separating those which will pass through the executor under the terms of the will and those which will pass by survivorship, by contract, or by trust directly to the beneficiaries without going through the probate estate. Following that procedure in the present case, Schedule I will be as follows:

SCHEDULE I

Assets	Estate Owner's Value
Solely owned assets:	
Cash	$ 4,000
Mutual fund	7,500
Parking lot (Erie, Pa.)	20,000
Personal effects	6,000
Partnership interest	88,700
Policy on wife (cash value)	800
Home (half interest)	21,000
Total probate estate	$148,000
Property passing by survivorship:	
Government "E" bonds (to wife)	5,000
Government "E" bonds (to children)	3,000
Property passing by trust, contract, or devise:	
Government "E" bonds (to wife)	2,000
Life insurance	66,000
Total nonprobate estate	$ 76,000

Retention or Conversion (Tentative). The next step will be a tentative determination as to whether the executor will convert the assets coming into his possession into cash or whether he will attempt to retain them. In this case, because the estate owner expressed a desire that his family retain all the assets he has except the cash, Schedule II will look like this:

SCHEDULE II

Probate Assets	Cash	Retention
Cash	$4,000	
Mutual fund		$ 7,500
Parking lot (Erie, Pa.)		20,000
Personal effects		6,000
Partnership interest		88,700
Policy on wife (cash value)		800
Home (half interest)		21,000

Calculating the Taxable Estate. 1. *Valuing the Partnership.* A subject which is of concern to the executor early in the administration is the position of the estate with reference to death taxes. Accordingly, very early, he will attempt to arrive at an estimate of the value of the property which will be included in the gross estate. It is obvious that the major problem here will relate to the valuation of the partnership interest for estate tax purposes. It may be assumed that the Internal Revenue Service will look closely at this retained partnership interest to determine whether there may be an element of good will which should be added into the valuation figure. Arriving at a value which resembles the future result of negotiations between Internal Revenue agents and counsel for the estate is a difficult problem, but if the analyst takes an average of the value arrived at through the use of three different methods, i.e., the book value, capitalization of earnings, and the ARM (Appeal and Review Memo No. 34) formula, he should come reasonably close to what will probably happen.

In this case, he might use the average earnings of $90,000, subtract therefrom the sum of $48,000 (as representing what would be an allowance for salaries, as though this were a corporation), and multiply the difference of $42,000 by a factor of 9, which gives a potential value of the partnership of $378,000. In applying the ARM formula, he again uses the earnings (adjusted by deducting salary allowance), subtracts $11,200 as representing a 10 percent return on the average invested capital of $112,000, and multiplies the difference by 5, which gives a figure of $154,000. This is probably what the Treasury will claim is the present capitalized value of the good will alone. If he then adds this capitalized good will value to the present book value of $177,400, he comes up with a possible valuation of the partnership of $331,400. If one adds the capitalized earnings value ($378,000) plus the ARM value ($331,400) plus the present book value ($177,400) and divides the total by three, he finds that the average figure for the partnership as a whole would be roughly $295,600, so that the estate owner's one half would thus carry a tax value of $147,800.[1]

2. *The Gross Estate.* The gross estate of the federal estate tax is as shown in Schedule III. The figures are self-explanatory, with the possible exception that only $4,000 of the $5,000 jointly held "E" bonds passing to the wife have been included in the gross estate. This is because only that portion of the value of joint property with right of survivorship that is attributable to the decedent's contribution toward the purchase price is includable in the gross estate. Here the wife contributed 20 percent to the total purchase price of these bonds, using funds which had come to

---

[1] Obviously, a critical element in the valuation is the selection of the "factors" to be used, both on the capitalization of earnings and the ARM method. Going into the details of how these are selected is beyond the scope of this chapter. It may be observed, however, that on the capitalization approach, the factor used is generally between 7 and 12, depending upon the stability of the particular industry and of the specific company. As to the ARM method, the "10 and 5" factors may vary from case to case such as allowing a 12 percent return and using a multiplier of 6 or 7. There are no standard rules which can be followed.

her from her mother, so only 80 percent of the value of these bonds (or $4,000) is includable in the gross estate.

SCHEDULE III

Cash on hand and in bank	$ 4,000
Mutual fund shares	7,500
Parking lot in Erie, Pa.	20,000
Personal effects	6,000
Partnership interest	147,800
Policy on wife (cash value)	800
Government "E" bonds (to wife)	4,000
Government "E" bonds (to children)	3,000
Government "E" bonds (to wife)	2,000
Home (half interest)	21,000
Life insurance	66,000
Total gross estate	$282,100

3. *Deductions.* The next step will be to determine the taxable estate, and the procedure will be as shown in Schedule IV. It will be observed that the marital deduction is less than the maximum allowable (one-half the adjusted gross estate), which is attributable to the fact that the residuary probate estate will not qualify because it goes to the wife for life only without general power of appointment and then to the children. The only assets qualifying for the marital deduction will be personal effects, $6,000; his share of equity in the home, $17,000; widow's allowance, $16,000; Series "E" bonds, $4,000; ordinary life insurance, $20,000; second ordinary life policy of $10,000; and government bonds, payable at death, $2,000.

SCHEDULE IV

Total gross estate (from Schedule III)		$282,100
Cost of administration	$9,450	
Current bills	900	
One half of accrued taxes on home	400	
Accrued taxes on Pennsylvania property	600	
State income tax	200	
Federal income tax	4,500	
Funeral and last expenses	2,500	
One half of mortgage on home	4,000	
Total deductions under Revenue Code Section 2053		22,550
Adjusted gross estate		$259,550
Marital deduction		75,000
		$184,550
Exemption		60,000
Taxable estate		$124,550

Cash Requirements. Having ascertained that the federal estate tax will come to $27,420, the total cash requirements in the estate are as follows:

SCHEDULE V

Liquidity (Cash) Needs	
Current bills payable	$ 900
Accrued taxes:	
Realty—Ohio (one half)	400
Realty—Pennsylvania	600
State income tax	200
Federal income tax	4,500
Funeral and last expenses	2,500
Widow's allowance	16,000
Cost of administration	9,450
State death tax	4,442
Federal estate tax	27,240*
Total cash requirements	$66,232

* The gross federal tax is $28,200, with the minimum being $27,240; thus, the difference of $960 is the maximum allowance credit against the federal tax for the amount of the state tax. Observe that in this case the actual state tax is almost five times the amount of the allowed federal credit.

Liquidating the Cash Requirements. From what source will this cash come? To begin with, reference to Schedule II shows that there is $4,000 in the bank, which the executor will have toward these costs. That schedule tentatively marked all the other assets for retention (following the estate owner's preference). It is clear by this time, however, that the actual retention of all those assets will be impossible. What can be done about the deficit? There are a number of alternatives, but for purposes of illustration, it may be assumed that the widow's allowance, instead of being paid in cash, will be satisfied by distributing to her a fractional part of the partnership interest; that the mutual fund shares will have to be sold; that the parking lot will have to be sold; and that the balance of the cash will have to come from the wife, who will cash in some of her "E" bonds, and use some of the lump-sum insurance proceeds. Outside of selling the personal effects and the partnership interest, there is no other answer.

The Family Income. In any event, after the funds are paid to the executor, who in turn pays the bills, the estate will be closed, and then the question arises of how the family will fare on the basis of the actual assets which are left and the income which can be expected from them. For the moment, in considering this income expectancy, assume that the partnership will continue to earn money and that the widow will be able to withdraw from those earnings the same amount as her husband anticipates she will be able to take, namely, $22,000 per year. On this basis, the wife's position will shape up along the line shown in Schedule VI.

In the category of fixed charges in this income schedule there are included three items: the monthly payment on the mortgage, the annual taxes, and the maintenance costs on the home.

This picture, however, is not complete. It shows only what will happen if everything works out *successfully* in the business and the wife is able to withdraw $1,833 per month. It will be noted that even under those

SCHEDULE VI

	Principal	Income
Personal effects (wife and husband)	$ 15,000	
Policy on wife (cash value)	800	
Home	42,000	
Partnership interest (tax value)	147,800	$22,000*
Lump-sum insurance proceeds (reinvested)	10,000	500
Insurance proceeds under option	36,000	2,400
Wife's Series "E" bonds (balance)	6,000	300
Wife's checking account	2,000	
Social security (approximately)		4,000†
Gross income		$29,200
Less fixed charges		3,580
		$25,620
Less income tax (federal and state)		8,060
Spendable income		$17,560
Income requirement		$18,000

* This figure is arrived at on the following assumptions given the analyst by the estate owner: the wife's share of the partnership earnings will remain at $52,000 per year; from this she will allocate $20,000 to hire a man to replace the estate owner; then she will permit $10,000 of her share to be plowed back into the business to assure future growth; and there will thus be left $22,000 to her as gross income.

† If the wife actively participates in the management of the business—and the estate owner assumes she will fill some kind of active role—then she will not be entitled to social security benefits for herself, although the benefits allowed to the children will be paid to her. Since the amounts will be available in the household budget, they are shown here as being additional income to the wife.

conditions the spendable income is lower than the income requirement, which is attributed primarily to the very large income tax. The reason this income tax figure is so large is that although the wife is actually *drawing* only $22,000 per year, she is taxed on $32,000, which is her net one-half share of the current partnership profits.

If a second step is taken in the analysis of the income picture and it is assumed that the worst were to happen to the business, namely, that it would be unable to pay anything to her, then her spendable income would amount to a little over $3,600 per year.

The Wife's Estate at Her Subsequent Death. At this stage of the analysis, then, the analyst has established what will happen in the husband's estate if he dies first and if the present arrangements are unaltered. Next, he will ascertain what will happen in the wife's estate at her subsequent death under the present program. He finds that her taxable estate will be very small, that the total cash requirements will amount to about $18,600, and that there will be adequate cash by virtue of the fact that in her estate there will be the remainder of the lump-sum insurance proceeds from her husband. After her estate is through probate, the children will then have (from both parents) the home, the personal effects, the remainder of the family income policy, the $3,000 of Series "E" bonds, and the partnership interest.

With regard to the partnership interest, however, it will be impossible to carry any further the fiction of retention by the family. At this stage, with both husband and wife being gone, there would be no adult member of the family with whom the survivor could make a contract, even if he were willing to do so. Certainly, no businessman in his right mind would carry on a partnership with three minors as partners, and it is very dubious whether the probate court would allow the guardian to do so. As a result, the partnership would have to be liquidated, at its liquidating value of $99,000, with a total of $49,500 going to the estate owner's family. This overall picture will leave the children with something around $143,000 in total assets, including the house, the personal effects, the family income policy, and the liquidated partnership, all producing an income of a little over $4,000, plus social security.

Reversing the Order of Death. Even now the analysis is not complete because it does not show what would happen if the order of deaths were reversed. If the wife dies first, her estate will be immaterial, since its sole assets will be her personal effects and half the home. Now the husband's estate must be run through on another set of schedules, but with the assets owned jointly with the wife now becoming a part of his probate estate and the partnership appearing in the estate at its liquidated value rather than at either its book value or its inflated tax value. Without running through the actual schedules again, because of limitations of space, the picture shows that the husband will have a gross estate of $224,000, with deductions of $24,770, leaving an adjusted gross estate of $199,230 and a taxable estate of $139,230, on which the federal estate tax will be $31,220 and the Ohio tax will come to $2,630. The total cash requirements in his estate will amount to $58,620. There will, however, be ample cash to take care of these from the cash on hand, the $10,000 of insurance on the wife's life, and cash from the liquidation of the partnership.

The children, after conclusion of the administration, will then have an asset picture as follows:

Cash	$ 4,880
Series "E" bonds	10,000
Mutual fund	7,500
Realty—Pennsylvania	20,000
Realty—home	42,000
Personal effects (husband and wife)	15,000
Life insurance proceeds (for children)	46,000

In addition to this, under the present arrangements, the $20,000 ordinary life insurance policy proceeds will go to Mr. White's parents.

FINDING THE OBSTACLES OR PROBLEMS

General Observations

Now the analysis is complete, thus concluding the *first step* in the overall estate planning procedure. The estate owner knows precisely what will happen in the event that both he and his wife die without making any change in their present arrangements, regardless of the order of deaths.

The next step, as mentioned at the outset of this chapter, is to enumerate the particular problems which the analysis has disclosed or, as stated in Chapter 55, to determine the obstacles. In other words, in what respects does the present estate plan fail to accomplish the estate owner's objectives? Before considering the actual problems in this case, it will be helpful to appreciate that the problems which will be found in *any* case will always fall in one of four different categories:

1. *Transfer Costs.* The first major problem area relates to the fact that transfer costs at some place or places in the overall picture are unnecessarily high. When the term "transfer costs" is used, it refers to the total of taxes and costs of administration. Note that the transfer costs are a problem not because they are large but because they are *unnecessarily* high and could be reduced to a more reasonable figure by using ideas that are consistent with the estate owner's objectives.

2. *Liquidation.* In a great many estates, even after the transfer costs are reduced to a reasonable level, there still are not sufficient liquid assets to meet all the cash requirements so as to be able to conserve the value of estate assets. This arises most frequently in the case of an owner of an interest in a closely held business where the objective is to retain that interest.

3. *Disposition of Assets.* Here the problem area deals with those basic questions of "who gets what, and when, and how?" Control of a closely held business is often found going to persons who are not qualified to enter into management, or other forms of property pass to individuals who are quite incapable of administering it. In addition, there are many cases of real injustices being done to various beneficiaries who are inadequately provided for.

4. *Family Income Problems.* This is an old and familiar field, but when encountered in estate planning, it has many new phases. While it is most common to find situations of the family income being insufficient, sometimes the income going to a given beneficiary is more than that beneficiary will need, giving rise to unnecessary income taxes. The analysis will show the relative dependence of the family upon the income from the business in order to help the estate owner ascertain the degree of risk entailed in his decision to retain that interest. Here also are the problems of how the family funds will be managed, and the source of education and emergency funds.

One of the primary advantages in simply enumerating the problems, after completing the analysis and before going into the planning, is that the analyst can thereby get the agreement of the estate owner and whoever else may be involved in the actual planning phase on what things in this picture need to have attention. Then, as the various estate planning ideas are considered, they can be related back to the agreed problems to ascertain how far any given proposal will go in solving each problem.

The Specific Problems

1. *As to Transfer Costs.* If these problem areas are now applied to the partnership case, they indicate: First of all, as to transfer costs, the only place where taxes are unreasonably high is in the estate of the husband where he dies first. This is occasioned by the fact that he is utilizing only $75,000 of the marital deduction against a possible maximum deduc-

tion of almost $129,775. This results in his estate paying an unnecessary federal estate tax of something over $13,000, which, if saved, would help to reduce the liquidity problem and also would help on the family income.

2. As to Liquidation. Next, in looking at the liquidation picture, it is apparent that if the husband dies first, there is a substantial deficit of liquid assets in the estate, resulting in a forced sale of assets which the estate owner has indicated he would like his family to have. Of course, to the extent that transfer costs are reduced, as mentioned above, the liquidation problem can be alleviated. However, that will not completely solve it, because even with the taxes reduced, there will still be a deficit. The liquidation problem arises primarily because of the retention of the partnership interest.

3. As to Disposition of Assets. Passing now to the third category of possible problems, the question is whether the present arrangement for division of assets is in good shape, taking into consideration the ages and business experience of the people involved and considering particularly the attendant risk. Here, several negative factors are apparent: First, under the present arrangement, if both husband and wife are gone, property will pass outright to minors, involving the necessity of a guardianship, with its obvious disadvantages.

Second, there is the admitted fact that the wife has no business experience and that in foisting upon her the responsibility of participating in the management of a business of which she knows nothing, the will places upon her, and also upon the surviving partner, a tremendous responsibility. The degree of that risk is even greater than the estate owner appreciates because, from a legal standpoint, both partners are jointly and severally liable. Thus, if the surviving partner were to make some unfortunate business decision involving substantial liabilities, the wife as a partner would be *personally* liable to the full extent of those liabilities. Furthermore, her personal liability would not be limited to business assets but would also subject all her own personal holdings, including even her home, to the claims of business creditors. A third, although minor point under this same heading, is that the $20,000 ordinary life policy is payable to the estate owner's parents rather than his children, if his wife predeceases him.

4. As to the Family Income. Finally, as to the family income situation, the analysis demonstrates that the income will be somewhat short of providing the family with the spendable income it will require, even if the partnership is able to continue its present earning scale. Coupled with this is the fact that if the business should fail, the family would lose the capital tied up in the business, and the income would be even further reduced. As one further factor, under the present arrangements there is no adequate provision for education and emergency funds.

So much for enumerating the problems. Considering all of them, anyone can readily see that the decision with reference to the partnership is actually the key to the whole situation. Of course, the various documents, including the wills and the insurance policies, need further consideration, but the starting point necessarily will have to be the problem of the partnership.

Up to this point, therefore, all the facts have been established, as well as all the obstacles or problems in the setup as it now stands. The case is now ready to proceed to the third step.

DESIGNING A PLAN

In this particular case, when the whole matter was presented to the estate owner, his accountant, and his counsel, it resulted in a long and serious discussion about the advisability of retaining the partnership. At the conclusion, all the parties were in accord that at least as of the present time, retention of the partnership would not be advisable. It was felt that the risk to the family was simply not justified.

The first planning procedure agreed upon, therefore, was that there should be a buy-and-sell agreement between the two partners, the price tentatively to be set at $150,000 for each partner's interest. It was agreed that the agreement would be funded by $300,000 of life insurance—$150,000 owned by each partner on the other's life. A collateral result of such a well-drawn buy-sell contract is that the IRS accepts, as binding, the agreed price.

Next, it was decided that the estate owner would need management of the estate funds both for his wife and for his children. Because of the age of the wife, it was also decided that the family would be better off if the insurance policies became a part of a trust arrangement, and that the estate owner should set up an insurance trust, which in turn would be split into marital (with full marital deduction) and nonmarital trusts. It was agreed that the nonmarital part would provide for income to the wife; that the trustee might advance principal as needed; that the trustee could use funds from the nonmarital portion for education and family emergencies; and finally, that after both husband and wife were gone, distribution of one half of each child's share should be made at age 28, with the balance being distributed to each at age 35.

As a companion to this insurance trust, the husband's will would provide that his interest in the home and his personal effects should go to his wife and that the balance of his estate (including the remainder of the cash received from the buy-and-sell agreement) should "pour over" into the insurance trust.

It was also agreed that the wife's will should leave everything to the husband, if he survived; but if he should not, then the wife's estate should also be left to the insurance trust. The result of this program would be that all the assets from both husband and wife, including all insurance proceeds, would wind up in a single trust for the benefit of the children, regardless of the order of death.

Testing the Plan

With a tentative program thus agreed upon, the next question was whether its operation would really improve the picture, and, if so, by how much. Therefore, the analyst made a "test run" to prove the economic results. This analysis showed that if the husband died first and the wife second, the new program would save approximately $3,000 in transfer costs. It was also found, however, that if the wife died first and the husband second, the transfer costs would be increased by about $26,000. The reason for this increase was that in this order of death, in the husband's estate at present there was no alternative except the liquidation of the partnership at $49,500; whereas under the new plan the children would have available the $150,000 proceeds from the buy-and-sell agreement, or an increase of $100,000.

The second significant thing which the revised analysis brought out was that the family income picture under the new plan showed spendable income of almost $15,500—completely independent of business income. This, admittedly, was about $2,500 less than the minimum needed. However, both the lawyer and the estate owner felt that since there would be over $190,000 in liquid assets in trust, this deficiency of income would not be too important because, to the extent of the deficiency, principal could be used.

Finally, it was observed that the new plan would completely eliminate all the liquidation problems in both the husband's estate and that of the wife, regardless of the order of death.

Implementing the Plan

With the tentative plan thus proved out and consequently accepted by all concerned, the next step was that of putting it into effect. The lawyer, of course, had the greatest amount of work to do in drafting the insurance trust and the wills. The drafts were checked out with the client and reviewed by the trust officer.

In the meantime, both of the partners were examined, and each partner applied for and purchased a $150,000 straight life policy on the life of the other partner. In addition to the trust agreement and the wills, the attorney also prepared a buy-and-sell agreement between the partners; and with the signing of all of these documents and the delivery of the policies, the entire job was completed.

Periodic Reviews

Although the client expressed complete satisfaction with the results of the estate planning job, he was cautioned, particularly by the lawyer, that the lapse of time, with its attendant changes in the family situation, in the valuation of the business, and in the nature and extent of his assets, could easily make this plan as obsolete as was his old one. It was consequently agreed that the plan should be reviewed at least every three years, and preferably every two years; and to that end the trust officer agreed that as these review times came around, he would see to it that the matter was called to the attention of the lawyer, the life underwriter, and the client so that an adequate follow-up was assured.

SELECTED REFERENCES

See citations at end of Chapter 55.

part X

Company Operations and Institutional Aspects

IN ITS ECONOMIC AND SOCIAL DIMENSIONS, life and health insurance is a highly pervasive institution. Its growth as a financial service institution has resulted primarily from its significant services to individuals and businesses. But, also of major importance is the strength and integrity of the institution that instills great confidence in those it serves.

The chapters in Part X are concerned with company operations and institutional aspects of the business. Regulation, taxation, investments, financial statements, claims administration, marketing and reinsurance are among the subjects covered. The similarities and differences in the Canadian and U.S. life insurance operations are presented.

61

Scope and Structure of
Life and Health Insurance

By BLAKE T. NEWTON, JR.

SCOPE OF COVERAGE AND BENEFITS

FIVE OUT of every six families in the United States own legal reserve life insurance; nearly 9 out of 10 Americans have private health insurance. In the single year of 1971, Americans received almost $27 billion in benefits from life and health insurance companies.

Ownership of life insurance in the United States at the beginning of 1972 reached an average of $21,800 for each family in the nation. This figure had more than doubled in a decade, while the average family's disposable income had risen 71 percent. Despite this increase in the ratio of protection to income, the average amount of life insurance equaled only slightly over two years' average disposable personal income as 1972 began.

Total life insurance in force with legal reserve companies was $1.5 trillion at the start of 1972. All other forms of insurance, including veterans' insurance issued by the federal government, and fraternal, assessment, and savings bank life insurance, provided another $68 billion of coverage.

Private health insurance at the beginning of 1972 provided protection in some degree for 168.5 million Americans under 65 years of age, or nearly 9 out of 10 of the civilian population of the United States under 65.

Life Insurance Growth

The life insurance business has grown markedly since the end of World War II. The total of insurance in force with legal reserve companies at the start of 1946 was $152 billion, about one tenth of the $1,505 billion in force at the beginning of 1972 (Figure 61–1).

Not all types of life insurance have participated equally in this growth. Industrial coverage increased 1.2 times up to 1955 but has remained at about the same level ever since. Group coverage, which emerged as a highly significant form of insurance during the war, has shown continuing growth during the postwar period, increasing more than 26 times.

Credit life insurance has multiplied more than 260 times. Individual ordinary insurance, still the most widely owned form of family protection, has had an increase of almost eight times.

The variations in growth among these four major types of coverage have important implications for company development. Ordinary life produces the largest ratio of assets to insurance in force. Group and credit life, which usually require relatively small policy reserves, produce a lesser ratio of assets to insurance in force. Industrial life is more costly to merchandise because it requires a relatively large sales force to service the many small policies involved.

FIGURE 61–1. Life Insurance in Force in the United States

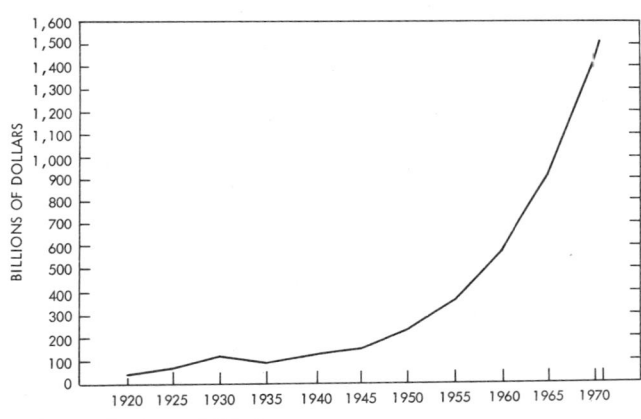

Source: Institute of Life Insurance.

Since ordinary and group life are by far the major forms of insurance in terms of total sales, it follows that these have provided the major areas of growth for companies both in assets and in insurance in force.

Life Insurance Purchases

American families bought $189.2 billion of new life insurance in 1971. Ten years earlier, purchases totaled $79 billion, or over two fifths of the recent rate. About three quarters of recent purchases have been of individual insurance (ordinary and industrial).

In 1971, Americans bought $132.7 billion of ordinary insurance, $7.5 billion of industrial, and $49 billion of group (Figure 61–2). These totals were represented in almost 26 million new policies and individual group certificates. Of these, 11 million were ordinary policies, 9 million were industrial policies, and 6 million were group certificates.

There has been a significant increase in the average size of policies purchased. In 1971, the average new ordinary policy was $11,670, nearly double the amount 10 years earlier.

Pension Plans

Insured pension plans are another important service of the life insurance business. At the beginning of 1972, there were 11.5 million people enrolled in plans administered by life companies. During 1971, the companies paid $1.5 billion in retirement benefits to 1.3 million people covered by such plans.

FIGURE 61–2. Recent Annual Growth of Life Insurance by Types

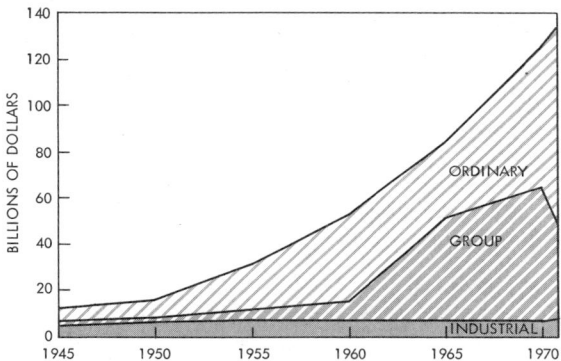

Source: Life Insurance Agency Management Association and Institute of Life Insurance.

Individual annuities are purchased from life companies to provide income on either a current or future basis. At the beginning of 1972, there were 1.8 million of these contracts in force, with annual income payable now or in the future totaling $1.4 billion.

The death payments or cash values of policies are sometimes requested by the policyowner or beneficiary as annuities under supplementary contracts. At the beginning of 1972, there were 612,000 such contracts in force, with annual income payments totaling $350 million.

While most annuities are intended to provide income in a predetermined amount, a relatively new service of life insurance companies is the so-called variable annuity. The income payments under these contracts vary according to the performance of a portfolio of common stock investments or a cost-of-living index. Variable annuities are sold on both a group and individual basis. At the beginning of 1972, there were 918,000 people covered by these contracts, mostly under group variable annuities.

Broader Financial Services

The greater affluence of American families as a consequence of the sustained economic growth of the past several decades has created the need for a more diverse approach to personal and family financial requirements. The life insurance business has been responding to this need through an expansion of its financial services to the public, notably through equity products.

In the latter part of the 1960s, some companies began offering mutual fund shares to their policyowners. As of 1972, about 280 life companies included mutual funds in their product lines. In some cases the funds were wholly owned affiliates of the companies, either through acquisition or origination; in other cases the shares were offered through arrangements with existing funds.

Variable annuities have been another equity-based vehicle developed to give people more financial flexibility during their retirement years. As of 1972, there were about 110 companies offering variable annuities on a group or individual basis.

An equity-based product under development in 1972 was variable life insurance. The reserves upon which a variable life policy is based would be invested in common stocks and other equities. The amount payable to beneficiaries would never drop below the face amount of the policy but could increase consonant with the performance of the common stock fund. However, the cash value of the policy could be adversely affected by a drop in value of the equity fund.

Health Insurance Growth

Although health insurance had its beginnings in the mid-19th century, modern forms of protection for hospital, surgical and medical expenses began emerging during the depression of the 1930s. Further developments were stimulated by World War II and the postwar economic expansion. The general trend has been steadily toward providing broader and more extensive coverages to meet the needs of the public, a trend that is continuing. However, legislation providing for national health insurance was seen as a strong possibility for 1973 or 1974, with the key question being whether the program would be government financed or rely in good measure on the traditional private mechanisms.

The five major forms of health insurance are hospital expense, surgical expense, basic medical expense, major medical expense, and disability income protection. Dental expense insurance is a recently introduced and rapidly growing form of coverage. In the decade ending in 1971, the number of people with hospital expense coverage increased 34 percent; the number with surgical coverage, 35 percent; the number with basic medical expense, 55 percent; the number with major medical expense, 136 percent; and the number with short-term disability insurance, over 35 percent.

Claims and other expenses vary not only with the types of coverage offered, but with geographic location. Costs of medical care vary considerably from region to region, and have been particularly high in metropolitan areas.

Although Medicare, which provides for medical expense payments for citizens over 65, is a government program, many covered retired persons carry supplemental health insurance through private companies. In addition, more than a dozen insurance companies act as fiscal agents of the government in the administration of Part B of Medicare.

Measured by premium payments, health insurance purchases have been increasing markedly. In 1971, premiums totaled $22.8 billion, an increase of $2.8 billion over the 1970 figure. Over the course of 10 years the increase in annual premiums amounted to $14.5 billion. During the same decade the average family increased the share of its disposable income devoted to health insurance (Figure 61–3). In 1971, American

FIGURE 61–3. Total Health Insurance Premiums as a Percentage of Disposable Income

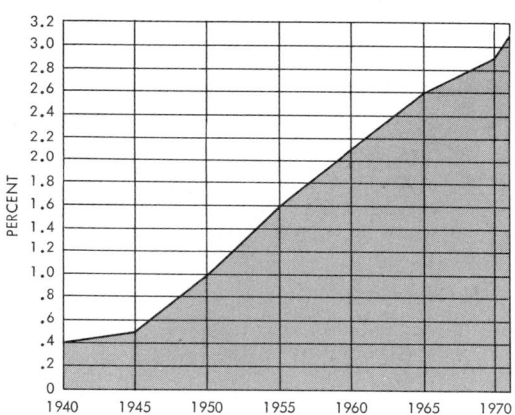

Source: Institute of Life Insurance.

families spent 3.1 cents out of every after-tax dollar for health insurance, compared to 2.3 cents 10 years earlier. Higher family incomes, permitting more adequate health coverage, are one reason for the increase. Another is the increasing demand for insurance offering more comprehensive protection and more liberal benefits, to keep pace with increasing use and rising costs of medical services.

Personal Insurance Benefits

Historically, life insurance companies have long paid more to living policyowners than to the survivors of those who have died. More than half of total payments continue to be in the form of so-called living benefits, despite the substantial dollar increase in death payments as ownership of life insurance has increased. Benefits to policyowners themselves come from a variety of sources. In 1971, they were, in decreasing order of size, policy dividends, surrender values, annuity payments, matured endowments, and disability payments (Figure 61–4).

Health insurance benefits have grown markedly since World War II, especially with the growth in group plans. Starting in 1945 with roughly equal benefit totals of $139 million each, insurance companies' group and individual plans diverged widely in their growth. By 1971, group insurance benefits had grown to about $8 billion for the year, while individual

FIGURE 61-4.   Life Insurance Payments, 1971

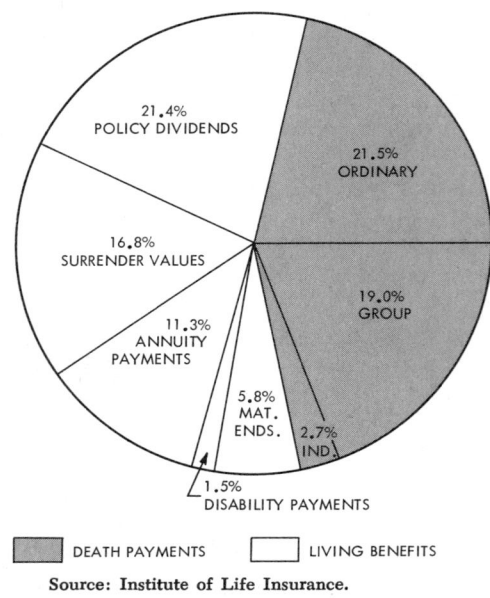

21.4%
POLICY DIVIDENDS

21.5%
ORDINARY

16.8%
SURRENDER VALUES

19.0%
GROUP

11.3%
ANNUITY
PAYMENTS

5.8%
MAT.
ENDS.

2.7%
IND.

1.5%
DISABILITY PAYMENTS

█ DEATH PAYMENTS   □ LIVING BENEFITS

Source: Institute of Life Insurance.

policy benefits amounted to some $1.5 billion. About $9.4 billion was additionally paid in health benefits during 1971 by Blue Cross/Blue Shield and other hospital-medical plans.

Health Insurance Purchases

A primary measure of progress in the health insurance business is the increasing number of persons insured. During 1971, an additional 4.5 million Americans came under the protection of private hospital expense plans, bringing the total number protected to 179.9 million. An additional 2.8 million persons had surgical expense insurance by the end of the year, for a total of 165.4 million covered. Regular medical expense insurance was extended to 3.7 million more persons, for a total of 144.4 million. More than 2.5 million more persons came under insurance companies' major medical expense plans, bringing the total number covered to 80.7 million. Some 41.2 million were covered by short-term disability income insurance at the end of 1971, giving them up to two years of coverage; 12 million people had long-term disability income insurance for longer periods of protection. (See Figure 61-5.)

INSURANCE COMPANIES AND CARRIERS

The company structures of the life insurance and health insurance business are varied. Most life insurance is issued by legal reserve companies of two basic types: mutual companies owned by their policyowners, and stock companies owned by stockholders. Health care bene-

FIGURE 61–5. Summary of Persons Covered by Type of Private Health Insurance, 1971

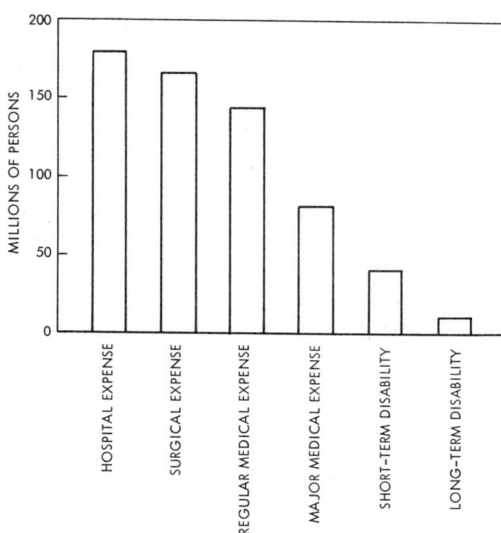

Source: Health Insurance Institute.

fits, by contrast, are offered by several different types of carriers: life, casualty, and health-only insurance companies; hospital and medical service plans such as Blue Cross and Blue Shield; prepaid group medical plans; and others.

Life Insurance Companies

The first American life insurance company was founded in 1759 under a somewhat unwieldy name: "The Corporation for Relief of Poor and Distressed Presbyterian Ministers and of the Poor and Distressed Widows and Children of Presbyterian Ministers." Still in business today under the more economical title of "Presbyterian Ministers' Fund," the company was one of an estimated 1,805 in business at the start of 1972. Much of this growth has come about recently; at the beginning of 1946, there were only 473 life companies in the United States.

As the increasing number of companies might suggest, the life insurance business today is highly competitive, and shows signs of becoming more so. For example, a decade ago mutual life insurance companies, which include most of the larger companies in the United States, had 60 percent of all life insurance in force, with stock companies carrying 40 percent. In the intervening 10 years, the proportions changed appreciably. At the beginning of 1972, the ratio of life insurance with mutual companies declined to 51 percent, with stock companies increasing to 49 percent.

Many newer and smaller firms specialize in providing coverage in a single state, or in a limited few. One result has been a spread of company home offices across the nation. By mid-1971, there were at least two company home offices in every state.

The great majority of U.S. life companies, including nearly all the newer ones, are stock companies. Over 91 percent of the companies in business at midyear 1971 were stockholder-owned. The typical mutual company is older as well as a great deal larger than the typical stock company.

A mutual company's funds are held for the exclusive benefit of policy-owners who elect the company's board of directors. By and large, mutual companies issue participating policies that pay annual dividends to policyowners. These dividends reduce the cost of the policy from the amount of the original premium.

A stock company's initial financing and continuing capital are pro-vided by its shareholders who assume ultimate management responsi-bility and receive a return on their investment. Stock companies primarily issue nonparticipating policies. The premiums for nonparticipating poli-cies generally are lower than for comparable policies paying dividends, and costs are fixed for the life of the policy. Some stock companies issue both participating and nonparticipating policies.

Aside from the legal reserve companies, all other life insurance com-panies accounted in 1971 for about 4 percent of all insurance in force. Chief among these other insurers are fraternals, which issue policies to members of fraternal organizations under special laws; assessment com-panies, issuing policies on which premiums are set and can be varied according to the companies' experience; savings banks, which in three states issue policies under special laws; and the federal government, which operates the veterans' insurance program.

Health Insurance Carriers

When health insurance coverage in this country originated over a century ago, casualty insurance companies were the only insurers. The majority of health business written by insurance companies is now writ-ten by life companies. The number of life companies issuing health insur-ance exceeds the number of casualty insurers in the health field. Slowest numerical growth has been among monoline insurers, chartered either as life or casualty companies and writing only health insurance. All three types may be operated either as mutual or stock companies, and except for the monolines, health insurance may be either a dominant or a small part of their total business.

Aside from insurance companies, the most widely known health in-surers are Blue Cross, Blue Shield, and other plans sponsored by hospitals or medical societies. These plans usually are organized on a state or regional basis. In several communities, group practice plans have been set up on a prepayment basis. Under these plans a group of physicians, surgeons, dentists, or optometrists contracts to provide required health care for a monthly or annual fee. Among these plans are the Health In-surance Plan of Greater New York and the Kaiser Foundation Health

Plan, based in California. Other independent plans, such as those sponsored by unions, employers, or fraternal societies, often provide care on a medical group practice basis. Some independent plans have members throughout the nation.

As the decade of the 1970s opened, various plans were drawn up which might better meet the nation's health care needs. These ranged from modest reform to virtually total replacement of the system with a government-operated plan. The private insurance sector proposed a middle-of-the-road approach called the "Healthcare" plan in which it would join forces with the government to upgrade health insurance coverage and alleviate shortages of medical personnel.

Under this plan, existing private health insurers (including insurance companies, Blue Cross/Blue Shield, and prepaid group practice plans) would be utilized to provide insurance benefits for the bulk of the population. At the same time, state pools of private insurers would be established to insure the benefits for the poor, the near-poor, and those who are uninsurable for reasons of health.

This private insurance approach was based on the following five principles:

1. Every American should have access to quality health care regardless of income.

2. The nation needs a new health care system which combines the strengths of our present system with new programs, reforms and additions, where the present system, for one reason or another, does not meet the nation's needs.

3. Such a new system should make maximum use of the private sector and judicious use of government funds.

4. The nation should make comprehensive health insurance coverage available to all of its people at the earliest date consistent with the availability of health care services.

5. Action should be taken simultaneously to improve the organization and delivery of health care and to improve the financing of health care.

ORGANIZATIONS IN THE BUSINESS

The many organizations in the life and health insurance business, or related to it, have been a source of its strength. They have contributed to growth, have served as a common ground for exchange of ideas and information, have helped find solutions to common problems, and have stimulated that competition which serves the public interest.

Because of the considerable interrelationships between life and health insurance, some of these organizations serve both areas. The major organizations are:

The *American Academy of Actuaries,* organized in 1965 to represent the whole of the actuarial profession in the United States, has established requirements of competence and conduct for its members.

The *American Life Insurance Association* was formed in 1973 through the merger of the two largest company associations, the American Life Convention and the Life Insurance Association of America. The ALIA, whose membership includes companies representing more than 95 percent of the assets of the business, will continue the functions of its predecessors in advancing the interests of policyowners and the business, particularly involving legislation, regulation, and economic research.

The *American Society of Chartered Life Underwriters* is the national professional organization whose membership is limited to those who have earned the Chartered Life Underwriter (C.L.U.) designation. It publishes the *C.L.U. Journal,* provides a variety of services for its nearly 20,000 members, and functions cooperatively through about 200 local chapters.

The *Health Insurance Association of America* is an organization of insurance companies of all types that write health coverages. It represents company views, provides forums for discussion, promotes high ethical standards, undertakes research, and represents member companies in legislation.

A division of the Health Insurance Association of America, the *Health Insurance Council* provides information and technical assistance on health insurance to the health care professions.

The *Health Insurance Institute* is a central source of health insurance information for the public and for such special audiences as the press, educators, labor unions, and employer groups. It represents insurance companies in the health field.

The *Home Office Life Underwriters Association* and the *Institute of Home Office Underwriters* are organizations to advance the sound underwriting of life insurance risks, and to seek out the most effective and most liberal standards for risk acceptance.

The *Institute of Life Insurance,* a public relations and research organization, provides a central source of life insurance information for the general public and for a variety of special sectors of the public, including the press, educators, and community organizations. It also performs or sponsors research in the statistical and basic social aspects of the business.

The *International Association of Health Underwriters* is an organization devoted to advancing the professional status of accident and health insurance agents.

The *Life Insurance Agency Management Association* is an organization of marketing executives of the life insurance companies. It engages in continuous research and training in marketing and life insurance.

The *Life Office Management Association* is an organization devoted to the continuing improvement of life insurance management through the exchange of experience and research findings of member companies, and through development of education programs for office employees.

The *Life Underwriter Training Council* is an organization sponsoring locally administered intermediate courses in sales techniques for life and health insurance agents.

An international organization of life insurance agents, the *Million Dollar Round Table,* seeks to set high standards for life agents through establishment of membership standards, in terms of both sales volume and ethics. It also provides a forum for the exchange of sales and technical information.

The *National Association of Life Underwriters* is an organization of life insurance agents, dedicated to support of legal reserve life insurance and to the advancement of agents' professional status through the quality of their service.

As the professional organization of life and health insurance actuaries, the *Society of Actuaries* qualifies an actuary for professional status, and studies problems in the technical and management aspects of the business.

Many other organizations in the life and health insurance business make continuing contributions to its effectiveness and public service. Notable among these are the organizations of companies' specialists in legal, medical, investment, public relations, and accounting and statistical areas.

In sum total, these organizations contribute to the advancement of life and health insurance in the interest of the policyowners. On the one hand, they serve to intensify competition among individual companies in the business; on the other, they provide the framework for extensive cooperation in research and methods. Both these functions operate to improve the service the business provides the public.

ORGANIZATIONS RELATED TO THE BUSINESS

The *American College of Life Underwriters* serves the higher education and certification needs of persons in life and health insurance and related fields. It functions as a nontraditional professional educational institution, acts as a national examining board for those aspiring to the Chartered Life Underwriter (C.L.U.) designation, and engages in learning research and economic security research activities.

The *American Risk and Insurance Association* is a learned society devoted to furthering the science of risk and insurance through education, research, literature, and communications. Its members include university teachers of insurance and many other persons with a scientific interest in insurance.

The *National Association of Insurance Commissioners* is an organization of state regulatory officials in insurance. It operates as an exchange medium for ideas and trends, and seeks standardization of the regulatory practices of the states.

ECONOMIC AND SOCIAL CONTRIBUTIONS

As investors and as employers, insurance companies make significant contributions to the health and stability of the nation's economy. Specifically, in their role as insurers providing money when the family most needs it, they directly support the health and stability of society's basic unit.

Companies are also demonstrating interest in major social problems. Under a special Urban Investment Program, companies provided $2 billion to finance construction of housing and job-creating enterprises for people living in blighted city neighborhoods.

As part of the business's continuing activities in the area of corporate social responsibility, a clearinghouse has been established under the sponsorship of major associations. It provides the business and the public with information on what companies are doing in various areas of social concern.

Guaranteeing Family Plans

The sum of benefit payments which life and health insurers paid in 1971 is impressive—almost $27 billion. To the individual or family receiving a share of this total, insurance benefits may be more than impressive; they may be a lifeline.

Life insurance payments are the principal assets available to most families on the death of the income producer, and cash values are a major source of family funds for emergencies. Health insurance payments are helping Americans meet an increasing share of their health costs, permitting a rising standard of health maintenance. Health insurance is also channeling an increasing share of total benefits to families stricken with unusually costly accidents or illnesses.

Investing in the National Economy

While the role of life and health insurance in providing for the financial welfare of individual families is widely recognized, the role of insurance companies in the growth of the national economy is not as widely recognized. The assets of life companies, which guarantee the meeting of obligations to policyowners as they come due, are in the meantime invested in a variety of ways, providing a major source of capital for the economy. The return on the investments helps to keep down the cost of protection for policyowners.

In 1971, life companies supplied 7 percent of the nation's capital flowing from all investment sources. At the beginning of 1972, life company investments totaled $222 billion.[1] Mortgage loans that finance the construction and purchase of housing, businesses, and industries comprise a major share of company investments. Other investments finance the construction or expansion of commerce and industry, governmental services, and utilities.[2]

Insurers as Employers

The entire insurance business in the United States employed 1,490,000 people in all its branches in 1971. It is estimated that about 750,000 persons of this total are involved in life and health insurance. Employment in the business continues to rise. However, increases in personnel in recent years have been relatively smaller than increases in sales, indicating larger unit sales and greater efficiency in handling the detailed records necessary in any insurance operation. Automation is particularly suitable for many phases of insurance work and has contributed to efficiency.

---

[1] *Life Insurance Fact Book, 1972.* New York, Institute of Life Insurance.
[2] For the distribution of life insurance company assets, see Chapter 68.

The median income of insurance personnel is substantially the same as that of all nonfarm, full-time workers in the United States. The median income of clerical workers in the insurance business tends to be somewhat lower than that for all clerical workers, while the median income of insurance sales, managerial, and professional workers is somewhat higher than the median income for all workers in these occupations.

WHAT OF THE FUTURE?

All the signs of the early seventies indicate that the future will see more vigorous scrutiny of the nation's established institutions and their role in society. In an effort to strengthen its role in economic and social growth and to measure up to public expectations, insurance companies have moved into new areas, as these examples will show:

—The business maintains a program of scientific research into attitudes of the public toward life and health insurance. The results are used by company managements in both short-range and long-range planning decisions.

—An effort is being undertaken to develop sensors that will help the business identify social and economic trends that bear on the institutional well-being of life and health insurance.

—Improved levels of expertise have become the rule in the home office and the field. Much of the credit goes to the associations of agents and home office specialists for having set high standards of ethics, as well as the development of educational standards for their members.

—The companies have been embarking on more venturesome approaches to insuring people who were once uninsurable, enabling many to obtain protection despite obvious risks. At the same time, new product lines have been added, notably those which provide for equity-linked services. The variable annuity and mutual fund are familiar examples; the variable life insurance policy, which has yet to be placed before the public on any significant basis, is an even more recent example.

—The growing force of organized consumerism, particularly with respect to the pricing of products and services, is increasingly touching the life insurance business. Several years ago, in response to the need for a more accurate method of comparing the cost of life insurance policies, an industry committee devised the "interest-adjusted" index. Despite a feeling in some quarters that this was only a first step, and that an even more accurate guideline would eventually be developed, many companies have begun to acquaint their agents and home office personnel with the "interest-adjusted" method in order that policyowner questions could be answered more fully.

SELECTED REFERENCES

Health Insurance Institute. *Source Book of Health Insurance Data, 1972–73.* New York, 1973.

Institute of Life Insurance. *Life Insurance Fact Book.* New York, 1972.

62

Regulation of
Life and Health Insurance

By W. LEE SHIELD*

THE PRINCIPLE that the business of insurance is "affected with the public interest" has been established for many years and is beyond challenge. Such statements have appeared frequently in judicial decisions and often are repeated by state legislatures in explanation of the purpose of insurance legislation. The insurance business consequently has found itself the object of thorough supervision and regulation by the several states exercising their police power with respect to the health and safety of their citizens.

Objectives of Regulation

An examination of certain characteristics of the life and health insurance business reveals the reasons for close governmental supervision. A policyowner secures from an insurer only a promise of future performance, a promise which may extend over a long period of time. An insurance policy is a contract wherein the party drafting it, the insurer, usually enjoys a superior economic position over the policyowner. A policy of life insurance is a highly technical document concerning the rights of persons long into the future, which obligations are to be carried out after the policyowner's death. An insurance relationship has some of the elements of a fiduciary relationship since it involves transfers of money between individuals and across time. Life and health insurance is of great economic and social importance in view of the magnitude of the funds accumulated by insurers and the number of people in need of basic protection against the risks of death and disability.

Throughout the history of the insurance business in the United States,

* The author expresses deep appreciation to Alexander K. Cieseilski and Robert J. Demichelis, Assistant General Counsels of the American Life Insurance Association, for their invaluable assistance in the preparation of this chapter.

statements of regulatory philosophy continually have reflected a strong endorsement of reasonable governmental supervision. Insurance Superintendent George W. Miller of New York made the statement as early as 1871 that, "The true object and aim of the government supervision should be to afford the fullest possible protection to the public, with the least possible annoyance or expense to, or interference with the companies." As recently as 1965, the Wisconsin legislature, in creating a committee to recodify the state's insurance laws, defined the basic purposes of the re-codification as "the protection of the public welfare and interest, especially with respect to insurance policyholders and shareholders, insurers, their agents and personnel."[1]

Two basic objectives of governmental regulation of life and health insurance are most commonly cited. The first is to ensure the stability and financial soundness of the insurance carrier, as a prerequisite to its capacity to perform. An insurer's successful operation is primarily concerned with the preservation of its capital, reserves, and investments, as its operation encompasses the creation of funds for the distribution of benefits in the future. The second is to ensure the reasonable and fair treatment of prospective and existing policyowners, insureds, and beneficiaries by both the insurer and the insurance agent. This objective is achieved by establishing specific standards in the solicitation of insurance and in the formulation of contractual provisions, primarily relating to the rights and benefits under an insurance policy.

A more complete enumeration of the purposes of an insurance code is included in the recently enacted Nevada Insurance Code, which took effect on January 1, 1972:

The purposes of this code are to:

(a) Protect policyholders and all having an interest under insurance policies;
(b) Implement the public interest in the business of insurance;
(c) Provide adequate standards of solidity of insurers, and of integrity and competence in conduct of their affairs in the home offices and in the field;
(d) Improve and thereby preserve state regulation of insurance;
(e) Insure that policyholders, claimants and insurers are treated fairly and equitably;
(f) Encourage full cooperation of the office of commissioner with other regulatory bodies, both of this and other states and of the Federal Government;
(g) Insure that the state has an adequate and healthy insurance market characterized by competitive conditions and the exercise of initiative;
(h) Prevent misleading, unfair and monopolistic practices in insurance operations; and
(i) Continue to provide the State of Nevada with a comprehensive modern and adequate body of law, in response to the McCarran Act (Public Law 15, 79th Congress, 15 U.S.C. §§1011 to 1015, inclusive), for the effective regulation and supervision of insurance business transacted with, or affecting interests of the people of this state.[2]

---

[1] Chapter 406, Wisconsin Laws, 1965.
[2] Chapter 660, Nevada Laws, 1971.

DEVELOPMENT OF STATE INSURANCE SUPERVISION

Governmental supervision of life insurance companies is as old as the modern life insurance policy itself, which evolved in the 1840s, and modern health insurance coverage which originated in the 1890s. The regulation of the life and health insurance business is the product of an evolutionary process which began with the adaptation of regulatory principles developed at the beginning of the last century in the fire and marine insurance business.

A number of present-day statutory requirements concerning insurers' financial soundness and policyowners' rights appeared for the first time more than a century ago: The filing, with the legislature (Massachusetts, 1807), or with a state official (New York, 1829), of an insurer's periodic reports of financial condition and statements of its affairs; recognition of an insurable interest in the life of the husband or father, for the wife and children, respectively, along with an exemption from the claims of creditors of proceeds payable to them if annual premiums did not exceed $300 (New York, 1840); procedures for incorporation of insurers (New York, 1849); establishment of a minimum deposit of securities (New York, 1851–53); minimum actuarial bases in valuing life insurance reserves and minimum nonforfeiture benefit standards (Massachusetts, 1858 and 1861); and licensing requirements for out-of-state insurers (Michigan and Wisconsin, just before 1860).

In order to implement these regulatory statutes, it became necessary to establish some form of state agency. The first insurance supervisory boards were created in the 1850s in New Hampshire, Massachusetts, Rhode Island, and Vermont. The first separate insurance department, independent of any established state agency, was created in Massachusetts in 1855, and the first full-time insurance commissioner was appointed in New York in 1859. Perhaps it was more than coincidental that one of the founders of modern life insurance, Elizur Wright, of Massachusetts, was one of the earliest insurance commissioners, serving from 1858 to 1867.

An important force in influencing the regulation of insurance has been the National Association of Insurance Commissioners, a voluntary organization of chief insurance supervisory officials of the several states. The NAIC was organized in 1871 and until 1935 was known as the National Convention of Insurance Commissioners (NCIC). As provided in its constitution, the main objective of the NAIC is to promote and encourage uniformity in legislation affecting insurance, as well as uniformity in the interpretation of such laws. The NAIC has been responsible for developing numerous uniform and model statutes, regulations, and procedures which in varying degrees have been accepted as the basic components of the insurance regulatory system throughout the United States. The early accomplishments of the NAIC include the adoption of a uniform set of annual statement blanks for use by life, fire, and marine insurers, and the approval of a model insurance regulatory statute in 1887; the recommendation of rules to curb insurers from doing business in any state where such insurers had not complied with its laws in 1895; the establishment of the Valuation of Securities Committee in 1907; and the establishment of the present zone system of examination in 1936. In more recent years the NAIC has adopted uniform and model laws such as the Individual Accident and Sickness Policy Provisions Law, group life definition and standard provisions bill, Standard Nonforfeiture and Valuation Laws, Fair Trade Practices Act, credit life and credit health insurance regulation bill, Unauthorized Insurers Service of Process Act, Insurance Holding Company System Regulatory Act, Variable Contract Law, and insider training bill.[3]

A profound influence on the regulation of the life insurance business in this country followed the investigation conducted by the Armstrong-Hughes Investigating Committee,[4] established by the New York legislature in 1905. That committee's recommendations were substantially enacted in the revision of the New York insurance laws in 1906. Some of the resultant legislation was limited in application to the State of New York, while other enactments proved to be of an experimental nature. For example, a standard life insurance policy form was required, but that provision was subsequently repealed in 1909; and the use of preliminary term valuation of policies was prohibited until that statute was repealed in 1920. Most of the legislative proposals made following the Armstrong investigation proved to be sound and were adopted by practically all the states. Such provisions related to company organization, election of directors, salaries and expenses of officers, authorized and prohibited investments, annual distribution of policyowner surplus, prohibition against deferred (tontine) dividends, prohibition against rebating, and provisions concerning the rights of policyowners generally.

Parallel in character to the life insurance investigation in New York was an investigation of accident and health insurance conducted by the 1910–11 New York legislature. Its recommendations served as a basis for the formulation by the NAIC in 1912 of standard provisions required in individual health insurance policies.

A further influence on the regulatory pattern was the investigation conducted by the Temporary National Economic Committee, which was created by the U.S. Congress to cooperate with the Securities and Exchange Commission in a comprehensive study of the nation's economy during 1938–41. Among other things, the TNEC report[5] made recommendations for strengthening state insurance departments, especially their examination procedures; for closer regulation of insurance agency practices; for standardized, simplified and fewer policy forms; for closer scru-

---

[3] For an exhaustive list of model bills and recommended regulations, see 1972 NAIC *Proceedings,* pp. XII through XX.

[4] Report of the Joint Committee of the Senate and Assembly of the State of New York, Appointed to Investigate the Affairs of Life Insurance Companies, in Exhibits, Reports and Index of Legislative Insurance Investigating Committee (Albany, 1906), Vol. VII.

[5] Temporary National Economic Committee, *Investigation of Concentration of Economic Power,* Monograph No. 28-A, 76th Cong., 3d sess. (Washington, D.C.: U.S. Government Printing Office, 1941).

tiny of the activities of company management; and for a fundamental change in the conduct of industrial life insurance.

MODERN STATE STATUTES AND REGULATIONS

A pattern of laws, currently described as "modern" insurance codes, thus has developed state by state. These codes usually cover four areas relating to (1) the insurance department, (2) the organization and licensing of insurance companies, (3) the licensing of agents and brokers, and (4) the required provisions of insurance contracts.

Insurance Department

State constitutions, as a rule, limit themselves to providing for the creation of an insurance department as one of several administrative agencies of the state which make up the executive branch of the government. The bulk of laws dealing with the organization, powers and duties of the insurance regulatory authority, therefore, have become an essential part of an insurance code.

In most states, the responsibility for the administration of the insurance laws is vested in an independent state agency, called the insurance department. The head of the insurance department is the commissioner, superintendent, or director of insurance, except in a few states where the duty is delegated to a multimember board or commission, or some subordinate division or bureau of a more comprehensive agency, such as the department of banking and insurance, department of commerce, or department of business regulation. In a very few states, the administration of insurance is entrusted to an officer of the state who has other responsibilities, such as the auditor, treasurer, or comptroller general of the state, serving as an ex-officio insurance commissioner. Several states elect the insurance official; however, in most states he is appointed by the governor, a commission, or other department or agency head.

The insurance commissioner has the authority to issue a license to do business to insurance companies, domestic and foreign. Concomitant with this authority is the power to revoke, suspend, or refuse to renew an insurance company's certificate of authority, for cause. In exercising control over the activities of insurers, the commissioner may impose penalties for violations of the law, with due process safeguards.

Supplementing his authority to review the insurers' annual statements, the commissioner is required to examine periodically, usually not less frequently than every three or five years at his discretion, the affairs of each insurer doing business in the state. Generally, the insurance department values an insurer's policy reserve liabilities. In all states, the insurance department examines and approves policy forms and other related documents, such as applications, riders, and supplemental contracts.

An important quasi-legislative prerogative of the commissioner is the power to make reasonable rules and regulations, necessary for, or as an aid to, the effectuation of any provision of the insurance code. Quasi-judicial powers also are granted by statute to the commissioner to conduct hearings, to compel testimony and production of evidence, and to issue orders, provided, of course, that due process safeguards are guaranteed.

Insurance Companies

The laws governing insurance companies may be divided into two categories; those dealing with the procedures for organization and incorporation of domestic insurers, and those relating to the insuring powers of both domestic and foreign insurers.

In the large majority of states the manner in which insurance companies, both stock and mutual, may be incorporated is an essential part of the insurance laws. In some states the business corporation statutes relating to domestic private corporations formed for profit are applicable to domestic stock and mutual insurers. Should any inconsistency arise, the express provisions of the insurance code usually prevail. Most insurance codes expressly permit mutualization of stock companies, but only a small number of states have provisions for conversion of a mutual company to a stock company. Most codes also provide procedures for bulk reinsurance, dissolution, and merger or consolidation of insurers. A set of basically uniform statutory provisions exists in most of the states regarding delinquent or insolvent companies and enables their rehabilitation or liquidation.

As prerequisites to being incorporated as an insurance company, the codes prescribe the amounts of minimum capital and surplus of a domestic stock insurer and the minimum surplus of a domestic mutual insurer as well as a minimum deposit of securities to be made with the insurance supervisory official. A significant statutory restriction is one which defines the classes of insurance that may be written by a single company. Usually, an insurer writing both life and health insurance and issuing annuity contracts is prohibited from exercising any further insuring powers, but may form or acquire a subsidiary to engage in various ancillary activities (and, in some states, in noninsurance-related operations).

With respect to insurers incorporated in other states, a typical insurance code prescribes the eligibility and requirements for admission to do an insurance business and establishes standards of solvency on a par with the standards fixed for domestic insurers. Various categories of insurers' assets, both "admitted" and "nonadmitted," as well as liabilities are enumerated. Detailed provisions specify various categories of authorized investments, along with quantitative and qualitative restrictions. Rules for the valuation of securities held by insurers, including corporate bonds and stocks, are also prescribed, generally following a uniform pattern established by the NAIC. These standards are used as a measure of an insurer's financial soundness and stability. The laws relating to authorized investments are applicable to domestic insurers and usually do not apply directly to foreign and alien insurers doing business in another state. The statutes generally provide that the investment portfolio of a foreign or alien insurer shall be as permitted by the laws of its state of domicile, if of a quality substantially as high as that required for similar funds held by domestic insurers of the same type.

All insurers doing business in the state are required to file annual statements with the insurance department providing information as to their operations and financial condition, and including various schedules and detailed items, as called for in the "annual statement blank" developed by the NAIC and used in all states. The contents of the annual statement are reviewed and examined by the respective states as a tool for auditing each insurer's financial condition.

The insurance laws of all states contain provisions applicable to insurers, agents and brokers operating in the state, prohibiting unfair or deceptive trade practices[6] or methods such as false advertising, misrepresentations, twisting, false financial statements, defamation, boycott, coercion, intimidation, unfair discrimination, and rebating. The insurance supervisory official is given the authority to obtain cease and desist orders from a court of competent jurisdiction to prevent the continuation of such practices if the insurer does not cease when ordered by the insurance department. Insurance codes prohibit insurers from doing an insurance business in the state without a certificate of authority. All states have enacted laws that subject unauthorized insurers to the jurisdiction of the courts of the state in suits by or on behalf of insureds or beneficiaries under insurance contracts. Additional statutory authority either prohibits unauthorized insurers from transacting business in the state or enables the insurance commissioner to obtain jurisdiction over an unauthorized insurer which may be soliciting insurance by mail or otherwise.

Agents' Qualification and Licensing

The agents' qualification and licensing statutes are an important part of the insurance laws. They require a license from the insurance department as a prerequisite to acting as an agent or broker, and prohibit licensed agents and brokers from sharing commissions with unlicensed persons. Exceptions from the licensing requirement commonly include a regular salaried employee of an insurer who assists the agent but receives no commission; and a person who, in the performance of ministerial duties, secures and forwards information for the purpose of group insurance, for enrolling individuals under group insurance coverages or for issuing group insurance certificates where no commission is paid for such services. In some states partnerships and corporations are ineligible for agents' or brokers' licenses.

Generally the license issued to an agent of a life insurance company permits the transaction of life and health insurance if the company is authorized to write both lines and if the agent is qualified accordingly. However, licenses authorizing the transaction of either life or health insurance only and requiring qualifications for one such line only, may usually be secured. In addition, some states make available limited licenses to sell credit life and credit health insurance only. Most states pro-

---

[6] The 1972 revision of the NAIC Model Unfair Trade Practices Act appears in Appendix X.

vide for a special license to be issued to life insurance agents prior to being permitted to sell variable annuity contracts. Since variable annuity contracts are subject to certain provisions of the federal securities laws, the agent must, of necessity, comply with those additional provisions before he legally can be authorized to sell such contracts. In exercising his authority to license insurance agents and brokers, the commissioner usually prescribes or approves study materials and develops examinations used in testing the qualifications of persons who are to be authorized to sell life and health insurance policies as well as fixed and variable annuity contracts.

One of the methods of determining a prospective licensee's competence and character, adopted generally in the states, is the requirement that the applicant successfully complete a training course conducted by the insurer. Typically, the states require the applicants for a license to pass an examination which is administered by the insurance department. A growing number of states exclude Chartered Life Underwriters (CLUs) from the written examination requirement. Also, through reciprocity, many states will dispense with the examination for nonresident agents if they are duly licensed in their state of domicile. In some states health insurance policies may be required to be countersigned by a licensed resident agent; only rarely is such a requirement applicable to life insurance policies.

Insurance Contracts

The laws bearing on the insurance contract and defining the rights and duties of the policyowners, insureds, and beneficiaries under such contracts are in derogation of the common-law doctrine of freedom of contract and are designed with a view to protecting the interests of the insuring public. They prescribe certain minimum standard policy provisions to be incorporated "in substance" in the policy, but permit the use of substitute provisions not less favorable to the policyowner, insured, or beneficiary. In the case of group life insurance, provisions may be used which are at least as favorable to the insured and more favorable to the policyowner. In addition to statutory standard policy provisions and the power of the commissioner to disapprove policy forms, the insurance buying public is further protected by the established rule of law which construes the insurance contract against the insurance company if the terms of the contract are determined to be ambiguous.

A great deal of similarity in the contents of insurance policies stems from the standard policy provisions law for ordinary (individual) and group life insurance, for individual, group and blanket health insurance, for nonforfeitures under life policies and annuity contracts, and for variable contracts and credit insurance. Standard provisions to be included in individual annuity contracts and in industrial policies are often separately spelled out, although specific provisions relating to the contents of a group annuity contract are frequently omitted.

The statutes require that ordinary life insurance policies must contain provisions relating to: (1) a grace period for premium payment; (2) policy incontestability; (3) policy and application as the entire contract, and statements as representations rather than warranties; (4) adjustment of benefits in the event of a misstatement of age; (5) apportionment of divisible surplus under participating policies; (6) nonforfeiture benefits and surrender values; (7) policy loans after the third year; (8) amounts of guaranteed installments if proceeds are paid in installments; and (9) reinstatement of policy.

Provisions prohibited in ordinary life insurance policies usually include (1) requiring the commencement of any suit against the insurer within any period shorter than the otherwise applicable statute of limitations; and (2) excluding or limiting liability for death caused in a specified manner or while the insured has a specified status, except for exclusion of risk of war, travel, specified hazardous occupation, foreign residency, or suicide during the first two policy years, if a provision is made for the return of the reserve in case of death within the permitted exclusion. Further, a number of statutes or regulations prohibit or limit the issuance of "special policies" of life insurance such as profit sharing, charter, or coupon policies, and various types of so-called tontine and semitontine policies.

Group life insurance, which in most states is subject to certain underwriting restrictions with eligibility limited to employer, trustee, labor union, and creditor groups, must contain provisions concerning: (1) a grace period; (2) incontestability; (3) attachment of, and statements in, the application; (4) misstatement of age; (5) facility of payment; (6) certificate of insurance; (7) conversion privilege on termination of eligibility; (8) conversion privilege on termination of policy; and (9) death pending conversion. (The three last-named provisions are inapplicable to creditor groups.)

The statutory required provisions in individual health insurance policies include those relating to: (1) the entire contract; (2) incontestability; (3) grace period; (4) reinstatement; (5) notice of claim; (6) claim forms; (7) proof of loss; (8) time of claim payment; (9) payment of claims; (10) physical examinations and autopsy; (11) legal actions; and (12) change of beneficiary. Other statutory provisions are classified as optional and may be included at the election of the insurer.

Most states also define persons eligible for group and blanket health insurance, and such contracts generally are required to contain the substance of applicable individual health insurance standard provisions.

The laws of almost all states contain the detailed requirements of the NAIC model bill on the regulation of credit life and credit accident and health insurance. Comprehensive regulations have been issued by most state insurance departments.

With regard to insurance contracts generally, the commissioner usually has the power to disapprove a policy form on the grounds that its provisions are unjust, unfair, inequitable, misleading or encouraging misrepresentation of the coverage, or that they are contrary to any provision of the insurance code or any departmental rule or regulation. In a substantial number of states, an additional specific ground for disapproval of an individual health insurance policy exists if the benefits provided therein are unreasonable in relation to the premium charged. Further, the laws of almost all states give the commissioner the specific power to disapprove a credit life or credit health insurance policy form if the premium rates charged or to be charged are excessive in relation to benefits.

CHALLENGES TO STATE REGULATION

Insurance supervision traditionally has been a function of state government. The entire body of state insurance laws which has developed is based upon the 1869 decision of the U.S. Supreme Court in *Paul* v. *Virginia*.[7] In that decision the court said: "Issuing a policy of fire insurance is not a transaction of commerce. . . . Such contracts are not interstate transactions. . . ." Although the legal issue involved only fire insurance companies, the court's broad holding applied equally to all lines of insurance, including life and health. This was made clear in 1913 when the Supreme Court reiterated its conclusion that insurance was not commerce in *New York Life Insurance Company* v. *Deer Lodge County*.[8]

On June 5, 1944, the Supreme Court of the United States, in *United States* v. *South-Eastern Underwriters Association*,[9] held that the business of insurance was commerce and when conducted across state lines, it was interstate commerce subject to the Sherman Antitrust Act and to the regulatory power of the federal government. The most important effect of the decision was that the concerted action whereby the fire and casualty insurance business promulgated uniform premium rates through rating bureaus became of doubtful legality. Boycott tactics became illegal. The decision threatened the foundation upon which state regulatory systems had been based.

All segments of the insurance business combined efforts with the NAIC to develop legislation to continue regulatory authority in the states. Early in 1945, the 79th Congress enacted Public Law 15, also known as the McCarran-Ferguson Act.[10] The legislative history of the Act is described in the following language from an opinion of the U.S. Supreme Court:

In 1944, this Court removed the supposed constitutional basis for exemption of insurance by holding, in *United States* v. *South-Eastern Underwriters Ass'n*. . . . , that the business of insurance was subject to federal regulation under the commerce power. Congress was quick to respond. It forthwith enacted the McCarran Act . . . which on its face demonstrates the purpose broadly to give support to the existing and future state systems for regulating and taxing the business of insurance, . . . and to assure that existing state power to regulate insurance would continue. . . . Thus, rather than encouraging Congress to enter the field of insurance, the South-Eastern decision spurred reiteration of its undeviating policy of abstention.[11]

The states responded quickly to the action of Congress. An all-industry committee was formed with representatives of practically all lines of in-

---

[7] 8 Wall. 168 (1869).
[8] 231 U.S. 495 (1913).
[9] 322 U.S. 533 (1944).
[10] 59 Stat. 33, 15 U.S.C. §§1011–1015 (1945).
[11] *Securities and Exchange Commission* v. *Variable Annuity Life Inc. Co.*, 359 U.S. 65, at page 99 (1959).

surance to work with the NAIC in developing state legislation. These efforts produced significant results. For example, by the end of the 1950s virtually all jurisdictions had enacted laws to prohibit unfair methods of competition and unfair practices in the insurance business. These laws were patterned closely after portions of the Federal Trade Commission Act. Most of the states have adopted service of process laws designed to enable claimants under insurance policies to bring actions in their state of residence against an insurer issuing such policies if the insurer were not licensed to do business in that state. Other examples of uniform state legislation have been referred to earlier in this chapter.

Of special significance in the property and liability insurance fields, the states enacted rate regulatory laws to provide supervision of the rating bureaus which have long been considered necessary in those lines of insurance for the pooling of loss and expense information to be used in the determination of premium rates. Laws of that type are not necessary in the life and health insurance business, since each insurer establishes its own premium rates on the basis of mortality and morbidity tables, nonforfeiture requirements, and individual experience. The competitive forces in these lines of insurance generally have produced equitable premium rates for the life and health insurance buying public.

Subsequent decisions of the U.S. Supreme Court have clarified further the extent of the states' authority to regulate insurance under the McCarran Act. In the field of insurance advertising, the Court held that under the McCarran Act the Federal Trade Commission does not have jurisdiction over insurance advertising of companies licensed in states which have enacted their own laws regulating such advertising.[12] This case involved the provision which stipulates that the Sherman Act, the Clayton Act, and the Federal Trade Commission Act shall apply to insurance to the extent that such business is not regulated by state law. The Court rejected the contention of the Federal Trade Commission that this provision should be construed to permit concurrent state and federal regulation. In a later case, a direct-mail insurer contested the regulatory authority of the Federal Trade Commission on the ground that the law of its domicile regulated the advertising it disseminated in states in which it was not licensed. The Court rejected this contention, holding that the McCarran Act meant regulation by the states in which the insurer's advertising activities were directed and had impact.[13]

Variable annuity contracts—which guarantee to the annuitant that upon reaching a specified age he will receive periodic payments, the amounts of which are not fixed and have no assured minimum but vary according to the success of the investments of the issuer of the annuity contract—were held to be securities under federal law and hence subject to the requirements of the Securities Act of 1933 and the Investment Company Act of 1940.[14] The Court reasoned that the issuer of a variable

---

[12] *Federal Trade Commission v. National Casualty Company,* 375 U.S. 560 (1958).
[13] *Federal Trade Commission v. Travelers Health Association,* 362 U.S. 293 (1960).
[14] *Securities and Exchange Commission v. Variable Annuity Life Ins. Co.,* 359 U.S. 65 (1959).

annuity assumed no true risk in the insurance sense and therefore was not exempt from federal regulation by reason of the McCarran Act.

In connection with a merger involving two life insurance companies which had received approval of a state insurance department, the Supreme Court held that the McCarran Act did not exempt the merger transaction from the provisions of federal securities laws. The Court made it clear that the McCarran Act exempts only the business of insurance from federal regulation, not all activities of insurance companies, and went on to point out that the "business of insurance" comprehends only the relationship between an insurer and its policyowners, not the relationship of an insurer and its shareholders. The Court emphasized: "The paramount federal interest in protecting shareholders is in this situation perfectly compatible with the paramount state interest in protecting policyholders."[15]

APPLICABLE FEDERAL LAWS
AND REGULATIONS

There is no immediate likelihood that the present system of state regulation will be discarded, but it is routinely necessary to review the growing federal interest in insurance, expressed both in statute and regulation. Constrained by the above judicial and statutory background, federal intervention for the most part has been indirect in nature. One exception lies in the jurisdiction of the Department of Defense over the solicitation and sale of life insurance to military personnel overseas. Actually, the department exercises jurisdiction over both domestic and overseas sales, as well as the utilization of military allotments in payment of premiums; but in recent years the department has placed almost complete reliance on the state insurance departments respecting coverages offered within the United States and the licensing of both companies and agents.

Perhaps the one most significant aspect of federal involvement in the life insurance business is in equity products and services, an area which many insurers entered voluntarily in the late sixties. Company views differed as to the advantages and disadvantages to both insurer and policyowner; however, by early 1971, nearly 200 life insurers were involved in some sort of equity products program.

The first major steps were taken well after litigation involving variable benefit contracts had been concluded.[16] Thus, a life insurer entering the variable annuity business knew it would be directly subject in such activities to the laws and regulations administered by the Securities and Exchange Commission, the Federal Reserve Board, and probably the National Association of Securities Dealers (a self-regulatory organization chartered, in effect, by the SEC). By such voluntary action an insurer accepts that (*a*) its variable annuity contract will be viewed as a security

---

[15] *Securities and Exchange Commission* v. *National Securities, Inc.*, 393 U.S. 453 (1969).

[16] *Securities and Exchange Commission* v. *Variable Annuity Life Insurance Co.*, 359 U.S. 65 (1959).

by the SEC, (*b*) its agents will be subject to federal examination and licensing, with the potential for revocation by the SEC or the NASD, (*c*) its sales literature will be subjected to standards of preclearance by people that follow a totally different standard for such matters, and (*d*) its internal operation will be directly regulated and ruled in a manner totally inconsistent with its past experiences. If the insurer, in order to conduct such a business, registers as a broker-dealer, it also invites scrutiny of its lending activities by the Federal Reserve Board. In short, the step into equities involves accepting the authority of the federal regulatory bodies over the insurance company operation in these areas.

While insurance companies in the equity products business have submitted themselves to regulation with respect to their securities operation, there have been a number of occasions where concessions were made to fit the insurance operation. The insurance business, through its trade associations, has worked with federal regulatory authorities and with Congress to achieve the amount of flexibility necessary to permit life insurers to exist under the unfamiliar rules designed for the securities industry. The SEC, FRB, and NASD have granted specific relief for life insurers. Congress has also recognized, at least in a limited area, the desirability of granting equality with banks by exempting certain tax-qualified plans from the federal securities laws. Problems may be expected to continue to arise, however, as regulations adopted or applied to govern the operations of a securities entity also impact on an insurance operation.

There are scores of federal agencies and departments which indirectly exert some measure of control on the business of insurance. In accordance with the terms of the McCarran Act, both the Federal Trade Commission and the Department of Justice retain partial jurisdiction over areas including false advertising, agreements to boycott, and unlawful acquisitions. The Federal Trade Commission has acted under this authority respecting false advertising by branding as misleading and deceptive eight practices involved in the sale of insurance by mail. This finding was the subject of a consumer bulletin first released in 1967 and republished in 1971 as the first of a "new series." Also, FTC has challenged a merger between insurance companies,[17] noting that some 580 mergers and acquisitions involving property-liability insurers had taken place between 1960 and 1969.[18]

The business of insurance, although substantially exempt from "The Age Discrimination in Employment Act of 1967," nevertheless is subject to the operation of wage and hour requirements as administered by the Department of Labor, the Welfare and Pension Plans Disclosure Act requirements, the provisions of the Equal Pay Act and The Civil Rights Act of 1964, both as an employer and in everyday business operations. If Congress had not accepted the premise that age and age-related factors are pivotal in designing employee pension and insurance plans, and

---

[17] FTC Complaint, Docket 8847, June 17, 1971.

[18] The most recent example of a successful effort by the Department of Justice to block an insurance company merger was the Chicago Title and Trust Company case. *United States* v. *Chicago Title and Trust Co.,* 241 F. Supp. 56 (N. D. Ill. 1965).

hence justifying the resulting exemption from the 1967 enactment, the effect on insurance would have been substantial.

THE FUTURE

Health care, already the subject of multiple congressional enactments including Medicare and Medicaid, exerts increasing influence in insurance regulation. Insurers already are deeply involved in the Medicare program as administrators of both hospitalization and professional care programs, and they currently are faced with a proposal for comprehensive national health insurance legislation. The health insurance business has developed its own proposal, known as "Healthcare," which is designed to provide access to quality health care for all persons regardless of their financial status. Under the plan, the quality of health care would be safeguarded and incentives provided to expand the available numbers of professional and paramedical personnel so that the health care delivery system would not be overloaded. Special attention to the development of comprehensive ambulatory care centers would aid in holding down treatment costs, while the co-payment system along with other safeguards against overutilization and abuse would be continued. This area of congressional consideration looms as a major expression of federal interest in insurance regulation.

Recent acts of Congress have threatened a departure from the concept that social security retirement benefits should constitute a basic floor of protection, and are of concern to the life insurance business. So are other proposals to extend the taxable wage base even farther above the national wage average, hence impinging on the area traditionally served by the private sector. These congressional considerations are linked inseparably with the future and growth of private pension plans. Proposals to regulate federally the operations of such plans, including establishment of vesting and funding standards, a guarantee of benefits, and a nationwide approach to "portability" of benefits, continue to be of considerable interest to the life insurance business.

Intensive efforts are being devoted to the development of variable benefit life insurance under which both death benefits and nonforfeiture benefits will vary, both upward and downward, to reflect the results in the underlying portfolio of investments subject only to a guarantee that the death benefit will never be less than the initial amount. As with the variable annuity, federal regulation will be substantially involved. The extent of such federal involvement and the resolution of certain federal income tax problems will determine the importance that this new product will attain in the immediate future.[19]

More than 100 years of experience suggests that the NAIC and state systems of insurance regulation are capable of resolving issues of national concern which have resulted from war, recession, inflation, civil disruption, and changes in social attitudes. The effectiveness of state regulation continues to depend upon the ability to regulate the solvency of insurers

---

[19] See Chapter 17 on variable life insurance for a discussion of the 1973 SEC ruling.

and achieve a goal of overall equity in supervision for both consumers and insurers.

SELECTED REFERENCES

Faulkner, Edwin J.   *Health Insurance*. New York: McGraw-Hill Book Co., 1960.

Huebner, S. S. and Black, Kenneth, Jr.   *Life Insurance*. 8th ed. New York: Appleton-Century-Crofts, Inc., 1972.

Kimball, Spencer L. and Denenberg, Herbert S.   *Insurance, Government, and Social Policy*. Homewood, Ill.: Richard D. Irwin, Inc., 1969.

McGill, Dan M.   *Life Insurance*. Homewood, Ill.: Richard D. Irwin, Inc., 1967.

Maclean, Joseph B.   *Life Insurance*. 9th ed. New York: McGraw-Hill Book Co., 1962.

Mayerson, Allen L.   *Introduction to Insurance*. New York: The Macmillan Co., 1962.

63

Company Organization and Management

By EDMUND L. ZALINSKI

LIFE AND HEALTH insurance is written by a great variety of carriers. Insurers include stock companies, mutual companies, fraternal associations, savings banks, state funds, and the U.S. government. Insurance companies range in size from the new company with few employees, to mature giants which are among the nation's largest business enterprises. Companies may be specialized, providing only a single type of coverage; in other instances, they may encompass virtually all insurance and annuity services, and may engage in equity-based products and other financial services fields as well.

This chapter primarily treats the private corporate form of insurance carrier of medium size. To a large extent, however, these comments are applicable as well to other types and sizes of companies, and throughout the chapter references to the latter will be made from time to time.

The activities of all life and health insurers demonstrate a common thread. Many aspects of management and organization tend to be similar, with differences largely the result of emphasis, nature of ownership, and magnitude.

Recently the holding company form has become increasingly popular, particularly with companies wishing to engage in financial service activities less directly concerned with life and health insurance.[1] In adopting the holding company form, an insurance company may organize as its "parent" an "upstream" entity chartered as a general business corporation. Another way to diversify, which, because of its organizational structure, is the only way available to a mutual company, is to form a "downstream" holding company that is a subsidiary of the insurer. By and large, life insurance companies that are affiliated with holding companies, whether upstream or downstream, are organized and operated in a manner similar to that outlined in this chapter.

---

[1] In 1969, the State of New York enacted legislation to regulate holding companies. See Chapter 190, Section 6, of the New York Insurance Law.

SPECIAL CHARACTERISTICS

Life insurance companies are unleveraged and require a combination of technical specialists in such fields of investments, law, accounting, actuarial science, selection of risks, and salesmanship. Management's task is that of maintaining a delicate, effective balance among an aggressive sales force, actuaries whose conservative design of products is characteristic, underwriters who appraise risks with independence, statutory regulations, and an overall operation that may be deemed sound while at the same time reflecting reasonable growth.

Life and health insurance is a service type of business employing large numbers of people, and differs from manufacturing concerns in that there is no raw material to be bought, inventoried, or processed. There is never any scarcity of supply or problem of manufacture, nor is a large investment in capital goods required.

Both banks and insurance companies handle other people's money. Banks operate on a relatively short-term basis, whereas insurance companies make contracts the fulfillment of which may depend upon the rate of interest earned, expenses incurred, and mortality and morbidity experience over 10, 20, 50, or even 100 years in the future. Insurance companies accumulate billions of dollars in assets to meet their long-term future obligations. Because of this, their investment activities are not only greater than those of most other types of business enterprise but are vital to safeguarding the interests of policyowners.

The importance of decisions by life insurance company management is magnified by the long-term nature of the business. Whereas the quality of management in most businesses can be determined by their annual profits, years—oftentimes measured in multiples of decades—may pass before the wisdom of life company management (or the lack of it) is revealed. That fact places a premium on the selection of capable insurance company management.

COMPANY FORMATION

Insight into the organization and management of companies may be gained by a brief review of the steps involved in organizing such a company. It is necessary to incorporate, secure a charter, draft bylaws, and obtain licenses from those jurisdictions in which the company intends to operate.

Company policy and management are profoundly influenced by state regulation, while at the same time state regulation itself has been greatly influenced by company management practices. State laws and regulations, on the one hand, have been adopted to prevent unsatisfactory management practices. On the other hand, the management practices followed by some companies have been found to serve the public interest so well that they were made mandatory for all companies. Generally speaking, state regulation is aimed at the protection of policyowners and the public, but is not especially concerned with the welfare of the stockholder. Specifically, the statutes of a typical insurance code affecting life and health insurance can be fitted into one of the following five categories:

1. Safeguarding the funds which are guaranteed to fulfill the obligations of the insurance contracts.
2. Preventing undertakings that are hazardous or contrary to the public interest.
3. Preventing deception or misunderstanding.
4. Assuring equity and preventing unfair discrimination among policyowners.
5. Obtaining tax revenue.

The availability of sufficient funds not only to launch the company but also to keep it going over a substantial number of years is a vital consideration in the formation of a new company. There is a continuous strain on the surplus caused by the large initial expense of acquiring business. Over 100 percent of the first-year premium is used to offset the cost of new business acquisition, including commissions, managerial compensation, medical and underwriting expenses, issuing and recording policies, establishing policy records, and the like. In addition, reserves must be set up for future liabilities—to a lesser extent for health insurance than for life insurance. This reserve and the excess initial expense must come from the company's capital and surplus.

Because the anticipated initial volume of business does not justify the employment of full-time technicians, new companies often rely on consulting firms and part-time assistance in order to save money. In addition, the executive staff may serve in several capacities. For example, the chief executive also might double as sales manager, actuary, accountant, or lawyer, depending on the nature of his past experience.

A new company's organization structure typically would be very simple, with few levels of authority and a minimum of departmentalization. Continued growth would lead to a larger number of officers and employees, greater specialization, more levels of authority, and increased departmentalization. Growth of the company would lead to more concentration on a more formalized system (and style) of management, and coordination of effort through effective policies, procedures, and communications.

New companies usually find it desirable to decide on the geographical area in which they intend to operate, the type of policies they intend to sell, the segment of the market they desire to develop, and the depth of desirable market penetration, all influenced heavily by their resources in money and manpower.

FORM OF ORGANIZATION

Companies engaged in life and health insurance for the most part apply the same basic principles of organization used by other forms of business enterprise. The exact combination depends upon many factors, particularly the circumstances surrounding the formation and growth of each concern. The simplest form, more likely to appear in smaller companies, might be described simply as a line organization. Here all authority rests with a single individual, usually the president. More common is line and staff, where executive officers rely upon advisory officers and departments, with specialized field of expertise. Where some staff officers also have "line" responsibilities for executing their recommendations, the situation is sometimes referred to as a functional organization.

Levels of Authority

In all forms of organized human activity, whether they be military, religious, cooperative, charitable, or for profit, there are various levels of authority. The individual or group possessing final authority delegates specific authority to others in subordinate positions to make decisions and take certain actions. Levels of authority are usually kept at a minimum to shorten lines of communication and to facilitate decision making and policy execution. It is important that both the authority and the responsibility for a given project or function be placed in one individual located as closely as possible to the actual point of execution. The failure to support responsibility with authority results in inefficiency and delay.

In the typical company, there are at least four major levels of authority. They may be described as directional, executive, managerial, and supervisory. Essential, therefore, is the fact that there must be a clear statement of functions for each level of authority, as well as a definite fixing of responsibility, in order to minimize the possibility of overlapping, tension, friction, or neglect of important functions.

Departmentalization

Companies make extensive use of the plan of departmentalization on a functional, product, and geographical basis. Functional departmentalization is exemplified, for example, by the actuarial department, which has the responsibility for a variety of related functions ranging from mortality studies to annual statement preparation. Product departmentalization is illustrated by the establishment of an *individual insurance* department and a *group insurance* department, within the same company. Geographical departmentalization is typified by the delegation of responsibility for insurance distribution in different territories to directors of agencies or field vice presidents.

Board of Directors

A stock company is owned and final authority held by its shareholders; in a mutual company the owners and primary source of control are the policyowners. The owners delegate their authority to a board of directors, which has the responsibility for both long-range planning and the periodic, short-term evaluation of results.

The board of directors is often composed of people in banking, commerce, and industry who have been selected either for their prestige or for their specialized knowledge. The authority of the board of directors and the numerous designations and duties of officers are spelled out in the company charter and bylaws. The board of directors usually meets monthly or quarterly; in the intervals between meetings, the board's affairs are handled by committees of the board and corporate officers.

Officers

The board of directors elects the chief executive officer of the company, who plans and directs all business activities. Usually, the chief executive officer of the company proposes policy, which the board either accepts, modifies, or rejects. He also appoints, with board approval, such other officers and department heads as are necessary to carry on the business of the company; and these, in turn, delegate a portion of their authority to unit managers, who are responsible for the daily operating results of a relatively small group of people performing similar or related functions.

Large companies frequently have a board chairman who is the chief executive officer and a president who is the chief administrative (or operations) officer. However, in smaller companies, frequently there is no board chairman, and the two offices are often combined, carrying the title either of chairman or president. In addition, there usually are several vice presidents, and other principal department heads such as actuary, controller, secretary, and treasurer. The particular duties or activities of top-ranking officers in different companies and departments depend upon company size, types of insurance offered for sale, methods of distribution, the pattern of organization that has been established, and the qualifications of the officers themselves. For example, the drafting of an insurance policy may be the responsibility of the actuarial or the legal department. Policyowner service may be handled by the agency department, by the actuary, or by a separate policyowner service department.

Committees

Considerable work in companies is done by committees which are found at board level and also at interdepartmental and intradepartmental levels.

The committees appointed by the board meet more frequently than the board and not only report to the board but also are on occasion empowered to act when the board is not in session. The most frequently appointed committees are an executive committee, which is the principal policymaking committee of the board; a finance committee, which concerns itself with investment policy and authorizes specific investment commitments; an auditing committee, which audits the accounts of the company periodically, normally through a professional auditing firm; and a nominating committee, which is concerned with the recommendation of replacements on the board of directors. In many instances the executive committee has the responsibility for making recommendations to the board on all financial and administrative matters, as well as those relating to the insurance business. Other board committees are sometimes appointed, such as an agency committee, a public relations committee, and others to deal with mortgages, real estate, and claims.

Interdepartmental committees often are useful in coordinating the efforts of interested departments toward the attainment of company objectives. The committee members normally report their findings to the officer responsible for their appointment, who then decides upon a course of action. Standing interdepartmental committees with representation from all interested departments may include an insurance committee, which advises on rates, products, benefits, and related items; an administrative committee, which considers questions of operating policy; a public relations or advertising committee; an agency committee, dealing with field problems; and a manpower and employee benefits committee to handle employee relations and other related matters.

Intradepartmental committees, as their name implies, are appointed by department heads for the purpose of coordinating the activities of departmental divisions or units for greater effectiveness. Excessive use of committees may limit the effectiveness of an organization and, therefore, the exact number of committees and their functions will vary according to the needs of each company and the desires of its directors and officers.

ORGANIZATION STRUCTURE

Organization Chart

It is a relatively simple matter to prepare an organization chart. Just as a balance sheet presents a photograph of corporate finances at a particular moment, so an organization chart presents a structural picture of a company at a given time. Similarly, an organization chart, as with a balance sheet, is only a partial representation of how functions and people are expected to interact. An organization chart shows only the primary and formal relationships of divisions and departments one to another. In any organization there exists a myriad of informal and often complex structures. These may be either ongoing or ad hoc. Informal organization is often as important as formal organization for effective operations. The organization chart must be constantly kept up to date as changes occur in personnel and duties, and as the organization's objectives grow and develop.

The organization chart presented in Figure 63-1 illustrates the typical organization pattern of a medium-sized company writing individual and group life and health insurance.

The number of departments and their functions vary from company to company, depending upon the company's needs. However, the major departments of an insurance company can be grouped in terms of line and staff relationships based upon the functions they perform and usually include actuarial, underwriting, agency, claims, legal, investment and finance, controlling and auditing, administration, systems, advertising and public relations.

Lines of Business

The typical company writing individual and group life and health insurance and annuities may be organized with all insurance operations departmentalized to follow product lines. Two separate major departments, group and individual, frequently are established under the direction of executive officers who are responsible for desired results and have direct control over the sales, actuarial, underwriting, claims and administration functions supportive to their respective lines of business.

Group Department

Group insurance is a highly competitive and rapidly changing business which may include such products as group life, group annuities, group

FIGURE 63–1. Organization Chart of a Medium-Sized Life and Health Insurance Company

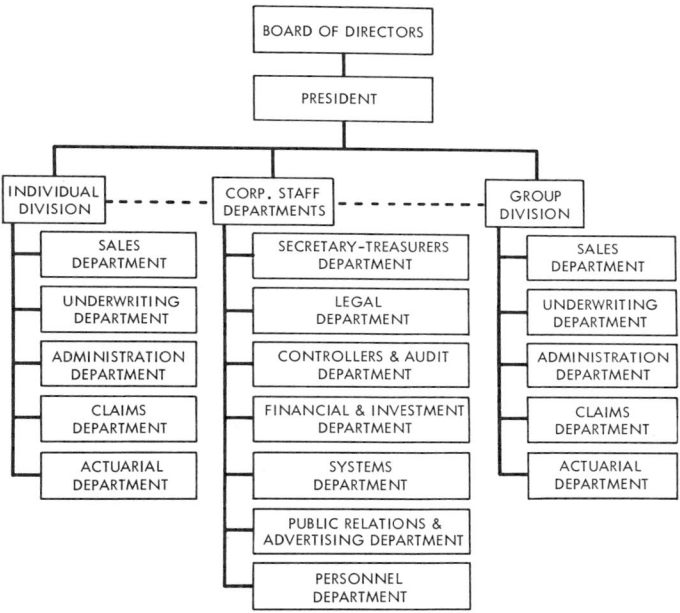

pensions, accidental death and disability, association groups, credit life and health, hospital-medical and long-term disability. A substantial investment of money, and a capable group executive with a properly balanced perspective on sales and underwriting problems, are requirements for companies which expect to compete successfully for group business. The group department must be alert to change, ready to seize aggressively ever-changing opportunities and able to search continually for new ways of selling group insurance. The principal source of business is the broker and agent who concentrate primarily in the selling of employee benefits programs.

Individual Department

Individual life business does not have the volatility of group lines. Profitability of individual life business is long range and is significantly influenced by first-year acquisition expenses and administrative costs. Consequently, great emphasis must be placed upon production at an appropriate rate of acquisition expense. That, in turn, demonstrates the need for a strong executive officer familiar with all factors which wield influence upon the profitability of individual life insurance.

One approach to the sale of individual health insurance is to regard it simply as another form of life insurance product; another approach is to establish a completely separate health insurance department. Often this is determined by the degree of emphasis the company wishes to place upon health insurance, in-house expertise, size of company, and the character of the investment it wishes to make in this line of business. Mass marketing of individual life and health products is rapidly developing as a significant distribution method.

Direct Supporting Operations

In companies where the concept of *profit centers* is pursued, each major department should be permitted and encouraged to exercise direct control over those functions which impact on profit. Therefore, the group department would be responsible for product development, underwriting, claims and administration relative to the business sold by the group sales force; and the individual department would be responsible for products, underwriting claims, and the administration relative to the business sold by the individual life sales force.

Sales Departments

The development of two separate field forces—group sales and individual sales—is natural and is characteristic of most major life insurance companies that write substantial amounts of both individual and group insurance. Most agents or agencies specialize either in the mass-marketed employee benefit field or in personal insurance, and the sales techniques required to secure the agent's business differ between the two specialties. There also are important differences in methods of compensation, field expense margins, and type of people required.

The individual sales department is responsible for the sale of new business, conservation of old business, and field service to policyowners. Its line functions include the recruitment and supervision of the company's agents and all other field personnel. Staff functions include planning the number and location of field offices, the preparation of cost and expense control information, the development of sales training and sales promotion programs, and the maintenance of detailed production records that are used to determine field management compensation.

The sales vice president maintains close cooperation between the line and staff officers of their respective departments. They must at the same time make certain that the view of the sales departments are considered by other company vice presidents in arriving at decisions which may affect the sales force and the products the company offers for sale, its underwriting policy, and service to policyowners. This is accomplished by individual conferences and also by membership of the sales vice presidents or their representatives on important interdepartmental standing committees.

The responsibility for production activities is usually divided by territory among a number of directors of agencies, who spend most of their time in the field directing the activities of managers or general agents under the overall supervision of the sales vice presidents.

At the head of each field office is an "agency manager" or "general agent," responsible for the selection and direction of agents and the supervision of all other agency employees. The manager is a company employee; whereas the general agent, as the name implies, is an independent contractor with a franchise to appoint field underwriters and promote company business in an assigned territory. In the case of smaller or newer companies with limited resources for financing sales development, the less costly general agency system frequently is used at the outset and is oftentimes continued indefinitely.

Managers or general agents are assisted in their work by assistant managers or supervisors, who may be specialists in recruiting, training, supervision, or some other phase of sales operation.

The office cashier is usually responsible for field office records, the direction of clerical work, service to policyowners, and the handling of all monies which clear through the field office. In many managerial companies the cashier is not directly responsible to the manager but, rather, reports to an officer in charge of sales administration in the home office, thus freeing the manager's time for sales activities. In the latter case, field clerical and administrative functions may be centralized on a regional basis when the company's size is such that regional centers are economically feasible.

Insurance is offered to the public by three types of agents: the "ordinary" company agent, the "combination" company agent, and the independent agent or broker. The ordinary company agent sells life and health insurance and group insurance, if they are offered by the company he represents. However, many ordinary company agents specialize in a particular market or in a particular income or business group. They may be general practitioners, or specialists in mass marketing, pensions, business insurance, or estate planning. The ordinary company agent usually collects only the first premium, renewal premiums being remitted directly to the company or through the cashier's office. The combination company agent, while selling most of the same products as his counterpart, receives a part of his compensation for conservation work and for collecting premiums from those of his policyowners who pay on a weekly or monthly basis. The independent agent or broker typically places his business with several companies and represents the client in dealing with the company; he frequently sells property, individual health, and group insurance in addition to individual life coverages.

Actuarial Departments

The actuarial departments see to it that the company's insurance operations are conducted on a sound basis. Periodic duties include policy design, calculation of premium rates and reserves, determination of dividend scales, drafting of new policies, securing policy approval from state insurance departments, mortality and lapse studies, and aiding in the establishment of commission scales and compensation plans for field management personnel. Routine duties embrace the maintenance of complete records of insurance in force and terminations, including lapses, surrenders, maturities, and changes; the calculation of dividends and loan values; and the like. The actuarial departments also prepare the gain and loss exhibit and, with other departments, are responsible for the correctness of the annual financial statements required by state insurance departments.

Underwriting Departments

The individual underwriting department selects and classifies individual risks. The lay underwriter reviews the application, the agent's statement, the physical examination, and the inspection report in order to determine the applicant's insurability. He is aided by the medical director (or, in large companies, the medical department), who establishes medical standards of insurability and appoints local examiners from among the practicing physicians in each locality. The medical director also reviews the medical reports of local examiners and helps the lay underwriters to decide whether the applicant is acceptable from the standpoint of health and physical condition. The final underwriting decision weighs the various factors affecting insurability—age, occupation, environment, finances, insurable interest, medical history, and physical findings.

Depending upon the size of the company and the size of their group insurance book of business, the group underwriting department may be organized by product line in order to recognize the variations in underwriting techniques required to compete in this volatile, highly competitive, and rapidly changing business.

Group business is underwritten on the basis of characteristics of the overall case as opposed to underwriting individual lives. In addition, the underwriting experience of group business usually can be evaluated on a case basis each year providing an opportunity for changes in coverage and rate adjustments where required. This is contrasted with the underwriting of individual policies which generally provides only a single opportunity for determining the applicant's insurability.

Administration Departments

Likewise, the approach to administration of group insurance is different from that of individual insurance. Administration of individual insurance, because it must be geared to the individual policyowner, results in considerably higher expense per thousand dollars of premium than group insurance administration. Premium rates for individual and group insurance take this into consideration and, accordingly, group administration is structured to handle large sums of premiums through corporate employers or associations at a relatively low expense. Because of these differences, two separate administrative departments may be developed.

Each administrative department provides facilities for handling the functions relative to policy issue, premium billing and collection, field compensation and commission accounting, and policyowner service, including policy changes, settlement options, reinstatements, conversions, transfers, and other similar transactions. Depending upon the size of the company, some administrative functions, such as policy issue and policy service, may be handled by the underwriting or actuarial departments.

Claims Departments

Claims handling in companies selling only individual life insurance is a relatively simple matter. It is usually not difficult to determine whether a policy has matured as a death claim or as an endowment, has lapsed, or has been surrendered if proper records have been maintained. Because of the intricacies of coverage provided by individual health policies, claims functions are usually handled from the home office. However, in the group insurance field the establishment of a separate group claims department with a regional claims organization throughout the territory in which the company operates frequently is desirable. Field claims offices are responsible for securing claims information, seeing that the necessary forms are obtained and forwarded to the home office for approval, and making certain that settlement release procedures are taken care of once claims have been approved. The home office claims department works closely with the contracts and law departments in the designing of policy contract language.

Staff Operations

Any function of a corporate nature, and certain staff functions not directly related to the profitability of either the group or individual departments, can be provided more economically at the corporate level rather than by being duplicated. These operations usually report directly to the president and include those departments which follow.

Legal Department. The legal department of a company has the responsibility of making certain that the company's insurance operations comply with federal and state laws and insurance departments' regulations. Usually, it assists in the preparation of policies and other forms, and aids in the determination of the company's contractual liabilities, as well as handling any litigation which may result. The legal department cooperates with the accounting and auditing departments in determining company liability for taxes. It also handles the legal phases of investing policyowners' funds, including the preparation of loan agreements and title work for mortgage loan and real estate investments.

Investment and Finance Department. The duties of the investment and finance department include both studying available offerings and carrying out the recommendations of the finance committee of the board of directors. Normally, annual cash income exceeds the amount of death and health claims and all other classes of payment, and these funds must be invested. In addition, there is a considerable reinvestment of funds due to turnover of existing investments, including bond maturities, repayments of mortgage loans, and sales of securities held.

Accounting and Auditing Departments. The accounting and auditing departments, under the direction of the controller, are responsible for establishing and supervising the company's accounting procedures. Accounting in an insurance company is frequently more complicated than in many other types of business because of the long-range nature of the product, the large variety of transactions, and the huge number of individual items which must be recorded.

Public Relations and Advertising Departments. The public relations and advertising departments are concerned not only with the advertising of company products but in seeing to it that good communications are maintained between the company and the various sectors of the public which it serves.

One of the most serious problems facing American business today is in the area of communications. Often the business is conducted on a far-flung, nationwide basis involving hundreds and even thousands of people many miles distant from one another. In addition, the company may be dealing with millions of policyowners and beneficiaries, and with contracts which will not mature for many years in the future. Every action and every statement of significance may have some effect upon the general public, the company's policyowners, its employees, its agents, its stockholders, and the insurance business. The skill and effectiveness with which all the various communication channels are used play an important role in determining the company's success.

Systems Department. The increasing usage of computers and other data processing equipment has resulted in the formation of a systems department in many companies. This department provides manual and computer systems design, definition, development, implementation, and maintenance services, and computer operations in support of these services for user departments within the company. Life insurance is essentially a service business engaged in processing a large volume of documents. Effective utilization of EDP equipment potentially is a great contributor to cost control and to increasing operating efficiency.

Other Departments. Large life insurance companies usually have a number of other departments. The personnel department, for example, plays a significant role in large life insurance companies employing thousands of people. It usually handles such matters as implementation of the company's personnel policy, procurement and termination of employees, the training of office employees, wage and salary administration, job evaluation, insurance and pension benefits, and so on.

Since large life insurance companies have substantial home office buildings and operate nationally, a real estate department also plays a significant role, including building maintenance, layout and remodeling, the negotiation of leases, the care of furniture and equipment, and related matters.

Also important in such companies are the secretary's and the treasurer's departments (often these are combined into one department). In connection with meetings of the board, the executive committee, or the stockholders, the secretary's department sends notices, prepares agenda, and keeps the minutes. With regard to stockholders' meetings, it also sends and tabulates the proxies, and arranges for judges of election and related matters. The treasurer's department frequently is responsible for such duties as negotiating and maintaining banking facilities and relationships, the collection and disbursement of funds, and the custodianship of securities and other valuable property. Purchasing is sometimes a division of the treasurer's department; in the very largest companies, it occupies departmental status.

Most insurance companies of any size also have a planning, or methods and procedures, department. This unit is responsible for studying the operations of other departments with a view to work simplification and economies of operation. It may report to the president, the controller, or to an administrative vice president if the company has one.

Additional facilities which are common to most large companies, regardless of the nature of their business, include addressograph, cafeteria or service dining rooms, expense control, mail, payroll, statistical, supply, tax, telegraph and teletype, transcribing, and transportation.

Other Financial Services

Through a subsidiary broker/dealer organization, many life insurers have broadened their activities to include the sale of equity products, either in conjunction with the life contract, as in the case of variable annuities, or separately, in the form of mutual funds. Companies may manage their own funds, sell funds managed by others, or some combination. The form of organization and the type of management vary widely among companies. In order for their agents to be able to offer customers a full line of insurance and financial services and as a means of adding to agents' earnings, some life companies have also formed a property and casualty subsidiary to write automobile, homeowners, and personal catastrophe policies.

SELECTED REFERENCES

Glover, John Desmond, Hower, Ralph M., and Tagiuri, Renato. *The Administrator.* 5th ed. Homewood, Ill.: Richard D. Irwin, Inc., 1973.

Huebner, S. S., and Black, Kenneth, Jr. *Life Insurance.* 8th ed. New York: Appleton-Century-Crofts, Inc., 1972.

Life Office Management Association. *Top Management Organization in Fifty Life Insurance Companies.* New York, 1960.

Mehr, Robert I. *Life Insurance: Theory and Practice.* 4th ed. Austin, Texas: Business Publications, Inc., 1970.

Neuschel, Richard F. "An Outsider Looks at the Major Management Problems of the Life Insurance Industry," *Proceedings of the Fifty-Seventh Annual Meeting,* American Life Convention, 1962, pp. 196–217.

64

Individual
Insurance Marketing

By BURKETT W. HUEY

ALTHOUGH life insurance had existed in the United States for nearly 100 years, it was not until the 1840s that it became a significant member of the American business community. Before the end of that decade, the industry experienced several profound changes including the founding of the first mutual companies, substantial reduction in ordinary life insurance rates, aggressive advertising campaigns in local newspapers, and, most significant of all, the appointment of the first full-time life insurance agent. The hiring of a representative to devote his entire business time and energy to selling individual life insurance recognized that life insurance is not bought. It must be sold and usually on a one-to-one basis. No matter how attractively a policy may be constructed and packaged, the consumer generally will not seek out the insurance company. This discovery has been the single most dominant factor in the successful marketing of individual life insurance in North America.

It is a matter of historical record that the agency distribution system is primarily responsible for the healthy growth of individual life insurance in the United States and Canada.[1] It remains to this day, far and away, the principal distribution system of the business. Attempts to replace this system with other methods of distribution have been largely unsuccessful because the other systems have failed to reach a significant segment of the total population.

---

[1] Terminology in insurance marketing is not always clear. The term "agency system" should be reasonably clear in its meaning as this chapter is read. The word "agent" has both a legal and a general connotation. "Life underwriter" or "health underwriter" are widely used terms and are most often, but not always, synonymous with "agent." For example, the trade association for most life agents is the National Association of Life Underwriters. The highly regarded professional designation in life and health insurance is "Chartered Life Underwriter" and about 75 percent of CLUs are involved in marketing, either individual or group life and health insurance. Agent and life underwriter will be used interchangeably in this chapter.

On the other hand, the agency system has succeeded in this area. By 1972, 7 out of every 10 people in the United States—145 million in all—had a share in the $1.5 trillion of life insurance issued by the 1,805 legal reserve life companies in the United States, and almost all of it was the result of the work of agents in the field. The average ordinary policy had a face value of $6,450, and the average amount of coverage for each insured family was $25,700, slightly more than 24 months of the family's total disposable personal income. Americans purchased three fourths of their new life insurance protection in 1971—over $140 billion—on an individual basis, usually through a life insurance agent. More than three out of every five adults (over age 18) in the United States, 62 percent in all, owned individual life insurance as the decade of the seventies began, and most of this business was sold through the agency system.

Still, for all its success, there are current indicators that the agency system will not remain the sole method of marketing life and health insurance to individuals and to family units. Other distribution systems, such as mail order, direct placement, salaried service representatives, over-the-counter sales, and savings bank life insurance, are gaining a larger share of the market. At present, because the rate of gain by these combined systems remains relatively small, they appear to be no more than supplementary to the basic system involving an individual client serviced directly by an individual agent. While there will be some changes, it appears that the agency system will remain, into the foreseeable future, the most effective distribution method for the product of life insurance.

History of Growth

While a small amount of life insurance was sold to the general market, life insurance got its real momentum in 1873 when a weekly premium product was introduced for the working classes. This product significantly broadened the economic base of life insurance policyowners. The weekly premium product made life insurance a product for the many. Even the name—industrial life insurance—identifies the market. By adopting methods pioneered in Great Britain, America became a nation where life insurance was a "working" man's product and not an exclusive privilege of the wealthier classes. As the working class grew in numbers, in influence and in affluence, a new product—group insurance—was developed as an additional answer to the growing need for protection. This new product featured higher amounts of protection and low premiums which were paid in part or in full by the employer as a fringe benefit. Premiums were based on term insurance rates. Today, group insurance is an expected form of noncash compensation for most Americans employed in business and industry.

While these two special products—group and industrial—were being marketed to many North American families, the more traditional individual ordinary life policies were being improved continually to meet the needs of a growing number of middle and upper income families and businesses. Sophisticated coverages utilizing pensions and profit sharing plans, key man plans, buy-and-sell agreements, estate planning, and various tax deferral arrangements became a part of total planning programs that protected nearly every financial need of families and businesses. Not only were final expenses and survivor benefits covered, but education, retirement, disability, mortgage cancellation, and contingencies arising in a policyowner's business also were provided by imaginative, innovative individual policies and programs.

Despite the development of consumer-appealing products, consumer studies show that only a small fraction of the purchases of individual life insurance is initiated by the buyer. While life insurance policies have changed, human nature has not. Most people still must be persuaded and motivated by an agent to buy. It is the agent's job to sell his product by tailoring insurance programs to fit individual needs and wants.

As the economy expands and average income levels increase, the question is not when the agent will evolve from salesman to counselor, but how far this evolution will extend. Already, many life underwriters have become financial service counselors; some charge fees for service, while many others remain in the traditional role of agents receiving compensation from commissions, renewals, and service fees. There is room in the marketplace today for both approaches, and as the future unfolds, the balance is likely to tip increasingly to the agent as a financial counselor.

THE CAREER OF SELLING LIFE INSURANCE

In several Latin-American countries, life insurance salesmen are called "intermediarios" or, in English, "intermediaries." This term, perhaps better than any other, describes the career of selling life insurance—acting as an intermediary between client and company, serving both in good faith.

The life underwriter must convince people to protect themselves and their loved ones against financial disaster. They are compensated solely on their own prospecting-selling-service abilities. They sell an intangible —an idea, or, in the word most commonly used within the business, a "need." For those who can accept the challenge of selling an "intangible" product to meet a "need," the life insurance sales career offers an almost perfect blend of the six career criteria most men seek: income, satisfaction, prestige, education and training, security, and opportunity.

Income

Today's life underwriter's income is directly related to his effort and ability. He has the power to determine his own income. He can set it as high as his ability, desire, enthusiasm, and ambition demands. Continuing surveys among well-educated life underwriters who function on a full-time career basis indicate that their incomes compare quite favorably with doctors, dentists, lawyers, CPAs, and the like. The income for professional career financial planners comes from first-year commissions, from renewal commissions that continue for a limited number of years, from service fees while the insurance is in force, and, in some cases, from consulting fees. Typically, over a 7- to 10-year period, the total renewal and service commissions equal the first-year premium. This system of renewal commissions and service fees means that even should a salesman continue to sell the same amount of premium each year, and assuming a constant persistency of business rate, his income will increase automatically.

In any textbook discussion centered around the marketing of life and health insurance, the reader would expect to find figures of agent earnings. Unfortunately, such figures are not available on an industrywide basis because many factors cause accurate information to be fragmented at best. For example, many life insurance agents receive income for selling and servicing products other than life insurance—products such as mutual funds, fire and casualty insurance, automobile insurance, and variable annuities. We know, also, that many companies have had difficulty in clearly distinguishing between true full-time life agents and those who have full-time contracts but spend only a part of their working time selling and servicing life insurance. Furthermore, a significant number of agents have full-time contracts with and receive income from several companies. It also is commonly known that many life insurance agents earn compensation from nonsales, but life insurance-related, activities such as training, supervision, and recruiting other agents. Many agents receive fees for consultation services and still others, many others, receive income for collecting premiums from policyowners.

Because of these many factors, it has not been possible to complete a valid, comprehensive national compensation study of agent earnings from life insurance sales. Still, individual companies and associations have attempted to conduct their own compensation studies. In late 1972 a most interesting survey, crossing company lines, was reported. Respondents were asked to indicate their total gross personal income in 1971 from all sources. The study, involving 5,333 of the nearly 11,000 members of the life insurance business's top sales organization—the Million Dollar Round Table—revealed the following:

Income	Percentage
Less than $10,000	0.3
$10,000– $20,000	7.9
$20,000– $30,000	21.8
$30,000– $40,000	20.1
$40,000– $50,000	17.1
$50,000– $75,000	17.8
$75,000–$100,000	7.6
$100,000–$150,000	4.6
$150,000–$250,000	1.6
Over $250,000	0.6

A 1972 survey of 1,535 members of the 100,000-member National Association of Life Underwriters and involving agents with a median of five years' field experience, revealed the following:

Income	Percentage
Less than $10,000	11.6
$10,000–$19,999	40.6
$20,000–$29,999	22.1
$30,000–$39,999	11.0
Over $40,000	14.7

The evidence indicates that while the starting income for a new agent typically is lower than the starting income for salesmen in other industries, for experienced agents the income is on a par and even slightly higher than that of experienced salesmen in other industries. The logical conclusion from the compensation evidence to date is that once established, there are better-than-average income opportunities for the life insurance agent.

Satisfaction and Prestige

In addition to monetary rewards, the agent as a financial planner has the opportunity to gain personal satisfaction from the social and economic contribution of his work. In his work, he has the satisfaction of knowing that he is contributing to the public welfare. He derives satisfaction from seeing life insurance—his product—at work, enabling a family to live comfortably, saving homes, educating children, providing business opportunities, meeting emergencies, and helping to create comfort and ease in retirement. In its more advanced phases, he sees his work making major contributions in the areas of estate planning, pension and retirement planning, business insurance planning, deferred compensation, and the like.

Education and Training

The life and health insurance business is education-oriented. While the training procedures differ from company to company, all life insurance salesmen are exposed to various sales techniques. The agent is taught how to present an idea to a prospective customer effectively and how to get the client to sign an application and pay the premium. During this initial training period, the agent receives direct assistance from a trainer or supervisor. Often the trainer will accompany an agent on sales calls where he will demonstrate various sales approaches and presentations. Later, the trainer will step aside and observe the new agent in action, until, finally, when the trainer feels that he has developed a trained salesman, the agent will be expected to make his sales calls on his own.

Career education and growing competence are ongoing concerns for the professional life insurance salesman. There are many company and industry educational opportunities available to the career agent. The Life Underwriter Training Council (LUTC) offers practical sales courses and many thousands of the more successful salesmen are graduates of this program.

Available also is a postgraduate-level program of advanced professional study leading to the diploma and designation of Chartered Life Underwriter (CLU) awarded by the American College of Life Underwriters at Bryn Mawr, Pennsylvania. If an agent is willing to study long and hard, the life insurance business offers attractive opportunities to learn. Experience is a great teacher, but a planned program of training, active supervision and higher education is a great teacher also; both avenues of learning are available to the career agent.

Security and Opportunity

As for security and opportunity, the life underwriter finds no style changes, seasonal slumps, income ceilings, seniority restrictions, territory cuts or shortage of materials to make his business life hazardous. There is no question of forced retirement or unemployment for life insurance salesmen. There are no market shortages. It is estimated that 1 out of every 13 persons—excluding those under age 15, those over age 65, and married women—will buy life insurance each year. There is always a market for the individual with the ability and the capacity to tell and to sell the life insurance story.

The agent has a potentially long earning span, with opportunity in many areas. His potential can be virtually unlimited in sales, and management also offers him a wide range for personal and professional growth.

Likes and Dislikes

Not everyone can be successful in marketing individual life and health insurance. It takes a quality that no one has been able to identify accurately. Successful life underwriters resemble each other only in their belief in life insurance and their missionary zeal in distributing it.

Among the disadvantages to a career in life insurance sales and service are late and long hours, and often relatively low compensation in the early years. There is the necessity of keeping precise records, a level of detail work that most salesmen seem to dislike. And there are the rebuffs that are everyday experiences for the life insurance salesman.

Approximately 1,000 experienced life insurance salesmen recently filled out a questionnaire telling how they felt about their job. Their replies are the best summary possible of the good and bad aspects of the career. Among the things they liked were "being my own boss, . . . the opportunity to meet new people, . . . being free to work with whom I choose, . . . the small capital outlay necessary to start in the business, . . . the service I do for society, . . . (and) the amount of recognition given for genuine achievement."

Among the aspects most disliked were "the amount of detail work required, . . . the ignorance of the public concerning life insurance, . . . the uncertainty while getting established, . . . (and) the amount of night work."

The Sales Process

As noted in other chapters, life insurance companies differ in many ways. These differences cut across all the activities and organization of companies, even to the segment of the marketplace they seek to serve. Some companies sell in all economic segments and sections of the nation and throughout the world. Others try to limit their market to certain income groups or their geographic coverage to particular states or provinces. The marketing direction of a company influences every activity within the organization—recruiting, training, product development, and the distribution system.

Virtually all companies working through the agency distribution system have similarities, particularly with respect to the basic steps through which the agent moves in his dealings with a client. A committee of the industrywide Life Insurance Agency Management Association has identified these steps as a "cycle" containing the following "spokes":

Preapproach. Specifically, how to obtain an interview with a prospect.

Approach. This covers the first three minutes of an interview. It is here that an agent creates interest and motivation.

Fixing the Problem. The time in which the agent, through various fact-finding methods, pinpoints the client's needs.

Designing the Solution. This takes place during the interview or at the agent's base of operations. Often it includes complex and sophisticated use of specialized insurance and financial knowledge and legal and accounting assistance.

Presenting the Solution. A spoken or graphic presentation by the agent to supply the answer to the client's needs.

Close. Motivating the client to act by answering objections, overcoming inertia, and offering a logical "wrap-up."

Follow Through. Arranging for a medical examination, initiating policy issue, and collecting the first premium.

Policy Delivery. The time in which the agent explains the policy, again outlines what the client must know to get the maximum benefits from his policy, and prepares the groundwork for future sales and service.

Commitment to Service. A pledge by the agent that he will stand ready to advise in the best interests of the client and the client's beneficiaries.

While agents may sell in widely varying markets, sell a broad range of products, and approach selling with varying philosophies, the sales process generally follows the "cycle" outlined here.

MARKETING METHODS

Life insurance and health insurance companies typically maintain an agency or marketing department, almost always headed by a senior management official. This unit performs many or all of the traditional marketing functions—research, product design, planning, advertising and sales promotion, administration, distribution, and the recruiting, training, and development of sales and sales management personnel. All these functions are aimed toward the primary objective of developing efficient sales and service of the company's life and health insurance products. This objective is accomplished through one or more of three basic marketing methods: career distributors, independent distributors, and special systems. Each method has its own distinctions and characteristics.

Career Distributors

Approximately 49 percent of the individual life insurance written in North America under the agency system currently is written through either the career agency or personal-producing general agency system.

About 33 percent is written through the combination or debit system, 10 percent by the independent brokerage system, and another 8 percent through exclusive multiple-line agents and through fraternal organization agents, both of which operate with methods similar to those of career agencies.

Career Agencies. Many of the major companies have established agencies or branches whose primary objective is the hiring and training of agents to sell life and health insurance. These agencies can be organized on a managerial basis where the manager is an employee of the company, retains no incidence of ownership in the agency, and has the normal employee benefit program including a retirement program. In the general agency system, the general agent has a vested right in the business that is written for the company in his agency during his tenure. The general agent retains a greater degree of proprietorship than does his managerial counterpart, but aside from this, there is relatively little difference between the two systems. Each recruits, selects, trains, and supervises individual agents. Each hires second-line management when necessary. In effect, each builds career agents and supervisors. The career general agent and/or manager is typically organized and trained to tap the middle and upper income markets.

Personal-Producing General Agents (*PPGA*). A large number of companies in life and health insurance emphasize distribution through the personal-producing general agent. For the most part, these companies are small to medium in size. The personal-producing general agent is primarily a salesman and typically he does not develop career agents. For many successful salesmen, this system has considerable appeal because the PPGA contract gives the individual a higher sales commission without the responsibility of recruiting, training, and supervising career agents. The PPGA may, however, build a sales organization, depending on his company's strategy. The relationship between the personal-producing general agent and the company can vary greatly from one company to another. He may be an independent contractor or a full-time representative. In addition to controlling his own sales activities, he also provides for his own office facilities, which is why he receives the override which normally is paid to the general agent in career general agency companies.

Combination or Debit Agencies. About one third of the individual life insurance written in the United States is written through the combination or debit system. Approximately 100 companies utilize this method. Some of the largest companies in the life insurance business were built on the combination or debit system.

"Combination" refers to the fact that agents sell both industrial and ordinary policies, and "debit" means that an amount of premium is "debited" to each agent. The agent is given an assigned territory and he is expected to collect the premiums of all the company's policyowners in that territory—the amount "debited" to him. In the earlier days of this system, most premiums were on a weekly basis. Today, most of the premiums are collected on a monthly basis and even semiannually or annually. The debit agent is expected to sell additional protection to policyowners in his assigned area and to develop new prospects inside and outside his assigned area. In most companies, the combination agent also sells ordinary policies inside and outside his assigned area. Traditionally, the combination agent's income is determined partially from a service fee for collections and partially from new sales commissions.

Almost all combination companies establish district offices in a given area, each office controlling a number of assigned territories or debits. A district manager is in charge of the area and typically is assisted by one or more staff, unit, or assistant managers. An employee-employer relationship exists between the company and the manager, and the company and the agent.

Exclusive Agent Multiple-Line.   About 5 percent of the individually owned life insurance in the United States is written by exclusive agent multiple-line companies. Multiple-line companies sell various lines of insurance protection, including automobile, fire, casualty, life, disability income, and health. As with ordinary life insurance companies, they develop experienced career agents to sell their products. Typically, the agent is hired and assigned a group of existing automobile policies. He services these policies and sells additional insurance and financial products —homeowner's, fire, personal property, variable annuities, and mutual funds—to policyowners. This system emphasizes the concept of "one-stop shopping"—the placing of all protection under one company.

While the "one-stop" concept has not developed to the extent many observers predicted, it is a fact that several companies featuring this marketing approach are among the fastest growing in the life insurance business in the early 1970s.

Fraternal Distributors.   Approximately 3.2 percent of the individually owned life insurance in the United States is written through fraternal associations. These companies operate in a manner similar to the ordinary career agencies but restrict their market to a particular population, often religious in nature.

Fraternal life insurance began in the United States in the latter half of the 19th century. By 1895, fraternal companies had about the same insurance in force as did all other life companies. In this century, non-fraternal companies have far outdistanced fraternals in insurance in force. However, in recent years, there has been a tendency for fraternals to compete aggressively with other types of companies in a wide range of markets.

Independent Distributors

Brokerage Distributors.   About 10 percent of the individually owned life insurance business in North America is written through brokerage operations. In the brokerage system, the company typically has a home office and field staff whose responsibility is to solicit life insurance from full-time property-casualty agents and others. Property-casualty agents provide the major source of brokerage business, but a meaningful portion also comes from career life insurance agents, frequently as "surplus business" or business which the agent could not place with his primary company. The motivation for career life underwriters to place brokerage business with companies other than a primary carrier is to take advantage of a product, commission, or underwriting specialty that a particular brokerage company has to offer. Also, there are life insurance general agents who represent a number of life companies, some of which are brokerage, and who place business on a regular basis with all these companies. They have no primary allegiance to any one company. Such general agents are best described as career life insurance brokers or independent agents.

Equity Sales Organizations. Still another source of individual life insurance sales through independent distributors is business generated by equity sales organizations and equity-related organizations. There are many mutual fund organizations that also sell life insurance. These organizations recruit, train, and supervise men primarily to sell mutual funds. Life insurance is a secondary line, but has been growing in importance in recent years.

Securities Dealers. In 1971, securities dealers were authorized to write individual life insurance. These firms are being tapped by brokerage companies as new sources of business.

Each of the last two systems—mutual fund organizations and securities dealers—writes a fractional amount of the total life insurance business written.

Special Systems

Individually owned life insurance is marketed through distribution systems other than career and independent agents. In most cases, these special systems do not involve an agent in the traditional sense.

Savings Bank Life Insurance. Savings bank life insurance as a means of distributing life insurance products started in Massachusetts at the beginning of the century. It is now written in three states—Massachusetts, New York, and Connecticut—and is the principal means through which savings banks are involved in life insurance marketing. Approximately one half of one percent of all the life insurance in the United States was written by these savings banks in the early 1970s.

The savings bank system, through an insurance company formed by member banks, is the insurer, competing directly with life insurance companies. Savings bank life insurance is written on both individual lives and groups, and is sold over-the-counter in savings banks that choose to participate. Sales come primarily through customer contacts at the banks and through communications media advertising.

By not paying a sales commission and appealing to a large market, it was hoped that insurance could be made available to low-income families at reduced rates through the savings bank distribution system. However, it appears that middle-income groups rather than lower income groups are the primary buyers of savings bank life insurance.

At the time savings bank life insurance was first proposed, other similar ideas were suggested also, including the notion that state governments act as insurers. Today Wisconsin is the only state that maintains such a program in life insurance, while four state funds are operated for health insurance and 18 function under workmen's compensation insurance laws.

The Wisconsin State Life Fund. The Wisconsin State Life Fund operates in essentially the same manner as savings banks and was established for the same purpose—to make life insurance more readily available to low-income families. Available only to state residents, it represents less than one percent of the life insurance in force in that state.

Savings and Loan Associations. Savings and loan associations generate sales of life insurance through various methods, most of which are still in the developmental stage. An example of this type of distribution is the mortgage cancellation package. Typically, this form of coverage is provided by an established life insurance company on a reducing term basis with the premium added to the monthly mortgage payment to the savings and loan association.

Credit Life Insurance. Credit life insurance is made available to consumers through many businesses. It covers the outstanding balance payable on installment purchases. It is sometimes marketed by traditional life companies, though in some instances a life insurance company is formed by a financial organization to handle credit life coverage. The great bulk of credit life is written on a group basis.

Mass Merchandising. The mass merchandising distribution method is sometimes referred to as mass advertising, and is perhaps the most controversial method of selling, although it represents only a small fraction of the total individually owned life insurance in force.

In mass advertising, a company appeals to a large number of consumers through massive direct mail or print media advertising campaigns utilizing newspapers, magazines, and "throw-aways." Amounts of coverage offered usually are small and often the markets and/or products are specific, some examples being travel policies, additions ("piggyback" policies) to existing health and disability plans such as Medicare, small amounts of life coverage for senior citizens, executive policies, accident and travel policies, and the like. Little underwriting is involved in these plans, and applicants often are required only to complete a short-form application and nonmedical questionnaire. Some companies writing these plans follow up with their insureds by providing their names to their agents, who are trained to present a more extensive insurance program tailored to meet particular needs. There are several small- to medium-sized companies that rely heavily on mail-order business and operate quite profitably in this area.

Salaried Sales Personnel. In selling large groups such as business concerns, associations, and social organizations, many companies may use a direct placement approach in which the sales presentation is made by a team of salaried home office employees in lieu of the traditional commissioned agent. This type of mass marketing is directed chiefly at organizations with large payrolls.

Employer-Employee Life and Health Insurance Plans. Employer-employee life and health insurance plans represent yet another form of mass marketing. Generally sponsored by the employer, the plan is paid through salary deductions. There are many types of coverage involved that can be sold by full-time agents or brokers or by a salaried sales organization from the home office. An agent, commissioned or salaried, can suggest that an employer arrange for his employees to receive individual insurance counseling through a company-sponsored program. The agent then arranges individual interviews and the insurance purchased is paid through salary deductions.

Pensions and profit sharing plans provide another area for individual marketing in the employee benefit field. In many companies, individual pension policies may be provided where an individual contract is issued to each member of the plan. Agents are involved in a substantial proportion of individual pension and profit sharing plans. In group plans, a master contract is provided and each individual covered receives a certificate describing the benefits.

Purchases of the individual contract pension or profit sharing plan also can be made by self-employed individuals under special tax provisions.

It is important to note that in the overall marketing strategy of a life insurance company, pension and profit sharing programs usually remain in the mainstream of the individual insurance marketing (agency) department operations. Generally, sales at this level call for greater sophistication on the part of the life underwriter and those who assist him with legal and technical assistance.

HEALTH INSURANCE

Unlike individual life insurance, health insurance is made available not only by private companies, but also by Blue Cross and Blue Shield associations, by independently funded plans, and by government organizations. Many public plans are compulsory and there is little competition from private carriers in these areas. Individual health insurance is marketed mainly by private insurance companies and to some extent by Blue Cross and Blue Shield associations. These latter organizations might be compared to exclusive general agency companies except that their representatives are salaried (rather than commissioned), are limited to a specific geographical area, and place little emphasis on individual prospecting and solicitation.

By far the largest proportion of health insurance provided by insurance companies is written by life companies. Both individual and group health insurance is marketed in a manner similar to individual and group life insurance. Casualty companies rely heavily on the independent agent and broker for individual and group health business.

SELECTED REFERENCES

Institute of Life Insurance. *Life Insurance Fact Book, 1972.* New York.

Life Insurance Agency Management Association. *Agent Development Library.* Hartford, Conn., 1969.

————. *The Life Insurance Career.* Hartford, Conn., 1969.

————. *Managing an Agency.* Hartford, Conn., 1969.

————. *This Man Could Be You.* Hartford, Conn., 1971.

Stalson, J. Owen. *Marketing Life Insurance: Its History in America.* (McCahan Foundation Series.) Homewood, Ill.: Richard D. Irwin, Inc., 1969.

65

Legal and Professional
Responsibilities of the
Life Underwriter

By FREDERICK R. H. WITHERBY and ROBERT J. FITZWILLIAM

IN A SINGLE crowded business day it is possible that a life underwriter[1] could do all of the following:

—Breakfast with a prospective client, take his application for an insurance policy, give him a conditional receipt for the first premium, and advance the premium payment out of his own pocket;
—Tell a client his company has rejected his application, but that the policy can be placed with another insurer;
—Sell shares in a mutual fund;
—Sell a variable annuity;
—Take a phone call from a life insurance client who is seeking fire insurance for his summer cottage;
—Attend the monthly luncheon of the local life underwriters association and vote to protest the sales method of a new charter policy company;
—Tell the office manager where to hang his newly framed C.L.U. diploma;
—Call a prospect about an H.R.-10 policy;
—Close the sale of an individual policy pension trust case;
—Phone a policyowner friend, remind him his renewal premium is overdue and agree to take care of it;
—Explain the workings of a long-term disability income policy to a client who had bought it but was doubtful about keeping it;
—Advise a client to surrender a policy with a "fly-by-night" outfit and take out new insurance in his own company;

---

[1] The terms "life underwriter" and "agent" are used interchangeably in this chapter. The general principles of agency law, of course, apply to the life insurance underwriter in his capacity as agent. *Association of Life Insurance Counsel Proceedings,* Vol. 14 (1959), p. 424, n. 5.

—Request from the home office an up-to-date statement of his own company benefits, including group insurance, retirement plan and its integration with social security;

—Call his accountant about his handling of unincorporated business tax;

—Spend a half hour with some younger men in the agency as part-time supervisor;

—Drive out to close a group insurance case and have a minor collision on the way.

That night he could go to sleep and literally never dream of all the far-reaching effects that might flow from his activities, or of the deeper questions that were raised in the course of his seemingly ordinary day. Probably the people he dealt with were equally unaware of anything unusual—his clients, his company, and a host of unascertained "third parties."

One Man, Many Parts

Who was the man who did all these things? He wore many hats, singly or in combination. For his social security and his fringe benefits, he was deemed to be an employee, and perhaps he was exempted as such from unincorporated business tax and workmen's compensation. While driving his car he was probably an independent contractor. He was an agent of his own company, and possibly of the company with which he "brokered" the surplus insurance. He probably was a broker for the fire insurance. As part-time supervisor he was an employee, but exempt from the federal wages and hours requirements as an "outside salesman," unless he worked too many hours. He was a professional counselor when he gave advice on the H.R.-10 retirement plan for the self-employed person, or acted as a pension expert. He was a registered representative in the sale of the mutual fund shares, and something else again in the sale of the variable annuity. He was a possible co-conspirator at his business lunch. As a Chartered Life Underwriter (C.L.U.) he held himself out as having greater skill and superior knowedge. He was, of course, a taxpayer. He was bonded. He was licensed by the state, or by several states, as an agent. He held a license as a broker, and was licensed as an insurance adviser and as a registered representative. He also more many more hats in his "private" life, apart from his business activities.

And our life underwriter was a human being, capable of making mistakes, capable of emotional reactions, and perhaps capable of yielding to temptations. It is the purpose of this chapter to examine many of the ways that things and people can go wrong in the world the life underwriter inhabits, and what bearing they have on his legal and professional responsibilities.

At the outset, it should be recognized that the vast majority of professional life underwriters, their companies, and their clients enjoy a beneficial relationship based upon competent service and mutual good faith. The exceptional circumstances that follow illustrate the significance of such competency and good faith in the purveyance of life insurance and other financial products and services.

COMPANY'S CONTRACT LIABILITY
FOR ACTS OF THE AGENT

Any standard law text will recite that within the scope of his authority, an agent has power to bind his principal. This is hardly surprising—the public thinks this is what he was chosen to do in the first place. A large insurance company cannot be everywhere at once; it retains the services of agents and employees to see that it is represented, and it acts through them. And because insurance is a business affected with the public interest, the government requires that its agents be licensed. Lest there be doubt as to whether he represents the company or the applicant, the law deems him to be the agent of the company.

This is not to say the state defines the authority of the agent; the company is left to struggle with that. The company spells out in the agent's contract where he may solicit, and the contract may prohibit him from making or altering contracts or waiving forfeitures or subjecting the company to liability without its consent. But this is strictly agent-company talk. Few prospects ever ask to see the agent's contract, or, for that matter, his license. The public accepts him at face value and, on the basis of advertisements on television and in the press, knows pretty well what to expect of him. For his part, the agent is largely a creature of his own design, with the help of company materials—the company logo on his stationery, his briefcase, the rate books and flipcharts and manuals and forms, and the graph paper on which he plots the prospect's life insurance needs.

As far as the client is concerned, the agent is the only "company" he ever sees, and perhaps the client can be forgiven for thinking that the agent has broad authority to bind the company. Most of the time it makes no difference what the client thinks; the application is taken and the policy goes into force and stays in force. But if the prospect had something wrong with his health, the insurance company—if it had known— would not have accepted him. Yet (as sometimes happens on rare occasions) perhaps the agent knew the truth, and fraudulently or mistakenly filled in false answers on the application. The agent's knowledge would be imputed to the company and the company would be bound, assuming that the insured took no part in the fraud.[2] The reason is that insurance is a contract *uberrimae fidei*—of the highest faith—and the applicant is chargeable with a basic minimum of fair dealing.[3] If he passes that test, the company is bound, for reasons of "social utility" or "reasonable expectations" or, in the legal view, the company "waived" a known right. Alternatively, in cloaking the agent in "ostensible" or "apparent" authority, it somehow misled the prospect and is therefore "estopped" to repudiate

---

[2] See discussion in *Proceedings, Legal Section, American Life Convention,* 1965, p. 130 and *Association of Life Insurance Counsel Proceedings,* 1960, p. 77.

[3] "Insurance policies are traditionally contracts *uberrimae fidei* and a failure by the insured to disclose conditions affecting the risk, of which he is aware, makes the contract voidable at the insurer's option." *Stipcich* v. *Metropolitan Life Ins., Co.,* 277 US 311 (1928).

its own agent. Stated differently, but for the fact that the agent was about his company's business, the event never would have happened, and if anyone is to be held accountable, it is the one with "superior knowledge" or technical know-how and experience. If the agent tells the applicant his previous illness was of no importance, then, as one court said, "the law does not require the applicant to go further and question the authority or judgment of the agent to decide the question, or whether the information is sufficiently important to merit consideration in the application."[4]

COMPANY'S TORT LIABILITY
FOR ACTS OF THE AGENT

The company's liability for the acts of the agent is not limited to contract, in issuing a policy it did not want to issue, or finding itself unable to rescind a policy for material misrepresentations by the applicant. The company's liability is also in tort. A corporation is a legal fiction, or an abstraction, and has no acts other than those of its officers, employees, or agents. If the acts of the agent can be imputed to the company, and if the acts constitute a tort, then the company is liable in addition to, and not merely instead of, the agent. Here again, various tests are used to determine whether the acts can be imputed to the company: Was the agent engaged in the company's business at the time? Was the act within the scope of his authority, either actual or apparent? Was the agent "armed by his principal with the means to do what he did"?[5] Did the company ratify the act? Did the company have control, for example, as to the manner in which the agent drove his automobile? Was the agent an employee or an "independent contractor"?

Assuming that the right mix of these elements can be found, the courts are increasingly willing to hold the company liable for the torts of the agent. The cases can range from nonfeasance to malfeasance, and from mere carelessness or omission to bodily assault. Thus, there have been cases[6] where an agent misled the insured as to the time within which a policy could be reinstated, and was negligent in forwarding the application; or an agent had the insured arrested for cursing him when he appeared to pay a weekly sick benefit; or an agent, sent to deny a claim for a sick benefit, thrust a spoon down the insured's throat and injured her; or an agent convinced a widow to settle out of court and breach her retainer agreement with the plaintiff-attorney; or an agent fraudulently misrepresented dividends; or an agent made slanderous remarks to a prospect about another policyowner's claim; or an agent driving his own car on company business struck and injured another; or an agent made threats and called a policyowner names; or a group of agents in a local life underwriters association conspired to prevent an out-of-state company from doing business in their state.

---

[4] *Farmers & Bankers Life Ins. Co.* v. *Baxley,* 215 P2d 941, 943 (Okla. 1950).

[5] *Bowman* v. *Home Life Ins. Co.,* 243 P2d 331, 335 (CA 3, 1957).

[6] See cases collected in *Association of Life Insurance Counsel Proceedings,* Vol. 21 (1969), p. 133.

In all these situations the agent's company was made a defendant, and although the outcome was not automatically in favor of the plaintiff, nevertheless it is significant that the company was subject to litigation. Whatever constitutes a tort of the agent could be the basis of an action against the company. An attorney normally will stretch his client's complaint against an agent to include the agent's company, or may ignore the agent, and go straight for the company.

In the contract cases where the company is bound by the act of its agent, the company pays contractual liability limited at least to the terms of an actual or implied agreement. In the tort cases, however, a new dimension is added; in addition to actual damages, which may be calculated in any of a number of ways, there is the ever-present element of exemplary, or punitive, damages for "humiliation," "insult," "mental suffering," "emotional stress," or "outrage." This punishment can cost a company many times the actual damages and inevitable fees. Punitive damages are not limited to the treble damages of the antitrust variety, but can be far in excess of that. Thus, in two recent California cases not involving soliciting agents, the compensatory damages awarded by the jury were $1,050 and $60,000, and the punitive damages were respectively $500,000 and $640,000, plus $10,000 punitive damages against the claims supervisor *personally.*[7] It should be remembered that general principles of agency law apply to life insurance agents, too.

Intentional infliction of mental suffering lay behind the *Wetherbee* and *Fletcher* cases. The "outrageous" conduct in the first case consisted of wrongfully inducing the insured not to cancel her disability policy, assuring her that it could not be cancelled while she was permanently disabled, whereas the company's subsequent conduct showed that it had no intention of living up to its assurances. The company also had sent the insured's doctor "an artfully worded letter which indicated its desire to assure plaintiff uninterrupted coverage," but which elicited a statement that the insured was not continuously confined within the house. The company's "eagerness to seize upon the admission by plaintiff's doctor as a ground for cancellation" was not in good faith and supported a finding of fraud. In the *Fletcher* case, the company's "bad faith refusals to make payments" and "false and threatening communications directed to plaintiff for the purpose of causing him to surrender his policy" were held to be the basis for damages for intentional infliction of emotional distress. The company's claims supervisor, who testified he would treat another identical claim the same way, was assessed $10,000 punitive damages personally.

On appeal, the final figures were scaled down in these cases, but other companies may not be so lucky. These cases apply what has been aptly called California's "outrage law," but the principle behind them is not new—just the magnitude. It may be only a matter of time before "outrage"

---

[7] *Wetherbee* v. *United Ins. Co. of America,* 95 Cal. Rptr. 678, *Fletcher* v. *Western National Life Ins. Co.,* 89 Cal. Rptr. 78. Massachusetts has recently adopted the doctrine; see *George* v. *Jordan Marsh Company,* 268 NE2d 915 (Sup. Jud. Ct. Mass., 1971).

damages are levied against companies in cases arising from acts of their agents.

Insurance is affected with a public interest, and an insurer owes the insured the duty of good faith and fair dealing. The violation of that duty is itself a tort.[8] The courts tend to consider what were the "reasonable expectations" of the insured in purchasing the insurance. It is clear that what an applicant "expects to get" is strongly influenced by what the soliciting agent tells him, both at the time the policy is taken and after, when the insured seeks an explanation of his coverage. How the agent conducts himself at such times may spell the difference between an emotionally upset insured and a polite but firm claimant—or the difference between tort and contract liability for the company and for the agent.

AGENT'S TORT LIABILITY FOR HIS ACTS

The fact that the company is held liable to a plaintiff by reason of the agent's actions does not necessarily mean that the agent gets off free. In contract cases there is little need to pursue the agent; the insured or beneficiary wants to hold the company to a policy that was issued, or should have been issued. Such a policy would be a contract between the company and the insured, and the agent would not be a party. Indeed, where his agency is known to the insured, he cannot be said to have made an individual undertaking for the loss covered by the company.[9]

In tort cases, however, the liability is not exclusive, and the agent cannot escape by pointing to his principal (though the plaintiff may ignore him and go after the company). The agent may even be singled out for punitive damages apart from those awarded against his company. Superficially, this may appear to be a double standard; the company is bound in tort by the agent acting within his authority, yet so far as the personal liability of the agent is concerned, the relationship is meaningless and the agent is also held liable. The reason is that the agent's liability does not arise from his agency, but from the common-law principle that every person must act so as not to injure others. It is no defense to say he was about his company's business.

There are many ways the agent could be held liable in tort to the insured and other third persons. What the agent may tend to forget, however, is his considerable liability to his own company. He may think he enjoys limited liability, and that, at most, he stands to have his contract terminated and his expected renewal commissions cut off. This is not all, however; he may find himself liable to his company for the liability it has suffered by reason of his conduct.

---

[8] Specifically applied to liability insurers, 14 Couch 2d 507, Sec. 51:3, this has been extended to a disability insurer by *Fletcher* v. *Western National Life Ins. Co.*, 89 Cal. Reptr. 78. The idea is not novel, and underlies the statutes that penalize an insurer for delay or vexatious refusal to pay. 16 Couch 2d 11, Sec. 58:7.

[9] By statute, an agent may be held personally liable on contracts of insurance made by him with a company not authorized to do business in the state; e.g., Sec. 171 of Chap. 175, Mass. Gen. Laws.

To begin with, agency is a relationship of trust and confidence. The agent represents the company. He owes it the duty of full disclosure. He may not act for it where his own interests are in conflict with the company's. Indeed, he is forbidden to act at all where his business is opposed to that of his principal. He is subject to a duty to act in accordance with his promises. He must know his company's business, including its rules and instructions. He owes the company the obligation of utmost good faith and loyalty. He may not proceed without or beyond his authority, particularly where he has been forbidden to act; and if in so proceeding his actions cause loss to the principal, he is fully accountable to the principal for the loss. The fiduciary relationship entitles the company to an accounting, even without the necessity of showing something due from the agent. The agent receives premiums as a fiduciary, and must account for them; they are a trust fund, and not a debt. If he fails to pay them over, it is a conversion. Even if he makes restitution, it will not cure the embezzlement, because it is a breach of a fiduciary duty.

The foregoing is a recitation of abstract principles of law which have been distilled over the centuries from many fact situations.[10] They contain few traps for most agents, but every now and then one of them will catch the agent by surprise. For example, an agent has more to worry about than just his "own" company; if he "brokers" a surplus policy to another insurer, that company, too, becomes his own company, and in most states he is licensed as agent of that company in order to place the business. In so doing, he must acquaint himself with perhaps new and different ground rules.

An agent is, of course, liable to his company for loans and advances it makes to him, though their nature will determine whether his liability is limited to his earned commissions. He must look to the company for compensation, and no case has yet held that he can collect from a prospect for commissions he lost when the prospect backed out. There may be instances where, as "advisor," "consultant," or "analyst," he can recover against a client for fees for his expert services, but no cases have been reported, probably because of the tendency of agents to forgive such fees if insurance is sold. This practice is considered an unlawful rebate in at least two states, New York and Ohio.[11]

It has become almost the rule, not the exception, that agents have added mutual funds to their insurance lines. Thus, a whole new world has opened of federal Securities and Exchange Commission and state blue-sky laws, National Association of Securities Dealers regulations, and myriad licensing and selling requirements. Life insurance and mutual funds interreact and combine to pose even more problems. With this expansion of rigid rules comes a corresponding increase of duties and responsibilities for the life underwriter. To complicate matters further, some life underwriters have offered premium financing to their clients; this subject, which can involve questions of usury, rebate, small loan laws,

---

[10] See, generally, 4 Couch 2d, Secs. 26:341–366.

[11] *Association of Life Insurance Counsel Proceedings,* Vol. 18 (1963), p 393, n. 68. But see Sec. 112-a of New York Insurance Law effective April 1, 1973.

truth-in-lending, and other regulations, is beyond the limits of this chapter.[12]

In the course of obtaining his license, the agent is made aware of many statutory duties and penalties to which he is subject. He can be fined, or his license can be revoked, for all sorts of conduct which can be characterized as untrustworthy, that is, misrepresentation, fraud, mishandling of money, defamation, discrimination, rebate, and so on. The liability he incurs for his acts done in violation of these statutes is to the public at large, in the form of penalties or other sanctions, and not by way of damages to any particular individual or to his company. As in tort and contract, his acts also may subject his company to statutory penalties. Virtually all licensed agents are aware that some states have stringent replacement control rules, which require written comparisons of the replacing and replaced policy to be kept on file for a period of years.

FIELD UNDERWRITER AS A PROFESSIONAL

Life insurance is a highly technical discipline. Agents can be well-educated and well-trained in the subject, can be "admitted to practice" only when duly licensed by the state, and are subject to penalties for "malpractice." As his skills grow, the agent's clients become increasingly aware of his professional competence. It may be too early to define an insurance professional exactly and to determine which individuals are included therein, but the trend toward professionalism is unmistakable and praiseworthy.

At the same time, professional stature poses risks. The higher the skill, the higher the responsibility. An army corpsman will not be held to the standards of a heart surgeon. The rookie agent will not be measured against the seasoned underwriter.

Clearly, the ordinary insurance solicitor only assumes those duties normally found in any agency relationship. In general this includes the obligation to deal with his principal in good faith and to carry out his instructions. No affirmative duty to advise is assumed by the mere creation of an agency relationship. However, this does not mean that the agent cannot assume additional duties either by express contract or a holding out. . . . This is an age of specialists and as more occupations divide into various specialties and strive towards "professional" status the law requires an ever higher standard of care in the performance of their duties. . . .

Whether defendant intended to act as a consultant and counseler as well as a solicitor of insurance is not clear. But it is clear that through the designations on his letterheads and the stickers he attached to policies issued by his office defendant held himself out to be an insurance expert. Under the evidence I am convinced that by his conduct and business practices defendant permitted a

---

[12] In view of the widespread practice of agents to advance the premium to the applicant, it may be well to point out that there are two twists. First, if the insured does not have to pay interest on this loan, the agent may be guilty of rebating (*Association of Life Insurance Counsel Proceedings*, Vol. 18 [1963], p. 398, n. 87). Second, if the loan is supported by a note, some states make it unlawful to negotiate the note before the policy is delivered (for example, Mo. Sec. 376.590; Nebraska, Sec. 44–369).

reasonable inference to be drawn by his customers, such as plaintiff, that he was a person highly skilled as an insurance advisor and that plaintiff relied upon him as such. . . .

I therefore conclude that defendant was under a duty to advise plaintiff as to his potential liability under the lease and to recommend insurance protection therefor. . . .

Judgment for plaintiff in the amount of $41,954.24, together with costs.[13]

. In the now famous case of *Gediman* v. *Anheuser Busch, Inc.*, 299 F2d 537 (CA2 1962), an employee retiring early "placed himself in defendant's hands"—the employer's—for advice on which election to make under his pension plan. Relying on a recommendation from the employer's pension consultants, the employee elected one which, upon his death by accident 15 months later, resulted in a substantial reduction of death benefit. In finding the employer liable for the difference the court said that the employee, Barsi,

should have been plainly warned that the risks incident to death, about which he had earlier been apprised with relation to the period prior to retirement, would continue until whatever date he picked for the distribution. Although we are sure everyone was acting in the best of faith, that needed statement was not forthcoming; instead, the memorandum made one of a dangerously lulling sort. Though the error was by defendant's advisers, defendant adopted it and, as between it and Barsi, is responsible on principles too familiar to require citation of authority.

The words "as between it and Barsi" leave no doubt the court thought the consultant was liable in turn to the employer for the advice given.

The higher the agent goes in his vocation, the greater his duty to use his special skill and give expert advice—indeed, he sometimes may come close to the unauthorized practice of law. As was said in *Hardt* v. *Brink:*

It has been suggested by defendant's counsel that this responsibility was more properly that of the plaintiff's lawyer. Although this may be true it does not follow that defendant, as a skilled insurance consultant, did not also have this responsibility. The evidence establishes that the potential liabilities of a tenant to a landlord as well as to others arising out of a lease agreement and insurance coverage available to protect against losses resulting therefrom are well known to experienced and prudent insurance agents and consultants.[14]

The life underwriter is also under an increasing duty to ascertain facts, such as the financial condition of the companies with which he places insurance for his insured; to find the "best buy" in coverage at the risk of making up the difference himself; and to know the circumstances of his client and whether a policy will qualify for technical tax treatment, such as a charitable deduction or a tax deferral. If the agent fails in his expertise, he can be in serious trouble, as witness the quintessential case of *Anderson* v. *Knox*.[15] The facts may be condensed as follows:

---

[13] *Hardt* v. *Brink*, 192 F. Supp. 879 (DC Wash 1961). Although the case involved fire insurance, its principles apply to any insurance solicitor.

[14] *Ibid.*

[15] 297 F2d 702 (CA9 1961), affirming 159 F. Supp. 795 and 162 F. Supp. 338 (DC Hawaii 1958).

Knox, the insured, lived with his wife and three children on Maui, where he worked as a field superintendent on a sugar plantation with a total income of less than $10,000. He was sent a letter from "a prominent member of the Honolulu business community" that his name had been given to Anderson, "an Insurance and Annuity Counselor," who will present a bank finance plan. Then the "bird dog," Kreidler, called and obtained three applications, for $50,000, $75,000 and $100,000 of additional insurance. Kreidler gave Anderson a buildup, calling him the greatest man in the insurance field. Anderson arrived at the plantation and gave a "torrent of words" presentation of the financed insurance, including complicated ledger sheets with the notation, "It is agreed that this schedule will not be shown, directly or indirectly, to any insurance competitor." The figures were based on the 40% tax bracket; Knox was in the 26% bracket. Knox bought the $100,000 plan, and even insurance on his wife, but growing worried he finally dropped the insurance, losing $13,309. The court awarded him that amount as actual damages, $2,500 for mental suffering, and $10,000 as punitive damages.

The Court of Appeals affirmed the decision in a lengthy opinion, stressing that the agent was built up as an expert; that Knox was obliged to take the program on faith, and relied on Anderson as "practically the only man alive who understood the plan fully"; that the program was unsuitable and costly, involved inflated commissions, twisting, and protection that "takes a strikingly deep nosedive during the first ten years"; that Anderson knew the dangers; and that "Anderson's representation of suitability, of his honest opinion thereof, was made with that reckless disregard of the truth which is the equivalent of intentional fraud and deceit." Said the court:

> The court could fairly infer from the circumstances here that Anderson's sole interest was in collecting his immense commission; that he felt no responsibility whatever, as he himself indicated, with respect to the truth or falsity of his representation of suitability. Indeed, the court might well regard seriously the argument that any insurance agent who would sell a man with Knox's limited income and prospects an insurance program that involved saddling him with a bank indebtedness of $125,000, an essentially term insurance type of protection, and dissipation of the accumulated cash values of his old insurance, must have known that he was not acting honestly in making the sale.[16]

In ending its opinion, the Court of Appeals, foreshadowing the *Wetherbee* and *Fletcher* decisions in California, found that Anderson intentionally inflicted mental suffering on Knox by his whole conduct, which included writing a letter to the insurer in a "manifest effort to prevent Knox from extricating himself at minimum expense from the situation in which he had been placed" by Anderson.[17]

In other days, activities of agents were usually tied in with their companies' business. Now, as they exercise the privileges of their professional status, agents join their local life underwriter associations—with the active encouragement of their companies—and open up another area of potential liability for themselves and for their companies. This liability

---

[16] 297 F2d 727.
[17] 297 F2d 731.

may be divorced from the business the agents and their companies considered themselves to be in, but it nevertheless is substantial and continuing. The pattern is typified by the so-called *Green Shield* case.[18] The facts are briefly as follows:

In January of 1962 Green Shield Life brought a civil antitrust suit against the Wichita General Agents and Managers Association, 24 large insurance companies, and 25 individual agents, and prayed for $12,000,000 treble damages in antitrust, $1,500,000 for libel and slander, and $3,000,000 in punitive damages. The nub of the complaint was Exhibit B, a five-page memorandum from the Wichita GAMA addressed to the members of the Wichita Association of Life Underwriters. Its preamble was that life insurance is a great benefit to mankind, that field forces should practice the Golden Rule, that the selling activities of Green Shield Life have caused a deluge of complaints, and now is the time for each agent to explain to 15 or 20 best friends and clients the background of Green Shield, to make certain that our business is being kept on a high and proper plane. The memo went on to say that Green Shield's dividend and profit illustrations are out of this world; the agents drive around in big Cadillacs, Lincolns, Thunderbirds, have airplanes and flying lessons for themselves at company expense, and have gone all out to spend everybody's money. The WALU agents were urged to make it clear that their interest is to protect the buying public from a get-rich-quick scheme. This case was settled, and dismissed with prejudice in April of 1964. Meanwhile, Green Shield's license to do business in Kansas was revoked on the matter of a certificate of title, and about 1964 Green Shield merged with another insurer.

In early 1965 five former Green Shield agents brought an action for treble damages against 52 life insurance companies, again for conspiracy to restrain plaintiffs' business, as witness the same Exhibit B memorandum. On motion for summary judgment, the United States District Court for the District of Kansas in September of 1966 entered judgment in favor of the companies, stating that the agents—who claimed treble damages totaling $4,800,000—had no independent standing, but were only representatives of Green Shield, whose action had been dismissed with prejudice on Green Shield's motion.

As long as private treble-damage action is available,[19] the mere existence of an association—hence the possibility for conspiracy—will continue to encourage suits of the Green Shield type, although liability insurance may help to keep the suits from reaching the courts.

RULES OF THE BUSINESS

The modern life underwriter is subject to a stupefying array of rules he must follow in the pursuit of his calling. He starts with all the explicit state statutes telling him what he may and may not do. Behind these laws is a state regulatory department charged with their enforcement, which has authority on more abstract grounds to decide whether the agent is trustworthy and fit to keep his license. To the extent that the state laws do not

---

[18] Not reported. Case No. W-2562, U.S. District Court for the District of Kansas (Wichita), January 25, 1962. See *Association of Life Insurance Counsel Proceedings,* Vol. 21 (1969), p. 161, n. 107.

[19] *Monarch Life Ins. Co.* v. *Loyal Protective Life Ins. Co.,* 326 F2d 841 (CA 2 1964).

cover an area of regulation, there are federal laws and their enforcement units. His company, or any other company for which he may temporarily act, has elaborate rules as to solicitation, underwriting, and handling of funds. If he sells mutual funds, there is another system of officials and mandates to obey; variable annuities partake of both worlds. He must be aware of the fundamental principles applied by the courts to his agency relationship, the statutes applicable to the products he sells, and the tax impact. He must be familiar with the customs and usages of his calling. He must steer carefully between his duty to advise and the unauthorized practice of law.

And yet, in the continuing process of self-education in which any professional must engage, there is a simple rule of conduct which will protect the agent and his principal from almost all liability, except for common error. It is, of course, the Golden Rule. If the agent becomes a Chartered Life Underwriter, he takes this professional pledge:

In all my relations with the insuring public, I agree to observe the following rule of professional conduct.

I shall, in the light of all the circumstances surrounding my client, which I shall make every conscientious effort to ascertain and to understand, give him that service which, had I been in the same circumstances, I would have applied to myself.

The C.L.U. Code of Ethics goes on to mention other guides to, and rules of, professional conduct.

Another Code of Ethics, that of the National Association of Life Underwriters, pledges the member "to keep the needs of my clients always uppermost. . . . To present accurately, honestly and completely every essential to my clients' decisions." This follows a preamble which recognizes that:

The position of the life underwriter is unique in that he is the liaison between his client and his company. As a life insurance advisor he owes a high professional duty toward his client, while, at the same time, he also occupies a position of trust and loyalty to his company. Only by observing the highest ethical balance can he avoid any conflict between these two obligations.

Which is to say that the agent should apply the Golden Rule to his company, as well as to his client. In fact, the insured and the company must also apply it to each other, for, as has long been held, insurance is a matter *uberrimae fidei.* No definition of utmost faith is more to the point than the Golden Rule.

It is not a distortion of the Rule to say that an agent must tell his client when he needs different, or higher, skills than he, the agent, can offer. When the matter is beyond the agent's competence, he must call in an expert. Or if it is a matter where he must not act at all, such as the practice of law, his is a most delicate path to tread—even with the help of "guideposts."

In 1953 the National Conference of Lawyers and Life Insurance Companies published an article entitled "Some Guideposts for Cooperation between Lawyers and Life Insurance Representatives,"[20] and in 1962 these were "revisited."[21] These articles have been given wide publicity in both insurance and bar association journals, and have been used in agency training courses and degree-granting studies. They incorporate a National Statement of Principles of Cooperation between Life Underwriters and Lawyers which, in various forms, dates back to 1940. Though the governing principles purport to control the conduct of both the lawyer and the agent, enforcement is done by local bar associations and courts, and the agents who at most have the right to protest to the local bar, cannot themselves discipline an attorney for violation of the principles. Moreover, even the guideposts recognize the difficulties facing an agent, who must decide at his peril whether a legal problem exists, and whether his advice to his client will give offense to lawyers who will be both his prosecutor and his judge:

> Since it is often necessary for the life underwriter to point up the legal problems which are generally incident to a possible estate plan in order to make an effective sales presentation, the line of demarcation between what is appropriate and what is not is sometimes hazy and indistinct. Recognizing this fact, the Conference believes that the following test with respect to "expectable consequences" may be helpful:

> If the expectable consequence of such discussion is to motivate the client to consult his lawyer for a review of his problems and to seek his advice, it will be in the permissive area. However, his presentation will offend, despite warnings to consult his lawyer, if it is so definitive, so final, or so apparently authoritative as to probably induce the client to by-pass his lawyer or to regard him as a mere scrivener to handle legal details. While the life insurance representative will be recognized as having the right to make definitive recommendations dealing solely with life insurance and the payment of policy proceeds, he should still refrain from giving legal opinions or legal advice either expressly or by implication.[22]

For an underwriter who has reached a professional standing, and who holds himself out as an expert advisor, it is absolutely necessary that he study the guideposts carefully. They are not a precise road map, but at least they will give him a good sense of direction, and a feel for the problems involved.

Lastly, there is the area largely without guideposts known as "consumerism." The traditional concept of *caveat emptor*, "let the buyer beware," is giving way to legislation for truth-in-lending, truth-in-selling,

---

[20] *C.L.U. Journal*, Vol. 8 (Winter 1953), p. 86.

[21] Frank P. Aschemeyer, "Cooperation between Life Insurance Representatives and Lawyers; 'Guideposts' Revisited," *C.L.U. Journal*, Vol. 17 (Winter 1963), p. 73. See Appendixes U and V, respectively, for the National Statement of Principles of Cooperation between Life Underwriters and Lawyers, and the Statement of Guiding Principles for Relationships between Life Underwriters and Trustmen.

[22] *Ibid.*, pp. 88–89.

and truth-in-securities. Truth-in-insurance probably will not be far behind. More and more the insurance business and its representatives will be required to disclose, inform, explain and simplify, and perhaps yield important concessions.[23]

Most proponents hold that the purpose of fuller disclosure is to put the consumer in possession of pertinent information before his purchase decision, so that he may know and intelligently compare his options.

Yet many believe it will still take a competent agent to determine how much disclosure is needed, and which information is pertinent. Currently, and perhaps for some time to come, actual service to clients will reflect the situation described in a 1910 decision.

It is a matter almost of common knowledge that a very small percentage of policy holders are actually cognizant of the provisions of their policies and many of them are ignorant of the names of the companies issuing the said policies. The policies are prepared by the experts of the companies, they are highly technical in their phraseology, they are complicated and voluminous—the one before us covering thirteen pages of the transcript—and in their numerous conditions and stipulations furnishing what sometimes may be veritable traps for the unwary. The insured usually confides implicitly in the agent securing the insurance. . . .[24]

If the agent has been guided consistently by the ethical rules to which he pledged himself when, for example, he was awarded his C.L.U. diploma, he will find that he will not go astray in serving the consumer public.

PROTECTION FOR THE LIFE UNDERWRITER

It has been observed that, "If men were angels, no government would be necessary." Nor would there be need for faithful performance bonds, liability coverage, and errors and omissions insurance. Therefore, even the most conscientious life underwriter should take the minimal precaution of obtaining appropriate insurance protection for himself, and thus devote his time and energies to his clients' needs. This coverage, variously referred to as errors and omissions insurance, malpractice insurance, or professional liability insurance, is available through the life underwriters association and through programs provided by insurance companies for their agents. It can protect against suits which are groundless, for even the most professional underwriter can be sued; but it usually excludes willful acts and hence punitive damages arising from such acts. Parallel coverage can be obtained to cover liability from association activities, as distinguished from an agent's business activities. Recently the National Association of Life Underwriters' professional liability insurance program

---

[23] The Pennsylvania Insurance Department announced in July 1972, a Proposed Regulation 30, which would require a detailed written proposal in the sale of every policy.

[24] *Raulet* v. *Northwestern Nat. Ins. Co.,* 107 Pac. 292, 298 (Sup. Ct. Calif. 1910).

has added coverage for mutual fund sales; variable annuity and variable life insurance sales are already covered.[25]

This chapter began with a day in the life of an agent who did many things that had deeper implications than he may have suspected. If he is like the vast majority of able and dedicated life underwriters, however, the unfortunate implications spelled out here should not affect him or the company with which he works, and at the end of his busy day he can sleep the sleep of the just.

SELECTED REFERENCES

American Life Convention. "Agency Law Handbook," *Proceedings of American Life Convention, Legal Section*, 1964, p. 565. Chicago, Ill.

————. *Proceedings of American Life Convention, Legal Section*, 1968, pp. 1–246. Chicago, Ill.

Aschemeyer, Frank P. "Cooperation between Life Insurance Representatives and Lawyers—'Guideposts' Revisited," *C.L.U. Journal*, Vol. 17 (Winter 1963), p. 73.

Burleson, Ira L. "Embezzlement and Malicious Prosecution—The Tintinnabulation of the Bells," *Association of Life Insurance Counsel Proceedings*, 1965, p. 61.

Chittick, Ralph J. "Responsibilities of Professionalism," *C.L.U. Journal*, Vol. 18 (Winter 1964), p. 29.

Demichelis, Robert J. "State Variable Annuity Laws and Regulations—Agents' Licensing," *Proceedings of American Life Convention, Legal Section*, 1968, p. 219.

Dillard, Robert L., Jr. "Survey of the Status of Agents under Social Legislation," *Proceedings of American Life Convention, Legal Section*, 1964, p. 177.

Douds, H. James. "Tort Liability of Life Insurance Agents—Further Trends," *Association of Life Insurance Counsel Proceedings*, 1969, p. 79.

Duckworth, J. Lon. "Knowledge of Representatives—Notice to Company," *Association of Life Insurance Counsel Proceedings*, 1960, p. 71.

Esterhai, John L. "The Insurance Company's Liability for the Torts of Its Soliciting Agents," *Association of Life Insurance Counsel Proceedings*, 1969, p. 133.

Hoeveler, William M. "Architects', Engineers' and Insurance Agents' Professional Liability," *Insurance Law Journal*, December 1966, p. 746, and *American Bar Association Journal*, 1966, p. 227.

Rowan, Gerald B. "Waiver or Estoppel because of Knowledge of Company's Agent as Affected by Parol Evidence Rule," *Proceedings of American Life Convention, Legal Section*, 1965, p. 130.

Steele, Allen M. "Legal Duties and Liabilities of the Life Insurance Agent," *Association of Life Insurance Counsel Proceedings*, 1959, p. 423.

Townsend, Oliver M. "Recent Trends in the Tort Liability of Life Insurance Agents," *Association of Life Insurance Counsel Proceedings*, 1962, p. 867.

---

[25] *National Underwriter*, August 7, 1971, p. 1. For a discussion of professional liability coverages, see *Association of Life Insurance Counsel Proceedings*, Vol. 16 (1962), p. 867 and Vol. 21 (1969), p. 79, more fully identified in the selected references.

66

Reinsurance

By WALTER W. STEFFEN

ALTHOUGH THE CONSUMER public seldom is aware of reinsurance, this invaluable technique is of major significance in the process of pooling risks to reduce the uncertainty of economic loss. The presence of reinsurance relationships between and among insurance companies has contributed to the extraordinary record of financial stability that characterizes the life and health insurance business.

Most of the following discussion is devoted to indemnity reinsurance. Assumption reinsurance, the second principal type of reinsurance in the life insurance field, is considered in the final pages of this chapter.

INDEMNITY REINSURANCE

Reinsurance Defined[1]

Reinsurance is an insurance agreement or contract under which one insurer, often called the *ceding company,* is indemnified against loss by another insurer, called the *reinsurer,* arising out of an insurance policy written by the original insurer. Thus, a reinsurance contract is a separate insurance agreement and presupposes the existence of an original policy.[2] This is emphasized by the terms of the usual reinsurance agreement, which state that it is an agreement solely between the insurer and the reinsurer, and creates no right or legal relationship whatever between the reinsurer and any insured or beneficiary of a policy issued by the insurer.[3]

---

[1] For an overview of reinsurance terminology, see the glossary of selected reinsurance terms at the end of this chapter.

[2] See Appendix Y for a specimen reinsurance agreement.

[3] There are two exceptions to the application of this indemnity principle. Reinsurance agreements specifically provide that reinsurance shall be paid without diminution because of the insolvency of the original insurer (in such an event the original insurer might pay less than the full amount of claims). It is also specifically provided in reinsurance agreements that both the insurer and the reinsurer share in any reduction in the amount of compromised claims or adjustment in the amount of claims involving a misstatement of age.

The reinsurance agreement is the master contract under which individual policies of reinsurance, called cessions are placed in effect and administered. The agreement is not necessarily limited in duration but may be terminated with respect to new business on proper notice by either party. It is customary to say that in placing reinsurance in effect, the original insurer is ceding reinsurance to the reinsurer.

Values of Reinsurance

Every life insurance company, in accordance with its financial strength, establishes a limit on the maximum claim it wishes to pay out of its own resources. This limit is called a retention. At the same time, a company wants its salesmen to be able to take an application for any amount the applicant is willing to seek. When such applications are for a sum over the company's retention, it handles the excess by means of reinsurance.

Through the use of reinsurance, then, an insurer is able to issue policies for amounts in excess of its retention limit. This is in the best interest of the insuring public, the insurer, and the reinsurer. It is an obvious convenience if an applicant can purchase a desired amount of insurance from one company rather than being forced to purchase a number of policies with varying conditions from a number of companies. Also, insurance protection will be distributed to a greater proportion of those needing protection if the life underwriters of many companies are in position to supply insurance protection to applicants requiring large amounts and to applicants who are not eligible for insurance at standard rates. Life underwriters benefit through the placing of additional insurance in an expanded market. The insurance industry benefits by reducing the waste arising out of policies which are applied for but not issued.

Further, the knowledge of the industry regarding classification of impaired risks is increased in the most economical manner. Reinsuring companies serve as a focal point for the collection of such risks where statistically significant volumes of consistently underwritten substandard business are accumulated and subjected to extensive analysis by an experienced staff. Improved underwriting standards are promulgated as a result of such analyses. This process is more efficient than if each insuring company found it necessary to attempt to perform its own underwriting research. Finally, the reinsurer benefits through the acquisition of business which is expected to prove profitable in the long run.

Retention Limit

The maximum amount of insurance which an insurer will carry on one life at its own risk without reinsurance protection is called the *retention limit of the insurer*. Fundamentally, the retention limit is set so as to avoid inconvenient fluctuations in earnings because of claims involving large amounts. Although determination of a retention limit is in part an actuarial problem, it also involves considerations not subject to precise quantitative analysis. Significant factors in setting a retention limit are the amount of the insurer's surplus, the expected mortality, the distribution of insurance in force per life, the distribution of new issues of insurance by size, the distribution of in-force insurance and new issues by age at issue and underwriting classification, underwriting skill, the degree of earnings stability desired, and the cost of the reinsurance ceded.

The statistical aspect of the problem is handled most conveniently, although incompletely, by a branch of actuarial mathematics known as the theory of risk. As a practical matter, however, the limit usually is set conservatively by studying the impact of retentions of different levels on the volumes of business which would be ceded at those levels. The retention limit is established to maintain the risk at a manageable level and to keep the volume of business ceded (and therefore the cost of reinsurance) within reasonable limits. After an appropriate retention limit for standard business issued at the central ages has been determined, the limit typically is graded down at the higher issue ages and for substandard risks. This is done primarily because classification of such risks is less certain than the classification of standard risks at the more common issue ages.

Reinsurance agreements provide that the ceding company may increase its limit of retention on new business and also specify the conditions under which amounts of existing reinsurance may be reduced because of the increased limit of retention. Amounts of reinsurance so reduced are said to be "recaptured."

Relationship of Insurer and Reinsurer

The outstanding characteristic of the relationship between insurer and reinsurer is that of utmost good faith. The frequently used description "gentlemen's agreement" is appropriate. The obligation of the insuring company to disclose information about the risk to the reinsurer even exceeds the obligation of the insured to disclose such information in his dealings with the original insurer. In return, the reinsurer follows in nearly every respect the fortunes of the insuring company on policies reinsured. Since it is impractical to attempt to cover all situations which may arise, the reinsurance agreement is drafted along broad and general lines. Binding arbitration of differences of opinion or interpretation is provided for by the reinsurance treaty. The arbitrators are not bound by any rules of established judicial procedure and are required to regard the treaty from the standpoints of practical business and equity rather than of strict law. Insurers and reinsurers generally take great pride in the fact that almost all differences of opinion are resolved by the parties to the agreement. Arbitration is extremely rare in the field of life reinsurance.

Life Reinsurance Plans

Reinsurance of ordinary business is usually accomplished on one of three plans: (1) risk premium reinsurance (RPR), sometimes referred to as yearly renewable term (YRT) or annual renewable term (ART); (2) coinsurance; and (3) modified coinsurance.

Risk Premium Reinsurance. The risk premium reinsurance (RPR) plan is used by the largest number of companies in this country. Under the RPR plan the insurer buys reinsurance for the net amount at risk allocable to amounts of insurance for which it requires reinsurance. The net amount at risk is the face amount payable upon the insured's death less the terminal reserve. This reflects the fact that the reserve will be released at death, thereby diminishing the insurer's net surplus loss. The relatively small terminal reserves involved on level term insurance of 20 years' or less duration and on decreasing term insurance of all durations are ignored as an administrative convenience.

The RPR premium scale is specified in the reinsurance agreement. Formerly, RPR premiums were based only on the attained age of the risk (with perhaps a 50 percent reduction in the first year as a recognition of the increased expenses of the insurer in the first year), but in the mid-1960s reinsurers began defining RPR premiums more precisely. At that time, RPR premiums were designed to take into account various items that affect the cost of reinsurance, such as the size of the reinsurance cession, the sex of the insured, whether the original policy was issued on a medical or on a nonmedical basis, and the length of time that has elapsed since issue of the policy.

To reflect savings realized by the reinsurer on larger reinsurance cessions, the RPR premium generally is made up of a basic rate per $1,000 of yearly net amount at risk plus a policy fee that remains constant irrespective of the amount of reinsurance. Some reinsurers have separate RPR premiums for male and female risks, while others recognize the better mortality of female risks by charging the male rate for an age three or four years younger than the actual age of the female risk. Because they do not participate in the underwriting savings generated by nonmedical issues but experience the increased mortality, some reinsurers charge a higher premium for reinsurance of nonmedically issued insurance. Since the mortality rate experienced by a group of insureds at a particular age is lowest when the group was selected recently, many reinsurers offer select and ultimate RPR premium scales which are lower at the earlier durations to reflect the lower mortality from risk selection. For the select period, the premium rate varies by the attained age of the risk and the number of years that have elapsed since the policy was originally issued. Thus, the reinsurance premium for a policy on a male now aged 35 will be lower for a policy that was issued at age 34 than it is for a policy issued at age 30.

Table 66–1 illustrates a sample calculation of reinsurance on an experience refunding basis for $10,000 of whole life insurance with reserves based on the 1958 CSO Table at 3 percent interest and the Commissioner's

TABLE 66–1. Illustrative Premium Computations for Risk Premium Reinsurance Plan

Attained Age	Gross Amount of Reinsurance	Terminal Reserve Thereon	Net Amount at Risk	Life Reinsurance Premium per $1,000	Policy Fee	Total Life Reinsurance Premium
35	$10,000	$ 0	$10,000	$2.09	$5.00	$25.90
36	10,000	149	9,851	2.55	5.00	30.12
37	10,000	300	9,700	2.96	5.00	33.71
38	10,000	455	9,545	3.33	5.00	36.78
39	10,000	613	9,387	3.64	5.00	39.17

Reserve Valuation Method. The first five policy years are shown for reinsurance of a male aged 35 at issue for a policy issued on a medically underwritten basis.

Customarily, further distinctions are made in reinsurance premium rates by sex, by underwriting classification, and according to whether or not the insurer is to receive experience refunds from the reinsurer in the event of favorable reinsurance experience. Nonrefund rates are lower than experience refund rates. It also usually is provided that the amount of insurance to be placed in the experience refund account on an individual life be limited to stabilize the insuring company's net reinsurance cost. Amounts in excess of this prescribed maximum most frequently are reinsured on the basis of lower nonrefund reinsurance premium rates—although certain other methods of net reinsurance cost stabilization are used by various reinsurers. In life reinsurance the experience refund typically depends solely on the experience in the reinsurance account of the individual original insurer. A system of pooled refunds based on the overall experience of the reinsurer sometimes is used for special categories of risks.

Because the RPR premiums contain no investment element, the premiums for risks subject to percentage extra mortality would be multiples of the standard reinsurance premiums were it not for the expense element. Although premiums for substandard risks must reflect the higher expenses associated with substandard business, the total expense is less than a multiple of the standard expense. Thus, substandard premiums are somewhat less than multiples of standard premiums. Table 66–2, showing ultimate (beyond the select period) RPR rates per $1,000 for a risk aged 35, will illustrate differences between male, female, refund, nonrefund, and standard and substandard premiums (no policy fee is included).

TABLE 66–2. Illustrative Risk Premium Reinsurance Premium Rates per $1,000 (35-year-old risk)

	Standard Mortality	200 Percent of Standard Mortality	300 Percent of Standard Mortality	400 Percent of Standard Mortality	500 Percent of Standard Mortality
Male refund	$3.81	$6.45	$9.09	$11.73	$14.37
Male nonrefund ...	3.06	5.18	7.30	9.42	11.54
Female refund	3.24	5.32	7.40	9.48	11.56
Female nonrefund ..	2.60	4.28	5.96	7.64	9.32

When the insured is assessed a flat extra premium, such as $5 per $1,000 per year, the extra premium allocable to amounts reinsured, less a commission and expense allowance, is paid to the reinsurer. Customarily, standard reserves are used to determine the net amount at risk on all substandard business. Reinsurance premiums are paid annually with a pro rata refund on termination at other than the policy anniversary. Of course, RPR premiums are payable during the continuance of the risk, even though the original policy may become paid up. It is customary for reinsurance claims to be payable in one sum, regardless of the mode of settlement selected under the provisions of the original policy. Typically, an insurance company pays premium tax on its premium income before deduction of premiums paid for reinsurance ceded and before addition of premiums received on reinsurance accepted. Therefore, a reinsurer reimburses the original insurer for the premium taxes allocable to the insurer's ceded premiums.

The RPR plan is widely used because of its many advantages. These advantages include:

1. The original insurer retains the investment element of the premium necessary to accumulate the policy reserve. Therefore, excess interest earning thereon will accrue to the insuring company, although there is the associated risk of investment losses. Also, to a young company the increased assets resulting from the retention of this investment element of the premium may be important as a measure of prestige.

2. Administratively, the plan is simple and easily understood. There are no dividends, commissions, or cash surrender values involved in the reinsurance transactions.

3. Since the reinsurance is all on the term plan, the computation of experience refunds also is simple and easily understood.

4. The reinsurer's investment in the business is modest so that, typically, business is eligible for recapture after it has been in force for five years and meets the other applicable recapture provisions of the reinsurance agreement. This five-year period gives the reinsurer an opportunity to recover its initial expense.

5. The expense of installing the reinsurance plan is minimal, since no extensive analysis of the insurer's price, commission, and benefit structure is required.

Accidental death benefits generally are reinsured with reinsurance of the life risk or, if there is no accompanying life reinsurance, alone. Because of the small reinsurance premium involved, it is important that the expense of administration of accidental death reinsurance without accompanying life reinsurance be kept at a minimum. One method of accomplishing this is the use of a cession card requiring little more than the name of the risk and the amount of reinsurance, without any other papers being forwarded to the reinsurer except in unusual circumstances. Another method is to apply a premium to the average amount of reinsurance in force for each calendar year, with only the total amount of such reinsurance in force at the end of each calendar year being reported to the reinsurer. Typically, a scale of rates varying by occupational class but not by attained age is used. In recognition of the insurer's increased expenses in the first year, the first-year premium rate generally is lower. The use of a flat rate is a great administrative convenience, but it may mean that at certain points in the original insurer's accidental death price structure the reinsurance premium may exceed the insurer's net premium income. This generally will be offset at other points of the insurer's accidental death price structure by reinsurance premiums substantially below the insurer's net premium income. Thus, this method works satisfactorily unless the insurer's distribution of business by issue age is unusual.

Coinsurance of accidental death benefits also is used, which eliminates the variance between the reinsurance premium and the insurer's premium but adds the complication of a more complex reinsurance premium scale. It should be remembered that antiselection by amount is a continuing feature of the studies of accidental death experience; therefore, the reinsurer's claim cost can be expected to be higher than the average claim cost of the original insurer. Because of the volatility of the accidental death coverage, experience refunds typically are a function of the reinsurer's overall experience rather than being based solely on the experience of the individual reinsurance account.

It is customary to coinsure waiver-of-premium and disability income benefits in proportion to the amount of life insurance reinsured.

Coinsurance Plan. Confusion sometimes exists regarding the coinsurance plan as used in life reinsurance. In life reinsurance the term "coinsurance" is used to denote a plan of indemnity reinsurance.[4] The coinsurance plan involves reinsurance on the basis of the plan issued by the original insurer to the insured, and the reinsurance premium is the premium charged by the original insurer. Where the original insurer grades its premiums by size of policy, the reinsurance premium is that for the highest amount "band" or that excluding any policy fee, depending upon the method of grading used by the original insurer. The reinsurer pays commissions and service fees according to the scale paid by the insurer. Service fees are frequently replaced by fully vested commissions of reduced amount, but with equivalent value, as an administrative convenience. An additional expense allowance, generally expressed as a percentage of the premium, also is paid by the reinsurer. The reinsurer thus accumulates the investment element of the premium and sets up the full reserve on the reinsured portion according to the valuation basis of the original insurer. The reinsurer grants cash surrender and other nonforfeiture values according to the provisions of the insurer's policy and follows the dividend scale of the insurer if the insurance is participating.

As is true in the case of RPR, premiums are paid annually, and the reinsurer customarily reimburses the insurer for premium taxes. When dividends are graded by size, the reinsurer typically reimburses the insurer on the assumption that all dividends on reinsured policies are at the highest amount "band" rate. The reinsurer does not participate in policy loans, thus making the coinsurance method inappropriate for business under which it is expected that full policy loans will be maintained.

Some of the advantages of the coinsurance plan are:

1. When applied to participating business, the insurer has the guarantee that the reinsurer will follow the changes in its dividend scale and that the reinsurance net cost will follow the insurer's net cost.
2. Where the original insurer establishes reserves on the net level pre-

---

[4] This can be contrasted with an arrangement where two insurers are liable jointly to an insured. The term "coinsurance" is used in different ways in health insurance and in property insurance.

mium basis, the additional surplus loss (a frequently quoted average figure for this loss being $21 per $1,000) necessitated by establishing the higher first-year reserve is absorbed by the reinsurer on the reinsured portion of the business.

3. Certain policies sometimes sold by younger companies may involve a substantial surplus drain. Reinsurance on the coinsurance plan provides a means of passing on to the reinsurer a portion of this drain on reinsured business.

4. It also might be said that the coinsurance plan passes on to the reinsurer the investment risk on reinsured policies. It is doubtful, however, that this would often be considered as an advantage. But in the case of very large policies which will ultimately represent "demand deposits" of unusually large magnitude in relation to the financial position of the insuring company, the coinsurance plan may be quite desirable for this reason.

The coinsurance plan has several disadvantages:

1. The assets of the original insurer do not grow as rapidly.
2. Administration is somewhat more complex, particularly for participating business.
3. The time limit on recapture is longer because of the reinsurer's greater investment in the business. If the initial investment is substantial and the return is to be delayed for a long period of time, recapture may not be granted at all.
4. The determination of profits and, therefore, the experience refund formula must be more complex because many more items contributing to a profit or loss on the business must be properly accounted for. In the computation of experience refunds, interest income is credited at the reinsurer's net earned rate less an allowance for capital losses in excess of capital gains.
5. An extensive analysis of the insurer's price structure is required in order to determine an appropriate expense allowance.

Modified Coinsurance Plan. The modified coinsurance plan is the same as the coinsurance plan, except that each year the current year's mean reserve on the reinsured portion, less the sum of the preceding year's mean reserve on the reinsured portion and the interest thereon, is returned to the insurer. To avoid substantial transfers of funds at year end, this mean reserve adjustment is frequently made in periodic installments throughout the year. The interest rate referred to is the insurer's net earned rate less an adjustment for capital losses in excess of capital gains. This modification of the coinsurance plan removes one of the major disadvantages of this plan, in that the original insurer's assets are not diminished. In fact, since the reserve returned usually exceeds the reinsurer's net income at early policy durations, the insurer's assets are increased in these cases.

Comparison of Reinsurance Plans. A comparison of the three plans of life reinsurance reveals certain similarities and also some differences. Table 66–3 sets out the distinctive features of RPR, coinsurance, and modified coinsurance as they apply to the specific situations shown in the left-hand column of the table.

TABLE 66–3.   Comparison of Distinctive Features of Risk Premium Reinsurance, Coinsurance, and Modified Coinsurance Plans

Specific Situations	Risk Premium Reinsurance	Coinsurance	Modified Coinsurance
Life Reinsurance Premium	Schedule in Agreement	Insurer's Gross Premium	Insurer's Gross Premium
Reimbursement of Insurer's Commissions	No	Yes	Yes
Expense Allowances	No	Yes	Yes
Premium Tax Reimbursement .	Yes	Yes	Yes
Experience Refund Provision . .	Yes	Yes	Yes
Recapture Privilege	Usually*	Negotiable*	Negotiable*
Dividend Reimbursement (Par Plan)	No	Yes	Yes
Death Claim Payment to Insurer	NAR†	Face	Face‡
Cash Surrender Reimbursement	No	Yes	Yes‡
Participation in Policy Loans . .	No	No	No
Supplementary Benefits: Disability	Coinsure	Yes	Yes
ADB	RPR or Coins.	RPR or Coins.	RPR or Coins.
Continuation of Life Reinsurance Premium: Paid-up Policy	Yes	No	No
Extended Insurance	Yes	No	No
Disability Claim	Yes	No	No

* Recapture privileges are an integral part of the reinsurance price structure; therefore, treaties are written with recapture privileges available after a few years or many years, or no recapture privileges at all.

† Net amount at risk = Face amount less terminal reserve in policy year of death according to insurer's reserve standard.

‡ Insurer returns to the reinsurer the previous year's mean reserve, plus interest thereon, at the end of the calendar year during which death or surrender occurs.

Automatic and Facultative Methods of Ceding Reinsurance

Reinsurance may be placed in effect either automatically or facultatively. When the facultative method is used, the insurer sends to the reinsurer copies of the application and all other evidence of insurability it has acquired. The reinsurer then classifies the risk (either immediately or upon receipt of such further evidence as it may require) and notifies the insurer of the basis on which it will accept the risk. When the automatic method is used, the insurer classifies the risk and notifies the reinsurer of the amount that has been ceded at the insurer's classification.

Automatic reinsurance agreements specify the conditions under which the insurer may use the automatic method. The typical automatic reinsurance agreement provides that the insurer may cede automatically a percentage, say 400 percent, of the amount of its retention limit on standard business and 400 percent of the amount actually retained on the current application on substandard business. It is customary to provide that the insurer must retain its retention limit for the age and underwriting classification assigned the risk to avail itself of the automatic facility. All reinsurance which does not fall within the category eligible for automatic binding must be handled on a facultative basis. It is also usual for the reinsurance agreement to provide that reinsurance shall be ceded facultatively when the total amount of insurance in force and applied for in all companies on a life exceeds, say, $2 million.

Most reinsurance agreements that require the reinsurer to accept certain reinsurance automatically also require, in return for such automatic facilities, that the insurer cede all of its excess to that reinsurer. Conversely, facultative agreements (no automatic facilities) do not obligate an insurer to cede reinsurance to a facultative reinsurer. An insurer may have one reinsurance agreement on an automatic basis (or two reinsurance agreements with two reinsurers, with the reinsurers splitting the excess, generally on the basis of the first letter of the insured's last name) and facultative agreements with several other reinsurers.

Much reinsurance that could be placed by the automatic method is, in practice, placed by the facultative method due to the preference of the insurer. The main advantage to the insurer of the automatic method is avoidance of any delay in issuing its policy. The advantage to the insurer of the facultative method is that it receives the reinsurer's underwriting opinion before the policy is issued. On occasion, the reinsurer may have had previous applications or may receive concurrent applications for reinsurance on the same life from different companies; for this reason, it may have more complete underwriting information than any single insurer.

By agreeing to accept business automatically, the reinsurer is relying on the underwriting judgment of the insurer and is bound to accept a case even though it may not agree with the underwriting decision. The reinsurer is protected by the requirement that the original insurer retain its full retention limit, which assures a measure of self-interest. In actual practice, when any question of proper underwriting classification exists, the insurer usually does not use its automatic facility but instead secures the reinsurer's underwriting opinion by submitting the case facultatively.

Individual Health Reinsurance

In the individual health insurance field, principal sum benefits and disability income benefits, particularly where there is a long maximum period of indemnity, frequently involve a substantial risk on an individual insured. Medical expense benefits rarely involve potential liabilities great enough to require reinsurance. A possible exception might be major medical benefits written by a young company with a modest surplus; most frequently, however, such a young company would restrict itself to basic hospitalization coverage if it entered the health insurance field at all.

Principal sum benefits are reinsured in the same manner as accidental death benefits issued with life insurance. The reinsurer's premium structure, as is true of the premium structure of the original insurer, will take into account differences in the two coverages. The most important of these differences is the different degree of selection exercised by the insured. Higher accidental death claim costs will, for example, be characteristic of policies providing accidental death coverage only. Reinsurance of such benefits may be either on the RPR plan or on the coinsurance plan.

Disability income benefits frequently are reinsured on the coinsurance plan. This is because of the great variety of benefits offered by the different companies and because of the influence of a particular company's underwriting and claims administration philosophy on loss ratios. Typically, the insurer's retention might vary by occupational class and indemnity limit. Reduced limits of retention usually are established for substandard disability income business. The rationale behind reduced retentions for more hazardous occupations and otherwise substandard lives is the same as in life insurance. Gradation of retention limits by indemnity limit is, of course, a direct reflection of the lesser risk on policies with shorter indemnity limits.

A second plan of disability income reinsurance, which has been used with increasing frequency in recent years, is a form of excess-of-loss coverage commonly referred to as extended waiting period reinsurance. Under this plan of reinsurance the original insurer pays the entire claim for the first 12, 24, 36, or 60 months of disability. Thereafter, the reinsurer indemnifies the original insurer for a portion, usually not to exceed 75 percent, of the continuing claim payments. This plan can be combined with coinsurance of disability income, the combination protecting the insurer both from large claims and long-duration claims. For example, the insurer could retain $300 per month for the first two years of a claim and $150 per month thereafter. The reinsurer's liability under a policy providing $600 per month would then be $300 per month for the first two years of a claim (coinsurance) and $450 per month beginning with the twenty-fifth monthly claim payment, until the insured recovered or died or the benefits expired. In this case the reinsurer has provided $300 of coinsurance from the policy issue date plus $150 of extended waiting period reinsurance after two years.

Nonproportional Reinsurance

With the exception of reinsurance of extended waiting period disability income benefits, the plans of reinsurance which have been discussed up to this point can be called proportional plans. The term "proportional" is appropriate, since the proportion of a claim for which the reinsurer will reimburse the insurer is known prior to the happening of the event insured against. Plans of reinsurance which do not meet this proportional definition can be called nonproportional plans. Almost all life reinsurance is on proportional plans.

It is apparent that extended waiting period disability income reinsurance is nonproportional—the reinsurer will have no liability if the claim terminates before the end of the extended waiting period. Thereafter the proportion of the total claim reimbursed by the reinsurer varies according to the length of the claim.

A very complete form of nonproportional reinsurance is commonly called *stop loss reinsurance*. Under this plan the reinsurer might indemnify the original insurer for, say, 90 percent of aggregate net claims in a calendar year in excess of, say, 120 percent of net expected claims for that year; the reinsurer's liability also is subject to a maximum amount. The attractiveness of this direct approach to the problem of mortality fluctuations is apparent. However, formidable practical and theoretical problems would prevent the reinsurer from covering war claims and would likely prevent the reinsurer from guaranteeing the price structure or the continuation of the reinsurance coverage. Insurers who have issued guaranteed renewable coverage without a war exclusion provision at guaranteed premium rates may find such incomplete reinsurance protection to be unsatisfactory. For this reason, stop loss reinsurance protection may never have wide application to life insurance, where the basic coverage is guaranteed renewable at a guaranteed premium.

Another form of nonproportional reinsurance, which has found considerable favor with life companies as a form of supplementary reinsurance protection, is known as *catastrophe* or *disaster reinsurance*. Under this plan the reinsurer pays losses in excess of a pre-established deductible or disaster retention when a specified number of claims result from a single accidental occurrence, such as more than three claims resulting from an airplane crash. The reinsurer's liability is subject to a maximum amount per accident. This form of nonproportional reinsurance has found considerable favor with life insurance companies as a form of supplementary reinsurance protection, because it is generally inexpensive, is easy to administer, and provides meaningful protection from large, single losses.

Group Reinsurance

Group underwriting controls, most particularly that control which relates the maximum amount of insurance on one life to the size of the group, serve to stabilize the financial experience of the insurer. The operation of any experience refund arrangement also stabilizes the insurer's experience, as an unfavorable claims experience is offset (partially, at least) by a reduction in experience refunds or dividends. Most group-writing companies therefore are willing to retain amounts of group coverage in addition to their individual ordinary limit of retention on a life. Amounts of group coverage in excess of that provided by the group schedule and issued on the basis of individual evidence of insurability, where required, can be reinsured according to individual ordinary reinsurance methods.

Most commonly, reinsurance of group-underwritten insurance is transacted on a quota-share basis, under which the insurer retains the same percentage of each certificate issued under a particular group policy. For example, if the insurer decided upon a 40 percent quota-share retention on a given group, it would retain 40 percent of each certificate issued under that policy, regardless of the amount of the certificate. The retention usually is set so that the insurer's retention on the largest certificate is equal to its maximum group retention. Since the reinsurer thereby has the same spread of risk as the insurer (generally, a large number of small amounts and a smaller number of the largest amounts), the group underwriting controls automatically protect the interests of both the insurer and the reinsurer, and administration of the insurance is kept simple. Alternatively, when amounts of group coverage in excess of a specified limit themselves form a group which conforms to the underwriting rules of the reinsurer, such excess amounts may be reinsured as a group.

ASSUMPTION REINSURANCE

Assumption reinsurance is the assumption by one company of all of the functions and obligations of one or more policies issued by another company. Generally, an assumption certificate outlining the takeover by the assuming company is sent to each policyowner whose policy has been assumed. An example of such a certificate is shown in Figure 66–1. In most cases, the insured will look to the assuming company in the future for all benefit payments under the policy, will pay all premiums to the assuming company, and will deal with the assuming company in the same manner as if it had originally written the policy.

FIGURE 66–1. Certificate of Assumption

Assumption reinsurance can arise in a least two ways: (1) a company wishes to sell a particular portion of its portfolio to another company; or, (2) a company finds itself in financial difficulty and arrangements are made to transfer its portfolio of insurance to a solvent company. In the latter situation, assumption reinsurance is often arranged by the commissioner of insurance in the state of domicile of the troubled company or some other interested party so that the protection offered to the insureds is maintained. This sort of assumption reinsurance is an interesting feature of U.S. life insurance.

Although close and constant care is exercised by the state insurance departments over the affairs of all domestic life insurance companies, occasionally, a life insurer, like many other financial institutions, will experience reverses and find itself in the position that it can no longer continue to operate. Such conditions are almost always brought to light before the insurer has exhausted all of its assets. At this time, arrangements are usually made for another company to take over the insolvent insurer's portfolio, assumption reinsurance is placed in effect, and the obligations to the policyowners are transferred, intact, to another, solvent insurer. Thus, owners of life insurance policies almost never find themselves without coverage and without a return of at least a substantial portion of their equity in their policy.

GLOSSARY OF IMPORTANT REINSURANCE TERMS

Assumption reinsurance. An agreement between two insurers under which one insurer disposes of its entire in-force portfolio, or a specific block thereof, and the other insurer assumes the functions and all obligations to the *insured* connected with the policies involved. Assumption certificates are issued by the assuming insurer to all insureds notifying them that it has replaced the original writing company and that it will be responsible for the obligations under the directly written policies previously issued by the original insurer.

Automatic reinsurance treaty. An agreement between an insurer and a reinsurer under which the insurer is obligated to cede and the reinsurer is obligated to accept as reinsurance the amounts written by the insurer in excess of its retention limits, within prescribed limits outlined in the agreement. The reinsurer's liability commences simultaneously with the insurer.

Catastrophe reinsurance. A form of nonproportional reinsurance under which a reinsurer indemnifies an insurer for losses in excess of a pre-established deductible arising from a single catastrophic occurrence. The reinsurer's liability is subject to a maximum amount per occurrence.

Coinsurance. A plan of indemnity reinsurance under which the reinsurer assumes the obligation on the amount reinsured in the same fashion as the insurer is obligated to the insured (excluding policy loans). For this risk the insurer usually pays to the reinsurer the gross premium (less commissions and expense allowances) it has collected from the insured on the amount reinsured. (It should be noted the reinsurer has no relationship with the insured or beneficiary.)

Excess of loss. A form of nonproportional reinsurance under which the reinsurer indemnifies the insurer for its share of a loss occurrence only after the loss to the insurer exceeds a stipulated amount or percentage, the reinsurer paying only the portion of the loss exceeding such amount or percentage.

Facultative reinsurance treaty. An indemnity reinsurance agreement under which there is no obligation on the part of the insurer to cede or the reinsurer to accept individual risks. The reinsurer retains the "faculty" to accept or reject each risk offered by the insurer. The reinsurer's liability commences after definite approval or acceptance of the risk.

Modified coinsurance. Same as coinsurance except the reinsurer lends the mean reserve to the insurer each year. (Each year the current year's mean reserve on the reinsured portion less the preceding year's mean reserve, plus interest thereon, is paid to the insurer, if this amount is positive, or returned to the reinsurer, if negative.)

Net amount at risk. This term is associated with the risk premium reinsurance (RPR) plan. It is the reinsurer's liability in the event of death, determined by deducting from the face amount reinsured the terminal reserve thereon, according to the insurer's valuation basis for the plan of insurance issued to the insured.

Nonproportional reinsurance. A plan of reinsurance under which the reinsurer provides protection in any one occurrence beyond the stipulated loss, deductible, or retention accepted by the reinsured regardless of the number of risks involved. The retention is stated in terms of the loss, either as a percentage or absolute amount, and as a function of either one event or a period of time during which several events producing losses take place, and is not proportionate or directly related to the risk assumed in the original policy issued to the insured. Catastrophe, stop-loss, excess of loss, or aggregate excess of loss reinsurance are examples of nonproportional reinsurance.

Proportional reinsurance. A plan of reinsurance under which the reinsurer provides protection in any one occurrence when the loss exceeds the retention or risk assumed by the reinsured. The retention is stated in terms of the risk assumed, either as a percentage or absolute amount, is the function of one event, and is proportionate or related to the risk assumed in the original policy issued to the insured. Risk premium reinsurance, coinsurance, and modified coinsurance are examples of proportional reinsurance.

Quota share. A plan of reinsurance under which an insurer and a reinsurer are liable for a stipulated percentage of each risk written under a defined category of business on a pro rata basis. This plan of reinsurance is particularly applicable to group-underwritten business.

Reinsurance (or indemnity reinsurance). A business transaction under which one party, called the reinsurer, in consideration of a premium paid to him, agrees to indemnify another party, called the reinsured, for part or all of the liability assumed by the latter party under a policy or policies of insurance which it has issued. The reinsured may also be referred to as the reassured, original company, insurer, primary insurer, direct writing company, or ceding company.

Reinsurance cession. Individual policies of reinsurance issued by the reinsurer to the reinsured setting out the administrative details of the reinsurance. One might consider the reinsurance cession as the counterpart of the policy issued by the insurer to the insured.

Reinsurer. The party to a reinsurance agreement who agrees to indemnify the other party to the agreement for losses arising out of an insurance policy written by the latter party.

Retention limit. The maximum amount of liability which a company will carry on one life or one event at its own risk without reinsurance protection.

Retrocession. A reinsurance transaction between reinsurers. This can best be defined by an example. Company B accepts reinsurance from Company A; Company B then obtains reinsurance from Company C for a portion of the business it has assumed from Company A. Company C is called a retrocessionaire—one who accepts reinsurance from a reinsurer.

Risk premium reinsurance (RPR). A plan of reinsurance under which an insurer purchases reinsurance for the net amount at risk allocable to amounts of insurance for which the insurer requires reinsurance.

SELECTED REFERENCES

Dougherty, Edward A. "Ordinary Life Insurance Limits," *Transactions of the Society of Actuaries,* Vol. V (1953), p. 125.

Feay, Herbert L. "Introduction to Nonproportional Reinsurance," *Transactions of the Society of Actuaries,* Vol. XII, No. 32 (1960), p. 22.

Kalmbach, L. J. "Life Reinsurance," in Life Office Management Association, *Life Office Management Readings in Life Insurance,* Vol. V, p. 251. New York, 1946.

McGill, Dan M. "Reinsurance of Life Risks," *Journal of the American Society of Chartered Life Underwriters,* Vol. XII, No. 2 (1958), p. 163.

Menge, Walter O. "The Life Reinsurance Market Today," *World Insurance Trends* (eds. Davis W. Gregg and Dan M. McGill). Philadelphia: University of Pennsylvania Press, 1959.

Ormsby, Charles A. "The Cost to Reinsure Individual Life Insurance Policies," *Transactions of the Society of Actuaries,* Vol. IV, No. 10 (1952), p. 448.

Rohm, John T. "Life Reinsurance," in *Proceedings: Conference of Actuaries in Public Practice,* Vol. V (1955), p. 100.

Werner, Edgar C. *Fundamentals of Reinsurance,* published by The College of Insurance, New York (1964).

67

Claims Administration

By PAUL R. CRAIG

IN ONE FORM or another, every life and health insurance contract contains a promise to pay. The payment of benefits—the final product of operations which may have extended over many decades—fulfills the primary purpose of insurance, namely, to provide protection against the hazards of untimely death, disability, accidents, sickness, or dependent old age. Claims administration is the process by which an insurance company meets its final obligations under the insurance contract.

NATURE AND FUNCTIONS OF CLAIMS ADMINISTRATION

A claims philosphy is necessary for consistent claims administration. Because the administration of claims is more of an art than an exact science, an insurance company must develop and communicate a claims philosophy that will give its claims personnel broad direction and guidance.

Claims administration in modern life and health insurance is not a static process. New policy wording, types of benefits, case law, and coverages constantly reflect new underwriting approaches. The experience gained under each, where favorable, creates pressure for liberal interpretations in claims administration. Competition is also a potent force in creating pressures for liberal claims policies.

In addition, marketing programs and policies change from time to time. These changes eventually involve the claims man with new and different groups of claimants, such as, for example, substandard risks, the elderly, and members of associations newly eligible for group insurance. The almost constant advances in underwriting standards to provide continually broader coverage for greater numbers of applicants result in ever-different claims problems. Further, the insurance business plays a major role in the financing of medical care and this has brought new responsibilities to claims people. Advances in medical technology create problems and opportunities that existing coverages did not contemplate.

In this dynamic climate of change, competition, and constant improvement, it is now more necessary than ever that a company evolve a claims philosophy. As a result of all of the forces working on the claims administrator, today's philosophy will probably be different from that developed in prior years. One company has developed a model claims philosophy along the following lines:

To endeavor to provide prompt, efficient, and courteous service. To endeavor at all times to perform faithfully the company's obligations, and to reflect an impression of the company as a fair, sound, and reputable organization. To endeavor to protect the company against fraud and misrepresentation, and to safeguard the policyowners' funds. To resolve the issue, in cases of reasonable doubt, in favor of the policyowner or beneficiary; and in cases of technical policy provisions, to look to the intent rather than the technical language of the provision. To endeavor to treat all policyowners with fairness, and to give all policyowners equal treatment in accordance with the provisions of their policies. To endeavor to develop the abilities of the company's employees, and to keep them knowledgeable concerning progressive developments in the industry. To endeavor at all times to maintain a high level of communication and understanding with other departments of the company and with other elements of the insurance industry.

ROLE OF THE CLAIMS ADMINISTRATOR

The claims administrator serves many sectors of the public. Principally, he deals with policyowners and policy beneficiaries. Beyond these, however, he has increasingly greater contacts with doctors, hospitals, lawyers, social workers, life underwriters, brokers, trust officers, state medical examiners, state insurance departments, rehabilitation experts, and many others.

Because of his unique position of fulfilling the obligations guaranteed by the contract and because of his many public contacts, the claims man probably is one of the greatest single forces available to a company for promoting good public relations. The residual impression left by a claims man extends far beyond his own company. It probably is a prime source for the creation of public opinion of the insurance business as a whole.

The claims administrator is a moving force within the company. Since he is close to the public, and since he carries out the provisions of the policy, he has the best available information as to whether or not the policies being sold really are meeting the needs of the insuring public who have purchased the coverages. He also is in an excellent position to observe the operation of contract provisions, including exceptions or exclusions, that may be more expensive to administer and cause more adverse public reaction than they are worth. In addition, he may identify contract wording which does not seem to permit the fulfillment of the intent of the policy. Since the claims administrator has firsthand information about the insureds and the product, he is a part of the company team engaged in regular creative development of improved products.

The typical insurance organization is composed of a number of distinct operations, each performing a specialized function. Claims operations usually are structured in one of two ways. There may be a separate department which handles all claims; or there may be several separate claims groups, each of which takes complete charge of only a given line of business—for example, group, ordinary life, industrial life, and individual health insurance.

The claims department itself normally keeps no individual policy records. Instead, it relies on other departments to maintain the necessary records and to provide funds for benefit payments. The claims department is usually responsible for approving or denying claims, paying benefits, accounting for benefit dollars disbursed, and recording claims statistics necessary for company operations.

In performing its several functions, the claims department generally is expected to be progressive, to fulfill the company's obligations promptly, to promote good public relations, and to be economical in its operations. Modern business systems have helped meet these obligations and have increasingly become a part of sound claims administration.

GENERAL CLAIMS PROCEDURES

The core of claims administration is the evaluation of proofs and the final approval or denial of the benefits claimed. Before this process can occur, however, there must have been a loss by the insured with corresponding potential liability by the insurer, and the claimant must have notified the insurer of his desire to assert the rights covering such event given him in the contract. To best facilitate this process, and to permit some uniformity of operations, insurers customarily provide forms for making claims.

Claim Proofs

In recent years, there has been much good work done through industry-wide cooperative efforts to promote uniform claim forms. Working with the American Medical Association, the American Hospital Association, and the American Dental Association, industry committees have taken the best of many forms, standardized their language, provided for a logical sequence of questions, and then promoted them for general use. Continued progress in this important field is and should continue to be actively supported.

In addition to claim forms, a company may require other evidence of loss to clarify a factual situation and to come to a proper decision. Such additional proofs may include death certificates, medical statements by attending physicians, hospital bills, and autopsy reports. The good claims administrator seeks constantly to reduce, simplify, and clarify the data which he requires from claimants and others.

The purpose of the claim form is to elicit the facts concerning the particular loss claimed in an easily usable form. Since there are many kinds of claims, it follows that there are forms used with questions that are pertinent to the particular classes of policies or claims involved. Nevertheless, efforts are made to keep the number of different forms at a minimum, and to use the same form for several types of claims where this is practical.

Claims Examination

Claims examination and evaluation is the principal job of the claims administrator. Methods of claims examination vary with the type of claim and with the claims philosophy of the company. However, there are certain basic procedures common to all claims. These procedures are briefly described below before the specific aspects of the administration of life and health insurance claims are considered.

Identification of the Insured. Identification of the insured as a first step is necessary so that the claims man can make use of the basic policy records. The factors involved usually are the policy number, the insured's name, and perhaps his age. On group insurance claims the claims administrator must go one step further. After identifying the policyholder, usually the employer, the claims administrator must identify the insured person under the group policy. Such identification is usually established through name and certificate number, or perhaps through the social security or employee number of the insured person.

Determination of Benefits Claimed. A determination of benefits claimed is usually evident if the appropriate claim statement or forms have been submitted. Within the broad categories of death, disability, or medical expense claims, the claims administrator must determine what specific benefits apply.

Determination of Policy Status. The status of the policy usually involves an examination of the company records concerning the policy, such as the application, the record of premium payment, and any record of policy loans and surrenders. In addition, if it is a group case, and if the policy is in force, it is necessary to determine that the certificate holder is currently insured. Where insurance does not appear to be in force, the claims examiner must be careful to look for any policy provision that might have extended the coverage. He also must determine whether or not the initial loss actually occurred at some earlier date when the insurance coverage was in effect.

Determination of the Extent, If Any, of Liability. In determining the extent of liability for individual policies, the examiner must be careful to note any additional amounts which might be due under the policy, such as, for example, policy dividends, interest, and paid-up additions. He also must recognize any necessary deductions from the proceeds, such as existing policy loans, loan interest due, or unpaid premiums. All coverages must be carefully checked at this stage, particularly amendments to group policies.

LIFE INSURANCE CLAIMS ADMINISTRATION

Life insurance policies generally provide fixed benefits for certain specific losses. All these benefits, which may be multiple benefits under some circumstances, are spelled out in the policy. On group life policies the benefits may vary for certain classes or salary grades of employees.

Claims for Death Benefits

Proofs of death which are acceptable to the company may consist of the claimant's statement on the claim form and a certificate of death or a statement by the physician attending the deceased at the time of death. On some group policies the employer also provides information about the coverage for the employee, such as the date last worked, reason for leaving work, and salary grade.

There is one prime qualifying situation on death claims arising out of the incontestable provision in individual or family life insurance contracts. If death has occurred within a specified period after the issuance of the policy (usually two years), and if there is proof of material misrepresentation by the policyowner in the application for the policy, the company may contest payment of the claim. Even though the policy itself may have passed the period of contestability, the claims administrator must be careful that there were no additional benefit riders added after the issuance of the policy which still may be within their own contestable period. Reinstatements also may give rise to new contestable periods and renew the suicide period in some jurisdictions. Should a claim be contestable, the claims man must examine the case thoroughly, and often must make a detailed investigation of past medical records through an interview with the family physician or review of hospital records. Such an investigation is to determine whether or not the statements made in the application were true and complete, and, if not, whether the application would have been accepted and the risk assumed if the true facts had been stated initially.

Accidental Death Claims

Special handling is required for accidental death claims. In these cases, it probably is necessary for the claims administrator to investigate beyond the initial claim proofs, although sometimes a simple newspaper clipping describing the accident might suffice. In analyzing the claim facts, the examiner must determine whether or not the death was "accidental" within the terms of the specific policy involved. Typical policy exclusions such as disease, infections, suicide while sane or insane, and war must be considered. Over the years, there have been differences of interpretation. and a variety of court decisions over the distinction between "accidental" and "accidental means." Some companies have eliminated the consideration of "means" in accidental death claims either by contract language or by claims administration policy. Where the distinction is still maintained, the examiner must be aware of the differences in court decisions and interpretations in the various states.

Multiple Indemnity Benefits for Accidental Death

The claims administrator must be certain that the qualifying policy conditions and limitations peculiar to multiple indemnity coverage are met. The potential liability on such cases can be sizable. An example of these limitations is the requirement that the insured must have suffered a covered loss of life, limb, or sight as a result of bodily injuries sustained solely through external violent and accidental means, directly and independently of all other causes.

Suicide

Most individual and family policies contain a suicide clause that limits the benefit amount payable when death is the result of suicide within a specified period (usually two years) after the issuance of the policy.

Claims involving death within that period which might have resulted from suicide, therefore, require careful consideration by the claims administrator. There is a variety of subtle means available to the insured intending suicide, and some medical examiners apparently are reluctant to commit themselves to a positive statement as to the cause of death when even a shadow of uncertainty exists. It is essential that the claims man exercise wisdom and judgment in evaluating the facts available to him, as well as the absence of facts, in every claim for "accidental death" benefits when the probability of suicide outweighs the probability of accident. Examples include death by motor vehicle accident, fall from a great height, asphyxiation, exposure, and drowning.

Hazardous Occupations

Occupations or avocations, such as aviation, generally no longer prohibit one from purchasing life insurance. However, if policies have such an exclusion, the claims man must check this carefully and look into the cause and circumstances of the insured's death. Should death result from skydiving, scuba diving, sports car racing, hunting, or some other hazardous hobby, and be found to fall within such an exclusion, the company usually only pays either an amount equal to the premiums paid for the policy, plus interest, or the cash surrender value of the policy. Such exclusions apply only to individual policies.

War

Deaths resulting from war, either declared or undeclared, normally are covered except under accidental death coverage. An exclusion may be included in policies issued during time of war.

Termination of Coverage

Death after termination of the insurance poses problems for the claims administrator in that he must make certain, under both individual and group policies, that there are no extensions of coverage set forth in the policy. For example, total disability may have occurred while the policy was in force, and thus the coverage of the basic policy may have been extended under the terms of the waiver-of-premium provision.

Apparent Errors in Age

Apparent errors in age should be checked by the claims administrator. In these cases the statement of the insured's age in the claim proofs may be different than that shown on the original application. Although the company probably would have issued a policy had the insured's correct age been known when the policy was applied for, the premium rate would have been different. When discrepancies in age appear to exist, the claims examiner should attempt to determine the correct age and then should have the policy recalculated on the basis of the true age at issue. This action may result either in a higher policy amount to be paid or in a reduced policy amount. However, modern claims practice is to waive minor reductions in face amount based on discrepancies in age. Age also has a bearing on accidental death coverage, since these benefits generally are restricted to those persons between the ages of 5 and 70.

HEALTH INSURANCE
CLAIMS ADMINISTRATION

Total and Permanent Disability Benefits

Life insurance policies often provide either for waiver of premiums or for both waiver of premiums and monthly income payments in the event of total and permanent disability. Disability income coverage also may be provided under separate individual or group contracts and either for "long-term" or for "short-term" durations. The source of most problems with disability claims lies in the construction to be placed on the words "total" and "permanent."

Historically, this coverage was intended to provide benefits only if the insured had become totally and permanently disabled for life. However, the original concept has been modified over the years. The policies typically define "total" disability as the inability of the insured to engage in any occupation for remuneration or profit. Because of court interpretations and changes in insurance operational philosophy, this definition of total disability generally is interpreted to mean the inability of the insured to carry on for profit his own occupation or some other occupation for which he is reasonably fitted by experience or training. Also, total disability need not be of a permanent nature or for life. Usually, the policies provide that total disability for a prescribed period, such as four or six months, is presumed to be permanent.

Group life contracts usually require that the disability must be total and permanent. This means that, to all appearances, total disability will continue for life or for an indefinite future period. Evidence of continuance of total disability is required annually under most group life contracts.

As in death claims, proof that the claimant is disabled is furnished to the claims administrator through claim forms. These forms contain statements by the claimant as to the nature and cause of his disability, its history, the type of work he did, when he last worked, and whether or not the accident or sickness resulted from his employment. A physician's statement indicating his diagnosis, the degree of disability, its history, and its progress and prognosis also is necessary. On some group claims the employer also completes a statement indicating the reason for termination of active work and the employee's insurance status.

From these reports and any results of investigation or medical examination deemed necessary by the insurer, the examiner must determine, on the basis of judgment and experience, whether or not the insured is totally and permanently disabled within the wording of the policy provision, applicable court decisions, and the company's prevailing claims philosophy.

Under individual policies, contestability is one of the prime qualifying situations in disability claims. There are several possible categories into which a disability claim may fall with respect to contestability. One is where both the life insurance policy and the disability provision are contestable and there is material misrepresentation (in the application) concerning a prior physical impairment or medical treatment which could result in the rescision of the policy. In another situation the life insurance policy is incontestable, but the disability provision remains contestable. Thus a material misrepresentation would make possible the rescision of only the disability provision where this provision is severable from the policy. Where both the policy and the disability provision are incontestable, neither coverage can be rescinded by the insurer. However, if disability results from bodily injury or disease sustained or contracted prior to the payment of the first premium on the policy, the claim may be denied under a preexisting exclusion clause of the disability provision and is not a matter of contestability but rather of the nonexistence of coverage.

Age limitations also affect the claimant's eligibility for benefits under disability claims. Generally, the policies stipulate that total disability must commence prior to a stated age of the insured, such as age 55 or 60.

Also, it is usually provided that the disability must commence while the person is insured, and that if the insurance has terminated, proof of the disability must be furnished within a definite period of time after the date of termination. Thus, if proofs are received by the insurer within the prescribed time after the insurance coverage has terminated, it is necessary to ascertain exactly when total disability commenced. If disability commenced prior to the time coverage ceased, the claim can, of course, be considered.

The right to require proof of continuing disability annually is generally provided for in most policies. However, the right is not always exercised when it is obvious from the nature of the injury or disease that the insured will continue to be totally and permanently disabled. When adequate information indicates that the insured has recovered, the examiner terminates benefits and restores the policy to a premium-paying basis.

Under most individual policies, if death occurs during the continuance of disability, all disability benefits terminate, and the face amount of the policy is payable. Under group policies the disability benefits also cease, and the face amount—or the difference between the face amount and the benefits already paid as installments under the disability coverage—is due.

Long-Term and Short-Term Disability Benefits

Loss-of-income claims present different problems. The monthly disability benefits provided under long-term disability coverage usually commence after a covered total disability has continued for a period ranging from one or two months to a year, to coordinate with a concurrent salary continuance plan or short-term disability coverage. Such long-term benefits are payable for a maximum period of 24 months during total disability caused by a nervous, mental, or emotional disease or disorder, and during the continuation of total disability caused by other conditions until the insured's 65th birthday.

During the first two years of total disability, the term "total disability" is usually defined as disability that prevents the insured from performing the duties of his occupation or employment. After the first two years, the term is usually redefined as disability that prevents the insured from performing the duties of any occupation or employment for which he is reasonably qualified by education, training, or experience. During the first two years of disability following onset of injury or disease, ability to work in a different occupation will not, of itself, defeat recovery of benefits. For example, a typist who sustains traumatic amputation of three fingers as a result of a meat grinding accident at home and thus is unable to type, is totally disabled and eligible for disability benefits, even though she might engage in a nontyping job.

Because of the substantial maximum benefits provided under long-term disability coverage, the claim administrator must exercise extraordinary care in evaluating and approving claims for long-term disability benefits. At the same time, he must be alert to situations where rehabilitation potential exists.

The National Rehabilitation Association defines rehabilitation as "an individualized process in which the disabled person, professionals, and others, through comprehensive, coordinated and integrated services, seek to minimize disability and its handicapping effects and to facilitate realization of maximum potential of the handicapped individual." The rehabilitation process does not necessarily require a large and elaborate program. Some patients require many different services; others only minimum care. In its broadest application, rehabilitation requires knowledge and skills of multiple professional specialists, working together as a team and utilizing community services. Rehabilitation has many stages. Services intended to be provided by the rehabilitation process fall into four specific categories: medical, psychological, social, and vocational. Significant elements of a successful rehabilitation program that must be considered are:

1. Early and thorough analysis of the claim for initial rehabilitation evaluation, including estimated maximum disability benefits, patient's age, cause of disability and motivation; and
2. Medical evaluation to establish rehabilitation potential, including attending physician's attitude, determination of who will evaluate (private rehabilitation center, state vocational rehabilitation agency, or private physician), agreement with patient to accept therapy and the formal program designed to rehabilitate him, and assistance of the patient to return to a job of maximum usefulness in the community.

The weekly disability benefits provided under short-term disability coverage usually commence after a covered disability resulting from sickness has continued for a period of a few days or a week, during which waiting period benefits are not payable. The purpose for this waiting period is to eliminate the many minor sickness claims which would result if there was no waiting period. The waiting period frequently is waived when disability results from accidental bodily injury.

The amount of disability benefits may be subject to offset or reduction for a period of covered disability during which the insured is known to be receiving concurrently such benefits as workmen's compensation, social security disability benefits, or other similar benefits, so that the aggregate benefits received during disability do not exceed a certain percentage of the insured's regular income.

To make sure that total disability has in fact continued, periodic additional medical proofs may be required. These additional proofs take the form of supplementary statements from the attending physician or examinations by a company physician.

Dismemberment Benefits

Dismemberment benefits are provided under some individual and group insurance policies for specific losses, such as the total and irrecoverable loss of the sight of one eye or both eyes, loss of both hands or both feet, or one hand and one foot, or the loss of either one hand or one foot. Proofs of loss are similar to those required for other benefits, except that special questions appear on the claim form to aid in determining whether the claim qualifies under applicable policy terms. Examples of these include: "Give date and exact point of severance," "State amount of vision in each eye," and "Is corrective operation contemplated?"

Unlike individual policies, group contracts generally require that the loss must occur within 90 days of the accident which caused the loss. On the other hand, individual policies normally require that the loss be sustained prior to the policy anniversary nearest the insured's 60th or 65th birthday. There generally is no such age limitation in a group policy.

Medical Expense Benefits

Health insurance policies, both group and individual, also may provide reimbursement for medical expenses incurred because of accidental bodily injury or disease. Some policies also cover dependents of the insured for medical expense benefits. One feature of medical expense policies is the variety of coverages involved. The most frequently sold coverages are hospitalization and surgical coverage, and major medical expense insurance—although there are many others available, such as medical treatment, diagnostic, dread disease, and dental coverages.

Individual health insurance policies generally are similar to group policies in the coverages provided. However, they are different in that they are individually underwritten, sometimes exclude payments for losses arising from specific physical conditions, and may be contested for a specified period of time. Individual policies also sometimes exclude losses that arise from hazardous occupations or avocations, or preexisting conditions. In addition, some include age limitations. Under both individual and group policies, benefits for maternity are usually provided on a reduced basis or are not provided at all.

Variability characterizes both group and individual health insurance policies. Combinations of benefits, benefit maximums, covered medical expenses, and qualifying language all vary from contract to contract. In group insurance, benefits and benefit limitations may be tailored to meet the specific needs of a particular customer. Each day sees innovations in health insurance, such as special group coverages and individual plans for the elderly to supplement Medicare. All of this means that the health insurance claims administrator must be flexible in his approach and creative in his method of handling these complicated claims—all the while adhering to the basic claims philosophy favored by his company.

For health insurance policies providing medical expense benefits, the claims administrator must determine what services were performed, which of these services were covered by the specific policy at hand, how much in the way of benefits is provided for those services, and to whom the policy benefits are payable.

Claim proofs for medical expense policies often consist of the claimant's statement, an attending physician's report, and, for group insurance, a policyholder's statement. In addition, the insurer requires itemized statements of services performed and the charges rendered for such services.

Unlike claims for most other types of benefits, medical expense claims require that the claims man determine whether the proofs in question apply to a new claim or to some prior claim. This determination involves such questions as: "Has there been an intervening recovery between claims?" or "Has there been a return to work?" or "Is the current condition different than previous conditions?" Claim proofs are used to aid the claims administrator in making this determination, although he often must get additional information to evaluate the claim properly. Once this decision has been made, the claims administrator then makes an examination of the claim and a determination of what benefits are due. During this examination of the claim the claims man should keep in mind the following typical conditions which generally are included in health insurance policies:

1. The attending physician in the case must be qualified according to the policy terms. Most policies state what types of physicians are acceptable under the particular policy. It may even be necessary for the claims man to check the applicable state law pertaining to licensing to make this determination.
2. The qualifications of any hospital or convalescent home involved must be checked, since most policies are very specific as to what institutions qualify under the contract.
3. The status of the hospital patient is usually important in claims for hospitalization benefits. Since many hospital-surgical-medical policies provide benefits only when there is inpatient care, the claims man must be careful to determine if the claimant is an inpatient. In examining the claim, however, he must remember that some policies also provide benefits for outpatient care under special conditions, such as, for example, emergency treatment following an accident or minor surgery.
4. Where hospital care has been furnished at government expense, the policy language must be studied thoroughly, since benefits generally are excluded in cases where the insured does not incur an obligation to pay.

Major Medical Expense Claims

Major medical expense insurance has become increasingly popular because these plans provide a broad coverage desired by the public. Major medical coverage is available under both individual and group policies. The rapid growth of this broad coverage, the growing demand of the public for better health care, and the ever-increasing cost of that care have challenged the claims man's ingenuity in dealing with the special problems of major medical coverage.

While the older forms of hospital, surgical, and medical coverages contained schedules listing maximum dollar benefits for surgical operations, laboratory tests, and other specified services, in major medical expense insurance the phrases "customary," "reasonable," and "necessary" have been substituted in the policy for many of the schedules previously used.[1] Although these give the claims man some opportunity for control of claim losses, they also place upon him the obligation to make subjective judgments as to whether or not a given fee meets the imprecise tests imposed by the policy. In effect, responsibility for the cost of the product has been shared by the underwriter with the claims man. To help meet that responsibility, the claims man uses, to varying degrees, "studies of relative values" and "normal cost guides."[2] There are such studies for surgical procedures, diagnostic services, anesthesia, radiology, psychiatry, and pharmacy. In addition to considering the medical necessity for the service furnished, whether or not the necessary service is covered, and whether or not the charge for the covered service is reasonable, the claims man must temper his judgment with regard to the age and income of the insured, medical complications, the geographic area in which the claim arose, and the physician's professional standing. In more difficult cases, he may seek the counsel of hospital utilization committees, or review committees set up by medical societies, or professional opinion from his company's medical department or a local consultant.

Duplicate Coverage

The insurance industry is concerned with duplicate coverage under health insurance policies because it is felt that overinsurance is not in the public interest. Overinsurance distorts the purpose of insurance, tends to encourage overutilization of service, and tends to increase the cost of medical care. Because of this concern, the insurance industry has actively promoted amendment of the Uniform Individual Accident and Sickness Policy Provisions Law. For the same reason, the industry has also developed a uniform coordination of benefits provision for group health insurance. The claims man must be alert to detect situations where such duplicate coverage might exist, such as in the case of working wives, for example.

The principle underlying coordination of benefits is that, when a person is covered under two or more benefit plans for any item of medical expense which is covered at least partially under at least one of the plans, all the plans will pay a benefit according to an established order of benefit determination so that all such items of expense will be paid in full. However, none of the plans will pay more through the operation

---

[1] It should be noted, however, that major medical policies still contain certain inside dollar limits.

[2] These are studies of medical services, with each service assigned a measure of value in relation to others in the same medical practice field to which appropriate dollar-conversion factors can be applied. Examples: California Medical Association Relative Value Studies, and Hospital Drug Reference: A Guide to Better Pharmaceutical and Drug Buying.

of the coordination of benefits provision than it would pay in the absence of it, and no benefits will be paid in excess of expenses. The standard coordination of benefits provision defines the plans, expenses, and claim determination period; explains the effect on benefits; and provides the right to exchange pertinent claims information to facilitate benefit payment.

Duration of Claims

Excessive duration of hospital claims is checked through the use of statistical "norms" which define the average or customary length of stay for common conditions. Claims for periods of hospitalization which exceed the "normal" stay among insureds of similar age, sex, and occupation with similar conditions may cause the claims man to call for further confirming evidence of the need for continued hospital confinement.

Disability claims for loss-of-income benefits may pose a problem similar to that presented by hospital confinements for an excessive duration. The claims man frequently uses the same kind of statistical norms to evaluate the proofs for such disability claims. Where longer than normal disablement is claimed, the claims man must look for further facts to help him come to an equitable decision on the claim. In his search for evidence, he may make use of investigations, additional medical proof, and interviews with the claimant or his employer.

CLAIMS PAYMENT

The process of paying benefits involves several steps. The payee or payees must be determined. In life insurance contracts the insured has named a beneficiary or beneficiaries to receive the death proceeds, and this designation usually is a part of the policy. The claims administrator should be particularly careful to note any change of beneficiary or any assignment of the policy to someone other than the beneficiary. In group policies the beneficiary designation is on file with the employer or with the insurer. Health insurance policies generally provide for benefit payments to the insured; however, some policies specify that benefits will be paid to the physician or hospital, or to any other person named by the insured. The claims man must be certain to determine the correct payee because erroneous payments may force the insurer into duplicating the payments at a later date.

The amount payable is calculated as a part of the claim examination; however, the claims examiner must be aware of whether or not interest is payable on the proceeds of a death claim. This determination already may have been made by a policy provision. If not, company practice must be followed. Interest may be payable at the legal rate in the beneficiary's state. Interest may be payable, for example, either from the date of death or from 30 days after the receipt of proof of death. The period during which interest is paid may be limited to six months or a year, and may depend on whether the delay was or was not caused by the claimant.

There are many methods of making actual benefit payments. Each of them must, however, encompass some means of accounting for the disbursement and of meeting the income-tax reporting requirements of the federal and state governments. The claims administrator also must remember that many states require the insurer, on claims for death benefits, to notify the state when payment has been made or, in some instances, to obtain the state's consent to payment prior to the time payment is effected. Depending upon the state involved, the circumstances, and the amount of the benefit payment, the state may sometimes waive this requirement.

Not all claims are payable. On health insurance policies where benefits are not payable because the loss is not covered, the insurer denies the claim but the policy remains in force. On individual health and life insurance policies, where a material misrepresentation is proved and the policy is still contestable, the policy may be rescinded and a return of premiums offered. Sometimes the individual health policy may be kept in force but revised through a rider or waiver excluding benefits for loss from a certain condition or excluding coverage for an uninsurable family member.

Where the claimant is dissatisfied with the decision of the company and resorts to legal action against the insurer, the claim is usually turned over to the insurer's law department.

OTHER PAYMENTS

The claims administrator also handles benefit payments that do not arise as claims. Matured endowments, for example, do not require the submission of claim proofs. Benefits are due on a given date, and it is the responsibility of the insurer to see that payment is made. The same is true of group annuities which become due as periodic installment payments commencing at a certain time and of individual annuities which mature on a certain date. The claims man's job here is to make certain that all is in order, that the correct payee receives the payments when due, and that the payments continue through the period specified in the policy. He also may be responsible for making periodic payments under optional methods of settlement, as where the owner or the beneficiary under a life insurance policy elects to have the policy proceeds paid in monthly installments as income benefits rather than in one lump sum.

AIDS IN CLAIMS ADMINISTRATION

There are many sources of aid available to the claims administrator. Certainly, the insurer's own law and medical departments furnish valuable technical support. In addition, the Health Insurance Council—with its many grass-roots state committees—is very helpful to the individual claims administrator and to the insurance business in providing information, arranging conferences on common problems, and interpreting and reporting the needs and attitudes of the many health care professions. Also, the Health Insurance Association of America and the Life Insurance Association of America are particularly helpful. The International Claim Association, another member organization of the Health Insurance Council, has as its objective "to promote goodwill, harmony, confidence, and cooperation generally among companies, and to devise and give effect to measures for the benefit of their policyholders, especially in matters relating to claims; and the observance of the amenities that should exist among companies and associations."

SELECTED REFERENCES

Clendening, Logan. *The Human Body.* New York: Alfred A. Knopf, Inc., 1945.

Dickerson, O. D. *Health Insurance.* Rev. ed. Homewood, Ill.: Richard D. Irwin, Inc., 1968.

Faulkner, Edwin J. *Health Insurance.* New York: McGraw-Hill Book Co., Inc., 1960.

Greider, Janice E., and Beadles, William T. *Law and the Life Insurance Contract.* Homewood, Ill.: Richard D. Irwin, Inc., 1968.

Harbaugh, Charles H. *Adjuster's Manual.* 6th ed. by P. V. Reinartz. Philadelphia: Chilton Co., 1958.

Insurance Accounting and Statistical Association. *Proceedings.* Kansas City, Mo., 1970.

International Claim Association. *Law Committee Reports.* Omaha, Nebr., n.d.

Rothenberg, E. E. (ed.). *Understanding Surgery.* New York: Trident Press, 1965.

Society of Actuaries. *Health Insurance Provided through Individual Policies.* Chicago, 1968.

Vance, William R. *Handbook on the Law of Insurance.* 3d ed. by Buist M. Anderson. St. Paul, Minn.: West Publishing Co., 1951.

68

Company Investments

By GEORGE T. CONKLIN, JR.

LIFE INSURANCE COMPANIES are the largest source of long-term capital in the American economy with over $204 billion[1] of invested assets at the end of 1971 and with gross new funds for investment up to $20 billion[2] annually. Their investments are also the most diversified of any type of financial institution. For example, life insurance companies hold working interests and royalties in oil wells; own barges, ships and automotive transportation equipment; and develop entire new urban communities, as well as invest in all the conventional media for long-term funds.

The commercial banking system is a much larger source of capital than life companies, but commercial banks are primarily lenders at short and intermediate term. Savings and loan associations come next with about $206 billion invested at the end of 1971, mainly in mortgages and with a somewhat larger but more variable flow of new funds for investment than life insurance companies. Mutual savings banks, also primarily mortgage lenders, had about $89 billion of invested assets at the end of 1971, and have roughly $10 billion a year for net new investments.[3] Private noninsured pension funds hold about $100 billion, which is invested primarily in existing securities, mainly common stocks.

The resources of the entire system of financial institutions grow in response to two quite different causes. The first is the level of real savings in the country. The second is inflationary or deflationary changes in the national money supply that exceed the ability of the economy to respond through changes in the level of productive activity alone. In recent years, the rate of growth in the domestic money supply has fluctuated dramatically. At times it has been well above the real needs of the economy, and at times it has been well below them as the monetary authorities attempted to restrain the inflation caused by previous periods of excessive monetary growth. The rate of growth of the assets held by financial institutions has fluctuated correspondingly.

---

[1] Net of policy loans. *Federal Reserve Bulletin*, March 1972, p. A39.
[2] *Life Insurance Fact Book, 1972* (New York: Institute of Life Insurance, 1972).
[3] *Federal Reserve Bulletin*, March 1972, pp. A39, A40.

Life insurance companies are unique among important financial institutions in that the enormous accumulations of capital held by them are composed principally of noninflationary long-term savings. They are not swollen by the inflationary consequences of excessive monetary expansion. However, there are ways in which policyowners and beneficiaries can withdraw some of their savings from life insurance companies when other sources of funds are unavailable or very costly. Therefore, the rate of growth in invested assets may slow down substantially during periods of tight money and high interest rates (see "Liquidity Needs" below).

This pool of savings represents mainly the accumulated reserves supporting life insurance policies and annuity contracts. The net level premium plan of ordinary whole life insurance, by which the annual premium for a life policy is held constant even though the real cost of the policy rises steadily with the advancing age of the insured, results in a substantial accumulation of savings in the early years of the contract when the premium charge exceeds the total cost of protection. These savings finance the later years of the contract, when the annual premium is far less than the true cost for the year. At the end of 1971 the aggregate reserves for ordinary life policies totaled $105.8 billion.[4]

Annuity contracts and supplementary contracts are funded by the payment to the life insurance company of a lump sum, or premiums over a fixed period of time, in exchange for a guaranteed income to commence either immediately or at some date in the future and to continue either for a fixed period of time or for the remaining life of the annuitant. At the end of 1971 the reserves supporting these contracts totaled $49.6 billion.[5]

Other sources of life insurance funds consist of the reserves behind group and industrial life policies, $16 billion; health insurance policies, $4 billion; funds set aside for policy dividends not yet paid, $4 billion; dividends paid but left on deposit with the company, $6.5 billion; separate accounts, $5 billion; miscellaneous obligations, $8 billion; and capital and surplus, $18 billion.[6]

CONSIDERATIONS INFLUENCING INVESTMENT POLICIES

Long-term and Predictable Nature of Liability and Cash Flow

Historically, life insurance and annuity contracts have been popular savings media in the United States, and the inflow of funds from policyowners has grown at a relatively stable rate. The return flow of savings to beneficiaries and annuitants is also reasonably stable and predictable, and the total resources of life companies have risen persistently throughout virtually the entire history of the business. This reasonably predictable flow of funds, plus the long-term nature of life insurance contracts,

---

[4] *Life Insurance Fact Book, 1972*, p. 66.

[5] *Ibid.*, p. 65.

[6] *Ibid.*, pp. 65, 66.

has led life insurance companies to emphasize the long-term outlook in their investment decisions. A life insurance company is much less exposed than other financial institutions to the risk of having to liquidate investments in a severely depressed market. Therefore, under normal circumstances, it can concentrate on the total return to be expected over the life of the commitment without being much concerned about interim fluctuations in market values.

Guaranteed Interest Rate on Policy Reserves

The premiums and considerations collected for life insurance and annuity contracts are not in themselves sufficient to pay the contractual benefits. Rather, they are calculated to be sufficient to pay the benefits *if* the accumulated reserves earn interest at a stipulated rate. This characteristic has led life insurance companies to be primarily long-term lenders at interest, and makes earning a sufficient return to cover the assumed rate a crucial consideration. During the period of very low rates of interest in the late 1930s and 1940s there was reason for concern that the industry might not be able to continue to earn the assumed rates. But in comparison with the historically high interest rates in more recent years, the assumed rates—which range from 2½ to 3½ percent—are highly conservative.

Limited Surplus

The surplus of the life insurance industry is limited. In order to deal fairly with succeeding generations of policyowners, premiums are calculated to be only slightly in excess of the true cost of insurance. (Or, in the case of participating policies, any substantial excess of premiums over experienced cost is returned in the form of policyowner dividends.) So, it is unusual for life insurance companies to accumulate any substantial surplus. The New York insurance law limits mutual companies to holding no more than 10 percent of their liabilities in surplus, and competitive factors generally result in a significantly lower figure than that. At the end of 1971, the capital and surplus of all life insurance companies amounted to 8 percent of total resources.[7] This limited margin by which total assets exceed total liabilities is a factor militating against running any risk of sizable losses that might impair surplus and thus cast a doubt upon the continued ability of the company to meet its contractual obligations.

Competition to Reduce Net Cost

On the other hand, the net cost of insurance is a primary competitive consideration in the industry, and in the long run a major determinant of the net cost of insurance is the rate of return on invested assets, along with mortality experience and the level of expenses and taxes. Thus, the dominant characteristic of the investment process of life insurance companies is a constant and unremitting search for the highest possible rate of return available at an acceptable level of risk.

---

[7] *Ibid.*, p. 66.

Regulation

The investments of a life insurance company are closely regulated by the separate laws of each state in which it is licensed to do business. The potential confusion to a company inherent in this situation is considerably reduced by three factors. First, since the Armstrong investigation in 1905 into various unsound practices that had crept into the industry, the state of New York has taken the lead in the regulation of the business, including investment policies and practices. Secondly, "foreign" companies (those domiciled in another state) are generally required to comply only "in substance" with specific state laws, not in every detail. Finally, the insurance commissioners of the individual states cooperate closely through the National Association of Insurance Commissioners (NAIC) in discharging their statutory responsibilities for the regulation of the industry's investments.

These laws and regulations take two general forms. First, they specify the types of investments that life insurance companies may make, and they generally specify maximum limits as to the percentage of assets or surplus for each type. For example, under the New York law, common stock investments are limited to the smaller of 10 percent of total assets or 100 percent of surplus.

Secondly, the laws and regulations specify standards of eligibility for specific investments. For example, under the New York law, an unsecured corporate bond is eligible if the issuing company has earned at least 1½ times its full fixed charges on average during the previous five years and in one of the two previous years at the time the test is made. However, some state laws specify modest percentages of total assets that may be invested without regard to the legal standards. These "basket" clauses give the companies some latitude for innovation, but the general effect of the laws is to hold the companies to reasonably strict standards of conservatism in investment policy.

The Going-Concern Method of Valuing Assets

State insurance commissioners, acting through the NAIC, also prescribe how life insurance companies shall value their investments for the purposes of determining their solvency and compliance with the state laws. The general principle involved is that a permanent, going concern like a life insurance company need not be overly concerned about the market price fluctuations of a fixed-income security that is reasonably certain to pay the income on schedule and to repay the principal at maturity. In accordance with this principle, life insurance companies have for many years carried their mortgages at the book value of the loan outstanding, as long as the loan is not in default. During the early 1950s the NAIC developed a valuation system for bonds according to which those in "good standing" would be carried at "amortized cost."[8] Thus,

---

[8] "Amortized cost" means simply that if the bond was purchased at a price different than the amount to be repaid at maturity, this premium or discount is to be written off over the life of the bond by charges against, or credits to, income.

the statement values of bonds are stabilized and insulated from market fluctuations as long as they remain in good standing.

The statement values of preferred stocks meeting qualifying tests are stabilized through being carried at cost. All common stocks, however, must be carried in the statement at year-end market values. This regulation has been an important factor in limiting common stock investments of life insurance companies, entirely aside from the various state laws directly limiting the holdings of common stocks to a relatively small percentage of assets.

Mandatory Securities Valuation Reserve

Recognizing that even apparently sound investments are not riskless and that losses occasionally occur, the NAIC also prescribed a "mandatory securities valuation reserve" to be built up by annual accruals out of income. The amount of the accruals with respect to each type of security varies according to the degree of risk to which they are deemed to be exposed, as do the maximum reserves that are to be held against each type of investment. This combination of stabilized carrying values and appropriate reserves is designed to reflect the fact that a life insurance company is a permanent, or at least a very long-lived, institution that need not concern itself greatly about what might be realized on investments if they were to be liquidated on the securities markets. A life insurance company is not precluded from capitalizing on market opportunities, but it usually has the option of holding its existing portfolio of securities until they mature or are redeemed.

Federal Income Tax

The federal income tax has an important impact on investment policy. Prior to 1958, when the present federal income tax for life insurance companies became effective, there existed a relationship between taxes and investment income that was the same for every company, was easily understood, and posed no portfolio management problems. The situation changed dramatically with the enactment of the present law, which is so complex as to make its impact upon a given investment transaction very difficult to ascertain, and subject to varying interpretations. The incidence of the tax furthermore is now peculiar to the particular company involved, and the tax results of one company cannot be generalized for another.

One undesirable and unintentional characteristic of the present income tax is that it is highly progressive, increasing as a function of the interest rate on the investment portfolio. The progressive characteristic of the tax results from the use of an approximate actuarial formula to compute adjusted life reserves for tax purposes, a formula that was never intended to be used when there is a substantial difference in interest rates. With interest rates in recent years rising to record levels, the present law has become an anachronism and results in seriously high marginal rates of taxation.

The present federal income tax law penalizes prudent risk-taking by life insurance companies compared to other savings and investing institutions. The law assumes that the return on an investment, no matter how speculative in nature, is wholly riskless, and no allowance can be charged against investment income for prospective investment losses as a bad debt reserve, or for losses that are actually realized. This is diametrically opposed to the tax treatment of commercial banks, savings banks, and savings and loan companies. Due to the progressive nature of the income tax, a security involving more risk and therefore a higher interest rate is taxed at a *higher* rate than a low-risk security or portfolio. Thus, a life insurance company not only gets no allowance for increased risk as a deduction from gross investment yield for tax purposes, but it is penalized in effect for taking the higher risk. The impact of this unique provision is magnified when the general level of interest rates is high.

The treatment of tax-free income in the life insurance income tax law also has an important and discriminatory effect upon life insurance investments. For other investors, tax-exempt interest is received entirely tax free and for corporate investors 85 percent of intercorporate dividends is received tax free. For life insurance companies, however, a proration of such income is made on the theory that a deduction for a portion of the income in question already has been granted in connection with reserve interest requirements. No such proration, for example, is made in connection with such income received by banks even though substantial deductions already have been given to the bank as a result of interest paid which would be comparable to the reserve interest deduction in life insurance.

The practical effect of this peculiarity of the law is virtually to eliminate life insurance companies as potential investors in municipal bonds. Thus, a 5 percent municipal bond provides an after-tax yield to a bank equivalent roughly to a 10 percent corporate bond, but to an average life insurance company, a 5 percent municipal bond would be roughly equivalent to a corporate bond yield in the general area of 6.5 percent. In a similar manner, preferred stocks are rendered much less attractive to life insurance companies than to other corporate investors, and as a result there is little life insurance company purchasing of preferred stocks.

Liquidity Needs

The flow of people's savings into the life insurance business has been large, and relatively stable and predictable, running between $8 and $10 billion a year. The total cash flow available for investment is much larger and less stable because it includes the proceeds from sales, maturities, calls and prepayments of investments as well as the inflow of new savings. The history of a relatively stable and predictable cash flow gave rise to an important determinant of life insurance investment policy, namely, the relative lack of need for liquidity. The lack of liquidity need is reflected in negligible holdings of cash and cash equivalent, and a concentration in the higher yielding nonmarketable area of investments.

Inflation and the behavior of interest rates and policy loans have caused many companies to reassess the need for liquidity in life insurance investment portfolios. The policy loan feature that is a characteristic of American life insurance was conceived primarily as a source of last resort for cash. The interest rate on policy loans, which is guaranteed for existing contracts, was therefore set as a penalty rate, well above other going rates at the time. But with the dramatic rise of interest rates in the last several years to levels far above historical experience, the policy loan interest rate, instead of being a penalty rate of last resort, has become an opportunity rate—the lowest rate available in the market. Thus under tight money conditions when short-term money is scarce and short-term interest rates rise well above the policy loan rate, policyowners avail themselves of their cash values through cheap interest rate loans. In 1966 and again in 1969–70, policy loans rose sharply, and coupled with this rise, the prepayments of existing loans declined sharply. The net result was a sharp curtailment of funds available for investment just when such investment would have been advantageous for the company and the majority of its policyowners. With substantial forward commitments outstanding, many life companies were forced to withdraw entirely from the market, and in some cases liquidation of existing investments was necessary at a time highly disadvantageous for sales.

As a consequence of this more recent experience, a reevaluation of liquidity needs has been under way in the life insurance business. To the extent that liquidity is deemed important, it will change the investment mix of life companies, limit their forward commitments, and tend to reduce their investment return as a necessary payment for liquidity.

At the same time, these events have given rise to a movement to modernize the anachronistic policy loan interest rate for future policies, either by raising the permissible rate substantially, or by making it a flexible rate geared to the general level of interest rates prevailing at any given time.

SPECIAL CHARACTERISTICS OF THE INVESTMENT PROCESS IN LIFE INSURANCE

Forward Commitments

Life insurance companies are primarily lenders at interest. Under normal circumstances, they have less need for liquidity and marketability than other types of financial institutions, and the stability of their cash flow makes it comparatively easy for them to look and plan ahead over relatively long periods of time. Most of their investments directly finance large productive undertakings such as factories, utility plants, office buildings and apartment houses. These projects also are planned well in advance, and their permanent financing usually is arranged before they are physically completed. Consequently, life insurance companies frequently enter into agreements to make investments a year or more in the future. These arrangements are called "forward commitments." The total backlog of such commitments outstanding frequently exceeds the industry's annual cash flow.[9] This unique characteristic of the life insurance

---

[9] This does not necessarily mean that the industry's or a given company's entire cash flow is committed for the next 12 months since a portion of those commitments will be for settlement, or "takedown," more than a year in the future.

investment process makes the planning of large productive undertakings far easier and more effective than it otherwise would be.

Direct Placements

One of the principal characteristics of life insurance investment policies has been their emphasis on the direct placement of corporate bonds. Direct placements are issues of securities with a maturity of over five years, the terms of which are negotiated directly between the borrower and the lender, and title to which passes directly from the borrower to the lender.

Life insurance companies played an important role in the development of the direct placement market, which up until the last few years has accounted for one third to one half of total corporate bond financing, the balance being offered to the general public through underwriters. Direct placements accounted for some 90 percent of industrial bond purchases of life insurance companies, and the life insurance companies often accounted for over 90 percent of all direct placements. But with the shrinkage in life insurance cash flow in the tight money periods of 1966 and 1969–70, and with the large increase in the supply of corporate bonds in the last few years, direct placements have declined in importance relative to public issues.

Direct placements offer great advantages to small borrowing corporations, both in the very sizable reduction in the total cost of financing and in the convenience and flexibility which they afford. Unlike the small borrower, the large corporate borrower has ready access to the public market at favorable financing costs; yet very often the large borrower also has chosen the direct placement over the public offering for several other reasons. In addition to flexibility and convenience, direct placements offer the ability to change provisions expeditiously when circumstances change, and the ability to secure a forward commitment fixing the financing costs of a project when it is first planned without having to draw down the funds until they are needed.

Diversification

All investments involve some risk, and the fundamental task of life insurance investment policy is to maximize yield while minimizing risk. One practical way of achieving both of these contradictory objectives as far as possible is to diversify investments, and life insurance companies practice diversification on a very wide scale. Even a company of moderate size will have investments in literally thousands of different situations. The risk that one or a few bad decisions could have a calamitous impact upon the company and its policyowners is virtually nonexistent.

Life insurance companies typically finance new productive enterprises directly to a much greater extent than they invest in existing securities on the secondary market. Therefore, changes in portfolio composition over time tend to reflect changes in the growth rates of the various sectors of our economy. For example, the industry's railroad bond holdings have only doubled since 1920 while holdings of public utility bonds have increased more than one hundredfold and holdings of industrial bonds a thousandfold.

DISTRIBUTION OF LIFE
INSURANCE COMPANY ASSETS[10]

Of the total of $222 billion of life insurance company assets held at the beginning of 1972, $210 billion, or 94.7 percent, were invested in mortgages, corporate stocks and bonds, government securities, policy loans, and real estate. Miscellaneous assets, including cash, amounted to 5.3 percent of the total. Figure 68–1 shows the distribution of assets of life insurance companies as of January 1, 1972.

**FIGURE 68–1.   Distribution of Assets of U.S. Life
Insurance Companies, January 1, 1972**

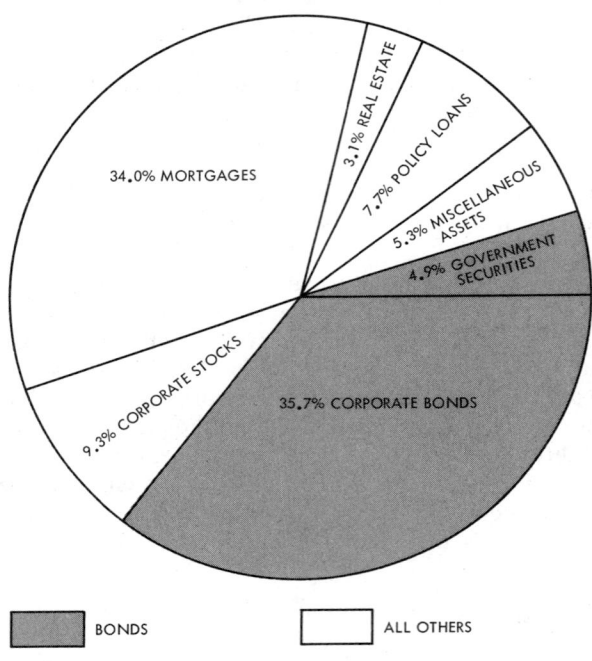

Source: Institute of Life Insurance.

In the early years of life insurance, cash was an important asset, often amounting to 15 percent or more of total assets. After 1900, cash declined as a percentage of assets to less than 1 percent in the period 1926–30. With the depression, demands on liquidity and a substantial increase in lapses, surrenders and policy loans, cash holdings rose after 1931 to 3.6 percent of assets in 1935. Since then the tendency was again steadily downward, and in the past 10 years has remained at less than 1 percent of assets. This low percentage of cash represents the desire of the companies to minimize nonearning assets, and the availability of interest-bearing short-term obligations to supply whatever liquidity is necessary.

---

[10] The source of statistics in this section is the *Life Insurance Fact Book, 1972* (New York: Institute of Life Insurance, 1972).

Mortgages

Mortgage debt on housing is probably one of the oldest forms of debt instrument. Therefore, it is not surprising that in the early years of life insurance, mortgages comprised as much as 90 percent of invested assets. While not as important as they once were, mortgages have continued to be a very important area of investment for life companies, generally amounting to more than one third of assets. The composition of mortgage holdings has changed materially over time. For many years, holdings of residential mortgages, particularly FHA and VA mortgages on one- to four-family dwellings dominated life insurance mortgage portfolios. In recent years, there has been a strong trend away from FHA and VA mortgages into the conventional uninsured areas, particularly in apartment mortgages and other large commercial mortgages. At the end of 1971, such conventional nonfarm mortgages totaled over $53.5 billion, or somewhat over two thirds of total mortgage holdings of $75.5 billion.

Corporate Bonds

A striking characteristic of life insurance investment portfolios in the early years of the business was the absence of any corporate bonds. The reason for this lay primarily in legal restrictions and in the lack of seasoning of such securities.

The first corporate bond investment took place in the railroad industry and since that time it has spread to public utilities and industrials; now, corporate bonds comprise a major investment outlet, approximating mortgage holdings.

Public Utility Bonds. The real development of a life insurance public utility portfolio started in the twenties when the electric utilities and the telephone industry began their great expansion. By 1937 they became the most important life insurance bond investment, passing the railroads. In 1950 they reached a peak of 16.5 percent of assets and totaled $10 billion. Since that time, while they have increased steadily in absolute amount, they have declined steadily as a percentage of assets, and now represent approximately 9 percent of assets. The primary reason for this relative decline in public utility bonds, which are predominantly publicly offered, has been their relatively unattractive yield to insurance companies. The life companies have preferred direct placements with higher yields and better call protection.

Railroad Bonds. At the height of railroad development, railroad bonds were the largest holdings of life insurance companies, reaching a peak of over one third of life insurance assets in 1906. They have declined sharply over the years as a percentage of assets, reflecting the relative decline of the railroads, and now comprise well under 2 percent of assets. Any new investments now are most likely to take the form of equipment trust certificates which are secured by a lien on rolling stock after a 20 percent down payment by the railroad and have 1- to 15-year maturities for rapid amortization.

Industrial and Miscellaneous Bonds. A heterogeneous category of bonds is comprised of industrial bonds; commercial bonds issued by department stores, food chains, and the like; finance bonds such as finance company obligations; and miscellaneous bonds of all types not elsewhere classified.

Life insurance companies had almost no bonds in this category until the thirties. As late as 1929 they totaled only 1.5 percent of assets. Beginning with the recovery from the 1932 depression, industrial and miscellaneous bonds rose steadily as a percentage of assets, and by 1951 industrials became the largest corporate bond holding, passing public utility bonds. At the end of 1971 such holdings totaled $55 billion and amounted to 25 percent of assets. A very large percentage of these bonds have been direct placements.

Government Securities

U.S. Government Bonds. With the unavailability of other investment outlets during World War II, life insurance companies invested heavily in U.S. government securities. At the end of the war, these bonds comprised an unprecedented 46.8 percent of assets. Since that time, reflecting the relative lack of attractiveness of U.S. government securities due to the pegging of their prices until 1951 and, more recently, the ceiling on interest rates of long-term governments and the higher rates on mortgages and direct placements, the holdings of U.S. government bonds have steadily declined until now they comprise about 2 percent of assets.

U.S. State and Local Bonds. Holdings of state and local municipal bonds have not been as attractive to life insurance companies as to other investors because of the peculiar characteristics of the life insurance federal income tax law. At the end of 1971, such holdings amounted to 1.5 percent of assets.

Securities of Foreign Governments and International Agencies. Foreign government bond investments, except Canadian issues, are strictly limited by law. Total foreign government investments at the end of 1971 totaled less than 1.5 percent of life insurance company assets, most of which consisted of Canadian holdings.

Equities

Equity investments have been strictly limited for life insurance companies, whether such equities be in the form of common stock or real estate. However, with the advent of inflation and greater institutional investment in equities, the laws have become somewhat less restrictive and the investment in equities has grown; but it still remains small relative to total assets.

Common Stocks. Common stocks historically have not been an important investment for the life insurance industry.[11] In the first place, there have been severe legal limitations placed upon the ability to invest in common stocks. In New York state, the most influential state with reference to life insurance regulation, investment in common stocks was made illegal after the Armstrong investigation; and it was not until 1951 that it was legalized to the minor extent of the lesser of 3 percent of assets

---

[11] See "Separate Accounts" discussed later in chapter.

or one third of surplus. Since that time, the legal permissible limits have generally increased for all states. As mentioned previously, New York state now permits common stock investment up to the lesser of 10 percent of assets or 100 percent of surplus.

In addition to the direct legal limitations, the surplus position of the business combined with the valuation requirement that common stocks be carried at year-end market value has limited the extent of interest in them. Thus, total holdings of common stocks at the end of 1971 totaled $17 billion or 7.5 percent of assets, well under the legally permissible percentage.

Preferred Stocks. Preferred stocks, for reasons similar to those affecting municipal bonds, generally have not been attractive as life insurance investments. As of the end of 1971 they totaled $3.8 billion, or 1.7 percent of assets.

Real Estate. As of the end of 1971, real estate holdings of the life insurance business totaled $6.9 billion, or somewhat over 3 percent of assets, having remained relatively constant at this figure for about 15 years. Nevertheless, as in the case of common stocks, there is increasing interest in investment in real estate equities and a tendency for legal limitations in this area to be liberalized. A number of companies have formed subsidiaries to invest in real estate equities.

Participation in real estate equities through mortgages has become a definite trend, either through the purchase of the land underlying a mortgage which is made on the improvement, or through the medium of participation of some type in the income from the property. Some lenders participate through being given an equity position in a project, though the percentage of income approach is more common. Both of these extra income inducements were mainly the result of stringent money conditions when rising bond market yields made the sluggish mortgage rate noncompetitive. Thus, by offering a participation not available in the bond market, funds were loosened for real estate investing.

An ongoing result of this condition was the joint venture—a partnership between a life company or subsidiary and a builder to develop and own real estate. The usual situation shows the builder finding land and performing the role of entrepreneur and the life insurance company furnishing equity funds. In many cases the long-term financing is secured from a third party. The returns possible are substantially larger than those available in the mortgage market.

Finally, a growing number of life insurance companies have established real estate investment trusts for which they serve as advisor and receive management advisory fees. These REITs are one example of the recent trend toward broadened financial services offered by the life insurance business.

Policy Loans

Policy loans have been discussed earlier in connection with factors determining life insurance investment policy. At the end of 1971, policy loans amounted to $17 billion, or 7.7 percent of assets, and they have been increasing as a percentage of assets for more than 15 years. The importance of policy loans varies considerably among companies depending upon the type of insurance written and the market served. For many companies, policy loans comprise a percentage of assets double the average for the life insurance business as a whole.

BROADENING RANGE OF FINANCIAL SERVICES OFFERED BY LIFE INSURANCE COMPANIES

In recent years the impact of inflation upon the savings habits of the American people has tended to erode the life insurance business's position as the major channel through which the savings stream flows. The business has responded to this challenge by developing a number of equity-oriented products with appeal to a wide range of savers under present conditions.

Separate Accounts

Until recent years, the life insurance business suffered from two severe handicaps in competing with uninsured pension funds for private pension business. The first, a tax disadvantage, was largely removed by a revision of the federal income tax law; the second was the legal limitation on investment in common stocks. The second limitation was removed through the development of the separate account.

The separate account is an asset account established by a life insurance company separate from other funds, and used primarily for group pension plans. Through these separate accounts, life companies can offer any type of investment funding that the pension buyer desires, whether wholly fixed income or wholly equity funds, or a combination of both. Separate account purchases of common stocks have dominated the life insurance companies' increased investment in common stocks since 1965. Separate account holdings of common stocks at the end of 1971 were $6.4 billion; this accounts for over one third of the total common stockholdings of $16.8 billion and for approximately two thirds of the net increase in industry common stockholdings since 1965.

Variable Annuities and Variable Life Insurance

In recent years there has been a strong trend for life insurance companies to offer variable annuities on both a group and an individual basis. The investment medium for such products is a common stock portfolio. This portfolio may be in a separate account within the asset structure of the insurance company or it may be in a mutual fund established and managed by the insurance company or its subsidiary.

In addition, the actuarial basis has been developed for variable life insurance contracts in which the face value of the life insurance will vary in accordance with the performance of an equity portfolio.

To the extent that the sale of these variable equity-based products grows, so will the life insurance investment in common stocks.

SELECTED REFERENCES

Brimmer, Andrew F. *Life Insurance Companies in the Capital Market.* East Lansing, Mich.: Michigan State University, 1962.

Denney, Rua, and Schoen. *Federal Income Taxation of Insurance Companies.* 2d ed. Scottdale, Pa.: Herald Press, 1966.

Fraine, Harold G. *Valuation of Securities Holdings of Life Insurance Companies.* Homewood, Ill.: Richard D. Irwin, Inc., 1962.

Institute of Life Insurance. *Life Insurance Fact Book, 1972.* New York, 1972.

Life Insurance Association of America. *Life Insurance Companies as Financial Institutions.* Englewood Cliffs, N.J.: Prentice-Hall, Inc., 1962.

Walter, James E. *Investment Process.* Cambridge, Mass.: Harvard University, Press, 1961.

69

Company Financial Statements

By B. FRANKLIN BLAIR

BECAUSE LIFE and health insurance companies differ fundamentally from most other forms of business enterprise, the annual financial reports of such insurance companies differ considerably from those of most other corporations. The purpose of this chapter is to describe the significant information contained in a typical report of such a company. For obvious reasons, this chapter does not cover the details of such a broad subject or mention unusual situations which pertain only to small segments of the insurance business.

ANNUAL STATEMENT FILED WITH INSURANCE DEPARTMENT

Each company must file an annual statement (on a calendar-year basis) with the insurance department of its home state and that of every other state in which it is licensed to do business. The annual statements must be on a standard form, called "convention blank" or "association blank," which (with a few relatively minor exceptions) is the same in every state and is prescribed by the National Association of Insurance Commissioners.[1] The NAIC has also set forth detailed instructions for completing this blank, so that all companies use as nearly identical methods as are practicable in making the various entries.

The convention blank form of annual statement measures about 12 inches by 18 inches and, for a large company, may contain well over one hundred pages of detailed tables. As a result, its circulation is limited, so that policyowners, stockholders, most home office personnel, or field underwriters (agents) rarely see this form. However, anyone who is sufficiently interested may go to a state insurance department and ex-

---

[1] See Chapter 62 for further information on the regulation of life and health insurance.

amine the form for any company doing business in that state, since these convention blanks are public documents.

Using the convention blank as a source of basic data, most (if not all) companies prepare an annual report to their policyowners and/or stockholders. Throughout this chapter the term "annual report" refers to such reports. Because the term "annual statement" is confusingly similar to "annual report," the official annual statement will be referred to throughout as the "convention blank."

In addition to filing the convention blank, each company is subject to regular audits, or "examinations," at three- to five-year intervals. The examinations are under the supervision of the insurance department of the home state, but representatives of other states participate in the examination on a "zone basis." During these comprehensive examinations the state examiners not only check the correctness of the company's convention blank but also investigate such matters as claims practices and other dealings with policyowners. Reports on these examinations are available to the public in the insurance departments of many states.

TECHNICAL TERMS

Explanations of a few technical terms which appear in the convention blank may make it easier to understand annual statements. These include the following:

Ledger Assets

Ledger assets are assets which have actually been entered on the books (ledgers) of the company because the transaction by which each of these assets was acquired has actually been completed. Cash and investments (including policy loans) are the main ledger assets.

Nonledger Assets

Nonledger assets are those assets which exist but have not yet been entered on the books of the company because the transaction by which each of these assets was acquired has not actually been completed. The more important ones are:

1. *Overdue Investment Income (Interest, Rents, Dividends).* This is usually relatively small except perhaps in periods of severe economic depression.

2. *Accrued Investment Income.* This is income which has "accrued" on each investment since the last interest due date preceding the date of the report. For example, on a bond with interest payable semiannually on May 1 and November 1, there would be two months' accrued interest on December 31.

3. *Net Premiums Overdue or Deferred on Insurance and Annuities.* Net premium as used in the convention blank means the *tabular* net premium, without any loading for expenses or profit. The net premiums overdue or deferred for the balance of the current policy year may be counted as assets when the reserves are calculated on the assumption that pre-

miums are paid annually. This is traditional in connection with ordinary insurance and annuities, and is recognized in the convention blank. Because the reserve liability set up is the same as though premiums for the full year had already been paid, the nonledger asset of net overdue and deferred premiums is needed as an offset.[2]

4. *Excess of Market Value over Book Value of Common Stocks.* This represents unrealized capital gain.

Admitted Assets

Admitted assets are those recognized as sound assets by the various state regulatory authorities and hence "admitted" to the balance sheet in the convention blank. The assets shown in an annual report are all admitted assets.

Nonadmitted Assets

Nonadmitted assets are those not recognized as sound or admitted assets. The common types of nonadmitted assets are:

1. *Furniture and Equipment.* The value after depreciation of furniture and equipment is treated as an asset in many other types of businesses but (except in the case of large-scale electronic data-processing equipment) it is not counted as a good asset by an insurance company because of the difficulty of realizing this value if the company is liquidated.

2. *Agents' Balances.* Advances to agents, even though secured by commission equities, are nonadmitted assets.

3. *Overdue and Accrued Interest on Certain Overdue Mortgages.*[3] Companies are allowed a certain amount of choice in determining the length of the period after which overdue and accrued interest on mortgages should be treated as a nonadmitted asset. This item has been negligible in recent years.

4. *Excess of Book Value over Admitted Asset Value of Securities.* Unrealized capital loss is represented here.

Some nonadmitted assets are ledger assets (e.g., agents' balances), and some are nonledger assets (e.g., overdue interest).

Amortized Basis

The amortized basis is used to determine the admitted asset value of most bonds which are not in default and have a good investment rating.[4] On this basis, which is independent of current market values, the values

---

[2] Overdue or deferred premiums are not assets in the usual sense, since they are not recoverable by law. Moreover, if and when they are collected, certain expenses such as commissions and premium taxes become payable by the company. It is therefore appropriate that they should be set up as an asset on a "net" basis, as specified by the NAIC.

[3] No item of overdue interest is carried as an asset on bonds in default, because the market value of such bonds reflects the probable value of any interest in default.

[4] The term "bonds" is used throughout this chapter in a broad sense, including such investments as debentures, notes, trust certificates, and Treasury bills.

of a bond at the end of successive years proceed by regular adjustments up or down (as the case may be) from the purchase price to the maturity value. The adjustments are so calculated that the interest received plus upward adjustments (called accrual of discount) or minus downward adjustments (called amortization of premium) represents the same percentage yield every year on the amortized value for that year.

Nonamortizable Securities

Nonamortizable securities are those which cannot be valued on the amortized basis.[5] This category includes securities without a fixed maturity date or a fixed interest rate, and securities not meeting quality criteria; it includes bonds in default and all stocks. According to the valuation rules currently in use by the NAIC, the admitted asset value in general is: (1) market value for (a) bonds in default, (b) common stocks, and (c) preferred stocks not meeting dividend and sinking fund payments; and (2) cost for other preferred stocks.

Accrued or Revenue Basis; Cash Basis

If income or disbursements reported include only items which have been actually received or disbursed and put through the books, the income or disbursements are said to be on a "cash basis." If, however, items are included which have not been actually received or disbursed, but which will be attributable to the current accounting period, the income or disbursements are said to be on an "accrued basis" or "revenue basis."

Examples of income items which have not actually been received are accrued interest and overdue premiums. Examples of disbursement items which have not actually been disbursed are claims in course of settlement and taxes payable in the following year on the current year's operations.

Supplementary Contracts

Supplementary contracts arise when policy proceeds are left under optional methods of settlement.

BALANCE SHEET

The most essential feature of a convention blank or an annual report is probably the statement of financial condition, or balance sheet. This consists of a statement of the assets of the company and a statement of the liabilities (or obligations) and the capital and surplus.

The excess of the assets over the liabilities consists of capital (in a stock company) and surplus funds (both special and unassigned). As will be discussed in more detail later, the relation of the capital and surplus to the liabilities is often used as a very rough indication of the financial stability of the company.

---

[5] The term "securities" has a specialized meaning in insurance company parlance. It covers bonds and stocks, but not mortgages.

Assets

In a typical company, investments (including policy loans) and cash represent 95 percent or more of the assets.[6] The other kinds of admitted assets usually represent only small percentages of the total admitted assets, and include the investment income and premium items mentioned in the description of nonledger assets and also large-scale electronic data-processing equipment.

Liabilities

Reserves. By far the largest part of the liabilities of a life or health insurance company is represented by the single category "reserves."[7] Minimum standards for the calculation of most reserves are prescribed by the regulatory authorities. Where minimum standards are not prescribed, a company must satisfy the authorities that the reserve basis used is adequate. The details of the basis of the reserves are reported in the convention blank. In a number of states the insurance department makes an independent calculation of the reserves of domestic companies. Therefore, the adequacy of the reserve item can ordinarily be taken for granted.

In general, the lower the interest rate used for valuation, the larger is the reserve. Therefore, a low valuation interest rate is usually regarded as conservative and indicative of a strong basis of valuation. Also, the reserves are larger on a net level premium basis than on a preliminary term basis, so that the net level premium basis is the more conservative. However, there are a number of other factors which cannot be determined from the convention blank—such as the margins in the gross premiums and the size of the nonforfeiture benefits guaranteed—which should be taken into consideration in appraising the conservatism of a valuation basis.

In this chapter, reserves are regarded as including amounts held by the company under supplementary contracts, both with and without life contingencies.

Other Liabilities. The "other liability" items may be grouped into the following broad categories:

1. *Dividends Left to Accumulate at Interest.* The liability shown will include accrued interest to the date of the statement.
2. *Premiums Received in Advance and Premium Deposit Funds.* On premiums received in advance, the liability is the then discounted value, at the rate of discount allowed, of the premiums received but not yet due.
3. *Policyowner Dividends for the Following Year.* In respect to participating business, the generally accepted practice (except on group insurance) is to set up as a liability the estimated amount of dividends to policyowners for the entire following calendar year. This is on the theory that dividends in a given calendar year should be paid out of surplus earned in the preceding calendar year.

---

[6] See Chapter 68 for analysis of company investments.
[7] See Chapter 12 for analysis of reserves.

4. *Claims in Course of Settlement.* This or some similar heading embraces the following liabilities:

   a) Claims due but unpaid. This liability should be very small or non-existent, since claims are usually paid as soon as the completed papers are received.

   b) Resisted claims. This is also usually a small item.

   c) Other claims in course of settlement. This includes claims which are still under investigation or for which complete papers have not been received.

   d) Estimated liability for claims incurred on or before December 31 but not reported by that date.

5. *Taxes Accrued, Payable in Following Year.*
6. *Miscellaneous Liabilities.* The following are typical examples of miscellaneous liabilities.

   a) Expenses (including commissions) due or accrued but not yet paid.

   b) Dividends due to policyowners but not yet paid because they are to be applied to reduce premiums which have not been paid.

   c) Investment income paid in advance. Any interest (usually on mortgages and policy loans) or rents due after December 31 but paid to the company on or before December 31 must be set up as a liability, so that the surplus is just the same as though the interest is not received until the year it is due.

   d) Liability for funded retirement plans for employees or agents. This liability may be included in the regular reserves mentioned above or as a miscellaneous liability.

7. *Mandatory Securities Valuation Reserve.* Beginning in 1951, the convention blank for life and health companies has included as a liability a "mandatory securities valuation reserve." The amount of this reserve is determined by rather complex rules established by the NAIC. The purpose is to accumulate a reserve over a period of years to protect against adverse fluctuations in the values of securities (bonds and stocks) and against losses on their sale. The reserve is built up by annual increments until it reaches a specified maximum. The amount of the increment for any one year depends on the values of the bonds and stocks held, and on the net capital gains on bonds and stocks during the year. Companies have been permitted, within limits, to add to the reserve more than the required increment.

   This reserve relates only to bonds and stocks. It is not intended to protect against depreciation in the values of other types of investments, such as mortgages and real estate; such investments have no effect on the size of this reserve.

8. *Special Liabilities.* Companies occasionally set up liability items of various kinds to cover special situations where there is greater uncertainty than usual as to whether there actually will be any additional liability, or where it is too difficult to determine exactly the amount of the extra liability to warrant including it in the regular items. Such items would be shown separately in the convention blank. In the annual

report, however, these special items would probably be included under "miscellaneous liabilities" unless they were unusually large.

Capital and Surplus

As indicated earlier, the excess of assets over liabilities consists of capital and surplus.[8] Capital, of course, appears only on the balance sheets of stock companies. Although it represents the interest of the stockholders in the company, it nevertheless is available for the protection of the policyowners. Their interests come before those of the stockholders if the company runs into any difficulties.

Surplus appears in the convention blank (and also in the annual reports of some companies) in one of two forms:

1. *Special Surplus Funds.* In some companies, part or all of the surplus is allocated to cover special contingencies. The types of contingencies which might be covered are illustrated by the following actual examples: "Voluntary Reserve for Strengthening of Policy Reserves," "Group Life Insurance Reserve for Epidemics," and "Special Reserve for Possible Loss or Fluctuation in the Value of Investments." A company may even carry its entire surplus in one special surplus fund to cover all unforeseen contingencies.
2. *Unassigned Surplus.* This represents either the entire surplus or the part not assigned to cover specific or general contingencies.

The earmarking of surplus to cover special contingencies can be changed from year to year. For example, a special reserve for investment fluctuation set up at the end of one year could be used during the following year to take care of mortality fluctuations.

SUMMARY OF OPERATIONS

The "summary of operations" in the convention blank presents an analysis on an *accrued* basis of the operating income of the company for the year and of the disposition of the income, excluding in both cases certain types of nonrecurring items, such as capital gains and losses. These nonrecurring items are included in the "surplus account," described later.

Income

Income ordinarily consists of the following items:

1. *Premiums from Policyowners.* This is usually by far the largest income item.
2. *Considerations for Supplementary Contracts (Settlement Options) and Dividends Left to Accumulate at Interest.* Death claims, maturities,

---

[8] There is some tendency in the annual reports of companies (in other types of business as well as in insurance) to treat portions (or all) of "surplus" as "contingency reserves" or "margins for contingencies." This tendency stems from the possible unfavorable connotation of "surplus," which implies an excess, or more than is needed. Thus, surplus might imply to policyowners that a life company was retaining larger funds than necessary and paying smaller dividends to them than it could.

and surrenders are included in the benefits paid, even when the proceeds are placed under a settlement option. Therefore the amount of such proceeds must also be included in income if the books are to balance. A similar situation exists with respect to dividends left to accumulate, because such dividends are included in dividends paid.

3. *Investment Income (Interest, Dividends, Rents, and Other Income Arising from Investments).* The convention blank calls for reporting investment income on a "net" basis, that is, *after* deducting investment expenses and taxes. (Federal income tax is not regarded as an investment tax.)

4. *Miscellaneous Income.* This is usually quite small in relation to total income; it includes minor items which do not fit clearly into one of the first three categories mentioned.

Deductions from Income

It might be expected that "income" would be followed by "outgo" in the summary of operations. However, the term "outgo" should not, strictly speaking, be used as the counterpart of "income." Much of the income of a life insurance company does not actually "go out" in the same year it is received but instead is retained for the benefit of policyowners and beneficiaries in the form of increased reserves and increased surplus (if the company is growing satisfactorily). Therefore, a more accurate term, such as "disposition of income" or "how the income was applied," is often used in annual reports to refer to the various items deducted from income to obtain the net gain from operations.

Many of the "deductions from income" are self-explanatory. The items may be grouped into the following major categories:

1. *Contractual Benefits to Policyowners and Beneficiaries.* These benefits include:

   a) Death benefits (including accidental death benefits).
   b) Matured endowments.
   c) Disability and health insurance benefits.
   d) Annuity payments (including annuity surrender values).
   e) Cash surrender values of insurance.
   f) Payments under supplementary contracts.
   g) Withdrawals of accumulated dividends.

   As mentioned earlier, the figures for benefits paid include policy proceeds left with the company under supplementary contracts as well as proceeds paid out in cash.

2. *Increase in Required Reserves Held for the Benefit of Policyowners and Beneficiaries.* This represents the increase in these reserves from the beginning of the year to the end of the year.

3. *Operating Expenses and Taxes.* This category excludes investment expenses and taxes (which are deducted from gross investment income) and also excludes federal income taxes. The principal types of disbursements included here are:

  a) Compensation of employees.
  b) Compensation of agents. A substantial part of the total expenses usually consists of commissions and other forms of compensation to agents (including brokers).
  c) General operating expense. This includes such expenses as rent, furniture, equipment, supplies, printing, postage, telephone, and advertising. In order to keep expenses on a comparable basis whether the home office is owned or rented, a company which owns a home office building is required to charge itself rent on a reasonable basis. As a result, home office rent is counted both as an expense and as an offsetting income item when the home office is owned. Except among the smaller companies, most companies own their home offices.
  d) Taxes, such as state taxes on premiums (which are a substantial amount), miscellaneous license fees, and social security taxes.

Net Gain from Operations and Dividends to Policyowners

In the last part of the summary of operations in the convention blank, the net gain from operations, dividends to policyowners, and federal income tax (excluding the tax on capital gains) are taken into consideration. Capital gains and losses are excluded in this last part, which is essentially as follows:

1. Net gain from operations before dividends to policyowners and federal income taxes—this net gain is equal to the income less the above deductions from income.
2. Dividends to policyowners.
3. Net gain from operations after dividends to policyowners and before federal income taxes (item 1 minus item 2).
4. Federal income taxes incurred.
5. Net gain from operations after dividends to policyowners and federal income taxes (item 3 minus item 4).

Treatment of Federal Income Tax

The federal income tax on an accrued basis is divided into the following three parts, each of which is treated differently in the convention blank:

1. Tax on current year's operations (excluding tax on capital gains)—this part is the same as item 4, mentioned in the preceding paragraph.
2. Tax on capital gains realized during the year—this part is deducted from the year's capital gains before the capital gains are brought into the surplus account, as described below.
3. Extraordinary amounts of taxes (or extraordinary refunds of taxes) relating to prior years.

The convention blank does not require the setting up of any liability for future income taxes on deferred income items.

SURPLUS ACCOUNT

In the convention blank the summary of operations is followed by an analysis of the surplus account, which reconciles the surplus at the beginning and end of the year. The method of reconciliation is as follows:

To the special, contributed and unassigned surplus at the beginning of the year, add any additions during the year, such as:

1. Net gain from operations *after* dividends to policyowners and federal income taxes (excluding tax on capital gains) and excluding capital gains and losses.
2. Net capital gains (realized and unrealized), less any federal income tax on realized gains.
3. Decrease in mandatory securities valuation reserve.
4. Increase in surplus of "separate account business" (this term is explained later).

From the sum, subtract any deductions from surplus during the year, such as:

1. Dividends to stockholders.
2. Net capital losses (realized and unrealized).
3. Extraordinary taxes relating to prior years.
4. Increase in reserves on account of change in valuation basis (reserve strengthening).
5. Increase in mandatory securities valuation reserve.
6. Decrease in surplus of separate account business.

The balance is equal to the special, contributed and unassigned surplus at the end of the year.

The surplus account is very helpful in giving an overall view of all factors affecting the company's surplus.

SEPARATE ACCOUNT BLANK

Life insurance companies now have the right, subject to certain prescribed conditions, to establish "separate accounts" for the handling of funds paid to a company in connection with pension or profit sharing plans or variable annuities.[9] Any investment income and any capital gains or losses on a separate account are credited or charged to the separate account. The insurance company in general makes no investment guarantees under a separate account.

At the present time, all detailed entries in respect to separate accounts are recorded in a special "separate account blank" completed by each insurance company doing any separate account business. Certain items and totals from the separate account blank are then included in the regular convention blank in order that the latter may show the financial picture for the entire company. Most companies with separate account business follow a similar procedure in their annual reports.

---

[9] See Chapter 40 for analysis of separate accounts pension funding.

EXHIBITS AND SCHEDULES IN
THE CONVENTION BLANK

Exhibits

Following the summary of operations and the surplus account in the convention blank is what is called the "gain and loss exhibit." The first part of this exhibit consists of a breakdown of each item in the summary of operations by *line of business,* as follows: (1) industrial, (2) ordinary, (3) group life insurance, (4) group annuities, (5) group health insurance, and (6) individual health insurance. The *ordinary* line is further subdivided into (1) life insurance, (2) disability, (3) accidental death benefits, (4) annuities, and (5) supplementary contracts.

The second part of the gain and loss exhibit is an analysis (by line of business, excluding health insurance) of the increase (or decrease) in the policy reserves from the beginning of the year to the end of the year.

There are many other exhibits and schedules in the convention blank which provide analyses of or further details in regard to items which appear only in total in the balance sheet or the summary of operations. The numbered exhibits cover the following subjects:

Exhibit 1.   Premium income and commissions.
Exhibits 2 and 3.   Investment income.
Exhibit 4.   Capital gains and losses on investments.
Exhibit 5.   General expenses.
Exhibit 6.   Taxes, licenses, and fees (excluding federal income taxes).
Exhibit 7.   Dividends to policyowners.
Exhibits 8, 9, and 10.   Policy and supplementary contract reserves.
Exhibit 11.   Policy claims.
Exhibit 12.   Reconciliation of ledger assets from the end of the previous year to the end of the current year.
Exhibits 13 and 14.   Ledger, nonledger, nonadmitted, and admitted assets.

There is also a "policy exhibit" analyzing the life insurance issued, terminated, and in force, and a corresponding "annuity exhibit." Following the exhibits, there is a page of "general interrogatories" about the company's history and operations.

Schedules

In general, the lettered schedules show even more detail than the numbered exhibits. Among the more important schedules are those dealing with invested assets: *Schedule A,* real estate; *Schedule B,* mortgages; *Schedule C,* collateral loans; *Schedule D,* bonds and stocks; and *Schedule BA,* other invested assets, such as transportation equipment, mineral rights, and oil royalties. These schedules show, in various classifications, the amounts owned at the end of the year and purchases and sales during the year. In *Schedules C, D,* and *BA,* each holding is listed individually.

Other important lettered schedules give detailed information on the following subjects:

Schedule E. Bank balances.

Schedule F. Resisted and compromised claims.

Schedule G. Salaries of ten highest paid persons and of all others receiving more than $30,000 a year.

Schedule J. Legal fees.

Schedule K. Expenses in connection with appearances before legislative bodies.

Schedule L. Proceedings at the last annual election of directors.

Schedule M. Dividends per $1,000 of insurance on certain plans of life insurance on (1) a 20-year historical basis and (2) a 20-year illustrative basis on the current scale.

Schedule T. Premiums received, analyzed by state—this schedule is helpful to the state taxing authorities in checking the payment of premium taxes.

ANNUAL REPORTS TO POLICYOWNERS AND STOCKHOLDERS

The scope and the amount of detail included in annual reports to policyowners and/or stockholders vary considerably from company to company (and even from year to year in many companies). In general, the annual reports present in condensed form the balance sheet, the summary of operations, and the surplus account. Frequently, a number of other items are presented, including information about any subsidiaries owned. Also, there is often considerable explanatory text, frequently of a sales promotion nature. The information given in the report serves its purpose only when it is read and understood, so companies try to make their reports readable and useful in promoting good public relations.

Where a stock life or health insurance company is owned by a holding company, the annual report to the stockholders will be addressed to the stockholders of the holding company; the insurance company's operations will be reported on only as part of the holding company's total operations. However, in some cases a wholly owned stock insurance company will issue a report to policyowners for public relations purposes.

Differences between Annual Report and Convention Blank

In addition to the fact that the information in an annual report is condensed, there are often other differences between the presentation of information in an annual report and the presentation in the convention blank, particularly in the summary of operations. The more common important areas of difference include the following:

1. In the convention blank, considerations for supplementary contracts are shown separately from premiums. In the annual report, considerations for supplementary contracts are often included in premiums.
2. In the convention blank, investment income is reported on a *net* basis, that is, *after* deducting investment expenses and taxes. Many companies, in their annual reports, follow the precedent of the convention

blank and show net investment income; but a number of companies show investment income on a *gross* basis, that is, *before* deducting investment expenses and taxes (in which case these investment expenses and taxes are included with other expenses and taxes in the "deductions from income"). Or a company may use some intermediate basis, deducting certain parts (but not all) of investment expenses and taxes to determine the investment income shown in its annual report.

3. In the convention blank, the "dividends to policyowners" item is the next to the last deduction in the summary of operations. However, many companies, in their annual reports, include dividends to policyowners with other benefit payments to policyowners and beneficiaries, so that such dividends appear instead as one of the first deductions from income. By following this procedure, these companies avoid showing the "net gain from operations before dividends to policyowners." The term "net gain" may carry an incorrect connotation, implying that the company, as distinguished from the policyowners, is profiting from the gain. Therefore, there is some feeling that using the term "net gain" is inadvisable. This applies particularly to "net gain before dividends," which is almost always a comparatively large figure in companies issuing participating insurance. The use in annual reports of the term "net gain after dividends" may also be avoided by using some title such as "transfer to surplus account" for what would otherwise be "net gain from operations after dividends to policyholders and federal income tax."

4. In the convention blank, all capital gains and losses are included in the surplus account. However, some companies, in their annual reports, include some or all of their net capital gains in regular income, generally as a separate and distinct item.

On the balance sheet, although items may be combined in the annual report, many states prohibit publishing a figure for total assets and liabilities different from those shown on the convention blank.

DIFFERENCES BETWEEN LIFE INSURANCE ACCOUNTING AND GENERALLY ACCEPTED ACCOUNTING PRACTICES

Financial reports of life and health insurance companies differ considerably from those of most other corporations largely because insurance companies have unique accounting problems, arising from the long-term nature of their insurance policies and from the assumptions which must be made with respect to mortality, morbidity, and investment return.[10] Major differences between the accounting practices of insurance com-

---

[10] "The results in any given year, as shown by a life insurance company's annual statement, are so much the product of estimates of future liabilities based on probabilities that the results themselves are essentially estimates instead of actualities." (Statement by American Life Convention, Life Insurance Association of America, and Life Insurance Conference, submitted on June 24, 1963, to Subcommittee on Securities of the Senate Banking and Currency Committee.)

panies and generally accepted accounting practices include the following points:

1. Commissions and other costs of acquiring premium income are charged to operations as they are incurred, rather than being deferred and charged to operations over the entire period that the premium income is received. As a result, there is usually a substantial drain on surplus for each new policy sold (particularly if reserves are set up on the net level premium basis). Consequently, an increase in the amount of new insurance sold may produce the result of a decrease in the net gain from operations, and a decrease in the new insurance sold may result in an increase in the net gain from operations. This practice differs from generally accepted accounting principles because revenue and costs are not being matched.
2. The asset values used for bonds are amortized values rather than cost or current market values.
3. The "nonadmitted assets," described earlier, are excluded from the assets as shown in the convention blank and in annual reports.
4. Contrary to generally accepted accounting practices, which would possibly restrict a portion of the total surplus for future value fluctuations, the mandatory securities valuation reserve is set up as a liability. Moreover, the amount of the mandatory securities valuation reserve is not directly related to the quality and current value of the securities.
5. No deferred liability is set up for future income tax liability on deferred income items such as:

   a) Unrealized net capital gains.
   b) Accelerated depreciation.
   c) Deferment of taxable income because of election to use net level premium reserves for tax purposes rather than the preliminary term reserves used in the convention blank.
   d) Untaxed income built up in the "policyholders surplus account" in stock life insurance companies.

"ADJUSTED" FIGURES FOR STOCK INSURANCE COMPANIES

A buyer or seller of capital stock in a life or health insurance company wants to have as good an idea as possible of what is a fair price. The book value of the stock may not necessarily be a good indicator of its fair market value, partly because there is usually a drain on surplus when new business is sold, and partly because in many companies (particularly the older ones) there is probably some understatement of surplus as a result of valuing assets low and liabilities high.

To attempt to arrive at a better indicator of reasonable prices for insurance company stocks and to obtain figures more consistent with those which would be obtained by the application of generally accepted accounting principles, many stock analysts and some insurance trade publications in the past have calculated "adjusted book values" and "adjusted earnings" for each company, taking into consideration by rough rules of thumb the assumed value of (1) the insurance in force and (2) the increase during the year in the insurance in force. The values assumed vary by the type of insurance.

"Conditional reserves" and their increase during the year may also be treated as equivalent to surplus in calculating "adjusted book values" and "adjusted earnings." These conditional reserves include the mandatory securities valuation reserve and amounts voluntarily set aside by management as reserves for possible future contingencies.

It should be strongly emphasized that rough rules of thumb for determining "adjusted book values" and "adjusted earnings" overlook many factors which have a marked effect on the proper value of the insurance in force. Among the more important of these factors are (1) the level of the gross premiums, (2) the interest rates assumed and earned, (3) the recent mortality experience, (4) the recent lapse rates, (5) the level of expenses, (6) the bases for valuing the insurance and annuity reserves, (7) the number of years the business has been in force, and (8) the quality of the assets.

The use of empirical schedules of the value of insurance is by no means the only method used to determine "adjusted book values" and "adjusted earnings." Recently considerable attention has been given to obtaining adjusted figures through the use of "natural reserves," substituting them for statutory reserves. Since 1970, several companies have issued their annual reports on this basis.

Natural reserves on nonparticipating insurance are based on the assumptions implicit in the gross premiums (after deducting the assumed profit margins in the premiums). Thus, these reserves take into account assumed mortality, interest, lapse rates, nonforfeiture values, and expenses. Because the heavy expenses in the first policy year are taken into account, the natural reserves are usually negative at the end of that year.

Thus the use of natural reserves has the effect of capitalizing first year expenses and recomputing reserves without regard to whether net level premium or preliminary term reserves are used in the convention blank. However, in addition to the amount of work and judgment involved in computing natural reserves, a number of other problems arise in actually using natural reserves, particularly on participating insurance and on plans where the cash value exceeds the natural reserve. Moreover, it is questionable whether a satisfactory method has yet been developed for recognizing any loss arising where it appears that subsequent experience will be markedly worse than the assumptions used in originally determining the natural reserves.

Despite strong sponsorship of the natural reserve method by a committee of the American Institute of Certified Public Accountants in 1971, it is too early to predict whether natural reserves will gain widespread use as a recognized method of obtaining figures in conformity with generally accepted accounting principles, particularly as applied to mutual companies.

It should be emphasized that the phrase "generally accepted accounting principles" is the special one adopted by the American Institute of

Certified Public Accountants to describe accounting methods accepted by that organization. It should not be inferred from the use of this phrase that other accounting methods, particularly those promulgated by insurance (or other) regulatory authorities, are somehow "not accepted." Each serves the purpose for which it was designed.

THE STRENGTH OF A COMPANY AS REVEALED BY ITS ANNUAL STATEMENT

How Realistic Are Balance Sheets?

"Value the assets low and the liabilities high." This epigram probably represents the basic policy of many of the life companies which have been established long enough to have the margins required for such a corporate policy. This does not mean that management arbitrarily fixes a low value on assets and a high value on liabilities, but simply that management generally tends, where a choice is presented, to choose the low value for an asset item and the high value for a liability item. State regulatory authorities often have encouraged this attitude in order to provide additional protection for the policyowners. Some examples of the application of such a policy will be presented.

Assets. Because of the definite rules of the NAIC on the valuation of securities and mortgages, conservatism in the valuation of specific assets is largely limited to two minor categories. These are:

1. *Real Estate, Particularly the Home Office and Real Estate Acquired by Foreclosure.* Real estate is supposed to be carried at its market value, but there is almost always leeway for judgment as to what is a fair market value at any time. Life companies usually tend to choose a conservative value; this tendency is furthered by the fact that it is common to write values down in deflationary periods but unusual to write them up in inflationary periods.

2. *Nonadmitted Assets.* Furniture and equipment are valuable assets in a going company (although they would probably have little value in the unlikely circumstance that the company had to be liquidated). The balances of most agents will eventually be collected. Therefore, treating furniture and equipment and agents' balances as nonadmitted assets tends to understate the true value of the assets.

The fact that no value is assigned to goodwill, to the agency force, or to future earnings on the insurance in force, is, of course, another instance of conservatism is determining the assets.

Liabilities. There is much more room for judgment in valuing the liabilities than in valuing the assets because the contingent nature of the major liabilities makes it necessary to assume interest rates for the calculation of present values as well as mortality and morbidity tables to measure any contingencies involved.

Unlike the convention blank, an annual report almost never gives any indication of the mortality and interest bases used in the calculation of reserves or of whether the life insurance reserves are calculated by the net level premium method or by a modified preliminary term method. As a result, it is almost impossible to tell from an annual report whether the reserve basis is at or near the prescribed minimum or whether the basis involves substantial margins of conservatism. Some trade publications, however, give information on the interest rates used in reserve calculations and also on the extent to which the net level premium method or other methods are used to determine the life insurance reserves. Conservatism also may be introduced by the methods used in the valuation of some of the minor liabilities.

An area in which companies differ considerably in setting up liabilities is the funding of retirement plans for employees and agents. As formal pension plans are almost a necessity for good employee relations, it is probable that sooner or later all life companies will set up formal funded plans. Viewed in this light, companies which have not set up reserves for past service credits could be regarded as having undervalued their future liability for this item. Another area where the liability may be understated is deferred income taxes, as mentioned earlier.

The mandatory securities valuation reserve is designed to involve a definite overstatement of liabilities. It introduces some inconsistencies between companies, since the relative size of the reserve is affected not only by the current investment portfolio but also by all capital gains and losses on securities from 1951 and by any voluntary increments.

Measures of the Strength of a Company

Although the entire picture—assets, liabilities, insurance in force, level of premiums, mortality experience, and so forth—is necessary in appraising the strength of a life company, nevertheless the single item which is of greatest significance as an indicator of the strength of a company is total surplus (including capital stock and special surplus funds as well as unassigned surplus). This figure is compared in most annual reports with the corresponding figure for the previous year, and the significant factors affecting the change from one year to the next are usually explained. It is particularly important that a suitable explanation be given if there is a decrease in surplus.

As an absolute figure, the amount of the surplus has little meaning. The surplus can only be evaluated in relation to some measuring rod. The two most commonly used relationships are (1) surplus as a percentage of liabilities and (2) surplus per $1,000 of insurance in force.

Surplus as a Percentage of Liabilities. Use of the ratio of surplus to liabilities has received the quasi approval of regulatory authorities, as evidenced by the fact that one large state limits surplus in life companies writing participating policies to $850,000 or 10 percent of "policy reserves and policy liabilities," if greater.[11] Nevertheless, this ratio is not completely satisfactory, because the surplus needed in relation to particular liabilities varies by type of business.

---

[11] The general purpose of this law is to prevent an undue accumulation of surplus at the expense of policyowners and to insure *annual* distribution of dividends.

For example, the reserves on both group and health insurance are usually quite small in relation to the amounts at risk. Therefore, a surplus of 10 percent of the reserves would be inadequate on group or health insurance. On the other hand, on types of business which do not involve mortality or morbidity contingencies—such types as supplementary contracts without life contingencies or dividends left to accumulate—surplus is needed only to protect against investment contingencies, so that a comparatively small surplus in relation to the liability would be satisfactory. Moreover, business with reserves on a minimum basis should probably have more surplus in relation to its liabilities than business with reserves on a very conservative basis. A comparatively small surplus in relation to the liability would also be satisfactory for separate account business because of the absence of investment guarantees on such business.

When surplus is expressed as a percentage of liabilities, no allowance is made for the proportions of the various types of liabilities. Therefore, this ratio is not entirely satisfactory for comparing companies which differ significantly in the composition of their business or in the basis of their reserves. Despite this drawback, the ratio is probably the most nearly satisfactory single criterion for measuring the financial strength of a company.

Because the mandatory securities valuation reserve is not a true liability, it can be argued that it should be subtracted from liabilities before calculating the ratio of surplus to liabilities. This refinement is theoretically justifiable but is probably unnecessary from a practical viewpoint.

Surplus per $1,000 of Insurance. Surplus per $1,000 of insurance in force has the advantage of giving greater weight to group insurance than does the ratio of surplus to liabilities. But surplus per $1,000 of insurance in force also has some disadvantages. This figure probably gives too great weight to group insurance. Also, it does not give any weight to annuities, supplementary contracts, health insurance, and the minor types of liabilities; all of these categories certainly need some surplus held for them. A minor disadvantage is the problem of how to handle reinsurance in calculating this figure. Business ceded to another company as reinsurance is usually included in the amount of insurance in force; but clearly, not much surplus is needed on business ceded to another company on the coinsurance basis.[12]

To a certain extent, the ratio of surplus to liabilities and the surplus per $1,000 of insurance are figures which complement each other. Probably a truer picture of a company can generally be obtained by looking at both figures than by looking at either figure alone.

Other Measures of Strength. Two ratios which are sometimes used as measures of the strength of a company involve "assets" instead of surplus. These ratios are (1) assets as a percentage of the liabilities and (2) assets per $1,000 of insurance in force.

Because the assets are equal to the liabilities plus the surplus, the figure for assets as a percentage of liabilities is simply 100 percent more than the

---

[12] See Chapter 66 for analysis of reinsurance.

figure for surplus as a percentage of liabilities. Therefore, similar results will be obtained whether comparisons are based on the ratio of surplus to liabilities or on the ratio of assets to liabilities.

On the other hand, the amount of assets per $1,000 of insurance in force is almost completely meaningless as a measure of the strength of a company. This figure does not reflect the strength of a company as much as it does the age and composition of the company's business.

SELECTED REFERENCES

American Institute of Certified Public Accountants. *Audits of Stock Life Insurance Companies.* New York, 1972.

Blair, B. Franklin. *Interpreting Life Insurance Company Annual Reports.* Bryn Mawr, Pa.: American College of Life Underwriters, 1968.

Bowles, Thomas F., Jr., and Coughtry, Lloyd S. "Certain Actuarial Considerations in Determining Life Insurance Company Equity Values," *Transactions of the Society of Actuaries,* Vol. XVII (1965), pp. 281–96.

Gold, M. L. "Valuing a Life Insurance Company," *Transactions of the Society of Actuaries,* Vol. XIV (1962), pp. 139–57.

Maclean, Joseph B. *Life Insurance.* 9th ed. New York: McGraw-Hill Book Co., Inc., 1962.

McDiarmid, Fergus J. "Valuation of Life Insurance Company Assets," *Transactions of the Society of Actuaries,* Vol. XVI (1964), pp. 390–408.

Noback, J. C. *Life Insurance Accounting.* Homewood, Ill.: Richard D. Irwin, Inc., 1969.

70

Taxation of Companies

By WILLIAM B. HARMAN, JR.

FEDERAL TAXATION

THE FEDERAL income taxation of life insurance companies has taken many different forms since 1913. From 1913 through 1920, life insurance companies were taxed on their total income, in a manner similar to other business corporations. After trying various investment income methods between 1921 and 1957, Congress reverted to a total income tax base in the Life Insurance Company Income Tax Act of 1959.[1]

It now appears fairly clear, after 15 years, that the 1959 Act has become the permanent method for taxing life insurance companies. As a result, one of the major problems confronting the life insurance business from the late forties to 1959—the development of a permanent and satisfactory federal income tax law—appears to have been resolved.

History of Federal Income Taxation
of Life Insurance Companies

The following is a very brief sketch of the various ways in which life insurance companies have been taxed under the federal income tax laws.

1913 to 1920—Total Income Base. Life insurance companies were taxed under the general provisions of the law applicable to ordinary corporations. There was no special section of the law devoted to life insurance companies. A life insurance company included in gross income its premium income, investment income, and capital gains. All deductions generally allowed to any corporation were allowed to life insurance companies. In addition, life insurance companies were allowed deductions for net additions to their reserve funds and claims payments under their insurance

---

[1] P. L. 86–69 was entitled "The Life Insurance Company Income Tax Act of 1959" although it was effective for the year 1958. The bill was passed by the Congress in 1959, and signed into law on June 25, 1959, by the President. The explanation of this misnomer in title is that it is customary to put in the title of a bill the year in which the bill is passed by the Congress rather than the particular year for which the bill becomes effective.

and annuity policies. In brief, life insurance companies were taxed on both underwriting and investment income—a total income base—for eight years.

1921 to 1957—Investment Income Base Only. From 1921 through 1957, life insurance companies were taxed only on their "free" or net investment income, that is, their investment income less (1) investment expenses and (2) interest on policy reserves. Investment income was limited to interest, dividends, and rents for most of this period. Investment expenses included expenses relating to the investment income, for example, investment department expenses, depreciation, and taxes. The major issue during this period was the determination of the amount of the policyowner reserve interest deduction, that is, the amount representing investment income needed for policy and contract obligations. This deduction was computed as follows:

1921 to 1931: Each company deducted 4 percent of its *own* insurance reserves.

1932 to 1941: Each company deducted 3.75 percent of its *own* insurance reserves.

1942 to 1948 (1942 formula): Each company deducted a fixed percentage of its net investment income. This percentage reflected (1) in part (35 percent), the portion of net investment income which the entire life insurance business added to its reserves during the preceding year; and (2) in part (65 percent), the portion of net investment income that the business would have needed for its reserves if all reserves had been on an arbitrary 3.75 percent basis. The percentage deduction allowed for each year and the tax liability of the life insurance business were as follows:

Year	Deduction Percentage (percent)	Tax Liability (millions)
1942	93.00	$27.4
1943	91.98	34.5
1944	92.61	34.5
1945	95.39	24.7
1946	95.95	21.8
1947	100.68	—
1948	102.42	—

In 1947 and 1948, the business paid no federal income tax since the reserve deduction percentage exceeded 100 percent of net investment income in each of these years. This was the beginning of the problem period which did not end until the 1959 act.

1949 to 1950 (stopgap formula): For these years, each company deducted a percentage of its net investment income—that portion of net investment income which the entire business needed during the preceding year for its reserves. These percentage deductions and the business tax liability for each year were as follows:

Year	Deduction Percentage (percent)	Tax Liability (millions)
1949	93.55	$42
1950	90.63	80

1951 to 1954 (1951 stopgap formula): For these years, the tax was 6.5 percent of each company's net investment income. This was the same, mathematically, as a tax at 52 percent on net investment income after deducting 87.5 percent of the first $1 million of net investment income and 85 percent of the remaining income.

1955 to 1957 (1955 stopgap formula): For these years, the deduction was 87.5 percent of the first $1 million of net investment income and 85 percent of the remaining income. The tax liability of life insurance companies was estimated to be $294 million in 1957.

1958 to Date—The Life Insurance Company Income Tax Act of 1959. Commencing with the year 1958, life insurance companies were subject to tax, at the regular corporate income tax rates, on their total income. Congress estimated that the revenue yield of the 1959 act would be approximately $500 million for the year 1958. This was approximately the same revenue yield as the 1942 formula would have produced if applied to the year 1958; if the 1955 formula had been applied to the year 1958, the estimated revenue yield would have been approximately $319 million.

The revenue yield under the 1959 Act was $455 million for the year 1958, and it has steadily increased to an amount of $1,143 million in 1968.[2] The revenue estimate for the year 1958 was approximately 10 percent larger than the tax liability reported by companies for the year. However, this revenue yield has been increased due to adjustments made by revenue agents upon audit and various court decisions interpreting the law. Thus, the original revenue estimate for $500 million was quite accurate and, possibly, even slightly low. The increase in tax liability of the life insurance business over the years is probably an accurate reflection of the growth of the business, e.g., assets have doubled between 1957 and 1970, investment yield rates have increased over this period, and mortality experience has not changed appreciably.

Basic Outline of the 1959 Act

The 1959 Act taxes a life insurance company at the corporate tax rates on its income from all sources. The elements that comprise taxable income of a life insurance company are summarized in Table 70–1.

The gain-from-operations tax base of a life insurance company is comparable to the taxable income base of other corporations. This base represents the total income of a life insurance company—all its receipt items have been included and it has been allowed to reduce this income by certain deductions and exclusions.

Gross Amounts. 1. *Premiums and Annuity Considerations.* A life insurance company has two basic sources of income—its receipts from its insurance business and its income from its investment operation. A company must include in its gross amounts all its premiums and other considerations received on its insurance and annuity contracts. These receipts

---

[2] These tax liability figures have been obtained from the Statistics of Income series published annually by the Internal Revenue Service. See Thomas G. Nash, Jr., *Federal Taxation of Life Insurance Companies* (New York: Matthew Bender, 1965), Appendix 4, Life Insurance Company Federal Statistics, for a detailed discussion of the revenue effect of the 1959 Act.

TABLE 70–1.   Outline of Items Comprising Gain (or Loss) from Operations

Gross Amounts	1. Premiums and annuity considerations 2. Gross investment income 3. All other items of gross income 4. Long-term capital gains 5. Decreases in reserves
Less	
Exclusion—Policyowners	Exclusion for policyowners' share of investment income
Less	
General Deductions	1. Ordinary corporate deductions 2. Investment and similar expense deductions 3. Deductions peculiar to insurance business
Equals	
Tentative Gain (or Loss) from Operations	
Less	
Special Deductions— Subject to Limitation	Special deductions for: 1. Policyowner dividends 2. Nonparticipating policies 3. Group life insurance and accident and health insurance
Equals	
Gain from Operations or Loss from Operations	Tax Base

include such items as fees, deposits, assessments, advance or prepaid premiums, and considerations received for assuming the liabilities of contracts issued by other insurance companies.

2. *Gross Investment Income.* The gross investment income of a life insurance company is comprised principally of interest, dividends, rents, and royalties. However, there are additional items included therein such as net short-term capital gains, commitment fees, prepayment charges, and a broad catchall category for any gross income derived from any trade or business other than the insurance business.

3. *All Other Items of Gross Income.* This is another basket or catchall provision to make certain no income item will escape being included in a life company's receipt items.

4. *Long-term Capital Gains.* Like other corporate taxpayers, life insurance companies must include the excess of net long-term capital gains over net short-term capital losses in its gross amount items. Again, like other corporations, life companies are permitted to use the alternative capital gains tax method if that method produces a lower tax than the regular method.

5. *Decreases in Reserves.* Life insurance companies are permitted to deduct amounts added to specified insurance reserves. When these reserves are released, such release, or decrease in reserves, results in an income item.

Exclusion—Policyowners. Simply stated, the exclusion for the policyowners' share of investment yield in the gain from operations base is equal to the required interest the company must add to its insurance reserves. Congress developed in the 1959 Act the so-called proration theory which is that the investment income (and deductions) of a life insurance company is divided into two parts (like a partnership)—one part being the policyowners' share, which is excluded from tax, and the other part being the company's share, which is subject to tax. The practical working of this "exclusion" is the same as a deduction for the interest requirements of a company to maintain its insurance reserves.[3] This can be illustrated by the following example:

Assume that a company's required interest is $3 million and its investment yield is $5 million. The policyowner's share is 60 percent ($3 million divided by $5 million), and the exclusion for the policyowners' share is $3 million ($5 million multiplied by 60 percent). The company's share is 40 percent (100 percent minus 60 percent equals 40 percent), or $2 million. This is the same as allowing a deduction for the required interest of $3 million ($5 million minus $3 million equals $2 million, the company's share).

General Deductions. 1. *Ordinary Corporate Deductions.* In general, a life insurance company is allowed all the deduction items permitted other corporate taxpayers; e.g., commisisons, wages, advertising, depreciation, and the like.

2. *Investment and Similar Expense Deductions.* A life insurance company is permitted to deduct its expenses related to the production of its gross investment income. These expenses include such items as investment expenses (for example, the expenses of the company's investment department), taxes and depreciation on its investment property, and depletion.

3. *Deductions Peculiar to the Insurance Business.* A life insurance company is permitted five deductions not granted to other noninsurance taxpayers because these deductions relate specifically to the life insurance business. These are deductions for death benefits and claims, additions to certain specified insurance reserves, assumption reinsurance payments, certain limited mutualization payments, and a so-called small business deduction (limited to $25,000).

---

[3] See *U.S.* v. *Atlas Life Insurance Company,* 85 S. Ct. 1379 (1965), for the case which tested the validity of the proration theory of the 1959 Act. The proration theory was developed by the Congress (and upheld by the U.S. Supreme Court) in order to meet certain objections relating to whether or not state and local bond interest and intercorporate dividends were unduly (or unconstitutionally) taxed. The 1959 Act permitted a deduction of only the company's share of municipal interest on the theory that the policyowners' share of such interest had been "excluded" from the tax base of the company.

Tentative Gain (or Loss) from Operations. It is necessary to determine the "tentative gain (or loss) from operations" because this figure is used in determining the limitation on the special deductions. This limitation is described later.

Special Deductions. A life insurance company is allowed three "special deduction" items which are:

1. Deduction for dividends to policyowners.
2. Deduction for nonparticipating policies—the larger of 3 percent of premiums or 10 percent of the increase in the reserves relating to these policies.
3. Deduction for group life insurance and accident and health insurance —this deduction is equal to 2 percent of premiums attributable to such policies.

These three items are usually referred to as "special" or "limited" deductions because the total of these three items is subject to a limitation. The sum of these three deductions cannot exceed (*a*) the difference between the gain from operations before these deductions and the taxable investment income base, plus (*b*) $250,000. The following example illustrates this rule:

Tentative gain from operations	$4,000,000
Less—taxable investment income	2,200,000
	$1,800,000
Plus—statutory amount	250,000
Limitation on special deduction	$2,050,000

Illustration of Gain from Operations Tax Base

The following example illustrates the gain from operations tax base of a life insurance company:

Gross amounts:		
Premiums and annuity considerations		$15,000,000
Investment income		3,000,000
		$18,000,000
Less exclusion for policyowners' share of investment income		2,000,000
		$16,000,000
Less deductions:		
Deductions peculiar to insurance business (for example, increase in insurance reserves, death benefits)	$7,000,000	
Investment and similar expenses	400,000	
General corporate deductions (for example, salaries, wages, depreciation)	3,000,000	10,400,000
Tentative gain from operations		$ 5,600,000
Less special deductions (subject to limitation)		1,800,000
Gain from operations		$ 3,800,000

Purpose of Determining Taxable
Investment Income Base

Once Congress had decided to place life insurance companies on a total income approach, the treatment of dividends to policyowners became a major issue. The income base for mutual or cooperative organizations is always difficult to determine because of the question of the amount of the rebate, patronage dividend, or policyowner dividend that should be allowed as a deduction at the corporate level. The real problem is to determine the portion of the policyowners' dividend which is the overcharge or redundant premium—which tax theorists agree is a proper deduction—and the earnings (or savings) portion which many persons[4] believe should be subject to tax at the corporate level.

The limitation provided by Congress was founded on the general principle that the deduction for policyowners' dividends could not reduce the gain from operations or total income base below an investment income tax base or floor. In effect, Congress was saying that all life companies should be on a total income approach; but, since mutual companies presented a particularly vexing problem because of policyowners' dividends, Congress would define the limitation in terms of investment income in order that these companies would not pay less tax under the total income method than they had been paying previously under an investment income approach. While this issue was framed in terms of a stock mutual company problem, the limitation on the deduction for policyowners' dividends applies to all participating policies—both individual and group —issued by mutual and stock life insurance companies.

In addition to the policyowners' dividends issue, a second important issue raised under the total income method was whether the long-term nature of the life insurance business justified certain special deductions for various contingencies inherent in the life insurance business. It was pointed out to Congress that a life company was subject to possible heavy losses from disasters where group policies were involved and for losses as the result of the uncertainties of the amount of claims for accident and health insurance. The stock companies emphasized they had to maintain larger capital and surplus accounts than their mutual company competitors because they did not have the redundant premium element inherent in participating insurance. This larger surplus had to come from aftertax profits. In order to be competitive with the mutual companies, the stock companies requested a special deduction based on nonparticipating contracts.

Congress recognized these arguments and provided two special deductions: one relating to nonparticipating contracts, and the second, a deduction for group life and group accident and health contracts.[5] These

---

[4] Representatives of mutual life insurance companies believe, in general, that a full deduction for policyowner dividends should be permitted.

[5] In 1962, this deduction was expanded to cover individual accident and health insurance.

two deductions were considered to be similar to the deduction for policy-owners' dividends in that the Congress provided that the sum of all three could not reduce a company's total income base more than $250,000 below its investment income floor.

Taxable Investment Income

The taxable investment income base of a company is illustrated in Table 70–2.

TABLE 70–2.   Outline of Items Comprising Taxable Investment Income

Gross Investment Income	1. Interest 2. Dividends 3. Rents and royalties 4. Prepaid charges, standby fees, etc. 5. Short-term capital gains 6. Income from any trade or business (other than insurance business)
Less	
Investment Deductions	1. Investment expenses 2. Real estate expenses 3. Depreciation 4. Depletion 5. Trade or business expenses related to the income from such sources
Equals	
Investment Yield	
Less	
Exclusion—Policyowners	Exclusion for policyowners' share of investment yield
Equals	
Company's Share of Investment Yield	The company's share is the balance after subtracting the policyowners' share
Plus	
Net Long-Term Capital Gains	All the long-term capital gains are attributable to the company
Less	
Reduction Items	1. Company's share of tax-exempt interest 2. Company's share of partially tax-exempt interest 3. Company's share of intercorporate dividends received 4. The small business deduction (limited to $25,000)
Equals	
Taxable Investment Income	

Gross Investment Income. Gross investment income in the taxable investment income base is the same as that determined in the gain from operations base.

Investment Deductions. As a general rule, the investment deductions in the taxable investment income base are the same as those in the gain from operations base. There is, however, a limitation on the amount of investment expenses that may be deducted under the taxable investment income base which is not present in the gain from operations base.

Investment Yield. Investment yield is the statutory name for the difference between the gross investment income and the investment deductions.

Exclusion—Policyowners. The exclusion for the policyowners' share of investment yield is equal to the "policy and other contract liability requirements." Basically, the purpose of this exclusion is to allow the company an "exclusion" (or deduction) for its policyowners' interest requirements. As in the gain from operations base, the Congress used a proration theory, with the investment yield divided into two parts—the policyowners' share and the company's share. The reserve interest rate used in determining the policyowners' share is based upon each company's average investment earnings on the theory that the competitive pressures within the insurance business will, in the long run, force various companies to build into their price structures for their policies a credit for interest on something like this basis.[6] It should be noted that the policyowners' share under the taxable investment income base is determined in a different manner than the policyowners' share under the gain from operations base. Generally speaking, the policyowners' share is larger in the taxable investment income base than under the gain from operations base.

The policy and other contract liability requirements are illustrated in Table 70–3. The adjusted reserves rate is the lower of the company's current earnings rate (that is, the company investment yield divided by its assets) or its average earnings rate (that is, the average of its earnings rate for the current year and the four preceding ones). For example, if the current earnings rate were 5.2 percent and the average earnings rate were 4.8 percent, the adjusted reserves rate would be the lower of the two, or 4.8 percent. The adjusted reserves rate is, in effect, the company's deduction rate.

The next step is to determine the adjusted life insurance reserves. The purpose of this adjustment is to determine the amount of the life insurance reserves as though they had been established originally using the adjusted reserves rate rather than the interest rate assumed by the company. This adjustment is computed by taking the difference between the deduction rate and the rate assumed by the company in establishing the reserves; the reserves then are adjusted downward by 10 percent for every 1 percent by which the deduction rate exceeds the assumed rate (or vice versa). For example, if the deduction rate is 4.8 percent, the assumed rate is 3 percent, and the reserves established by the company are $1 million, then the adjusted life reserves are $820,000 (the difference between the deduc-

---

[6] See Senate Report No. 291, 86th Cong., 1st sess. (1955), pages 4–6 and 14–17, for a complete explanation of the congressional theory underlying the determination of the policyowners' share in the taxable investment income base.

TABLE 70–3.   Items Includable in Policy and Other Contract Liability Requirements

Interest on Life Insurance Reserves	Adjusted life insurance reserves times Adjusted reserves rate
Plus	
Interest on Pension Plan Reserves	Mean of pension plan reserves times Current earnings rate
Plus	
Interest Paid	1. Interest on indebtedness 2. Amounts in nature of interest on insurance and annuity contracts not involving life reserves 3. Discount on prepaid premiums 4. Interest on special contingency reserves
Equals	
Policy and Other Contract Liability Requirements	

tion rate and the assumed rate is 1.8 percent; and the reserves of $1 million must be adjusted downward by 10 percent for each 1 percent of difference; thus, a reduction of 18 percent is made which reduces the reserves to $820,000).

Once the adjusted life insurance reserves are determined, then the amount of investment earnings allocable to life reserves is computed by multiplying the adjusted life reserves by the deduction rate. This is the first item of the policyowners' requirements.

The second item that comprises the policyowners' requirements is the amount of investment earnings allocable to pension plan reserves. These reserves are the life insurance reserves that are accumulated under qualified pension and profit sharing plans. The amount of this item is determined by multiplying the amount of the pension plan reserves by the company's current earnings rate. This is on the theory that a life company, in order to be competitive with trusteed pension plans, must credit to its pension reserves an amount at least equal to the company's earning rate.

The third item of the policyowners' requirements is the interest paid on indebtedness; discount on prepaid premiums; interest paid on insurance and annuity contracts for which no provision is made in the life insurance reserves; and the interest on special contingency reserves under contracts of group term life insurance and group accident and health which are established and maintained for the provision of insurance on retired lives, for premium stabilization, or for a combination thereof. These interest payments are similar in nature to interest paid or credited on deposits by a bank.

Company's Share.   The company's share of the investment yield is the balance of the investment yield after subtracting or excluding the policyowners' share.

Net Long-Term Capital Gain. The net long-term capital gain item is the same as that included in the gain from operations base.

Reduction Items. A company is allowed to reduce its share of investment yield by four so-called reduction items. These are described below.

1. *Tax-exempt Interest.* A company is allowed a deduction for the amount of tax-exempt interest (state and municipal interest) included in its base. For example, if a company had $1,000 of municipal interest included in its gross investment income, and the company's share of investment yield was 30 percent, there would be $300 of municipal interest in its share for which it could take a deduction.

2. and 3. *Partially Tax-exempt Interest and the Company's Share of Intercorporate Dividends Received.* Deductions are permitted for these items to the extent included in the company's share and to the extent permitted other taxpayers.

4. *Small Business Deduction.* The small business deduction is the same as that allowed in the gain from operations base, and is equal to 10 percent of investment yield, or $25,000, whichever is smaller.

Illustration of Taxable Investment Income Tax Base

The following example illustrates the taxable investment income tax base of a life insurance company:

Gross investment income:		
Interest		$2,100,000
Dividends		500,000
Rents and Royalties		400,000
Total		$3,000,000
Less—deductions:		
Investment expenses	$180,000	
Depreciation, real estate taxes	70,000	
Depletion	10,000	260,000
Investment yield		$2,740,000
Company's share (25%)		$ 685,000
Net long-term capital gain		20,000
Total		$ 705,000
Less—reduction items:		
Tax-exempt interest and		
dividends received deduction	$480,000	
Small business deduction	25,000	505,000
Taxable Investment Income		$ 200,000

Life Insurance Company Taxable Income

The gain from operations tax base of a life insurance company differs from the taxable income base of other corporate taxpayers in one major respect. Only part of this gain from operations may be subject to tax currently, with the tax on the remainder of the base being deferred to a later year. With respect to other business corporations, all their taxable income base is subject to tax currently.

Therefore, it is necessary to determine what part, if any, of a company's gain from operations will qualify for tax deferral. This tax deferral arises only when the gain from operations base is in *excess* of the "taxable investment income" base. When this occurs, the current tax base of a life insurance company is (1) the taxable investment income base, plus (2) one half of the difference between the gain from operations base and the taxable investment income base. The other one half of this difference becomes the tax-deferred base. It should be observed that the sum of the current tax base and the deferred tax base will equal the gain from operations.

When the gain from operations base is *less than,* or *equal to,* the taxable investment income base, the current tax base is equal to the gain from operations base. In other words, there is no deferred tax base in these instances.

The above explanation is summarized in Table 70–4.

TABLE 70–4.   Illustration of Current, Deferred and Total Tax Bases of Life Insurance Companies

Case	Current Tax Base	Deferred Tax Base*	Total Tax Base
I. Gain from operations *less than* taxable investment income base†	Gain from operations	None	Gain from operations
II. Gain from operations *equal to* taxable investment income base	Gain from operations	None	Gain from operations
III. Gain from operations *greater than* taxable investment income base	Taxable investment income plus ½ (Gain from operations minus taxable investment income)	½ (Gain from operations minus taxable investment income)	Gain from operations

* For simplicity, this table ignores the fact that two of the three special deductions must be added to the deferred tax base. See chapter section "Tax-Deferred Account."

† It should be noted that most mutual life insurance companies fall within Case I. This is because their gain from operations is generally $250,000 less than taxable investment income, due to the limitation on policyowner dividends.

Tax-Deferred Account

The tax-deferred account is technically called the policyowners' surplus account. This name is based on the idea that the purpose of the tax deferral is to provide a contingency reserve or surplus for the protection of the policyowners; hence, the name policyowners' surplus. This name is a misnomer in that the contingency reserve belongs to the company and not to the policyowners. It may be used, however, for the benefit of policyowners.

There are three items that are added to the policyowners' surplus account. The first is the deferred or untaxed amount of the gain from operations. The other items are two of the "special deductions"—the deduction for nonparticipating policies and the deduction for group life and accident and health insurance. Since the purpose of these two deductions was to give the companies a "cushion" against possible catastrophic losses, Congress concluded that these deductions should create only deferment, and not elimination, of tax. Thus, these deductions are included in the tax-deferred account.

A company will incur tax on its deferred-tax base in several situations. One is if the company distributes dividends to its stockholders in excess of its previously taxed income. Others are when the amount in the tax-deferred account exceeds a statutory ceiling or the company ceases to be a life insurance company.

CONTROLLED FOREIGN CORPORATIONS

Prior to 1963, the earnings of foreign subsidiaries that were American controlled were not subject to tax by the United States until these earnings were returned to the American owners, usually in the form of dividends. Thus, there was no current U.S. tax on the earnings at the time they arose, but only a U.S. tax at time of distribution, which was usually years later. This tax effect is generally referred to as "tax deferral."

President Kennedy, in his 1961 tax message to Congress, recommended removing tax deferral in the case of what have been called "tax havens," for example, countries such as Switzerland, Liechtenstein, and Bermuda, which have low or nonexistent income tax structures. The tax message cited insurance as being one of the activities that typically sought out tax haven methods of operation. The Revenue Act of 1962 eliminated, in general, the tax deferral for "tax haven" operations by U.S. controlled corporations (sections 951 through 964 of the Internal Revenue Code).

The approach taken in the law was that certain categories of income of American-controlled foreign corporations, even though undistributed, had to be included in the income of the American shareholders in the year earned by the foreign corporation. One of the specified categories of income was "income derived from the insurance of United States risks." This term is defined, under section 953 of the Code, to mean the income derived from the following insurance transactions:

Life insurance and annuity contracts. The issuing or reinsurance of any insurance contract or annuity in connection with the lives of residents of the United States.

Accident and health insurance contracts. The issuing or reinsurance of any insurance contract in connection with the health of residents of the United States.

Property-liability insurance contracts. The issuing or reinsurance of any insurance contract in connection with property in the United States, or in connection with liability arising out of activity in the United States.

Avoidance arrangements. Any arrangement whereby the controlled foreign corporation exchanged contracts described above for contracts on foreign or non-U.S. risks.

Apparently, following the passage of the Life Insurance Company Income Tax Act of 1959, some life insurance companies had developed certain arrangements to avoid the newly imposed tax on underwriting gains. One of these arrangements shifted the income from the insurance of U.S. risks to controlled foreign subsidiaries, usually located in tax haven countries, through a reinsurance agreement. In other instances, the insurance was placed directly with a foreign insurance company which was controlled by either an American insurance company or other American business. The net result of these various arrangements was to shift the income from the insurance of U.S. risks to a foreign corporation which was beyond the then current taxing powers of the United States. These tax avoidance schemes were the basic cause of insurance being specifically singled out in President Kennedy's tax message in 1961 and the inclusion of "income derived from the insurance of United States risks" in the tax law. The Revenue Act of 1962 has apparently closed this so-called foreign insurance tax loophole.

INTEREST EQUALIZATION TAX

In 1964, Congress enacted the Interest Equalization Tax Act for the purpose of aiding the U.S. balance-of-payments position. The interest equalization tax is a temporary excise tax which raises the cost to foreigners of obtaining capital in the U.S. capital market to a level more closely aligned with the costs prevailing in capital markets of other industrialized nations. This tax has been extended four times. It has become a "permanent" tax, at least until the U.S. balance-of-payments situation improves.

The tax rates imposed are designed to reduce the net rate of return to the U.S. buyer on the foreign securities involved by about 1 percent per annum, in order to decrease the volume of foreign securities sold in the U.S. market. The tax applies to foreign stock and to foreign debt obligations with maturities of one year or more.

The interest equalization tax law contains a number of exemptions which deal with specific types of situations. Basically, these exemptions have one aspect in common—the acquisition of the foreign securities was due to factors other than the interest rate differential between American and foreign security markets. It was on this ground that insurance companies were able to obtain an exemption for the foreign investments made by their foreign branches.

Many domestic or U.S. life insurance companies engage in business in foreign countries through branch operations (as opposed to foreign subsidiaries). This is particularly true in the case of many U.S. companies which have branch operations in Canada. In the conduct of this foreign branch operation, the companies collect premiums in a foreign country, reinvest the premiums in stock and debt obligations payable in that foreign currency, and pay their liabilities arising under the insurance contract in the same currency as that in which the premiums are collected. These transactions do not affect the balance-of-payments accounts of the United States. If the interest equalization tax were applied to such investment transactions, it would impose an unreasonable burden on the insurance companies by requiring them, in order to avoid the tax, to invest their reserves in U.S. securities, and thereby expose themselves to a foreign exchange risk between the time of investment of the premiums and the time the claims under the policies were payable.

In view of this, a specific exemption was provided in the law for insurance companies. This exemption, in general, permits life insurance companies to acquire, tax-free, stock and debt obligations of foreign issuers and obligors in an amount equal to 110 percent of their reserves against foreign risks.

POLICIES ISSUED BY FOREIGN INSURERS

Section 4371 of the Internal Revenue Code of 1954 imposes an excise tax on insurance policies issued by foreign insurers to U.S. persons. The tax rates are as follows:

Type of Policy	Tax on Each $1 or Fraction of Premium Paid (cents)
1. Casualty insurance policies, indemnity, fidelity or surety bonds	4
2. Life insurance, annuity, and sickness and accident policies	1
3. Reinsurance policies covering contracts mentioned in (1) and (2) ..	1

The excise tax does not apply if the foreign insurer is actually doing business in the United States and the insurance policy is signed by an officer or agent of the foreign insurer in a state within which such insurer is authorized to do business. The tax must be remitted by the person who makes the payment of the premiums to the foreign insurer (this is usually the U.S. broker).

It should be observed that foreign insurers not engaged in business in the United States are not subject to federal income tax. While the legislative history of the excise tax on policies issued by foreign insurers to U.S. citizens is unclear, this excise tax may have been imposed by Congress as a tax "in lieu" of income taxes. Moreover, it may have been imposed as a form of competitive protection for domestic insurance companies. Probably these two reasons, plus the fact it raises a small amount of revenue,[7] explain the underlying rationale of this tax.

STATE TAXATION[8]

Premium Tax

In order to trace the origin of taxation of insurance companies at the state level, it is necessary to review the history of the regulation of in-

---

[7] $18,482,000 in fiscal year 1969 and $8,614,000 in fiscal year 1970.

[8] The basic material appearing under the headings of State Taxation and Local Taxation was prepared from drafts written by Robert J. Demichelis, Associate General Counsel, American Life Insurance Association.

surance in the United States. In many jurisdictions the earliest insurance regulation was found in tax statutes. The most significant method of taxing insurance companies was developed in the early years of insurance operations in this country, and it has become known as the premium tax.

The origin of a tax on premiums received by insurance companies can be traced back to 1824 when New York imposed a tax at a rate of 10 percent on premiums collected by fire insurance agents in that state representing foreign insurance companies. During the next few years, taxes on insurance premiums spread to other states, which action can be attributed in part to retaliation against the New York tax. In 1837 the tax rate in New York was reduced to 2 percent. By the turn of the century most states were using some form of tax measured by premium receipts as the primary mode of taxing insurance companies. State premium taxes paid by life insurance companies totaled $660,000,000 in 1971 and now constitute the second largest tax paid by the insurance business, exceeded only in amount by the federal income tax.

Generally speaking, the premium tax can be described as the imposition of a flat rate of tax to a base of gross premiums received by an insurer from the sale of insurance contracts on risks within the boundaries of a particular state. The base to which the rate is applied begins with the premium specified in the contract. Most states permit deductions for policyowner dividends. No state, however, permits deductions for company expenses incurred in the transaction of business or for claims paid under insurance contracts.[9] Reinsurance premiums are ordinarily excluded from the premium tax base of the reinsurer. The tax base thus can be described generally as adjusted gross premium receipts.

Tax rates levied by the states on life and health insurance premiums range from 0 to 4 percent, with most states using a rate of 2 to 2.5 percent. A majority of states make no distinction in the rate of tax levied upon life and health insurance premiums. Some states, however, impose a different rate of tax on health insurance premiums received by life insurers and property-liability insurers. A large majority of states do not levy a tax on annuity considerations. Several states levy a tax on annuity considerations at a rate lower than that levied on either life or health insurance premiums. In addition, one quarter of the states that tax annuity considerations have specifically exempted from the premium tax those premiums and considerations received in connection with federally qualified pension and profit sharing plans.

Some states offer a reduced rate of tax or credits against the premium tax based upon the amount or type of investment an insurer may have in that particular state. Such rate reductions or tax credits usually are based upon the relationship of the insurer's investment in the particular state to the insurer's total assets, the amount of reserves on policies issued in that state, or to the amount of premiums written. Several states offer a rate

---

[9] In 1971, Missouri amended its premium tax statute to permit a life insurance company to deduct, from gross premiums received on health insurance policies issued to employer and labor union groups, the amount of health benefit payments actually made. The deduction for health benefit payments is phased in over a four-year period, with these payments being fully deductible for all calendar years after 1974.

reduction based upon the establishment of a regional office or home office. The rationale of these rate credits is to encourage foreign insurers to invest in local securities or to establish a local office in order to stimulate the state's economy. A review of experience under this type of statutory provision, however, indicates that tax credits related to a percentage of an insurer's total investments have proven to be an ineffectual inducement in attracting foreign capital to the state, unless such investments otherwise meet the insurer's established standards for quality and rate of return consistent with its overall investment policy. This type of statutory provision usually works to the advantage of domestic insurers, except perhaps in those states which provide a credit for ad valorem taxes and a reduced rate for a foreign insurer which maintains a regional office in the state.

Numerous inequities have found their way into the existing premium tax system. Exemptions from tax vary from state to state and may be based upon a particular organizational form or on a particular line of insurance. For example, fraternal benefit societies enjoy a widespread exemption from premium tax. The majority of states do not impose taxes on nonprofit hospital and medical plans such as Blue Cross/Blue Shield. Efforts to tax noninsured employee welfare and benefit plans have been unsuccessful. Many institutions organized for charitable, religious, or educational purposes also provide insurance to their members or subscribers, and such institutions usually receive either complete exemption from tax or other favorable treatment under state tax statutes.

While the premium tax law began as a regulatory measure, from a practical standpoint it has assumed the position of an important revenue measure, since the evidence shows that the tax collected on premiums has for many years greatly exceeded the annual expenses of the operation of state insurance departments. The major advantages of the premium tax are its ability to produce steadily increasing revenue and its relative ease of computation and administration. Over the years, the premium tax has been criticized by various segments of the insurance business because it does not reflect ability to pay; it tends to favor participating business, when the laws permit dividends to be deducted from taxable premiums; and it places taxable insurers at a disadvantage as compared with various forms of tax-exempt insurers and self-insurers. Some critics of the premium tax have pointed out that the tax base for life insurers bears no similarity to the tax base of other financial institutions, such as banks and savings and loan associations, or general business corporations. These critics of the premium tax generally advocate the repeal of the premium tax and the imposition of a state net income tax, patterned after the 1959 act, on life insurance companies.

Probably the most significant difference in taxation of insurance premiums occurs in the treatment of foreign and domestic insurers. Over half of the states utilize some technique to achieve a tax rate differential favoring domestic insurers. These techniques take various forms—exemption from taxes, lower tax rates, or various tax credits. These domestic preferences are based on a rationale that a state should afford preferential tax treatment to its domestic industry in order to enable such industry to furnish its services to residents of the state in competition with services offered by out-of-state companies. Curiously enough, there are three states[10] in which domestic insurers are subject to higher premium tax rates than foreign insurers.

The principle of tax differentials between foreign and domestic insurers has been upheld by the United States Supreme Court.[11] An attack was made upon a South Carolina premium tax imposed annually on foreign insurers as a condition of being licensed to do an insurance business, where no similar tax was required of domestic insurers. The Court held that such tax had not prevented foreign insurers from competing with local insurers and, moreover, Congress had declared that the continued regulation and taxation by the several states of the business of insurance is in the public interest,[12] and such business shall be subject to the laws of the several states which relate to its regulation or taxation. It should be noted that, in those states which have exempted domestic insurers from premium tax, the differential in the tax burden has been somewhat tempered by requiring the domestic insurers to pay a corporate income tax, a capital stock tax, or some other type of tax or fee, where the tax or fee is not imposed on foreign insurers.

While the number of states which impose an income tax on business corporations continues to grow each year, most states still exempt from the income tax insurers that are subject to the state premium tax law. Some states, however, do impose an income tax on their domestic insurers in lieu of a premium tax. Only a half dozen states subject foreign insurers to an income tax, and in these states special formulas have been devised for determining the taxable income of foreign insurers.

The most recent development in state premium taxation has been the trend toward accelerating the dates for payment of premium taxes. In over one third of the states, insurers must pay the premium tax on an estimated basis, usually in quarterly advance installments, but sometimes on a semiannual basis. These payment methods are often similar to those imposed on other business corporations which must pay state income tax on an estimated basis. A state usually benefits from a one-time windfall during the first year following enactment, but an insurer is continually deprived of the additional investment earnings which would otherwise have been available were such funds not paid over to the state in advance.

Retaliatory Taxes

Retaliatory tax laws need explanation since they are unique to the field of insurance company taxation. A retaliatory tax provision can be best explained by the following illustration. Assume that state X imposes a premium tax of 1 percent and state N imposes a premium tax of 3 percent. If a life insurance company domiciled in state X does business in state N, it must pay the 3 percent rate to state N; if a life insurance company domiciled in state N does business in state X, it must pay the 1 percent

---

[10] Connecticut, Massachusetts, and New York.

[11] *Prudential Insurance Co.* v. *Benjamin,* 328 U.S. 408 (1946).

[12] 59 Stat. 33, commonly known as Public Law 15 of 1945, or the McCarran Act.

rate plus an additional 2 percent by reason of the retaliatory law of state X. Retaliatory laws were first enacted in this country over 100 years ago. They were designed to protect domestic insurers from burdens of various kinds imposed upon them by other states as conditions for being permitted to do business in those states. Thus, retaliatory statutes are defensive in nature. The theory of the retaliatory law (viewed from the domestic state) is that foreign insurers doing business in the domestic state shall suffer the same burdens as a domestic insurer of that state doing business in the state of origin of the foreign insurer. These laws have been held to be not invalid as discriminatory or in violation of the Constitution.

For the most part, the retaliatory laws are broad in scope and permit retaliation with respect to almost every phase of an interstate insurance business. Their purpose is to equalize the tax burdens imposed on insurers operating beyond their state of domicile. Such a determination can only be made upon comparison of the total burdens imposed on an insurer doing business in the taxing state, with the total burdens imposed on an insurer operating in its own state of domicile. The essential ingredient for retaliation is a comparison of the respective burdens between the states concerned. Retaliatory statutes generally are not considered to be revenue measures and any increase in revenue is incidental to the regulatory function.

Retaliatory statutes not only protect the domestic insurers where they do business in another state but they usually protect the foreign insurers from any increase in tax burdens. This is because the domestic companies of the state proposing a premium tax increase emphasize strongly the increased tax burden they would incur in other states because of the retaliatory laws. This argument is usually most effective. While some persons recently have questioned the merits of the retaliatory laws, the majority view is that these laws have been extremely helpful in maintaining the rate of premium taxation at the present levels. Without these laws, many fear the various state premium tax rates would have been increased substantially in recent years.

Other State Taxes

The primary method for taxation of life insurance companies at the state level is a tax on premium income. Although life insurers are, in theory, subject to many of the taxes imposed by a state on business corporations, most of these taxes are made inapplicable to life insurers by virtue of an "in lieu" provision included in the state premium tax statutes. The principle underlying the "in lieu" provision is that the system of premium taxation is singularly applicable to insurance companies and not to other classes of corporations. Therefore, insurers need to be relieved of other forms of state corporate taxation.

While state "in lieu" provisions vary, they generally provide that the premium tax shall be in lieu of all other taxes—state, county, or municipal —except for ad valorem taxes imposed upon real property and tangible personal property held by insurance companies. In addition, most of the states provide that the premium tax shall be "in lieu" of licenses and fees which otherwise might be required of insurers or their agents by any political subdivision in the state. The scope of this provision has been limited in its application by the courts to taxes of a similar nature, such as a gross receipts or income tax, but not to sales and use taxes and ad valorem property taxes.

Real estate taxes paid by life insurance companies in 1971 totaled $172 million. This is the largest "other" tax paid by life insurance companies at the state level. In 1971, life insurance companies paid $121 million in other taxes, licenses, and fees, including both state and local government levies.

LOCAL TAXATION

Any discussion of state taxation of life insurers would be incomplete without a brief mention of municipal and local taxes. Although most states have by statute preempted the right to regulate and tax insurance companies, about one third of the states, primarily in the South, authorize local governments and other political subdivisions to impose taxes on insurers. Most of the municipalities so authorized have exercised this right and now impose a wide variety of license fees and occupation taxes on both life insurance companies and their agents. The compliance and jurisdictional problems caused by these local taxes have created considerable administrative problems for most insurers.

SELECTED REFERENCES

Denney, Richard L., Rua, Anthony P., and Schoen, Robert J. *Federal Income Taxation of Insurance Companies.* 2d ed. New York: The Ronald Press Co., 1966.

Harman, William B., Jr. "Controlled Foreign Corporations—Section 953," *Tax Management,* No. 235. Washington, D.C.: Bureau of National Affairs, 1970.

_____. "The Pattern of Life Insurance Company Taxation under the 1959 Act," *Fifteenth Annual Tulane Tax Institute.* New York: The Journal of Taxation, Inc., 1965.

Knickerbocker, Daniel C., Jr., Walker, Paul H., and Levy, David. "Life Insurance Companies—Taxable Income," *Tax Management,* No. 246. Washington, D.C.: Bureau of National Affairs, 1971.

Levy, David, Knickerbocker, Daniel C., Jr., and Walker, Paul H. "Life Insurance Companies—Special Problems; Separate Accounts," *Tax Management,* No. 247. Washington, D.C.: Bureau of National Affairs, 1971.

Nash, Thomas G., Jr. *Federal Taxation of Life Insurance Companies.* 2 Vols. New York: Matthew Bender, 1965.

Prentice-Hall, Inc. *Federal Taxes, Excise Taxes Volume.* Loose-leaf reference service. Englewood Cliffs, N.J.

Walker, Paul H., Levy, David, and Knickerbocker, Daniel C., Jr. "Life Insurance Companies—Definition and Accounting," *Tax Management,* No. 245. Washington, D.C.: Bureau of National Affairs, 1971.

71

Canadian Life Insurance— Important Variations

By J. W. BURNS

THE DEVELOPMENT of the institution of life insurance in Canada has, to a large extent, paralleled that in the United States. The result is a marked similarity between plans of insurance and policy forms, investment practices, company organization and management, methods and techniques of selection and training of agents, and other agency operations. Nevertheless, there are important variations in practice between the life insurance companies of these two great nations. Some of these stem from certain fundamental legislative differences; others may be attributed to economic and geographic considerations.

Canadian life insurance companies have been aggressively managed and have gone beyond their national boundaries. A number of companies do business in the United States and the United Kingdom, and several do business in other countries. More than 2 million people in 30 different countries own policies in Canadian companies in an amount in excess of $32 billion, so that life insurance constitutes one of Canada's most important "exports." At the same time, Canadians own life insurance to the extent of 197 percent of their national income, which is the highest percentage in the world.

Canadian life insurance companies are subject to several corporate restrictions not generally applicable in other countries. Chief among these are the following:

1. They may not acquire more than 30 percent of the common stock of any corporation, nor may they invest their life insurance funds in the stock of another Canadian life insurance company. However, they do have the power to invest in the fully paid shares of foreign life companies; domestic casualty companies; property development companies; mutual funds; corporations providing advisory, management, or sales services in relation to a mutual fund or to variable life or annuity policies owned or issued by the company or a foreign life subsidiary of the company; and any corporation whose business is reasonably ancillary to the business of life insurance.

2. If securities are shown in the balance sheet at book values, the current practice which is encouraged by the federal Department of Insurance is to provide in the liabilities for any excess of book values over maximum statutory values. Maximum statutory values mean amortized values in the case of securities issued or guaranteed by the government of Canada, any province of Canada, the United Kingdom, or the United States, and market values for all other securities. This is in contrast to the situation in the United States, where companies must use amortized values for virtually all bonds and market values in the case of other securities. Companies in the United States, however, maintain a mandatory security valuation reserve in their liabilities.

Life insurance in Canada developed principally through stock companies. A high degree of policyowner participation in earnings has been traditional, because stock companies have for many years made use of their statutory powers to sell participating as well as nonparticipating insurance. Companies are required to keep separate accounts for participating and nonparticipating insurance. Shareholders in small companies are limited by statute to a maximum of 10 percent of the earnings on participating business. A sliding scale further reduces the shareholders' interest as the company becomes larger, so that shareholders are limited to 2½ percent of earnings on participating insurance when the mean participating fund exceeds $1 billion. Many companies have voluntarily limited shareholder interest in participating earnings to 5 percent, even when the sliding scale in the statute would allow them more. In recent years, five Canadian stock life insurance companies have converted from a stock basis to a mutual basis.

By 1970, each provincial insurance department had authorized the licensing of mutual fund salesmen for the sale of life insurance, and correspondingly each provincial securities commission had authorized the licensing of life insurance agents for the sale of mutual funds. For the past decade, life companies have been authorized to provide variable life or annuity policies. Primarily used for the funding of group pension plans, variable policies are also issued in individual form as well.

Also worthy of note is the fact that interest rates have been consistently higher in Canada than in the United States, and this is frequently reflected in premium rates and dividend scales.

GOVERNMENT REGULATION
OF LIFE INSURANCE

Government supervision of life insurance is much the same in Canada as it is in the United States, but it has developed along somewhat different lines. The significant feature in Canada is the dual control exercised by the federal and provincial (equivalent to state) governments.

Insurance legislation was historically the subject of long and involved constitutional conflict between the federal and provincial authorities.[1]

---

[1] In re Insurance Act (1932), A.C. 45.

This conflict has been resolved practically, if not strictly constitutionally; and it may be said that the primary responsibility of the federal government is the solvency of the Canadian, British, and foreign insurance companies licensed or registered by it for the protection of the insuring public. This responsibility is authorized by and administered under the Department of Insurance Act, the Foreign Insurance Companies Act (1932), and the Canadian and British Insurance Companies Act (1932),[2] which, when read together, represent the codified insurance laws of Canada as distinguished from the provincial laws. They are the only general acts of the Parliament of Canada relating directly to insurance.

With regard to all companies licensed or registered by it, whether domestic or foreign, the federal government is concerned with such matters as the maintenance in Canada of adequate assets, the types of investments made, the proper accounting, and the conditions under which an insurance company may be declared insolvent and prevented from further transactions or business. With regard to domestic companies, the federal government is also concerned with more specific matters, such as the methods of incorporation, the powers of directors and officers, and the manner in which they may be elected or appointed. That regulation of insurance in Canada has functioned efficiently is evidenced by the fact that no Canadian legal reserve life insurance company has ever occasioned the loss of a dollar to any policyowner through failure to carry out its obligations under its policy contracts. The same is true for more than the past 80 years with respect to Canadian policyowners insured with companies from other countries doing business in Canada.

Generally, the role of the provincial departments of insurance is to parallel the supervision of the federal department for those companies operating under provincial charter exclusively. In addition, the provincial governments are concerned, in respect to all insurance, with the regulation of the terms, conditions, and incidents of the contracts of all insurers, and with the licensing and regulation of agents, brokers, and adjusters.

The so-called Uniform Life Insurance Act of the Provinces of Canada[3] (applicable in all provinces except Quebec) contains provisions relating to the rights and status of beneficiaries, their designation by the insured, the destination of the insurance money, and, generally, all provisions respecting life insurance contracts other than those relating to the incorporation, licensing, and regulation of insurers. In all provinces except Newfoundland, the Uniform Act is contained in a separate part of a general insurance act; in Newfoundland, it is a separate enactment. Revisions and amendments have been substantially uniform in all provinces on the recommendation of the Association of Superintendents of Insurance for the provinces of Canada. A comprehensive revision was adopted in final form by the superintendents in 1959; after enactment by all provinces (except Quebec), it came into force on July 1, 1962. It applies not only to contracts made after this date but also to those made at an earlier date.

---

[2] Revised Statutes of Canada, 1970, C.I-17, C.I-16, C.I-15.

[3] References herein will be made to Ontario legislation, Revised Statutes of Ontario, 1970, C.224.

The only exception to this pattern of uniformity is the Province of Quebec, where the law relating to life insurance contracts is to be found mainly in the Quebec Civil Code, the Husbands' and Parents' Life Insurance Act,[4] and the Quebec Insurance Act.[5] Quebec is largely a French-speaking province which, under the Canadian Constitution, is guaranteed the right to its own law, which stems from that of France.

POLICY CONTRACT

Canadian policies, in form and substance, are essentially comparable to American policies. But whereas the latter are subject to strict legislative control regarding required provisions and their wording, Canadian policies are governed by statute law only as to the substance of some of their provisions. The result is that some provisions of Canadian policies are different from corresponding provisions of American ones.

Every individual policy[6] subject to the Uniform Act must set forth the name or a sufficient description of the insured (i.e., the applicant) and of the person whose life is insured; the amount, or the method of determining the amount, of the insurance money payable and the conditions under which it becomes payable; and the amount, or the method of determining the amount, of the premium and the period of grace within which it may be paid. Quebec law requires essentially the same policy contents, including a declaration of the commencement and duration of the risk and the signing and dating by the insurer.[7]

In addition, the Uniform Act requires every policy to include the conditions upon which the policy, if it lapses, may be reinstated. The policy must show whether the insurance is participating or nonparticipating; if it provides surrender, loan, paid-up, or extended options, they must be set forth in the policy.

Legally, a policy need contain no further provisions, and even these mandatory terms and conditions are not required to be in the form of standard provisions. This also applies to other subject matter dealt with in the Uniform Act, such as incontestability and suicide. Life insurance companies therefore are permitted complete freedom of expression in drafting policy contracts, provided the intent of the statutory provisions of the law is not changed except in a manner more favorable to the insured.

It should be noted that while the Uniform Act is not as confining as the various state insurance codes with respect to required provisions and their wording, it does provide that the provisions in the application, the policy, any document attached to the policy when issued, and any amendment to the contract agreed upon in writing after the policy is issued constitute the entire contract.[8] Thus, for instance, while the written application or a

---

4 Revised Statutes of Quebec, 1964, C.296.

5 *Ibid.*, C.295.

6 For contents of group life insurance policy, see Uniform Act, S.150.

7 Quebec Civil Code, Art.2587.

8 Uniform Act, S.148(2).

copy thereof need not be attached to the policy, it is made a part of the contract whether or not it is attached.

Beneficiaries

Prior to the 1962 revision of the Uniform Act, there were three classes of beneficiaries: beneficiaries for value, preferred beneficiaries, and ordinary beneficiaries. A "beneficiary for value" acquired a vested interest in the policy. If the insured named a "preferred beneficiary," a trust was created in favor of that beneficiary, and the insurance money therefore was beyond the insured's control, subject to certain exceptions. The insured could change the beneficiary to another member of the preferred class, but he could not go outside that class without the consent of a named preferred beneficiary. The preferred class was defined as the spouse, child, grandchild, or parent of the life insured. All others were "ordinary beneficiaries," who were similar to revocable beneficiaries in the United States.

The most significant change in the 1962 revision was the elimination of the beneficiary for value, the preferred beneficiary and the trust in his favor, and the ordinary beneficiary. In substitution for these types of designation, beneficiaries may be appointed revocably or irrevocably. Any beneficiary for value or preferred beneficiary, designated as such prior to July 1, 1962, does, however, retain his rights as they then existed. These rights will continue to be governed by the previous law unless and until a beneficiary for value ceases to be a beneficiary of that class, or until a preferred beneficiary by death or by a release of interest has ceased to retain the rights which the previous law gave to that class of beneficiary.[9] In the case of a preferred beneficiary, this means that if he consents to a change to a beneficiary outside the "preferred" class, the new law will apply to the policy. Also, if a preferred beneficiary releases his interest to the insured and the insured reappoints him as beneficiary, the provisions of the new law will apply.

The designation of an irrevocable beneficiary must be effected in the contract or by a declaration in writing (other than a declaration in a will), which declaration must be filed with the company during the lifetime of the person whose life is insured.[10] If, however, an irrevocable designation is contained in a will or in a declaration that is not so filed, the beneficiary will be deemed to have been designated revocably.[11] Once a beneficiary has been designated irrevocably, the insured may not, while the beneficiary is living, alter or revoke the designation or deal with the policy in any way without the consent of the beneficiary, but the insured remains entitled to dividends.

It is important to note that the result of the provisions just mentioned is that an irrevocable designation must be a conscious and positive act. This differs from the situation in the United States, where a designation is

---

9 *Ibid.*, S.146(2), (3).
10 *Ibid.*, S.165(1).
11 *Ibid.*, S.165(2).

deemed to be irrevocable unless the power to revoke the designation is expressly enunciated.

If any beneficiary is named in a contract, the insurance money is free from the claims of the insured's creditors from the time it becomes payable. If, on the other hand, the beneficiary is a spouse, child, grandchild, or parent of the person whose life is insured, or if any beneficiary is designated irrevocably, the insurance money is free from the claims of the insured's creditors, both before and after the time it becomes payable.[12]

The Province of Nova Scotia deviated somewhat from the uniform provision regarding irrevocable beneficiaries. The significance of this deviation is that where an insured makes an irrevocable designation of beneficiary, the insured must sign a statement acknowledging that he understands the effect of the irrevocable designation, and the agent must also sign a statement certifying that he has fully explained to the insured (not in the presence of the beneficiary) the nature and effect of the irrevocable designation.[13]

In contrast to the purely contractual practice in the United States of including a "spendthrift" provision in settlement agreements elected by an insured, this matter is specifically dealt with by statute in the common-law provinces of Canada.[14]

There are three classes of beneficiaries in Quebec: those designated under a marriage contract whose rights are determined in the light of the particular contract involved, those who obtain their rights from Article 1029 of the Civil Code, and those, corresponding to preferred beneficiaries, who are nominated under the Husbands' and Parents' Life Insurance Act, and who consist of the wife, their children, his children, or her children.[15] An implied trust is created in favor of these so-called "preferred" beneficiaries by virtue of which the insurance money does not go into the insured's estate and is not subject to his debts or those of the persons benefited. Once a preferred beneficiary has been named, changes may be made within the class, but consent of the beneficiary is required for a change outside the class.

Other beneficiaries in Quebec who have accepted the benefit obtain by law a vested interest. Some authorities are inclined to the view that this interest may be made subject to divestment by reserving in the appointment of beneficiary the right to make subsequent changes.[16] The law on this matter, however, is not settled.

Incontestability

The insurance policy itself is not incontestable. Incontestability applies to statements by the insured (applicant) and the person whose life is insured in the application and on the medical examination, and written statements or answers furnished as evidence of insurability (e.g., state-

[12] *Ibid.*, S.170.

[13] Revised Statutes of Nova Scotia, 1967, C.148, S. 150(3).

[14] Uniform Act, S.191.

[15] Revised Statutes of Quebec, 1964, C.296, S.2.

[16] *Adam* v. *Ouellette* (1947), S.C.R. 283. There is still some controversy on this point.

ments respecting airplane travel). Consequently, the question of what constitutes a "contest" of the policy, over which there has been considerable controversy in the United States, does not arise. War and aviation exclusion clauses and other provisions relating to coverage can be enforced without question even after the contestable period has expired.

If the insured or the person whose life is insured fails to disclose or misrepresents any material fact within his knowledge, the contract is voidable by the insurer.[17] Quebec law does not place any limit on the period during which a statement may be contested. In practice, a two-year incontestability clause is generally used in policies subject to Quebec law.

The provision regarding incontestability does not apply to the disability benefit or to a misstatement of age. Insurers usually take advantage of the disability benefit exception, and concealment or misstatement of a material fact renders this benefit liable to forfeiture on discovery. The provision regarding incontestability does apply, however, to the accidental means death benefit.

Reinstatement

The reinstatement provision in the Uniform Act is similar to the corresponding provision in United States policies. This statutory provision has no counterpart in the laws governing a Quebec contract, the rights in this regard being covered entirely by agreement between the parties.

There are two additional provisions in the Uniform Act respecting reinstatement which are of particular interest, since they establish the law on questions which have caused some difficulty in the United States. The first provides that in the case of reinstated policies, the two-year incontestability period, insofar as it affects the rights of the insurer, runs from the date of reinstatement. In a similar manner, the period of time fixed by the policy contract, during which the contract shall be void in the event of suicide, also commences with the date of reinstatement instead of the original date of the policy.[18]

There is no comparable law in Quebec. The Civil Code provides that insurance effected by a person on his own life is void if he dies by suicide;[19] but in practice, companies pay suicide claims if the policy has been in force for two years or more.

Cash Values and Nonforfeiture Provisions

Insurers in Canada are not compelled by law to include in their policies cash values and the various loan and nonforfeiture benefits. Nevertheless, it is the invariable practice of most companies to show tables of cash values, paid-up insurance values, and, usually, extended insurance values, which are for the most part comparable to those required by law in the United States. If there is default in the payment of premiums under a

---

[17] Uniform Act, S.157.
[18] *Ibid.*, S.163(2),(3),(4).
[19] Civil Code, Art.2593.

policy that has acquired a cash value, the automatic nonforfeiture benefit usually is a premium loan.

Juvenile Insurance

The revision of the Uniform Act increased from 15 to 16 the age at which a minor may apply for a policy, but broadened the powers of the minor to give him the right to apply for insurance on the life of any person, and to deal other than as beneficiary with any policy in which he has an interest, e.g., a policy assigned to him by someone else.[20] A new provision gives a minor beneficiary of the age of 18 years the capacity to receive insurance money and give a good discharge therefor.[21] This has overcome problems that had arisen where policy proceeds were payable to a minor child or a minor wife.

Quebec law provides that a minor of 15 or over may insure his own life. He may not, however, on his own deal with such policy.[22] Moreover, there is no procedure in the case of third-party contracts for the naming of successor owners.

Both the Uniform Act and the law of Quebec have removed the limits on the benefits payable in policies insuring children. Any limitations now become a matter of underwriting and of contract.

Miscellaneous Provisions

The Uniform Act also contains important procedural provisions which contribute to the efficient handling and payment of claims. For instance, where the insurer admits the validity of the contract but is not satisfied with the sufficiency of the proof furnished by the claimant of his right to the proceeds, or of the maturity of the contract, or of the age of the life insured, or of the name and age of the beneficiary, either the insurer or the claimant may ask the court to decide the issue.[23] The court may either declare the proof sufficient, or direct that further proof be furnished. In any event, payment by the insurer in accordance with the court's order operates as a complete discharge. A similar procedure is available where the person whose life is insured has not been heard of for seven years, in which case either the insurer or the claimant may seek a declaration from the court as to presumption of death.[24]

In cases where the claim has been properly proved and the insurer admits liability but is unable to make payment because there are adverse claimants, or the person entitled to the money cannot be located, or there is no person capable of giving and authorized to give a valid discharge who is willing to do so, the insurer may apply for an order to pay the money into court.[25] If the beneficiary is a minor, the insurer may, after one month from the maturity of the contract, pay the money directly into court

---

[20] Uniform Act, S.176.
[21] *Ibid.,* S.177.
[22] Revised Statutes of Quebec, 1964, C. 295, S. 219.
[23] Uniform Act, S.183.
[24] *Ibid.,* S.184.
[25] *Ibid.,* S.189.

without applying for an order.[26] Somewhat similar relief is granted to an insurer in Quebec where there are contending claimants.[27] A declaration of presumption of death also may be obtained in Quebec.[28]

The revision of the Uniform Act has effected two other significant changes. In addition to setting out who is deemed to have an insurable interest in the life insured, a provision has been added declaring that a policy is not void for lack of insurable interest if the person whose life is insured has consented in writing to the insurance being placed on his life.[29] In the case of a child under age 16, a parent can give this consent.

The Uniform Act continues to provide that unless the application or policy provides otherwise, the policy does not take effect until it is delivered and the first premium is paid.[30] A provision has been added, however, whereby a policy is deemed to have been delivered when the company has delivered it to an agent for unconditional delivery to the insured.[31] This, of course, does not preclude the company from attaching conditions to the delivery of the policy, such as a condition that the agent deliver it only if the life insured is in good health. In such a case the provision would not apply.

TAXATION OF LIFE INSURANCE

Long-awaited tax reform at the Canadian federal level came into effect on January 1, 1972. Although the changes were major in scope, including, for the first time, a tax on capital gains, few related only to the taxation of life insurance. In fact, tax reform for insurers and policyowners had preceded and had come into effect on January 1, 1969.

The Canadian system is such that the provinces also impose their own income taxes. Quebec administers and collects its own corporation and personal taxes and Ontario does the same with its corporation tax. Otherwise, the taxes are administered and collected for the provinces with the federal taxes by the federal government. The tax reforms have generally been adopted by all the jurisdictions.

Tax reform included the surrender by the federal government at the end of 1971 of estate tax and gift tax. Both taxes were withdrawn and the fields opened to the provinces, with the federal government offering to administer and collect them. Effective January 1, 1972, all provinces (except Alberta) had in force gift tax legislation very similar in form and designed to take advantage of the federal offer.

As to succession duties, British Columbia, Ontario, and Quebec were already raising their own. Saskatchewan, Manitoba, New Brunswick, Prince Edward Island, Nova Scotia, and Newfoundland adopted similar legislation with effect from January 1, 1972, but the system soon showed signs of foundering.

---

[26] *Ibid.*, S.195(1).
[27] Revised Statutes of Quebec, 1964, C.64, S.68.
[28] Quebec Civil Code, Art.2593(a).
[29] Uniform Act, S.144.
[30] *Ibid.*, S.154(1).
[31] *Ibid.*, S.154(2).

Alberta did not move to impose either tax. Prince Edward Island has completely reversed its position and abolished the taxes with refunds. New Brunswick has announced its withdrawal at the end of the year with immediate relief for farmers and fishermen. Nova Scotia will vacate the fields on March 31, 1974. Ontario appears, with increasing and continuous alleviation, to be committed to an announced policy of phasing out the levies as the capital gains tax matures.

The position has, therefore, been one of rapid and continuing change. It is presently rather chaotic and certainly no tidy pattern can be traced. Whatever might be written would have only temporary accuracy and consequently no attempt is being made to provide more detail in this edition of the *Handbook*.

Federal Income Tax[32]

In many respects, the taxation of life insurance policies in Canada is similar to that afforded by United States tax law. Life insurance premiums normally are not deductible expenses for income tax purposes in Canada. The so-called "dividends" paid to participating policyowners are not taxed as income to the policyowner, but the interest on accumulated dividends is taxable. Where policy proceeds become payable on death, the amount received is clearly a capital receipt and is not subject to income tax.

However, where a policyowner receives a disposition of proceeds from a life insurance policy, other than an annuity contract (e.g., maturity or surrender), he is subject to income tax on the amount by which the proceeds of the disposition exceeds the adjusted cost basis of the policy to the policyowner at the time of disposition. The adjusted cost basis at any particular time is the amount by which the aggregate of the cost to him of acquiring all his interests in the policy exceeds prior "tax-free" dispositions. The receipt of a dividend is considered to be a disposition.

Where the proceeds of a policy are left on deposit or are payable under some other settlement option, the full interest portion of such payments will be subject to income tax. The $1,000 interest exclusion, granted by Section 101(d)(1) of the United States Internal Revenue Code of 1954 to a surviving spouse under an agreement to pay the proceeds as a life income or in installments, has no counterpart in Canadian income tax laws.

There is no transfer-for-value rule applicable to insurance proceeds in Canada. If a policy or any interest in a policy has been transferred for a valuable consideration, the transferee receives the whole of the proceeds free of income tax.

Policy proceeds frequently are used by a Canadian business to continue, either on a contractual or on a voluntary basis, all or part of an employee's salary to his dependents for a reasonable period of time. Such payments, when paid voluntarily, are not strictly deductible, since they do not constitute a legitimate business expense.[33] According to current depart-

---

[32] References herein will be made to the Canadian Income Tax Act, Revised Statutes of Canada, 1970, C.I-5, described as the Income Tax Act.

[33] Income Tax Act, S.12(1)(a).

ment practice, however, a voluntary lump-sum payment of less than a year's salary to the widow of an officer of a company is deductible.

These death benefit payments, whether voluntary or contractual, are taxable as income in the hands of the recipient where such payment is made to the widow of the officer or employee. The amount of the death benefit included in income is reduced by an amount equal to the deceased employee's remuneration for the last year of employment, or $10,000, whichever is the lesser. If the amount actually received as a death benefit is less than either of these amounts, the exemption will be limited to the amount so received.[34]

As in the United States, the split-dollar plan is regarded, for Canadian income tax purposes, as though interest-free loans actually are made by the employer to the employee in amounts equal to the annual increase in the cash surrender value of the policy. The Canadian Income Tax Act, however, introduces a variation with respect to a shareholder-employee. If the corporation makes a loan to him, the amount thereof is deemed to have been received as a taxable dividend, unless the loan is repaid within a year from the end of the taxation year of the corporation in which the loan was made.[35] This means that the split-dollar plan has little attraction for a shareholder-employee, even though he may, on repaying the loan to his company, deduct the amount repaid in the year of repayment.[36]

Group insurance in Canada enjoys a position similar to that in the United States. The premiums paid by an employer are deductible as a business expense. If the insurance is group term life insurance, the premiums paid by the employer are not taxable in the hands of the employee, except to a limited extent.[37] The portion of the premium paid by an employer for any group term life insurance which is applicable to insurance on a taxpayer's life in excess of $25,000 is required to be included in the income of the taxpayer, if such insurance was effected in respect of, in the course of, or by virtue of his office or employment, or former office or employment.[38]

Annuities

The general rule is that whereas a taxpayer, in computing his income, is not entitled to deduct the expenses, premiums, or other costs of an annuity contract, only the interest portion of annuity payments is taxable.[39] Any gain that arises up to the time the annuity vests also, in effect, becomes taxable because the basic rule is that the capital element or the consideration for the contract is the sum of the premiums.

There are two exceptions to this principle. First, where premium contributions have been exempt from income tax, as for example, under a registered superannuation or pension plan, or under a registered retirement savings plan, any payments from that plan are taxable in full.

---

[34] *Ibid.*, S.139(1)(j)(i).
[35] *Ibid.*, S.8(2).
[36] *Ibid.*, S.11(1)(da).
[37] *Ibid.*, S.5(1)(a).
[38] *Ibid.*, S.6(1)(db).
[39] *Ibid.*, S.6(1)(aa) and S.11(1)(k).

Second, any amount received as a refund of premiums on the death of the holder of a life annuity contract is not subject to income tax.

There is one further variation where, on maturity or surrender, a lump-sum payment is elected rather than a life annuity. With respect to contracts entered into on or after June 14, 1963, the general rule above would apply; that is, the entire interest element would be taxable. However, with respect to life annuity contracts entered into before that date, only the interest element accruing after the second anniversary date to occur after October 22, 1968, will be subject to tax.[40]

Contributions by an employer and employee to a registered pension plan are deductible from their respective taxable incomes within certain defined limits.[41] Payments may be received from such a plan on three occasions, namely, retirement, termination of service, or death. In the case of retirement, the pension benefits are fully taxable as received.[42]

On termination of service the employee has the option, depending upon the terms and provisions of the plan, of taking a lump-sum settlement, taking a paid-up deferred annuity, continuing the contract on a premium-paying basis, or a combination of the foregoing. If he elects to take the benefits in a lump sum, he may either add the amount received to his income in that year and pay tax at the applicable rate, or pay a special tax based on various averaging provisions. Alternatively, he may transfer the amount received to another registered retirement savings plan, a deferred profit sharing plan, or a registered pension plan, and the amount so transferred will not be included in computing his income if transferred within the same taxation year or within 60 days thereafter.[43]

If the employee elects to receive a paid-up deferred annuity on termination of service, he has two alternatives. He may pay the income tax on the present value of the deferred annuity, in which case the company may amend or rewrite the policy, which is treated thereafter as an ordinary annuity contract. Or the employee may continue the paid-up deferred annuity subject to the tax liability and eventually pay tax on the total monthly income, or on the single sum at maturity or on the death benefit when he dies, or on the surrender value if he subsequently surrenders the policy.

Finally, if the employee, upon withdrawal from a registered pension plan, continues his original individual policy on a premium-paying basis, he pays income tax on the present value of the deferred annuity. The policy, which is thereafter considered for tax purposes as though it had never been in the plan, may be rewritten by the company on its usual type of policy form.

A lump-sum payment out of a pension plan upon the death of an employee ordinarily is income in the year received, but the recipient taxpayer (whether the employee's estate or a named beneficiary) may exclude such payment from his income for that year and instead pay tax based on various averaging provisions. If the payments on death are made

---

[40] *Ibid.*, S.7(5).
[41] *Ibid.*, S.11(1)(g) and S.11(1)(i).
[42] *Ibid.*, S.6(1)(a)(iv).
[43] *Ibid.*, S.11(1)(u).

in the form of an annuity to the widow,[44] it appears that she pays income tax each year only on the amounts received.

One of the exceptions to the general principle concerning the taxation of annuity payments is when they constitute benefits under a registered retirement savings plan. These plans were authorized by amendment to the federal Income Tax Act in 1957[45] and are intended to achieve greater equality of tax treatment; thus professional and other self-employed persons who are not eligible to participate in a registered pension plan are allowed to obtain similar tax advantages.

The principal features of a registered retirement savings plan are:

1. No benefits are payable prior to maturity other than refund of premiums and payment of interest if the annuitant fails to survive to retirement age.
2. The taxpayer may elect an annuity for his life, with no guaranteed period or a guaranteed period not exceeding 15 years.
3. The taxpayer may elect a joint life and last survivor annuity for the benefit of the taxpayer and his or her spouse, with or without a guaranteed period, not exceeding 15 years, and under which provision may also be made for payments to be reduced on the first death.
4. Premiums are deductible, within certain defined limits, in computing earned income only.
5. The contract matures not later than the annuitant's 71st birthday.
6. Annuity payments are fully taxable as and when received.
7. If life insurance is part of the plan, only the portion of the premium considered to be the cost of the annuity (which is determined through the use of a somewhat complicated formula) is deductible.
8. Once annuity payments commence, no further premiums may be deducted.
9. The plan includes a provision stipulating that no annuity payable thereunder is capable, either in whole or in part, of surrender, commutation, or assignment.
10. The plan may be revised or amended to provide for the payment or transfer of any funds, on behalf of an annuitant, to another registered retirement savings plan or to a pension fund.
11. If a plan is deregistered by means of the surrendering of the policy, the cash value becomes fully taxable in the hands of the individual in the year in which he receives it. This cash received is added to all his other income for the year and raises the rate of tax accordingly.
12. Contracts in existence prior to 1957 may also qualify.
13. Commencing in 1972, taxpayers may defer tax on certain unused payments through the purchase of an "income-averaging annuity."

Life insurance in Canada is provided solely by private insurance companies and fraternal benefit associations. From 1908 to 1967, the federal government, under the jurisdiction of the Government Annuities Act, sold individual and group annuities. However, since November of 1967, the federal government has ceased to sell new annuities and the annuities

---

[44] Optional methods of settlement on death are allowed, but on a restricted basis.
[45] Income Tax Act, S.79(B).

branch is now only administering existing individual contracts. It is also allowing additions to existing group annuity contracts.

TAXATION OF LIFE INSURANCE COMPANIES

In the case of income derived from other-than-life insurance operations, life insurance companies are taxed on business income at normal tax rates, applying the general provisions relating to domestic insurance companies which operate wholly in the other-than-life insurance field.

In the case of income derived from life insurance operations, the federal income tax is in two parts. The first part of the tax is levied on life insurance business income in Canada at normal corporate rates. The second part of the tax is levied on life insurance investment income in Canada at the rate of 15 percent. This second part is a tax paid by the companies on behalf of their policyowners in place of the tax that would otherwise be levied, at personal income tax rates on investment income in the hands of the policyowners.

In addition, the taxing statutes of all Canadian provinces require life insurance companies to pay income tax. Under the Ontario and Quebec Acts, this is payable directly to these provinces; in the other provinces, payment is made through federal income tax returns and collection machinery. Taxable federal life insurance business income is apportioned by provinces on the basis of premium income and the portions are subject to the relevant provincial income taxes. However, offset is allowed against the federal income tax otherwise payable and this serves virtually to eliminate double taxation.

Premium tax statutes were enacted by all provinces in 1957. Prior to that time, life insurance companies paid premium taxes to the federal government in accordance with the provisions of the federal-provincial tax-sharing agreements in effect between the government of Canada and the provinces (except Quebec). The rate under the provincial statutes is 2 percent on insurance premiums less insurance dividends. Annuity considerations are not taxed. The tax returns in each province are not identical in form but produce taxable income on a consistent basis.

There are, in addition to the above, various miscellaneous taxes and fees imposed by federal, provincial, and municipal authorities which affect the operation of a life insurance company doing business in Canada. These include transfer fees on the sale of securities and various business and property taxes, all of which appear to have their counterparts in the United States.

SELECTED REFERENCES

Canadian and British Insurance Companies Act, 1932. Ottawa, Can.: The Queen's Printer, 1932.

The Life Insurance Laws of Quebec. Toronto: Stone & Cox, Ltd., 1965.

McVitty, E. H. *A Commentary on the Life Insurance Laws of Canada.* Toronto: Life Insurance Institute of Canada, 1970.

The Revised Uniform Life Insurance Act of the Provinces of Canada except Quebec. Toronto: Stone & Cox, Ltd., 1972.

72

A Brief History*

By PAUL A. NORTON

INSURANCE is as old as man's quest for financial security. The germ of the idea traces back four thousand years, to the time when the cargoes of Babylonian caravans and Phoenician ships were pledged as security for loans. Later, we know that during the period of the Roman Empire, religious and fraternal societies paid out benefits upon the death of their members. But despite this ancient lineage, life insurance as we know it today is a relatively new development. It evolved from a great transformation in Western life which began in the 19th century: the decline of an agrarian society and the rise of an industrial one. Industrialization—with its cities, factories, cash economy, and an urban "saving" class—set the stage for life insurance as a large-scale, national institution. Life insurance, it can truly be said, is a product of modern industrial democracy.

LIFE INSURANCE

The growth of the insurance business in America well illustrates this point. Up to the 19th century, only a handful of life insurance policies had been written in this country. Some were granted by the Presbyterian Ministers' Fund, which was formed in 1759 as the first life insurance company in America, and a few others by the Insurance Company of North America, originally chartered in 1794. (A chronology of historic dates in the development of life and health insurance in the United States is found in Appendix A.) The remainder were issued by individual insurers. Working out of coffeehouses where colonial merchants congregated, these individual underwriters (the term "underwriter" arose when a person willing to take a portion of the risk wrote his name beneath the contract, and was thus said to have underwritten, or guaranteed, the insurance) at first underwrote marine insurance only. Occasionally, however, they wrote policies covering the risk of capture by pirates and eventually added

---

* This historical review will be devoted chiefly to the long steady development of life insurance, with a brief section at the end on the history of health insurance. The principal developments and important growth of health insurance did not occur until recent decades, when it became more closely allied with life insurance.

policies covering death during a voyage. Yet such policies were small in number; and by the end of the 18th century, few Americans had ever been protected, at any stage of their lives, by life insurance.

Actually, early America had little need for such protection. In 1800 the United States was overwhelmingly a land of farmers. Only six cities—Philadelphia, New York, Boston, Charleston, Baltimore, and Salem—numbered populations above 8,000. Of the total population—a scant five million persons—fully nine tenths were chiefly engaged in agriculture. In this agrarian society the farm itself afforded family protection. The crops and herds provided food; the woodlot, fuel; the nearby wilderness, game animals; and the home stood as an enduring shelter for the aged and the infirm. The security of every individual was the concern of family and friends. Small wonder, then, that in this society, life insurance made little progress.

Industrialization Sets the Stage

But in the early 19th century, America, like western Europe before it, began to undergo a fundamental change. Stimulated by the War of 1812, which shut off European imports, the nation began to industrialize. As factories sprang up throughout New England and the Middle states, the sons and daughters of farmers rushed to man them, and towns and cities began an explosive growth. Within a few short years, while the population of the entire United States increased 334 percent, that of towns and cities—attracting farmers from far and wide—shot up over 1,000 percent (from 525,000 in 1810 to 6.2 million in 1860).[1] This migration profoundly altered the structure of American social life and set in motion an urban society urgently in need of life insurance.

In transplanting himself from farm to city, the new urban dweller left his traditional security behind. Gone was the certainty of food and shelter and the surety that relatives—now often days' distance away—would offer assistance in time of need. In these circumstances, many of the new urbanites became receptive to the idea of "outside" insurance. Fortunately, they now had the means to buy such protection. Unlike the agrarian society from which they came, where the barter system had prevailed, city workers were paid in coin. They lived in a cash society, and the more frugal and self-reliant among them were now able to *buy* security and financial protection for their families.

Early Years

Responding to this need for a new kind of security, scores of new life insurance companies were organized in the early decades of the 1800s. Many of these were unsoundly financed and soon dropped out of existence; others, however, met with considerable success. The great advantage of these companies over the earlier individual underwriters was that policyowners generally could rely upon them to meet their obligations.

---

[1] Figures include population of cities and towns of 2,500 and over. See Bureau of the Census, U.S. Department of Commerce, *Historical Statistics of the United States, 1789–1945* (Washington, D.C.: U.S. Government Printing Office, 1949).

Too often the coffeehouse underwriters not only disputed claims but were unable to pay even those they freely acknowledged. With the organization of the stock companies in the early 1800s, life insurance at last began to be organized on a systematic, businesslike basis.

In spite of substantial progress, life insurance was not yet out of its infancy. As late as 1840, there was only $4,690,000 worth of life insurance in force throughout the United States. The business, however, was on the brink of its first great forward stride. Its immense growth truly began in what for insurance companies could be called the "golden forties."

For the nation as a whole the 1840s represented a period of great ferment and growth. It saw the first inrush of German, Irish, and Scandinavian immigrants; the building of a vast network of turnpikes and canals linking the eastern seaboard with the fast-growing trans-Appalachian states; the Mexican War; the acquisition of Oregon, Texas, New Mexico, and California; and, most important for the future of life insurance, a tremendous acceleration of the process of urbanization and industrialization which had commenced such a short time before. As the industrial system took hold, life insurance became more essential—and more popular —than ever before. Greatly contributing to this growth were two important changes within the life insurance business itself: the start of mutual companies and the development of more aggressive sales techniques, particularly the rise of the agency system.

Rise of Mutuals

The idea of mutuality—whereby policyowners share in the divisible surplus of the business—was not new. For years, there had been mutual life insurance companies in England; and in America, mutuals in the fire insurance field were not uncommon. But it was not until 1843 that the first life mutual began business in this country—the Mutual Life Insurance Company of New York. Formed in 1842 by Morris Robinson, a former Canadian and ex-banker, its first policies were issued in February of 1843. It was soon followed by the New England Mutual Life Insurance Company, which began issuing policies later in 1843 (although it was chartered in 1835); State Mutual (1844); Mutual Benefit and New York Life (1845); Connecticut Mutual (1846); Penn Mutual (1847); and many more.

New Sales Techniques

By this time, too, insurance was being sold more aggressively than ever before. Unlike earlier firms, which often waited for customers to come to them, the new mutuals, along with their competitors, the stock companies, now began employing new sales techniques. Promotion circulars were sent out; advertisements extolling the virtues of life insurance were placed in magazines and newspapers; and above all, scores of new agents were hired to seek out prospects.

By today's standards, relations between these early agents and their companies were casual indeed. The agent received no formal contract, his appointment being made verbally or by letter; and he was given no training whatever. Armed with little more than a form sheet listing his duties and a rate and commission schedule (the commission was usually 5 percent or 10 percent on first-year premiums and 5 percent for a limited period on renewals), the agent set out to market insurance. In the 1840s, this was no easy task. The product he was selling was still unfamiliar to most people and, compared to today, enormously high in cost ($25 to $30 per $1,000 on a participating policy at age 30—at a time when the average factory worker was earning $1.50 a day). The agent, moreover, was prevented from selling large policies even to those able to afford them, since most companies had policy limits between $5,000 and $10,000.

Mid-Century Growth

Despite its high cost and limited coverage, life insurance was being sold. By 1850, insurance in force had reached $97.1 million; and by the outbreak of the Civil War, this figure had leaped to $173.3 million, a spectacular rise of over 3,000 percent within two decades.

Not even the war seriously interrupted the progress of the business. Before the war's end, insurance in force was increasing at a faster rate than ever, and in the immediate postwar period the increase reached a fabulous 50 percent a year. Every year saw the formation of new companies—24 began business within the two-year period 1866–67, and in New York State alone, the number reporting to the State Insurance Department rose from 17 to 71 between 1862 and 1870.

This period also saw a number of other notable changes: the widespread application of nonforfeiture provisions (first recognized as a policyowner's right by New York Life in 1860); the beginnings of fraternal insurance (imported from England along with its friendly societies—the Odd Fellows, Foresters, and others); the growth of the general agency system, which came into use in the early 1860s and by 1865 was the "generally accepted method for the organization of the selling of life insurance";[2] the decline of term insurance (which predominated up to the 1840s) and the ascendancy of the level premium, whole life type; and an outstanding actuarial accomplishment, the construction of a new mortality table by Sheppard Homans of Mutual Life. Homans' achievement lay in his discovery that mortality rates in America were higher at the younger and older ages and much lower at the middle ages than in England. His table, the first American Experience Mortality Table, was widely used for three quarters of a century. By the close of the 1860s the insurance business had witnessed its first great period of growth. Insurance in force stood at what was then the colossal figure of $2 billion.

Business in Crisis

Yet the situation was not as bright as it seemed. Much of this growth had not been as healthy as it might have been, a reflection of a basic change in the tone of American business and political life which began in the postwar era.

---

[2] R. Carlyle Buley, *The American Life Convention: 1906–1952* (New York: Appleton-Century-Crofts, Inc., 1953), Vol. I, p. 80.

America's postbellum period was a raw and lusty age. Encouraged by the Civil War, with its unprecedented demand for manufactured goods of every description, Americans feverishly set out to turn their nation into an industrial colossus overnight. Hastily, railroads were flung across mountains; the earth was opened for its wealth of iron ore, copper, and coal; cables were strung from continent to continent; and new industries sprang up overnight. But in the process—in an excess of raw, creative energy—the rules of the game were often forgotten. During the Grant administrations the ethics of business and political life reached a low ebb. Politicians figured in "salary grabs," brazen tax frauds, and land steals. Corruption reached almost to the doors of the White House itself, for in the Credit Mobilier scandal, Vice President Schuyler Colfax was a leading figure. And in business, "defalcations, stock-watering, wildcat investment schemes, railway wrecking were accepted parts of commercial life."[3]

Quite naturally, the life insurance business—which by now had begun to play a leading role in American social and economic life—was not immune to these influences. In the competitive race to sell insurance, the policyowner was often forgotten, and the "earlier emphasis upon . . . life insurance as a great cooperative scheme, an eleemosynary principle with unlimited liberating possibilities which would alleviate, even eliminate, human distress,"[4] was largely overlooked. Instead, many life insurance practitioners came to look upon the business chiefly as a means of accumulating power and prestige. With this philosophy, sound business practices were frequently forgotten. Commissions were recklessly raised, advertising claims were grotesquely inflated, agencies raided one another to lure away star salesmen, showy offices were erected which sometimes cost more than the total assets of the company, dividends were declared that had not been earned, risks were accepted carelessly, scant concern was shown for proper methods of premium and reserve calculations, and a few shakily financed companies even went so far as to frighten "enough policyholders into forfeiting so that liabilities could be scaled down to somewhere near the assets on hand."[5]

By the 1870s, life insurance companies were paying heavily for their sins. Public disclosure of abuses caused numerous Americans to take a searching look at the business; and because of their concern at what they saw, new business fell off alarmingly. Before long, company after company began to fail. Thirty-three life insurance firms went to the wall between 1870 and 1872. Another 48 followed during the 1873–77 period—a time of general depression which contributed to the industry's decline—and by 1882, only 55 companies remained of the 129 which had been doing business in 1870. Without a doubt, the 70s, as an authority in the field once observed, "must be accounted the most trying period in the history of American life insurance."[6]

---

[3] Samuel Eliot Morison and Henry Steele Commager, *The Growth of the American Republic* (New York: Oxford University Press, 1940), Vol. I, pp. 74–75.

[4] Buley, *The American Life Convention, 1906–1952*, p. 91.

[5] *Ibid.*, p. 92.

[6] John A. McCall, President, New York Life Insurance Company, quoted in *ibid.*, p. 90.

To some extent, the downfall of many firms was occasioned not only by extravagance, inefficiency, or dishonesty, but by the strict enforcement of state insurance laws, particularly those relating to reserves and the admittance of assets. These laws—indeed, the state insurance departments· themselves—were relatively new, the outcome of a long campaign waged a few years earlier by Elizur Wright, "the father of life insurance in America."

Beginnings of State Regulation

In the early years of the 19th century, state regulation of life insurance in America had been almost totally unknown. What few rules existed were set forth in the charters of individual companies. But in the 1840s, Wright, a schoolteacher, newspaper editor, and fiery abolitionist, became concerned with the hit-or-miss methods used by most insurance companies in calculating their reserves. With prodigious effort, he compiled a series of net valuation tables (involving in all nearly 200,000 calculations), which showed what reserve should be held at the end of each year during the life of various policies. Wright thought that life insurance companies should be legally obligated to maintain adequate reserves, and in 1858 almost single-handedly lobbied a version of his legal reserve principle through the Massachusetts legislature. This, plus Wright's appointment in that same year as head of the Massachusetts state insurance department,[7] marks the beginning of effective state regulation of life insurance in this country. Other states soon passed similar regulatory laws; and within a decade, 35 states had established special insurance departments or delegated the supervision of insurance to an official specifically appointed for that purpose.

New Policies, New Methods, New Growth

This closer state supervision, combined with the pruning-out of weaker companies during the depressed 70s, had, by the 1880s, restored much of the industry's vigor. Meanwhile, the economy in general had recovered as well. Industrial expansion had gained new momentum; money in circulation had greatly increased; the population had risen to 50 million (up from 17 million in 1840); the West was being rapidly peopled; and more important still, the population of cities—where the need for life insurance was greatest and most clearly recognized—had risen to 22½ percent of the total population, compared with 8½ percent two decades earlier. In this atmosphere of confidence and growth the life insurance business resumed its forward surge.

Increasingly, after 1880, life insurance was liberalized, and its benefits were shared more broadly throughout the nation. As the West grew, older companies expanded, and new ones sprang up to provide protection for the mounting number of cattlemen, miners, and farmers who were turning this region into a settled part of the nation. In the East, and in other

---

[7] In 1852, Massachusetts set up a board of insurance commissioners composed of the secretary, treasurer, and auditor of the state. They were replaced in 1855 by a formally organized insurance department, generally regarded as the first in the United States.

parts of the country as well, industrial insurance, first introduced in America by the Prudential in 1875 to meet the insurance needs of low-income groups, began to be much more widely sold. Simultaneously, older types of insurance were greatly improved. As Americans began to travel more, travel restrictions were removed (this had started with the policies of the Home Life of New York in 1886). Cash and surrender values were written into ordinary life policies. Thirty days' grace on premium payments became more common. Policies were beginning to appear containing statements of incontestability. The insuring of substandard risks became more widespread (this had been pioneered by Connecticut General in 1865), and in 1896 the first policies were issued providing waiver of premiums if the insured should become totally disabled. Along with these changes, insurance in force steadily mounted. It rose from $1,522,000,000 in 1880 to $3,522,000,000 in 1890 and by the end of the century had leaped to $7.5 billion. At this point the life insurance business in America had reached a size unequaled in any other country in the world.

Armstrong Investigation

Its size, in fact, soon proved a momentary disadvantage. At the turn of the century, with the nation in an era of "frenzied finance," and with the "muckrakers" exposing questionable business practices—some real and some imagined—the power and influence, as well as the operating methods, of the life insurance business were subjected to careful scrutiny. Were life insurance companies, many wondered, fit custodians for so much of the nation's wealth? Despite the many reputable firms, there were reasons for thinking that some, at least, were not. More than a few, it appeared, had engaged in shady practices. As the public became aware of these evils, there arose outraged cries for an investigation of the entire business, and in 1905 a part of this difficult task was handed to a group of carefully chosen men, the Armstrong Investigating Committee, which was charged with investigating the life insurance business in New York.

It is to the credit of the committee that the business as a whole was not victimized. From the outset, Charles Evans Hughes, Chief Counsel for the committee, made it clear that the purpose of the investigation was not to condemn, but to protect and strengthen the business by ridding it of undesirable practices.

The New York Insurance Code, adopted in 1906, included nearly all of the committee's recommendations. The Code called for closer regulation by the state insurance department of the election of company officers; the prohibition of investments in common stocks, subsequently modified; a limitation on the amount that could be spent in securing new business; and the outlawing of the deferred dividend system. All in all, the Armstrong Investigation amounted to a sober, responsible housecleaning of the industry—a boon not only to the public but to the business as well. In fact, the stoutest defenders of the committee's regulations were responsible insurance companies themselves, which quite naturally wished to allay the suspicion that the business was peopled wholly by self-seekers.

For a time following the Armstrong Investigation, new insurance fell off sharply, but this slackening was of short duration. Soon, public confidence was restored; and throughout the next quarter of a century, encouraged partly by Americans' favorable experience with government life insurance during World War I, new business, insurance in force, and assets steadily climbed. In 1929 alone, a record $20 billion of new insurance was written; and in that year, insurance in force passed the $100-billion mark.

As with other periods of progress, this one had been accompanied by numerous beneficial advances within the business. Among them were the introduction of group insurance (just prior to World War I), the inclusion in policies of disability clauses and double indemnity benefits, and the development of optional settlements of policy proceeds. The business also prospered because of the steadily growing use of life insurance for business purposes and because of the reduced cost of insurance—owing to favorable mortality experience, high interest rates, and relative freedom from capital losses.

Depression Decade

It was from this position of strength that the insurance business entered the depression decade of the 1930s. When the stock market crashed in the autumn of 1929, it brought on the worst economic setback in United States history. By 1932, stocks were worth little more than a tenth of their 1929 values, about 13 million people were unemployed, and the national income had been cut in half.

For a time the effect on the life insurance business was severe. Sharp decreases in the amount of new insurance written were seen in 1931 and 1932; and in the latter year, for the first time in a generation, total insurance in force declined. Meanwhile, owing chiefly to suicides, the business suffered high mortality experience (suicides rose to 30 percent above normal during the early years of the 30s), and disability claims and losses enormously increased. Lapses and surrenders were also high; and owing to defaults in mortgage payments and to lower interest rates, earnings fell off sharply.

Nevertheless, compared with most American businesses, life insurance fared exceedingly well. Of a total of about 350 companies, only 20 went into the hands of receivers. Of these, not one was of major size. The actual insurance involved in these failures amounted to only a little more than 1 percent of the total insurance in force in all companies. But even this was reinsured by solvent companies, so that the actual loss to policyowners was practically nil. This unequaled record of strength and stability, under the harshest economic conditions, is one of which the business may well be proud.

Modern Quest for Security

Curiously enough, in one way the depression probably proved a boon to the life insurance business. So deep and long-lasting were its effects that Americans, more earnestly than ever before, began a determined search for financial security, a quest which persists to the present day. The Social Security Act, signed by the President in August 1935, is a part of this trend. Amended in 1939 to provide survivors' benefits, the Act, in effect, provides a large volume of government life insurance. Yet, far from satisfying Americans' insurance needs and cutting into private insurance sales, it in fact re-emphasized the value of financial protection and helped whet the nation's appetite for more. The result of this search for security has been a spectacular increase in life insurance in force, particularly in the years since World War II.

In their efforts to build themselves a more or less "insured society," Americans in recent years have increasingly used life insurance as one of the major tools. Today, the skilled, full-time practitioners of the life insurance art transact the far greater portion of the life insurance business. Over the years, life insurance companies have placed increasing emphasis on the education and training of their agents. This training is now conducted on three levels: the training courses, running from six months to two years, offered by individual companies; the courses offered by the Life Underwriter Training Council; and the rigorous advanced training program conducted in colleges, study groups, and insurance company classrooms under the auspices of the American College of Life Underwriters. The latter organization was formed in 1927 to raise the standards of career education and has been a notable success. Its graduates, designated as Chartered Life Underwriters (C.L.U.), generally are the industry's most deeply informed, thoroughly professional underwriters.

The introduction of new policies in recent years, most notably the family plan; the enormous growth of low-cost group insurance, which tripled in the decade 1960–70; the great rise of annuities, together with the mounting use of insured pension plans and credit life insurance—all demonstrate the wide-ranging usefulness of life insurance to a broadening range of people. And this usefulness has been expanded still further by the insurance business's recent movement into the field of variable products. Well over 50,000 agents have been licensed by the National Association of Securities Dealers, Inc. The Institute of Life Insurance has reported that about 100 life insurance companies have announced plans to sell variable annuities and over 230 companies have indicated their intention to offer mutual funds. These products, along with others, like the proposed variable benefit life insurance, are all examples of the insurance industry's continuing effort to serve the full range of a family's needs for financial security. Though selling whole life insurance will remain the primary purpose of life insurance companies in coming years, the selling of variable and equity plans is likely to become an increasingly important part of the insurance industry's operations.

Today, with nearly nine out of ten American families carrying at least some protection, and with over $1.5 trillion of life insurance in force at the beginning of 1972, Americans, it is clear, are recognizing the urgent need for insurance in our modern industrial society—a society, it is important to note, that life insurance itself has helped to create.

Premium Payments and National Progress

Along with its protection side, America's life insurance business traditionally has played another—and highly important—role: investing in the nation's economy. For a century or more, life insurance funds, the savings of millions of frugal Americans, have been poured back into the economy. During the early national period, when Americans were vigorously tying their land together through a network of turnpikes and canals, an ally was found in the life insurance business, which helped buy the bonds to pay for these improvements. Again, when the Civil War threatened to sunder the nation, the industry responded by making huge purchases of government bonds, helping to bolster the Union's credit and thereby stimulating industry. In the same century, when research and ingenuity made possible new conveniences, life insurance companies gave freely of their support to a succession of vital public utilities undertakings: gas, light, water, telephone, telegraph, and electric power.

There has been scarcely a field in which life insurance funds have not figured prominently. Through mortgage loans, particularly during the housing crises following the Civil War and World Wars I and II, life insurance money has provided homes for millions of Americans. On occasion, insurance funds have even helped feed the world. Money lent farmers during World War I permitted farm mechanization, which in turn ameliorated the food shortage that accompanied the war. Municipalities have received life insurance assistance, too. As populations increased, the demand for municipal services—roads, hospitals, and schools—grew apace, and insurance companies helped provide the capital for them.

But increasingly, the biggest beneficiary of the life insurance dollar has been American industry. Where once, as we have seen, life insurance had to wait upon industrial development, the life insurance business has since become a great storehouse of investment capital feeding our industrial growth. Through the purchase of industrial bonds, through the use of the "sale and lease-back" device, which frees corporate capital for other purposes, and by the investment of funds in preferred and common stocks, life insurance companies have energized American business and quickened our national growth.

Of course, while it is important that businesses operate on a sound financial basis, they also need to function in a healthy social and political environment, and the life insurance business certainly has recognized this. Under its Urban Investment Program, which was announced at the White House in 1968, the life insurance business has pledged to invest $2 billion in city core areas to improve housing conditions and to finance job-creating enterprises. By mid-1971, the companies participating in this program had loaned or committed about 90 percent of that total, making possible some 110,000 housing units and providing more than 60,000 new jobs.

Today, life insurance plays an indispensable role in contemporary life. With its systematic means of funneling funds into the economy, plus its protection side—an ingenious means of guarding millions of Americans against financial hazard—life insurance has earned an honored place at the center of the American scene. In sum, life insurance, the product of man's eternal quest for security, has proved itself one of the most useful institutions ever devised by man.

EXPANSION OF GROUP INSURANCE

The expansion of the group insurance market over the past several decades has been one of the more dramatic trends in the whole field of insurance. The origin of this expansion lay in the hardships of the depression and the effects of the industrial wage and price controls that were imposed during World War II. During the depression countless Americans became increasingly aware of the rapidly rising costs of medical care and of the benefits of life insurance both as security and as a source of savings. This awareness resulted in a dramatic increase of interest in group insurance, an interest that was only intensified by the controls on wages. Since fringe benefits, including insurance provisions, were not controlled, group life and health insurance became a major element of the collective bargaining process. In the postwar period, the continuing rise in medical costs, the appearance of a booming full-employment economy, the growing strength of labor unions and the entrance of most large insurance companies into the group field, each contributed to a steady growth of all forms of group insurance.

Annual sales of group life insurance, for instance, have increased from under $1 billion in 1940 to $49 billion in 1971. By the latter year, there was over $581 billion of group life insurance in force on the lives of more than 81 million individuals. And that total represented over one third of all life insurance in force in the United States.

Still, the growth of group life insurance is only part of the story. That of group health insurance has been equally dramatic. The most popular forms of group health insurance are group hospital and group surgical expense plans. The earliest instance of such a plan was an arrangement in the early years of the depression between a group of schoolteachers and Baylor Hospital in Dallas by which the teachers provided themselves with hospital care on a prepayment basis. This was not only the origin of the Blue Cross service concept of hospital care, but also foreshadowed the reimbursement policy that major insurance companies would develop for hospital and surgical care. Today, more than 175 million Americans are protected by hospital expense insurance and over 90 percent of these also have surgical expense coverage.

In addition to hospital and surgical expense, other forms of group health insurance include regular medical expense, major medical expense, and disability income protection. Although not as many people are covered by these kinds of protection, their numbers are, nevertheless, growing at a dramatic rate.

HEALTH INSURANCE

The history of health insurance in the United States, though reaching back more than one hundred years, is one of halting early developments and experiments and rapidly accelerating later developments and growth, particularly since the mid-1930s.

The companies that first began issuing accident insurance, and later such coverages as employers' liability and workmen's compensation, were chiefly multiple-line casualty insurance companies. In the decades of the 1930s and 1940s, many life insurance companies entered the health insurance field, and by 1950, they were providing slightly over one half of all individual health insurance coverage. Thus in 1950, life insurance companies were protecting one of every two persons who were covered by private health insurance, and by 1970, three out of every five.

The first company to offer health insurance against the cost of medical care was the Massachusetts Health Insurance Company of Boston, organized in 1847. Three years later, the Franklin Health Assurance Company of Massachusetts was organized to issue the first accident insurance.

One of the most hazardous activities of the latter half of the 19th century was travel, especially by rail and steamboat, and the early growth of health insurance was mainly in coverage against such travel accidents. The first company formed to offer accident insurance on a basis resembling its modern form was the Travelers Insurance Company of Hartford, organized in 1863, which first provided insurance against railway mishaps, and later against all types of accidents.

The success of accident insurance paved the way for the first ventures into sickness and disability income insurance, and the first individual policies offering disability insurance appeared in 1890. The first decade of the new century saw the introduction of surgical benefits and hospital expense benefits (in some individual disability income policies); and in 1907 the first noncancellable, guaranteed renewable disability income policy was issued.

During the 1920s, many liberalizations were made under pressure of competition and without adequate experience or statistical data. The combination of overliberal benefits, excessive amounts of indemnity on individual risks, and the adverse economic conditions of the depression following 1929 brought about a retrenchment at that time.[8] With the beginning of economic recovery, however, this trend was reversed. The late 40s saw the beginning of a truly surging growth, still continuing, in health insurance coverage and in the extension of its benefits.

One reason for this rapid advance in health insurance, in addition to the entrance of more life insurance companies into the field, was the establishment of Blue Cross/Blue Shield and other independent hospital-medical expense plans. These latter are on a group insurance basis; and where, prior to the 1930s, most health insurance was under individual plans, the greater amount of coverage today is under group policies. Group health insurance now figures prominently among employee benefits offered by industry.

The first city-wide Blue Cross plan was inaugurated by a group of hospitals in Sacramento, California, in 1932. The first of the Blue-Shield-type plans was begun in 1939.

In 1971, total premium payments from health insurance policies rose to almost $23 billion. Of this total, $10 billion represented subscription income of Blue Cross/Blue Shield organizations and other hospital-medical plans. As an indication of the acceleration in coverage that has occurred in recent years, the growth in premium income received by all private insurers between 1961 and 1971 was about 154 percent. Significant developments in health insurance coverage during the past two decades

---

[8] E. L. Bartleson et al., *Health Insurance Provided through Individual Policies* (Chicago: Society of Actuaries, 2d ed., 1968).

have included major medical expense policies, long-term disability income coverage, guaranteed renewable hospital-surgical expense coverages, the mass enrollment plans, and the development by the federal government of the Medicare and Medicaid programs.

The Medicare program, for people over age 65, became effective on July 1, 1966. The program is made up of two parts: first, compulsory hospital insurance that is financed by contributions from employees, employers, and the self-employed; second, medical insurance to help pay for medical services and supplies not covered under the hospital benefits. The medical insurance coverage is voluntary and can be secured only by enrollment. It is financed by monthly premiums shared equally by those who enroll in the plan and by the federal government. During 1971, about 20 million persons were enrolled in each of the sections under the Medicare program.

Medicaid, which refers to Title 19 of the Federal Social Security Act, became effective on January 1, 1966. Under this program, federal matching funds help individual states to expand their public assistance programs in order to help those persons, regardless of age, whose income and resources are regarded as insufficient to pay for health care.

Accompanying the recent growth in health insurance, and affecting both its need by the general public and its premium costs, have been the great advances made in recent decades in medical science and continued rising costs of medical care of all kinds. Many formerly incurable or crippling diseases have been brought under control by the medical profession; more medical care in and out of hospitals is available; but also, the cost of medical care continues to rise rapidly. This rapid increase in cost, together with the uneven distribution of medical services among all Americans, has prompted a growing interest in a broader program of national health insurance. A number of bills have already been introduced in Congress that would create such a system.

The awakening of more and more people to the need for comprehensive health insurance has paralleled the growing recognition of life insurance as the cornerstone of the American family's financial security. Whether it be through private or public vehicles, the future of health insurance is clearly one of continued rapid growth.

SELECTED REFERENCES

Anderson, O. D. *Uneasy Equilibrium: Private and Public Financing of Health Services in the U.S., 1875–1965.* New Haven, Conn.: College and University Press, 1968.

Bartleson, E. L., et al. *Health Insurance Provided through Individual Policies.* 2d ed. Chicago: Society of Actuaries, 1968.

Buley, R. Carlyle. *The American Life Convention: 1906–1952.* 2 vols. New York: Appleton-Century-Crofts, Inc., 1953.

Eilers, R. D. *Regulation of Blue Cross and Blue Shield Plans.* Homewood, Ill.: Richard D. Irwin, Inc., 1963.

Eilers, R. D., and Crowe, R. M. *Group Insurance Handbook.* Homewood, Ill.: Richard D. Irwin, Inc., 1965.

Health Insurance Council. *The Health Insurance Story.* New York, n.d.

Health Insurance Institute. *Source Book of Health Insurance Data, 1972–73.* New York, 1973.

Huebner, S. S., and Black, K. *Life Insurance.* 8th ed. New York: Appleton-Century-Crofts, Inc., 1972.

Maclean, Joseph B. *Life Insurance.* 9th ed. New York: McGraw-Hill Book Co., Inc., 1962.

O'Donnell, Terence. *History of Life Insurance in Its Formative Years.* Chicago: American Conservation Co., 1936.

Stalson, J. Owen. *Marketing Life Insurance: Its History in America.* 1942 ed. reprinted as a volume in the McCahan Foundation Book Series in 1969 by Richard D. Irwin, Inc., Homewood, Ill.

A

**Historic Dates in the
Development of Life and
Health Insurance in the
United States**

LIFE INSURANCE[1]

1759. The first life insurance company in the United States, "The Corporation for Relief of Poor and Distressed Presbyterian Ministers and of the Poor and Distressed Widows and Children of Presbyterian Ministers," was established in Philadelphia by the Synod of the Presbyterian Church. This company, now Presbyterian Ministers' Fund, is the oldest life insurance company in continued existence in the world.

1794. The Insurance Company of North America chartered; was the first general insurance company to sell life insurance in America. In five years only six policies were issued and the company discontinued its life insurance business in 1804.

1807. Israel Whelen of Philadelphia appointed agent for the Pelican Life Insurance Company of London. Probably first agent for level premium life insurance in America.

1812. Pennsylvania Company for Insurance on Lives and Granting Annuities incorporated; first corporation to be organized in America for the sole purpose of issuing life insurance policies and annuities. First policy issued 1813. It discontinued issuing life policies in 1872.

1830. New York Life Insurance and Trust Company started, notable as first American life company to employ agents. This company later discontinued its life insurance business and was subsequently merged with the Bank of New York.

1835. Charter granted New England Mutual Life Insurance Company of Boston. First mutual company to be chartered in America. Did not actually begin business until December 1843.

---

[1] Reprinted with permission from the *Fact Book*, 1972, Institute of Life Insurance, 277 Park Avenue, New York, N.Y. 10017.

1836. The Girard Life Insurance, Annuity and Trust Company of Philadelphia established upon a new principle, that of granting policyholders participation in profits, although it was a stock company. The first dividends were allotted in 1844 as additions of insurance to policies in force three or more years. This company later became a trust company only.

1840. The legislature of the state of New York enacted a law which provided that the proceeds of a policy made out to a widow as beneficiary would be paid to her and were exempt from claims of creditors. This strengthened immeasurably the protective power of a life insurance policy.

1842. The Mutual Life Insurance Company of New York was chartered. First policy issued February 1, 1843, marking the beginning of mutual life insurance as it is known today.

1848. First policy loans granted about this time.

1849. New York's first general insurance law passed.

1851. New Hampshire established the first regulatory body to examine the affairs of insurance companies.

1853. Policy valuation tables, which had been worked on by Elizur Wright for nine years, published.

1859. New York state established an insurance department.

1861. Massachusetts first state to require nonforfeiture values as part of life policies.

1861. First war risk insurance written by life companies in Civil War.

1864. Incontestable clause first written into policies by an American company.

1868. American Experience Table of Mortality published as a part of New York law. Covering experience 1843–1858, it was the first mortality table based on experience of insured lives in America.

1869. Earliest organization of life insurance agents recorded in Chicago.

1871. First convention of State Insurance Commissioners, in New York City, in May.

1873. First weekly premium policy issued in the United States.

1875. Industrial insurance agency system introduced in the United States.

1880. Cash surrender values first established by law in Massachusetts.

1905. Armstrong investigation of life insurance by New York State Legislature, resulting in many changes in insurance laws.

1906. New York insurance laws revised.

1909. Standard provisions for life insurance policies adopted in New York State.

1911. First group life insurance for employees of an employer.

1917. Life insurance for servicemen of World War I offered by government under War Risk Insurance Act; such insurance is now known as U.S. Government Life Insurance.

1918. American Men Ultimate Mortality Table published. Covered experience 1900–1915.

1928. First examinations held for Chartered Life Underwriters, resulting in awards of CLU designations to qualified life insurance personnel.

1935. Social Security Act enacted. Subsequently amended at various times to include benefits for survivors and dependents and for disabled workers and their dependents, to extend coverage as to employments covered, to lower minimum retirement age, to raise benefit levels, to revise contribution schedules, to increase earnings base, and, in 1965, to establish "Medicare," a broad program of health insurance for people aged 65 or older.

1938. The 1937 Standard Annuity Mortality Table published. Based primarily on experience 1932–1936.

1939. Temporary National Economic Committee investigation of life insurance.

1940. National Service Life Insurance Act, providing insurance for men and women in service in World War II, adopted by Congress.

1941. Commissioners 1941 Standard Ordinary Table of Mortality published, based on experience 1930–1940.

1944. U.S. Supreme Court held insurance to be commerce.

1948. Legislation permitting "Standard Nonforfeiture and Valuation" methods of computation effective in nearly all states.

1954. Federal Employees' Group Life Insurance Act providing group life insurance and accidental death and dismemberment insurance to civilian officers and employees of the United States government through private insurance companies.

1958. Commissioners 1958 Standard Ordinary Table of Mortality based on experience 1950–1954 published.

1965. Servicemen's Group Life Insurance Act, providing members on active duty in the uniformed services with group life insurance underwritten by private insurers through a contract with the Veterans Administration.

HEALTH INSURANCE[2]

1798. U.S. Marine Hospital Service established by U.S. Congress. Compulsory deductions for hospital service were made from seamen's wages.

1847. Organization of Massachusetts Health Insurance Company of Boston. First U.S. company organized to issue insurance against the costs of medical care.

1850. Franklin Health Assurance Company of Massachusetts organized; first insurance company authorized to issue accident insurance in the United States.

1863. Founding of Travelers In-

---

[2] Reprinted with permission from *Source Book of Health Insurance Data,* 1970, Health Insurance Institute, 1701 K Street, N.W., Washington, D.C. 20006.

surance Company of Hartford. The company offered accident insurance for railway mishaps; then all forms of accident protection. It was the first company to issue accident insurance on a basis resembling its present form.

1890. Introduction of individual insurance policies offering disability income protection from certain specified diseases.

1903. Limited surgical benefits included in some individual disability income policies.

1905. Hospital expense benefits first offered in some individual disability income policies in the form of a benefit increase while the disabled insured person was hospitalized.

1907. First noncancellable and guaranteed renewable disability income policy offered in the United States.

1912. Uniform Standard Provisions Law promulgated by the National Association of Insurance Commissioners.

1921. First noncancellable and guaranteed renewable disability policy issued to contain a stated maximum indemnity period for total disability due to sickness with no aggregate limit.

1932. First citywide Blue Cross plan tried out with a group of hospitals in Sacramento, Calif.

1937. Organization of Health Service Plan Commission (Blue Cross Commission).

1939. Establishment of the California Physicians' Service, the first Blue Shield-type plan formed.

1946. Organization of Blue Shield Medical Care Plans, Inc. (Blue Shield Commission).

1946. Formation of the Health Insurance Council, a federation of eight insurance associations organized to give technical and practical assistance on health insurance to the providers of medical care.

1948. First noncancellable and guaranteed renewable hospital-surgical-medical policy issued providing protection to age 65.

1949. First major medical group insurance contract issued. Liberty Mutual Insurance Company issued this contract to the Elfun Society—management personnel of General Electric Company.

1952. First noncancellable and guaranteed renewable hospital-surgical-medical policy issued providing protection for the lifetime of the policyholder.

1955. First guaranteed renewable lifetime hospital-surgical policy designed for older age people.

1958. First comprehensive major medical individual insurance policy issued.

1959. Continental Casualty Company issued first comprehensive group dental insurance plan written by an insurance company.

1961. First state enrollment plan made available by Connecticut to persons 65 and over on a state basis and under special enabling legislation allowing the pooling of risks by a group of insurance companies (Associated Connecticut Health Insurance Companies).

1962. First lifetime noncancellable and guaranteed renewable hospital-surgical policy offered by

Standard Security Life Insurance Company of New York.

1962. First fully paid-up guaranteed renewable lifetime major medical insurance introduced by American Life Insurance Company of New York and Georgia International Life Insurance Company.

1966. Program of governmental health insurance, Medicare, for people age 65 and over, became effective July 1.

B Application for Life Insurance Policy, Including Medical Examiner's Report

Part I of Application for Insurance in

Life Insurance Company of ▓▓▓▓▓

THE QUESTIONS AND ITEMS HEREIN APPLY TO THE PROPOSED INSURED		

1 Name (Print) *John Doe* ☒ Male ☐ Female

2 (a) Date of birth Month *Jan.* Day *10* Year *38* **(b) Place of birth** City or town *Phila., Pa.* State Country *U.S.A.*

3 Age nearest birthday *35*

4 ☐ Single ☐ Divorced ☐ Widowed ☒ Married ☐ Separated

5 (a) Occupation. If more than one give all. *Lawyer* **(b) How long so employed?** *5 years*

(c) Describe fully your exact duties. *Usual duties*

(d) Name of employer *Self-employed*

(e) If so employed less than two years, give former occupation.

6 Addresses (No.) (Street) (City) (State) (Zip No.) (Yrs.)
Residence *98 WinchesterAve. Phila., Pa. 19136 10*
Business *45 Main St Phila., Pa. 19103 5*

7 Premium notices to: ☐ Residence address ☐ Business address or (Name and address)

8 (a) Complete list of all life insurance on your life.

Company	Year issued	Amount of insurance Personal	Amount of insurance Business	Amount of disability income	Amount of accidental death benefit
Totals *NONE*					

(b) Complete list of all other insurance providing indemnity for sickness or accident.

Company	Amount of monthly indemnity Non-cancellable Sickness	Accident	Other Sickness	Accident	How long payable
NONE					

(c) Total death benefit—accident and sickness insurance $

9 Do you intend to change your occupation, or to travel or reside outside of the United States or Canada within the next year? Give full details. *No*

10 Have you ever been declined or postponed for life, disability, sickness or accident insurance, or offered insurance differing in plan, amount, or premium rate from that for which you applied? Give full details and names of companies. *No*

11 Are any other applications for life, disability, sickness or accident insurance on your life pending or contemplated? Give amounts, companies, and all benefits applied for. *No*

12 (a) Have you flown in any aircraft as a pilot, student pilot, officer or member of the crew within the last five years, or do you intend to do so in the future? ☐ Yes ☒ No

(b) Have you flown more than 100 hours a year as a passenger within the last two years, or do you intend to do so in the future? ☐ Yes ☒ No

(If answer to 12 (a) or (b) is "Yes", complete Aviation Supplement.)

13 Life insurance policy applied for:
(a) Amount and plan *$50,000. Whole Life*
(b) Additional benefits:
☒ Disability—waiver only ☐ Automatic premium loan
☐ Disability—waiver & income ☒ Guaranteed purchase option
☒ Accidental death $50,000. on basic life insurance policy
$ on level term agreement
☐ Term dividend option—balance of dividends applied as in 15 (b).
Protected premium agreement ☐ Death only ☐ Death or disability

14 Income protection insurance policy applied for:
(a) Monthly indemnity $ **(b) Plan**
(c) Maximum duration of monthly indemnity payments:
Sickness year (s) Accident year (s)
(d) Elimination period during which benefits are not payable:
Sickness days Accident days
(e) Additional benefits:
☐ Principal sum amount $
☐ Monthly hospital indemnity $
☐ Partial disability ☐ Accident only ☐ Accident & sickness

15 (a) Premiums payable
Life insurance / Income protection
☒ Yearly ☐
☐ Half-yearly ☐
☐ Quarterly ☐
☐ Monthly ☐

(b) Dividend election
Life insurance / Income protection
☐ Pay in cash ☐
☐ Reduce premium ☐
☐ Buy paid-up additions ☐
☒ Accumulate at interest

16 Has full first premium been paid?
Life insurance ☒ Yes ☐ No Income protection ☐ Yes ☐ No

17 Owner (life insurance only). The owner of all life insurance will be the insured unless another owner is designated here.

The owner of all income protection insurance will be the insured.

18 Beneficiary and relationship to proposed insured (not applicable to income protection insurance unless principal sum is applied for).
Insured's wife, Mary A. Doe

Amendments (Reserve for Home Office use)

№ 360738

Signed at (City and State) *Phila., Pa.*
On (Date) *February 1* 19 *73*
Signature of agent *Richard Roe*

Proposed insured *John Doe*
Applicant if other than proposed insured

Form 9896 12-63

Application for Life Insurance Policy, Including Medical Examiner's Report (continued)

THIS SPACE FOR HOME OFFICE USE ONLY

☐ N. R.

Final disposition
of application

SUPPLEMENTARY STATEMENT BY PROPOSED INSURED OR APPLICANT

Is the insurance now applied for intended to replace insurance or annuities in this Company? ☐ Yes ☐ No
If yes, give policy numbers of insurance or annuities being replaced.

Is the insurance now applied for intended to replace insurance or annuities in any other company? ☐ Yes ☐ No
If yes, give names of companies and amounts and plans of insurance or annuities being replaced.

Has the person to be insured participated in skin or scuba diving, sky diving, automobile, ☐ Yes ☐ No
motorboat or motorcycle racing or any other similar sport, hobby or avocation within
the last five years or does the person to be insured intend to do so in the future?
If yes, give details.

Signature of proposed insured or applicant

TO BE COMPLETED BY THE AGENT

1 (a) Do you have knowledge or reason to believe that replacement of existing insurance or annuity contracts may be involved? If yes, give details. ☐ Yes ☐ No
(b) If the insurance now applied for is intended to replace insurance or annuities in this or any other company, have you submitted to the applicant a written proposal setting forth all the facts, advantages and disadvantages in making the replacement? ☐ Yes ☐ No

2 Is proposed insured a U.S. citizen? ☐ Yes ☐ No

3 Are you personally acquainted with the proposed insured?
☐ Yes ☐ No
If yes, how long have you known him? | Are you related?

4 What do you estimate proposed insured's worth and annual income to be?

Worth	Earned income	Other income
$	$	$

5 Social Security or other taxpayer identifying number of:

(a) Proposed insured
(b) Owner, if other than proposed insured

6 What settlement has been obtained with this application and receipted for on the conditional receipt?

7 (a) Amount and mode of payment of initial premium:
Life insurance $
☐ Yearly
☐ Half-yearly
☐ Quarterly
☐ Monthly
☐ A.P.P.
☐ Other (specify in detail)

Income protection $
☐ Yearly
☐ Half-yearly
☐ Quarterly
☐ Monthly
☐ A.P.P.
☐ Other (specify in detail)

(b) What occupational class has been used in calculating the premium for income protection?

8 TO BE COMPLETED ON NON-MEDICAL LIFE INSURANCE APPLICATIONS:
Has proposed insured applied for non-medical life insurance to any other company during the past twelve months? ☐ Yes ☐ No
If yes, give companies, amounts and dates.

COMPLETE IF PROPOSED INSURED IS A MALE AGE 17 THROUGH 26

9 Draft classification

10 Has he been alerted or called for future duty? ☐ Yes ☐ No

11 Has he completed his military service? ☐ Yes ☐ No

12 If in service or planning to enter, including reserves or ROTC
(a) What is his branch?
(b) What is his rating or rank?
(c) Is he or will he be a career man? ☐ Yes ☐ No

COMPLETE IF PROPOSED INSURED IS A FEMALE

13 If married, amount of husband's life insurance

14 Husband's occupation

15 If she is divorced or separated, give date and cause.

COMPLETE IF PROPOSED INSURED IS A DEPENDENT CHILD

16 Amount of life insurance on the applicant

17. (a) Applicant's occupation   (b) Relationship to proposed insured

18 List the following for minor brothers and sisters of the proposed insured:

Name	Age	Amount of life insurance

Credit: (Please print)

Agency Number

Signature of Agent

Recommended

Signature of General Agent or Manager

Application for Life Insurance Policy, Including Medical Examiner's Report (continued)

Part II of Application for Insurance in

Life Insurance Company of

To be completed in the handwriting of the examiner
(or of an authorized company representative on non-medical applications)

THE QUESTIONS AND ITEMS HEREIN APPLY TO THE PROPOSED INSURED

1 Name (Print)   *John Doe*

2 Date of birth	Month *Jan.*	Day 10	Year 1938

3 Are you now in good health? If not, give details.   *Yes*

4 (a) Family history

	Age if living	State of health	Age at death	Cause of death
Father	65	Good		
Mother	60	Good		
Brothers and sisters No. living	0			
No. dead	0			

(b) Is there any history of diabetes or nervous or mental disorder in your family? Give details.   *No*

(c) Have you been associated within the last five years with any persons, including members of your family, having tuberculosis? Give details.   *No*

5 Have you ever applied for or received from any source sickness, accident or disability benefits or a pension? Give reasons, dates, and durations of disabilities.   *No*

6 Do you now use or have you ever used alcoholic beverages? State kinds and amounts used daily or weekly.   *No*

7 Have you ever been under treatment for the alcoholic or drug habit? Give details.   *No*

8 Have you ever taken or been advised by a physician or other practitioner to take insulin or any other medicine for diabetes?   *No*

9 Are you now taking or have you within the last two years taken any drug or any medicine prescribed by a physician or other practitioner? Give details.   *No*

10 Have you ever undergone or been advised by a physician or other practitioner to undergo any surgical operation? Give details including reasons and dates.   *No*

11 Have you ever been in any hospital or sanitarium for treatment or observation? Give details including reasons and dates.   *No*

12 Have you ever had or been advised by a physician or other practitioner to have any special examinations or tests such as x-rays, electrocardiograms, heart studies, blood studies or urine tests? Give details including reasons and dates.   *No*

13 When and for what reason did you last consult a physician or other practitioner?

14 Give names and addresses of all physicians and other practitioners consulted within the last five years, including reasons for and dates of all consultations.   *1970 - Cold - Dr. Smythe - Medical Bldg. 17th + Chesnut Sts. Phila., Pa.*

15 Have you ever had or been told by a physician or other practitioner that you had any of the following: (Answer "Yes" or "No" opposite each part of this question.)

(a) Dizziness, fainting spells, convulsions or fits, nervous or mental disorder, severe or persistent headache, stroke, insanity or epilepsy?	*No*	(f) Diabetes, goitre, thyroid disorder, skin disorder, tumors, lumps or growths, cancer, enlargement of any glands, or syphilis?	*No*	
(b) Kidney disorder or stone; urinary, bladder or prostate disorder; sugar, albumin, pus, blood or casts in urine?	*No*	(g) Hernia, varicose veins, deformity or paralysis?	*No*	
(c) Shortness of breath, spitting blood, night sweats, frequent or persistent cough, disorder of the lungs, asthma, tuberculosis or pleurisy?	*No*	(h) Recurrent indigestion, cramps or colic, chronic diarrhea, passage of blood, colitis, stomach or duodenal ulcer, gall bladder disorder, gall stones, liver disorder or jaundice?	*No*	
(d) Pain, pressure or any discomfort in the chest, palpitation, heart trouble, angina pectoris, coronary disorder, heart murmur, high blood pressure, swelling of legs or ankles?	*No*	(i) Impairment of vision not fully corrected by glasses or any impairment of hearing?	*No*	
(e) Rheumatic fever, chorea, rheumatism or arthritis?	*No*	(j) Any disease, disorder, ailment, impairment, injury or amputation not listed above?	*No*	

16 If any parts of question 15 are answered "Yes", give full details below.

Part of question 15	Full details including duration, severity, dates, and after effects	Physicians, practitioners, hospitals, etc. (Names and addresses)

17 (a) Height in shoes 5 feet 11 inches	(b) Weight fully dressed 165 pounds	(c) Have you lost any weight within the last two years? 0 pounds lost	(d) How long has your present weight been maintained? 5 yrs.

18 Were you weighed and measured when this form was completed? *Yes*	19 Ask of Married Women: Are you now pregnant? If so, give expected date of delivery

I have read this completed Part II and represent that to the best of my knowledge and belief all statements and answers herein are complete, true and correctly recorded.

Signed at   *Phila., Pa*
City and State

on   *February 1*   19 *73*
Date

Completed and witnessed by   *Richard Spitz M.D.*   M.D. or Agent

Proposed insured   *John Doe*

Form 9897 12.63

Application for Life Insurance Policy, Including Medical Examiner's Report (concluded)

MEDICAL EXAMINER'S REPORT

20 GENERAL APPEARANCE:

21 G'RTH: Chest at full inspiration .... inches
Chest at full expiration .... inches
Abdomen one inch below umbilicus .... inches

22 BLOOD PRESSURE:

		Highest	Lowest
Record three or more separate readings including the highest and the lowest. The applicant should be seated and the pressures taken over a period of at least five minutes.	Systolic		
	Diastolic (disappearance of all sound)		

23 HEART: Make examination of the heart and chest with stethoscope against bare skin.
Auscultate all valve areas before and after exercise (25 vigorous hops on each foot), sitting and recumbent, including the left lateral position.

(a) Heart rate	per minute		
If irregular complete the following:	At rest	After exercise	2 min. after exercise
Heart rate			
Number of irregularities			
Type of irregularity			

(b) Is the heart enlarged?
If so, indicate position of apex or left border.

(c) Are heart sounds normal?

(d) If a murmur is present, describe its timing, location, transmission, and the effect of exercise and respiration.

24 LUNGS: Are the lungs and thoracic cage normal?
If not, give details.

25 ABDOMEN: Describe scars, tenderness, rigidity, masses or other abnormality. If hernia, give size and reducibility.

26 NEUROLOGICAL: Describe neurological condition including patellar and pupillary reflexes and Romberg's sign.

27 Is the thyroid normal?
If enlarged, is it nodular or diffuse?

28 Describe any abnormalities of:
(a) Veins (varicosities—location, extent, ankle edema, ulceration)
(b) Lymphatic glands
(c) Teeth and gums
(d) Throat and tonsils

29 URINALYSIS:

(a) Date and hour voided

Date .... 19......	
Time .... a.m.	
	p.m.

(b) Specific gravity
(If under 1.015 obtain another specimen)

(c) Albumin present?

(d) Sugar present?

A portion of the specimen of urine should be sent to the home office if:
(1) Insurance age is 40 or younger and amount of life insurance applied for is more than $50,000;
(2) Insurance age is 41-60 and amount of life insurance applied for is more than $30,000;
(3) Insurance age is 61 or older;
(4) Albumin or sugar is present or has ever been found or suspected in the past;
(5) There is a history of any genito-urinary disease; or
(6) Diastolic blood pressure is 95 or over.

30 Are you forwarding a specimen of urine to the home office?
If so, give reason.

31 (a) Where was this examination made?
□ Examiner's office
□ Agent's office
□ Proposed insured's residence
□ Proposed insured's place of business

(b) If not at examiner's office, were the facilities suitable for a satisfactory examination?

32 After reviewing the answers and as a result of your examination, do you find any evidence of any past or present disease not specifically mentioned in this application?

If proposed insured is a female, also answer question 33, giving details.
33 (a) Has she ever had any tumors or disease of the breasts?

(b) Has she ever had any uterine or ovarian disease?

(c) Is menstruation normal?

(d) Were labors normal?
In case of Cesarean section, was she sterilized?

ADDITIONAL EXPLANATORY REMARKS

Medical Fee Voucher may be used to submit confidential information to the Medical Director

№ 480908 VOUCHER NUMBER

I certify that the statements and answers made by the proposed insured, in answer to the questions in Part II of the application on the reverse side of this form, are correctly recorded therein; that I have made a full and careful physical examination of the proposed insured; and that the answers to the questions on both sides of this form are in my own handwriting.

....M.D.

Name of Agent   (Address of Examiner)

Form 9897 12.63

C

Specimen Inspection Report—Life Form and Health Form

RETAIL CREDIT COMPANY
LIFE REPORT

CONFIDENTIAL

Acct. No.

Dist., Agcy., or Br.

OFFICE

Date:

Pol. No.

NAME:

Date

INSURANCE HISTORY

Acct. No.   Amt. or Type Coverage   Fam. or Indiv.

Address:
Occupation on
Inq. & Employer:

Date of Birth: A   Health App'd for $ Per   ☐ Hospitalization   ☐ Major Medical Exp.

				NO	YES	
	1.	**SIGNIFICANT FEATURES:**				
	2.	On what date was this inspection made?				
IDENTITY	3—A.	How many years has each of your sources known applicant?	A.			
	B.	How many days since you or your sources have seen applicant? *(If not within two weeks, explain fully.)*	B.			
AGE	4.	Is there any reason to doubt accuracy of birth date given?				
FINANCES	5—A.	What is estimate of net worth?	A. $			
	B.	What is annual earned income from work or business?	B. $			
	C.	Has applicant any income from investments, rentals, pension, etc.? *(If so, state source, amount.)*	C.			
OCCUPA-TION	6—A.	Does the occupation or job differ in name from that given in heading of this report?	A.			
	B.	Does applicant change jobs frequently?	B.			
	C.	Any part-time or off-season occupation? Does applicant plan work or travel in foreign countries?	C.			
	D.	Does applicant or employer sell or manufacture beer, wine or liquor?	D.			
DRIVING RECORD	7.	Is applicant a fast, reckless, or careless driver?				IF YES, See Questions on Back.
AVIATION SPORTS-AVOCATIONS	8—A.	Has applicant taken flying lessons, either as member of armed forces or as civilian, owned or piloted a plane, or flown in planes not operated by scheduled airlines?	A.			
	B.	Does applicant engage in hazardous sports or avocations (racing, skin or scuba diving, sky diving, snow-mobiling, big game hunting, mountain climbing, cave exploring, dune buggy, etc.)?	B.			
HEALTH	9—A.	Is there anything unhealthy about appearance, such as being very thin or having excess weight?	A.			
	B.	Any deformity, amputation, blindness, deafness, or other defects?	B.			
	10.	Do you learn of any illness, operation, or injury, past or present?				IF YES, See Questions on Back.
	11.	Do you learn applicant was ever rejected for military service or discharged for medical reasons?				
	12.	Do you learn of any member of family (blood relation) having had heart trouble, cancer, diabetes, tuberculosis or mental trouble? *(If so, who and which disease.)*				
HABITS	13—A.	Is applicant a steady, frequent drinker (daily, almost daily, several times a week)?	A.			
	IF SO, { B.	How often?	B.			
	C.	How many drinks does applicant take on these occasions?	C.			
	D.	What does applicant usually drink?	D.			
	14.	Does applicant now or has applicant in the past used intoxicants to excess?				IF YES, See Questions on Back.
ENVIRON-MENT	15.	Anything adverse about living conditions or neighborhood?				IF YES, See Questions on Back.
REPUTA-TION	16.	Do any of following apply to this applicant: Heavy debts? Domestic trouble? Drug habit? Connection with illegal liquor? Irregular beneficiary?				
	17.	Is there any criticism of character, morals, or general reputation?				
	18.	*IF FAMILY POLICY:* Anything adverse on health or physical condition of other family members? (If so, cover in Remarks.)	Answer only if Family Policy	☐ NO ☐ YES		

SPECIMEN REPORT

REMARKS: 19. COMMENT BELOW ON TOPICS LISTED AT LEFT. ALSO, GIVE DETAILS OF "YES" OR INCOMPLETE ANSWERS.

A. BUSINESS:
Employer's name, line and size of business? Name of applicant's job? How long so employed? Cover any indication of frequent job changes or instability of employment.

B. ANSWER HANDY GUIDE QUESTIONS, IF APPLICABLE.

C. PERSONAL: Married, single, or divorced? Any children? Type of associates. IF WOMAN, "name of father or husband; his occupation, worth and income.

RETAIL CREDIT COMPANY

Signature of person making report

Form 1—10-70 U.S.A.   OVER—SEE ADDITIONAL QUESTIONS ON BACK   LIFE REPORT

Specimen Inspection Report—Life Form and Health Form (continued)

#19 Continued

DETAILS OF APPEARANCE:

20—A. How does applicant appear unhealthy (complexion, weight, or what)?_____ B. Describe. (If overweight or underweight, give details.)

DETAILS OF HEALTH HISTORY ON APPLICANT:

21. Nature of illness, operation or injury?_____

22. Approximate date it occurred?_____
23—A. How long confined or "laid up"?_____
    B. Completely recovered?_____
24—A. Attended by Dr. (Name)_____
    Address _____
    B. Confined to hospital?_____ If so, name and address:
    Name _____
    Address _____
25. Any effect on present health?_____ Details:

SPECIMEN REPORT

DETAILS OF DRIVING RECORD:

26. When, where, and under what circumstances does applicant drive in a fast or reckless manner? (Open highway, congested areas, etc.—if known to drive considerably in excess of speed limit, cover.)

27. Any evidence of unsupervised racing?_____ Give details:

ANSWER THESE IF LEARNED IN INVESTIGATION

28. Any arrests?_____ (Approximate dates)_____
29. Charges? _____
    If convicted, approximate dates?_____
30. Any accidents?_____ If so, approximate dates and details:

31. License ever suspended or revoked?_____ If so, cause, date and whether applicant drove without a license?

DETAILS OF ENVIRONMENT:

32. LIVING CONDITIONS:
    A. Over-crowded, dirty, unsanitary, etc.?_____
       (If so, give details.)
    B. If apartment, dark or dirty halls, broken or littered stairs, etc.? (If so, give details.)

33. NEIGHBORHOOD: Deteriorating physically, poor sanitation, vice and crime, vandalism, etc.? (If so, give details.)

DETAILS OF DRINKING HABITS: Give these additional details to show drinking habits as definitely as possible:

34. Classify excessive drinking: ☐ Present   ☐ Past

		How often? (Once a week, once a month, etc.)
A. Getting "drunk," stupefied, entirely out of control of usual faculties?	A. ☐	A._____
B. Loud, boisterous, or obviously under influence, although still in possession of most of faculties?	B. ☐	B._____
C. Mild excess, just getting "feeling good"; exhilaration or stimulation?	C. ☐	C._____

35. Do (did) these occasions last for an evening, a day, two days, a week, or for how long?
36. How long has (had) applicant been drinking to this extent?
37. WHEN WAS THE LAST OCCASION OF THIS SORT?
38. If applicant is an excessive drinker at present, does applicant drive a car during periods of excess?
39. Has applicant ever taken any "cure" for liquor habit? (If so, when? Any subsequent lapse?)
40. Tell how applicant drinks, if social or solitary, or if because of domestic or other trouble, how it affects applicant (jovial, belligerent, etc.), whether ever arrested, and details to give clear picture of drinking habits; if habits have changed, tell how and how long since change; if reformed, what led to reformation (ill health, domestic trouble or what)?

FIELD REPRESENTATIVE: Do not write in this space.
(Use Continuation of Report, Form 5166, for additional remarks.)

1-B—10-70

Specimen Inspection Report —Life Form and Health Form (continued)

RETAIL CREDIT COMPANY
HEALTH REPORT

CONFIDENTIAL

Acct. No.	Dist., Agcy., or Br.		OFFICE
Date:	Pol. No.		
NAME:		INSURANCE HISTORY	

Address:
Duties on
Inq. & Employer:

| Date | Acct. No. | Amt. or Type Coverage | Fam. or Indiv. |

Date of Birth: Indem. App'd $ Per   Carried $ Per   Life App'd $ ☐ Hosp. ☐ M. M. Ex.

1. SIGNIFICANT FEATURES:

2. On what date was this inspection made?

3—A. How many years has each of your sources known applicant?   A.   **IDENTITY**
   B. How many days since you or your sources have seen applicant? (If not within   B.
   two weeks, explain fully.)

   AGE

4. Is there any reason to doubt accuracy of birth date given?

5—A. What is annual earned income from work or business? (If professional or self-   A. $ **EARNED INCOME**
   employed, give net and gross.)
   B. In addition to above, what amount (if any) does applicant also receive from   B. $
   commissions, year-end bonus, etc. (If none, so state.)
   C. Are your answers to two preceding questions exact figures or estimates? (State   C.
   which.)

   D. If exact figures, who gave them (employer, banker, or who)?   D.
   E. If not exact figures, who gave estimates reported above?   E.
   F. Is there any reason to question sufficiency of earned income for amount of   F.
   insurance applied and carried? (If so, explain in Remarks.)

6—A. How much annual income does applicant have from investments, rentals,   A. $ **UNEARNED INCOME—**
   pensions, etc.?   **WORTH**
   B. What is estimate of net worth?   B. $

		NO	YES		
7—A. Do duties or job differ in name from that given in heading of this report?	A.				**DUTIES**
B. Does applicant change jobs frequently?	B.				
C. Has applicant any part-time or off-season occupation? Does applicant plan work or travel in foreign countries?	C.				
8. Is applicant a fast, reckless, or careless driver?				IF YES, see Questions on Back.	DRIVING
9—A. Has applicant taken flying lessons, either as member of armed forces or as civilian, owned, or piloted a plane, or flown in planes not operated by scheduled airlines?	A.				AVIATION—SPORTS— AVOCATIONS
B. Does applicant engage in hazardous sports or avocations (racing, skin or scuba diving, sky diving, snow-mobiling, big game hunting, mountain climbing, cave exploring, dune buggy, etc.)?	B.				
10—A. Is there anything unhealthy about applicant's appearance, such as being very thin or having excess weight?	A.			IF YES, see Questions on Back.	HEALTH
B. Has applicant any deformity, amputation, blindness, deafness, or other defects?	B.				
11. Do you learn of any illness, operation, or injury, past or present?				IF YES, see Questions on Back.	
12. Do you learn applicant was ever rejected for military service or discharged for medical reasons?					
13. Do you learn of any member of applicant's family (blood relation) having had heart trouble, cancer, diabetes, tuberculosis or mental trouble? (If so, who and which disease.)					
14—A. Is applicant a steady, frequent drinker (daily, almost daily, several times a week)?	A.				HABITS
IF SO, { B. How often?	B.				
C. How many drinks does applicant take on these occasions?	C.				
D. What does applicant usually drink?	D.				
15. Does applicant now or has applicant in the past used intoxicants to excess?				IF YES, see Questions on Back.	
16. Anything adverse about living conditions or neighborhood?				IF YES, see Questions on Back.	ENVIRON- MENT
17. Do any of the following apply to this applicant: Unfair business practices or dealings? Heavy debts? Domestic trouble? Drug habit? Connection with illegal liquor? Irregular beneficiary?					REPUTATION
18. Is there any criticism of character, morals, or general reputation?					

REMARKS: 19. **COMMENT BELOW ON TOPICS LISTED AT LEFT. ALSO GIVE DETAILS OF "YES" OR INCOMPLETE ANSWERS.**

A. BUSINESS:
Employer's name and line of business? Name of applicant's job? Number of employees? How long so employed? Cover any indication of frequent job changes or instability of employment. If self-employed, is business operated from home?

B. DUTIES:
Tell exactly what applicant does. What articles or materials sold or handled? Any outside duties, such as travel, selling, or driving delivery vehicle? How much of time so spent?

C. PERSONAL:
Married, single, or divorced? Any children? If woman, name of father or husband; his occupation, worth and income.

RETAIL CREDIT COMPANY

Signature of person making report

Form 82—10-70 U.S.A.   **OVER—SEE ADDITIONAL QUESTIONS ON BACK**   HEALTH REPORT

Specimen Inspection Report —Life Form and Health Form (concluded)

#19 Continued

DETAILS OF APPEARANCE:

20—A. How does applicant appear unhealthy (complexion, weight, or what)?_____B. Describe. (If overweight or underweight, give details.)

DETAILS OF HEALTH HISTORY:

21. Nature of illness, operation or injury? _____

22. Approximate date it occurred?_____

23—A. How long confined or "laid up"?_____

B. Completely recovered? _____

24—A. Attended by Dr. (Name)_____

Address _____

B. Confined to hospital?_____If so, name and address:

Name _____

Address _____

25. Any effect on present health?_____Details:

SPECIMEN REPORT

DETAILS OF DRIVING RECORD:

26. When, where, and under what circumstances does applicant drive in a fast or reckless manner? (Open highway, congested areas, etc.—if known to drive considerably in excess of speed limit, cover.)

27. Any evidence of unsupervised racing?_____ Give details:

ANSWER THESE IF LEARNED IN INVESTIGATION

28. Any arrests?_____(Approximate dates)_____

29. Charges? _____

If convicted, approximate dates?_____

30. Any accidents?_____If so, approximate dates and details:

31. License ever suspended or revoked?_____If so, cause, date and whether applicant drove without a license?

DETAILS OF ENVIRONMENT:

22. LIVING CONDITIONS:
A. Over-crowded, dirty, unsanitary, etc.?_____(If so, give details.)

B. If apartment, dark or dirty halls, broken or littered stairs, etc.? (If so, give details.)

23. NEIGHBORHOOD: Deteriorating physically, poor sanitation, vice and crime, vandalism, etc.? (If so, give details.)

DETAILS OF DRINKING HABITS: Give these additional details to show drinking habits as definitely as possible:

34. Classify excessive drinking: ☐ Present   ☐ Past

A. Getting "drunk," stupefied, entirely out of control of usual faculties?

B. Loud, boisterous, or obviously under influence, although still in possession of most of faculties?

C. Mild excess, just getting "feeling good"; exhilaration or stimulation?

How often? (Once a week, once a month, etc.)

A. ☐   A._____

B. ☐   B._____

C. ☐   C._____

35. Do (did) these occasions last for an evening, a day, two days, a week, or for how long?

36. How long has (had) applicant been drinking to this extent?

37. WHEN WAS THE LAST OCCASION OF THIS SORT?

38. If applicant is an excessive drinker at present, does applicant drive a car during periods of intoxication?

39. Has applicant ever taken any "cure" for liquor habit? (If so, when? Any subsequent lapse?)

40. Tell how applicant drinks, if social or solitary, or if because of domestic or other trouble, how it affects applicant (jovial, belligerent, etc.), whether ever arrested, and details to give clear picture of drinking habits; if habits have changed, tell how and how long since change; if reformed, what led to reformation (ill health, domestic trouble or what)?

FIELD REPRESENTATIVE: Do not write in this space.
(Use Continuation of Report, Form 5166, for additional remarks.)

82R—10-70

D

Specimen Individual Life Insurance Contract (Straight Life)

INSURED John Doe		35 **INSURING AGE**
POLICY NUMBER 3,000,000		2-09-73 **POLICY DATE**
FACE AMOUNT $50,000		

███████████ LIFE INSURANCE COMPANY OF ████████ agrees to pay the face amount to the beneficiary upon receipt of due proof of the Insured's death, subject to the provisions on this and the following pages of this policy.

Signed at the Home Office of the Company in ████████████.

Attest

Paul D. Smith

Registrar   President

A GUIDE TO THE PROVISIONS OF THIS POLICY

	Page
Change of Plan Provisions	9
Definitions	2
Dividend Provisions	2
Endorsements	4
General Provisions	6
Loan Provisions	6
Ownership and Beneficiary Provisions	2
Policy Specifications	3
Premium Provisions	2
Settlement Option Provisions	7, 8
Surrender Value and Nonforfeiture Provisions	5

Supplementary agreements, if any, and a copy of the application appear between pages 8 and 9.

Life Policy. Payable at Death.
Premiums Payable during Premium Period or until Prior Death.
Yearly Dividend.

Specimen Individual Life Insurance Contract (Straight Life) (continued)

Page 2

DEFINITIONS

Where dates are shown in the form of numerals separated by dashes, the numerals represent month-day-year in that order.

Policy years, policy months and policy anniversaries are measured from the policy date unless otherwise indicated.

The policy anniversary nearest a particular birthday of the Insured means that policy anniversary on which the insuring age specified on page 3, increased by the number of policy years elapsed since the policy date, is equal to the Insured's age on that particular birthday.

The phrase "written request" means a request in writing satisfactory to the Company and filed at its home office in ▮▮▮▮▮▮▮▮

The phrase "in full force" means that the insurance provided by this policy is in force and that no unpaid premium is more than 31 days overdue.

OWNERSHIP AND BENEFICIARY PROVISIONS

OWNER. The owner of this policy is the Insured unless another owner is designated in the application. While the Insured is living, the owner, without the consent of any other person or party, may exercise all rights and privileges granted by this policy or allowed by the Company and may agree with the Company to any change in, amendment to or cancellation of this policy. If an owner other than the Insured dies while the Insured is living, all rights and privileges of the owner will vest in the executor or administrator of the owner unless otherwise provided.

BENEFICIARY. The beneficiary is designated in the applica-

tion and this designation will remain in effect until changed by the owner.

While the Insured is living, the owner may change any designation of beneficiary by written request. A change when filed at the home office will take effect as of the date the request was signed, whether or not the Insured or the owner is alive at the time of filing, subject to any payment or other action by the Company before filing. Any reference in any beneficiary designation to a beneficiary living or surviving will, unless otherwise provided, mean living at the Insured's death. The interest of any beneficiary who dies before the Insured will vest in the owner unless otherwise provided.

PREMIUM PROVISIONS

PAYMENT OF PREMIUMS. While the Insured is living, premiums are payable as provided in the "Schedule of Total Premiums and Due Dates" on page 3, in accordance with the frequency elected in the application. Upon written request and with the consent of the Company, premiums may be made payable yearly, half-yearly, quarterly or monthly at the applicable premium rates in use on the issue date. All premiums are payable in advance either at the home office, or to an agent of the Company upon delivery of a receipt signed by the president or a vice president of the Company and duly countersigned by the agent. If any premium is not paid on or before its due date or before the expiration of its grace period, this policy will terminate and have no further value except as provided by the nonforfeiture provisions.

GRACE PERIOD. A grace period of 31 days from the due date is allowed for the payment of every premium after the first. During the grace period this policy will continue in full force. If the Insured dies during the grace period, such portion of any overdue premium as is applicable to the period from the due date to the date of death will be deducted from the proceeds of this policy.

PREMIUM REFUND AT DEATH. At the Insured's death, such portion of the last premium due and paid as is applicable to a period beyond the date of death will be paid as a part of the proceeds of this policy, provided such premium was not waived under a supplementary agreement providing waiver of premium.

DIVIDEND PROVISIONS

DIVIDENDS. The share of divisible surplus accruing upon this policy will be determined yearly by the Company. Upon payment of the premium for the full second policy year, and at the end of the second and each later policy year, any share of divisible surplus apportioned to this policy will be credited as a dividend.

DIVIDEND OPTIONS. While this policy is in force except as extended term insurance, each dividend credited will be applied, as elected in the application, under one of the following options:

(a) Paid in cash.

(b) Applied toward the payment of a premium on this policy at the time when the balance of the premium is paid.

(c) Used to purchase a participating paid-up addition to this policy. Any existing paid-up additions will be paid as a part of the proceeds of this policy at the Insured's death, or may be surrendered for their cash value upon written request at any time while the Insured is living if not required as security for indebtedness on this policy.

(d) Left with the Company to accumulate with interest at such yearly rate, not less than 2¾%, as the Company may each year determine. Any existing dividend accumulations will be paid as a part of the proceeds of this policy at the Insured's death, or may be withdrawn in cash upon written request at any time while the Insured is living.

Any election of a dividend option will remain in effect until another election, applicable only to subsequent dividends, is made. If no election is in effect, dividends will be held to accumulate under option (d). Any dividend credited while this policy is in force as extended term insurance will be paid in cash.

DIVIDEND AT DEATH. Any dividend apportioned to this policy by the Company for the period from the beginning of the policy year in which the Insured dies to the date of death will be paid as a part of the proceeds of this policy.

PAID-UP PRIVILEGE. On any policy anniversary when the cash value of any paid-up additions, together with any dividend accumulations and any dividend due and unpaid, equals the present value of the future premiums, adjusted to a net basis as determined by the Company, for all benefits provided by this policy, the Company will, upon written request, endorse this policy as a fully paid-up policy of the same kind and amount, subject to any unpaid indebtedness.

ENDOWMENT PRIVILEGE. At any time when the cash value of this policy and of any paid-up additions, together with any dividend accumulations and any dividend due and unpaid, equals the face amount of this policy, the Company will, upon written request, pay as a matured endowment the face amount less any indebtedness.

Specimen Individual Life Insurance Contract (Straight Life) (continued)

POLICY SPECIFICATIONS

BASIC POLICY PLAN	STRAIGHT LIFE		
PREMIUM PERIOD	LIFE	2-09-73	ISSUE DATE
INSURED	JOHN DOE	35	INSURING AGE
POLICY NUMBER	3,000,000	2-09-73	POLICY DATE
FACE AMOUNT	$50,000		
CLASSIFICATION	STANDARD		

SCHEDULE OF BENEFITS AND YEARLY PREMIUMS

The Yearly Premiums shown in this schedule are the amounts payable on and after the Policy Date if premiums are paid yearly. The period of Years Payable commences on the Policy Date.

FORM NUMBER	BENEFIT	YEARLY PREMIUM	YEARS PAYABLE
A100	BASIC POLICY	$1,115.00	LIFE
A400	ACCIDENTAL DEATH BENEFIT—AMOUNT $50,000	43.50	35
A500	DISABILITY WAIVER OF PREMIUM	28.50	25
A600	OPTION TO PURCHASE ADDITIONAL INSURANCE	32.25	5
	TOTAL YEARLY PREMIUM ON POLICY DATE	$1,219.25	

A200 35170 A20   A810A709M

SCHEDULE OF TOTAL PREMIUMS AND DUE DATES

This schedule shows the amounts and due dates of the total premiums payable for all benefits included in the policy, based on the frequency of premium payments elected in the application. If the frequency of premium payments is changed, the amounts of the premiums and their due dates will change accordingly.

FIRST PREMIUM: $1,219.25 DUE 2-09-73

LATER PREMIUMS: $1,219.25 DUE EVERY 12 MONTHS BEGINNING 2-09-74, THEN
(due on the same
day of the month $1,187.00 DUE EVERY 12 MONTHS BEGINNING 2-09-78, THEN
as the Policy Date) $1,158.50 DUE EVERY 12 MONTHS BEGINNING 2-09-98, THEN
                      $1,115.00 DUE EVERY 12 MONTHS BEGINNING 2-09-08

Page 3

Specimen Individual Life Insurance Contract (Straight Life) (continued)

Page 4

ENDORSEMENTS

To be made by the Company only

Specimen Individual Life Insurance Contract (Straight Life) (continued)

SURRENDER VALUE AND NONFORFEITURE PROVISIONS

SURRENDER VALUE. The surrender value of this policy will be paid by the Company upon written request while the Insured is living.

The surrender value will be the cash value of this policy and of any paid-up additions, determined in accordance with the "Basis of Computation" provision, plus any dividend accumulations and any dividend due and unpaid, less any indebtedness.

The Company may defer the payment of any surrender value for a period not exceeding 6 months from receipt of written request, but if the payment is deferred for 30 days or more the amount payable will bear interest at the yearly rate of 2¾% during the deferment.

NONFORFEITURE PROVISIONS—EXTENDED TERM INSURANCE OR PAID-UP INSURANCE. *(Extended term insurance is available only if the classification of this policy is "standard".)* If a premium is not paid by the end of its grace period, the surrender value, if any, will be applied as a net single premium to provide insurance commencing on the due date of the unpaid premium on whichever of the following two bases is applicable:

(1) Extended term insurance, for such period as the surrender value will purchase, of an amount equal to the face amount of this policy plus any paid-up additions, any dividend accumulations and any dividend due and unpaid, less any indebtedness; or

(2) Paid-up life insurance of such amount as the surrender value will purchase.

If the classification of this policy, as specified on page 3, is "standard", extended term insurance will automatically become effective, but paid-up life insurance may be elected in place of extended term insurance by written request not later than 60 days after the due date of the unpaid premium and while the Insured is living. If the classification of this policy, as specified on page 3, is other than "standard", paid-up life insurance will automatically become effective and extended term insurance will not be available.

While this policy is in force as extended term insurance or paid-up life insurance it will be credited with any dividends apportioned thereto by the Company.

BASIS OF COMPUTATION. The net single premiums and present values referred to in this policy are computed on the

basis of the Commissioners 1958 Standard Ordinary Mortality Table, except that net single premiums for extended term insurance are computed on the basis of the Commissioners 1958 Extended Term Insurance Table. These computations are based on continuous functions with interest at the yearly rate of 2½%.

While this policy is in full force its cash value on any policy anniversary will be computed by the Standard Nonforfeiture Value Method and will be the excess, if any, of the then net single premium for the face amount of this policy over the then present value of the applicable nonforfeiture factors, as determined from the Table of Values and based on the face amount of the policy, for each of the policy years remaining in the premium period. While this policy is in force as extended term insurance or paid-up life insurance its cash value on any policy anniversary will be the then net single premium for such insurance. The cash value on any policy anniversary of any paid-up additions will be the then net single premium for the additions but will not be less than the dividends used to purchase them.

The net single premiums and present values used in computing cash values and nonforfeiture benefits as of any policy anniversary will be those applicable at the Insured's then attained age, which is the insuring age specified on page 3 increased by the number of years elapsed since the policy date.

The cash value at any time during a policy year, and nonforfeiture benefits based thereon, will be determined by the Company with due allowance for the time elapsed in such year and the date to which premiums are paid, except that (a) within 60 days after the due date of the first unpaid premium the cash value will be computed as of such due date and (b) if all premiums required under this policy have been paid, or if this policy is in force as extended term insurance or paid-up life insurance, the cash value within 30 days after a policy anniversary will not be less than the cash value computed as of such anniversary.

Any fraction of a dollar in the amount of cash value per $1,000 of insurance, apart from any paid-up additions, will be taken as a whole dollar. Any supplementary agreement attached to this policy will not increase the cash values or nonforfeiture benefits unless otherwise provided in the agreement. The cash values and nonforfeiture benefits under this policy are equal to or greater than those required by any statute of the state in which this policy is delivered.

TABLE OF VALUES

	End of Policy Year	Cash or Loan Value*	Paid-Up Life Insurance*	Extended Term Insurance†		End of Policy Year	Cash or Loan Value*	Paid-Up Life Insurance*	Extended Term Insurance†	
				Years	Days				Years	Days
AGE 35	1	$ 7	$ 17	2	12	13	$228	$411	16	301
	2	24	55	5	328	14	246	435	16	300
STRAIGHT LIFE	3	41	91	8	224	15	265	459	16	297
	4	59	128	10	269	16	284	483	16	275
64 – 35170	5	77	163	12	110	17	303	506	16	236
	6	96	199	13	212	18	322	528	16	184
	7	115	234	14	203	19	342	551	16	134
	8	133	265	15	81	20	361	571	16	60
	9	153	298	15	315	25	456	664	14	337
	10	172	329	16	100	30	548	741	13	175
	11	190	356	16	184					
	12	209	384	16	257					

Policy Years	Nonforfeiture Factor*
1-10	$19.53
LATER	18.28

* For each $1000 of face amount of this policy.

† Extended term insurance is not available if the classification of this policy, as specified on page 3, is other than "standard".

The values shown in the table are computed upon the bases: (a) that all premiums to maintain this policy in full force until the end of the policy year stated have been paid, and (b) that there is no indebtedness on this policy and that no paid-up additions or accumulated or other dividends stand to the credit of this policy.

Values for policy years subsequent to the twentieth not stated in the table will be determined by the methods used to obtain the values stated and will be furnished on request.

Specimen Individual Life Insurance Contract (Straight Life) (continued)

Page 6

LOAN PROVISIONS

POLICY LOANS. At any time while this policy is in force other than as extended term insurance the Company will loan an amount which, together with any existing indebtedness. does not exceed the loan value. Any premium due and unpaid at the time the loan is made must be paid either in cash or by deduction from the proceeds of the loan. A loan agreement satisfactory to the Company will be required.

AUTOMATIC PREMIUM LOANS. If elected either in the application or by written request while the policy is in full force, this automatic premium loan provision will be operative during any period while premiums are payable yearly, half-yearly or quarterly but will never apply to any premium payable monthly. If the frequency of premium payments is changed to monthly while this provision is operative. the provision will then become and remain inoperative until the frequency of premium payments is changed to yearly, half-yearly or quarterly at which time the provision will again become operative unless revoked by written request. An election of this provision may be revoked by written request at any time, but only with respect to premiums payable thereafter.

While this provision is operative any premium which remains unpaid on the last day of its grace period will be paid automatically by a loan on that date. provided that the loan together with any existing indebtedness would not exceed the loan value of this policy. This provision will not change the frequency of premium payments. If the amount necessary to pay the full premium due, in accordance with the frequency of premium payments then in effect, together with existing indebtedness would exceed the loan value, the nonforfeiture provisions will apply.

LOAN VALUE. The loan value of this policy is the amount which, with interest to the next premium due date, or to the next policy anniversary if no further premiums are payable, will equal the cash value, on such date or anniversary, of this policy and of any paid-up additions which are outstanding at the time the loan value is determined.

MISCELLANEOUS LOAN PROVISIONS. Interest on loans will accrue from day to day at the yearly rate of 5%, due on each policy anniversary. Any interest not paid when due will be added to the loan and will bear interest on the same terms.

All or any part of a loan may be repaid at any time while the Insured is living unless a nonforfeiture provision has become operative since the loan was made. When a loan is repaid in full, any accrued interest will be due.

If at any time the total indebtedness equals or exceeds the cash value of this policy and of any paid-up additions, this policy will terminate and have no further value 31 days after notice has been mailed to the owner and any assignee of record at their addresses last known to the Company.

This policy will be the only security for any loans granted under these loan provisions.

The Company may defer the making of any loan, except a loan to pay premiums to the Company, for a period not exceeding 6 months from receipt of written request for the loan.

Indebtedness, wherever referred to in this policy, means all existing loans on this policy with accrued interest.

Interest rate on loans amended to 6% - see Rider A810

GENERAL PROVISIONS

THE CONTRACT. This policy is issued in consideration of the application for this policy and of the payment to the Company of the required premiums.

This policy and the application, a copy of which is attached at issue, constitute the entire contract.

All statements made by or on behalf of the Insured will, in the absence of fraud, be deemed representations and not warranties. No statement will invalidate this policy or be used in defense of a claim hereunder unless it is contained in the application.

No alteration or waiver of any of the provisions of this policy will be valid unless made in writing and signed by the president or a vice president of the Company. No agent may bind the Company by making any promise not contained in this policy.

SUICIDE. If the Insured, whether sane or insane, commits suicide within 2 years after the issue date, the amount payable by the Company will be limited to the amount of the premiums paid.

MISSTATEMENT OF AGE OR SEX. If the age or sex of the Insured has been misstated, any amount payable under this policy will be such as the premium paid would have purchased using the correct age and sex.

INCONTESTABILITY. This policy will be incontestable after it has been in force during the lifetime of the Insured for 2 years after the issue date. except for non-payment of premium and except as to any provision or agreement for benefits in event of disability.

REINSTATEMENT. This policy may be reinstated at any time within 5 years after default in payment of premium, if it has not been surrendered for its surrender value, upon evidence of insurability satisfactory to the Company and payment of overdue premiums with interest at the yearly rate of 5%, and also upon payment or reinstatement of any indebtedness on this policy which existed at the date of default increased by interest to the date of reinstatement in accordance with the loan provisions.

ASSIGNMENT. The owner may assign this policy but no assignment will be of any effect so far as the Company is concerned until the original or a duplicate thereof is filed at the home office. The interest of any beneficiary and of any owner will be subject to any assignment so made. The Company assumes no responsibility for the validity or sufficiency of any assignment. All assignments will be subject to any indebtedness on this policy.

PAYMENTS BY THE COMPANY. Sums payable by the Company under this policy are payable at the home office. In making any payment any indebtedness to the Company on this policy will be deducted and the Company may require the return of this policy.

If the proceeds of this policy which become payable at the Insured's death are paid in one sum, interest will be paid on the proceeds from the date of the Insured's death to the date of payment, but for a period not to exceed one year, at such yearly rate, not less than 2¾%, as the Company may each year determine.

Specimen Individual Life Insurance Contract (Straight Life) (continued)

SETTLEMENT OPTION PROVISIONS

Instead of being paid in one sum the net amount (called proceeds in these settlement option provisions) payable under this policy at the Insured's death or at the maturity of an endowment or as a surrender value may, at the time the proceeds become payable, be settled for the benefit of the person entitled thereto (called payee in these settlement option provisions) under one of the following options subject to the following terms and conditions.

OPTION 1—PROCEEDS AT INTEREST. The Company will retain the proceeds and pay interest thereon to the payee yearly, half-yearly, quarterly or monthly as designated in the election of the option. The interest per $1,000 of the proceeds remaining with the Company will be $27.50 if payable yearly, $13.66 if payable half-yearly, $6.81 if payable quarterly or $2.26 if payable monthly.

OPTION 2—INSTALMENTS OF A SPECIFIED AMOUNT. The Company will pay the proceeds to the payee in equal yearly, half-yearly, quarterly or monthly instalments in the amount designated in the election of the option with the consent of the Company. The instalments will continue until the proceeds and interest as herein provided are exhausted, and the final instalment will be for the balance only of the proceeds and interest. Once each year interest at the yearly rate of 2¾% on the average amount of the proceeds remaining with the Company during the preceding 12 months will be added to the proceeds.

OPTION 3—INSTALMENTS FOR A SPECIFIED PERIOD. The Company will pay the proceeds to the payee in the number of equal monthly instalments certain designated in the election of the option. The amount of each instalment will be determined in accordance with the table entitled "Option 3—Instalments for a Specified Period." If provided in the election, the proceeds will be paid in yearly, half-yearly or quarterly instalments, which are determined by multiplying the monthly instalments by 11.852, 5.966 or 2.993 respectively.

OPTION 4—LIFE INCOME. The Company will apply the proceeds to provide equal monthly instalments to the payee during the payee's life, either without instalments certain or with 120 or 240 instalments certain or with instalments certain until the proceeds are refunded, as designated in the election of the option. The amount of each instalment will be determined in accordance with the table entitled "Option 4—Life Income." The phrase "with instalments certain until the proceeds are refunded" means with instalments certain until the sum of the instalments paid equals the amount of proceeds settled under this option.

OPTION 5—JOINT AND SURVIVOR LIFE INCOME. The Company will apply the proceeds to provide equal monthly instalments during the joint lives of the payee and one other person, on whose lives the option is based, and during the life of the survivor, either without instalments certain or with 120 or 240 instalments certain, as designated in the election of the option. The amount of each instalment will be determined in accordance with the table entitled "Option 5—Joint and Survivor Life Income."

DATE OF FIRST PAYMENT. The first interest payment under option 1 will be payable at the end of the first payment interval. The first instalment under option 2, 3, 4 or 5 will be payable immediately.

ADDITIONAL INTEREST AND PARTICIPATION. Interest payments under option 1, the interest added each year to proceeds remaining under option 2 and the instalments payable under option 3 will be increased by such additional interest as the Company may each year determine. The instalments payable under options 4 and 5 will be increased by such share of divisible surplus as the Company may each year apportion thereto.

WITHDRAWAL OR COMMUTATION. If expressly provided in the election of the option but not otherwise, the payee will have the right to withdraw in sums not less than $100 each any part of the amount remaining with the Company under option 1 or 2 or to take in one sum the commuted value of any remaining instalments certain under option 3, 4 or 5, the commuted value being computed at the yearly rate of 2¾% compound interest for option 3 and at the yearly rate of 3% compound interest for options 4 and 5. In no event will there be any right of commutation under option 4 or 5 of any instalments other than instalments certain. If the payee exercises his right of withdrawal or commutation, the Company may defer payment of the amount withdrawn or commuted for a period not exceeding 6 months.

SETTLEMENT AT DEATH OF PAYEE. After the death of the payee, any amount remaining unpaid under option 1 or 2, including accrued interest, and any remaining instalments certain under option 3 or 4 will be paid as may be directed, with the consent of the Company, in the election of the option. After the death of the survivor of the payee and the other person any remaining instalments certain under option 5 will be paid as may be directed, with the consent of the Company, in the election of the option.

AVAILABILITY AND LIMITATIONS. An option is available if the proceeds are payable to a natural person in his own right, and is available with the consent of the Company if the proceeds are payable to a corporation, partnership, association, fiduciary or assignee.

If on the date the proceeds become payable the policy is subject to an assignment as collateral security, any previously elected optional method of settlement will not apply to the amount payable to the assignee and such amount will be payable in one sum.

The Company will not settle the proceeds of this policy or any share thereof under any option if the amount of the proceeds or share is less than $1,000. If the periodic payment under an option would be less than $10, the Company may change the frequency of payment so that the amount of each payment will be at least $10.

ELECTION. The election of an option to apply to the proceeds which become payable to the beneficiary by reason of the Insured's death may be made by the owner at any time before the Insured's death. If no election is in force at the Insured's death, the beneficiary may make an election when the proceeds become payable. The election of an option to apply to the surrender value of this policy may be made by the owner when the surrender value becomes payable. The election of an option to apply to the proceeds which become payable at maturity of the endowment, if this policy is on an endowment plan, may be made by the owner on or before the maturity date. If no election has been made by the owner on or before the maturity date and if the proceeds at maturity are payable to a person other than the owner, such person may make an election on the maturity date.

The election or revocation of any option must be made by written request. When filed at the home office an election or revocation will take effect as of the date it was signed, whether or not the person making it is alive at the time of filing, subject to any payment or other action by the Company before filing.

MISCELLANEOUS. If the proceeds are settled under an option, the Company will have the right to require the return of this policy and to issue in its place a certificate expressing the terms of the option elected.

If the proceeds are settled under option 4 or 5, written proof satisfactory to the Company of the date of birth of each person upon whose life the option is based must be furnished.

The proceeds settled under an option will be and remain a part of the general funds of the Company without any duty or requirement of segregation or separate investment.

Specimen Individual Life Insurance Contract (Straight Life) (continued)

Page 8

OPTION 3—INSTALMENTS FOR A SPECIFIED PERIOD

Monthly Instalments for Each $1,000 of the Proceeds of This Policy Settled Under Option 3

Number of Monthly Instalments Certain	Amount of Each Monthly Instalment	Number of Monthly Instalments Certain	Amount of Each Monthly Instalment	Number of Monthly Instalments Certain	Amount of Each Monthly Instalment	Number of Monthly Instalments Certain	Amount of Each Monthly Instalment	Number of Monthly Instalments Certain	Amount of Each Monthly Instalment	Number of Monthly Instalments Certain	Amount of Each Monthly Instalment
12	$84.37	**72**	$15.03	**132**	$8.75	**192**	$6.41	**252**	$5.20	**312**	$4.46
24	42.76	**84**	13.06	**144**	8.13	**204**	6.11	**264**	5.02	**324**	4.35
36	28.89	**96**	11.57	**156**	7.60	**216**	5.85	**276**	4.86	**336**	4.24
48	21.96	**108**	10.42	**168**	7.15	**228**	5.61	**288**	4.72	**348**	4.15
60	17.80	**120**	9.50	**180**	6.75	**240**	5.39	**300**	4.59	**360**	4.06

OPTION 4—LIFE INCOME

Monthly Instalments for Each $1,000 of the Proceeds of This Policy Settled Under Option 4

Age of Payee*		Number of Monthly Instalments Certain				Age of Payee*		Number of Monthly Instalments Certain				Age of Payee*		Number of Monthly Instalments Certain			
Male	Female	None	120	240	Until Proceeds Are Refunded	Male	Female	None	120	240	Until Proceeds Are Refunded	Male	Female	None	120	240	Until Proceeds Are Refunded
	5**	$2.79	$2.79	$2.78	$2.78	30	35	$3.35	$3.35	$3.33	$3.31	60	65	$5.72	$5.50	$4.88	$5.15
	6	2.80	2.80	2.79	2.79	31	36	3.39	3.38	3.36	3.34	61	66	5.89	5.64	4.94	5.26
	7	2.81	2.81	2.80	2.80	32	37	3.42	3.42	3.39	3.37	62	67	6.07	5.77	4.99	5.38
	8	2.82	2.82	2.81	2.81	33	38	3.46	3.45	3.43	3.41	63	68	6.26	5.92	5.05	5.51
	9	2.83	2.83	2.82	2.82	34	39	3.50	3.49	3.46	3.44	64	69	6.47	6.07	5.10	5.64
5**	10	2.84	2.84	2.84	2.83	35	40	3.54	3.53	3.50	3.48	65	70	6.68	6.22	5.15	5.78
6	11	2.85	2.85	2.85	2.84	36	41	3.58	3.57	3.54	3.52	66	71	6.91	6.38	5.20	5.92
7	12	2.87	2.87	2.86	2.85	37	42	3.63	3.62	3.58	3.56	67	72	7.15	6.54	5.24	6.07
8	13	2.88	2.88	2.87	2.87	38	43	3.68	3.66	3.62	3.60	68	73	7.41	6.70	5.28	6.23
9	14	2.89	2.89	2.89	2.88	39	44	3.73	3.71	3.66	3.64	69	74	7.69	6.86	5.32	6.40
10	15	2.91	2.91	2.90	2.89	40	45	3.78	3.76	3.71	3.68	70	75	7.98	7.03	5.35	6.57
11	16	2.92	2.92	2.92	2.91	41	46	3.83	3.82	3.75	3.73	71	76	8.29	7.20	5.35	6.76
12	17	2.94	2.94	2.93	2.92	42	47	3.89	3.87	3.80	3.78	72	77	8.62	7.37	5.35	6.95
13	18	2.95	2.95	2.95	2.94	43	48	3.95	3.93	3.85	3.83	73	78	8.98	7.54	5.35	7.16
14	19	2.97	2.97	2.96	2.95	44	49	4.01	3.99	3.90	3.88	74	79	9.35	7.71	5.35	7.37
15	20	2.99	2.99	2.98	2.97	45	50	4.08	4.05	3.96	3.94	75	80	9.76	7.87	5.35	7.60
16	21	3.01	3.00	3.00	2.99	46	51	4.15	4.12	4.01	4.00	76	81	10.19	8.03	5.35	7.83
17	22	3.02	3.02	3.01	3.01	47	52	4.23	4.19	4.07	4.06	77	82	10.65	8.19	5.35	8.08
18	23	3.04	3.04	3.03	3.02	48	53	4.31	4.27	4.12	4.12	78	83	11.14	8.34	5.35	8.35
19	24	3.06	3.06	3.05	3.04	49	54	4.39	4.34	4.18	4.19	79	84	11.66	8.49	5.35	8.62
20	25	3.08	3.08	3.07	3.06	50	55	4.48	4.43	4.24	4.25	80	85†	12.22	8.62	5.35	8.92
21	26	3.11	3.10	3.10	3.08	51	56	4.57	4.51	4.30	4.33	81		12.83	8.75	5.35	9.23
22	27	3.13	3.13	3.12	3.11	52	57	4.67	4.60	4.37	4.40	82		13.47	8.87	5.35	9.55
23	28	3.15	3.15	3.14	3.13	53	58	4.77	4.70	4.43	4.48	83		14.16	8.98	5.35	9.89
24	29	3.18	3.18	3.16	3.15	54	59	4.89	4.80	4.49	4.56	84		14.90	9.08	5.35	10.26
25	30	3.20	3.20	3.19	3.18	55	60	5.00	4.90	4.56	4.65	85†		15.69	9.17	5.35	10.65
26	31	3.23	3.23	3.21	3.20	56	61	5.13	5.01	4.62	4.74						
27	32	3.26	3.26	3.24	3.23	57	62	5.26	5.13	4.69	4.84						
28	33	3.29	3.29	3.27	3.25	58	63	5.41	5.25	4.75	4.94						
29	34	3.32	3.32	3.30	3.28	59	64	5.56	5.37	4.81	5.04						

* On birthday nearest to due date of first instalment.
** Ages 5 and under.
† Ages 85 and over.

OPTION 5—JOINT AND SURVIVOR LIFE INCOME

Monthly Instalments for Each $1,000 of the Proceeds of This Policy Settled Under Option 5

WITHOUT INSTALMENTS CERTAIN

Age of Other Person* / Age of Payee*

Male	Female	Male 45 / Female 50	50 / 55	55 / 60	56 / 61	57 / 62	58 / 63	59 / 64	60 / 65	61 / 66	62 / 67	63 / 68	64 / 69	65 / 70	66 / 71	67 / 72	68 / 73	69 / 74	70 / 75	75 / 80
45	50	$3.60	$3.72	$3.83	$3.85	$3.87	$3.88	$3.90	$3.92	$3.93	$3.94	$3.95	$3.96	$3.96	$3.97	$3.98	$3.98	$3.98	$3.98	$3.99
50	55	3.72	3.88	4.03	4.06	4.08	4.11	4.14	4.16	4.19	4.21	4.23	4.25	4.26	4.28	4.29	4.30	4.31	4.32	4.35
51	56	3.74	3.91	4.07	4.10	4.13	4.16	4.19	4.21	4.24	4.26	4.29	4.31	4.33	4.34	4.36	4.37	4.38	4.40	4.43
52	57	3.76	3.94	4.11	4.14	4.17	4.21	4.24	4.27	4.30	4.32	4.35	4.37	4.39	4.41	4.43	4.45	4.46	4.47	4.52
53	58	3.79	3.97	4.15	4.19	4.22	4.25	4.29	4.32	4.35	4.38	4.41	4.43	4.46	4.48	4.50	4.52	4.54	4.55	4.61
54	59	3.81	4.00	4.19	4.23	4.27	4.30	4.34	4.37	4.41	4.44	4.47	4.50	4.53	4.55	4.58	4.60	4.62	4.64	4.71
55	60	3.83	4.03	4.23	4.27	4.31	4.35	4.39	4.43	4.47	4.50	4.54	4.57	4.60	4.63	4.65	4.68	4.70	4.72	4.80
56	61	3.85	4.06	4.27	4.32	4.36	4.40	4.44	4.49	4.53	4.56	4.60	4.64	4.67	4.70	4.73	4.76	4.79	4.81	4.91
57	62	3.87	4.08	4.31	4.36	4.41	4.45	4.50	4.54	4.58	4.63	4.67	4.71	4.74	4.78	4.81	4.85	4.88	4.90	5.01
58	63	3.88	4.11	4.35	4.40	4.45	4.50	4.55	4.60	4.64	4.69	4.73	4.78	4.82	4.86	4.90	4.93	4.97	5.00	5.13
59	64	3.90	4.14	4.39	4.44	4.50	4.55	4.60	4.65	4.70	4.75	4.80	4.85	4.89	4.94	4.98	5.02	5.06	5.09	5.24
60	65	3.92	4.16	4.43	4.49	4.54	4.60	4.65	4.71	4.76	4.82	4.87	4.92	4.97	5.02	5.06	5.11	5.15	5.19	5.36
61	66	3.93	4.19	4.47	4.53	4.58	4.64	4.70	4.76	4.82	4.88	4.94	4.99	5.05	5.10	5.15	5.20	5.25	5.29	5.48
62	67	3.94	4.21	4.50	4.56	4.63	4.69	4.75	4.82	4.88	4.94	5.00	5.06	5.12	5.18	5.24	5.29	5.34	5.39	5.61
63	68	3.95	4.23	4.54	4.60	4.67	4.73	4.80	4.87	4.94	5.00	5.07	5.14	5.20	5.26	5.32	5.38	5.44	5.50	5.74
64	69	3.96	4.25	4.57	4.64	4.71	4.78	4.85	4.92	4.99	5.06	5.14	5.21	5.28	5.34	5.41	5.47	5.54	5.60	5.87
65	70	3.96	4.26	4.60	4.67	4.74	4.82	4.89	4.97	5.05	5.12	5.20	5.28	5.35	5.42	5.50	5.57	5.64	5.70	6.00
70	75	3.98	4.32	4.72	4.81	4.90	5.00	5.09	5.19	5.29	5.39	5.50	5.60	5.70	5.81	5.91	6.01	6.12	6.22	6.70
75	80	3.99	4.35	4.80	4.91	5.01	5.13	5.24	5.36	5.48	5.61	5.74	5.87	6.00	6.14	6.28	6.42	6.56	6.70	7.41

WITH 120 MONTHLY INSTALMENTS CERTAIN

Age of Other Person* / Age of Payee*

Male	Female	Male 45 / Female 50	50 / 55	55 / 60	56 / 61	57 / 62	58 / 63	59 / 64	60 / 65	61 / 66	62 / 67	63 / 68	64 / 69	65 / 70	66 / 71	67 / 72	68 / 73	69 / 74	70 / 75	75 / 80
45	50	$3.60	$3.72	$3.82	$3.84	$3.86	$3.88	$3.89	$3.90	$3.92	$3.93	$3.94	$3.95	$3.95	$3.96	$3.96	$3.97	$3.97	$3.98	$4.00
50	55	3.72	3.87	4.02	4.05	4.08	4.10	4.13	4.15	4.17	4.20	4.21	4.23	4.25	4.26	4.28	4.29	4.30	4.31	4.35
51	56	3.74	3.90	4.06	4.09	4.12	4.15	4.18	4.20	4.23	4.25	4.27	4.29	4.31	4.33	4.34	4.36	4.37	4.38	4.43
52	57	3.76	3.93	4.10	4.14	4.17	4.20	4.23	4.26	4.28	4.31	4.33	4.36	4.38	4.40	4.41	4.43	4.45	4.46	4.51
53	58	3.78	3.96	4.15	4.18	4.21	4.25	4.28	4.31	4.34	4.37	4.40	4.42	4.44	4.47	4.49	4.51	4.52	4.54	4.60
54	59	3.80	3.99	4.19	4.22	4.26	4.30	4.33	4.37	4.40	4.43	4.46	4.49	4.51	4.54	4.56	4.58	4.60	4.62	4.69
55	60	3.82	4.02	4.23	4.27	4.31	4.35	4.38	4.42	4.46	4.49	4.52	4.55	4.58	4.61	4.64	4.66	4.68	4.70	4.78
56	61	3.84	4.05	4.27	4.31	4.35	4.39	4.44	4.48	4.51	4.55	4.59	4.62	4.65	4.68	4.71	4.74	4.77	4.79	4.88
57	62	3.86	4.08	4.31	4.35	4.40	4.44	4.49	4.53	4.57	4.61	4.65	4.69	4.73	4.76	4.79	4.82	4.85	4.88	4.98
58	63	3.88	4.10	4.35	4.39	4.44	4.49	4.54	4.59	4.63	4.67	4.72	4.76	4.80	4.84	4.87	4.90	4.94	4.97	5.08
59	64	3.89	4.13	4.38	4.44	4.49	4.54	4.59	4.64	4.69	4.74	4.78	4.83	4.87	4.91	4.95	4.99	5.02	5.06	5.19
60	65	3.90	4.15	4.42	4.48	4.53	4.59	4.64	4.69	4.75	4.80	4.85	4.90	4.94	4.99	5.03	5.07	5.11	5.15	5.30
61	66	3.92	4.17	4.46	4.51	4.57	4.63	4.69	4.75	4.80	4.86	4.91	4.97	5.02	5.07	5.11	5.16	5.20	5.24	5.41
62	67	3.93	4.20	4.49	4.55	4.61	4.67	4.74	4.80	4.86	4.92	4.98	5.03	5.09	5.14	5.19	5.24	5.29	5.34	5.52
63	68	3.94	4.21	4.52	4.59	4.65	4.72	4.78	4.85	4.91	4.98	5.04	5.10	5.16	5.22	5.28	5.33	5.38	5.43	5.64
64	69	3.95	4.23	4.55	4.62	4.69	4.76	4.83	4.90	4.97	5.03	5.10	5.17	5.23	5.29	5.36	5.41	5.47	5.53	5.75
65	70	3.95	4.25	4.58	4.65	4.73	4.80	4.87	4.94	5.02	5.09	5.16	5.23	5.30	5.37	5.43	5.50	5.56	5.62	5.87
70	75	3.98	4.31	4.70	4.79	4.88	4.97	5.06	5.15	5.24	5.34	5.43	5.53	5.62	5.71	5.80	5.89	5.98	6.07	6.46
75	80	4.00	4.35	4.78	4.88	4.98	5.08	5.19	5.30	5.41	5.52	5.64	5.75	5.87	5.99	6.11	6.22	6.34	6.46	6.99

WITH 240 MONTHLY INSTALMENTS CERTAIN

Age of Other Person* / Age of Payee*

Male	Female	Male 45 / Female 50	50 / 55	55 / 60	56 / 61	57 / 62	58 / 63	59 / 64	60 / 65	61 / 66	62 / 67	63 / 68	64 / 69	65 / 70	66 / 71	67 / 72	68 / 73	69 / 74	70 / 75	75 / 80
45	50	$3.60	$3.71	$3.80	$3.81	$3.83	$3.84	$3.85	$3.87	$3.88	$3.89	$3.89	$3.90	$3.91	$3.91	$3.92	$3.92	$3.93	$3.93	$3.95
50	55	3.71	3.85	3.99	4.01	4.03	4.06	4.08	4.09	4.11	4.13	4.14	4.15	4.17	4.18	4.19	4.20	4.20	4.21	4.23
51	56	3.73	3.88	4.02	4.05	4.07	4.10	4.12	4.14	4.16	4.18	4.19	4.21	4.22	4.23	4.24	4.25	4.26	4.27	4.29
52	57	3.75	3.91	4.06	4.09	4.12	4.14	4.16	4.19	4.21	4.23	4.24	4.26	4.27	4.29	4.30	4.31	4.32	4.33	4.35
53	58	3.76	3.94	4.10	4.13	4.16	4.18	4.21	4.23	4.26	4.28	4.30	4.31	4.33	4.34	4.36	4.37	4.38	4.39	4.42
54	59	3.78	3.96	4.13	4.16	4.20	4.22	4.25	4.28	4.30	4.33	4.35	4.37	4.38	4.40	4.41	4.43	4.44	4.45	4.48
55	60	3.80	3.99	4.17	4.20	4.23	4.27	4.29	4.32	4.35	4.37	4.40	4.42	4.44	4.45	4.47	4.48	4.50	4.51	4.54
56	61	3.81	4.01	4.20	4.24	4.27	4.31	4.34	4.37	4.40	4.42	4.45	4.47	4.49	4.51	4.53	4.54	4.56	4.57	4.60
57	62	3.83	4.03	4.23	4.27	4.31	4.34	4.38	4.41	4.44	4.47	4.50	4.52	4.54	4.56	4.58	4.60	4.61	4.63	4.67
58	63	3.84	4.06	4.27	4.31	4.34	4.38	4.42	4.45	4.48	4.52	4.54	4.57	4.59	4.62	4.64	4.65	4.67	4.68	4.73
59	64	3.85	4.08	4.29	4.34	4.38	4.42	4.46	4.49	4.53	4.56	4.59	4.62	4.64	4.67	4.69	4.71	4.73	4.74	4.79
60	65	3.87	4.09	4.32	4.37	4.41	4.45	4.49	4.53	4.57	4.60	4.63	4.66	4.69	4.72	4.74	4.76	4.78	4.80	4.85
61	66	3.88	4.11	4.35	4.40	4.44	4.48	4.53	4.57	4.61	4.64	4.68	4.71	4.74	4.77	4.79	4.81	4.83	4.85	4.91
62	67	3.89	4.13	4.37	4.42	4.47	4.52	4.56	4.60	4.64	4.68	4.72	4.75	4.78	4.81	4.84	4.86	4.88	4.90	4.96
63	68	3.89	4.14	4.40	4.45	4.50	4.54	4.59	4.63	4.68	4.72	4.76	4.79	4.83	4.86	4.88	4.91	4.93	4.95	5.02
64	69	3.90	4.15	4.42	4.47	4.52	4.57	4.62	4.66	4.71	4.75	4.79	4.83	4.86	4.90	4.93	4.95	4.98	5.00	5.07
65	70	3.91	4.17	4.44	4.49	4.54	4.59	4.64	4.69	4.74	4.78	4.83	4.86	4.90	4.94	4.97	4.99	5.02	5.04	5.12
70	75	3.93	4.21	4.51	4.57	4.63	4.68	4.74	4.80	4.85	4.90	4.95	5.00	5.04	5.08	5.12	5.15	5.19	5.21	5.30
75	80	3.95	4.23	4.54	4.60	4.67	4.73	4.79	4.85	4.91	4.96	5.02	5.07	5.12	5.16	5.20	5.24	5.27	5.30	5.41

* On birthday nearest to due date of first instalment. The amount of the monthly instalment for any combination of ages not shown in this table will be furnished on request.

Specimen Individual Life Insurance Contract (Straight Life) (continued)

CHANGE OF PLAN PROVISIONS

At any time while this policy is in full force it may be exchanged upon written request for a policy of the same face amount on another insurance plan, subject to the following terms and conditions:

(1) The new policy may be on any life or endowment plan which (a) is customarily issued by the Company on the issue date of this policy for the same face amount and in the same class of risk as this policy, (b) has a level face amount and a level premium, (c) provides cash values computed on the same basis of mortality and interest as that specified under "Basis of Computation" in this policy and (d) does not mature within 5 years after the date of change.

(2) The new policy will be written as of the policy date and at the insuring age specified in this policy, on the policy form and at the premium rate in use by the Company on the issue date of this policy for the same class of risk. The new policy will be subject to any indebtedness outstanding against this policy.

(3) Evidence of insurability satisfactory to the Company will be required if the change is to a plan having a longer term of insurance than this policy or a smaller cash value on the date of change.

(4) If the classification of this policy is "standard" and the cash value of the new policy is larger than the cash value of this policy on the date of change, a cost of change will be charged by the Company as follows:

(a) If the change is made within 5 years after the policy date, the cost of change will be the difference in premiums for the two plans from the policy date to the date of change (reduced by such dividend adjustment, if any, as the Company may determine) with interest at the yearly rate of 5% compounded yearly from the due date of each premium to the date of change.

(b) If the change is made more than 5 years after the policy date, the cost of change will be the difference between the cash values of the two plans on the date of change, plus 5% of such difference.

(5) If the classification of this policy is "standard" and the cash value of the new policy is smaller than the cash value of this policy on the date of change, the difference between these cash values will be allowed by the Company as a credit. Unless otherwise provided with the consent of the Company, this credit will first be applied in reduction of any indebtedness to the Company on this policy and any balance will be paid by the Company in one sum.

(6) If the classification of this policy is other than "standard", the amount of any cost charged or credit allowed will be as determined by the Company.

(7) If any paid-up additions to this policy are outstanding on the date of change, the net single premium for the outstanding paid-up additions will be applied to purchase paid-up additions conforming to the provisions of the new policy. Any dividend accumulations and any dividend due and unpaid on the date of change will be credited to the new policy.

(8) A supplementary agreement included in this policy may be continued in the new policy, at the applicable premium rate in use by the Company on the issue date of the supplementary agreement, provided the supplementary agreement would have been issued with a policy on the new plan on that date. Evidence of insurability satisfactory to the Company will be required if the supplementary agreement provides a waiver of premium benefit or states that such evidence will be required in event of a change of plan. A charge determined by the Company may be required if a supplementary agreement is continued in the new policy.

(9) A change of plan other than as provided in these provisions will be made only with the consent of the Company and subject to such requirements as the Company may determine.

Specimen Individual Life Insurance Contract (Straight Life) (continued)

SUPPLEMENTARY AGREEMENT FOR
ACCIDENTAL DEATH BENEFIT

Attached to and made a part of this policy

The Company agrees to pay the amount of accidental death benefit specified in the "Schedule of Benefits and Yearly Premiums" on page 3 upon receipt of due proof that (a) the Insured's death resulted directly and independently of all other causes from accidental bodily injury evidenced by a visible contusion or wound on the exterior of the body (except in case of accidental drowning or internal injury revealed by an autopsy), (b) the cause of death was not one listed below in the "Exclusions from Coverage" and (c) death occurred within 90 days after the injury was sustained and before the policy anniversary nearest the Insured's 70th birthday or the prior termination of this supplementary agreement. The amount of accidental death benefit will be paid as a part of the proceeds of this policy.

EXCLUSIONS FROM COVERAGE. This accidental death benefit will not be payable if the Insured's death resulted directly or indirectly, wholly or partly, from:

(1) any physical or mental disease or ailment, or any infection other than an infection sustained through an accidental cut or wound, even though the proximate or precipitating cause of death was accidental bodily injury;

(2) suicide while sane or insane;

(3) any intentionally self-inflicted injury while sane or insane;

(4) any medicine, drug, sedative, poison, chemical, chemical compound, gas or fumes, whether voluntarily, involuntarily, accidentally or otherwise taken, administered, absorbed or inhaled;

(5) committing or attempting to commit any assault or felony;

(6) being in or on or descending from an aircraft of any kind if the Insured was a pilot, officer or member of its crew or was giving or receiving any training or instruction or had any duty aboard or requiring descent from the aircraft; or

(7) insurrection or war or service in the military, naval or air forces of any country, combination of countries or international organization while such country, combination of countries or international organization was engaged in war. "War" means declared or undeclared war and any act incidental thereto and includes resistance to armed aggression.

PREMIUMS. The yearly premiums for this accidental death benefit and the number of years the premiums are payable are specified in the "Schedule of Benefits and Yearly Premiums" on page 3. The premiums for this benefit based on the frequency of premium payments elected in the application are included in the total premiums for this policy specified in the "Schedule of Total Premiums and Due Dates" on page 3.

AUTOPSY. The Company will have the right and opportunity to examine the Insured's body and to perform an autopsy unless prohibited by law.

TERMINATION. This supplementary agreement will terminate (a) upon written request, (b) 31 days after the due date of any unpaid premium or (c) in all events on the policy anniversary nearest the Insured's 70th birthday or upon the prior surrender, maturity, expiry or other termination of this policy.

Attached by ███████████████ LIFE INSURANCE COMPANY OF ███████████ on the issue date of this policy.

Paul D. Smith

President

Specimen Individual Life Insurance Contract (Straight Life) (continued)

SUPPLEMENTARY AGREEMENT FOR WAIVER OF PREMIUM BENEFIT IN EVENT OF TOTAL DISABILITY

Attached to and made a part of this policy

The Company agrees to waive the payment of premiums becoming due under this policy, subject to the terms and conditions stated below, if the Insured becomes totally disabled as defined below.

TOTAL DISABILITY. The Insured will be deemed to be totally disabled if he is unable, because of his bodily injury or sickness, to perform any and every duty of his regular occupation and is not engaged in any gainful occupation for which he is reasonably fitted by education, training and experience; except that, after a period of such total disability has continued for 5 years, the Insured will be deemed to be totally disabled only if he is unable, because of his bodily injury or sickness, to engage in any and every gainful occupation for which he is reasonably fitted by education, training and experience.

A period of total disability commencing while this supplementary agreement is in full force and due to causes which are the same as or related to the causes of any prior period of total disability during which premiums were waived in accordance with this supplementary agreement will be regarded as a continuation of the prior period of total disability; except that, if the Insured has engaged for a continuous period of at least 6 months in any gainful occupation for which he is reasonably fitted by education, training and experience, any subsequent period of total disability will be regarded as a new period of total disability for the purposes of this supplementary agreement.

The total and irrecoverable loss of the sight of both eyes, or of the use of both hands or of both feet or of one hand and one foot, will be considered total disability as defined in this supplementary agreement.

WAIVER OF PREMIUM BENEFIT. Upon receipt of due proof that the Insured is totally disabled as defined above and that the total disability commenced while this supplementary agreement was in full force and prior to the policy anniversary nearest the Insured's 60th birthday and has continued uninterruptedly for a period of 6 months, the Company will waive the payment of (or will refund if already paid) each premium under this policy becoming due after the commencement of such total disability and during the continuation thereof prior to the policy anniversary nearest the Insured's 65th birthday, according to the frequency of premium payments in effect at the commencement of such total disability; except that no premium will be waived if its due date is more than 1 year prior to the date written notice of total disability is filed at the home office of the Company.

If total disability resulting in waiver of premiums continues uninterruptedly until the policy anniversary nearest the Insured's 65th birthday and this policy provides for premium payments on and after such policy anniversary, no further premium payments will be required and the benefits thereafter provided under this policy will be the same as if this policy had been issued on the single premium basis.

EXCLUSIONS FROM COVERAGE. No premiums will be waived if the total disability resulted directly or indirectly, wholly or partly, from:

(1) any intentionally self-inflicted injury while sane or insane;

(2) bodily injury or sickness occurring before this supplementary agreement took effect; or

(3) service in the military, naval or air forces of any country, combination of countries or international organization while such country, combination of countries or international organization was engaged in war. "War" means declared or undeclared war and any act incidental thereto and includes resistance to armed aggression.

NOTICE AND PROOF OF TOTAL DISABILITY. Written notice and proof of total disability under this supplementary agreement must be filed at the home office of the Company while the Insured is living and during the continuation of total disability and not later than 6 months after the policy anniversary nearest the Insured's 60th birthday. Failure to file written notice and proof within the time specified will not invalidate a claim if it is shown that written notice and proof were filed as soon as was reasonably possible.

Proof of the continuation of total disability must be furnished to the Company when requested but such proof will not be required more often than once a year after total disability has continued for 2 full years. As part of any proof of total disability the Company may require medical examinations of the Insured by physicians designated by the Company.

Upon cessation of total disability or upon failure to furnish proof of the continuation of total disability when requested, no further premiums will be waived and all premiums thereafter due under this policy will be payable according to its provisions.

PREMIUMS. The yearly premiums for this waiver of premium benefit and the number of years the premiums are payable are specified in the "Schedule of Benefits and Yearly Premiums" on page 3. The premiums for this benefit based on the frequency of premium payments elected in the application are included in the total premiums for this policy specified in the "Schedule of Total Premiums and Due Dates" on page 3.

If any premium under this policy is due and unpaid at the time written notice of total disability is filed at the home office of the Company, premiums will be waived only if the written notice is filed within 1 year of the due date of the first unpaid premium and either:

(1) the total disability commenced on or before the due date of the first unpaid premium, or

(2) the total disability commenced after the due date of the first unpaid premium but within its grace period, in which case the unpaid premium will be payable to the Company, or may be deducted from any payment by the Company under this policy, together with interest at the yearly rate of 5%.

TERMINATION. This supplementary agreement will terminate (a) upon written request, (b) 31 days after the due date of any unpaid premium (except as otherwise provided under "Premiums" in this supplementary agreement) or (c) in all events on the policy anniversary nearest the Insured's 60th birthday or upon the prior surrender, maturity, expiry or other termination of this policy.

MISCELLANEOUS. While premiums are being waived under this supplementary agreement, any cash values, loan values and dividends provided for in this policy will be the same as if the waived premiums had been paid as they became due.

Any sum which is payable by the Company on account of the waiver of a premium previously paid and which is unpaid at the Insured's death will be paid as a part of the proceeds of this policy.

Attached by ██████████████ LIFE INSURANCE COMPANY OF ████████████ on the issue date of this policy.

Paul D. Smith

President

Specimen Individual Life Insurance Contract (Straight Life) (continued)

SUPPLEMENTARY AGREEMENT PROVIDING
OPTION TO PURCHASE ADDITIONAL INSURANCE

Attached to and made a part of this policy

The Company agrees, subject to the terms and conditions stated below and while this supplementary agreement is in full force:

(1) To permit the purchase, without evidence of insurability, of an additional policy on the life of the Insured:

(a) during each Regular Option Period that is not cancelled by a prior purchase during an Alternate Option Period and

(b) during each Alternate Option Period, and also

(2) To provide term insurance on the life of the Insured commencing on the first day of each Alternate Option Period and expiring on the day immediately preceding the termination date of such Alternate Option Period.

OPTION PERIODS. Regular Option Periods are the periods which commence on the 60th day preceding, and terminate on, those policy anniversaries, subsequent to the policy date of this policy, which are nearest the Insured's 25th, 28th, 31st, 34th, 37th and 40th birthdays.

An Alternate Option Period commences on the date of the occurrence, subsequent to the policy date of this policy, of any of the following events:

(1) the marriage of the Insured,

(2) the birth of a living child of the Insured's marriage, or

(3) the legal adoption by the Insured of a child less than 18 years old.

The termination date of any Alternate Option Period is the 90th day following the date of the event establishing such Period, except that (a) if such 90th day is the 29th, 30th or 31st day of a month the termination date will be the 1st day of the following month, and (b) any Alternate Option Period which commences within 90 days prior to the date on which this supplementary agreement terminates will terminate on that date.

The exercise of a right to purchase an additional policy during an Alternate Option Period will cancel the next Regular Option Period which has not already been cancelled by exercise of such a right during a previous Alternate Option Period. If both a Regular Option Period and an Alternate Option Period terminate on the same date, the right to purchase an additional policy may be exercised with respect to either the Regular Option Period or the Alternate Option Period, but not both.

AMOUNT OF ADDITIONAL POLICY. The face amount of the additional policy that may be purchased during a Regular Option Period or during an Alternate Option Period, except as provided below, will be the face amount of this policy or $15,000, whichever is less. If this policy provides a basic face amount or an ultimate face amount, such basic face amount or ultimate face amount will be construed as its face amount in determining the face amount of the additional policy that may be purchased.

If two or more children are born or adopted on the same date, the face amount of the additional policy that may be purchased during the ensuing Alternate Option Period will be the amount determined as above multiplied by the number of children so born or adopted.

CONDITIONS OF PURCHASE OF ADDITIONAL POLICY.

(1) Proper written application and payment of the first premium for an additional policy must be submitted to the Company at its home office during a Regular Option Period or Alternate Option Period.

(2) The issue date of an additional policy applied for during a Regular Option Period may be, as designated in the application therefor, any date during such Regular Option Period except the 29th, 30th or 31st day of any month. The issue date of an additional policy applied for during an Alternate Option Period will be the termination date of such Alternate Option Period.

(3) An additional policy will become effective on its issue date if the Insured is then living. If the Insured dies before such date any premiums paid for the additional policy will be refunded.

(4) An additional policy may be on any life or endowment plan which has a level face amount and a level premium and which, on the issue date of the additional policy, is customarily issued by the Company at the Insured's then attained age in the amount to be purchased and in the same class of risk as this policy. The premium for an additional policy will be based on the age of the Insured at the Insured's birthday nearest the issue date of the additional policy and on the premium rates in use by the Company on that date for the class of risk in which this policy was issued.

(5) If on the issue date of an additional policy this policy contains a supplementary agreement for waiver of premium in event of disability and if premiums for the additional policy are payable for 20 years or more, the additional policy will contain a supplementary agreement for waiver of premium in event of total disability on the form then in use by the Company. If on the issue date of an additional policy this policy contains a supplementary agreement providing an accidental death benefit, the additional policy will contain a supplementary agreement for accidental death benefit on the form then in use by the Company and in an amount equal to the face amount of the additional policy. The premium for any such supplementary agreement will be based on the age of the Insured at the Insured's birthday nearest the issue date of the additional policy and on the premium rates in use by the Company on that date for the class of risk in which this policy was issued.

(6) An additional policy will contain any restrictions, riders or endorsements limiting the Company's liability that this policy contains or that the Company, on the issue date of the new policy, customarily includes in all new policies of the same plan and face amount as the additional policy which are issued on the lives of persons of the same age, sex and class of risk as the Insured.

(7) The periods of years stated in the suicide and incontestability provisions of an additional policy will be measured from the issue date of this policy. An endorsement to this effect will be included in the additional policy.

TERM INSURANCE. Beginning on the date of any marriage, birth or adoption that establishes an Alternate Option Period and expiring on the day immediately preceding the termination date of such Alternate Option Period, term insurance will be in force on the life of the Insured in an amount equal to the face amount of the additional policy that may be purchased during such Alternate Option Period in accordance with the terms of this supplementary agreement. If this policy contains a supplementary agreement for accidental death benefit, and if such accidental death benefit becomes payable by reason of the Insured's death occurring while term insurance is in force under this provision, the amount of term insurance otherwise payable under this provision will be doubled. If the Insured dies while any term insurance provided by this supplementary agreement is in force, the amount of such term insurance will be paid as a part of the proceeds of this policy.

PREMIUMS. The yearly premiums for this supplementary agreement and the number of years the premiums are payable are specified in the "Schedule of Benefits and Yearly Premiums" on page 3. The premiums for this supplementary agreement based on the frequency of premium payments elected in the application are included in the total premiums for this policy specified in the "Schedule of Total Premiums and Due Dates" on page 3.

(Continued on reverse side)

Specimen Individual Life Insurance Contract (Straight Life) (continued)

TERMINATION. The right to purchase an additional policy during any Regular Option Period or Alternate Option Period, if not exercised during such period, will terminate on the termination date thereof.

This supplementary agreement will terminate (a) upon written request, (b) 31 days after the due date of any unpaid premium, (c) upon the cancellation of the last Regular Option Period by exercise of the right to purchase an additional policy during an Alternate Option Period or (d) in all events on the policy anniversary nearest the Insured's 40th birthday or upon the prior surrender, maturity or other termination of this policy.

MISCELLANEOUS. Proof satisfactory to the Company of any marriage, birth or adoption which establishes an Alternate Option Period will be required before the Company will issue any additional policy that may be purchased during such Alternate Option Period or will pay any term insurance benefit upon the death of the Insured during such Alternate Option Period. The term "marriage" as used in this supplementary agreement means a marriage in which a marriage ceremony has been performed by a person legally authorized to do so.

Reinstatement of this policy and this supplementary agreement after default in payment of premium will not reinstate any right to purchase an additional policy with respect to any Regular Option Period or Alternate Option Period which terminated before the date of reinstatement.

Attached by ▉▉▉▉▉▉▉▉▉▉ LIFE INSURANCE COMPANY OF ▉▉▉▉▉▉▉ on the issue date of this policy.

Paul D. Smith
President

Specimen Individual Life Insurance Contract (Straight Life) (continued)

INCOME PURCHASE OPTION

The Settlement Option Provisions on page 7 of this policy are hereby amended by adding the following provision:

PURCHASE OF ADDITIONAL INCOME UNDER OPTION 4. Upon the maturity of this policy as an endowment or its surrender at any time on or after the 10th policy anniversary when this policy is in full force and the age of the Insured on his nearest birthday is not under 55 or over 75, if the proceeds are applied under option 4 to provide monthly income based on and payable during the life of the Insured, the owner may at the same time purchase, by a single payment to the Company, additional monthly income under option 4 based on and payable during the life of the Insured.

The number of monthly instalments certain, if any, will be the same for the additional monthly income purchased by the single payment as for the monthly income provided by the settlement of the policy proceeds under option 4. All of the terms, conditions and limitations relating to the use of option 4 will apply to the single payment and the additional monthly income purchased thereby in the same manner and on the same terms as to the policy proceeds and the monthly income provided by such proceeds.

The total monthly income payable under this policy after purchase of such additional monthly income may not exceed either (a) $10 for each $1,000 of the face amount of this policy, not including the amount of insurance under any supplementary agreement included in this policy, or (b) the amount which, together with the total monthly income provided under all other policies issued by this Company on the life of the Insured and on which this privilege of purchasing additional income under option 4 has been or is being exercised, equals $1,000.

Purchase of the additional monthly income may be made by written request accompanied by a single payment equal to 1.05 times the amount of proceeds that would be required to provide the additional monthly income, determined in accordance with the table on page 8 of this policy entitled "Option 4—Life Income."

Attached by ▮▮▮▮▮▮▮▮▮▮▮▮ LIFE INSURANCE COMPANY OF ▮▮▮▮▮▮▮▮▮▮ on the issue date of this policy unless otherwise stated below.

Paul D. Smith
President

Specimen Individual Life Insurance Contract (Straight Life) (concluded)

AMENDMENT OF MISCELLANEOUS LOAN PROVISIONS

The provisions of this policy entitled "Miscellaneous Loan Provisions" are hereby amended on the issue date by modifying the first sentence thereof to read as follows: "Interest on loans will accrue from day to day at the yearly rate of 6%, due on each policy anniversary."

Attached by ████████████████ LIFE INSURANCE COMPANY OF ████████████ on the issue date of this policy.

Paul D. Smith

President

E

Death Rates and Expectation of Life under Various Mortality and Annuity Tables*

	American Experience (1843–58)		Commissioners 1941 Standard Ordinary (1930–40)		Commissioners 1958 Standard Ordinary (1950–54)		Annuity Table for 1949—Male (1939–49)		United States Total Population (1959–61)	
Age	Deaths per 1000	Expectation of Life-Years	Deaths per 1000	Expectation of Life-Years	Deaths per 1000	Expectation of Life-Years	Deaths per 1000	Expectation of Life-Years	Deaths per 1000	Expectation of Life-Years
0	154.70	41.45	22.58	62.33	7.08	68.30	4.04	73.18	25.93	69.89
1	63.49	47.94	5.77	62.76	1.76	67.78	1.58	72.48	1.70	70.75
2	35.50	50.16	4.14	62.12	1.52	66.90	.89	71.59	1.04	69.87
3	23.91	50.98	3.38	61.37	1.46	66.00	.72	70.65	.80	68.94
4	17.70	51.22	2.99	60.58	1.40	65.10	.63	69.70	.67	67.99
5	13.60	51.13	2.76	59.76	1.35	64.19	.57	68.75	.59	67.04
6	11.37	50.83	2.61	58.92	1.30	63.27	.53	67.78	.52	66.08
7	9.75	50.41	2.47	58.08	1.26	62.35	.50	66.82	.47	65.11
8	8.63	49.90	2.31	57.22	1.23	61.43	.49	65.85	.43	64.14
9	7.90	49.33	2.12	56.35	1.21	60.51	.48	64.89	.39	63.17
10	7.49	48.72	1.97	55.47	1.21	59.58	.48	63.92	.37	62.19
11	7.52	48.08	1.91	54.58	1.23	58.65	.49	62.95	.37	61.22
12	7.54	47.45	1.92	53.68	1.26	57.72	.50	61.98	.40	60.24
13	7.57	46.80	1.98	52.78	1.32	56.80	.51	61.01	.48	59.26
14	7.60	46.16	2.07	51.89	1.39	55.87	.52	60.04	.59	58.29
15	7.63	45.50	2.15	50.99	1.46	54.95	.54	59.07	.71	57.33
16	7.66	44.85	2.19	50.10	1.54	54.03	.55	58.10	.82	56.37
17	7.69	44.19	2.25	49.21	1.62	53.11	.57	57.13	.93	55.41
18	7.73	43.53	2.30	48.32	1.69	52.19	.58	56.17	1.02	54.46
19	7.77	42.87	2.37	47.43	1.74	51.28	.60	55.20	1.08	53.52
20	7.80	42.20	2.43	46.54	1.79	50.37	.62	54.23	1.15	52.58
21	7.86	41.53	2.51	45.66	1.83	49.46	.65	53.27	1.22	51.64
22	7.91	40.85	2.59	44.77	1.86	48.55	.67	52.30	1.27	50.70
23	7.96	40.17	2.68	43.88	1.89	47.64	.70	51.33	1.28	49.76
24	8.01	39.49	2.77	43.00	1.91	46.73	.73	50.37	1.27	48.83
25	8.06	38.81	2.88	42.12	1.93	45.82	.77	49.41	1.26	47.89
26	8.13	38.12	2.99	41.24	1.96	44.90	.81	48.44	1.25	46.95

* Reprinted with permission from the *Fact Book*, 1972, Institute of Life Insurance, 277 Park Avenue, New York, N.Y. 10017.

Death Rates and Expectation of Life under Various Mortality and Annuity Tables (continued)

Age	American Experience (1843–58) Deaths per 1000	Expectation of Life-Years	Commissioners 1941 Standard Ordinary (1930–40) Deaths per 1000	Expectation of Life-Years	Commissioners 1958 Standard Ordinary (1950–54) Deaths per 1000	Expectation of Life-Years	Annuity Table for 1949–Male (1939–49) Deaths per 1000	Expectation of Life-Years	United States Total Population (1959–61) Deaths per 1000	Expectation of Life-Years
27	8.20	37.43	3.11	40.36	1.99	43.99	.85	47.48	1.26	46
28	8.26	36.73	3.25	39.49	2.03	43.08	.90	46.52	1.30	45
29	8.34	36.03	3.40	38.61	2.08	42.16	.95	45.56	1.36	44
30	8.43	35.33	3.56	37.74	2.13	41.25	1.00	44.61	1.43	43
31	8.51	34.63	3.73	36.88	2.19	40.34	1.07	43.65	1.51	42
32	8.61	33.92	3.92	36.01	2.25	39.43	1.14	42.70	1.60	41
33	8.72	33.21	4.12	35.15	2.32	38.51	1.21	41.75	1.70	40
34	8.83	32.50	4.35	34.29	2.40	37.60	1.30	40.80	1.81	39
35	8.95	31.78	4.59	33.44	2.51	36.69	1.39	39.85	1.94	38
36	9.09	31.07	4.86	32.59	2.64	35.78	1.49	38.90	2.09	37
37	9.23	30.35	5.15	31.75	2.80	34.88	1.61	37.96	2.28	36
38	9.41	29.62	5.46	30.91	3.01	33.97	1.73	37.02	2.49	35
39	9.59	28.90	5.81	30.08	3.25	33.07	1.87	36.08	2.73	34
40	9.79	28.18	6.18	29.25	3.53	32.18	2.03	35.15	3.00	33
41	10.01	27.45	6.59	28.43	3.84	31.29	2.22	34.22	3.30	33
42	10.25	26.72	7.03	27.62	4.17	30.41	2.48	33.30	3.62	32
43	10.52	26.00	7.51	26.81	4.53	29.54	2.80	32.38	3.97	31
44	10.83	25.27	8.04	26.01	4.92	28.67	3.19	31.47	4.35	30
45	11.16	24.54	8.61	25.21	5.35	27.81	3.63	30.57	4.76	29
46	11.56	23.81	9.23	24.43	5.83	26.95	4.12	29.68	5.21	28
47	12.00	23.08	9.91	23.65	6.36	26.11	4.66	28.80	5.73	27
48	12.51	22.36	10.64	22.88	6.95	25.27	5.25	27.93	6.33	26
49	13.11	21.63	11.45	22.12	7.60	24.45	5.88	27.07	7.00	26
50	13.78	20.91	12.32	21.37	8.32	23.63	6.56	26.23	7.74	25
51	14.54	20.20	13.27	20.64	9.11	22.82	7.28	25.40	8.52	24
52	15.39	19.49	14.30	19.91	9.96	22.03	8.04	24.58	9.29	23
53	16.33	18.79	15.43	19.19	10.89	21.25	8.84	23.78	10.05	22
54	17.40	18.09	16.65	18.48	11.90	20.47	9.68	22.99	10.82	22
55	18.57	17.40	17.98	17.78	13.00	19.71	10.56	22.20	11.61	21
56	19.89	16.72	19.43	17.10	14.21	18.97	11.49	21.44	12.49	20
57	21.34	16.05	21.00	16.43	15.54	18.23	12.46	20.68	13.52	19
58	22.94	15.39	22.71	15.77	17.00	17.51	13.48	19.93	14.73	19
59	24.72	14.74	24.57	15.13	18.59	16.81	14.54	19.20	16.11	18
60	26.69	14.10	26.59	14.50	20.34	16.12	15.66	18.48	17.61	17
61	28.88	13.47	28.78	13.88	22.24	15.44	16.87	17.76	19.17	17
62	31.29	12.86	31.18	13.27	24.31	14.78	18.20	17.06	20.82	16
63	33.94	12.26	33.76	12.69	26.57	14.14	19.67	16.37	22.52	15
64	36.87	11.67	36.58	12.11	29.04	13.51	21.28	15.68	24.31	15
65	40.13	11.10	39.64	11.55	31.75	12.90	23.07	15.01	26.22	14
66	43.71	10.54	42.96	11.01	34.74	12.31	25.03	14.36	28.28	13
67	47.65	10.00	46.56	10.48	38.04	11.73	27.19	13.71	30.53	13
68	52.00	9.47	50.46	9.97	41.68	11.17	29.58	13.08	33.01	12
69	56.76	8.97	54.70	9.47	45.61	10.64	32.20	12.46	35.73	11
70	61.99	8.48	59.30	8.99	49.79	10.12	35.09	11.86	38.66	11
71	67.67	8.00	64.27	8.52	54.15	9.63	38.27	11.28	41.82	10
72	73.73	7.55	69.66	8.08	58.65	9.15	41.77	10.71	45.30	10

ath Rates and Expectation of Life under Various Mortality and Annuity Tables
ncluded)

	American Experience (1843–58)		Commissioners 1941 Standard Ordinary (1930–40)		Commissioners 1958 Standard Ordinary (1950–54)		Annuity Table for 1949—Male (1939–49)		United States Total Population (1959–61)	
	Deaths per 1000	Expectation of Life-Years	Deaths per 1000	Expectation of Life-Years	Deaths per 1000	Expectation of Life-Years	Deaths per 1000	Expectation of Life-Years	Deaths per 1000	Expectation of Life-Years
	80.18	7.11	75.50	7.64	63.26	8.69	45.62	10.15	49.15	9.74
	87.03	6.68	81.81	7.23	68.12	8.24	49.85	9.61	53.42	9.21
	94.37	6.27	88.64	6.82	73.37	7.81	54.50	9.09	57.99	8.71
	102.31	5.88	96.02	6.44	79.18	7.39	59.61	8.58	62.96	8.21
	111.06	5.49	103.99	6.07	85.70	6.98	65.22	8.10	68.67	7.73
	120.83	5.11	112.59	5.72	93.06	6.59	71.37	7.63	75.35	7.26
	131.73	4.74	121.86	5.38	101.19	6.21	78.11	7.17	83.02	6.81
	144.47	4.39	131.85	5.06	109.98	5.85	85.50	6.74	92.08	6.39
	158.60	4.05	142.60	4.75	119.35	5.51	93.59	6.32	102.19	5.98
	174.30	3.71	154.16	4.46	129.17	5.19	102.44	5.92	112.44	5.61
	191.56	3.39	166.57	4.18	139.38	4.89	112.11	5.54	121.95	5.25
	211.36	3.08	179.88	3.91	150.01	4.60	122.67	5.18	130.67	4.91
	235.55	2.77	194.13	3.66	161.14	4.32	134.18	4.84	143.80	4.58
	265.68	2.47	209.37	3.42	172.82	4.06	146.71	4.51	158.16	4.26
	303.02	2.18	225.63	3.19	185.13	3.80	160.33	4.20	173.55	3.97
	346.69	1.91	243.00	2.98	198.25	3.55	175.12	3.90	190.32	3.70
	395.86	1.66	261.44	2.77	212.46	3.31	191.15	3.62	208.35	3.45
	454.55	1.42	280.99	2.58	228.14	3.06	208.49	3.36	227.09	3.22
	532.47	1.19	301.73	2.39	245.77	2.82	227.19	3.12	245.98	3.02
	634.26	.98	323.64	2.21	265.93	2.58	247.33	2.88	264.77	2.85
	734.18	.80	346.66	2.03	289.30	2.33	268.96	2.67	282.84	2.69
	857.14	.64	371.00	1.84	316.66	2.07	292.12	2.47	299.52	2.55
	1,000.00	.50	396.21	1.63	351.24	1.80	316.83	2.28	314.16	2.43
			447.19	1.37	400.56	1.51	343.12	2.10	329.15	2.32
			548.26	1.08	488.42	1.18	370.97	1.94	344.50	2.21
			724.67	.78	668.15	.83	400.35	1.79	360.18	2.10
			1,000.00	.50	1,000.00	.50	431.20	1.65	376.16	2.01
							463.41	1.52	392.42	1.91
							496.87	1.40	408.91	1.83
							531.39	1.29	425.62	1.75
							566.76	1.20	442.50	1.67
							602.71	1.10	459.51	1.60
							638.96	1.02	476.62	1.53
							675.14	.94	493.78	1.46
							710.90	.86	510.95	1.40
							745.82	.75	528.10	1.35
							1,000.00	.50	545.19	1.29

F

Selected Compound
Interest Values at
Various Interest Rates

			2½ Percent	
	Amount of 1	Amount of 1 per Annum	Present Value of 1	Present Value of 1 per Annum
Year	How $1 Left at Compound Interest Will Grow	How $1 Deposited at Beginning of Each Year Will Grow	What $1 Due in the Future Is Worth	What $1 Payable at Beginning of Each Year Is Worth
1	1.02500	1.02500	.97561	1.00000
2	1.05062	2.07562	.95181	1.97561
3	1.07689	3.15252	.92860	2.92742
4	1.10381	4.25633	.90595	3.85602
5	1.13141	5.38774	.88385	4.76197
6	1.15969	6.54743	.86230	5.64583
7	1.18869	7.73612	.84127	6.50813
8	1.21840	8.95452	.82075	7.34939
9	1.24886	10.20338	.80073	8.17014
10	1.28008	11.48347	.78120	8.97081
11	1.31209	12.79555	.76214	9.75206
12	1.34489	14.14044	.74356	10.51421
13	1.37851	15.51895	.72542	11.25776
14	1.41297	16.93193	.70773	11.98318
15	1.44830	18.38022	.69047	12.69091
16	1.48451	19.86473	.67362	13.38138
17	1.52162	21.38635	.65720	14.05500
18	1.55966	22.94601	.64117	14.71220
19	1.59865	24.54466	.62553	15.35336
20	1.63862	26.18327	.61027	15.97889
21	1.67958	27.86286	.59539	16.58916
22	1.72157	29.58443	.58086	17.18455
23	1.76461	31.34904	.56670	17.76541
24	1.80873	33.15776	.55288	18.33211
25	1.85394	35.01171	.53939	18.88499
26	1.90029	36.91200	.52623	19.42438
27	1.94780	38.85980	.51340	19.95061
28	1.99650	40.85630	.50088	20.46401
29	2.04641	42.90270	.48866	20.96489
30	2.09757	45.00027	.47674	21.45355
40	2.68506	69.08762	.37243	25.73034
50	3.43711	99.92146	.29094	29.07137
60	4.39979	139.39138	.22728	31.68137
70	5.63210	189.91622	.17755	33.72030
80	7.20957	254.59228	.13870	35.31311
90	9.22886	337.38311	.10836	36.55741
100	11.81372	443.36237	.08465	37.52946

To calculate the present value of $1 at 2½ percent interest payable at the beginning of each month, multiply the figure in the right-hand column for the period of the monthly payments by 11.86526. For example, if the period of monthly payments is 20 years, the value is 15.97840 × 11.86526, which is 189.58787.

Selected Compound Interest Values at Various Interest Rates (continued)

	3 Percent			
	Amount of 1	*Amount of 1 per Annum*	*Present Value of 1*	*Present Value of 1 per Annum*
Year	*How $1 Left at Compound Interest Will Grow*	*How $1 Deposited at Beginning of Each Year Will Grow*	*What $1 Due in the Future Is Worth*	*What $1 Payable at Beginning of Each Year Is Worth*
1	1.03000	1.03000	.97087	1.00000
2	1.06090	2.09090	.94260	1.97087
3	1.09273	3.18363	.91514	2.91347
4	1.12551	4.30914	.88849	3.82861
5	1.15927	5.46841	.86261	4.71710
6	1.19405	6.66246	.83748	5.57971
7	1.22987	7.89234	.81309	6.41719
8	1.26677	9.15911	.78941	7.23028
9	1.30477	10.46388	.76642	8.01969
10	1.34392	11.80780	.74409	8.78611
11	1.38423	13.19203	.72242	9.53020
12	1.42576	14.61779	.70138	10.25262
13	1.46853	16.08632	.68095	10.95400
14	1.51259	17.59891	.66112	11.63496
15	1.55797	19.15688	.64186	12.29607
16	1.60471	20.76159	.62317	12.93794
17	1.65285	22.41444	.60502	13.56110
18	1.70243	24.11687	.58739	14.16612
19	1.75351	25.87037	.57029	14.75351
20	1.80611	27.67649	.55368	15.32380
21	1.86029	29.53678	.53755	15.87747
22	1.91610	31.45288	.52189	16.41502
23	1.97359	33.42647	.50669	16.93692
24	2.03279	35.45926	.49193	17.44361
25	2.09378	37.55304	.47761	17.93554
26	2.15659	39.70963	.46369	18.41315
27	2.22129	41.93092	.45019	18.87684
28	2.28793	44.21885	.43708	19.32703
29	2.35657	46.57542	.42435	19.76411
30	2.42726	49.00268	.41199	20.18845
40	3.26204	77.66330	.30656	23.80822
50	4.38391	116.18077	.22811	26.50166
60	5.89160	167.94504	.16973	28.50583
70	7.91782	237.51189	.12630	29.99712
80	10.64089	331.00391	.09398	31.10679
90	14.30047	456.64937	.06993	31.93248
100	19.21863	625.50636	.05203	32.54687

To calculate the present value of $1 at 3 percent interest payable at the beginning of each month, multiply the figure in the right-hand column for the period of the monthly payments by 11.83895. For example, if the period of monthly payments is 20 years, the value is 15.32380 × 11.83895, which is 181.41770.

Selected Compound Interest Values at Various Interest Rates (continued)

	Amount of 1	*Amount of 1 per Annum*	*Present Value of 1*	*Present Value of 1 per Annum*
Year	*How $1 Left at Compound Interest Will Grow*	*How $1 Deposited at Beginning of Each Year Will Grow*	*What $1 Due in the Future Is Worth*	*What $1 Payable at Beginning of Each Year Is Worth*
1	1.03500	1.03500	.96618	1.00000
2	1.07122	2.10622	.93351	1.96618
3	1.10872	3.21494	.90194	2.89969
4	1.14752	4.36247	.87144	3.80164
5	1.18769	5.55015	.84197	4.67308
6	1.22926	6.77941	.81350	5.51505
7	1.27228	8.05169	.78599	6.32855
8	1.31681	9.36850	.75941	7.11454
9	1.36290	10.73139	.73373	7.87396
10	1.41060	12.14199	.70892	8.60769
11	1.45997	13.60196	.68495	9.31661
12	1.51107	15.11303	.66178	10.00155
13	1.56396	16.67699	.63940	10.66333
14	1.61869	18.29568	.61778	11.30274
15	1.67535	19.97103	.59689	11.92052
16	1.73397	21.70502	.57671	12.51741
17	1.79468	23.49969	.55720	13.09412
18	1.85749	25.35718	.53836	13.65132
19	1.92250	27.27968	.52016	14.18968
20	1.98979	29.26947	.50257	14.70984
21	2.05943	31.32890	.48557	15.21240
22	2.13151	33.46041	.46915	15.69797
23	2.20611	35.66653	.45329	16.16712
24	2.28333	37.94986	.43796	16.62041
25	2.36324	40.31310	.42315	17.05837
26	2.44596	42.75906	.40884	17.48151
27	2.53157	45.29063	.39501	17.89035
28	2.62017	47.91080	.38165	18.28536
29	2.71188	50.62268	.36875	18.66702
30	2.80679	53.42947	.35628	19.03577
40	3.95926	87.50954	.25257	22.10250¹
50	5.58493	135.58284	.17905	24.27656
60	7.87809	203.39497	.12693	25.81780
70	11.11283	299.05069	.08999	26.91041
80	15.67574	433.98252	.06379	27.68498
90	22.11218	624.31720	.04522	28.23409
100	31.19141	892.80306	.03206	28.62337

To calculate the present value of $1 at 3½ percent interest payable at the beginning of each month, multiply the figure in the right-hand column for the period of the monthly payments by 11.81285. For example, if the period of monthly payments is 20 years, the value is 14.70984 × 11.81285, which is 173.76513.

Selected Compound Interest Values at Various Interest Rates (continued)

		4 Percent		
	Amount of 1	Amount of 1 per Annum	Present Value of 1	Present Value of 1 per Annum
Year	How $1 Left at Compound Interest Will Grow	How $1 Deposited at Beginning of Each Year Will Grow	What $1 Due in the Future Is Worth	What $1 Payable at Beginning of Each Year Is Worth
1	1.04000	1.04000	.96154	1.00000
2	1.08160	2.12160	.92456	1.96154
3	1.12486	3.24646	.88900	2.88609
4	1.16986	4.41632	.85480	3.77509
5	1.21665	5.63298	.82193	4.62990
6	1.26532	6.89829	.79031	5.45182
7	1.31593	8.21423	.75992	6.24214
8	1.36860	9.58280	.73069	7.00205
9	1.42331	11.00611	.70259	7.73274
10	1.48024	12.48635	.67556	8.43533
11	1.53945	14.02581	.64958	9.11090
12	1.60103	15.62684	.62460	9.76048
13	1.66507	17.29191	.60057	10.38507
14	1.73168	19.02359	.57748	10.98565
15	1.80094	20.82453	.55526	11.56312
16	1.87298	22.69751	.53391	12.11839
17	1.94790	24.64541	.51337	12.65230
18	2.02582	26.67123	.49363	13.16567
19	2.10685	28.77808	.47464	13.65930
20	2.19112	30.96920	.45639	14.13394
21	2.27877	33.24797	.43883	14.59033
22	2.36992	35.61789	.42196	15.02916
23	2.46472	38.08260	.40573	15.45112
24	2.56330	40.64591	.39012	15.85684
25	2.66584	43.31174	.37512	16.24696
26	2.77247	46.08421	.36069	16.62208
27	2.88337	48.96758	.34682	16.98277
28	2.99870	51.96629	.33348	17.32959
29	3.11865	55.08494	.32065	17.66306
30	3.24340	58.32834	.30832	17.98371
40	4.80102	98.82654	.20829	20.58448
50	7.10668	158.77377	.14071	22.34147
60	10.51963	247.51031	.09506	23.52843
70	15.57162	378.86208	.06422	24.33030
80	23.04980	573.29478	.04338	24.87201
90	34.11933	861.10267	.02931	25.23797
100	50.50495	1287.12865	.01980	25.48520

To calculate the present value of $1 at 4 percent interest payable at the beginning of each month, multiply the figure in the right-hand column for the period of the monthly payments by 11.78696. For example, if the period of monthly payments is 20 years, the value is 14.13394 × 11.78696, which is 166.59618.

Selected Compound Interest Values at Various Interest Rates (continued)

		5 Percent		
	Amount of 1	*Amount of 1 per Annum*	*Present Value of 1*	*Present Value of 1 per Annum*
Year	*How $1 Left at Compound Interest Will Grow*	*How $1 Deposited at Beginning of Each Year Will Grow*	*What $1 Due in the Future Is Worth*	*What $1 Payable at Beginning of Each Year Is Worth*
1	1.05000	1.05000	.95238	1.00000
2	1.10250	2.15250	.90703	1.95238
3	1.15762	3.31012	.86384	2.85941
4	1.21551	4.52563	.82270	3.72325
5	1.27628	5.80191	.78353	4.54595
6	1.34010	7.14201	.74622	5.32948
7	1.40710	8.54911	.71068	6.07569
8	1.47746	10.02656	.67684	6.78637
9	1.55133	11.57789	.64461	7.46321
10	1.62889	13.20679	.61391	8.10782
11	1.71034	14.91713	.58468	8.72173
12	1.79586	16.71298	.55684	9.30641
13	1.88565	18.59863	.53032	9.86325
14	1.97993	20.57856	.50507	10.39357
15	2.07893	22.65749	.48102	10.89864
16	2.18287	24.84037	.45811	11.37966
17	2.29202	27.13238	.43630	11.83777
18	2.40662	29.53900	.41552	12.27407
19	2.52695	32.06595	.39573	12.68959
20	2.65330	34.71925	.37689	13.08532
21	2.78596	37.50521	.35894	13.46221
22	2.92526	40.43048	.34185	13.82115
23	3.07152	43.50200	.32557	14.16300
24	3.22510	46.72710	.31007	14.48857
25	3.38635	50.11345	.29530	14.79864
26	3.55567	53.66913	.28124	15.09394
27	3.73346	57.40258	.26785	15.37519
28	3.92013	61.32271	.25509	15.64303
29	4.11614	65.43885	.24295	15.89813
30	4.32194	69.76079	.23138	16.14107
40	7.03999	126.83976	.14205	18.01704
50	11.46740	219.81540	.08720	19.16872
60	18.67919	371.26290	.05354	19.87575
70	30.42643	617.95494	.03287	20.30981
80	49.56144	1019.79026	.02018	20.57628
90	80.73037	1674.33767	.01239	20.73987
100	131.50126	2740.52641	.00760	20.84031

To calculate the present value of $1 at 5 percent interest payable at the beginning of each month, multiply the figure in the right-hand column for the period of the monthly payments by 11.73579. For example, if the period of monthly payments is 20 years, the value is 13.08532 × 11.73569, which is 153.56657.

Selected Compound Interest Values at Various Interest Rates (concluded)

	6 Percent			
	Amount of 1	Amount of 1 per Annum	Present Value of 1	Present Value of 1 per Annum
Year	How $1 Left at Compound Interest Will Grow	How $1 Deposited at Beginning of Each Year Will Grow	What $1 Due in the Future Is Worth	What $1 Payable at Beginning of Each Year Is Worth
1	1.06000	1.06000	.94340	1.00000
2	1.12360	2.18360	.89000	1.94340
3	1.19102	3.37462	.83962	2.83339
4	1.26248	4.63709	.79209	3.67301
5	1.33823	5.97532	.74726	4.46511
6	1.41852	7.39384	.70496	5.21236
7	1.50363	8.89747	.66506	5.91732
8	1.59385	10.49132	.62741	6.58238
9	1.68948	12.18079	.59190	7.20979
10	1.79085	13.97164	.55839	7.80169
11	1.89830	15.86994	.52679	8.36009
12	2.01220	17.88214	.49697	8.88687
13	2.13293	20.01507	.46884	9.38384
14	2.26090	22.27597	.44230	9.15268
15	2.39656	24.67253	.41727	10.29498
16	2.54035	27.21288	.39365	10.71225
17	2.69277	29.90565	.37136	11.10590
18	2.85434	32.75999	.35034	11.47726
19	3.02560	35.78559	.33051	11.82760
20	3.20714	38.99273	.31180	12.15812
21	3.39956	42.39229	.29416	12.46992
22	3.60354	45.99583	.27751	12.76408
23	3.81975	49.81558	.26180	13.04158
24	4.04893	53.86451	.24698	13.30338
25	4.29187	58.15638	.23300	13.55036
26	4.54938	62.70577	.21981	13.78336
27	4.82235	67.52811	.20737	14.00317
28	5.11169	72.63980	.19563	14.21053
29	5.41839	78.05819	.18456	14.40616
30	5.74349	83.80168	.17411	14.59072
40	10.28572	164.04768	.09722	15.94907
50	18.42015	307.75606	.05429	16.70757
60	32.98769	565.11587	.03031	17.13111
70	59.07593	1026.00810	.01693	17.36762
80	105.79599	1851.39588	.00945	17.49968
90	189.46451	3329.53970	.00528	17.57342
100	339.30208	5976.67014	.00295	17.61460

To calculate the present value of $1 at 6 percent interest payable at the beginning of each month, multiply the figure in the right-hand column for the period of the monthly payments by 11.68540. For example, if the period of monthly payments is 20 years, the value is 12.15812 × 11.68540, which is 142.07250.

G

Net Level Premiums at
2½ and 3 Percent,
Curtate Functions, under
the 1958 CSO Table at
Quinquennial Ages for
Various Plans of Insurance

Age Nearest Birthday (Males)	Ordinary Life		20-Payment Life		20-Year Endowment		20-Year Term	
	2½%	3%	2½%	3%	2½%	3%	2½%	3%
5	$ 8.28	$ 6.03	$14.17	$11.32	$38.93	$36.89	–	–
10	8.05	6.98	15.73	12.78	39.01	36.97	–	–
15	9.29	8.15	17.52	14.49	39.16	37.12	$ 1.85	$ 1.83
20	10.75	9.56	19.48	16.40	39.28	37.25	2.13	2.11
25	12.55	11.28	21.68	18.57	39.44	37.41	2.63	2.60
30	14.80	13.47	24.23	21.15	39.78	37.75	3.58	3.53
35	17.67	16.29	27.24	24.23	40.44	38.42	5.27	5.18
40	21.38	19.96	30.84	27.95	41.62	39.62	8.06	7.91
45	26.16	24.70	35.15	32.44	43.54	41.57	12.38	12.15
50	32.38	30.91	40.50	38.00	46.61	44.69	18.96	18.61
55	40.57	39.09	47.39	45.13	51.49	49.63	28.53	28.01
60	51.50	50.02	56.66	54.64	59.10	57.33	41.72	41.00
65	66.21	64.75	69.54	67.75	70.76	69.10	–	–
70	85.94	84.48	87.62	86.00	88.09	86.53	–	–

H

пп

Securities and Exchange Commission Policy on Variable Life Contracts*

The Commission today announced its determinations on regulation of variable life insurance.

The Commission's action stems from public hearings last year on rules proposed by the American Life Convention and the Life Insurance Association of America. Their proposed rules would have exempted certain variable life insurance contracts, issuers and related persons from the Securities Act, the Securities Exchange Act, the Investment Company Act and the Investment Advisers Act.

In brief, the Commission determined that:

1. The investment character of variable life contracts would make them securities so that any public offering of the type of contracts contemplated in the hearings would have to be registered under the Securities Act.

2. People selling these variable life contracts generally would have to register as broker/dealers under the Securities Exchange Act.

3. The separate account of a company engaged in issuing and selling these variable life contracts would fall under the definition of an investment company under the Investment Company Act. However, the Commission determined to exempt by rule such accounts from the elaborate regulatory requirements of the act in deference to state regulation of insurance and because of complex administrative problems that would arise in providing the substantial exemptions from the act that would be necessary to make feasible operations of these accounts.

4. An insurance company or other entity providing investment advice incidental to the issuance of variable life contracts would be an investment adviser under the Investment Advisers Act. However, the Commission determined to exempt by rule from the act insurance companies or affiliated companies acting as advisers to these accounts essentially for the reasons cited in adopting the Investment Company Act exemption.

In determining not to adopt an exemptive rule with respect to variable life contracts under the Securities Act, the Commission in its release said:

---

* Announcement released January 31, 1973.

The important investment features of the contract—the opportunity to participate in the investment experience of the separate account in order to achieve increased life insurance benefits including death protection and cash value—require that contract holders be afforded the protections of full disclosure which would be developed by registration of the contracts under the Securities Act. The Commission has had extensive experience with the registration of complex investment contracts under the Securities Act and is confident that adequate disclosure can be developed for variable life insurance to achieve the truth-in-securities afforded by registration under the Statute. Such disclosure would cover, for example, the operation of the contract, the investment policies of the separate account, the extent of the contract holder's participation in the investment experience, the nature of the investment risk borne by the contract holder and a clear discussion of such costs as sales charges, administrative and mortality charges, risk charges and management fees.

At the same time, the Commission in its release said it had decided not to exempt these contracts from the provisions of the Securities Exchange Act

. . . because the complex nature of the investment elements of variable life insurance make it particularly important that the disclosures provided by Securities Act registration be communicated by salesmen and firms subject to regulation by the Commission, and no justification was established at the hearing for relief from the confirmation requirement.

In adopting the proposed exemptions for variable life contracts in the form of Rule 3c–4, under the Investment Company Act and Rule 202–1 under the Investment Advisers Act, the Commission release stated:

The Commission is persuaded to take this course for several reasons, even though some of the protections of the Investment Company Act would be relevant to variable life insurance. The principal reason is that to reconcile the regulatory scheme of the Act with state regulation of insurance—which unquestionably is applicable to variable life insurance—would, at the very least, be difficult. It probably could not be done without interfering to some degree with the orderly development of state regulation. In deference, therefore, to the established Congressional policy of preserving state regulation of insurance, the Commission concludes that the exemption should be granted. In addition, application of the Investment Company Act to variable life insurance would create complex administrative problems, since substantial exemptions from the Act would be required in order to make feasible the operation of a separate account to fund variable life insurance contracts. In particular, the Commission is persuaded by the active participation of the National Association of Insurance Commissioners in the hearing and the Model Variable Contract Law and Regulation adopted by them which the Commission views as the beginning of the development of a uniform state regulatory structure designed specifically to meet the requirements of variable life insurance and the needs of variable life insurance contract holders beyond the disclosure which the Securities Act would provide. Based on the representations made in the memoranda submitted by the National Association of Insurance Commissioners, the Commission believes that they are qualified to develop and administer the type of regulation particularly appropriate to the operation of variable life insurance separate accounts. Application of many of the provisions of the Investment Company Act in this context would only duplicate the regulation developed by the state insurance commissioners.

Consistent with the representations made by the National Association of Insurance Commissioners, we expect the states to move expeditiously to develop, refine and adopt regulations with respect to variable life insurance. Further, we expect that such regulations will provide material protections to purchasers substantially equivalent to the relevant protections that would be available under the Investment Company Act. In particular, we believe it important that the regulations provide for the valuation of portfolio securities in a uniform manner; that they assure that contract holders be furnished annual statements containing information similar in nature to the information that would be provided by a registered investment company through annual reports and proxy statements; that they provide protection against unauthorized or improper changes in investment policies and against excessive management, administrative and sales charges; and that transaction with affiliates be restricted in a manner similar to Section 17 (15 U.S.C. 80a–17) of the Investment Company Act and the rules thereunder. The Commission will closely monitor the development of state law in this area to assure its adequacy in providing these protections and, if in the future it appears that substantial deficiencies exist and are not likely to be remedied, the Commission will then consider whether it is necessary or appropriate to modify or rescind Rule 3c–4.

Effective date of the rules is February 12.

Last February 15, in response to a petition from American Life Convention and the Life Insurance Association of America, the Commission issued a notice and an order for a rule making proceeding under the Administrator Procedure Act and the Commission's Rules of Practice. The public hearing began last April 10 and concluded on June 7, after receiving more than 2,300 pages of testimony, supplemented by hundreds of pages of exhibits and other data. The Commission is releasing, in conjunction with its release on its policy determinations today, a report detailing the issues and recommendations of the Division of Investment Management Regulation, as well as a letter to petitioners advising them of the Commission's determinations.

I

The 1950 Uniform Individual Accident and Sickness Policy Provisions Law—NAIC

Section 1. DEFINITION OF ACCIDENT AND SICKNESS INSURANCE POLICY.

The term "policy of accident and sickness insurance" as used herein includes any policy or contract covering the kind or kinds of insurance described in .... (*insert here the section of law authorizing accident and sickness insurance*).

(*Note: If the insurance law of the state in which this draft is proposed for enactment does not have a section specifically authorizing the various types of insurance which may be written, this section should be modified to define accident and sickness insurance as "insurance against loss resulting from sickness or from bodily injury or death by accident, or both."*)

Section 2. FORM OF POLICY.

(A) No policy of accident and sickness insurance shall be delivered or issued for delivery to any person in this state unless:

(1) the entire money and other considerations therefor are expressed therein; and

(2) the time at which the insurance takes effect and terminates is expressed therein; and

(3) it purports to insure only one person, except that a policy may insure, originally or by subsequent amendment, upon the application of an adult member of a family who shall be deemed the policyholder, any two or more eligible members of that family, including husband, wife, dependent children or any children under a specified age which shall not exceed nineteen years and any other person dependent upon the policyholder; and

(*Note: In states having community property systems derived from the civil law it is suggested that in the foregoing subparagraph the words "an adult member" be replaced with "the head."*)

1145

(4) the style, arrangement and over-all appearance of the policy give no undue prominence to any portion of the text, and unless every printed portion of the text of the policy and of any endorsements or attached papers is plainly printed in light-faced type of a style in general use, the size of which shall be uniform and not less than ten-point with a lower-case unspaced alphabet length not less than one hundred and twenty-point (the "text" shall include all printed matter except the name and address of the insurer, name or title of the policy, the brief description if any, and captions and subcaptions); and

(5) the exceptions and reductions of indemnity are set forth in the policy and, except those which are set forth in section 3 of this act, are printed, at the insurer's option, either included with the benefit provision to which they apply, or under an appropriate caption such as "EXCEPTIONS," or "EXCEPTIONS AND REDUCTIONS," provided that if an exception or reduction specifically applies only to a particular benefit of the policy, a statement of such exception or reduction shall be included with the benefit provision to which it applies; and

(6) each such form, including riders and endorsements, shall be identified by a form number in the lower left-hand corner of the first page thereof; and

(7) it contains no provision purporting to make any portion of the charter, rules, constitution, or by-laws of the insurer a part of the policy unless such portion is set forth in full in the policy, except in the case of the incorporation of, or reference to, a statement of rates or classification of risks, or short-rate table filed with the (*Commissioner*).

(B) If any policy is issued by an insurer domiciled in this state for delivery to a person residing in another state, and if the official having responsibility for the administration of the insurance laws of such other state shall have advised the (*Commissioner*) that any such policy is not subject to approval or disapproval by such official, the (*Commissioner*) may by ruling require that such policy meet the standards set forth in subsection (A) of this section and in section 3.

Section 3.   ACCIDENT AND SICKNESS POLICY PROVISIONS.

(A) *Required Provisions*

Except as provided in paragraph (C) of this section each such policy delivered or issued for delivery to any person in this state shall contain the provisions specified in this subsection in the words in which the same appear in this section; provided, however, that the insurer may, at its option, substitute for one or more of such provisions corresponding provisions of different wording approved by the (*Commissioner*) which are in each instance not less favorable in any respect to the insured or the beneficiary. Such provisions shall be preceded individually by the caption appearing in this subsection or, at the option of the insurer, by such appropriate individual or group captions or subcaptions as the (*Commissioner*) may approve.

(1) A provision as follows:

Entire Contract; Changes. This policy, including the endorsements and the attached papers, if any, constitutes the entire contract of insurance. No change in this policy shall be valid until approved by an executive officer of the insurer and unless such approval be endorsed hereon or attached hereto. No agent has authority to change this policy or to waive any of its provisions.

(*Note: When enacted in states which prohibit amendment of a policy form by means other than attached printed rider upon a separate piece of paper the new law should contain (but not as a required policy provision) an added section defining "endorsement" in such a manner as to make the new law consistent with current statutes.*)

(2) A provision as follows:

Time Limit on Certain Defenses. (a) After three years from the date of issue of this policy no misstatements, except fraudulent misstatements, made by the applicant in the application for such policy shall be used to void the policy or to deny a claim for loss incurred or disability (as defined in the policy) commencing after the expiration of such three year period.

(The foregoing policy provision shall not be so construed as to affect any legal requirement for avoidance of a policy or denial of a claim during such initial three year period, nor to limit the application of section 3 (B), (1), (2), (3), (4) and (5) in the event of misstatement with respect to age or occupation or other insurance.)

A policy which the insured has the right to continue in force subject to its terms by the timely payment of premium (1) until at least age 50 or, (2) in the case of a policy issued after age 44, for at least five years from its date of issue, may contain in lieu of the foregoing the following provision (from which the clause in parentheses may be omitted at the insurer's option) under the caption "INCONTESTABLE":

After this policy has been in force for a period of three years during the lifetime of the insured (excluding any period during which the insured is disabled), it shall become incontestable as to the statements contained in the application.)

(b) No claim for loss incurred or disability (as defined in the policy) commencing after three years from the date of issue of this policy shall be reduced or denied on the ground that a disease or physical condition not excluded from coverage by name or specific description effective on the date of loss had existed prior to the effective date of coverage of this policy.

(3) A provision as follows:

Grace Period. A grace period of .... (*insert a number not less than "7" for weekly premium policies, "10" for monthly premium policies and "31" for all other policies*) days will be granted for the payment of each premium falling due after the first premium, during which grace period the policy shall continue in force.

(A policy which contains a cancellation provision may add, at the end of the above provision,

subject to the right of the insurer to cancel in accordance with the cancellation provision hereof.

A policy in which the insurer reserves the right to refuse any renewal shall have, at the beginning of the above provision,

Unless not less than five days prior to the premium due date the insurer has delivered to the insured or has mailed to his last address as shown by the records of the insurer written notice of its intention not to renew this policy beyond the period for which the premium has been accepted.)

(4) A provision as follows:

Reinstatement. If any renewal premium be not paid within the time granted the insured for payment, a subsequent acceptance of premium by the insurer or by any agent duly authorized by the insurer to accept such premium, without requiring in connection therewith an application for reinstatement, shall reinstate the policy; provided, however, that if the insurer or such agent requires an application for reinstatement and issues a conditional receipt for the premium tendered, the policy will be reinstated upon approval of such application by the insurer or, lacking such approval, upon the forty-fifth day following the date of such conditional receipt unless the insurer has previously notified the insured in writing of its disapproval of such application. The reinstated policy shall cover only loss resulting from accidental injury as may be sustained after the date of reinstatement and loss due to such sickness as may begin more than ten days after such date. In all other respects the insured and insurer shall have the same rights thereunder as they had under the policy immediately before the due date of the defaulted premium, subject to any provisions endorsed hereon or attached hereto in connection with the reinstatement. Any premium accepted in connection with a reinstatement shall be applied to a period for which premium has not been previously paid, but not to any period more than sixty days prior to the date of reinstatement.

(The last sentence of the above provision may be omitted from any policy which the insured has the right to continue in force subject to its terms by the timely payment of premiums (1) until at least age 50 or, (2) in the case of a policy issued after age 44, for at least five years from its date of issue.)

(5) A provision as follows:

Notice of Claim. Written notice of claim must be given to the insurer within twenty days after the occurrence or commencement of any loss covered by the policy, or as soon thereafter as is reasonably possible. Notice given by or on behalf of the insured or the beneficiary to the insurer at .... (*insert the location of such office as the insurer may designate for the purpose*), or to any authorized agent of the insurer, with information sufficient to identify the insured, shall be deemed notice to the insurer.

(In a policy providing a loss-of-time benefit which may be payable for at least two years, an insurer may at its option insert the following between the first and second sentences of the above provision:

Subject to the qualifications set forth below, if the insured suffers loss of time on account of disability for which indemnity may be payable for at least two years, he shall, at least once in every six months after having given notice of claim, give to the insurer notice of continuance of said disability, except in the event of legal incapacity. The period of six months following any filing of proof by the insured or any payment by the insurer on account of such claim or any denial of liability in whole or in part by the insurer shall be excluded in applying this provision. Delay in the giving of such notice shall not impair the insured's right to any indemnity which would otherwise have accrued during the period of six months preceding the date on which such notice is actually given.)

(6) A provision as follows:

Claim Forms. The insurer, upon receipt of a notice of claim, will furnish to the claimant such forms as are usually furnished by it for filing proofs of loss. If such forms are not furnished within fifteen days after the giving of such notice the claimant shall be deemed to have complied with the requirements of this policy as to proof of loss upon submitting, within the time fixed in the policy for filing proofs of loss, written proof covering the occurrence, the character and the extent of the loss for which claim is made.

(7) A provision as follows:

Proofs of Loss. Written proof of loss must be furnished to the insurer at its said office in case of claim for loss for which this policy provides any periodic payment contingent upon continuing loss within ninety days after the termination of the period for which the insurer is liable and in case of claim for any other loss within ninety days after the date of such loss. Failure to furnish such proof within the time required shall not invalidate nor reduce any claim if it was not reasonably possible to give proof within such time, provided such proof is furnished as soon as reasonably possible and in no event, except in the absence of legal capacity, later than one year from the time proof is otherwise required.

(8) A provision as follows:

Time of Payment of Claims. Indemnities payable under this policy for any loss other than loss for which this policy provides any periodic payment will be paid immediately upon receipt of due written proof of such loss. Subject to due written proof of loss, all accrued indemnities for loss for which this policy provides periodic payment will be paid

.... (*insert period for payment which must not be less frequently than monthly*) and any balance remaining unpaid upon the termination of liability will be paid immediately upon receipt of due written proof.

(9) A provision as follows:

Payment of Claims. Indemnity for loss of life will be payable in accordance with the beneficiary designation and the provisions respecting such payment which may be prescribed herein and effective at the time of payment. If no such designation or provision is then effective, such indemnity shall be payable to the estate of the insured. Any other accrued indemnities unpaid at the insured's death may, at the option of the insurer, be paid either to such beneficiary or to such estate. All other indemnities will be payable to the insured.

(The following provisions, or either of them, may be included with the foregoing provision at the option of the insurer:

If any indemnity of this policy shall be payable to the estate of the insured, or to an insured or beneficiary who is a minor or otherwise not competent to give a valid release, the insurer may pay such indemnity, up to an amount not exceeding $............ (*insert an amount which shall not exceed $1,000*), to any relative by blood or connection by marriage of the insured or beneficiary who is deemed by the insurer to be equitably entitled thereto. Any payment made by the insurer in good faith pursuant to this provision shall fully discharge the insurer to the extent of such payment.

Subject to any written direction of the insured in the application or otherwise all or a portion of any indemnities provided by this policy on account of hospital, nursing, medical, or surgical services may, at the insurer's option and unless the insured requests otherwise in writing not later than the time of filing proofs of such loss, be paid directly to the hospital or person rendering such services; but it is not required that the service be rendered by a particular hospital or person.)

(10) A provision as follows:

Physical Examinations and Autopsy. The insurer at its own expense shall have the right and opportunity to examine the person of the insured when and as often as it may reasonably require during the pendency of a claim hereunder and to make an autopsy in case of death where it is not forbidden by law.

(11) A provision as follows:

Legal Actions. No action at law or in equity shall be brought to recover on this policy prior to the expiration of sixty days after written proof of loss has been furnished in accordance with the requirements of this policy. No such action shall be brought after the expiration of three years after the time written proof of loss is required to be furnished.

(12) A provision as follows:

Change of Beneficiary. Unless the insured makes an irrevocable designation of beneficiary, the right to change of beneficiary is reserved to the insured and the consent of the beneficiary or beneficiaries shall not be requisite to surrender or assignment of this policy or to any change of beneficiary or beneficiaries, or to any other changes in this policy.

(The first clause of this provision, relating to the irrevocable designation of beneficiary, may be omitted at the insurer's option.)

(B) *Other Provisions*

Except as provided in paragraph (C) of this section, no such policy delivered or issued for delivery to any person in this state shall contain provisions respecting the matters set forth below unless such provisions are in the words in which the same appear in this section; provided, however, that the insurer may, at its option, use in lieu of any such provision a corresponding provision of different wording approved by the (*Commissioner*) which is not less favorable in any respect to the insured or the beneficiary. Any such provision contained in the policy shall be preceded individually by the appropriate caption appearing in this subsection or, at the option of the insurer, by such appropriate individual or group captions or subcaptions as the (*Commissioner*) may approve.

(1) A provision as follows:

Change of Occupation. If the insured be injured or contract sickness after having changed his occupation to one classified by the insurer as more hazardous than that stated in this policy or while doing for compensation anything pertaining to an occupation so classified, the insurer will pay only such portion of the indemnities provided in this policy as the premium paid would have purchased at the rates and within the limits fixed by the insurer for such more hazardous occupation. If the insured changes his occupation to one classified by the insurer as less hazardous than that stated in this policy, the insurer, upon receipt of proof of such change of occupation, will reduce the premium rate accordingly, and will return the excess pro-rata unearned premium from the date of change of occupation or from the policy anniversary date immediately preceding receipt of such proof, whichever is the more recent. In applying this provision, the classification of occupational risk and the premium rates shall be such as have been last filed by the insurer prior to the occurrence of the loss for which the insurer is liable or prior to date of proof of change in occupation with the state official having supervision of insurance in the state where the insured resided at the time this policy was issued; but if such filing was not required, then the classification of occupational risk and the premium rates shall be those last made effective by the insurer in such state prior to the occurrence of the loss or prior to the date of proof of change in occupation.

(2) A provision as follows:

Misstatement of Age. If the age of the insured has been misstated, all amounts payable under this policy shall be such as the premium paid would have purchased at the correct age.

(3) A provision as follows:

Other Insurance in This Insurer. If an accident or sickness or accident and sickness policy or policies previously issued by the insurer to the insured be in force concurrently herewith, making the aggregate indemnity for .... (*insert type of coverage or coverages*) in excess of $................. (*insert maximum limit of indemnity or indemnities*) the excess insurance shall be void and all premiums paid for such excess shall be returned to the insured or to his estate.

Or, in lieu thereof:

Insurance effective at any one time on the insured under a like policy or policies in this insurer is limited to the one such policy elected by the insured, his beneficiary or his estate, as the case may be, and the insurer will return all premiums paid for all other such policies.

(4) A provision as follows:

Insurance with Other Insurers. If there be other valid coverage, not with this insurer, providing benefits for the same loss on a provision of service basis or on an expense incurred basis and of which this insurer has not been given written notice prior to the occurrence or commencement of loss, the only liability under any expense incurred coverage of this policy shall be for such proportion of the loss as the amount which would otherwise have been payable hereunder plus the total of the like amounts under all such other valid coverages for the same loss of which this insurer had notice bears to the total like amounts under all valid coverages for such loss, and for the return of such portion of the premiums paid as shall exceed the pro-rata portion for the amount so determined. For the purpose of applying this provision when other coverage is on a provision of service basis, the "like amount" of such other coverage shall be taken as the amount which the services rendered would have cost in the absence of such coverage.

(If the foregoing policy provision is included in a policy which also contains the next following policy provision there shall be added to the caption of the foregoing provision the phrase "—EXPENSE INCURRED BENEFITS." The insurer may, at its option, include in this provision a definition of "other valid coverage," approved as to form by the (*Commissioner*), which definition shall be limited in subject matter to coverage provided by organizations subject to regulation by insurance law or by insurance authorities of this or any other state of the United States or any province of Canada, and by hospital or medical service organizations, and to any other coverage the inclusion of which may be approved by the (*Commissioner*). In the absence of such definition such term shall not include group insurance, automobile medical payments insurance, or coverage provided by hospital or medical service organizations or by union welfare plans or employer or employee benefit organizations. For the purpose of applying the foregoing policy provision with respect to any insured, any amount of benefit provided for such insured pursuant to any compulsory benefit statute (including any workmen's compensation or employer's liability statute) whether provided by a governmental agency or otherwise shall in all cases be deemed to be "other valid coverage" of which the insurer has had notice. In applying the foregoing policy provision no third party liability coverage shall be included as "other valid coverage.")

(5) A provision as follows:

Insurance with Other Insurers. If there be other valid coverage, not with this insurer, providing benefits for the same loss on other than an expense incurred basis and of which this insurer has not been given written notice prior to the occurrence or commencement of loss, the only liability for such benefits under this policy shall be for such proportion of the indemnities otherwise provided hereunder for such loss as the like indemnities of which the insurer had notice (including the indemnities under this policy) bear to the total amount of all like indemnities for such loss, and for the return of such portion of the premium paid as shall exceed the pro-rata portion for the indemnities thus determined.

If the foregoing policy provision is included in a policy which also contains the next preceding policy provision there shall be added to the caption of the foregoing provision the phrase "—OTHER BENEFITS." The insurer may, at its option, include in this provision a definition of "other valid coverage," approved as to form by the (*Commissioner*), which definition shall be limited in subject matter to coverage provided by organizations subject to regulation by insurance law or by insurance authorities of this or any other state of the United States or any province of Canada, and to any other coverage the inclusion of which may be approved by the (*Commissioner*). In the absence of such definition such term shall not include group insurance, or benefits provided by union welfare plans or by employer or employee benefit organizations. For the purpose of applying the foregoing policy provision with respect to any insured, any amount of benefit provided for such insured pursuant to any compulsory benefit statute (including any workmen's compensation or employer's liability statute) whether provided by a governmental agency or otherwise shall in all cases be deemed to be "other valid coverage" of which the insurer has had notice. In applying the foregoing policy provision no third party liability coverage shall be included as "other valid coverage."

(6) A provision as follows:

Relation of Earnings to Insurance. If the total monthly amount of loss of time benefits promised for the same loss under all valid loss of time coverage upon the insured, whether payable on a weekly or monthly basis, shall exceed the monthly earnings of the insured at the time disability commenced or his average monthly earnings for the period of two years immediately preceding a disability for which claim is made, whichever is the greater, the insurer will be liable only for such proportionate amount of such benefits under this policy as the amount of such monthly earnings or such average monthly earnings of the insured bears to the total amount of monthly benefits for the same loss under all such coverage upon the insured at the time such disability commences and for the return of such part of the premiums paid during such two years as shall exceed the pro-rata amount of the premiums for the benefits actually paid hereunder; but this shall not operate to reduce the total monthly amount of benefits payable under all such coverage upon the insured below the sum of two hundred dollars or the sum of the monthly benefits specified in such coverages, whichever is the lesser, nor shall it operate to reduce benefits other than those payable for loss of time.

The foregoing policy provision may be inserted only in a policy which the insured has the right to continue in force subject to its terms by the timely payment of premiums (1) until at least age 50 or, (2) in the case of a policy issued after age 44, for at least five years from its date of issue. The insurer may, at its option, include in this provision a definition of "valid loss of time coverage," approved as to form by the (*Commissioner*), which definition shall be limited in subject matter to coverage provided by governmental agencies or by organizations subject to regulation by insurance law or by insurance authorities of this or any other state of the United States or any province of Canada, or to any other coverage the inclusion of which may be approved by the (*Commissioner*) or any combination of such coverages. In the absence of such definition such term shall not include any coverage provided for such insured pursuant to any compulsory benefit statute (including any workmen's compensation or employer's liability statute), or benefits provided by union welfare plans or by employer or employee benefit organizations.)

(7) A provision as follows:

Unpaid Premium.   Upon the payment of a claim under this policy, any premium then due and unpaid or covered by any note or written order may be deducted therefrom.

(8) A provision as follows:

Cancellation.   The insurer may cancel this policy at any time by written notice delivered to the insured, or mailed to his last address as shown by the records of the insurer, stating when, not less than five days thereafter, such cancellation shall be effective; and after the policy has been continued beyond its original term the insured may cancel this policy at any time by written notice delivered or mailed to the insurer, effective upon receipt or on such later date as may be specified in such notice. In the event of cancellation, the insurer will return promptly the unearned portion of any premium paid. If the insured cancels, the earned premium shall be computed by the use of the short-rate table last filed with the state official having supervision of insurance in the state where the insured resided when the policy was issued. If the insurer cancels, the earned premium shall be computed pro-rata. Cancellation shall be without prejudice to any claim originating prior to the effective date of cancellation.

(*Note: In some states by statute termination of the in force status of the policy alone may not prejudice any claim for loss arising during and out of a disability which commenced while the policy was in force. The language here is susceptible of an interpretation consistent with such statutes.*)

(9) A provision as follows:

Conformity with State Statutes.   Any provision of this policy which, on its effective date, is in conflict with the statutes of the state in which the insured resides on such date is hereby amended to conform to the minimum requirements of such statutes.

(10) A provision as follows:
Illegal Occupation. The insurer shall not be liable for any loss to which a contributing cause was the insured's commission of or attempt to commit a felony or to which a contributing cause was the insured's being engaged in an illegal occupation.

(11) A provision as follows:
Intoxicants and Narcotics. The insurer shall not be liable for any loss sustained or contracted in consequence of the insured's being intoxicated or under the influence of any narcotic unless administered on the advice of a physician.
(*Note: Paragraphs* (10) *and* (11) *are suggested for states which desire such provisions.*)

(C) *Inapplicable or Inconsistent Provisions*

If any provision of this section is in whole or in part inapplicable to or inconsistent with the coverage provided by a particular form of policy the insurer, with the approval of the (*Commissioner*), shall omit from such policy any inapplicable provision or part of a provision, and shall modify any inconsistent provision or part of the provision in such manner as to make the provision as contained in the policy consistent with the coverage provided by the policy.

(D) *Order of Certain Policy Provisions*

The provisions which are the subject of subsections (A) and (B) of this section, or any corresponding provisions which are used in lieu thereof in accordance with such subsections, shall be printed in the consecutive order of the provisions in such subsections or, at the option of the insurer, any such provision may appear as a unit in any part of the policy, with other provisions to which it may be logically related, provided the resulting policy shall not be in whole or in part unintelligible, uncertain, ambiguous, abstruse, or likely to mislead a person to whom the policy is offered, delivered or issued.

(E) *Third Party Ownership*

The word "insured," as used in this act, shall not be construed as preventing a person other than the insured with a proper insurable interest from making application for and owning a policy covering the insured or from being entitled under such a policy to any indemnities, benefits and rights provided therein.

(F) *Requirements of Other Jurisdictions*

(1) Any policy of a foreign or alien insurer, when delivered or issued for delivery to any person in this state, may contain any provision which is not less favorable to the insured or the beneficiary than the provisions

of this act and which is prescribed or required by the law of the state under which the insurer is organized.

(2) Any policy of a domestic insurer may, when issued for delivery in any other state or country, contain any provision permitted or required by the laws of such other state or country.

(G) Filing Procedure

The (*Commissioner*) may make such reasonable rules and regulations concerning the procedure for the filing or submission of policies subject to this act as are necessary, proper or advisable to the administration of this act. This provision shall not abridge any other authority granted the (*Commissioner*) by law.

Section 4.   CONFORMING TO STATUTE.

(A) Other Policy Provisions

No policy provision which is not subject to section 3 of this act shall make a policy, or any portion thereof, less favorable in any respect to the insured or the beneficiary than the provisions thereof which are subject to this act.

(B) Policy Conflicting with This Act

A policy delivered or issued for delivery to any person in this state in violation of this act shall be held valid but shall be construed as provided in this act. When any provision in a policy subject to this act is in conflict with any provision of this act, the rights, duties and obligations of the insurer, the insured and the beneficiary shall be governed by the provisions of this act.

Section 5.   APPLICATION.

(A) The insured shall not be bound by any statement made in an application for a policy unless a copy of such application is attached to or endorsed on the policy when issued as a part thereof. If any such policy delivered or issued for delivery to any person in this state shall be reinstated or renewed, and the insured or the beneficiary or assignee of such policy shall make written request to the insurer for a copy of the application, if any, for such reinstatement or renewal, the insurer shall within fifteen days after the receipt of such request at its home office or any branch office of the insurer, deliver or mail to the person making such request, a copy of such application. If such copy shall not be so delivered or mailed, the insurer shall be precluded from introducing such application as evidence in any action or proceeding based upon or involving such policy or its reinstatement or renewal.

(B) No alteration of any written application for any such policy shall be made by any person other than the applicant without his written consent, except that insertions may be made by the insurer, for administrative purposes only, in such manner as to indicate clearly that such insertions are not to be ascribed to the applicant.

(C) The falsity of any statement in the application for any policy covered by this act may not bar the right to recovery thereunder unless such false statement materially affected either the acceptance of the risk or the hazard assumed by the insurer.

(*Note: Section 5, or any subsection thereof, is suggested for use in states which have no comparable statutes relating to the application.*)

Section 6. NOTICE, WAIVER.

The acknowledgment by any insurer of the receipt of notice given under any policy covered by this act, or the furnishing of forms for filing proofs of loss, or the acceptance of such proofs, or the investigation of any claim thereunder still not operate as a waiver of any of the rights of the insurer in defense of any claim arising under such policy.

Section 7. AGE LIMIT.

If any such policy contains a provision establishing, as an age limit or otherwise, a date after which the coverage provided by the policy will not be effective, and if such date falls within a period for which premium is accepted by the insurer or if the insurer accepts a premium after such date, the coverage provided by the policy will continue in force subject to any right of cancellation until the end of the period for which premium has been accepted. In the event the age of the insured has been misstated and if, according to the correct age of the insured, the coverage provided by the policy would not have become effective, or would have ceased prior to the acceptance of such premium or premiums, then the liability of the insurer shall be limited to the refund, upon request, of all premiums paid for the period not covered by the policy.

Section 8. NON-APPLICATION TO CERTAIN POLICIES.

Nothing in this act shall apply to or affect (1) any policy of workmen's compensation insurance or any policy of liability insurance with or without supplementary expense coverage therein; or (2) any policy or contract of reinsurance; or (3) any blanket or group policy of insurance; or (4) life insurance, endowment or annuity contracts, or contracts supplemental thereto which contain only such provisions relating to accident and sickness insurance as (a) provide additional benefits in case of death or dismemberment or loss of sight by accident, or as (b) operate to safeguard such contracts against lapse, or to give a special surrender value or special benefit or an annuity in the event that the insured or annuitant shall become totally and permanently disabled, as defined by the contract or supplemental contract.

(*Note: This provision may, if desired, be modified in individual states so as to be consistent with current statutes of such states.*)

Section 9. VIOLATION.

Any person, partnership or corporation willfully violating any provision of this act or order of the (*Commissioner*) made in accordance with this act, shall forfeit to the people of the state a sum not to exceed $.............. for each such violation, which may be revoked by a civil action. The (*Commissioner*) may also suspend or revoke the license of an insurer or agent for any such willful violation.

(Note: This provision is to be used only in those states which do not have similar legislation now in effect.)

Section 10.   JUDICIAL REVIEW.

Any order or decision of the (*Commissioner*) under this act shall be subject to review by appeal (writ of certiorari) to the .... Court at the instance of any party in interest. The filing of the appeal (petition for such writ) shall operate as a state of any such order or decision until the Court directs otherwise. The Court may review all the facts and, in disposing of the issue before it, may modify, affirm or reverse the order or decision of the (*Commissioner*) in whole or in part.

(Note: This provision is to be used only in those states which do not have similar legislation now in effect.)

Section 11.   REPEAL OF INCONSISTENT ACTS.

(Note: This section should contain suitable language to repeal acts or parts of acts presently enacted and inconsistent with this act. The repealing section should contain an appropriate exception with regard to section 12 of this act.)

Section 12.   EFFECTIVE DATE OF ACT.

This act shall take effect on the .... day of ...., 19..... A policy, rider or endorsement, which could have been lawfully used or delivered or issued for delivery to any person in this state immediately before the effective date of this act may be used or delivered or issued for delivery to any such person during five years after the effective date of this act without being subject to the provisions of sections 2, 3, or 4 of this act.

J

Seventh Status Report on Overinsurance for the Subcommittee on Overinsurance of the Accident and Health Committee, National Association of Insurance Commissioners, November 22, 1963

I. INTRODUCTORY

In December 1959, the National Association of Insurance Commissioners requested that the Health Insurance Association of America undertake a study of overinsurance. In response to such request, HIAA has heretofore submitted a series of six "Status Reports on Overinsurance" to the NAIC.

The first, submitted on May 13, 1960, described the nature of the over-insurance problem and provided the findings resulting from an over-insurance survey conducted by the Health Insurance Council. *Proceedings of the National Association of Insurance Commissioners*, 1960, Vol. 11, pp. 549–64.

The second, submitted on November 23, 1960, contained a summary of court decisions permitting multiple recovery of hospital or medical expenses, some recommended principles for a new "Relation of Earnings to Insurance" provision, and a draft provision to implement such principles. *Proceedings of the National Association of Insurance Commissioners*, 1961, Vol. 1, pp. 331–38.

The third, submitted on November 22, 1961, enumerated the limitations of underwriting control of overinsurance, described the deficiencies of the "Insurance With Other Insurers" provisions, and offered the text of a new provision designed to overcome such deficiencies. *Proceedings of the National Association of Insurance Commissioners,* 1962, Vol. 1, pp. 90–96.

The fourth, submitted on June 8, 1962, provided the text of a proposed revision of the overinsurance portions of the Uniform Individual Accident and Sickness Policy Provisions Law, described in relationship between such revision and the principles contained in earlier status reports, and offered a series of illustrative hypothetical claims to show the manner in which the proposed revision would be administered. *Proceedings of the National Association of Insurance Commissioners,* 1962, Vol. 11, pp. 370–87.

The fifth, submitted on October 19, 1962 offered the views of HIAA on two questions (overinsurance criteria and premium refunds) which arose during the June 1962 NAIC meeting, as well as additional illustrative hypothetical claims. *Proceedings of the National Association of Insurance Commissioners,* 1963, Vol. 1, pp. 85–94.

The sixth, submitted on May 31, 1963, offered additional recommendations for amendments of the overinsurance provisions of the Uniform Individual Accident and Sickness Policy Provisions Law. It also provided a compilation of evidence that overinsurance is a sufficiently serious problem to justify the remedial legislation, such compilation having been requested by the NAIC at its December 1962 meetings. *Proceedings of the National Association of Insurance Commissioners,* 1963, Vol. 11.

II. RECOMMENDATIONS FOR REMEDIAL LEGISLATION

Exhibit A of this Report contains our revised recommendations for amendment of the overinsurance provisions of the Uniform Individual Accident and Sickness Policy Provisions Law. It reflects the areas of agreement reached at the July 30 and October 16 conferences between the NAIC Subcommittee on Overinsurance and an HIAA representative. It therefore differs from the amendments offered in Exhibit A of the Sixth Status Report in that the definition of "allowable expense" has been amended by the addition of "110% of" in line 57, and the reference to a pro rata return of premium has been deleted. The Instructions for Section 2 have been modified by the addition of a sentence contained in the Instructions for Section 4 but heretofore omitted by oversight from the Instructions for Section 2: "The Insurer may require, as part of the proof of claim, the information necessary to administer this provision." The Instructions for Section 2 have also been modified, as requested by the NAIC Subcommittee on Overinsurance, in three other ways:

1. The words "guaranteed renewable and noncancellable as well as guaranteed renewable" have been added in parentheses in lines 86–87 to indicate that each enacting state is to make its own decision as to the availability of Section 2 for use in policies renewable at the option of the insurer.

2. The words "except for individual policies individually underwritten" have been added to lines 90–91 as requested by the NAIC Subcommittee.

3. The words "but an insurer may at its option include a subrogation clause in its policy" have been placed in parentheses in lines 104–5 to indicate that each enacting state is to make its own decision as to whether subrogation provisions are to be permitted.

HIAA acceptance of the above modification of the definition of "allowable expense" should not be construed as a lack of continued concern regarding the objections discussed earlier. Such acceptance simply means that a majority of the industry is of the opinion that the need for effective overinsurance provisions is so immediate that acquiescence in the NAIC Subcommittee's support of such modified definition is necessary in order to have a bill for the 1964 session of the several state legislatures.

Similarly, although the attached revision of Exhibit A complies with the NAIC Subcommittee's request to make the availability of Section 2 in contracts renewable at the option of the insurer an issue to be determined by each enacting state, it is urged that the parenthetical expression be deleted from lines 86–87 so as not to encourage refusals to renew. By reason of policies with special limitations upon the insurer's right to refuse renewal, as for example those policies the renewal of which will not be refused by reason of deterioration of health, it is no longer easy to classify all policies as noncancellable, guaranteed renewable or renewable at the option of the insurer. Even within the last named type of policy, health insurers have for many years voluntarily sought to limit refusals to renew by constricting the occasions for the exercise of such reserved right. The Subcommittee is therefore urged to reconsider its position on this point.

III. RECOMMENDATION FOR IMPLEMENTING REGULATION

At the October 16 meeting of the NAIC Subcommittee on Overinsurance, the HIAA representative was directed to submit a further modification of the Sixth Status Report which, if adopted, would require insurers electing to use either the new hospital-medical-surgical or the new loss-of-time overinsurance provision to place in the application and on the face of the policy a brief statement to the effect that the benefits of the policy could be reduced by reason of the overinsurance provision contained therein. Exhibit B of this report is offered to comply with such request. It is cast in the form of a recommended regulation for promulgation simultaneously with the enactment of Exhibit A in any particular state. It is believed that Exhibit A is responsive to the October 16 request of the NAIC Subcommittee.

The requirement contained in Exhibit B will be effective if it is confined, at the insurer's option, to the application or the policy, and need not extend to both. Many insurers use one application for several policies some of which will, and some of which will not, contain an overinsurance provision. To require the statement in the application, and thus a special application for each policy containing the overinsurance provision, would be an additional and unnecessary expense for insurers which use a statement in the policy itself as well as a "ten-day free look" provision.

Other insurers can satisfy the requirement with equal efficacy by a statement in the application rather than in the policy.

We urge that either form of compliance be permitted as indicated in Exhibit B.

Respectfully submitted,
S/d *John Hanna*
John P. Hanna
General Counsel

EXHIBIT A.   Proposed Revision of Sections 3(B)(3), 3(B)(4), 3(B)(5) and 3(B)(6) of the Uniform Individual Accident and Sickness Policy Provisions Law

1.   Section 1. (Insert reference to statutory section which contains
2. Section 3(B)(3) of the Uniform Individual Accident and Sickness Policy
3. Provisions Law) is amended as follows:
4. [OTHER INSURANCE IN THIS INSURER] *OVERINSURANCE:* If an
5. accident or sickness or accident and sickness policy or policies pre-
6. viously issued by the insurer to the insured be in force concurrently
7. herewith, making the aggregate indemnity for . . . . (insert
8. type of coverage or coverages) in excess of $. . . . . (insert
9. maximum limit of indemnity or indemnities) the excess shall be void and
10. all premiums paid for such excess shall be returned to the insured or to
11. his estate.
12. or, in lieu thereof:
13. Insurance effective at any one time on the insured under *this policy* and a
14. like policy or policies in this insurer is limited to the one [such] policy
15. elected by the insured, his beneficiary or his estate, as the case may be,
16. and the insurer will return all premiums paid for all other such policies.
17.   Section 2. (Insert reference to statutory section which contains
18. Section 3(B)(4) of the Uniform Individual Accident and Sickness Policy
19. Provisions Law), is hereby repealed and the following is enacted in lieu
20. thereof.
21. OVERINSURANCE: If, with respect to a person covered under this policy,
22. benefits for allowable expense incurred during a claim determination
23. period under this policy together with benefits for allowable expense
24. during such period under all other valid coverage (without giving effect
25. to this provision or to any "overinsurance provision" applying to such
26. other valid coverage), exceed the total of such person's allowable expense
27. during such period, this insurer shall be liable only for such proportionate
28. amount of the benefits for allowable expense under this policy during such
29. period as
30.   (*i*) the total allowable expense during such period
31. bears to
32.   (*ii*) the total amount of benefits payable during such
33.   period for such expense under this policy and all
34.   other valid coverage (without giving effect to this
35.   provision or to any "overinsurance provision"
36.   applying to such other valid coverage)
37. less in both (i) and (ii) any amount of benefits for allowable expense
38. payable under other valid coverage which does not contain an "over-
39. insurance provision." In no event shall this provision operate to increase
40. the amount of benefits for allowable expense payable under this policy
41. with respect to a person covered under this policy above the amount which
42. would have been paid in the absence of this provision. This insurer may
43. pay benefits to any insurer providing other valid coverage in the event

Exhibit A (continued)

44. of overpayment by such insurer. Any such payment shall discharge the
45. liability of this insurer as fully as if the payment had been made directly
46. to the insured, his assignee or his beneficiary. In the event that this
47. insurer pays benefits to the insured, his assignee or his beneficiary, in
48. excess of the amount which would have been payable if the existence of
49. other valid coverage had been disclosed, this insurer shall have a right
50. of action against the insured, his assignee or his beneficiary, to recover
51. the amount which would not have been paid had there been a disclosure of
52. the existence of the other valid coverage. The amount of other valid
53. coverage which is on a provision of service basis shall be computed
54. as the amount the services rendered would have cost in the absence of
55. such coverage.
56. For purposes of this provision:
57.   (*i*) "allowable expense" means 110% of any necessary,
58.   reasonable and customary item of expense which is
59.   covered, in whole or in part, as a hospital, surgical,
60.   medical or major medical expense under this policy
61.   or under any other valid coverage.
62.   (*ii*) "claim determination period" with respect to any covered
63.   person means the initial period of . . . .
64.   (insert period of not less than thirty days) and each
65.   successive period of a like number of days, during
66.   while allowable expense covered under this policy is
67.   incurred on account of such person. The
68.   first such period begins on the date when
69.   the first such expense is incurred, and
70.   successive periods shall begin when such
71.   expense is incurred after expiration of a
72.   prior period.
73. or, in lieu thereof:
74.   "claim determination period" with respect
75.   to any covered person means each . . . .
76.   (insert calendar or policy period of not less
77.   than a month) during which allowable expense
78.   covered under this policy is incurred on
79.   account of such person,
80.   (*iii*) "overinsurance provision" means this pro-
81.   vision and any other provision which may re-
82.   duce an insurer's liability because of the
83.   existence of benefits under other valid cov-
84.   erage.
85. *INSTRUCTIONS*
86. The foregoing policy provision may be inserted in all (guaranteed renew-
87. able and non-cancellable as well as guaranteed renewable) policies pro-
88. viding hospital, surgical, medical or major medical benefits. The
89. insurer may make this provision applicable to either or both (a) other
90. valid coverage with other insurers and (b), except for individual policies
91. individually underwritten, other valid coverage with the same insurer.
92. The insurer shall include in this provision a definition of "other valid
93. coverage" approved as to form by the (commissioner). Such term may
94. include hospital, surgical, medical or major medical benefits provided
95. by group, blanket or franchise coverage, individual and family-type
96. coverage, Blue Cross-Blue Shield coverage and other prepayment plans,
97. group practice and individual practice plans, uninsured benefits provided
98. by labor-management trusteed plans, or union welfare plans, or by em-
99. ployer or employee benefit organizations, benefits provided under govern-
100. mental programs, workmen's compensation insurance or any coverage
101. required or provided by any other statute, and medical payments under
102. automobile liability and personal liability policies. Other valid coverage

Exhibit A (continued)

103. shall not include payments made under third party liability coverage as a
104. result of a determination of negligence (, but an insurer may at its option
105. include a subrogation clause in its policy). The insurer may require, as
106. part of the proof of claim, the information necessary to administer this
107. provision.
108.　　　Section 3. (Insert reference to statutory section which contains
109. Section 3(B)(5) of the Uniform Individual Accident and Sickness Policy Pro-
110. visions Law) is hereby repealed.
111.　　　Section 4. (Insert reference to statutory section which contains
112. Section 3(B)(6) of the Uniform Individual Accident and Sickness Policy Pro-
113. visions Law) is hereby repealed and the following is enacted in lieu thereof:
114. OVERINSURANCE: After the loss-of-time benefit of this policy has been
115. payable for 90 days, such benefit will be adjusted, as provided below, if
116. the total amount of unadjusted loss-of-time benefits provided in all valid
117. loss-of-time coverage upon the insured should exceed. . . . % of the in-
118. sured's earned income; provided, however, that if the information con-
119. tained in this application discloses that the total amount of loss-of-time
120. benefits under this policy and under all other valid loss-of-time coverage
121. expected to be effective upon the insured in accordance with the application
122. for this policy exceeded . . . % of the insured's earned income at the time
123. of such application, such higher percentage will be used in place of . . . %.
124. Such adjusted loss-of-time benefit under this policy for any month shall
125. be only such proportion of the loss-of-time benefit otherwise payable
126. under this policy as
127.　　　(i) the product of the insured's earned income
128.　　　　　and. . . . % (or, if higher, the alternative
129.　　　　　percentage described at the end of the first
130.　　　　　sentence of this provision)
131. bears to
132.　　　(ii) the total amount of loss-of-time benefits pay-
133.　　　　　able for such month under this policy and all
134.　　　　　other valid loss-of-time coverage on the in-
135.　　　　　sured (without giving effect to the "overinsurance
136.　　　　　provision" in this or any other coverage)
137. less in both (i) and (ii) any amount of loss-of-time benefits payable under
138. other valid loss-of-time coverage which does not contain an "overinsur-
139. ance provision." In making such computation, all benefits and earnings
140. shall be converted to a consistent (insert "weekly" if the loss-of-time
141. benefit of this policy is payable weekly, "monthly" if such benefit is pay-
142. able monthly, etc.) basis. If the numerator of the foregoing ratio is zero
143. or is negative, no benefit shall be payable under this policy. In no event
144. shall this provision (i) operate to reduce the total combined amount of loss-
145. of-time benefits for such month payable under this policy and all other valid
146. loss-of-time coverage below the lesser of $300 and the total combined
147. amount of loss-of-time benefits determined without giving effect to any
148. "overinsurance provision," nor (ii) operate to increase the amount of
149. benefits payable under this policy above the amount which would have been paid
150. in the absence of this provision, nor (iii) take into account or operate to
151. reduce any benefit other than the loss-of-time benefit.
152. For purposes of this provision:
153.　　　(i) "earned income," except where otherwise specified,
154.　　　　　means the greater of the monthly earnings of the
155.　　　　　insured at the time disability commences and his
156.　　　　　average monthly earnings for a period of two years
157.　　　　　immediately preceding the commencement of such
158.　　　　　disability, and shall not include any investment in-
159.　　　　　come or any other income not derived from the in-
160.　　　　　sured's vocational activities.
161.　　　(ii) "overinsurance provision" shall include this pro-

Exhibit A (concluded)

162.   vision and any other provision with respect to any
163.   loss-of-time coverage which may have the effect
164.   of reducing an insurer's liability if the total amount
165.   of loss-of-time benefits under all coverage exceeds
166.   a stated relationship to the insured's earnings.
167. INSTRUCTIONS. The foregoing provision may be included only in a
168. policy which provides a loss-of-time benefit which may be payable for
169. at least 52 weeks, which is issued on the basis of selective underwriting
170. of each individual application, and for which the application includes a
171. question designed to elicit information necessary either to determine
172. the ratio of the total loss-of-time benefits of the insured to the insured's
173. earned income or to determine that such ratio does not exceed the per-
174. centage of earnings, not less than 60%, selected by the insurer and
175. inserted in lieu of the blank factor above. The insurer may require, as
176. part of the proof of claim, the information necessary to administer this
177. provision. If the application indicates that other loss-of-time coverage
178. is to be discontinued, the amount of such other coverage shall be excluded
179. in computing the alternative percentage in the first sentence of the over-
180. insurance provision. The policy shall include a definition of "valid loss-
181. of-time coverage," approved as to form by the (commissioner), which
182. definition may include coverage provided by governmental agencies and
183. by organizations subject to regulation by insurance law and by insurance
184. authorities of this or any other state of the United States or of any other
185. country or subdivision thereof, coverage provided for such insured pur-
186. suant to any disability benefits statute or any workmen's compensation
187. or employer's liability statute, benefits provided by labor-management
188. trusteed plans or union welfare plans or by employer or employee-bene-
189. fit organizations, or by salary continuance or pension programs, and any
190. other coverage the inclusion of which may be approved by the (commis-
191. sioner).
192.   Section 5. This Act shall take effect on the . . . . day
193. of . . . . , 19 . . . . A policy, rider or endorsement
194. which could have been lawfully used or delivered or issued for delivery
195. to any person in this state immediately before the effective date of this
196. Act may be used or delivered or issued for delivery to any such person
197. during five years after the effective date of this Act.

EXHIBIT B. Proposed Regulation Re Overinsurance Provisions

 1.   Each individual health insurance policy, issued in this State on or
 2. after (insert the effective date contained in Section 5 of Exhibit A), which
 3. contains the overinsurance provisions authorized in (insert reference to
 4. statutory section which contains Section 3(B)(4) of the Uniform Individual
 5. Accident and Sickness Policy Provisions Law) or (insert reference to
 6. statutory section which contains Section 3(B)(6) of the Uniform Individual
 7. Accident and Sickness Policy Provisions Law) as amended by (insert
 8. session laws citation to Exhibit A) or, at the option of the insurer, the
 9. application for such policy, shall contain, or have attached to or be stamped
10. or endorsed to add, a statement to the effect that benefits under the policy
11. are subject to reduction if the insured has benefits under any other cov-
12. erage of the type described in the overinsurance provision causing over-
13. insurance as defined in such provision. If the insurer elects to include
14. such statement in the policy, rather than in the application, the policy
15. shall also contain, or have attached to or be stamped or endorsed to add,
16. an additional statement to the effect that during a period of ten days from
17. the date the policy is delivered to the policyholder, it may be surrendered
18. to the insurer together with a written request for cancellation of the policy
19. and in such event the insurer will refund any premium paid therefor
20. including any policy fees or other charges.

K

National Association of Insurance Commissioners Model Group Life Insurance Bill

GROUP LIFE INSURANCE DEFINITION

I. No policy of group life insurance shall be delivered in this state unless it conforms to one of the following descriptions:

1. A policy issued to an employer, or to the trustees of a fund established by an employer, which employer or trustees shall be deemed the policyholder, to insure employees of the employer for the benefit of persons other than the employer, subject to the following requirements:

   a) The employees eligible for insurance under the policy shall be all of the employees of the employer, or all of any class or classes thereof determined by conditions pertaining to their employment. The policy may provide that the term "employees" shall include the employees of one or more subsidiary corporations, and the employees, individual proprietors, and partners of one or more affiliated corporations, proprietors or partnerships if the business of the employer and of such affiliated corporations, proprietors or partnerships is under common control through stock ownership or contract. The policy may provide that the term "employees" shall include the individual proprietor or partners if the employer is an individual proprietor or a partnership. The policy may provide that the term "employees" shall include retired employees. No director of a corporate employer shall be eligible for insurance under the policy unless such person is otherwise eligible as a bona fide employee of the corporation by performing services other than the usual duties of a director. No individual proprietor or partner shall be eligible for insurance under the policy unless he is actively engaged in and devotes a substantial part of his time to the conduct of the business of the proprietor or partnership.

b) The premium for the policy shall be paid by the policyholder, either wholly from the employer's funds or funds contributed by him, or partly from such funds and partly from funds contributed by the insured employees. No policy may be issued on which the entire premium is to be derived from funds contributed by the insured employees. A policy on which part of the premium is to be derived from funds contributed by the insured employees may be placed in force only if at least 75 percent of the then eligible employees, excluding any as to whom evidence of individual insurability is not satisfactory to the insurer, elect to make the required contributions. A policy on which no part of the premium is to be derived from funds contributed by the insured employees must insure all eligible employees, or all except any as to whom evidence of individual insurability is not satisfactory to the insurer.

c) The policy must cover at least 10 employees at date of issue.

d) The amounts of insurance under the policy must be based upon some plan precluding individual selection either by the employees or by the employer or trustees.

2. A policy issued to a creditor, who shall be deemed the policyholder, to insure debtors of the creditor, subject to the following requirements:

a) The debtors eligible for insurance under the policy shall be all of the debtors of the creditor whose indebtedness is repayable either (i) in installments or (ii) in one sum at the end of a period not in excess of eighteen months from the initial date of debt, or all of any class or classes thereof determined by conditions pertaining to the indebtedness or to the purchase giving rise to the indebtedness. The policy may provide that the term "debtors" shall include the debtors of one or more subsidiary corporations, and the debtors of one or more affiliated corporations, proprietors or partnerships if the business of the policyholder and of such affiliated corporations, proprietors or partnerships is under common control through stock ownership, contract or otherwise. No debtor shall be eligible unless the indebtedness constitutes an irrevocable obligation to repay which is binding upon him during his lifetime, at and from the date the insurance becomes effective upon his life.

b) The premium for the policy shall be paid by the policyholder, either from the creditor's funds, or from charges collected from the insured debtors, or from both. A policy on which part or all of the premium is to be derived from the collection from the insured debtors of identifiable charges not required of uninsured debtors shall not include, in the class or classes of debtors eligible for insurance, debtors under obligations outstanding at its date of issue without evidence of individual insurability unless at least 75 percent of the then eligible debtors elect to pay the required charges. A policy on which no part of the premium is to be derived from the collection of such identifiable charges must insure all eligible debtors, or all except any as to whom evidence of individual insurability is not satisfactory to the insurer.

c) The policy may be issued only if the group of eligible debtors is then receiving new entrants at the rate of at least 100 persons yearly, or may reasonably be expected to receive at least 100 new entrants during the first policy year, and only if the policy reserves to the insurer the right to require evidence of individual insurability if less than 75 percent of the new entrants become insured. The policy may exclude from the classes eligible for insurance classes of debtors determined by age.

d) The amount of insurance on the life of any debtor shall at no time exceed the amount owed by him which is repayable in installments to the creditor, or $10,000., whichever is less. Where the indebtedness is repayable in one sum to the creditor, the insurance on the life of any debtor shall in no instance be in effect for a period in excess of eighteen months except that such insurance may be continued for an additional period not exceeding six months in the case of default, extension or recasting of the loan. The amount of the insurance on the life of any debtor shall at no time exceed the amount of the unpaid indebtedness, or $10,000., whichever is less.

e) The insurance shall be payable to the policyholder. Such payment shall reduce or extinguish the unpaid indebtedness of the debtor to the extent of such payment."

3. A policy issued to a labor union, which shall be deemed the policyholder, to insure members of such union for the benefit of persons other than the union or any of its officials, representatives or agents, subject to the following requirements:

a) The members eligible for insurance under the policy shall be all of the members of the union, or all of any class or classes thereof determined by conditions pertaining to their employment, or to membership in the union, or both.

b) The premium for the policy shall be paid by the policyholder, either wholly from the union's funds, or partly from such funds and partly from funds contributed by the insured members specifically for their insurance. No policy may be issued on which the entire premium is to be derived from funds contributed by the insured members specifically for their insurance. A policy on which part of the premium is to be derived from funds contributed by the insured members specifically for their insurance may be placed in force only if at least 75 percent of the then eligible members, excluding any as to whom evidence of individual insurability is not satisfactory to the insurer, elect to make the required contributions. A policy on which no part of the premium is to be derived from funds contributed by the insured members specifically for their insurance must insure all eligible members, or all except any as to whom evidence of individual insurability is not satisfactory to the insurer.

c) The policy must cover at least 25 members at date of issue.

d) The amounts of insurance under the policy must be based upon some plan precluding individual selection either by the members or by the union.

4. A policy issued to the trustees of a fund established by two or more employers in the same industry or by one or more labor unions, or by one or more employers and one or more labor unions, which trustees shall be deemed the policyholder, to insure employees of the employers or members of the unions for the benefit of persons other than the employers or the unions, subject to the following requirements:

a) The persons eligible for insurance shall be all of the employees of the employers or all of the members of the unions, or all of any class or classes thereof determined by conditions pertaining to their employment, or to membership in the unions, or to both. The policy may provide that the term "employees" shall include retired employees, and the individual proprietor or partners if an employer is an individual proprietor or a partnership. No director of a corporate employer shall be eligible for insurance under the policy unless such person is otherwise eligible as a bona fide employee of the corporation by performing services other than the usual duties of a director. No individual proprietor or partner shall be eligible for insurance under the policy unless he is actively engaged in and devotes a substantial part of his time to the conduct of the business of the proprietor or partnership. The policy may provide that the term "employees" shall include the trustees or their employees, or both, if their duties are principally connected with such trusteeship.

b) The premium for the policy shall be paid by the trustees wholly from funds contributed by the employer or employers of the insured persons, or by the union or unions, or by both. No policy may be issued on which any part of the premium is to be derived from funds contributed by the insured persons specifically for their insurance. The policy must insure all eligible persons, or all except any as to whom evidence of individual insurability is not satisfactory to the insurer.

c) The policy must cover at date of issue at least 100 persons and not less than an average of five persons per employer unit; and if the fund is established by the members of an association of employers the policy may be issued only if (i) either (a) the participating employers constitute at date of issue at least 60 percent of those employer members whose employees are not already covered for group life insurance or (b) the total number of persons covered at date of issue exceeds 600; and (ii) the policy shall not require that, if a participating employer discontinues membership in the association, the insurance of his employees shall cease solely by reason of such discontinuance.

d) The amounts of insurance under the policy must be based upon some plan precluding individual selection either by the insured persons or by the policyholder, employers, or unions.

II. No such policy of group life insurance may be issued to an employer, or labor union or to the trustees of a fund established in whole or in part by an employer or a labor union, which provides term insurance under any group life insurance policy or policies issued to the employer or employers of such person or to a labor union or labor unions of which such person is a member or to the trustees of a fund or funds established in whole or in part by such employer or employers or such labor union or labor unions, exceeds $20,000, unless 150 percent of the annual compensation of such person from his employer or employers exceeds $20,000, in which event all such term insurance shall not exceed $40,000 or 150 percent of such annual compensation, whichever is the lesser.

L

Specimen Group Term Life Insurance Policy

GROUP
TERM
LIFE
INSURANCE
POLICY

ABC MUTUAL LIFE INSURANCE
COMPANY OF
HARRISBURG, PENNSYLVANIA
(A Mutual Company)

No. G L 1000-1

Hereby insures certain

THE JOHN DOE COMPANY

herein known as the policyholder, and agrees to pay the benefits provided herein.

This policy is issued in consideration of the application of the policyholder and the payment in advance of the premiums computed and payable as herein provided. The first premium is due and payable as of June 1, 1973 , which shall be the date of issue of this policy, to cover the period from that date until July 1, 1973 . Subsequent premiums shall be due and payable monthly , beginning on said last mentioned date, during the continuance of this policy.

The provisions and conditions on the subsequent pages hereof shall form a part of the policy as fully as if recited in detail above the signatures hereto affixed.

In Witness Whereof, ABC MUTUAL LIFE INSURANCE COMPANY OF HARRISBURG, herein called the Company, has caused this policy to be executed as of its date of issue.

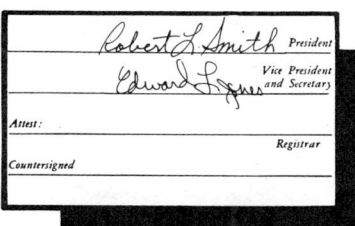

President

Vice President
and Secretary

Attest:

Registrar

Countersigned

Specimen Group Term Life Insurance Policy (continued)

Article I - Life Insurance Benefit

The Company, upon receipt of due proof of death of any covered person, agrees to pay the proceeds of the life insurance in force on the life of such covered person under this policy.

Article IA - Schedule of Insurance

The amount of insurance on each covered person shall be determined as follows:

Classification of Covered Persons	Amount of Insurance
1. President, Vice Presidents, Treasurer, or Secretary	$25,000
2. Each other eligible employee	$15,000

Reduction Formula

Each covered person age 65 or over on the date his insurance becomes effective shall be insured on that date for 50% of the amount for which he would otherwise be eligible.

The amount of insurance for which a covered person was insured prior to attainment of age 65 will be reduced by 50% on the date of such attainment.

No covered person, the amount of whose insurance has been or is being reduced by reason of his having attained an age at which a reduction in the amount of his insurance is specified, shall be eligible for any increase in the amount of his insurance on or after the date such a reduction commences or is effected.

Specimen Group Term Life Insurance Policy (continued)

Article II - Definitions

A "covered person" as used herein means an employee who is eligible for insurance under Article III and whose insurance has become effective under Article IV.

"Wages" or "earnings" of a covered person as used herein shall mean his regular basic pay exclusive of overtime, bonuses or any other form of additional compensation.

A masculine personal pronoun as used herein includes the feminine, wherever the context requires.

"Active, full-time employee" as used herein means an employee of the policyholder who is working regularly throughout the entire duration of the policyholder's work week, and in any event not less than thirty hours per week, at any of the policyholder's business establishments or at some other location to which the policyholder's business requires the employee to travel, and whose principal source of earned income is his wages or earnings received from the policyholder.

Specimen Group Term Life Insurance Policy (continued)

Article III - Eligibility

Each active, full-time employee of the policyholder on the date of issue of this policy shall be eligible for insurance hereunder on said date of issue.

Each person who becomes an active, full-time employee of the policyholder after the date of issue of this policy shall be eligible for insurance hereunder on the day following the completion of   one month of   continuous service as an active, full-time employee with the policyholder.

No employee shall be eligible for coverage in more than one classification or as an employee of more than one employer herein.

If the employment of any employee as an active, full-time employee be terminated and he shall subsequently be reemployed as an active, full-time employee, his employment shall be deemed to commence on the last date of hiring and previous employment shall be ignored, provided, however, that this provision shall not apply to a previously insured employee who is rehired within a twelve-month period following the termination of his employment.

Part-time and temporary employees shall not be eligible for insurance hereunder.

(12 months)

Specimen Group Term Life Insurance Policy (continued)

Article III - A-Associated Companies

Employees of such companies, corporations, firms or individuals subsidiary to or affiliated with the policyholder as are listed below and referred to herein as associated companies shall be considered employees of the policyholder for the purposes of this policy:

The Richard Roe Company

Specimen Group Term Life Insurance Policy (continued)

Article IV - Effective Date of Insurance

1. If an employee is not required to contribute to the cost of insurance under this policy, such employee will become insured on the date he becomes eligible, provided he is actually at work on a full-time basis on that date, otherwise such employee will become insured on the date upon which he actually returns to work for the policy-holder on a full-time basis.

2. If an employee is required to contribute to the cost of his insurance under this policy, such employee, if eligible, may elect to be insured hereunder by completing a payroll deduction authorization for the amount he must contribute toward the payment of premiums. The insurance of each such employee who has so elected shall become effective on

    (a)   the date the employee becomes eligible, if the policyholder receives the employee's authorization on or prior to such date, or

    (b)   the date the policyholder receives the employee's authorization, if it is received within 31 days after the date he becomes eligible, or

    (c)   the date the company accepts as satisfactory, evidence of insurability furnished at the employee's own expense, if his authorization is received by the policyholder more than 31 days after the date he becomes eligible, or if the employee is again electing the insurance after having previously canceled his payroll deduction authorization;

provided, that if such employee is not actually at work on a full-time basis on the date his insurance would otherwise become effective, such employee's insurance will become effective on the date he returns to active, full-time employment.

3. Any increase in the amount of an employee's insurance due to a change in his insurance classification under Article IA will take effect automatically on the date his class changes, provided he is then actually at work on a full-time basis, or if the employee is not actually at work on that date, the increase will take effect on the date he actually returns to full-time work. Any decrease in the amount of an employee's insurance due to a change in his insurance classification under Article IA will take effect automatically on the date his class changes irrespective of whether or not he is then actually at work.

4. Any increase in the amount of an employee's insurance due to a reason other than a change in insurance classification will take effect automatically on the effective date of such increase provided he is then actually at work on a full-time basis, or if the employee is not actually at work on that date, the increase will take effect on the date he actually returns to full-time work. Any decrease in the amount of an employee's insurance due to a reason other than a change in insurance classification will take effect automatically on the effective date of such decrease irrespective of whether or not he is then actually at work.

Specimen Group Term Life Insurance Policy (continued)

Article V - Individual Terminations

The insurance on any covered person shall cease automatically on the earliest of the following, subject to Articles V-A, Conversion Privilege, and IX, Continuation of Insurance:

(a) the date of termination of employment, or

(b) the date he ceases to be an active, full-time employee, or

(c) the date he ceases to be eligible, or

(d) the date of termination of this policy, or

(e) at the end of the last period for which the employee has made the required contribution if he has notified the policyholder of cancellation of the payroll deduction authorization or otherwise failed to make his contribution.

Specimen Group Term Life Insurance Policy (continued)

Article V-A - Conversion Privilege

1. If all or any part of a covered person's insurance terminates because of termination of employment or membership in an eligible class, he shall have the privilege of converting the insurance thus terminated, without evidence of insurability, to an individual policy of life insurance only, subject to the following conditions:

(a) written application for the policy and payment of the first premium thereon must be made within thirty-one days after such termination of his insurance, and

(b) the individual policy shall be upon any form then customarily issued by the Company at the age and for the amount applicable, except term insurance, provided that such policy shall not contain disability benefits nor other supplementary benefits, and

(c) the individual policy shall be effective at the end of the thirty-one day period after such termination of insurance, and

(d) the premium payable shall be at the then current rate of the Company applicable to the class of risk to which the covered person belongs and his age at birthday nearest to the effective date of the individual policy applied for.

2. If a covered person's insurance terminates because this policy terminates with respect to all covered persons or to any eligible class of which he is a member, and if he has been insured by this policy for five years prior to such termination, he shall have the privilege of converting to an individual policy in the same manner as if his insurance had terminated under Section 1 above, except that the amount of the individual policy shall not exceed the lesser of

(a) the amount for which his life had been insured by this policy on the date it terminated, reduced by the amount of any group life insurance issued by or reinstated with this Company or any other insurer for which he may then be eligible or for which he would become eligible within thirty-one days after such termination, or

(b) $2,000.

If a covered person shall die during the thirty-one day period following the termination of his insurance in either manner aforesaid, the Company will pay the amount of insurance, if any, to which he would have been entitled under an individual policy at the expiration of such thirty-one day period, as a claim under this group policy, and in the event any premium has been paid for such individual policy, such premium will be refunded.

Specimen Group Term Life Insurance Policy (continued)

Article VI - Beneficiary

Each covered person shall designate a beneficiary to whom the proceeds under this policy shall be payable. If at the death of such covered person there be no named beneficiary, or if such beneficiary does not survive such covered person, the proceeds shall be payable, at the option of the Company, to any one or more of the following surviving relatives of such covered person, wife, husband, mother, father, child or children, or to the executor or administrator of the deceased covered person. During such covered person's lifetime, he shall be entitled to change the beneficiary on written notice to the Company (on forms provided by the Company); such change shall take effect on receipt of such notice by the Company but shall relate back to the date of such notice without prejudice to the Company for any money paid prior to receipt of such notice.

If any beneficiary if a minor or physically, mentally or otherwise incapable of giving a valid release for any payment due, the Company may, at its option, and until claim is made by the duly appointed guardian or committee for such beneficiary, make payment to any person or institution who appears to the Company to have assumed responsibility for the care, custody or support of such beneficiary. Such payments will be made in instalments in the amount specified in any optional method of settlement previously elected or in the absence of such optional method of settlement in instalments not in excess of $100 monthly.

Payment in the manner and to the persons described above shall to the extent thereof release the Company of all further liability.

Optional Methods of Settlement

Upon written election by the covered person during his lifetime, or in the absence of such election, on election by the beneficiary at such covered person's death, the Company in lieu of payment in one sum will pay the proceeds in such number of equal monthly instalments certain, in accordance with the table below, as may be designated in the election of the option, the amount of each instalment to be determined from the table and the first instalment to be payable immediately:

Number of monthly instalments certain	Amounts of each instalment certain per $1,000 of proceeds
12	$84.37
24	42.76
36	28.89
48	21.96
60	17.80
120	9.50
180	6.75
240	5.39

If any instalment payment would amount to less than $10, this option shall not be available. Yearly, half-yearly or quarterly instalments will be paid in lieu of monthly instalments certain if so provided in the election of this option. Such instalments may be computed by multiplying the monthly instalment by 11.852, 5.966 or 2.993, respectively. Instalments certain shall participate in such proportion of the divisible surplus as the Company may allot and set apart thereto. After the death of any payee, any remaining instalments certain will be paid in such manner as may be directed in the election of the option with the consent of the Company.

Specimen Group Term Life Insurance Policy (continued)

Article VII - Premiums

Payment of Premiums   All premiums are payable by the policyholder in advance at the Home
Office of the Company in Harrisburg, Pennsylvania, or to any authorized agent of the Company.
Except as otherwise provided, this policy shall terminate and become void on nonpayment of
premium.

Grace Period   A grace period of thirty-one days, without interest, will be allowed for the
payment of every premium after the first during which period this policy shall continue in force,
except that if the policyholder shall give the Company written notice in advance of an earlier date
of termination, then this policy shall terminate on such earlier date. The policyholder shall be
liable to the Company for the payment of the pro rata premium for the time this policy was in
force during the grace period.

Calculation of Premium   The method of premium calculation described below is guaranteed for
twelve months from the date of issue of this policy, but may be changed thereafter by the Company
as of any premium due date, except that an increase in premium rates may not be made more
often than once in any twelve-month period.

On the date of issue of this policy an average premium rate will be established as follows:

Determine the tabular premium in accordance with the Table of Monthly Premiums
shown below separately for those male persons and those female persons covered
on such date. To the sum of the male tabular premium plus 60% of the female
tabular premium add $.20 per $1,000 on the first $40,000 of insurance. The
monthly premium so determined is reduced by the Advance Expense Adjustment
Percentage in accordance with the schedule shown below to produce the total
monthly premium. The rate per $1,000 is established by dividing the total premium
by the total amount of insurance inforce on male and female persons. The rate per
$1,000 may be increased by the Company to reflect any additional hazards.

On each anniversary of the date of issue after the first, an average premium rate will be
established as follows:

Determine the tabular premium in accordance with the Table of Monthly Premiums
then in effect. Such tabular premium is modified by any loadings or discounts then
in effect. The monthly premium so determined is reduced by an advance expense
adjustment percentage in accordance with the schedule then in use by the Company
to produce the total monthly premium. The rate per $1,000 is established by dividing
the total premium by the total amount of insurance inforce. The rate per $1,000 may
be increased by the Company to reflect any additional hazards.

The premium payable under this policy on any premium due date shall be calculated by multiplying
the amount of insurance then inforce by the average premium rate then applicable.

Specimen Group Term Life Insurance Policy (continued)

Advance Expense Adjustment

Total Monthly Premium before Adjustment	Percentage	Total Monthly Premium before Adjustment	Percentage
Under $200	0%	Under $200	0%
$ 200 - 224	1%	$ 1,700 - 1,999	18%
225 - 249	2%	2,000 - 2,499	19%
250 - 299	3%	2,500 - 2,999	20%
300 - 349	4%	3,000 - 3,499	21%
350 - 399	5%	3,500 - 3,999	22%
400 - 449	6%	4,000 - 4,999	23%
450 - 499	7%	5,000 - 5,999	24%
500 - 549	8%	6,000 - 7,499	25%
550 - 599	9%	7,500 - 9,499	26%
600 - 649	10%	9,500 - 11,999	27%
650 - 699	11%	12,000 - 14,999	28%
700 - 799	12%	15,000 - 19,999	29%
800 - 899	13%	20,000 - 26,999	30%
900 - 999	14%	27,000 - 34,999	31%
1,000 - 1,199	15%	35,000 - 44,999	32%
1,200 - 1,399	16%	45,000 - 59,999	33%
1,400 - 1,699	17%	60,000 - 79,999	34%
		80,000 and over	35%

Table of Monthly Premiums

Age of Insured Nearest Birthday	Premium per $1,000	Age of Insured Nearest Birthday	Premium per $1,000	Age of Insured Nearest Birthday	Premium per $1,000
15	$.19	42	$ .53	69	$ 5.34
16	.20	43	.58	70	5.81
17	.21	44	.63	71	6.32
18	.22	45	.68	72	6.84
19	.23	46	.74	73	7.38
20	.23	47	.81	74	7.95
21	.24	48	.89	75	8.56
22	.24	49	.97	76	9.24
23	.25	50	1.06	77	10.00
24	.25	51	1.16	78	10.86
25	.25	52	1.26	79	11.81
26	.25	53	1.38	80	12.83
27	.26	54	1.51	81	13.93
28	.26	55	1.65	82	15.07
29	.26	56	1.80	83	16.26
30	.27	57	1.97	84	17.50
31	.27	58	2.14	85	18.80
32	.28	59	2.32	86	20.16
33	.29	60	2.51	87	21.60
34	.30	61	2.72	88	23.13
35	.32	62	2.96	89	24.79
36	.34	63	3.21	90	26.62
37	.36	64	3.48	91	28.68
38	.38	65	3.78	92	31.03
39	.41	66	4.11	93	33.75
40	.45	67	4.48	94	36.95
41	.49	68	4.89	95	40.98

Specimen Group Term Life Insurance Policy (continued)

Article VIII - General Provisions

Dividends   This policy shall participate in the divisible surplus of the Company to such extent and under such terms and conditions as may be determined annually be the Company. Any such divisible surplus shall be paid in cash or applied to the reduction of the premium due or to become due, except that in the event of contribution by the covered persons hereunder any excess of the divisible surplus over the policyholder's contribution shall be used by the policyholder for the benefit of such persons.

The Entire Contract; Changes   This policy, the policyholder's application (a copy of which is attached hereto) and the covered person's individual applications, if any, shall constitute the entire contract of insurance. No agent has authority to waive or amend any provision of this policy. No amendment shall be valid unless signed by the president or a vice president of the Company. Any statements in any application hereunder shall be deemed representations and not warranties and no statement shall be used as a defense to a claim unless contained in a written application.

Incontestability   The validity of this policy shall not be contested, except for the nonpayment of premiums, after it has been in force one year from its date of issue. The validity of the insurance on any covered person shall not be contested, except for the nonpayment of premiums, after such person's insurance has been in force hereunder for one year during his lifetime. No statement by any covered person relating to his insurability shall be used by the Company to deny liability hereunder unless it is contained in a written application signed by him and a copy of such application is furnished to him or to his beneficiary.

Misstatement of Age   If the age of any covered person has been misstated, the insurance payable will be the amount to which such covered person is entitled under Article IA, Schedule of Insurance, at his true age, but adjustments in premium payments will be made so that the policyholder shall pay the Company the actual premiums at the true age of the covered person.

Assignment   The insurance under this policy shall not be assignable.

Records   The policyholder shall maintain records of those covered by name, age, amount for which persons are covered, dates of entry and of termination, change of status, beneficiary designations and other pertinent information. Such information shall be furnished to the Company as needed or requested on authorized Company forms. The Company shall have the right of inspection of such records at any reasonable time. Clerical errors shall not deprive persons of coverage but no such errors shall continue such coverage beyond the termination date described in Article V, Individual Terminations.

Certificate   The Company will issue each covered person hereunder an individual certificate describing the benefits and conversion privilege under this policy and the beneficiary to whom the proceeds are payable. Such certificate shall in no way change or amend any provision under this policy.

Discontinuance of this Policy   The Company may discontinue this policy as of any date on which a premium is due and payable by giving at least 31 days written notice to the policyholder if on any date
    (a) the number of covered persons is less than 10 or
    (b) the percentage of covered persons within any class of eligible employees
       is less than 75%
The policyholder may discontinue this policy as of a date on which premium is due and payable by giving written notice to the Company in advance of that date. Failure on the part of the policyholder to pay premiums within the Grace Period shall be deemed to be notice by the policyholder to the Company to discontinue this policy at the expiration of such Grace Period.

Discontinuance of this policy shall be without prejudice to any claim originating prior to the date on which this policy is discontinued.

Specimen Group Term Life Insurance Policy (continued)

<u>Maximum Covered Person's Contribution</u>   The maximum contribution of any person covered hereunder for insurance on his life, shall be $.60 per month per $1,000 of such insurance.

Specimen Group Term Life Insurance Policy (continued)

Article IX - Continuation of Insurance

Under the following circumstances, a covered person's insurance may be continued in force after the date it would otherwise terminate under Article V, Individual Terminations.

A.   Payment of Premiums by Policyholder

If the policyholder elects to continue the payment of premiums for such covered person's insurance in case of leave of absence, layoff or other temporary interruption of active full-time employment, the employment and insurance of such covered person will be deemed to continue until whichever of the following events shall first occur: (1) the date the policyholder stops paying the premium for such covered person's insurance, or (2) the expiration of a period of 3 months following the first day of such leave of absence, layoff or other temporary interruption, provided that such insurance may be continued until a later date by mutual agreement between the policyholder and the Company. In electing to continue payment of premiums under this Section A the policyholder shall act in such a way as to preclude individual selection.

B.   Waiver of Premium for Total Disability

1. If a covered person while insured hereunder and prior to his 60th birthday becomes totally disabled as defined herein, his insurance will continue in force during the period he remains continuously and totally disabled but not to exceed a period of one year from the date the policyholder stops paying the premium for such insurance.

2. If, prior to a covered person's 60th birthday and within one year after the policyholder stops paying the premium for such person's insurance, due proof is submitted to the Home Office of the Company that total disability has existed continuously for a period of nine months as to such covered person, the insurance for such covered person will be continued in force, without further payment of premiums, during the continuance of such total disability, subject to the yearly submission of due proof of the continuance of such total disability within three months preceding each anniversary of the receipt of the original proof of such disability, and submission to examination by a physician as herein provided. Insurance of a covered person under this paragraph 2 shall terminate upon the happening of any one of the following events: (a) cessation of total disability, (b) failure to submit required proof of the continuance of total disability, or (c) failure to submit to examination by a physician as herein provided.

3. In the event of termination of such insurance under paragraphs 1 or 2, the covered person shall be entitled to the rights set forth in Article V-A, Conversion Privilege, in the same manner as if employment had been then terminated, unless he returns to work and is again insured under this policy.

4. The Company shall have the right during the continuance of insurance under any of the terms of this Section B to have a physician of its choice examine the covered person, provided that no examination will be requested more often than once a year after the covered person's insurance has been in force under this Section B for two full years.

C.   Definitions

The term "total disability" as used herein shall mean the complete inability of

Specimen Group Term Life Insurance Policy (concluded)

the covered person to engage in any and every gainful occupation as a result of accidental bodily injury, sickness or disease originating after the date such covered
person's insurance became effective. The loss of both hands or of both feet or of
one hand and one foot or of the sight of both eyes after a covered person's insurance
becomes effective, shall be considered total disability even though such person may
be able to pursue a gainful occupation, and no further proof of disability will be required. Loss of hands or feet means severance at or above the wrist or ankle joint.
Loss of sight must be total and irrecoverable.

D.   Miscellaneous Provisions

There shall be no continuation of insurance under the terms of this Article after
the exercise of the right of conversion unless the individual policy of life insurance
issued in accordance therewith is surrendered to the Company without claim other
than for return of the premiums paid on such policy, less dividends and indebtedness,
if any.

No payment shall be made on account of the death of any covered person whose
insurance is continued under the terms of this Article unless written notice of death of
the covered person is received by the Company at its Home Office within twelve months
after the date of death.

The amount of insurance which will be continued for a covered person under the
provisions of this Article will be the amount provided in Article IA, Schedule of Insurance,
for such person, provided that the amount shall in no event be in excess of the amount in
force for the covered person on the date premium payments were stopped for such person,
and provided further that if such covered person retires or attains an age at which the
amount of insurance reduces or ceases under the terms of this policy, the amount of insurance in force for such covered person under this Article shall also reduce or cease
at such retirement or age.

If any covered person ceases to be totally disabled and returns to work for the
policyholder, the insurance on such covered person will be continued in force only on
resumption of payment of premiums by the policyholder for such covered person. If
any covered person ceases to be totally disabled but does not immediately return to
work for the policyholder, the covered person's insurance shall automatically terminate,
subject to the rights set forth under Article V-A, Conversion Privilege.

The benefits in this Article are provided without any additional premium.

M

Specimen Group Life Employee's Certificate Booklet

> THE JOHN DOE COMPANY
> (herein called the Policyholder)

YOUR

GROUP INSURANCE

PLAN

Specimen Group Life Employee's Certificate Booklet (continued)

ABC MUTUAL LIFE INSURANCE
COMPANY
OF HARRISBURG, PENNSYLVANIA
(herein called the Company)

HEREBY CERTIFIES that the benefits provided by the group policy(ies) are available to employees in an Eligible Class.

The eligibility requirements are set forth in the section of this booklet entitled Eligibility and Effective Date. Under no circumstances may any insurance become effective prior to the applicable Effective Date.

The description of your insurance is set forth in general terms in this certificate booklet; the complete terms of the group insurance coverage(s) are set forth in the Group Insurance Policy(ies). Nothing contained in this certificate booklet shall alter or amend the terms of said Policy(ies).

This certificate booklet replaces and supersedes any other certificate which may have been issued previously.

ABC Mutual Life
Insurance Company

Robert L. Smith
President

Specimen Group Life Employee's Certificate Booklet (continued)

SCHEDULE

Effective Date of the Plan - June 1, 1973

Group Policy No. - GL1000-1

Beneficiary - As on file with the Company

THE JOHN DOE COMPANY
(herein called the Policyholder)

Eligible Classes - 1. President, Vice Presidents,
Treasurer, and Secretary
2. Each other employee

Waiting Period - One month of continuous, active service

S1030

Specimen Group Life Employee's Certificate Booklet (continued)

SCHEDULE OF BENEFITS

FOR EMPLOYEES
Life Insurance

Class 1 . . . . $25,000
Class 2 15,000

The amount of Life Insurance will be reduced 50%
for all covered persons age 65 or over when insured,
and for covered persons attaining age 65 while insured.

No covered person, the amount of whose insurance
has been or is being reduced by reason of his having
attained an age at which a reduction in the amount
of his insurance is specified, shall be eligible for
any increase in the amount of his insurance on or
after the date such a reduction commences or is
effected.

**INCREASES AND DECREASES IN
AMOUNTS OF INSURANCE**

The Group Insurance Policy describes the circumstances under which the amount of your insurance
will be increased or decreased and the date such
change becomes effective.

Any increase in the amount of insurance will take
effect without obtaining your application provided
you are actually at work on a full-time basis on
the date the change becomes effective. If you are
not at work on the date the increase becomes effective, the increase will take effect on the date you
return to full-time work.

Any decrease in the amount of insurance will take
effect on the date the change becomes effective.

Specimen Group Life Employee's Certificate Booklet (continued)

ELIGIBILITY AND EFFECTIVE DATE

ELIGIBILITY

Employees . . .

If, on the Effective Date of the Plan, as shown in the Schedule, you were an active, full-time employee of an Eligible Class, as shown in the Schedule, you were eligible to participate on that date.

If, after the Effective Date of the Plan, you become an active, full-time employee of an Eligible Class, you will be eligible to participate on the day following your completion of the Waiting Period as shown in the Schedule.

EFFECTIVE DATE OF INSURANCE

Employees . . .

If you enroll on or before your eligibility date, you will become insured as of that date. If you enroll after your eligibility date, but within 31 days thereafter, you will become insured on the date you enroll. If you fail to enroll within 31 days of your eligibility date, you will become insured on the date the Company accepts as satisfactory, evidence of insurability, furnished at your own expense.

Specimen Group Life Employee's Certificate Booklet (continued)

TERMINATION OF INSURANCE

The insurance of any employee will terminate on the date upon which any of the following events first occurs:

—termination of employment

—termination of eligibility

—termination of the policy

—termination of any required contributions.

DEFINITIONS

"Employee" as used herein means any employee who is or becomes eligible for insurance in accordance with the eligibility requirements of the Group Policy.

"Total Disability" of an employee as used herein means the complete inability to engage in any and every gainful occupation as a result of accidental bodily injury or sickness.

"Wages" or "Earnings" of a covered person as used herein shall mean his regular basic pay exclusive of overtime, bonuses or any other form of additional compensation.

A masculine personal pronoun as used herein includes the feminine, wherever the context requires.

"Active, full-time employee" as used herein means an employee of the policyholder who is working regularly throughout the entire duration of the policyholder's work week, and in any event not less than thirty hours per week, at any of the policyholder's business establishments or at some other location to which the policyholder's business requires the employee to travel, and whose principal source of earned income is his wages or earnings received from the policyholder.

G 10 110

Specimen Group Life Employee's Certificate Booklet (continued)

LIFE
INSURANCE
FOR
EMPLOYEES

Benefits . . .

The amount for which you are insured, as shown in the Schedule of Benefits, is payable in the event of your death at any time, at any place, and from any cause while insured.

Naming Your Beneficiary . . .

You name your beneficiary when you apply for insurance. You may change this designation at any time by making written request on the form provided by ABC Mutual.

Payment of Benefits , . .

The life insurance benefit is usually payable in a lump sum. However, at your request, the proceeds may be paid in fixed monthly instalments. If you make no such election, your beneficiary may do so after your death.

If You Become Disabled . . .

If while insured you become totally disabled prior to age 60, your Life Insurance, subject to any reduction for age or due to retirement, will remain in force as long as you remain so disabled, provided you submit proof within 12 months after the policyholder stops paying premiums for your insurance that the total disability has existed continuously for 9 months. Subsequent proof of such disability must be submitted annually thereafter. No further premium payment will be required during the continuance of this disability after ABC Mutual accepts proof of the disability.

Conversion Privilege . . .

If your employment terminates or you cease to be a member of a class eligible for insurance, you have a 31-day period commencing when your insurance terminates in which to convert your Group Life Insurance to any individual policy of Life Insurance (except term insurance) without disability or other supplementary benefits then being offered by ABC Mutual. This individual policy will be issued without medical examination and will become effective 31 days after the termination of your Group Life Insurance.

Specimen Group Life Employee's Certificate Booklet (continued)

If the Group Life Policy is terminated for all employees or for the class to which you belong, and you have been continuously insured for at least five years prior to such termination, you will be entitled to a conversion privilege as though your employment had terminated on that date, except that the amount of Life Insurance you may convert will be the lesser of $2,000 or the amount of insurance to which you were entitled under the Group Life Policy less the amount of any life insurance for which you are or become eligible within 31 days under any other Group Life Policy.

If the amount of your insurance is reduced by reason of your retirement or the attainment of an age at which a reduction is specified in the Group Life Policy this conversion privilege will apply to the amount by which your insurance is reduced.

If you die during the 31-day period provided under this Conversion Privilege, the Life Insurance Benefit will be payable as a claim under the Group Life Policy.

Specimen Group Life Employee's Certificate Booklet (concluded)

GENERAL PROVISIONS

Life Insurance Only

If at the death of a covered person there is no named beneficiary, or if such beneficiary does not survive the covered person, the proceeds shall be payable, at the option of ABC Mutual, to any of the following surviving relatives of such covered person: wife, husband, mother, father, child or children, or to the executor or administrator of the deceased covered person.

If any beneficiary or any covered person is a monor or is physically, mentally or otherwise incapable of giving a valid release for any payment due, ABC Mutual may, at its option, and until claim is made by the duly appointed guardian or committee for such beneficiary or such covered person, make payment to any person or institution who appears to ABC Mutual to have assumed responsibility for the care, custody or support of such beneficiary or covered person. Such payments will be made in instalments in the amount specified in any optional method of settlement previously elected or in the absence of such election, in installments not in excess of $100 monthly.

Assignment— The insurance under the Group Policy shall not be assignable.

Modification of Plan— The policyholder reserves the right to discontinue or modify this Plan at any time.

N

Model Blanket
Accident and Sickness
Insurance Bill

Section 1. *Blanket Accident and Sickness Insurance Defined.* Blanket accident and sickness insurance is hereby declared to be that form of accident, sickness or accident and sickness insurance covering groups of persons as enumerated in one of the following paragraphs (*a*) to (*i*) inclusive:

(*a*) Under a policy or contract issued to any common carrier or to any operator, owner or lessee of a means of transportation, who or which shall be deemed the policyholder, covering a group of persons who may become passengers defined by reference to their travel status on such common carrier or such means of transportation.

(*b*) Under a policy or contract issued to an employer, who shall be deemed the policyholder, covering any group of employees, dependents or guests, defined by reference to specified hazards incident to an activity or activities or operations of the policyholder.

(*c*) Under a policy or contract issued to a college, school or other institution of learning, a school district or districts, or school jurisdictional unit, or to the head, principal or governing board of any such educational unit, who or which shall be deemed the policyholder, covering students, teachers or employees.

(*d*) Under a policy or contract issued to any religious, charitable, recreational, educational, or civic organization, or branch thereof, which shall be deemed the policyholder, covering any group of members or participants defined by reference to specified hazards incident to an activity or activities or operations sponsored or supervised by such policyholder.

(*e*) Under a policy or contract issued to a sports team, camp or sponsor thereof, which shall be deemed the policyholder, covering members, campers, employees, officials or supervisors.

(*f*) Under a policy or contract issued to any volunteer fire department, first aid, civil defense, or other such volunteer organization, which shall be deemed the policyholder, covering any group of members or participants defined by reference to specified hazards incident to an activity or activities or operations sponsored or supervised by such policyholder.

(g) Under a policy or contract issued to a newspaper or other publisher, which shall be deemed the policyholder, covering its carriers.

(h) Under a policy or contract issued to an association, including a labor union, which shall have a constitution and by-laws and which has been organized and is maintained in good faith for purposes other than that of obtaining insurance, which shall be deemed the policyholder, covering any group of members or participants defined by reference to specified hazards incident to an activity or activities or operations sponsored or supervised by such policyholder.

(i) Under a policy or contract issued to cover any other risk or class of risks which, in the discretion of the Commissioner, may be properly eligible for blanket accident and sickness insurance. The discretion of the Commissioner may be exercised on an individual risk basis or class of risks, or both.

Section 2. Required Provisions.   Any insurer authorized to write accident and sickness insurance in this state shall have the power to issue blanket accident and sickness insurance. No such blanket policy, except as provided in Section 5 of this Act, may be issued or delivered in this state unless a copy of the form thereof shall have been filed in accordance with Section _____[1]. Every such blanket policy shall contain provisions which in the opinion of the Commissioner are not less favorable to the policyholder and the individual insured than the following:

(a) A provision that the policy, including endorsements and a copy of the application, if any, of the policyholder and the persons insured shall constitute the entire contract between the parties, and that any statement made by the policyholder or by a person insured shall in absence of fraud, be deemed a representation and not a warranty, and that no such statements shall be used in defense to a claim under the policy, unless contained in a written application. Such person, his beneficiary, or assignee, shall have the right to make written request to the insurer for a copy of such application and the insurer shall, within 15 days after the receipt of such request at its home office or any branch office of the insurer, deliver or mail to the person making such request a copy of such application. If such copy shall not be so delivered or mailed, the insurer shall be precluded from introducing such application as evidence in any action based upon or involving any statements contained therein.

(b) A provision that written notice of sickness or of injury must be given to the insurer within twenty days after the date when such sickness or injury occurred. Failure to give notice within such time shall not invalidate nor reduce any claim if it shall be shown not to have been reasonably possible to give such notice and that notice was given as soon as was reasonably possible.

(c) A provision that the insurer will furnish either to the claimant or to the policyholder for delivery to the claimant such forms as are usually furnished by it for filing proof of loss. If such forms are not furnished

---

[1] Insert number of the section of the insurance laws applicable to the filing and approval of Accident and Sickness Policy forms.

before the expiration of fifteen days after giving of such notice, the claimant shall be deemed to have complied with the requirements of the policy as to proof of loss upon submitting, within the time fixed in the policy for filing proof of loss, written proof covering the occurrence, the character and the extent of the loss for which claim is made.

(d) A provision that in the case of claim for loss of time for disability, written proof of such loss must be furnished to the insurer within ninety days after the commencement of the period for which the insurer is liable, and that subsequent written proofs of the continuance of such disability must be furnished to the insurer at such intervals as the insurer may reasonably require, and that in the case of claim for any other loss, written proof of such loss must be furnished to the insurer within ninety days after the date of such loss. Failure to furnish such proof within such time shall not invalidate nor reduce any claim if it shall be shown not to have been reasonably possible to furnish such proof and that such proof was furnished as soon as was reasonably possible.

(e) A provision that all benefits payable under the policy other than benefits for loss of time will be payable immediately upon receipt of due written proof of such loss, and that, subject to due proof of loss, all accrued benefits payable under the policy for loss of time will be paid not less frequently than monthly during the continuance of the period for which the insurer is liable, and that any balance remaining unpaid at the termination of such period will be paid immediately upon receipt of such proof.

(f) A provision that the insurer at its own expense, shall have the right and opportunity to examine the person of the insured when and so often as it may reasonably require during the pendency of claim under the policy and also the right and opportunity to make an autopsy where it is not prohibited by law.

(g) A provision that no action at law or in equity shall be brought to recover under the policy prior to the expiration of sixty days after written proof of loss has been furnished in accordance with the requirements of the policy and that no such action shall be brought after the expiration of three years after the time written proof of loss is required to be furnished.

Section 3. Application and Certificates Not Required. An individual application need not be required from a person covered under a blanket accident and sickness policy or contract, nor shall it be necessary for the insurer to furnish each person a certificate.

Section 4. Facility of Payment. All benefits under any blanket accident and sickness policy or contract shall be payable to the person insured, or to his designated beneficiary or beneficiaries, or to his estate, except that if the person insured be a minor or otherwise not competent to give a valid release, such benefits may be made payable to his parent, guardian or other person actually supporting him. Provided further, however, that the policy may provide that all or a portion of any indemnities provided by any such policy on account of hospital, nursing, medical or surgical services may, at the option of the insurer and unless the insured requests otherwise in writing not later than the time of filing proofs of such loss, be paid directly to the hospital or person rendering such services; but the policy may not require that the service be rendered by a particular hospital or person. Payment so made shall discharge the obligation of the insurer with respect to the amount of insurance so paid.

Section 5. Binders.   An insurer authorized to write accident and sickness insurance in this state may issue blanket accident and sickness coverages without prior approval of the policy form, provided that:

(*a*) The group is one eligible for coverage pursuant to the provisions of this Act; and

(*b*) A covering note or binder is issued to bind the insurance; and

(*c*) The covering note or binder contains in summary form: (*i*) the class or classes of persons eligible for coverage; (*ii*) the benefits to be provided; and (*iii*) the exceptions and reductions to such benefits, if any; and

(*d*) Within 30 days after the date on which the covering note or binder is issued the insurer shall submit to the Commissioner for approval a policy form drafted to provide the coverage provided by such covering note or binder and make such revisions in the policy submitted as the Commissioner may lawfully require.

(*e*) The Commissioner may exempt from the policy filing and approval requirements of Section _____² for so long as he deems proper, any blanket accident and sickness policy or contract to which in his opinion such requirements may not practicably be applied, or may dispense with such filing and approval as, in his opinion, is not desirable nor necessary for the protection of the public.

Section 6. Repeal of Inconsistent Act.   [Note: This section should contain suitable language to repeal acts or parts of acts presently enacted and inconsistent with this act.]

---

² Insert number of the section of the insurance laws applicable to the filing and approval of Accident and Sickness policy forms.

O

Model Franchise
Accident and Health
Insurance Bill

Accident and sickness insurance on a franchise plan is hereby declared to be that form of accident and sickness insurance issued to:

1. Five or more employees of any corporation, co-partnership, or individual employer or any governmental corporation, agency or department thereof; or
2. Ten or more members, employees, or employees of members of any trade or professional association or of a labor union or of any other association having had an active existence for at least two years where such association or union has a constitution or by-laws and is formed in good faith for purposes other than that of obtaining insurance;

where such persons, with or without their dependents, are issued the same form of an individual policy varying only as to amounts and kinds of coverage applied for by such persons under an arrangement whereby the premiums on such policies may be paid to the insurer periodically by the employer, with or without payroll deductions, or by the association or union for its members, or by some designated person acting on behalf of such employer or association or union. The term "employees" as used herein shall be deemed to include the officers, managers and employees and retired employees of the employer and the individual proprietor or partners if the employer is an individual proprietor or partnership.

P

NAIC Model Rules and Regulations for Group Coverage Discontinuance and Replacement

Section (1). AUTHORITY. These rules and regulations are adopted and promulgated by [title of supervisory authority] pursuant to section [s_____] of [the _____ Insurance Code].

Section (2). SCOPE. They are applicable to all insurance policies and subscriber contracts issued or provided by an insurance company or a non-profit service corporation on a group or group type basis covering persons as employees of employers or as members of unions [or associations].

Section (3). DEFINITION. The term "group type basis" means a benefit plan, other than "salary savings" or "salary budget" plans utilizing individual insurance policies or subscriber contracts, which meets the following conditions:

a) Coverage is provided through insurance policies or subscriber contracts to classes of employees or members defined in terms of conditions pertaining to employment or membership.

b) The coverage is not available to the general public and can be obtained and maintained only because of the covered person's membership in or connection with the particular organization or group.

c) There are arrangements for bulk payment of premiums or subscription charges to the insurer or non-profit service corporation.

d) There is sponsorship of the plan by the employer, union, [or association].

Section (4). EFFECTIVE DATE OF DISCONTINUANCE FOR NON-PAYMENT OF PREMIUM OR SUBSCRIPTION CHARGES. a) If a policy or contract subject to these rules and regulations provides for automatic discontinuance of the policy or contract after a premium or subscription charge has remained unpaid through the grace period allowed for such payment, the carrier shall be liable for valid claims for covered losses insured prior to the end of the grace period.

b) If the actions of the carrier after the end of the grace period indicate that it considers the policy or contract as continuing in force beyond the end of the grace period (such as, by continuing to recognize claims subsequently incurred), the carrier shall be liable for valid claims for losses beginning prior to the effective date of written notice of discontinuance to the policyholder or other entity responsible for making premium payments or submitting subscription charges to the carrier. The effective date of discontinuance shall not be prior to midnight at the end of the third scheduled work day after the date upon which the notice is delivered.

Section (5). REQUIREMENTS FOR NOTICE OF DISCONTINU-ANCE.   *a*) Any notice of discontinuance so given by the carrier shall include a request to the group policyholder or other entity involved to notify employees covered under the policy or subscriber contract of the date as of which the group policy or contract will discontinue and to advise that, unless otherwise provided in the policy or contract, the carrier shall not be liable for claims for losses incurred after such date. Such notice of discontinuance shall also advise, in any instance in which the plan involves employee contributions, that if the policyholder or other entity continues to collect contributions for the coverage beyond the date of discontinuance, the policyholder or other entity may be held solely liable for the benefits with respect to which the contributions have been collected.

b) The carrier will prepare and furnish to the policyholder or other entity at the same time a supply of a notice form to be distributed to the employees or members concerned indicating such discontinuance and the effective date thereof, and urging the employees or members to refer to their certificates or contracts in order to determine what rights, if any, are available to them upon such discontinuance.

Section (6). EXTENSION OF BENEFITS.   *a*) Every group policy or other contract subject to these rules and regulations hereafter issued, or under which the level of benefits is hereafter altered, modified, or amended, must provide a reasonable provision for extension of benefits in the event of total disability at the date of discontinuance of the group policy or contract, as required by the following paragraphs of this section.

b) In the case of a group life plan which contains a disability benefit extension of any type (e.g., premium waiver extension, extended death benefit in event of total disability, or payment of income for a specified period during total disability), the discontinuance of the group policy shall not operate to terminate such extension.

c) In the case of a group plan providing benefits for loss of time from work or specific indemnity during hospital confinement, discontinuance of the policy during a disability shall have no effect on benefits payable for that disability or confinement.

d) In the case of hospital or medical expense coverages other than dental and maternity expense, a reasonable extension of benefits or accrued liability provision is required. Such a provision will be considered "reasonable" if it provides an extension of at least 12 months under "major medical" and "comprehensive medical" type coverages, and under other types of hospital or medical expense coverages provides either an extension of at least 90 days or an accrued liability for expenses incurred during a period of disability or during a period of at least 90 days starting with a specific event which occurred while coverage was in force (e.g., an accident).

e) Any applicable extension of benefits or accrued liability shall be described in any policy or contract involved as well as in group insurance certificates. The benefits payable during any period of extension or accrued liability may be subject to the policy's or contract's regular benefit limits (e.g., benefits ceasing at exhaustion of a benefit period or of maximum benefits).

Section (7). CONTINUANCE OF COVERAGE IN SITUATIONS INVOLVING REPLACEMENT OF ONE CARRIER BY ANOTHER.

a) This section shall indicate the carrier responsible for liability in those instances in which one carrier's contract replaces a plan of similar benefits of another.

b) Liability of Prior Carrier. The prior carrier remains liable only to the extent of its accrued liabilities and extensions of benefits. The position of the prior carrier shall be the same whether the group policyholder or other entity secures replacement coverage from a new carrier, self-insures, or foregoes the provision of coverage.

c) Liability of Succeeding Carrier

1. Each person who is eligible for coverage in accordance with the succeeding carrier's plan of benefits (in respect of classes eligible and actively at work and non-confinement rules) shall be covered by that carrier's plan of benefits.

2. Each person not covered under the succeeding carrier's plan of benefits in accordance with paragraph (1) above must nevertheless be covered by the succeeding carrier in accordance with the following rules if such individual was validly covered (including benefit extension) under the prior plan on the date of discontinuance and if such individual is a member of the class or classes of individuals eligible for coverage under the succeeding carrier's plan. Any reference in the following rules to an individual who was or was not totally disabled is a reference to the individual's status immediately prior to the date the succeeding carrier's coverage becomes effective.

   a) The minimum level of benefits to be provided by the succeeding carrier shall be the applicable level of benefits of the prior carrier's plan reduced by any benefits payable by the prior plan.

   b) Coverage must be provided by the succeeding carrier until at least the earliest of the following dates:

      i) the date the individual becomes eligible under the succeeding carrier's plan as described in paragraph (1) above.

      ii) in the case of an individual who was not totally disabled, for each type of coverage, the date the individual's coverage would terminate in accordance with the succeeding carrier's plan provisions applicable to individual termination of coverage (e.g., at termination of employment or ceasing to be an eligible dependent, as the case may be).

iii) in the case of an individual who was totally disabled, and in the case of a type of coverage for which Section (6) requires an extension or accrued liability, the end of any period of extension or accrued liability which is required of the prior carrier by Section (6) or, if the prior carrier's policy or contract is not subject to that section, would have been required of that carrier had its policy or contract been subject to Section (6) at the time the prior plan was discontinued and replaced by the succeeding carrier's plan.

3. In the case of a pre-existing conditions limitation included in the succeeding carrier's plan, the level of benefits applicable to pre-existing conditions of persons becoming covered by the succeeding carrier's plan in accordance with this subsection during the period of time this limitation applies under the new plan shall be the lesser of

   a) the benefits of the new plan determined without application of the pre-existing conditions limitation; and

   b) the benefits of the prior plan.

4. The succeeding carrier, in applying any deductibles or waiting periods in its plan, shall give credit for the satisfaction or partial satisfaction of the same or similar provisions under a prior plan providing similar benefits. In the case of deductible provisions, the credit shall apply for the same or overlapping benefit periods and shall be given for expenses actually incurred and applied against the deductible provisions of the prior carrier's plan during the 90 days preceding the effective date of the succeeding carrier's plan but only to the extent these expenses are recognized under the terms of the succeeding carrier's plan and are subject to a similar deductible provision.

5. In any situation where a determination of the prior carrier's benefit is required by the succeeding carrier, at the succeeding carrier's request the prior carrier shall furnish a statement of the benefits available or pertinent information, sufficient to permit verification of the benefit determination or the determination itself by the succeeding carrier. For the purposes of this section, benefits of the prior plan will be determined in accordance with all of the definitions, conditions, and covered expense provisions of the prior plan rather than those of the succeeding plan. The benefit determination will be made as if coverage had not been replaced by the succeeding carrier.

Section (8). EFFECTIVE DATE. These rules and regulations shall take effect on [at least 120 days after promulgation].

Q

Revenue Ruling 64–328, 1964–2 CBU, Pertaining To Split-Dollar Life Insurance

Advice has been requested regarding the tax effects of a so-called "split dollar" arrangement between an employer, Y corporation, and its employee, B.

Under the "split dollar" arrangement, the employer and employee join in purchasing an insurance contract, in which there is a substantial investment element, on the life of the employee. The employer provides the funds to pay part of the annual premium to the extent of the increase in the cash surrender value each year, and the employee pays the balance of the annual premium. The employer is entitled to receive, out of the proceeds of the policy, an amount equal to the cash surrender value, or at least a sufficient part thereof to equal the funds it has provided for premium payments. The employee has the right to name the beneficiary of the balance of any proceeds payable by reason of his death. In practical effect, athough the employee must pay a substantial part of the first premium, after the first year his share of the premium decreases rapidly, and in some cases it even becomes zero after a relatively few years. He thus obtains valuable insurance protection (decreasing each year, but still substantial for a long time) with a relatively small outlay for premiums in the early years, and at little or no cost to him in later years.

Two major types of "split dollar" arrangements are considered: the endorsement system and the collateral assignment system. In the endorsement system, the employer owns the policy and is responsible for the payment of the annual premiums. The employee is then required to reimburse the employer for his share, if any, of the premiums. Under the collateral assignment system, the employee in form owns the policy and pays the entire premium thereon. The employer in form makes annual loans, without interest (or below the fair rate of interest), to the employee of amounts equal to the yearly increases in the cash surrender value, but not exceeding the annual premiums. The employee executes an assignment of his policy to the employer as collateral security for the loans. The loans are generally payable at the termination of employment or the death of the employee.

A similar problem, involving the endorsement system, was considered in Revenue Ruling 55–713, C.B. 1955–2, 23, wherein it was stated that, in substance, the arrangement is in all essential respects the same as if the employer had made annual loans without interest to the employee, of an amount equal to the annual increases in the cash surrender value of the policies. That ruling concluded that the mere making available of money without interest does not result in taxable income to the payee or a deduction to the payer.

The proper tax treatment of such life insurance arrangements between employers and employees has been reconsidered in the light of the statements in the House and Senate Committee Reports pertaining to the Revenue Act of 1964, Public Law 88–272, C.B. 1964–1 (Part 2), 6, that legislation to provide the proper tax treatment of "split dollar" life insurance arrangements had been deferred because it was believed that "the issues involved in this problem, and the proper solution, including the possibility of administrative action, are in need of further study by the Treasury Department." H.R. Report No. 749,88th Congress, C.B. 1964–1 (Part 2), 125, at 186; S. Report No. 830,88th Congress, C.B. 1964–1 (Part 2), 505, at 582. The problem has been given such further study, and the conclusion has been reached that Revenue Ruling 55–713 incorrectly analyzed the substance of the "split dollar" arrangement in stating that the substance of the arrangement is in all essential respects the same as if the employer incorporation makes annual loans without interest to the employee.

Even if the arrangement is cast under the collateral assignment system, it should not be treated in substance as involving a loan from employer to employee, since generally the employee is not expected to repay the funds provided by the employer except out of the proceeds of the policy or from funds available to the employee by reason of the surrender or loan value of the policy. Instead, the substance is, whether the endorsement or collateral assignment system, is used, that the employer provides the funds representing the investment element in the life insurance contract, which would, in arm's length dealings, entitle it to the earnings accruing to that element. The effect of the arrangement for the sharing of the cost of annual life insurance premiums, however, is that the earnings on the investment element in the contract are applied to provide current life insurance protection to the employee from year to year, without cost to the employee, to the extent that the earnings are sufficient to do so.

The table below illustrates the practical working of the arrangement in the case of an "accelerated ten payment life policy" issued on the life of an employee aged 45, in the face amount of $100,000. (The figures in the first six columns were taken or derived from an actual policy contained in a case before the Internal Revenue Service.)

The cost of insurance per $1,000 shown in column (7) is taken from the table contained in Revenue Ruling 55–747, C.B. 1955–2, 228, at page 229. This table reflects 1-year term costs based upon table 38, U.S. Life and Actuarial Tables, and 2 1/2 percent interest.

It is implicit in the illustration, that in each year the "split dollar" arrangement is in effect, the employer allows the annual earnings on the investment element in the policy to provide for the employee, to the extent that they are sufficient to do so, the cost of the current life insurance protection which the employee should bear were the parties to divide the annual premium costs in accordance with their respective interests in the policy, in an arm's length manner where neither party is attempting to confer a benefit upon the other. Taking the third year of the accelerated payment life policy set out in the illustration as an example, the employer pays the annual premium to the extent of the increase in the cash value, $7,690. The employee is obligated to pay only $209.50, although he receives current insurance protection in the $567.56. The employer confers the benefit of the difference between these amounts ($358.06) by in effect allowing earnings on the investment element to be applied in payment of the cost of the employee's current insurance protection. If the parties were to divide the annual premium in accordance with their respective interests in the

Accelerated 10 Payment Life Policy

(1) Policy Year	(2) Cash Value per $100,000	(3) Gross Premiums	(4) Amount Provided by Employer, Y	(5) Amount Paid by Employee, B	(6) Proceeds Payable to Employee B's Beneficiary	(7) Cost of Insurance per $1,000	(8) Value of Insurance to Employee, B(6)X(7)	(9) Value Provided by Employer, Y(8) — (5)
1	$7,291.00	$7,899.50	$7,291.00	$608.50	$92,709.00	$6.30	$584.07	0
2	14,775.00	7,899.50	7,484.00	415.50	85,225.00	6.78	577.83	$162.33
3	22,465.00	7,899.50	7,690.00	209.50	77,535.00	7.32	567.56	358.06
4	30,375.00	7,899.50	7,899.50	0	69,625.00	7.89	549.34	549.34
5	35,791.00	5,268.50	5,268.50	0	64,209.00	8.53	547.70	547.70
6	41,356.00	5,268.50	5,268.50	0	58,644.00	9.22	540.70	540.70
7	47,080.00	5,268.50	5,268.50	0	52,920.00	9.97	527.61	527.61
8	52,977.00	5,268.50	5,268.50	0	47,023.00	10.79	507.38	507.38
9	59,062.00	5,268.50	5,268.50	0	40,938.00	11.69	478.57	478.57
10	65,356.00	5,268.50	5,268.50	0	34,644.00	12.67	438.94	438.94
11	66,385.00	0	0	0	33,615.00	13.74	461.87	461.87
15	70,462.00	0	0	0	29,538.00	20.73	612.32	612.32
20	75,373.00	0	0	0	24,627.00	31.51	776.00	776.00

The figures in column (8) represent the figures in column (6) multiplied by the corresponding figures in column (7) and divided by $1,000.

policy, the employer would pay $7,331.94, and the employee would pay $567.56. Even after the 10-year premium paying period, earnings on the investment element in the contract are used to provide the cost of the employee's insurance protection.

In the typical "split dollar" arrangement, then, the purpose is, and the effect is, to provide an economic benefit to the employee represented by the amount of the annual premium cost that he should bear and of which he is relieved. It is well settled that the providing of life insurance results in an economic benefit to the insured. See, for example, *Burnet v. Frederick B. Wells*, 289 U.S. 670 (1933), Ct. D. 688, C.B. XII–1, 261 (1933). An employee who receives an economic benefit under an arrangement with his employer generally must include in his gross income the value of the benefit received. *Commissioner v. John H. Smith*, 324 U.S. 177 (1945), Ct. D. 1633, C.B. 1945, 49; *Commissioner v. Philip J. Lo-Bue*, 351 U.S. 243 (1956), Ct. D. 1798, C.B. 1956–2, 967. In a situation such as this, in which the economic benefit to the employee is a continuing annual benefit so long as the "split dollar" arrangement is kept in force, the amount to be included annually is the annual value of the benefit received by the employee under the arrangement, which is held to be an amount equal to the 1-year term cost of the declining life insurance protection to which the employee is entitled from year to year, less the portion, if any, provided by the employee. The cost of life insurance protection per $1,000, as shown in the table contained in Revenue Ruling 55–747, *supra*, may be used to compute the 1-year term cost.

It is further held that the employer is not entitled to any deduction for its share of the annual premiums since it "is directly or indirectly a beneficiary under such policy" within the meaning of section 264(a)(1) of the Internal Revenue Code of 1954. G.C.M. 7997, C.B. IX–1, 210 (1930), *Wyoming National Bank of Wilkes-Barre v. Commissioner*, B.T.A. Memorandum Opinion entered January 27, 1933. *Cf., Omaha Elevator Company v. Commissioner*, 6 B.T.A. 817 (1927).

It is further held that the provisions of section 101(a) of the Code apply to the proceeds of the policy payable upon the death of *B*, both as to the portion received by *Y* corporation and as to the portion received by the designated beneficiary of *B*.

The same income tax results obtain if the transaction is cast in some other form resulting in a similar benefit to the employee.

In view of the foregoing, Revenue Ruling 55–713, C.B. 1955–2, 23, is revoked. The revocation is effective as to policies purchased under "split dollar" arrangements or utilized to establish such arrangements after November 13, 1964.

R

Provisions of Disability Buy-and-Sell Agreement (Close Corporation)

AGREEMENT made this ———— day of ———————————, 19———,

between ——————————————— of ———————————————,

——————————————————— of ———————————————,

and ——————————————— of ———————————————,

(hereinafter referred to as "Shareholders"), ———————————————

———————————————————, a corporation of the State

of ——————————————— (hereinafter referred to as "Corporation"),

and ——————————————————, a corporation of the State

of ——————————— (hereinafter referred to as "Trustee"), as trustee;

WHEREAS, the Shareholders own the following number of shares in the Corporation:

NAME OF SHAREHOLDER	NUMBER OF SHARES
———————————————	———————————————
———————————————	———————————————
———————————————	———————————————

WHEREAS, the Shareholders and the Corporation desire to ensure continuity of management of the corporation and, therefore, desire that in the event of the death or long-term disability of a shareholder his shares of stock in the Corporation shall be sold to the Corporation and in the event that a Shareholder wishes to sell his shares, he shall first offer them to the Corporation; and

WHEREAS, the Corporation to fund its obligations hereunder has or will acquire policies of life and health insurance on the lives of the Shareholders;

NOW, THEREFORE, in consideration of the premises and the convenants and agreements herein set forth, the parties hereto for themselves, their heirs, executors, administrators, successors and assigns do covenant and agree as follows:

1. Each of the Shareholders will deposit with the Trustee any shares of the Corporation now and hereafter standing in his name, together with an assignment thereof executed in blank. Such deposit and assignment shall in no way affect the right of the Shareholder to vote such shares, to collect dividends thereon, and to exercise all other rights as Shareholder except as forbidden or restricted by this Agreement.

2. The Trustee shall receive the deposit of shares as aforesaid and hold the same subject to the terms of this Agreement.

3. In the event that a Shareholder is "totally disabled" as that term is defined in Paragraph 4(*a*) hereof for a period of two years and 90 days and, at the conclusion of said two years and 90 days is "totally disabled" as that term is defined in Paragraph 4(*b*) hereof, the said Shareholder shall sell his shares to the Corporation and the Corporation shall buy his shares on the terms and conditions and at the price set forth herein, said price to be determined as of the date the Shareholder is first deemed "totally disabled" under Paragraph 4(*a*) hereof.

(*This paragraph establishes a mandatory disability buy-and-sell agreement. The buy-out is "triggered" after a shareholder is "totally disabled" for two years and 90 days. A shorter period than two years increases the possibility of the shareholder's recovery and consequent problems. A longer "trigger period" increases the probability that the disabled shareholder will not recover but also increases the period of time during which the disabled shareholder must rely on the solvency of the corporation.*)

(*The buy-out price is determined as of the date the disabled shareholder was first "totally disabled." In this way, the disabled shareholder does not partcipate in either the growth or decline of the corporation subsequent to his disability.*)

4. *a*) For the purposes of the salary continuation clause of this Agreement, a Shareholder shall be deemed to be "totally disabled" when he is deemed to be totally disabled by the _____ Life Insurance Company (hereinafter referred to as "The Insurance Company") for the purposes of its health insurance policy #_____, and he shall continue to be deemed to be so totally disabled for the purposes of the said salary continuation clause until The Insurance Company ceases to recognize him as totally disabled for the purposes of the said policy.

b) For the purposes of the disability buy-out for which this Agreement makes provision, a Shareholder shall be deemed to be "totally disabled" if The Insurance Company deems him to be totally disabled for the purposes of its life insurance policy #_____.

(*Save for disappearance, whether a human being is alive or dead is easy enough for competent medical authorities to determine. Sometimes, one of the most difficult questions for medical experts to agree upon or for a Court of law to determine is when a human being is or is not "totally disabled" for the purposes of agreements such as this. For that reason, the burden for making that decision is thrust upon The Insurance Company. The definition of disability in The Insurance Company's disability income policies and life insurance waiver of premium rider is different. This difference is recognized in Paragraph 4 and throughout this sample agreement.*)

5. Upon the death of a Shareholder the Corporation shall buy and the executor or administrator of the deceased's estate (hereinafter referred to as

"Legal Representative") shall sell the deceased Shareholder's shares to the Corporation at the price and upon the terms and conditions set forth herein.

(This is a conventional mandatory buy and sell clause. Variance from it could weaken the agreement as a device for "fixing" federal estate tax values.)

6. If a shareholder wishes to sell his shares during his lifetime, he shall give the corporation and each of the other shareholders written notice of his desire to do so. (A certified or registered mail receipt evidencing delivery of such notice at the Corporation's principal place of business or to a Shareholder at his usual place of abode shall be sufficient evidence of delivery of said notice for the purposes of this agreement). The Corporation shall have the right to purchase the withdrawing Shareholder's interest at any time within 60 days of the delivery of said notice to it and all of the other Shareholders, at a price determined in accordance with Paragraph 7 hereof as of the day of the delivery of said notice by the said Shareholder.

If the Corporation decides to exercise said right to purchase said interest at said price, it shall give notice of its election to do so in writing to the Shareholder within said 60 days and shall pay said purchase price in cash or at its election in _____ equal monthly notes, the first of which shall be due _____ days after the Corporation gives said notice. Thereafter, one of said notes shall be due and shall be paid by the Corporation on the first day of each month until all of the notes are paid. Each of said notes shall bear interest at the rate of _____ percentum per annum (not less than 4%—IRC 483). The Corporation may pay said notes in full or in part at any time or from time to time after their delivery, with the consent of the payee.

Upon said payment in cash or by notes, the selling Shareholder and his successors in interest shall have no further right, title or interest in or to the Corporation.

If the Corporation does not elect to purchase the interest of such a Shareholder within said 60 days, the Corporation shall be liquidated forthwith.

If the Corporation elects to purchase the interest of such a Shareholder set forth herein, the said Shareholder shall not do business, solicit clients or customers or in any other way compete with the Corporation within _____ miles from the principal office of the Corporation at the time of said purchase for a period of _____ years from the date of his withdrawal. This agreement not to compete is to protect the goodwill of the Corporation.

(This provision is one of the most important in a buy and sell agreement. It is the so-called life option which is generally deemed to be vital in fixing the value of the deceased's interest in the business for federal estate tax purposes (R.R. 59–60; May v. McGowan, etc.). It is also highly important as a practical matter because in the 20, 30, 40 ? years of a Corporation's existence it is quite possible that it will be used.)

(This particular provision provides for the exercise of the option within 60 days (perhaps it is not the right time in your case) or liquidation of corporation (perhaps liquidation not appropriate in your case). The option price is the same as that which would be paid if either the death or disability buy-out were invoked at the same point in time. If a price higher than the death price could be paid under this provision, many authorities believe the buy and sell agreement would lose much of its utility for purposes of fixing value for federal estate tax purposes. The shareholders might wish to set a lower price such as 75 percent of the price established under Paragraph 7 so as to penalize a withdrawing shareholder. If the "life option" price is less than the "death" price, the

agreement will be as effective in "fixing" the value of the business interest for federal estate tax purposes as though the prices were identical.)

(Provision is made for the purchase price to be paid in installments. Care should be used to comply with the installment buy-out rules of IRC 453. The provision for interest is mandatory since the Revenue Act of 1964 if the agreement is to avoid the problems created by IRC 483. A minimum rate of 4 percent must be used.)

(The provision contains a covenant not to compete. This must be carefully drawn to comply with local law so as not to be overreaching and hence null and void. The tax consequences of such a clause should be carefully considered. It can convert capital gain payments into ordinary income. If it is vague it can be expected to lead to litigation. The statement that the agreement not to compete is to protect goodwill in an attempt to maintain the characterization of capital gain or loss payments for goodwill as being such and to avoid transmutation of these payments into ordinary income deductible by the Corporation and taxable to the withdrawing Shareholder.)

7. Unless and until changed as set forth herein, the value of and purchase price to be paid for the shares of a Shareholder shall be _____ Dollars ($___) per share.

On or about the first day of the month of _____ in each succeeding calendar year the Shareholders and the Corporation will in writing either reaffirm the purchase price in effect hereunder in the immediately preceding calendar year or agree upon a new purchase price, sign an original and five copies of the writing, each of which shall be considered an original for the purposes of this agreement and each Shareholder, the Corporation and the Trustee shall receive one such original.

If the Shareholders and the Corporation do not either so reaffirm or agree upon the purchase price, their failure to do so will not void this agreement, but, rather, the price set forth above or the last purchase price reaffirmed or agreed upon by the Shareholders and the Corporation in a writing signed by all of them shall be fully binding upon them, their legal Representatives, heirs, successors and assigns except that if the Shareholders and the Corporation do not so reaffirm or agree upon the purchase price for three consecutive years and one of Shareholder's shares are offered to the Corporation under paragraph 3, 5 or 6 of this agreement and the parties cannot agree on a purchase price, the purchase price shall be determined as of the date of said offer by the independent certified public accountant regularly retained by the Corporation to audit its books. If no such accountant is available, the purchase price shall be determined by any other certified public account selected by the mutual agreement of the parties and his compensation shall be charged ½ to the seller and ½ to the buyer.

Anything to the contrary herein notwithstanding except in the event of a sale and purchase made during the lifetime of the selling Shareholder, in no event shall the purchase price to be paid for all the shares of a Shareholder in the Corporation be less than the death proceeds and avails paid under the policies of life insurance taken out by the Corporation on the life of the deceased Shareholder described in Schedule A which is attached to and made a part hereof.

(Most writers on the subject of buy-outs agree that a simple valuation clause such as this one is to be preferred over such ambiguous terms as "book value," "net worth," or "net worth and goodwill." A variation of this simple approach would be to provide that if the parties do not set a new value, the preceding year's value shall be increased by 5 percent.)

8. The Corporation, in order to fund its obligation to purchase the shares of a Shareholder, has acquired or will acquire a policy or policies of life insurance and health insurance on the life of each Shareholder. These policies are more particularly described in Schedule A.

Additional policies of life insurance and health insurance subject to this agreement may be acquired by the Corporation on the lives of Shareholders. Such policies and the description thereof shall be added to Schedule A. As to each of such life policies, the Corporation either has or will:

a) request that its automatic premium loan provision, if any, be made effective, and

b) request that dividends be applied to purchase paid-up additional insurance, and

c) designate itself as owner of the policy and make the Trustee the beneficiary thereof.

Except as provided below, as to each of said health insurance policies designated in Schedule A as a noncancellable business disability policy, the Corporation and the Shareholders shall take all necessary steps to:

a) vest all right, title and interest therein in the Corporation (and the insured Shareholder jointly for the first _____ [five?] years of continuous disability, thereafter the insured) and

b) to designate the Corporation as the sole payee of any benefits thereunder (for the first _____ [five] years of continuous disability, thereafter the insured).

As to each of said health insurance policies designated in Schedule A as an optionally renewable key man business disability policy, issued on the life of a Shareholder by The Insurance Company, the Corporation and the Shareholders shall take all necessary steps to:

a) vest all right, title and interest therein in the Corporation, and

b) designate the Trustee as the sole payee of any benefits thereunder.

(*This insurance provision should be carefully thought out by counsel. When a trustee is used in a buy-out, usually the buying entity owns the funding life insurance policies and the trustee is designated as beneficiary of their death proceeds as is done in this sample agreement. If the parties desire to have the trustee carry out the disability buy-out and it is willing to do so (not done in this sample agreement), it may be advisable to have the trustee own the life insurance policies so as to be able to use their cash values in the disability buy-out.*)

(*The long-term noncancellable disability policies issued by The Insurance Company within its normal issue and participation limits are to be owned by the Corporation and insured jointly during the period of years having to do with the disability buy-out, typically: "the first five years of continuous disability." This is because under The Insurance Company's business insurance policy (perhaps unique in the industry) the owner may designate and change the loss payee just as the beneficiary of a typical modern life insurance policy may be designated and changed from time to time by its owner. Joint ownership would call for joint action to change the loss payee for "the first _____ years of continuous disability" and thus makes sure the Corporation will receive these benefits. If a period longer than the buy-out period is insured, for example, lifetime, the owner of the policy after the buy-out period and the loss payee after the buy-out period will be made the insured [e.g., "thereafter the In-*

sured"]. *Under this arrangement, the Corporation will pay the premiums allocable to the "first five [?] years of continuous disability" and the insured will pay the premiums allocable to any excess period of benefits. The Corporation will receive the benefits paid to it income tax free (IRC 104(a)(3); Castner Garage Ltd, 43 B.T.A.1, acq.). The insured will receive the benefits paid to him under the policy after the buy-out period income tax free [IRC 104 (a)(3)].)*

(If shorter term policies are used, say with five year maximum benefit periods in this example, then of course, the Corporation should be named as the sole owner and loss payee of the noncancellable business disability policies [(a) and (b), bottom of preceding page].)

(The benefits of the optionally renewable key man business disability policies issued by The Insurance Company providing disability income benefits in excess of The Insurance Company's normal limits are to be used to indemnify an entity for the loss of the services of its key man through disability or to effect the buy-out of a disabled businessman's interest in a business. These benefits are not to be paid to the disabled insured directly or indirectly as salary continuation benefits. For this reason the corporation will be the owner and the trustee will be the loss payee of these policies. The Insurance Company will not issue such coverage unless this is done and will cancel such coverage if there is a subsequent change in the arrangement.)

9. Excepting for automatic premium loans, the Corporation shall not in any way encumber any policy described in Schedule A, change its beneficiary designation or elect any settlement option other than a lump-sum payment of its death proceeds without the written consent of all the parties to this agreement except that it may request the life insurance company which issued the policy to apply the dividends allotted on said policy under any of the options of said policy or in any manner permitted by said life insurance company.

10. Upon the death of a Shareholder, the Trustee shall forthwith make claim under all policies on the life of the deceased Shareholder in which it is designated as beneficiary of the death proceeds thereof to the life insurance companies issuing said policies. The Trustee shall hold said proceeds for the purposes set forth herein.

If such proceeds are equal to the purchase price, the Trustee shall pay over such proceeds to the Legal Representative of the deceased Shareholder's estate.

If such proceeds are less than the purchase price, the Trustee shall pay over such proceeds to said Legal Representative and, in addition, the Corporation shall pay an amount equal to the difference between such proceeds and the purchase price to said Legal Representative. Such additional amount may be paid in cash or, at the option of the Corporation, in promissory notes, the first of which shall fall due and be paid by the Corporation on the first anniversary of the death of the Shareholder, and one of which shall fall due and be payable by the Corporation on the first day of each month thereafter until all of said notes are paid. Each of said notes shall bear interest at the rate of _____ per-centum per annum. The Corporation may pay said notes in full or in part at any time or from time to time after their delivery.

Upon payment of such proceeds and additional amount, if any, to the said Legal Representative, the said Legal Representative and the Trustee shall execute and deliver to the Corporation such instruments as are necessary to transfer full and complete title to the deceased Shareholder's shares to the Corporation. If an additional amount is paid by the Corporation's promissory note, the Corporation shall forthwith assign to the Legal Representative as collateral security for the payment of said note such number of said shares as will equal in value (as determined under this agreement) the unpaid portion of said note. Upon the final payment of said note, the said shares shall be released from the collateral assignment and returned to the Corporation.

Any of the provisions hereof to the contrary notwithstanding, if the Legal Representative shall request the Trustee to do so, the Trustee shall request the insurance company or companies issuing the policy or policies on the deceased Shareholder's life described in Schedule A to designate the Trustee as the primary beneficiary for one year from the date of the insured's death under the interest option of said policy or policies with full and partial power to withdraw and to designate the beneficiary or beneficiaries requested by the Legal Representative as secondary beneficiaries under the options and in the manner requested by the Legal Representative and permitted by the said insurance company or companies. Upon the transfer of the deceased Shareholder's shares to the Corporation, the trustee shall release its right, title and interest under said interest option in favor of the secondary beneficiary or beneficiaries. If the Legal Representative does make such a request and if the Trustee complies with such request, the Corporation shall receive a credit towards the purchase price for the total amount of the death proceeds and avails so released in favor of the secondary beneficiary or beneficiaries to the same extent and in the same manner as if the released proceeds had been paid in one sum to the Legal Representative.

In the event that the deceased Shareholder's shares are not transferred to the Corporation within the first 11 months of the year during which the Trustee is primary beneficiary, the Trustee shall withdraw the entire proceeds plus any other amount allocated to the contract by the insurance company and retain the same until the shares are transferred to the Corporation, at which time it shall pay over the same to the said Legal Representative.

(*The only unusual thing about this paragraph is the right of the Legal Representative to have the death proceeds portion of the purchase price paid under a settlement option. The IRC 101(d) "$1,000 widow's exemption" would not apply to these payments.*)

(*If there are to be installment payments, remember to put in a provision for at least 4 percent interest unless the parties are willing to accept the arrangement spelled out in IRC 483 and regulations. It is the opinion of the author that the deceased shareholder's beneficiary should not have to accept an interest rate below that which a bank would charge for similar notes.*)

11. *a*) Ninety days after a Shareholder is "totally disabled" within the meaning of that term as it is defined in Paragraph 4(*a*) hereof, the Corporation shall cease to pay said Shareholder his normal salary, and in lieu thereof the Corporation shall pay him so long as he is so totally disabled, but no longer than five years, a monthly amount equal to the monthly amount received by it under the noncancellable policies of which the Corporation is the owner issued by The Insurance Company on the life of the Shareholder.

b) In the event that a Shareholder is "totally disabled" within the meaning of that term as it is defined in Paragraph 4(*b*) hereof, at the conclusion of two years and 90 days of being continuously "totally disabled" within the meaning of that term as it is defined in Paragraph 4(*a*) hereof, the Corporation will pay the Shareholder 20 percent of the price established under paragraphs 3 and 7 hereof; if such disability continues for a third year, at the conclusion of said year the Corporation will pay the Shareholder 20 percent of said price plus one year's interest at the rate of ___ percent a year (make no less than 4 percent to avoid imputed interest under IRC 483) on 80 percent of said price; if such disability continues for a fourth year, at the conclusion of said year the

Corporation will pay the Shareholder 20 percent of said price plus one year's interest at the rate of ___ percent a year on 60 percent of said price; if said disability continues for a fifth year, at the conclusion of said year, the Corporation will pay the Shareholder the remaining 40 percent of said price plus one year's interest at the rate of ___ percent a year on 40 percent of said price; if the Shareholder is so continuously "totally disabled" for two years and 90 days or more and then ceases to be so "totally disabled," the payments to be made under this subparagraph 9(b) shall be reduced to $___ per month plus interest on the outstanding balance of said price at the rate of ___ percent a year such payments to be made by the Corporation to said Shareholder until the entire price has been paid; all of the principal payments made under this subparagraph 9(b) shall be applied against the said price.

c) If the Shareholder is alive at the conclusion of five years and 90 days of being so continuously "totally disabled," he shall have a ___ month option to purchase the policy or policies of life insurance on his life from the Corporation. The price of each policy shall be the gift tax value of said policy on the date of the exercise of said option as determined by the issuing insurance company.

d) If the Trustee receives benefits under an optionally renewable key man business disability policy issued by The Insurance Company it shall deposit such benefits at interest.

If the Corporation makes payments under (b) above to a disabled Shareholder the Trustee shall pay an amount or amounts of such benefits and interest to the Corporation equal to the payments it has made under (b) above to the disabled Shareholder.

If benefits are paid under an optionally renewable key man business disability policy issued by The Insurance Company and the insured recovers before the conclusion of two years and 90 days as set forth in (b) above, the Trustee shall pay over to the Corporation any benefits it has received as a result of the insured's disability plus interest, if any, and the Corporation shall add such payment to its surplus.

e) Anything to the contrary in this Agreement notwithstanding, if a Shareholder dies while receiving payments under (b), of this paragraph, the purchase price of his shares shall be the greater of the death proceeds of the life insurance policies on his life described in Schedule A and owned by the Corporation or the purchase price established under Paragraph 7 hereof and the said death proceeds shall be applied to pay the amount, if any, by which said purchase price exceeds the sum of the principal amounts paid under (b).

f) In the event that the payments made on the said purchase price by the Corporation under (b) and (e) of this paragraph are less than the purchase price, the Corporation shall pay an additional amount equal to the difference between such payments and the purchase price to the said Shareholder. Such additional amount may be paid in cash or, at the option of the Corporation, in a series of promissory notes the first of which shall fall due and be paid by the Corporation at the conclusion of the period set forth in (b) of this paragraph and one of which shall fall due and be paid by the Corporation on the first day of each month thereafter until all of said notes are paid. Each of said notes shall be in the amount of $___ and shall bear interest at the rate of ___ per centum per annum.

g) Upon payment to the said Shareholder of the first payment required by subparagraph (b), the said Shareholder and Trustee shall execute and deliver to the Corporation such instruments as are necessary to transfer full and complete title to the said Shareholder's shares to the Corporation. If additional amounts are to be paid by the Corporation, the Corporation shall forthwith assign to the disabled shareholder as collateral security for the said payments, such number of said shares as will equal in value (as determined under this agreement) the unpaid portion of such additional amounts. As additional payments of the purchase price are made by the corporation, the number of said assigned shares which equal in value the amount of each such payment shall be released from the collateral assignment and returned to the Corporation.

(11(a) *is a salary continuation provision. Under it, the disabled Shareholder will receive his normal salary during the first 90 days of disability. Thereafter, the Corporation will receive payments from The Insurance Company under its NC51 policies on the disabled Shareholder's life. It will pay exactly the same amount to the Shareholder as it receives. The Corporation will receive the payments made to it income tax free as noted above. The payments it makes to the disabled Shareholder will be deductible by it and $100 a week excluded from the Shareholder's gross income if there is a plan (Reg. 1.162–10 third sentence; IRC 105(d); Reg. 1.105–5(a)). The tax savings resulting from the difference between the income tax-free benefits to the Corporation and the after-tax cost of the tax deductible payments to the disabled Shareholder of the same dollar amount will be used to help fund the buy-out. In the sample agreement this is five years.)*

(11(b) *is the disability buy-out. It is an installment buy-out. It is phrased in terms of percentage installments. Due regard is given to IRC 453 and IRC 483. Insofar as the buy-out payments constitute capital gain to a Shareholder, he may elect to add one-half of the payment to his other ordinary income or pay the flat capital gain tax (IRC 1201 as amended by the Tax Reform Act of 1969). In the sample agreement in the sixth year the disabled Shareholder will receive the payments from the noncancellable business disability contract directly and income tax free since he paid the premium out of his own after tax dollars for the benefits in excess of five years of continuous disability. In the sixth year, he will receive his largest buy-out installment. This arrangement should give him a better tax result than a lump-sum payment or level installment payments. The Corporation's advisers may wish to adjust the arithmetic in the agreement to get the best possible result for the Corporation and its Shareholders.)*

(11(c) *is optional. Obviously a policy of life insurance on a man who has been disabled for five or more years will usually be worth a great deal more than its cash value. First, so long as the insured is disabled, premiums will be waived and the buildup in the policy's cash value plus dividends will be available to the disabled insured and his family for their benefit. Second, the probability of an early demise of a man disabled for five years will usually be greater than for a healthy man.)*

(11(d) *or something accomplishing the same result is* mandatory *as a quid pro quo for the issuance of The Insurance Company's A&H41 contract in excess of the Insurance Company's normal limits. Note that under its language, none of the benefits paid to the trustee may be used to make salary continuation payments to the disabled Shareholder.)*

(11(e) *and* (f) *cover the death of a disabled Shareholder during the disability buy-out.)*

(11(g) *provides for the transfer to the Corporation of all shares of the disabled owner at the time the buy-out is "triggered." Sufficient shares are then assigned by the Corporation to the Shareholder to provide security for the remaining payments to be made by the Corporation.)*

12. In the event that a Shareholder is "totally disabled within the meaning of that term as it is defined in Paragraph 4(a) or 4(b) hereof, he shall give the highest officer of the Corporation other than himself his proxy to vote his

shares each year that he is so disabled in accordance with the majority vote of the shares of the Corporation other than said shares.

13. *a*) If at the time of the purchase of shares under Paragraphs 10 or 11 hereof a corporation cannot purchase or redeem its own shares except out of surplus under the law of the Corporation's state of incorporation, and if the Corporation does not have sufficient surplus to enable it to fulfill its obligations hereunder, then the Corporation and the Shareholders including the Legal Representative of a Shareholder shall take all possible steps permitted under the law of the Corporation's state of incorporation to recapitalize and to increase said surplus to an amount sufficient to enable the corporation to fulfill its obligation hereunder including, but not limited to, the reduction of the par value of capital stock of the Corporation and the increase of the book value of all the assets of the Corporation including its good will, if any, to their market value on the books of the corporation.

b) If after taking all possible steps in accordance with (*a*) the Corporation does not have sufficient surplus to enable it to fulfill its obligations hereunder.

(*i*) the Corporation shall purchase as many shares as it is possible for it to do under the law of its state of incorporation, and

(*ii*) the remaining Shareholder or Shareholders shall purchase any and all shares which the Corporation was obliged to purchase hereunder and which it did not so purchase.

(*A corporation may not have sufficient "surplus" to effect a stock redemption and thus the expectations of the parties would be frustrated. Paragraph 13 is designed to solve this problem. Under it, either enough "surplus" will be made available or the remaining shareholders must take over the corporations obligation. There are many different ways of expressing this concept.*)

14. If all of the Shareholders die or are disabled within a 30-day period, this agreement shall terminate. The proceeds of the life insurance policy or policies on each deceased Shareholder's life described in Schedule A shall be paid to the Corporation by the Trustee, the Trustee shall transfer all of its right, title and interest to all of the life insurance policies still in force to the Corporation, and the Corporation shall transfer to the insured named therein each of the non-cancellable health insurance policies described in Schedule A which is still in force and shall cancel all of the optionally renewable key man business disability policies which are still in force.

15. This agreement shall terminate upon:

a) Its complete execution upon the death or disability of all but one of the Shareholders.

b) The lapse of the policies described in Schedule A without value.

c) The bankruptcy or insolvency of the Corporation.

d) The sale of all of the shares of all but one of the Shareholders.

e) The written agreement of all of the Shareholders and the Corporation to terminate it.

Upon the termination of this agreement, the Trustee shall deliver the shares of any surviving Shareholder which are in its possession to said Shareholder and shall take all steps necessary to forthwith transfer all right, title and interest in any life insurance policy or noncancellable disability income policy owned by it and described in Schedule A to the Corporation and to cancel any optionally renewable disability income policy owned by it and described in Schedule A.

16. If a shareholder sells his shares of stock during his life pursuant to the terms of this agreement other than the disability buy-out provisions of the agreement, he shall have a 60-day option from the date of said sale to purchase the policy or policies on his life described in Schedule A from the then owner save that in the event of such sale, any optionally renewable disability income policy on said Shareholder's life shall be canceled.

17. The Trustee shall be entitled to receive, as compensation for its services hereunder, fees as follows:

_____

_____

_____

18. The Trustee may be removed by the joint action of the Corporation and the Shareholders. The Trustee, or any successor Trustee, may resign and discharge itself of the trust created hereunder, but such resignation shall not be effective for 45 days after written notice is given to all of the other parties hereto then alive or in legal existence. In case of removal or resignation, the Trustee shall deliver to its successor all right, title and interest in any policy or policies owned by it and described in Schedule A. to its successor. Upon the death, resignation or removal of the Trustee, a successor Trustee shall be appointed as soon as practicable by the joint action of the Corporation and the Shareholders. For purposes of this Paragraph 18, the term "Shareholder" shall be deemed to include the Executor or Administrator of the estate of a deceased Shareholder, and to include any individual with respect to whom payments pursuant to Paragraph 11(b) of this Agreement have commenced but have not been completed.

19. This agreement shall be governed by the laws of the State of _____.

20. No insurance company which has issued a policy or policies described in Schedule A shall be under any obligation with respect to the performance of the terms or provisions hereof. Such company or companies shall only be liable as set forth in its policies.

21. This agreement shall be binding upon the parties hereto, their Legal Representatives, heirs, and assigns and the parties hereto do hereby covenant and agree that they, their Legal Representatives, heirs, and assigns will execute any and all papers or documents that may be required of them in accordance with this agreement.

IN WITNESS WHEREOF, the parties have hereunto set their hands and seals or caused these presents to be signed by their proper corporate officers and caused their proper corporation seals to be affixed hereto, the day and year first above written.

Witness   _____

                                 _____

                                 _____

                                 _____

Attest: Company

_____   By: _____
              (Title)   (Title)

Corporate Seal.

Attest: Company

_____   By: _____
              (Title)   (Title)

Corporate Seal.

S

Specimen Agreement for Change of Beneficiary

Specimen Agreement for Change of Beneficiary

SEE REVERSE SIDE FOR EXPLANATION OF NUMBERED BENEFICIARY DESIGNATIONS

CHANGE OF BENEFICIARY

To be used for Policies (not providing Income) Numbered 422897 and higher.

Policy Number 3,000,000

Insured   John Doe

The beneficiary under the above numbered policy, issued by ██████████ LIFE INSURANCE COMPANY OF ██████████, is hereby REVOCABLY changed so that any proceeds becoming payable by reason of Insured's death will be paid to the person or persons indicated below.

1. ☐ Insured's executors or administrators.

2. ☐ Insured's .... , ... , if living.

3. ☐ Insured's .... , ... , if living, otherwise Insured's .... ,
.... , if living.

4. ☐ Insured's .... , ... , if living, otherwise Insured's .... ,
.... , if living, otherwise Insured's .... ,
.... , if living.

5. ☐ Insured's .... , ... , if living, otherwise Insured's .... ,
.... and .... , share and share alike,
if living, or the survivor if living.

6. ☐ Insured's .... , ... , if living, otherwise such of Insured's ....
.... as may be living, share and share alike.

7. ☐ Insured's .... , ... , if living, otherwise such lawful children of Insured as
may be living, share and share alike.

8. ☐ Insured's wife, ... , ... , if living, otherwise such children of Insured by his said
wife as may be living, share and share alike.

9. ☐ Insured's .... , and .... ,
share and share alike, if living, or the survivor if living.

10. ☐ Insured's .... , and .... ,
share and share alike, if living, or the survivor if living, otherwise Insured's ....
.... , if living.

11. ☐ Insured's .... , and .... ,
share and share alike, if living, or the survivor if living, otherwise Insured's ....
.... and .... ,
share and share alike, if living, or the survivor if living.

12. ☒ Insured's wife , Mary Doe , if living, otherwise such lawful children of Insured as
may be living, share and share alike, provided that if any lawful child of Insured is then deceased leaving then living a lawful child or children, the share which would have been paid to such deceased child of Insured if such child had continued to live will be paid, share and share alike, to his or her then living lawful children.

13. ☐ Such of Insured's ....
.... , as may be living, share and share alike.

14. ☐ Such of Insured's lawful children as may be living, share and share alike.

15. ☐ Insured's .... , ... , if living at the expiration of a period of 30 days following Insured's death, otherwise such lawful children of Insured as may be then living, share and share alike, and if there shall be then living no lawful child of Insured to Insured's executors or administrators.

16. ☐ .... ,
of .... , or ....
successor or successors in trust, trustee(s) under trust agreement dated ....
executed by ....

(Page 1)

11995 4.70

Specimen Agreement for Change of Beneficiary (concluded)

If the Insured is the owner of the policy and all beneficiaries designated in this instrument to receive the proceeds of the policy at Insured's death are then deceased, the proceeds of the policy will be paid to the Insured's executors or administrators.

If someone other than the Insured is the owner of the policy and all beneficiaries designated in this instrument to receive the proceeds of the policy at Insured's death are then deceased, the proceeds of the policy will be paid to the owner if then living, otherwise to the executors or administrators of the owner.

Any reference in this instrument to a beneficiary living or surviving will, unless otherwise provided herein, mean living at the Insured's death.

Any election of a method of settlement previously made is hereby revoked as to the policy.

Wherever the word "policy" is used herein, it will be interpreted to mean "policies" if more than one policy is included.

Any moneys due a minor hereunder will be paid to the legally appointed guardian of the minor. If written notice of the existence of a legally appointed guardian has not been received by the Company at its home office, any moneys due a minor hereunder will be paid to the minor wherever the law of the minor's domicile permits.

The Company, in determining the beneficiaries comprising any class mentioned in this instrument, or any facts relating to any beneficiaries mentioned in this instrument, either as a class or otherwise, their names, addresses, ages and dates of death, may rely solely upon an affidavit by any one of the beneficiaries, and is hereby relieved and discharged from all liability and responsibility in making payments in accordance therewith.

If a trustee under instrument of trust is designated as beneficiary and the trust is not in effect at Insured's death, then, unless otherwise provided herein, the proceeds of the policy will be paid to the Insured's executors or administrators, or, if someone other than the Insured is the owner of the policy, to the owner, his executors or administrators. The Insurance Company will not be bound or obligated in any way by any of the terms, provisions or conditions of any instrument of trust, and any payment to the designated beneficiary will constitute a full and complete discharge of the Insurance Company for the payment so made.

If any policy under this instrument is numbered 422897 to 1,999,999, the Company is requested to waive all provisions of such policy requiring endorsement of a beneficiary change, election of an option, or revocation of an existing election, and to endorse the policy, if not previously so endorsed, as follows:

"The beneficiary of this policy has been changed according to written request filed with the Company.

"Every change of beneficiary, election of an option and revocation of an existing election must be made by written request, and when filed with the Company at its home office, will take effect as of the date signed, whether or not the Insured is alive at the time of filing, subject to any payment or other action by the Company before filing. All provisions of this policy requiring endorsement of change of beneficiary, election of an option and revocation of an existing election are canceled."

EXECUTED ...., 19 .....
Date

.... (SEAL)
(Signature of Insured or Owner)

I HEREBY CONSENT TO THIS INSTRUMENT

.... (SEAL)
(Signature of consenting person or party)

ENDORSEMENT INSTRUCTIONS

Send the policy to the home office for endorsement of change of beneficiary and R. S. No. 288 only if numbered 422897 to 1,999,999 and not previously so endorsed. After executing, send both copies to the home office of the Company for recording. After recording, a verified copy will be returned for filing with the policy.

Explanation of Numbered Beneficiary Designations (on reverse side)
1. Insured's estate
2. One primary
3. One primary and one secondary
4. One primary and two secondaries successively
5. One primary and two secondaries equally or the survivor
6. One primary and three or more secondaries equally
7. Spouse (primary) and unnamed lawful children of Insured equally (secondary)
8. Wife (primary) and unnamed children by named wife equally (secondary)
9. Two primaries equally or the survivor
10. Two primaries equally or the survivor, and one secondary
11. Two primaries equally or the survivor, and two secondaries equally or the survivor
12. Spouse (primary) and unnamed lawful children and grandchildren of Insured per stirpes
13. Three or more primaries equally or the survivors
14. Insured's lawful children equally
15. Common Disaster clause, spouse otherwise unnamed lawful children of Insured, equally
16. Trustee (inter vivos)

SEE DIVIDER "A" OF UNDERWRITER'S MANUAL OR BLUE CARD NO. 10815 AS A GUIDE IN COMPLETING FORM.

HOME OFFICE USE ONLY: Original signed copy is filed with the ██████████████ LIFE INSURANCE
COMPANY OF ███████████.

....
Registrar
(Page 2)   Date

11995   4.70

T

Specimen Agreement for Election of Method of Settlement

Specimen Agreement for Election of Method of Settlement

ELECTION OF METHOD OF SETTLEMENT

To be used for Life Insurance Policies and Annuities Numbered 422897 and higher.

Policy Number 3,000,000

Insured   John Doe

The beneficiary under the above numbered policy, issued by ███████████ LIFE INSURANCE COMPANY OF ████████ is hereby REVOCABLY changed as follows:

If the proceeds of the policy shall become payable by reason of Insured's death, the Company will make settlement of said proceeds as follows:

I. If Insured's wife, Mary Doe
(born   ), shall be living at Insured's death, the Company will retain said proceeds, if not less than $1,000, under option 1 contained in the policy and pay interest thereon monthly   to said wife if living when said interest payments shall respectively become payable, with right in her at any time while receiving interest under option 1 to withdraw said proceeds in whole or in parts. If said proceeds shall be less than $1,000, the Company at Insured's death will pay same, in a lump sum, to said wife if then living.

Said wife shall have the right at any time while receiving interest under option 1 to direct that such of said proceeds as may then remain with the Company, if not less than $1,000, shall be applied for her benefit under option 2, 3 or 4 contained in the policy. Said wife shall have the right at any time while receiving (a) instalments under option 2 to withdraw the then balance of said proceeds in whole or in parts, or (b) instalments certain under option 3 or 4 to commute for a lump sum the then unpaid instalments certain.

If said wife shall die while receiving instalments under option 2 or instalments certain under option 3 or 4, any remaining instalments or instalments certain will be paid, when the same shall respectively become payable, share and share alike, to such lawful children of Insured as may be living at the death of said wife, provided that if any lawful child of Insured shall be then deceased leaving then living a lawful child or children, the share of said proceeds which would have been paid to such deceased child of Insured in instalments if such child had continued to live or the commuted value of the share of the unpaid instalments certain which such deceased child of Insured would have received if such child had continued to live will be paid, in a lump sum, share and share alike, to his or her then living lawful children. Each child of Insured shall have the right at any time while receiving (a) instalments or share thereof under option 2 to withdraw the then balance of his or her share in whole or in parts, or (b) instalments certain or share thereof under option 3 or 4 to commute for a lump sum the then unpaid instalments certain or share thereof which such child may be entitled to receive.

II. If said wife shall be deceased at Insured's death or shall thereafter die while receiving interest under option 1, the Company at the death of the survivor of Insured and said wife will apportion such of said proceeds as may then remain with the Company, share and share alike, to such lawful children of Insured as may be then living, provided that if any lawful child of Insured shall be then deceased leaving then living a lawful child or children, the share which would have been apportioned to such deceased

10510 4.69   (Page 1)

Specimen Agreement for Election of Method of Settlement (continued)

child of Insured if such child had continued to live will be paid, in a lump sum, share and share alike, to his or her then living lawful children.

The share apportioned to each child of Insured, if not less than $1,000, will be retained under option 1 contained in the policy and interest paid thereon **monthly** to such child if living when said interest payments shall respectively become payable, with right in such child at any time while receiving interest under option 1 to withdraw his or her share in whole or in parts. If the share apportioned to each child of Insured shall be less than $1,000, the Company at the time of such apportionment will pay same, in a lump sum, to such child.

Each child of Insured shall have the right at any time while receiving interest under option 1 to direct that such of his or her share as may then remain with the Company, if not less than $1,000, shall be applied for his or her benefit under option 2, 3 or 4 contained in the policy. Each child of Insured shall have the right at any time while receiving (a) instalments under option 2 to withdraw the then balance of his or her share in whole or in parts, or (b) instalments certain under option 3 or 4 to commute for a lump sum the then unpaid instalments certain which such child may be entitled to receive.

III. If any child of Insured shall die while receiving interest or instalments, or share thereof, the Company at such child's death will pay the then balance of his or her share of said proceeds or the commuted value of the share of the then unpaid instalments certain which such child would have received if he or she had continued to live, in a lump sum, share and share alike, to his or her then living lawful children, and if there shall be then living no lawful child of such child of Insured so dying, share and share alike, to such lawful children of Insured as may be then living, provided that if any lawful child of Insured shall be then deceased leaving then living a lawful child or children, the share which would have been paid to such deceased child of Insured if such child had continued to live will be paid, share and share alike, to his or her then living lawful children, and if there shall be then living no lawful child of Insured and no lawful child of a deceased lawful child of Insured the Company will pay same in accordance with the terms of Section V hereof.

IV. If said wife shall be deceased at Insured's death or shall thereafter die while receiving interest or instalments, and if at the death of the survivor of Insured and said wife there shall be living no lawful child of Insured and no lawful child of a deceased lawful child of Insured, the Company will pay such of said proceeds as may then remain with the Company or the commuted value of the then unpaid instalments certain in accordance with the terms of Section V hereof.

V. Any sum or sums to be settled in accordance with the terms of this Section V will be paid at the death of the last survivor of Insured, said wife and Insured's lawful children (there being then living no lawful child of any deceased lawful child of Insured), in a lump sum, to the executors or administrators of the last survivor of Insured, said wife and Insured's lawful children.

Any interest accrued but not due at the death of any beneficiary hereunder who would have been entitled thereto if such beneficiary had continued to live will be paid to the next succeeding beneficiary or beneficiaries.

(Page 1a)

Specimen Agreement for Election of Method of Settlement (concluded)

Any election of a method of settlement previously made is hereby revoked as to the policy.

If this instrument is used in connection with an annuity contract, the words "policy" and "Insured" used herein will be interpreted to mean "contract" and "Annuitant" respectively.

Wherever the word "policy" or "contract" is used herein, it will be interpreted to mean "policies" or "contracts" if more than one policy or contract is included.

Notwithstanding any provision contained herein, the minimum amount of each instalment payable under any option 2 settlement herein will be at the rate of (a) $4 if a monthly instalment, (b) $12 if a quarterly instalment, (c) $24 if a half-yearly instalment, or (d) $48 if a yearly instalment, for each $1,000 of the sum applied under such option 2 settlement at the time it becomes operative. If any instalment under such option 2 settlement is less than such minimum amount, the Company will have the right to increase such instalment to such minimum amount.

To the extent permitted by law, it is hereby provided that no beneficiary entitled under the terms of this instrument to receive any part of the proceeds of the policy or any interest, instalment or other payment will be permitted to commute, anticipate, encumber, alienate or assign the same or any part thereof except as may be otherwise expressly provided herein and that no interest, principal or other payments under this instrument will be in any way subject to the beneficiary's debts, contracts or engagements nor to any judicial processes to levy upon or attach the same for payment thereof.

Any moneys due or any right granted to a minor hereunder will be paid to or must be exercised by the legally appointed guardian of the minor. If written notice of the existence of a legally appointed guardian has not been received by the Company at its home office, any moneys due or any right granted to a minor hereunder will be paid to or may be exercised by the minor wherever the law of the minor's domicile permits.

The Company, in determining the beneficiaries comprising any class mentioned in this instrument, or any facts relating to any beneficiaries mentioned in this instrument, either as a class or otherwise, their names, addresses, ages and dates of death, may rely solely upon an affidavit by any one of the beneficiaries, and is hereby relieved and discharged from all liability and responsibility in making payments in accordance therewith.

The Company will have the right to require the return of the policy and to issue in its place a certificate or certificates if any proceeds are left with the Company under this method of settlement.

The Insurance Company will not be bound or obligated in any way by any of the terms, provisions or conditions of any instrument of trust, and any payment to the designated beneficiary will constitute a full and complete discharge of the Insurance Company for the payment so made.

If any policy under this instrument is numbered 422897 to 1,999,999, the Company is requested to waive all provisions of such policy requiring endorsement of a beneficiary change, election of an option, or revocation of an existing election, and to endorse the policy, if not previously so endorsed, as follows:

"The beneficiary of this policy has been changed according to written request filed with the Company.

"Every change of beneficiary, election of an option and revocation of an existing election must be made by written request, and when filed with the Company at its home office, will take effect as of the date signed, whether or not the Insured is alive at the time of filing, subject to any payment or other action by the Company before filing. All provisions of this policy requiring endorsement of change of beneficiary, election of an option and revocation of an existing election are canceled."

EXECUTED .... , 19 ......
Date

.... (SEAL)
(Signature of Insured or Owner)

(Affix Corporate Seal)   I HEREBY CONSENT TO THIS INSTRUMENT

.... (SEAL)
(Signature of consenting person or party)

NOTE: If a Corporate Owner executes this instrument, the Corporate Seal must be affixed.

ENDORSEMENT INSTRUCTIONS

Send the policy to the home office for endorsement of change of beneficiary and R. S. No. 288 only if numbered 422897 to 1,999,999 and not previously so endorsed. After executing, send both copies to the home office of the Company for recording. After recording, a verified copy will be returned for filing with the policy.

HOME OFFICE USE ONLY: Original signed copy is filed with the ████████████████ LIFE INSURANCE
COMPANY OF ███████████

....
Registrar   Date

10510 4.69   (Page 2)

U

National Statement of
Principles of Cooperation
between Life
Underwriters and Lawyers

In February 1948, the National Conference of Lawyers and Life Underwriters issued its *National Statement of Principles of Cooperation between
Life Underwriters and Lawyers*. That Statement reads:

Foreword

The National Conference of Lawyers and Life Underwriters was constituted
on July 17, 1946, by representatives of The American Bar Association and The
National Association of Life Underwriters upon due authorization by the governing bodies of the two Associations. Its purpose shall be to promote cooperation and understanding between life underwriters and lawyers and to eliminate,
as far as possible, misunderstandings and causes for complaint by either against
the other in relation to any practices which do not appear to be in the public
interest.

.   .   .   .   .

In 1940, a National Statement of Principles of Cooperation between Life
Underwriters and Lawyers was published. The present Statement is intended
to supersede the 1940 Statement. It, like its predecessor, is intended as a guide
to the professional conduct of attorneys and life underwriters in respect to one
another and in relation to the public.

Statement

In recent years, much of the actual negotiation of the sale of life insurance
contracts involves estate planning. The acquisition of life insurance has become a complex problem by its ever increasing relation to plans of testamentary
disposition, wills and living trusts, to partnerships and close corporation contracts, and to problems of taxation. The solution of such problems requires a
man to make far-reaching decisions. These decisions often are, or upon the
happening of death become, irrevocable. The American public should therefore
receive not only expert insurance service and disinterested advice but also

skilled and disinterested legal guidance and advice when necessary; both are often required in problems arising out of negotiation for and use of life insurance, and when this is the case, the simultaneous and harmonious attention of a representative of each profession in solving the problems of the same client will provide the safest and most efficient service.

Fair dealing with the public and an observance of laws which have been enacted throughout the United States require that all legal service and advice should at all times be given by an individual trained in the law and duly licensed to practice; anyone who gives legal advice should be solely devoted to the interest of his client and permit no personal consideration whatsoever to weaken his exclusive loyalty to his client.

In this connection, it might well be remembered that the courts consider communications between an attorney and his client as privileged, that is, they do not compel their disclosure; while communications between a life underwriter and his client are not so considered. This distinction should, for the protection of the public, be borne in mind by the members of both professions.

For the guidance of life underwriters and of lawyers, and to insure that the public shall be protected by receiving authorized and disinterested legal advice on life insurance problems, such as those hereinabove referred to, the National Conference states:

I.

The National Conference considers it to be in the interest of cooperation between life underwriters and lawyers and of better service to the public, that all lawyers be guided by the opinion of the American Bar Association's Standing Committee on Professional Ethics and Grievances, dated February 10, 1940, issued in reply to an inquiry from that Association's Standing Committee on Unauthorized Practice of Law. That opinion in full is as follows:

"In the opinion of the Committee, the Lawyer's conduct in each of the following situations is ethically improper and should be condemned:

"1. A life underwriter recommends a certain transaction, for example, the purchase of business life insurance. The client presents the proposed transaction to his attorney for approval or disapproval. The attorney then demands of the life underwriter, as a condition for his approval, a share in the life underwriter's commission.

"2. An attorney promises a life underwriter to recommend him to the attorney's clients, provided the life underwriter will pay to the attorney a share of his commissions resulting from any business obtained from the lawyer's clients.

"It should be noted, in this connection, that in most of the states participation in commissions on life insurance contracts by any person other than a duly licensed life insurance agent, has been condemned by statute or by court decision and has been declared unethical for life underwriters by their professional organizations.

"3. A life underwriter proposes a certain life insurance plan to a prospective client; the client submits the proposed plan to his attorney for his legal opinion. The attorney approves the plan, but for reasons of personal advantage to himself advises the client to divert the business and to purchase the necessary life insurance not through the underwriter who submitted the plan but through another underwriter whom the attorney recommends although the interests of the client do not require such substitution.

"4. An attorney promises an underwriter that if he, the underwriter, will induce his clients to refer legal business to the attorney, the attorney will pay to the underwriter a share of the fees resulting from such business.

"5. To advertise himself and to promote his sale of life insurance, a life underwriter desires to use a lawyer's legal opinion in relation to a specific plan by using the lawyer's name and opinion in a general circular or as a selling document. At the underwriter's request, a lawyer furnishes such an opinion knowing (*a*) that the attorney's name will be thus advertised and utilized by the underwriter and (*b*) that the opinion may mislead the person to whom it is exhibited to his detriment unless it is adapted to the facts of his particular case. This form of business solicitation by life underwriters has been condemned by their profession and by this Association's Committee on Unauthorized Practice of the Law."

II.

The National Conference considers it to be in the interest of cooperation between life underwriters and lawyers and of better service to the public, that all life underwriters be guided by the following principles:

1. A life underwriter has no right to practice law or to give legal advice or to hold himself out as having such rights. He should not attempt to do so directly or indirectly. Therefore, he must never prepare for execution by his client legal documents of any kind, such as wills or codicils thereto, trust agreements, corporation charters, minutes, by-laws, or business insurance agreements. When submitting an involved mode of settlement, or one which may affect a client's prior disposition of property by his Last Will and Testament, the life underwriter should suggest that the same be submitted to the client's attorney for approval.

In estate planning, all transfers of property, except simple modes of settlement under life insurance policies or changes of beneficiary thereof, should be recommended subject to the approval of the client's attorney. Since these decisions should in the final analysis be subject to the approval of the client's attorney, it is important for the life underwriter to collaborate with his client's attorney as early as possible in the negotiations so as to afford his client the safest and most effective service.

It is improper for a life underwriter, in submitting to his client an estate planning report, to attach thereto or insert therein any forms of legal instruments or of specific legal clauses.

2. A life underwriter should never dissuade a client from seeking the advice of legal counsel. It is improper for a life underwriter to attempt to divert legal business from one attorney to another.

3. It is improper for a life underwriter to furnish attorneys who will give legal advice to the life underwriter's clients or prospective clients.

4. A life underwriter must never share or participate in an attorney's fee; a life underwriter must not pay directly or indirectly any part of his commission to an attorney or any other person not a life underwriter, whether or not such sharing in commissions is known to the insured.

It should be noted, in this connection, that in most of the states participation in commissions on life insurance contracts by any person other than a duly licensed life insurance agent, has been condemned by statute or by court decision and has been declared unethical for life underwriters by their professional organizations.

5. A life underwriter may properly obtain legal advice or a written legal opinion from an attorney for his own guidance; it is improper conduct, however, to circularize any such legal opinion, or to use it as a selling document.

Nothing herein contained is intended to restrict or limit the life underwriter's legitimate activities in measuring the client's need for life insurance, determining the amount and type needed, developing a comprehensive life insurance program in relation with the client's other plans and affairs, and selling such insurance; the ethics of his profession require him not to recommend the purchase of additional insurance unless needed. Such activities are for the benefit of those insured and their dependents only insofar as they are consistent with the foregoing statement of principles.

III.

The National Conference of Lawyers and Life Underwriters recommends to state, district and local bar associations and to state and local associations of life underwriters that cooperative action be taken by them to secure adherence to the principles contained in this Statement and to dispose of misunderstandings between the two groups. The National Conference is authorized to act in an advisory capacity as a clearing house for suggestions and complaints, to aid in establishing, as far as may be practical, a country-wide recognition of these principles, and to aid in the setting up of similar conference groups in the various states and localities. It gladly offers its services in this respect to state, district and local associations of the bar and life underwriters.

V

Statement of Guiding Principles for Relationships between Life Underwriters and Trustmen

In September, 1968, the Executive Committee of the National Association of Life Underwriters and the Executive Committee of the Trust Division of the American Bankers Association issued a *Statement of Guiding Principles for Relationships between Life Underwriters and Trustmen.* That statement reads:

Life Insurance–Trust Relationships Logical. The existence and continuance of active and cooperative relations between life underwriters and trustmen are not only logical but also mutually beneficial because life underwriters and trustmen deal frequently with closely related aspects of the same estates. Consequently, life underwriters and trustmen should have a clear understanding of the basic principles and practices underlying these relationships.

Relationships Focus in Estate Analysis and Insurance Settlement. Life Insurance–Trust relationships focus principally on human and financial aspects of estate analysis. Life underwriters analyze estate assets to determine insurance needs and trustmen analyze estate assets to determine trust needs. In the analysis of the same estate it is desirable for the life underwriter and the trustman to coordinate their efforts so that each may bring to bear upon the analysis his special points of emphasis. Such an analysis usually leads to the realization of the need for a will or trust and a determination of how best to deal with life insurance. Since the mode of settlement of the life insurance is an integral part of the general estate plan, it is desirable in such cases for the life underwriter and the trustman to cooperate toward reaching a recommendation concerning the disposition of the life insurance proceeds which can be presented to the individual's lawyer for consideration.

Life Insurance–Trust Mode of Settlement. The life insurance trust might be likened to a mode of settlement, but, unlike the others, it is a method that requires the introduction of a trustee involving continuous flexible management of the insurance proceeds vested in the trustee. Every mode of settlement has is special function and no single mode is equally appropriate for all cases. Conse-

1231

quently, life underwriters should acquaint their clients with the special and distinctive functions of trusts and modes of settlement and help them select the method best suited to their needs. Trustmen should present the life insurance trust as one, but not as the only method of settlement.

The Use of the Terms "Option" and "Trusts." When not payable in lump sum there are two principal methods of distributing life insurance proceeds— (1) through the optional settlements of the life insurance policies, and (2) through trusts administered by trustee. The term "trust" implies a fiduciary obligation that is enforceable in a court of equity as distinguished from a contractual obligation that is enforceable in a court of law. For the sake of clarity and common understanding of terms a mode of settlement of insurance should be referred to as a "trust" or "trust settlement," only in those cases in which the relation between the life insurance company or the trust institution and the beneficiary is, in fact, an equitable relationship of trustee and beneficiary and not a legal relationship of debtor and creditor such as exists under policy "options."

Life Insurance Options. Both life underwriters and trustmen realize the value and advantages of the optional settlements provided in life insurance policies.

Insurance Trusts. The life insurance trust is a method of settlement especially to be considered in the following situations:

1. When flexibility of administration and the exercise of discretionary powers are needed to meet situations which cannot be foreseen or requirements of beneficiaries that cannot be provided for beforehand;
2. When, in connection with business insurance, there is need for an impartial and responsible third party to carry out the plan under which the insurance was effected;
3. When the immaturity, inexperience, or incompetence of the beneficiaries creates a need for the services of an experienced and objective financial adviser;
4. When the primary purpose of the insurance is to safeguard the estate against complications and shrinkage due to debts, taxes, and administration expenses.

Advice of Life Underwriters and Trustmen Restricted to Their Respective Fields. While life underwriters should be familiar with the basic principles of trust, and trustmen with the basic principles of life insurance, neither life underwriters nor trustmen should give specific information or advice on matters that lie within the province of the other. Instead of offering specific advice or information on trust matters, the underwriter should consult with or call into conference a trustman of the individual's choice; and instead of offering specific advice or information on life insurance matters, the trustman should consult with or call in a life underwriter of the individual's choice.

Life Underwriters and Trustmen Mutually Cooperative. Life underwriters and trustmen are both engaged in the processes of estate creation, conservation, administration and distribution for the same persons. The best interests of the individual and his beneficiaries should be paramount. In promoting the best interests of the individual, the life underwriter and the trustman will work together in mutual respect and cooperation.

W

Personal Life Insurance Trust Agreements[*]

I. A REVOCABLE TRUST AGREEMENT

TRUST AGREEMENT made the 16th day of July, 1971 between the Grantor, JOHN DOE of New York, New York and the Trustee, ABLE TRUST COMPANY, a New York corporation with an office at New York, New York.

WITNESSETH:

1. TRUST PROPERTY. The Grantor has designated the Trustee as beneficiary of the dead proceeds of the insurance policies upon Grantor's life (and the proceeds of, or benefits under, savings, pension, profit sharing, retirement, stock bonus or similar benefit plans provided by Grantor's employer) described in Schedule A while retaining possession of said policies (and evidences of such benefit plans). The Trustee accepts such designation and agrees to hold all such proceeds and additions in trust for the purposes and subject to the terms and conditions of this agreement. The Grantor or any other person may at any time transfer to the trust by further beneficiary designation or by gift, devise, bequest, appointment or otherwise any additional property acceptable to the Trustee. The death proceeds of such insurance (and the proceeds of, or benefits under, such benefit plans), together with any additions, are termed "the trust estate."

2. RIGHTS IN POLICIES (AND BENEFIT PLANS). With respect to any insurance policies (and benefit plans), the death proceeds of which the Grantor has made or may hereafter make subject to this trust, the Grantor reserves all the rights of the owner of such policies (and his interests in such employer benefit plans) and, without the consent or approval of the Trustee or any other person, may sell, assign or hypothecate such policies (and benefit plans) and may exercise any option or privilege granted by such policies (or benefit plans), including, without limitation, the right to change the beneficiaries, to borrow any sum in accordance with the provisions of such policies (or benefit plans), to surrender or convert such policies, to receive all payments,

---

[*] These life insurance trust agreements are liberally based upon those compiled by the Manufacturers Hanover Trust Company for distribution to members of the Bar, with numerous changes made by Virgil N. Woolfolk, Esq., author of Chapter 56. No form is usable without careful consideration by an attorney to see that it carries out the intended results of the grantor and the trustee, both as to the disposition of the income and principal of the trust estate and as to the tax results to be expected.

dividends, loan or surrender values, benefits or privileges of any kind which may accrue on account of such policies (or benefit plans) during the Grantor's lifetime, and generally all the incidents of ownership of such policies. The Trustee shall assent to or join in the execution of any instrument requested by the Grantor to enable the Grantor to exercise the rights so reserved.

3.   REVOCABILITY.   The Grantor hereby reserves the continuing right and power, by instrument (other than a will or codicil thereto) executed and acknowledged by the Grantor and delivered to the Trustee during the Grantor's lifetime, to revoke this trust agreement in whole or in part, or to alter or amend any term or provision thereof in any way, except that the Grantor shall have no power to diminish the compensation of the Trustee or to increase the duties of the Trustee without its written consent. The addition of additional property to the trust in accordance with Article 1 shall not be deemed to increase the duties or obligations of the Trustee.

4.   COLLECTION OF PROCEEDS.   Upon being advised of the maturity of any such policy (or benefit plan) by reason of Grantor's death, the Trustee shall collect the proceeds thereof which shall become payable to it. To facilitate the receipt of such proceeds, the Trustee is authorized to execute and deliver receipts and other instruments, to compromise or adjust disputed claims in such manner as it deems equitable, and to take such steps as it deems appropriate for collection thereof, but the Trustee shall not be obliged to institute any legal proceedings for collection unless there are funds in the trust estate sufficient for that purpose, or unless the Trustee is indemnified to its satisfaction against any loss, liability, cost or expense, including attorney's fees. The Trustee is authorized to use any such funds in the trust estate to pay the costs and expenses of legal proceedings for the collection of such proceeds, and shall be entitled to reimbursement from the trust estate for any advances made for such purposes. Upon payment to the Trustee of the amount found to be due under each policy (or benefit plan) subject to this trust, the payor shall be relieved of all further liability thereon, and no payor shall be responsible for the application of any proceeds paid to the Trustee or for the carrying out of any of the provisions of this agreement.

5.   DISPOSITIVE PROVISIONS.   During the life of the Grantor, any and all dividends, disability benefits or other payments which may be received by the Trustee shall be forthwith paid to the Grantor. Upon the death of the Grantor, the Trustee shall hold and dispose of the trust estate as follows:

> (*Here insert provisions for disposition of the income and principal of the trust estate after Grantor's death.*)

6.   TERMINATION OF SMALL TRUST.   Anything in this agreement to the contrary notwithstanding, if, at any time after Grantor's death, the principal of any trust or separate share hereunder has a fair market value of less than $_____, the Trustee may in its sole discretion (but shall not be required to) terminate such trust or separate share and distribute the entire principal thereof and all accrued and undistributed income thereon, outright and free of trust, to the person or persons then entitled to receive the income and in the same proportions, if more than one. If income is then being distributed among a class, the same discretions granted to the Trustee concerning the distributions of the income of such trust shall apply to the distribution of principal under this Article. The Trustee shall not be accountable to any persons other than those to whom such distribution is made.

7.   DIRECTIONS GOVERNING DISPOSITIVE PROVISIONS.   Anything in this agreement to the contrary notwithstanding:

A.   Unless the contrary is expressly stated, each gift made herein of any estate or interest shall be contingent upon survivorship at the time such gift vests in possession, all distributions or divisions to or among "descendants" or "issue" shall be made *per stirpes* and not *per capita.*

B.   Any person occupying any status by adoption, and descendants of the blood or adopted descendants of such person, shall take under this agreement to the same extent as if occupying such status by blood.

C.   In case any beneficiary of this agreement and the Grantor, or any income beneficiary and remainderman of any trust, shall die in such circumstances that there is no sufficient evidence that they died otherwise than simultaneously, it shall be conclusively deemed that such beneficiary predeceased the Grantor or that such remainderman predeceased such income beneficiary, as the case may be.

(Consider whether this presumption should be reversed as to the Grantor and Grantor's spouse.)

D.   Income shall be paid at least quarterly unless accumulation of income is authorized. Whenever provision is made for payment of principal or income to any person, the same may instead be applied for the benefit of such person. Application of principal or income for the benefit of a person under legal disability may be made directly, or in the discretion of the Trustee, by payment to his or her parent or spouse or his or her guardian or committee in whatever jurisdiction appointed, or to any one with whom such person resides, and the receipt of the one to whom payment is made shall be a full acquittance in respect of any property so applied.

E.   The Trustee shall be free to exercise liberally any power to make discretionary payments of principal or income and shall not be restrained by the interests of persons other than the person to whom a given payment is to be made. In exercising its discretion, however, the Trustee shall consider the income of said person, and in so doing may rely upon any statement of income furnished by or on behalf of that person. The decision of the Trustee as to the purpose, time and amount of any such payment shall be conclusive upon all beneficiaries of this agreement.

F.   If upon the termination of any trust any property would vest free of trust in a minor, then the Trustee may, but need not, retain the same as donee of a power during minority to manage property vested in an infant, and apply the income and principal for the maintenance, education and support of such minor, accumulating any income not so applied, until such minor attains majority or until such minor's prior death, when all remaining principal and accumulated income shall be paid to such minor or to his or her estate.

G.   No part of any income received by the Trustee on property originally transferred or subsequently added to this trust shall be deemed to be principal by reason of the fact that it may have accrued prior to the time of such transfer or addition.

8.   POWERS OF THE TRUSTEE.   Without limiting any other powers granted by this agreement or authorized by law, the Trustee shall have the following powers and discretion which shall extend to the trust estate, to any income until its distribution, and to property held as donee of a power during minority to manage property vested in an infant, and which the Trustee may exercise in its sole and absolute discretion whenever and as often as it may deem advisable without application to or approval by any court:

A.   To retain and to purchase or otherwise acquire stocks, whether common or preferred, bonds, obligations, or any other property, real or personal, of whatsoever nature, wheresoever situated, without duty to diversify and whether or not the same may be authorized by law for the investment of trust funds.

B.   To sell at public or private sale, exchange, mortgage, lease without statutory or other limitation as to duration, partition, grant options on, alter, improve, demolish buildings or otherwise deal with any property, real or personal, upon any terms and whether for cash or upon credit.

C.   To exercise in person or by proxy all voting, conversion, subscription or other rights incident to the ownership of any property, including the right to participate in any corporate reorganization, merger or other transaction and to retain any property received thereunder and the right to delegate discretionary power.

D.   To compromise or arbitrate claims; to prepay or accept prepayment of any debt and to enforce or abstain from enforcing, extend, modify or release any right or claim or to hold any claim after maturity without extension, with or without consideration.

E.   To hold separate shares *in solido,* and to hold property in bearer form or in the name of a nominee or nominees.

F.   To execute and deliver deeds or other instruments, with or without covenants, warranties and representations and with or without consideration, including releases which shall discharge the recipient from responsibility for property receipted for thereby.

G.   To abstain from rendering or filing any inventory or periodic account in any court.

H.   To make division or distribution in cash or in kind or partly in each.

I.   To purchase any property at such price as the Trustee shall determine from, and to lend money at such rate of interest as the Trustee shall determine to, the executor or administrator of the Grantor's estate, whether or not the Trustee shall be acting as an executor or administrator thereof in a separate capacity.

J.   Generally, to exercise in good faith and with reasonable care all investment and administrative powers and discretion of an absolute owner which may lawfully be conferred upon a fiduciary.

9.   RESIGNATION OF TRUSTEE AND APPOINTMENT OF SUCCESSORS.   Any Trustee may resign at any time by delivering or mailing written and acknowledged notice of such resignation to the Grantor, or if the Grantor be dead or under any legal disability, to each beneficiary of the income not under any legal disability and each beneficiary not under any legal disability who would be entitled to a share of the principal if the trust were to terminate at the time of mailing or delivering such notice. Such resignation shall take effect upon the date specified in such notice, not less than 30 days after such mailing or delivery, and upon the date so specified all duties of the Trustee so resigning shall cease. In case of any vacancy in the office of Trustee, a successor Trustee may be appointed by written instrument signed and acknowledged by the Grantor, or if the Grantor be dead or under any legal disability, signed and acknowledged by a majority of those beneficiaries not under any legal disability who either are entitled to the income or would be entitled to the principal if the trust were to terminate at the time of such appointment, and such appointment shall take effect upon the acceptance thereof by the Trustee so appointed. Such instrument of appointment may specify the commissions of the successor Trustee so appointed. All provisions of this agreement shall apply to any successor Trustee as if originally named herein.

10. COMMISSIONS.

*(Here insert provisions for the compensation of the
Trustee, both before and after Grantor's death.)*

11. BOND. No Trustee or donee of a power during minority to manage property vested in an infant shall be required to give bond for any purpose.

12. ACCOUNTINGS. The Trustee may settle its account of any trust hereunder at any time by agreement or judicially. An agreement made with those beneficiaries who are subject to no legal disability and who at the time are entitled to the income or would be entitled to the principal if the same were then distributable, shall bind all persons, whether or not then in being or of legal capacity, then or thereafter entitled to any principal or income of the trust accounted for, and shall release and discharge the Trustee for the acts and proceedings embraced in the account as effectively as a judicial settlement.

13. ESTATE TAXES. In case any claim that the trust estate or any part thereof shall be chargeable with any estate, legacy, succession, transfer, inheritance or similar tax or duty, or a share thereof, by reason of the death of any person, the Trustee may pay the amount thereof to the legal representative of the estate of said person or direct to any collector of such taxes and may subject itself and the trust estate to the jurisdiction of any court within or without the State of New York in order to determine or apportion such taxes, irrespective of the domicile of said person at his or her death; provided, however, that this paragraph shall not be deemed of itself to create any liability for such taxes or any part thereof. (In making such payments to Grantor's legal representative, the Trustee is directed not to distribute the proceeds of or benefits under any savings, pension, profit sharing, retirement, stock bonus or similar benefit plan which would be excludable from Grantor's gross estate for Federal estate tax purposes if payable to any beneficiary other than Grantor's legal representative.) The Trustee may rely upon the statement of said legal representative as to the liability of any trust or separate share for a share of any such tax as to the correctness of the assessment, method of apportionment, and the amount payable by any trust or share hereunder and may make payment to the legal representative of the estate of said decedent without further duty of inquiry or obligation to see to the application thereof by such legal representative, and such payment shall be a full and complete discharge to the Trustee with respect thereto.

*(Consider whether taxes should be apportioned among
separate shares if there are more than one.)*

14. DEFINITION OF TERMS. The word "Trustee" and the pronouns therefor as used in this agreement shall be construed as masculine, feminine or neuter and in the singular or plural, as the sense requires.

15. EFFECTIVE DATE AND GOVERNING LAW. This trust agreement shall not take effect until both the Grantor and the Trustee have executed it, and shall be construed, regulated and administered in all respects in accordance with the laws of the State of New York.

WITNESS the due execution hereof by the parties hereto as of the day and year first above written.

_____

Grantor

ABLE TRUST COMPANY

BY _____

(ATTEST)

(ACKNOWLEDGEMENTS)

SCHEDULE A

of Trust Agreement dated July 16, 1971 made between JOHN DOE, as Grantor, and ABLE TRUST COMPANY, as Trustee.

———:0:—•—

The Grantor has revocably designated the Trustee as beneficiary of the death proceeds of the insurance policies upon Grantor's life (and the death proceeds of or benefits under certain benefit plans) as follows:

Policy or Certificate Number	Company Name (or Benefit Plan Identification)	Face Amount

_____
Grantor

ABLE TRUST COMPANY

By _____
Trustee

II. AN IRREVOCABLE TRUST AGREEMENT

TRUST AGREEMENT made the 16th day of July, 1971 between the Grantor, JOHN DOE of New York, New York, and the Trustee, ABLE TRUST COMPANY, a New York corporation with an office at New York, New York.

WITNESSETH:

1. TRUST PROPERTY.   The Grantor has designated the Trustee as beneficiary of the proceeds of the insurance policies upon the Grantor's life described in Schedule A, and has assigned all the Grantor's incidents of ownership thereof and delivered said policies to the Trustee. The Trustee accepts such designation,

assignment and delivery, and agrees to hold said policies and all such proceeds and additions in trust for the purposes and subject to the terms and conditions of this agreement. The Grantor or any other person may at any time transfer to the trust by further beneficiary designation, assignment and delivery, or by gift, devise, bequest, appointment or otherwise, any additional property acceptable to the Trustee. Said policies, proceeds, and additions are termed "the trust estate."

2. RIGHTS IN POLICIES. With respect to any insurance policies which are or may become subject to this trust, the Trustee shall have all the rights of the owner of such policies and, without the consent or approval of the Grantor or of any other person, may sell, assign or hypothecate such policies and may exercise any option or privilege granted by such policies, including, without limitation, the right to change the beneficiaries of such policies, to borrow any sum in accordance with the provisions of such policies, to surrender or convert such policies, to receive all payments, dividends, loan or surrender values, benefits or privileges of any kind which may accrue on account of such policies during the Grantor's lifetime, and generally all the incidents of ownership of such policies. The grantor shall assent to or join in the execution of any instrument requested by the Trustee to enable it to exercise the rights transferred to it.

3. PRIOR TO MATURITY OF POLICIES. Prior to the maturity of any such policy by reason of the Grantor's death or otherwise, the Trustee shall use its best efforts, upon receiving timely written notice that any premiums, dues, assessments or other charges due or to become due upon said policy will not be or have not been paid within the allowable grace period, to borrow against the cash value of said policy or of any other policy or policies then a part of the trust estate, to convert said policy to extended term, paid-up or any other form of insurance to the extent the cash value of said policy will permit, or to surrender said policy or any other policy or policies then a part of the trust estate for the cash surrender value or values thereof and to use cash so received and the income therefrom for the payment of premiums, dues, assessments and other charges then or thereafter becoming due upon any policy or policies from time to time a part of the trust estate; if any such action has to be taken, the Trustee shall be entitled to receive out of the trust estate additional reasonable compensation for its time and study devoted to deciding upon and carrying out the particular alternative taken. Except as directed in the preceding sentence, the Trustee shall not be obliged to pay any premiums, dues, assessments or other charges which may become due and payable on any policies, or to see that such payments are made, or to notify the Grantor or any other person that such payments are or will become due, and the Trustee shall not be liable for any failure by the Grantor or any other person to make such payments. Neither the Trustee nor the Grantor shall be deemed, because of this agreement, to have entered into any covenant to keep such policies in force.

4. IRREVOCABILITY. The Grantor has been advised of the difference between a revocable and an irrevocable trust, and declares this trust agreement, and the estates and interests hereby created, to be irrevocable.

5. COLLECTION OF PROCEEDS. Upon being advised of the maturity of any policy then a part of the trust estate by reason of Grantor's death or otherwise, the Trustee shall collect the proceeds thereof which shall become payable to it. To facilitate the receipt of such proceeds, the Trustee is authorized to execute and deliver receipts and other instruments, to compromise or adjust disputed claims in such manner as it deems equitable, and to take such steps as it deems appropriate for collection thereof, but the Trustee shall not be obliged to institute any legal proceedings for collection unless there are funds in the trust estate sufficient for that purpose, or unless the Trustee is indemnified to

its satisfaction against any loss, liability, cost or expense, including attorney's fees. The Trustee is authorized to use any such funds in the trust estate to pay the costs and expenses of legal proceedings for the collection of such proceeds, and shall be entitled to reimbursement from the trust estate for any advances made for such purposes. Upon payment to the Trustee of the amount found to be due under each policy subject to this trust, the payor shall be relieved of all further liability thereon and no payor shall be responsible for the application of any proceeds paid to the Trustee or for the carrying out of any of the provisions of this agreement.

6.   DISPOSITIVE PROVISIONS.   The Trustee shall hold and dispose of the trust estate as follows:

> *(Here insert provisions for the disposition of the income and principal of the trust estate.)*

7.   TERMINATION OF SMALL TRUST.

> *(Here insert language similar to Article 6, the Revocable Trust form.)*

8.   DIRECTIONS GOVERNING DISPOSITIVE PROVISIONS.

> *(Here insert language similar to Article 7, the Revocable Trust form.)*

9.   POWERS OF THE TRUSTEE.

> *(Here insert language similar to Article 8, the Revocable Trust form.)*

10.   RESIGNATION OF TRUSTEE AND APPOINTMENT OF SUCCESSORS.   Any Trustee may resign at any time by delivering or mailing written and acknowledged notice of such resignation to each beneficiary of the income not under any legal disability and each beneficiary not under any legal disability who would be entitled to a share of the principal if the trust were to terminate at the time of mailing or delivering such notice. Such resignation shall take effect upon the date specified in such notice, not less than 30 days after such mailing or delivery, and upon the date so specified all duties of the Trustee so resigning shall cease. In case of any vacancy in the office of Trustee, a successor Trustee may be appointed by written instrument signed and acknowledged by a majority of those beneficiaries not under any legal disability who either are entitled to the income or would be entitled to the principal if the trust were to terminate at the time such appoinment, and such appointment shall take effect upon the acceptance thereof by the Trustee so appointed. Such instrument of appointment may specify the commissions of the successor Trustee so appointed. All provisions of this trust agreement shall apply to any successor Trustee as if originally named herein.

11.   COMMISSIONS.

> *(Here insert provisions for the compensation of the Trustee, both before and after Grantor's death.)*

12.   BOND.   No Trustee or donee of a power during minority to manage property vested in an infant shall be required to give bond for any purpose.

13. ACCOUNTINGS. The Trustee may settle its account of any trust hereunder at any time by agreement or judicially. An agreement made with those beneficiaries who are subject to no legal disability and who at the time are entitled to the income or would be entitled to the principal if the same were then distributable, shall bind all persons, whether or not then in being or of legal capacity, then or thereafter entitled to any principal or income of the trust accounted for, and shall release and discharge the Trustee for the acts and proceedings embraced in the account as effectively as a judicial settlement.

14. ESTATE TAXES. In case any claim that the trust estate or any part thereof shall be chargeable with any estate, legacy, succession, transfer, inheritance or similar tax or duty, or a share thereof, by reason of the death of any person, the Trustee may pay the amount thereof to the legal representative of the estate of said person or direct to any collector of such taxes and may subject itself and the trust estate to the jurisdiction of any court within or without the State of New York in order to determine or apportion such taxes, irrespective of the domicile of said person at his or her death; provided, however, that this paragraph shall not be deemed of itself to create any liability for such taxes or any part thereof. The Trustee may rely upon the statement of said legal representative as to the liability of any trust or separate share for a share of any such tax as to the correctness of the assessment, method of apportionment, and the amount payable by any trust or share hereunder and may make payment to the legal representative of the estate of said decedent without further duty of inquiry or obligation to see to the application thereof by such legal representative, and such payment shall be a full and complete discharge to the Trustee with respect thereto.

15. DEFINITION OF TERMS. The word "Trustee" and the pronouns therefor as used in this agreement shall be construed as masculine, feminine or neuter and in the singular or plural, as the sense requires.

16. EFFECTIVE DATE AND GOVERNING LAW. This trust agreement shall not take effect until both the Grantor and the Trustee have executed it, and shall be construed, regulated and administered in all respects in accordance with the laws of the State of New York.

WITNESS the due execution hereof by the parties hereto as of the day and year first above written.

_____

Grantor

ABLE TRUST COMPANY

BY _____

(ATTEST)

(ACKNOWLEDGEMENTS)

SCHEDULE A

of Trust Agreement dated July 16, 1971 made between JOHN DOE, as Grantor, and ABLE TRUST COMPANY, as Trustee.

——:0:——

Policy Number   *Company Name*   *Face Amount*

_____

Grantor

ABLE TRUST COMPANY

By _____
                                        Trustee

X

NAIC Model Act
Relating to Unfair
Methods of Competition
and Unfair and Deceptive
Acts and Practices in the
Business of Insurance
(Revised 1972)

Section 1—Declaration of Purpose

The purpose of this Act is to regulate trade practices in the business of insurance in accordance with the intent of Congress as expressed in the Act of Congress of March 9, 1945 (Public Law 15, 79th Congress), by defining, or providing for the determination of, all such practices in this state which constitute unfair methods of competition or unfair or deceptive acts or practices and by prohibiting the trade practices so defined or determined.

Section 2—Definitions

When used in this Act:

a) "Person" shall mean any individual, corporation, association, partnership, reciprocal exchange, inter-insurer, Lloyds insurer, fraternal benefit society, and any other legal entity engaged in the business of insurance, including agents, brokers and adjusters. "Person" shall also mean medical service plans and hospital service plans as defined in Section ————. For purposes of this Act, medical and hospital service plans shall be deemed to be engaged in the business of insurance.

(Drafting Note: This definition could also include dental, optometric, and other service plans. The enabling statutes of all service plans should also be amended to make them subject to this Act.)

b) ("Commissioner") shall mean the (Commissioner) of Insurance of this state.

c) "Insurance policy" or "insurance contract" shall mean any contract of insurance, indemnity, medical or hospital service, suretyship, or annuity issued, proposed for issuance, or intended for issuance by any person.

(Drafting Note: Each state may wish to consider the advisability of defining "insurance" for purposes of this Act if its present insurance code is not satisfactory in this regard. In some cases a cross reference will be sufficient. "Service contract" is intended to cover the product issued by medical and hospital service plans and should be changed to conform to the laws of each state.)

Section 3—Unfair Methods of Competition and Unfair or Deceptive Acts or Practices Prohibited

No person shall engage in this state in any trade practice which is defined in this Act as, or determined pursuant to Section 7 of this Act to be, an unfair method of competition or an unfair or deceptive act or practice in the business of insurance.

Section 4—Unfair Methods of Competition and Unfair or Deceptive Acts or Practices Defined

The following are hereby defined as unfair methods of competition and unfair or deceptive acts or practices in the business of insurance:

(1) *Misrepresentations and false advertising of insurance policies.* Making issuing, circulating, or causing to be made, issued or circulated, any estimate, illustrations, circular, statement, sales presentation, omission, or comparison which:

a) misrepresents the benefits, advantages, conditions, or terms of any insurance policy; or

b) misrepresents the dividends or share of the surplus to be received on any insurance policy; or

c) makes any false or misleading statements as to the dividends or share of surplus previously paid on any insurance policy; or

d) is misleading or is a misrepresentation as to the financial condition of any person, or as to the legal reserve system upon which any life insurer operates; or

e) uses any name or title of any insurance policy or class of insurance policies misrepresenting the true nature thereof; or

f) is a misrepresentation for the purpose of inducing or tending to induce the lapse, forfeiture, exchange, conversion, or surrender of any insurance policy; or

g) is a misrepresentation for the purpose of effecting a pledge or assignment of or effecting a loan against any insurance policy; or

h) misrepresents any insurance policy as being shares of stock.

(2) *False information and advertising generally.* Making, publishing, disseminating, circulating or placing before the public, or causing, directly or indirectly, to be made, published, disseminated, circulated, or placed before the public, in a newspaper, magazine or other publication, or in the form of a notice, circular, pamphlet, letter or poster or over any radio or television station, or in any other way, an advertisement, announcement or statement containing any assertion, representation or statement with respect to the business of insurance or with respect to any person in the conduct of his insurance business, which is untrue, deceptive or misleading.

(3) *Defamation.* Making, publishing, disseminating, or circulating, directly or indirectly, or aiding, abetting or encouraging the making, publishing, disseminating or circulating of any oral or written statement or any pamphlet, circular, article or literature which is false, or maliciously critical of or derogatory to the financial condition of any person, and which is calculated to injure such person.

(4) *Boycott, coercion and intimidation.* Entering into any agreement to commit, or by any concerted action committing any act of boycott, coercion or

intimidation resulting in or tending to result in reasonable restraint of, or monopoly in, the business of insurance.

(5) *False statements and entries.*

a) Knowingly filing with any supervisory or other public official, or knowingly making, publishing, disseminating, circulating or delivering to any person, or placing before the public; or knowingly causing, directly or indirectly, to be made, published, disseminated, circulated, delivered to any person, or placed before the public, any false material statement of fact as to the financial condition of a person.

b) Knowingly making any false entry of a material fact in any book, report or statement of any person, or knowingly omitting to make a true entry of any material fact pertaining to the business of such person in any book, report or statement of such person.

(6) *Stock operations and advisory board contracts.* Issuing or delivering or permitting agents, officers or employees to issue or deliver, agency company stock or other capital stock, or benefit certificates or shares in any common-law corporation, or securities or any special or advisory board contracts or other contracts of any kind promising returns and profits as an inducement to insurance.

(7) *Unfair discrimination.*

a) Making or permitting any unfair discrimination between individuals of the same class and equal expectation of life in the rates charged for any contract of life insurance or of life annuity or in the dividends or other benefits payable thereon, or in any other of the terms and conditions of such contract.

b) Making or permitting any unfair discrimination between individuals of the same class and of essentially the same hazard in the amount of premium, policy fees, or rates charged for any policy or contract of accident or health insurance or in the benefits payable thereunder, or in any of the terms or conditions of such contract, or in any other manner whatever.

(Drafting Note: In the event that unfair discrimination in connection with accident and health coverage is treated in other statutes, this paragraph should be omitted.)

(8) *Rebates.*

a) Except as otherwise expressly provided by law, knowingly permitting or offering to make or making any contract of life insurance, life annuity or accident and health insurance, or agreement as to such contract other than as plainly expressed in the insurance contract issued thereon, or paying or allowing, or giving or offering to pay, allow, or give, directly or indirectly, as inducement to such insurance or annuity, any rebate of premiums payable on the contract, or any special favor or advantage in the dividends or other benefits thereon, or any valuable consideration or inducement whatever not specified in the contract; or giving, or selling, or purchasing or offering to give, sell, or purchase as inducement to such insurance contract or annuity or in connection therewith, any stocks, bonds, or other securities of any insurance company or other corporation, association, or partnership, or any dividends or profits accrued thereon, or anything of value whatsoever not specified in the contract.

b) Nothing in clause (7) or paragraph (a) of clause (8) of this subsetion shall be construed as including within the definition of discrimination or rebates any of the following practices:

(i) in the case of any contract of life insurance or life annuity, paying bonuses to policyholders or otherwise abating their premiums in whole or in part out of surplus accumulated from nonparticipating insurance, provided that any such bonuses or abatement of premiums shall be fair and equitable to policyholders and for the best interests of the company and its policyholders;

(ii) in the case of life insurance policies issued on the industrial debit plan, making allowance to policyholders who have continuously for a specified period made premium payments directly to an office of the insurer in an amount which fairly represents the saving in collection expenses;

(iii) readjustment of the rate of premium for a group insurance policy based on the loss or expense thereunder, at the end of the first or any subsequent policy year of insurance thereunder, which may be made retroactive only for such policy year.

(Drafting Note: Each state may wish to examine its rating laws to assure that they contain sufficient provision against rebating. If they do not, this section might be expanded to cover all lines of insurance.)

(9) *Unfair claim settlement practices.* Committing or performing with such frequency as to indicate a general business practice any of the following:

a) misrepresenting pertinent facts or insurance policy provisions relating to coverages at issue;

b) failing to acknowledge and act reasonably promptly upon communications with respect to claims arising under insurance policies;

c) failing to adopt and implement reasonable standards for the prompt investigation of claims arising under insurance policies;

d) refusing to pay claims without conducting a reasonable investigation based upon all available information;

e) failing to affirm or deny coverage of claims within a reasonable time after proof of loss statements have been completed;

f) not attempting in good faith to effectuate prompt, fair and equitable settlements of claims in which liability has become reasonably clear;

g) compelling insureds to institute litigation to recover amounts due under an insurance policy by offering substantially less than the amounts ultimately recovered in actions brought by such insured;

h) attempting to settle a claim for less than the amount to which a reasonable man would have believed he was entitled by reference to written or printed advertising material accompanying or made part of an application;

i) attempting to settle claims on the basis of an application which was altered without notice to, or knowledge or consent of, the insured;

j) making claims payments to insureds or beneficiaries not accompanied by a statement setting forth the coverage under which payments are being made;

k) making known to insureds or claimants a policy of appealing from arbitration awards in favor of insureds or claimants for the purpose of compelling them to accept settlements or compromises less than the amount awarded in arbitration;

l) delaying the investigation or payment of claims by requiring an insured, claimant, or the physician of either to submit a preliminary claim report and then requiring the subsequent submission of formal proof of loss forms, both of which submissions contain substantially the same information;

m) failing to promptly settle claims, where liability has become reasonably clear, under one portion of the insurance policy coverage in order to influence settlements under other portions of the insurance policy coverage;

n) failing to promptly provide a reasonable explanation of the basis in the insurance policy in relation to the facts or applicable law for denial of a claim or for the offer of a compromise settlement.

(*10*) *Failure to maintain complaint handling procedures.* Failure of any person to maintain a complete record of all the complaints which it has received since the date of its last examination under Section ———. This record shall indicate the total number of complaints, their classification by line of insurance, the nature of each complaint, the disposition of these complaints, and the time it took to process each complaint. For purposes of this subsection, "complaint" shall mean any written communication primarily expressing a grievance.
(Drafting Note: Each state may wish to consider exempting agents and brokers from this subsection.)

(*11*) *Misrepresentation in insurance applications.* Making false or fraudulent statements or representations on or relative to an application for an insurance policy, for the purpose of obtaining a fee, commission, money, or other benefit from any insurers, agent, broker, or individual.

(*12*) *Any violation of any one of Section* ———, ———.
(Drafting Note: Insert section numbers of any other sections of the Insurance Law which it is deemed desirable or necessary to include as an unfair trade practice.)

Section 5—Favored Agent or Insurer; Coercion of Debtors

a) No person may (i) require, as a condition precedent to the lending of money or extension of credit, or any renewal thereof, that the person to whom such money or credit is extended or whose obligation the creditor is to acquire or finance, negotiate any policy or contract of insurance through a particular insurer or group of insurers or agent or broker or group of agents or brokers; or

(ii) unreasonably disapprove the insurance policy provided by a borrower for the protection of the property securing the credit or lien; or

(iii) require directly or indirectly that any borrower, mortgagor, purchaser, insurer, broker, or agent pay a separate charge, in connection with the handling of any insurance policy required as security for a loan on real estate, or pay a separate charge to substitute the insurance policy of one insurer for that of another; or

(iv) use or disclose information resulting from a requirement that a borrower, mortgagor or purchaser furnish insurance of any kind on real property being conveyed or used as collateral security to a loan, when such information is to the advantage of the mortgagee, vendor, or lender, or is to the detriment of the borrower, mortgagor, purchaser, insurer, or the agent or broker complying with such a requirement.

b) (i) Paragraph (a) (iii) does not include the interest which may be charged on premium loans or premium advancements in accordance with the security instrument.

(ii) For purposes of paragraph (*a*) (ii), such disapproval shall be deemed unreasonable if it is not based solely on reasonable standards uniformly applied, relating to the extent of coverage required and the financial soundness and the services of an insurer. Such standards shall not discriminate against any particular type of insurer, nor shall such standards call for the disapproval of an insurance policy because such policy contains coverage in addition to that required.

(iii) The (Commissioner) may investigate the affairs of any person to whom this subsection applies to determine whether such person has violated this subsection. If a violation of this subsection is found, the person in violation shall be subject to the same procedures and penalties as are applicable to other provisions of this Act.

(iv) For purposes of this section, "person" includes any individual, corporation, association, partnership, or other legal entity.

Section 6—Power of (Commissioner)

The (Commissioner) shall have power to examine and investigate into the affairs of every person engaged in the business of insurance in this state in order to determine whether such person has been or is engaged in any unfair method of competition or in any unfair or deceptive act or practice prohibited by Section 3 of this Act.

Section 7—Defined and Undefined Practices: Hearings, Witnesses,
Appearances, Production of Books and Service of Process

a) Whenever the (Commissioner) shall have reason to believe that any such person has been engaged or is engaging in this state in any unfair method of competition or any unfair or deceptive act or practice whether or not defined in Sections 4 or 5, and that a proceeding by him in respect thereto would be to the interest of the public, he shall issue and serve upon such person a statement of the charges in that respect and a notice of a hearing thereon to be held at a time and place fixed in the notice, which shall not be less than _____ days after the date of the service thereof.

b) At the time and place fixed for such hearing, such person shall have an opportunity to be heard and to show cause why an order should not be made by the (Commissioner) requiring such person to cease and desist from the acts, methods or practices so complained of. Upon good cause shown, the (Commissioner) shall permit any person to intervene, appear and be heard at such hearing by counsel or in person.

c) Nothing contained in this Act shall require the observance of any such hearing of formal rules of pleading or evidence.

d) The (Commissioner), upon such hearing, may administer oaths, examine and cross-examine witnesses, receive oral and documentary evidence, and shall have the power to subpoena witnesses, compel their attendance, and require the production of books, papers, records, correspondence, or other documents which he deems relevant to the inquiry. The (Commissioner), upon such hearing, may, and upon the request of any party shall, cause to be made a stenographic record of all the evidence and all the proceedings had at such hearing. If no stenographic record is made and if a judicial review is sought, the (Commissioner) shall prepare a statement of the evidence and proceeding for use on review. In case of a refusal of any person to comply with any subpoena issued hereunder or to testify with respect to any matter concerning which he may be lawfully interrogated, the _____ court of _____ county or the county where such party resides, on application of the (Commissioner), may issue an order requiring such person to comply with such subpoena and to testify; and any failure to obey any such order of the court may be punished by the court as a contempt thereof.

e) Statements of charges, notices, orders, and other processes of the (Commissioner) under this Act may be served by anyone duly authorized by the (Commissioner), either in the manner provided by law for service of process in civil actions, or by registering and mailing a copy thereof to the person affected by such statement, notice, order, or other process at his or its residence or principal office or place of business. The verified return by the person so serving such statement, notice, order, or other process, setting forth the manner of such service, shall be proof of the same, and the return postcard receipt for such statement, notice, order or other process, registered and mailed as aforesaid, shall be proof of the service of the same.

Section 8—Cease and Desist and Penalty Orders and Modifications Thereof

a) If, after such hearing, the (Commissioner) shall determine that the person charged has engaged in an unfair method of competition or an unfair or deceptive act or practice, he shall reduce his findings to writing and shall issue and cause to be served upon the person charged with the violation a copy of such findings and an order requiring such person to cease and desist from engaging in such method of competition, act or practice and if the act or practice is a violation of Sections 4 or 5, the (Commissioner) may at his discretion order any one or more of the following:

(A) payment of a monetary penalty of not more than $1,000 for each and every act or violation; but not to exceed an aggregate penalty of $10,000, unless the person knew or reasonably should have known he was in violation of this Act, in which case the penalty shall be not more than $5,000 for each and every act or violation, but not to exceed an aggregate penalty of $50,000 in any six-month period;

(B) suspension or revocation of the person's license if he knew or reasonably should have known he was in violation of this Act.

b) Until the expiration of the time allowed under Section 9 of this Act for filing a petition for review (by appeal or writ of certiorati) if no such petition has been duly filed within such time, or, if a petition for review has been filed within such time, then until the transcript of the record in the proceeding has been filed in the _____ court, as hereinafter provided, the (Commissioner) may at any time, upon such notice and in such manner as he shall deem proper, modify or set aside in whole or in part any order issued by him under this section.

c) After the expiration of the time allowed for filing such a petition for review, if no such petition has been duly filed within such time, the (Commissioner) may at any time, after notice and opportunity for hearing, reopen and alter, modify or set aside, in whole or in part, any order issued by him under this section, whenever in his opinion conditions of fact or of law have so changed as to require such action or if the public interest shall so require.

Section 9—Judicial Review of Orders

a) Any person subject to an order of the (Commissioner) under Section 8 or Section 11 may obtain a review of such order by filing in the _____ court of _____ county, within _____ days from the date of the service of such order, a written petition praying that the order of the (Commissioner) be set aside. A copy of such petition shall be forthwith served upon the (Commissioner), and thereupon the (Commissioner) forthwith shall certify and file in such court a transcript of the entire record in the proceeding, including all the evidence taken and the report and order of the (Commissioner). Upon such filing of the petition and transcript such court shall have jurisdiction of the proceeding and of the question determined therein, shall determine whether the filing of such petition shall operate as a stay of such order of the (Commissioner), and shall have power to make and enter upon the pleadings, evidence, and proceedings set forth in such transcript a decree modifying, affirming or reversing the order of the (Commissioner), in whole or in part. The findings of the (Commissioner) as to the facts, if supported by _____ evidence, shall be conclusive.

(Drafting Note: Insert appropriate language to accommodate to local procedure the effect given the Commissioner's determination.)

b) To the extent that the order of the (Commissioner) is affirmed, the court shall thereupon issue its own order commanding obedience to the terms of such order of the (Commissioner). If either party shall apply to the court for leave to adduce additional evidence, and shall show to the satisfaction of the court that such additional evidence is material and that there were reasonable grounds for the failure to adduce such evidence in the proceeding before the (Commissioner), the court may order such additional evidence to be taken before the (Commissioner) and to be adduced upon the hearing in such manner and upon such terms and conditions as to the court may seem proper. The (Commissioner), may modify his findings of fact, or make new findings by reason of the additional evidence so taken, and he shall file such modified or new findings which if supported by _____ evidence shall be conclusive, and his recommendation if any, for the modification or setting aside of his original order, with the return of such additional evidence.

(Drafting Note: Insert appropriate language to accommodate to local procedure the effect given the Commissioner's determination. In a state where the final judgment, order or decree would not be subject to review by an appellate court, provision therefor should be here inserted.)

   c) An order issued by the (Commissioner) under section 8 shall become final:

> (1) upon the expiration of the time allowed for filing a petition for review if no such petition has been duly filed within such time, except that the (Commissioner) may thereafter modify or set aside his order to the extent provided in Section 8(*b*); or
>
> (2) upon the final decision of the court if the court directs that the order of the (Commissioner) be affirmed or the petition for review dismissed.

   d) No order of the (Commissioner) under this Act or order of a court to enforce the same shall in any way relieve or absolve any person affected by such order from any liability under any other laws of this state.

Section 10—Judicial Review by Intervenor

   If, after any hearing under Section 7 or Section 11, the report of the (Commissioner) does not charge a violation of this Act, then any intervenor in the proceedings may, within _____ days after the service of such report, cause a petition (notice of appeal) (petition for writ of certiorari) to be filed in the _____ court of _____ county for a review of such report. Upon such review, the court shall have authority to issue appropriate orders and decrees in connection therewith, including, if the court finds that it is to the interest of the public, orders enjoining and restraining the continuance of any method of competition, act or practice which it finds, notwithstanding such report of the (Commissioner), constitutes a violation of this Act and containing penalties pursuant to Section 8.

(Drafting Note: The type of procedure should conform to state procedure. See also note to Section 9 concerning review by appellate courts.)

Section 11—Penalty for Violation of Cease and Desist Orders

   Any person who violates a cease and desist order of the (Commissioner) under Section 8, while such order is in effect, may after notice and hearing and upon order of the (Commissioner) be subject at the discretion of the (Commissioner) to any one or more of the following:

> *a*) a monetary penalty of not more than $10,000 for each and every act or violation; or
>
> *b*) suspension or revocation of such person's license.

Section 12—Regulations

The (Commissioner) may, after notice and hearing, promulgate reasonable rules and regulations as are necessary or proper to identify specific methods of competition or acts or practices which are prohibited by Sections 4 or 5, but the regulations shall not enlarge upon or extend the provisions of Sections 4 and 5. Such regulations shall be subject to review in accordance with Section ——————.

(Drafting Note: Insert section number providing for review of administrative orders.)

Section 13—Provisions of Act Additional to Existing Law

The powers vested in the (Commissioner) by this Act shall be additional to any other powers to enforce any penalties, fines or forfeitures authorized by law with respect to the methods, acts and practices hereby declared to be unfair or deceptive.

Section 14—Immunity from Prosecution

If any person shall ask to be excused from attending and testifying or from producing any books, papers, records, correspondence or other documents at any hearing on the ground that the testimony or evidence required of him may tend to incriminate him or subject him to a penalty or forfeiture, and shall notwithstanding be directed to give such testimony or produce such evidence, he must none the less comply with such direction, but he shall not thereafter be prosecuted or subjected to any penalty or forfeiture for or on account of any transaction, matter or thing concerning which he may testify or produce evidence thereto, and no testimony so given or evidence produced shall be received against him upon any criminal action, investigation or proceeding, provided, however, that no such individual so testifying shall be exempt from prosecution or punishment for any perjury committed by him while so testifying and the testimony or evidence so given or produced shall be admissible against him upon any criminal action, investigation or proceeding concerning such perjury, nor shall he be exempt from the refusal, revocation or suspension of any license, permission or authority conferred, or to be conferred, pursuant to the Insurance Law of this state. Any such individual may execute, acknowledge and file in the office of the (Commissioner) a statement expressly waiving such immunity or privilege in respect to any transaction, matter or thing specified in such statement and thereupon the testimony of such person or such evidence in relation to such transaction, matter or thing may be received or produced before any judge or justice, court, tribunal, grand jury or otherwise, and if so received or produced such individual shall not be entitled to any immunity or privilege on account of any testimony he may so give or evidence so produced.

Section 15—Separability Provision

If any provision of this Act, or the application of such provision to any person or circumstances, shall be held invalid, the remainder of the Act, and the application of such provision to person or circumstances other than those as to which it is held invalid, shall not be affected thereby.

Y

Reinsurance Agreement

_____

of

_____

hereinafter referred to as the "REINSURED," and

THE _____ LIFE INSURANCE COMPANY

of

_____ , _____ ,

hereinafter referred to as the "_____."

REINSURANCE COVERAGE

1. On the basis hereinafter stated, the REINSURED'S excess of individual ordinary Life, Waiver of Premium Disability, and Accidental Death insurance issued directly by the REINSURED on lives having surnames which commence with letters of the alphabet from ____ to ____, inclusive, shall be reinsured with the _____ automatically in accordance with the REINSURED'S individual ordinary underwriting rules or shall be submitted to the _____ on a facultative basis.

2. Subject to the prior approval of the _____ in the case of facultative reinsurance, the liability of the _____ shall begin simultaneously with that of the REINSURED. In no event shall the reinsurance be in force and binding unless the insurance issued directly by the REINSURED is in force and unless the issuance and delivery of such insurance constituted the doing of business in a state of the United States of America or a country in which the REINSURED was properly licensed.

3. The Life and Accidental Death reinsurance under this agreement shall be term insurance for the amount at risk on the portion of the original insurance which is reinsured with the _____. The amount of reinsurance shall be the death benefit provided by the portion of the original insurance which is reinsured with the _____. The amount at risk shall be the amount of reinsurance less the terminal reserve thereon, such difference taken to the nearest dollar. The terminal reserve shall be disregarded on all Accidental Death insurance and on Life insurance if the original insurance is on a level term plan of twenty years or less or on a decreasing term plan.

4. Reinsurance of Disability insurance shall follow the original forms of the REINSURED.

5. Accidental Death reinsurance in amounts less than $500 or Life reinsurance in amounts less than the amount at risk upon $1,000 of insurance shall not be placed in effect under this agreement.

6. The amount of reinsurance under this agreement shall be maintained in force without reduction so long as the amount of insurance carried by the REINSURED on the life remains in force without reduction, except as provided in the "PAYMENT OF REINSURANCE PREMIUMS" and "INCREASE IN LIMIT OF RETENTION" articles.

AUTOMATIC AND FACULTATIVE REINSURANCE

1. When the REINSURED retains its limit of retention, as shown in Schedule A, on a risk specified in paragraph 1 of the "REINSURANCE COVERAGE" article, it may cede and the _____ shall accept automatically reinsurance of Life, Disability, and Accidental Death insurance in amounts not to exceed those shown in Schedule B.

2. Reinsurance shall not be ceded automatically hereunder on any life if the sum of the amount of insurance already in force on that life in the REINSURED and the amount applied for from the REINSURED on the current application exceeds the sum of the amount shown in Schedule B and the REINSURED'S maximum limit of retention for the mortality class, plan of insurance, and age at issue on the current application, nor shall reinsurance be ceded automatically hereunder on any life if the sum of the amount of insurance already in force on that life and the amount applied for currently, in all companies, is in excess of the following amounts:

Ages	Life Insurance Waiver of Premium	Accidental Death
0–20	$ 750,000	$150,000
21–60	2,000,000	150,000

3. Reinsurance on a risk specified in paragraph 1 of the "REINSURANCE COVERAGE" article which may not be ceded automatically under the terms of this agreement or which the REINSURED prefers not to cede automatically shall be submitted upon a facultative basis. Reinsurance on a risk not specified in paragraph 1 of that article may be submitted upon a facultative basis.

PLACING REINSURANCE IN EFFECT

1. To effect automatic reinsurance, the REINSURED shall mail a preliminary notification in substantial accord with Schedule C, Part I, to the _____. The REINSURED shall mail the notification within three working days after it has taken final underwriting action.

2. When the REINSURED submits a risk to the _____ for reinsurance upon a facultative basis, an application for such reinsurance shall be made on a form in substantial accord with Schedule C, Part II. Copies of the original applications, all medical examinations, microscopical reports, inspection reports, and all other information which the REINSURED may have pertaining to the insurability of the risk shall accompany the application. Upon receipt of such application, the _____ shall immediately examine the papers and shall notify the REINSURED of its underwriting action as soon as possible.

3. Within ten working days after the original policy has been reported delivered and paid for, the REINSURED shall mail a reinsurance cession in duplicate to the _____ in substantial accord with Schedule C, Part III. If reinsurance is ceded automatically, the REINSURED shall enter on the cession the insured's build, sex, occupation, impairments, if any, and blood pressure if a medically-examined case; if the risk is substandard, copies of all underwriting information shall accompany the cession. The cession shall be completed by the _____ and one copy returned to the REINSURED.

4. To effect Accidental Death reinsurance apart from life reinsurance, the REINSURED shall mail to the _____ consecutively numbered cards in substantial accord with Schedule C, Part IV. The REINSURED shall send the cards within ten working days after the original policy has been reported delivered and paid for.

COMPUTATION OF REINSURANCE PREMIUMS

1. The premium to be paid to the _____ for Life reinsurance shall be the sum of: (*a*) the appropriate premium rate from the schedule of premiums in Schedule D applied to the appropriate amount at risk reinsured; plus (*b*) the appropriate policy fee as shown in Schedule D; plus (*c*) any flat extra premium charged the insured on the face amount initially reinsured less total allowances in the amount of 75 percent of any first year permanent flat extra premium and 10 percent of any renewal flat extra premium.

2. The portions of the reinsurance premiums described in subparagraphs (*a*) and (*c*) of the preceding paragraph shall hereinafter be referred to as the basic premium.

3. The premium to be paid the _____ for reinsurance of Supplemental Benefits shall be as shown in Schedule D.

4. For technical reasons relating to the uncertain status of deficiency reserve requirements by the various state insurance departments, the Life reinsurance rates cannot be guaranteed for more than one year. On all reinsurance ceded at these rates, however, the _____ anticipates continuing to accept premiums on the basis of the rates shown in Schedule D.

5. When reinsurance is term insurance, premiums for renewal years shall be payable for so long as the reinsurance remains in force.

PAYMENT OF REINSURANCE PREMIUMS

1. The _____ shall send the REINSURED each month a statement in duplicate showing all outstanding first-year policies for which the _____'S records have been completed and a statement in duplicate showing all renewal reinsurance premiums on reinsurance policies having anniversaries in the preceding month.

2. One copy of each statement received from the _____ shall be returned to the _____ not later than fifteen days after the statement was received with notice of any adjustments made necessary by changes in reinsurance during such month. The REINSURED shall remit with such statement the premiums due the _____ as adjusted. Premiums for reinsurance hereunder are payable at the Home Office of the _____ and shall be paid on an annual basis without regard to the manner of payment stipulated in the policy issued by the REINSURED.

3. The payment of reinsurance premiums in accordance with the provisions of the preceding paragraph shall be a condition precedent to the liability of the _____ under reinsurance covered by this agreement. In the event that

reinsurance premiums are not paid as provided in the preceding paragraph, the _____ shall have the right to terminate the reinsurance under all policies having reinsurance premiums in arrears. If the _____ elects to exercise its right of termination, it shall give the REINSURED thirty days' notice of its intention to terminate such reinsurance. If all reinsurance premiums in arrears, including any which may become in arrears during the thirty-day period, are not paid before the expiration of such period, the _____ shall thereupon be relieved of future liability under all reinsurance for which premiums remain unpaid. Policies on which reinsurance premiums subsequently fall due will automatically terminate if reinsurance premiums are not paid when due as provided in paragraph 2 of this Article. The reinsurance so terminated may be reinstated at any time within sixty days of the date of termination upon payment of all reinsurance premiums in arrears; but, in the event of such reinstatement, the _____ shall have no liability in connection with any claims incurred between the date of termination and the date of reinstatement of the reinsurance. The _____'S right to terminate reinsurance as herein provided shall be without prejudice to its right to collect premiums for the period reinsurance was in force prior to the expiration of the thirty-day notice period.

SETTLEMENT OF CLAIMS

1. The REINSURED shall give the _____ prompt notice of any claim. Proofs obtained by the REINSURED shall be accepted as sufficient by the _____, and copies of such proofs shall be furnished to the _____ when requested. It is agreed, however, that if the amount of Supplemental Benefits reinsured with the _____ in connection with any claim for such benefits is in excess of the amount of such benefits retained by the REINSURED, all papers in connection with such claim are to be submitted to the _____ for its recommendation before payment is made.

2. The _____ shall accept the decision of the REINSURED in settling the claim and shall pay, at its Home Office, its portion to the REINSURED when the REINSURED settles with the claimant. It is understood and agreed that the payment of a death claim by the _____ shall be made in one sum regardless of the mode of settlement under the policy of the REINSURED. In settlement of a Waiver of Premium Disability claim, the _____ shall pay its share of the gross premium waived to the REINSURED.

3. If the REINSURED should contest or compromise any claim or suit, and the amount thereby be reduced, the _____ shall share in the reduction in the proportion that the net liability of the _____ bore to the sum of the retained net liability of the REINSURED and the net liability of other reinsurers immediately prior to such reduction. Any unusual expenses incurred by the REINSURED in defending or investigating the claim or in taking up or rescinding a policy reinsured hereunder, aside from the routine investigations and other expenses incidental to the settlement of claims, shall be shared in the same proportion.

4. In the event the amount of insurance provided by a policy or policies reinsured hereunder is increased or reduced because of a misstatement of age or sex established after the death of the insured, the _____ shall share in the increase or reduction in the proportion that the net liability of the _____ bore to the sum of the retained net liability of the REINSURED and the net liability of other reinsurers immediately prior to such increase or reduction. The reinsurance policy or policies of the _____ shall be rewritten from commencement on the basis of the adjusted amounts using premiums and reserves at the

correct ages and sex. The adjustment for the difference in premiums shall be made without interest.

5.   The _____ shall return to the REINSURED any basic life reinsurance premiums and any reinsurance premiums for Supplemental benefits, without interest thereon, paid to the _____ for any period beyond the date of death of a life reinsured hereunder.

EXTENDED AND PAID-UP INSURANCE

1.   If an original policy of the REINSURED which is reinsured hereunder lapses and extended or paid-up insurance is granted in accordance with its provisions, the REINSURED shall notify the _____ by means of an amended cession in duplicate that such extended or paid-up insurance has been granted. The _____ shall share in any adjustment in amount in the proportion that the amount of reinsurance of the _____ on that policy bears to the total amount of that policy retained by the REINSURED and reinsured with other reinsurers. If the continuing amount of reinsurance hereunder would be less than $1,000, such reinsurance shall be canceled.

2.   The reinsurance premium shown on the amended cession shall be computed on the basis of the reinsurance premiums applicable to the policy prior to the change. The _____ shall complete the amended cession and return one copy to the REINSURED.

EXPERIENCE REFUNDS

1.   The experience refund account shall include all new Life reinsurance on a life so long as the total amount of reinsurance on that life in the _____ does not exceed the experience refund account limit of . . . . All amounts of new Life reinsurance not included in the experience refund account shall be included in the nonrefund account.

2.   An experience refund shall be made annually by the _____ with respect to Life reinsurance in the experience refund account and with respect to all Supplemental Benefits reinsurance if the operation of the formula in use produces such a refund. A description of the method by which experience refunds were computed for the calendar year preceding the effective date of this agreement is set forth in Schedule E. The _____ reserves the right to change the basis of computation from time to time.

3.   Life reinsurance shall not be transferred from the experience refund account to the nonrefund account or vice versa. The rule for allocating future new reinsurance between the two accounts may be changed by agreement between the parties.

PREMIUM TAX REIMBURSEMENT

When the _____ is not required to pay state premium taxes upon reinsurance premiums received from the REINSURED, it shall reimburse the REINSURED for any such taxes the latter may be required to pay with respect to that part of the premiums received under the REINSURED'S original policies which is remitted to the _____ as reinsurance premiums.

POLICY CHANGES

If a change is made in the policy issued by the REINSURED to the insured which affects reinsurance hereunder, the REINSURED shall immediately notify the _____ of such change.

REINSTATEMENTS

If a policy reinsured hereunder lapses for nonpayment of premium and is reinstated in accordance with its terms and the rules of the REINSURED, the _____ shall automatically reinstate its reinsurance under such policy. The REINSURED shall mail notice of the reinstatement to the _____ not later than the tenth working day after the reinstatement of the original policy. The REINSURED shall pay the _____ all reinsurance premiums in arrears in connection with the reinstatement with interest at the same rate and in the same manner as the REINSURED received under its policy.

EXPENSES

The REINSURED shall bear the expense of all medical examinations, inspection fees, and other charges incurred in connection with the original policy.

REDUCTIONS

1. If a portion of the insurance issued by the REINSURED on a life reinsured hereunder is terminated, reinsurance on that life hereunder shall be reduced as hereinafter provided to restore, as far as possible, the retention level of the REINSURED on the risk, provided, however, that the REINSURED shall not assume on any policy being adjusted as provided in this article an amount of insurance in excess of its retention limit at the time of issue of that policy for the retention category of the policy. The reduction in reinsurance shall first be applied to the reinsurance, if any, of the specific policy under which insurance terminated. The reinsurance of the _____ shall be reduced by an amount which is the same proportion of the amount of reduction so applied as the reinsurance of the _____ on the policy bore to the total reinsurance on the policy. The balance, if any, of the reduction shall be applied to reinsurance of other policies on the life, the further reduction, if any, in the reinsurance of the _____ again being determined on a proportional basis.

2. The _____ shall return to the REINSURED any basic life reinsurance premiums and any reinsurance premiums for Supplemental benefits, without interest thereon, paid to the _____ for any period beyond the date of reduction of reinsurance hereunder.

INSPECTION OF RECORDS

The _____ shall have the right at any reasonable time to inspect, at the office of the REINSURED, all books and documents relating to the reinsurance under this agreement.

INCREASE IN LIMIT OF RETENTION

1. The REINSURED may increase its limit of retention and may elect, subject to the other provisions of this Article, to: (*a*) continue unchanged reinsurance then in force under this agreement; (*b*) make reductions in both standard and substandard reinsurance then in force under this agreement; or (*c*) make reductions in standard reinsurance then in force under this agreement. The increased limit of retention shall be effective with respect to new reinsurance on the date specified by the REINSURED subsequent to written notice to the _____. Such written notice shall specify the new limit of retention, the effective date thereof, and the election permitted by the first sentence of this paragraph. If the REINSURED makes election (*b*) or (*c*), the

amount of reinsurance shall be reduced, except as hereinafter provided, to the excess, if any, over the REINSURED'S new limit of retention.

2.   No reduction shall be made in the amount of any reinsurance policy unless the REINSURED retained its maximum limit of retention for the plan, age, and mortality classification at the time the policy was issued, nor shall reductions be made unless held by the REINSURED at its own risk without benefit of any proportional or nonproportional reinsurance other than catastrophe accident reinsurance. No reduction shall be made in any class of reinsurance fully reinsured. The plan, age, and mortality classification at issue shall be used to determine the REINSURED'S new retention on any life on which reinsurance policies are reduced in accordance with the provisions of this article.

3.   The reduction in each reinsurance policy shall be effective upon the reinsurance renewal date of that policy first following the effective date of the increased limit of retention or upon the fifth reinsurance renewal date of the reinsurance policy, if later. If there is reinsurance in other reinsurers on a life on whom a reinsurance policy will be reduced hereunder, the _____ shall share in the reduction in the proportion that the amount of reinsurance of the _____ on the life bore to the amount of reinsurance of other reinsurers on the life.

4.   In the event the REINSURED overlooks any reduction in the amount of a reinsurance policy which should have been made on account of an increase in the REINSURED'S limit of retention, the acceptance by the _____ of reinsurance premiums under such circumstances and after the effective date of the reduction shall not constitute or determine a liability on the part of the _____ for such reinsurance. The _____ shall be liable only for a refund of premiums so received, without interest.

OVERSIGHTS

It is understood and agreed that, if failure to comply with any terms of this agreement is shown to be unintentional and the result of misunderstanding or oversight on the part of either the REINSURED or the _____, both the REINSURED and the _____ shall be restored to the positions they would have occupied had no such misunderstanding or oversight occurred.

ARBITRATION

1.   It is the intention of the parties that customs and usages of the business of reinsurance shall be given full effect in the interpretation of this agreement. The parties shall act in all things with the highest good faith. A dispute or difference between the parties with respect to the operation or interpretation of this agreement on which an amicable understanding cannot be reached shall be decided by arbitration. The arbitrators are empowered to decide all questions or issues and shall be free to reach their decision from the standpoint of equity and customary practices of the insurance and reinsurance industry rather than from that of the strict law.

2.   The court of arbitration shall be held in the city where the Home Office of the REINSURED is located and shall consist of three arbitrators who must be officers of life insurance companies other than the parties to this agreement or their affiliates or subsidiaries. The REINSURED shall appoint one arbitrator and the _____ the second. These two arbitrators shall then select the third before arbitration begins. Should one of the parties decline to appoint an arbitrator or should the two arbitrators be unable to agree upon the choice of a third, such appointment shall be left to the president of the American Life Insurance Association.

3. The arbitrators shall decide by a majority of votes, and from their written decision there can be no appeal. The cost of arbitration, including the fees of the arbitrators, shall be borne by the losing party unless the arbitrators decide otherwise.

INSOLVENCY

1. In the event of the insolvency of the REINSURED, all reinsurance shall be payable directly to the liquidator, receiver, or statutory successor of said REINSURED, without diminution because of the insolvency of the REINSURED.

2. In the event of insolvency of the REINSURED, the liquidator, receiver, or statutory successor shall give the _____ written notice of the pendency of a claim on a policy reinsured within a reasonable time after such claim is filed in the insolvency proceeding. During the pendency of any such claim, the _____ may investigate such claim and interpose in the name of the REINSURED (its liquidator, receiver, or statutory successor), but at its own expense, in the proceeding where such claim is to be adjudicated any defense or defenses which the _____ may deem available to the REINSURED or its liquidator, receiver, or statutory successor.

3. The expense thus incurred by the _____ shall be chargeable, subject to court approval, against the REINSURED as part of the expense of liquidation to the extent of a proportionate share of the benefit which may accrue to the REINSURED solely as a result of the defense undertaken by the _____. Where two or more reinsurers are participating in the same claim and a majority in interest elect to interpose a defense or defenses to any such claim, the expense shall be apportioned in accordance with the terms of the reinsurance agreement as though such expense had been incurred by the REINSURED.

PARTIES TO AGREEMENT

This is an agreement for indemnity reinsurance solely between the REINSURED and the _____. The acceptance of reinsurance hereunder shall not create any right or legal relation whatever between the _____ and the insured or the beneficiary under any policy reinsured hereunder.

EXECUTION AND DURATION OF AGREEMENT

The provisions of this reinsurance agreement shall apply with respect to policies issued by the REINSURED and bearing policy dates on and after the _____ day of _____ but in no event shall this agreement become effective unless and until it has been duly executed by two officers of the _____ at its Home Office in _____, _____. This agreement shall be unlimited as to its duration but may be terminated at any time, insofar as it pertains to the handling of new reinsurance thereafter, by either party giving three months' notice of termination in writing. The _____ shall continue to accept reinsurance during the three months aforesaid and shall remain liable on all reinsurance granted under this agreement until the termination or expiry of the insurance reinsured.

IN WITNESS WHEREOF the said

---

and the said

THE _____ _____ LIFE INSURANCE COMPANY

of _____, _____,

have by their respective officers executed and delivered these presents in duplicate on the dates shown below.

By _____

Date _____

Date _____

THE _____ _____ LIFE
INSURANCE COMPANY

By _____

Second Vice President

Date _____

_____

Assistant Secretary

Date _____

SCHEDULE A

Retention Limits of the REINSURED

Life

_____

Waiver of Premium Disability

_____

Accidental Death

_____

SCHEDULE B

Maximum Amounts which the REINSURED may cede Automatically:

Life

_____

On substandard risks, the REINSURED shall not cede automatically more than the smaller of the amounts shown above and ____% of the amount retained on the current application.

The REINSURED may cede automatically Waiver of Premium Disability insurance in amounts not to exceed the amount applicable to the amount of Life insurance ceded.

Ages	Accidental Death Benefits Standard—Table F	Tables H–P None

If the REINSURED, before having concluded the necessary reinsurance, shall become liable under a conditional receipt for a death claim of an amount which, together with the amount retained by the REINSURED under previously issued policies, if any, exceeds its own limit of retention, the ———— shall accept reinsurance automatically for an amount not to exceed: $————, REINSURED'S limit of retention applicable to the mortality class, plan of insurance, and age at issue for which a premium was collected and less the amount of Life and Accidental Death insurance, if any, previously ceded by the REINSURED to the ————. The REINSURED shall submit copies of its conditional receipt to the ———— and shall notify the ———— immediately of any change therein.

Reinsurance Agreement (continued)

RISK PREMIUM REINSURANCE AUTOMATIC NOTIFICATION OR FACULTATIVE APPLICATION

To The ▆▆▆▆▆▆ Life Insurance Company   PART 1

☐ AUTOMATIC
☐ FACULTATIVE

☐ MALE
☐ FEMALE

Name of Insured _____   Birth Date _____   State of Birth _____   State of Residence _____

	LIFE	DISABILITY	ACCIDENTAL DEATH	PLAN OF NEW INSURANCE
Previous insurance in force	$_____	$_____	$_____	
of which we retain	_____	_____	_____	
Rating, if substandard	_____	_____	_____	IF TERM RIDER IN-
New insurance applied for	_____	_____	_____	CLUDED PLEASE IN-
of which we propose to retain	_____	_____	_____	DICATE AMOUNT
Rating, if substandard	_____	_____	_____	ISSUED.
Amount reinsured or applied for	_____	_____	_____	_____

W.P. ☐   Inc. ☐

Will policy contain aviation exclusion provision?_____ Have you recently asked us for quotation on this risk? _____Is case being submitted elsewhere for reinsurance?_____
If a member of M.I.B. please indicate codes which will be reported to the Bureau:
Additional evidence being obtained which will be forwarded later:

Date_____   Reinsured Company _____

Dated at _____   By _____

Reinsurance Agreement (concluded)

FORMAL RISK PREMIUM REINSURANCE CESSION

☐ MEDICAL
☐ NONMEDICAL
☐ AUTOMATIC
☐ FACULTATIVE

To The ▮▮▮▮▮ Life Insurance Company   **PART 2**

☐ MALE
☐ FEMALE

Name of Insured	Birth Date	State of Birth	State of Residence

Policy Number _____   Policy Date _____   Short Term from _____   RESERVE BASIS:
☐ Nearest Birthday   Mort. Table, Int. Rate, Modification
☐ Last Birthday
Issue Age _____

	LIFE	DISABILITY	ACCIDENTAL DEATH	PLAN OF NEW INSURANCE
Previous Insurance in force	$	$	$	
of which we retain				
Rating, if substandard				IF TERM RIDER IN-CLUDED PLEASE IN-DICATE AMOUNT ISSUED.
New Insurance issued				
of which we retain				
Rating, if substandard				
Reinsurance ceded to The Lincoln				

W.P. ☐   Inc. ☐

Will policy contain aviation exclusion provision? _____ Have you recently asked us for quotation on this risk? _____ Is case being submitted elsewhere for reinsurance? _____
If a member of M.I.B. please indicate codes which will be reported to the Bureau:

Date _____   Reinsured Company _____

Dated at _____   By _____

SHORT TERM: Age _____
                Premium $_____   **DETAILS OF THE REINSURANCE**

Policy Year	Terminal Reserve	Amount of Risk	Age	Premiums					Policy Fee	Total Premium
				Standard	Table Extra	Flat Extra	Disability	Accidental Death		
19										
19										
19										
19										
19										
19										

Show net amounts at risk for 6 years.   Show all premiums net of commission

Complete for Standard Automatic Cases
Where Papers are not to be Forwarded

Height _____ Weight _____ Sex _____
Blood Pressure (not required in nonmedical cases) _____
Occupation _____
Impairments _____

WITHDRAW CASE ON ACCOUNT OF:
☐ Application filed incomplete
☐ Policy not delivered
☐ Amount delivered was within our retention
☐ Reinsured elsewhere

	DISABILITY	ACCIDENTAL DEATH
Form No.		
Terminal age		
Number of renewal premiums payable		

In event of Disability

Lincoln's liability $_____ annually for waiver of original premium

Lincoln's liability $_____ annually for monthly income

The above cession is accepted subject to the terms and conditions of the contract of Indemnity reinsurance now in force between the Reinsured Company and

THE ▮▮▮▮▮ LIFE INSURANCE COMPANY

By _____

                                                      Assistant Secretary

▮▮▮ POLICY No. _____

Dated at ▮▮▮ this _____ day of _____, 19_____

SCHEDULE C, PART IV
Cession Card
Front

CESSION NUMBER		POL. NO. ORIG. CO.		STATE		DATE OF POLICY
REINS. PREM. 1ST	S.T. PREMIUM	ORIGINAL COMPANY				SHORT TERM FROM
REN.	P.R. PREMIUM	NAME				PRO RATA FROM
BIRTH DATE				LIFE		**DOUBLE INDEMNITY**
OCCUPATION		PREVIOUS INS.				
		AMT. RETAINED				
DUTIES		CURRENT INS.				
CLASSIFICATION		AMT. CURRENT INS. RETAINED				
		AMT. DOUBLE INDEMNITY CEDED TO THE ▬▬▬▬ LIFE INS. CO.				
FORM 813 4-61	TERMINATED					
	REVISED					

Reverse

YEAR	DATE PAID	PREMIUM	MEMO.									
1												
2												
3												
4												
5												
6												
7												
8												
9												
10												
11												
12												

Reinsurance Agreement (continued)

SCHEDULE D

THE ▮▮▮▮▮▮▮▮▮▮ LIFE INSURANCE COMPANY
Premiums for $1000 of Risk Premium Reinsurance (RPR-ER-Male)
Age Nearest Birthday

Premiums for Non-Medical Business	Annual Policy Fee To Be Added To Total Life Reinsurance Premium	
Use actual attained age with duration increased by 1, 2, or 4 years for age groups at issue 31-35, 36-40, 41-45, respectively.	$2.00 per M first year gross risk reinsured, with maximum of $5.00 per year first five years and $2.50 per year thereafter.	**ER-M**

STANDARD

Age at Issue	POLICY YEAR											Attained Age
	One	Two	Three	Four	Five	Six	Seven	Eight	Nine	Ten	Thereafter	
0	$7.15	$2.43	$2.24	$2.10	$1.99	$1.91	$1.84	$1.79	$1.75	$1.73	$1.73	10
1	2.43	2.24	2.10	1.99	1.91	1.84	1.79	1.75	1.73	1.73	1.76	11
2	2.24	2.10	1.99	1.91	1.84	1.79	1.75	1.73	1.73	1.76	1.83	12
3	2.10	1.99	1.91	1.84	1.79	1.75	1.73	1.73	1.76	1.83	1.93	13
4	1.99	1.91	1.84	1.79	1.75	1.73	1.73	1.76	1.83	1.93	2.06	14
5	1.91	1.84	1.79	1.75	1.73	1.73	1.76	1.83	1.93	2.06	2.22	15
6	1.84	1.79	1.75	1.73	1.73	1.76	1.83	1.93	2.06	2.22	2.37	16
7	1.79	1.75	1.73	1.73	1.76	1.83	1.93	2.06	2.22	2.35	2.51	17
8	1.75	1.73	1.73	1.76	1.83	1.93	2.06	2.22	2.35	2.48	2.65	18
9	1.73	1.73	1.76	1.83	1.93	2.06	2.22	2.35	2.47	2.59	2.79	19
10	1.73	1.76	1.83	1.93	2.06	2.22	2.35	2.46	2.58	2.70	2.92	20
11	1.76	1.83	1.93	2.06	2.22	2.35	2.45	2.56	2.69	2.83	3.04	21
12	1.83	1.93	2.06	2.22	2.35	2.44	2.54	2.66	2.80	2.94	3.13	22
13	1.93	2.06	2.22	2.34	2.43	2.52	2.63	2.75	2.90	3.02	3.20	23
14	2.06	2.22	2.33	2.42	2.49	2.59	2.71	2.84	2.97	3.06	3.26	24
15	2.22	2.32	2.40	2.47	2.55	2.66	2.79	2.91	3.01	3.07	3.31	25
16	2.31	2.38	2.44	2.52	2.60	2.73	2.84	2.94	3.02	3.07	3.34	26
17	2.36	2.40	2.47	2.55	2.65	2.77	2.86	2.95	3.02	3.06	3.36	27
18	2.37	2.41	2.48	2.58	2.68	2.78	2.86	2.94	3.00	3.03	3.37	28
19	2.37	2.41	2.48	2.58	2.67	2.76	2.84	2.91	2.95	2.95	3.39	29
20	2.34	2.39	2.45	2.55	2.62	2.71	2.79	2.85	2.87	2.87	3.41	30
21	2.29	2.33	2.39	2.48	2.54	2.65	2.74	2.79	2.81	2.84	3.45	31
22	2.22	2.25	2.30	2.40	2.49	2.60	2.70	2.74	2.79	2.83	3.51	32
23	2.12	2.16	2.22	2.36	2.46	2.57	2.68	2.73	2.79	2.84	3.58	33
24	2.00	2.09	2.19	2.35	2.46	2.57	2.68	2.74	2.81	2.87	3.64	34
25	1.90	2.05	2.19	2.37	2.49	2.60	2.70	2.77	2.85	2.94	3.81	35
26	1.85	2.04	2.21	2.41	2.54	2.66	2.75	2.83	2.93	3.03	3.97	36
27	1.82	2.05	2.26	2.47	2.60	2.72	2.81	2.91	3.02	3.14	4.15	37
28	1.82	2.08	2.32	2.54	2.68	2.79	2.89	3.00	3.13	3.28	4.34	38
29	1.83	2.12	2.39	2.62	2.76	2.87	2.98	3.12	3.27	3.48	4.58	39
30	1.86	2.17	2.46	2.71	2.84	2.96	3.10	3.26	3.47	3.74	4.81	40
31	1.89	2.23	2.53	2.80	2.93	3.08	3.24	3.45	3.71	4.06	5.10	41
32	1.93	2.29	2.62	2.90	3.05	3.22	3.43	3.71	4.05	4.41	5.44	42
33	1.98	2.36	2.72	3.01	3.19	3.41	3.66	4.03	4.39	4.78	5.83	43
34	2.03	2.45	2.83	3.14	3.39	3.65	3.96	4.35	4.77	5.21	6.27	44
35	2.09	2.55	2.96	3.33	3.64	3.95	4.26	4.72	5.19	5.68	6.76	45
36	2.16	2.66	3.15	3.56	3.94	4.25	4.64	5.04	5.63	6.17	7.27	46
37	2.24	2.79	3.34	3.82	4.24	4.63	5.04	5.54	6.08	6.68	7.81	47
38	2.32	2.94	3.56	4.09	4.60	5.03	5.49	6.01	6.59	7.25	8.43	48
39	2.42	3.11	3.80	4.41	4.97	5.47	5.95	6.51	7.15	7.88	9.09	49
40	2.53	3.29	4.07	4.74	5.37	5.94	6.43	7.09	7.77	8.59	9.81	50
41	2.66	3.53	4.40	5.04	5.69	6.36	6.94	7.64	8.36	9.26	10.64	51
42	2.81	3.78	4.75	5.40	6.08	6.84	7.50	8.28	9.06	10.08	11.54	52
43	2.98	4.03	5.10	5.82	6.56	7.38	8.14	9.00	9.88	11.02	12.56	53
44	3.16	4.28	5.44	6.28	7.12	7.98	8.84	9.81	10.82	12.11	13.69	54
45	3.37	4.54	5.80	6.82	7.75	8.64	9.61	10.70	11.87	13.34	14.96	55
46	3.58	4.81	6.18	7.40	8.44	9.37	10.44	11.65	12.98	14.62	16.37	56
47	3.79	5.11	6.62	8.01	9.18	10.16	11.32	12.63	14.08	15.84	17.92	57
48	3.99	5.44	7.10	8.66	9.94	11.04	12.26	13.64	15.17	17.01	19.60	58
49	4.19	5.79	7.64	9.34	10.75	11.97	13.24	14.68	16.25	18.14	21.40	59

EFFECTIVE NOVEMBER 1, 1964

Reinsurance Agreement (continued)

THE ████████████ LIFE INSURANCE COMPANY
Premiums for $1000 of Risk Premium Reinsurance (RPR-ER-Male)
Age Nearest Birthday

Premiums for Non-Medical Business	Annual Policy Fee To Be Added To Total Life Reinsurance Premium
Use actual attained age with duration increased by 1, 2, or 4 years for age groups at issue 31-35, 36-40, 41-45, respectively.	$2.00 per M first year gross risk reinsured, with maximum of $5.00 per year first five years and $2.50 per year thereafter.

STANDARD

Age at Issue	One	Two	Three	Four	Five	Six	Seven	Eight	Nine	Ten	Thereafter	Attained Age
50	$4.38	$6.17	$8.22	$10.04	$11.60	$12.97	$14.29	$15.76	$17.32	$19.21	$23.30	60
51	4.60	6.59	8.86	10.80	12.50	14.04	15.40	16.91	18.45	20.34	25.30	61
52	4.90	7.06	9.54	11.60	13.46	15.16	16.56	18.18	19.71	21.64	27.41	62
53	5.28	7.59	10.28	12.46	14.50	16.34	17.80	19.56	21.10	23.09	29.61	63
54	5.72	8.17	11.08	13.38	15.58	17.59	19.10	21.05	22.90	24.71	31.93	64
55	6.25	8.81	11.92	14.35	16.74	18.89	20.46	22.66	24.28	26.49	34.36	65
56	6.83	9.52	12.82	15.40	17.98	20.24	21.90	24.00	26.09	28.46	36.90	66
57	7.44	10.31	13.80	16.58	19.34	21.64	23.39	26.08	28.06	30.66	39.63	67
58	8.10	11.19	14.84	17.88	20.80	23.10	24.96	27.84	30.21	33.06	42.58	68
59	8.79	12.16	15.94	19.30	22.37	24.59	26.60	29.65	32.53	35.69	45.81	69
60	9.52	13.21	17.12	20.84	24.05	26.13	28.30	31.50	35.02	38.54	49.39	70
61	10.30	14.34	18.38	22.38	25.69	27.71	30.12	33.48	37.62	41.50	53.30	71
62	11.14	15.53	19.74	23.76	27.14	29.32	32.10	35.70	40.25	44.44	57.59	72
63	12.04	16.79	21.20	25.03	28.40	30.96	34.24	38.14	42.91	47.38	62.24	73
64	13.00	18.12	22.75	26.16	29.46	32.62	36.54	40.81	45.62	50.30	67.29	74
65	14.03	19.51	24.40	27.15	30.34	34.31	39.00	43.71	48.36	53.22	72.70	75
66	15.12	20.92	26.10	28.40	31.65	36.52	42.04	47.30	52.83	60.08	79.32	76
67	16.27	22.29	27.78	30.30	34.02	39.76	46.06	52.04	57.70	67.07	86.68	77
68	17.49	23.63	29.46	32.84	37.44	44.00	51.08	57.21	66.58	75.00	94.74	78
69	18.78	24.93	31.12	36.02	41.91	49.25	56.49	65.59	74.39	83.59	103.74	79
70	20.12	26.20	32.78	39.86	47.44	55.52	64.10	73.18	82.76	92.85	113.89	80
71	21.72	27.74	34.76	43.97	53.19	62.07	71.54	82.01	92.25	106.07	125.39	81
72	23.76	29.92	37.42	47.99	58.47	68.31	78.93	91.01	105.09	119.82	137.61	82
73	26.21	32.73	40.76	51.03	63.27	74.23	86.28	100.16	116.49	134.10	150.92	83
74	29.10	36.17	44.76	55.79	67.60	79.85	93.59	109.46	128.04	148.91	164.24	84
75	32.42	40.24	49.44	59.56	71.45	85.15	100.86	118.93	139.75	164.24	177.85	85
											191.62	86
											205.48	87
											219.36	88
											235.36	89
											251.62	90
											271.13	91
											293.25	92
											314.94	93
											338.00	94
											363.52	95
											404.98	96
											479.80	97
											549.98	98
											660.94	99

Reinsurance Agreement (continued)

THE ██████████████ LIFE INSURANCE COMPANY

Additional Premiums for $1000 of Risk Premium Reinsurance on Substandard Risks (RPR-ER-Male)
Age Nearest Birthday

SUBSTANDARD

ER-M

EXTRA PREMIUMS FOR EACH TABLE OF RATING. FOR RATINGS HIGHER THAN TABLE ONE APPLY APPROPRIATE MULTIPLE

Age at Issue	POLICY YEAR											Attained Age
	One	Two	Three	Four	Five	Six	Seven	Eight	Nine	Ten	Thereafter	
0	$ .44	$ .44	$ .44	$ .44	$ .44	$ .44	$ .44	$ .44	$ .44	$ .44	$ .44	10
1	.44	.44	.44	.44	.44	.44	.44	.44	.44	.44	.44	11
2	.44	.44	.44	.44	.44	.44	.44	.44	.44	.44	.44	12
3	.44	.44	.44	.44	.44	.44	.44	.44	.44	.44	.44	13
4	.44	.44	.44	.44	.44	.44	.44	.44	.44	.44	.44	14
5	.44	.44	.44	.44	.44	.44	.44	.44	.44	.44	.44	15
6	.44	.44	.44	.44	.44	.44	.44	.44	.44	.44	.44	16
7	.44	.44	.44	.44	.44	.44	.44	.44	.44	.44	.44	17
8	.44	.44	.44	.44	.44	.44	.44	.44	.44	.44	.44	18
9	.44	.44	.44	.44	.44	.44	.44	.44	.44	.44	.44	19
10	.44	.44	.44	.44	.44	.44	.44	.44	.44	.44	.44	20
11	.44	.44	.44	.44	.44	.44	.44	.44	.44	.44	.44	21
12	.44	.44	.44	.44	.44	.44	.44	.44	.44	.44	.44	22
13	.44	.44	.44	.44	.44	.44	.44	.44	.44	.44	.44	23
14	.44	.44	.44	.44	.44	.44	.44	.44	.44	.44	.44	24
15	.44	.44	.44	.44	.44	.44	.44	.44	.44	.44	.44	25
16	.44	.44	.44	.44	.44	.44	.44	.44	.44	.44	.45	26
17	.44	.44	.44	.44	.44	.44	.44	.44	.44	.45	.46	27
18	.44	.44	.44	.44	.44	.44	.44	.44	.45	.46	.47	28
19	.44	.44	.44	.44	.44	.44	.44	.45	.46	.47	.48	29
20	.44	.44	.44	.44	.44	.44	.45	.46	.47	.48	.49	30
21	.44	.44	.44	.44	.44	.45	.46	.47	.48	.49	.50	31
22	.44	.44	.44	.44	.45	.46	.47	.48	.49	.50	.52	32
23	.44	.44	.44	.45	.46	.47	.48	.49	.50	.52	.55	33
24	.44	.44	.45	.46	.47	.48	.49	.50	.52	.55	.60	34
25	.44	.45	.46	.47	.48	.49	.50	.52	.55	.60	.66	35
26	.44	.45	.46	.47	.48	.49	.51	.53	.58	.66	.72	36
27	.44	.45	.46	.47	.48	.49	.51	.56	.64	.72	.77	37
28	.44	.45	.46	.47	.48	.50	.54	.62	.69	.77	.81	38
29	.45	.46	.47	.47	.48	.52	.60	.67	.74	.81	.88	39
30	.45	.46	.47	.48	.51	.57	.64	.71	.79	.88	.94	40
31	.45	.46	.47	.51	.56	.62	.68	.75	.85	.94	.98	41
32	.45	.47	.51	.56	.61	.67	.74	.82	.90	.98	1.02	42
33	.45	.48	.54	.60	.65	.72	.80	.88	.95	1.02	1.07	43
34	.45	.49	.57	.64	.70	.78	.86	.93	1.00	1.07	1.13	44
35	.45	.51	.60	.68	.77	.85	.92	.98	1.05	1.13	1.23	45
36	.45	.53	.64	.74	.84	.90	.96	1.03	1.12	1.23	1.36	46
37	.46	.56	.69	.80	.88	.94	1.01	1.10	1.21	1.36	1.49	47
38	.48	.60	.74	.84	.93	1.00	1.08	1.19	1.33	1.49	1.64	48
39	.50	.64	.78	.88	.98	1.06	1.16	1.30	1.46	1.64	1.80	49
40	.53	.68	.82	.93	1.04	1.14	1.28	1.43	1.60	1.80	1.97	50
41	.56	.72	.86	.99	1.12	1.25	1.40	1.57	1.76	1.97	2.16	51
42	.59	.76	.92	1.06	1.22	1.37	1.54	1.72	1.92	2.16	2.36	52
43	.62	.80	.98	1.16	1.33	1.50	1.68	1.88	2.10	2.36	2.57	53
44	.65	.84	1.06	1.26	1.45	1.64	1.84	2.06	2.30	2.57	2.79	54
45	.68	.90	1.15	1.38	1.59	1.79	2.00	2.24	2.51	2.79	3.02	55
46	.71	.96	1.25	1.50	1.74	1.95	2.19	2.45	2.73	3.02	3.25	56
47	.74	1.03	1.35	1.63	1.90	2.14	2.39	2.66	2.95	3.25	3.49	57
48	.77	1.10	1.46	1.77	2.08	2.33	2.60	2.88	3.18	3.49	3.73	58
49	.80	1.17	1.58	1.94	2.27	2.54	2.82	3.11	3.42	3.73	3.98	59

EFFECTIVE NOVEMBER 1, 1964

Reinsurance Agreement (continued)

THE ██████████████ LIFE INSURANCE COMPANY

Additional Premiums for $1000 of Risk Premium Reinsurance on Substandard Risks (RPR-ER-Male)
Age Nearest Birthday

SUBSTANDARD   ER-M

EXTRA PREMIUMS FOR EACH TABLE OF RATING. FOR RATINGS HIGHER THAN TABLE ONE APPLY APPROPRIATE MULTIPLE

Age at Issue	One	Two	Three	Four	Five	Six	Seven	Eight	Nine	Ten	Thereafter	Attained Age
50	$ .83	$1.26	$1.73	$2.12	$2.47	$2.75	$3.04	$3.34	$3.66	$3.98	$4.22	60
51	.87	1.38	1.90	2.31	2.68	2.97	3.26	3.57	3.89	4.22	4.47	61
52	.96	1.52	2.08	2.51	2.90	3.19	3.50	3.81	4.13	4.47	4.72	62
53	1.08	1.68	2.26	2.72	3.12	3.41	3.73	4.05	4.37	4.72	4.97	63
54	1.20	1.84	2.45	2.93	3.34	3.64	3.95	4.27	4.60	4.97	5.22	64
55	1.33	2.00	2.64	3.14	3.56	3.88	4.16	4.48	4.84	5.22	5.60	65
56	1.46	2.17	2.84	3.36	3.78	4.06	4.36	4.70	5.08	5.60	6.15	66
57	1.61	2.35	3.04	3.57	3.95	4.24	4.56	4.91	5.42	6.15	6.55	67
58	1.76	2.53	3.25	3.73	4.12	4.42	4.75	5.24	5.96	6.55	7.10	68
59	1.91	2.71	3.40	3.89	4.28	4.60	5.05	5.77	6.36	7.10	7.75	69
60	2.07	2.86	3.54	4.04	4.44	4.87	5.58	6.18	6.90	7.75	8.50	70
61	2.23	3.01	3.68	4.19	4.69	5.39	5.99	6.71	7.54	8.50	9.20	71
62	2.40	3.16	3.82	4.43	5.20	5.81	6.51	7.32	8.26	10.05	10.05	72
63	2.58	3.31	4.04	4.94	5.62	6.32	7.11	8.01	8.94	10.05	10.95	73
64	2.77	3.52	4.53	5.36	6.12	6.90	7.77	8.67	9.76	10.95	11.95	74
65	3.00	3.99	4.96	5.84	6.68	7.53	8.41	9.47	10.64	11.95	12.90	75
66	3.45	4.43	5.42	6.38	7.29	8.14	9.19	10.33	11.62	12.90	13.50	76
67	3.90	4.86	5.92	6.94	7.88	8.90	10.03	11.30	12.56	13.50	13.90	77
68	4.30	5.31	6.42	7.50	8.61	9.72	10.97	12.23	13.20	13.90	14.20	78
69	4.69	5.72	6.94	8.20	9.41	10.64	11.89	12.90	13.66	14.20	14.35	79
70	5.03	6.18	7.58	8.97	10.32	11.56	12.60	13.42	14.05	14.35	14.40	80
71	5.43	6.76	8.31	9.85	11.22	12.30	13.19	13.90	14.29	14.40	14.40	81
72	5.94	7.43	9.15	10.74	12.00	12.95	13.75	14.23	14.40	14.40	14.40	82
73	6.55	8.18	10.03	11.56	12.71	13.60	14.17	14.40	14.40	14.40	14.40	83
74	7.27	9.04	10.92	12.37	13.45	14.11	14.40	14.40	14.40	14.40	14.40	84
75	8.10	10.06	11.86	13.23	14.05	14.40	14.40	14.40	14.40	14.40	14.40	85
											14.40	86
											14.40	87
											14.40	88
											14.40	89
											14.40	90
											14.40	91
											14.40	92
											14.40	93
											14.40	94
											14.40	95
											14.40	96
											14.40	97
											14.40	98
											14.40	99

EFFECTIVE NOVEMBER 1, 1964

Reinsurance Agreement (continued)

THE ███████████████ LIFE INSURANCE COMPANY
Premiums for $1000 of Risk Premium Reinsurance (RPR-NR-Male)
Age Nearest Birthday

Premiums for Non-Medical Business	Annual Policy Fee To Be Added To Total Life Reinsurance Premium
Use actual attained age with duration increased by 1, 2, or 4 years for age groups at issue 31-35, 36-40, 41-45, respectively.	$2.00 per M first year gross risk reinsured, with maximum of $5.00 per year first five years and $2.50 per year thereafter.

NR-M

STANDARD

Age at Issue	One	Two	Three	Four	Five	Six	Seven	Eight	Nine	Ten	Thereafter	Attained Age
0	$6.50	$1.70	$1.50	$1.38	$1.30	$1.22	$1.15	$1.09	$1.05	$1.02	$1.00	10
1	1.70	1.50	1.38	1.30	1.22	1.15	1.09	1.05	1.02	1.00	1.04	11
2	1.50	1.38	1.30	1.22	1.15	1.09	1.05	1.02	1.00	1.04	1.10	12
3	1.38	1.30	1.22	1.15	1.09	1.05	1.02	1.00	1.04	1.10	1.18	13
4	1.30	1.22	1.15	1.09	1.05	1.02	1.00	1.04	1.10	1.18	1.28	14
5	1.22	1.15	1.09	1.05	1.02	1.00	1.04	1.10	1.18	1.28	1.40	15
6	1.15	1.09	1.05	1.02	1.00	1.04	1.10	1.18	1.28	1.40	1.52	16
7	1.09	1.05	1.02	1.00	1.04	1.10	1.18	1.28	1.40	1.51	1.63	17
8	1.05	1.02	1.00	1.04	1.10	1.18	1.28	1.40	1.51	1.61	1.74	18
9	1.02	1.00	1.04	1.10	1.18	1.28	1.40	1.51	1.61	1.70	1.86	19
10	1.00	1.04	1.10	1.18	1.28	1.40	1.51	1.61	1.69	1.78	1.97	20
11	1.04	1.10	1.18	1.28	1.40	1.51	1.61	1.68	1.77	1.87	2.09	21
12	1.10	1.18	1.28	1.40	1.51	1.60	1.67	1.76	1.85	1.94	2.21	22
13	1.18	1.28	1.40	1.51	1.59	1.66	1.75	1.83	1.92	2.00	2.32	23
14	1.28	1.40	1.50	1.58	1.65	1.74	1.81	1.89	1.97	2.05	2.43	24
15	1.40	1.49	1.57	1.64	1.72	1.79	1.86	1.94	2.02	2.09	2.51	25
16	1.48	1.56	1.63	1.70	1.76	1.83	1.90	1.98	2.05	2.09	2.56	26
17	1.55	1.62	1.68	1.73	1.79	1.86	1.93	2.00	2.05	2.05	2.60	27
18	1.61	1.66	1.70	1.75	1.81	1.88	1.95	2.00	2.01	2.01	2.62	28
19	1.64	1.67	1.70	1.75	1.81	1.88	1.94	1.96	1.96	1.97	2.63	29
20	1.64	1.65	1.67	1.74	1.79	1.85	1.89	1.90	1.92	1.95	2.66	30
21	1.60	1.60	1.62	1.70	1.74	1.79	1.84	1.87	1.90	1.95	2.71	31
22	1.54	1.54	1.57	1.64	1.69	1.75	1.81	1.86	1.91	1.97	2.77	32
23	1.46	1.47	1.52	1.59	1.66	1.73	1.81	1.88	1.94	2.00	2.84	33
24	1.38	1.42	1.49	1.58	1.66	1.74	1.84	1.91	1.98	2.06	2.94	34
25	1.31	1.39	1.48	1.60	1.69	1.78	1.88	1.96	2.04	2.15	3.06	35
26	1.28	1.39	1.51	1.65	1.75	1.85	1.94	2.03	2.14	2.26	3.18	36
27	1.26	1.41	1.56	1.72	1.83	1.92	2.02	2.13	2.25	2.41	3.32	37
28	1.26	1.44	1.62	1.80	1.91	2.01	2.12	2.24	2.40	2.59	3.47	38
29	1.27	1.48	1.69	1.88	2.00	2.11	2.23	2.39	2.58	2.79	3.66	39
30	1.29	1.54	1.77	1.97	2.10	2.22	2.38	2.57	2.78	3.03	3.87	40
31	1.32	1.60	1.85	2.06	2.20	2.37	2.56	2.77	3.02	3.32	4.13	41
32	1.36	1.67	1.94	2.16	2.36	2.54	2.76	3.01	3.31	3.64	4.43	42
33	1.40	1.74	2.05	2.30	2.53	2.74	2.97	3.30	3.63	3.99	4.78	43
34	1.45	1.83	2.17	2.46	2.72	2.96	3.23	3.60	3.98	4.39	5.17	44
35	1.51	1.93	2.31	2.65	2.95	3.22	3.52	3.93	4.36	4.82	5.61	45
36	1.57	2.04	2.48	2.86	3.21	3.51	3.86	4.29	4.77	5.28	6.07	46
37	1.64	2.16	2.66	3.10	3.50	3.85	4.23	4.69	5.19	5.74	6.56	47
38	1.71	2.29	2.86	3.36	3.82	4.22	4.64	5.12	5.66	6.27	7.12	48
39	1.81	2.44	3.08	3.64	4.16	4.63	5.07	5.59	6.18	6.85	7.73	49
40	1.92	2.61	3.33	3.96	4.53	5.06	5.52	6.12	6.75	7.51	8.39	50
41	2.03	2.80	3.62	4.19	4.75	5.48	6.02	6.65	7.29	8.12	9.15	51
42	2.17	3.00	3.91	4.49	5.07	5.94	6.57	7.25	7.94	8.86	9.98	52
43	2.32	3.23	4.23	4.88	5.51	6.44	7.15	7.91	8.70	9.74	10.93	53
44	2.49	3.49	4.58	5.34	6.07	6.98	7.77	8.65	9.56	10.75	11.98	54
45	2.68	3.76	4.93	5.88	6.73	7.56	8.44	9.45	10.53	11.89	13.16	55
46	2.88	4.05	5.31	6.46	7.45	8.20	9.16	10.31	11.55	13.07	14.49	56
47	3.07	4.35	5.73	7.05	8.16	8.92	9.95	11.20	12.56	14.21	15.95	57
48	3.26	4.65	6.17	7.64	8.87	9.72	10.82	12.14	13.57	15.29	17.54	58
49	3.45	4.96	6.65	8.24	9.58	10.59	11.75	13.11	14.57	16.32	19.26	59

EFFECTIVE NOVEMBER 1, 1964

Reinsurance Agreement (continued)

THE ███████████████ LIFE INSURANCE COMPANY
Premiums for $1000 of Risk Premium Reinsurance (RPR-NR-Male)
Age Nearest Birthday

Premiums for Non-Medical Business	Annual Policy Fee To Be Added To Total Life Reinsurance Premium
Use actual attained age with duration increased by 1, 2, or 4 years for age groups at issue 31-35, 36-40, 41-45, respectively.	$2.00 per M first year gross risk reinsured, with maximum of $5.00 per year first five years and $2.50 per year thereafter.

NR-M

STANDARD

Age at Issue	POLICY YEAR											Attained Age
	One	Two	Three	Four	Five	Six	Seven	Eight	Nine	Ten	Thereafter	
50	$3.62	$5.28	$7.16	$8.84	$10.28	$11.55	$12.76	$14.12	$15.56	$17.31	$20.97	60
51	3.83	5.64	7.72	9.48	11.03	12.57	13.82	15.19	16.60	18.35	22.77	61
52	4.11	6.05	8.34	10.20	11.88	13.62	14.92	16.32	17.76	19.53	24.67	62
53	4.45	6.54	9.02	11.00	12.83	14.71	16.06	17.53	19.03	20.87	26.65	63
54	4.86	7.09	9.77	11.87	13.88	15.84	17.24	18.81	20.39	22.36	28.74	64
55	5.35	7.71	10.58	12.82	15.03	17.01	18.46	20.16	21.88	23.99	30.92	65
56	5.87	8.37	11.42	13.82	16.23	18.20	19.72	21.60	23.51	25.81	33.21	66
57	6.40	9.08	12.28	14.86	17.42	19.40	21.02	23.14	25.33	27.87	35.67	67
58	6.95	9.81	13.14	15.92	18.60	20.60	22.37	24.79	27.33	30.16	38.32	68
59	7.50	10.56	14.00	17.02	19.77	21.81	23.76	26.54	29.53	32.68	41.23	69
60	8.06	11.36	14.87	18.15	20.94	23.02	25.19	28.40	31.91	35.43	44.45	70
61	8.66	12.21	15.80	19.28	22.10	24.30	26.76	30.39	34.40	38.29	47.97	71
62	9.32	13.14	16.85	20.37	23.25	25.69	28.55	32.55	36.92	41.12	51.83	72
63	10.04	14.16	18.01	21.42	24.38	27.21	30.57	34.86	39.46	43.93	56.02	73
64	10.82	15.26	19.29	22.44	25.51	28.84	32.81	37.35	42.03	46.73	60.56	74
65	11.67	16.44	20.68	23.43	26.62	30.59	35.28	39.99	44.64	49.50	66.16	75
66	12.60	17.68	22.20	24.66	28.10	32.88	38.32	43.28	48.01	55.56	72.18	76
67	13.66	18.99	23.82	26.54	30.48	36.04	42.19	47.67	55.08	62.21	78.88	77
68	14.84	20.35	25.57	29.08	33.80	40.08	46.90	54.12	61.64	69.47	86.21	78
69	16.14	21.78	27.44	32.25	38.02	44.98	52.68	60.51	68.76	77.32	94.40	79
70	17.56	23.26	29.43	36.07	43.18	50.76	58.81	67.33	76.32	85.78	103.64	80
71	19.24	25.03	31.71	40.10	48.49	56.74	65.53	75.50	85.08	97.75	114.10	81
72	21.32	27.28	34.44	43.96	53.36	62.44	72.21	83.69	96.53	110.10	125.23	82
73	23.80	30.03	37.63	47.65	57.79	67.83	78.84	91.90	106.71	122.84	137.34	83
74	26.66	33.28	41.26	51.18	61.78	72.93	85.44	100.12	116.95	135.96	149.46	84
75	29.92	37.01	45.35	54.53	65.32	77.74	91.99	108.37	127.25	149.46	161.84	85
											174.37	86
											186.99	87
											199.62	88
											214.18	89
											228.97	90
											246.73	91
											266.86	92
											286.60	93
											307.58	94
											330.80	95
											368.53	96
											436.62	97
											500.48	98
											601.46	99

EFFECTIVE NOVEMBER 1, 1964

Reinsurance Agreement (continued)

THE ███████████ LIFE INSURANCE COMPANY

Additional Premiums for $1000 of Risk Premium Reinsurance on Substandard Risks (RPR-NR-Male)
Age Nearest Birthday

SUBSTANDARD   NR-M

EXTRA PREMIUMS FOR EACH TABLE OF RATING. FOR RATINGS HIGHER THAN TABLE ONE APPLY APPROPRIATE MULTIPLE

Age at Issue	One	Two	Three	Four	Five	Six	Seven	Eight	Nine	Ten	Thereafter	Attained Age
0	$ .35	$ .35	$ .35	$ .35	$ .35	$ .35	$ .35	$ .35	$ .35	$ .35	$ .35	10
1	.35	.35	.35	.35	.35	.35	.35	.35	.35	.35	.35	11
2	.35	.35	.35	.35	.35	.35	.35	.35	.35	.35	.35	12
3	.35	.35	.35	.35	.35	.35	.35	.35	.35	.35	.35	13
4	.35	.35	.35	.35	.35	.35	.35	.35	.35	.35	.35	14
5	.35	.35	.35	.35	.35	.35	.35	.35	.35	.35	.35	15
6	.35	.35	.35	.35	.35	.35	.35	.35	.35	.35	.35	16
7	.35	.35	.35	.35	.35	.35	.35	.35	.35	.35	.35	17
8	.35	.35	.35	.35	.35	.35	.35	.35	.35	.35	.35	18
9	.35	.35	.35	.35	.35	.35	.35	.35	.35	.35	.35	19
10	.35	.35	.35	.35	.35	.35	.35	.35	.35	.35	.35	20
11	.35	.35	.35	.35	.35	.35	.35	.35	.35	.35	.35	21
12	.35	.35	.35	.35	.35	.35	.35	.35	.35	.35	.35	22
13	.35	.35	.35	.35	.35	.35	.35	.35	.35	.35	.35	23
14	.35	.35	.35	.35	.35	.35	.35	.35	.35	.35	.35	24
15	.35	.35	.35	.35	.35	.35	.35	.35	.35	.35	.35	25
16	.35	.35	.35	.35	.35	.35	.35	.35	.35	.35	.36	26
17	.35	.35	.35	.35	.35	.35	.35	.35	.35	.36	.37	27
18	.35	.35	.35	.35	.35	.35	.35	.35	.36	.37	.38	28
19	.35	.35	.35	.35	.35	.35	.35	.36	.37	.38	.38	29
20	.35	.35	.35	.35	.35	.35	.36	.37	.38	.38	.39	30
21	.35	.35	.35	.35	.35	.36	.37	.38	.38	.39	.40	31
22	.35	.35	.35	.35	.36	.37	.38	.38	.39	.40	.42	32
23	.35	.35	.35	.36	.37	.38	.38	.39	.40	.42	.44	33
24	.35	.35	.36	.37	.38	.38	.39	.40	.42	.44	.48	34
25	.35	.35	.37	.38	.38	.39	.40	.42	.44	.48	.53	35
26	.35	.35	.37	.38	.39	.40	.41	.43	.47	.53	.59	36
27	.35	.35	.38	.39	.39	.40	.42	.46	.52	.59	.64	37
28	.35	.36	.39	.39	.40	.42	.45	.51	.57	.64	.68	38
29	.35	.37	.39	.40	.41	.44	.50	.56	.62	.68	.75	39
30	.35	.39	.40	.41	.43	.48	.55	.60	.67	.75	.81	40
31	.35	.40	.41	.44	.48	.54	.58	.64	.73	.81	.85	41
32	.35	.41	.44	.48	.53	.58	.64	.71	.78	.85	.90	42
33	.35	.42	.48	.53	.57	.63	.70	.77	.84	.90	.96	43
34	.36	.44	.51	.57	.63	.70	.77	.84	.90	.96	1.03	44
35	.38	.46	.55	.62	.70	.77	.84	.89	.96	1.03	1.13	45
36	.39	.49	.59	.68	.77	.83	.88	.95	1.03	1.13	1.26	46
37	.41	.52	.64	.74	.82	.87	.94	1.02	1.13	1.26	1.40	47
38	.43	.56	.70	.79	.87	.94	1.02	1.12	1.25	1.40	1.57	48
39	.45	.61	.74	.84	.94	1.01	1.11	1.24	1.39	1.57	1.75	49
40	.48	.65	.80	.90	1.01	1.11	1.24	1.39	1.55	1.75	1.90	50
41	.51	.69	.83	.96	1.08	1.21	1.35	1.52	1.70	1.90	2.07	51
42	.54	.73	.88	1.02	1.17	1.32	1.48	1.65	1.84	2.07	2.25	52
43	.58	.76	.94	1.11	1.27	1.43	1.60	1.80	2.01	2.25	2.44	53
44	.62	.80	1.01	1.20	1.38	1.56	1.75	1.96	2.18	2.44	2.65	54
45	.65	.86	1.09	1.31	1.51	1.70	1.90	2.13	2.38	2.65	2.87	55
46	.66	.90	1.17	1.40	1.63	1.82	2.05	2.29	2.55	2.82	3.09	56
47	.68	.95	1.24	1.50	1.74	1.96	2.19	2.44	2.71	2.98	3.32	57
48	.69	.99	1.32	1.60	1.88	2.10	2.35	2.60	2.87	3.15	3.54	58
49	.71	1.04	1.40	1.72	2.01	2.25	2.50	2.76	3.03	3.30	3.78	59

EFFECTIVE NOVEMBER 1, 1964

Reinsurance Agreement (continued)

THE ████████████████ LIFE INSURANCE COMPANY

Additional Premiums for $1OOO of Risk Premium Reinsurance on Substandard Risks (RPR-NR-Male)
Age Nearest Birthday

SUBSTANDARD   NR-M

EXTRA PREMIUMS FOR EACH TABLE OF RATING. FOR RATINGS HIGHER THAN TABLE ONE APPLY APPROPRIATE MULTIPLE

Age at Issue	One	Two	Three	Four	Five	Six	Seven	Eight	Nine	Ten	Thereafter	Attained Age
50	$ .72	$ 1.10	$ 1.51	$ 1.84	$ 2.15	$ 2.39	$ 2.64	$ 2.91	$ 3.18	$ 3.46	$ 4.05	60
51	.75	1.20	1.65	2.00	2.32	2.57	2.82	3.09	3.37	3.65	4.29	61
52	.83	1.31	1.79	2.16	2.50	2.75	3.02	3.28	3.56	3.85	4.53	62
53	.93	1.44	1.94	2.33	2.68	2.93	3.20	3.47	3.75	4.05	4.77	63
54	1.02	1.57	2.09	2.50	2.85	3.11	3.37	3.65	3.93	4.24	5.01	64
55	1.13	1.70	2.24	2.67	3.03	3.30	3.54	3.81	4.11	4.44	5.26	65
56	1.26	1.87	2.44	2.89	3.25	3.49	3.75	4.04	4.37	4.82	5.66	66
57	1.40	2.04	2.64	3.11	3.44	3.69	3.97	4.27	4.72	5.35	5.90	67
58	1.55	2.23	2.86	3.28	3.63	3.89	4.18	4.61	5.24	5.76	6.39	68
59	1.70	2.41	3.03	3.46	3.81	4.09	4.49	5.14	5.66	6.32	6.98	69
60	1.86	2.57	3.19	3.64	4.00	4.38	5.02	5.56	6.21	6.98	7.74	70
61	2.03	2.74	3.35	3.81	4.27	4.90	5.45	6.11	6.86	7.74	8.46	71
62	2.21	2.91	3.51	4.08	4.78	5.35	5.99	6.73	7.60	8.46	9.35	72
63	2.40	3.08	3.76	4.59	5.23	5.88	6.61	7.45	8.31	9.35	10.29	73
64	2.60	3.31	4.26	5.04	5.75	6.49	7.30	8.15	9.17	10.29	11.35	74
65	2.85	3.79	4.71	5.55	6.35	7.15	7.99	9.00	10.11	11.35	12.26	75
66	3.15	4.21	5.15	6.06	6.93	7.73	8.73	9.81	11.04	12.26	12.82	76
67	3.42	4.62	5.62	6.59	7.49	8.46	9.53	10.74	11.93	12.82	13.20	77
68	3.71	5.04	6.10	7.12	8.18	9.23	10.42	11.62	12.54	13.20	13.49	78
69	4.04	5.43	6.59	7.79	8.94	10.11	11.30	12.26	12.98	13.49	13.63	79
70	4.39	5.82	7.20	8.52	9.80	10.98	11.97	12.75	13.35	13.63	13.68	80
71	4.81	6.26	7.89	9.36	10.66	11.68	12.53	13.20	13.58	13.68	13.68	81
72	5.33	6.82	8.61	10.20	11.40	12.30	13.06	13.52	13.68	13.68	13.68	82
73	5.95	7.51	9.41	10.98	12.07	12.92	13.46	13.68	13.68	13.68	13.68	83
74	6.67	8.32	10.32	11.75	12.78	13.40	13.68	13.68	13.68	13.68	13.68	84
75	7.48	9.25	11.27	12.57	13.35	13.68	13.68	13.68	13.68	13.68	13.68	85
											13.68	86
											13.68	87
											13.68	88
											13.68	89
											13.68	90
											13.68	91
											13.68	92
											13.68	93
											13.68	94
											13.68	95
											13.68	96
											13.68	97
											13.68	98
											13.68	99

EFFECTIVE NOVEMBER 1, 1964

Reinsurance Agreement (continued)

THE LIFE INSURANCE COMPANY
Premiums for $1000 of Risk Premium Reinsurance (RPR-ER-Female)
Age Nearest Birthday

Premiums for Non-Medical Business	Annual Policy Fee To Be Added To Total Life Reinsurance Premium	
Use actual attained age with duration increased by 1, 2, or 4 years for age groups at issue 31-35, 36-40, 41-45, respectively.	$2.00 per M first year gross risk reinsured, with maximum of $5.00 per year first five years and $2.50 per year thereafter.	**ER-F**

STANDARD

Age at Issue	POLICY YEAR											Attained Age
	One	Two	Three	Four	Five	Six	Seven	Eight	Nine	Ten	Thereafter	
0	$7.15	$2.43	$2.24	$2.10	$1.99	$1.91	$1.84	$1.79	$1.75	$1.72	$1.70	10
1	2.43	2.24	2.10	1.99	1.91	1.84	1.79	1.75	1.72	1.70	1.70	11
2	2.24	2.10	1.99	1.91	1.84	1.79	1.75	1.72	1.70	1.70	1.76	12
3	2.10	1.99	1.91	1.84	1.79	1.75	1.72	1.70	1.70	1.73	1.85	13
4	1.99	1.91	1.84	1.79	1.75	1.72	1.70	1.70	1.73	1.79	1.96	14
5	1.91	1.84	1.79	1.75	1.72	1.70	1.70	1.73	1.78	1.86	2.06	15
6	1.84	1.79	1.75	1.72	1.70	1.70	1.73	1.77	1.85	1.93	2.15	16
7	1.79	1.75	1.72	1.70	1.70	1.73	1.76	1.84	1.92	2.00	2.24	17
8	1.75	1.72	1.70	1.70	1.72	1.75	1.83	1.91	1.99	2.05	2.32	18
9	1.72	1.70	1.70	1.71	1.74	1.82	1.90	1.98	2.04	2.09	2.40	19
10	1.70	1.70	1.70	1.73	1.81	1.89	1.97	2.03	2.08	2.13	2.47	20
11	1.69	1.69	1.72	1.80	1.87	1.95	2.01	2.07	2.12	2.16	2.54	21
12	1.68	1.70	1.77	1.84	1.92	1.99	2.05	2.10	2.14	2.18	2.60	22
13	1.68	1.73	1.81	1.89	1.96	2.03	2.08	2.12	2.17	2.20	2.64	23
14	1.68	1.75	1.85	1.93	2.00	2.06	2.10	2.15	2.19	2.22	2.66	24
15	1.68	1.77	1.88	1.96	2.03	2.07	2.13	2.17	2.21	2.24	2.68	25
16	1.69	1.79	1.90	1.99	2.03	2.11	2.15	2.19	2.22	2.26	2.69	26
17	1.70	1.81	1.93	1.99	2.07	2.13	2.17	2.20	2.24	2.28	2.71	27
18	1.71	1.83	1.93	2.03	2.09	2.15	2.18	2.22	2.26	2.30	2.74	28
19	1.72	1.83	1.96	2.04	2.11	2.16	2.20	2.24	2.28	2.34	2.79	29
20	1.73	1.85	1.98	2.06	2.12	2.18	2.22	2.26	2.32	2.38	2.84	30
21	1.74	1.87	1.99	2.08	2.14	2.20	2.24	2.30	2.36	2.44	2.90	31
22	1.75	1.88	2.01	2.09	2.16	2.22	2.28	2.34	2.42	2.50	2.97	32
23	1.76	1.89	2.02	2.11	2.18	2.26	2.32	2.40	2.48	2.57	3.05	33
24	1.77	1.90	2.04	2.13	2.21	2.29	2.37	2.45	2.54	2.66	3.14	34
25	1.78	1.92	2.05	2.15	2.24	2.34	2.42	2.51	2.63	2.76	3.24	35
26	1.79	1.93	2.08	2.18	2.29	2.39	2.48	2.60	2.73	2.87	3.37	36
27	1.80	1.95	2.10	2.23	2.34	2.45	2.57	2.70	2.83	2.99	3.52	37
28	1.81	1.96	2.14	2.27	2.39	2.53	2.66	2.79	2.95	3.13	3.68	38
29	1.82	1.99	2.17	2.32	2.46	2.62	2.75	2.91	3.08	3.29	3.85	39
30	1.83	2.01	2.21	2.38	2.54	2.71	2.86	3.03	3.24	3.48	4.03	40
31	1.84	2.03	2.26	2.45	2.62	2.81	2.98	3.19	3.42	3.69	4.21	41
32	1.85	2.06	2.32	2.52	2.72	2.93	3.13	3.36	3.62	3.92	4.40	42
33	1.86	2.10	2.38	2.61	2.82	3.07	3.30	3.55	3.85	4.16	4.60	43
34	1.87	2.13	2.44	2.70	2.95	3.23	3.48	3.77	4.08	4.40	4.81	44
35	1.88	2.17	2.52	2.81	3.09	3.41	3.69	4.00	4.31	4.66	5.04	45
36	1.89	2.21	2.60	2.93	3.26	3.61	3.91	4.22	4.56	4.93	5.30	46
37	1.90	2.26	2.70	3.08	3.44	3.82	4.13	4.46	4.83	5.19	5.59	47
38	1.91	2.31	2.82	3.24	3.63	4.03	4.36	4.72	5.08	5.47	5.88	48
39	1.92	2.39	2.96	3.42	3.83	4.26	4.61	4.97	5.35	5.75	6.20	49
40	1.95	2.48	3.10	3.60	4.04	4.50	4.85	5.23	5.63	6.06	6.51	50
41	1.99	2.57	3.25	3.79	4.26	4.73	5.11	5.50	5.93	6.37	6.88	51
42	2.04	2.68	3.42	3.99	4.48	4.99	5.37	5.80	6.23	6.73	7.24	52
43	2.10	2.80	3.59	4.19	4.71	5.24	5.66	6.09	6.58	7.08	7.70	53
44	2.17	2.92	3.76	4.41	4.95	5.52	5.95	6.43	6.93	7.47	8.19	54
45	2.25	3.05	3.96	4.63	5.22	5.80	6.28	6.77	7.31	7.87	8.75	55
46	2.33	3.20	4.15	4.88	5.48	6.13	6.61	7.15	7.70	8.30	9.30	56
47	2.44	3.35	4.37	5.13	5.79	6.45	6.98	7.53	8.12	8.76	9.93	57
48	2.55	3.53	4.60	5.42	6.10	6.81	7.36	7.94	8.58	9.25	10.54	58
49	2.68	3.71	4.86	5.70	6.44	7.18	7.76	8.39	9.06	9.77	11.21	59

EFFECTIVE NOVEMBER 1, 1964

Reinsurance Agreement (continued)

THE ███████████████ LIFE INSURANCE COMPANY

Premiums for $1000 of Risk Premium Reinsurance (RPR-ER-Female)

Age Nearest Birthday

Premiums for Non-Medical Business	Annual Policy Fee To Be Added To Total Life Reinsurance Premium	
Use actual attained age with duration increased by 1, 2, or 4 years for age groups at issue 31-35, 36-40, 41-45, respectively.	$2.00 per M first year gross risk reinsured, with maximum of $5.00 per year first five years and $2.50 per year thereafter.	**ER-F**

STANDARD

Age at Issue	One	Two	Three	Four	Five	Six	Seven	Eight	Nine	Ten	Thereafter	Attained Age
50	$2.82	$3.92	$5.12	$6.02	$6.79	$7.58	$8.20	$8.87	$9.57	$10.27	$11.98	60
51	2.98	4.14	5.41	6.36	7.17	8.01	8.68	9.37	10.07	10.87	12.90	61
52	3.15	4.38	5.71	6.72	7.59	8.48	9.17	9.87	10.66	11.54	13.92	62
53	3.34	4.63	6.05	7.12	8.04	8.97	9.66	10.45	11.32	12.34	15.10	63
54	3.55	4.92	6.42	7.56	8.52	9.45	10.24	11.10	12.11	13.37	16.51	64
55	3.79	5.25	6.83	8.02	9.00	10.03	10.88	11.88	13.12	14.57	18.18	65
56	4.07	5.62	7.27	8.49	9.55	10.66	11.65	12.87	14.29	15.97	20.04	66
57	4.41	6.02	7.72	9.02	10.17	11.41	12.61	14.01	15.65	17.59	22.19	67
58	4.77	6.45	8.23	9.62	10.88	12.35	13.73	15.33	17.23	19.46	24.70	68
59	5.17	6.91	8.80	10.30	11.77	13.44	15.01	16.87	19.05	21.48	27.49	69
60	5.59	7.43	9.43	11.13	12.80	14.69	16.51	18.64	21.02	23.55	30.42	70
61	6.06	7.97	10.18	12.09	13.98	16.15	18.23	20.56	23.04	25.75	33.26	71
62	6.51	8.58	11.03	13.18	15.34	17.82	20.10	22.52	25.18	28.13	36.17	72
63	6.98	9.26	11.99	14.44	16.90	19.63	22.00	24.60	27.49	30.72	39.34	73
64	7.48	10.00	13.09	15.88	18.58	21.48	24.02	26.85	30.02	33.57	42.80	74
65	8.00	10.84	14.34	17.42	20.31	23.44	26.21	29.32	32.81	37.12	46.53	75
66	8.59	11.78	15.69	19.01	22.14	25.57	28.62	32.05	36.28	41.11	50.76	76
67	9.22	12.79	17.07	20.70	24.14	27.92	31.29	35.44	40.18	45.77	55.48	77
68	9.89	13.83	18.54	22.54	26.35	30.52	34.59	39.24	44.73	50.99	60.63	78
69	10.59	14.93	20.15	24.60	28.80	33.74	38.30	43.68	49.81	56.75	66.39	79
70	11.32	16.16	21.97	26.89	31.83	37.36	42.63	48.64	55.45	63.38	72.89	80
71	12.16	17.60	24.03	29.72	35.25	41.58	47.47	54.14	61.92	71.67	82.76	81
72	13.22	19.26	26.55	32.91	39.23	46.31	52.83	60.45	69.99	80.78	93.57	82
73	14.49	21.26	29.39	36.61	43.68	51.52	58.98	68.30	78.85	90.25	105.64	83
74	15.97	23.53	32.68	40.75	48.59	57.51	66.61	76.92	88.07	100.06	118.25	84
75	17.67	26.14	36.36	45.32	54.20	64.92	74.99	85.89	97.63	110.22	131.61	85
											144.67	86
											158.22	87
											172.20	88
											188.29	89
											205.07	90
											225.04	91
											247.80	92
											270.85	93
											295.75	94
											323.53	95
											366.51	96
											441.42	97
											514.23	98
											627.89	99

EFFECTIVE NOVEMBER 1, 1964

Reinsurance Agreement (continued)

THE ▮▮▮▮▮▮▮▮▮▮ LIFE INSURANCE COMPANY

Additional Premiums for $1000 of Risk Premium Reinsurance on Substandard Risks (RPR-ER-Female)
Age Nearest Birthday

SUBSTANDARD   ER-F

EXTRA PREMIUMS FOR EACH TABLE OF RATING. FOR RATINGS HIGHER THAN TABLE ONE APPLY APPROPRIATE MULTIPLE

Age at Issue	One	Two	Three	Four	Five	Six	Seven	Eight	Nine	Ten	Thereafter	Attained Age
0	$ .44	$ .44	$ .44	$ .44	$ .44	$ .44	$ .44	$ .44	$ .44	$ .44	$ .44	10
1	.44	.44	.44	.44	.44	.44	.44	.44	.44	.44	.44	11
2	.44	.44	.44	.44	.44	.44	.44	.44	.44	.44	.44	12
3	.44	.44	.44	.44	.44	.44	.44	.44	.44	.44	.44	13
4	.44	.44	.44	.44	.44	.44	.44	.44	.44	.44	.44	14
5	.44	.44	.44	.44	.44	.44	.44	.44	.44	.44	.44	15
6	.44	.44	.44	.44	.44	.44	.44	.44	.44	.44	.44	16
7	.44	.44	.44	.44	.44	.44	.44	.44	.44	.44	.44	17
8	.44	.44	.44	.44	.44	.44	.44	.44	.44	.44	.44	18
9	.44	.44	.44	.44	.44	.44	.44	.44	.44	.44	.44	19
10	.44	.44	.44	.44	.44	.44	.44	.44	.44	.44	.44	20
11	.44	.44	.44	.44	.44	.44	.44	.44	.44	.44	.44	21
12	.44	.44	.44	.44	.44	.44	.44	.44	.44	.44	.44	22
13	.44	.44	.44	.44	.44	.44	.44	.44	.44	.44	.44	23
14	.44	.44	.44	.44	.44	.44	.44	.44	.44	.44	.44	24
15	.44	.44	.44	.44	.44	.44	.44	.44	.44	.44	.44	25
16	.44	.44	.44	.44	.44	.44	.44	.44	.44	.44	.44	26
17	.44	.44	.44	.44	.44	.44	.44	.44	.44	.44	.44	27
18	.44	.44	.44	.44	.44	.44	.44	.44	.44	.44	.44	28
19	.44	.44	.44	.44	.44	.44	.44	.44	.44	.44	.45	29
20	.44	.44	.44	.44	.44	.44	.44	.44	.44	.45	.46	30
21	.44	.44	.44	.44	.44	.44	.44	.44	.45	.46	.47	31
22	.44	.44	.44	.44	.44	.44	.44	.45	.46	.47	.48	32
23	.44	.44	.44	.44	.44	.44	.45	.46	.47	.48	.49	33
24	.44	.44	.44	.44	.44	.45	.46	.47	.48	.49	.50	34
25	.44	.44	.44	.44	.45	.46	.47	.48	.49	.50	.52	35
26	.44	.44	.44	.45	.46	.47	.48	.49	.50	.52	.55	36
27	.44	.44	.45	.46	.47	.48	.49	.50	.52	.55	.60	37
28	.44	.45	.46	.47	.48	.49	.50	.52	.55	.60	.66	38
29	.44	.45	.46	.47	.48	.49	.51	.53	.58	.66	.72	39
30	.44	.45	.46	.47	.48	.49	.51	.56	.64	.72	.77	40
31	.44	.45	.46	.47	.48	.50	.54	.62	.69	.77	.81	41
32	.45	.46	.47	.47	.48	.52	.60	.67	.74	.81	.88	42
33	.45	.46	.47	.48	.51	.57	.64	.71	.79	.88	.94	43
34	.45	.46	.47	.51	.56	.62	.68	.75	.85	.94	.98	44
35	.45	.47	.51	.56	.61	.67	.74	.82	.90	.98	1.02	45
36	.45	.48	.54	.60	.65	.72	.80	.88	.95	1.02	1.07	46
37	.45	.49	.57	.64	.70	.78	.86	.93	1.00	1.07	1.13	47
38	.45	.51	.60	.68	.77	.85	.92	.98	1.05	1.13	1.23	48
39	.45	.53	.64	.74	.84	.90	.96	1.03	1.12	1.23	1.36	49
40	.46	.56	.69	.80	.88	.94	1.01	1.10	1.21	1.36	1.49	50
41	.48	.60	.74	.84	.93	1.00	1.08	1.19	1.33	1.49	1.64	51
42	.50	.64	.78	.88	.98	1.06	1.16	1.30	1.46	1.64	1.80	52
43	.53	.68	.82	.93	1.04	1.14	1.28	1.43	1.60	1.77	1.93	53
44	.54	.72	.86	.99	1.12	1.25	1.40	1.57	1.73	1.87	2.05	54
45	.56	.76	.92	1.06	1.22	1.37	1.54	1.69	1.83	1.97	2.19	55
46	.58	.80	.98	1.16	1.33	1.50	1.65	1.79	1.93	2.08	2.33	56
47	.61	.84	1.06	1.26	1.45	1.61	1.75	1.88	2.03	2.19	2.48	57
48	.64	.88	1.15	1.36	1.53	1.70	1.84	1.99	2.15	2.31	2.64	58
49	.67	.93	1.22	1.43	1.61	1.80	1.94	2.10	2.27	2.44	2.80	59

EFFECTIVE NOVEMBER 1, 1964

Reinsurance Agreement (continued)

THE ████████████ LIFE INSURANCE COMPANY

Additional Premiums for $1000 of Risk Premium Reinsurance on Substandard Risks (RPR-ER-Female)
Age Nearest Birthday

SUBSTANDARD   ER-F

EXTRA PREMIUMS FOR EACH TABLE OF RATING. FOR RATINGS HIGHER THAN TABLE ONE APPLY APPROPRIATE MULTIPLE

Age at Issue	POLICY YEAR											Attained Age
	One	Two	Three	Four	Five	Six	Seven	Eight	Nine	Ten	Thereafter	
50	$ .71	$ .98	$ 1.28	$ 1.51	$ 1.70	$ 1.90	$ 2.05	$ 2.22	$ 2.39	$ 2.57	$ 3.00	60
51	.75	1.04	1.35	1.59	1.79	2.00	2.17	2.34	2.52	2.72	3.23	61
52	.79	1.10	1.43	1.68	1.90	2.12	2.29	2.47	2.67	2.89	3.48	62
53	.83	1.16	1.51	1.78	2.01	2.24	2.42	2.61	2.83	3.09	3.78	63
54	.87	1.23	1.61	1.89	2.13	2.36	2.56	2.78	3.03	3.34	4.13	64
55	.95	1.31	1.71	2.01	2.25	2.51	2.72	2.97	3.28	3.64	4.55	65
56	1.02	1.41	1.82	2.12	2.39	2.67	2.91	3.22	3.57	3.99	4.97	66
57	1.10	1.51	1.93	2.26	2.54	2.85	3.15	3.50	3.91	4.40	5.22	67
58	1.19	1.61	2.06	2.41	2.72	3.09	3.43	3.83	4.31	4.87	5.60	68
59	1.29	1.73	2.20	2.58	2.94	3.36	3.75	4.22	4.76	5.37	6.15	69
60	1.40	1.86	2.36	2.78	3.20	3.67	4.13	4.66	5.26	5.89	6.55	70
61	1.52	1.99	2.55	3.02	3.50	4.04	4.56	5.14	5.76	6.44	7.10	71
62	1.63	2.15	2.76	3.30	3.84	4.46	5.03	5.63	6.30	7.03	7.75	72
63	1.75	2.32	3.00	3.61	4.23	4.87	5.50	6.15	6.87	7.68	8.50	73
64	1.87	2.50	3.27	3.97	4.65	5.37	5.99	6.71	7.51	8.39	9.20	74
65	2.00	2.71	3.59	4.36	5.08	5.81	6.51	7.32	8.20	9.20	10.05	75
66	2.15	2.95	3.92	4.75	5.54	6.32	7.11	8.01	8.94	10.05	10.95	76
67	2.31	3.20	4.27	5.18	6.04	6.90	7.77	8.67	9.76	10.95	11.95	77
68	2.47	3.46	4.64	5.64	6.59	7.53	8.41	9.47	10.64	11.95	12.90	78
69	2.65	3.73	5.04	6.15	7.20	8.14	9.19	10.33	11.62	12.90	13.50	79
70	2.83	4.04	5.49	6.72	7.88	8.90	10.03	11.30	12.56	13.50	13.90	80
71	3.04	4.40	6.01	7.43	8.61	9.72	10.97	12.23	13.20	13.90	14.20	81
72	3.31	4.82	6.64	8.20	9.41	10.64	11.89	12.90	13.66	14.20	14.35	82
73	3.62	5.32	7.35	8.97	10.32	11.56	12.60	13.42	14.05	14.35	14.40	83
74	3.99	5.88	8.17	9.85	11.22	12.30	13.19	13.90	14.29	14.40	14.40	84
75	4.42	6.54	9.09	10.74	12.00	12.95	13.75	14.23	14.40	14.40	14.40	85
											14.40	86
											14.40	87
											14.40	88
											14.40	89
											14.40	90
											14.40	91
											14.40	92
											14.40	93
											14.40	94
											14.40	95
											14.40	96
											14.40	97
											14.40	98
											14.40	99

EFFECTIVE NOVEMBER 1, 1964

Reinsurance Agreement (continued)

THE ████████████████ LIFE INSURANCE COMPANY

Premiums for $1000 of Risk Premium Reinsurance (RPR-NR-Female)
Age Nearest Birthday

Premiums for Non-Medical Business	Annual Policy Fee To Be Added To Total Life Reinsurance Premium
Use actual attained age with duration increased by 1, 2, or 4 years for age groups at issue 31-35, 36-40, 41-45, respectively.	$2.00 per M first year gross risk reinsured, with maximum of $5.00 per year first five years and $2.50 per year thereafter.

NR-F

STANDARD

Age at Issue	One	Two	Three	Four	Five	Six	Seven	Eight	Nine	Ten	Thereafter	Attained Age
					POLICY YEAR							
0	$6.50	$1.70	$1.50	$1.38	$1.30	$1.22	$1.15	$1.09	$1.05	$1.02	$1.00	10
1	1.70	1.50	1.38	1.30	1.22	1.15	1.09	1.05	1.02	1.00	1.00	11
2	1.50	1.38	1.30	1.22	1.15	1.09	1.05	1.02	1.00	1.00	1.03	12
3	1.38	1.30	1.22	1.15	1.09	1.05	1.02	1.00	1.00	1.00	1.07	13
4	1.30	1.22	1.15	1.09	1.05	1.02	1.00	1.00	1.00	1.01	1.14	14
5	1.22	1.15	1.09	1.05	1.02	1.00	1.00	1.00	1.01	1.03	1.22	15
6	1.15	1.09	1.05	1.02	1.00	1.00	1.00	1.01	1.03	1.06	1.30	16
7	1.09	1.05	1.02	1.00	1.00	1.00	1.01	1.03	1.06	1.09	1.39	17
8	1.05	1.02	1.00	1.00	1.00	1.01	1.03	1.06.	1.08	1.13	1.48	18
9	1.02	1.00	1.00	1.00	1.01	1.03	1.05	1.07	1.12	1.17	1.57	19
10	1.00	1.00	1.00	1.01	1.02	1.04	1.06	1.11	1.16	1.20	1.67	20
11	.99	.99	1.00	1.01	1.03	1.05	1.10	1.15	1.19	1.22	1.75	21
12	.98	.99	1.00	1.02	1.04	1.09	1.14	1.18	1.21	1.24	1.83	22
13	.98	.99	1.01	1.03	1.08	1.13	1.17	1.20	1.23	1.26	1.90	23
14	.98	1.00	1.02	1.07	1.12	1.16	1.19	1.22	1.25	1.28	1.96	24
15	.98	1.00	1.05	1.11	1.15	1.18	1.21	1.24	1.27	1.30	2.01	25
16	.98	1.02	1.09	1.13	1.17	1.20	1.23	1.26	1.29	1.32	2.06	26
17	.99	1.04	1.11	1.15	1.19	1.22	1.25	1.28	1.31	1.34	2.10	27
18	1.00	1.06	1.12	1.17	1.21	1.24	1.27	1.30	1.33	1.36	2.13	28
19	1.01	1.07	1.14	1.18	1.22	1.26	1.29	1.32	1.35	1.39	2.17	29
20	1.02	1.08	1.15	1.20	1.24	1.28	1.31	1.34	1.38	1.43	2.22	30
21	1.03	1.10	1.17	1.22	1.26	1.30	1.33	1.37	1.42	1.48	2.28	31
22	1.04	1.11	1.18	1.23	1.28	1.32	1.36	1.41	1.47	1.55	2.35	32
23	1.05	1.12	1.20	1.25	1.29	1.34	1.40	1.46	1.54	1.62	2.43	33
24	1.06	1.13	1.21	1.27	1.32	1.38	1.44	1.52	1.60	1.72	2.51	34
25	1.07	1.15	1.23	1.29	1.35	1.42	1.50	1.58	1.70	1.82	2.60	35
26	1.08	1.16	1.25	1.32	1.39	1.48	1.56	1.68	1.80	1.94	2.70	36
27	1.09	1.17	1.27	1.35	1.45	1.54	1.66	1.77	1.91	2.08	2.82	37
28	1.10	1.19	1.30	1.40	1.50	1.63	1.74	1.88	2.05	2.23	2.96	38
29	1.11	1.21	1.34	1.45	1.58	1.71	1.85	2.02	2.19	2.40	3.10	39
30	1.12	1.24	1.38	1.52	1.66	1.82	1.98	2.15	2.36	2.57	3.25	40
31	1.13	1.26	1.44	1.59	1.75	1.94	2.11	2.31	2.52	2.75	3.41	41
32	1.14	1.29	1.49	1.67	1.86	2.06	2.26	2.47	2.69	2.95	3.58	42
33	1.15	1.33	1.55	1.76	1.97	2.21	2.41	2.63	2.89	3.16	3.77	43
34	1.16	1.36	1.63	1.87	2.10	2.35	2.57	2.82	3.09	3.38	3.97	44
35	1.17	1.41	1.71	1.98	2.23	2.51	2.75	3.02	3.30	3.61	4.17	45
36	1.18	1.45	1.80	2.09	2.37	2.68	2.94	3.22	3.52	3.85	4.39	46
37	1.19	1.50	1.89	2.22	2.53	2.86	3.14	3.43	3.76	4.08	4.62	47
38	1.20	1.55	1.99	2.36	2.69	3.05	3.34	3.67	3.98	4.33	4.87	48
39	1.21	1.61	2.10	2.51	2.87	3.25	3.57	3.88	4.22	4.60	5.15	49
40	1.23	1.68	2.23	2.67	3.05	3.47	3.78	4.11	4.49	4.88	5.47	50
41	1.26	1.76	2.36	2.83	3.25	3.67	4.00	4.38	4.76	5.16	5.83	51
42	1.29	1.85	2.50	3.01	3.44	3.89	4.26	4.64	5.04	5.49	6.25	52
43	1.34	1.95	2.65	3.18	3.65	4.14	4.52	4.91	5.36	5.82	6.70	53
44	1.39	2.05	2.80	3.38	3.88	4.39	4.78	5.23	5.68	6.20	7.17	54
45	1.45	2.16	2.97	3.59	4.12	4.65	5.09	5.54	6.05	6.59	7.70	55
46	1.52	2.29	3.15	3.81	4.36	4.95	5.40	5.90	6.43	6.99	8.23	56
47	1.61	2.43	3.35	4.04	4.64	5.25	5.75	6.27	6.83	7.41	8.83	57
48	1.71	2.59	3.55	4.30	4.92	5.59	6.11	6.66	7.24	7.83	9.44	58
49	1.83	2.75	3.79	4.57	5.25	5.95	6.49	7.07	7.65	8.28	10.09	59

EFFECTIVE NOVEMBER 1, 1964

Reinsurance Agreement (continued)

THE ███████████ LIFE INSURANCE COMPANY
Premiums for $1000 of Risk Premium Reinsurance (RPR-NR-Female)
Age Nearest Birthday

Premiums for Non-Medical Business	Annual Policy Fee To Be Added To Total Life Reinsurance Premium
Use actual attained age with duration increased by 1, 2, or 4 years for age groups at issue 31-35, 36-40, 41-45, respectively.	$2.00 per M first year gross risk reinsured, with maximum of $5.00 per year first five years and $2.50 per year thereafter.

NR-F

STANDARD

Age at Issue	One	Two	Three	Four	Five	Six	Seven	Eight	Nine	Ten	Thereafter	Attained Age
50	$1.95	$2.94	$4.03	$4.87	$5.59	$6.32	$6.89	$7.47	$8.10	$8.71	$10.78	60
51	2.09	3.14	4.31	5.20	5.95	6.71	7.29	7.91	8.52	9.20	11.62	61
52	2.24	3.36	4.60	5.53	6.32	7.11	7.72	8.33	9.00	9.78	12.54	62
53	2.41	3.61	4.91	5.89	6.71	7.53	8.14	8.80	9.57	10.46	13.60	63
54	2.61	3.87	5.24	6.25	7.11	7.94	8.60	9.36	10.24	11.33	14.87	64
55	2.83	4.15	5.58	6.65	7.51	8.40	9.15	10.01	11.09	12.38	16.37	65
56	3.06	4.45	5.95	7.03	7.95	8.94	9.78	10.84	12.11	13.59	18.02	66
57	3.33	4.78	6.30	7.45	8.46	9.55	10.59	11.83	13.28	15.05	19.98	67
58	3.61	5.10	6.69	7.93	9.04	10.34	11.55	12.97	14.70	16.76	22.23	68
59	3.90	5.44	7.14	8.48	9.78	11.27	12.66	14.35	16.37	18.63	24.74	69
60	4.19	5.82	7.63	9.14	10.65	12.35	14.00	15.97	18.19	20.55	27.36	70
61	4.50	6.22	8.22	9.96	11.65	13.65	15.57	17.74	20.05	22.59	29.93	71
62	4.80	6.67	8.92	10.88	12.86	15.17	17.29	19.55	22.04	24.67	32.55	72
63	5.12	7.19	9.72	11.99	14.28	16.84	19.05	21.49	24.07	27.24	35.40	73
64	5.46	7.79	10.68	13.28	15.83	18.55	20.94	23.47	26.58	29.91	38.52	74
65	5.85	8.49	11.79	14.71	17.43	20.38	22.86	25.92	29.19	32.90	42.34	75
66	6.30	9.31	13.02	16.18	19.14	22.26	25.26	28.47	32.12	36.67	46.20	76
67	6.83	10.22	14.31	17.76	20.91	24.59	27.75	31.34	35.81	41.06	50.48	77
68	7.42	11.19	15.68	19.40	23.10	27.03	30.56	34.94	40.09	45.85	55.17	78
69	8.07	12.23	17.14	21.44	25.41	29.77	34.07	39.12	44.77	50.70	60.42	79
70	8.78	13.38	19.95	23.61	28.01	33.20	38.15	43.69	49.52	56.61	66.33	80
71	9.62	14.80	20.90	26.05	31.24	37.18	42.61	48.34	55.29	64.52	75.31	81
72	10.66	16.40	23.11	29.07	34.99	41.53	47.15	53.97	62.99	72.67	85.16	82
73	11.90	18.22	25.82	32.57	39.09	45.96	52.64	61.45	70.92	81.07	96.14	83
74	13.33	20.39	28.93	36.39	43.29	51.31	59.91	69.17	79.11	89.73	107.61	84
75	14.96	22.86	32.34	40.32	48.33	58.37	67.42	77.15	87.55	98.64	119.76	85
											131.65	86
											143.98	87
											156.70	88
											171.34	89
											186.61	90
											204.79	91
											225.50	92
											246.48	93
											269.13	94
											294.41	95
											333.52	96
											401.69	97
											467.95	98
											571.39	99

EFFECTIVE NOVEMBER 1, 1964

Reinsurance Agreement (continued)

THE ████████████ LIFE INSURANCE COMPANY

Additional Premiums for $1000 of Risk Premium Reinsurance on Substandard Risks (RPR-NR-Female)
Age Nearest Birthday

SUBSTANDARD

NR-F

EXTRA PREMIUMS FOR EACH TABLE OF RATING. FOR RATINGS HIGHER THAN TABLE ONE APPLY APPROPRIATE MULTIPLE

Age at Issue	POLICY YEAR											Attained Age
	One	Two	Three	Four	Five	Six	Seven	Eight	Nine	Ten	Thereafter	
0	$ .35	$ .35	$ .35	$ .35	$ .35	$ .35	$ .35	$ .35	$ .35	$ .35	$ .35	10
1	.35	.35	.35	.35	.35	.35	.35	.35	.35	.35	.35	11
2	.35	.35	.35	.35	.35	.35	.35	.35	.35	.35	.35	12
3	.35	.35	.35	.35	.35	.35	.35	.35	.35	.35	.35	13
4	.35	.35	.35	.35	.35	.35	.35	.35	.35	.35	.35	14
5	.35	.35	.35	.35	.35	.35	.35	.35	.35	.35	.35	15
6	.35	.35	.35	.35	.35	.35	.35	.35	.35	.35	.35	16
7	.35	.35	.35	.35	.35	.35	.35	.35	.35	.35	.35	17
8	.35	.35	.35	.35	.35	.35	.35	.35	.35	.35	.35	18
9	.35	.35	.35	.35	.35	.35	.35	.35	.35	.35	.35	19
10	.35	.35	.35	.35	.35	.35	.35	.35	.35	.35	.35	20
11	.35	.35	.35	.35	.35	.35	.35	.35	.35	.35	.35	21
12	.35	.35	.35	.35	.35	.35	.35	.35	.35	.35	.35	22
13	.35	.35	.35	.35	.35	.35	.35	.35	.35	.35	.35	23
14	.35	.35	.35	.35	.35	.35	.35	.35	.35	.35	.35	24
15	.35	.35	.35	.35	.35	.35	.35	.35	.35	.35	.35	25
16	.35	.35	.35	.35	.35	.35	.35	.35	.35	.35	.35	26
17	.35	.35	.35	.35	.35	.35	.35	.35	.35	.35	.35	27
18	.35	.35	.35	.35	.35	.35	.35	.35	.35	.35	.35	28
19	.35	.35	.35	.35	.35	.35	.35	.35	.35	.35	.36	29
20	.35	.35	.35	.35	.35	.35	.35	.35	.35	.36	.37	30
21	.35	.35	.35	.35	.35	.35	.35	.35	.36	.37	.38	31
22	.35	.35	.35	.35	.35	.35	.35	.35	.37	.38	.38	32
23	.35	.35	.35	.35	.35	.35	.35	.37	.38	.38	.39	33
24	.35	.35	.35	.35	.35	.35	.36	.38	.38	.39	.40	34
25	.35	.35	.35	.35	.35	.36	.38	.38	.39	.40	.42	35
26	.35	.35	.35	.35	.35	.37	.38	.39	.40	.42	.44	36
27	.35	.35	.35	.35	.36	.38	.39	.40	.42	.44	.48	37
28	.35	.35	.35	.35	.38	.39	.40	.42	.44	.48	.53	38
29	.35	.35	.35	.36	.39	.40	.41	.43	.47	.53	.59	39
30	.35	.35	.35	.38	.39	.40	.42	.46	.52	.59	.64	40
31	.35	.35	.36	.39	.40	.42	.45	.51	.57	.64	.68	41
32	.35	.35	.37	.40	.41	.44	.50	.56	.62	.68	.75	42
33	.35	.35	.39	.41	.43	.48	.55	.60	.67	.75	.81	43
34	.35	.35	.41	.44	.48	.54	.58	.64	.73	.81	.85	44
35	.35	.35	.43	.48	.53	.58	.64	.71	.78	.85	.90	45
36	.35	.36	.45	.52	.57	.63	.70	.77	.84	.90	.96	46
37	.35	.38	.47	.56	.63	.70	.77	.84	.90	.96	1.03	47
38	.35	.39	.50	.59	.67	.76	.84	.89	.96	1.03	1.13	48
39	.35	.40	.53	.63	.72	.81	.88	.95	1.03	1.13	1.26	49
40	.35	.42	.56	.67	.76	.87	.94	1.02	1.12	1.22	1.37	50
41	.35	.44	.59	.71	.81	.92	1.00	1.10	1.19	1.29	1.46	51
42	.35	.46	.63	.75	.86	.97	1.07	1.16	1.26	1.37	1.56	52
43	.35	.49	.66	.80	.91	1.04	1.13	1.23	1.34	1.46	1.68	53
44	.35	.51	.70	.85	.97	1.10	1.20	1.31	1.42	1.55	1.79	54
45	.36	.54	.74	.90	1.03	1.16	1.27	1.39	1.51	1.65	1.93	55
46	.38	.57	.79	.95	1.09	1.24	1.35	1.48	1.61	1.75	2.06	56
47	.40	.61	.84	1.01	1.16	1.31	1.44	1.57	1.71	1.85	2.21	57
48	.43	.65	.89	1.08	1.23	1.40	1.53	1.67	1.81	1.96	2.36	58
49	.46	.69	.95	1.14	1.31	1.49	1.62	1.77	1.91	2.07	2.52	59

EFFECTIVE NOVEMBER 1, 1964

Reinsurance Agreement (concluded)

THE ■■■■■■■■■■■■ LIFE INSURANCE COMPANY

Additional Premiums for $1000 of Risk Premium Reinsurance on Substandard Risks (RPR-NR-Female)
Age Nearest Birthday

SUBSTANDARD

NR-F

EXTRA PREMIUMS FOR EACH TABLE OF RATING. FOR RATINGS HIGHER THAN TABLE ONE APPLY APPROPRIATE MULTIPLE

Age at Issue	POLICY YEAR											Attained Age
	One	Two	Three	Four	Five	Six	Seven	Eight	Nine	Ten	Thereafter	
50	$ .49	$ .74	$ 1.01	$ 1.22	$ 1.40	$ 1.58	$ 1.72	$ 1.87	$ 2.03	$ 2.18	$ 2.70	60
51	.52	.79	1.08	1.30	1.49	1.68	1.82	1.98	2.13	2.30	2.91	61
52	.56	.84	1.15	1.38	1.58	1.78	1.93	2.08	2.25	2.45	3.14	62
53	.60	.90	1.23	1.47	1.68	1.88	2.04	2.20	2.39	2.62	3.40	63
54	.65	.97	1.31	1.56	1.78	1.99	2.15	2.34	2.56	2.83	3.72	64
55	.71	1.04	1.40	1.66	1.88	2.10	2.29	2.50	2.77	3.10	4.09	65
56	.77	1.11	1.49	1.76	1.99	2.24	2.45	2.71	3.03	3.40	4.51	66
57	.83	1.20	1.58	1.86	2.12	2.39	2.65	2.96	3.32	3.76	5.00	67
58	.90	1.28	1.67	1.98	2.26	2.59	2.89	3.24	3.68	4.19	5.26	68
59	.98	1.36	1.79	2.12	2.45	2.82	3.17	3.59	4.09	4.66	5.66	69
60	1.05	1.46	1.91	2.29	2.66	3.09	3.50	3.99	4.55	5.14	5.90	70
61	1.13	1.56	2.06	2.49	2.91	3.41	3.89	4.44	5.01	5.65	6.39	71
62	1.20	1.67	2.23	2.72	3.22	3.79	4.32	4.89	5.51	6.17	6.98	72
63	1.28	1.80	2.43	3.00	3.57	4.21	4.76	5.37	6.02	6.81	7.74	73
64	1.37	1.95	2.67	3.32	3.96	4.64	5.24	5.87	6.65	7.48	8.46	74
65	1.46	2.12	2.95	3.68	4.36	5.10	5.72	6.48	7.30	8.23	9.35	75
66	1.58	2.33	3.26	4.05	4.79	5.57	6.32	7.12	8.03	9.17	10.29	76
67	1.71	2.56	3.58	4.44	5.23	6.15	6.94	7.84	8.95	10.27	11.35	77
68	1.86	2.80	3.92	4.85	5.78	6.76	7.64	8.74	10.02	11.35	12.26	78
69	2.02	3.06	4.29	5.36	6.35	7.44	8.52	9.78	11.04	12.26	12.82	79
70	2.20	3.35	4.99	5.90	7.00	8.30	9.53	10.74	11.93	12.82	13.20	80
71	2.41	3.70	5.23	6.51	7.81	9.23	10.42	11.62	12.54	13.20	13.49	81
72	2.67	4.10	5.78	7.27	8.75	10.11	11.30	12.26	12.98	13.49	13.63	82
73	2.98	4.56	6.46	8.14	9.77	10.98	11.97	12.75	13.35	13.63	13.68	83
74	3.33	5.10	7.23	9.10	10.66	11.68	12.53	13.20	13.58	13.68	13.68	84
75	3.74	5.72	8.09	10.08	11.40	12.30	13.06	13.52	13.68	13.68	13.68	85
											13.68	86
											13.68	87
											13.68	88
											13.68	89
											13.68	90
											13.68	91
											13.68	92
											13.68	93
											13.68	94
											13.68	95
											13.68	96
											13.68	97
											13.68	98
											13.68	99

EFFECTIVE NOVEMBER 1, 1964

SCHEDULE D *(Continued)*

Waiver of Premium Disability and Payor Benefits

The premium which the REINSURED charges the insured on the amount reinsured less total allowances of 75 percent first year and 10 percent in renewal years.

Accidental Death Benefits

Based on the classification of the occupational manual of the REINSURED:

| | Rates per Thousand | |
Classification	First Year	Renewal
Standard	$0.25	$0.90
1½ × Standard	0.40	1.25
2 × Standard	0.50	1.60
3 × Standard	0.75	2.35
5 × Standard	1.25	3.80

SCHEDULE E

Experience Refund Formula

I.   Provided that the REINSURED has earned Experience Refund Risk Premium Reinsurance Life premiums during the calendar year (*a*) of at least $15,000, or (*b*) of at least $1,000 and an automatic experience refund reinsurance agreement under the terms of which 50 percent or more of its excess is ceded to the ———— (the requirement of $1,000 earned premiums will be waived for the first experience refund computation), Experience Refunds will be computed according to the following formula:

$$ER = \frac{1}{2}\,(EP + A - E - C - LP), \text{ if positive}$$
$$= 0, \text{ otherwise,}$$

where ER = Experience Refund;

EP = Earned Experience Refund Risk Premium Reinsurance Life premiums for the calendar year, defined as one-half the sum of such premiums for the current and preceding calendar years. Premiums for a calendar year are the collected premiums appropriately adjusted for renewal premiums on reinsurance with November and December anniversaries (the word "premiums," as used here, means basic premiums exclusive of policy fees);

A = A production adjustment equal to one-half the premiums for the calendar year less one-half the premiums for the preceding calendar year (the sum of any negative production adjustments shall not exceed the sum of previously-credited positive production adjustments);

E = An expense and contingency charge as specified in III;

C = Incurred claims for the calendar year, including claim expenses incurred by the REINSURED for which it is reimbursed by the ————;

LP = Losses of prior years which have not been amortized or forgiven.

(LC = Loss of the current year to be carried forward in computing the experience refund of certain subsequent calendar years, in symbols:

$$LC = C + E - EP - A, \text{ if positive}$$
$$= 0, \text{ otherwise})$$

A loss arising from reinsurance under the agreement will be forgiven if not amortized by the end of the third year following the year of loss. Losses which expire first will be amortized first.

II.   If the REINSURED does not meet the qualifications in I, above, Experience Refunds will be computed on a pooled basis provided there are no unamortized and unforgiven losses of prior years during which Experience Refunds of the REINSURED were computed on a nonpooled basis. For companies with such losses, Experience Refunds will be computed according to the formula specified in I until such losses are amortized or forgiven. For each pool company, the "excess" defined as $EP^\circ - E - C$ will be computed. EP° is defined as earned Risk Premium Reinsurance Life premiums reduced by 50% of the decrease, if any, of the premiums for the calendar year from those for the preceding calendar year. Such reductions shall not exceed the amount of production adjustments previously granted. The aggregate pool refund shall be 50% of the sum of the excesses unless such sum is negative, in which case the aggregate refund shall be zero and the aggregate excess will be treated as a claim in computing the refund of the succeeding calendar year. A company with a positive excess will share in the aggregate refund in proportion to its excess. E is as specified in III. Should the _____ so choose, an experience refund may be paid even though the aggregate pool refund computed as above is zero. In such instances the _____ shall have the right to appropriately adjust future aggregate pool refunds.

III.   Except as hereinafter provided, the expense and contingency charge shall be the percentage of the earned Experience Refund Risk Premium Reinsurance Life premiums specified in the following table:

EP	Percent
$95,000.01 or greater	6.0
85,000.01 to $95,000	6.5
75,000.01 to 85,000	7.0
65,000.01 to 75,000	7.5
55,000.01 to 65,000	8.0
45,000.01 to 55,000	8.5
35,000.01 to 45,000	9.0
25,000.01 to 35,000	9.5
0.01 to 25,000	10.0

The expense and contingency charge applicable to Experience Refund Risk Premium Life reinsurance under an automatic reinsurance agreement providing that at least 80% of the REINSURED'S excess will be reinsured with the _____ shall be 6%. Any future change in the reinsurance agreement which reduces the portion of the REINSURED'S excess ceded to the _____ to less than 80 percent shall not cause the expense charge to be increased on business ceded prior to the date of such change.

IV.   Experience Refunds for Supplemental Benefits will be computed on a pooled basis.

V.   The _____ reserves the right to change the basis of Experience Refund computation from time to time.

indexes

Index of Names

A

Abelle, Barnie E., 780
Allen, Everett T., Jr., 528–29, 547
Alvord, Morgan H., 613, 614
Anderson, Buist M., 112n, 1021
Anderson, James C. H., 156
Anderson, O. D., 1101
Angle, John C., 333
Appleman, John Alan, 716
Archibald, J. C., 449
Arends, Verne J., 587
Aronsohn, Alan J. B., 702
Aschemeyer, Frank P., 988n, 990

B

Barnhart, E. Paul, 332
Bartleson, Edwin L., 289, 302, 319, 332,
    347, 1100n, 1101
Batchelder, Joseph E., III, 675
Beadles, William T., 27, 38, 55, 120, 1021
Becker, Gary S., 21
Belth, Joseph M., 46n, 52, 156, 186n, 218,
    220n, 224
Best Company, A. M., 223–24
Biggs, John H., 255
Black, Kenneth, Jr., 17, 26, 65, 77, 91, 105,
    172, 193, 371, 950, 963, 1102
Blair, B. Franklin, 1054
Blaug, Mark, 18n, 25
Boeckner, Robert G., 140
Bohner, Theodore J., 906
Boothroyd, Herbert J., 471
Bowe, William J., 891
Bower, William J., 906
Bowles, Thomas F., Jr., 1054
Bragg, John M., 238, 332
Brimmer, Andrew F., 1035
Bronson, Dorrance C., 613, 638n, 643
Brosterman, Robert, 815
Brown, John E., 24n
Brown, Lawrence R., Jr., 833
Brown, Robert A., Jr., 730
Buley, R. Carlyle, 1092n, 1093n, 1101

Burleson, Ira L., 990
Burns, Eveline M., 767
Burns, J. W., 1075
Bush, J. S., 865
Butcher, Marjorie V., 139

C

Cagan, Phillip, 14n
Caine, N. R., 718n
Campbell, Paul A., 240, 255
Casey, William J., 272
Casner, Andrew James, 865, 891
Chandler, Brooks, 275, 449
Chasman, Herbert, 731, 747, 906
Cheit, Earl F., 351n
Chittick, Ralph J., 990
Cieseilski, Alexander K., 936n
Clendening, Logan, 1021
Cody, Donald D., 449, 471
Cohen, Jerome B., 272
Cohen, Sidney, 209
Cohen, Wilbur J., 767
Colson, Earl M., 891
Commager, Henry Steele, 1093n
Conklin, George T., Jr., 1022
Cooley, Richard P., 303
Cooper, B. S., 20
Corson, John J., 767
Coughtry, Lloyd S., 1054
Cox, Norwood, 865
Craig, Paul R., 1007
Craven, George, 891
Crowe, Robert M., 371, 391, 411, 432, 449,
    470, 493, 509

D

Darnton, John M., 613
Davis, Gene C., 855
Dawson, Miles, 121n
de Mere, Chevalier, 122
Demichelis, Robert J., 936n, 990, 1069n
Denenberg, Herbert S., 950
Denney, Richard L., 1035, 1074

Deric, Arthur J., 509
deRoode, Albert, 518n
DeWaerdye, Ltd., 227
Dibrell, Charles G., Jr., 832
Dickerson, O. D., 288, 302, 319, 411, 432, 470, 661, 1021
Dillard, Robert L., Jr., 990
Dillavou, Essel R., 702
Dopheide, Fred J., 866
Dorn, Lowell M., 332
Dornfeld, Kivie, 661, 726n, 730
Douds, H. James, 990
Dougherty, Edward A., 1005
Dray, Mark S., 747
Dublin, Louis I., 20, 26, 209
Duckworth, J. Lon, 990

E

Eaton, Berrien C., Jr., 747
Eilers, Robert D., 371, 391, 411, 432, 449, 470, 493, 509, 1101
Esterhai, John L., 990

F

Farr, James F., 855
Fassel, Elgin G., 182
Faulkner, Edwin J., 289, 302, 411, 950, 1021
Feay, Herbert L., 1006
Feinberg, Paul H., 675
Ferrari, J. Robert, 45n, 52
Fischer, Carl H., 157, 635n, 638n
Fisher, H. F., 156
Fitzwilliam, Robert J., 976
Follmann, J. F., Jr., 432, 779
Ford, Curtis B., 906
Fraine, Harold G., 1035
Fraser, J. C., 238
Friedman, Morris, 722n, 727n, 730

G

Gaumnitz, Erwin A., 139
George, Albert, Jr., 878n, 881
Gibbs, Lawrence B., 747
Gingery, Stanley W., 411
Ginsburg, Joseph, 747
Glover, John Desmond, 963
Gold, M. L., 1054
Golden, Jerome S., 227
Goodman, Isidore, 573
Goodman, Mary Ellen, 16
Graham, Bernard, 272
Green, Edward A., 449
Gregg, Davis W., 3, 16, 351, 352n, 371, 391, 452n, 470, 493, 509
Greider, Janice E., 38, 106, 120, 1021
Griffin, Frank L., Jr., 528, 643
Guertin, Alfred N., 175, 223–24

Guilfoyle, A. F., 865
Gybbons, William, 55

H

Hall, Charles P., Jr., 413
Hamilton, James A., 643
Hanson, Arthur W., 272
Harbaugh, Charles H., 1021
Harman, William B., Jr., 1055, 1074
Harmelin, William, 661, 718, 722n, 727n, 730
Harper, Floyd S., 139, 156
Harris, Homer I., 815
Hart, Philip A., 215n, 224
Hedinger, F. R., 432
Hicks, Ernest L., 626
Hinckley, Charles C., 575, 582n, 586
Hoeveler, William M., 990
Hofflander, Al E., 26
Horsley, Walter H., 747
Hoskins, J. E., 182, 332
Houseman, Raymond F., 643
Hower, Ralph M., 963
Huebner, Solomon S., 24, 26, 34, 38, 52, 65, 77, 91, 105, 172, 186n, 193, 654n, 661, 718, 719n, 798, 950, 963, 1102
Huey, Burkett W., 964
Huey, W. R., Jr., 892
Hunter, Douglas B., 614

I

Ilse, Louise Wolters, 371, 411

J

Jackson, Paul H., 493, 627
Jackson, Robert T., 193
Jacobs, Raymond H., 272
Jacobson, James B., 494
Jenkins, Wilmer A., 332
Johnson, Mack H., 891
Jones, H. Bradley, 747
Jordan, C. W., 172
Jordan, Robert H., 193

K

Kahn, Douglas A., 891
Kalmbach, L. J., 1006
Katona, George, 14n, 51n
Kedzie, D. P., 411
Keffer, Ralph, 493
Kellison, Stephen G., 139
Kiker, B. F., 18n
Kimball, Spencer L., 950
Kirkpatrick, T. H., 320
Klarman, H. E., 779
Knecht, Lawrence G., 907
Knickerbocker, Daniel C., Jr., 1074
Krueger, Harry, 120

L

Lacovara, P. P., 865
Larson, Robert E., 139
Lassiter, Roy L., Jr., 19 n, 25 n
Latimer, Murray Webb, 519 n, 643
Levy, David, 1074
Lew, Edward, 197
Linton, M. Albert, 45, 52, 65, 219
Lloyd, Alex, 747
Long, John D., 344 n, 347
Lotka, Alfred J., 20, 26
Lucas, Vane B., 39
Lynch, William B., 675–76

M

McCabe, Thomas C., 717
McCaffrey, Charles B., 661–62
McCahan, David, 411, 449
McCall, John A., 1093 n
McClelland, H. F., 256
McConnell, John W., 767
McCuistion, John J., 333
McDiarmid, Fergus J., 1054
MacDonald, Roy A., 347
McGill, Dan M., 52, 77, 105, 156, 172,
      193, 528, 547, 595, 613, 626, 643,
      815, 832, 843, 950, 1006
MacGregor, Douglas, 6 n
MacIntyre, Duncan M., 493
Maclean, Joseph B., 77, 193, 832, 950,
      1054, 1102
MacNeill, Earl S., 855
McVitty, E. H., 1088
Marples, William F., 528, 547
Marshall, Edward W., 193
Maslow, Abraham H., 4–7 n, 16
Mayerson, Allen L., 950
Mehr, Robert I., 38, 52, 65, 77–78, 91,
      172, 193, 815, 963
Melone, Joseph J., 513, 528–29 n, 547, 626
Menge, Walter O., 157, 1006
Mertens, Jacobs, 891
Metzger, B. L., 561
Miller, George W., 937
Miller, Morton D., 332, 392
Miller, Walter N., 238
Milliken, Charles B., 747
Milliman, Wendell, 509
Mitchell, William H., 717
Monroe, Stuart A., 703, 717
Moore, Russell F., 675
Moorehead, E. J., 176 n, 211, 224
Morison, Samuel Eliot, 1093 n
Murray, Roger F., 14 n
Myers, Robert J., 432, 767–69, 779

N

Nash, Thomas G., Jr., 1057 n, 1074

Nesbitt, Cecil J., 139
Neuschel, Richard F., 963
Newton, Blake T., Jr., 923
Noback, J. C., 1054
Nolan, Stephen, 689
Norton, Paul A., 1089

O

O'Byrne, John C., 702
O'Donnell, Terence, 1102
Olsen, James J., 332
O'Neill, Albert C., Jr., 747
Ormsby, Charles A., 1006
Osborn, Grant M., 779
Osler, Robert W., 661, 730

P

Pascal, Blaise, 122
Pedoe, Arthur, 139, 209
Pennell, John S., 702
Pericles, 8
Pharr, J. B., 170 n, 172
Phillips, James T., 302
Pickrell, Jesse F., 371, 412, 470, 493, 509
Pillsbury, John S., Jr., 215
Piro, Robert J., 906
Plowden-Wardlaw, Thomas C., 717
Plumb, John J., 257
Powell, Loran E., 798 n

R

Rabel, William H., 450
Rabkin, Jacob, 891
Randall, Gerald J., 689
Ray, George E., 574, 747
Ray, Jordan B., 19 n, 25 n
Redeker, Harry S., 854 n, 881
Reid, Charles K., III, 881
Rice, D. P., 20
Richardson, Charles F. B., 173, 182
Riggs, Arthur J., 643
Rocco, Carolyn F., 906
Rohm, John T., 1006
Rosenbloom, Samuel, 238
Rotgin, Philip N., 586, 747
Rothenberg, E. E., 1021
Rothschild, V. H., II, 675
Rottenberg, Simon, 23 n
Rowan, Gerald B., 990
Rua, Anthony P., 1035, 1074
Rustigan, Edward C., 574
Ryan, John F., 335 n

S

Samuelson, Paul A., 6 n
Sarnoff, Paul E., 105
Schlesinger, E. S., 865
Schmidt, William H., 158
Schoen, Robert J., 1035, 1074

Schultz, Theodore W., 18n
Schwarzschild, Stuart, 45n, 46n, 52, 224
Shattuck, Mayo A., 855
Shepherd, B. E., 182
Shepherd, Pearce, 210
Sherman, Gerald H., 882
Shield, W. Lee, 936
Shur, Walter, 121
Sibigtroth, Joseph C., 239
Siegel, Conrad M., 613
Silverstein, Leonard L., 882
Simmons, Sherwin P., 881
Smith, J. Carlton, 661
Smith, J. Henry, 335n
Smyers, John D., 675
Somers, Anne R., 432
Somers, Herman M., 432, 767, 779
Speiser, Stuart M., 18n, 21n, 23n, 26
Spencer, Charles D., & Associates, Inc., 561
Spencer, Thaxter P., 562
Squier, Lee Welling, 517n
Stalson, J. Owen, 975, 1102
Stamm, Charles H., III, 306n
Steele, Allen M., 990
Steffen, Walter W., 991
Stein, Mel, 157
Sternhell, Charles M., 121, 238
Stonecipher, David A., 238

T

Tarver, Norman H., 586
Taylor, Robert C., 748
Thayer, Paul W., 798n
Thies, Winthrop D., 748
Thomas, Gordon W., 433
Thomas, James E., 689
Thompson, John S., Jr., 290
Tilton, Earle B., 347
Tournier, Paul, 3–4n
Townsend, Frederick S., 182
Townsend, Oliver M., 990
Trachtman, Joseph, 855
Tremayne, Bertram W., Jr., 717

Trowbridge, Charles L., 528, 643
Turnbull, John G., 351n
Turner, Samuel H., 239

V

Vance, William R., 112n, 120, 1021
Vogel, Julius, 92

W

Waggoner, Leland T., 120, 797
Walker, Harry, 227, 239, 256
Walker, Paul H., 1074
Walter, James E., 1035
Washington, G. T., 675
Webster, Andrew C., 210
Weisbrod, Burton A., 18n, 22n
Werner, Edgar C., 1006
White, Byron F., 881
White, Edwin H., 702
White, Edwin W., 717
Wickman, J. M., 337n, 347
Williams, Arthur L., 59n
Williams, C. Arthur, Jr., 66, 183, 351n
Williams, William G., 372
Wilson, K. B., 314n
Witherby, Frederick R. H., 976
Witte, Edwin E., 768
Wolfe, Don M., 661
Wood, Glenn L., 183
Woolfolk, V. N. 856
Workman, L. C., 139, 156
Wormser, Rene A., 855
Worthy, K. Martin, 748
Wren, Harold G., 855

Y

Yates, H. Powell, 256, 317n
Yochem, Donald E., 347

Z

Zalinski, Edmund L., 951
Zimet, P., 891
Zischke, James B., 548, 561

Index of Subjects

A

ABA assignment form, 829–30
Accident and sickness insurance, history and development of, 276–77
Accidental death benefits
  claims administration, 1011
  multiple indemnity, 1011
  reinsurance, 996–97
  rider, 27
Accounting methods
  life insurance versus generally accepted, 1048–49
  nonqualified deferred compensation plans, 666–67
Accrued benefits not yet due, reserve for, 325–26
Accumulated earnings tax
  key man life insurance, 656
  professional corporations, 746
Accumulation of capital, 14–15
Accumulation of funds at interest, 191
Accumulation type gross premium formula, 147
Acquisition expenses, 145–46, 154
Active life reserves, 320–21, 323–24
Actuarial costs of trust fund plans, 636–38
Actuarial valuation of trust fund plans, 637
Actuaries' trust fund plan responsibility, 638–39
Acute illnesses, history of, as risk selection factor, 339
AD&D; see Group accidental death and dismemberment insurance and Voluntary accidental death and dismemberment insurance
Additional compensation arrangements
  estate tax consequences, 885–86
  income tax consequences, 879–80
Additional risk-averaging method in group insurance experience rating, 481
Administrative expenses of variable annuities, 251
Administrative services agreements in group insurance, 488

Age
  apparent errors in, 1012
  formation of insurance contract, 106
  misstatement of, 88, 117
  mortality rate factor, 128
  pension plan eligibility requirement, 531
  risk selection, 194, 196–97
Agency distribution system, 964–65; see also Individual insurance marketing and Sales process
  basic steps in, 970
Agent compensation expenses, 145–46, 154
Agents' qualifications and licensing state laws governing, 942–43
Agents' reports as risk selection tool, 205, 347
Alcohol, use of, as risk selection factor, 201–2, 343
Alimony payments, tax consequences of, 878–79
American Academy of Actuaries, 931
American College of Life Underwriters, 933
American Express Company plan, 519
American Institute of Certified Public Accountants Accounting Principles Board opinions on pension plan cost accounting, 527–28
American Life Insurance Association, 931–32
American Risk and Insurance Association, 933
American Society of Chartered Life Underwriters, 932
Amortization schedule, 135, 137
Analysis of costs and benefits; see Contract analysis
Annual claims cost of individual health insurance, 321–23
Annual-premium annuities, 818–82
Annual-premium deferred annuities, 85–86, 155–56

Annual renewable term (ART) reinsurance, 993
Annual report of life insurance companies, 1037, 1047–48
Annual statement, company; *see* Financial statements, company
Annual statements of group reserves, 483–84
Annuities
 amortization schedule, 135, 137
 annual-premium basis, 81–82
 assignment clause, 88
 beneficiary designation and change, 88
 Canadian tax aspects, 1085–88
 cash refund, 83–84
 certain, 84, 134
 change in ownership clause, 87
 classification of, 80–87
 computation, 79–80
 contracts of, 53, 78–91
 date benefits begin as basis, 85–86
 deferred, 82, 85–86
 defined, 134
 disposition of proceeds as basis, 82–85
 dividend options, 88
 estate tax aspects, 90, 887–88
 fixed, 87
 formulas applicable to, 80
 grace period, 88
 gross premiums for, 153–56
 growth of, 925
 guaranteed minimum, 83–84
 immediate, 85
 income tax treatment, 89
 incontestability clause, 88
 information required in contract, 87
 installment refund, 83
 investment income, 79–80
 joint and last survivorship, 86
 joint life, 87
 life, 134
  no refund, 82–83
  period certain, 83
 life insurance distinguished, 78
 limitations of, 90–91
 liquidation of capital through, 88–89
 method of paying premiums as basis, 80–82
 misstatement-of-age clause, 88
 money concepts relating to, 134–37
 nontransferability, 88
 number of lives covered by, 86–87
 ownership clause, 87
 participating basis, 88
 periodic income under, 79–80
 policy loan privileges, 88
 policy provisions, 87–88
 principal of, 79
 principle of, 78-80

Annuities—*Cont.*
 refund, 83
 retirement contracts, 97
 retirement income provided by, 88–89
 savings element of, 40
 self-employed persons, 563
 settlement options, 88
 single-premium deferred annuities, 82, 85–86
 single-premium life contract, 78–81
 straight life, 83
 survivorship benefit, 79–80
 tax advantages, 89–90
 temporary life, 84–85
 units in which pay-out benefits expressed, 87, 244–46
 uses of, 88–90
 variable, 87; *see also* Variable annuities
 waiver-of-premium benefit, 88
Annuities certain, 84, 134
Annuity with contingencies, 385
Annuity due, 85
Annuity purchase plans, 533
Annuity units, 87, 244–46
Application form, 110–11
Applications
 group insurance, 457
 individual health insurance, 304–6
 key man life insurance, 651
 risk selection tool, 204–5, 345
Armstrong Investigation, 174, 180, 939, 1095–96
Asset charge in gross premiums on variable life insurance, 233
Asset share, 175
 calculation, 176
 individual health insurance gross premiums, 329
Assets of life insurance companies; *see* Life insurance companies
Assignment, 119, 828–31
 absolute, 828, 831
 annuities, 88
 beneficiary change, need for, 829, 831
 collateral, 828
 form, 829–30
 group insurance, 458–60
 group survivor income benefit insurance, 386
 group term life insurance, 376
 notice to insurance company, 829
 self-employed persons' pensions and profit sharing, 570
 types, 828
Assumed investment return (AIR), 243–44
Assumption reinsurance, 1003–4
Attending physicians' statements as risk selection tool, 206, 345–46

Audits, 1037
  group insurance, 458
Automatic premium loans, 47, 181–82
  advantage and disadvantage, 182
Automatic quota share agreements, 448
Automatic reinsurance agreements, 999–
  1000, 1004
Average monthly wage (AMW) concept
  in social security, 756–57
Average reserves, 158
Averages, law of, 121
Aviation as risk selection factor, 199–200

B

Balance sheet; *see* Financial statements,
  company
Baltimore & Ohio Railroad Company plan,
  519
Band system of gross premium calculation,
  146
Basic earnings, 23
Basic medical expense coverages in group
  medical expense insurance, 419–23
Baylor University Hospital plan, 413
Belonging needs, 5
Beneficiary designation and change, 819–
  28
  annuities, 88
  assignment of policy, 829, 831
  business organizations, 822–23
  Canadian life insurance, 1079–80
  change, reasons for and methods of
    making, 825–26
  class designation, 821–22
  contingent beneficiaries, 820
  current, importance of keeping, 831
  group life insurance, 462–63
  group term life insurance, 375–76
  identity of beneficiary, 821–22
  individual health insurance, 315–16
  insurable interest, 820–21; *see also* In-
    surable interest
  insured's estate, 821
  irrevocable beneficiaries, 819–20
  key man life insurance, 652
  method of, 825–26
  minors, 824–25
  per capita, 822
  per stirpes, 822
  primary beneficiaries, 820
  revocable beneficiaries, 819–20
  specifically named persons, 821
  stock redemption plan, 714–15
  testamentary trustee, 823–24
  trust companies, 823–25
  trustees, 823–25
  veterans' life insurance, 786
  will provisions, 823–24

Benefit comparisons, 211–24; *see also*
  Contract analysis
Benefits; *see also specific types of plans*
  deferred compensation plans, 671, 673–
    75
  deposit administration pension plans,
    615–16
  federal employees' group life insurance
    plan, 388
  group creditor disability insurance, 409–
    10
  group creditor life insurance, 454
  group health insurance, tax aspects of,
    469
  group insurance, 357–58, 437
    nonduplication clause, 464–65
  group life insurance, 453–54
  group medical expense insurance inte-
    gration patterns for, 425–30
  group survivor income benefit insur-
    ance, 385
  group term life insurance, tax aspects
    of, 466–67
  health insurance, 927–28
  individual disability income insurance,
    279–81, 286–87
  individual health insurance, 309–10
  life insurance, 927
  long-term disability income insurance,
    404–6
  Medicare
    hospital insurance, 771–72
    supplementary medical insurance,
      773–74
  pension plans, 522–26
  scope of, 923–28
  self-employed persons' pensions and
    profit sharing, 569
  servicemen's group life insurance plan,
    390–91
  short-term disability income insurance,
    396–400
  social security; *see* Social security bene-
    fits
  trust fund plans, 632–34
Blood pressure; *see* High blood pressure
Blue Cross Association, 418
  emergence of, 414
  plans, 414–17, 930–31
    basic medical expense coverages,
      419–23
    broad medical expense coverages,
      423–30
    establishment of, 1100
    experience rating lacking, 478
    hospital expense insurance, 420–21
Blue Shield plans, 414–17, 930–31
  basic medical expense coverages, 419–
    23

Blue Shield Plans—*Cont.*
 broad medical expense coverages, 423–
  30
 establishment of, 1100
 experience rating lacking, 478
 surgical expense insurance, 421–23
Blue sky laws, 269–70
Bond purchase plans of self-employed persons, 564
Broad medical expense coverages in group medical expense insurance, 423–30
Brokerage distributors, 972–73
Brokers, 499–500
Business continuation; *see also specific type of business*
 corporations, 703–17
 disability of members of business, protection against, 718–30; *see also specific type of business*
 income protection for, 718–30; *see also specific type of business*
 insurance for, 34
 partnership, 695–701
 professional individuals, 701–2
 proprietorship, 690–95
 unincorporated business interest, 690–702
Business expediency concept, 517
Business health insurance, income tax treatment of premiums of, 871
Business insurance, 33–34
 buy-and-sell agreements funded by, 647
Business interests, 51
Business life insurance
 income tax treatment of premiums, 871
 proceeds as corporate distributions, 874–75
Business organizations
 beneficiary designation, 822–23
 mutual funds and, 271
Business trip insurance, 388
Business uses of life insurance, 50
Buy-and-sell agreements
 business insurance funding of, 647
 disability portion of, check list for, 727–29
 disposing of corporate stock interests through, 710–16
 advantages of, 716
 partnership interest sale, 698–701
 sale of proprietorship to key man, 691–92, 694–95
 settlement options to fund, 842–43
Buy-out agreements
 check list of important points for, 728–29
 disability insurance to fund, 287–88
Buy-out method of continuing partnership, 698–99

C

Cammack-Jenkins type of gross premiums formula, 329
Canadian life insurance, 1075–88
 annuities, 1085–88
 claims administration, 1082–83
 corporate restrictions, 1075–76
 federal income tax, 1084–85
 policy contract provisions, 1078–83
  beneficiaries, 1079–80
  cash values, 1081–82
  forms, 1078–79
  incontestability, 1080–81
  insurable interest, 1083
  juvenile insurance, 1082
  miscellaneous provisions, 1082–83
  nonforfeiture provisions, 1081–82
  reinstatement, 1081
 regulation of, 1076–78
 taxation of companies, 1088
 taxation of life insurance, 1083–88
  annuities, 1085–88
  federal income tax, 1084–85
 variable life insurance, 227–30
Cancellable insurance
 individual disability income insurance, 285
 individual health insurance, 317
 individual medical expense insurance, 298
Cardiovascular diseases, 199
Career agencies, 971
Career of selling life insurance, 966–70; *see also* Life underwriting as a career
Carriers of life and health insurance, 928–29
Cash dividends, 191
Cash refund annuity, 83–84
Cash surrender values
 Canadian life insurance, 1081–82
 defined, 42
 delay clause, 178
 federal income tax treatment, 49
 group paid-up life insurance, accumulation in, 381
 individual disability income insurance, 288
 schedules in contracts, 42
 Standard Nonforfeiture Law provisions, 177–78
 variable life insurance, 232
Cash value insurance
 reserves and, 170–71
 return of, provision for, 103
 term riders, 56
Cash value life insurance, 39
 business uses of, 50
 gifts of, 49–50

Cash value life insurance—*Cont.*
  maintenance of credit, 46
  mortality rate, 44
Catastrophe reinsurance, 1002, 1004
Catastrophes
  group medical expense insurance, 424
  group reinsurance for risk of, 446–47
  individual health insurance, 331
Ceding company, 991
Cessions, 992, 1005
Change in ownership clause in annuity
    policy, 87
Change of beneficiary; *see* Beneficiary des-
    ignation and change
Change of plan provision, 120
  individual health insurance, 311–12
  special policies including, 103
  term insurance, 60
  veterans' life insurance, 785
Charitable bequests, settlement options
    for, 842
Charitable contributions, federal income
    tax, consequences of, 877
Charitable foundations, 852
Charitable gifts of life insurance, 902–6;
    see also Gifts of life insurance
Chartered Life Underwriter (CLU), 968
  Code of Ethics, 987
  professional pledge, 987
Children
  payor clauses for benefit of, 119–20
  settlement options for income for, 840–
    41
Children in school
  endowment insurance coverage, 96–97
  income provided for, 32
Chronic illnesses as risk selection factor,
    338–39
Civil Rights Act of 1964, 455, 948
Claim costs
  gross premiums for individual health
    insurance, 328
  group insurance experience rating, 478
Claim forms provision in individual health
    insurance, 314
Claim procedures for group insurance, 462
Claim provisions in group insurance, 462–
    65
Claim reserves in group insurance, 484
Claims administration, 1007–21
  aids in, 1020–21
  Canadian life insurance, 1082-83
  defined, 1007
  function of, 1007–8
  general procedures, 1009–10
    claim proofs, 1009
    claims examination, 1009–10
  health insurance, 1013–19
    coordination of benefits, 1018–19

Claims administration—*Cont.*
    dismemberment benefits, 1016
    duplicate coverage, 1018–19
    duration of claims, 1019
    long-term disability benefits, 1014–16
    major medical expense claims, 1017–
      18
    medical expense benefits, 1016–17
    short-term disability benefits, 1014–16
    total and permanent disability bene-
      fits, 1013–14
  life insurance, 1010–12
    accidental death claims, 1011
    apparent errors in age, 1012
    death benefits, 1010–11
    hazardous occupations, 1012
    multiple indemnity benefits for acci-
      dental death, 1011
    suicide, 1011–12
    termination of coverage, 1012
    war deaths, 1012
  nature of, 1007–8
  payment of claims, 1019–20
  payments other than claims, 1020
  philosophy of, 1007–8
  role of, 1008–9
Claims in course of settlement, reserve for,
    325
Claims records as risk selection tool, 346–
    47
Clauses in insurance contracts; *see* Con-
    tracts *or* specific types of clauses
Clayton Act, 946
Clifford trust, 863
Close corporation, 703–4; *see also* Cor-
    porations
Closed-end investment company, 258
Codes of Ethics, 987
Coin tossing illustration, 122–25
Coinsurance, 933, 997–99, 1004
  advantages, 997–98
  disadvantages, 998
  group medical expense insurance, 424
  individual medical expense insurance,
    292
  major medical expense insurance, 296–
    97
  modified, 993, 998–99, 1004
Collateral assignment system, 680–82
Collateral assignments; *see* Assignment
College education insurance, 32–33
College Retirement Equities Fund
    (CREF), 242
Combination agencies, 971–72
Combination plans, 525, 557–58
  funding of, 590–91
Commissions to agents and brokers of
    group insurance, 501–3; *see also*
    Group insurance

Common disaster clause, 826–27
Common stocks
  assets of life insurance companies, 1032–33
  investment in, 1034
  separate accounts for, 1034
  valuation, 1026
Company financial statements; *see* Financial statements, company
Company organization and management, 951–63
  accounting and auditing departments, 961–62
  actuarial departments, 959–60
  administration departments, 960–61
  advertising department, 962
  agency manager, 959
  agents, 959
  board of directors, 954–55
  cashier, 959
  claims departments, 961
  combination company agent, 959
  committees, 955–56
  departmentalization, 954
  direct supporting operations, 958
  form of organization, 953–56
  formation of company, 952–53
  general agent, 959
  group insurance department, 957
  group sales departments, 958
  holding company, 951
  independent agent or broker, 959
  individual insurance department, 957–58
  individual sales department, 958
  investment and finance department, 961
  legal department, 961
  levels of authority, 954
  line and staff, 954
  lines of business, 956–57
  miscellaneous departments, 962–63
  miscellaneous financial services, 963
  officers, 955
  ordinary company agent, 959
  organization chart, 956–57
  public relations department, 962
  sales departments, 958–59
  special characteristics, 952
  staff operations, 961–63
  statutes relating to, 952–53
  structure of organization, 956–63
  systems department, 962
  types of companies, 951
  underwriting departments, 960
Company pension and profit-sharing benefits, 51
Competition
  gross premiums for nonparticipating life insurance, 140, 142

Competition—*Cont.*
  pension plans of large and small employers, 521
  to reduce net cost of insurance, 1024
  variable annuity pricing, 251
Comprehensive medical expense insurance, 297
  group medical expense insurance, 425–27, 429
Compromise settlement of disability insurance, 287
Computers, use in programming, 803–5
Concealment of material facts, 110–11
Conditional premium receipts
  approval type, 108
  binding type, 108
  individual health insurance, 306
  insurability type, 107
Confining disability defined, 279
Conformity with state statutes provision
  individual health insurance, 317–18
Consideration clause in individual health insurance, 307
Constructive receipt doctrine, 664–65
Consultants, 499–500
Consumer investigative reports as risk selection tool, 205–6
Consumer Price Index (CPI), 227, 229, 240–41, 254
Consumerism, 988–89
Consumption, 19
Contest of claims under group life insurance, 462
Contingency loading, 147
Contingency reserves in group insurance, 484
Contingent beneficiaries, 820
Continuance table for individual health insurance, 321–22, 325
Continuation of protection provisions federal employees' group life insurance plan, 389–90
  group accidental death and dismemberment insurance, 386
  group health insurance, 462
  group life insurance, 461–62
  group ordinary life insurance, 384
  group survivor income benefit insurance, 385–86
  group term life insurance, 373–75
  servicemen's group life insurance plan, 391
  voluntary accidental death and dismemberment insurance, 387
Contract analysis
  benefits other than death benefits, 212–13
  checklist of factors requiring attention, 218–19

Contract analysis—*Cont.*
  collateral contract features, 220–21
  dividend histories, 213–14
  dividend scales, 213–14
  endowment and whole life contracts, 220
  interest-adjusted method, 215–18, 220
  new contracts that are dissimilar, 219–21
  new contracts that are similar, 213–19
  new contracts with contracts in force, 221–23
  participating and nonparticipating contracts, 212, 220
  proposed methods, 215, 218
  purposes for, 211
  replacement insurance, 221–23
  term and permanent contracts, 219–20
  traditional method, 214–15, 220
Contract liability of company for acts of agent, 979–81
Contracts; *see also specific topics and clauses*
  age required for execution of, 106
  analysis, 211–24; *see also* Contract analysis
  annuities, 53, 78–91
  assignment clause, 119
  automatic premium loans, 181–82
  Canadian life insurance, 1078–83
  capacity to enter into, 106–7
  change of plan provision, 120
  competent parties to, 106–7
  concealment of facts, 110–11
  consideration for, 108–9
  deposit administration pension plans, 618–20
  endowment insurance, 75–77
  entire contract provision, 116
  estoppel, doctrine of, 112
  form required by law, 109
  formation of, 106–9
  grace period provision, 116–17
  group creditor life insurance, 379–80
  group insurance, 437, 455–65
  incontestable clause, 112–16
  individual disability income insurance, 277–82
  individual health insurance, 306–18
  individual life insurance, 53; *see also specific form of insurance*
  insurable interest requirement, 109–10
  key man life insurance, 651–52
  legal concepts governing, 106–20; *see also specific subtopics hereunder*
  minors, 107
  misrepresentation, 110–11
  misstatement-of-age provision, 117
  mutual assent to, 107–8

Contracts—*Cont.*
  nonqualified deferred compensation plans, 663
  offer and acceptance, 107
  ownership provision, 119
  payor clause, 119–20
  provisions of, 106–20; *see also specific subtopics*
  reformation of, 115
  reinstatement provision, 117–18
  reinsurance, 991–92; *see also* Reinsurance
  rights under, 816
  special policies, 92–105
  state laws governing requirements for and provisions of, 943–45
  suicide provision, 118–19
  tax deferred annuities, 578
  term insurance, 55–65
  Uniform Standard Policy Provisions Law requirements, 116–18
  variable annuities, 247–48
  variable life insurance, 230–33
  veterans' life insurance, 784
  waiver, doctrine of, 111–12
  war clauses, 119
  warranties, 111
  whole life insurance, 66–74
Controlled foreign corporations, federal income taxation of, 1067–68
Conversion privileges
  family policy, 101
  group health insurance, 461
  group life insurance, 460–61
  group term life insurance, 374
  mutual funds, 265–66
  retroactive, 58–59
  term insurance, 58–60
  veterans' life insurance, 785
  whole life insurance, 71
Conversion rates, 243
Convertible term insurance, 58–60
  retroactive conversion, 58–59
Corporations, 703–17
  buy-and-sell agreements
    advantages of, 716
    kinds of, 710
  closely held, 703–4
  creation of, 703
  cross-purchase agreement, 710–15
  death of principal stockholder, problems caused by, 704–5
  death of stockholder, effect of, 704
  defined, 703
  disability income insurance for continuance of, 725–27
  disability of stockholder, effect of, 720–21

Corporations—*Cont.*
   solutions to problems with disability
      income insurance, 725–27
   solutions to problems without disabil-
      ity income insurance, 722–23
   disposing of stock interest through for-
      mal agreement, 710–16
   equal stockholder situation, 706
   estate liquidity problems, 709–10
   family retention of stock interest, 707–
      10
      estate liquidity problem, 709–10
      valuation, 708–9
   majority stockholder situation, 706
   mandatory buy-and-sell agreement,
      710–11
   minority stockholder situation, 705–6
   nature of, 703–4
   parties to agreements, 711
   partnership distinguished, 703–4
   risk faced by, 703
   situations analysis, importance of, 706–
      7
   situations among stockholders, 705–6
   special family situations, 715–16
   stock redemption agreement, 710–15
   stock redemption versus cross-purchase,
      711–15
      beneficiary designation, 714–15
      enforceability, 711–12
      estate tax status, 715
      funding, 712
      income tax basis, 713–14
      premium payments, 712–13
      transfer of insurance policies, 713
   stock share, basic elements of, 705–7
   stockholders of, 703
   valuation of stock for estate tax pur-
      poses, 711
   valuation of stock interest, 708–9
Cosmetic surgery, individual medical ex-
      pense insurance for, 300
Cost accounting
   group insurance, 477; *see also* Experi-
      ence rating
   pension plans, 527–28
Cost analysis, 211–24; *see also* Contract
      analysis
Cost control procedure
   group medical expense insurance, 417
   short-term disability income insurance,
      401–3
Cost of insurance; *see also* Premiums
   deferred compensation plans, 669–75
   federal employees' group life insurance
      plan, 389
   group medical expense insurance, 431
   servicemen's group life insurance plan,
      391

Cost of insurance—*Cont.*
   term insurance versus straight life in-
      surance, 63–64
Cost-of-living adjustments, increasing term
      rider for, 57
Cost-of-living plans, 229, 254
Costs of pension plans; *see* Pension plans
Cost plus plans of group insurance, 488
County medical society plans, 414
Court decisions cited
   Alsup v. *Travelers Insurance Co.,* 456n
   Anderson v. *Knox,* 984–85
   Ashcraft v. *Commissioner,* 878n
   Atlantic Oil v. *Patterson,* 874n
   Avery v. *Commissioner,* 656n
   Blair, Estate of W. A., 657n
   Bogene, Inc. 727n
   Boseman v. *Connecticut General Life
      Insurance Co.,* 456n
   Bowman v. *Home Life Ins. Co.,* 979n
   Brodie, Renton K., 665
   Castner Garage, Ltd., 659n, 870n
   Claggett, S. O., 745n
   Cockrill v. *O'Hara,* 658n
   Commissioner v. *Charleston National
      Bank,* 876n
   Detroit Bank & Trust Co. v. *United
      States,* 862n, 893n
   Doerken, Estate of Edward, 657n
   Ducros, Francis H. W., 874n
   Emeloid Co., The v. *Commissioner,*
      656n
   Farmers & Bankers Life Ins. Co. v. *Bax-
      ley,* 979n
   Federal Trade Commission v. *National
      Casualty Company,* 946n
   Federal Trade Commission v. *Travelers
      Health Association,* 946n
   *First National Bank and Trust Company
      of Tulsa* v. *Jones,* 876n
   First National Bank of Oregon v. *United
      States,* 893n
   Fletcher v. *Western National Life Ins.
      Co.,* 980, 981n, 985
   Forrest v. *Mutual Benefit Life Insurance
      Company,* 114n
   Gediman v. *Anheuser Busch, Inc.,* 984
   George v. *Jordan Marsh Company,*
      980n
   Glassner v. *Commissioner,* 875n
   Golden v. *Commissioner,* 875n
   Gray v. *Penn Mutual Life Insurance
      Co.,* 817
   Green Shield case, 986
   Hardt v. *Brink,* 984
   Hubert Transfer and Storage, 879n
   Hunton, Eppa, IV, 877n
   Hyland v. *Commissioner,* 664

Court decisions cited—*Cont.*
  Keckley v. *Conshocton Glass Company*, 653n
  Kintner case, 731–32
  Klein v. *Commissioner*, 875n
  Landfield Finance Co. v. *United States*, 877n
  Larkin case, 726
  Legallet case, 714–15
  McCamant, T. O., 877n
  Magee v. *Equitable Life Assurance Society*, 456n
  Metropolitan Life Insurance Company v. *Conway*, 115n
  Monahan v. *Metropolitan Life Insurance Company*, 113n
  Monarch Life Ins. Co. v. *Loyal Protective Life Ins. Co.*, 986n
  Morrissey v. *Commissioner*, 731
  Morse, Eliot C., 665
  Musette v. *Monarch Life Insurance Company*, 112n
  Mushro case, 715
  Mutual Benefit Life v. *Ellis*, 818n
  Nashville Trust Company v. *Commissioner*, 818n
  New York Life Insurance Company v. *Deer Lodge County*, 945
  Patton's Will, In re, 657n
  Paul v. *Virginia*, 450n, 945
  Pelton v. *Commissioner*, 731n
  Prudential Insurance Co. v. *Benjamin*, 1072n
  Raulet v. *Northwestern Nat. Ins. Co.*, 989n
  Reed's Estate, In re, 657n
  Reilly v. *Penn Mutual Life Insurance Company*, 653n
  Rivers v. *Capital Life Insurance Co.*, 456n
  Roubik v. *Commissioner*, 733n
  St. Louis Refrigerating and Cold Storage Co. v. *United States*, 877n
  Scherer, Estate of, 657n
  Securities and Exchange Commission v. *National Securities, Inc.* 947n
  Securities and Exchange Commissions v. *Variable Annuity Life Ins. Co.*, 946n, 947n
  Skouras v. *Commissioner*, 818n
  Stipcich v. *Metropolitan Life Ins. Co.*, 978n
  Twin City Tile and Marble Co., 879n
  Union Mutual Life Insurance Company v. *Wilkinson*, 112n
  United States v. *Atlas Life Insurance Company*, 1059n
  United States v. *Chicago Title and Trust Co.*, 948n

Court decisions cited—*Cont.*
  United States v. *Empey*, 733n
  United States v. *Holder*, 733n
  United States v. *Kurzner*, 733n
  United States v. *O'Neill*, 733n
  United States v. *South-Eastern Underwriters Association*, 450n, 945
  United States v. *Supplee-Biddle Hardward Company*, 653n
  Weatherbee v. *United Ins. Co. of America*, 980, 985
  Wurzberg v. *New York Life Insurance Company*, 653n
"Create and save" method, 37
Credit, maintenance of, 46
Credit insurance, 34, 394–95
Credit life insurance, 974
  group; *see* Group creditor life insurance
Creditor-debtor groups for group insurance, 355–56
Creditor-debtor situations
  federal income tax consequences, 875
  assignments, 875–76
  death proceeds, 877
  deductibility of premiums, 875–76
Creditor exemption statutes; *see* Exemption statutes
Creditor protection through insurance, 34, 37–38
Creditors as group insurance market, 497–98
Creditors' claims, exemption of life insurance from, 48–49
Cross-purchase agreement, 710–15; 724, 727; *see also* Corporations
Custodial accounts of self-employed persons, 563
Custodial gifts of life insurance for minors, 900–902
  manner of making, 901
Customer groups in group insurance market, 497

D

Death benefits
  claims administration, 1010–11
  deferred compensation plans, 671, 673
  deposit administration pension plans, 616–17
  graded policy, 104, 209
  pension plans, 537
  profit sharing plans, 554–55
  tax aspects, 866–68, 877–79
  veterans, 790–93
Death estate, creation of, 37
Death taxes, exemption of life insurance proceeds from, 38
Debit agencies, 971–72
Decision-making ability, 17

Decreasing term policies, 56, 93–95
Deductibles
    group medical expense insurance, 424
    individual medical expense insurance,
        292
    major medical expense insurance, 296
Deferred annuities
    annual-premium, 85–86, 155–56
    deferred period, 86
    gross premiums for, 155–56
        expense assumptions, 155–56
        formulas for, 155–56
        interest assumptions, 155
    group; *see* Group deferred annuities
    guarantee feature, 86
    installment premium, 85–86
    liquidation period, 86
    pay-out period, 86
    periods of, 86
    single-premium, 82, 85–86, 155
    tax advantages, 90
    variable, 244–45
Deferred compensation plans, 511 ff.; *see
    also specific topics and* Pension plans
    defined, 662–63
    funding of, 50
    key man life insurance to fund, 651
    nonqualified, 662–75; *see also* Nonqual-
        ified deferred compensation plans
    qualified, 662–63
Deferred wage concept, 518–19
Deficiency reserves, 169–70
    individual health insurance, 326
Defined benefit plans, 533, 535, 609–10
Defined contribution plans, 533–35, 610
Definitions clause in individual health in-
    surance, 307
Dental care, initial premium rates for, 476
Department of Defense supervision of
    overseas military personnel insurance
    purchases, 947
Department of Justice jurisdiction, 948
Departure from social mores as risk se-
    lection factor, 202
Dependency and Indemnity Compensation
    (DIC) for veterans, 790–91
Dependency period income
    programming for, 809–10
    settlement options for, 839
Dependent coverage in group term life in-
    surance, 376–77
Deposit administration pension plans,
    614–26
    accumulation of funds, 625–26
    benefits, 615–16
    contract holder, 618
    contract provisions, 618–20
    contributory, 618–19
    death benefits, 616–17

Deposit administration pension plans—
        Cont.
    disability benefits, 617
    discontinuance of contributions, 620
    discontinuance provisions, 617–18
    eligibility, 615
    employee contributions, 615
    experience rating, 620–21
    fund maintained for active employees,
        619
    guarantees, 619–22
    inclusion of plan specifications, 618
    maximums, 618
    minimums, 618
    nature of, 614–15
    origin, 614
    retirement age, 615
    separate account facility, 623–24
    specifications, 615–18
    supplementary deposit administration,
        622–23
    underwriting, 618
    withdrawal benefits, 616
Direct marketing of group insurance, 501
Direct placements, 1029
Direct-rated deposit administration con-
    tract, 621 n
Disability benefits
    deferred compensation plans, 674–75
    deposit administration pension plans,
        617
    pension plans, 538
    trust fund plans, 633
Disability compensation and pension to
    veterans, 789–90
Disability, defined, 277–79, 395–96, 403–
    4
Disability income insurance, 33
    business continuation as purpose, 718–
        30; *see also specific type of busi-
        ness*
    claims administration, 1013–14
    corporation, continuance of, 725–27
    group; *see* Group disability income in-
        surance
    individual; *see* Individual disability in-
        come insurance
    individual life coverage, 48
    partnership, continuance of, 724–25
    proprietorship, continuance of, 723–24
    purpose of, 30
    social security benefits; *see* Social secur-
        ity benefits
    state statutory plans; *see* Statutory dis-
        ability income plans
    tax aspects, 870
    veterans' life insurance, 787
Disability income payments under state
    plans as risk selection factor, 344

Disability income reinsurance, 1001
Disabled life reserves, 320, 324–25
Disaster reinsurance, 1002
Discounted or present value of money, 133–34
Discounting
 for interest, 137
 for mortality, 137
Disposable personal income, 12n
 augmented, 12–13
Diversification of investments, 1029
Dividend class, defined, 187
Dividend distribution; *see* Policy dividends
Dividend histories, 213–14
Dividend options, 191–92
 accumulated funds at interest, 48, 191
 annuities, 88
 cash, 191
 fifth, 192
 individual life insurance, 47–48
 paid-up additions, 47–48, 191
 reduced premiums, 191
 straight refund of premium overcharge, 47
 tax deferred annuities, 583
 term insurance, 191
 types, 47–48
 whole life insurance, 71
Dividend reserves for group insurance, 484
Dividend scales, 190–91, 213–14; *see also* Policy dividends
Divorce decrees, federal income tax consequences of, 878–79
Doctor fee benefits, 294
Double indemnity, 27
 group accidental death and dismemberment insurance, 386
Driving record as risk selection factor, 202
Drug use as risk selection factor, 201–2, 343

E

Earning power, 51
Earnings schedules, 358
Economic contributions of insurance companies, 933–35
Economic security
 in America, 8–12
  definition, 8
  expenditures 1950–70, 10–12
  group aspect of, 9–10
  individual aspect of, 9
  social aspect of, 10
  tripod of, 9–10
 attitude of man toward, 13
 criteria of, 3

Economic security—*Cont.*
 defined, 3–4, 6–7
 dimensions of, 3
 etymology, 3
 future dimensions of, 13–16
 goal for persons, 3
 instincts for, 3–4
 insurance in relation to, 1
 issues and unanswered questions, 12–16
 man's need for, 1, 6–8
 motivation for, 14
 national income allocation to public programs, 13–14
 patterns and philosophies, 3–16
 preference for, 3
 underdeveloped nation versus affluent society, 3
Economics, defined, 6
Education insurance
 benefits to veterans' orphans, wives, and widows, 791–92
 endowment policies, 76, 96–97
 income for family of decedent, 32
 programming for, 809
 settlement options for, 841
Eligibility
 deposit administration pension plans, 615
 federal employees' group life insurance plan, 388–89
 group creditor life insurance, 378, 453
 group insurance, 355–57, 436–37, 460
 group life insurance, 453
 Medicare
  hospital insurance, 770
  supplementary medical insurance, 773
 pension plan requirements, 530–32; *see also* Pension plans
 servicemen's group life insurance plan, 390
 tax deferred annuities, 576–78
Elimination period in individual disability income insurance, 279–80
Emergency funds
 accident benefits, 293
 programming, 809
 settlement option for, 839
Employee contributions; *see* Pension plans *or specific type*
Employee insurance; *see various types of group insurance*
Employer-employee life and health insurance plans, 974–75
Employer groups for group insurance
 individual, 355, 496–97
 multiple, 355, 441
Employer trusts in group insurance market, 497
Endorsement system, 681–83, 687

Endowment insurance
  contracts, 75–77
  economic concept of, 75
  education of children, 76, 96–97
  functions of, 76
  limitations of, 76–77
  mathematical concept of, 75
  misuse of, 76–77
  old age protection, 76
  payor clause, 76
  proceeds, federal income tax treatment
    of, 49
  pure endowment, defined, 75
  purposes of, 76
  retirement funds, 75–76
  savings element of, 40, 70
  types of policies, 75
  whole life compared, 220
Entire contract provision, 116
  group insurance, 456
  individual health insurance, 311–12,
    314
Entity method for sale of partnership in-
    terest, 699–701, 724
Equal Pay Act, 948
Equation type gross premium formula,
    147
Equitable Life Assurance Society, 519
Equity-linked life insurance; *see* Variable
    life insurance
Equity sales organizations, 973
Equity-type assets, 50–51
Establishment funds, 393
Estate clearance fund
  need for, 30–31
  settlement option for, 837–38
Estate creation by insurance, 37
Estate impairment
  evaluation of items of, 849
  forces of, 845–46
Estate planning, 795 ff., 844–55
  advantages of, 853
  analysis of case, 907–16
  business interests, 848
  cautions regarding, 844
  consultation required for, 849
  common disaster clause, 827
  current plan, 847–48
  defined, 798, 844
  design of plan, 849–52, 919–20
  domicile, 847
  evaluating estate impairment items, 849
  execution of legal documents, 852
  factual basis for, 846–49, 907–16
  family facts, 847
  gifts, 852
    contemplated, 848
  illustration of, 907–20
  implementation of, 920

Estate planning—*Cont.*
  joint ownership with right of survivor-
    ship, 852
  life insurance vehicle, 850–51
  marital deduction, 827, 850
  mutual funds for, 271
  objectives, 848
  old versus new concept, 845
  periodic review, 853, 920
  pour-over trust, 851–52
  probate procedure, 910–16
  problems, determination of, 916–19
  process of, 846–53
  programming in relation to, 798
  property profile, 847
  "Some Guideposts for Cooperation Be-
    tween Lawyers and Life Insurance
    Representatives," 854
  tax planning distinguished, 844
  team of professionals involved in, 853–
    55
  testing the plan, 852, 919–20
  tools utilized in, 849–52
  trusts, inter vivos and testamentary,
    851–52
  will preparation and use, 850
Estate tax 845
  additional compensation arrangements,
    885–86
  annuities, function of, 90
  gifts of insurance, 887, 904
    three-year measuring period, 887
  group term life insurance, 886
  identity of beneficiary, 883
  incidents of ownership, 883–84
  key man life insurance, 657–58
  life insurance, 38, 882–88
  owner of policy, 883–86
    definition of ownership, 884
    relationship to compensation arrange-
      ments, 885–86
    transfer of ownership, 884–85
  partnership interest purchase and sale,
    701
  payor of premiums, 886–87
  premium payment test, 887
  proprietorship valuation, 693–94
  qualified retirement plans, relationship
    to, 887–88
  split-dollar plans, 686–87, 886
  stock redemption plan, 715
  tax deferred annuities, 583
  transfer of ownership, 884–85
    in contemplation of death, 883
  valuation of corporate stock, 711
  value of insurance includable for, 882–
    83
Esteem needs, 5–6
  economic security and, 7

Estoppel
  defined, 112
  doctrine of, 112
Evidence of insurability in group insurance, 460
Exceptions provisions in individual health insurance, 310
Excess amounts pooling method in group insurance experience rating, 481
Exchange privilege in mutual funds, 265–66
Exclusions
  group creditor disability insurance, 410–11
  individual disability income insurance, 281–82
  individual health insurance, 310
  individual medical expense insurance, 299–300
  long-term disability income insurance, 406–7
  short-term disability income insurance, 400
Exclusive agent multiple-line, 972
Exemption of insurance from claims of creditors, 48–49
Exemption statutes, 37–38, 827
Expectation of life, 56, 132
Expenses
  gross premiums
    deferred annuities, 155–56
    individual health insurance, 328
    nonparticipating insurance, 145–46
    participating insurance, 151
    single-premium immediate annuities, 154–55
    variable life insurance, 233
  group insurance experience rating, 478
  pension plan cost considerations, 542
Experience rating
  deposit administration pension plans, 620–21
  group insurance, 361, 477–83
    additional risk-averaging method, 481
    Blue Cross/Blue Shield operations, 478
    claims costs, 478
    credibility factors, 480
    dividends, 483
    excess amounts pooling method, 481
    expenses, 478
    extra contingency reserve method, 481
    factors, 478
    formulas, 479–81
    high limits, treatment of, 481
    illustrative calculations, 488–93
    loss-limit method, 481
    renewal rating, 479, 481–82
    reserves, 485–86
    retrospective rate credits, 483

Experience rating—*Cont.*
    risk-averaging formula, 479–80
    risk-charge formula, 480–81
    transfer cases, rating of, 482–83
Experience tables
  adaptation to specific policy, 330
  adjustments in, 327
  individual health insurance, 320
  sources, 330
Extended care benefit of medical expense insurance, 294–95
Extended term insurance, Standard Nonforfeiture Law, 178–79
Extra contingency reserve method in group insurance experience rating, 481
Extra numerical mortality, 206–7

F

Face amount certificate company, 258
Facility of payment clause
  group life insurance, 463
  group term life insurance, 376
Facultative quota share agreements, 448–49
Facultative reinsurance agreements, 999–1000, 1004
Fair Credit Reporting Act, 305, 455
Fair Labor Standards Act, 455
Family business, 690
Family gifts of life insurance, 892–902;
  see also Gifts of life insurance
Family policies, 100–101
  conversion privilege, 101
  coverage, 101
  death of head of family, 101
  income policy, 56, 93–95
  maintenance policy, 57, 93–94
  premiums, 100–101
  reserves, 169
  riders for, 101
  scope of, 100
  wife's prior death, 101
Federal Employees' Group Life Insurance Plan (FEGLI), 388–90
  amounts, 388
  benefit structure, 388
  continuing protection provisions, 389–90
  cost, 389
  eligibility and enrollment, 388–89
  insurers for, 389
Federal Employees Health Benefits Plan, 422
Federal estate tax; *see* Estate tax
Federal gift tax; *see* Gift tax
Federal income tax; *see also* Taxation, company
  annuities, 89

Federal income tax—*Cont.*
  charitable gifts of life insurance, 903
  financial statement treatment, 1044
  group health insurance, 469
  group ordinary life insurance, 383–84
  group paid-up life insurance, 381
  group term life insurance, 465–67, 880
  health insurance, 870–71
    business, 871
    disability income payments, 870
    medical reimbursement, 870
    personal, 871
    premiums, 871
  investments of life insurance companies, 1026–27
  key man life insurance, 655–56
  life insurance 38, 49, 866–71
    additional compensation payments, 879–80
    alimony payments, 878–79
    business, 871, 874–75
    charitable contributions, 877
    contingent payees, 867–70
    creditor-debtor situations, 875–77
    death benefits, 866–68
    divorce decrees, 878–79
    insurable interest lacking, 874
    interest exclusion, 867
    interest option, 867–68
    instalment options, 867–69
    living benefits, 868–70
    lump-sum payments, 866–68
    personal, 870–71
    premiums, 870–71
    proceeds as corporate distributions, 874–75
    separation agreements, 878–79
    transfer for value, 872–74
  limited-payment life insurance, 73
  mutual funds, 267–68
  nonqualified deferred compensation plans, 663–68
  partnership, 696
  partnership interest purchase and sale, 699, 701
  pension plans, 522, 548–49
  professional corporations; *see* Professional corporations
  profit sharing plans, 548–49
  rate of return on investment, 46
  short-term disability income insurance waiting period, 396–99
  split dollar life insurance, 880
  split-dollar plans, 684–86
  stock redemption plan, 713–14
  tax deferred annuities; *see* Tax deferred annuities
  variable life insurance, 237
Federal tax liens, 827–28

Federal Trade Commission Act, 946
Federal Trade Commission jurisdiction, 948
Fifth dividend option, 192
Final-pay plans, 254
Financial statements, company, 1036–54
  accounting principles, life insurance versus generally accepted, 1048–49
  accrued basis, 1039, 1042
  "adjusted" figures for stock insurance companies, 1049–51
  admitted assets, 1038
  amortized basis, 1038–39
  annual report, 1037, 1047–48
    convention blank distinguished, 1037, 1047–48
  annual statement filed with insurance department, 1036–37, *see also specific subtopics hereunder*
    annual report distinguished, 1037, 1047–48
    association blank form, 1036
    convention blank form, 1036–37
    audits, 1037
  balance sheet, 1039–42
    assets, 1040
    capital, 1042
    liabilities, 1040–42
    surplus, 1042
  cash basis, 1039
  convention blank, 1036–37; *see also specific subtopics hereunder*
  exhibits in convention blank, 1046
  ledger assets, 1037
  nonadmitted assets, 1038
  nonamortizable securities, 1039
  nonledger assets, 1037–38
  revenue basis, 1039
  schedules in convention blank, 1046–47
  separate account blank, 1045
  strength of company revealed by, 1051–54
  summary of operations, 1042–44
    deductions from income, 1043–44
    dividends to policy owners, 1044
    federal income tax, 1044
    income, 1042–43
    net gain from operations, 1044
  supplementary contracts, 1039
  surplus account, 1045
  terminology explained, 1037–39
Financing methods; *see specific type of insurance or plan*
First dollar coverage in group medical expense insurance, 416–17
First Investment Annuity Company (FIAC), 242
First year death claims, 27

Fixed-benefit life insurance (FBLI), 230
Fixed-dollar annuities, 87
  limitations of, 90–91
Fixed-dollar assets, 50
Fixed-premium insurance, 230–31
Foreign insurers' policies, federal income
  tax consequences, 1069
Foreign residence as risk selection factor,
  200–201
Forfeiture provisions in nonqualified de-
  ferred compensation plans, 667–68
Formation of contract of insurance, 106–9;
  see also Contracts *or specific type of
  insurance*
Forward commitments, 1028–29
Franchise disability insurance, 283
Franchise health insurance, 354
Fraternal life insurance, 972
Fringe benefits, 23
Funded pension plans; *see* Trust fund
  plans
Funding instruments; *see* Funding of pension plans
Funding of pension plans; *see also specific type of plan*
  allocated funding instruments, 596
  combination plans, 590-91
  deferred compensation agreements,
    668–69
  deposit administration contracts, 614–
    23, 625–26
  funding agency, 525
  funding instrument, 525
  group deferred annuities, 605–13; *see
    also* Group deferred annuities
  group permanent contracts, 597–605;
    see also Group permanent contracts
  individual policy plans, 587–90
  life insurance for retired employees,
    486–87
  policy of, 525
  separate accounts, 623–24
  settlement options used in connection
    with, 843
  stock redemption plans, 734–35
  tax deferred annuities, 583–84
  trust fund plans, 627–43
Future contingent payments, reserve for,
  326

G

Gambling
  essence of, 29
  insurance versus, 29–30
  risk of loss to individual, 29
Gentlemen's agreements, 449, 993
Gift tax, 845
  annual exclusion, 889–90

Gift Tax—*Cont.*
  charitable gifts of life insurance, 904
  exemptions, 889–90
  inadvertent gift, 891
  incomplete gifts of insurance, 888
  life insurance, 888–91
  lifetime exclusion, 889–90
  marital deduction, 890, 900
  marital status of donor, 890
  rates, 889
  savings available by family gifts of life
    insurance, 892–94
  split-dollar plans, 687–88
  split gift approach, 890
  tax deferred annuities, 583
  taxable value, 888–89
  value for purposes of, 888–89
Gift-to-minors trust, 890 n
Gifts in estate planning, 852
Gifts of insurance
  estate tax consequences, 887
    three-year measuring period, 887
  limited-payment policies, 73
  settlement options for, 842
  tax aspects, 888–91; *see also* Gift tax
Gifts of life insurance, 49–50, 892–906
  charitable gifts, 902–6
    additional personal life insurance
      combined with, 905–6
    advantages of, 902–3
    bequest at death, 904–5
    existing policy given, 905
    group support, 905
    insurance in lieu of current cash, 904
    tax advantages, 903–4
  custodianship for minors, 900–902
  direct gifts, 896–98
  family gifts, 892–902
    proceeds payable to named benefi-
      ciaries, 893
    proceeds payable to the estate, 893
    tax savings available, 892–94
  future interests, problem of, 897, 899
  marital deduction, 900
  minors, 896–97
    custodianship, 900–902
    trust, 899–900
  nontax advantages of, 894–96
  settlement options, problem of, 897–98
  surrender by donee, 897
  tax advantages to donee, 894
  trusts, 898–900
Going-concern method of valuing assets,
  1025–26
Government benefit schemes, 749 ff.; *see
  also specific types*
Governmental supervision; *see* Regulation
  and State statutes and laws

Governmentally operated hospitals individual medical expense insurance, 299–300
Grace period
annuity policy, 88
contract clause for, 116–17
group insurance, 458
individual health insurance, 312–13
variable life insurance, 232–33
Gradation
dividends, 67 n
premiums, 67
Graded death benefit, 104, 209
Graded-premium contracts, 74
Graded-premium plan, 98
Gross premiums; *see also specific topics*
annuities, 153–56
Cammack-Jenkins type of formula, 329
Hoskins asset share method of calculating, 329
individual health insurance, 320, 328–29
nonparticipating life insurance, 140–49
participating policies, 149–52
significance of, 156
variable life insurance, 233–34
Group accidental death and dismemberment insurance (AD&D), 353, 386–87
continuing protection, provisions for, 386
double indemnity feature, 386
limitations, 387
nature of, 386
twenty-four hour coverage, 386
Group annuities
single-premium plans, 81
variable, 243, 254
Group buyer, 498–99
Group credit disability income insurance, 394–95
Group credit life insurance, 395
Group creditor disability insurance, 409–11
benefits, determination and duration of, 409–10
exclusions, 410–11
limitations, 410–11
nature of, 409
preexisting conditions clause, 410
risk selection, 445–46
Group creditor life insurance, 372, 378–80
benefits, 454
contract provisions, 379–80
creditor modifications of conventional term plan, 379–80
declining amount of insurance, 379
eligible creditors, 378
eligible groups, 453

Group creditor life insurance—*Cont.*
insuring clause, 379
loans, 378–79
premium rates, 380
purchases insured, 379
regulation, 380
risk selection, 380, 445–46
statement of insurance, issuance of, 380
termination reasons, 379–80
Group deferred annuities, 596–97
allocated concept as basis, 596–97
classical, 605–8
benefit formula, 606
countertrend, 608
future service, 605
past service, 605–6
strengths, 606
trend, 608
weaknesses, 606–8
funding for the individual employee, 609–12
costs, 611–12
defined benefit plans, 609–10
defined contribution plans, 610
past service, 610
pattern of, 612
money purchase plans, 608–9
variations of, 612–13
Group, defined, 356–57
Group disability income insurance, 352, 354, 392–412
development of, 392–95
growth of, 393–95
long-term disability income, 403–7; *see also* Long-term disability income
nature of, 392–95
purpose of, 392–93
risk selection, 443–44
short-term disability income, 395–403; *see also* Short-term disability income
Group health insurance, 349 ff.; *see also* Group insurance
benefits, tax aspects of, 469
continuance of policy benefit after termination of coverage, 462
contracts, 455–65; *see also* Group insurance
conversion privilege, 461
extended rate guarantees, 477
initial premium rates, 474–76
payment to providers of group health services, 464
physical examination and autopsy, 464
premiums, tax aspects of, 469
recognition of expenses by size of case, 476–77
regulation, 454–55
risk selection, 334

Group health insurance—*Cont.*
 scope of coverage, 365–67
 taxation, 469
 types, 352, 354
Group hospital expense insurance, 420–21
Group insurance; *see also specific type of Group insurance*
 actively at work, 459
 administrative services agreements, 488
 amendment of contract, 457
 application for, 457
 assignments, 458–60
 basic features, 354–60
 benefit levels, 437
 benefit schedules, 357–58
 certificate for group, 459
 claim procedures, 462
 claim provisions, 462–65
 collective bargaining as factor, 370
 compensation to agents and brokers, 501–3
  commission levels, 502
  group permanent commission, 503
  small case commission, 503
  types of commissions, 502–3
 contracts, 437, 455–65
 contributory plans, 360
 cost accounting, 477
 cost plus plans, 488
 creditor-debtor groups, 34, 355–56
 defined, 9
 distinguished from all other types of insurance, 351–52
 dividends, 483
 effective date of coverage, 457
 eligibility period, 460
 eligibility requirements, 436–37
 eligible groups, 355–57
  actively at work, 437
 employer groups, multiple, 441
 entire contract clause, 456
 evidence of insurability, 460
 expansion limits, 15
 expansion of, 1098–99
 experience rating, 361, 477–83; *see also* Experience rating
 financing methods, 358–60
  contributory, 360
  noncontributory, 358–60
 formation of contract, 456–57
 fundamental characteristics of, 351–71
 grace period, 458
 growth of, 9–10, 351, 364–67
  forces underlying, 367–71
 inception of coverage, 459–60
 individual employer groups, 355
 individual insurance contrasted, 352–53
 inflation as factor, 379
 insured's provisions, 459–65

Group insurance—*Cont.*
 insuring agreements, 456
 labor union groups, 355
 legal concepts, 450–65
 minimum number in group, 356–57
 minimum premium plans, 487–88
 minimum proportion of group, 357
 miscellaneous groups, 356
 modified premium-dividend plans, 488
 multiple-employer groups, 355
 negotiated trusteeships, 355
 noncontributory plans, 358–60
 nonduplication of benefits, 464–65
 organizational structure of company, 506–7
 parties to contract, 456
 plan design, 436–37
 policyholder report and audit, 458
 policyholder's provisions, 457–59
 preexisting conditions, 463–64
 premiums, 457–58
 premiums theory, 472
 probationary period, 459–60
 product design, 471–72
 professional associations, 441
 public employee groups, 438
 records required, 458
 regulation, 450–55, 496
 reinsurance, 446–49
 renewal rating, 479, 481–82
 reserves, 483–86
 retired employees, 438
 retrospective premium plans, 488
 retrospective rate credits, 483
 risk selection, 361–62, 433–41
 sales process, 503–6; *see also* Sales process
 scope of coverage, 364–67
 seasonal employees, 438
 selection of group, 360–63; *see also* Group selection
 significance of, 371
 size specifications, 356–57
 small groups, 438–39
 State Insurance Department regulation, 451
 state statutes governing, 452
 stop-loss plans, 488
 system design, 472
 Taft-Hartley Trusts, 439–40
 taxation, 465–69
 termination of contract, 457
 transfer cases, rating of, 482–83
 union groups, 440
 voluntary trade associations, 355, 440–41
Group insurance administrators, 500
Group insurance marketing, 494–509
 administrators, 500

Group insurance marketing—*Cont.*
  advantages, 495
  associations of individuals, 497
  brokers, 499–500
  characteristics, 496
  consultants, 499–500
  creditors, 497–98
  customer groups, 497
  description of market, 496–98
  direct, 501
  employer trusts, 497
  entry into, 507–9
    problems to be considered, 508–9
    reasons for, 507–8
  group buyer, 498–99
  growth, 494–96
  importance, 494–96
  individual employers, 496–97
  insurance company agents, 500
  joint employer-union groups, 497
  labor unions, 497
  mail, 501
  mass media, 501
  nature of the market, 494–98
  new product development, 495
  penetration of market, 495
  regulatory factors, 496
  relative size of different types of groups, 498
  representatives, 500–501
  system of, 498–501
  voluntary trade associations, 497
Group life insurance, 349 ff.; *see also* Group insurance *and other specific types*
  beneficiary designation and change, 462–63
  benefits, 453–54
  contest of claims, 462
  continuance of policy benefit after termination of coverage, 461–62
  contracts, 455–65; *see also* Group insurance
  conversion privilege, 460–61
  eligible groups, 453
  facility of payment clause, 463
  federal employees', 388–90
  funding for retired employees, 486–87
  incontestable clause, 462
  initial premium rates, 472–74
  misstatement of age, 462
  premiums, 454
  regulation, 452–54
  risk selection, 442
  scope of coverage, 364–65
  servicemen's plan, 390–91
  settlement options, 463
  state laws governing, 944
  types of, 352–53, 372

Group medical expense insurance, 352, 354, 413–32
  assignment of benefits agreement, 417
  basic coverages, 419–23
  benefit integration patterns, 425–30
  blanket approach, 424–25
  broad coverages, 423–30
  catastrophic illnesses, 424
  coinsurance, 424
  competition, 414–15
  comprehensive medical expense insurance, 425–27, 429
  coöperation, 431–32
  cost control procedure, 417
  costs, 431
  deductibles, 424
  development of, 413–18
  evolving group concepts, 418–19
  first dollar versus major medical, 416–17
  growth, 414–15
  hospital expense insurance, 420–21
  indemnity versus service benefits
    consumer view, 416
    third party view, 415–16
  initial premium rates, 475–76
  major medical expense insurance, 424–25
  merging philosophies, 415–17
  nature of, 413–18
  origins, 413–14
  other group health insurance benefits, 423
  other medical expense charges, 423
  percentage participation, 424
  prepaid group practice, 417–18
  prospective future developments, 430–32
  rates, 417
  risk selection, 444–45
  "sniffle" costs, 416
  surgical expense insurance, 421–23
  UCR (usual, customary and reasonable) basis, 417, 421, 428
Group ordinary life insurance, 27, 383–84
  advantages, of, 384
  continuing protection, provisions for, 384
  limitations, 384
  nature of, 383
  tax aspects, 383–84, 468–69
Group paid-up life insurance, 372, 380–82
  advantages of, 382
  allocation of cost, 381
  cash surrender values, treatment of, 381
  continuing protection, provisions for, 381–82
  limitations, 382

Group paid-up life insurance— *Cont.*
nature of, 380–81
risk selection, 442
tax aspects, 381, 468
Group permanent contracts, 596–97
allocated concepts as basis, 596–97
function of, 597
original plans, 597
retirement income contract, 597–603
whole life and conversion fund, 603–5
Group permanent life insurance, 352–53
regulation, 452
risk selection, 442
tax aspects, 467–68
Group permanent retirement income contract, 597–603
Group permanent whole life and conversion fund, 603–5
Group reinsurance, 1002–3
Group representatives, 500–501
Group selection, 360–63
administration, simplicity and efficiency of, 363
automatic determination of benefits, 362
basic objectives of rules of, 361
flow of persons through group, 362
insurance incidental to group, 362
minimum proportion of group, 362–63
objective of, 361–62
sharing of cost, 363
theory of, 361–63
departures from, 363
Group surgical expense insurance, 421–23
relative value schedule, 422
Group survivor income benefit insurance (SIBI), 372, 384–86, 442
advantages, 386
assignment, 386
benefits, 385
continuing protection, provisions for, 385–86
coverage, 385
limitations, 386
nature of, 384–85
regulation, 452–53
Group term life insurance, 352–53, 372–78
advantages to employee, 377–78
advantages to employer, 377
assignment, 376
beneficiary designation and change, 375–76
benefits, tax aspects of, 466–67
characteristics of, 372–73
continuation of insurance at election of employer, 374
continuing protection, provisions for, 373–75
conversion privilege, 374

Group term life insurance—*Cont.*
dependent coverage, 376–77
employee coverage, 373–76
estate tax consequences, 886
extension-of-pay concept, 373
facility of payment clause, 376
limitations, 378
premiums, tax aspects of, 465–66
principal attribute of, 373
professional corporations, 737, 739
reduction formula, 375
regulation, 452–54
reserves, 454
risk selection, 442
settlement options, 375–76
taxation, 465–67, 880
thirty-one-day continuation of protection, 374
waiver-of-premium benefit, 374–75
Growth of health insurance, 926–27
Growth of life insurance, 923–24, 965–66
Guaranteed fixed-dollar investments, 257
Guaranteed insurability rider, 95–96
characteristics of, 96
Guaranteed minimum annuities, 83–84
life annuity-no refund distinguished, 84
Guaranteed minimum death benefit insurance, 230
variable life insurance cost, 234
Guaranteed renewability provisions
individual disability income insurance, 282, 285–86
individual health insurance, 307–8
individual medical expense insurance, 298
Guaranteed valuation of principal, 42
Guaranteed value at death, 38

H

H-R 10 plans, 249; *see also* Self-employed persons
H-R 10 variable annuities, 253–54
Habit
dominance of, 3
risk selection factor, 343
Hazardous occupations, claims administration for, 1012
Health care supplements, 283
Health insurance; *see* Group health insurance; Individual health insurance; *or other specific topics*
Health Insurance Association of America, 932, 1020
model group accident and sickness law, 454–55
Health insurance carriers; *see also* Life insurance companies
development of, 930–31

Health insurance carriers—*Cont.*
future outlook, 935
types, 929
Health Insurance Council, 932, 1020
Health Insurance Institute, 932
Health insurance marketing, 975
Health Insurance Plan of Greater New York, 930
Health Maintenance Organization (HMO), 418 n
Health services of state and local governments, 779
Healthcare plans, 931, 949
Hierarchy of needs, 4–6
High blood pressure
individual health insurance premiums, 337
individual health insurance risk selection factor, 340
High early cash value policy, 98–99
History, 1089–1102
group insurance expansion, 1098–99
health insurance, 1099–1101
life insurance, 1089–98
Armstrong Investigation, 1095–96
beginnings of state regulation, 1094
crisis situations, 1092–94
depression decade, 1096
early years, 1090–91
industrialization, 1090
mid-century growth, 1092
mutuals, rise of, 1091
new policies, methods and growth, 1094–95
new sales techniques, 1091–92
premium payments and national progress, 1097–98
security, quest for, 1096–97
Holding companies, 951
Home Office Life Underwriters Association, 932
Hoskins asset share method of gross premiums formula, 329
Hospital, defined, 299
Hospital expense benefits
group insurance, 420–21
individual health insurance, 326
individual medical expense insurance, 292–93
purpose of insurance for, 29–30
Hospital indemnity benefit, 295
Hospital insurance under Medicare; *see* Medicare
Hospital plans, 413–14
Hospital service associations, 413–14
Human capital; *see also* Human life values
concept of, 18–21
estimating, 19
investment in, 18–19

Human capital—*Cont.*
significance of, 18–19
valuation of, significance of, 19–20
Human depreciation concept, 517–18
Human life values, 17–26; *see also* Human capital
appraisal of, 23–25
calculation of, 24–25
concept of, 21–25
defined, 21–22
development of concept of, 24
discount factors, 22
early efforts to estimate, 20–21
insurance in relation to, 35
"life will" concept, derivation of, 35
mortality as discount factor, 22
programming approach, 798–99
property values and, 22–23
Human needs; *see* Needs of man
Human resources; *see* Human capital

I

Illnesses as risk selection factor, 198–99
Immediate annuity, 85
variable, 243–44
Immediate participation guarantee contract, 621–22
Impairment exclusion riders in individual health insurance, 335–36
In-hospital medical expense benefit, 294
"In lieu" tax provisions, 1073–74
Incentive earnings, 23
Incidents of ownership, 38, 689, 883–84, 893
Income for family of decedent
children in school, 32
college education insurance, 32–33
insurance purchased for, 31–33
living expenses for widow, 32
mortgage payments, 32–33
readjustment period income, 31
settlement options for, 839–40
special family needs, 32–33
Income protection for business continuation, 718–30; *see also* Business continuation
Income tax; *see* Federal income tax
Incontestable clause, 112–16
annuities, 88
Canadian life insurance, 1080–81
development of use of, 113–14
fraud and, 115–16
group life insurance, 462
individual health insurance, 312, 314
interpretation of, 113–14
purpose of, 115–16
reformation of contracts, 115
reinstated policy, effect upon, 118
wording, 113

Increasing term policies, 56–57
  cost-of-living adjustments, 57
  uses for, 57
Indemnity benefits in group medical expense insurance, 415–16
Indemnity reinsurance, 991–1003, 1005; *see also* Reinsurance
Individual annuities, 53 ff.; *see also* Annuities *or specific topics*
Individual disability income insurance, 275–89
  benefit amounts, 280–81
  benefit payments, administration of, 286–87
  benefit period, 279–80
  business interest purchase, 287
  business overhead insurance, 287
  cancellable contracts, 285
  cash surrender values, 288
  compromise settlements, 287
  confining disability defined, 279
  coverage, extent of, 277–78
  definition of disability, 277–79
  development of, 276–77
  disability defined, 277–79
  elimination period, 279–80
  exclusions, 281–82
  franchise disability, 283
  full coverage contract with increased premium, 285
  functions, 275
  guaranteed insurability provisions, 282
  guaranteed renewable with right of insurer to change premiums by class, 285–86
  health care supplements, 283
  "his occupation" periods, 278–79
  history of, 276–77
  impairment rider, 285
  industrial disability, 283
  inflation benefits, 288
  insurance with other insurers provision, 281
  insuring agreement, 277–79
  legal contests, 287
  modified premium plans, 283–84
  mortgage protection, 283
  needs for, 275–76
  noncancellable policies, 286
  nonconfining disability defined, 279
  nonoccupational coverage, 283
  other insurance with this insurer provision, 281
  overinsurance provisions, 281
  partial disability defined, 279
  payment duration, 279-80
  purpose, 284
  rehabilitation, use of, 287

Individual disability income insurance— *Cont.*
  relation of earnings to insurance provision, 281
  renewal provisions, 285–86
  return of premium provisions, 288
  risk selection, 284–85
  special forms, 282–84
  standard risks, 284
  substandard risks, 277, 284–85
  total disability defined, 278–79
  waiver-of-premium benefit, 280
  waiver of premium disability income benefits under life policies, 282–83
Individual employers for group insurance; *see* Employer groups for group insurance
Individual health insurance, 273 ff.; *see also specific topics*
  additional family members, 308–9
  annual claims cost, 321–23
  applications for, 304–6
  beneficiary designation or change, 315–16
  benefit clause, 309–10
  cancellation provision, 317
  catastrophes, provision for, 331
  claim forms provision, 314
  conditional coverage receipt, 306
  conformity with state statutes provision, 317–18
  consideration clause, 307
  continuance table, 321–22, 325
  contract principles applicable, 303–4
  contract provisions, 306–11
    uniform, 311–18
  definitions clause, 307
  disability income insurance, 275–89
  distinguishing feature, 303
  eligibility for coverage, 308–9
  entire contract and changes provision, 311–12, 314
  exceptions provisions, 310
  exclusions, 310
  experience tables, 320
    adjustments in, 327
  extra premiums, 336–37
  face of contract, 306–7
  filing back of contract, 306–7
  formation of contract, 304–6
  grace period provision, 312–13
  gross premiums, 320, 328–29
  gross premiums for noncancellable policies, 328–29
    calculation methods, 329
    claims, 328
    expenses, 328
    interest, 328–29
    mortality, 328–29

Individual health insurance—*Cont.*
  termination rate, 328
  guaranteed renewable clause, 307–8
  hospital benefits, 326
  impairment exclusion riders, 335–36
  incontestability provision, 312, 314
  insurance with other insurers, 316–17
  insuring clause, 307
  legal actions provision, 315
  legal concepts, 303–19
  limited policy, 306–7
  loss ratios, 327
  loss-of-time benefits, 321, 323
  major medical benefits, 326–27
  misstatement of age provision, 316
  modification of coverage, 337–38
  net premiums, 320–23
  noncancellable provisions, 307–8
  nonrenewal right, 308
  notice of claim provision, 314
  occupation change provision, 316
  offer and acceptance, 304–6
  other insurance in this insurer provision,
    316
  package policy, 309
  payment of claims provision, 315
  payment of premiums clause, 308
  physical examinations and autopsy pro-
    vision, 315
  practical considerations, 326–27
  practical problems in rate making, 329–
    31
  preexisting conditions clause, 310–11
  premiums, 320–23, 328–29
  proof of loss provision, 314
  reductions provisions, 310
  regulation, 331–32
  reinstatement provision, 313–14
  relation of earnings to insurance pro-
    vision, 317
  renewability clause, 307–8
  renewal of, nature upon, 318–19
  reserves, 320, 323–27
    accrued benefits not yet due, 325–26
    active life, 320–21, 323–24
    claims in course of settlement, 325
    deficiency, 326
    disabled life, 320, 324–25
    future contingent payments, 326
    unreported claims, 325
  risk selection, 333–47
  schedule policy, 309–10
  Standard Provisions Law of 1912, 311
  state laws governing, 944
  substandard premiums, 329
  substandard risks, 335–38
  surgical benefits, 326
  10-day right to examine policy, 306
  termination clause, 309

Individual health insurance—*Cont.*
  time limit on certain defenses provision,
    312, 314
  time of payment of claim provision, 314
  uniform policy provisions, 311–18
    optional, 316–18
    required, 311–16
  unpaid premium provision, 317
  variables in, 303
  verification of claims assumptions, 327
  waiver-of-premium benefits, 323
Individual health reinsurance, 1000–1001
Individual insurance, 9
  debtor-creditor protection, 34
  group insurance contrasted, 352–53
  growth rate, 9–10
  income tax treatment of premiums, 870–
    71
  scope of benefits, 927
Individual insurance marketing, 964–75
  agency distribution system, 964–65
  brokerage distributors, 972–73
  career agencies, 971
  career distributors, 970–72
  career of selling life insurance, 966–70;
    see also Life underwriting as a
    career
  combination agencies, 971–72
  credit life insurance, 974
  debit agencies, 971–72
  employer-employee life and health in-
    surance plans, 974–75
  equity sales organizations, 973
  exclusive agent multiple-line, 972
  fraternal distributors, 972
  history of growth, 965–66
  independent distributors, 972–73
  mass merchandising, 974
  methods of, 970–75
  pension plans, 975
  personal-producing   general   agents
    (PPGA), 971
  profit sharing plans, 975
  salaried sales personnel, 974
  savings and loan associations, 974
  savings bank life insurance, 973
  securities dealers, 973
  special systems, 973–75
  Wisconsin State Life Fund, 973–74
Individual life insurance, 53 ff.; *see also*
    Insurance *or specific topics*
  contracts of, 53 ff.; *see also specific form
    of insurance*
  savings functions of, 39–52; *see also*
    Savings functions of insurance
Individual medical expense insurance,
    290–302
  basic coverages, 291
  cancellability, 298

Individual medical expense insurance—
  Cont.
  characteristics of, 297–301
  coinsurance, 292, 296–97
  comprehensive medical expense insur-
    ance, 297
  cosmetic surgery, 300
  coverages, 290
  deductible, 292
  development, 290–91
  doctor fee benefit, 294
  elective procedures, 299
  emergency accident benefit, 293
  exclusions, 299–300
  expenses not associated with injury or
    sickness, 300
  extended care benefit, 294–95
  forms of, 291–97
  governmentally operated hospitals, 299–
    300
  growth in, 291, 301
  guaranteed renewability, 298
  hospital defined, 299
  hospital expense benefit, 292–93
    daily, 292
    emergency accident, 293
    miscellaneous, 292
  hospital indemnity benefit, 295
  increasing importance of, 291, 301
  in-hospital medical expense benefit, 294
  major medical coverage, 292, 295–97
  maternity benefits, 300
  nursing expense benefit, 294
  percentage-participation-sharing of risk,
    292, 296–97
  preexistence exclusion, 300–301
  probationary period, 298–301
  regular medical benefit, 294
  renewability, 297–98
  risk selection 300–301
  successive periods of hospitalization, 299
  surgical expense benefit, 293–94
  term for which written, 297–98
  types of expenses covered, 290
Individual policy pension plans
  advantage of, 587
  funding of, 587–90
  growth of, 587
  nature of, 588–89
  nonqualified plans, 594–95
  retirement income/endowment insur-
    ance, 589
  term insurance, 589
  trust agreement, 591–92
    master or prototype, 591
  types of policies, 589
  whole life insurance, 589–90
Individual variable annuities, 243, 253
Industrial disability insurance, 283

Inertia, law of, 3
Inflation, 241, 254, 662, 1027
  group insurance, 370
  individual disability income insurance,
    288
Inflation hedges, 51
Informal pension plan payments, federal
  income tax consequences of, 879–80
Initial premium rates; *see* Premiums *or
  specific type of insurance*
Initial reserves, calculation of, 162, 165
Initial term insurance, 56
Insecurity of man, 4
Inspection reports, 205–6, 346
Installment premium deferred annuities,
  85–86
Installment refund annuity, 83
Instincts of man, 3–4
  self-preservation, 5
Institute of Home Office Underwriters, 932
Institute of Life Insurance, 932
Institutional aspects of insurance companies, 921 ff.; *see also* Life insurance
  companies *or specific topics*
Institutionalized security arrangements
  motivation of individuals, effect upon,
    14
  needs of man, provision for, 14
Institutions, mutual funds and, 271–72
Insurable income as risk selection factor,
  343–44
Insurable interest, 820–21
  application of, 109–10
  Canadian life insurance, 1083
  concept of, 203
  defined, 30
  key man life insurance, 653
  requirement of, 109–10
  risk selection factor, 202–4
  tax consequences of lack of, 874
Insurance; *see also specific types*
  annuity distinguished, 78
  future outlook, 949–50
  gambling versus, 29–30
  human life value in relation to, 35
  important aspects of, 78
  risk involved, 29
  scope of coverage and benefits, 923–28
  state laws governing contract require-
    ments and provisions for, 943–45
Insurance codes
  areas covered by, 940–45; *see also* State
    statutes and laws
  purposes of, 937
Insurance company agents, 500
Insurance company operations, 921 ff.; *see
  also* Life insurance companies *or specific topics*

Insurance company organizational structure, 506–7
Insurance with other insurers provision
  individual disability income insurance, 281
  individual health insurance, 316–17
Insured pension plans, 525–26
  growth of, 925
Insuring clause
  group creditor life insurance, 379
  group insurance, 456
  individual disability income insurance, 277
  individual health insurance, 307
Inter vivos trusts
  defined, 857
  estate planning, 851–52
Interest-adjusted method of cost comparisons, 215–18, 220
Interest assumptions for gross premiums; *see* Yield
Interest earnings, 133
Interest Equalization Tax Act, 1068–69
Interest rate
  individual life insurance, 44–46
  policy loans, 47
  reserves as affected by changes in, 166–67
  10 times rule of thumb, 166–67
Interim term insurance, 100
International Association of Health Underwriters, 932
International Claim Association, 1020
Investment advisor, 260–61
Investment annuity, 242, 578
Investment Company Act of 1940, 235, 249, 258, 259n, 260, 263–65, 267, 269–70, 946
Investment Company Amendments Act of 1970; *see* Investment Company Act of 1940
Investment income, 133, 662
  pension plan cost consideration, 542
Investment management fees for variable annuities, 251
Investments, company, 1022–35
  common stocks, 1034
  competition to reduce net cost, 1024
  considerations influencing policies of, 1023–28
  direct placements, 1029
  distribution of life insurance company assets, 1030–34; *see also* Life insurance companies
  diversification, 1029
  federal income tax, 1026–27
  forward commitments, 1028–29
  going-concern method of valuing assets, 1025–26

Investments, company—*Cont.*
  guaranteed interest rate on policy reserves, 1024
  limited surplus, 1024
  liquidity needs, 1027–28
  long-term outlook, 1023–24
  mandatory securities valuation reserve, 1026
  predictable nature, 1023–24
  regulation of, 1025
  separate accounts, 1034
  special characteristics of, 1028–29
  variable annuities, 1034
  variable life insurance, 1034
Irrevocable beneficiaries, 819–20
Irrevocable trusts, 857; *see also* Trusts

J

Joint and last survivorship annuities, 86
Joint life annuities, 87
Joint life policy, 104–5
Joint ownership with right of survivorship as estate planning tool, 852
Jumping juvenile policy, 95
  reserves, 169
Juvenile educational endowment policy, 96–97
Juvenile insurance
  Canadian life insurance, 1082
  group insurance, 459
  risk selection factor, 196–97

K

Kaiser Foundation Health Plan, 930–31
Kaiser Permanente Plans, 418
Keogh Act, 253–54, 522
  custodial accounts under, 267
  split funded plans under, 267
Keogh-Smathers Act, 90
Key man
  additional compensation to, tax consequences of, 879–80
  defined, 33, 647–48
  sale of proprietorship to, 691–92
Key man disability insurance, 660–61
Key man health insurance, 658–61
  indemnification for loss, 659
    illustration, 659
    limitations, 660
    motive, 659–60
  need for, 658
  purpose of, 658
Key man insurance protection, 33, 50
Key man life insurance, 647–61
  accumulated earnings tax, 656
  accumulation of business emergency fund, 649–50
  application for, 651
  beneficiary designation and change, 652

Key man life insurance—*Cont.*
  deferred compensation plans funded by, 651
  defined, 647
  disposition upon key man's leaving firm, 653
  estate tax
    taxation of proceeds, 657
    value of key man's stock, 657–58
  evidence of character and stability, 650
  existing life insurance, use of, 652–53
  federal income tax
    deductibility of premiums, 655–56
    increase in cash values, 655–56
    taxability of proceeds, 656
  human factor in business success, 647–48
  indemnity in case of financial or human loss, 648–50, 658–59
  insurable interest, 653
  motivation for purchase of, 647
  nature of, 647–48
  ownership of policy, 651–52
  payment of premiums, 651
  policy provisions, 651–52
  services of, 648–51
  strengthening of credit of firms, 650–51
  supporting collateral for loans, 650–51
  type of policy for, 652
  valuation of key man for purpose of, 653–55
  waiver of premium provision, 652

L

Labor agreements in trust fund plans, 635–36
Labor Management Relations Act of 1947, 355, 439
Large numbers, law of, 28–29, 121, 123–25
Laws; *see* State statutes and laws
Legal actions provision in individual health insurance, 315
Legal concepts, 106–20; *see also* Contracts *or specific topics*
Legal contest of disability insurance, 287
Legal responsibilities of life underwriter; *see* Responsibilities of life underwriter
Letter of intention, 265
Level premium concept
  net premium versus gross premium, 68–69
  protection function of insurance, 69–70
  savings element of, 69
  straight life insurance, 67–68
  term insurance, 67–68
  whole life insurance, 67–70
  yearly renewable term insurance, 68–69

Level premium insurance
  features of, 173
  split-dollar plans, 677
Level premium life insurance, 40–42
  yearly renewable term premium distinguished, 41
Level premium reserves, 159–65
  annual premium calculation, 161
  initial, 162, 165
  interest data, 160–61
  mean, 162, 165
  mortality data, 160–61
  prospective calculation, 159, 161–63
  retrospective calculation, 159, 162, 164
  terminal, 161–62, 165
Level term coverage, 57, 93
Liabilities of life underwriter; *see* Responsibility of life underwriter
Lien system, 209
Life annuities, 134
Life annuity-no refund, 82–83
  guaranteed minimum annuity distinguished, 84
Life annuity-period certain, 83
Life estate, creation of, 37
Life expectancy contract, 55–56
Life insurance; *see* Group life insurance; Insurance; Variable life insurance; *or other specific topics*
Life Insurance Agency Management Association, 932
Life Insurance Association of America, 1020
Life insurance companies
  assets of
    common stocks, 1032–33
    corporate bonds, 1031–32
    distribution of, 1030–34
    equities, 1032–33
    government securities, 1032
    industrial bonds, 1031–32
    mortgages, 1031
    policy loans, 1033–34
    preferred stocks, 1033
    public utility bonds, 1031
    railroad bonds, 1031
    real estate, 1033
    valuation, 1025–26
  broadened financial services provided by, 52, 925–26
  economic contributions of, 933–35
  fair dealing, duty of, 981
  future outlook, 935
  good faith, duty of, 981
  history and development of, 929–30
  investments of; *see* Investments, company
  regulation of, 43
  social contributions of, 933–35

Life insurance companies—*Cont.*
  solvency measure, 171
  state laws governing, 941–42
  types, 928, 930
  waiver of premium disability income
    benefits offered by, 282–83
Life Insurance Company Income Tax Act
    of 1959, 144, 166, 237, 1055, 1057,
    1067
  exclusion for policyowner's share, 1059
  general deductions, 1059–60
  gross amounts, 1057–59
  illustration of gain from operations tax
    base, 1060
  special deductions, 1060
  tentative gain or loss from operations,
    1060
Life insurance trusts, 857–65; *see also*
    Trusts
Life Office Management Association, 932
Life reinsurance plans, 993–99; *see also*
    Reinsurance
Life underwriter
  career as; *see* Life underwriting as a
    career
  legal and professional responsibilities
    of; *see* Responsibilities of life un-
    derwriter
  liability insurance program, 989–90
  mutual fund sales by, 272
  professional status of, 983–86
  protection for, 989–90
Life Underwriter Training Council (LUTC),
    932, 968
Life underwriting as a career, 966–70
  disadvantages of, 969
  education for, 968
  good aspects of, 969
  income earned, 966–68
  opportunity, 969
  prestige, 968
  sales process, 969–70
  satisfaction, 968
  security, 969
  training for, 968
"Life will" concept, 34–36
  property will distinguished, 36
Limited-payment life insurance, 66–67
  gifts of, 73
  limitation of, 73
  tax treatment, 73
  uses of, 72–73
Limited-payment whole life insurance,
    savings element of, 40
Liquidation
  partnership, 696–97, 722
  proprietorship, 692
Liquidity, 44

Liquidity—*Cont.*
  investments of life insurance companies,
    1027–28
Loading, 175, 188
  gross premiums on single-premium im-
    mediate annuities, 154
  variable annuities, 251
Loan privileges; *see* Policy loans
Loans
  key man life insurance, 650–51
  policy; *see* Policy loans
  premium, 181–82
  self-employed persons' pensions and
    profit sharing, 570
Local taxes, 1074
Long Island Lighting Company pension
    plan, 242
Longevity; *see* Old age, economic prob-
    lems of
Long-term disability income, 403–7
  benefits
    amount, 404–6
    duration, 404
    integration with social security, 406
  claims administration, 1014–16
  definition of disability, 403–4
  exclusions, 406–7
  initial premium rates, 475
  limitations, 406–7
  maternity benefits, 404
  pension accrual benefit, 405
  rehabilitation provision, 405–6
  risk selection, 443–44
  termination of coverage, 407
  waiting period, 404–6
Loss limit method in group insurance ex-
    perience rating, 481
Loss-of-income claims, 1014, 1019
Loss-of-time insurance, 331
  individual health insurance, 321, 323
Loss ratios, 327
Love and acceptance needs, 5
  economic security and, 7

M

McCarran-Ferguson Act, 249, 450, 945–
    47
Mail marketing of group insurance, 501
Maintenance of credit, 46
Maintenance expenses, 145–46, 154
Major medical benefits
  group medical expense insurance, 416–
    17
  individual health insurance, 326–27
Major medical expense insurance, 292,
    295–97
  claims administration, 1017–18
  coinsurance, 296–97
  deductible, 296

Major medical expense insurance—*Cont.*
each illness approach, 296
group medical expense insurance, 424–25
initial premium rates, 475–76
inside limits, 297
percentage-participation, 296–97
total maximum, 297
Man distinguished from animals, 17
Management company, 260–61
Management of companies; *see* Company organization and management
Marine insurance, legal concepts relating to, 110
Marital deduction, 827
estate planning factor, 850
gift tax aspects, 890, 900
Marketing
group insurance; *see* Group insurance marketing
health insurance, 975
individual insurance, 964–75; *see also* Individual insurance marketing methods of; *see* Individual insurance marketing
Married women as risk selection factor, 197
Mass media marketing of group insurance, 501
Mass merchandising, 974
Maternity
individual medical expense insurance, 300
long-term disability income insurance, 404
short-term disability income insurance, 396, 399
Mean reserves, calculation of, 162, 165
Medicaid, 444, 775, 949, 1101
Medical examination requirement, 111, 198–99
individual health insurance, 346
risk selection tool, 346
Medical expense insurance, 33
claims administration, 1016–17
group; *see* Group medical expense insurance
individual; *see* Individual medical expense insurance
professional corporations, 739–40
tax aspects, 870
Medical Information Bureau for exchange of information in risk selection, 206
Medical service associations, 413–14
Medicare, 295, 297–98, 301, 431, 438, 444, 496, 769–75, 926, 949, 1101
development and history of, 769–70
hospital insurance (HI) under, 770–72

Medicare—*Cont.*
administration, 772
benefits, 771–72
coverage, 770
eligibility, 770
financing, 772
supplementary medical insurance (SMI) under, 772–75
administration, 774–75
benefits, 773–74
coverage, 773
eligibility, 773
financing, 774
Metropolitan Life Insurance Company, 388–90, 519
Military personnel; *see topics relating to* Servicemen *or* Veterans
Military service as risk selection factor, 200
Million Dollar Round Table, 932
Minimum deposit plans, 99 n
Minimum premium plans for group insurance, 487–88
Minors
beneficiary designation, 824–25
contracts of, 107
gifts of life insurance to, 896–97
custodianship, 900–902
trust, 899–900
Misrepresentation, 110–11
Misstatement-of-age provision, 117
annuities, 88
group life insurance, 462
individual health insurance, 316
Model Group Anti-Duplication Provision, 464–65
Modified life contracts, 73–74
Modified premium-dividend plans for group insurance, 488
Modified premium policies, 98, 102
individual disability income insurance, 283–84
Money concepts, 132–39
accumulated value of money, 133
annuities, 134–37
discounted or present value of money, 133–34
Money purchase plans, 533, 608–9
Montgomery and Ward Company negotiations, 393
Moral hazard as risk selection factor, 344–45
Mortality, 125–32, 137–39
age, 128
cash value life insurance, 44
defined, 127
determination of rates, 127–28
discount factor in human life value, 22
expectation of life, 132
factors affecting, 128–30

Mortality—*Cont.*
general population versus insured lives, 128
graduation of rates, 129
gross premiums
individual health insurance, 328–29
nonparticipating life insurance, 143
single-premium immediate annuities, 153-54
variable life insurance, 233
level premium reserves, 160–61
life insurance versus annuity mortality, 128
patterns of, pricing systems in relation to, 207
period of observation, 129
pricing systems in relation to, 206–9
probability of death, 125–27
rates; *see specific subtopics hereunder*
risk selection factor, 196
safety factors, 129–30
sex, 128–29
standard versus substandard insurance, 128
statistics, 28
term insurance, 44, 61–62
Mortality tables
basis of, 128
Commissioners Standard Ordinary Mortality Table, 131
defined, 130
gross premiums for participating insurance, 150–51
number living and number dying, 130–31
probabilities computed from, 130
reserves as affected by changes in, 167
risk selection basis, 194
ultimate, 129
Mortgage payment protection, 32–33
individual disability income insurance, 283
programming for, 809
settlement option for, 838–39
Motivation, 4
economic security, 14
Multiemployer pension plans, 521
Multiemployer trust fund plans, 640–41
Multiple-employer groups; *see* Employer groups for group insurance
Multiple owners of insurance, 818
Multiple protection policy, 93
Multiple table extra premiums, 208
Mutual companies, 928, 930
defined, 184
dividend fund determination, 186
rise of, 1091
Mutual fund company
balanced fund, 260

Mutual fund company—*Cont.*
bond funds, 260
classification by investment objective, 259-60
conservation of principal fund, 260
custodian, 261
definition, 258–59
growth funds, 259
income funds, 259
investment advisor, 260–61
investment objectives, 259–60
national distributor, 261
organization of, 260–61
purpose, 258–59
regulated investment company, qualification as, 267–68
regulation of, 269–70
securities laws governing, 269–70
special features and services, 264–67
specialty funds, 259
structure of, 260–61
underwriter, 261
Mutual funds, 225 ff., 257–72, 982
asked price, 262
bid price, 262
blue sky laws, 269–70
business organizations and, 271
capital gains distributions in additional shares, 264, 266
tax liability, 268
continuous purchases for cash, 263–64
contractual plan, 263–64
conversion privilege, 265–66
custodial accounts under Keogh Act, 267
early history preceding, 257
estate planning, 271
exchange privilege, 265–66
families of, 265–66
financial planning and, 270–72
front-end loading, 264
growth of industry, 258
income taxes and, 267–68
institutions and, 271–72
life underwriters' sales of, 272
lump-sum cash purchase, 262
net asset value per share, 262
offer of, 926
open account, 263
periodic purchase plans, 263–64
personal needs, programming, 270–71
pricing shares of, 262
prototype corporate retirement plans, 267
purchase methods, 262–65
quantity discounts, 264–65
redemption privilege, 265
refund rights, 264
regular account, 262–63

Mutual funds—*Cont.*
reinvestment of income dividends, 264, 266
tax liability, 268
right of accumulation, 265
single cash purchase, 262
spread load, 264
state laws governing, 269–70
voluntary accumulation plan, 263
withdrawal plans, 266–67

N

National Association of Blue Shield Plans (NABSP), 414, 418, 425
National Association of Insurance Commissioners (NAIC), 451, 933, 938–39
Code of Ethical Practices, 455
Model Variable Contract Law and Regulation, 232, 237
National Association of Life Underwriters, 933
Code of Ethics, 987
National Association of Securities Dealers, Inc. (NASD), 269
National Convention of Insurance Commissioners (NCIC), 938
National Health Insurance Partnership Act of 1971, 431
National income, allocation to public security programs, 13–14
National Labor Relations Board ruling on pensions, 520–21
National Service Life Insurance (NSLI); *see* Veterans' life insurance
Natural reserves, 170
Needs for insurance, 30–34; *see also* Protection functions of insurance
Needs of man, 4; *see also specific needs*
economic security and, 6–8
hierarchy of, 4–6
institutionalized security arrangements, effect of, 14
prepotency, 4–5
satisfaction of, 4, 15
Negotiated trusteeships for group insurance, 355
Net premiums for individual health insurance, 320–23
Netherlands, variable life insurance in, 227–28
1958 CSO Mortality Table, 131
No-evidence limits of group permanent retirement income contracts, 598–99
"No load" funds, 261
Noncancellable policies
individual disability income insurance, 286
individual health insurance, 307–8
gross premiums for, 328–29

Nonconfining disability defined, 279
Nonforfeiture legislation, historical development of, 173–74
Nonforfeiture values, 173–83
Canadian life insurance, 1081–82
cash surrender values, 177–78
concepts underlying, 174–77
extended term insurance, 178–79
minimum legal requirements, 175–76
provisions, 173
reduced paid-up insurance, 179–80
state statutes, 61
term insurance, 61
variable life insurance, 232
whole life insurance contracts, 71
Nonlevel valuation premiums
full preliminary term reserve method, 165
modified preliminary term reserves, 165–66
reserves based on, 165–66
Nonoccupational coverage
individual disability income insurance, 283
short-term disability income insurance, 396–400
Nonparticipating insurance
defined, 184
gross premiums for, 140–49
accumulation type formula, 147
adequacy, 141
background, 140–41
band system of calculation, 146
basic considerations and requirements, 141–42
calculation, steps in, 148
competition and company objectives, 142
competitive atmosphere, 140
equation type formula, 147
equity, 141
expenses, types and variations in, 145–46
factors and assumptions for factors, 142–47
formulas, 147
interest assumptions, selection of, 143–44
legal limitations, 141–42
mortality rates and experience, 143
participating insurance comparison, 149–50
policy fee system of calculation, 146
profit factor, 146–47
testing of, 148–49
withdrawals, 144–45
participating compared, 212, 220
premium calculation, 184–85
term policies, 61

Nonparticipating insurance—*Cont.*
  variations in contracts for, 102–3
Nonparticipating life insurance, 47
Nonproportional reinsurance, 1001–2, 1005
Nonqualified deferred compensation plans, 662–75
  annual premium deposit, 669
  bare promise versus commercial annuity, 666
  cash versus accrual accounting, 666–67
  constructive receipt doctrine, 664–65
  contingent rights, 667–68
  contract provisions, 663
  cost considerations, 669–75
  death benefit, 671, 673
  disability benefits, 674–75
  economic benefit, 665–66
  employee benefits, 671, 673
  forfeiture provisions, 667–68
  funding of, 668–69
    intra-company, 668–69
    life insurance, 669
  income tax considerations, 663–68
  individual policies for, 594–95
  professional corporations, 736
  retirement benefit, 673–74
  vesting of rights, 667–68
  waiver of premium provision, 674–75
Nonrenewal rights in individual health insurance, 308
Notice of claim provision in individual health insurance, 314
Nursing expense benefit, 294

O

Occupation change provision in individual health insurance, 316
Occupations
  rating classes, 342
  risk selection factor, 199, 341–43
  short-term disability income insurance, 400
Old age, economic problems of, 513–16
  capacity to save, 515–16
  employment opportunities, 514–15
  increasing longevity, 513–14
  nature of risk of excessive longevity, 514
Old-age, survivors, and disability insurance (OASDI); *see* Social security benefits
Older persons as risk selection factor, 197
Open-end investment company; *see* Mutual fund company *and* Mutual funds
Ordinary life insurance, 66
  group; *see* Group ordinary life insurance
  state laws governing, 943–44
Organization of companies; *see* Company organization and management

Organizational structure of insurance company, 506–7
  departmental functions, 507
  field, 506–7
  general considerations, 506
  home office, 506
Organizations in life and health insurance business, 931–33
Organizations related to life and health insurance business, 933
Other insurance with this insurer provision
  individual disability income insurance, 281
  individual health insurance, 316
Overhead expenses, 145
  defined, 287
  insurance in event of disability, 287
Overinsurance, 1018–19
  individual disability income insurance, 281
Overweight
  individual health insurance premiums, 337
  risk selection factor, 197–98
Ownership investments, 51
Ownership provision, 119, 816–19
  annuity policy, 87
  key man life insurance, 651–52
  multiple owners, 818
  third party ownership, 816–17
    case law, 817–18
  transfers of ownership, 817–19

P

Package policy for individual health insurance, 309
Paid-up additions, 47–48
Paid-up-at-65 insurance contract, 73
Paid-up insurance option, 191
  whole life insurance, 71
Paid-up life insurance, group; *see* Group paid-up life insurance
Partial disability, defined, 279
Participating insurance
  advantage of, 102
  annuities, 88
  defined, 184
  gross premiums, 149–52
    assumptions for, 150–51
    calculation of scale of, 152
    dividends in relation to, 149
    expenses, 151
    general considerations, 151
    interest margin, 150
    interrelationships, 151–52
    mortality tables, 150–51
    nonparticipating insurance comparison, 149–50

Participating insurance—*Cont.*
 testing of, 152
 nonparticipating compared, 212, 220
 premium caculation, 185
 principle of, 149
 term policies, 61
 units of initial coverage of $1,000, 102
 variations in contracts for, 101–2
Participating life insurance, 47
Partnership, 695–701
 agreement of, 695–96
 buy-out method, 698–99
 buy-sell method, 698
  funding of, 699–701
 corporation distinguished, 703–4
 cross-purchase arrangement, 699, 701, 724
 death of partner, 697, 704
 defined, 695
 disability income insurance for continuance of, 724–25
 disability of partner, effect of, 720
  solutions to problems with disability income insurance, 724–25
  solutions to problems without disability income insurance, 721–22
 entity arrangement for sale, 699–701, 724
 estate tax considerations, 701
 federal income tax aspects, 696
  purchase and sale of interest, 699, 701
 heirs' sale to outsiders, 697–98
 liquidation of, 696–97, 722
  alternatives to, 697–98
 professional, 702
  corporate form compared, 742–43
 reorganization after death of partner, 697
 sale of business, 698
 shared responsibility, 695
 withdrawal of partner, planning for, 696
Payment of claims, 1019–20
 individual health insurance, 315
 variable life insurance, 235
Payment of premiums
 cross-purchase agreement, 712–13
 individual health insurance, 308
 key man life insurance, 651
 stock redemption plan, 712
Payor clause, 119–20; *see also* Waiver-of-premium provision
 endowment insurance, 76
Pension accrual benefit, 405
Pension administration contract, 621n
Pension plans; *see also specific types*
 accounting for costs of, 527–28
 actuarial cost considerations, 541–46
  benefits paid, 541–42
  choice of assumptions, 542–43

Pension plans—*Cont.*
  cost assumptions, 541–42
  estimated cost versus ultimate cost, 541
  expenses, 542
  investment income, 542
 actuarial cost methods, 543–46
  accrued benefit cost method, 544–45
  aggregate cost methods, 546
  choice of, 544
  projected benefit cost method with or without supplemental liability, 545–46
 basic features, 529–41
 benefits; *see also specific type hereunder*
  funding plan, 524–26
  levels of, 522–23
  security of, 523–24
  vesting of, 523–24
 business expediency concept, 517
 combination, 525
 combination with profit sharing, 557–58
 competition between small and large employers, 521
 contributory, 539–40
 cost considerations; *see* "actuarial cost considerations" *hereunder*
 coverage of, 521–22
 current scope of, 521–26
 death benefits, 537
  profit sharing plans distinguished, 554–55
 deferred wage concept, 518–19
 design of, 529–41
 development of, 519–21
 disability benefits, 538
 disclosure laws, 526–27
  federal, 526–27
  state, 527
 early plans, establishment of, 516–18
 eligibility requirements, 530–32
  deferment of employee's participation, 530
  earnings, 531
  employment classification, 531–32
  exclusion of employees, 530
  Internal Revenue Code requirements, 530
  maximum age, 531
  minimum age, 531
  profit sharing plans distinguished, 550
  years of service, 530–31
 employee contributions, 539–40
 employee turnover, effect of, 593
 employer contribution requirements, 550–51
  allocation formulas, 551–52
 employer's options and actions, 593–94

Pension plans—*Cont.*
estate tax aspects, 887–88
factors to be considered, 529
financing policy, 525
funding instruments; *see* Funding of pension plans
funding plan benefits, 524–26
general provisions, 540–41
growth of, 519–20, 925
human depreciation concept, 517–18
income tax treatment, 522
inflexibility of, 556
informal, tax consequences of, 879–80
insured, 525–26
integration with social security, 552, 553n
investment experience, effect of, 592
investment of funds of, 556–57
labor's drive for, 520–21
marketing of, 975
multiemployer, 521
nature of, 513–28
profit sharing plan differences, 549–56
prohibited group of employees, 529
purpose of, 549–50
qualification of, 525
qualified, 520, 529–30
rationale of, 516–19
reinsurance scheme establishment, proposal for, 524
retirement ages
early, 532–33
floating normal, 532
late, 533
normal, 532
staggered normal, 532
retirement benefits, 533–36
annuity purchase formula, 533
defined benefit formulas, 533, 535
defined contribution formulas, 533–35
determination of earnings, 533–34
flat amount formula, 535
flat amount per year of service formula, 535
flat percentage of earnings formula, 535
integrated formulas, 536
maximum, 536
minimum, 536
money purchase formula, 533
percentage of earnings per year of service formula, 535
profit sharing plans distinguished, 553–54
social security integration with, 536, 552, 553n
variable benefit formulas, 535–36
security of benefits, 523–24

Pension plans—*Cont.*
self-employed persons; *see* Self-employed persons
severance of employment benefits, 538–39
profit sharing plans distinguished, 555–56
split funding, 624–25
tax advantages, 548–49
trust fund, 525–26
vesting of benefits, 523–24, 538–39
veterans
death, 791
disability, 789–90
wartime developments, 519–20
Per capita beneficiary designation, 822
Per stirpes beneficiary designation, 822
Percentage participation; *see* Coinsurance
Periodic-payment variable annuities, 245–46
Permanent flat extra premiums, 207
Permanent life insurance, 39–40n
business emergency fund accumulation, 649–50
group, 352–53
Personal health insurance, income tax treatment of premiums on, 871
Personal holding company tax, 745
Personal insurance; *see* Individual insurance
Personal-producing general agents (PPGA), 971
Physical examination and autopsy
group health insurance, 464
individual health insurance, 315
Physiological needs, 5
economic security and, 7
Policy dividends
comparisons, 213–14
defined, 47, 184
distribution of, 187–91
expense element, 188
federal income tax treatment, 49
financial statement entry, 1044
gradation, 67n
gross premiums in relation to, 149
group insurance, 483
group permanent retirement income contracts, 600–601
health insurance, 192–93
investment element, 187–88
mortality element, 187
nature of, 184–86
practical considerations, 190–91
source of funds for payment of, 185
statutory requirements, 189–90
terminal, 188–89
three-factor formula, 188
three-factor method, 187–88

Policy dividends—*Cont.*
  veterans' life insurance, 785
Policy fee system of gross premium calculation, 146
Policy loans, 180–81
  annuities, 88
  assets of life insurance companies, 1033–34
  group creditor life insurance, 378–79
  individual life insurance, 47
  interest rate, 47
  maximum rate of interest on, 180–81
  variable life insurance, 232
  whole life insurance, 71
Policy proceeds; *see* Proceeds of insurance
Policy provisions; *see* Contracts *or specific provisions*
Pooling of risks, 28–29
Position schedules, 358
Pour-over trust, 859 n
  in estate planning, 851–52
Powers of appointment, 852
Preexisting conditions
  group creditor disability insurance, 410
  group insurance, 463–64
  individual health insurance, 310–11
  individual medical expense insurance, 300–301
Preferred risk contracts, 74, 196
Preferred stocks
  assets of life insurance companies, 1033
  valuation, 1026
Preliminary term insurance, 56
Preliminary term reserves
  full, 165
  modified, 165–66
Premium loans, automatic, 181–82
Premium tax, 1069–72
Premiums; *see also* Cost of insurance *and* Level premium concept
  accidental death and dismemberment insurance
    initial rates, 474
  annuities classification basis, 80–82
  calculation, 184–85
  conditional receipts for, 107–8
  dental care, initial rates for, 476
  estate tax aspects, 886–87
  family policies, 100–101
  females, 67
  gradation, 67
  graded plans, 74, 98
  gross, 140–57; *see also* Gross premiums
  group creditor life insurance, 380
  group health insurance
    extended rate guarantees, 477
    initial rates, 474–76
    recognition of expenses by size of case, 476–77

Premiums—*Cont.*
  tax aspects, 469
  group insurance, 457–58, 472
  group life insurance, 454
    initial rates, 472–74
  group medical expense insurance, initial rates for, 475–76
  group permanent retirement income contracts, 599
  group term life insurance, tax aspects of, 465–66
  individual health insurance, 320–23, 328–29
  interim term insurance, 100
  joint life insurance, 105
  level, 40–42
  limited-payment life insurance, 66–67
  long-term disability income insurance, initial rates for, 475
  males, 67
  minimization of initial outlay for, 98–100
  modified life contracts, 73
  modified plans, 102
  modified policies, 98
  mortality as basis for, 206–9
  nonparticipating insurance, 184–85
  participating insurance, 185
  receipts for, 107–8
  reduced, 191
  return of, provision for, 103
  semicompulsory nature of payments of, 42–43
  short-term disability income insurance, initial rates for, 474–75
  step-rate plans, 98, 102
  straight life insurance, 66
  substandard risks, 207–9
    individual health insurance, 336–37
  tax aspects, 870–71, 878
  term insurance, 63
  whole life insurance, reduction in rates of, 74
  yearly renewable term, 41
Premiums paid in advance for group insurance reserves, 484
Prepaid group practice plans, medical expense insurance for, 417–18
Price comparisons; *see* Contract analysis
Primary beneficiaries, 820
Principal of annuities, 79
Principal of insurance
  guaranteed valuation of, 42
  safety of, 43
Private annuities, 852
Private insurance and social insurance distinguished, 351–52
Private pension plans; *see* Pension plans *and other related topics*

Probability, 137–39
  addition rule, 122–23
  of death; *see* Mortality *and* Mortality
    rates
  definition, 122
  distribution of insurance claims, 125
  insurers' use of, 28
  multiplication rule, 123
  origin of theory of, 122
  rules of, 122–23
  theory of, 121–25
Probationary period
  group insurance, 459–60
  individual medical expense insurance,
    298–301
Proceeds of insurance
  annuities classified on basis of disposi-
    tion of, 82–85
  exemption statutes, 37–38
  tax treatment, 38
Production factors, 22
Professional associations' group insurance,
    441, 497
Professional corporations, 90, 562, 572–73,
    731–48
  accumulation of earnings tax, 746
  capital provided by, 734
  centralized management, 741
  comparison of flexibility of corporate
    versus unincorporated qualified
    plans, 738–39
  continuity of life, 741, 744
  ease of transferability, 741, 744
  85% dividend credit, 736
  employee fringe benefits, 736–40
  federal tax question, 731–33
  $5,000 tax-free death benefit, 736
  funding stock redemption plan, 734–35
  future outlook, 747
  group term life insurance, 737, 739
  history of events leading to formation
    of, 731–33
  limited liability, 740–41
  marginal efficiency of profits, 740
  medical expense benefits, 739–40
  new taxpayer, creation of, 734–36
  nonqualified deferred compensation
    plans, 736
  one-man, 744
  partnership form compared, 742–43
  personal holding company tax, 745
  problem areas, 744–46
  qualified retirement plans, 736–37
  reasonableness of compensation, 745–
    46
  requirements of Internal Revenue Ser-
    vice, 733
  salary continuation plans, 740

Professional corporations—*Cont.*
  split-dollar life insurance, 735–36
  state law, 732
  tax,advantages of, 733–40
Professional individuals' business contin-
    uation problems, 701–2
Professional responsibilities of life under-
    writer; *see* Responsibilities of life un-
    derwriter
Professional Services Index (PSI), 421
Profit
  gross premium factor of nonparticipat-
    ing insurance, 146–47
  limitation on, 186
  objectives of, 147
Profit sharing, defined, 548
Profit sharing plans, 548–58
  combination with pension plans, 557–58
  death benefits, 554–55
  defined, 548–49
  distributions prior to separation from
    service, 556
  eligibility requirements, 550
  employee turnover, effect of, 593
  employer contribution requirements,
    550–51
    allocation formulas, 551–52
  estate tax aspects, 887–88
  flexibility of, 556
  forfeiture reallocation provisions, 556
  investment experience, effect of, 593
  investment of funds of, 556–57
  marketing of, 975
  pension plan differences, 549–56
  purpose of, 549–50
  qualified, 548–49
  retirement benefits, 553–54
  self-employed persons; *see* Self-em-
    ployed persons
  severance of employment benefits, 555–
    56
  tax advantages, 548–49
Programming, 32n, 797–815
  ability to pay, 813–14
  analysis of needs, 808–11
  analysis of relevant factors, 800
  cash needs, 808–9
  chart, preparation of
    health insurance, 812–13
    life insurance, 810–11
  computer, use of, 803–5
  defined, 797–98
  estate conservation, 799, 807–8
  estate creation, 799, 807–8
  estate distribution, 799, 807–8
  estate planning in relation to, 798
  flexibility, need for, 815
  future outlook, 815

Programming—*Cont.*
  goals of client, determination of, 800–801
  health insurance, 811–13
  human life value approach to, 798–99
  illustrative confidential programming survey and analysis form, 801–8
  income needs, 808–10
  key concepts of, 813–15
  life insurance, 805–6
  personal needs through mutual funds, 270–71
  planning calculator, 803
  preparation of specific plan to meet client's goals, 801–5
  problems of, 797
  process of, 799–808
  review, need for, 814
  self-disclosure, 814
  service, concept of, 814
  settlement options for monthly income, 815
  social security benefits, charting of, 811
Proof of loss provision in individual health insurance, 314
Property status of life insurance, 36–38
Property values and human life values, 22–23
Property will and "life will" concept distinguished, 36
Proportional reinsurance, 1001, 1005
Proprietorship, 690–95
  buy-and-sell agreement, 691–92, 694–95
  death, planning for sale at, 692–93
    estate administration, 693
    life insurance, 692–93
    will provisions, 693
  defined, 690
  disability hazard, 691
  disability income insurance for continuance of, 723–24
  disability of owner, effect of, 719
    solutions to problems with disability income insurance, 723–24
    solutions to problems without disability income insurance, 721
  family business, 690
  keeping business in family, 692
  liquidation of, 692
  mature (in 50s), 691
  reporting gain from sale of, 694
  sale to key man, 691–92, 694–95
  valuation of, 693–94
Prospective calculation of level premium reserves, 159, 161–63
Protection functions of insurance, 27–38
  business insurance, 33–34
  creditor protection, 37–38

Protection functions of insurance—*Cont.*
  disability income, 33
  efficiency of, 44
  estate clearance fund, 30–31
  immediate estate creation, 37
  income for family of decedent, 31–33; *see also* Income for family of decedent
  level premium concept, 69–70
  medical expenses, 33
  significance of, 38
Protection needs, 5
Prototype corporate retirement plans, 267
Prototype pension plans, 591
Providers of group health services, payment to, group health insurance clause for, 464
Provisions of policies; *see* Contracts *or specific provisions*
Prudential Insurance Company, 391
Public employee groups, 438
Public security programs, national income allocable too, 13–14
Purchase rates of variable annuities, 251–52
Purchases of health insurance, 928
Purchases of life insurance, 924
Pure endowment defined, 75
Purpose of life insurance, 29

Q

Qualified deferred compensation plans, 662–63
Qualified pension plans, 520, 529–30; *see also* Pension plans
  comparison of flexibility of corporate versus unincorporated forms, 738–39
Qualified profit sharing plans, 548–49
Qualified retirement plans for professional corporations, 736–37
Quantity discounts in mutual funds, 264–65

R

Rate of interest on policy loans, 180–81
Rate making as individual health insurance problem, 329–31
Rate of return
  gross premiums of variable life insurance, 233
  individual life insurance, 44–46
  stability of, 45
  tax treatment, 44–46
  variables affecting, 45
Rate-up in age, 208–9
Rating; *see* Experience rating
Readjustment period income
  income for famliy of decedent, 31

Readjustment period income—*Cont.*
  programming for, 809
  settlement options for, 839
Rebating, 982–83 n
Recognition effect, 14
Record requirements
  group insurance policyholders, 458
  trust fund plans, 630–31
  variable annuities, 252
Redemption privilege of mutual funds, 265
Reduced paid-up insurance, nonforfeiture values of, 179–80
Reduction of insurance
  group term life insurance, 375
  individual health insurance, 310
Reflexes, dominance of, 3
Refund annuity, 83
Regulated investment company, 267–68
Regulation, 936–50; *see also* State statutes and laws
  beginnings of, 1094
  Canadian life insurance, 1076–78
  federal agencies involved in, 947–49
  goals of, 450–51
  group creditor life insurance, 380
  group health insurance, 454–55
  group insurance, 450–55, 496
  group life insurance, 452–54
  group permanent life insurance, 452
  group survivor income benefit insurance, 452
  group term life insurance, 452–54
  individual health insurance, 331–32
  investments of life insurance companies, 1025
  life insurance companies, 43
  mutual fund companies, 269–70
  objectives of, 936–37
  state insurance supervision, development of, 938–40
  variable annuities, 248–53
  variable life insurance, 235–37
Rehabilitation
  defined, 287
  use of, 287
Rehabilitation provisions in long-term disability income insurance, 405–6
Reinstatement provision, 117–18
  Canadian life insurance, 1081
  individual health insurance, 313–14
  variable life insurance, 232–33, 235
  veterans' life insurance, 784–85
Reinsurance, 991–1006
  accidental death and dismemberment insurance, 388
  agreement for, 991–92
  arbitration of differences, 993
  assumption, 1003–4

Reinsurance—*Cont.*
  automatic methods of ceding reinsurance, 999–1000, 1004
  automatic quota share agreements, 448
  catastrophe, 1002, 1004
  ceding company, 991
  cessions, 992, 1005
  coinsurance, 993, 997–99, 1004
    advantages, 997–98
    disadvantages, 998
    modified, 993, 998–99, 1004
  comparison of plans, 998–99
  defined, 446, 991–92, 1005
  disability income, 1001
  disaster, 1002
  excess of loss, 1004
  facultative methods of ceding reinsurance, 999–1000, 1004
  facultative quota share agreements, 448–49
  gentlemen's agreements, 449
  good faith requirement, 993
  group, 1002–3
  group insurance, 446–49
    agreement, 448–49
    catastrophic accident risk, 446–47
    excess, 446
    pro rata, 446
    sharing business for nonrisk reasons, 448
    sharing portion of normal risk, 447–48
  Hartford method of handling dividends, 449
  indemnity, 991–1003, 1005; *see also specific subtopics hereinunder*
  individual health, 1000–1001
  life reinsurance plans, 993–99
  New York method of handling dividends, 449
  nonproportional, 1001–2, 1005
  proportional, 1001, 1005
  quota share, 1005
  recapture privileges, 993, 999
  reinsurer defined, 991, 1005
  relationship of insurer and reinsurer, 993
  retention, 992
  retention limit, 992–93, 1005
  retrocession, 1005
  risk premium reinsurance, 993–97, 999, 1005
    accidental death benefits, 996–97
    advantages, 996
    net amount at risk, 1004
  significance of, 991
  stop loss, 1002
  values of, 992

Relation of earnings to insurance premium
individual disability income insurance, 281
individual health insurance, 317
Relative value schedule (RVS) in group surgical expense insurance, 422
Renewability clause in individual health insurance, 307–8
Renewable term insurance, 57–58
Renewal of insurance
individual disability income insurance, 285–86
individual health insurance, nature of, 318–19
individual medical expense insurance, 297–98
Renewal rating in group insurance experience rating, 479, 481–82
Replacement insurance, 221–23
Report of the Joint Special Committee on Life Insurance Costs, 215, 220 n
Report to policyholders, 1037, 1047–48
group insurance, 458
variable annuities, 252
variable life insurance, 235
Representations, 111
Reserves, 158–72; *see also specific topics*
average, 158
balance sheet account, 1040
cash values and, 170–71
changes in assumptions, effect of, 166–68
continuous functions, 168
curtate functions, 166
deficiency, 169–70
defined, 42, 171
disabled life, 169
group insurance, 483–86
annual statements, 483–84
claim reserves, 484
contingency reserves, 484
dividends, 484
experience rating, 485–86
premiums, 484
premiums paid in advance, 484
unearned premiums, 484
group term life insurance, 454
guaranteed interest rate on, 1024
individual health insurance, 320, 323–27
interest rate changes, 166–67
level premium, 159–65, 169
mortality table changes, effect of, 167
natural, 170, 1050
nonlevel valuation premiums as basis, 165–66
securities valuation, 1026
solvency measure, 171
statutory, 170–71

Reserves—*Cont.*
tax deferred annuities, 583
tax treatment, 45 n
valuation of, 42
valuation single premium, 168–69
valuation standards, 171
Residence ownership, 51
Residence requirement as risk selection factor, 200–201
Resisted claims, reserve for, 326
Resources, 22
Responsibilities of life underwriter, 976–90
activities during business day, 976–77
company's contract liability, 978–79
company's tort liability, 979–81
contract liability of company, 978–79
full disclosure, 982
Golden Rule, 987
one man, many parts, 977
professional stature, 983–86
rules of the business, 986–89
"Some Guideposts for Cooperation between Lawyers and Life Insurance Representatives," 987–88
statutory duties and penalties, 983
tort liability of company, 979–81
tort liability for own acts, 981–83
Retaliatory taxes, 1072–73
Retired employees
funding of life insurance for, 486–87
group insurance, 438
Retirement age
deposit administration pension plans, 615
pension plans, 532–33; *see also* Pension plans
self-employed persons' pensions and profit sharing, 570
Retirement annuity contracts, 97
Retirement benefits
deferred compensation plans, 673–74
pension plans, 533–36; *see also* Pension plans
profit sharing plans, 553–54
trust fund plans, 633–34
Retirement income, programming for, 810
Retirement income contracts, 75–76, 98; *see also* Endowment insurance *and* Variable annuities
Retroactive conversion, term insurance, 58–59
Retrospective calculation of level premium reserves, 159, 162, 164
Retrospective premium plans for group insurance, 488
Retrospective rate credits for group insurance, 483
Return of premium provisions in individual disability income insurance, 288

Reversionary annuity, 385
Revocable beneficiaries, 819–20
Revocable trusts, 857; *see also* Trusts
Right of accumulation privilege in mutual funds, 265
Risk appraisal; *see* Risk selection
Risk-averaging formula in group insurance experience rating, 479–80
Risk-charge formula in group insurance experience rating, 480–81
Risk of loss, 29–30
Risk manager, 499
Risk premium reinsurance (RPR), 993–97, 999, 1005
    accidental death benefits, 996–97
    advantages, 996
    net amount at risk, 1004
Risk selection
    defined, 194
    deposit administration pension plans, 618
    group creditor disability insurance, 445–46
    group creditor life insurance, 380, 445–46
    group disability income insurance, 443–44
    group health insurance, 334
    group insurance, 361–62, 433–41
        administrative control and cooperation, 435
        amounts precluding selection, 434
        composition of group, 435–36
        economic conditions, 436
        environment, 436
        flow of persons through group, 435
        geographic area, 436
        high expectation of persistency, 435
        industry factors, 436
        insurance incidental to the group, 434
        maximum amounts, 434
        minimum number in group, 434
        nondiscriminatory classifications, 434
        nonstatutory factors, 434–36
        percentage of enrollment, 434
        policyholder sharing of cost, 435
        professional associations, 441
        public employee groups, 438
        retired employees, 438
        seasonal employees, 438
        size of group, 435
        small groups, 438–39
        statutory requirements, 433–34
        Taft-Hartley trusts, 439–40
        transferred business from another carrier, 436
        union groups, 440

Risk selection—*Cont.*
        variations by type of coverage, 441–46
        variations by type of policyholder, 437–41
        voluntary trade associations, 440–41
    group life insurance, 442
    group medical expense insurance, 444–45
    group paid-up life insurance, 442
    group permanent life insurance, 442
    group survivor income benefit insurance, 442
    group term life insurance, 442
    individual disability income insurance, 284–85
        antiselection, 284
        applicant qualifications, 284
        factors, 284
        standard risks, 284
        substandard risks, 284–85
    individual health insurance, 333–47
        acute illness, history of, 339
        agents' reports, 347
        alcoholism, 343
        applicant's health, 338–41
        application as source of information, 345
        attending physician's statement, 345–46
        blood pressure, 340
        build of applicant, 341
        chronic conditions, 338–40
        claims records, 346–47
        classes of risks, 334
        disability income payments under state plans, 344
        drugs, use of, 343
        factors, 338–45
        habits, 343
        height and weight, 341
        "his occupation" provision, 342
        individual life insurance compared, 335–36
        inspection reports, 346
        medical examination, 346
        medical and personal history, 338–41
        moral hazard, 344–45
        nature, 333–34
        occupation, 341–43
        outcomes, 335
        portion of income insurable, 343–44
        risk class, 334
        sources of information, 345–47
        standard class, 334–35
        substandard risks, 335–38
    individual life insurance, 194–206
        agents' reports, 205
        alcohol, use of, 201–2

Risk selection—*Cont.*
 antiselection, effect of, 194–95
 application for insurance, 204–5
 attending physicians' statements, 206
 aviation, 199–200
 avocation, 199–200
 build of persons, 197–98
 consumer investigative reports, 205–6
 departure from social mores, 202
 driving record, 202
 drugs, use of, 201–2
 evidence of physical insurability, 204–5
 factors of, 196–204
 family history, 197
 financial considerations, 202–4
 foreign residence, 200–201
 height and weight of persons, 197–98
 illnesses, 198–99
 individual company objectives, 195
 individual health insurance compared, 335–36
 inspection reports, 205–6
 insurable interest requirement, 202–4
 medical history and impairments, 198–99
 Medical Information Bureau exchange of information, 206
 military service, 200
 mortality classes, 196
 mortality tables as basis, 194
 objectives of, 194–96
 occupation, 199
 recent immigration, 201
 significance, 209
 social objectives, 196
 special questionnaires, 204
 standard risks, 195
 substandard risks, 195
 tools of, 204–6
 unacceptable risks, 195
individual medical expense insurance, 300–301
long-term disability income insurance, 443–44
short-term disability income insurance, 401–3, 443
variable life insurance, 234

S

Safety needs, 5
 economic security and, 7
Safety of insurance principal, 43
Salaried sales personnel, 974
Salary continuation plans of professional corporations, 740
Sales expenses for variable annuities, 251
Sales process, 503–6

Sales process—*Cont.*
 basic steps in, 970
 conservation of policyholder, 505–6
 cycle of, 970
 enrollment of eligible employees, 505
 installation of case, 505
 issue work completion, 505
 life underwriting as a career, 969–70
 motivating factors, 503–4
 new techniques, 1091–92
 selection of carrier, 504–5
 service calls, 505
 steps leading to purchase, 504–5
"Save and create" method, 37
Savings bank life insurance, 973
Savings functions of insurance, 39–52
 business uses of life insurance, 50
 cash surrender values, 42
 characteristics of, 43–49
 disability income coverage, 48
 dividend options, 47–48
 dollar value, 44
 efficiency of protection element, 44
 endowment insurance, 70
 exemption from claims of creditors, 48–49
 federal income tax treatment, 48
 gifts of life insurance, 49–50
 guaranteed valuation of principal, 42
 interest rate, 44–46
 level premium concept, 40–42, 69
 liquidity, 44
 maintenance of credit, 46
 nature of, 39–43
 policy loan privilege, 47
 rate of return, 44–46
 reserves valuation, 42
 safety of principal, 43
 semicompulsory nature of premium payments, 42–43
 special characteristics, 47–49
 special uses of, 49–50
 supplementary benefits, 48
 surrender options, 48
 tax status of return on invested funds, 44–46
 waiver of premium benefit, 48
 whole life insurance, 70
 yield on insurance, 44–46
Savings-investment program, 50–51
 balance in, 51
Savings and loan associations, 974
Schedule policy of individual health insurance, 309–10
Scope of coverage, 923–28
Seasonal employees' group insurance, 438
Securities Act of 1933; *see* Securities laws
Securities Exchange Act of 1934; *see* Securities laws

Securities and Exchange Commission
  mutual funds regulation, 269–70
  variable life insurance regulation, 235–37
Securities dealers, 973
Securities laws, 946
  mutual fund regulation, 269–70
  variable annuities regulated by, 248–49
  variable life insurance, regulation of, 235–37
Securities valuation reserve, 1026, 1041
Security; *see* Economic security
Security expenditures; *see* Economic security system in America
Security-oriented activities, 6
Selection of group; *see* Group selection
Selection of risks; *see* Risk selection
Self-actualization needs, 6
Self-Employed Individuals Tax Retirement Act of 1962, 267, 562
Self-employed persons
  pensions and profit sharing plans, 522, 562–74
    annuity plans, 563
    assignments, 570
    basis of contributions, 565
    benefit formula, 569
    bond purchase plans, 564
    cessation of business activity, 572
    contribution limits, 565–66
    contributions of property, 566–67
    controlled business, defined, 564–65
    coverage requirements, 568–69
    custodial accounts, 563
    death, effect of, 571
    deduction limits, 565–66
    definitions of terms, 564–65
    design, 568–70
    entry date, 569
    excess contributions, defined and treatment, 567–68
    funding methods, choice of, 563–64
    incorporation of business, 572–73
    law providing for, 562
    life insurance protection cost, 566
    loans, 570
    methods of payment, 570
    nature of, 563–73
    owner-employee, defined, 564
    partner-employee, defined, 564
    premature distributions, 571
    prior service, 569
    prohibited transactions, 571
    required employee contributions, 567
    retirement age, 570
    self-employed person, defined, 564
    shared employees, 569
    significance of, 573

Self-employed persons—*Cont.*
    social security integration with, 570
    tax aspects, 571–72
    termination of employment, 570–71
    three-year average rule for insurance, 568
    trust arrangement, 563
    vehicles for, choice of, 563–64
    vesting, 569
    voluntary employee contributions, 567
    waiver of participation, 569
Self-fulfillment needs, 5–6, 15
  economic security and, 7–8
Separate account blank, 1045
Separate accounts, 186, 1034
  funding of pension plans, 623–24
  variable annuities, 249–50
  variable life insurance, 234–35
Separation agreements, federal income tax consequences of, 878–79
Service benefits of group medical expense insurance, 415–16
Service Disabled Veterans Insurance (SDVI), 781
Servicemen's group life insurance plan (SGLI), 390–91, 787–88
  administration of, 390, 780–81
  amounts, 390–91
  benefit structure, 390–91
  continuing protection provisions, 391
  cost, 391
  eligibility and enrollment, 390
  insurer, 391
  law authorizing, 390
Servicemen's medical care programs, 775–76
Servicemen's social security benefits, 792
Settlement agreements, 843
Settlement options, 833–43
  annuities, 88
  basic company rules for use of, 843
  cash funds, 837–39
  defined, 833–36, 858
  development, 833
  educational funds, 841
  election of, 842–43
  fixed-amount option, 835
  fixed-period option, 835
  function, 833
  general rules, 842–43
  gifts of life insurance, 897–98
  group life insurance, 463
  group term life insurance, 375–76
  growth in use of, 833
  income for children, 840–41
  income for family of decedent, 839–40
  interest option, 835
  joint and survivorship life income option, 836

Settlement Options—*Cont.*
life income options, 835–36
living life insurance trusts, 857–59
lump sum settlement, 833–34
disadvantages of, 834
programming for, 815
refund life income option, 836
requesting settlement agreements, 843
special arrangements and policies, 836
special purpose funds, 842
tax aspects, 866–70
types of, 833–36
use of, 836–42
veterans' life insurance, 786–87
Severance of employment benefits
pension plans, 538–39
profit sharing plans, 555–56
self-employed persons' plans, 570–71
Sex
gross premiums on nonparticipating life
insurance, 143
mortality rate factor, 128–29
risk selection, 194, 197
Sherman Act, 946
Short-term disability income, 395–403
amounts of, 399–400
benefits
amount, 399–400
duration, 396–99
claims administration, 1014–16
cost control procedures, 401–3
definition of disability, 395–96
employer cooperation, 403
exclusions, 400
initial premium rates, 474–75
limitations, 400
maternity benefits, 396, 399
nonoccupational coverage, 396–400
occupational supplement, 400
risk selection, 401–3, 443
tax aspects, 396–99
termination of coverage, 400–401
waiting period, 396–99, 401–2
SIBI; *see* Group survivor income benefit
insurance
Simultaneous death clauses, 826–27
Single-premium deferred annuities, 82,
155–56
Single-premium deferred variable annuity,
244–45
Single-premium immediate annuities
gross premiums for, 153–55
expense assumptions, 154–55
formulas, 154–55
interest assumptions, 154
mortality assumptions, 153–54
substandard annuities, 155
Single-premium immediate variable annuity, 243–44

Single-premium life annuity contract, 78–
81
Single-premium reserves, 168–69
Small general lines brokers, 499
Small groups' group insurance, 438–39
Social contributions of insurance companies, 933–35
Social insurance, 9
characteristics of, 351 n–352 n
expansion, limits of, 15
growth rate, 10
Social security benefits, 15, 32, 51, 515,
751–68
amounts, 756–58
average monthly wage (AMW) concept, 756–57
basic principles of system, 763–65
beneficiary categories, 754–56
coverage provisions, 751–53
development and history of system,
765–67
disability benefits, 754–55
earnings-related benefits, 764
earnings test, 758–60
financial impact of program, 751
financing provisions, 760–63
floor-of-protection concept, 763–64
formula for, 757–58
gap fund for, 839–40
individual equity versus social adequacy
of, 764
insured status conditions, 753–54
integration of long-term disability income insurance, 406
integration of pension plan with, 536,
552, 553 n
integration of retirement benefits with,
536
integration of self-employed persons'
pensions and profit sharing with,
570
law governing, 751
lump-sum death payments, 756
military personnel, 792
old-age beneficiaries, 754
payments abroad, 760
presumptive need as basis, 763
programming with, 811
scope of program, 751
self-supporting contributory financing,
764–65
special age-72 benefits, 756
supplementary benefits, 755
survivor benefits, 755–56
Society of Actuaries, 933
Sole proprietorship; *see* Proprietorship
Special policies, 74
advantage of, 92
change of plan provisions, 103

Special policies—*Cont.*
  classification of, 93
  contracts for, 92–105
  current insurance needs exceeding probable future insurance needs, 93–95
  current insurance needs less than probable future insurance needs, 95–96
  decreasing term coverage, 93–95
  family income policy, 93–95
  family maintenance policy, 93–94
  family policies, 100–101
  graded death benefit policy, 104
  graded premium plans, 98
  guaranteed insurability rider, 95–96
  high early cash value policy, 98–99
  inflexibility of, 92
  interim term insurance, 100
  joint life policy, 104–5
  jumping juvenile policies, 95
  juvenile educational endowment policy, 96–97
  level term coverage, 93
  markets for, 92
  minimization of initial premium outlay, 98–100
  miscellaneous, 101–5
  modified premium plans, 98
  multiple protection policy, 93
  need for, 92–93
  nonparticipating contract variations, 102–3
  participating contract variations, 101–2
  retirement annuity contract, 97
  retirement income contract, 98
  retirement orientation, 976–98
  return of premiums or cash value, 103
  savings orientation, 96–97
  step-rate premium plans, 98
  tailor-made term insurance, 103–4
Special questionnaires as risk selection tool, 204
Specialty brokers or consultants, 499–500
Spendthrift clauses, 827
Split dollar life insurance
  estate tax consequences, 886
  tax aspects, 880
Split dollar plans, 676–89
  background, 676–77
  basic patterns, 677–78
    variations in, 678–80
  collateral assignment system, 680–82
  defined, 676
  endorsement system, 681–83, 687
  estate taxation, 686–87
  examples of, 688–89
  execution of written plan agreement, 683–84

Split dollar plans—*Cont.*
  federal income tax, 684–86
  gift taxation, 687–88
  level premium insurance, 677
  major systems of, 680–82
  professional corporations, 735–36
  putting package together, 682–84
  term insurance, 677
Split funding of pension plans, 624–25
Split gift approach, 890
Split life insurance, 99 n, 100 n
Sprinkling trusts, 852
Standard Nonforfeiture Law, 143, 175–77
  cash surrender values, 177–78
Standard Provisions Law of 1912, 311
Standard risks, 195
  individual disability income insurance, 284
Standard Valuation Law, 143
State insurance departments
  duties of, 451
  group insurance regulation, 451
  laws governing, 940–41
  variable annuities regulation, 249–50
State statutes and laws
  age for formation of insurance contract, 106–7
  agents' qualification and licensing, 942–43
  automatic premium loan provisions, 181
  challenges to, 945–47
  company formation, 952–53
  contracts of insurance, requirements for and provisions of, 943–45
  creditor exemption, 827
  deficiency reserves, 141–42
  development of insurance supervision under, 938–40
  disability income payments, 344
  disability income plans; *see* Statutory disability income plans
  dividend options, 189
  dividend requirements, 189–90
  exemption from claims of creditors, 49
  exemption statutes, 37–38
  gross premiums, limitations on, 141–42
  group insurance regulation under, 452
  group insurance for trade associations, 440
  group risk selection, 433–34
  incontestable provision requirement, 113–14
  individual health insurance policies, 311–18
  initial premium rates for group life insurance, 472
  insurance companies, incorporation, operation, and powers of, 941–42

State statutes and laws—*Cont.*
insurance departments, authority, powers, and duties of, 940–41
interest rates on policy loans, 180–81
investments of life insurance companies, regulation of, 1025
life insurance company regulation, 43
limitation on profits, 186
minimum cash value, 142
mutual funds, 269–70
nonforfeiture values, 61, 173–74
policy loan interest rate, 181
replacement insurance, 221–23
requirements for insurance, 30
separation of accounts, 186
supervisory scope of, 938–39
tax treatment of insurance proceeds, 38
taxes; *see* Taxation *and* Taxation, company
temporary disability insurance, 778–79
variable annuities, 250
warranties governed by, 111
welfare and pension plan disclosure, 527
workmen's compensation, 776–78
State taxes; *see* Taxation *and* Taxation, company
Statutory disability income plans, 407–9
California, 407–8
Hawaii, 408
New Jersey, 408
New York, 408
Puerto Rico, 408–9
Rhode Island, 407–8
Statutory reserves, 170–71
Step-rate premium plan, 98
individual disability income insurance, 283
Step-rate premium policies, 102
Stock companies, 928, 930
"adjusted" figures for, 1049–51
defined, 184
dividend fund determination, 186
Stock redemption agreement, 710–15, 727; *see also* Corporations
funding of, 734-35
Stop-loss plans for group insurance, 488
Stop loss reinsurance, 1002
Straight life annuity, 83
Straight life insurance, 66–67
accumulation of retirement savings through, 72
cost compared with term insurance, 63–64
level premium concept, 67–68
limitations of, 72
nature of, 70
permanent protection afforded by, 71–72

Straight life insurance—*Cont.*
premature death protection, 72
savings element of, 39–40
term insurance compared, 219–20
uses of, 71–72
Strength of company, measures of, 1051–54
Substandard annuities, gross premiums for, 155
Substandard premiums for individual health insurance, 329
Substandard pricing methods
individual life insurance, 207–9
lien system, 209
multiple table extra premiums, 208
permanent flat extra premiums, 207
rate-up in age, 208–9
temporary flat extra premiums, 207–8
Substandard risks, 195
disability insurance for, 277
graded death benefit policy for, 104
individual disability income insurance, 284–85
individual health insurance, 335–38
evaluating experience, 338
extra premiums, 336–37
impairment exclusion riders, 335–36
modification of coverage, 337–38
Suicide
claims administration, 1011–12
contract provision, 118–19
Summary of operations; *see* Financial statements, company
Supplementary contracts, 1039
Supplementary deposit administration plan, 622–23
Supplementary medical insurance under Medicare; *see* Medicare
Surgical expense benefits
individual health insurance, 326
individual medical expense insurance, 293–94
Surgical expense group insurance, 421–23
Surplus
balance sheet account, 1042
basis for ascertainment of, 159
convention blank account, 1045
determination of, 186
limited nature of, 1024
separation of accounts between participating and nonparticipating business, 186
strength of company measured by, 1052–53
Surrender options in individual life insurance, 48
Survivor benefits under social security; *see* Social security benefits

Survivor income benefit insurance, group;
see Group survivor income benefit insurance
Survivors' benefit group life insurance,
353

T

Taft-Hartley Act, 355, 439
Taft-Hartley Trusts in group insurance,
439–40
Tailor-made term insurance, 103–4
Target benefit plan, 254
Tax deferred annuities, 575–86
additional income tax benefits, 582
adjustments for contributions to tax-
free retirement plan in previous
years, 580–81
advantages, 575–76
basic principles of, 585–86
benefit, defined, 578
benefits available, 575–76
budgetary constraints, 581
contracts, 578
dividend option, 583
eligible employees, 577–78
eligible employers, 576–77
estate tax exclusion, 583
exclusion allowance formula, 578–79
$5,000 income exclusion, 582
formula, 581
funding problems, 583–84
gift tax exclusion, 583
government employers other than public
schools, 577
includable compensation, 579–80
income taxation upon receipt under,
584–85
Internal Revenue Code description, 576
life insurance incidental to, with or
without, 584–85
part-time employees, 580
practical considerations, 581
reduction in salary of employee, 583–84
regulations governing, 576
reserves, 583
tax exempt status, determination of,
576–77
terminal retirement funding, 585
termination of employment, 585
variable, 253
years of service, 580
Tax exempt employers' retirement plans,
575–86; see also Tax deferred annuities
Tax planning and estate planning distinguished, 844
Tax Reform Act of 1969, 852, 865, 877
Taxation, 38; see also Taxation, company
and specific taxes

Taxation—*Cont.*
annuities, 89–90
Canadian life insurance, 1083–88
funded life insurance trusts, 862–64
group ordinary life insurance, 468–69
group paid-up life insurance, 468
group permanent life insurance, 467–68
group term life insurance, 465–67
irrevocable unfunded life insurance
trust, 861
return on invested funds, 44–46
self-employed persons' pensions and
profit sharing, 571–72
Taxation, company
Canadian life insurance companies,
1088
controlled foreign corporations, 1067–
68
federal income tax, 1055–67; see also
Life Insurance Company Income
Tax Act of 1959
history of, 1055–57
life insurance company taxable income, 1065–66
tax-deferred account, 1066–67
taxable investment income base, purpose of determining, 1061–62
taxable investment income items,
1062–65
foreign insurers, policies issued by,
1069
interest equalization tax, 1068–69
local taxes, 1074
state taxes, 1069–74
"in lieu" provisions, 1073–74
premium tax, 1069–72
retaliatory taxes, 1072–73
Teachers Insurance and Annuity Association (TIAA), 241–42
Teachers Insurance and Annuity Associa-
tion-College Retirement Equities
Fund (TIAA-CREF), 608–9
Temporary disability insurance (TDI)
programs, 778–79
Temporary flat extra premiums, 207–8
Temporary life annuities, 84–85
Temporary National Economic Committee
(TNEC) report, 939–40
Term expectancy contract, 55–56
Term insurance, 99
advantages to insured, 63–65
"built-in" values lacking, 65
"buy term and invest the difference"
concept, 65
change of plan provision, 60
contracts, 55–65
convertible, 58–60
cost-of-living adjustments, 57
cost of straight life compared, 63–64

Term insurance—*Cont.*
  decreasing term rider, 56
  defined, 55
  disadvantages to insured, 63–65
  dividend option, 191
  duration, 55–56
  extended, 178–79
  ideal form of, 60
  increasing term rider, 56–57
  initial, 56
  interim, 100
  level premium concept, 67–68
  level term riders, 57
  life expectancy contract, 55–56
  low-outlay aspect, 63
  mortality rate, 44, 61–62
  nature of, 55–63
  net outlay, 63–64
  nonforfeiture values, 61
  nonparticipating, 61
  nonrenewable but automatically convertible, 60
  participating, 61
  policy features, 61
  preliminary, 56
  premiums, 63
  renewable, 57–58
  retroactive conversion, 58–59
  riders for, 56
  split-dollar plans, 677
  straight life compared, 219–20
  tailor-made policy, 103–4
  temporary nature of protection, 64
  waiver of premium provision, 61
Term life insurance, 39
  group; *see* Group term life insurance
Terminal dividends, 188–89
Terminal reserves, 167, 169
  calculation of, 161–62, 165
Termination expenses, 145–46
Termination of coverage
  claims administration, 1012
  group creditor life insurance, 379–80
  group insurance, 457
  individual health insurance, 309
  long-term disability income insurance, 407
  short-term disability income insurance, 400–401
Termination rate for gross premiums on individual health insurance, 328
Testamentary trustee as beneficiary designation, 823–24
Testamentary trusts
  defined, 857
  estate planning vehicle, 851–52
Third party owners, 816–17
  transfers by, 817–18

Thirty-one-day continuation of protection provisions
  group survivor income benefit insurance, 386
  group term life insurance, 374
Thrift institutions, 39
Thrift savings plans, 558–61
  advantages of, 560–61
  characteristics of, 558–59
  investment provisions, 560
  satellite, 560
  standard, 559–60
  voluntary, 560
Time limit on certain defenses provision in individual health insurance, 312, 314
Time of payment of claim provision in individual health insurance, 314
Tort liability
  agent for own acts, 981–83
  company for agent's acts, 979–81
Total disability benefits, claims administration of, 1013–16
Total disability, defined, 278–79
Trade associations; *see* Voluntary trade associations
Traditional method of cost comparison, 214–15, 220
Transfer cases, rating of, in group insurance experience rating, 482–83
Transfer-for-value rule
  estate tax on life insurance, 885
  exception to, 872
  tax consequences, 872–74
  violations of, 873–74
Travel accident insurance, 388
Trust agreements
  estate planning vehicle, 851–52
  life insurance proceeds disposition under, 823–24
Trust companies as beneficiary designation, 823–25
Trust fund pension plans, 525–26, 627–43
  accounting system for, 631
  actuarial aspects, 636–38
  actuarial valuation, 637
  adjustments to benefits after retirement, 634
  agreement for, 591–92
  amendments, 631
  benefit formula, 632–33
  current problem areas, 641–42
  death after retirement, 633
  death before retirement, 633–34
  disability retirement, 633
  disclosure requirements, 639
  early retirement, 633
  flexibility, 643

Trust fund pension plans—*Cont.*
  funding methods, 636–37
    aggregate cost method, 636
    entry age normal cost method, 636
    frozen initial liability method, 636
    unit credit method, 636
  general rules included in document of, 632
  investment of fund, 629
    restrictions on, 629
  investment performance, measurement of, 638
  labor agreement, 635–36
  mergers, 631–32
  miscellaneous provisions in trust agreement, 631
  past service, 635
  payments from trust, 630
  plan document, 632–36
  popularity of, 627, 642–43
  powers of trustee, 630
  prototype, 591
  record keeping requirements, 630–31
  responsibilities, 638–41
    actuary, 638–39
    employer, 639
    multiemployer plans, 640–41
    union, 640
  self-employed persons, 563
  significance of, 642–43
  termination, 631–32
  termination of plan, 634–35
  trust agreement, 629–32
  trustee's liability, 631
  valuation of assets, 637–38
  vested rights, 634
Trustees, 856–57
  beneficiary designation, 823–25
Trusts, 856–65; *see also specific types*
  classification of, 857
  defined, 856–57
  funded life insurance trusts, 862–65
  gifts of life insurance in, 898–900; *see also* Gifts of life insurance
  inter vivos, 857
  irrevocable, 857
  life insurance trusts, 857
    funded, 862–65
    unfunded, 859–62, 865
    uses of, 857–59
  parties involved in, definition of, 856–57
  revocable, 857
  short-term trusts, 863
  testamentary, 857
  types, 857–64; *see also specific types*
  unfunded life insurance trust, 859
    irrevocable, 861–62, 865
    revocable, 859–61

Truth-in-insurance, 989
Twenty-four hour coverage in accidental death and dismemberment insurance, 386–87

U

UCR (usual, customary and reasonable) basis for coverage in group medical expense insurance, 417, 421, 428
Unacceptable risks, 195
Underwriter; *see* Life underwriter
Underwriting; *see* Risk selection
Unearned premium reserves in group insurance, 484
Uniform Individual Accident and Sickness Policy Provisions Law, 311–18, 1018
Uniform Policy Provisions Law, individual disability income insurance benefits, 286
Uniform Standard Policy Provisions Law, requirements of, 116–18
Unincorporated business interest, business continuation insurance for, 690–702
Uninsurable risks, 195
Union groups
  group insurance, 355, 440, 497
  trust fund plans, 640
Unit investment trusts, 258
United Kingdom, variable life insurance in, 228, 230
United Mine Workers of America welfare fund establishment, 517
United States Government Life Insurance (USGLI), 781, 783
  programming with, 806
Unpaid premium provision in individual health insurance, 317
Unreported claims, reserve for, 325
Urban Investment Program, 933

V

Valuation
  bonds, 1025–26
  common stocks, 1026
  company assets, 1025–26
  corporate stock for estate tax purposes, 711
  corporation stock interest, 708–9
  key man for insurance, 653–55
  life insurance for estate tax purposes, 882–83
  life insurance for gift tax purposes, 888–89
  preferred stocks, 1026
  proprietorship, 693–94
Variable annuities, 87, 225 ff., 240–56, 925–26, 946–47, 1034
  administration of, 252–53
  administrative expenses, 251

Variable annuities—*Cont.*
 assumed investment return, 243–44
 competition, effects of, 251
 concept of, 241
 consumer protection provided by, 247
 consumer service provided by, 247
 contract provisions, 247–48
 corporate structure and management of, 250
 cost-of-living plans, 254
 defined, 243
 early plans, 241–42
 federal regulation, 248–49, 947–48
 final-pay plan, 254
 function of, 254
 group, 243, 254
 guarantees provided by, 246–47
 H-R 10, 253–54
 individual, 243, 253
 installation of, 252–53
 investment annuity as departure from, 242
 investment management fees, 251
 nature of, 240–42
 periodic-payment, 245–46
 potential markets for, 253–54
 pricing aspects of, 251–52
 purchase rates, 251–52
 record requirements, 252
 regulatory environment, 248–53
 reports to policyowners, 252
 retirement planning approach, 240–41
 sales expenses, 251
 separate accounts, role of, 250
 significance of, 255
 single-premium deferred, 244–45
 single-premium immediate, 243–44
 state regulation, 249–50
 target benefit plan, 254
 tax-deferred, 253
 types, 243–46
 unique characteristics of, 243
 units, 244–46
Variable dollar assets, 50–51
 types of, 50–51
Variable life insurance (VLI), 225 ff., 227–39, 926, 1034
 accounting methods, 234–35
 cash surrender values, 232
 contract design, 230–33
 defined, 227
 development in other countries, 227–229
 development in United States, 229–30
 "Dutch" design of, 227–28, 230–31
 endowment-type plans, 227–28
 federal income tax aspects, 237
 fixed premium, 230–31
 grace period, 232–33

Variable life insurance—*Cont.*
 gross premiums, 233–34
 guaranteed minimum death benefit, 230
 legal aspects, 235–37
 nonforfeiture options, 232
 one contract, 230
 outlook for, 237–38
 payment of claims, 235
 policy loan provisions, 232
 regulatory aspects, 235–37
 reinstatement provision, 232–33, 235
 reporting to policyowners, 235
 risk selection, 234
 securities laws, application of, 235–37
 special contract provisions, 232–33
 withdrawal provision, 232
Verification of claims assumptions for individual health insurance, 327
Vesting nonqualified deferred compensation plans, 667–68
 pension plans, 523–24, 538–39
Veterans' compensation benefits, 788–89
 death, 790–91
 disability, 789
Veterans' death benefits, 792–93
Veterans' life insurance, 780–87
 beneficiary designation and change, 786
 change of plan, 785
 conversion, 785
 data and statistics concerning program of, 780–82
 disability coverage, 787
 dividends, 785
 general policy provisions, 784
 guaranteed values, 784
 history, 781, 783–84
 programming with, 806
 reinstatement, 784–85
 settlement options, 786–87
 waiver of premium provisions, 787
Veterans' medical care programs, 775–76
Veterans' orphans', wives' and widows' education benefits, 791–92
Veterans' pension benefits, 788–91
 death, 791
 disability, 789–90
Veterans Reopened Insurance, 783
Voluntary accidental death and dismemberment
 insurance, 387–88
 claims administration, 1016
 continuing protection provisions, 387
 initial premium rates, 474
 limitations, 387–88
 nature of, 387
 reinsurance treaties, 388
 travel accident or business trip coverage, 388

Voluntary accidental death and dismemberment—*Cont.*
twenty-four hour coverage, 387
Voluntary trade associations, group insurance for, 355, 440–41, 497

W

Wage and hour requirements, 948
Waiting periods
long-term disability income insurance, 404–6
short-term disability income insurance, 396–99, 401–2
Waiver
defined, 112
doctrine of, 111–12
Waiver-of-premium provisions, 119–20
annuities, 88
deferred compensation plans, 674–75
group term life insurance, 374–75
individual disability income insurance, 280
individual health insurance, 323
individual life insurance, 48
key man life insurance, 652
term insurance, 61
veterans' life insurance, 787
Waiver of premium disability income benefits under life policies, 282–83
War clauses, 119, 200
results clause, 119
status clause, 119
War deaths, claims administration for, 1012
Warranties, 111
Weight; *see* Overweight
Welfare and Pension Plan Disclosure Act, 455, 526–27, 639, 948
Whole life insurance; *see also specific topics*
contracts, 66–74
conversion privileges, 71
defined, 66
dividend options, 71
endowments compared, 220
flexible provisions in contracts of, 71
graded-premium contracts, 74
level premium concept, 67–70
limited-payment life contracts, 66–67
loan privileges, 71
modified life contract, 73–74
nonforfeiture options, 71
paid-up insurance option, 71

Whole life insurance—*Cont.*
preferred risk contracts, 74
reduced premium rates, 74
savings element of, 39–40, 70
specials, 74
straight life contracts, 66–67
types of contracts, 66–67
Wholesale life insurance, 353
Widows
life income for, programming for, 810
living expenses provided for, 32
settlement option for life income for, 840
Wills, 35–36, 845
charitable bequests of life insurance, 904–5
estate planning with, 850
insurance proceeds trustees designated in, 823–24
Wisconsin State Life Fund, 973–74
Withdrawal benefits in deposit administration pension plans, 616
Withdrawal plans for mutual funds, 266–67
Withdrawal provisions in variable life insurance, 232
Withdrawal rates for gross premiums on nonparticipating life insurance, 144–45
Workmen's compensation programs, 776–78
Wrongful death cases, 21
mortality as discount factor, 22

Y

Yearly renewable term insurance, 58
gross premiums versus net premiums, 68–69
level premium concept, 68–69
Yearly renewable term premium and level premium distinguished, 41
Yearly renewable term (YRT) reinsurance, 993
Yield
gross premiums
deferred annuities, 155
individual health insurance, 328–29
nonparticipating life insurance, 143–44
participating insurance, 150
single-premium immediate annuities, 154
individual life insurance, 44–46
level premium reserves, 160–61